RSMeans
Repair & Remodeling Cost Data
20th Annual Edition

1999

Senior Editor
Howard M. Chandler

Contributing Editors
Thomas J. Akins
Barbara Balboni
John H. Chiang, PE
Paul C. Crosscup
Jennifer L. Curran
Stephen E. Donnelly
J. Robert Lang
Robert C. McNichols
Robert W. Mewis
Melville J. Mossman, PE
John J. Moylan
Jeannene D. Murphy
Peter T. Nightingale
Jesse R. Page
Stephen C. Plotner
Michael J. Regan
Kornelis Smit
William R. Tennyson, II
Phillip R. Waier, PE

Manager, Engineering Operations
John H. Ferguson, PE

President
Durwood S. Snead

Vice President and General Manager
Roger J. Grant

Vice President, Sales and Marketing
John M. Shea

Production Manager
Michael Kokernak

Production Coordinator
Marion E. Schofield

Technical Support
Michele S. Able
Wayne D. Anderson
Thomas J. Dion
Michael H. Donelan
Gary L. Hoitt
Paula Reale-Camelio
Kathryn S. Rodriguez
James N. Wills

Art Director
Helen A. Marcella

Book & Cover Design
Norman R. Forgit

R.S. Means Company, Inc. ("R.S. Means"), its authors, editors and engineers, apply diligence and judgment in locating and using reliable sources for the information published. **However, R.S. Means makes no express or implied warranty or guarantee in connection with the content of the information contained herein, including the accuracy, correctness, value, sufficiency, or completeness of the data, methods and other information contained herein. R.S. Means makes no express or implied warranty of merchantability or fitness for a particular purpose.** R.S. Means shall have no liability to any customer or third party for any loss, expense, or damage including consequential, incidental, special or punitive damages, including lost profits or lost revenue, caused directly or indirectly by any error or omission, or arising out of, or in connection with, the information contained herein.

No part of this publication may be reproduced, stored in a retrieval system, or transmitted in any form or by any means without prior written permission of R.S. Means Company, Inc.

Editorial Advisory Board

James E. Armstrong
Energy Consultant
EnergyVision

William R. Barry
Chief Estimator
Mitchell Construction Company

Robert F. Cox, PhD
Assistant Professor
ME Rinker Sr. School of Bldg. Constr.
University of Florida

Roy F. Gilley, AIA
Principal
Gilley-Hinkel Architects

Kenneth K. Humphreys, PhD, PE, CCE
Secretary-Treasurer
International Cost Engineering Council

Patricia L. Jackson, PE
Vice President, Project Management
Aguirre Corporation

Martin F. Joyce
Vice President, Utility Division
Bond Brothers, Inc.

First Printing

Foreword

R.S. Means Co., Inc. is owned by CMD Group, a leading worldwide provider of proprietary construction information. CMD Group is comprised of three synergistic product groups crafted to be the complete resource for reliable, timely and actionable construction market data. In North America, CMD Group encompasses: Architects' First Source, an innovative product selection and specification solution in print and on the Internet; Construction Market Data (CMD), the source for construction activity information, as well as early planning reports for the design community; Associated Construction Publications, with 14 magazines, one of the largest editorial networks dedicated to U.S. highway and heavy construction coverage; Manufacturer's Survey Associates (MSA), a leading estimating and quantity survey firm in the U.S.; R.S. Means, the authority on construction cost data in North America; CMD Canada, the leading supplier of project information, industry news and forecasting data products for the Canadian construction industry; and BIMSA/Mexico, the dominant distributor of information on building projects and construction throughout Mexico. Worldwide, CMD Group includes Byggfakta Scandinavia, providing construction market data to Denmark, Estonia, Finland, Norway and Sweden; and Cordell Building Information Services, the market leader for construction and cost information in Australia.

Our Mission

Since 1942, R.S. Means Company, Inc. has been actively engaged in construction cost publishing and consulting throughout North America.

Today, over fifty years after the company began, our primary objective remains the same: to provide you, the construction and facilities professional, with the most current and comprehensive construction cost data possible.

Whether you are a contractor, an owner, an architect, an engineer, a facilities manager, or anyone else who needs a quick construction cost estimate, you'll find this publication to be a highly useful and necessary tool.

Today, with the constant flow of new construction methods and materials, it's difficult to find the time to look at and evaluate all the different construction cost possibilities. In addition, because labor and material costs keep changing, last year's cost information is not a reliable basis for today's estimate or budget.

That's why so many construction professionals turn to R.S. Means. We keep track of the costs for you, along with a wide range of other key information, from city cost indexes . . . to productivity rates . . . to crew composition . . . to contractor's overhead and profit rates.

R.S. Means performs these functions by collecting data from all facets of the industry, and organizing it in a format that is instantly accessible to you. From the preliminary budget to the detailed unit price estimate, you'll find the data in this book useful for all phases of construction cost determination.

The Staff, the Organization, and Our Services

When you purchase one of R.S. Means' publications, you are in effect hiring the services of a full-time staff of construction and engineering professionals.

Our thoroughly experienced and highly qualified staff works daily at collecting, analyzing, and disseminating comprehensive cost information for your needs. These staff members have years of practical construction experience and engineering training prior to joining the firm. As a result, you can count on them not only for the cost figures, but also for additional background reference information that will help you create a realistic estimate.

The Means organization is always prepared to help you solve construction problems through its five major divisions: Construction and Cost Data Publishing, Electronic Products and Services, Consulting Services, Insurance Division, and Educational Services.

Besides a full array of construction cost estimating books, Means also publishes a number of other reference works for the construction industry. Subjects include construction estimating and project and business management; special topics such as HVAC, roofing, plumbing, and hazardous waste remediation; and a library of facility management references.

In addition, you can access all of our construction cost data through your computer with Means CostWorks '99 CD-ROM, an electronic tool that offers over 50,000 lines of Means construction cost data.

What's more, you can increase your knowledge and improve your construction estimating and management performance with a Means Construction Seminar or In-House Training Program. These two-day seminar programs offer unparalleled opportunities for everyone in your organization to get updated on a wide variety of construction-related issues.

Means also is a worldwide provider of construction cost management and analysis services for commercial and government owners and of claims and valuation services for insurers.

In short, R.S. Means can provide you with the tools and expertise for constructing accurate and dependable construction estimates and budgets in a variety of ways.

Robert Snow Means Established a Tradition of Quality That Continues Today

Robert Snow Means spent years building his company, making certain he always delivered a quality product.

Today, at R.S. Means, we do more than talk about the quality of our data and the usefulness of our books. We stand behind all of our data, from historical cost indexes... to construction materials and techniques... to current costs.

If you have any questions about our products or services, please call us toll-free at 1-800-334-3509. Our customer service representatives will be happy to assist you.

Table of Contents

Foreword	ii
How the Book Is Built: An Overview	iv
Quick Start	v
How To Use the Book: The Details	vi
Unit Price Section	1
Assemblies Section	351
Reference Section	499
Reference Numbers	500
Change Orders	554
Crew Listings	558
Historical Cost Indexes	582
City Cost Indexes	583
Location Factors	602
Abbreviations	607
Index	610
Other Means Publications and Reference Works	Yellow Pages
Installing Contractor's Overhead & Profit	Inside Back Cover

UNIT PRICES

GENERAL REQUIREMENTS	1
SITE WORK	2
CONCRETE	3
MASONRY	4
METALS	5
WOOD & PLASTICS	6
THERMAL & MOISTURE PROTECTION	7
DOORS & WINDOWS	8
FINISHES	9
SPECIALTIES	10
EQUIPMENT	11
FURNISHINGS	12
SPECIAL CONSTRUCTION	13
CONVEYING SYSTEMS	14
MECHANICAL	15
ELECTRICAL	16

ASSEMBLIES

FOUNDATIONS	1
SUBSTRUCTURES	2
SUPERSTRUCTURES	3
EXTERIOR CLOSURE	4
ROOFING	5
INTERIOR CONSTRUCTION	6
CONVEYING SYSTEMS	7
MECHANICAL	8
ELECTRICAL	9
SPECIAL CONSTRUCTION	11
SITE WORK	12

REFERENCE INFORMATION

- REFERENCE NUMBERS
- CREWS
- COST INDEXES
- INDEX

How the Book Is Built: An Overview

A Powerful Construction Tool

You have in your hands one of the most powerful construction tools available today. A successful project is built on the foundation of an accurate and dependable estimate. This book will enable you to construct just such an estimate.

For the casual user the book is designed to be:

- quickly and easily understood so you can get right to your estimate
- filled with valuable information so you can understand the necessary factors that go into the cost estimate

For the regular user, the book is designed to be:

- a handy desk reference that can be quickly referred to for key costs
- a comprehensive, fully reliable source of current construction costs and productivity rates, so you'll be prepared to estimate any project
- a source book for preliminary project cost, product selections, and alternate materials and methods

To meet all of these requirements we have organized the book into the following clearly defined sections.

Quick Start

This one-page section (see following page) can quickly get you started on your estimate.

How To Use the Book: The Details

This section contains an in-depth explanation of how the book is arranged . . . and how you can use it to determine a reliable construction cost estimate. It includes information about how we develop our cost figures and how to completely prepare your estimate.

Unit Price Section

All cost data has been divided into the 16 divisions according to the MasterFormat system of classification and numbering as developed by the Construction Specifications Institute (CSI) and Construction Specifications Canada (CSC). For a listing of these divisions and an outline of their subdivisions, see the Unit Price Section Table of Contents.

Estimating tips are included at the beginning of each division.

Assemblies Section

The cost data in this section has been organized in an "Assemblies" format. These assemblies are the functional elements of a building and are arranged according to the 12 divisions of the UniFormat classification system. For a complete explanation of a typical "Assemblies" page, see "How To Use the Assemblies Cost Tables."

Reference Section

This section includes information on Reference Numbers, Change Orders, Crew Listings, Historical Cost Indexes, City Cost Indexes, Location Factors, and a listing of Abbreviations. It is visually identified by a vertical gray bar on the edge of pages.

Reference Numbers: At the beginning of selected major classifications in the Unit Price Section are "reference numbers" shown in bold squares. These numbers refer you to related information in the Reference Section.

In this section, you'll find reference tables, explanations, and estimating information that support how we develop the unit price data. Also included are alternate pricing methods, technical data, and estimating procedures, along with information on design and economy in construction. You'll also find helpful tips on what to expect and what to avoid when estimating and constructing your project.

It is recommended that you refer to the Reference Section if a "reference number" appears within the major classification you are estimating.

Change Orders: This section includes information on the factors that influence the pricing of change orders.

Crew Listings: This section lists all the crews referenced in the book. For the purposes of this book, a crew is composed of more than one trade classification and/or the addition of power equipment to any trade classification. Power equipment is included in the cost of the crew. Costs are shown both with bare labor rates and with the installing contractor's overhead and profit added. For each, the total crew cost per eight-hour day and the composite cost per labor-hour are listed.

Historical Cost Indexes: These indexes provide you with data to adjust construction costs over time. If you know costs for a project completed in the past, you can use these indexes to calculate a rough estimate of what it would cost to construct the same project today.

City Cost Indexes: Obviously, costs vary depending on the regional economy. You can adjust the "national average" costs in this book to 305 major cities throughout the U.S. and Canada by using the data in this section. How to use information is included.

Location Factors, to quickly adjust the data to over 930 zip code areas, are included.

Abbreviations: A listing of the abbreviations used throughout this book, along with the terms they represent, is included.

Index

A comprehensive listing of all terms and subjects in this book to help you find what you need quickly when you are not sure where it falls in MasterFormat.

The Scope of This Book

This book is designed to be as comprehensive and as easy to use as possible. To that end we have made certain assumptions and limited its scope in three key ways:

1. We have established material prices based on a "national average."
2. We have computed labor costs based on a 30-city "national average" of union wage rates.
3. We have targeted the data for projects of a certain size range.

For a more detailed explanation of how the cost data is developed, see "How To Use the Book: The Details."

Project Size

This book is aimed primarily at residential, commercial and industrial repair/remodeling projects costing $10,000 to $1,000,000.

With reasonable exercise of judgment the figures can be used for any repair/remodeling work. *However, for civil engineering structures such as bridges, dams, highways, or the like, please refer to* **Means Heavy Construction Cost Data.**

Quick Start

If you feel you are ready to use this book and don't think you need the detailed instructions that begin on the following page, this Quick Start section is for you.

These steps will allow you to get started estimating in a matter of minutes.

1 First, decide whether you require a Unit Price or Assemblies type estimate. Unit price estimating requires a breakdown of the work to individual items. Assemblies estimates combine individual items or components into building systems.

If you need to estimate each line item separately, follow the instructions for **Unit Prices.**

If you can use an estimate for the entire assembly or system, follow the instructions for **Assemblies.**

2 Find each cost data section you need in the Table of Contents (either for Unit Prices or Assemblies).

Unit Prices: The cost data for Unit Prices has been divided into 16 divisions according to the CSI MasterFormat.

Assemblies: The cost data for Assemblies has been divided into 12 divisions according to the UniFormat.

3 Turn to the indicated section and locate the line item or assemblies table you need for your estimate. Portions of a sample page layout from both the Unit Price Listings and the Assemblies Cost Tables appear below.

Unit Prices: If there is a reference number listed at the beginning of the section, it refers to additional information you may find useful. See the referenced section for additional information.

- Note the crew code designation. You'll find full descriptions of crews in the Crew Listings including labor-hour and equipment costs.

Assemblies: The Assemblies (*not* shown in full here) are generally separated into three parts: 1) an illustration of the system to be estimated; 2) the components and related costs of a typical system; and 3) the costs for similar systems with dimensional and/or size variations.

4 Determine the total number of units your job will require.

Unit Prices: Note the unit of measure for the material you're using is listed under "Unit."

- Bare Costs: These figures show unit costs for materials and installation. Labor and equipment costs are calculated according to crew costs and average daily output. Bare costs do not contain allowances for overhead, profit or taxes.
- "Labor-hours" allows you to calculate the total labor-hours to complete that task. Just multiply the quantity of work by this figure for an estimate of activity duration.

Assemblies: Note the unit of measure for the assembly or system you're estimating is listed in the System Components section.

5 Then multiply the total units by . . .

Unit Prices: "Total Incl. O&P" which stands for the total cost including the installing contractor's overhead and profit. (See the "How To Use the Unit Price Pages" for a complete explanation.)

Assemblies: The "Total" in the right-hand column, which is the total cost including the installing contractor's overhead and profit. (See the "How To Use the Assemblies Cost Tables" section for a complete explanation.)

Material and equipment cost figures include a 10% markup. For labor markups, see the inside back cover of this book. If the work is to be subcontracted, add the general contractor's markup, approximately 10%.

6 The price you calculate will be an estimate for either an individual item of work, or for a completed assembly or *system*.

7 Compile a list of all items or assemblies included in the total project. Summarize cost information, and add project overhead.

Localize costs by using the City Cost Indexes or Location Factors found in the Reference Section.

For a more complete explanation of the way costs are derived, please see the following sections.

Editors' Note: We urge you to spend time reading and understanding all of the supporting material and to take into consideration the reference material such as Crews Listing and the "reference numbers."

Unit Price Pages

Assemblies Pages

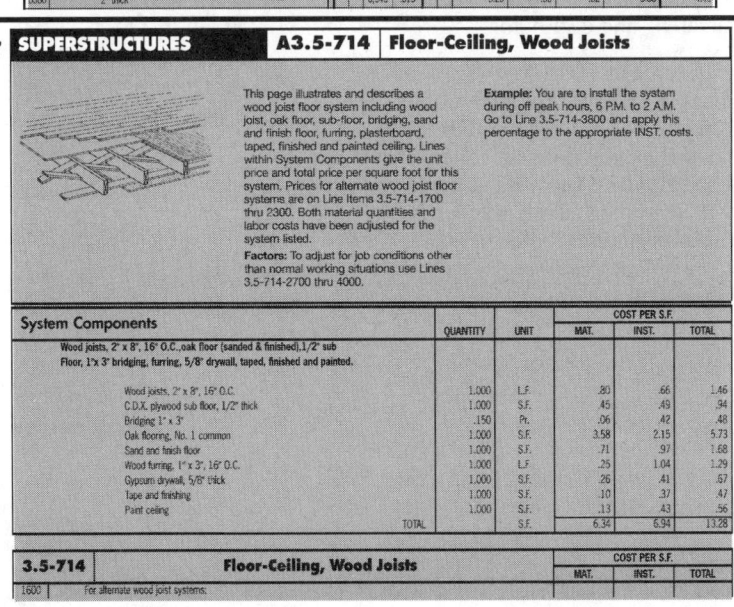

How to Use the Book: The Details

What's Behind the Numbers? The Development of Cost Data

The staff at R.S. Means continuously monitors developments in the construction industry in order to ensure reliable, thorough and up-to-date cost information.

While *overall* construction costs may vary relative to general economic conditions, price fluctuations within the industry are dependent upon many factors. Individual price variations may, in fact, be opposite to overall economic trends. Therefore, costs are continually monitored and complete updates are published yearly. Also, new items are frequently added in response to changes in materials and methods.

Costs—$ (U.S.)

All costs represent U.S. national averages and are given in U.S. dollars. The Means City Cost Indexes can be used to adjust costs to a particular location. The City Cost Indexes for Canada can be used to adjust U.S. national averages to local costs in Canadian dollars.

Material Costs

The R.S. Means staff contacts manufacturers, dealers, distributors, and contractors all across the U.S. and Canada to determine national average material costs. If you have access to current material costs for your specific location, you may wish to make adjustments to reflect differences from the national average. Included within material costs are fasteners for a normal installation. R.S. Means engineers use manufacturers' recommendations, written specifications and/or standard construction practice for size and spacing of fasteners. Adjustments to material costs may be required for your specific application or location. Material costs do not include sales tax.

Labor Costs

Labor costs are based on the average of wage rates from 30 major U.S. cities. Rates are determined from labor union agreements or prevailing wages for construction trades for the current year. Rates along with overhead and profit markups are listed on the inside back cover of this book.

- If wage rates in your area vary from those used in this book, or if rate increases are expected within a given year, labor costs should be adjusted accordingly.

Labor costs reflect productivity based on actual working conditions. These figures include time spent during a normal workday on tasks other than actual installation, such as material receiving and handling, mobilization at site, site movement, breaks, and cleanup.

Productivity data is developed over an extended period so as not to be influenced by abnormal variations and reflects a typical average.

Equipment Costs

Equipment costs include not only rental, but also operating costs for equipment under normal use. The operating costs include parts and labor for routine servicing such as repair and replacement of pumps, filters and worn lines. Normal operating expendables such as fuel, lubricants, tires and electricity (where applicable) are also included. Extraordinary operating expendables with highly variable wear patterns such as diamond bits and blades are excluded. These costs are included under materials. Equipment rental rates are obtained from industry sources throughout North America—contractors, suppliers, dealers, manufacturers, and distributors.

Crew Equipment Cost/Day—The power equipment required for each crew is included in the crew cost. The daily cost for crew equipment is based on dividing the weekly bare rental rate by 5 (number of working days per week), and then adding the hourly operating cost times 8 (hours per day). This "Crew Equipment Cost/Day" is listed in Subdivision 016.

General Conditions

Cost data in this book is presented in two ways: Bare Costs and Total Cost including O&P (Overhead and Profit). General Conditions, when applicable, should also be added to the Total Cost including O&P. The costs for General Conditions are listed in Division 1 of the Unit Price Section and the Reference Section of this book. General Conditions for the *Installing Contractor* may range from 0% to 10% of the Total Cost including O&P. For the *General* or *Prime Contractor*, costs for General Conditions may range from 5% to 15% of the Total Cost including O&P, with a figure of 10% as the most typical allowance.

Overhead and Profit

Total Cost including O&P for the *Installing Contractor* is shown in the last column on both the Unit Price and the Assemblies pages of this book. This figure is the sum of the bare material cost plus 10% for profit, the base labor cost plus total overhead and profit, and the bare equipment cost plus 10% for profit. Details for the calculation of Overhead and Profit on labor are shown on the inside back cover and in the Reference Section of this book. (See the "How to Use the Unit Price Pages" for an example of this calculation.)

Factors Affecting Costs

Costs can vary depending upon a number of variables. Here's how we have handled the main factors affecting costs.

Quality—The prices for materials and the workmanship upon which productivity is based represent sound construction work. They are also in line with U.S. government specifications.

Overtime—We have made no allowance for overtime. If you anticipate premium time or work beyond normal working hours, be sure to make an appropriate adjustment to your labor costs.

Productivity—The productivity, daily output, and labor-hour figures for each line item are based on working an eight-hour day in daylight hours in moderate temperatures. For work that extends beyond normal work hours or is performed under adverse conditions, productivity may decrease. (See the section in "How To Use the Unit Price Pages" for more on productivity.)

Size of Project—The size, scope of work, and type of construction project will have a significant impact on cost. Economies of scale can reduce costs for large projects. Unit costs can often run higher for small projects. Costs in this book are intended for the size and type of project as previously described in "How the Book Is Built: An Overview." Costs for projects of a significantly different size or type should be adjusted accordingly.

Location—Material prices in this book are for metropolitan areas. However, in dense urban areas, traffic and site storage limitations may increase costs. Beyond a 20-mile radius of large cities, extra trucking or transportation charges may also increase the material costs slightly. On the other hand, lower wage rates may be in effect. Be sure to consider both these factors when preparing an estimate, particularly if the job site is located in a central city or remote rural location.

In addition, highly specialized subcontract items may require travel and per diem expenses for mechanics.

Other factors—
- season of year
- contractor management
- weather conditions
- local union restrictions
- building code requirements
- availability of:
  - adequate energy
  - skilled labor
  - building materials
- owner's special requirements/restrictions
- safety requirements
- environmental considerations

Unpredictable Factors—General business conditions influence "in-place" costs of all items. Substitute materials and construction methods may have to be employed. These may affect the installed cost and/or life cycle costs. Such factors may be difficult to evaluate and cannot necessarily be predicted on the basis of the job's location in a particular section of the country. Thus, where these factors apply, you may find significant, but unavoidable cost variations for which you will have to apply a measure of judgment to your estimate.

Rounding of Costs

In general, all unit prices in excess of $5.00 have been rounded to make them easier to use and still maintain adequate precision of the results. The rounding rules we have chosen are in the following table.

Prices from . . .	Rounded to the nearest . . .
$.01 to $5.00	$.01
$5.01 to $20.00	$.05
$20.01 to $100.00	$.50
$100.01 to $300.00	$1.00
$300.01 to $1,000.00	$5.00
$1,000.01 to $10,000.00	$25.00
$10,000.01 to $50,000.00	$100.00
$50,000.01 and above	$500.00

Final Checklist

Estimating can be a straightforward process provided you remember the basics. Here's a checklist of some of the items you should remember to do before completing your estimate.

Did you remember to . . .

- factor in the City Cost Index for your locale
- take into consideration which items have been marked up and by how much
- mark up the entire estimate sufficiently for your purposes
- read the background information on techniques and technical matters that could impact your project time span and cost
- include all components of your project in the final estimate
- make use of Minimum Labor/Equipment Charges for Small Quantities (see the following page for more details)
- double check your figures to be sure of your accuracy
- call R.S. Means if you have any questions about your estimate or the data you've found in our publications

Remember, R.S. Means stands behind its publications. If you have any questions about your estimate . . . about the costs you've used from our books . . . or even about the technical aspects of the job that may affect your estimate, feel free to call the R.S. Means editors at 1-781-585-7898 or 1-800-448-8182.

Using Minimum Labor/Equipment Charges for Small Quantities

When preparing a repair and remodeling estimate, it is a good idea to carefully evaluate the "Minimum" Labor and Equipment figures listed within the Unit Price section of the book.

An estimate that has a bottom line Labor or Equipment cost LESS THAN the "Minimum" amounts listed at the bottom of specific sections of cost figures should be adjusted upward to the "Minimum" figures shown. The "Minimum" figures are included as a guide for that area of construction. Bid figures for any job must be adjusted and allowances made for the contractor to recover the expense connected with losing a portion of a normal work day. This allowance is usually needed to allow for set-up cost, cleanup and/or travel time.

Materials add a cost to an estimate over and above Labor and Equipment costs; therefore, Material costs should never be confused with this adjustment to "Minimum" Labor and Equipment figures. When Labor and Equipment costs have been developed for a specific item, ALWAYS ADJUST FIGURES UP TO THE "MINIMUM" AMOUT SHOWN."

086 | Wood & Plastic Windows

086 100	Wood Windows	CREW	DAILY OUTPUT	LABOR-HOURS	UNIT	1999 BARE COSTS				TOTAL INCL O&P
						MAT.	LABOR	EQUIP.	TOTAL	
120 0010	CASEMENT WINDOW Including frame, screen, and exterior trim										120
0100	Avg. quality, bldrs. model, 2'-0" x 3'-0" H, standard glazed	1 Carp	10	.800	Ea.	158	22		180	210
8100	Metal clad, deluxe, insulating glass, 2'-0" x 3'-0" high		10	.800		163	22		185	216
8120	2'-0" x 4'-0" high		9	.889		196	24.50		220.50	256
9000	Minimum labor/equipment charge	1 Carp	3	2.667	Job		73		73	122
124 0010	DOUBLE HUNG Including frame, screen, and exterior trim										124
0100	Avg. quality, bldrs. model, 2'-0" x 3'-0" high, standard glazed	1 Carp	10	.800	Ea.	105	22		127	153
0150	Insulating glass		10	.800		149	22		171	201
0200	3'-0" x 4'-0" high, standard glazed		9	.889		138	24.50		162.50	193
0250	Insulating glass		9	.889		182	24.50		206.50	241
0300	4'-0" x 4'-6" high, standard glazed		8	1		169	27.50		196.50	232

Example:

Establish the bid price to replace a casement window unit. Assume installation of a 2' x 5' Metal Clad Window with Insulating Glass.

Solution:

Step One: —Develop Material Cost and Labor Cost separately.

Material Cost for Line Number [086-120-8120] = $196

Labor Cost for Line Number [086-120-8120] = $24.50

Total Incl. O&P for Line Number [086-120-8120] =

[Material + 10%] + [Labor + 67.4%] =
 [$196 + $20] + [$24.50 + $16.50]   = [$216] + [$41] = $257.00

Step Two: —Evaluate Minimum Labor and Equipment Figure.

Minimum Labor/Equipment Figure for this section = $73 (Compare to $24.50)

Minimum Labor/Equipment Figure Incl. O&P for this section = $122.00

Add Material Cost plus a 10% markup to the Minimum Labor/Equipment Cost listed in the Total Incl. O&P Column [$196 + 10% ($196)] + [$122] =
 [$216] + [$122] = $338

ANSWER: $338.00 is the correct figure to use. This sum takes into consideration the Minimum Labor/Equipment figure (with O&P included), plus Material Cost (with 10% for profit).

Unit Price Section

Table of Contents

Div No.		Page
	General Requirements	5
010	Overhead & Miscellaneous Data	6
013	Submittals	8
014	Quality Control	8
015	Construction Facilities & Temporary Controls	9
016	Material & Equipment	15
017	Contract Closeout	21
	Site Work	23
020	Subsurface Investigation & Demolition	24
021	Site Preparation & Excavation Support	43
022	Earthwork	43
023	Tunneling, Piles & Caissons	49
025	Paving & Surfacing	51
026	Piped Utilities	56
027	Sewerage & Drainage	58
028	Site Improvements	60
029	Landscaping	63
	Concrete	69
031	Concrete Formwork	70
032	Concrete Reinforcement	75
033	Cast-In-Place Concrete	76
034	Precast Concrete	83
035	Cementitious Decks & Toppings	84
037	Concrete Restoration & Cleaning	84
	Masonry	85
041	Mortar & Masonry Accessories	86
042	Unit Masonry	89
044	Stone	95
045	Masonry Restoration, Cleaning & Refractories	97
	Metals	101
050	Metal Materials, Coatings & Fastenings	102
051	Structural Metal Framing	104
052	Metal Joists	107
053	Metal Decking	107
054	Cold Formed Metal Framing	108
055	Metal Fabrications	111
057	Ornamental Metal	114
058	Expansion Control	114
	Wood & Plastics	117
060	Fasteners & Adhesives	118
061	Rough Carpentry	119
062	Finish Carpentry	130
063	Wood Treatment	136
064	Architectural Woodwork	136
066	Plastic Fabrications	141
	Thermal & Moisture Protection	143
071	Waterproofing & Dampproofing	144
072	Insulation & Fireproofing	145
073	Shingles & Roofing Tiles	152
074	Preformed Roofing & Siding	155
075	Membrane Roofing	158
076	Flashing & Sheet Metal	161
077	Roof Specialties & Accessories	166
078	Skylights	168
079	Joint Sealers	169
	Doors & Windows	171
081	Metal Doors & Frames	172
082	Wood & Plastic Doors	174
083	Special Doors	181
084	Entrances & Storefronts	187
085	Metal Windows	189
086	Wood & Plastic Windows	192
087	Hardware	197
088	Glazing	204
089	Glazed Curtain Walls	206
	Finishes	209
091	Metal Support Systems	210
092	Lath, Plaster & Gypsum Board	210
093	Tile	216
094	Terrazzo	218
095	Acoustical Treatment & Wood Flooring	219
096	Flooring & Carpet	221
097	Special Flooring & Floor Treatment	225
098	Special Coatings	225
099	Painting & Wall Coverings	225
	Specialties	239
101	Visual Display Boards, Compartments & Cubicles	240
102	Louvers, Corner Protection & Access Flooring	242
103	Fireplaces, Exterior Specialties & Flagpoles	242
104	Identifying & Pedestrian Control Devices	244
105	Lockers, Protective Covers & Postal Specialties	245
106	Partitions & Storage Shelving	247
107	Telephone Specialties	249
108	Toilet & Bath Accessories & Scales	249
	Equipment	251
110	Equipment	252
111	Mercantile, Commercial & Detention Equipment	253
114	Food Service, Residential, Darkroom, Athletic Equipment	256
115	Industrial & Process Equipment	263
116	Laboratory, Planetarium, Observatory Equipment	263
	Furnishings	265
125	Window Treatment	266
126	Furniture & Accessories	266
	Special Construction	269
130	Special Construction	270
131	Pre-Eng. Structures, Aquatic Facilities & Ice Rinks	272
137	Security Access & Surveillance	272
	Conveying Systems	275
141	Dumbwaiters	276
142	Elevators	276
144	Lifts	280
145	Material Handling Systems	280
146	Hoists & Cranes	280
	Mechanical	283
151	Pipe & Fittings	284
152	Plumbing Fixtures	301
153	Plumbing Appliances	305
154	Fire Protection	307
155	Heating	307
156	HVAC Piping Specialties	317
157	Air Conditioning & Ventilation	318
	Electrical	327
160	Raceways	328
161	Conductors & Grounding	332
162	Boxes & Wiring Devices	335
163	Motors, Starters, Boards & Switches	336
164	Transformers & Bus Ducts	339
165	Power Systems & Capacitors	340
166	Lighting	340
167	Electric Utilities	343
168	Special Systems	343

How to Use the Unit Price Pages

The following is a detailed explanation of a sample entry in the Unit Price Section. Next to each bold number below is the item being described with appropriate component of the sample entry following in parenthesis. Some prices are listed as bare costs, others as costs that include overhead and profit of the installing contractor. In most cases, if the work is to be subcontracted, the general contractor will need to add an additional markup (R.S. Means suggests using 10%) to the figures in the column "Total Incl. O&P."

1 Division Number/Title (025/Paving & Surfacing)

Use the Unit Price Section Table of Contents to locate specific items. The sections are classified according to the CSI MasterFormat.

2 Line Numbers (025 104 0160)

Each unit price line item has been assigned a unique 10-digit code based on the 5-digit CSI MasterFormat classification.

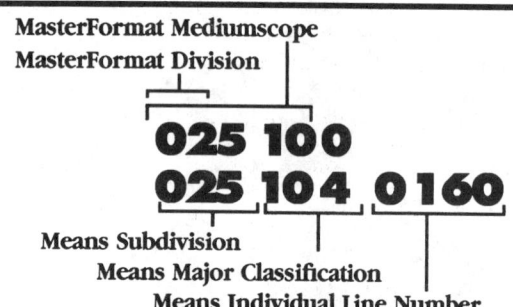

- MasterFormat Mediumscope
- MasterFormat Division
- **025 100**
- **025 104 0160**
- Means Subdivision
- Means Major Classification
- Means Individual Line Number

3 Description (Asphaltic Concrete Pavement, Etc.)

Each line item is described in detail. Sub-items and additional sizes are indented beneath the appropriate line items. The first line or two after the main item (in boldface) may contain descriptive information that pertains to all line items beneath this boldface listing.

4 Reference Number Information

 You'll see reference numbers shown in bold squares at the beginning of some major classifications. These refer to related items in the Reference Section, visually identified by a vertical gray bar on the edge of pages.

The relation may be: (1) an estimating procedure that should be read before estimating, (2) an alternate pricing method, or (3) technical information.

The "R" designates the Reference Section. The numbers refer to the MasterFormat classification system.

It is strongly recommended that you review all reference numbers that appear within the major classification you are estimating.

Example: The square number above is directing you to refer to the reference number R025-110. This particular reference number shows how the unit price lines for asphaltic concrete pavement were formulated and costs derived.

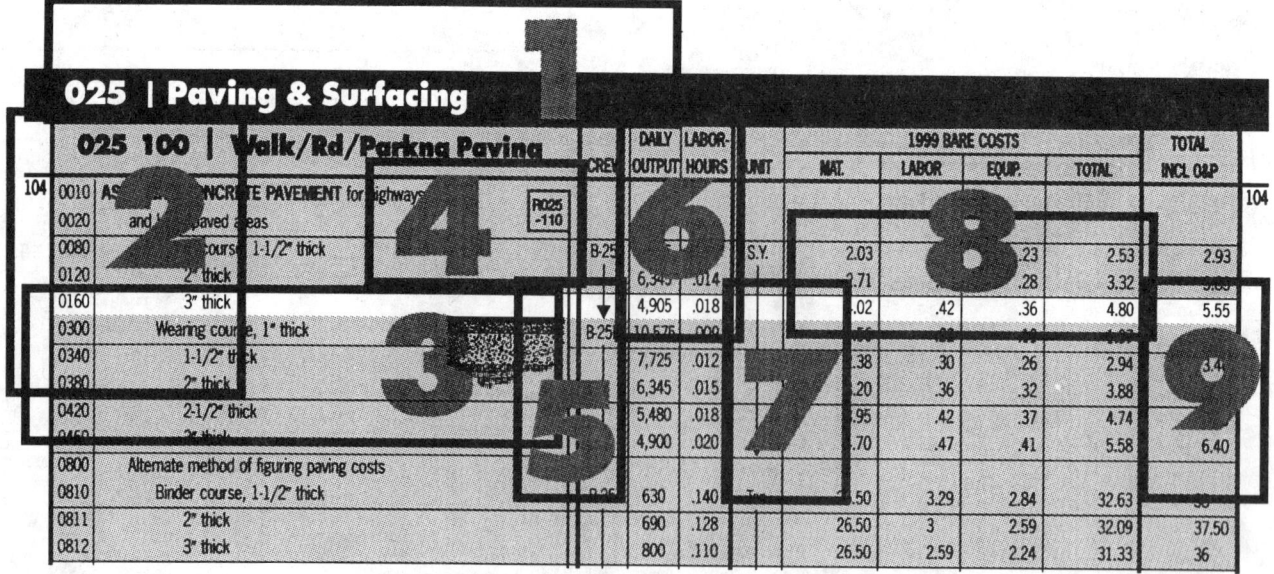

Crew (B-25)

The "Crew" column designates the typical trade or crew used to install the item. If an installation can be accomplished by one trade and requires no power equipment, that trade and the number of workers are listed (for example, "1 Clab"). If an installation requires a composite crew, a crew code designation is listed (for example, "B-25"). You'll find full details on all composite crews in the Crew Listings.
- For a complete list of all trades utilized in this book and their abbreviations, see the inside back cover.

Crews

Crew No.	Bare Costs		Incl. Subs O & P		Cost Per Labor-Hour	
Crew B-25	Hr.	Daily	Hr.	Daily	Bare Costs	Incl. O&P
1 Labor Foreman	$23.45	$187.60	$39.25	$314.00	$23.53	$38.74
7 Laborers	21.45	1201.20	35.90	2010.40		
3 Equip. Oper. (med.)	28.40	681.60	45.20	1084.80		
1 Asphalt Paver, 130 H.P		1299.00		1428.90		
1 Tandem Roller, 10 Ton		245.10		269.60		
1 Roller, Pneumatic Wheel		244.20		268.60	20.32	22.35
88 L.H., Daily Totals		$3858.70		$5376.30	$43.85	$61.09

Productivity: Daily Output (4905)/Labor-Hours (.018)

The "Daily Output" represents the typical number of units the designated crew will install in a normal 8-hour day. To find out the number of days the given crew would require to complete the installation, divide your quantity by the daily output. For example:

Quantity	÷	Daily Output	=	Duration
10000 S.Y.	÷	4905 S.Y./ Crew Day	=	2.04 Crew Days

The "Labor-Hours" figure represents the number of labor-hours required to install one unit of work. To find out the number of labor-hours required for your particular task, multiply the quantity of the item times the number of labor-hours shown. For example:

Quantity	x	Productivity Rate	=	Duration
10000 S.Y.	x	.018 Labor-Hours/ S.Y.	=	180 Labor-Hours

Unit (S.Y.)

The abbreviated designation indicates the unit of measure upon which the price, production, and crew are based (S.Y. = Square Yard). For a complete listing of abbreviations refer to the Abbreviations Listing in the Reference Section of this book.

Bare Costs:
Mat. (Bare Material Cost) (4.02)

The unit material cost is the "bare" material cost with no overhead and profit included. *Costs shown reflect national average material prices for January of the current year and include delivery to the job site. No sales taxes are included.*

Labor (.42)

The unit labor cost is derived by multiplying bare labor-hour costs for Crew B-25 by labor-hour units. The bare labor-hour cost is found in the Crew Section under B-25. (If a trade is listed, the hourly labor cost—the wage rate—is found on the inside back cover.)

Labor-Hour Cost Crew B-25	x	Labor-Hour Units	=	Labor
$23.53	x	.018	=	$.42

Equip. (Equipment) (.36)

Equipment costs for each crew are listed in the description of each crew. Tools or equipment whose value justifies purchase or ownership by a contractor are considered overhead as shown on the inside back cover. The unit equipment cost is derived by multiplying the bare equipment hourly cost by the labor-hour units.

Equipment Cost Crew B-25	x	Labor-Hour Units	=	Equip.
$20.32	x	.018	=	$.36

Total (4.80)

The total of the bare costs is the arithmetic total of the three previous columns: mat., labor, and equip.

Material	+	Labor	+	Equip.	=	Total
$4.02	+	$.42	+	$.36	=	$4.80

Total Costs Including O&P

This figure is the sum of the bare material cost plus 10% for profit; the bare labor cost plus total overhead and profit (per the inside back cover or, if a crew is listed, from the crew listings); and the bare equipment cost plus 10% for profit.

Material is Bare Material Cost + 10% = $4.02 + $.40	=	$4.42
Labor for Crew B-25 = Labor-Hour Cost ($38.74) x Labor-Hour Units (.018)	=	$ .70
Equip. is Bare Equip. Cost + 10% = $.36 + $.04	=	$ .40
Total (Rounded)	=	$5.55

Division 1
General Requirements

Estimating Tips

The General Requirements of any contract are very important to both the bidder and the owner. These lay the ground rules under which the contract will be executed and have a significant influence on the cost of operations. Therefore, it is extremely important to thoroughly read and understand the General Requirements both before preparing an estimate and when the estimate is complete, to ascertain that nothing in the contract is overlooked. Caution should be exercised when applying items listed in Division 1 to an estimate. Many of the items are included in the unit prices listed in the other divisions such as mark-ups on labor and company overhead.

010 Overhead & Miscellaneous Data
- Before determining a final cost estimate, it is a good practice to review all the items listed in subdivision 010 to make final adjustments for items that may need customizing to specific job conditions.
- Historic preservation projects may require specialty labor and methods, as well as extra time to protect existing materials that must be preserved and/or restored. Some additional expenses may be incurred in architectural fees for facility surveys and other special inspections and analyses.
- When estimating historic preservation projects (depending on the condition of the existing structure and the owner's requirements), a 15-20% contingency or allowance is recommended, regardless of the stage of the drawings.

013 Submittals
- Requirements for initial and periodic submittals can represent a significant cost to the General Requirements of a job. Thoroughly check the submittal specifications when estimating a project to determine any costs that should be included.

014 Quality Control
- All projects will require some degree of Quality Control. This cost is not included in the unit cost of construction listed in each division. Depending upon the terms of the contract, the various costs of inspection and testing can be the responsibility of either the owner or the contractor. Be sure to include the required costs in your estimate.

015 Construction Facilities & Temporary Controls
- Barricades, access roads, safety nets, scaffolding, security and many more requirements for the execution of a safe project are elements of direct cost. These costs can easily be overlooked when preparing an estimate. When looking through the major classifications of this subdivision, determine which items apply to each division in your estimate.

016 Material & Equipment
- This subdivision contains transportation, handling, storage, protection and product options and substitutions. Listed in this cost manual are average equipment rental rates for all types of equipment. This is useful information when estimating the time and materials requirement of any particular operation in order to establish a unit or total cost.
- A good rule of thumb is that weekly rental is 3 times daily rental and that monthly rental is 3 times weekly rental.
- The figures in the column for Crew Equipment Cost represent the rental rate used in determining the daily cost of equipment in a crew. It is calculated by dividing the weekly rate by 5 days and adding the hourly operating cost times 8 hours.

017 Contract Closeout
- When preparing an estimate, read the specifications to determine the requirements for Contract Closeout thoroughly. Final cleaning, record documentation, operation and maintenance data, warranties and bonds, and spare parts and maintenance materials can all be elements of cost for the completion of a contract. Do not overlook these in your estimate.

018 Maintenance
- If maintenance and repair are included in your contract, they require special attention. To estimate the cost to remove and replace any unit usually requires a site visit to determine the accessibility and the specific difficulty at that location. Obstructions, dust control, safety, and often overtime hours must be considered when preparing your estimate.

Reference Numbers
Reference numbers are shown in bold squares at the beginning of some major classifications. These numbers refer to related items in the Reference Section. The reference information may be an estimating procedure, an alternate pricing method or technical information.

Note: Not all subdivisions listed here necessarily appear in this publication.

010 | Overhead & Miscellaneous Data

010 000 | Overhead

			CREW	DAILY OUTPUT	LABOR-HOURS	UNIT	1999 BARE COSTS MAT.	LABOR	EQUIP.	TOTAL	TOTAL INCL O&P	
004	0011	**ARCHITECTURAL FEES**	R010 -010									004
	0020	For new construction										
	0060	Minimum				Project					4.90%	
	0090	Maximum									16%	
	0100	For alteration work, to $500,000, add to fee									50%	
	0150	Over $500,000, add to fee									25%	
016	0011	**CONSTRUCTION MANAGEMENT FEES**										016
	0060	For work to $10,000				Project					10%	
	0070	To $25,000									9%	
	0090	To $100,000									6%	
	0100	To $500,000									5%	
	0110	To $1,000,000									4%	
020	0010	**CONTINGENCIES** Allowance to add at conceptual stage				Project					20%	020
	0050	Schematic stage									15%	
	0100	Preliminary working drawing stage									10%	
	0150	Final working drawing stage									2%	
028	0010	**ENGINEERING FEES**	R010 -030									028
	0020	Educational planning consultant, minimum				Contrct					4.10%	
	0100	Maximum									10.10%	
	0400	Elevator & conveying systems, minimum									2.50%	
	0500	Maximum									5%	
	1000	Mechanical (plumbing & HVAC), minimum									4.10%	
	1100	Maximum									10.10%	
	1200	Structural, minimum				Project					1%	
	1300	Maximum				"					2.50%	
032	0010	**FACTORS** Cost adjustments	R011 -010									032
	0100	Add to construction costs for particular job requirements										
	0500	Cut & patch to match existing construction, add, minimum				Costs	2%	3%				
	0550	Maximum					5%	9%				
	0800	Dust protection, add, minimum					1%	2%				
	0850	Maximum					4%	11%				
	1100	Equipment usage curtailment, add, minimum					1%	1%				
	1150	Maximum					3%	10%				
	1400	Material handling & storage limitation, add, minimum					1%	1%				
	1450	Maximum					6%	7%				
	1700	Protection of existing work, add, minimum					2%	2%				
	1750	Maximum					5%	7%				
	2000	Shift work requirements, add, minimum						5%				
	2050	Maximum						30%				
	2300	Temporary shoring and bracing, add, minimum					2%	5%				
	2350	Maximum					5%	12%				
	2400	Work inside prisons, add, minimum						30%				
	2450	Maximum				Costs		50%				
036	0011	**FIELD PERSONNEL**										036
	0020											
	0180	Project manager, minimum				Week		1,180		1,180	1,860	
	0200	Average						1,320		1,320	2,085	
	0220	Maximum						1,490		1,490	2,350	
	0240	Superintendent, minimum						1,125		1,125	1,775	
	0260	Average						1,245		1,245	1,965	
	0280	Maximum						1,405		1,405	2,215	
040	0010	**INSURANCE** Builders risk, standard, minimum	R010 -040			Job					.22%	040
	0050	Maximum									.59%	
	0200	All-risk type, minimum	R010 -060								.25%	
	0250	Maximum									.62%	

Important: See the Reference Section for critical supporting data - Reference Nos., Crews, & City Cost Indexes

010 | Overhead & Miscellaneous Data

010 000 | Overhead

			CREW	DAILY OUTPUT	LABOR-HOURS	UNIT	1999 BARE COSTS MAT.	LABOR	EQUIP.	TOTAL	TOTAL INCL O&P	
040	0400	Contractor's equipment floater, minimum [R010-040]				Value					.50%	040
	0450	Maximum				"					1.50%	
	0600	Public liability, average [R010-060]				Job					1.55%	
	0810	Workers' compensation & employer's liability										
	2000	Range of 35 trades in 50 states, excl. wrecking, minimum				Payroll		2%				
	2100	Average						18.30%				
	2200	Maximum						132.92%				
042	0010	**JOB CONDITIONS** Modifications to total										042
	0020	project cost summaries										
	0100	Economic conditions, favorable, deduct				Project					2%	
	0200	Unfavorable, add									5%	
	0300	Hoisting conditions, favorable, deduct									2%	
	0400	Unfavorable, add									5%	
	0500	General Contractor management, experienced, deduct									2%	
	0600	Inexperienced, add									10%	
	0700	Labor availability, surplus, deduct									1%	
	0800	Shortage, add									10%	
	0900	Material storage area, available, deduct									1%	
	1000	Not available, add									2%	
	1100	Subcontractor availability, surplus, deduct									5%	
	1200	Shortage, add									12%	
	1300	Work space, available, deduct									2%	
	1400	Not available, add									5%	
048	0010	**MAIN OFFICE EXPENSE** Average for General Contractors										048
	0020	As a percentage of their annual volume										
	0030	Annual volume to $50,000, minimum				% Vol.					20%	
	0040	Maximum									30%	
	0060	To $100,000, minimum									17%	
	0070	Maximum									22%	
	0080	To $250,000, minimum									16%	
	0090	Maximum									19%	
	0110	To $500,000, minimum									14%	
	0120	Maximum									16%	
	0130	To $1,000,000, minimum									8%	
	0140	Maximum									10%	
052	0010	**MARK-UP** For General Contractors for change										052
	0100	of scope of job as bid										
	0200	Extra work, by subcontractors, add				%					10%	
	0250	By General Contractor, add									15%	
	0400	Omitted work, by subcontractors, deduct									5%	
	0450	By General Contractor, deduct									7.50%	
	0600	Overtime work, by subcontractors, add									15%	
	0650	By General Contractor, add									10%	
	1000	Installing contractors, on his own labor, minimum									58.80%	
	1100	Maximum									112%	
058	0010	**OVERHEAD** As percent of direct costs, minimum [R010-050]				%					5%	058
	0050	Average									15%	
	0100	Maximum [R010-070]									30%	
062	0010	**OVERHEAD & PROFIT** Allowance to add to items in this [R010-050]										062
	0020	book that do not include Subs O&P, average				%					30%	
	0100	Allowance to add to items in this book that										
	0110	do include Subs O&P, minimum				%					5%	
	0150	Average									10%	
	0200	Maximum									15%	

010 | Overhead & Miscellaneous Data

010 000 | Overhead

			CREW	DAILY OUTPUT	LABOR-HOURS	UNIT	1999 BARE COSTS MAT.	LABOR	EQUIP.	TOTAL	TOTAL INCL O&P	
062	0290	Typical, by size of project, under $50,000	R010-050			%				40%		062
	0310	$50,000 to $100,000								35%		
	0320	$100,000 to $500,000								25%		
	0330	$500,000 to $1,000,000								20%		
070	0010	**PERMITS** Rule of thumb, most cities, minimum				Job					.50%	070
	0100	Maximum				"					2%	
082	0010	**SMALL TOOLS** As % of contractor's work, minimum	R010-050			Total					.50%	082
	0100	Maximum				"					2%	
086	0010	**TAXES** Sales tax, State, average	R010-090			%	4.71%					086
	0050	Maximum					7.25%					
	0200	Social Security, on first $68,400 of wages	R010-100					7.65%				
	0300	Unemployment, MA, combined Federal and State, minimum						2.60%				
	0350	Average						7%				
	0400	Maximum						8.50%				

013 | Submittals

013 300 | Survey Data

			CREW	DAILY OUTPUT	LABOR-HOURS	UNIT	1999 BARE COSTS MAT.	LABOR	EQUIP.	TOTAL	TOTAL INCL O&P	
306	0010	**SURVEYING** Conventional, topographical, minimum	A-7	3.30	7.273	Acre	16	175		191	300	306
	0100	Maximum	A-8	.60	53.333		48	1,250		1,298	2,075	
	0300	Lot location and lines, minimum, for large quantities	A-7	2	12		25	288		313	495	
	0320	Average	"	1.25	19.200		45	460		505	795	
	0400	Maximum, for small quantities	A-8	1	32		72	745		817	1,275	
	1100	Crew for building layout, 2 person crew	A-6	1	16	Day		410		410	650	
	1200	3 person crew	A-7	1	24			575		575	930	
	1300	4 person crew	A-8	1	32			745		745	1,200	

013 400 | Shop Drawings

			CREW	DAILY OUTPUT	LABOR-HOURS	UNIT	MAT.	LABOR	EQUIP.	TOTAL	INCL O&P	
408	0010	**RENDERINGS** Color, matted, 20" x 30", eye level,										408
	0020	1 building, minimum				Ea.	1,500			1,500	1,650	
	0050	Average					2,500			2,500	2,750	
	0100	Maximum					3,500			3,500	3,850	
	1000	5 buildings, minimum					3,000			3,000	3,300	
	1100	Maximum					6,000			6,000	6,600	

014 | Quality Control

014 100 | Testing Services

			CREW	DAILY OUTPUT	LABOR-HOURS	UNIT	1999 BARE COSTS MAT.	LABOR	EQUIP.	TOTAL	TOTAL INCL O&P	
108	0010	**FIELD TESTING**										108
	1800	Compressive strength, cylinders, delivered to lab				Ea.					13	
	1900	Picked up by lab, minimum									15	
	1950	Average									20	
	2000	Maximum									30	
	2200	Compressive strength, cores (not incl. drilling)									40	

014 | Quality Control

014 100 | Testing Services

		CREW	DAILY OUTPUT	LABOR-HOURS	UNIT	MAT.	LABOR	EQUIP.	TOTAL	TOTAL INCL O&P	
108	2300 Patching core holes				Ea.					24	108
	4730 Soil testing										
	4735 Soil density, nuclear method, ASTM D2922-71				Ea.					38.67	
	4740 Sand cone method ASTM D1556064									30.17	
	4750 Moisture content									5.33	
	4780 Permeability test, double ring infiltrometer									550	
	4800 Permeability, variable or constant head, undisturbed									205	
	4850 Recompacted									233.33	
	4900 Proctor compaction, 4" standard mold									125	
	4950 6" modified mold									75	
	5100 Shear tests, triaxial, minimum									450	
	5150 Maximum									600	
	5550 Technician for inspection, per day, earthwork									215	
	5650 Bolting									270	
	5750 Roofing									250	
	5790 Welding									260	
	5820 Non-destructive testing, dye penetrant				Day					320	
	5840 Magnetic particle									320	
	5860 Radiography									480	
	5880 Ultrasonic									330	
	6000 Welding certification, minimum				Ea.					100	
	6100 Maximum				"					275	
	7000 Underground storage tank										
	7500 Hydrostatic tank tightness test per tank, min.				Ea.					500	
	7510 Maximum				"					1,000	
	7600 Vadose zone (soil gas) sampling, 10-40 samples, min.				Day					1,500	
	7610 Maximum				"					2,500	
	7700 Ground water monitoring incl. drilling 3 wells, min.				Total					5,000	
	7710 Maximum				"					7,000	
	8000 X-ray concrete slabs				Ea.					200	

015 | Construction Facilities & Temporary Controls

015 100 | Temporary Utilities

		CREW	DAILY OUTPUT	LABOR-HOURS	UNIT	MAT.	LABOR	EQUIP.	TOTAL	TOTAL INCL O&P	
104	0010 **TEMPORARY UTILITIES**										104
	0100 Heat, incl. fuel and operation, per week, 12 hrs. per day	1 Skwk	100	.080	CSF Flr	5	2.24		7.24	9.25	
	0200 24 hrs. per day	"	60	.133		7.55	3.74		11.29	14.50	
	0350 Lighting, incl. service lamps, wiring & outlets, minimum	1 Elec	34	.235		2.03	7.50		9.53	13.85	
	0360 Maximum	"	17	.471		4.42	15		19.42	28	
	0400 Power for temp lighting only, per month, min/month 6.6 KWH								.75	1.18	
	0450 Maximum/month 23.6 KWH								2.85	2.85	
	0600 Power for job duration incl. elevator, etc., minimum								47	51.70	
	0650 Maximum								110	121	

015 200 | Temporary Construction

		CREW	DAILY OUTPUT	LABOR-HOURS	UNIT	MAT.	LABOR	EQUIP.	TOTAL	TOTAL INCL O&P	
204	0010 **PROTECTION** Stair tread, 2" x 12" planks, 1 use	1 Carp	75	.107	Tread	3.87	2.91		6.78	9.15	204
	0100 Exterior plywood, 1/2" thick, 1 use		65	.123		1.23	3.36		4.59	6.95	
	0200 3/4" thick, 1 use		60	.133		1.75	3.64		5.39	8	

015 | Construction Facilities & Temporary Controls

015 200 | Temporary Construction

			CREW	DAILY OUTPUT	LABOR-HOURS	UNIT	1999 BARE COSTS				TOTAL INCL O&P
							MAT.	LABOR	EQUIP.	TOTAL	
208	0010	**TEMPORARY CONSTRUCTION** See also division 015-300									208

015 250 | Construction Aids

			CREW	DAILY OUTPUT	LABOR-HOURS	UNIT	MAT.	LABOR	EQUIP.	TOTAL	TOTAL INCL O&P
251	0010	**STAGING AIDS** and fall protection equipment									251
	0100	Sidewall staging bracket, tubular, buy				Ea.	30.50			30.50	33.50
	0110	Cost each per day, based on 250 days use				Day	.12			.12	.13
	0200	Guard post, buy				Ea.	15			15	16.50
	0210	Cost each per day, based on 250 days use				Day	.06			.06	.07
	0300	End guard chains, buy per set				Ea.	25			25	27.50
	0310	Cost per set per day, based on 250 days use				Day	.12			.12	.13
	1010	Cost each per day, based on 250 days use				"	.03			.03	.03
	1100	Wood bracket, buy				Ea.	11.50			11.50	12.60
	1110	Cost each per day, based on 250 days use				Day	.05			.05	.05
	2010	Cost per pair per day, based on 250 days use				"	.32			.32	.35
	2100	Steel siderail jack, buy per pair				Pair	69			69	76
	2110	Cost per pair per day, based on 250 days use				Day	.28			.28	.30
	3010	Cost each per day, based on 250 days use				"	.17			.17	.19
	3100	Aluminum scaffolding plank, 20" wide x 24' long, buy				Ea.	660			660	730
	3110	Cost each per day, based on 250 days use				Day	2.65			2.65	2.91
	4000	Nylon full body harness, lanyard and rope grab				Ea.	233			233	257
	4010	Cost each per day, based on 250 days use				Day	.93			.93	1.03
	4100	Rope for safety line, 5/8" x 100' nylon, buy				Ea.	35			35	38.50
	4110	Cost each per day, based on 250 days use				Day	.14			.14	.15
	4200	Permanent U-Bolt roof anchor, buy				Ea.	30.50			30.50	33.50
	4300	Temporary (one use) roof ridge anchor, buy				"	18.60			18.60	20.50
	5000	Installation (setup and removal) of staging aids									
	5010	Sidewall staging bracket	2 Carp	64	.250	Ea.		6.80		6.80	11.45
	5020	Guard post with 2 wood rails	"	64	.250			6.80		6.80	11.45
	5030	End guard chains, set	1 Carp	64	.125			3.41		3.41	5.70
	5100	Roof shingling bracket		96	.083			2.27		2.27	3.81
	5200	Ladder jack	↓	64	.125			3.41		3.41	5.70
	5300	Wood plank, 2x10x16'	2 Carp	80	.200			5.45		5.45	9.15
	5310	Aluminum scaffold plank, 20" x 24'	"	40	.400			10.90		10.90	18.30
	5410	Safety rope	1 Carp	40	.200			5.45		5.45	9.15
	5420	Permanent U-Bolt roof anchor (install only)	2 Carp	40	.400			10.90		10.90	18.30
	5430	Temporary roof ridge anchor (install only)	1 Carp	64	.125	↓		3.41		3.41	5.70
254	0014	**SCAFFOLDING, STEEL TUBULAR** Rent, 1 use per mo., no plank R015-100									254
	0015	Set up and take down									
	0090	Building exterior, wall face, 1 to 5 stories	3 Carp	24	1	C.S.F.	24.50	27.50		52	72
	0200	6 to 12 stories	4 Carp	21.20	1.509		24.50	41		65.50	95.50
	0310	13 to 20 stories	5 Carp	20	2		24.50	54.50		79	118
	0460	Building interior, wall face area, up to 16' high	3 Carp	25	.960		24.50	26		50.50	70.50
	0560	16' to 40' high		23	1.043	↓	24.50	28.50		53	74
	0800	Building interior floor area, up to 30' high		312	.077	C.C.F.	1.87	2.10		3.97	5.60
	0900	Over 30' high	4 Carp	275	.116	"	1.87	3.18		5.05	7.35
	0910	Steel tubular, heavy duty shoring, buy									
	0920	Frames 5' high 2' wide				Ea.	75			75	82.50
	0925	5' high 4' wide					85			85	93.50
	0930	6' high 2' wide				↓	86			86	94.50
	0935	6' high 4' wide					101			101	111
	0940	Accessories									
	0945	Cross braces				Ea.	16			16	17.60
	0950	U-head, 8" x 8"					16			16	17.60
	0955	J-head, 4" x 8"	↓			↓	12			12	13.20

015 | Construction Facilities & Temporary Controls

015 250 | Construction Aids

				CREW	DAILY OUTPUT	LABOR-HOURS	UNIT	1999 BARE COSTS MAT.	LABOR	EQUIP.	TOTAL	TOTAL INCL O&P	
254	0960	Base plate, 8" x 8"					Ea.	13			13	14.30	254
	0965	Leveling jack	R015 -100					30.50			30.50	33.50	
	1000	Steel tubular, regular, buy											
	1100	Frames 3' high 5' wide					Ea.	58			58	64	
	1150	5' high 5' wide						67			67	73.50	
	1200	6'-4" high 5' wide						84			84	92.50	
	1350	7'-6" high 6' wide						145			145	160	
	1500	Accessories cross braces						15			15	16.50	
	1550	Guardrail post						15			15	16.50	
	1600	Guardrail 7' section						7.25			7.25	8	
	1650	Screw jacks & plates						24			24	26.50	
	1700	Sidearm brackets						28			28	31	
	1750	8" casters						33			33	36.50	
	1800	Plank 2" x 10" x 16'-0"						42.50			42.50	47	
	1900	Stairway section						235			235	259	
	1910	Stairway starter bar						21			21	23.50	
	1920	Stairway inside handrail						53			53	58.50	
	1930	Stairway outside handrail						73			73	80.50	
	1940	Walk-thru frame guardrail						28			28	31	
	2000	Steel tubular, regular, rent/mo.											
	2100	Frames 3' high 5' wide					Ea.	3.75			3.75	4.13	
	2150	5' high 5' wide						3.75			3.75	4.13	
	2200	6'-4" high 5' wide						3.75			3.75	4.13	
	2250	7'-6" high 6' wide						7			7	7.70	
	2500	Accessories, cross braces						.60			.60	.66	
	2550	Guardrail post						1			1	1.10	
	2600	Guardrail 7' section						.75			.75	.83	
	2650	Screw jacks & plates						1.50			1.50	1.65	
	2700	Sidearm brackets						1.50			1.50	1.65	
	2750	8" casters						6			6	6.60	
	2800	Outrigger for rolling tower						3			3	3.30	
	2850	Plank 2" x 10" x 16'-0"						5			5	5.50	
	2900	Stairway section						10			10	11	
	2910	Stairway starter bar						.10			.10	.11	
	2920	Stairway inside handrail						5			5	5.50	
	2930	Stairway outside handrail						5			5	5.50	
	2940	Walk-thru frame guardrail						2			2	2.20	
	3000	Steel tubular, heavy duty shoring, rent/mo.											
	3250	5' high 2' & 4' wide					Ea.	5			5	5.50	
	3300	6' high 2' & 4' wide						5			5	5.50	
	3500	Accessories, cross braces						1			1	1.10	
	3600	U - head, 8" x 8"						1			1	1.10	
	3650	J - head, 4" x 8"						1			1	1.10	
	3700	Base plate, 8" x 8"						1			1	1.10	
	3750	Leveling jack						2			2	2.20	
255	0011	**SCAFFOLDING SPECIALTIES**											255
	1200	Sidewalk bridge, heavy duty steel posts & beams, including											
	1210	parapet protection & waterproofing											
	1220	8' to 10' wide, 2 posts		3 Carp	15	1.600	L.F.	42	43.50		85.50	119	
	1230	3 posts		"	10	2.400	"	63	65.50		128.50	180	
	1500	Sidewalk bridge using tubular steel											
	1512	scaffold frames, including planking		3 Carp	55	.436	L.F.	4.72	11.90		16.62	25	
	1600	For 2 uses per month, deduct from all above						50%					
	1700	For 1 use every 2 months, add to all above						100%					
	1900	Catwalks, 32" wide, no guardrails, 6' span, buy					Ea.	120			120	132	

015 | Construction Facilities & Temporary Controls

015 250 | Construction Aids

			DAILY	LABOR-		1999 BARE COSTS				TOTAL
		CREW	OUTPUT	HOURS	UNIT	MAT.	LABOR	EQUIP.	TOTAL	INCL O&P
255	2000	10' span, buy				Ea.	190			190	209
	2800	Hand winch-operated masons									
	2810	scaffolding, no plank moving required									
	2900	98' long, 10'-6" high, buy				Ea.	19,700			19,700	21,700
	3000	Rent per month					790			790	865
	3100	28'-6" high, buy					25,700			25,700	28,200
	3200	Rent per month					1,025			1,025	1,125
	3400	196' long, 28'-6" high, buy					49,700			49,700	54,500
	3500	Rent per month					2,000			2,000	2,175
	3600	64'-6" high, buy					73,000			73,000	80,000
	3700	Rent per month					2,900			2,900	3,200
	3720	Putlog, standard, 8' span, with hangers, buy					61			61	67
	3730	Rent per month					10			10	11
	3750	12' span, buy					92			92	101
	3755	Rent per month					15			15	16.50
	3760	Trussed type, 16' span, buy					210			210	231
	3770	Rent per month					20			20	22
	3790	22' span, buy					252			252	277
	3795	Rent per month					30			30	33
	4000	7 step					405			405	450
	4100	Rolling towers, buy, 5' wide, 7' long, 10' high					1,150			1,150	1,250
	4200	For 5' high added sections, to buy, add					188			188	207
	4300	Complete incl. wheels, railings, outriggers,									
	4350	21' high, to buy				Ea.	1,925			1,925	2,125
	4400	21' high, rent per month				"	138			138	152
256	0010	**SWING STAGING**, 500 lb cap., 2' wide to 24' long, hand operated hoist									
	0020	steel cable type, with 60' cables, buy				Ea.	3,650			3,650	4,000
	0030	Rent per month				"	450			450	495
	0600	Lightweight (not for masons) 24' long for 150' height.									
	0610	manual type, buy				Ea.	3,900			3,900	4,300
	0620	Rent per month					520			520	575
	0700	Powered, electric or air, to 150' high, buy					13,500			13,500	14,800
	0710	Rent per month					840			840	925
	0780	To 300' high, buy					14,300			14,300	15,700
	0800	Rent per month					910			910	1,000
	1000	Bosun's chair or work basket 3' x 3.5', to 300' high, electric, buy					7,250			7,250	7,975
	1010	Rent per month					450			450	495
	2200	Move swing staging (setup and remove)	E-4	2	16	Move		500	41	541	990
257	0010	**PUMP STAGING**, aluminum	R015-200								
	0200	24' long pole section, buy				Ea.	335			335	365
	0300	18' long pole section, buy					258			258	284
	0400	12' long pole section, buy					174			174	192
	0500	6' long pole section, buy					92			92	101
	0600	6' long splice joint section, buy					68			68	75
	0700	Pump jack					111			111	123
	0900	Foldable brace					48.50			48.50	53
	1000	Workbench/back safety rail support					59			59	64.50
	1100	Scaffolding planks/workbench, 14" wide x 24' long					545			545	600
	1200	Plank end safety rail					183			183	202
	1250	Safety net, 22' long					267			267	294
	1300	System in place, 50' working height, per use based on 50 uses	2 Carp	84.80	.189	C.S.F.	4.95	5.15		10.10	14.05
	1400	100 uses		84.80	.189		2.48	5.15		7.63	11.30
	1500	150 uses		84.80	.189		1.66	5.15		6.81	10.40

015 | Construction Facilities & Temporary Controls

015 300 | Barriers & Enclosures

		Description	CREW	DAILY OUTPUT	LABOR-HOURS	UNIT	MAT.	LABOR	EQUIP.	TOTAL	TOTAL INCL O&P	
302	0010	**BARRICADES** 5' high, 3 rail @ 2" x 8", fixed	2 Carp	30	.533	L.F.	10.80	14.55		25.35	36.50	302
	0150	Movable	"	20	.800	"	10.80	22		32.80	48.50	
	0300	Stock units, 6' high, 8' wide, plain, buy				Ea.	430			430	475	
	0350	With reflective tape, buy				"	525			525	580	
	0400	Break-a-way 3" PVC pipe barricade										
	0410	with 3 ea. 1' x 4' reflectorized panels, buy				Ea.	305			305	335	
	0500	Plywood with steel legs, 32" wide					70			70	77	
	0600	Telescoping Christmas tree, 9' high, 5 flags, buy					121			121	133	
	0800	Traffic cones, PVC, 18" high					8.70			8.70	9.55	
	0850	28" high					12.35			12.35	13.55	
	0900	Barrels, 55 gal., with flasher	1 Clab	96	.083		52	1.79		53.79	60	
	1000	Guardrail, wooden, 3' high, 1" x 6", on 2" x 4" posts	2 Carp	200	.080	L.F.	.99	2.18		3.17	4.75	
	1100	2" x 6", on 4" x 4" posts	"	165	.097		1.79	2.65		4.44	6.40	
	1200	Portable metal with base pads, buy					15			15	16.50	
	1250	Typical installation, assume 10 reuses	2 Carp	600	.027		1.58	.73		2.31	2.96	
304	0010	**FENCING** Chain link, 11 ga, 5' high	2 Clab	100	.160	L.F.	4.04	3.43		7.47	10.20	304
	0100	6' high		75	.213		3.37	4.58		7.95	11.35	
	0200	Rented chain link, 6' high, to 500' (up to 12 mo.)		100	.160		2.19	3.43		5.62	8.15	
	0250	Over 1000' (up to 12 mo.)		110	.145		1.59	3.12		4.71	6.95	
	0350	Plywood, painted, 2" x 4" frame, 4' high	A-4	135	.178		4.06	4.71		8.77	12.25	
	0400	4" x 4" frame, 8' high	"	110	.218		7.05	5.80		12.85	17.35	
	0500	Wire mesh on 4" x 4" posts, 4' high	2 Carp	100	.160		5.55	4.37		9.92	13.45	
	0550	8' high	"	80	.200		8.35	5.45		13.80	18.35	
306	0010	**WINTER PROTECTION** Reinforced plastic on wood										306
	0100	framing to close openings	2 Clab	750	.021	S.F.	.35	.46		.81	1.16	
	0200	Tarpaulins hung over scaffolding, 8 uses, not incl. scaffolding		1,500	.011		.16	.23		.39	.56	
	0250	Tarpaulin polyester reinf. w/ integral fastening system 11 mils thick		1,600	.010		.73	.21		.94	1.16	
	0300	Prefab fiberglass panels, steel frame, 8 uses		1,200	.013		.70	.29		.99	1.25	

015 400 | Security

		Description	CREW	DAILY OUTPUT	LABOR-HOURS	UNIT	MAT.	LABOR	EQUIP.	TOTAL	TOTAL INCL O&P	
480	0010	**WATCHMAN** Service, monthly basis, uniformed person, minimum				Hr.					7.80	480
	0100	Maximum									14.15	
	0200	Person and command dog, minimum									10.30	
	0300	Maximum									15.30	
	0500	Sentry dog, leased, with job patrol (yard dog), 1 dog				Week					195	
	0600	2 dogs				"					275	
	0800	Purchase, trained sentry dog, minimum				Ea.					800	
	0900	Maximum				"					2,000	

015 500 | Access Roads

		Description	CREW	DAILY OUTPUT	LABOR-HOURS	UNIT	MAT.	LABOR	EQUIP.	TOTAL	TOTAL INCL O&P	
552	0010	**ROADS AND SIDEWALKS** Temporary										552
	2200	Sidewalks, 2" x 12" planks, 2 uses	1 Carp	350	.023	S.F.	.55	.62		1.17	1.65	
	2300	Exterior plywood, 2 uses, 1/2" thick		750	.011		.30	.29		.59	.82	
	2400	5/8" thick		650	.012		.35	.34		.69	.95	
	2500	3/4" thick		600	.013		.42	.36		.78	1.07	

015 600 | Temporary Controls

		Description	CREW	DAILY OUTPUT	LABOR-HOURS	UNIT	MAT.	LABOR	EQUIP.	TOTAL	TOTAL INCL O&P	
602	0010	**TARPAULINS** Cotton duck, 10 oz. to 13.13 oz. per S.Y., minimum				S.F.	.38			.38	.42	602
	0050	Maximum					.55			.55	.61	
	0100	Polyvinyl coated nylon, 14 oz. to 18 oz., minimum					.45			.45	.50	
	0150	Maximum					.65			.65	.71	
	0200	Reinforced polyethylene 3 mils thick, white					.10			.10	.11	
	0300	4 mils thick, white, clear or black					.12			.12	.13	

015 | Construction Facilities & Temporary Controls

015 600 | Temporary Controls

		CREW	DAILY OUTPUT	LABOR-HOURS	UNIT	1999 BARE COSTS				TOTAL INCL O&P	
						MAT.	LABOR	EQUIP.	TOTAL		
602	0400 5.5 mils thick, clear				S.F.	.09			.09	.10	602
	0500 White, fire retardant					.16			.16	.18	
	0600 7.5 mils, oil resistant, fire retardant					.17			.17	.19	
	0700 8.5 mils, black					.22			.22	.24	
	0720 Steel reinforced polyethylene, 4 mils thick					.50			.50	.55	
	0730 Polyester reinforced w/ integral fastening system 11 mils thick					1			1	1.10	
	0740 Mylar polyester, non-reinforced, 7 mils thick				↓	1.10			1.10	1.21	

015 800 | Project Signs

| 804 | 0010 **SIGNS** Hi-intensity reflectorized, no posts, buy | | | | S.F. | 12.05 | | | 12.05 | 13.25 | 804 |

015 900 | Field Offices & Sheds

904	0010 **OFFICE** Trailer, furnished, no hookups, 20' x 8', buy	2 Skwk	1	16	Ea.	5,075	450		5,525	6,325	904
	0250 Rent per month					134			134	148	
	0300 32' x 8', buy	2 Skwk	.70	22.857		7,825	640		8,465	9,700	
	0350 Rent per month					158			158	174	
	0400 50' x 10', buy	2 Skwk	.60	26.667		13,400	750		14,150	16,000	
	0450 Rent per month					273			273	300	
	0500 50' x 12', buy	2 Skwk	.50	32		15,800	900		16,700	18,900	
	0550 Rent per month					315			315	345	
	0700 For air conditioning, rent per month, add				↓	35.50			35.50	39	
	0800 For delivery, add per mile				Mile	1.50			1.50	1.65	
	1200 Storage boxes, 20' x 8', buy	2 Skwk	1.80	8.889	Ea.	3,200	249		3,449	3,950	
	1250 Rent per month					66.50			66.50	73.50	
	1300 40' x 8', buy	2 Skwk	1.40	11.429		3,325	320		3,645	4,200	
	1350 Rent per month					85			85	93.50	

016 | Material & Equipment

016 400 | Equipment Rental

			UNIT	HOURLY OPER. COST	RENT PER DAY	RENT PER WEEK	RENT PER MONTH	CREW EQUIPMENT COST/DAY
406	0010	**CONCRETE EQUIPMENT RENTAL**						
	0100	without operators						
	0200	Bucket, concrete lightweight, 1/2 C.Y.	Ea.	.14	25	75	225	16.10
	0600	Cart, concrete, self propelled, operator walking, 10 C.F.		1.24	66.50	200	600	49.90
	0700	Operator riding, 18 C.F.		2.42	107	320	960	83.35
	0800	Conveyer for concrete, portable, gas, 16" wide, 26' long		3.61	167	500	1,500	128.90
	0900	46' long		3.71	227	680	2,050	165.70
	1000	56' long		3.86	250	750	2,250	180.90
	1150	11 H.P., 8" to 18" cores		.67	93.50	280	840	61.35
	1200	Finisher, concrete floor, gas, riding trowel, 48" diameter		2.68	100	300	900	81.45
	1300	Gas, manual, 3 blade, 36" trowel		2.27	56.50	170	510	52.15
	1400	4 blade, 48" trowel		2.37	50	150	450	48.95
	1500	Float, hand-operated (Bull float) 48" wide		.10	6.65	20	60	4.80
	1600	Grinder, concrete and terrazzo, electric, floor		1.34	58.50	175	525	45.70
	1700	Wall grinder		.62	35	105	315	25.95
	1800	Mixer, powered, mortar and concrete, gas, 6 C.F., 18 H.P.		.93	58.50	175	525	42.45
	1900	10 C.F., 25 H.P.		1.34	50	150	450	40.70
	2120	Pump, concrete, truck mounted, 4" line, 80' boom		11.95	915	2,750	8,250	645.60
	2140	5" line, 110' boom		13.29	1,100	3,275	9,825	761.30
	2160	Mud jack, 50 C.F. per hr.		3.17	70	210	630	67.35
	2180	225 C.F. per hr.		6.28	310	925	2,775	235.25
	2600	Saw, concrete, manual, gas, 18 H.P.		2.83	76.50	230	690	68.65
	2650	Self-propelled, gas, 30 H.P.		5.58	110	330	990	110.65
	2700	Vibrators, concrete, electric, 60 cycle, 2 H.P.		.31	23.50	70	210	16.50
	2800	3 H.P.		.36	33.50	100	300	22.90
	2900	Gas engine, 5 H.P.		.67	33.50	100	300	25.35
	3000	8 H.P.		.93	50	150	450	37.45
408	0010	**EARTHWORK EQUIPMENT RENTAL** Without operators						
	0055	Fence post auger, truck mounted	Ea.	10	465	1,400	4,200	360
	0100	Backhoe, diesel hydraulic, crawler mounted, 1/2 C.Y. cap.		11.43	410	1,225	3,675	336.45
	0120	5/8 C.Y. capacity		15.53	450	1,350	4,050	394.25
	0140	3/4 C.Y. capacity		17.39	515	1,550	4,650	449.10
	0150	1 C.Y. capacity		22.20	615	1,850	5,550	547.60
	0200	1-1/2 C.Y. capacity		26.59	835	2,500	7,500	712.70
	0300	2 C.Y. capacity		42.85	1,125	3,400	10,200	1,023
	0320	2-1/2 C.Y. capacity		59.38	2,025	6,100	18,300	1,695
	0340	3-1/2 C.Y. capacity		79.44	2,525	7,600	22,800	2,156
	0341	Attachments						
	0342	Bucket thumbs		.46	293	880	2,650	179.70
	0345	Grapples		.31	300	900	2,700	182.50
	0350	Gradall type, truck mounted, 3 ton @ 15' radius, 5/8 C.Y.		26.47	710	2,125	6,375	636.75
	0370	1 C.Y. capacity		28.22	965	2,900	8,700	805.75
	0400	Backhoe-loader, wheel type, 40 to 45 H.P., 5/8 C.Y. capacity		7.31	237	710	2,125	200.50
	0450	45 H.P. to 60 H.P., 3/4 C.Y. capacity		8.60	250	750	2,250	218.80
	0470	112 H.P.,1-3/4 C.Y. loader, 1/2 C.Y. backhoe		15.55	385	1,150	3,450	354.40
	0480	Attachments						
	0482	Compactor, 20,000 lb		1.29	188	565	1,700	123.30
	0485	Hydraulic hammer, 750 ft-lbs		.41	305	915	2,750	186.30
	0486	Hydraulic hammer, 1000 ft-lbs		.46	345	1,030	3,100	209.70
	1200	Compactor, roller, 2 drum, 2000 lb., operator walking		1.88	130	390	1,175	93.05
	1250	Rammer compactor, gas, 1000 lb. blow		.57	45	135	405	31.55
	1300	Vibratory plate, gas, 13" plate, 1000 lb. blow		.71	41.50	125	375	30.70
	1350	24" plate, 5000 lb. blow		1.75	63.50	190	570	52
	1860	Grader, self-propelled, 25,000 lb.		14.83	580	1,740	5,225	466.65
	1910	30,000 lb.		17.82	720	2,165	6,500	575.55
	1920	40,000 lb.		20.50	860	2,575	7,725	679
	1930	55,000 lb.		33.48	1,300	3,865	11,600	1,041

GENERAL REQUIREMENTS 1

016 | Material & Equipment

016 400 | Equipment Rental

			UNIT	HOURLY OPER. COST	RENT PER DAY	RENT PER WEEK	RENT PER MONTH	CREW EQUIPMENT COST/DAY	
408	1950	Hammer, pavement demo., hyd., gas, self-prop., 1000 to 1250 lb.	Ea.	18.59	410	1,225	3,675	393.70	408
	2000	Diesel 1300 to 1500 lb.		9.01	455	1,360	4,075	344.10	
	2050	Pile driving hammer, steam or air, 4150 ft.-lb. @ 225 BPM		1.80	288	865	2,600	187.40	
	2100	8750 ft.-lb. @ 145 BPM		3.24	410	1,235	3,700	272.90	
	2150	15,000 ft.-lb. @ 60 BPM		4.22	480	1,440	4,325	321.75	
	2200	24,450 ft.-lb. @ 111 BPM		4.65	585	1,760	5,275	389.20	
	2250	Leads, 15,000 ft.-lb. hammers	L.F.	.02	2.67	8	24	1.75	
	2300	24,450 ft.-lb. hammers and heavier	"	.04	3	9	27	2.10	
	2350	Diesel type hammer, 22,400 ft.-lb.	Ea.	6.17	480	1,440	4,325	337.35	
	2400	41,300 ft.-lb.		9.57	755	2,265	6,800	529.55	
	2450	141,000 ft.-lb.		19.68	1,450	4,325	13,000	1,022	
	2500	Vib. elec. hammer/extractor, 200 KW diesel generator, 34 H.P.		9.33	610	1,835	5,500	441.65	
	2550	80 H.P.		18.23	925	2,780	8,350	701.85	
	2600	150 H.P.		31.36	1,625	4,840	14,500	1,219	
	2700	Extractor, steam or air, 700 ft.-lb.		1.44	172	515	1,550	114.50	
	2750	1000 ft.-lb.		1.85	240	720	2,150	158.80	
	3000	Roller, tandem, gas, 3 to 5 ton		6.23	172	515	1,550	152.85	
	3050	Diesel, 8 to 12 ton		9.01	288	865	2,600	245.10	
	3100	Towed type, vibratory, gas 12.5 H.P., 2 ton		3.86	137	410	1,225	112.90	
	3150	Sheepsfoot, double 60" x 60"		4.74	145	435	1,300	124.90	
	3200	Pneumatic tire diesel roller, 12 ton		8.65	292	875	2,625	244.20	
	3250	21 to 25 ton		15.97	345	1,030	3,100	333.75	
	3300	Sheepsfoot roller, self-propelled, 4 wheel, 130 H.P.		20.96	650	1,955	5,875	558.70	
	3320	300 H.P.		26.68	765	2,300	6,900	673.45	
	3350	Vibratory steel drum & pneumatic tire, diesel, 18,000 lb.		11.48	435	1,300	3,900	351.85	
	3400	29,000 lb.		12.72	535	1,600	4,800	421.75	
	3450	Scrapers, towed type, 9 to 12 C.Y. capacity		3.19	86.50	260	780	77.50	
	3500	12 to 17 C.Y. capacity		5.93	258	775	2,325	202.45	
	3550	Scrapers, self-propelled, 4 x 4 drive, 2 engine, 14 C.Y. capacity		60.87	1,875	5,650	17,000	1,617	
	3600	2 engine, 24 C.Y. capacity		73.95	2,200	6,600	19,800	1,912	
	3650	Self-loading, 11 C.Y. capacity		27.32	785	2,350	7,050	688.55	
	3700	22 C.Y. capacity		33.07	1,200	3,600	10,800	984.55	
	3710	Screening plant 110 hp. w / 5' x 10'screen		15.97	435	1,300	3,900	387.75	
	3720	5' x 16' screen		17.61	515	1,550	4,650	450.90	
	3850	Shovels, see Cranes division 016-460							
	3860	Shovel/backhoe bucket, 1/2 C.Y.	Ea.	1.13	76.50	230	690	55.05	
	3870	3/4 C.Y.		3.19	128	385	1,150	102.50	
	3880	1 C.Y.		3.50	172	515	1,550	131	
	3890	1-1/2 C.Y.		4.21	210	630	1,900	159.70	
	3910	3 C.Y.		7.52	400	1,200	3,600	300.15	
	4110	Tractor, crawler, with bulldozer, torque converter, diesel 75 H.P.		10.97	365	1,100	3,300	307.75	
	4150	105 H.P.		14.68	500	1,500	4,500	417.45	
	4200	140 H.P.		17	615	1,850	5,550	506	
	4260	200 H.P.		29.87	1,000	3,000	9,000	838.95	
	4310	300 H.P.		38.83	1,375	4,100	12,300	1,131	
	4360	410 H.P.		47.48	1,675	5,000	15,000	1,380	
	4380	700 H.P.		95.58	3,325	10,000	30,000	2,765	
	4400	Loader, crawler, torque conv., diesel, 1-1/2 C.Y., 80 H.P.		12.51	415	1,250	3,750	350.10	
	4450	1-1/2 to 1-3/4 C.Y., 95 H.P.		14.96	465	1,400	4,200	399.70	
	4510	1-3/4 to 2-1/4 C.Y., 130 H.P.		18.80	600	1,800	5,400	510.40	
	4530	2-1/2 to 3-1/4 C.Y., 190 H.P.		30.64	1,025	3,100	9,300	865.10	
	4560	3-1/2 to 5 C.Y., 275 H.P.		42.81	1,325	4,000	12,000	1,142	
	4610	Tractor loader, wheel, torque conv., 4 x 4, 1 to 1-1/4 C.Y., 65 H.P.		9.33	283	850	2,550	244.65	
	4620	1-1/2 to 1-3/4 C.Y., 80 H.P.		11.89	375	1,125	3,375	320.10	
	4650	1-3/4 to 2 C.Y., 100 H.P.		12.47	405	1,215	3,650	342.75	
	4710	2-1/2 to 3-1/2 C.Y., 130 H.P.		18.81	500	1,500	4,500	450.50	
	4730	3 to 4-1/2 C.Y., 170 H.P.		20.86	685	2,050	6,150	576.90	
	4760	5-1/4 to 5-3/4 C.Y., 270 H.P.		38.31	1,025	3,100	9,300	926.50	

Important: See the Reference Section for critical supporting data - Reference Nos., Crews, & City Cost Indexes

016 | Material & Equipment

016 400 | Equipment Rental

		UNIT	HOURLY OPER. COST	RENT PER DAY	RENT PER WEEK	RENT PER MONTH	CREW EQUIPMENT COST/DAY
4810	7 to 8 C.Y., 375 H.P.	Ea.	56.88	1,375	4,125	12,400	1,280
4870	12-1/2 C.Y., 690 H.P.		115.60	2,400	7,200	21,600	2,365
4880	Wheeled, skid steer, 10 C.F., 30 H.P. gas		4.53	125	375	1,125	111.25
4890	1 C.Y., 78 H.P., diesel		6.28	300	900	2,700	230.25
4891	Attachments for all skid steer loaders						
4892	Auger	Ea.	.12	83.50	250	750	50.95
4893	Backhoe		.15	110	330	990	67.20
4894	Broom		.16	107	320	960	65.30
4895	Forks		.08	38.50	115	345	23.65
4896	Grapple		.12	86.50	260	780	52.95
4897	Concrete hammer		.25	180	540	1,625	110
4898	Tree spade		.36	128	385	1,150	79.90
4899	Trencher		.41	240	720	2,150	147.30
4900	Trencher, chain, boom type, gas, operator walking, 12 H.P.		2.16	133	400	1,200	97.30
4910	Operator riding, 40 H.P.		6.36	267	800	2,400	210.90
5100	Diesel, 6' deep, 20" wide		15.65	735	2,200	6,600	565.20
5150	Ladder type, diesel, 5' deep, 8" wide		9.41	375	1,125	3,375	300.30
5200	Diesel, 8' deep, 16" wide		17.61	660	1,975	5,925	535.90
5250	Truck, dump, tandem, 12 ton payload		17.41	375	1,125	3,375	364.30
5300	Three axle dump, 16 ton payload		20.28	465	1,400	4,200	442.25
5450	Flatbed, single axle, 1-1/2 ton rating		10.87	142	425	1,275	171.95
5500	3 ton rating		11.43	147	440	1,325	179.45
5550	Off highway rear dump, 25 ton capacity		20.50	890	2,675	8,025	699
5600	35 ton capacity		32.27	1,300	3,900	11,700	1,038
0010	**GENERAL EQUIPMENT RENTAL** Without operators						
0150	Aerial lift, scissor type, to 15' high, 1000 lb. cap., electric	Ea.	1.18	85	255	765	60.45
0160	To 25' high, 2000 lb. capacity		1.80	128	385	1,150	91.40
0170	Telescoping boom to 40' high, 750 lb. capacity, gas		6.42	385	1,150	3,450	281.35
0180	1000 lb. capacity		7.98	435	1,300	3,900	323.85
0190	To 60' high, 750 lb. capacity		8.47	525	1,575	4,725	382.75
0195	Air compressor, portable, 6.5 CFM, electric		.12	33.50	100	300	20.95
0196	gasoline		.13	41.50	125	375	26.05
0200	Air compressor, portable, gas engine, 60 C.F.M.		5.41	55	165	495	76.30
0300	160 C.F.M.		6.80	71.50	215	645	97.40
0400	Diesel engine, rotary screw, 250 C.F.M.		6.49	122	365	1,100	124.90
0500	365 C.F.M.		9.29	167	500	1,500	174.30
0550	375 to 450 C.F.M. Compressor		9.80	233	700	2,100	218.40
0600	600 C.F.M.		15.99	242	725	2,175	272.90
0700	750 C.F.M.		17.57	247	740	2,225	288.55
0800	For silenced models, small sizes, add		3%	5%	5%	5%	
0900	Large sizes, add		5%	7%	7%	7%	
0920	Air tools and accessories						
0930	Breaker, pavement, 60 lb.	Ea.	.19	30	90	270	19.50
0940	80 lb.		.21	35	105	315	22.70
0950	Drills, hand (jackhammer) 65 lb.		.23	25	75	225	16.85
0960	Track or wagon, swing boom, 4" drifter		10.57	380	1,135	3,400	311.55
0980	Dust control per drill		2.11	11.65	35	105	23.90
0990	Hammer, chipping, 12 lb.		.12	20	60	180	12.95
1000	Hose, air with couplings, 50' long, 3/4" diameter		.15	5	15	45	4.20
1100	1" diameter		.15	6.65	20	60	5.20
1525	Pneumatic nailer w/accessories		.12	31.50	95	285	19.95
1550	Spade, 25 lb.		.08	8.35	25	75	5.65
1560	Tamper, single, 35 lb.		.10	23.50	70	210	14.80
1570	Triple, 140 lb.		1.80	41.50	125	375	39.40
1580	Wrenches, impact, air powered, up to 3/4" bolt		.25	21.50	65	195	15
1590	Up to 1-1/4" bolt		.35	43.50	130	390	28.80
1700	Carts, brick, hand powered, 1000 lb. capacity		1.11	21.50	65	195	21.90
1800	Gas engine, 1500 lb., 7-1/2' lift		1.65	95	285	855	70.20

016 | Material & Equipment

016 400 | Equipment Rental

			UNIT	HOURLY OPER. COST	RENT PER DAY	RENT PER WEEK	RENT PER MONTH	CREW EQUIPMENT COST/DAY	
420	1850	Drill, rotary hammer, electric, 1-1/2" diameter	Ea.	.15	23.50	70	210	15.20	420
	1860	Carbide bit for above			5.65	17	51	3.40	
	2020	Forklift, wheeled, for brick, 18', 3000 lb., 2 wheel drive, gas		9.28	167	500	1,500	174.25	
	2040	28', 4000 lb., 4 wheel drive, diesel		6.39	200	600	1,800	171.10	
	2100	Generator, electric, gas engine, 1.5 KW to 3 KW		1.13	38.50	115	345	32.05	
	2200	5 KW		1.49	56.50	170	510	45.90	
	2300	10 KW		2.39	137	410	1,225	101.10	
	2400	25 KW		6.81	152	455	1,375	145.50	
	2500	Diesel engine, 20 KW		4.35	110	330	990	100.80	
	2600	50 KW		6.86	123	370	1,100	128.90	
	2700	100 KW		11.34	188	565	1,700	203.70	
	2800	250 KW		28.99	325	980	2,950	427.90	
	2850	Hammer, hydraulic, for mounting on boom, to 500 ft.-lb.		.98	128	385	1,150	84.85	
	2860	500 to 1200 ft.-lb.		2.52	267	800	2,400	180.15	
	2900	Heaters, space, oil or electric, 50 MBH		.12	26.50	80	240	16.95	
	3000	100 MBH		.12	31.50	95	285	19.95	
	3100	300 MBH		.12	50	150	450	30.95	
	3150	500 MBH		.15	66.50	200	600	41.20	
	3200	Hose, water, suction with coupling, 20' long, 2" diameter		.06	10	30	90	6.50	
	3210	3" diameter		.06	15	45	135	9.50	
	3250	Discharge hose with coupling, 50' long, 2" diameter		.05	6.65	20	60	4.40	
	3260	3" diameter		.05	8.35	25	75	5.40	
	3300	Ladders, extension type, 16' to 36' long			15	45	135	9	
	3400	40' to 60' long			31.50	95	285	19	
	3410	Level, laser type, for pipe laying, self leveling			102	305	915	61	
	3430	Manual leveling			78.50	235	705	47	
	3440	Rotary beacon with rod and sensor			103	310	930	62	
	3460	Builders level with tripod and rod			30	90	270	18	
	3500	Light towers, towable, with diesel generator, 2000 watt		1.55	117	350	1,050	82.40	
	3600	4000 watt		1.97	137	410	1,225	97.75	
	3700	Mixer, powered, plaster and mortar, 6 C.F., 7 H.P.		.82	53.50	160	480	38.55	
	3800	10 C.F., 9 H.P.		1.22	76.50	230	690	55.75	
	3850	Nailer, pneumatic		.08	23.50	70	210	14.65	
	3900	Paint sprayers complete, 8 CFM		.08	41.50	125	375	25.65	
	4000	17 CFM		.08	60	180	540	36.65	
	4020	Pavers, bituminous, rubber tires, 8' wide, 52 H.P., gas		14.94	575	1,725	5,175	464.50	
	4030	8' wide, 64 H.P., diesel		15.45	1,000	3,025	9,075	728.60	
	4050	Crawler, 10' wide, 78 H.P., gas		22.20	1,400	4,200	12,600	1,018	
	4060	10' wide, 87 H.P., diesel		22.80	1,075	3,200	9,600	822.40	
	4070	Concrete paver, 12' to 24' wide, 250 H.P.		24.27	1,525	4,550	13,700	1,104	
	4080	Placer-spreader-trimmer, 24' wide, 300 H.P.		32.02	1,775	5,325	16,000	1,321	
	4100	Pump, centrifugal gas pump, 1-1/2", 4 MGPH		.46	31.50	95	285	22.70	
	4500	Submersible electric pump, 1-1/4", 55 GPM		.36	36.50	110	330	24.90	
	4600	1-1/2", 83 GPM		.39	40	120	360	27.10	
	4700	2", 120 GPM		.41	45	135	405	30.30	
	4800	3", 300 GPM		.72	55	165	495	38.75	
	4900	4", 560 GPM		1.18	68.50	205	615	50.45	
	5000	6", 1590 GPM		5.36	207	620	1,850	166.90	
	5100	Diaphragm pump, gas, single, 1-1/2" diameter		.49	25	75	225	18.90	
	5500	Trash pump, self-priming, gas, 2" diameter		1.24	40	120	360	33.90	
	5700	Salamanders, L.P. gas fired, 100,000 B.T.U.		.70	21.50	65	195	18.60	
	5720	Sandblaster, portable, open top, 3 C.F. capacity		.19	50	150	450	31.50	
	5740	Accessories for above		.06	16.65	50	150	10.50	
	5750	Sander, floor		.12	38.50	115	345	23.95	
	5760	Edger		.10	26.50	80	240	16.80	
	5800	Saw, chain, gas engine, 18" long		.54	38.50	115	345	27.30	
	5900	36" long		1.13	73.50	220	660	53.05	
	6000	Masonry, table mounted, 14" diameter, 5 H.P.		1.82	50	150	450	44.55	

Important: See the Reference Section for critical supporting data - Reference Nos., Crews, & City Cost Indexes

016 | Material & Equipment

016 400 | Equipment Rental

			UNIT	HOURLY OPER. COST	RENT PER DAY	RENT PER WEEK	RENT PER MONTH	CREW EQUIPMENT COST/DAY	
420	6050	Saw, portable cut-off, 8 H.P.	Ea.	.82	58.50	175	525	41.55	420
	6100	Circular, hand held, electric, 7-1/4" diameter		.16	20	60	180	13.30	
	6200	12" diameter		.27	36.50	110	330	24.15	
	6300	Steam cleaner, 100 gallons per hour		.43	51.50	155	465	34.45	
	6310	200 gallons per hour		.70	58.50	175	525	40.60	
	6340	Tar Kettle/Pot, 400 gallon		.49	70	210	630	45.90	
	6350	Torch, cutting, acetylene-oxygen, 150' hose		7.53	25	75	225	75.25	
	6360	Hourly operating cost includes tips and gas		7.62				60.95	
	6410	Toilet, portable chemical			15	45	135	9	
	6420	Recycle flush type			18.35	55	165	11	
	6430	Toilet, fresh water flush, garden hose,			21.50	65	195	13	
	6440	Hoisted, non-flush, for high rise			18.35	55	165	11	
	6450	Toilet, trailers, minimum			33.50	100	300	20	
	6460	Maximum			100	300	900	60	
	7020	Transit with tripod			33.50	100	300	20	
	7030	Trench box, 3000 lbs. 6'x8'		.80	100	300	900	66.40	
	7040	7200 lbs. 6'x20'		1.46	172	515	1,550	114.70	
	7050	8000 lbs., 8' x 16'		1.61	182	545	1,625	121.90	
	7060	9500 lbs., 8'x20'		1.82	188	565	1,700	127.55	
	7065	11,000 lbs., 8'x24'		1.87	242	725	2,175	159.95	
	7070	12,000 lbs., 10' x 20'		1.98	250	750	2,250	165.85	
	7100	Truck, pickup, 3/4 ton, 2 wheel drive		10.62	73.50	220	660	128.95	
	7200	4 wheel drive		12.06	81.50	245	735	145.50	
	7620	Vacuum truck, hazardous material, 2500 gallon		13.89	300	900	2,700	291.10	
	7625	5,000 gallon		15.02	335	1,000	3,000	320.15	
	7650	Vacuum, H.E.P.A., 16 gal., wet/dry		.93	51.50	155	465	38.45	
	7655	55 gal, wet/dry		.80	51.50	155	465	37.40	
	7660	Water tank, portable			20	60	180	12	
	7690	Large production vacuum loader, 3150 CFM		11.86	715	2,150	6,450	524.90	
	7700	Welder, electric, 200 amp		.81	31.50	95	285	25.50	
	7800	300 amp		1.09	68.50	205	615	49.70	
	8100	Wheelbarrow, any size			8.35	25	75	5	
	8200	Wrecking ball, 4000 lb.		.41	61.50	185	555	40.30	
460	0010	**LIFTING AND HOISTING EQUIPMENT RENTAL** R022-250							460
	0100	without operators							
	0120	Aerial lift truck R016-410	Ea.	16.19	735	2,200	6,600	569.50	
	0140	Boom truck		15.35	220	660	1,975	254.80	
	0300	101' jib, 10,250 lb. capacity, 270 FPM		35.34	1,550	4,650	14,000	1,213	
	0600	Crawler, cable, 1/2 C.Y., 15 tons at 12' radius		19	535	1,600	4,800	472	
	0900	Crawler, cable, 1-1/2 C.Y., 40 tons at 12' radius		30.54	765	2,300	6,900	704.30	
	1000	2 C.Y., 50 tons at 12' radius		35.59	935	2,800	8,400	844.70	
	1100	3 C.Y., 75 tons at 12' radius		43.66	965	2,900	8,700	929.30	
	1200	100 ton capacity, standard boom		41.43	1,325	4,000	12,000	1,131	
	1300	165 ton capacity, standard boom		64.77	2,175	6,500	19,500	1,818	
	1400	200 ton capacity, 150' boom		120.73	2,325	7,000	21,000	2,366	
	1500	450' boom		135.50	3,000	9,000	27,000	2,884	
	1600	Truck mounted, cable operated, 6 x 4, 20 tons at 10' radius		14.07	665	2,000	6,000	512.55	
	1700	25 tons at 10' radius		20.80	1,075	3,200	9,600	806.40	
	1900	40 tons at 12' radius		29.34	765	2,300	6,900	694.70	
	2000	8 x 4, 60 tons at 15' radius		44.87	900	2,700	8,100	898.95	
	2050	82 tons at 15' radius		45.56	1,625	4,900	14,700	1,344	
	2100	90 tons at 15' radius		48.95	1,025	3,100	9,300	1,012	
	2200	115 tons at 15' radius		51.15	1,875	5,600	16,800	1,529	
	2300	150 tons at 18' radius		76.61	1,575	4,700	14,100	1,553	
	2350	165 tons at 18' radius		77.65	2,200	6,600	19,800	1,941	
	2400	Truck mounted, hydraulic, 12 ton capacity		22.93	435	1,300	3,900	443.45	
	2500	25 ton capacity		23.67	600	1,800	5,400	549.35	

016 | Material & Equipment

016 400 | Equipment Rental

			UNIT	HOURLY OPER. COST	RENT PER DAY	RENT PER WEEK	RENT PER MONTH	CREW EQUIPMENT COST/DAY	
460	2550	33 ton capacity	Ea.	24.37	835	2,500	7,500	694.95	460
	2560	40 ton hydraulic truck crane		24.42	860	2,575	7,725	710.35	
	2600	55 ton capacity		34.14	865	2,600	7,800	793.10	
	2700	80 ton capacity		37.29	1,325	4,000	12,000	1,098	
	2800	Self-propelled, 4 x 4, with telescoping boom, 5 ton		10.18	315	950	2,850	271.45	
	2900	12-1/2 ton capacity		16.42	435	1,300	3,900	391.35	
	3000	15 ton capacity		18.20	485	1,450	4,350	435.60	
	3050	20 ton capacity		18.01	500	1,500	4,500	444.10	
	3100	25 ton capacity		20.99	635	1,900	5,700	547.90	
	3550	Helicopter, small, lift to 1250 lbs. maximum		257.50	2,425	7,250	21,800	3,510	
	3600	Hoists, chain type, overhead, manual, 3/4 ton		.06	6	18	54	4.10	
	3900	10 ton		.25	25	75	225	17	
	4000	Hoist and tower, 5000 lb. cap., portable electric, 40' high		4.03	172	515	1,550	135.25	
	4100	For each added 10' section, add			11.65	35	105	7	
	4200	Hoist and single tubular tower, 5000 lb. electric, 100' high		5.41	237	710	2,125	185.30	
	4300	For each added 6'-6" section, add		.73	20	60	180	17.85	
	4400	Hoist and double tubular tower, 5000 lb., 100' high		5.77	250	750	2,250	196.15	
	4500	For each added 6'-6" section, add		.06	16.65	50	150	10.50	
	4550	Hoist and tower, mast type, 6000 lb., 100' high		5.34	275	825	2,475	207.70	
	4570	For each added 10' section, add		.15	15	45	135	10.20	
	4600	Hoist and tower, personnel, electric, 2000 lb., 100' @ 125 FPM		10.04	685	2,050	6,150	490.30	
	4700	3000 lb., 100' @ 200 FPM		10.79	735	2,200	6,600	526.30	
	4800	3000 lb., 150' @ 300 FPM		11.47	790	2,370	7,100	565.75	
	4900	4000 lb., 100' @ 300 FPM		12.33	885	2,650	7,950	628.65	
	5000	6000 lb., 100' @ 275 FPM		12.93	925	2,775	8,325	658.45	
	5100	For added heights up to 500', add	L.F.		1.67	5	15	1	
	5200	Jacks, hydraulic, 20 ton	Ea.	.15	2.67	8	24	2.80	
	5500	100 ton	"	.19	20	60	180	13.50	
	6000	Jacks, hydraulic, climbing with 50' jackrods							
	6010	and control consoles, minimum 3 mo. rental							
	6100	30 ton capacity	Ea.	.06	100	300	900	60.50	
	6150	For each added 10' jackrod section, add			3	9	27	1.80	
	6300	50 ton capacity			158	475	1,425	95	
	6350	For each added 10' jackrod section, add			3.33	10	30	2	
	6500	125 ton capacity			415	1,250	3,750	250	
	6550	For each added 10' jackrod section, add			26.50	80	240	16	
	6600	Cable jack, 10 ton capacity with 200' cable			83.50	250	750	50	
	6650	For each added 50' of cable, add			8.35	25	75	5	

017 | Contract Closeout

		017 100	Final Cleaning	CREW	DAILY OUTPUT	LABOR-HOURS	UNIT	1999 BARE COSTS				TOTAL INCL O&P	
								MAT.	LABOR	EQUIP.	TOTAL		
104	0010		**CLEANING UP** After job completion, allow, minimum				Job					.30%	104
	0040		Maximum				"					1%	
	0052		Cleanup of floor area, continuous, per day	A-5	16	1.125	M.S.F.	1.65	24	2.69	28.34	45.50	
	0100		Final	"	11.50	1.565	"	2.63	33.50	3.74	39.87	63	

For information about Means Estimating Seminars, see yellow pages 11 and 12 in back of book

Division Notes

		CREW	DAILY OUTPUT	LABOR-HOURS	UNIT	1999 BARE COSTS				TOTAL INCL O&P
						MAT.	LABOR	EQUIP.	TOTAL	

Division 2
Site Work

Estimating Tips

020 Subsurface Investigation & Demolition

In preparing estimates on structures involving earthwork or foundations, all information concerning soil characteristics should be obtained. Look particularly for hazardous waste, evidence of prior dumping of debris, and previous stream beds.

- The costs shown for selective demolition do not include rubbish handling or disposal. These items should be estimated separately using Means data or other sources.
- Historic preservation often requires that the contractor remove materials from the existing structure, rehab them and replace them. The estimator must be aware of any related measures and precautions that must be taken when doing selective demolition, and cutting and patching. Requirements may include special handling and storage, as well as security.

021 Site Preparation & Excavation Support

- If possible visit the site and take an inventory of the type, quantity and size of the trees. Certain trees may have a landscape resale value or firewood value. Stump disposal can be very expensive, particularly if they cannot be buried at the site. Consider using a bulldozer in lieu of hand cutting trees.
- Estimators should visit the site to determine the need for haul road, access, storage of materials, and security considerations. When estimating for access roads on unstable soil, consider using a geotextile stabilization fabric. It can greatly reduce the quantity of crushed stone or gravel. Sites of limited size and access can cause cost overruns due to lost productivity. Theft and damage is another consideration if the location is isolated. A temporary fence or security guards may be required. Investigate the site thoroughly.

022 Earthwork

- Estimating the actual cost of performing earthwork requires careful consideration of the variables involved. This includes items such as type of soil, whether or not water will be encountered, dewatering, whether or not banks need bracing, disposal of excavated earth, length of haul to fill or spoil sites, etc. If the project has large quantities of cut or fill, consider raising or lowering the site to reduce costs while paying close attention to the effect on site drainage and utilities if doing this.
- If the project has large quantities of fill, creating a borrow pit on the site can significantly lower the costs. It is very important to consider what time of year the project is scheduled for completion. Bad weather can create large cost overruns from dewatering, site repair and lost productivity from cold weather.

025 Paving & Surfacing

- When estimating paving, keep in mind the project schedule. If an asphaltic paving project is in a colder climate and runs through to the spring, consider placing the base course in the autumn, then topping it in the spring just prior to completion. This could save considerable costs in spring repair. Keep in mind that prices for asphalt and concrete are generally higher in the cold seasons.

026 Piped Utilities
027 Sewerage & Drainage

- Never assume that the water, sewer and drainage lines will go in at the early stages of the project. Consider the site access needs before dividing the site in half with open trenches, loose pipe, and machinery obstructions. Always inspect the site to establish that the site drawings are complete. Check off all existing utilities on your drawing as you locate them. If you find any discrepancies, mark up the site plan for further research. Differing site conditions can be very costly if discovered later in the project.

029 Landscaping

- The timing of planting and guarantee specifications often dictate the costs for establishing tree and shrub growth and a stand of grass or ground cover. Establish the work performance schedule to coincide with the local planting season. Maintenance and growth guarantees can add from 20% to 100% to the total landscaping cost. The cost to replace trees and shrubs can be as high as 5% of the total cost depending on the planting zone, soil conditions and time of year.

Reference Numbers

Reference numbers are shown in bold squares at the beginning of some major classifications. These numbers refer to related items in the Reference Section. The reference information may be an estimating procedure, an alternate pricing method or technical information.

Note: Not all subdivisions listed here necessarily appear in this publication.

020 | Subsurface Investigation & Demolition

020 120 | Std Penetration Tests

			CREW	DAILY OUTPUT	LABOR-HOURS	UNIT	MAT.	LABOR	EQUIP.	TOTAL	TOTAL INCL O&P	
123	0010	**BORINGS** Initial field stake out and determination of elevations	A-6	1	16	Day		410		410	650	123
	0100	Drawings showing boring details				Total		170		170	245	
	0200	Report and recommendations from P.E.						375		375	540	
	0300	Mobilization and demobilization, minimum	B-55	4	6			129	160	289	390	
	0350	For over 100 miles, per added mile		450	.053	Mile		1.15	1.42	2.57	3.47	
	0600	Auger holes in earth, no samples, 2-1/2" diameter		78.60	.305	L.F.		6.60	8.15	14.75	19.85	
	0650	4" diameter		67.50	.356			7.65	9.45	17.10	23	
	0800	Cased borings in earth, with samples, 2-1/2" diameter		55.50	.432		12.50	9.30	11.50	33.30	42	
	0850	4" diameter		32.60	.736		20	15.85	19.60	55.45	70	
	1000	Drilling in rock, "BX" core, no sampling	B-56	34.90	.458			11.15	17.25	28.40	37	
	1050	With casing & sampling		31.70	.505		12.50	12.30	18.95	43.75	55	
	1200	"NX" core, no sampling		25.92	.617			15	23	38	50	
	1250	With casing and sampling		25	.640		16	15.55	24	55.55	69.50	
	1400	Drill rig and crew with truck mounted auger	B-55	1	24	Day		515	640	1,155	1,575	
	1450	With crawler type drill	B-56	1	16	"		390	600	990	1,300	
	1500	For inner city borings add, minimum									10%	
	1510	Maximum									20%	
125	0010	**DRILLING, CORE** Reinforced concrete slab, up to 6" thick slab										125
	0020	Including bit, layout and set up										
	0100	1" diameter core	B-89A	28	.571	Ea.	2.28	14.15	2.19	18.62	28.50	
	0150	Each added inch thick, add		300	.053		.40	1.32	.20	1.92	2.87	
	0300	3" diameter core		23	.696		5	17.20	2.66	24.86	37	
	0350	Each added inch thick, add		186	.086		.90	2.13	.33	3.36	4.89	
	0500	4" diameter core		19	.842		5	21	3.23	29.23	43.50	
	0550	Each added inch thick, add		170	.094		1.15	2.33	.36	3.84	5.55	
	0700	6" diameter core		14	1.143		8.30	28.50	4.38	41.18	61	
	0750	Each added inch thick, add		140	.114		1.40	2.83	.44	4.67	6.75	
	0900	8" diameter core		11	1.455		11.30	36	5.55	52.85	78.50	
	0950	Each added inch thick, add		95	.168		1.90	4.17	.65	6.72	9.75	
	1100	10" diameter core		10	1.600		15.10	39.50	6.15	60.75	89.50	
	1150	Each added inch thick, add		80	.200		2.50	4.95	.77	8.22	11.85	
	1300	12" diameter core		9	1.778		18.10	44	6.80	68.90	100	
	1350	Each added inch thick, add		68	.235		3	5.80	.90	9.70	14	
	1500	14" diameter core		7	2.286		22	56.50	8.75	87.25	128	
	1550	Each added inch thick, add		55	.291		3.80	7.20	1.11	12.11	17.40	
	1700	18" diameter core		4	4		28.50	99	15.30	142.80	213	
	1750	Each added inch thick, add		28	.571		5	14.15	2.19	21.34	31.50	
	1760	For horizontal holes, add to above								30%	30%	
	1770	Prestressed hollow core plank, 6" thick										
	1780	1" diameter core	B-89A	52	.308	Ea.	1.50	7.60	1.18	10.28	15.65	
	1790	Each added inch thick, add		350	.046		.25	1.13	.18	1.56	2.35	
	1800	3" diameter core		50	.320		3.30	7.90	1.23	12.43	18.20	
	1810	Each added inch thick, add		240	.067		.55	1.65	.26	2.46	3.64	
	1820	4" diameter core		48	.333		4.40	8.25	1.28	13.93	20	
	1830	Each added inch thick, add		216	.074		.75	1.83	.28	2.86	4.19	
	1840	6" diameter core		44	.364		5.45	9	1.39	15.84	22.50	
	1850	Each added inch thick, add		175	.091		.90	2.26	.35	3.51	5.15	
	1860	8" diameter core		32	.500		7.30	12.40	1.92	21.62	30.50	
	1870	Each added inch thick, add		118	.136		1.25	3.36	.52	5.13	7.55	
	1880	10" diameter core		28	.571		9.85	14.15	2.19	26.19	37	
	1890	Each added inch thick, add		99	.162		1.35	4	.62	5.97	8.80	
	1900	12" diameter core		22	.727		12	18	2.79	32.79	46.50	
	1910	Each added inch thick, add		85	.188		2	4.66	.72	7.38	10.75	
	1950	Minimum charge for above, 3" diameter core		7	2.286	Total		56.50	8.75	65.25	104	
	2000	4" diameter core		6.80	2.353			58	9	67	107	

020 | Subsurface Investigation & Demolition

020 120 | Std Penetration Tests

			CREW	DAILY OUTPUT	LABOR-HOURS	UNIT	MAT.	LABOR	EQUIP.	TOTAL	TOTAL INCL O&P	
125	2050	6" diameter core	B-89A	6	2.667	Total		66	10.20	76.20	121	125
	2100	8" diameter core		5.50	2.909			72	11.15	83.15	132	
	2150	10" diameter core		4.75	3.368			83.50	12.90	96.40	153	
	2200	12" diameter core		3.90	4.103			102	15.70	117.70	186	
	2250	14" diameter core		3.38	4.734			117	18.15	135.15	215	
	2300	18" diameter core		3.15	5.079			126	19.45	145.45	231	
	3010	Bits for core drill, diamond, premium, 1" diameter				Ea.	112			112	123	
	3020	3" diameter					274			274	300	
	3040	4" diameter					305			305	335	
	3050	6" diameter					490			490	535	
	3080	8" diameter					715			715	785	
	3120	12" diameter					1,100			1,100	1,200	
	3180	18" diameter					1,800			1,800	1,975	
	3240	24" diameter					2,400			2,400	2,650	

020 550 | Site Demolition

			CREW	DAILY OUTPUT	LABOR-HOURS	UNIT	MAT.	LABOR	EQUIP.	TOTAL	TOTAL INCL O&P	
554	0010	**SITE DEMOLITION** No hauling, abandon catch basin or manhole	B-6	7	3.429	Ea.		80	31.50	111.50	167	554
	0020	Remove existing catch basin or manhole, masonry		4	6			140	54.50	194.50	290	
	0030	Catch basin or manhole frames and covers, stored		13	1.846			43	16.85	59.85	89.50	
	0040	Remove and reset		7	3.429			80	31.50	111.50	167	
	0100	Roadside delineators, remove only	B-80	175	.183			4.29	3.08	7.37	10.45	
	0110	Remove and reset	"	100	.320			7.50	5.40	12.90	18.25	
	0400	Minimum labor/equipment charge	B-6	4	6	Job		140	54.50	194.50	290	
	0600	Fencing, barbed wire, 3 strand	2 Clab	430	.037	L.F.		.80		.80	1.34	
	0650	5 strand	"	280	.057			1.23		1.23	2.05	
	0700	Chain link, posts & fabric, remove only, 8' to 10' high	B-6	445	.054			1.26	.49	1.75	2.61	
	0800	Guiderail, corrugated steel, remove only	B-80A	100	.240			5.15	1.80	6.95	10.55	
	0850	Remove and reset	"	40	.600			12.85	4.49	17.34	26.50	
	0860	Guide posts, remove only	B-80B	120	.267	Ea.		6.10	2.36	8.46	12.65	
	0870	Remove and reset	B-55	50	.480	"		10.35	12.75	23.10	31	
	0890	Minimum labor/equipment charge	2 Clab	4	4	Job		86		86	144	
	0900	Hydrants, fire, remove only	B-21A	5	8	Ea.		213	78	291	425	
	0950	Remove and reset	"	2	20	"		530	196	726	1,075	
	0990	Minimum labor/equipment charge	2 Plum	2	8	Job		261		261	410	
	1000	Masonry walls, block or tile, solid, remove	B-5	1,800	.031	C.F.		.74	.58	1.32	1.85	
	1100	Cavity wall		2,200	.025			.60	.48	1.08	1.51	
	1200	Brick, solid		900	.062			1.48	1.16	2.64	3.71	
	1300	With block back-up		1,130	.050			1.18	.93	2.11	2.95	
	1400	Stone, with mortar		900	.062			1.48	1.16	2.64	3.71	
	1500	Dry set		1,500	.037			.89	.70	1.59	2.23	
	1600	Median barrier, precast concrete, remove and store	B-3	430	.112	L.F.		2.59	4.07	6.66	8.75	
	1610	Remove and reset	"	390	.123	"		2.85	4.49	7.34	9.60	
	1650	Minimum labor/equipment charge	A-1	4	2	Job		43	17.15	60.15	91	
	1710	Pavement removal, bituminous roads, 3" thick	B-38	690	.058	S.Y.		1.41	1.48	2.89	3.94	
	1750	4" to 6" thick		420	.095			2.32	2.43	4.75	6.45	
	1800	Bituminous driveways		640	.063			1.52	1.59	3.11	4.24	
	1900	Concrete to 6" thick, hydraulic hammer, mesh reinforced		255	.157			3.83	4	7.83	10.65	
	2000	Rod reinforced		200	.200			4.88	5.10	9.98	13.60	
	2100	Concrete, 7" to 24" thick, plain		33	1.212	C.Y.		29.50	31	60.50	82.50	
	2200	Reinforced		24	1.667	"		40.50	42.50	83	114	
	2250	Minimum labor/equipment charge		6	6.667	Job		163	170	333	455	
	2300	With hand held air equipment, bituminous, to 6" thick	B-39	1,900	.025	S.F.		.57	.09	.66	1.05	
	2320	Concrete to 6" thick, no reinforcing		1,200	.040			.91	.15	1.06	1.68	
	2340	Mesh reinforced		1,400	.034			.78	.13	.91	1.43	
	2360	Rod reinforced		765	.063			1.43	.24	1.67	2.62	
	2390	Minimum labor/equipment charge	B-38	6	6.667	Job		163	170	333	455	

020 | Subsurface Investigation & Demolition

020 550 | Site Demolition

			DAILY	LABOR-		\<1999 BARE COSTS\>				TOTAL	
										INCL O&P	
			CREW	OUTPUT	HOURS	UNIT	MAT.	LABOR	EQUIP.	TOTAL	
554	2400	Curbs, concrete, plain	B-6	360	.067	L.F.		1.56	.61	2.17	3.23	554
	2500	Reinforced		275	.087			2.04	.80	2.84	4.23	
	2600	Granite		360	.067			1.56	.61	2.17	3.23	
	2700	Bituminous		528	.045			1.06	.41	1.47	2.20	
	2790	Minimum labor/equipment charge		6	4	Job		93.50	36.50	130	193	
	2900	Pipe removal, sewer/water, no excavation, 12" diameter		175	.137	L.F.		3.21	1.25	4.46	6.65	
	2930	15" diameter		150	.160			3.74	1.46	5.20	7.75	
	2960	24" diameter		120	.200			4.67	1.82	6.49	9.65	
	3000	36" diameter		90	.267			6.25	2.43	8.68	12.90	
	3200	Steel, welded connections, 4" diameter		160	.150			3.51	1.37	4.88	7.25	
	3300	10" diameter		80	.300			7	2.74	9.74	14.50	
	3390	Minimum labor/equipment charge		3	8	Job		187	73	260	385	
	3500	Railroad track removal, ties and track	B-13	330	.170	L.F.		3.94	1.66	5.60	8.35	
	3600	Ballast	B-14	500	.096	C.Y.		2.18	.44	2.62	4.10	
	3700	Remove and re-install, ties & track using new bolts & spikes		50	.960	L.F.		22	4.38	26.38	41	
	3800	Turnouts using new bolts and spikes		1	48	Ea.		1,100	219	1,319	2,050	
	3890	Minimum labor/equipment charge		5	9.600	Job		218	44	262	410	
	4000	Sidewalk removal, bituminous, 2-1/2" thick	B-6	325	.074	S.Y.		1.73	.67	2.40	3.57	
	4050	Brick, set in mortar		185	.130			3.03	1.18	4.21	6.30	
	4100	Concrete, plain, 4"		160	.150			3.51	1.37	4.88	7.25	
	4200	Mesh reinforced		150	.160			3.74	1.46	5.20	7.75	
	4290	Minimum labor/equipment charge	B-39	12	4	Job		91	15.05	106.05	168	
558	0010	HYDRODEMOLITION, concrete pavement, 4000 PSI, 2" depth	B-5	500	.112	S.F.		2.66	2.09	4.75	6.65	558
	0120	4" depth		450	.124			2.95	2.32	5.27	7.40	
	0130	6" depth		400	.140			3.32	2.61	5.93	8.30	
	0410	6000 PSI, 2" depth		410	.137			3.24	2.55	5.79	8.15	
	0420	4" depth		350	.160			3.80	2.99	6.79	9.55	
	0430	6" depth		300	.187			4.43	3.49	7.92	11.15	
	0510	8000 PSI, 2" depth		330	.170			4.03	3.17	7.20	10.10	
	0520	4" depth		280	.200			4.74	3.73	8.47	11.90	
	0530	6" depth		240	.233			5.55	4.36	9.91	13.90	

020 600 | Building Demolition

			CREW	DAILY OUTPUT	LABOR-HOURS	UNIT	MAT.	LABOR	EQUIP.	TOTAL	INCL O&P	
604	0010	BUILDING DEMOLITION Large urban projects, incl. 20 Mi. haul										604
	0012	No foundation or dump fees, C.F. is volume of building standing, steel	B-8	21,500	.003	C.F.		.07	.11	.18	.24	
	0050	Concrete		15,300	.004			.10	.15	.25	.33	
	0080	Masonry		20,100	.003			.08	.11	.19	.25	
	0100	Mixture of types, average		20,100	.003			.08	.11	.19	.25	
	0500	Small bldgs, or single bldgs, no salvage included, steel	B-3	14,800	.003			.08	.12	.20	.25	
	0600	Concrete		11,300	.004			.10	.15	.25	.33	
	0650	Masonry		14,800	.003			.08	.12	.20	.25	
	0700	Wood		14,800	.003			.08	.12	.20	.25	
	1000	Single family, one story house, wood, minimum				Ea.				2,300	2,700	
	1020	Maximum								4,000	4,800	
	1200	Two family, two story house, wood, minimum								3,000	3,600	
	1220	Maximum								5,800	7,000	
	1300	Three family, three story house, wood, minimum								4,000	4,800	
	1320	Maximum								7,000	8,400	
	1400	Gutting building, see division 020-716										
	5000	For buildings with no interior walls, deduct				Ea.				50%		
608	0010	DISPOSAL ONLY Urban buildings with salvage value allowed										608
	0020	Including loading and 5 mile haul to dump										
	0200	Steel frame	B-3	430	.112	C.Y.		2.59	4.07	6.66	8.75	
	0300	Concrete frame		365	.132			3.05	4.79	7.84	10.25	

020 | Subsurface Investigation & Demolition

020 600 | Building Demolition

			CREW	DAILY OUTPUT	LABOR-HOURS	UNIT	MAT.	LABOR	EQUIP.	TOTAL	TOTAL INCL O&P	
608	0400	Masonry construction	B-3	445	.108	C.Y.		2.50	3.93	6.43	8.45	608
	0500	Wood frame	↓	247	.194	↓		4.50	7.10	11.60	15.20	
612	0010	**DUMP CHARGES** Typical urban city, tipping fees only										612
	0100	Building construction materials				Ton					55	
	0200	Trees, brush, lumber									45	
	0300	Rubbish only									50	
	0500	Reclamation station, usual charge				↓					80	
620	0010	**RUBBISH HANDLING** The following are to be added to the										620
	0020	demolition prices										
	0400	Chute, circular, prefabricated steel, 18" diameter	B-1	40	.600	L.F.	19.35	13.25		32.60	43.50	
	0440	30" diameter	"	30	.800	"	25	17.70		42.70	57	
	0600	Dumpster, weekly rental, 1 dump/week, 6 C.Y. capacity (2 Tons)				Ea.					300	
	0700	10 C.Y. capacity (4 Tons)									385	
	0800	30 C.Y. capacity (10 Tons)									650	
	0840	40 C.Y. capacity (13 Tons)				↓					775	
	0900	Alternate pricing for dumpsters										
	0910	Delivery, average for all sizes				Ea.					55	
	0920	Haul, average for all sizes									130	
	0930	Rent per day, average for all sizes									2.75	
	0940	Rent per month, average for all sizes				↓					25	
	0950	Disposal fee per ton, average for all sizes				Ton					45	
	1000	Dust partition, 6 mil polyethylene, 4' x 8' panels, 1" x 3" frame	2 Carp	2,000	.008	S.F.	.40	.22		.62	.81	
	1080	2" x 4" frame	"	2,000	.008	"	.50	.22		.72	.92	
	2000	Load, haul to chute & dumping into chute, 50' haul	2 Clab	24	.667	C.Y.		14.30		14.30	24	
	2040	100' haul		16.50	.970			21		21	35	
	2080	Over 100' haul, add per 100 L.F.		35.50	.451			9.65		9.65	16.20	
	2120	In elevators, per 10 floors, add	↓	140	.114			2.45		2.45	4.10	
	3000	Loading & trucking, including 2 mile haul, chute loaded	B-16	45	.711			15.70	9.85	25.55	37	
	3040	Hand loading truck, 50' haul	"	48	.667			14.75	9.20	23.95	34.50	
	3080	Machine loading truck	B-17	120	.267			6.15	4.86	11.01	15.45	
	3120	Wheeled 50' and ramp dump loaded	2 Clab	24	.667			14.30		14.30	24	
	5000	Haul, per mile, up to 8 C.Y. truck	B-34B	1,165	.007			.15	.38	.53	.67	
	5100	Over 8 C.Y. truck	"	1,550	.005	↓		.11	.29	.40	.50	

020 700 | Selective Demolition

			CREW	DAILY OUTPUT	LABOR-HOURS	UNIT	MAT.	LABOR	EQUIP.	TOTAL	TOTAL INCL O&P	
702	0010	**CEILING DEMOLITION** R020-510										702
	0200	Drywall, furred and nailed	2 Clab	800	.020	S.F.		.43		.43	.72	
	0220	On metal frame		760	.021			.45		.45	.76	
	0240	On suspension system, including system		720	.022			.48		.48	.80	
	1000	Plaster, lime and horse hair, on wood lath, incl. lath		700	.023			.49		.49	.82	
	1020	On metal lath		570	.028			.60		.60	1.01	
	1100	Gypsum, on gypsum lath		720	.022			.48		.48	.80	
	1120	On metal lath		500	.032			.69		.69	1.15	
	1200	Suspended ceiling, mineral fiber, 2'x2' or 2'x4'		1,500	.011			.23		.23	.38	
	1250	On suspension system, incl. system		1,200	.013			.29		.29	.48	
	1500	Tile, wood fiber, 12" x 12", glued		900	.018			.38		.38	.64	
	1540	Stapled		1,500	.011			.23		.23	.38	
	1580	On suspension system, incl. system		760	.021			.45		.45	.76	
	2000	Wood, tongue and groove, 1" x 4"		1,000	.016			.34		.34	.57	
	2040	1" x 8"		1,100	.015			.31		.31	.52	
	2400	Plywood or wood fiberboard, 4' x 8' sheets	↓	1,200	.013	↓		.29		.29	.48	
	9000	Minimum labor/equipment charge	1 Clab	2	4	Job		86		86	144	
704	0010	**CUTOUT DEMOLITION** Conc., elev. slab, light reinf., under 6 C.F.	B-9C	65	.615	C.F.		13.45	2.78	16.23	25.50	704
	0050	Light reinforcing, over 6 C.F.	"	75	.533	"		11.65	2.41	14.06	22	

020 | Subsurface Investigation & Demolition

020 700 | Selective Demolition

		CREW	DAILY OUTPUT	LABOR-HOURS	UNIT	MAT.	LABOR	EQUIP.	TOTAL	TOTAL INCL O&P
704 0200	Slab on grade to 6" thick, not reinforced, under 8 S.F.	B-9	85	.471	S.F.		10.30	2.12	12.42	19.55
0250	Not reinforced, over 8 S.F.		175	.229	"		4.99	1.03	6.02	9.50
0600	Walls, not reinforced, under 6 C.F.		60	.667	C.F.		14.55	3.01	17.56	28
0650	Not reinforced, over 6 C.F.		65	.615	"		13.45	2.78	16.23	25.50
1000	Concrete, elevated slab, bar reinforced, under 6 C.F.	B-9C	45	.889			19.40	4.01	23.41	37
1050	Bar reinforced, over 6 C.F.	"	50	.800			17.50	3.61	21.11	33.50
1200	Slab on grade to 6" thick, bar reinforced, under 8 S.F.	B-9	75	.533	S.F.		11.65	2.41	14.06	22
1250	Bar reinforced, over 8 S.F.	"	105	.381	"		8.30	1.72	10.02	15.85
1400	Walls, bar reinforced, under 6 C.F.	B-9C	50	.800	C.F.		17.50	3.61	21.11	33.50
1450	Bar reinforced, over 6 C.F.	"	55	.727	"		15.90	3.28	19.18	30
2000	Brick, to 4 S.F. opening, not including toothing									
2040	4" thick	B-9C	30	1.333	Ea.		29	6	35	55.50
2060	8" thick		18	2.222			48.50	10	58.50	92.50
2080	12" thick		10	4			87.50	18.05	105.55	166
2400	Concrete block, to 4 S.F. opening, 2" thick		35	1.143			25	5.15	30.15	47.50
2420	4" thick		30	1.333			29	6	35	55.50
2440	8" thick		27	1.481			32.50	6.70	39.20	61.50
2460	12" thick		24	1.667			36.50	7.50	44	69.50
2600	Gypsum block, to 4 S.F. opening, 2" thick	B-9	80	.500			10.95	2.26	13.21	21
2620	4" thick		70	.571			12.50	2.58	15.08	24
2640	8" thick		55	.727			15.90	3.28	19.18	30
2800	Terra cotta, to 4 S.F. opening, 4" thick		70	.571			12.50	2.58	15.08	24
2840	8" thick		65	.615			13.45	2.78	16.23	25.50
2880	12" thick		50	.800			17.50	3.61	21.11	33.50
4000	For toothing masonry, see Division 045-290									
6000	Walls, interior, not including re-framing,									
6010	openings to 5 S.F.									
6100	Drywall to 5/8" thick	A-1	24	.333	Ea.		7.15	2.86	10.01	15.10
6200	Paneling to 3/4" thick		20	.400			8.60	3.43	12.03	18.15
6300	Plaster, on gypsum lath		20	.400			8.60	3.43	12.03	18.15
6340	On wire lath		14	.571			12.25	4.90	17.15	26
7000	Wood frame, not including re-framing, openings to 5 S.F.									
7200	Floors, sheathing and flooring to 2" thick	A-1	5	1.600	Ea.		34.50	13.75	48.25	72.50
7310	Roofs, sheathing to 1" thick, not including roofing		6	1.333			28.50	11.45	39.95	60.50
7410	Walls, sheathing to 1" thick, not including siding		7	1.143			24.50	9.80	34.30	52
8500	Minimum labor/equipment charge		4	2	Job		43	17.15	60.15	91
706 0010	**DOOR DEMOLITION**									
0200	Doors, exterior, 1-3/4" thick, single, 3' x 7' high	1 Clab	16	.500	Ea.		10.75		10.75	17.95
0220	Double, 6' x 7' high		12	.667			14.30		14.30	24
0500	Interior, 1-3/8" thick, single, 3' x 7' high		20	.400			8.60		8.60	14.35
0520	Double, 6' x 7' high		16	.500			10.75		10.75	17.95
0700	Bi-folding, 3' x 6'-8" high		20	.400			8.60		8.60	14.35
0720	6' x 6'-8" high		18	.444			9.55		9.55	15.95
0900	Bi-passing, 3' x 6'-8" high		16	.500			10.75		10.75	17.95
0940	6' x 6'-8" high		14	.571			12.25		12.25	20.50
1500	Remove and reset, minimum	1 Carp	8	1			27.50		27.50	45.50
1520	Maximum	"	6	1.333			36.50		36.50	61
2000	Frames, including trim, metal	A-1	8	1			21.50	8.60	30.10	45.50
2200	Wood	2 Carp	32	.500			13.65		13.65	23
2201	Alternate pricing method	A-1	200	.040	L.F.		.86	.34	1.20	1.82
2950	Minimum labor/equipment charge	1 Clab	4	2	Job		43		43	72
3000	Special doors, counter doors	2 Carp	6	2.667	Ea.		73		73	122
3100	Double acting		10	1.600			43.50		43.50	73
3200	Floor door (trap type)		8	2			54.50		54.50	91.50
3300	Glass, sliding, including frames		12	1.333			36.50		36.50	61
3400	Overhead, commercial, 12' x 12' high		4	4			109		109	183

Important: See the Reference Section for critical supporting data - Reference Nos., Crews, & City Cost Indexes

020 | Subsurface Investigation & Demolition

020 700 | Selective Demolition

			CREW	DAILY OUTPUT	LABOR-HOURS	UNIT	MAT.	LABOR	EQUIP.	TOTAL	TOTAL INCL O&P	
706	3440	20' x 16' high	2 Carp	3	5.333	Ea.		146		146	244	706
	3500	Residential, 9' x 7' high	R020 -510	8	2			54.50		54.50	91.50	
	3540	16' x 7' high		7	2.286			62.50		62.50	104	
	3600	Remove and reset, minimum		4	4			109		109	183	
	3620	Maximum		2.50	6.400			175		175	292	
	3700	Roll-up grille		5	3.200			87.50		87.50	146	
	3800	Revolving door		2	8			218		218	365	
	3900	Storefront swing door		3	5.333			146		146	244	
	9000	Minimum labor/equipment charge	1 Carp	4	2	Job		54.50		54.50	91.50	
708	0010	**ELECTRICAL DEMOLITION**	R020 -510									708
	0020	Conduit to 15' high, including fittings & hangers										
	0100	Rigid galvanized steel, 1/2" to 1" diameter	1 Elec	242	.033	L.F.		1.05		1.05	1.63	
	0120	1-1/4" to 2"	R020 -708	200	.040			1.28		1.28	1.97	
	0140	2" to 4"		151	.053			1.69		1.69	2.61	
	0200	Electric metallic tubing (EMT) 1/2" to 1"		394	.020			.65		.65	1	
	0220	1-1/4" to 1-1/2"		326	.025			.78		.78	1.21	
	0240	2" to 3"		236	.034			1.08		1.08	1.67	
	0400	Wiremold raceway, including fittings & hangers										
	0420	No. 3000	1 Elec	250	.032	L.F.		1.02		1.02	1.58	
	0440	No. 4000	"	217	.037	"		1.18		1.18	1.82	
	0500	Channels, steel, including fittings & hangers										
	0520	3/4" x 1-1/2"	1 Elec	308	.026	L.F.		.83		.83	1.28	
	0540	1-1/2" x 1-1/2"	"	269	.030	"		.95		.95	1.47	
	0600	Copper bus duct, indoor, 3 phase										
	0610	Including hangers & supports										
	0620	225 amp	2 Elec	135	.119	L.F.		3.78		3.78	5.85	
	0640	400 amp		106	.151			4.82		4.82	7.45	
	0660	600 amp		86	.186			5.95		5.95	9.15	
	0680	1000 amp		60	.267			8.50		8.50	13.15	
	0700	1600 amp		40	.400			12.75		12.75	19.70	
	0720	3000 amp		10	1.600			51		51	79	
	0800	Plug-in switches, 600V 3 ph, incl. disconnecting										
	0820	wire, pipe terminations, 30 amp	1 Elec	15.50	.516	Ea.		16.45		16.45	25.50	
	0840	60 amp		13.90	.576			18.35		18.35	28.50	
	0850	100 amp		10.40	.769			24.50		24.50	38	
	0860	200 amp		6.20	1.290			41		41	63.50	
	0940	1200 amp	2 Elec	2	8			255		255	395	
	0960	1600 amp	"	1.70	9.412			300		300	465	
	1010	Safety switches, 250 or 600V, incl. disconnection										
	1050	of wire & pipe terminations										
	1100	30 amp	1 Elec	12.30	.650	Ea.		21		21	32	
	1120	60 amp		8.80	.909			29		29	45	
	1140	100 amp		7.30	1.096			35		35	54	
	1160	200 amp		5	1.600			51		51	79	
	1210	Panel boards, incl. removal of all breakers,										
	1220	pipe terminations & wire connections										
	1230	3 wire, 120/240V, 100A, to 20 circuits	1 Elec	2.60	3.077	Ea.		98		98	152	
	1240	200 amps, to 42 circuits		1.30	6.154			196		196	305	
	1260	4 wire, 120/208V, 125A, to 20 circuits		2.40	3.333			106		106	164	
	1270	200 amps, to 42 circuits		1.20	6.667			213		213	330	
	1300	Transformer, dry type, 1 ph, incl. removal of										
	1320	supports, wire & pipe terminations										
	1340	1 kVA	1 Elec	7.70	1.039	Ea.		33		33	51	
	1360	5 kVA		4.70	1.702			54.50		54.50	84	
	1420	75 kVA		1.25	6.400			204		204	315	

020 | Subsurface Investigation & Demolition

020 700 | Selective Demolition

		CREW	DAILY OUTPUT	LABOR-HOURS	UNIT	1999 BARE COSTS MAT.	LABOR	EQUIP.	TOTAL	TOTAL INCL O&P
1440	3 Phase to 600V, primary									
1460	3 kVA	1 Elec	3.85	2.078	Ea.		66.50		66.50	102
1480	15 kVA	2 Elec	4.20	3.810			122		122	188
1500	30 kVA	"	3.50	4.571			146		146	225
1530	112.5 kVA	R-3	2.90	6.897			218	47	265	390
1560	500 kVA		1.40	14.286			450	97	547	805
1570	750 kVA		1.10	18.182			575	123	698	1,025
1600	Pull boxes & cabinets, sheet metal, incl. removal									
1620	of supports and pipe terminations									
1640	6" x 6" x 4"	1 Elec	31.10	.257	Ea.		8.20		8.20	12.70
1660	12" x 12" x 4"		23.30	.343			10.95		10.95	16.95
1720	Junction boxes, 4" sq. & oct.		80	.100			3.19		3.19	4.93
1740	Handy box		107	.075			2.39		2.39	3.69
1760	Switch box		107	.075			2.39		2.39	3.69
1780	Receptacle & switch plates		257	.031			.99		.99	1.53
1800	Wire, THW-THWN-THHN, removed from									
1810	in place conduit, to 15' high									
1830	#14	1 Elec	65	.123	C.L.F.		3.93		3.93	6.05
1840	#12		55	.145			4.64		4.64	7.15
1850	#10		45.50	.176			5.60		5.60	8.65
1880	#4	2 Elec	53	.302			9.65		9.65	14.90
1890	#3		50	.320			10.20		10.20	15.80
1910	1/0		33.20	.482			15.35		15.35	24
1920	2/0		29.20	.548			17.50		17.50	27
1930	3/0		25	.640			20.50		20.50	31.50
1980	400 kcmil		17	.941			30		30	46.50
1990	500 kcmil		16.20	.988			31.50		31.50	48.50
2000	Interior fluorescent fixtures, incl. supports									
2010	& whips, to 15' high									
2100	Recessed drop-in 2' x 2', 2 lamp	2 Elec	35	.457	Ea.		14.60		14.60	22.50
2120	2' x 4', 2 lamp		33	.485			15.45		15.45	24
2140	2' x 4', 4 lamp		30	.533			17		17	26.50
2160	4' x 4', 4 lamp		20	.800			25.50		25.50	39.50
2180	Surface mount, acrylic lens & hinged frame									
2200	1' x 4', 2 lamp	2 Elec	44	.364	Ea.		11.60		11.60	17.95
2220	2' x 2', 2 lamp		44	.364			11.60		11.60	17.95
2260	2' x 4', 4 lamp		33	.485			15.45		15.45	24
2280	4' x 4', 4 lamp		40	.400			12.75		12.75	19.70
2300	Strip fixtures, surface mount									
2320	4' long, 1 lamp	2 Elec	53	.302	Ea.		9.65		9.65	14.90
2340	4' long, 2 lamp		50	.320			10.20		10.20	15.80
2360	8' long, 1 lamp		42	.381			12.15		12.15	18.80
2380	8' long, 2 lamp		40	.400			12.75		12.75	19.70
2400	Pendant mount, industrial, incl. removal									
2410	of chain or rod hangers, to 15' high									
2420	4' long, 2 lamp	2 Elec	35	.457	Ea.		14.60		14.60	22.50
2440	8' long, 2 lamp	"	27	.593	"		18.90		18.90	29
2460	Interior incandescent, surface, ceiling									
2470	or wall mount, to 12' high									
2480	Metal cylinder type, 75 Watt	2 Elec	62	.258	Ea.		8.25		8.25	12.70
2500	150 Watt	"	62	.258	"		8.25		8.25	12.70
2520	Metal halide, high bay									
2540	400 Watt	2 Elec	15	1.067	Ea.		34		34	52.50
2560	1000 Watt		12	1.333			42.50		42.50	65.50
2580	150 Watt, low bay		20	.800			25.50		25.50	39.50
2600	Exterior fixtures, incandescent, wall mount									

020 | Subsurface Investigation & Demolition

020 700 | Selective Demolition

			CREW	DAILY OUTPUT	LABOR-HOURS	UNIT	MAT.	LABOR	EQUIP.	TOTAL	TOTAL INCL O&P	
708	2620	100 Watt	2 Elec	50	.320	Ea.		10.20		10.20	15.80	708
	2640	Quartz, 500 Watt		33	.485			15.45		15.45	24	
	2660	1500 Watt		27	.593			18.90		18.90	29	
	2680	Wall pack, mercury vapor										
	2700	175 Watt	2 Elec	25	.640	Ea.		20.50		20.50	31.50	
	2720	250 Watt	"	25	.640	"		20.50		20.50	31.50	
	9000	Minimum labor/equipment charge	1 Elec	4	2	Job		64		64	98.50	
712	0010	**FLOORING DEMOLITION**										712
	0200	Brick with mortar	2 Clab	475	.034	S.F.		.72		.72	1.21	
	0400	Carpet, bonded, including surface scraping		2,000	.008			.17		.17	.29	
	0480	Tackless		9,000	.002			.04		.04	.06	
	0600	Composition, acrylic or epoxy		400	.040			.86		.86	1.44	
	0700	Concrete, scarify skin	A-1	225	.036			.76	.31	1.07	1.62	
	0800	Resilient, sheet goods	2 Clab	1,400	.011			.25		.25	.41	
	0820	For gym floors		900	.018			.38		.38	.64	
	0900	Vinyl composition tile, 12" x 12"		1,000	.016			.34		.34	.57	
	2000	Tile, ceramic, thin set		675	.024			.51		.51	.85	
	2020	Mud set		625	.026			.55		.55	.92	
	2200	Marble, slate, thin set		675	.024			.51		.51	.85	
	2220	Mud set		625	.026			.55		.55	.92	
	2600	Terrazzo, thin set		450	.036			.76		.76	1.28	
	2620	Mud set		425	.038			.81		.81	1.35	
	2640	Cast in place		300	.053			1.14		1.14	1.91	
	3000	Wood, block, on end	1 Carp	400	.020			.55		.55	.91	
	3200	Parquet		450	.018			.49		.49	.81	
	3400	Strip flooring, interior, 2-1/4" x 25/32" thick		325	.025			.67		.67	1.12	
	3500	Exterior, porch flooring, 1" x 4"		220	.036			.99		.99	1.66	
	3800	Subfloor, tongue and groove, 1" x 6"		325	.025			.67		.67	1.12	
	3820	1" x 8"		430	.019			.51		.51	.85	
	3840	1" x 10"		520	.015			.42		.42	.70	
	4000	Plywood, nailed		600	.013			.36		.36	.61	
	4100	Glued and nailed		400	.020			.55		.55	.91	
	8000	Remove flooring, bead blast, minimum	A-1A	1,000	.008			.22	.13	.35	.52	
	8100	Maximum		400	.020			.56	.33	.89	1.29	
	8150	Mastic only		1,500	.005			.15	.09	.24	.35	
	9000	Minimum labor/equipment charge	A-1	4	2	Job		43	17.15	60.15	91	
714	0010	**FRAMING DEMOLITION**										714
	1020	Concrete, average reinforcing, beams, 8" x 10"	B-9	120	.333	L.F.		7.30	1.50	8.80	13.85	
	1040	10" x 12"		110	.364			7.95	1.64	9.59	15.10	
	1060	12" x 14"		90	.444			9.70	2	11.70	18.45	
	1200	Columns, 8" x 8"		120	.333			7.30	1.50	8.80	13.85	
	1240	10" x 10"		120	.333			7.30	1.50	8.80	13.85	
	1280	12" x 12"		110	.364			7.95	1.64	9.59	15.10	
	1320	14" x 14"		100	.400			8.75	1.80	10.55	16.65	
	1400	Girders, 14" x 16"		55	.727			15.90	3.28	19.18	30	
	1440	16" x 18"		40	1			22	4.51	26.51	41.50	
	1600	Slabs, elevated, 6" thick		600	.067	S.F.		1.46	.30	1.76	2.77	
	1640	8" thick		450	.089			1.94	.40	2.34	3.69	
	1680	10" thick		360	.111			2.43	.50	2.93	4.61	
	1900	Add for heavy reinforcement									25%	
	1910	Minimum labor/equipment charge	A-1	1	8	Job		172	68.50	240.50	365	
	2000	Steel framing, beams, 4" x 6"	B-13	500	.112	L.F.		2.60	1.10	3.70	5.50	
	2020	4" x 8"		400	.140			3.25	1.37	4.62	6.85	
	2080	8" x 12"		250	.224			5.20	2.20	7.40	10.95	

020 | Subsurface Investigation & Demolition

020 700 | Selective Demolition

			CREW	DAILY OUTPUT	LABOR-HOURS	UNIT	MAT.	LABOR	EQUIP.	TOTAL	TOTAL INCL O&P	
714	2200	Columns, 6" x 6"	B-13	400	.140	L.F.		3.25	1.37	4.62	6.85	714
	2240	8" x 8"	R020-510	350	.160			3.72	1.57	5.29	7.85	
	2280	10" x 10"		320	.175			4.07	1.72	5.79	8.60	
	2400	Girders, 10" x 12"		225	.249			5.80	2.44	8.24	12.20	
	2440	10" x 14"		200	.280			6.50	2.75	9.25	13.70	
	2480	10" x 16"		165	.339			7.90	3.33	11.23	16.65	
	2520	10" x 24"	▼	125	.448	▼		10.40	4.39	14.79	22	
	2950	Minimum labor/equipment charge	A-1	1	8	Job		172	68.50	240.50	365	
	3000	Wood framing, beams, 6" x 8"	B-2	275	.145	L.F.		3.18		3.18	5.30	
	3040	6" x 10"		220	.182			3.97		3.97	6.65	
	3080	6" x 12"		185	.216			4.72		4.72	7.90	
	3120	8" x 12"		140	.286			6.25		6.25	10.45	
	3160	10" x 12"	▼	110	.364			7.95		7.95	13.30	
	3400	Fascia boards, 1" x 6"	1 Clab	500	.016			.34		.34	.57	
	3440	1" x 8"		450	.018			.38		.38	.64	
	3480	1" x 10"	▼	400	.020	▼		.43		.43	.72	
	3520	For trim boards, see division 020-720										
	3800	Headers over openings, 2 @ 2" x 6"	1 Clab	110	.073	L.F.		1.56		1.56	2.61	
	3840	2 @ 2" x 8"		100	.080			1.72		1.72	2.87	
	3880	2 @ 2" x 10"	▼	90	.089			1.91		1.91	3.19	
	4200	Joists, 2" x 4"	2 Clab	1,000	.016			.34		.34	.57	
	4230	Joists, 2" x 6"		970	.016			.35		.35	.59	
	4240	2" x 8"		940	.017			.37		.37	.61	
	4250	2" x 10"		910	.018			.38		.38	.63	
	4280	2" x 12"		880	.018			.39		.39	.65	
	5400	Posts, 4" x 4"		800	.020			.43		.43	.72	
	5440	6" x 6"		400	.040			.86		.86	1.44	
	5480	8" x 8"		300	.053			1.14		1.14	1.91	
	5500	10" x 10"		240	.067			1.43		1.43	2.39	
	5800	Rafters, ordinary, 2" x 6"		850	.019			.40		.40	.68	
	5840	2" x 8"		837	.019			.41		.41	.69	
	5900	Hip & valley, 2" x 6"		500	.032			.69		.69	1.15	
	5940	2" x 8"		420	.038	▼		.82		.82	1.37	
	6200	Stairs and stringers, minimum		40	.400	Riser		8.60		8.60	14.35	
	6240	Maximum		26	.615	"		13.20		13.20	22	
	6600	Studs, 2" x 4"		2,000	.008	L.F.		.17		.17	.29	
	6640	2" x 6"	▼	1,600	.010	"		.21		.21	.36	
	9000	Minimum labor/equipment charge	1 Clab	4	2	Job		43		43	72	
	9500	See Div. 020-620 for rubbish handling										
716	0010	**GUTTING** Building interior, including disposal, dumpster fees not included										716
	0500	Residential building										
	0560	Minimum	B-16	400	.080	SF Flr.		1.77	1.11	2.88	4.16	
	0580	Maximum	"	360	.089	"		1.97	1.23	3.20	4.62	
	0900	Commercial building										
	1000	Minimum	B-16	350	.091	SF Flr.		2.02	1.26	3.28	4.75	
	1020	Maximum		250	.128	"		2.83	1.77	4.60	6.65	
	3000	Minimum labor/equipment charge	▼	4	8	Job		177	111	288	415	
717	0010	**HAZARDOUS WASTE CLEANUP/PICKUP/DISPOSAL**										717
	0100	For contractor equipment, i.e. dozer,										
	0110	front end loader, dump truck, etc., see div. 016-408										
	1000	Solid pickup										
	1100	55 gal. drums				Ea.					200	
	1120	Bulk material, minimum				Ton					150	
	1130	Maximum				"					500	
	1200	Transportation to disposal site										

020 | Subsurface Investigation & Demolition

020 700 | Selective Demolition

		Description	CREW	DAILY OUTPUT	LABOR-HOURS	UNIT	MAT.	LABOR	EQUIP.	TOTAL	TOTAL INCL O&P
717	1220	Truckload = 80 drums or 25 C.Y. or 18 tons									
	1260	Minimum				Mile					2.30
	1270	Maximum				"					4
	3000	Liquid pickup, vacuum truck, stainless steel tank									
	3100	Minimum charge, 4 hours									
	3110	1 compartment, 2200 gallon				Hr.					100
	3120	2 compartment, 5000 gallon				"					100
	3400	Transportation in 6900 gallon bulk truck				Mile					4.30
	3410	In teflon lined truck				"					5
	5000	Heavy sludge or dry vacuumable material				Hr.					100
	6000	Dumpsite disposal charge, minimum				Ton					100
	6020	Maximum				"					400
718	0010	**HVAC DEMOLITION** R020-510									
	0100	Air conditioner, split unit, 3 ton	Q-5	2	8	Ea.		236		236	370
	0150	Package unit, 3 ton	Q-6	3	8			245		245	385
	0300	Boiler, electric	Q-19	2	12			365		365	565
	0340	Gas or oil, steel, under 150 MBH	Q-6	3	8			245		245	385
	0380	Over 150 MBH	"	2	12			365		365	575
	1000	Ductwork, 4" high, 8" wide	1 Clab	200	.040	L.F.		.86		.86	1.44
	1020	10" wide		190	.042			.90		.90	1.51
	1040	14" wide		180	.044			.95		.95	1.60
	1100	6" high, 8" wide		165	.048			1.04		1.04	1.74
	1120	12" wide		150	.053			1.14		1.14	1.91
	1140	18" wide		135	.059			1.27		1.27	2.13
	1200	10" high, 12" wide		125	.064			1.37		1.37	2.30
	1220	18" wide		115	.070			1.49		1.49	2.50
	1240	24" wide		110	.073			1.56		1.56	2.61
	1300	12"-14" high, 16"-18" wide		85	.094			2.02		2.02	3.38
	1320	24" wide		75	.107			2.29		2.29	3.83
	1340	48" wide		71	.113			2.42		2.42	4.05
	1400	18" high, 24" wide		67	.119			2.56		2.56	4.29
	1420	36" wide		63	.127			2.72		2.72	4.56
	1440	48" wide		59	.136			2.91		2.91	4.87
	1500	30" high, 36" wide		56	.143			3.06		3.06	5.15
	1520	48" wide		53	.151			3.24		3.24	5.40
	1540	72" wide		50	.160			3.43		3.43	5.75
	1550	Duct heater, electric strip	1 Elec	8	1	Ea.		32		32	49.50
	1850	Minimum labor/equipment charge	1 Clab	3	2.667	Job		57		57	95.50
	2200	Furnace, electric	Q-20	2	10	Ea.		292		292	465
	2300	Gas or oil, under 120 MBH	Q-9	4	4			114		114	183
	2340	Over 120 MBH	"	3	5.333			152		152	244
	2800	Heat pump, package unit, 3 ton	Q-5	2.40	6.667			197		197	310
	2840	Split unit, 3 ton		2	8			236		236	370
	3000	Mechanical equipment, light items. Unit is weight, not cooling.		.90	17.778	Ton		525		525	820
	3600	Heavy items		1.10	14.545	"		430		430	670
	9000	Minimum labor/equipment charge	Q-6	3	8	Job		245		245	385
720	0010	**MILLWORK AND TRIM DEMOLITION** R020-510									
	1000	Cabinets, wood, base cabinets	2 Clab	80	.200	L.F.		4.29		4.29	7.20
	1020	Wall cabinets	"	80	.200	"		4.29		4.29	7.20
	1060	Remove and reset, base cabinets	2 Carp	18	.889	Ea.		24.50		24.50	40.50
	1070	Wall cabinets	"	20	.800	"		22		22	36.50
	1100	Steel, painted, base cabinets	2 Clab	60	.267	L.F.		5.70		5.70	9.55
	1120	Wall cabinets		60	.267	"		5.70		5.70	9.55
	1200	Casework, large area		320	.050	S.F.		1.07		1.07	1.80
	1220	Selective		200	.080	"		1.72		1.72	2.87
	1500	Counter top, minimum		200	.080	L.F.		1.72		1.72	2.87

020 | Subsurface Investigation & Demolition

020 700 | Selective Demolition

		CREW	DAILY OUTPUT	LABOR-HOURS	UNIT	MAT.	LABOR	EQUIP.	TOTAL	TOTAL INCL O&P
1510	Maximum	2 Clab	120	.133	L.F.		2.86		2.86	4.79
1550	Remove and reset, minimum	2 Carp	50	.320			8.75		8.75	14.60
1560	Maximum	"	40	.400	↓		10.90		10.90	18.30
2000	Paneling, 4' x 8' sheets, 1/4" thick	2 Clab	2,000	.008	S.F.		.17		.17	.29
2100	Boards, 1" x 4"		700	.023			.49		.49	.82
2120	1" x 6"		750	.021			.46		.46	.77
2140	1" x 8"		800	.020	↓		.43		.43	.72
3000	Trim, baseboard, to 6" wide		1,200	.013	L.F.		.29		.29	.48
3040	12" wide	↓	1,000	.016			.34		.34	.57
3080	Remove and reset, minimum	2 Carp	400	.040			1.09		1.09	1.83
3090	Maximum	"	300	.053			1.46		1.46	2.44
3100	Ceiling trim	2 Clab	1,000	.016			.34		.34	.57
3120	Chair rail		1,200	.013			.29		.29	.48
3140	Railings with balusters		240	.067	↓		1.43		1.43	2.39
3160	Wainscoting	↓	700	.023	S.F.		.49		.49	.82
9000	Minimum labor/equipment charge	1 Clab	4	2	Job		43		43	72
0010	**MOVING EQUIPMENT,** Remove and reset, 100' distance,									
0020	No obstructions, no assembly or leveling unless noted									
0100	Annealing furnace, 24' overall	B-67	4	4	Ea.		112	43	155	225
0200	Annealing oven, small		14	1.143			32	12.20	44.20	64.50
0240	Very large		1	16			450	171	621	905
0400	Band saw, small		12	1.333			37.50	14.25	51.75	75
0440	Large		8	2			56	21.50	77.50	113
0500	Blue print copy machine		7	2.286			64	24.50	88.50	129
0600	Bonding mill, 6"		7	2.286			64	24.50	88.50	129
0620	12"		6	2.667			74.50	28.50	103	151
0640	18"		4	4			112	43	155	225
0660	24"	↓	2	8			224	85.50	309.50	450
0700	Boring machine (jig)	B-68	7	3.429			97	24.50	121.50	181
0800	Bridgeport mill, standard	B-67	14	1.143			32	12.20	44.20	64.50
1000	Calibrator, 6 unit	"	14	1.143			32	12.20	44.20	64.50
1100	Comparitor, bench top	2 Clab	14	1.143			24.50		24.50	41
1140	Floor mounted	B-67	7	2.286			64	24.50	88.50	129
1200	Computer, desk top	2 Clab	25	.640			13.75		13.75	23
1300	Copy machine	"	25	.640			13.75		13.75	23
1500	Deflasher	B-67	14	1.143			32	12.20	44.20	64.50
1600	Degreaser, small		14	1.143			32	12.20	44.20	64.50
1640	Large 24' overall	↓	1	16			450	171	621	905
1700	Desk with chair	2 Clab	25	.640			13.75		13.75	23
1800	Dial press	B-67	7	2.286			64	24.50	88.50	129
1900	Drafting table	2 Clab	14	1.143			24.50		24.50	41
2000	Drill press, bench top	"	14	1.143			24.50		24.50	41
2040	Floor mounted	B-67	14	1.143			32	12.20	44.20	64.50
2080	Industrial radial	"	7	2.286			64	24.50	88.50	129
2100	Dust collector, portable	2 Clab	25	.640			13.75		13.75	23
2140	Stationary, small	B-67	7	2.286			64	24.50	88.50	129
2180	Stationary, large	"	2	8			224	85.50	309.50	450
2300	Electric discharge machine	B-68	7	3.429	↓		97	24.50	121.50	181
2400	Environmental chamber walls, including assembly	4 Clab	18	1.778	L.F.		38		38	64
2600	File cabinet	2 Clab	25	.640	Ea.		13.75		13.75	23
2800	Grinder/sander, pedestal mount	B-67	14	1.143			32	12.20	44.20	64.50
3000	Hack saw, power	2 Clab	24	.667			14.30		14.30	24
3100	Hydraulic press	B-67	14	1.143			32	12.20	44.20	64.50
3500	Laminar flow tables	"	14	1.143			32	12.20	44.20	64.50
3600	Lathe, bench	2 Clab	14	1.143			24.50		24.50	41
3640	6"	B-67	14	1.143	↓		32	12.20	44.20	64.50

020 | Subsurface Investigation & Demolition

020 700 | Selective Demolition

		CREW	DAILY OUTPUT	LABOR-HOURS	UNIT	MAT.	LABOR	EQUIP.	TOTAL	TOTAL INCL O&P
3680	10"	B-67	13	1.231	Ea.		34.50	13.15	47.65	69.50
3720	12"		12	1.333			37.50	14.25	51.75	75
4000	Milling machine		8	2			56	21.50	77.50	113
4100	Molding press, 25 ton		5	3.200			89.50	34	123.50	181
4140	60 ton		4	4			112	43	155	225
4180	100 ton		2	8			224	85.50	309.50	450
4220	150 ton		1.50	10.667			298	114	412	600
4260	200 ton		1	16			450	171	621	905
4300	300 ton		.75	21.333			595	228	823	1,200
4700	Oil pot stand		14	1.143			32	12.20	44.20	64.50
5000	Press, 10 ton		14	1.143			32	12.20	44.20	64.50
5040	15 ton		12	1.333			37.50	14.25	51.75	75
5080	20 ton		10	1.600			45	17.10	62.10	90.50
5120	30 ton		8	2			56	21.50	77.50	113
5160	45 ton		6	2.667			74.50	28.50	103	151
5200	60 ton		4	4			112	43	155	225
5240	75 ton		2.50	6.400			179	68.50	247.50	360
5280	100 ton		2	8			224	85.50	309.50	450
5500	Raised floor, including assembly	2 Carp	250	.064	S.F.		1.75		1.75	2.92
5600	Rolling mill, 6"	B-67	7	2.286	Ea.		64	24.50	88.50	129
5640	9"		6	2.667			74.50	28.50	103	151
5680	12"		4	4			112	43	155	225
5720	13"		3.50	4.571			128	49	177	258
5760	18"		2	8			224	85.50	309.50	450
5800	25"		1	16			450	171	621	905
6000	Sander, floor stand		14	1.143			32	12.20	44.20	64.50
6100	Screw machine		7	2.286			64	24.50	88.50	129
6200	Shaper, 16"		14	1.143			32	12.20	44.20	64.50
6300	Shear, power assist		4	4			112	43	155	225
6400	Slitter, 6"		14	1.143			32	12.20	44.20	64.50
6440	8"		13	1.231			34.50	13.15	47.65	69.50
6480	10"		12	1.333			37.50	14.25	51.75	75
6520	12"		11	1.455			40.50	15.55	56.05	82
6560	16"		10	1.600			45	17.10	62.10	90.50
6600	20"		8	2			56	21.50	77.50	113
6640	24"		6	2.667			74.50	28.50	103	151
6800	Snag and tap machine		7	2.286			64	24.50	88.50	129
6900	Solder machine (auto)		7	2.286			64	24.50	88.50	129
7000	Storage cabinet metal, small	2 Clab	36	.444			9.55		9.55	15.95
7040	Large		25	.640			13.75		13.75	23
7100	Storage rack open, small		14	1.143			24.50		24.50	41
7140	Large		7	2.286			49		49	82
7200	Surface bench, small	B-67	14	1.143			32	12.20	44.20	64.50
7240	Large	"	5	3.200			89.50	34	123.50	181
7300	Surface grinder, large wet	B-68	5	4.800			136	34	170	254
7500	Time check machine	2 Clab	14	1.143			24.50		24.50	41
8000	Welder, 30 KVA (bench)		14	1.143			24.50		24.50	41
8100	Work bench with chair		25	.640			13.75		13.75	23
0010	**PLUMBING DEMOLITION**									
1020	Fixtures, including 10' piping									
1100	Bath tubs, cast iron	1 Plum	4	2	Ea.		65		65	102
1120	Fiberglass		6	1.333			43.50		43.50	68
1140	Steel		5	1.600			52		52	81.50
1200	Lavatory, wall hung		10	.800			26		26	41
1220	Counter top		8	1			32.50		32.50	51
1300	Sink, steel or cast iron, single		8	1			32.50		32.50	51

020 | Subsurface Investigation & Demolition

020 700 | Selective Demolition

		CREW	DAILY OUTPUT	LABOR-HOURS	UNIT	MAT.	1999 BARE COSTS LABOR	EQUIP.	TOTAL	TOTAL INCL O&P	
1320	Double	1 Plum	7	1.143	Ea.		37.50		37.50	58.50	
1400	Water closet, floor mounted		8	1			32.50		32.50	51	
1420	Wall mounted		7	1.143			37.50		37.50	58.50	
1500	Urinal, floor mounted		4	2			65		65	102	
1520	Wall mounted		7	1.143			37.50		37.50	58.50	
1600	Water fountains, free standing		8	1			32.50		32.50	51	
1620	Recessed		6	1.333			43.50		43.50	68	
2000	Piping, metal, to 2" diameter		200	.040	L.F.		1.30		1.30	2.04	
2050	2" to 4" diameter		150	.053			1.74		1.74	2.72	
2100	4" to 8" diameter	2 Plum	100	.160			5.20		5.20	8.15	
2150	8" to 16" diameter	"	60	.267			8.70		8.70	13.60	
2240	Toilet partitions, see division 020-732										
2250	Water heater, 40 gal.	1 Plum	6	1.333	Ea.		43.50		43.50	68	
6000	Remove and reset fixtures, minimum		6	1.333			43.50		43.50	68	
6100	Maximum		4	2			65		65	102	
9000	Minimum labor/equipment charge		2	4	Job		130		130	204	
0010	**ROOFING AND SIDING DEMOLITION**	R020 -510									
1000	Deck, roof, concrete plank	B-13	1,680	.033	S.F.		.77	.33	1.10	1.64	
1100	Gypsum plank		3,900	.014			.33	.14	.47	.70	
1150	Metal decking		3,500	.016			.37	.16	.53	.78	
1200	Wood, boards, tongue and groove, 2" x 6"	2 Clab	960	.017			.36		.36	.60	
1220	2" x 10"		1,040	.015			.33		.33	.55	
1280	Standard planks, 1" x 6"		1,080	.015			.32		.32	.53	
1320	1" x 8"		1,160	.014			.30		.30	.50	
1340	1" x 12"		1,200	.013			.29		.29	.48	
1350	Plywood, to 1" thick		2,000	.008			.17		.17	.29	
2000	Gutters, aluminum or wood, edge hung	1 Clab	240	.033	L.F.		.72		.72	1.20	
2100	Built-in		100	.080	"		1.72		1.72	2.87	
2500	Roof accessories, plumbing vent flashing		14	.571	Ea.		12.25		12.25	20.50	
2600	Adjustable metal chimney flashing		9	.889	"		19.05		19.05	32	
2650	Coping, sheet metal, up to 12" wide		240	.033	L.F.		.72		.72	1.20	
2660	Concrete, up to 12" wide	2 Clab	160	.100	"		2.15		2.15	3.59	
3000	Roofing, built-up, 5 ply roof, no gravel	B-2	1,600	.025	S.F.		.55		.55	.91	
3001	Including gravel		890	.045			.98		.98	1.64	
3100	Gravel removal, minimum		5,000	.008			.17		.17	.29	
3120	Maximum		2,000	.020			.44		.44	.73	
3400	Roof insulation board, up to 2" thick		3,900	.010			.22		.22	.38	
3450	Roll roofing, cold adhesive	1 Clab	12	.667	Sq.		14.30		14.30	24	
4000	Shingles, asphalt strip, 1 layer	B-2	3,500	.011	S.F.		.25		.25	.42	
4100	Slate		2,500	.016			.35		.35	.59	
4300	Wood		2,200	.018			.40		.40	.66	
4500	Skylight to 10 S.F.	1 Clab	8	1	Ea.		21.50		21.50	36	
5000	Siding, metal, horizontal		444	.018	S.F.		.39		.39	.65	
5020	Vertical		400	.020			.43		.43	.72	
5200	Wood, boards, vertical		400	.020			.43		.43	.72	
5220	Clapboards, horizontal		380	.021			.45		.45	.76	
5240	Shingles		350	.023			.49		.49	.82	
5260	Textured plywood		725	.011			.24		.24	.40	
9000	Minimum labor/equipment charge		2	4	Job		86		86	144	
0010	**SAW CUTTING**, Asphalt, up to 3" deep	B-89	1,050	.015	L.F.	.24	.37	.29	.90	1.18	
0020	Each additional inch of depth		1,800	.009		.06	.22	.17	.45	.60	
0400	Concrete slabs, mesh reinforcing, up to 3" deep		980	.016		.33	.40	.31	1.04	1.35	
0420	Each additional inch of depth		1,600	.010		.44	.24	.19	.87	1.08	
0800	Concrete walls, hydraulic saw, plain, per inch of depth	B-89B	250	.064		.30	1.57	2.11	3.98	5.15	
0820	Rod reinforcing, per inch of depth		150	.107		.42	2.61	3.52	6.55	8.55	

020 | Subsurface Investigation & Demolition

020 700 | Selective Demolition

			CREW	DAILY OUTPUT	LABOR-HOURS	UNIT	MAT.	1999 BARE COSTS LABOR	EQUIP.	TOTAL	TOTAL INCL O&P	
728	1200	Masonry walls, hydraulic saw, brick, per inch of depth	B-89B	300	.053	L.F.	.30	1.31	1.76	3.37	4.37	728
	1220	Block walls, solid, per inch of depth	↓	250	.064		.31	1.57	2.11	3.99	5.20	
	2000	Brick or masonry w/hand held saw, per inch of depth	A-1	125	.064		.24	1.37	.55	2.16	3.17	
	5000	Wood sheathing to 1" thick, on walls	1 Carp	200	.040			1.09		1.09	1.83	
	5020	On roof	"	250	.032	↓		.87		.87	1.46	
	9000	Minimum labor/equipment charge	A-1	2	4	Job		86	34.50	120.50	182	
	9950	See also div. 020-125 core drilling										
730	0010	**TORCH CUTTING** Steel, 1" thick plate	1 Clab	32	.250	L.F.		5.35		5.35	9	730
	0040	1" diameter bar	"	210	.038	Ea.		.82		.82	1.37	
	1000	Oxygen lance cutting, reinforced concrete walls										
	1040	12" to 16" thick walls	1 Clab	10	.800	L.F.		17.15		17.15	28.50	
	1080	24" thick walls	"	6	1.333	"		28.50		28.50	48	
	1090	Minimum labor/equipment charge	A-1	1	8	Job		172	68.50	240.50	365	
	1100	See also division 051-240										
732	0010	**WALLS AND PARTITIONS DEMOLITION** R020-510										732
	0100	Brick, 4" to 12" thick	B-9C	220	.182	C.F.		3.97	.82	4.79	7.55	
	0200	Concrete block, 4" thick		1,000	.040	S.F.		.87	.18	1.05	1.66	
	0280	8" thick	↓	810	.049			1.08	.22	1.30	2.05	
	0300	Exterior stucco 1" thick over netting	B-9	3,200	.013			.27	.06	.33	.52	
	1000	Drywall, nailed	1 Clab	1,000	.008			.17		.17	.29	
	1020	Glued and nailed		900	.009			.19		.19	.32	
	1500	Fiberboard, nailed		900	.009			.19		.19	.32	
	1520	Glued and nailed		800	.010			.21		.21	.36	
	2000	Movable walls, metal, 5' high		300	.027			.57		.57	.96	
	2020	8' high	↓	400	.020			.43		.43	.72	
	2200	Metal or wood studs, finish 2 sides, fiberboard	B-1	520	.046			1.02		1.02	1.71	
	2250	Lath and plaster		260	.092			2.04		2.04	3.42	
	2300	Plasterboard (drywall)		520	.046			1.02		1.02	1.71	
	2350	Plywood	↓	450	.053			1.18		1.18	1.97	
	3000	Plaster, lime and horsehair, on wood lath	1 Clab	400	.020			.43		.43	.72	
	3020	On metal lath		335	.024			.51		.51	.86	
	3400	Gypsum or perlite, on gypsum lath		410	.020			.42		.42	.70	
	3420	On metal lath		300	.027	↓		.57		.57	.96	
	3800	Toilet partitions, slate or marble		5	1.600	Ea.		34.50		34.50	57.50	
	3820	Hollow metal	↓	8	1	"		21.50		21.50	36	
	5000	Wallcovering, vinyl	1 Pape	700	.011	S.F.		.29		.29	.47	
	5040	Designer	"	480	.017	"		.42		.42	.68	
	9000	Minimum labor/equipment charge	1 Clab	4	2	Job		43		43	72	
734	0010	**WINDOW DEMOLITION** R020-510										734
	0200	Aluminum, including trim, to 12 S.F.	1 Clab	16	.500	Ea.		10.75		10.75	17.95	
	0240	To 25 S.F.		11	.727			15.60		15.60	26	
	0280	To 50 S.F.		5	1.600			34.50		34.50	57.50	
	0320	Storm windows, to 12 S.F.		27	.296			6.35		6.35	10.65	
	0360	To 25 S.F.		21	.381			8.15		8.15	13.70	
	0400	To 50 S.F.		16	.500	↓		10.75		10.75	17.95	
	0600	Glass, minimum		200	.040	S.F.		.86		.86	1.44	
	0620	Maximum		150	.053	"		1.14		1.14	1.91	
	1000	Steel, including trim, to 12 S.F.		13	.615	Ea.		13.20		13.20	22	
	1020	To 25 S.F.		9	.889			19.05		19.05	32	
	1040	To 50 S.F.		4	2			43		43	72	
	2000	Wood, including trim, to 12 S.F.		22	.364			7.80		7.80	13.05	
	2020	To 25 S.F.		18	.444			9.55		9.55	15.95	
	2060	To 50 S.F.	↓	13	.615			13.20		13.20	22	
	5020	Remove and reset window, minimum	1 Carp	6	1.333	↓		36.50		36.50	61	

020 | Subsurface Investigation & Demolition

020 700 | Selective Demolition

		CREW	DAILY OUTPUT	LABOR-HOURS	UNIT	MAT.	1999 BARE COSTS LABOR	EQUIP.	TOTAL	TOTAL INCL O&P	
5040	Average	1 Carp	4	2	Ea.		54.50		54.50	91.50	
5080	Maximum		2	4			109		109	183	
9000	Minimum labor/equipment charge	1 Clab	4	2	Job		43		43	72	

020 750 | Concrete Removal

		CREW	DAILY OUTPUT	LABOR-HOURS	UNIT	MAT.	LABOR	EQUIP.	TOTAL	TOTAL INCL O&P
0010	**FOOTINGS AND FOUNDATIONS DEMOLITION**									
0200	Floors, concrete slab on grade,									
0240	4" thick, plain concrete	B-9C	500	.080	S.F.		1.75	.36	2.11	3.33
0280	Reinforced, wire mesh		470	.085			1.86	.38	2.24	3.53
0300	Rods		400	.100			2.18	.45	2.63	4.16
0400	6" thick, plain concrete		375	.107			2.33	.48	2.81	4.43
0420	Reinforced, wire mesh		340	.118			2.57	.53	3.10	4.88
0440	Rods		300	.133			2.91	.60	3.51	5.55
1000	Footings, concrete, 1' thick, 2' wide	B-5	300	.187	L.F.		4.43	3.49	7.92	11.15
1080	1'-6" thick, 2' wide		250	.224			5.30	4.18	9.48	13.35
1120	3' wide		200	.280			6.65	5.25	11.90	16.70
1140	2' thick, 3' wide		175	.320			7.60	5.95	13.55	19.05
1200	Average reinforcing, add								10%	10%
1220	Heavy reinforcing, add								20%	20%
2000	Walls, block, 4" thick	1 Clab	180	.044	S.F.		.95		.95	1.60
2040	6" thick		170	.047			1.01		1.01	1.69
2080	8" thick		150	.053			1.14		1.14	1.91
2100	12" thick		150	.053			1.14		1.14	1.91
2200	For horizontal reinforcing, add								10%	10%
2220	For vertical reinforcing, add								20%	20%
2400	Concrete, plain concrete, 6" thick	B-9	160	.250			5.45	1.13	6.58	10.40
2420	8" thick		140	.286			6.25	1.29	7.54	11.85
2440	10" thick		120	.333			7.30	1.50	8.80	13.85
2500	12" thick		100	.400			8.75	1.80	10.55	16.65
2600	For average reinforcing, add								10%	10%
2620	For heavy reinforcing, add								20%	20%
9000	Minimum labor/equipment charge	A-1	2	4	Job		86	34.50	120.50	182
0010	**MASONRY DEMOLITION**									
1000	Chimney, 16" x 16", soft old mortar	A-1	24	.333	V.L.F.		7.15	2.86	10.01	15.10
1020	Hard mortar		18	.444			9.55	3.81	13.36	20
1080	20" x 20", soft old mortar		12	.667			14.30	5.70	20	30.50
1100	Hard mortar		10	.800			17.15	6.85	24	36
1140	20" x 32", soft old mortar		10	.800			17.15	6.85	24	36
1160	Hard mortar		8	1			21.50	8.60	30.10	45.50
1200	48" x 48", soft old mortar		5	1.600			34.50	13.75	48.25	72.50
1220	Hard mortar		4	2			43	17.15	60.15	91
2000	Columns, 8" x 8", soft old mortar		48	.167			3.58	1.43	5.01	7.55
2020	Hard mortar		40	.200			4.29	1.72	6.01	9.10
2060	16" x 16", soft old mortar		16	.500			10.75	4.29	15.04	22.50
2100	Hard mortar		14	.571			12.25	4.90	17.15	26
2140	24" x 24", soft old mortar		8	1			21.50	8.60	30.10	45.50
2160	Hard mortar		6	1.333			28.50	11.45	39.95	60.50
2200	36" x 36", soft old mortar		4	2			43	17.15	60.15	91
2220	Hard mortar		3	2.667			57	23	80	121
3000	Copings, precast or masonry, to 8" wide									
3020	Soft old mortar	A-1	180	.044	L.F.		.95	.38	1.33	2.02
3040	Hard mortar	"	160	.050	"		1.07	.43	1.50	2.27
3100	To 12" wide									
3120	Soft old mortar	A-1	160	.050	L.F.		1.07	.43	1.50	2.27

020 | Subsurface Investigation & Demolition

020 750 | Concrete Removal

		Crew	Daily Output	Labor-Hours	Unit	Mat.	Labor	Equip.	Total	Total Incl O&P	
758	3140	Hard mortar	A-1	140	.057	L.F.		1.23	.49	1.72	2.59	758
	4000	Fireplace, brick, 30" x 24" opening										
	4020	Soft old mortar	A-1	2	4	Ea.		86	34.50	120.50	182	
	4040	Hard mortar		1.25	6.400			137	55	192	291	
	4100	Stone, soft old mortar		1.50	5.333			114	46	160	242	
	4120	Hard mortar		1	8	↓		172	68.50	240.50	365	
	5000	Veneers, brick, soft old mortar		140	.057	S.F.		1.23	.49	1.72	2.59	
	5020	Hard mortar		125	.064			1.37	.55	1.92	2.90	
	5100	Granite and marble, 2" thick		180	.044			.95	.38	1.33	2.02	
	5120	4" thick		170	.047			1.01	.40	1.41	2.13	
	5140	Stone, 4" thick		180	.044			.95	.38	1.33	2.02	
	5160	8" thick		175	.046	↓		.98	.39	1.37	2.07	
	5400	Alternate pricing method, stone, 4" thick		60	.133	C.F.		2.86	1.14	4	6.05	
	5420	8" thick		85	.094	"		2.02	.81	2.83	4.27	
	9000	Minimum labor/equipment charge	↓	2	4	Job		86	34.50	120.50	182	

020 800 | Haz. Mat'l Abatement

810	0010	**ASBESTOS ABATEMENT EQUIPMENT** and supplies, buy	R020 -820									810
	0200	Air filtration device, 2000 C.F.M.				Ea.	2,500			2,500	2,750	
	0250	Large volume air sampling pump, minimum					450			450	495	
	0260	Maximum					1,000			1,000	1,100	
	0300	Airless sprayer unit, 2 gun					2,000			2,000	2,200	
	0350	Light stand, 500 watt				↓	250			250	275	
	0400	Personal respirators										
	0410	Negative pressure, 1/2 face, dual operation, min.				Ea.	22.50			22.50	25	
	0420	Maximum					24			24	26.50	
	0450	P.A.P.R., full face, minimum					400			400	440	
	0460	Maximum					700			700	770	
	0470	Supplied air, full face, incl. air line, minimum					450			450	495	
	0480	Maximum					600			600	660	
	0500	Personnel sampling pump, minimum					450			450	495	
	0510	Maximum					750			750	825	
	1500	Power panel, 20 unit, incl. G.F.I.					1,800			1,800	1,975	
	1600	Shower unit, including pump and filters					1,125			1,125	1,250	
	1700	Supplied air system (type C)					10,000			10,000	11,000	
	1750	Vacuum cleaner, HEPA, 16 gal., stainless steel, wet/dry					1,000			1,000	1,100	
	1760	55 gallon					2,200			2,200	2,425	
	1800	Vacuum loader, 9-18 ton/hr					90,000			90,000	99,000	
	1900	Water atomizer unit, including 55 gal. drum					230			230	253	
	2000	Worker protection, whole body, foot, head cover & gloves, plastic					30			30	33	
	2500	Respirator, single use					9			9	9.90	
	2550	Cartridge for respirator					36			36	39.50	
	2570	Glove bag, 7 mil, 50" x 64"					8.50			8.50	9.35	
	2580	10 mil, 44" x 60"					8.40			8.40	9.25	
	3000	HEPA vacuum for work area, minimun					1,000			1,000	1,100	
	3050	Maximum					4,500			4,500	4,950	
	6000	Disposable polyethelene bags, 6 mil, 3 C.F.					1.15			1.15	1.27	
	6300	Disposable fiber drums, 3 C.F.					6.50			6.50	7.15	
	6400	Pressure sensitive caution lables, 3" x 5"					.12			.12	.13	
	6450	11" x 17"					.25			.25	.28	
	6500	Negative air machine, 1800 C.F.M.	↓			↓	775			775	855	
820	0010	**ASBESTOS ABATEMENT WORK AREA** Containment and preparation.										820
	0100	Pre-cleaning, HEPA vacuum and wet wipe, flat surfaces	A-10	12,000	.005	S.F.		.16		.16	.27	
	0200	Protect carpeted area, 2 layers 6 mil poly on 3/4" plywood	"	1,000	.064		1.50	1.95		3.45	4.90	
	0300	Separation barrier, 2" x 4" @ 16", 1/2" plywood ea. side, 8' high	2 Carp	400	.040	↓	1.25	1.09		2.34	3.21	

020 | Subsurface Investigation & Demolition

020 800 | Haz. Mat'l Abatement

			CREW	DAILY OUTPUT	LABOR-HOURS	UNIT	MAT.	LABOR	EQUIP.	TOTAL	TOTAL INCL O&P	
820	0310	12' high	2 Carp	320	.050	S.F.	1.40	1.36		2.76	3.83	820
	0320	16' high		200	.080		1.50	2.18		3.68	5.30	
	0400	Personnel decontam. chamber, 2" x 4" @ 16", 3/4" ply ea. side		280	.057		2.50	1.56		4.06	5.35	
	0450	Waste decontam. chamber, 2" x 4" studs @ 16", 3/4" ply ea. side	↓	360	.044	↓	3	1.21		4.21	5.35	
	0500	Cover surfaces with polyethelene sheeting										
	0501	Including glue and tape										
	0550	Floors, each layer, 6 mil	A-10	8,000	.008	S.F.	.10	.24		.34	.52	
	0551	4 mil		9,000	.007		.06	.22		.28	.43	
	0560	Walls, each layer, 6 mil		6,000	.011		.09	.33		.42	.64	
	0561	4 mil	↓	7,000	.009		.07	.28		.35	.53	
	0570	For heights above 12', add						20%				
	0575	For heights above 20', add						30%				
	0580	For fire retardant poly, add					100%					
	0590	For large open areas, deduct					10%	20%				
	0600	Seal floor penetrations with foam firestop to 36 Sq. In.	2 Carp	200	.080	Ea.	6.25	2.18		8.43	10.55	
	0610	36 Sq. In. to 72 Sq. In.		125	.128		12.50	3.49		15.99	19.60	
	0615	72 Sq. In. to 144 Sq. In.		80	.200		25	5.45		30.45	36.50	
	0620	Wall penetrations, to 36 square inches		180	.089		6.25	2.43		8.68	10.95	
	0630	36 Sq. In. to 72 Sq. In.		100	.160		12.50	4.37		16.87	21	
	0640	72 Sq. In. to 144 Sq. In.	↓	60	.267	↓	25	7.30		32.30	39.50	
	0800	Caulk seams with latex	1 Carp	230	.035	L.F.	.15	.95		1.10	1.76	
	0900	Set up neg. air machine, 1-2k C.F.M. /25 M.C.F. volume	1 Asbe	4.30	1.860	Ea.		56.50		56.50	94	
830	0010	**DEMOLITION IN ASBESTOS CONTAMINATED AREA**										830
	0200	Ceiling, including suspension system, plaster and lath	A-9	2,100	.030	S.F.		.93		.93	1.55	
	0210	Finished plaster, leaving wire lath		585	.109			3.34		3.34	5.55	
	0220	Suspended acoustical tile		3,500	.018			.56		.56	.93	
	0230	Concealed tile grid system		3,000	.021			.65		.65	1.08	
	0240	Metal pan grid system		1,500	.043			1.30		1.30	2.17	
	0250	Gypsum board		2,500	.026	↓		.78		.78	1.30	
	0260	Lighting fixtures up to 2' x 4'		72	.889	Ea.		27		27	45	
	0400	Partitions, non load bearing										
	0410	Plaster, lath, and studs	A-9	690	.093	S.F.	.55	2.83		3.38	5.30	
	0450	Gypsum board and studs	"	1,390	.046	"		1.40		1.40	2.34	
	9000	For type C (supplied air) respirator equipment, add				%					10%	
840	0010	**BULK ASBESTOS REMOVAL**										840
	0020	Includes disposable tools and 1 suit and respirator/day/worker										
	0100	Beams, W 10 x 19	A-9	235	.272	L.F.		8.30		8.30	13.80	
	0110	W 12 x 22		210	.305			9.30		9.30	15.45	
	0120	W 14 x 26		180	.356			10.85		10.85	18.05	
	0130	W 16 x 31		160	.400			12.20		12.20	20.50	
	0140	W 18 x 40		140	.457			13.95		13.95	23	
	0150	W 24 x 55		110	.582			17.75		17.75	29.50	
	0160	W 30 x 108		85	.753			23		23	38	
	0170	W 36 x 150	↓	72	.889	↓		27		27	45	
	0200	Boiler insulation		480	.133	S.F.	.06	4.07		4.13	6.80	
	0210	With metal lath add				%				50%		
	0300	Boiler breeching or flue insulation	A-9	520	.123	S.F.		3.76		3.76	6.25	
	0310	For active boiler, add				%				100%		
	0400	Duct or AHU insulation	A-10B	440	.073	S.F.		2.22		2.22	3.70	
	0500	Duct vibration isolation joints, up to 24 Sq. In. duct	A-9	56	1.143	Ea.		35		35	58	
	0520	25 Sq. In. to 48 Sq. In. duct		48	1.333			40.50		40.50	67.50	
	0530	49 Sq. In. to 76 Sq. In. duct		40	1.600	↓		49		49	81	
	0600	Pipe insulation, air cell type, up to 4" diameter pipe		900	.071	L.F.		2.17		2.17	3.61	
	0610	4" to 8" diameter pipe		800	.080			2.44		2.44	4.06	
	0620	10" to 12" diameter pipe		700	.091			2.79		2.79	4.64	
	0630	14" to 16" diameter pipe	↓	550	.116	↓		3.55		3.55	5.90	

Important: See the Reference Section for critical supporting data - Reference Nos., Crews, & City Cost Indexes

020 | Subsurface Investigation & Demolition

020 800 | Haz. Mat'l Abatement

			CREW	DAILY OUTPUT	LABOR-HOURS	UNIT	MAT.	LABOR	EQUIP.	TOTAL	TOTAL INCL O&P	
840	0650	Over 16" diameter pipe	A-9	650	.098	S.F.		3		3	5	840
	0700	With glove bag up to 3" diameter pipe		100	.640	L.F.	3.15	19.55		22.70	36	
	1000	Pipe fitting insulation up to 4" diameter pipe		320	.200	Ea.		6.10		6.10	10.15	
	1100	6" to 8" diameter pipe		304	.211			6.40		6.40	10.70	
	1110	10" to 12" diameter pipe		192	.333			10.15		10.15	16.90	
	1120	14" to 16" diameter pipe		128	.500			15.25		15.25	25.50	
	1130	Over 16" diameter pipe		176	.364	S.F.		11.10		11.10	18.45	
	1200	With glove bag, up to 8" diameter pipe		40	1.600	Ea.	6.55	49		55.55	88	
	2000	Scrape foam fireproofing from flat surface		2,400	.027	S.F.		.81		.81	1.35	
	2100	Irregular surfaces		1,200	.053			1.63		1.63	2.71	
	3000	Remove cementitious material from flat surface		1,800	.036			1.08		1.08	1.80	
	3100	Irregular surface		1,400	.046			1.39		1.39	2.32	
	4000	Scrape acoustical coating/fireproofing, from ceiling		3,200	.020			.61		.61	1.02	
	5000	Remove VAT from floor by hand		2,400	.027			.81		.81	1.35	
	5100	By machine	A-11	4,800	.013			.41	.01	.42	.69	
	5150	For 2 layers, add				%				50%		
	6000	Remove contaminated soil from crawl space by hand	A-9	400	.160	C.F.		4.88		4.88	8.10	
	6100	With large production vacuum loader	A-12	700	.091	"		2.79	.75	3.54	5.45	
	7000	Radiator backing, not including radiator removal	A-9	1,200	.053	S.F.		1.63		1.63	2.71	
	8000	Cement-asbestos transite board	2 Asbe	2,000	.008		.08	.24		.32	.50	
	8100	Transite shingle siding	A-10D	750	.043		.08	1.22	.93	2.23	3.09	
	8200	Shingle roofing	A-10B	2,000	.016		.07	.49		.56	.89	
	8250	Built-up, no gravel, non-friable	B-2	1,400	.029		.07	.62		.69	1.12	
	8300	Asbestos millboard	2 Asbe	1,000	.016		.08	.49		.57	.89	
	9000	For type C (supplied air) respirator equipment, add				%					10%	
850	0010	**WASTE PACKAGING, HANDLING, & DISPOSAL**										850
	0100	Collect and bag bulk material, 3 C.F. bags, by hand	A-9	400	.160	Ea.	1.15	4.88		6.03	9.35	
	0200	Large production vacuum loader	A-12	880	.073		.80	2.22	.60	3.62	5.25	
	1000	Double bag and decontaminate	A-9	960	.067		2.30	2.03		4.33	5.90	
	2000	Containerize bagged material in drums, per 3 C.F. drum	"	800	.080		6.50	2.44		8.94	11.20	
	3000	Cart bags 50' to dumpster	2 Asbe	400	.040			1.22		1.22	2.03	
	5000	Disposal charges, not including haul, minimum				C.Y.					50	
	5020	Maximum				"					175	
	5100	Remove refrigerant from system	1 Plum	40	.200	Lb.		6.50		6.50	10.20	
	9000	For type C (supplied air) respirator equipment, add				%					10%	
860	0010	**DECONTAMINATION CONTAINMENT AREA DEMOLITION** and clean-up										860
	0100	Spray exposed substrate with surfactant (bridging)										
	0200	Flat surfaces	A-9	6,000	.011	S.F.	.35	.33		.68	.93	
	0250	Irregular surfaces		4,000	.016	"	.30	.49		.79	1.14	
	0300	Pipes, beams, and columns		2,000	.032	L.F.	.55	.98		1.53	2.23	
	1000	Spray encapsulate polyethelene sheeting		8,000	.008	S.F.	.30	.24		.54	.74	
	1100	Roll down polyethelene sheeting		8,000	.008	"		.24		.24	.41	
	1500	Bag polyethelene sheeting		400	.160	Ea.	.75	4.88		5.63	8.95	
	2000	Fine clean exposed substrate, with nylon brush		2,400	.027	S.F.		.81		.81	1.35	
	2500	Wet wipe substrate		4,800	.013			.41		.41	.68	
	2600	Vacuum surfaces, fine brush		6,400	.010			.31		.31	.51	
	3000	Structural demolition										
	3100	Wood stud walls	A-9	2,800	.023	S.F.		.70		.70	1.16	
	3500	Window manifolds, not incl. window replacement		4,200	.015			.46		.46	.77	
	3600	Plywood carpet protection		2,000	.032			.98		.98	1.62	
	4000	Remove custom decontamination facility	A-10A	8	3	Ea.	12.50	92		104.50	167	
	4100	Remove portable decontamination facility	3 Asbe	12	2	"	12.50	61		73.50	115	
	5000	HEPA vacuum, shampoo carpeting	A-9	4,800	.013	S.F.	.05	.41		.46	.74	
	9000	Final cleaning of protected surfaces	A-10A	8,000	.003	"		.09		.09	.15	

020 | Subsurface Investigation & Demolition

020 800 | Haz. Mat'l Abatement

		CREW	DAILY OUTPUT	LABOR-HOURS	UNIT	1999 BARE COSTS MAT.	LABOR	EQUIP.	TOTAL	TOTAL INCL O&P
870	0010	**ENCAPSULATION WITH SEALANTS**									
	0100	Ceilings and walls, minimum	A-9	21,000	.003	S.F.	.25	.09		.34	.43
	0110	Maximum		10,600	.006		.40	.18		.58	.75
	0200	Columns and beams, minimum		13,300	.005		.25	.15		.40	.52
	0210	Maximum		5,325	.012		.45	.37		.82	1.11
	0300	Pipes to 12" diameter including minor repairs, minimum		800	.080	L.F.	.35	2.44		2.79	4.45
	0310	Maximum		400	.160	"	1	4.88		5.88	9.20
880	0010	**REMOVAL OF UNDERGROUND STORAGE TANKS** R020-880									
	0011	Petroleum storage tanks, non-leaking									
	0100	Excavate & load onto trailer									
	0110	3000 gal. to 5000 gal. tank	B-14	4	12	Ea.		273	54.50	327.50	510
	0120	6000 gal to 8000 gal tank	B-3A	3	13.333			305	238	543	765
	0130	9000 gal to 12000 gal tank	"	2	20			455	355	810	1,150
	0190	Known leaking tank add				%				100%	100%
	0200	Remove sludge, water and remaining product from bottom									
	0201	of tank with vacuum truck									
	0300	3000 gal to 5000 gal tank	A-13	5	1.600	Ea.		43.50	105	148.50	185
	0310	6000 gal to 8000 gal tank		4	2			54.50	131	185.50	231
	0320	9000 gal to 12000 gal tank		3	2.667			72.50	175	247.50	305
	0390	Dispose of sludge off-site, average				Gal.					4
	0400	Insert solid carbon dioxide "dry ice" to produce inert gas									
	0401	For cleaning/transporting tanks (1.5 lbs./100 gal. cap)	1 Clab	500	.016	Lb.	1.20	.34		1.54	1.89
	1020	Haul tank to certified salvage dump, 100 miles round trip									
	1023	3000 gal. to 5000 gal. tank				Ea.				550	630
	1026	6000 gal. to 8000 gal. tank								650	750
	1029	9,000 gal. to 12,000 gal. tank								875	1,000
	1100	Disposal of contaminated soil to landfill									
	1110	Minimum				C.Y.					100
	1111	Maximum				"					300
	1120	Disposal of contaminated soil to									
	1121	bituminous concrete batch plant									
	1130	Minimum				C.Y.					50
	1131	Maximum				"					100
	2010	Decontamination of soil on site incl poly tarp on top/bottom									
	2011	Soil containment berm, and chemical treatment									
	2020	Minimum	B-11C	100	.160	C.Y.	5.60	3.99	2.19	11.78	15.05
	2021	Maximum	"	100	.160		7.25	3.99	2.19	13.43	16.90
	2050	Disposal of decontaminated soil, minimum									60
	2055	Maximum									125
890	0010	**OSHA TESTING**									
	0100	Certified technician, minimum				Day					300
	0110	Maximum				"					500
	0200	Personal sampling, PCM analysis, minimum	1 Asbe	8	1	Ea.	2.75	30.50		33.25	53.50
	0210	Maximum	"	4	2	"	3	61		64	104
	0300	Industrial hygienist, minimum				Day					400
	0310	Maximum				"					550
	1000	Cleaned area samples	1 Asbe	8	1	Ea.	2.50	30.50		33	53.50
	1100	PCM analysis		8	1		30	30.50		60.50	83.50
	1110	Maximum		4	2		3.09	61		64.09	104
	1200	TEM analysis, minimum									400
	1210	Maximum									1,000

021 | Site Preparation & Excavation Support

021 200 | Structure Moving

			CREW	DAILY OUTPUT	LABOR-HOURS	UNIT	MAT.	LABOR	EQUIP.	TOTAL	TOTAL INCL O&P	
204	0010	**MOVING BUILDINGS** One day move, up to 24' wide										204
	0020	Reset on new foundation, patch & hook-up, average move				Total					8,700	
	0040	Wood or steel frame bldg., based on ground floor area	B-4	185	.259	S.F.		5.70	2.57	8.27	12.25	
	0060	Masonry bldg., based on ground floor area	"	137	.350			7.65	3.47	11.12	16.60	
	0200	For 24' to 42' wide, add									15%	
	0220	For each additional day on road, add	B-4	1	48	Day		1,050	475	1,525	2,275	
	0240	Construct new basement, move building, 1 day										
	0300	move, patch & hook-up, based on ground floor area	B-3	155	.310	S.F.	5.75	7.15	11.30	24.20	30.50	

021 520 | Shores

			CREW	DAILY OUTPUT	LABOR-HOURS	UNIT	MAT.	LABOR	EQUIP.	TOTAL	TOTAL INCL O&P	
524	0010	**SHORING** Existing building, with timber, no salvage allowance	B-51	2.20	21.818	M.B.F.	645	475	78	1,198	1,600	524
	1000	With 35 ton screw jacks, per box and jack		3.60	13.333	Jack	40	291	47.50	378.50	580	
	1090	Minimum labor/equipment charge		2	24	Ea.		525	86	611	970	
	1100	Masonry openings in walls, see div. 020-704										

021 560 | Underpinning

			CREW	DAILY OUTPUT	LABOR-HOURS	UNIT	MAT.	LABOR	EQUIP.	TOTAL	TOTAL INCL O&P	
564	0010	**UNDERPINNING FOUNDATIONS** Including excavation,										564
	0020	forming, reinforcing, concrete and equipment										
	0100	5' to 16' below grade, 100 to 500 C.Y.	B-52	2.30	24.348	C.Y.	168	615	188	971	1,425	
	0200	Over 500 C.Y.		2.50	22.400		152	565	173	890	1,300	
	0400	16' to 25' below grade, 100 to 500 C.Y.		2	28		185	705	216	1,106	1,625	
	0500	Over 500 C.Y.		2.10	26.667		175	670	206	1,051	1,550	
	0700	26' to 40' below grade, 100 to 500 C.Y.		1.60	35		202	880	270	1,352	2,000	
	0800	Over 500 C.Y.		1.80	31.111		185	785	240	1,210	1,775	
	0900	For under 50 C.Y., add					10%	40%				

021 610 | Sheet Piling

			CREW	DAILY OUTPUT	LABOR-HOURS	UNIT	MAT.	LABOR	EQUIP.	TOTAL	TOTAL INCL O&P	
614	0010	**SHEET PILING** Steel, not incl. wales, 22 psf, 15' excav., left in place	B-40	10.81	5.920	Ton	795	163	178	1,136	1,350	614
	0100	Drive, extract & salvage		6	10.667	"	211	294	320	825	1,100	
	1200	15' deep excavation, 22 psf, left in place		983	.065	S.F.	9.25	1.80	1.96	13.01	15.40	
	1300	Drive, extract & salvage		656	.098	"	2.37	2.69	2.93	7.99	10.45	
	2100	Rent steel sheet piling and wales, first month				Ton	230			230	253	
	2200	Per added month				"	23			23	25.50	
	3900	Wood, solid sheeting, incl. wales, braces and spacers,										
	3910	drive, extract & salvage, 8' deep excavation	B-31	330	.121	S.F.	1.52	2.79	.46	4.77	6.85	
	4520	Left in place, 8' deep, 55 S.F./hr.		440	.091	"	2.73	2.09	.35	5.17	6.90	
	4990	Minimum labor/equipment charge		2	20	Job		460	76	536	855	
	5000	For treated lumber add cost of treatment to lumber										
	5010	See division 063-102										

022 | Earthwork

022 200 | Excav./Backfill/Compact.

			CREW	DAILY OUTPUT	LABOR-HOURS	UNIT	MAT.	LABOR	EQUIP.	TOTAL	TOTAL INCL O&P	
204	0010	**BACKFILL** By hand, no compaction, light soil	1 Clab	14	.571	C.Y.		12.25		12.25	20.50	204
	0100	Heavy soil		11	.727			15.60		15.60	26	
	0300	Compaction in 6" layers, hand tamp, add to above		20.60	.388			8.35		8.35	13.95	
	0400	Roller compaction operator walking, add	B-10A	100	.120			3.13	.93	4.06	6.05	
	0500	Air tamp, add	B-9C	190	.211			4.60	.95	5.55	8.75	
	0600	Vibrating plate, add	A-1	60	.133			2.86	1.14	4	6.05	

022 | Earthwork

022 200 | Excav./Backfill/Compact.

			CREW	DAILY OUTPUT	LABOR-HOURS	UNIT	MAT.	LABOR	EQUIP.	TOTAL	TOTAL INCL O&P	
204	0800	Compaction in 12" layers, hand tamp, add to above	1 Clab	34	.235	C.Y.		5.05		5.05	8.45	204
	1000	Air tamp, add	B-9	285	.140			3.07	.63	3.70	5.85	
	1100	Vibrating plate, add	A-1	90	.089			1.91	.76	2.67	4.03	
	1200	Trench, dozer, no compaction, 60 HP	B-10L	425	.028			.74	.72	1.46	1.99	
	1300	Dozer backfilling, bulk, up to 300' haul, no compaction	B-10B	1,200	.010			.26	.70	.96	1.19	
	1400	Air tamped	B-11B	240	.067			1.66	4.35	6.01	7.50	
	1900	Dozer backfilling, trench, up to 300' haul, no compaction	B-10B	900	.013			.35	.93	1.28	1.59	
	2000	Air tamped	B-11B	235	.068			1.70	4.44	6.14	7.65	
	2350	Spreading in 8" layers, small dozer	B-10B	1,060	.011			.30	.79	1.09	1.35	
	2450	Compacting with vibrating plate, 8" lifts	A-1	73	.110			2.35	.94	3.29	4.96	
208	0010	**BACKFILL, STRUCTURAL** Dozer or F.E. loader										208
	0020	From existing stockpile, no compaction										
	2000	75 H.P., 50' haul, sand & gravel	B-10L	1,100	.011	C.Y.		.28	.28	.56	.77	
	2020	Common earth		975	.012			.32	.32	.64	.87	
	2040	Clay		850	.014			.37	.36	.73	.99	
	2400	300' haul, sand & gravel		370	.032			.85	.83	1.68	2.28	
	2420	Common earth		330	.036			.95	.93	1.88	2.56	
	2440	Clay		290	.041			1.08	1.06	2.14	2.91	
	3000	105 H.P., 50' haul, sand & gravel	B-10W	1,350	.009			.23	.31	.54	.71	
	3020	Common earth		1,225	.010			.26	.34	.60	.78	
	3040	Clay		1,100	.011			.28	.38	.66	.88	
	3300	300' haul, sand & gravel		465	.026			.67	.90	1.57	2.08	
	3320	Common earth		415	.029			.75	1.01	1.76	2.33	
	3340	Clay		370	.032			.85	1.13	1.98	2.61	
212	0010	**BORROW** Buy and load at pit, haul 2 miles round trip										212
	0020	and spread, with 200 H.P. dozer, no compaction										
	0100	Bank run gravel	B-15	600	.047	C.Y.	5.50	1.11	2.87	9.48	11	
	0200	Common borrow		600	.047		3.75	1.11	2.87	7.73	9.10	
	0300	Crushed stone, (1.40 tons per CY), 1-1/2"		600	.047		17.75	1.11	2.87	21.73	24.50	
	0320	3/4"		600	.047		17.75	1.11	2.87	21.73	24.50	
	0340	1/2"		600	.047		18.25	1.11	2.87	22.23	25	
	0360	3/8"		600	.047		19	1.11	2.87	22.98	26	
	0400	Sand, washed, concrete		600	.047		11.50	1.11	2.87	15.48	17.65	
	0500	Dead or bank sand		600	.047		3.75	1.11	2.87	7.73	9.10	
	0600	Select structural fill		600	.047		7.50	1.11	2.87	11.48	13.20	
	0700	Screened loam		600	.047		18.25	1.11	2.87	22.23	25	
	0800	Topsoil, weed free		600	.047		14.15	1.11	2.87	18.13	20.50	
	0900	For 5 mile haul, add	B-34B	200	.040			.88	2.21	3.09	3.87	
222	0010	**COMPACTION, STRUCTURAL** Steel wheel tandem roller, 5 tons	B-10E	8	1.500	Hr.		39	19.10	58.10	84	222
	0050	Air tamp, 6" to 8" lifts, common fill	B-9	250	.160	C.Y.		3.50	.72	4.22	6.65	
	0060	Select fill	"	300	.133			2.91	.60	3.51	5.55	
	0600	Vibratory plate, 8" lifts, common fill	A-1	200	.040			.86	.34	1.20	1.82	
	0700	Select fill	"	216	.037			.79	.32	1.11	1.68	
	9000	Minimum labor/equipment charge	1 Clab	4	2	Job		43		43	72	
226	0010	**COMPACTION**										226
	5000	Riding, vibrating roller, 6" lifts, 2 passes	B-10Y	3,000	.004	C.Y.		.10	.12	.22	.30	
	5020	3 passes		2,300	.005			.14	.15	.29	.39	
	5040	4 passes		1,900	.006			.16	.19	.35	.47	
	5060	12" lifts, 2 passes		5,200	.002			.06	.07	.13	.17	
	5080	3 passes		3,500	.003			.09	.10	.19	.25	
	5100	4 passes		2,600	.005			.12	.14	.26	.34	
	5600	Sheepsfoot or wobbly wheel roller, 6" lifts, 2 passes	B-10G	2,400	.005			.13	.23	.36	.47	
	5620	3 passes		1,735	.007			.18	.32	.50	.64	
	5640	4 passes		1,300	.009			.24	.43	.67	.86	
	5680	12" lifts, 2 passes		5,200	.002			.06	.11	.17	.22	
	5700	3 passes		3,500	.003			.09	.16	.25	.32	

Reference note: R022-220 (shown at rows 0800 and 0010 of section 222)

022 | Earthwork

022 200 | Excav./Backfill/Compact.

			CREW	DAILY OUTPUT	LABOR-HOURS	UNIT	MAT.	LABOR	EQUIP.	TOTAL	TOTAL INCL O&P	
226	5720	4 passes	B-10G	2,600	.005	C.Y.		.12	.21	.33	.43	226
	7000	Walk behind, vibrating plate 18" wide, 6" lifts, 2 passes	B-18	200	.120			2.65	.26	2.91	4.73	
	7020	3 passes	A-1	185	.043			.93	.37	1.30	1.96	
	7040	4 passes		140	.057			1.23	.49	1.72	2.59	
	7200	12" lifts, 2 passes		560	.014			.31	.12	.43	.64	
	7220	3 passes		375	.021			.46	.18	.64	.97	
	7240	4 passes		280	.029			.61	.25	.86	1.30	
	7500	Vibrating roller 24" wide, 6" lifts, 2 passes	B-10A	420	.029			.75	.22	.97	1.44	
	7520	3 passes		280	.043			1.12	.33	1.45	2.17	
	7540	4 passes		210	.057			1.49	.44	1.93	2.90	
	7600	12" lifts, 2 passes		840	.014			.37	.11	.48	.72	
	7620	3 passes		560	.021			.56	.17	.73	1.08	
	7640	4 passes		420	.029			.75	.22	.97	1.44	
	8000	Rammer tamper, 6" to 11", 4" lifts, 2 passes	A-1	130	.062			1.32	.53	1.85	2.79	
	8050	3 passes		97	.082			1.77	.71	2.48	3.74	
	8100	4 passes		65	.123			2.64	1.06	3.70	5.60	
	8200	8" lifts, 2 passes		260	.031			.66	.26	.92	1.39	
	8250	3 passes		195	.041			.88	.35	1.23	1.86	
	8300	4 passes		130	.062			1.32	.53	1.85	2.79	
	8400	13" to 18", 4" lifts, 2 passes		390	.021			.44	.18	.62	.93	
	8450	3 passes		290	.028			.59	.24	.83	1.25	
	8500	4 passes		195	.041			.88	.35	1.23	1.86	
	8600	8" lifts, 2 passes		780	.010			.22	.09	.31	.47	
	8650	3 passes		585	.014			.29	.12	.41	.62	
	8700	4 passes		390	.021			.44	.18	.62	.93	
	9000	Water, 3000 gal. truck, 3 mile haul	B-45	1,888	.008		.20	.21	.39	.80	.99	
	9010	6 mile haul		1,444	.011		.20	.28	.52	1	1.24	
	9020	12 mile haul		1,000	.016		.20	.40	.74	1.34	1.69	
	9030	6000 gal. wagon, 3 mile haul	B-59	2,000	.004		.20	.09	.26	.55	.65	
	9040	6 mile haul	"	1,600	.005		.20	.11	.33	.64	.76	
238	0010	**EXCAVATING, BULK BANK MEASURE** Common earth piled R022-240										238
	0020	For loading onto trucks, add								15%	15%	
	0200	Backhoe, hydraulic, crawler mtd., 1 C.Y. cap. = 75 C.Y./hr. R022-250	B-12A	600	.027	C.Y.		.71	.91	1.62	2.13	
	1200	Front end loader, track mtd., 1-1/2 C.Y. cap. = 70 C.Y./hr.	B-10N	560	.021			.56	.63	1.19	1.59	
	1500	Wheel mounted, 3/4 C.Y. cap. = 45 C.Y./hr.	B-10R	360	.033			.87	.68	1.55	2.15	
	9000	Minimum labor/equipment charge	B-10L	2	6	Job		156	154	310	420	
242	0010	**EXCAVATING, BULK, DOZER** Open site										242
	2000	75 H.P., 50' haul, sand & gravel	B-10L	460	.026	C.Y.		.68	.67	1.35	1.84	
	2200	150' haul, sand & gravel		230	.052			1.36	1.34	2.70	3.67	
	2400	300' haul, sand & gravel		120	.100			2.61	2.57	5.18	7.05	
	3000	105 H.P., 50' haul, sand & gravel	B-10W	700	.017			.45	.60	1.05	1.38	
	3200	150' haul, sand & gravel		310	.039			1.01	1.35	2.36	3.11	
	3300	300' haul, sand & gravel		140	.086			2.24	2.98	5.22	6.90	
	4000	200 H.P., 50' haul, sand & gravel	B-10B	1,400	.009			.22	.60	.82	1.02	
	4200	150' haul, sand & gravel		595	.020			.53	1.41	1.94	2.40	
	4400	300' haul, sand & gravel		310	.039			1.01	2.71	3.72	4.61	
	5040	Clay	B-10M	1,025	.012			.31	1.10	1.41	1.70	
	5400	300' haul, sand & gravel	"	470	.026			.67	2.41	3.08	3.72	
250	0010	**EXCAVATING, STRUCTURAL** Hand, pits to 6' deep, sandy soil	1 Clab	8	1	C.Y.		21.50		21.50	36	250
	0100	Heavy soil or clay		4	2			43		43	72	
	0300	Pits 6' to 12' deep, sandy soil		5	1.600			34.50		34.50	57.50	
	0500	Heavy soil or clay		3	2.667			57		57	95.50	
	0700	Pits 12' to 18' deep, sandy soil		4	2			43		43	72	
	0900	Heavy soil or clay		2	4			86		86	144	
	1100	Hand loading trucks from stock pile, sandy soil		12	.667			14.30		14.30	24	
	1300	Heavy soil or clay		8	1			21.50		21.50	36	

For expanded coverage of these items see Means Heavy Construction Cost Data 1999

022 | Earthwork

022 200 | Excav./Backfill/Compact.

		CREW	DAILY OUTPUT	LABOR-HOURS	UNIT	1999 BARE COSTS				TOTAL INCL O&P
						MAT.	LABOR	EQUIP.	TOTAL	
250 1500	For wet or muck hand excavation, add to above				%		50%		50%	250
2000	Machine excavation, for spread and mat footings, elevator pits,									
2001	and small building foundations									
2035	Common earth, hydraulic backhoe, 3/4 C.Y. bucket	B-12F	90	.178	C.Y.		4.75	4.99	9.74	13.05
2040	1 C.Y. bucket	B-12A	108	.148			3.96	5.05	9.01	11.90
2050	1-1/2 C.Y. bucket	B-12B	144	.111			2.97	4.95	7.92	10.15
2060	2 C.Y. bucket	B-12C	200	.080			2.14	5.10	7.24	9.05
2070	Sand and gravel, 3/4 C.Y. bucket	B-12F	100	.160			4.27	4.49	8.76	11.75
2080	1 C.Y. bucket	B-12A	120	.133			3.56	4.56	8.12	10.65
2090	1-1/2 C.Y. bucket	B-12B	160	.100			2.67	4.45	7.12	9.15
3000	2 C.Y. bucket	B-12C	220	.073			1.94	4.65	6.59	8.20
3010	Clay, till, or blasted rock, 3/4 C.Y. bucket	B-12F	80	.200			5.35	5.60	10.95	14.70
3020	1 C.Y. bucket	B-12A	95	.168			4.50	5.75	10.25	13.50
3030	1-1/2 C.Y. bucket	B-12B	130	.123			3.29	5.50	8.79	11.30
3040	2 C.Y. bucket	B-12C	175	.091			2.44	5.85	8.29	10.35
9000	Minimum labor/equipment charge	1 Clab	4	2	Job		43		43	72
254 0010	**EXCAVATING, TRENCH** or continuous footing, common earth									254
0020	No sheeting or dewatering included									
1400	By hand with pick and shovel 2' to 6' deep, light soil	1 Clab	8	1	C.Y.		21.50		21.50	36
1500	Heavy soil	"	4	2			43		43	72
1700	For tamping backfilled trenches, air tamp, add	A-1	100	.080			1.72	.69	2.41	3.63
1900	Vibrating plate, add	B-18	230	.104			2.31	.23	2.54	4.11
2100	Trim sides and bottom for concrete pours, common earth		1,500	.016	S.F.		.35	.03	.38	.63
2300	Hardpan		600	.040	"		.88	.09	.97	1.58
9000	Minimum labor/equipment charge	1 Clab	4	2	Job		43		43	72
258 0010	**EXCAVATING, UTILITY TRENCH** Common earth									258
0050	Trenching with chain trencher, 12 H.P., operator walking									
0100	4" wide trench, 12" deep	B-53	800	.010	L.F.		.27	.12	.39	.56
0150	18" deep		750	.011			.29	.13	.42	.60
0200	24" deep		700	.011			.31	.14	.45	.64
0300	6" wide trench, 12" deep		650	.012			.33	.15	.48	.69
0350	18" deep		600	.013			.36	.16	.52	.76
0400	24" deep		550	.015			.40	.18	.58	.82
0450	36" deep		450	.018			.48	.22	.70	1.01
0600	8" wide trench, 12" deep		475	.017			.46	.20	.66	.96
0650	18" deep		400	.020			.54	.24	.78	1.14
0700	24" deep		350	.023			.62	.28	.90	1.30
0750	36" deep		300	.027			.73	.32	1.05	1.51
0900	Minimum labor/equipment charge		2	4	Job		109	48.50	157.50	227
1000	Backfill by hand including compaction, add									
1050	4" wide trench, 12" deep	A-1	800	.010	L.F.		.21	.09	.30	.45
1100	18" deep		530	.015			.32	.13	.45	.68
1150	24" deep		400	.020			.43	.17	.60	.91
1300	6" wide trench, 12" deep		540	.015			.32	.13	.45	.67
1350	18" deep		405	.020			.42	.17	.59	.90
1400	24" deep		270	.030			.64	.25	.89	1.34
1450	36" deep		180	.044			.95	.38	1.33	2.02
1600	8" wide trench, 12" deep		400	.020			.43	.17	.60	.91
1650	18" deep		265	.030			.65	.26	.91	1.36
1700	24" deep		200	.040			.86	.34	1.20	1.82
1750	36" deep		135	.059			1.27	.51	1.78	2.69
2000	Chain trencher, 40 H.P. operator riding									
2050	6" wide trench and backfill, 12" deep	B-54	1,200	.007	L.F.		.18	.18	.36	.48
2100	18" deep		1,000	.008			.22	.21	.43	.58
2150	24" deep		975	.008			.22	.22	.44	.60

Important: See the Reference Section for critical supporting data - Reference Nos., Crews, & City Cost Indexes

022 | Earthwork

022 200 | Excav./Backfill/Compact.

			CREW	DAILY OUTPUT	LABOR-HOURS	UNIT	MAT.	LABOR	EQUIP.	TOTAL	TOTAL INCL O&P	
258	2200	36" deep	B-54	900	.009	L.F.		.24	.23	.47	.64	258
	2250	48" deep		750	.011			.29	.28	.57	.77	
	2300	60" deep		650	.012			.33	.32	.65	.89	
	2400	8" wide trench and backfill, 12" deep		1,000	.008			.22	.21	.43	.58	
	2450	18" deep		950	.008			.23	.22	.45	.60	
	2500	24" deep		900	.009			.24	.23	.47	.64	
	2550	36" deep		800	.010			.27	.26	.53	.72	
	2600	48" deep		650	.012			.33	.32	.65	.89	
	2700	12" wide trench and backfill, 12" deep		975	.008			.22	.22	.44	.60	
	2750	18" deep		860	.009			.25	.25	.50	.67	
	2800	24" deep		800	.010			.27	.26	.53	.72	
	2850	36" deep		725	.011			.30	.29	.59	.80	
	3000	16" wide trench and backfill, 12" deep		835	.010			.26	.25	.51	.69	
	3050	18" deep		750	.011			.29	.28	.57	.77	
	3100	24" deep	▼	700	.011	▼		.31	.30	.61	.82	
	3200	Compaction with vibratory plate, add								50%	50%	
	9000	Minimum labor/equipment charge	A-1	4	2	Job		43	17.15	60.15	91	
262	0010	**FILL** Spread dumped material, by dozer, no compaction	B-10B	1,000	.012	C.Y.		.31	.84	1.15	1.43	262
	0100	By hand	1 Clab	12	.667	"		14.30		14.30	24	
	9000	Minimum labor/equipment charge	"	4	2	Job		43		43	72	
266	0011	**HAULING** Excavated or borrow material, loose cubic yards										266
	0015	no loading included, highway haulers										
	0020	6 C.Y. dump truck, 1/4 mile round trip, 5.0 loads/hr.	B-34A	195	.041	C.Y.		.91	1.87	2.78	3.53	
	0200	4 mile round trip, 1.8 loads/hr.	"	70	.114			2.53	5.20	7.73	9.80	
	0310	12 C.Y. dump truck, 1/4 mile round trip 3.7 loads/hr.	B-34B	288	.028			.61	1.54	2.15	2.69	
	0500	4 mile round trip, 1.6 loads/hr.	"	125	.064			1.41	3.54	4.95	6.20	
	0600	16.5 C.Y. dump trailer, 1 mile round trip, 2.6 loads/hr.	B-34C	280	.029			.63	2	2.63	3.23	
	1100	4 mile round trip, 1.6 loads/hr.	"	172	.047			1.03	3.25	4.28	5.25	
	1150	20 C.Y. dump trailer, 1 mile round trip, 2.5 loads/hr.	B-34D	325	.025			.54	1.73	2.27	2.79	
	1240	4 mile round trip, 1.5 loads/hr.		195	.041			.91	2.88	3.79	4.65	
	1300	Hauling in medium traffic, add								20%	20%	
	1400	Heavy traffic, add								30%	30%	
	1600	Grading at dump, or embankment if required, by dozer	B-10B	1,000	.012	▼		.31	.84	1.15	1.43	
	1800	Spotter at fill or cut, if required	1 Clab	8	1	Hr.		21.50		21.50	36	
	4700	Highway hauling beyond 20 miles, per loaded mile, minimum				Mile					1	
	4750	Maximum				"					2	
270	0010	**HORIZONTAL BORING** Casing only, 100' minimum,										270
	0020	not incl. jacking pits or dewatering										
	0100	Roadwork, 1/2" thick wall, 24" diameter casing	B-42	14	4.571	L.F.	45	110	80	235	325	
	0200	36" diameter		12	5.333		75	129	93.50	297.50	405	
	0300	48" diameter		12	5.333		105	129	93.50	327.50	435	
	0500	Railroad work, 24" diameter		10	6.400		45	155	112	312	435	
	0600	36" diameter		9.50	6.737		75	163	118	356	490	
	0700	48" diameter	▼	9	7.111		105	172	125	402	545	
	0900	For ledge, add								145	175	
	1000	Small diameter boring, 3", sandy soil	B-82	900	.018		13	.43	.05	13.48	15.05	
	1040	Rocky soil	"	500	.032	▼	13	.78	.10	13.88	15.70	
274	0010	**MOBILIZATION OR DEMOBILIZATION** Up to 50 miles										274
	0020	Dozer, loader, backhoe or excavator, 70 H.P.- 250 H.P.	B-34K	6	1.333	Ea.		29.50	152	181.50	216	
	0100	Above 250 H.P		4	2			44	228	272	325	
	0300	Scraper, towed type (incl. tractor), 6 C.Y. capacity		3.75	2.133			47	244	291	345	
	0400	10 C.Y.		3.50	2.286			50.50	261	311.50	370	
	0600	Self-propelled scraper, 15 C.Y.	▼	3.30	2.424			53.50	277	330.50	395	

For expanded coverage of these items see *Means Heavy Construction Cost Data 1999*

022 | Earthwork

022 200 | Excav./Backfill/Compact.

			CREW	DAILY OUTPUT	LABOR-HOURS	UNIT	MAT.	LABOR	EQUIP.	TOTAL	TOTAL INCL O&P
274	0700	24 C.Y.	B-34K	3	2.667	Ea.		59	305	364	430
	0900	Shovel or dragline, 3/4 C.Y.		3.60	2.222			49	254	303	360
	1000	1-1/2 C.Y.		3	2.667			59	305	364	430
	1100	Delivery charge for small equipment on flatbed trailer, minimum									40
	1150	Maximum									100
	3000	For large pieces of equipment, allow for knockdown, assembly									
	3001	and lead and tail vehicles for highway transport									
286	0010	**LOAM OR TOPSOIL** Remove and stockpile on site									
	0700	Furnish and place, truck dumped, screened, 4" deep	B-10S	1,300	.009	S.Y.	2.28	.24	.25	2.77	3.17
	0800	6" deep		820	.015	"	2.92	.38	.39	3.69	4.26
	0810	Minimum labor/equipment charge		2	6	Ea.		156	160	316	430
	0900	Fine grading and seeding, incl. lime, fertilizer & seed,									
	1000	With equipment	B-14	1,000	.048	S.Y.	.30	1.09	.22	1.61	2.38
	2000	Minimum labor/equipment charge	1 Clab	4	2	Job		43		43	72

022 300 | Pavement Base

304	0010	**BASE** Prepare and roll sub-base, small areas to 2500 S.Y.	B-32A	1,500	.016	S.Y.		.42	.66	1.08	1.40
	0100	Large areas over 2500 S.Y.	B-32	3,700	.009	"		.23	.45	.68	.86
	9000	Minimum labor/equipment charge	1 Clab	4	2	Job		43		43	72
308	0010	**BASE COURSE** For roadways and large paved areas									
	0050	Crushed 3/4" stone base, compacted, 3" deep	B-36B	5,200	.012	S.Y.	3.07	.31	.63	4.01	4.57
	0100	6" deep		5,000	.013		6.15	.32	.65	7.12	8.05
	0200	9" deep		4,600	.014		9.25	.35	.71	10.31	11.50
	0300	12" deep		4,200	.015		12.55	.38	.78	13.71	15.30
	0301	Crushed 1-1/2" stone base, compacted to 4" deep		6,000	.011		3.78	.27	.54	4.59	5.20
	0302	6" deep		5,400	.012		5.80	.30	.60	6.70	7.50
	0303	8" deep		4,500	.014		7.55	.36	.73	8.64	9.75
	0304	12" deep		3,800	.017		11.60	.43	.86	12.89	14.40
	0310	Minimum labor/equipment charge	B-36	1	40	Job		985	1,150	2,135	2,875
	0350	Bank run gravel, spread and compacted									
	0370	6" deep	B-32	6,000	.005	S.Y.	2.34	.14	.28	2.76	3.11
	0390	9" deep		4,900	.007		3.44	.17	.34	3.95	4.44
	0400	12" deep		4,200	.008		4.68	.20	.40	5.28	5.90
	8900	For small and irregular areas, add						50%	50%		
	9000	Minimum labor/equipment charge	1 Clab	3	2.667	Job		57		57	95.50

022 400 | Soil Stabilization

408	0010	**GROUTING, PRESSURE** Cement and sand, 1:1 mix, minimum	B-61	124	.323	Bag	7.90	7.40	2.88	18.18	24
	0100	Maximum		51	.784	"	7.90	18.05	7	32.95	46.50
	0200	Cement and sand, 1:1 mix, minimum		250	.160	C.F.	15.85	3.68	1.43	20.96	25
	0300	Maximum		100	.400		24	9.20	3.57	36.77	45
	0400	Epoxy cement grout, minimum		137	.292		100	6.70	2.60	109.30	124
	0500	Maximum		57	.702		100	16.15	6.25	122.40	143
	0600	Structural epoxy grout				Gal.	45			45	49.50
	0700	Alternate pricing method: (Add for materials)									
	0710	5 person crew and equipment	B-61	1	40	Day		920	355	1,275	1,925

022 700 | Slope/Erosion Control

704	0010	**EROSION CONTROL** Jute mesh, 100 S.Y. per roll, 4' wide, stapled	B-80A	2,400	.010	S.Y.	.72	.21	.07	1	1.23
	0100	Plastic netting, stapled, 2" x 1" mesh, 20 mil	B-1	2,500	.010		.40	.21		.61	.80
	0200	Polypropylene mesh, stapled, 6.5 oz./S.Y.		2,500	.010		1	.21		1.21	1.46
	0300	Tobacco netting, or jute mesh #2, stapled		2,500	.010		.07	.21		.28	.44

022 | Earthwork

022 700 | Slope/Erosion Control

			CREW	DAILY OUTPUT	LABOR-HOURS	UNIT	1999 BARE COSTS				TOTAL INCL O&P	
							MAT.	LABOR	EQUIP.	TOTAL		
704	1000	Silt fence, polypropylene, 3' high, ideal conditions	2 Clab	1,600	.010	L.F.	.35	.21		.56	.75	704
	1100	Adverse conditions	"	950	.017	"	.28	.36		.64	.91	
	1200	Place and remove hay bales	A-2	3	8	Ton	50	172	57.50	279.50	405	
	1250	Hay bales, staked	"	1,800	.013	L.F.	6	.29	.10	6.39	7.20	
716	0010	**STONE WALL** Including excavation, concrete footing and										716
	0020	stone 3' below grade. Price is exposed face area.										
	0200	Decorative random stone, to 6' high, 1'-6" thick, dry set	D-1	35	.457	S.F.	7.60	11.25		18.85	27	
	0300	Mortar set		40	.400		9.25	9.85		19.10	26.50	
	0500	Cut stone, to 6' high, 1'-6" thick, dry set		35	.457		11.50	11.25		22.75	31.50	
	0600	Mortar set		40	.400		13.50	9.85		23.35	31	
	0800	Retaining wall, random stone, 6' to 10' high, 2' thick, dry set		45	.356		9.50	8.75		18.25	25	
	0900	Mortar set		50	.320		11.50	7.85		19.35	25.50	
	1100	Cut stone, 6' to 10' high, 2' thick, dry set		45	.356		14.75	8.75		23.50	31	
	1200	Mortar set		50	.320		15.75	7.85		23.60	30.50	
	9000	Minimum labor/equipment charge		2	8	Job		197		197	325	

022 800 | Soil Treatment

			CREW	DAILY OUTPUT	LABOR-HOURS	UNIT	MAT.	LABOR	EQUIP.	TOTAL	INCL O&P	
804	0010	**TERMITE PRETREATMENT**										804
	0020	Slab and walls, residential	1 Skwk	1,200	.007	SF Flr.	.19	.19		.38	.51	
	0100	Commercial, minimum		2,496	.003		.16	.09		.25	.32	
	0200	Maximum		1,645	.005		.13	.14		.27	.37	
	0390	Minimum labor/equipment charge		4	2	Job		56		56	93	
	0400	Insecticides for termite control, minimum		14.20	.563	Gal.	10	15.80		25.80	37	
	0500	Maximum		11	.727	"	17.10	20.50		37.60	53	

023 | Tunneling, Piles & Caissons

023 100 | Tunnel Construction

			CREW	DAILY OUTPUT	LABOR-HOURS	UNIT	1999 BARE COSTS				TOTAL INCL O&P	
							MAT.	LABOR	EQUIP.	TOTAL		
150	0010	**MICROTUNNELING** Not including excavation, backfill, shoring,										150
	0020	or dewatering, average 50'/day, slurry method										
	0100	24" to 48" outside diameter, minimum				L.F.					600	
	0110	Adverse conditions, add				%					50%	
	1000	Rent microtunneling machine, average monthly lease				Month					80,000	
	1010	Operating technician				Day					600	
	1100	Mobilization and demobilization, minimum				Job					40,000	
	1110	Maximum				"					400,000	

023 550 | Pile Driving

			CREW	DAILY OUTPUT	LABOR-HOURS	UNIT	MAT.	LABOR	EQUIP.	TOTAL	INCL O&P	
554	0010	**MOBILIZATION** Set up & remove, air compressor, 600 C.F.M.	A-5	3.30	5.455	Ea.		117	13.05	130.05	210	554
	0100	1200 C.F.M.	"	2.20	8.182			176	19.55	195.55	315	
	0200	Crane, with pile leads and pile hammer, 75 ton	B-19	.60	106			2,950	2,400	5,350	7,650	
	0300	150 ton	"	.36	177			4,900	4,000	8,900	12,800	
558	0011	**PILING SPECIAL COSTS** pile caps, see Division 033-130										558
	0500	Cutoffs, concrete piles, plain	1 Pile	5.50	1.455	Ea.		39.50		39.50	70.50	
	0600	With steel thin shell, add		38	.211			5.75		5.75	10.20	
	0700	Steel pile or "H" piles		19	.421			11.45		11.45	20.50	
	0800	Wood piles		38	.211			5.75		5.75	10.20	
	1000	Testing, any type piles, test load is twice the design load										

For expanded coverage of these items see *Means Heavy Construction Cost Data 1999*

023 | Tunneling, Piles & Caissons

023 550 | Pile Driving

			CREW	DAILY OUTPUT	LABOR-HOURS	UNIT	1999 BARE COSTS				TOTAL INCL O&P	
							MAT.	LABOR	EQUIP.	TOTAL		
558	1050	50 ton design load, 100 ton test				Ea.				14,000	15,000	558
	1100	100 ton design load, 200 ton test								18,000	19,000	
	1200	200 ton design load, 400 ton test				↓				24,500	27,000	

023 600 | Driven Piles

			CREW	DAILY OUTPUT	LABOR-HOURS	UNIT	MAT.	LABOR	EQUIP.	TOTAL	TOTAL INCL O&P	
604	0010	**PILES, CONCRETE** 200 piles, 60' long										604
	0020	unless specified otherwise, not incl. pile caps or mobilization										
	0800	Cast in place friction pile, 50' long, fluted,										
	0810	tapered steel, 4000 psi concrete, no reinforcing										
	0900	12" diameter, 7 ga.	B-19	600	.107	V.L.F.	11.65	2.94	2.40	16.99	20.50	
	1200	18" diameter, 7 ga.	"	480	.133	"	17.50	3.68	2.99	24.17	29	
	1300	End bearing, fluted, constant diameter,										
	1320	4000 psi concrete, no reinforcing										
	1340	12" diameter, 7 ga.	B-19	600	.107	V.L.F.	12.20	2.94	2.40	17.54	21	
	1400	18" diameter, 7 ga.		480	.133		19.50	3.68	2.99	26.17	31	
	3100	Precast, prestressed, 40' long, 10" thick, square		700	.091		7.70	2.52	2.05	12.27	15.05	
	3200	12" thick, square		680	.094		8.55	2.60	2.11	13.26	16.15	
	3400	14" thick, square	↓	600	.107		9.80	2.94	2.40	15.14	18.45	
	4000	18" thick, square	B-19A	520	.123	↓	17.80	3.40	2.71	23.91	28.50	
608	0010	**PILES, STEEL** Not including mobilization or demobilization										608
	0100	Step tapered, round, concrete filled										
	0110	8" tip, 60 ton capacity, 30' depth	B-19	760	.084	V.L.F.	5	2.32	1.89	9.21	11.55	
	0120	60' depth		740	.086		5.65	2.39	1.94	9.98	12.40	
	0250	"H" Sections, 50' long, HP8 x 36	↓	640	.100		10.60	2.76	2.25	15.61	18.85	
	1300	HP14 X 102	B-19A	510	.125		26.50	3.46	2.77	32.73	38	
	2600	Pipe piles, 50' lg. 8" diam., 29 lb. per L.F., no concrete	B-19	500	.128		9.45	3.53	2.87	15.85	19.60	
	2700	Concrete filled		460	.139		10.05	3.84	3.12	17.01	21	
	3500	14" diameter, 46 lb. per L.F., no concrete		430	.149		16.15	4.11	3.34	23.60	28.50	
	3600	Concrete filled		355	.180		19.05	4.97	4.05	28.07	34	
	4100	18" diameter, 59 lb. per L.F., no concrete		355	.180		21.50	4.97	4.05	30.52	36.50	
	4200	Concrete filled	↓	310	.206	↓	28	5.70	4.64	38.34	46	
612	0010	**PILES, WOOD** Friction or end bearing, not including										612
	0050	mobilization or demobilization										
	0100	Untreated piles, up to 30' long, 12" butts, 8" points	B-19	625	.102	V.L.F.	5.25	2.83	2.30	10.38	13.15	
	0200	30' to 39' long, 12" butts, 8" points	"	700	.091	"	5.25	2.52	2.05	9.82	12.35	
	0800	Treated piles, 12 lb. per C.F.,										
	0810	friction or end bearing, ASTM class B										
	1000	Up to 30' long, 12" butts, 8" points	B-19	625	.102	V.L.F.	9.45	2.83	2.30	14.58	17.70	
	1100	30' to 39' long, 12" butts, 8" points	"	700	.091	"	9.35	2.52	2.05	13.92	16.85	

023 800 | Caissons

			CREW	DAILY OUTPUT	LABOR-HOURS	UNIT	MAT.	LABOR	EQUIP.	TOTAL	TOTAL INCL O&P	
804	0010	**CAISSONS** Incl. excav., concrete, 50 lbs. reinf. per C.Y., not										804
	0020	incl. mobilization, boulder removal, disposal										
	0100	Open style, machine drilled, to 50' deep, in stable ground, no										
	0110	casings or ground water, 18" diam., 0.065 C.Y./L.F.	B-43	200	.240	V.L.F.	4.82	5.65	8.90	19.37	24.50	
	0200	24" diameter, 0.116 C.Y./L.F.		190	.253	"	8.65	5.95	9.35	23.95	29.50	
	0210	4' bell diameter, add		20	2.400	Ea.	51.50	56.50	89	197	248	
	0500	48" diameter, 0.465 C.Y./L.F.		100	.480	V.L.F.	34.50	11.30	17.75	63.55	76	
	0510	9' bell diameter, add		2	24	Ea.	540	565	890	1,995	2,500	
	1210	Open style, machine drilled, to 25' deep, in wet ground,										
	1220	pulled casing and pumping										
	1400	24" diameter, 0.116 C.Y./L.F.	B-48	125	.448	V.L.F.	8.65	10.80	15.80	35.25	44.50	
	1410	4' bell diameter, add	"	19.80	2.828	Ea.	51.50	68	100	219.50	278	
	1700	48" diameter, 0.465 C.Y./L.F.	B-49	55	1.600	V.L.F.	34.50	40	46	120.50	155	
	1710	9' bell diameter, add	"	3.30	26.667	Ea.	540	670	765	1,975	2,525	

023 | Tunneling, Piles & Caissons

023 800 | Caissons

		CREW	DAILY OUTPUT	LABOR-HOURS	UNIT	MAT.	LABOR	EQUIP.	TOTAL	TOTAL INCL O&P	
804	2310	Open style, machine drilled, to 25' deep, in soft rocks and	R023 -810								804
	2320	medium hard shales									
	2500	24" diameter, 0.116 C.Y./L.F.	B-49	30	2.933	V.L.F.	8.65	73.50	84	166.15	224
	2510	4' bell diameter, add		10.90	8.073	Ea.	51.50	203	232	486.50	645
	2800	48" diameter, 0.465 C.Y./L.F.		10	8.800	V.L.F.	34.50	221	253	508.50	680
	2810	9' bell diameter, add		1.10	80	Ea.	405	2,000	2,300	4,705	6,300
	3600	For rock excavation, sockets, add, minimum		120	.733	C.F.		18.40	21	39.40	53.50
	3650	Average		95	.926			23.50	26.50	50	67.50
	3700	Maximum		48	1.833			46	52.50	98.50	134
	3900	For 50' to 100' deep, add				V.L.F.				7%	7%
	4000	For 100' to 150' deep, add								25%	25%
	4100	For 150' to 200' deep, add								30%	30%
	4200	For casings left in place, add				Lb.	.50			.50	.55
	4300	For other than 50 lb. reinf. per C.Y., add or deduct				"	.50			.50	.55
	4400	For steel "I" beam cores, add	B-49	8.30	10.602	Ton	960	266	305	1,531	1,825
	4500	Load and haul excess excavation, 2 miles	B-34B	178	.045	C.Y.		.99	2.48	3.47	4.35
	4600	For mobilization, 50 mile radius, rig to 36"	B-43	2	24	Ea.		565	890	1,455	1,900
	4650	Rig to 84"	B-48	1.75	32			770	1,125	1,895	2,500
	4700	For low headroom, add								50%	
	4750	For difficult access, add								25%	

025 | Paving & Surfacing

025 100 | Walk/Rd/Parkng Paving

		CREW	DAILY OUTPUT	LABOR-HOURS	UNIT	MAT.	LABOR	EQUIP.	TOTAL	TOTAL INCL O&P	
104	0010	ASPHALTIC CONCRETE PAVEMENT for highways	R025 -110								104
	0020	and large paved areas									
	0080	Binder course, 1-1/2" thick	B-25	7,725	.011	S.Y.	2.03	.27	.23	2.53	2.93
	0120	2" thick		6,345	.014		2.71	.33	.28	3.32	3.83
	0160	3" thick		4,905	.018		4.02	.42	.36	4.80	5.55
	0300	Wearing course, 1" thick	B-25B	10,575	.009		1.56	.22	.19	1.97	2.29
	0340	1-1/2" thick		7,725	.012		2.38	.30	.26	2.94	3.40
	0380	2" thick		6,345	.015		3.20	.36	.32	3.88	4.46
	0420	2-1/2" thick		5,480	.018		3.95	.42	.37	4.74	5.45
	0460	3" thick		4,900	.020		4.70	.47	.41	5.58	6.40
	0800	Alternate method of figuring paving costs									
	0810	Binder course, 1-1/2" thick	B-25	630	.140	Ton	26.50	3.29	2.84	32.63	38
	0811	2" thick		690	.128		26.50	3	2.59	32.09	37.50
	0812	3" thick		800	.110		26.50	2.59	2.24	31.33	36
	0813	4" thick		850	.104		26.50	2.44	2.10	31.04	36
	0850	Wearing course, 1" thick	B-25B	575	.167		29	4	3.54	36.54	42.50
	0851	1-1/2" thick		630	.152		29	3.65	3.23	35.88	41.50
	0852	2" thick		690	.139		29	3.33	2.95	35.28	40.50
	0853	2-1/2" thick		745	.129		29	3.08	2.73	34.81	40
	0854	3" thick		800	.120		29	2.87	2.54	34.41	39.50
	1000	Pavement replacement over trench, 2" thick	B-37	90	.533	S.Y.	3.25	12.15	1.70	17.10	25.50
	1050	4" thick		70	.686		6.45	15.60	2.18	24.23	35.50
	1080	6" thick		55	.873		10.25	19.85	2.78	32.88	47.50
120	0010	CONCRETE PAVEMENT Including joints, finishing, and curing	R025 -110								120
	0020	Fixed form, 12' pass, unreinforced, 6" thick	B-26	3,000	.029	S.Y.	14.55	.71	.63	15.89	17.90

For expanded coverage of these items see *Means Heavy Construction Cost Data 1999*

025 | Paving & Surfacing

025 100 | Walk/Rd/Parkng Paving

			CREW	DAILY OUTPUT	LABOR-HOURS	UNIT	MAT.	LABOR	EQUIP.	TOTAL	TOTAL INCL O&P	
120	0100	8" thick	B-26	2,750	.032	S.Y.	20.50	.77	.69	21.96	24.50	120
	0400	12" thick		1,800	.049		27	1.18	1.05	29.23	33	
	0450	Minimum labor/equipment charge	1 Cefi	1	8	Job		209		209	335	
	0700	Finishing, broom finish small areas	2 Cefi	120	.133	S.Y.		3.49		3.49	5.55	
	1000	Curing, with sprayed membrane by hand	2 Clab	1,500	.011	"	.22	.23		.45	.62	
124	0011	**PAVING** Asphaltic concrete, parking lots & driveways										124
	0020	6" stone base, 2" binder course, 1" topping	B-25C	9,000	.005	S.F.	1.13	.13	.17	1.43	1.65	
	0300	Binder course, 1-1/2" thick		35,000	.001		.23	.03	.04	.30	.36	
	0400	2" thick		25,000	.002		.30	.05	.06	.41	.48	
	0500	3" thick		15,000	.003		.47	.08	.10	.65	.76	
	0600	4" thick		10,800	.004		.62	.11	.14	.87	1.02	
	0800	Sand finish course, 3/4" thick		41,000	.001		.15	.03	.04	.22	.26	
	0900	1" thick		34,000	.001		.19	.03	.05	.27	.32	
	1000	Fill pot holes, hot mix, 2" thick	B-16	4,200	.008		.38	.17	.11	.66	.82	
	1100	4" thick		3,500	.009		.56	.20	.13	.89	1.10	
	1120	6" thick		3,100	.010		.75	.23	.14	1.12	1.37	
	1140	Cold patch, 2" thick	B-51	3,000	.016		.45	.35	.06	.86	1.14	
	1160	4" thick		2,700	.018		.86	.39	.06	1.31	1.66	
	1180	6" thick		1,900	.025		1.33	.55	.09	1.97	2.49	
128	0010	**SIDEWALKS, DRIVEWAYS, & PATIOS** No base										128
	0020	Asphaltic concrete, 2" thick	B-37	720	.067	S.Y.	2.74	1.52	.21	4.47	5.75	
	0100	2-1/2" thick	"	660	.073	"	3.47	1.65	.23	5.35	6.80	
	0110	Bedding for brick or stone, mortar, 1" thick	D-1	300	.053	S.F.	.32	1.31		1.63	2.52	
	0120	2" thick	"	200	.080		.79	1.97		2.76	4.13	
	0130	Sand, 2" thick	B-18	8,000	.003		.16	.07	.01	.24	.30	
	0140	4" thick	"	4,000	.006		.32	.13	.01	.46	.58	
	0300	Concrete, 3000 psi, CIP, 6 x 6 - W1.4 x W1.4 mesh,										
	0310	broomed finish, no base, 4" thick	B-24	600	.040	S.F.	1.02	1		2.02	2.76	
	0350	5" thick		545	.044		1.36	1.10		2.46	3.30	
	0400	6" thick		510	.047		1.58	1.18		2.76	3.67	
	0450	For bank run gravel base, 4" thick, add	B-18	2,500	.010		.14	.21	.02	.37	.54	
	0520	8" thick, add	"	1,600	.015		.28	.33	.03	.64	.91	
	0550	Exposed aggregate finish, add to above, minimum	B-24	1,875	.013		.11	.32		.43	.65	
	0600	Maximum	"	455	.053		.35	1.32		1.67	2.56	
	0950	Concrete tree grate, 5' square	B-6	25	.960	Ea.	265	22.50	8.75	296.25	340	
	0960	Cast iron tree grate with frame, 2 piece, round, 5' diameter		25	.960		685	22.50	8.75	716.25	800	
	0980	Square, 5' side		25	.960		700	22.50	8.75	731.25	815	
	1700	Redwood, prefabricated, 4' x 4' sections	2 Carp	316	.051	S.F.	4.53	1.38		5.91	7.30	
	1750	Redwood planks, 1" thick, on sleepers	"	240	.067	"	3.17	1.82		4.99	6.55	
	9000	Minimum labor/equipment charge	D-1	2	8	Job		197		197	325	

025 150 | Unit Pavers

			CREW	DAILY OUTPUT	LABOR-HOURS	UNIT	MAT.	LABOR	EQUIP.	TOTAL	TOTAL INCL O&P	
154	0010	**ASPHALT BLOCKS**, 6"x12"x1-1/4", w/bed & neopr. adhesive	D-1	135	.119	S.F.	3	2.92		5.92	8.15	154
	0100	3" thick		130	.123		4.20	3.03		7.23	9.60	
	0300	Hexagonal tile, 8" wide, 1-1/4" thick		135	.119		3.20	2.92		6.12	8.35	
	0400	2" thick		130	.123		4.48	3.03		7.51	9.95	
	0500	Square, 8" x 8", 1-1/4" thick		135	.119		3	2.92		5.92	8.15	
	0600	2" thick		130	.123		4.20	3.03		7.23	9.60	
	9000	Minimum labor/equipment charge	1 Bric	2	4	Job		110		110	183	
158	0010	**BRICK PAVING** 4" x 8" x 1-1/2", without joints (4.5 brick/S.F.)	D-1	110	.145	S.F.	2.04	3.58		5.62	8.15	158
	0100	Grouted, 3/8" joint (3.9 brick/S.F.)		90	.178		2.43	4.37		6.80	9.90	
	0200	4" x 8" x 2-1/4", without joints (4.5 bricks/S.F.)		110	.145		2.69	3.58		6.27	8.85	
	0300	Grouted, 3/8" joint (3.9 brick/S.F.)		90	.178		2.48	4.37		6.85	10	

025 | Paving & Surfacing

025 150 | Unit Pavers

		CREW	DAILY OUTPUT	LABOR-HOURS	UNIT	MAT.	LABOR	EQUIP.	TOTAL	TOTAL INCL O&P	
158	0500 Bedding, asphalt, 3/4" thick	B-25	5,130	.017	S.F.	.26	.40	.35	1.01	1.32	158
	0540 Course washed sand bed, 1" thick	B-18	5,000	.005		.18	.11	.01	.30	.39	
	0580 Mortar, 1" thick	D-1	300	.053		.36	1.31		1.67	2.57	
	0620 2" thick		200	.080		.36	1.97		2.33	3.66	
	1500 Brick on 1" thick sand bed laid flat, 4.5 per S.F.		100	.160		2.96	3.94		6.90	9.75	
	2000 Brick pavers, laid on edge, 7.2 per S.F.		70	.229		2.06	5.60		7.66	11.55	
	2500 For 4" thick concrete bed and joints, add		595	.027		.75	.66		1.41	1.93	
	2800 For steam cleaning, add	A-1	950	.008		.05	.18	.07	.30	.44	
	9000 Minimum labor/equipment charge	1 Bric	2	4	Job		110		110	183	
166	0010 **STONE PAVERS**										166
	1300 Slate, natural cleft, irregular, 3/4" thick	D-1	92	.174	S.F.	1.80	4.28		6.08	9.10	
	1350 Random rectangular, gauged, 1/2" thick		105	.152		3.90	3.75		7.65	10.50	
	1400 Random rectangular, butt joint, gauged, 1/4" thick		150	.107		4.19	2.62		6.81	8.95	
	1450 For sand rubbed finish, add					2.50			2.50	2.75	
	1550 Granite blocks, 3-1/2" x 3-1/2" x 3-1/2"	D-1	92	.174		5.25	4.28		9.53	12.90	
	1600 4" to 12" long, 3" to 5" wide, 3" to 5" thick	"	98	.163		4.38	4.02		8.40	11.45	

025 250 | Curbs

		CREW	DAILY OUTPUT	LABOR-HOURS	UNIT	MAT.	LABOR	EQUIP.	TOTAL	TOTAL INCL O&P	
254	0010 **CURBS** Asphaltic, machine formed, 8" wide, 6" high, 40 L.F./ton	B-27	1,000	.032	L.F.	.58	.70	.07	1.35	1.90	254
	0100 8" wide, 8" high, 30 L.F. per ton		900	.036		.67	.78	.08	1.53	2.13	
	0150 Asphaltic berm, 12" W, 3"-6" H, 35 L.F./ton, before pavement		700	.046		.80	1	.10	1.90	2.68	
	0200 12" W, 1-1/2" to 4" H, 60 L.F. per ton, laid with pavement	B-2	1,050	.038		.49	.83		1.32	1.93	
	0300 Concrete, wood forms, 6" x 18", straight	C-2A	500	.096		2.11	2.54		4.65	6.55	
	0400 6" x 18", radius	"	200	.240		2.22	6.35		8.57	13	
	0415 Machine formed, 6" x 18", straight	B-69A	2,000	.024		3.04	.57	.23	3.84	4.53	
	0416 6" x 18", radius	"	900	.053		3.17	1.27	.50	4.94	6.10	
	0550 Precast, 6" x 18", straight	B-29	700	.080		6.25	1.86	.91	9.02	10.95	
	0600 6" x 18", radius	"	325	.172		7.75	4	1.96	13.71	17.25	
	1000 Granite, split face, straight, 5" x 16"	D-13	500	.096		10	2.51	.78	13.29	16	
	1100 6" x 18"	"	450	.107		13.15	2.79	.87	16.81	20	
	1300 Radius curbing, 6" x 18", over 10' radius	B-29	260	.215		16.10	5	2.45	23.55	28.50	
	1400 Corners, 2' radius		80	.700	Ea.	54	16.25	7.95	78.20	95.50	
	1600 Edging, 4-1/2" x 12", straight		300	.187	L.F.	5	4.34	2.12	11.46	15	
	1800 Curb inlets, (guttermouth) straight		41	1.366	Ea.	120	31.50	15.55	167.05	202	
	2000 Indian granite (belgian block)										
	2100 Jumbo, 10-1/2"x7-1/2"x4", grey	D-1	150	.107	L.F.	1.75	2.62		4.37	6.25	
	2150 Pink		150	.107		2.15	2.62		4.77	6.70	
	2200 Regular, 9"x4-1/2"x4-1/2", grey		160	.100		1.70	2.46		4.16	5.95	
	2250 Pink		160	.100		2	2.46		4.46	6.25	
	2300 Cubes, 4"x4"x4", grey		175	.091		1.65	2.25		3.90	5.55	
	2350 Pink		175	.091		1.75	2.25		4	5.65	
	2400 6"x6"x6", pink		155	.103		3.60	2.54		6.14	8.15	
	2500 Alternate pricing method for indian granite										
	2550 Jumbo, 10-1/2"x7-1/2"x4" (30lb), grey				Ton	100			100	110	
	2600 Pink					125			125	138	
	2650 Regular, 9"x4-1/2"x4-1/2" (20lb), grey					120			120	132	
	2700 Pink					140			140	154	
	2750 Cubes, 4"x4"x4" (5lb), grey					200			200	220	
	2800 Pink					225			225	248	
	2850 6"x6"x6" (25lb), pink					140			140	154	
	2900 For pallets, add					15			15	16.50	
258	0010 **EDGING**										258
	0050 Aluminum alloy, including stakes, 1/8" x 4", mill finish	B-1	390	.062	L.F.	1.75	1.36		3.11	4.21	

For expanded coverage of these items see *Means Heavy Construction Cost Data 1999*

025 | Paving & Surfacing

025 250 | Curbs

		CREW	DAILY OUTPUT	LABOR-HOURS	UNIT	MAT.	LABOR	EQUIP.	TOTAL	TOTAL INCL O&P
0051	Black paint	B-1	390	.062	L.F.	2.03	1.36		3.39	4.51
0052	Black anodized	↓	390	.062		2.34	1.36		3.70	4.86
0100	Brick, set horizontally, 1-1/2 bricks per L.F.	D-1	370	.043		.90	1.06		1.96	2.75
0150	Set vertically, 3 bricks per L.F.	"	135	.119		1.90	2.92		4.82	6.90
0200	Corrugated aluminum, roll, 4" wide	1 Carp	650	.012		.28	.34		.62	.87
0250	6" wide	"	550	.015		.35	.40		.75	1.05
0600	Railroad ties, 6" x 8"	2 Carp	170	.094		2.30	2.57		4.87	6.85
0650	7" x 9"		136	.118		2.55	3.21		5.76	8.20
0750	2" x 4"	↓	330	.048		2.67	1.32		3.99	5.15
0800	Steel edge strips, incl. stakes, 1/4" x 5"	B-1	390	.062		2.75	1.36		4.11	5.30
0850	3/16" x 4"		390	.062	↓	2.17	1.36		3.53	4.67
9000	Minimum labor/equipment charge	1 Carp	4	2	Job		54.50		54.50	91.50

025 450 | Surfacing

		CREW	DAILY OUTPUT	LABOR-HOURS	UNIT	MAT.	LABOR	EQUIP.	TOTAL	TOTAL INCL O&P
0010	**SURFACE TREATMENT**									
3000	Pavement overlay, polypropylene									
3040	6 oz. per S.Y., ideal conditions	B-63	10,000	.004	S.Y.	1	.09	.01	1.10	1.26
3080	Adverse conditions		1,000	.040		1.34	.90	.11	2.35	3.09
3120	4 oz. per S.Y., ideal conditions		10,000	.004		.70	.09	.01	.80	.93
3160	Adverse conditions		1,000	.040		.90	.90	.11	1.91	2.61
3200	Tack coat, emulsion, .05 gal per S.Y., 1000 S.Y	B-45	2,500	.006		.15	.16	.30	.61	.76
3240	10,000 S.Y.		10,000	.002		.12	.04	.07	.23	.28
3280	.15 gal per S.Y., 1000 S.Y.		2,500	.006		.41	.16	.30	.87	1.04
3320	10,000 S.Y.	↓	10,000	.002	↓	.33	.04	.07	.44	.51
5000	Reclamation, pulverizing and blending with existing base									
5040	Aggregate base, 4" thick pavement, over 15,000 S.Y.	B-73	2,400	.027	S.Y.		.69	1.42	2.11	2.69
5080	5,000 S.Y. to 15,000 S.Y.		2,200	.029			.76	1.55	2.31	2.94
5120	8" thick pavement, over 15,000 S.Y.		2,200	.029			.76	1.55	2.31	2.94
5160	5,000 S.Y. to 15,000 S.Y.	↓	2,000	.032			.83	1.71	2.54	3.23
5180	Add for mobilization and demobilization				Ea.				1,600	
5200	Cold planing & cleaning, 1" to 3" asphalt pavmt., over 25,000 S.Y.	B-71	6,000	.009	S.Y.		.23	.66	.89	1.10
5280	5,000 S.Y. to 10,000 S.Y.	"	4,000	.014	"		.35	.99	1.34	1.65
5291	See also concrete pavement, div. 025-120									
5300	Asphalt pavement removal from conc. base, no haul									
5320	Rip, load & sweep 1" to 3"	B-70	8,000	.007	S.Y.		.17	.14	.31	.44
5330	3" to 6" deep	"	5,000	.011			.28	.23	.51	.70
5340	Profile grooving, asphalt pavement load & sweep, 1" deep	B-71	12,500	.004			.11	.32	.43	.53
5350	3" deep	↓	9,000	.006			.15	.44	.59	.73
5360	6" deep		5,000	.011	↓		.28	.79	1.07	1.32
5500	Recycle asphalt pavement at site									
5520	Remove, rejuvenate and spread 4" deep	B-72	2,500	.026	S.Y.	2	.64	2.88	5.52	6.40
5521	6" deep	"	2,000	.032	"	3	.81	3.60	7.41	8.55
0010	**SEALCOATING** 2 coat coal tar pitch emulsion over 10,000 S.Y.	B-45	5,000	.003	S.Y.	.43	.08	.15	.66	.77
0030	1000 to 10,000 S.Y.	"	3,000	.005		.43	.13	.25	.81	.97
0100	Under 1000 S.Y.	B-1	1,050	.023		.43	.51		.94	1.33
0300	Petroleum resistant, over 10,000 S.Y.	B-45	5,000	.003		.50	.08	.15	.73	.84
0320	1000 to 10,000 S.Y.	"	3,000	.005		.50	.13	.25	.88	1.04
0400	Under 1000 S.Y.	B-1	1,050	.023		.50	.51		1.01	1.40
0600	Non-skid pavement renewal, over 10,000 S.Y.	B-45	5,000	.003		.60	.08	.15	.83	.95
0620	1000 to 10,000 S.Y.	"	3,000	.005		.60	.13	.25	.98	1.15
0700	Under 1000 S.Y.	B-1	1,050	.023		.60	.51		1.11	1.51
0800	Prepare and clean surface for above	A-2	8,545	.003	↓		.06	.02	.08	.12
1000	Hand seal asphalt curbing	B-1	4,420	.005	L.F.	.30	.12		.42	.53
1900	Asphalt surface treatment, single course, small area									
1901	0.30 gal/S.Y. asphalt material, 20#/S.Y. aggregate	B-91	5,000	.013	S.Y.	.70	.32	.30	1.32	1.62
1910	Roadway or large area	↓	10,000	.006	↓	.64	.16	.15	.95	1.13

025 | Paving & Surfacing

025 450 | Surfacing

		CREW	DAILY OUTPUT	LABOR-HOURS	UNIT	1999 BARE COSTS MAT.	LABOR	EQUIP.	TOTAL	TOTAL INCL O&P	
458	1950 Asphalt surface treatment, dbl. course for small area	B-91	3,000	.021	S.Y.	1.30	.54	.50	2.34	2.85	458
	1960 Roadway or large area		6,000	.011		1.17	.27	.25	1.69	2	
	1980 Asphalt surface treatment, single course, for shoulders		7,500	.009		.75	.22	.20	1.17	1.40	
	2080 Sand sealing, sharp sand, asphalt emulsion, small area		10,000	.006		.50	.16	.15	.81	.97	
	2120 Roadway or large area		18,000	.004		.43	.09	.08	.60	.71	
	3000 Sealing random cracks, min 1/2" wide, to 1-1/2", 1,000 L.F.	B-77	2,800	.014	L.F.	.40	.31	.14	.85	1.12	
	3040 10,000 L.F.		4,000	.010	"	.31	.22	.10	.63	.81	
	3080 Alternate method, 1,000 L.F.		200	.200	Gal.	9	4.38	2	15.38	19.40	
	3120 10,000 L.F.		325	.123	"	7.25	2.70	1.23	11.18	13.80	
	3200 Multi-cracks (flooding), 1 coat, small area	B-92	460	.070	S.Y.	1.92	1.53	.77	4.22	5.50	
	3240 Large area		2,850	.011		1.70	.25	.12	2.07	2.42	
	3280 2 coat, small area		230	.139		6	3.05	1.55	10.60	13.40	
	3320 Large area		1,425	.022		5.45	.49	.25	6.19	7.10	
	3360 Alternate method, small area		115	.278	Gal.	8.50	6.10	3.09	17.69	23	
	3400 Large area		715	.045	"	8	.98	.50	9.48	11	
	3600 Waterproofing, membrane, tar and fabric, small area	B-63	233	.172	S.Y.	4.80	3.88	.48	9.16	12.25	
	3640 Large area		1,435	.028		4.42	.63	.08	5.13	6	
	3680 Preformed rubberized asphalt, small area		100	.400		6.50	9.05	1.11	16.66	23.50	
	3720 Large area		367	.109		5.90	2.46	.30	8.66	10.90	
	9000 Minimum labor/equipment charge	1 Clab	2	4	Job		86		86	144	
459	0010 **SLURRY SEAL**										459
	0100 Slurry seal, type I, 8 lbs agg./S.Y., 1 coat, small or irregular area	B-90	2,800	.023	S.Y.	.70	.53	.48	1.71	2.16	
	0150 Roadway or large area		10,000	.006		.70	.15	.13	.98	1.16	
	0200 Type II, 12 lbs aggregate/S.Y., 2 coats, small or irregular area		2,000	.032		1.40	.75	.67	2.82	3.49	
	0250 Roadway or large area		8,000	.008		1.40	.19	.17	1.76	2.03	
	0300 Type III, 20 lbs aggregate/S.Y., 2 coats, small or irregular area		1,800	.036		1.65	.83	.74	3.22	3.99	
	0350 Roadway or large area		6,000	.011		1.65	.25	.22	2.12	2.47	
	0400 Slurry seal, thermoplastic coal-tar, type I, small or irregular area		2,400	.027		1.45	.62	.56	2.63	3.23	
	0450 Roadway or large area		8,000	.008		1.45	.19	.17	1.81	2.09	
	0500 Type II, small or irregular area		2,400	.027		1.85	.62	.56	3.03	3.67	
	0550 Roadway or large area		7,800	.008		1.85	.19	.17	2.21	2.54	
	0600 Average mobilization cost				Ea.				3,500	3,500	

025 800 | Pavement Marking

		CREW	DAILY OUTPUT	LABOR-HOURS	UNIT	MAT.	LABOR	EQUIP.	TOTAL	TOTAL INCL O&P	
804	0010 **LINES ON PAV'T** Acrylic waterborne, white or yellow, 4" wide	B-78	20,000	.002	L.F.	.09	.05	.03	.17	.21	804
	0200 6" wide		11,000	.004		.09	.10	.05	.24	.31	
	0500 8" wide		10,000	.005		.11	.10	.05	.26	.35	
	0600 12" wide		4,000	.012		.20	.26	.13	.59	.80	
	0620 Arrows or gore lines		2,300	.021	S.F.	.50	.46	.22	1.18	1.56	
	0640 Temporary paint, white or yellow		15,000	.003	L.F.	.15	.07	.03	.25	.33	
	0660 Removal	1 Clab	300	.027			.57		.57	.96	
	0680 Temporary tape	2 Clab	1,500	.011		1.12	.23		1.35	1.61	
	0710 Thermoplastic, white or yellow, 4" wide	B-79	15,000	.003		.56	.06	.05	.67	.77	
	0730 6" wide		14,000	.003		.81	.06	.05	.92	1.04	
	0740 8" wide		12,000	.003		1.09	.07	.06	1.22	1.38	
	0750 12" wide		6,000	.007		1.62	.15	.11	1.88	2.15	
	0760 Arrows		660	.061	S.F.	1.50	1.33	1.03	3.86	5	
	0770 Gore lines		2,500	.016		1	.35	.27	1.62	1.98	
	0780 Letters		660	.061		1.25	1.33	1.03	3.61	4.73	
	0790 Layout of pavement marking	A-2	25,000	.001	L.F.		.02	.01	.03	.04	
	0800 Parking stall, paint, white	B-78	440	.109	Stall	1.84	2.38	1.16	5.38	7.25	
	1000 Street letters and numbers	"	1,600	.030	S.F.	.50	.65	.32	1.47	1.99	

For expanded coverage of these items see *Means Heavy Construction Cost Data 1999*

026 | Piped Utilities

			DAILY	LABOR-		1999 BARE COSTS				TOTAL	
026 010	**Piped Utilities**	CREW	OUTPUT	HOURS	UNIT	MAT.	LABOR	EQUIP.	TOTAL	INCL O&P	
012 0010	**BEDDING** For pipe and conduit, not incl. compaction										012
0050	Crushed or screened bank run gravel	B-6	150	.160	C.Y.	6.90	3.74	1.46	12.10	15.35	
0100	Crushed stone 3/4" to 1/2"		150	.160		17.75	3.74	1.46	22.95	27.50	
0200	Sand, dead or bank		150	.160		3.75	3.74	1.46	8.95	11.90	
0500	Compacting bedding in trench	A-1	90	.089			1.91	.76	2.67	4.03	
014 0010	**EXCAVATION AND BACKFILL** See division 022-204 & 254	R022 -240									014
0100	Hand excavate and trim for pipe bells after trench excavation										
0200	8" pipe	1 Clab	155	.052	L.F.		1.11		1.11	1.85	
0300	18" pipe		130	.062	"		1.32		1.32	2.21	
0400	Underground tape, detectable aluminum, 2"		150	.053	C.L.F.	3.70	1.14		4.84	6	
0500	6"		140	.057	"	9.25	1.23		10.48	12.25	
9000	Minimum labor/equipment charge		4	2	Job		43		43	72	
026 050	**Manholes & Cleanouts**										
054 0010	**UTILITY VAULTS** Precast concrete, 6" thick										054
0050	5' x 10' x 6' high, I.D.	B-13	2	28	Ea.	1,250	650	275	2,175	2,775	
0350	Hand hole, precast concrete, 1-1/2" thick										
0400	1'-0" x 2'-0" x 1'-9", I.D., light duty	B-1	4	6	Ea.	330	133		463	585	
0450	4'-6" x 3'-2" x 2'-0", O.D., heavy duty	B-6	3	8	"	870	187	73	1,130	1,350	
026 650	**Water Systems**										
686 0010	**PIPING, WATER DISTRIBUTION SYSTEMS** Pipe laid in trench,	R151 -050									686
0020	excavation and backfill not included										
1400	Ductile Iron, cement lined, class 50 water pipe, 18' lengths										
1410	Mechanical joint, 4" diameter	B-20	144	.167	L.F.	6.95	4.05		11	14.40	
9000	Minimum labor/equipment charge	1 Clab	4	2	Job		43		43	72	
026 700	**Water Wells**										
704 0010	**WELLS** Domestic water	R151 -050									704
0100	Drilled, 4" to 6" diameter	B-23	120	.333	L.F.	7.30	16.30		23.60	30	
0200	8" diameter	"	95.20	.420	"	9.20	20.50		29.70	38	
1400	Remove & reset pump, minimum	B-21	4	7	Ea.		175	34	209	330	
1420	Maximum	"	2	14	"		350	68	418	655	
1500	Pumps, installed in wells to 100' deep, 4" submersible										
1510	1/2 H.P.	Q-1	3.22	4.969	Ea.	425	146		571	700	
1520	3/4 H.P.		2.66	6.015		475	177		652	800	
1600	1 H.P.		2.29	6.987		525	205		730	900	
1700	1-1/2 H.P.	Q-22	1.60	10		580	294	277	1,151	1,400	
1800	2 H.P.		1.33	12.030		620	355	335	1,310	1,600	
1900	3 H.P.		1.14	14.035		775	410	390	1,575	1,925	
2000	5 H.P.		1.14	14.035		1,250	410	390	2,050	2,450	
2050	Remove and install motor only, 4 H.P.		1.14	14.035		585	410	390	1,385	1,725	
5000	Wells to 180 ft. deep, 4" submersible, 1 HP	B-21	1.10	25.455		400	635	123	1,158	1,625	
5500	2 HP		1.10	25.455		675	635	123	1,433	1,925	
6000	3 HP		1	28		700	700	136	1,536	2,075	
7000	5 HP		.90	31.111		725	780	151	1,656	2,275	
9000	Minimum labor/equipment charge		1.80	15.556	Job		390	75.50	465.50	730	
026 800	**Fuel Distribution**										
804 0010	**GAS STATION PRODUCT LINE**										804
0020	Primary containment pipe, fiberglass-reinforced										

026 | Piped Utilities

026 800 | Fuel Distribution

			CREW	DAILY OUTPUT	LABOR-HOURS	UNIT	1999 BARE COSTS MAT.	LABOR	EQUIP.	TOTAL	TOTAL INCL O&P	
804	0030	Plastic pipe 15' & 30' lengths										804
	0040	2" diameter	Q-6	425	.056	L.F.	2.97	1.73		4.70	5.95	
	0050	3" diameter		400	.060		4.40	1.83		6.23	7.70	
	0060	4" diameter	▼	375	.064	▼	5.75	1.96		7.71	9.40	
	0100	Fittings										
	0110	Elbows, 90° & 45°, bell-ends, 2"	Q-6	24	1	Ea.	31	30.50		61.50	82	
	0120	3" diameter		22	1.091		35	33.50		68.50	90.50	
	0130	4" diameter		20	1.200		42	36.50		78.50	104	
	0200	Tees, bell ends, 2"		21	1.143		36.50	35		71.50	95	
	0210	3" diameter		18	1.333		40	41		81	108	
	0220	4" diameter		15	1.600		52	49		101	134	
	0230	Flanges bell ends, 2"		24	1		20	30.50		50.50	70	
	0240	3" diameter		22	1.091		22	33.50		55.50	76	
	0250	4" diameter		20	1.200		25	36.50		61.50	85	
	0260	Sleeve couplings, 2"		21	1.143		7.75	35		42.75	63	
	0270	3" diameter		18	1.333		10.75	41		51.75	76	
	0280	4" diameter		15	1.600		15.50	49		64.50	93.50	
	0290	Threaded adapters 2"		21	1.143		10.95	35		45.95	66.50	
	0300	3" diameter		18	1.333		16.50	41		57.50	82	
	0310	4" diameter		15	1.600		23	49		72	102	
	0320	Reducers, 2"		27	.889		14.15	27		41.15	58	
	0330	3" diameter		22	1.091		16.50	33.50		50	70	
	0340	4" diameter	▼	20	1.200	▼	25	36.50		61.50	85	
	1010	Gas station product line for secondary containment (double wall)										
	1100	Fiberglass reinforced plastic pipe 25' lengths										
	1120	Pipe, plain end, 3"	Q-6	375	.064	L.F.	3.98	1.96		5.94	7.45	
	1130	4" diameter		350	.069		4.95	2.10		7.05	8.75	
	1140	5" diameter		325	.074		5.50	2.26		7.76	9.60	
	1150	6" diameter	▼	300	.080	▼	9.45	2.45		11.90	14.25	
	1200	Fittings										
	1230	Elbows, 90° & 45°, 3"	Q-6	18	1.333	Ea.	37	41		78	105	
	1240	4" diameter		16	1.500		70	46		116	149	
	1250	5" diameter		14	1.714		145	52.50		197.50	242	
	1260	6" diameter		12	2		150	61		211	261	
	1270	Tees, 3"		15	1.600		53	49		102	135	
	1280	4" diameter		12	2		85	61		146	189	
	1290	5" diameter		9	2.667		158	81.50		239.50	300	
	1300	6" diameter		6	4		165	122		287	375	
	1310	Couplings, 3"		18	1.333		24	41		65	90.50	
	1320	4" diameter		16	1.500		65	46		111	144	
	1330	5" diameter		14	1.714		135	52.50		187.50	231	
	1340	6" diameter		12	2		140	61		201	250	
	1350	Cross-over nipples, 3"		18	1.333		5.75	41		46.75	70.50	
	1360	4" diameter		16	1.500		6.75	46		52.75	79.50	
	1370	5" diameter		14	1.714		10	52.50		62.50	93	
	1380	6" diameter		12	2		10.50	61		71.50	107	
	1400	Telescoping, reducers, concentric 4" x 3"		18	1.333		19.15	41		60.15	85	
	1410	5" x 4"		17	1.412		50	43		93	123	
	1420	6" x 5"	▼	16	1.500	▼	120	46		166	204	

026 850 | Gas Distribution System

			CREW	DAILY OUTPUT	LABOR-HOURS	UNIT	MAT.	LABOR	EQUIP.	TOTAL	INCL O&P	
854	0010	**PIPING, GAS SERVICE & DISTRIBUTION, POLYETHYLENE**										854
	0020	not including excavation or backfill										
	1000	60 psi coils, comp cplg @ 100', 1/2" diameter, SDR 9.3	B-20A	608	.053	L.F.	.35	1.36		1.71	2.59	
	1040	1-1/4" diameter, SDR 11	▼	544	.059	▼	.57	1.52		2.09	3.09	

For expanded coverage of these items see Means Heavy Construction Cost Data 1999

026 | Piped Utilities

026 850 | Gas Distribution System

		Crew	Daily Output	Labor-Hours	Unit	\\ MAT.	1999 Bare Costs \\ LABOR	\\ EQUIP.	\\ TOTAL	Total Incl O&P	
854	1100	2" diameter, SDR 11	B-20A	488	.066	L.F.	.72	1.70		2.42	3.53	854
	1160	3" diameter, SDR 11		408	.078		1.51	2.03		3.54	4.93	
	1500	60 PSI 40' joints with coupling, 3" diameter, SDR 11	B-21A	408	.098		1.51	2.61	.96	5.08	6.90	
	1540	4" diameter, SDR 11		352	.114		3.33	3.02	1.11	7.46	9.75	
	1600	6" diameter, SDR 11		328	.122		10.90	3.24	1.19	15.33	18.50	
	1640	8" diameter, SDR 11		272	.147		14.55	3.91	1.44	19.90	24	
	9000	Minimum labor/equipment charge	B-20	2	12	Job		292		292	485	

027 | Sewerage & Drainage

027 150 | Sewage Systems

			Crew	Daily Output	Labor-Hours	Unit	MAT.	LABOR	EQUIP.	TOTAL	Total Incl O&P	
152	0010	**CATCH BASINS OR MANHOLES** not including footing, excavation,										152
	0020	backfill, frame and cover										
	0050	Brick, 4' inside diameter, 4' deep	D-1	1	16	Ea.	263	395		658	940	
	0100	6' deep		.70	22.857		370	560		930	1,325	
	0150	8' deep		.50	32		475	785		1,260	1,825	
	0200	For depths over 8', add		4	4	V.L.F.	100	98.50		198.50	273	
	1110	Precast, 4' I.D., 4' deep	B-22	4.10	7.317	Ea.	315	185	49.50	549.50	705	
	1120	6' deep		3	10		425	253	68	746	960	
	1130	8' deep		2	15		470	380	102	952	1,250	
	1140	For depths over 8', add		16	1.875	V.L.F.	78.50	47.50	12.75	138.75	179	
	1600	Frames & covers, C.I., 24" square, 500 lb.	B-6	7.80	3.077	Ea.	213	72	28	313	385	
	1700	26" D shape, 600 lb.	"	7	3.429	"	214	80	31.50	325.50	405	
	3320	Frames and covers, existing, raised for paving 2", including										
	3340	row of brick, concrete collar, up to 12" wide frame	B-6	18	1.333	Ea.	31	31	12.15	74.15	98.50	
162	0010	**PIPING, DRAINAGE & SEWAGE, CONCRETE**	R027 -110									162
	0020	Not including excavation or backfill										
	1000	Non-reinforced pipe, extra strength, B&S or T&G joints										
	1010	6" diameter	B-14	265.04	.181	L.F.	3.47	4.12	.83	8.42	11.55	
	1020	8" diameter		224	.214		3.81	4.87	.98	9.66	13.35	
	1040	12" diameter		200	.240		5.20	5.45	1.09	11.74	15.95	
	2000	Reinforced culvert, class 3, no gaskets										
	2010	12" diameter	B-14	210	.229	L.F.	8.10	5.20	1.04	14.34	18.65	
	2020	15" diameter	"	175	.274	"	9.90	6.25	1.25	17.40	22.50	
164	0010	**PIPING, STORM DRAINAGE, CORRUGATED METAL**	R151 -050									164
	0020	Not including excavation or backfill										
	2000	Corrugated metal pipe, galvanized and coated										
	2020	Bituminous coated with paved invert, 20' lengths										
	2040	8" diameter, 16 ga.	B-14	330	.145	L.F.	7.10	3.31	.66	11.07	14.10	
	2080	12" diameter, 16 ga.	"	210	.229	"	11.90	5.20	1.04	18.14	23	
168	0010	**PIPING, DRAINAGE & SEWAGE, POLYVINYL CHLORIDE**										168
	0020	Not including excavation or backfill										
	2000	10' lengths, S.D.R. 35, B&S, 4" diameter	B-20	375	.064	L.F.	2.17	1.56		3.73	4.99	
	2040	6" diameter		350	.069		3.95	1.67		5.62	7.15	
	2080	8" diameter		335	.072		3.94	1.74		5.68	7.25	
	2120	10" diameter	B-21	330	.085		3.81	2.12	.41	6.34	8.15	
172	0010	**PIPING, DRAINAGE & SEWAGE, VITRIFIED CLAY** C700										172
	0020	Not including excavation or backfill,										

Important: See the Reference Section for critical supporting data - Reference Nos., Crews, & City Cost Indexes

027 | Sewerage & Drainage

027 150 | Sewage Systems

				DAILY	LABOR-		1999 BARE COSTS				TOTAL
			CREW	OUTPUT	HOURS	UNIT	MAT.	LABOR	EQUIP.	TOTAL	INCL O&P
4030	Extra strength, compression joints, C425										
5000	4" diameter x 4' long		B-20	265	.091	L.F.	1.77	2.20		3.97	5.60
5020	6" diameter x 5' long		"	200	.120		2.89	2.92		5.81	8.05
5040	8" diameter x 5' long		B-21	200	.140		4.08	3.51	.68	8.27	11.05
5060	10" diameter x 5' long		"	190	.147		6.70	3.69	.71	11.10	14.25
9000	Minimum labor/equipment charge		1 Clab	4	2	Job		43		43	72

027 400 | Septic Systems

			CREW	DAILY OUTPUT	LABOR HOURS	UNIT	MAT.	LABOR	EQUIP.	TOTAL	INCL O&P
0010	**SEPTIC TANKS** Not incl. excav. or piping, precast, 1,000 gallon		B-21	8	3.500	Ea.	450	87.50	17	554.50	660
0020	1,250 gallon			8	3.500		550	87.50	17	654.50	770
0060	1,500 gallon			7	4		650	100	19.40	769.40	905
0100	2,000 gallon			5	5.600		870	140	27	1,037	1,225
0140	2,500 gallon			5	5.600		1,000	140	27	1,167	1,350
0180	4,000 gallon			4	7		3,000	175	34	3,209	3,625
0220	5,000 gal., 4 piece		B-13	3	18.667		5,575	435	183	6,193	7,075
0300	15,000 gallon, 4 piece		B-13B	1.70	32.941		11,000	765	465	12,230	13,900
0400	25,000 gallon, 4 piece			1.10	50.909		16,500	1,175	720	18,395	20,900
0500	40,000 gallon, 4 piece			.80	70		27,000	1,625	990	29,615	33,500
0520	50,000 gallon, 5 piece		B-13C	.60	93.333		31,100	2,175	1,875	35,150	39,900
0540	75,000 gallon, cast in place		C-14C	.25	448		37,800	11,700	148	49,648	61,500
0560	100,000 gallon		"	.15	746		46,800	19,500	246	66,546	85,000
0600	High density polyethylene, 1,000 gallon		B-21	6	4.667		800	117	22.50	939.50	1,100
0700	1,500 gallon			4	7		1,000	175	34	1,209	1,425
0900	Galley, 4' x 4' x 4'			16	1.750		175	44	8.50	227.50	275
1000	Distribution boxes, concrete, 7 outlets		2 Clab	16	1		75	21.50		96.50	119
1100	9 outlets		"	8	2		225	43		268	320
1150	Leaching field chambers, 13' x 3'-7" x 1'-4", standard		B-13	16	3.500		665	81.50	34.50	781	900
1200	Heavy duty, 8' x 4' x 1'-6"			14	4		320	93	39	452	545
1300	13' x 3'-9" x 1'-6"			12	4.667		910	108	46	1,064	1,225
1350	20' x 4' x 1'-6"			5	11.200		750	260	110	1,120	1,375
1420	Leaching pit, 6', dia, 3' deep complete						500			500	550
1600	Leaching pit, 6'-6" diameter, 6' deep		B-21	5	5.600		450	140	27	617	755
1620	8' deep			4	7		530	175	34	739	915
1700	8' diameter, H-20 load, 6' deep			4	7		730	175	34	939	1,125
1720	8' deep			3	9.333		900	234	45.50	1,179.50	1,425
2000	Velocity reducing pit, precast conc., 6' diameter, 3' deep			4.70	5.957		225	149	29	403	525
2200	Excavation for septic tank, 3/4 C.Y. backhoe		B-12F	145	.110	C.Y.		2.95	3.10	6.05	8.10
2400	4' trench for disposal field, 3/4 C.Y. backhoe		"	335	.048	L.F.		1.28	1.34	2.62	3.50
2600	Gravel fill, run of bank		B-6	150	.160	C.Y.	5.50	3.74	1.46	10.70	13.80
2800	Crushed stone, 3/4"		"	150	.160	"	18.30	3.74	1.46	23.50	28

027 660 | Relining Exist. Pipelines

			CREW	DAILY OUTPUT	LABOR HOURS	UNIT	MAT.	LABOR	EQUIP.	TOTAL	INCL O&P
0010	**LINING PIPE** with cement, incl. bypass and cleaning										
0020	Less than 10,000 L.F., urban, 6" to 10"		C-17E	130	.615	L.F.	5.80	17.50	.47	23.77	36
0050	10" to 12"			125	.640		7.15	18.20	.49	25.84	38.50
0070	12" to 16"			115	.696		7.35	19.80	.53	27.68	41.50
0100	16" to 20"			95	.842		8.60	24	.64	33.24	49.50
0200	24" to 36"			90	.889		9.25	25.50	.68	35.43	53
0300	48" to 72"			80	1		14.80	28.50	.76	44.06	64
0500	Rural, 6" to 10"			180	.444		5.80	12.65	.34	18.79	28
0550	10" to 12"			175	.457		7.15	13	.35	20.50	30
0570	12" to 16"			160	.500		7.45	14.25	.38	22.08	32
0600	16" to 20"			135	.593		7.90	16.85	.45	25.20	37
0700	24" to 36"			125	.640		9.40	18.20	.49	28.09	41
0800	48" to 72"			100	.800		14.80	23	.61	38.41	54.50
1000	Greater than 10,000 L.F., urban, 6" to 10"			160	.500		5.80	14.25	.38	20.43	30.50

For expanded coverage of these items see *Means Heavy Construction Cost Data 1999*

027 | Sewerage & Drainage

027 660 | Relining Exist. Pipelines

		CREW	DAILY OUTPUT	LABOR-HOURS	UNIT	MAT.	LABOR	EQUIP.	TOTAL	TOTAL INCL O&P	
1050	10" to 12"	C-17E	155	.516	L.F.	7.05	14.70	.39	22.14	32.50	
1070	12" to 16"		140	.571		7.35	16.25	.43	24.03	35.50	
1100	16" to 20"		120	.667		7.90	18.95	.51	27.36	40.50	
1200	24" to 36"		115	.696		9.40	19.80	.53	29.73	44	
1300	48" to 72"		95	.842		14.80	24	.64	39.44	56.50	
1500	Rural, 6" to 10"		215	.372		5.80	10.60	.28	16.68	24.50	
1550	10" to 12"		210	.381		7.15	10.85	.29	18.29	26	
1570	12" to 16"		185	.432		7.35	12.30	.33	19.98	29	
1600	16" to 20"		150	.533		7.90	15.15	.41	23.46	34	
1700	24" to 36"		140	.571		9.40	16.25	.43	26.08	38	
1800	48" to 72"		120	.667		14.90	18.95	.51	34.36	48.50	

(1999 BARE COSTS columns: MAT., LABOR, EQUIP., TOTAL)

028 | Site Improvements

028 100 | Irrigation Systems

		CREW	DAILY OUTPUT	LABOR-HOURS	UNIT	MAT.	LABOR	EQUIP.	TOTAL	TOTAL INCL O&P
0010	**SPRINKLER IRRIGATION SYSTEM** For lawns									
0100	Golf course with fully automatic system	C-17	.05	1,600	9 holes	75,000	45,500		120,500	158,000
0200	24' diam. head at 15' O.C incl. piping, auto oper., minimum	B-20	70	.343	Head	16.50	8.35		24.85	32
0300	Maximum		40	.600		38	14.60		52.60	66.50
0500	60' diam. head at 40' O.C. incl. piping, auto oper., minimum		28	.857		50	21		71	90
0600	Maximum		23	1.043		140	25.50		165.50	197
0800	Residential system, custom, 1" supply		2,000	.012	S.F.	.25	.29		.54	.77
0900	1-1/2" supply		1,800	.013	"	.28	.32		.60	.85

028 300 | Fences & Gates

		CREW	DAILY OUTPUT	LABOR-HOURS	UNIT	MAT.	LABOR	EQUIP.	TOTAL	TOTAL INCL O&P
0010	**FENCE, CHAIN LINK INDUSTRIAL**, schedule 40									
0020	3 strands barb wire, 2" post @ 10' O.C., set in concrete, 6' H									
0200	9 ga. wire, galv. steel	B-80	240	.133	L.F.	7	3.13	2.25	12.38	15.30
0300	Aluminized steel		240	.133		9	3.13	2.25	14.38	17.50
0800	6 ga. wire, 6' high but omit barbed wire, galv. steel		250	.128		11	3	2.16	16.16	19.40
0900	Aluminized steel		250	.128		15.40	3	2.16	20.56	24.50
0920	8' H, 6 ga. wire, 2-1/2" line post, galv. steel		180	.178		17.95	4.17	3	25.12	30
0940	Aluminized steel		180	.178		22	4.17	3	29.17	34.50
1100	Add for corner posts, 3" diam., galv. steel		40	.800	Ea.	55	18.75	13.50	87.25	106
1200	Aluminized steel		40	.800		66	18.75	13.50	98.25	118
1400	Gate for 6' high fence, 1-5/8" frame, 3' wide, galv. steel		10	3.200		80	75	54	209	271
1500	Aluminized steel		10	3.200		110	75	54	239	305
3100	Overhead slide gate, chain link, 6' high, to 18' wide		38	.842	L.F.	82.50	19.75	14.20	116.45	139
3110	Cantilever type		48	.667		38	15.65	11.25	64.90	80
3120	8' high		24	1.333		55	31.50	22.50	109	137
3130	10' high		18	1.778		65	41.50	30	136.50	173
3150	Tennis courts, 11 ga. wire, 1-3/4" mesh, 2-1/2" line posts									
3170	1-5/8" top rail, 3" corner and gate posts									
3190	10' high, galvanized steel	B-80	190	.168	L.F.	10	3.95	2.84	16.79	20.50
3210	Vinyl covered 9 ga. wire		190	.168	"	11	3.95	2.84	17.79	21.50
3240	Corner posts for above, 3" diameter, 10' high		30	1.067	Ea.	105	25	18	148	177
3300	Residential, 11 ga. wire, 1-5/8" line post @ 10' O.C.									
3310	1-3/8" top rail									
3350	4' high, galvanized steel	B-80	475	.067	L.F.	5.50	1.58	1.14	8.22	9.90

028 | Site Improvements

028 300 | Fences & Gates

			CREW	DAILY OUTPUT	LABOR-HOURS	UNIT	MAT.	LABOR	EQUIP.	TOTAL	TOTAL INCL O&P	
308	3400	Aluminized	B-80	475	.067	L.F.	5.55	1.58	1.14	8.27	9.95	308
	3600	Gate, 3' wide, 1-3/8" frame, galv. steel		10	3.200	Ea.	45	75	54	174	232	
	3700	Aluminized		10	3.200	"	50	75	54	179	238	
	3900	3' high, galvanized steel		620	.052	L.F.	3.25	1.21	.87	5.33	6.55	
	4000	Aluminized		620	.052	"	4	1.21	.87	6.08	7.35	
	4200	Gate, 3' wide, 1-3/8" frame, galv. steel		12	2.667	Ea.	40	62.50	45	147.50	197	
	4300	Aluminized		12	2.667		45	62.50	45	152.50	202	
	7795	Cantilever, manual, exp. roller, (pr) 40' wide x 8' high	B-22	1	30		2,075	760	204	3,039	3,775	
	7800	30' wide x 8' high		1	30		1,750	760	204	2,714	3,400	
	7805	24' wide x 8' high		1	30		1,300	760	204	2,264	2,900	
	7810	Motor operators for gates, (no elec wiring), 3' wide swing	2 Skwk	.50	32		765	900		1,665	2,350	
	7815	Up to 20' wide swing		.50	32		2,400	900		3,300	4,125	
	7820	Up to 45' sliding		.50	32		2,425	900		3,325	4,175	
	7825	Overhead gate, 6' to 18' wide, sliding/cantilever		45	.356	L.F.	88.50	9.95		98.45	114	
	7830	Gate operators, digital receiver		7	2.286	Ea.	176	64		240	299	
	7835	Two button transmitter		24	.667		34.50	18.70		53.20	69	
	7840	3 button station		14	1.143		41	32		73	98	
	7845	Master slave system		4	4		150	112		262	350	
	8000	Components only, fabric, galvanized, 4' high	B-80	585	.055	L.F.	2	1.28	.92	4.20	5.30	
	8040	6' high		430	.074	"	2.63	1.75	1.25	5.63	7.15	
	8200	Posts, line post, 4' high		34	.941	Ea.	7	22	15.85	44.85	61	
	8240	6' high		26	1.231	"	7.75	29	21	57.75	79	
	8400	Top rails, 1-3/8" O.D.		1,000	.032	L.F.	1	.75	.54	2.29	2.92	
	8440	1-5/8" O.D.		1,000	.032	"	1.10	.75	.54	2.39	3.03	
	9000	Minimum labor/equipment charge		2	16	Job		375	270	645	910	
320	0010	**FENCE, MISC. METAL** Chicken wire, posts @ 4', 1" mesh, 4' high	B-80	410	.078	L.F.	1.10	1.83	1.32	4.25	5.65	320
	0100	2" mesh, 6' high		350	.091		1	2.14	1.54	4.68	6.30	
	0200	Galv. steel, 12 ga., 2" x 4" mesh, posts 5' O.C., 3' high		300	.107		1.50	2.50	1.80	5.80	7.75	
	0300	5' high		300	.107		2	2.50	1.80	6.30	8.30	
	0400	14 ga., 1" x 2" mesh, 3' high		300	.107		1.60	2.50	1.80	5.90	7.85	
	0500	5' high		300	.107		2.20	2.50	1.80	6.50	8.50	
	1000	Kennel fencing, 1-1/2" mesh, 6' long, 3'-6" wide, 6'-2" high	2 Clab	4	4	Ea.	250	86		336	420	
	1050	12' long		4	4		300	86		386	475	
	1200	Top covers, 1-1/2" mesh, 6' long		15	1.067		50	23		73	93.50	
	1250	12' long		12	1.333		80	28.50		108.50	136	
	1300	For kennel doors, see division 083-729										
	4500	Security fence, prison grade, set in concrete, 12' high	B-80	25	1.280	L.F.	20	30	21.50	71.50	95	
	4600	16' high	"	20	1.600		24.50	37.50	27	89	118	
	5000	Snow fence on steel posts 10' O.C., 4' high	B-1	500	.048		1.55	1.06		2.61	3.49	
	5300	Tubular picket, steel, 6' sections, 1-9/16" posts, 4' high	B-80	300	.107		15.50	2.50	1.80	19.80	23	
	5400	2" posts, 5' high		240	.133		21.50	3.13	2.25	26.88	31	
	5600	2" posts, 6' high		200	.160		24.50	3.75	2.70	30.95	35.50	
	5700	Staggered picket 1-9/16" posts, 4' high		300	.107		14	2.50	1.80	18.30	21.50	
	5800	2" posts, 5' high		240	.133		23	3.13	2.25	28.38	33	
	5900	2" posts, 6' high		200	.160		24	3.75	2.70	30.45	35	
	6200	Gates, 4' high, 3' wide	B-1	10	2.400	Ea.	135	53		188	238	
	6300	5' high, 3' wide		10	2.400		175	53		228	282	
	6400	6' high, 3' wide		10	2.400		180	53		233	287	
	6500	4' wide		10	2.400		210	53		263	320	
324	0010	**FENCE, RAIL** Picket, No. 2 cedar, Gothic, 2 rail, 3' high	B-1	160	.150	L.F.	4.40	3.32		7.72	10.40	324
	0050	Gate, 3'-6" wide		9	2.667	Ea.	38	59		97	140	
	0600	Open rail, rustic, No. 1 cedar, 2 rail, 3' high		160	.150	L.F.	3.95	3.32		7.27	9.90	
	0650	Gate, 3' wide		9	2.667	Ea.	44	59		103	147	
	1200	Stockade, No. 2 cedar, treated wood rails, 6' high		160	.150	L.F.	5.50	3.32		8.82	11.60	
	1250	Gate, 3' wide		9	2.667	Ea.	45	59		104	148	

For expanded coverage of these items see Means Site Work and Landscape Cost Data 1999

028 | Site Improvements

028 300 | Fences & Gates

		CREW	DAILY OUTPUT	LABOR-HOURS	UNIT	MAT.	LABOR	EQUIP.	TOTAL	TOTAL INCL O&P	
324	3300	Board, shadow box, 1" x 6", treated pine, 6' high	B-1	160	.150	L.F.	8.10	3.32		11.42	14.50	324
	3400	No. 1 cedar, 6' high		150	.160		16	3.54		19.54	23.50	
	3900	Basket weave, No. 1 cedar, 6' high		160	.150		15.90	3.32		19.22	23	
	3950	Gate, 3'-6" wide		8	3	Ea.	101	66.50		167.50	223	
	4000	Treated pine, 6' high		150	.160	L.F.	8.70	3.54		12.24	15.45	
	4200	Gate, 3'-6" wide		9	2.667	Ea.	47.50	59		106.50	151	
	8000	Posts only, 4' high		40	.600		11.75	13.25		25	35	
	8040	6' high		30	.800		16.20	17.70		33.90	47.50	
	9000	Minimum labor/equipment charge	1 Clab	2	4	Job		86		86	144	

028 400 | Walk/Road/Parkg Appurt

		CREW	DAILY OUTPUT	LABOR-HOURS	UNIT	MAT.	LABOR	EQUIP.	TOTAL	TOTAL INCL O&P	
404	0010	GUIDE/GUARD RAIL Corrugated steel, galv. steel posts, 6'-3" O.C.	B-80	850	.038	L.F.	10	.88	.63	11.51	13.15	404
	0200	End sections, galvanized, flared		50	.640	Ea.	40	15	10.80	65.80	80.50	
	0300	Wrap around end		50	.640	"	60	15	10.80	85.80	102	
	0400	Timber guide rail, 4" x 8" with 6" x 8" wood posts, treated		960	.033	L.F.	12	.78	.56	13.34	15.10	
408	0010	PARKING BARRIERS Timber with saddles, treated type										408
	1000	Wheel stops, precast concrete incl. dowels, 6" x 10" x 6'-0"	B-2	120	.333	Ea.	25.50	7.30		32.80	40.50	
	1300	Pipe bollards, conc filled/paint, 8' L x 4' D hole, 6" diam.	B-6	20	1.200		165	28	10.95	203.95	240	
	1400	8" diam.		15	1.600		250	37.50	14.60	302.10	355	
	1500	12" diam.		12	2		325	46.50	18.25	389.75	455	
412	0010	SIGNS Stock, 24" x 24", no posts, .080" alum. reflectorized	B-80	70	.457	Ea.	25	10.70	7.70	43.40	53.50	412
	0100	High intensity		70	.457		45	10.70	7.70	63.40	75.50	
	0300	30" x 30", reflectorized		70	.457		48	10.70	7.70	66.40	79	
	0400	High intensity		70	.457		64	10.70	7.70	82.40	96.50	
	0600	Guide and directional signs, 12" x 18", reflectorized		70	.457		15.50	10.70	7.70	33.90	43	
	0700	High intensity		70	.457		15	10.70	7.70	33.40	42.50	
	0900	18" x 24", stock signs, reflectorized		70	.457		24	10.70	7.70	42.40	52.50	
	1000	High intensity		70	.457		38	10.70	7.70	56.40	68	
	1200	24" x 24", stock signs, reflectorized		70	.457		25	10.70	7.70	43.40	53.50	
	1300	High intensity		70	.457		45	10.70	7.70	63.40	75.50	
	1500	Add to above for steel posts, galvanized, 10'-0" upright, bolted		200	.160		28	3.75	2.70	34.45	40	
	1600	12'-0" upright, bolted		140	.229		30	5.35	3.85	39.20	46	
	1800	Highway road signs, aluminum, over 20 S. F., reflectorized		350	.091	S.F.	12	2.14	1.54	15.68	18.40	
	2000	High intensity		350	.091		15	2.14	1.54	18.68	21.50	
	2200	Highway, suspended over road, 80 S.F. min., reflectorized		165	.194		15	4.55	3.27	22.82	27.50	
	2300	High intensity		165	.194		20	4.55	3.27	27.82	33	
416	0010	STEPS Incl. excav., borrow & concrete base, where applicable										416
	0100	Brick steps	B-24	35	.686	LF Riser	7.60	17.10		24.70	36.50	
	0200	Railroad ties	2 Clab	25	.640		2.75	13.75		16.50	26	
	0300	Bluestone treads, 12" x 2" or 12" x 1-1/2"	B-24	30	.800		16.35	20		36.35	51	
	0490	Minimum labor/equipment charge	D-1	2	8	Job		197		197	325	
	0500	Concrete, cast in place, see division 033-130										
	0600	Precast concrete, see division 034-804										

028 700 | Site/Street Furnishings

		CREW	DAILY OUTPUT	LABOR-HOURS	UNIT	MAT.	LABOR	EQUIP.	TOTAL	TOTAL INCL O&P	
704	0010	BENCHES Park, precast concrete, w/backs,wood rails, 4' long	2 Clab	5	3.200	Ea.	310	68.50		378.50	455	704
	0100	8' long		4	4		635	86		721	840	
	0300	Fiberglass, without back, one piece, 4' long		10	1.600		355	34.50		389.50	450	
	0400	8' long		7	2.286		700	49		749	850	
	0500	Steel barstock pedestals w/backs, 2" x 3" wood rails, 4' long		10	1.600		630	34.50		664.50	755	
	0510	8' long		7	2.286		745	49		794	900	
	0520	3" x 8" wood plank, 4' long		10	1.600		635	34.50		669.50	760	
	0530	8' long		7	2.286		740	49		789	895	

Important: See the Reference Section for critical supporting data - Reference Nos., Crews, & City Cost Indexes

028 | Site Improvements

028 700 | Site/Street Furnishings

			CREW	DAILY OUTPUT	LABOR-HOURS	UNIT	MAT.	LABOR	EQUIP.	TOTAL	TOTAL INCL O&P	
704	0540	Backless, 4" x 4" wood plank, 4' square	2 Clab	10	1.600	Ea.	615	34.50		649.50	735	704
	0550	8' long		7	2.286		585	49		634	725	
	0600	Aluminum pedestals, with backs, aluminum slats, 8' long		8	2		150	43		193	237	
	0610	15' long		5	3.200		250	68.50		318.50	390	
	0620	Portable, aluminum slats, 8' long		8	2		170	43		213	259	
	0630	15' long		5	3.200		275	68.50		343.50	420	
	0800	Cast iron pedestals, back & arms, wood slats, 4' long		8	2		460	43		503	575	
	0820	8' long		5	3.200		765	68.50		833.50	955	
	0840	Backless, wood slats, 4' long		8	2		400	43		443	510	
	0860	8' long		5	3.200		675	68.50		743.50	860	
	1700	Steel frame, fir seat, 10' long		10	1.600		150	34.50		184.50	223	
	9000	Minimum labor/equipment charge		2	8	Job		172		172	287	
716	0010	**PLANTERS** Concrete, sandblasted, precast, 48" diameter, 24" high	2 Clab	15	1.067	Ea.	425	23		448	510	716
	0100	Fluted, precast, 7' diameter, 36" high		10	1.600	"	1,150	34.50		1,184.50	1,300	
	0300	Fiberglass, circular, 36" diameter, 24" high		15	1.067	Ea.	315	23		338	385	
	0400	60" diameter, 24" high		10	1.600	"	645	34.50		679.50	770	
	9000	Minimum labor/equipment charge	1 Clab	2	4	Job		86		86	144	

029 | Landscaping

029 100 | Shrub/Tree Transplanting

			CREW	DAILY OUTPUT	LABOR-HOURS	UNIT	MAT.	LABOR	EQUIP.	TOTAL	TOTAL INCL O&P	
104	0010	**TREE GUYING** Including stakes, guy wire and wrap										104
	0100	Less than 3" caliper, 2 stakes	2 Clab	35	.457	Ea.	15	9.80		24.80	33	
	0200	3" to 4" caliper, 3 stakes	"	21	.762	"	17.60	16.35		33.95	47	
	1000	Including arrowhead anchor, cable, turnbuckles and wrap										
	1100	Less than 3" caliper, 3" anchors	2 Clab	20	.800	Ea.	45	17.15		62.15	78	
	1200	3" to 6" caliper, 4" anchors		15	1.067		65	23		88	110	
	1300	6" caliper, 6" anchors		12	1.333		80	28.50		108.50	136	
	1400	8" caliper, 8" anchors		9	1.778		80	38		118	152	
108	0010	**TREE REMOVAL**										108
	0100	Dig & lace, shrubs, broadleaf evergreen, 18"-24"	B-1	55	.436	Ea.		9.65		9.65	16.15	
	0200	2'-3'	"	35	.686			15.15		15.15	25.50	
	0300	3'-4'	B-6	30	.800			18.70	7.30	26	38.50	
	0400	4'-5'	"	20	1.200			28	10.95	38.95	58	
	1000	Deciduous, 12"-15"	B-1	110	.218			4.83		4.83	8.10	
	1100	18"-24"		65	.369			8.15		8.15	13.65	
	1200	2'-3'		55	.436			9.65		9.65	16.15	
	1300	3'-4'	B-6	50	.480			11.20	4.38	15.58	23	
	2000	Evergreeen, 18"-24"	B-1	55	.436			9.65		9.65	16.15	
	2100	2'-0" to 2'-6"		50	.480			10.60		10.60	17.75	
	2200	2'-6" to 3'-0"		35	.686			15.15		15.15	25.50	
	2300	3'-0" to 3'-6"		20	1.200			26.50		26.50	44.50	
	3000	Trees, deciduous, small, 2'-3'		55	.436			9.65		9.65	16.15	
	3100	3'-4'	B-6	50	.480			11.20	4.38	15.58	23	
	3200	4'-5'		35	.686			16.05	6.25	22.30	33.50	
	3300	5'-6'		30	.800			18.70	7.30	26	38.50	
	4000	Shade, 5'-6'		50	.480			11.20	4.38	15.58	23	
	4100	6'-8'		35	.686			16.05	6.25	22.30	33.50	
	4200	8'-10'		25	.960			22.50	8.75	31.25	46.50	

For expanded coverage of these items see *Means Site Work and Landscape Cost Data 1999*

029 | Landscaping

029 100 | Shrub/Tree Transplanting

		CREW	DAILY OUTPUT	LABOR-HOURS	UNIT	1999 BARE COSTS MAT.	LABOR	EQUIP.	TOTAL	TOTAL INCL O&P	
4300	2" caliper	B-6	12	2	Ea.		46.50	18.25	64.75	96.50	108
5000	Evergreen, 4'-5'		35	.686			16.05	6.25	22.30	33.50	
5100	5'-6'		25	.960			22.50	8.75	31.25	46.50	
5200	6'-7'		19	1.263			29.50	11.50	41	61	
5300	7'-8'		15	1.600			37.50	14.60	52.10	77.50	
5400	8'-10'	↓	11	2.182	↓		51	19.90	70.90	106	

029 200 | Soil Preparation

		CREW	DAILY OUTPUT	LABOR-HOURS	UNIT	MAT.	LABOR	EQUIP.	TOTAL	TOTAL INCL O&P	
0010	**LAWN BED PREPARATION**										204
0100	Rake topsoil, site material, harley rock rake, ideal	B-6	33	.727	M.S.F.		17	6.65	23.65	35.50	
0200	Adverse	"	7	3.429			80	31.50	111.50	167	
0300	Screened loam, york rake and finish, ideal	B-62	24	1			23.50	4.64	28.14	43.50	
0400	Adverse	"	20	1.200			28	5.55	33.55	52	
1000	Remove topsoil & stock pile on site, 75 HP dozer, 6" deep, 50' haul	B-10L	30	.400			10.45	10.25	20.70	28	
1050	300' haul		6.10	1.967			51.50	50.50	102	139	
1100	12" deep, 50' haul		15.50	.774			20	19.85	39.85	54.50	
1150	300' haul	↓	3.10	3.871			101	99.50	200.50	272	
1200	200 HP dozer, 6" deep, 50' haul	B-10B	125	.096			2.50	6.70	9.20	11.45	
1250	300' haul		30.70	.391			10.20	27.50	37.70	46.50	
1300	12" deep, 50' haul		62	.194			5.05	13.55	18.60	23	
1350	300' haul	↓	15.40	.779	↓		20.50	54.50	75	93	
1400	Alternate method, 75 HP dozer, 50' haul	B-10L	860	.014	C.Y.		.36	.36	.72	.98	
1450	300' haul	"	114	.105			2.75	2.70	5.45	7.40	
1500	200 HP dozer, 50' haul	B-10B	2,660	.005			.12	.32	.44	.54	
1600	300' haul	"	570	.021	↓		.55	1.47	2.02	2.51	
1800	Rolling topsoil, hand push roller	1 Clab	3,200	.002	S.F.		.05		.05	.09	
1850	Tractor drawn roller	B-66	10,666	.001	"		.02	.02	.04	.05	
2000	Root raking and loading, residential, no boulders	B-6	53.30	.450	M.S.F.		10.50	4.11	14.61	22	
2100	With boulders		32	.750			17.55	6.85	24.40	36.50	
2200	Municipal, no boulders		200	.120			2.80	1.09	3.89	5.80	
2300	With boulders	↓	120	.200			4.67	1.82	6.49	9.65	
2400	Large commercial, no boulders	B-10B	400	.030			.78	2.10	2.88	3.57	
2500	With boulders	"	240	.050			1.30	3.50	4.80	5.95	
3000	Scarify subsoil, residential, skid steer loader w/scarifiers, 50 HP	B-66	32	.250			6.80	6.25	13.05	17.70	
3050	Municipal, skid steer loader w/scarifiers, 50 HP	"	120	.067			1.81	1.67	3.48	4.73	
3100	Large commercial, 75 HP, dozer w/scarifier	B-10L	240	.050	↓		1.30	1.28	2.58	3.51	
3500	Screen topsoil from stockpile, vibrating screen, wet material (organic)	B-10P	200	.060	C.Y.		1.56	4.33	5.89	7.30	
3550	Dry material	"	300	.040	↓		1.04	2.88	3.92	4.85	
3600	Mixing with conditioners, manure and peat	B-10R	550	.022	↓		.57	.44	1.01	1.41	
3650	Mobilization add for 2 days or less operation	B-34K	3	2.667	Job		59	305	364	430	
3800	Spread conditioned topsoil, 6" deep, by hand	B-1	360	.067	S.Y.	3.15	1.47		4.62	5.95	
3850	300 HP dozer	B-10M	27	.444	M.S.F.	340	11.60	42	393.60	440	
4000	Spread soil conditioners, alum. sulfate, 1#/S.Y., hand push spreader	A-1	17,500	.001	S.Y.	.90	.01		.91	1.01	
4050	Tractor spreader	B-66	700	.011	M.S.F.	100	.31	.29	100.60	111	
4100	Fertilizer, 0.2#/S.Y., push spreader	A-1	17,500	.001	S.Y.	.05	.01		.06	.08	
4150	Tractor spreader	B-66	700	.011	M.S.F.	5.55	.31	.29	6.15	6.90	
4200	Ground limestone, 1#/S.Y., push spreader	A-1	17,500	.001	S.Y.	.08	.01		.09	.11	
4250	Tractor spreader	B-66	700	.011	M.S.F.	11.90	.31	.29	12.50	13.85	
4300	Lusoil, 3#/S.Y., push spreader	A-1	17,500	.001	S.Y.	.40	.01		.41	.46	
4350	Tractor spreader	B-66	700	.011	M.S.F.	44.50	.31	.29	45.10	50	
4400	Manure, 18#/S.Y., push spreader	A-1	2,500	.003	S.Y.	2.35	.07	.03	2.45	2.72	
4450	Tractor spreader	B-66	280	.029	M.S.F.	261	.78	.72	262.50	289	
4500	Perlite, 1" deep, push spreader	A-1	17,500	.001	S.Y.	7.25	.01		7.26	8	
4550	Tractor spreader	B-66	700	.011	M.S.F.	805	.31	.29	805.60	885	
4600	Vermiculite, push spreader	A-1	17,500	.001	S.Y.	2.20	.01		2.21	2.44	
4650	Tractor spreader	B-66	700	.011	M.S.F.	244	.31	.29	244.60	270	

029 | Landscaping

029 200 | Soil Preparation

		CREW	DAILY OUTPUT	LABOR-HOURS	UNIT	MAT.	LABOR	EQUIP.	TOTAL	TOTAL INCL O&P	
204	5000	Spread topsoil, skid steer loader and hand dress	B-62	270	.089	C.Y.	14.15	2.08	.41	16.64	19.45	204
	5100	Articulated loader and hand dress	B-100	320	.038		14.15	.98	1.59	16.72	18.95	
	5200	Articulated loader and 75HP dozer	B-10M	500	.024		14.15	.63	2.26	17.04	19.10	
	5300	Road grader and hand dress	B-11L	1,000	.016		14.15	.40	.58	15.13	16.90	
	6000	Tilling topsoil, 20 HP tractor, disk harrow, 2" deep	B-66	50,000	.001	S.Y.					.01	
	6050	4" deep		40,000	.001			.01	.01	.02	.02	
	6100	6" deep		3,000	.003			.07	.07	.14	.19	
	6150	26" rototiller, 2" deep	A-1	1,250	.006			.14	.05	.19	.29	
	6200	4" deep		1,000	.008			.17	.07	.24	.37	
	6250	6" deep		750	.011			.23	.09	.32	.48	
	7000	Lawn maintenance see Division 029-700										
208	0010	**PLANT BED PREPARATION**										208
	0100	Backfill planting pit, by hand, on site topsoil	2 Clab	18	.889	C.Y.		19.05		19.05	32	
	0200	Prepared planting mix	"	24	.667			14.30		14.30	24	
	0300	Skid steer loader, on site topsoil	B-62	340	.071			1.65	.33	1.98	3.07	
	0400	Prepared planting mix	"	410	.059			1.37	.27	1.64	2.55	
	1000	Excavate planting pit, by hand, sandy soil	2 Clab	16	1			21.50		21.50	36	
	1100	Heavy soil or clay	"	8	2			43		43	72	
	1200	1/2 C.Y. backhoe, sandy soil	B-11C	150	.107			2.66	1.46	4.12	5.95	
	1300	Heavy soil or clay	"	115	.139			3.47	1.90	5.37	7.75	
	2000	Mix planting soil, incl. loam, manure, peat, by hand	2 Clab	60	.267		25	5.70		30.70	37	
	2100	Skid steer loader	B-62	150	.160		25	3.74	.74	29.48	34.50	
	3000	Pile sod, skid steer loader	"	2,800	.009	S.Y.		.20	.04	.24	.37	
	3100	By hand	2 Clab	400	.040			.86		.86	1.44	
	4000	Remove sod, F.E. loader	B-10S	2,000	.006			.16	.16	.32	.43	
	4100	Sod cutter	B-12K	3,200	.005			.13	.25	.38	.49	
	4200	By hand	2 Clab	240	.067			1.43		1.43	2.39	

029 300 | Lawns & Grasses

		CREW	DAILY OUTPUT	LABOR-HOURS	UNIT	MAT.	LABOR	EQUIP.	TOTAL	TOTAL INCL O&P	
304	0010	**SEEDING** Mechanical seeding, 215 lb./acre	B-66	1.50	5.333	Acre	485	145	134	764	915	304
	0100	44 lb./M.S.Y.	"	2,500	.003	S.Y.	.15	.09	.08	.32	.40	
	0600	Limestone hand push spreader, 50 lbs. per M.S.F.	1 Clab	180	.044	M.S.F.	3.25	.95		4.20	5.20	
	9000	Minimum labor/equipment charge	"	4	2	Job		43		43	72	
316	0010	**SODDING** 1" deep, bluegrass sod, on level ground, over 8 M.S.F.	B-63	22	1.818	M.S.F.	200	41	5.05	246.05	294	316
	0200	4 M.S.F.		17	2.353	"	220	53	6.55	279.55	335	
	0300	1000 S.F.		3.50	11.429	Ea.	250	258	32	540	735	
	0500	Sloped ground, over 8 M.S.F.		6	6.667	M.S.F.	200	151	18.55	369.55	490	
	0600	4 M.S.F.		5	8		220	181	22	423	565	
	0700	1000 S.F.		4	10		250	226	28	504	680	
	1000	Bent grass sod, on level ground, over 6 M.S.F.		20	2		460	45	5.55	510.55	585	
	1100	3 M.S.F.		18	2.222		500	50	6.20	556.20	640	
	1200	Sodding 1000 S.F. or less		14	2.857		550	64.50	7.95	622.45	720	
	1500	Sloped ground, over 6 M.S.F.		15	2.667		460	60.50	7.40	527.90	615	
	1600	3 M.S.F.		13.50	2.963		500	67	8.25	575.25	670	
	1700	1000 S.F.		12	3.333		300	75.50	9.25	384.75	465	

029 500 | Trees/Plants/Grnd Cover

		CREW	DAILY OUTPUT	LABOR-HOURS	UNIT	MAT.	LABOR	EQUIP.	TOTAL	TOTAL INCL O&P	
504	0010	**GROUND COVER** Plants, pachysandra, in prepared beds	B-1	15	1.600	C	34	35.50		69.50	96.50	504
	0200	Vinca minor, 1 yr, bare root		12	2	"	40	44		84	118	
	0600	Stone chips, in 50 lb. bags, Georgia marble		520	.046	Bag	3.36	1.02		4.38	5.40	
	0700	Onyx gemstone		260	.092		13.10	2.04		15.14	17.85	
	0800	Quartz		260	.092		5.50	2.04		7.54	9.45	
	0900	Pea gravel, truckload lots		28	.857	Ton	24.50	18.95		43.45	58.50	
520	0010	**PLANTING** Moving shrubs on site, 12" ball	B-62	28	.857	Ea.	20	3.98		23.98	37.50	520
	0100	24" ball	"	22	1.091	"		25.50	5.05	30.55	47.50	

For expanded coverage of these items see *Means Site Work and Landscape Cost Data 1999*

029 | Landscaping

029 500 | Trees/Plants/Grnd Cover

			CREW	DAILY OUTPUT	LABOR-HOURS	UNIT	MAT.	LABOR	EQUIP.	TOTAL	TOTAL INCL O&P
520	0300	Moving trees on site, 36" ball	B-6	3.75	6.400	Ea.		150	58.50	208.50	310
	0400	60" ball	"	1	24	"		560	219	779	1,150
524	0010	**SHRUBS** Broadleaf evergreen, planted in prepared beds									
	0100	Andromeda, 15"-18", container	B-1	96	.250	Ea.	14	5.55		19.55	24.50
	0200	Azalea, 15" - 18", container		96	.250		19	5.55		24.55	30.50
	0300	Barberry, 9"-12", container		130	.185		11.45	4.08		15.53	19.45
	0400	Boxwood, 15"-18", B & B		96	.250		16.25	5.55		21.80	27
	0500	Euonymus, emerald gaiety, 12" to 15", container		115	.209		12.25	4.62		16.87	21.50
	0600	Holly, 15"-18", B & B		96	.250		16.75	5.55		22.30	27.50
	0900	Mount laurel, 18" - 24", B & B		80	.300		48	6.65		54.65	64
	1000	Paxistema, 9 - 12" high		130	.185		9	4.08		13.08	16.75
	1100	Rhododendron, 18"-24", container		48	.500		25	11.05		36.05	46
	1200	Rosemary, 1 gal container		600	.040		35	.88		35.88	40
	2000	Deciduous, amelanchier, 2'-3', B & B		57	.421		55	9.30		64.30	76
	2100	Azalea, 15"-18", B & B		96	.250		18.25	5.55		23.80	29.50
	2300	Bayberry, 2'-3', B & B		57	.421		22.50	9.30		31.80	40
	2600	Cotoneaster, 15"-18", B & B		80	.300		14	6.65		20.65	26.50
	2800	Dogwood, 3'-4', B & B	B-17	40	.800		21	18.45	14.60	54.05	69
	2900	Euonymus, alatus compacta, 15" to 18", container	B-1	80	.300		20	6.65		26.65	33
	3200	Forsythia, 2'-3', container	"	60	.400		16	8.85		24.85	32.50
	3300	Hibiscus, 3'-4', B & B	B-17	75	.427		24	9.85	7.75	41.60	51
	3400	Honeysuckle, 3'-4', B & B	B-1	60	.400		17	8.85		25.85	33.50
	3500	Hydrangea, 2'-3', B & B	"	57	.421		20	9.30		29.30	37.50
	3600	Lilac, 3'-4', B & B	B-17	40	.800		38	18.45	14.60	71.05	88
	3900	Privet, bare root, 18"-24"	B-1	80	.300		5	6.65		11.65	16.60
	4100	Quince, 2'-3', B & B	"	57	.421		9	9.30		18.30	25.50
	4200	Russian olive, 3'-4', B & B	B-17	75	.427		17	9.85	7.75	34.60	43.50
	4400	Spirea, 3'-4', B & B	B-1	70	.343		14	7.60		21.60	28
	4500	Viburnum, 3'-4', B & B	B-17	40	.800		17.50	18.45	14.60	50.55	65.50
528	0010	**SHRUBS AND TREES** Evergreen, in prepared beds, B & B									
	0100	Arborvitae pyramidal, 4'-5'	B-17	30	1.067	Ea.	35	24.50	19.45	78.95	101
	0150	Globe, 12"-15"	B-1	96	.250		10	5.55		15.55	20.50
	0300	Cedar, blue, 8'-10'	B-17	18	1.778		111	41	32.50	184.50	225
	0500	Hemlock, canadian, 2-1/2'-3'	B-1	36	.667		14.25	14.75		29	40
	0550	Holly, Savannah, 8' - 10' H		9.68	2.479		500	55		555	640
	0600	Juniper, andorra, 18"-24"		80	.300		14	6.65		20.65	26.50
	0620	Wiltoni, 15"-18"		80	.300		14.50	6.65		21.15	27
	0640	Skyrocket, 4-1/2'-5'	B-17	55	.582		38.50	13.40	10.60	62.50	76
	0660	Blue pfitzer, 2'-2-1/2'	B-1	44	.545		16	12.05		28.05	37.50
	0680	Ketleerie, 2-1/2'-3'		50	.480		28	10.60		38.60	49
	0700	Pine, black, 2-1/2'-3'		50	.480		29.50	10.60		40.10	50.50
	0720	Mugo, 18"-24"		60	.400		30	8.85		38.85	48
	0740	White, 4'-5'	B-17	75	.427		44	9.85	7.75	61.60	73
	0800	Spruce, blue, 18"-24"	B-1	60	.400		28	8.85		36.85	46
	0840	Norway, 4'-5'	B-17	75	.427		56	9.85	7.75	73.60	86
	0900	Yew, densiforma, 12"-15"	B-1	60	.400		22.50	8.85		31.35	40
	1000	Capitata, 18"-24"		30	.800		21	17.70		38.70	52.50
	1100	Hicksi, 2'-2-1/2'		30	.800		26	17.70		43.70	58
536	0010	**TREES** Deciduous, in prep. beds, balled & burlapped (B&B)									
	0100	Ash, 2" caliper	B-17	8	4	Ea.	100	92	73	265	340
	0200	Beech, 5'-6'		50	.640		200	14.75	11.65	226.40	257
	0300	Birch, 6'-8', 3 stems		20	1.600		110	37	29	176	214
	0500	Crabapple, 6'-8'		20	1.600		64	37	29	130	163
	0600	Dogwood, 4'-5'		40	.800		61	18.45	14.60	94.05	113

029 | Landscaping

029 500 | Trees/Plants/Grnd Cover

			CREW	DAILY OUTPUT	LABOR-HOURS	UNIT	MAT.	LABOR	EQUIP.	TOTAL	TOTAL INCL O&P	
536	0700	Eastern redbud 4'-5'	B-17	40	.800	Ea.	115	18.45	14.60	148.05	173	536
	0800	Elm, 8'-10'		20	1.600		70	37	29	136	170	
	0900	Ginkgo, 6'-7'		24	1.333		60	30.50	24.50	115	143	
	1000	Hawthorn, 8'-10', 1" caliper		20	1.600		80	37	29	146	181	
	1100	Honeylocust, 10'-12', 1-1/2" caliper		10	3.200		80	74	58.50	212.50	273	
	1300	Larch, 8'		32	1		50	23	18.20	91.20	113	
	1400	Linden, 8'-10', 1" caliper		20	1.600		95	37	29	161	198	
	1500	Magnolia, 4'-5'		20	1.600		55	37	29	121	153	
	1600	Maple, red, 8'-10', 1-1/2" caliper		10	3.200		125	74	58.50	257.50	325	
	1700	Mountain ash, 8'-10', 1" caliper		16	2		120	46	36.50	202.50	248	
	1800	Oak, 2-1/2"-3" caliper		3	10.667		159	246	194	599	795	
	2100	Planetree, 9'-11', 1-1/4" caliper		10	3.200		90	74	58.50	222.50	284	
	2200	Plum, 6'-8', 1" caliper		20	1.600		42	37	29	108	139	
	2300	Poplar, 9'-11', 1-1/4" caliper		10	3.200		51.50	74	58.50	184	242	
	2500	Sumac, 2'-3'		75	.427		24	9.85	7.75	41.60	51	
	2700	Tulip, 5'-6'		40	.800		48	18.45	14.60	81.05	99	
	2800	Willow, 6'-8', 1" caliper		20	1.600		63	37	29	129	162	
	9000	Minimum labor equipment charge	1 Clab	4	2	Job		43		43	72	

For information about Means Estimating Seminars, see yellow pages 11 and 12 in back of book

For expanded coverage of these items see *Means Site Work and Landscape Cost Data 1999*

Division Notes

	CREW	DAILY OUTPUT	LABOR-HOURS	UNIT	1999 BARE COSTS				TOTAL INCL O&P
					MAT.	LABOR	EQUIP.	TOTAL	

Division 3
Concrete

Estimating Tips
General
- Carefully check all the plans and specifications. Concrete often appears on drawings other than structural drawings, including mechanical and electrical drawings for equipment pads. The cost of cutting and patching is often difficult to estimate. See Division 020 for demolition costs.
- Always obtain concrete prices from suppliers near the job site. A volume discount can often be negotiated depending upon competition in the area. Remember to add for waste, particularly for slabs and footings on grade.

031 Concrete Formwork
- A primary cost for concrete construction is forming. Most jobs today are constructed with prefabricated forms. The selection of the forms best suited for the job and the total square feet of forms required for efficient concrete forming and placing are key elements in estimating concrete construction. Enough forms must be available for erection to make efficient use of the concrete placing equipment and crew.
- Concrete accessories for forming and placing depend upon the systems used. Study the plans and specifications to assure that all special accessory requirements have been included in the cost estimate such as anchor bolts, inserts and hangers.

032 Concrete Reinforcement
- Ascertain that the reinforcing steel supplier has included all accessories, cutting, bending and an allowance for lapping, splicing and waste. A good rule of thumb is 10% for lapping, splicing and waste. Also, 10% waste should be allowed for welded wire fabric.

033 Cast-in-Place Concrete
- When estimating structural concrete, pay particular attention to requirements for concrete additives, curing methods and surface treatments. Special consideration for climate, hot or cold, must be included in your estimate. Be sure to include requirements for concrete placing equipment and concrete finishing.

034 Precast Concrete
035 Cementitious Decks & Toppings
- The cost of hauling precast concrete structural members is often an important factor. For this reason, it is important to get a quote from the nearest supplier. It may become economically feasible to set up precasting beds on the site if the hauling costs are prohibitive.

Reference Numbers
Reference numbers are shown in bold squares at the beginning of some major classifications. These numbers refer to related items in the Reference Section. The reference information may be an estimating procedure, an alternate pricing method or technical information.

Note: Not all subdivisions listed here necessarily appear in this publication.

031 | Concrete Formwork

031 100 | Struct C.I.P. Formwork

			DAILY	LABOR-		1999 BARE COSTS				TOTAL	
		CREW	OUTPUT	HOURS	UNIT	MAT.	LABOR	EQUIP.	TOTAL	INCL O&P	
125	0010 **SLAB TEXTURE STAMPING,** buy										125
	0020 Approx. 3 S.F.- 5 S.F. each, minimum				Ea.	40			40	44	
	0030 Average				"	44			44	48.50	
	0120 Per S.F. of tool, average				S.F.	48			48	53	
	0200 Commonly used chemicals for texture systems										
	0210 Hardeners w/colors average				S.F.	.40			.40	.44	
	0220 Release agents w/colors, average					.15			.15	.17	
	0225 Clear, average					.10			.10	.11	
	0230 Sealers, clear, average					.10			.10	.11	
	0240 Colors, average					.12			.12	.13	
132	0010 **EXPANSION JOINT** Keyed, cold, 24 ga, incl. stakes, 3-1/2" high	1 Carp	200	.040	L.F.	.80	1.09		1.89	2.71	132
	0050 4-1/2" high		200	.040		.90	1.09		1.99	2.82	
	0100 5-1/2" high		195	.041		1.12	1.12		2.24	3.10	
	0150 7-1/2" high		190	.042		1.35	1.15		2.50	3.41	
	0300 Poured asphalt, plain, 1/2" x 1"	1 Clab	450	.018		.31	.38		.69	.98	
	0350 1" x 2"		400	.020		1.13	.43		1.56	1.96	
	0500 Neoprene, liquid, cold applied, 1/2" x 1"		450	.018		1.50	.38		1.88	2.29	
	0550 1" x 2"		400	.020		5.70	.43		6.13	6.95	
	0700 Polyurethane, poured, 2 part, 1/2" x 1"		400	.020		1.75	.43		2.18	2.65	
	0750 1" x 2"		350	.023		6.90	.49		7.39	8.40	
	0900 Rubberized asphalt, hot or cold applied, 1/2" x 1"		450	.018		.58	.38		.96	1.28	
	0950 1" x 2"		400	.020		1.13	.43		1.56	1.96	
	1100 Hot applied, fuel resistant, 1/2" x 1"		450	.018		1	.38		1.38	1.74	
	1150 1" x 2"		400	.020		1.38	.43		1.81	2.24	
	2000 Premolded, bituminous fiber, 1/2" x 6"	1 Carp	375	.021		.36	.58		.94	1.36	
	2050 1" x 12"		300	.027		1.71	.73		2.44	3.10	
	2250 Cork with resin binder, 1/2" x 6"		375	.021		1.75	.58		2.33	2.90	
	2300 1" x 12"		300	.027		5.15	.73		5.88	6.85	
	2500 Neoprene sponge, closed cell, 1/2" x 6"		375	.021		1.73	.58		2.31	2.87	
	2550 1" x 12"		300	.027		6.40	.73		7.13	8.20	
	2750 Polyethylene foam, 1/2" x 6"		375	.021		.38	.58		.96	1.39	
	2800 1" x 12"		300	.027		2.10	.73		2.83	3.53	
	3000 Polyethylene backer rod, 3/8" diameter		460	.017		.02	.47		.49	.81	
	3050 3/4" diameter		460	.017		.07	.47		.54	.86	
	3100 1" diameter		460	.017		.13	.47		.60	.93	
	3500 Polyurethane foam, with polybutylene, 1/2" x 1/2"		475	.017		.80	.46		1.26	1.65	
	3550 1" x 1"		450	.018		1.40	.49		1.89	2.35	
	3750 Polyurethane foam, regular, closed cell, 1/2" x 6"		375	.021		.65	.58		1.23	1.68	
	3800 1" x 12"		300	.027		2.40	.73		3.13	3.86	
	4000 Polyvinyl chloride foam, closed cell, 1/2" x 6"		375	.021		1.62	.58		2.20	2.75	
	4050 1" x 12"		300	.027		5.05	.73		5.78	6.75	
	4250 Rubber, gray sponge, 1/2" x 6"		375	.021		2.58	.58		3.16	3.81	
	4300 1" x 12"		300	.027		10.35	.73		11.08	12.60	
	4500 Lead wool for joints, 1 ton lots				Lb.	2			2	2.20	
	4550 Retail				"	2.20			2.20	2.42	
	5000 For installation in walls, add						75%				
	5250 For installation in boxouts, add						25%				
138	0010 **FORMS IN PLACE, BEAMS AND GIRDERS** R031-040										138
	0020 See also Elevated Slabs, division 031-150										
	0500 Beams & girders, exterior spandrel, plywood, 12" wide, 1 use R031-050	C-2	225	.213	SFCA	2.29	5.70		7.99	12	
	0650 4 use		310	.155		.74	4.13		4.87	7.70	
	1000 Exterior spandrel, 18" wide, 1 use		250	.192		2.07	5.10		7.17	10.85	
	1150 4 use		315	.152		.68	4.06		4.74	7.55	
	1500 Exterior spandrel, 24" wide, 1 use		265	.181		1.88	4.83		6.71	10.15	
	1650 4 use		325	.148		.61	3.94		4.55	7.25	

Important: See the Reference Section for critical supporting data - Reference Nos., Crews, & City Cost Indexes

031 | Concrete Formwork

031 100 | Struct C.I.P. Formwork

			CREW	DAILY OUTPUT	LABOR-HOURS	UNIT	MAT.	LABOR	EQUIP.	TOTAL	TOTAL INCL O&P	
138	2000	Interior beam, 12" wide, 1 use	C-2	300	.160	SFCA	2.23	4.27		6.50	9.60	138
	2150	4 use		377	.127		.73	3.39		4.12	6.50	
	2500	Interior beam, 24" wide, 1 use		320	.150		1.93	4		5.93	8.85	
	2650	4 use		395	.122		.62	3.24		3.86	6.10	
	3000	Beam and Girder, encasing steel frame, hung, plywood, 1 use		325	.148		2.23	3.94		6.17	9.05	
	3150	4 use		430	.112		.72	2.98		3.70	5.80	
	9000	Minimum labor/equipment charge	2 Carp	2	8	Job		218		218	365	
142	0010	**FORMS IN PLACE, COLUMNS**										142
	0020											
	0500	Round fiberglass, 4 use per mo., rent, 12" diameter	C-1	160	.200	L.F.	2.10	5.15		7.25	10.95	
	0550	16" diameter		150	.213		2.25	5.50		7.75	11.75	
	0600	18" diameter		140	.229		2.50	5.90		8.40	12.65	
	0650	24" diameter		135	.237		3.20	6.15		9.35	13.75	
	0700	28" diameter		130	.246		3.50	6.35		9.85	14.50	
	0800	30" diameter		125	.256		4.10	6.60		10.70	15.55	
	0850	36" diameter		120	.267		4.70	6.90		11.60	16.70	
	1500	Round fiber tube, 1 use, 8" diameter		155	.206		1.84	5.35		7.19	11	
	1550	10" diameter		155	.206		2.57	5.35		7.92	11.80	
	1600	12" diameter		150	.213		3.10	5.50		8.60	12.65	
	1650	14" diameter		145	.221		3.97	5.70		9.67	13.90	
	1700	16" diameter		140	.229		5.40	5.90		11.30	15.85	
	1750	20" diameter		135	.237		8.05	6.15		14.20	19.10	
	1800	24" diameter		130	.246		9.80	6.35		16.15	21.50	
	1850	30" diameter		125	.256		14.25	6.60		20.85	27	
	1900	36" diameter		115	.278		19.05	7.20		26.25	33	
	1950	42" diameter		100	.320		39	8.25		47.25	56.50	
	2000	48" diameter		85	.376		48.50	9.75		58.25	70	
	2200	For seamless type, add					15%					
	3000	Round, steel, 4 use per mo., rent, regular duty, 12" diameter	C-1	145	.221	L.F.	2.70	5.70		8.40	12.50	
	3050	16" diameter		125	.256		2.95	6.60		9.55	14.30	
	3100	Heavy duty, 20" diameter		105	.305		3.20	7.90		11.10	16.70	
	3150	24" diameter		85	.376		3.30	9.75		13.05	19.95	
	3200	30" diameter		70	.457		3.55	11.80		15.35	23.50	
	3250	36" diameter		60	.533		4.05	13.80		17.85	27.50	
	3300	48" diameter		50	.640		6.05	16.55		22.60	34	
	3350	60" diameter		45	.711		7.25	18.40		25.65	39	
	4000	Column capitals, steel, 4 uses/mo., 24" col, 4' cap diameter		12	2.667	Ea.	17.85	69		86.85	135	
	4050	5' cap diameter		11	2.909		19.40	75		94.40	148	
	4100	6' cap diameter		10	3.200		22	82.50		104.50	162	
	4150	7' cap diameter		9	3.556		24	92		116	181	
	4500	For second and succeeding months, deduct					50%					
	5000	Plywood, 8" x 8" columns, 1 use	C-1	165	.194	SFCA	1.56	5		6.56	10.10	
	5050	2 use		195	.164		.90	4.24		5.14	8.10	
	5100	3 use		210	.152		.62	3.94		4.56	7.30	
	5150	4 use		215	.149		.51	3.85		4.36	7	
	5500	12" x 12" columns, 1 use		180	.178		1.58	4.59		6.17	9.45	
	5550	2 use		210	.152		.87	3.94		4.81	7.55	
	5600	3 use		220	.145		.63	3.76		4.39	7	
	5650	4 use		225	.142		.51	3.68		4.19	6.70	
	6000	16" x 16" columns, 1 use		185	.173		1.63	4.47		6.10	9.30	
	6050	2 use		215	.149		.87	3.85		4.72	7.40	
	6100	3 use		230	.139		.65	3.60		4.25	6.70	
	6150	4 use		235	.136		.53	3.52		4.05	6.50	
	6500	24" x 24" columns, 1 use		190	.168		1.75	4.35		6.10	9.25	
	6550	2 use		216	.148		.96	3.83		4.79	7.45	

For expanded coverage of these items see *Means Concrete & Masonry Cost Data 1999*

031 | Concrete Formwork

031 100 | Struct C.I.P. Formwork

			CREW	DAILY OUTPUT	LABOR-HOURS	UNIT	1999 BARE COSTS MAT.	LABOR	EQUIP.	TOTAL	TOTAL INCL O&P	
142	6600	3 use	C-1	230	.139	SFCA	.66	3.60		4.26	6.75	142
	6650	4 use	R031-040	238	.134		.57	3.47		4.04	6.45	
	7000	36" x 36" columns, 1 use	R031-060	200	.160		1.73	4.13		5.86	8.80	
	7050	2 use		230	.139		.97	3.60		4.57	7.05	
	7100	3 use		245	.131		.69	3.38		4.07	6.40	
	7150	4 use		250	.128		.56	3.31		3.87	6.15	
	7500	Steel framed plywood, 4 use per mo., rent, 8" x 8"		340	.094		2.50	2.43		4.93	6.80	
	7550	10" x 10"		350	.091		2.25	2.36		4.61	6.45	
	7600	12" x 12"		370	.086		2.13	2.23		4.36	6.10	
	7650	16" x 16"		400	.080		2	2.07		4.07	5.65	
	7700	20" x 20"		420	.076		1.90	1.97		3.87	5.40	
	7750	24" x 24"		440	.073		1.80	1.88		3.68	5.15	
	7755	30" x 30"		440	.073		1.80	1.88		3.68	5.15	
	9000	Minimum labor/equipment charge	2 Carp	2	8	Job		218		218	365	
150	0010	**FORMS IN PLACE, ELEVATED SLABS**	R031-020									150
	1000	Flat plate plywood to 15' high, 1 use		C-2 470	.102	S.F.	2.49	2.72		5.21	7.30	
	1150	4 use	R031-050	560	.086		.81	2.29		3.10	4.72	
	1500	15' to 20' high ceilings, 4 use		495	.097		1.01	2.59		3.60	5.45	
	2000	Flat slab with drop panels, to 15' high, 1 use		449	.107		2.57	2.85		5.42	7.60	
	2150	4 use		544	.088		1.13	2.35		3.48	5.20	
	2250	15' to 20' high ceilings, 4 use		480	.100		1.37	2.67		4.04	5.95	
	3500	Floor slab, with 20" metal pans, 1 use		415	.116		3.45	3.08		6.53	8.95	
	3650	4 use		500	.096		1.20	2.56		3.76	5.60	
	4500	With 30" fiberglass domes, 1 use		405	.119		4.31	3.16		7.47	10.05	
	4550	4 use		470	.102		2.09	2.72		4.81	6.85	
	5000	Box out for slab openings, over 16" deep, 1 use		190	.253	SFCA	1.94	6.75		8.69	13.40	
	5050	2 use		240	.200	"	1.07	5.35		6.42	10.10	
	5500	Shallow slab box outs, to 10 S.F.		42	1.143	Ea.	9.75	30.50		40.25	62	
	5550	Over 10 S.F. (use perimeter)		600	.080	L.F.	1.30	2.13		3.43	5	
	6000	Bulkhead forms for slab, with keyway, 1 use, 2 piece		500	.096		1.56	2.56		4.12	6	
	6100	3 piece (see also edge forms)		460	.104		2.09	2.78		4.87	6.95	
	6200	Bulkhead forms for slab, w/keyway expanded metal										
	6210	In lieu of 2 piece form	C-1	1,100	.029	L.F.	1.12	.75		1.87	2.49	
	6215	In lieu of 3 piece form		960	.033		1.12	.86		1.98	2.67	
	6220	6" high, 4 uses		1,100	.029		1.35	.75		2.10	2.75	
	6500	Curb forms, wood, 6" to 12" high, on elevated slabs, 1 use		180	.178	SFCA	1.44	4.59		6.03	9.30	
	6550	2 use		205	.156		1.14	4.03		5.17	8	
	6600	3 use		220	.145		.83	3.76		4.59	7.20	
	6650	4 use		225	.142		.68	3.68		4.36	6.90	
	7000	Edge forms to 6" high, on elevated slab, 4 use		500	.064	L.F.	.36	1.65		2.01	3.17	
	7500	Depressed area forms to 12" high, 4 use		300	.107		.43	2.76		3.19	5.10	
	7550	12" to 24" high, 4 use		175	.183		.58	4.73		5.31	8.55	
	8000	Perimeter deck and rail for elevated slabs, straight		90	.356		9.10	9.20		18.30	25.50	
	8050	Curved		65	.492		12.50	12.70		25.20	35.50	
	8500	Void forms, round fiber, 3" diameter		450	.071		1.08	1.84		2.92	4.27	
	8650	8" diameter		375	.085		3.46	2.21		5.67	7.50	
	9000	Minimum labor/equipment charge	2 Carp	2	8	Job		218		218	365	
154	0010	**FORMS IN PLACE, EQUIPMENT FOUNDATIONS** 1 use	C-2	160	.300	SFCA	1.69	8		9.69	15.25	154
	0150	4 use	"	205	.234	"	.55	6.25		6.80	11.05	
	9000	Minimum labor/equipment charge	1 Carp	3	2.667	Job		73		73	122	
158	0010	**FORMS IN PLACE, FOOTINGS** Continuous wall, plywood, 1 use	C-1 R031-050	375	.085	SFCA	1.93	2.21		4.14	5.80	158
	0150	4 use	"	485	.066	"	.63	1.70		2.33	3.54	
	1500	Keyway, 4 use, tapered wood, 2" x 4"	1 Carp R031-060	530	.015	L.F.	.19	.41		.60	.90	
	1550	2" x 6"	"	500	.016	"	.27	.44		.71	1.03	

031 | Concrete Formwork

031 100 | Struct C.I.P. Formwork

			CREW	DAILY OUTPUT	LABOR-HOURS	UNIT	MAT.	LABOR	EQUIP.	TOTAL	TOTAL INCL O&P	
158	3000	Pile cap, square or rectangular, plywood, 1 use (R031-050)	C-1	290	.110	SFCA	1.85	2.85		4.70	6.80	158
	3150	4 use		383	.084		.60	2.16		2.76	4.27	
	5000	Spread footings, plywood, 1 use (R031-060)		305	.105		1.49	2.71		4.20	6.20	
	5150	4 use		414	.077		.49	2		2.49	3.88	
	9000	Minimum labor/equipment charge	1 Carp	3	2.667	Job		73		73	122	
162	0010	FORMS IN PLACE, GRADE BEAM Plywood, 1 use	C-2	530	.091	SFCA	1.36	2.41		3.77	5.55	162
	0150	4 use	"	605	.079	"	.44	2.12		2.56	4.03	
	9000	Minimum labor/equipment charge	2 Carp	2	8	Job		218		218	365	
170	0010	FORMS IN PLACE, SLAB ON GRADE										170
	1000	Bulkhead forms with keyway, wood, 1 use, 2 piece	C-1	510	.063	L.F.	.65	1.62		2.27	3.42	
	1400	Bulkhead forms w/keyway, 1 piece expanded metal, left in place										
	1410	In lieu of 2 piece form	C-1	1,375	.023	L.F.	1.12	.60		1.72	2.24	
	1420	In lieu of 3 piece form		1,200	.027		1.12	.69		1.81	2.38	
	1430	In lieu of 4 piece form		1,050	.030		1.12	.79		1.91	2.55	
	2000	Curb forms, wood, 6" to 12" high, on grade, 1 use		215	.149	SFCA	1.17	3.85		5.02	7.75	
	2150	4 use		275	.116	"	.38	3.01		3.39	5.45	
	3000	Edge forms, wood, 4 use, on grade, to 6" high		600	.053	L.F.	.24	1.38		1.62	2.57	
	3050	7" to 12" high		435	.074	SFCA	.63	1.90		2.53	3.87	
	3500	For depressed slabs, 4 use, to 12" high		300	.107	L.F.	.61	2.76		3.37	5.30	
	3550	To 24" high		175	.183		.79	4.73		5.52	8.75	
	4000	For slab blockouts, to 12" high, 1 use		200	.160		.62	4.13		4.75	7.60	
	4050	To 24" high, 1 use		120	.267		.78	6.90		7.68	12.40	
	4100	Plastic (extruded), to 6" high, multiple use, on grade		800	.040		.22	1.03		1.25	1.97	
	5000	Screed, 24 ga. metal key joint, see Div 031-132										
	5020	Wood, incl. wood stakes, 1" x 3"	C-1	900	.036	L.F.	.40	.92		1.32	1.98	
	5050	2" x 4"		900	.036		1.15	.92		2.07	2.81	
	6000	Trench forms in floor, wood, 1 use		160	.200	SFCA	1.90	5.15		7.05	10.75	
	6150	4 use		185	.173	"	.67	4.47		5.14	8.25	
	9000	Minimum labor/equipment charge	1 Carp	2	4	Job		109		109	183	
182	0010	FORMS IN PLACE, WALLS (R031-010)										182
	0100	Box out for wall openings, to 16" thick, to 10 S.F.	C-2	24	2	Ea.	19.60	53.50		73.10	111	
	0150	Over 10 S.F. (use perimeter)	"	280	.171	L.F.	1.76	4.57		6.33	9.60	
	0250	Brick shelf, 4" w, add to wall forms, use wall area abv shelf (R031-050)										
	0260	1 use (R031-060)	C-2	240	.200	SFCA	1.98	5.35		7.33	11.15	
	0350	4 use		300	.160	"	.79	4.27		5.06	8	
	0500	Bulkhead forms, with keyway, 1 use, 2 piece		265	.181	L.F.	2.50	4.83		7.33	10.85	
	0550	3 piece		175	.274	"	3.10	7.30		10.40	15.65	
	0600	Bulkhead forms w/keyway, 1 piece expanded metal, left in place										
	0610	In lieu of 2 piece form	C-1	800	.040	L.F.	1.05	1.03		2.08	2.88	
	0620	In lieu of 3 piece form	"	525	.061	"	1.05	1.58		2.63	3.79	
	0700	Buttress forms, to 8' high, 1 use	C-2	350	.137	SFCA	2.97	3.66		6.63	9.35	
	0850	4 use		480	.100	"	.98	2.67		3.65	5.55	
	1000	Corbel (haunch) forms, to 12" wide, add to wall forms, 1 use		150	.320	L.F.	1.61	8.55		10.16	16.05	
	1150	4 use		180	.267	"	.52	7.10		7.62	12.45	
	2000	Job built plyform wall forms, to 8' high, 1 use, below grade		300	.160	SFCA	1.89	4.27		6.16	9.20	
	2150	4 use, below grade		435	.110		.62	2.94		3.56	5.60	
	2400	Over 8' to 16' high, 1 use		280	.171		3.60	4.57		8.17	11.60	
	2550	4 use		395	.122		.68	3.24		3.92	6.15	
	2700	Over 16' high, 1 use		235	.204		2.34	5.45		7.79	11.65	
	2850	4 use		330	.145		.76	3.88		4.64	7.35	
	3000	For architectural finish, add		1,820	.026		.58	.70		1.28	1.82	
	3500	Polystyrene (expanded) wall forms										
	3510	To 8' high, 1 use, left in place	1 Carp	295	.027	SFCA	1.55	.74		2.29	2.94	

For expanded coverage of these items see *Means Concrete & Masonry Cost Data 1999*

031 | Concrete Formwork

031 100 | Struct C.I.P. Formwork

			CREW	DAILY OUTPUT	LABOR-HOURS	UNIT	MAT.	LABOR	EQUIP.	TOTAL	TOTAL INCL O&P	
182	4000	Radial wall forms, smooth curved, 1 use	C-2	245	.196	SFCA	2.30	5.20		7.50	11.30	182
	4150	4 use		335	.143		.75	3.82		4.57	7.20	
	4200	Wall forms, smooth curved, below grade, job built plyform		225	.213		2.78	5.70		8.48	12.55	
	4210	2 use		225	.213		1.54	5.70		7.24	11.20	
	4220	3 use		225	.213		1.25	5.70		6.95	10.85	
	4230	4 use		225	.213		.90	5.70		6.60	10.50	
	4600	Retaining wall forms, battered, to 8' high, 1 use		300	.160		1.78	4.27		6.05	9.10	
	4750	4 use		390	.123		.54	3.28		3.82	6.10	
	4900	Over 8' to 16' high, 1 use		240	.200		1.94	5.35		7.29	11.10	
	5050	4 use		320	.150		.63	4		4.63	7.40	
	5750	Liners for forms (add to wall forms), A.B.S. plastic										
	5800	Aged wood, 4" wide, 1 use	1 Carp	250	.032	SFCA	4.75	.87		5.62	6.65	
	5820	2 use		400	.020		2.63	.55		3.18	3.80	
	5840	4 use		750	.011		1.60	.29		1.89	2.25	
	5850											
	5900	Fractured rope rib, 1 use	1 Carp	250	.032	SFCA	7.40	.87		8.27	9.60	
	6000	4 use		750	.011		2.45	.29		2.74	3.19	
	6100	Ribbed look, 1/2" & 3/4" deep, 1 use		300	.027		5.15	.73		5.88	6.85	
	6200	4 use		800	.010		1.65	.27		1.92	2.28	
	6300	Rustic brick pattern, 1 use		250	.032		4.80	.87		5.67	6.75	
	6400	4 use		750	.011		1.60	.29		1.89	2.25	
	6500	Striated, random, 3/8" x 3/8" deep, 1 use		300	.027		5.10	.73		5.83	6.80	
	6600	4 use		800	.010		1.65	.27		1.92	2.28	
	7500	Lintel or sill forms, 1 use		30	.267		2.30	7.30		9.60	14.75	
	7560	4 use		37	.216		.75	5.90		6.65	10.70	
	7800	Modular prefabricated plywood, to 8' high, 1 use per month	C-2	910	.053		.97	1.41		2.38	3.41	
	7860	4 use per month		970	.049		.31	1.32		1.63	2.55	
	8000	To 16' high, 1 use per month		550	.087		1.23	2.33		3.56	5.25	
	8060	4 use per month		610	.079		.40	2.10		2.50	3.95	
	8100	Over 16' high, 1 use per month		550	.087		1.48	2.33		3.81	5.50	
	8160	4 use per month		610	.079		.48	2.10		2.58	4.04	
	8600	Pilasters, 1 use		270	.178		2.20	4.74		6.94	10.35	
	8660	4 use		385	.125		.72	3.32		4.04	6.35	
	9100	Minimum labor/equipment charge	2 Carp	2	8	Job		218		218	365	
	9475	For elevated walls, add						10%				
	9480	For battered walls, 1 side battered, add					10%	10%				
	9485	For battered walls, 2 sides battered, add					15%	15%				
186	0010	**GAS STATION FORMS** Curb fascia, with template,										186
	0050	12 ga. steel, left in place, 9" high	1 Carp	50	.160	L.F.	6.80	4.37		11.17	14.80	
	1000	Sign or light bases, 18" diameter, 9" high		9	.889	Ea.	38	24.50		62.50	82.50	
	1050	30" diameter, 13" high		8	1	"	64.50	27.50		92	117	
	1990	Minimum labor/equipment charge		2	4	Job		109		109	183	
	2000	Island forms, 10' long, 9" high, 3'- 6" wide	C-1	10	3.200	Ea.	175	82.50		257.50	330	
	2050	4' wide		9	3.556		190	92		282	365	
	2500	20' long, 9" high, 4' wide		6	5.333		310	138		448	570	
	2550	5' wide		5	6.400		325	165		490	635	
	9000	Minimum labor/equipment charge	1 Carp	3	2.667	Job		73		73	122	
190	0010	**SCAFFOLDING** See division 015-254										190
192	0010	**SHORES** Erect and strip, by hand, horizontal members										192
	0500	Aluminum joists and stringers	2 Carp	60	.267	Ea.		7.30		7.30	12.20	
	0600	Steel, adjustable beams		45	.356			9.70		9.70	16.25	
	0700	Wood joists		50	.320			8.75		8.75	14.60	
	0800	Wood stringers		30	.533			14.55		14.55	24.50	
	1000	Vertical members to 10' high		55	.291			7.95		7.95	13.30	

031 | Concrete Formwork

031 100 | Struct C.I.P. Formwork

		CREW	DAILY OUTPUT	LABOR-HOURS	UNIT	1999 BARE COSTS MAT.	LABOR	EQUIP.	TOTAL	TOTAL INCL O&P
1050	To 13' high	2 Carp	50	.320	Ea.		8.75		8.75	14.60
1100	To 16' high		45	.356			9.70		9.70	16.25
1500	Reshoring		1,400	.011	S.F.	.17	.31		.48	.71
1600	Flying truss system	C-17D	9,600	.009	SFCA		.25	.06	.31	.47
1760	Horizontal, aluminum joists, 6' to 30' spans, buy				L.F.	10.75			10.75	11.80
1770	Aluminum stringers, 12' & 16' spans				"	16.50			16.50	18.15
1810	Horizontal, steel beam, adjustable, 4' to 7' span				Ea.	110			110	121
1830	6' to 10' span					142			142	156
1920	9' to 15' span					260			260	286
1940	12' to 20' span					300			300	330
1970	Steel stringer, 6' to 15' span				L.F.	8.10			8.10	8.90
3000	Rent for job duration, aluminum, first month				SF Flr.	.25			.25	.28
3050	Steel				"	.20			.20	.22
3500	Vertical, adjustable steel, 5'-7" to 9'-6" high, 10,000# cap., buy				Ea.	59			59	65
3550	7'-3" to 12'-10" high, 7800# capacity					71			71	78
3600	8'-10" to 12'-4" high, 10,000# capacity					79			79	87
3650	8'-10" to 16'-1" high, 3800# capacity					86			86	94.50
4000	Frame shoring systems, aluminum, 10,000# per leg,									
4050	6' wide, 5' & 6' high				Ea.	235			235	259
4100	5' to 7' post with base, jack screw & top plate				Set	52			52	57
5010	Steel, 10,000# per leg									
5040	2' & 4' wide, 3', 4', 5' & 6' high				Ea.	97			97	107
5250	6' extension tube with adjusting collar					91			91	100
5550	Base plate					9.75			9.75	10.75
5600	12" adjustable leg					39			39	43
5650	Top plate					21			21	23
5750	Flying truss system				SFCA	9			9	9.90
0010	**WATERSTOP** PVC, ribbed 3/16" thick, 4" wide	1 Carp	155	.052	L.F.	.74	1.41		2.15	3.17
0050	6" wide		145	.055	"	1.28	1.51		2.79	3.93
0500	Ribbed, PVC, with center bulb, 9" wide, 3/16" thick		135	.059	L.F.	1.76	1.62		3.38	4.65
0550	3/8" thick		130	.062	"	2.20	1.68		3.88	5.25

032 | Concrete Reinforcement

032 100 | Reinforcing Steel

		CREW	DAILY OUTPUT	LABOR-HOURS	UNIT	1999 BARE COSTS MAT.	LABOR	EQUIP.	TOTAL	TOTAL INCL O&P
0010	**REINFORCING IN PLACE** A615 Grade 60									
0102	Beams & Girders, #3 to #7	4 Rodm	3,200	.010	Lb.	.28	.30		.58	.86
0152	#8 to #18		5,400	.006		.27	.18		.45	.62
0202	Columns, #3 to #7		3,000	.011		.28	.32		.60	.89
0252	#8 to #18		4,600	.007		.27	.21		.48	.68
0402	Elevated slabs, #4 to #7		5,800	.006		.29	.17		.46	.62
0502	Footings, #4 to #7		4,200	.008		.28	.23		.51	.73
0552	#8 to #18		7,200	.004		.27	.14		.41	.54
0602	Slab on grade, #3 to #7		4,200	.008		.27	.23		.50	.71
0702	Walls, #3 to #7		6,000	.005		.28	.16		.44	.60
0752	#8 to #18		8,000	.004		.27	.12		.39	.52
2000	Unloading & sorting, add to above	C-5	100	.560	Ton		16.60	5.50	22.10	35
2200	Crane cost for handling, add to above, minimum		135	.415			12.30	4.07	16.37	26
2210	Average		92	.609			18.05	5.95	24	38

For expanded coverage of these items see *Means Concrete & Masonry Cost Data 1999*

032 | Concrete Reinforcement

032 100 | Reinforcing Steel

		CREW	DAILY OUTPUT	LABOR-HOURS	UNIT	MAT.	LABOR	EQUIP.	TOTAL	TOTAL INCL O&P	
107											107
2220	Maximum	C-5	35	1.600	Ton		47.50	15.70	63.20	100	
2400	Dowels, 2 feet long, deformed, #3	2 Rodm	520	.031	Ea.	.22	.94		1.16	1.92	
2410	#4		480	.033		.40	1.01		1.41	2.26	
2420	#5		435	.037		.62	1.12		1.74	2.69	
2430	#6		360	.044		.89	1.35		2.24	3.41	
2450	Longer and heavier dowels		725	.022	Lb.	.44	.67		1.11	1.69	
2500	Smooth dowels, 12" long, 1/4" or 3/8" diameter		140	.114	Ea.	.67	3.47		4.14	7	
2520	5/8" diameter		125	.128		1.18	3.89		5.07	8.30	
2530	3/4" diameter		110	.145		1.46	4.42		5.88	9.55	
2700	Dowel caps, 5" long, 1/2" to 3/4" diameter		800	.020		.21	.61		.82	1.33	
2720	1-1/4" diameter		750	.021		.26	.65		.91	1.46	
9000	Minimum labor/equipment charge	1 Rodm	4	2	Job		61		61	110	

032 200 | Welded Wire Fabric

		CREW	DAILY OUTPUT	LABOR-HOURS	UNIT	MAT.	LABOR	EQUIP.	TOTAL	TOTAL INCL O&P	
207	0010	**WELDED WIRE FABRIC** ASTM A185										207
	0050	Sheets									
	0100	6 x 6 - W1.4 x W1.4 (10 x 10) 21 lb. per C.S.F.	2 Rodm	35	.457	C.S.F.	6.90	13.90		20.80	32.50	
	0200	6 x 6 - W2.1 x W2.1 (8 x 8) 30 lb. per C.S.F.		31	.516		10.40	15.70		26.10	40	
	0300	6 x 6 - W2.9 x W2.9 (6 x 6) 42 lb. per C.S.F.		29	.552		14.70	16.75		31.45	46	
	0400	6 x 6 - W4 x W4 (4 x 4) 58 lb. per C.S.F.		27	.593		21.50	18		39.50	56	
	0500	4 x 4 - W1.4 x W1.4 (10 x 10) 31 lb. per C.S.F.		31	.516		10.45	15.70		26.15	40	
	0600	4 x 4 - W2.1 x W2.1 (8 x 8) 44 lb. per C.S.F.		29	.552		12.80	16.75		29.55	44	
	0650	4 x 4 - W2.9 x W2.9 (6 x 6) 61 lb. per C.S.F.		27	.593		18.75	18		36.75	53	
	0700	4 x 4 - W4 x W4 (4 x 4) 85 lb. per C.S.F.		25	.640		28.50	19.45		47.95	66	
	0750	Rolls										
	0800	2 x 2 - #14 galv. @ 21 lb., beam & column wrap	2 Rodm	6.50	2.462	C.S.F.	14.80	75		89.80	151	
	0900	2 x 2 - #12 galv. for gunite reinforcing	"	6.50	2.462	"	21	75		96	158	
	0950	Material prices for above include 10% lap										
	1000	Specially fabricated heavier gauges in sheets	4 Rodm	50	.640	C.S.F.		19.45		19.45	35	
	1010	Material only, minimum				Ton	520			520	570	
	1020	Average					725			725	800	
	1030	Maximum					930			930	1,025	
	9000	Minimum labor/equipment charge	1 Rodm	4	2	Job		61		61	110	
240	0010	**FIBROUS REINFORCING**										240
	0100	Synthetic fibers				Lb.	3.78			3.78	4.15	
	0110	1-1/2 lb. per C.Y., add to concrete				C.Y.	5.85			5.85	6.40	
	0150	Steel fibers				Lb.	.46			.46	.51	
	0155	25 lb. per C.Y., add to concrete				C.Y.	11.50			11.50	12.65	
	0160	50 lb. per C.Y., add to concrete					23			23	25.50	
	0170	75 lb. per C.Y., add to concrete					35.50			35.50	39	
	0180	100 lb. per C.Y., add to concrete					46			46	50.50	

033 | Cast-In-Place Concrete

033 100 | Structural Concrete

		CREW	DAILY OUTPUT	LABOR-HOURS	UNIT	MAT.	LABOR	EQUIP.	TOTAL	TOTAL INCL O&P	
118	0010	**CONCRETE ADMIXTURES & SURFACE TREATMENTS**										118
	0040	Abrasives, aluminum oxide, over 20 tons				Lb.	.88			.88	.97	
	0070	Under 1 ton					.92			.92	1.01	
	0100	Silicon carbide, black, over 20 tons					1.20			1.20	1.32	

033 | Cast-In-Place Concrete

033 100 | Structural Concrete

		CREW	DAILY OUTPUT	LABOR-HOURS	UNIT	1999 BARE COSTS MAT.	LABOR	EQUIP.	TOTAL	TOTAL INCL O&P	
118	0120 Under 1 ton				Lb.	1.25			1.25	1.38	118
	0200 Air entraining agent, .7 to 1.5 oz. per bag, 55 gallon lots				Gal.	7.40			7.40	8.10	
	0220 5 gallon lots					8.45			8.45	9.25	
	0300 Bonding agent, acrylic latex (200-250 S.F. per gallon)					26			26	28.50	
	0320 Epoxy resin (70-80 S.F. per gallon)				▼	50			50	55	
	0400 Calcium chloride, 100 lb. bags, FOB plant, truckload lots				Ton	330			330	365	
	0420 Less than truckload lots				Bag	19.75			19.75	21.50	
	0500 Carbon black, liquid, 2 to 8 lbs. per bag of cement				Lb.	2.85			2.85	3.14	
	0600 Colors, integral, 2 to 10 lb. per bag of cement, minimum					1.30			1.30	1.43	
	0610 Average					2.07			2.07	2.28	
	0620 Maximum				▼	3.69			3.69	4.06	
	0700 Curing compound, (200 to 400 S.F. per gallon), 55 gal. lots				Gal.	9.90			9.90	10.90	
	0720 5 gallon lots					8.40			8.40	9.25	
	0800 Premium grade, (450 S.F. per gallon), 55 gal. lots					12.80			12.80	14.10	
	0820 5 gallon lots					14.25			14.25	15.70	
	0900 Dustproofing compound, (200-600 S.F./gal.), 55 gallon lots					7.75			7.75	8.55	
	0920 5 gallon lots				▼	8.90			8.90	9.80	
	1000 Epoxy dustproof coating, colors, (300-400 S.F. per coat),										
	1010 or transparent, (400-600 S.F. per coat)				Gal.	56			56	61.50	
	1100 Hardeners, metallic, 55 lb. bags, natural (grey)				Lb.	.76			.76	.84	
	1200 Colors, average					.95			.95	1.05	
	1300 Non-metallic, 55 lb. bags, natural (grey), minimum					.31			.31	.34	
	1310 Maximum					.35			.35	.39	
	1320 Non-metallic, colors, minimum					.43			.43	.47	
	1340 Maximum					.69			.69	.76	
	1400 Non-metallic, non-slip, 100 lb. bags, minimum					.43			.43	.47	
	1420 Maximum				▼	.85			.85	.94	
	1500 Solution type, (300 to 400 S.F. per gallon)				Gal.	5.80			5.80	6.40	
	1600 Sealer, hardener and dustproofer, clear, 450 S.F., minimum					6.30			6.30	6.90	
	1620 Maximum					14			14	15.40	
	1700 Colors (300-400 S.F. per gallon)				▼	36			36	39.50	
	1750										
	1800 Set accelerator for below freezing, 1 to 1-1/2 gal. per C.Y.				Gal.	5.25			5.25	5.80	
	1900 Set retarder, 2 to 4 fl. oz. per bag of cement				"	10.75			10.75	11.80	
	2000 Waterproofing, integral 1 lb. per bag of cement				Lb.	.72			.72	.79	
	2100 Powdered metallic, 40 lbs. per 100 S.F., minimum					.95			.95	1.05	
	2120 Maximum				▼	1.95			1.95	2.15	
	2200 Water reducing admixture, average				Gal.	8.75			8.75	9.65	
126	0010 **CONCRETE, READY MIX** Regular weight R033-020										126
	0020 2000 psi				C.Y.	56.50			56.50	62	
	0100 2500 psi R033-060					57			57	63	
	0150 3000 psi					61			61	67	
	0200 3500 psi R033-070					61			61	67	
	0300 4000 psi					62.50			62.50	68.50	
	0350 4500 psi					63.50			63.50	69.50	
	0400 5000 psi					67.50			67.50	74	
	0411 6000 psi					77			77	84.50	
	0412 8000 psi					125			125	138	
	0413 10,000 psi					178			178	196	
	0414 12,000 psi					215			215	236	
	1000 For high early strength cement, add					10%					
	2000 For all lightweight aggregate, add				▼	45%					
	3000 For integral colors, 2500 psi, 5 bag mix										
	3100 Red, yellow or brown, 1.8 lb. per bag, add				C.Y.	13.05			13.05	14.35	
	3200 9.4 lb. per bag, add					70.50			70.50	77.50	
	3400 Black, 1.8 lb. per bag, add				▼	15.50			15.50	17.05	

For expanded coverage of these items see *Means Concrete & Masonry Cost Data 1999*

033 | Cast-In-Place Concrete

033 100 | Structural Concrete

			CREW	DAILY OUTPUT	LABOR-HOURS	UNIT	1999 BARE COSTS MAT.	LABOR	EQUIP.	TOTAL	TOTAL INCL O&P	
126	3500	7.5 lb. per bag, add	R033 -020			C.Y.	65			65	71.50	126
	3700	Green, 1.8 lb. per bag, add					31			31	34	
	3800	7.5 lb. per bag, add	R033 -060				149			149	163	
130	0010	**CONCRETE IN PLACE** Including forms (4 uses), reinforcing	R033 -010									130
	0050	steel, including finishing unless otherwise indicated										
	0300	Beams, 5 kip per L.F., 10' span	R033 -100	C-14A	15.62	12.804	C.Y.	207	350	44	601	870
	0350	25' span		"	18.55	10.782		188	296	37	521	750
	0500	Chimney foundations, industrial, minimum	R033 -130	C-14C	32.22	3.476		126	91	1.15	218.15	293
	0510	Maximum		"	23.71	4.724		147	123	1.56	271.56	375
	0700	Columns, square, 12" x 12", minimum reinforcing	R042 -055	C-14A	11.96	16.722		210	460	57	727	1,075
	0720	Average reinforcing			10.13	19.743		310	540	67.50	917.50	1,325
	0740	Maximum reinforcing			9.03	22.148		390	605	76	1,071	1,550
	0800	16" x 16", minimum reinforcing			16.22	12.330		178	340	42	560	815
	0820	Average reinforcing			12.57	15.911		293	435	54.50	782.50	1,125
	0840	Maximum reinforcing			10.25	19.512		410	535	66.50	1,011.50	1,425
	0900	24" x 24", minimum reinforcing			23.66	8.453		149	232	29	410	585
	0920	Average reinforcing			17.71	11.293		242	310	38.50	590.50	835
	0940	Maximum reinforcing			14.15	14.134		335	385	48.50	768.50	1,075
	1000	36" x 36", minimum reinforcing			33.69	5.936		143	163	20.50	326.50	455
	1020	Average reinforcing			23.32	8.576		230	235	29.50	494.50	680
	1040	Maximum reinforcing			17.82	11.223		315	310	38.50	663.50	910
	1200	16" diameter, minimum reinforcing			31.49	6.351		211	174	21.50	406.50	550
	1220	Average reinforcing			19.12	10.460		340	287	36	663	900
	1240	Maximum reinforcing			13.77	14.524		470	400	49.50	919.50	1,250
	1300	20" diameter, minimum reinforcing			41.04	4.873		200	134	16.65	350.65	465
	1320	Average reinforcing			24.05	8.316		315	228	28.50	571.50	760
	1340	Maximum reinforcing			17.01	11.758		430	320	40	790	1,050
	1400	24" diameter, minimum reinforcing			51.85	3.857		188	106	13.20	307.20	400
	1420	Average reinforcing			27.06	7.391		305	203	25.50	533.50	705
	1440	Maximum reinforcing			18.29	10.935		425	300	37.50	762.50	1,000
	1500	36" diameter, minimum reinforcing			75.04	2.665		176	73	9.10	258.10	325
	1520	Average reinforcing			37.49	5.335		265	146	18.25	429.25	560
	1540	Maximum reinforcing			22.84	8.757		380	240	30	650	855
	1900	Elevated slabs, flat slab, 125 psf Sup. Load, 20' span		C-14B	38.45	5.410		138	148	17.75	303.75	420
	1950	30' span			50.99	4.079		126	112	13.40	251.40	340
	2100	Flat plate, 125 psf Sup. Load, 15' span			30.24	6.878		146	188	22.50	356.50	500
	2150	25' span			49.60	4.194		120	115	13.75	248.75	340
	2300	Waffle const., 30" domes, 125 psf Sup. Load, 20' span			37.07	5.611		178	154	18.40	350.40	475
	2350	30' span			44.07	4.720		162	129	15.50	306.50	415
	2500	One way joists, 30" pans, 125 psf Sup. Load, 15' span			27.38	7.597		209	208	25	442	610
	2550	25' span			31.15	6.677		196	183	22	401	550
	2700	One way beam & slab, 125 psf Sup. Load, 15' span			20.59	10.102		168	276	33	477	685
	2750	25' span			28.36	7.334		154	201	24	379	535
	2900	Two way beam & slab, 125 psf Sup. Load, 15' span			24.04	8.652		157	237	28.50	422.50	605
	2950	25' span			35.87	5.799		133	159	19	311	435
	3100	Elevated slabs including finish, not										
	3110	including forms or reinforcing										
	3150	Regular concrete, 4" slab		C-8	2,613	.021	S.F.	.77	.52	.25	1.54	1.96
	3200	6" slab			2,585	.022		1.21	.52	.25	1.98	2.45
	3250	2-1/2" thick floor fill			2,685	.021		.52	.50	.24	1.26	1.66
	3300	Lightweight, 110# per C.F., 2-1/2" thick floor fill			2,585	.022		.64	.52	.25	1.41	1.83
	3400	Cellular concrete, 1-5/8" fill, under 5000 S.F.			2,000	.028		.45	.67	.32	1.44	1.96
	3450	Over 10,000 S.F.			2,200	.025		.35	.61	.29	1.25	1.71
	3500	Add per floor for 3 to 6 stories high			31,800	.002			.04	.02	.06	.09
	3520	For 7 to 20 stories high			21,200	.003			.06	.03	.09	.13

033 | Cast-In-Place Concrete

033 100 | Structural Concrete

			CREW	DAILY OUTPUT	LABOR-HOURS	UNIT	MAT.	LABOR	EQUIP.	TOTAL	TOTAL INCL O&P	
130	3800	Footings, spread under 1 C.Y.	C-14C	38.07	2.942	C.Y.	89.50	77	.97	167.47	230	130
	3850	Over 5 C.Y.		81.04	1.382		82.50	36	.46	118.96	152	
	3900	Footings, strip, 18" x 9", plain		41.04	2.729		80.50	71.50	.90	152.90	210	
	3950	36" x 12", reinforced		61.55	1.820		83	47.50	.60	131.10	172	
	4000	Foundation mat, under 10 C.Y.		38.67	2.896		113	75.50	.96	189.46	254	
	4050	Over 20 C.Y.		56.40	1.986		101	52	.66	153.66	199	
	4200	Grade walls, 8" thick, 8' high	C-14D	45.83	4.364		97.50	119	14.90	231.40	320	
	4250	14' high		27.26	7.337		124	199	25	348	500	
	4260	12" thick, 8' high		64.32	3.109		89.50	84.50	10.65	184.65	252	
	4270	14' high		40.01	4.999		99.50	136	17.10	252.60	355	
	4300	15" thick, 8' high		80.02	2.499		85.50	68	8.55	162.05	217	
	4350	12' high		51.26	3.902		89	106	13.35	208.35	291	
	4500	18' high		48.85	4.094		99	111	14	224	310	
	4520	Handicap access ramp, railing both sides, 3' wide	C-14H	14.58	3.292	L.F.	94.50	89	2.57	186.07	257	
	4525	5' wide		12.22	3.928		108	106	3.06	217.06	300	
	4530	With cheek walls and rails both sides, 3' wide		8.55	5.614		96.50	151	4.38	251.88	365	
	4535	5' wide		7.31	6.566		97	177	5.10	279.10	410	
	4650	Slab on grade, not including finish, 4" thick	C-14E	60.75	1.449	C.Y.	73.50	39	.62	113.12	149	
	4700	6" thick	"	92	.957	"	70.50	25.50	.41	96.41	122	
	4751	Slab on grade, incl. troweled finish, not incl. forms										
	4760	or reinforcing, over 10,000 S.F., 4" thick slab	C-14F	3,425	.021	S.F.	.79	.52	.01	1.32	1.72	
	4820	6" thick slab		3,350	.021		1.16	.53	.01	1.70	2.14	
	4840	8" thick slab		3,184	.023		1.59	.56	.01	2.16	2.66	
	4900	12" thick slab		2,734	.026		2.38	.65	.01	3.04	3.70	
	4950	15" thick slab		2,505	.029		2.99	.71	.01	3.71	4.46	
	5000	Slab on grade, incl. textured finish, not incl. forms										
	5001	or reinforcing, 4" thick slab	C-14G	2,873	.019	S.F.	.79	.48	.01	1.28	1.65	
	5010	6" thick		2,590	.022		1.24	.53	.01	1.78	2.24	
	5020	8" thick		2,320	.024		1.62	.59	.02	2.23	2.76	
	5200	Lift slab in place above the foundation, incl. forms,										
	5210	reinforcing, concrete and columns, minimum	C-14B	2,113	.098	S.F.	4.74	2.69	.32	7.75	10.10	
	5250	Average		1,650	.126		5.20	3.45	.41	9.06	12	
	5300	Maximum		1,500	.139		5.80	3.79	.45	10.04	13.25	
	5500	Lightweight, ready mix, including screed finish only,										
	5510	not including forms or reinforcing										
	5550	1:4 for structural roof decks	C-14B	260	.800	C.Y.	91.50	22	2.62	116.12	141	
	5600	1:6 for ground slab with radiant heat	C-14F	92	.783		86.50	19.40	.41	106.31	127	
	5650	1:3:2 with sand aggregate, roof deck	C-14B	260	.800		91.50	22	2.62	116.12	141	
	5700	Ground slab	C-14F	107	.673		91.50	16.70	.35	108.55	128	
	5900	Pile caps, incl. forms and reinf., sq. or rect., under 5 C.Y.	C-14C	54.14	2.069		86	54	.68	140.68	187	
	5950	Over 10 C.Y.		75	1.493		83.50	39	.49	122.99	159	
	6000	Triangular or hexagonal, under 5 C.Y.		53	2.113		79	55	.70	134.70	181	
	6050	Over 10 C.Y.		85	1.318		83.50	34.50	.43	118.43	150	
	6200	Retaining walls, gravity, 4' high see division 022-708	C-14D	66.20	3.021		81	82	10.35	173.35	238	
	6250	10' high		125	1.600		72	43.50	5.45	120.95	158	
	6300	Cantilever, level backfill loading, 8' high		70	2.857		88	77.50	9.75	175.25	238	
	6350	16' high		91	2.198		85.50	59.50	7.50	152.50	202	
	6800	Stairs, not including safety treads, free standing, 3'-6" wide	C-14H	83	.578	LF Nose	5.75	15.60	.45	21.80	33.50	
	6850	Cast on ground		125	.384	"	4.05	10.35	.30	14.70	22	
	7000	Stair landings, free standing		200	.240	S.F.	2.25	6.50	.19	8.94	13.60	
	7050	Cast on ground		475	.101	"	1.30	2.73	.08	4.11	6.10	
	9000	Minimum labor/equipment charge	2 Carp	1	16	Job		435		435	730	
134	0010	**CURING** Burlap, 4 uses assumed, 7.5 oz.	2 Clab	55	.291	C.S.F.	2.55	6.25		8.80	13.25	134
	0100	12 oz.		55	.291		3.74	6.25		9.99	14.55	
	0200	Waterproof curing paper, 2 ply, reinforced		70	.229		4.71	4.90		9.61	13.40	
	0300	Sprayed membrane curing compound		95	.168		2.42	3.61		6.03	8.70	

References: R033-010, R033-100, R033-130, R042-055

For expanded coverage of these items see *Means Concrete & Masonry Cost Data 1999*

033 | Cast-In-Place Concrete

033 100 | Structural Concrete

			CREW	DAILY OUTPUT	LABOR-HOURS	UNIT	MAT.	LABOR	EQUIP.	TOTAL	TOTAL INCL O&P	
134	0710	Electrically, heated pads, 15 watts/S.F., 20 uses, minimum				S.F.	.16			.16	.18	134
	0800	Maximum				"	.27			.27	.29	
	9000	Minimum labor/equipment charge	1 Clab	5	1.600	Job		34.50		34.50	57.50	
160	0010	**GUNITE**										160
	0020	Applied in 1" layers, no mesh included	C-8	2,000	.028	S.F.	.92	.67	.32	1.91	2.47	
	0300	Typical in place, including mesh, 2" thick, minimum	C-16	1,000	.072		1.68	1.83	.65	4.16	5.65	
	0350	Maximum		500	.144		2.60	3.67	1.29	7.56	10.45	
	0500	4" thick, minimum		750	.096		2.49	2.45	.86	5.80	7.80	
	0550	Maximum		350	.206		3.86	5.25	1.85	10.96	15.10	
	0900	Prepare old walls, no scaffolding, minimum	C-10	1,000	.024		.57	.59		1.16	1.58	
	0950	Maximum	"	275	.087		1.80	2.15		3.95	5.45	
	1100	For high finish requirement or close tolerance, add, minimum						50%				
	1150	Maximum						110%				
	9000	Minimum labor/equipment charge	C-10	1	24	Job		590		590	955	
168	0010	**PATCHING CONCRETE**										168
	0100	Floors, 1/4" thick, small areas, regular grout	1 Cefi	170	.047	S.F.	.07	1.23		1.30	2.03	
	0150	Epoxy grout	"	100	.080	"	.52	2.09		2.61	3.91	
	0300	Slab on Grade, cut outs, up to 50 C.F.	2 Cefi	50	.320	C.F.	4.52	8.35		12.87	18.30	
	2000	Walls, including chipping, cleaning and epoxy grout										
	2100	Minimum	1 Cefi	65	.123	S.F.	.12	3.22		3.34	5.30	
	2150	Average		50	.160		.19	4.18		4.37	6.85	
	2200	Maximum		40	.200		.35	5.25		5.60	8.75	
	2510	Underlayment, P.C based self-leveling, 4100 psi, pumped, 1/4"	C-8	20,000	.003		1.16	.07	.03	1.26	1.43	
	2520	1/2"		19,000	.003		2.09	.07	.03	2.19	2.46	
	2530	3/4"		18,000	.003		3.25	.07	.04	3.36	3.73	
	2540	1"		17,000	.003		4.41	.08	.04	4.53	5	
	2550	1-1/2"		15,000	.004		6.75	.09	.04	6.88	7.60	
	2560	Hand mix, 1/2"	C-18	4,000	.002		2.09	.05	.01	2.15	2.39	
	2610	Topping, P.C. based self-level/dry 6100 psi, pumped, 1/4"	C-8	20,000	.003		1.76	.07	.03	1.86	2.09	
	2620	1/2"		19,000	.003		3.17	.07	.03	3.27	3.64	
	2630	3/4"		18,000	.003		4.93	.07	.04	5.04	5.55	
	2660	1"		17,000	.003		6.70	.08	.04	6.82	7.50	
	2670	1-1/2"		15,000	.004		10.20	.09	.04	10.33	11.45	
	2680	Hand mix, 1/2"	C-18	4,000	.002		3.17	.05	.01	3.23	3.57	
	9000	Minimum labor/equipment charge	1 Cefi	4.50	1.778	Job		46.50		46.50	74	
172	0010	**PLACING CONCRETE** and vibrating, including labor & equipment R033-090										172
	0050	Beams, elevated, small beams, pumped	C-20	60	1.067	C.Y.		24.50	12	36.50	54	
	0100	With crane and bucket	C-7	45	1.600			37	19.85	56.85	83	
	0200	Large beams, pumped	C-20	90	.711			16.45	8	24.45	36	
	0250	With crane and bucket	C-7	65	1.108			26	13.75	39.75	57.50	
	0400	Columns, square or round, 12" thick, pumped	C-20	60	1.067			24.50	12	36.50	54	
	0450	With crane and bucket	C-7	40	1.800			42	22.50	64.50	93.50	
	0600	18" thick, pumped	C-20	90	.711			16.45	8	24.45	36	
	0650	With crane and bucket	C-7	55	1.309			30.50	16.25	46.75	68	
	0800	24" thick, pumped	C-20	92	.696			16.10	7.85	23.95	35	
	0850	With crane and bucket	C-7	70	1.029			24	12.75	36.75	53.50	
	1000	36" thick, pumped	C-20	140	.457			10.60	5.15	15.75	23	
	1050	With crane and bucket	C-7	100	.720			16.75	8.95	25.70	37.50	
	1400	Elevated slabs, less than 6" thick, pumped	C-20	140	.457			10.60	5.15	15.75	23	
	1450	With crane and bucket	C-7	95	.758			17.65	9.40	27.05	39.50	
	1500	6" to 10" thick, pumped	C-20	160	.400			9.25	4.50	13.75	20.50	
	1550	With crane and bucket	C-7	110	.655			15.20	8.10	23.30	34	
	1600	Slabs over 10" thick, Pumped	C-20	180	.356			8.25	4	12.25	18	

033 | Cast-In-Place Concrete

033 100 | Structural Concrete

			CREW	DAILY OUTPUT	LABOR-HOURS	UNIT	MAT.	LABOR	EQUIP.	TOTAL	TOTAL INCL O&P	
172	1650	With crane and bucket	C-7	130	.554	C.Y.		12.90	6.85	19.75	28.50	172
	1900	Footings, continuous, shallow, direct chute	C-6	120	.400			9.05	.62	9.67	15.65	
	1950	Pumped	C-20	150	.427			9.90	4.80	14.70	21.50	
	2000	With crane and bucket	C-7	90	.800			18.60	9.90	28.50	41.50	
	2100	Footings, continuous, deep, direct chute	C-6	140	.343			7.75	.53	8.28	13.45	
	2150	Pumped	C-20	160	.400			9.25	4.50	13.75	20.50	
	2200	With crane and bucket	C-7	110	.655			15.20	8.10	23.30	34	
	2400	Footings, spread, under 1 C.Y., direct chute	C-6	55	.873			19.70	1.36	21.06	34	
	2450	Pumped	C-20	65	.985			23	11.10	34.10	49.50	
	2500	With crane and bucket	C-7	45	1.600			37	19.85	56.85	83	
	2600	Footings, spread, over 5 C.Y., direct chute	C-6	120	.400			9.05	.62	9.67	15.65	
	2650	Pumped	C-20	150	.427			9.90	4.80	14.70	21.50	
	2700	With crane and bucket	C-7	100	.720			16.75	8.95	25.70	37.50	
	2900	Foundation mats, over 20 C.Y., direct chute	C-6	350	.137			3.10	.21	3.31	5.40	
	2950	Pumped	C-20	400	.160			3.71	1.80	5.51	8.10	
	3000	With crane and bucket	C-7	300	.240			5.60	2.98	8.58	12.40	
	3200	Grade beams, direct chute	C-6	150	.320			7.20	.50	7.70	12.50	
	3250	Pumped	C-20	180	.356			8.25	4	12.25	18	
	3300	With crane and bucket	C-7	120	.600			13.95	7.45	21.40	31	
	3500	High rise, for more than 5 stories, pumped, add per story	C-20	2,100	.030			.71	.34	1.05	1.54	
	3510	With crane and bucket, add per story	C-7	2,100	.034			.80	.43	1.23	1.78	
	3700	Pile caps, under 5 C.Y., direct chute	C-6	90	.533			12.05	.83	12.88	21	
	3750	Pumped	C-20	110	.582			13.45	6.55	20	29	
	3800	With crane and bucket	C-7	80	.900			21	11.15	32.15	47	
	3850	Pile cap, 5 C.Y. to 10 C.Y., direct chute	C-6	175	.274			6.20	.43	6.63	10.70	
	3900	Pumped	C-20	200	.320			7.40	3.60	11	16.15	
	3950	With crane and bucket	C-7	150	.480			11.15	5.95	17.10	25	
	4000	Over 10 C.Y., direct chute	C-6	215	.223			5.05	.35	5.40	8.75	
	4050	Pumped	C-20	240	.267			6.20	3	9.20	13.50	
	4100	With crane and bucket	C-7	185	.389			9.05	4.83	13.88	20	
	4300	Slab on grade, 4" thick, direct chute	C-6	110	.436			9.85	.68	10.53	17.10	
	4350	Pumped	C-20	130	.492			11.40	5.55	16.95	25	
	4400	With crane and bucket	C-7	110	.655			15.20	8.10	23.30	34	
	4600	Over 6" thick, direct chute	C-6	165	.291			6.55	.45	7	11.40	
	4650	Pumped	C-20	185	.346			8	3.90	11.90	17.50	
	4700	With crane and bucket	C-7	145	.497			11.55	6.15	17.70	25.50	
	4900	Walls, 8" thick, direct chute	C-6	90	.533			12.05	.83	12.88	21	
	4950	Pumped	C-20	100	.640			14.80	7.20	22	32.50	
	5000	With crane and bucket	C-7	80	.900			21	11.15	32.15	47	
	5050	12" thick, direct chute	C-6	100	.480			10.85	.75	11.60	18.80	
	5100	Pumped	C-20	110	.582			13.45	6.55	20	29	
	5200	With crane and bucket	C-7	90	.800			18.60	9.90	28.50	41.50	
	5300	15" thick, direct chute	C-6	105	.457			10.30	.71	11.01	17.90	
	5350	Pumped	C-20	120	.533			12.35	6	18.35	27	
	5400	With crane and bucket	C-7	95	.758			17.65	9.40	27.05	39.50	
	5600	Wheeled concrete dumping, add to placing costs above										
	5610	Walking cart, 50' haul, add	C-18	32	.281	C.Y.		6.10	1.56	7.66	11.90	
	5620	150' haul, add		24	.375			8.15	2.08	10.23	15.90	
	5700	250' haul, add		18	.500			10.85	2.77	13.62	21	
	5800	Riding cart, 50' haul, add	C-19	80	.112			2.44	1.04	3.48	5.25	
	5810	150' haul, add		60	.150			3.25	1.39	4.64	7	
	5900	250' haul, add		45	.200			4.33	1.85	6.18	9.30	
	9000	Minimum labor/equipment charge	C-6	2	24	Job		540	37.50	577.50	940	
184	0010	**STAIR TREAD INSERTS** Cast iron, abrasive, 3" wide	1 Carp	90	.089	L.F.	5.60	2.43		8.03	10.20	184
	0020	4" wide		80	.100		6.85	2.73		9.58	12.05	

For expanded coverage of these items see Means Concrete & Masonry Cost Data 1999

033 | Cast-In-Place Concrete

033 100 | Structural Concrete

			CREW	DAILY OUTPUT	LABOR-HOURS	UNIT	1999 BARE COSTS MAT.	LABOR	EQUIP.	TOTAL	TOTAL INCL O&P	
184	0040	6" wide	1 Carp	75	.107	L.F.	8.40	2.91		11.31	14.10	184
	0050	9" wide		70	.114		12.45	3.12		15.57	18.90	
	0100	12" wide	↓	65	.123		18.65	3.36		22.01	26	
	0300	Cast aluminum, compared to cast iron, deduct					10%					
	0500	Extruded aluminum safety tread, 3" wide	1 Carp	75	.107		4.75	2.91		7.66	10.05	
	0550	4" wide		75	.107		6.40	2.91		9.31	11.90	
	0600	6" wide		75	.107		10.75	2.91		13.66	16.65	
	0650	9" wide to resurface stairs	↓	70	.114	↓	15.15	3.12		18.27	22	
	1700	Cement filled pan type, plain	1 Cefi	115	.070	S.F.	2.15	1.82		3.97	5.25	
	1750	Non-slip	"	100	.080	"	3.23	2.09		5.32	6.90	
196	0010	**WINTER PROTECTION** For heated ready mix, add, minimum				C.Y.	3.75			3.75	4.13	196
	0050	Maximum				"	4.75			4.75	5.20	
	0100	Protecting concrete and temporary heat, add, minimum	2 Clab	6,000	.003	S.F.	.15	.06		.21	.27	
	0150	Maximum, see also division 010-094	"	2,000	.008	"	.65	.17		.82	1	
	0200	Temporary shelter for slab on grade, wood frame and polyethylene										
	0201	sheeting, minimum	2 Carp	10	1.600	M.S.F.	275	43.50		318.50	380	
	0210	Maximum	"	3	5.333	"	330	146		476	610	
	0300	See also Division 033-134										

033 450 | Concrete Finishing

			CREW	DAILY OUTPUT	LABOR-HOURS	UNIT	MAT.	LABOR	EQUIP.	TOTAL	TOTAL INCL O&P	
454	0010	**FINISHING FLOORS** Monolithic, screed finish	1 Cefi	900	.009	S.F.		.23		.23	.37	454
	0050	Darby finish		750	.011			.28		.28	.44	
	0100	Screed and float finish		725	.011			.29		.29	.46	
	0150	Screed, float, and broom finish		630	.013			.33		.33	.53	
	0200	Screed, float, and hand trowel		600	.013			.35		.35	.56	
	0250	Machine trowel		550	.015	↓		.38		.38	.61	
	0370	Minimum labor/equipment charge	↓	4	2	Job		52.50		52.50	83.50	
	0380											
	0400	Integral topping and finish, using 1:1:2 mix, 3/16" thick	C-10	1,000	.024	S.F.	.06	.59		.65	1.01	
	0450	1/2" thick		950	.025		.15	.62		.77	1.16	
	0500	3/4" thick		850	.028		.23	.69		.92	1.37	
	0600	1" thick		750	.032		.30	.79		1.09	1.60	
	0800	Granolithic topping, laid after, 1:1:1-1/2 mix, 1/2" thick		590	.041		.16	1		1.16	1.80	
	0820	3/4" thick		580	.041		.24	1.02		1.26	1.91	
	0850	1" thick		575	.042		.32	1.03		1.35	2.02	
	0950	2" thick		500	.048	↓	.65	1.18		1.83	2.62	
	9100	Minimum labor/equipment charge	↓	2	12	Job		295		295	475	
458	0010	**FINISHING WALLS** Break ties and patch voids	1 Cefi	540	.015	S.F.	.03	.39		.42	.65	458
	0050	Burlap rub with grout	"	450	.018		.03	.46		.49	.77	
	0300	Bush hammer, green concrete	B-39	1,000	.048		.03	1.09	.18	1.30	2.04	
	0350	Cured concrete	"	650	.074		.03	1.68	.28	1.99	3.11	
	0700	Sandblast, light penetration	C-10	1,100	.022		.20	.54		.74	1.09	
	0750	Heavy penetration		375	.064	↓	.40	1.57		1.97	2.98	
	9000	Minimum labor/equipment charge	↓	2	12	Job		295		295	475	

034 | Precast Concrete

034 100 | Structural Precast

		CREW	DAILY OUTPUT	LABOR-HOURS	UNIT	1999 BARE COSTS MAT.	LABOR	EQUIP.	TOTAL	TOTAL INCL O&P	
104	0011 BEAMS, "L" shaped, 20' span, 12" x 20"	C-11	32	2.250	Ea.	1,350	67.50	48.50	1,466	1,675	104
	1000 Inverted tee beams, add to above, small beams				L.F.	15%					
	1050 Large beams				"	5.55			5.55	6.10	
	1200 Rectangular, 20' span, 12" x 20"	C-11	32	2.250	Ea.	925	67.50	48.50	1,041	1,200	
	1250 18" x 36"		24	3		1,700	90	64.50	1,854.50	2,100	
	1300 24" x 44"		22	3.273		2,450	98	70.50	2,618.50	2,950	
	1400 30' span, 12" x 36"		24	3		2,175	90	64.50	2,329.50	2,600	
	1450 18" x 44"		20	3.600		3,050	108	77.50	3,235.50	3,625	
	1500 24" x 52"		16	4.500		4,325	135	97	4,557	5,100	
	1600 40' span, 12" x 52"		20	3.600		4,025	108	77.50	4,210.50	4,700	
	1650 18" x 52"		16	4.500		4,900	135	97	5,132	5,750	
	1700 24" x 52"		12	6		6,000	180	129	6,309	7,075	
	2000 "T" shaped, 20' span, 12" x 20"		32	2.250		1,600	67.50	48.50	1,716	1,950	
	2050 18" x 36"		24	3		2,550	90	64.50	2,704.50	3,050	
	2100 24" x 44"		22	3.273		3,600	98	70.50	3,768.50	4,200	
	2200 30' span, 12" x 36"		24	3		3,650	90	64.50	3,804.50	4,225	
	2250 18" x 44"		20	3.600		4,975	108	77.50	5,160.50	5,750	
	2300 24" x 52"		16	4.500		5,150	135	97	5,382	6,000	
	2500 40' span, 12" x 52"		20	3.600		6,850	108	77.50	7,035.50	7,825	
	2550 18" x 52"		16	4.500		7,500	135	97	7,732	8,600	
	2600 24" x 52"		12	6		9,150	180	129	9,459	10,600	
112	0010 COLUMNS Rectangular to 12' high, small columns	C-11	120	.600	L.F.	66.50	18	12.95	97.45	120	112
	0050 Large columns	"	96	.750	"	105	22.50	16.20	143.70	175	
136	0010 SLABS Prestressed roof/floor members, solid, grouted, 4" thick (R034-030)	C-11	3,600	.020	S.F.	4.65	.60	.43	5.68	6.65	136
	0050 6" thick		4,500	.016		4.48	.48	.35	5.31	6.20	
	0100 8" thick, hollow		5,600	.013		4.83	.39	.28	5.50	6.30	
	0150 10" thick		8,800	.008		5.70	.25	.18	6.13	6.90	
	0200 12" thick		8,000	.009		4.78	.27	.19	5.24	5.95	

034 500 | Architectural Precast

		CREW	DAILY OUTPUT	LABOR-HOURS	UNIT	MAT.	LABOR	EQUIP.	TOTAL	TOTAL INCL O&P	
504	0011 WALL PANELS Material only										504
	2200 Fiberglass reinforced cement with urethane core										
	2210 R20, 8' x 8', minimum	E-2	750	.075	S.F.	8.30	2.22	1.35	11.87	14.70	
	2220 Maximum	"	600	.093	"	15.50	2.78	1.69	19.97	24	

034 800 | Precast Specialties

		CREW	DAILY OUTPUT	LABOR-HOURS	UNIT	MAT.	LABOR	EQUIP.	TOTAL	TOTAL INCL O&P	
802	0010 LINTELS										802
	0800 Precast concrete, 4" wide, 8" high, to 5' long	D-1	175	.091	L.F.	5.60	2.25		7.85	9.85	
	0850 5'-12' long	D-4	190	.168		5.85	4.13	.58	10.56	13.85	
	1000 6" wide, 8" high, to 5' long		185	.173		8.35	4.24	.59	13.18	16.80	
	1050 5'-12' long		190	.168		6.95	4.13	.58	11.66	15.05	
	1200 8" wide, 8" high, to 5' long		185	.173		9.60	4.24	.59	14.43	18.15	
	1250 5'-12' long		190	.168		8.85	4.13	.58	13.56	17.15	
	1400 10" wide, 8" high, to 14' long		180	.178		31.50	4.36	.61	36.47	43	
	1450 12" wide, 8" high, to 19' long		185	.173		33.50	4.24	.59	38.33	44.50	
804	0010 STAIRS, Precast concrete treads on steel stringers, 3' wide	C-12	75	.640	Riser	53.50	17.30	5.90	76.70	94	804
	0300 Front entrance, 5' wide with 48" platform, 2 risers		16	3	Flight	276	81	27.50	384.50	470	
	0350 5 risers		12	4		315	108	37	460	565	
	0500 6' wide, 2 risers		15	3.200		315	86.50	29.50	431	520	
	0550 5 risers		11	4.364		335	118	40.50	493.50	610	
	1200 Basement entrance stairs, steel bulkhead doors, minimum	B-51	22	2.182		460	47.50	7.80	515.30	595	
	1250 Maximum	"	11	4.364		680	95.50	15.60	791.10	925	

For expanded coverage of these items see *Means Concrete & Masonry Cost Data 1999*

035 | Cementitious Decks & Toppings

035 200 | Lightweight Concrete

			CREW	DAILY OUTPUT	LABOR-HOURS	UNIT	MAT.	LABOR	EQUIP.	TOTAL	TOTAL INCL O&P	
212	0010	**INSULATING** Lightweight cellular concrete roof fill R035-010										212
	0020	Portland cement and foaming agent	C-8	50	1.120	C.Y.	72	27	12.90	111.90	137	
	0100	Poured vermiculite or perlite, field mix,										
	0110	1:6 field mix	C-8	50	1.120	C.Y.	100	27	12.90	139.90	168	
	0200	Ready mix, 1:6 mix, roof fill, 2" thick		10,000	.006	S.F.	.56	.13	.06	.75	.90	
	0250	3" thick		7,700	.007	"	.84	.18	.08	1.10	1.30	
306	0010	**WOOD FIBER** Lightweight cement system										306
	0050	Plank, beveled, 1" thick	2 Carp	1,000	.016	S.F.	1.85	.44		2.29	2.77	
	0100	Plank, T & G, 1-1/2" thick		975	.016		2.15	.45		2.60	3.12	
	0150	2" thick		950	.017		2.90	.46		3.36	3.96	
	0200	2-1/2" thick		925	.017		3	.47		3.47	4.09	
	0300	3-1/2" thick		875	.018		5	.50		5.50	6.35	
	0350	4" thick		850	.019		5.50	.51		6.01	6.90	
	1000	Bulb tee, sub-purlin and grout, 6' span, add	E-1	5,000	.005		1.62	.14	.02	1.78	2.06	
	1100	8' span	"	4,200	.006		1.67	.17	.02	1.86	2.17	

037 | Concrete Restoration & Cleaning

037 300 | Concrete Rehabilitation

			CREW	DAILY OUTPUT	LABOR-HOURS	UNIT	MAT.	LABOR	EQUIP.	TOTAL	TOTAL INCL O&P	
330	0010	**CRACK REPAIR**, including chipping, sand blasting and cleaning										330
	0100	Epoxy injection, up to 1/4" wide	B-9	80	.500	L.F.	1.25	10.95	2.26	14.46	22	
	0110	Over 1/4" wide		60	.667		2.50	14.55	3.01	20.06	30.50	
	0200	Latex injection, up to 1/4" wide		100	.400		.75	8.75	1.80	11.30	17.45	
	0210	Latex injection, over 1/4" wide		75	.533		1.50	11.65	2.41	15.56	24	

For information about Means Estimating Seminars, see yellow pages 11 and 12 in back of book

Division 4 Masonry

Estimating Tips

041 Mortar & Masonry Accessories

- The terms *mortar* and *grout* are often used interchangeably, and incorrectly. Mortar is used to bed masonry units, seal the entry of air and moisture, provide architectural appearance, and allow for size variations in the units. Grout is used primarily in reinforced masonry construction and is used to bond the masonry to the reinforcing steel. Common mortar types are M(2500 psi), S(1800 psi), N(750 psi), and O(350 psi), and conform to ASTM C270. Grout is either fine or coarse, conforms to ASTM C476, and in-place strengths generally exceed 2500 psi. Mortar and grout are different components of masonry construction and are placed by entirely different methods. An estimator should be aware of their unique uses and costs.

042 Unit Masonry

- The most common types of unit masonry are brick and concrete masonry. The major classifications of brick are building brick (ASTM C62), facing brick (ASTM C216) and glazed brick, fire brick and pavers. Many varieties of texture and appearance can exist within these classifications, and the estimator would be wise to check local custom and availability within the project area. On repair and remodeling jobs, matching the existing brick may be the most important criteria.
- Brick and concrete block are priced by the piece and then converted into a price per square foot of wall. Openings less than two square feet are generally ignored by the estimator because any savings in units used is offset by the cutting and trimming required.
- It is often difficult and expensive to find and purchase small lots of historic brick. Costs can vary widely. Many design issues affect costs, selection of mortar mix, and repairs or replacement of masonry materials. Cleaning techniques must be reflected in the estimate.
- All masonry walls, whether interior or exterior, require bracing. The cost of bracing walls during construction should be included by the estimator and this bracing must remain in place until permanent bracing is complete. Permanent bracing of masonry walls is accomplished by masonry itself, in the form of pilasters or abutting wall corners, or by anchoring the walls to the structural frame. Accessories in the form of anchors, anchor slots and ties are used, but their supply and installation can be by different trades. For instance, anchor slots on spandrel beams and columns are supplied and welded in place by the steel fabricator, but the ties from the slots into the masonry are installed by the bricklayer. Regardless of the installation method the estimator must be certain that these accessories are accounted for in pricing.

Reference Numbers

Reference numbers are shown in bold squares at the beginning of some major classifications. These numbers refer to related items in the Reference Section. The reference information may be an estimating procedure, an alternate pricing method or technical information.

Note: Not all subdivisions listed here necessarily appear in this publication.

041 | Mortar & Masonry Accessories

041 000 | Mortar

				CREW	DAILY OUTPUT	LABOR-HOURS	UNIT	1999 BARE COSTS MAT.	LABOR	EQUIP.	TOTAL	TOTAL INCL O&P	
008	0010	**CEMENT** Gypsum 80 lb. bag, T.L. lots					Bag	11.25			11.25	12.40	008
	0050	L.T.L. lots						11.75			11.75	12.95	
	0100	Masonry, 70 lb. bag, T.L. lots						5.80			5.80	6.40	
	0150	L.T.L. lots						5.60			5.60	6.15	
	0200	White, 70 lb. bag, T.L. lots						15.85			15.85	17.45	
	0250	L.T.L. lots						16.40			16.40	18.05	
016	0010	**GROUTING** Bond bms. & lintels, 8" dp., pumped, not incl. block											016
	0020	8" thick, 0.2 C.F. per L.F.		D-4	1,400	.023	L.F.	.66	.56	.08	1.30	1.74	
	0050	10" thick, 0.25 C.F. per L.F.			1,200	.027		.83	.65	.09	1.57	2.08	
	0060	12" thick, 0.3 C.F. per L.F.			1,040	.031		.99	.75	.11	1.85	2.44	
	0200	Concrete block cores, solid, 4" thk., by hand, 0.067 C.F./S.F.		D-8	1,100	.036	S.F.	.22	.92		1.14	1.76	
	0210	6" thick, pumped, 0.175 C.F. per S.F.		D-4	720	.044		.58	1.09	.15	1.82	2.59	
	0250	8" thick, pumped, 0.258 C.F. per S.F.			680	.047		.85	1.15	.16	2.16	3.01	
	0300	10" thick, pumped, 0.340 C.F. per S.F.			660	.048		1.13	1.19	.17	2.49	3.37	
	0350	12" thick, pumped, 0.422 C.F. per S.F.			640	.050		1.40	1.23	.17	2.80	3.74	
	0500	Cavity walls, 2" space, pumped, no shoring, 0.167 C.F./S.F.			1,700	.019		.55	.46	.06	1.07	1.44	
	0550	3" space, 0.250 C.F./S.F.			1,200	.027		.83	.65	.09	1.57	2.08	
	0600	4" space, 0.333 C.F. per S.F.			1,150	.028		1.10	.68	.10	1.88	2.43	
	0700	6" space, 0.500 C.F. per S.F.			800	.040		1.65	.98	.14	2.77	3.58	
	0800	Door frames, 3' x 7' opening, 2.5 C.F. per opening			60	.533	Opng.	8.25	13.05	1.82	23.12	32.50	
	0850	6' x 7' opening, 3.5 C.F. per opening			45	.711	"	11.60	17.40	2.43	31.43	44	
	2000	Grout, C476, for bond beams, lintels and CMU cores			350	.091	C.F.	3.31	2.24	.31	5.86	7.65	
	9000	Minimum labor/equipment charge		1 Bric	2	4	Job		110		110	183	
020	0010	**LIME** Masons, hydrated, 50 lb. bag, T.L. lots					Bag	5.40			5.40	5.95	020
	0050	L.T.L. lots					"	5.65			5.65	6.20	
	0200	Finish, double hydrated, 50 lb. bag, T.L. lots					Bag	6.50			6.50	7.15	
	0250	L.T.L. lots					"	7.40			7.40	8.15	
024	0010	**MORTAR**											024
	0100	Type M, 1:1:6 mix		1 Brhe	143	.056	C.F.	3.17	1.21		4.38	5.50	
	0200	Type N, 1:3 mix			143	.056		2.96	1.21		4.17	5.25	
	0300	Type O, 1:3 mix			143	.056		2.97	1.21		4.18	5.25	
	0400	Type PM, 1:1:6 mix, 2500 psi			143	.056		3.17	1.21		4.38	5.50	
	0500	Type S, 1/2:1:4 mix			143	.056		3.36	1.21		4.57	5.70	
	2000	With portland cement and lime											
	2100	Type M, 1:1/4:3 mix		1 Brhe	143	.056	C.F.	3.82	1.21		5.03	6.20	
	2200	Type N, 1:1:6 mix, 750 psi			143	.056		3.11	1.21		4.32	5.40	
	2300	Type O, 1:2:9 mix (Pointing Mortar)			143	.056		3.02	1.21		4.23	5.30	
	2400	Type PL, 1:1/2:4 mix, 2500 psi			143	.056		3.47	1.21		4.68	5.80	
	2500	Type K, 1:3:12 mix, 75 psi			143	.056		2.98	1.21		4.19	5.30	
	2600	Type S, 1:1/2:4 mix, 1800 psi			143	.056		3.47	1.21		4.68	5.80	
	2700	Mortar for glass block			143	.056		7.25	1.21		8.46	9.95	
	2800	Gypsum cement mortar						5.60			5.60	6.15	
	2900	Mortar for Fire Brick, 80 lb. bag, T.L. Lots					Bag	12.60			12.60	13.85	

041 500 | Masonry Accessories

				CREW	DAILY OUTPUT	LABOR-HOURS	UNIT	MAT.	LABOR	EQUIP.	TOTAL	TOTAL INCL O&P	
504	0010	**ANCHOR BOLTS** Hooked type with nut and washer, 1/2" diam., 8" long		1 Bric	200	.040	Ea.	.52	1.10		1.62	2.40	504
	0030	12" long			190	.042		1.22	1.16		2.38	3.26	
	0040	5/8" diameter, 8" long			180	.044		1.25	1.23		2.48	3.41	
	0050	12" long			170	.047		1.38	1.30		2.68	3.66	
	0060	3/4" diameter, 8" long			160	.050		1.70	1.38		3.08	4.17	
	0070	12" long			150	.053		2.11	1.47		3.58	4.76	
508	0010	**CONTROL JOINT** Rubber, 4" and wider wall		1 Bric	400	.020	L.F.	2.40	.55		2.95	3.55	508
	0050	PVC, 4" wall			400	.020		1.36	.55		1.91	2.41	
	0100	Rubber, 6" wall			320	.025		4.30	.69		4.99	5.85	
	0120	PVC, 6" wall			320	.025		1.62	.69		2.31	2.92	

041 | Mortar & Masonry Accessories

041 500 | Masonry Accessories

			CREW	DAILY OUTPUT	LABOR-HOURS	UNIT	MAT.	LABOR	EQUIP.	TOTAL	TOTAL INCL O&P	
508	0140	Rubber, 8" and wider wall	1 Bric	280	.029	L.F.	4.40	.79		5.19	6.15	508
	0160	PVC, 8" wall		280	.029		1.67	.79		2.46	3.15	
	0180	12" wall	▼	240	.033	▼	2.79	.92		3.71	4.59	
512	0010	**REINFORCING** Steel bars A615, placed horiz., #3 & #4 bars	1 Bric	450	.018	Lb.	.27	.49		.76	1.10	512
	0020	#5 & #6 bars		800	.010		.27	.28		.55	.75	
	0050	Placed vertical, #3 & #4 bars		350	.023		.27	.63		.90	1.33	
	0060	#5 & #6 bars	▼	650	.012	▼	.27	.34		.61	.85	
	0500	Joint reinforcing, ladder type, mill std galvanized										
	0600	9 ga. sides, 9 ga. ties, 4" wall	1 Bric	30	.267	C.L.F.	6.90	7.35		14.25	19.80	
	0650	6" wall		30	.267		7.30	7.35		14.65	20	
	0700	8" wall		25	.320		7.65	8.85		16.50	23	
	0750	10" wall		20	.400		8.15	11.05		19.20	27.50	
	0800	12" wall	▼	20	.400	▼	8.60	11.05		19.65	28	
	1000	Truss type										
	1100	9 ga. sides, 9 ga. ties, 4" wall	1 Bric	30	.267	C.L.F.	9.85	7.35		17.20	23	
	1150	6" wall		30	.267		9.95	7.35		17.30	23	
	1200	8" wall		25	.320		10.40	8.85		19.25	26	
	1250	10" wall		20	.400		10.70	11.05		21.75	30	
	1300	12" wall		20	.400		11.25	11.05		22.30	30.50	
	1500	3/16" sides, 9 ga. ties, 4" wall		30	.267		12.85	7.35		20.20	26.50	
	1550	6" wall		30	.267		13.10	7.35		20.45	26.50	
	1600	8" wall		25	.320		13.45	8.85		22.30	29.50	
	1650	10" wall		20	.400		13.95	11.05		25	33.50	
	1700	12" wall		20	.400		14.50	11.05		25.55	34	
	2000	3/16" sides, 3/16" ties, 4" wall		30	.267		18.40	7.35		25.75	32.50	
	2050	6" wall		30	.267		18.65	7.35		26	32.50	
	2100	8" wall		25	.320		19.30	8.85		28.15	36	
	2150	10" wall		20	.400		20	11.05		31.05	41	
	2200	12" wall	▼	20	.400	▼	21.50	11.05		32.55	42	
	2500	Cavity truss type, galvanized										
	2600	9 ga. sides, 9 ga. ties, 4" wall	1 Bric	25	.320	C.L.F.	9.80	8.85		18.65	25.50	
	2650	6" wall		25	.320		10.35	8.85		19.20	26	
	2700	8" wall		20	.400		10.40	11.05		21.45	30	
	2750	10" wall		15	.533		10.75	14.70		25.45	36.50	
	2800	12" wall		15	.533		11.35	14.70		26.05	37	
	3000	3/16" sides, 9 ga. ties, 4" wall		25	.320		13.45	8.85		22.30	29.50	
	3050	6" wall		25	.320		13.70	8.85		22.55	29.50	
	3100	8" wall		20	.400		14.05	11.05		25.10	34	
	3150	10" wall		15	.533		14.50	14.70		29.20	40.50	
	3200	12" wall	▼	15	.533	▼	15.15	14.70		29.85	41	
	3500	For hot dip galvanizing, add					50%					
520	0010	**WALL TIES** To brick veneer, galv., corrugated, 7/8" x 7", 22 Ga.	1 Bric	10.50	.762	C	4.47	21		25.47	40	520
	0100	24 Ga.		10.50	.762		3.97	21		24.97	39.50	
	0150	16 Ga.		10.50	.762		13.45	21		34.45	50	
	0200	Buck anchors, galv., corrugated, 16 gauge, 2" bend, 8" x 2"		10.50	.762		93	21		114	137	
	0250	8" x 3"	▼	10.50	.762	▼	99	21		120	144	
	0300	Adjustable, rectangular, 4-1/8" wide										
	0350	Anchor and tie, 3/16" wire, mill galv.										
	0400	2-3/4" eye, 3-1/4" tie	1 Bric	1.05	7.619	M	315	210		525	695	
	0500	2-3/4" eye, 4-3/4" tie		1.05	7.619		345	210		555	730	
	0520	2-3/4" eye, 5-1/2" tie		1.05	7.619		355	210		565	740	
	0550	4-3/4" eye, 3-1/4" tie		1.05	7.619		350	210		560	735	
	0570	4-3/4" eye, 4-3/4" tie		1.05	7.619		380	210		590	765	
	0580	4-3/4" eye, 5-1/2" tie		1.05	7.619	▼	390	210		600	780	
	0600	Cavity wall, Z type, galvanized, 6" long, 1/4" diameter	▼	10.50	.762	C	17.45	21		38.45	54	

For expanded coverage of these items see *Means Concrete & Masonry Cost Data 1999*

041 | Mortar & Masonry Accessories

041 500 | Masonry Accessories

		CREW	DAILY OUTPUT	LABOR-HOURS	UNIT	1999 BARE COSTS MAT.	LABOR	EQUIP.	TOTAL	TOTAL INCL O&P	
520	0650	3/16" diameter	1 Bric	10.50	.762	C	9.50	21		30.50	45.50	520
	0800	8" long, 1/4" diameter		10.50	.762		23.50	21		44.50	61	
	0850	3/16" diameter		10.50	.762		10.45	21		31.45	46.50	
	1000	Rectangular type, galvanized, 1/4" diameter, 2" x 6"		10.50	.762		38.50	21		59.50	77.50	
	1050	2" x 8" or 4" x 6"		10.50	.762		29	21		50	66.50	
	1100	3/16" diameter, 2" x 6"		10.50	.762		17.45	21		38.45	54	
	1150	2" x 8" or 4" x 6"		10.50	.762		19.40	21		40.40	56.50	
	1200	Mesh wall tie, 1/2" mesh, hot dip galvanized										
	1400	16 gauge, 12" long, 3" wide	1 Bric	9	.889	C	68.50	24.50		93	116	
	1420	6" wide		9	.889		105	24.50		129.50	156	
	1440	12" wide		8.50	.941		167	26		193	226	
	1500	Rigid partition anchors, plain, 8" long, 1" x 1/8"		10.50	.762		48	21		69	88	
	1550	1" x 1/4"		10.50	.762		94	21		115	138	
	1580	1-1/2" x 1/8"		10.50	.762		66.50	21		87.50	108	
	1600	1-1/2" x 1/4"		10.50	.762		158	21		179	208	
	1650	2" x 1/8"		10.50	.762		83	21		104	127	
	1700	2" x 1/4"		10.50	.762		225	21		246	283	
	2000	Column flange ties, wire, galvanized										
	2300	3/16" diameter, up to 3" wide	1 Bric	10.50	.762	C	54	21		75	94.50	
	2350	To 5" wide		10.50	.762		59	21		80	100	
	2400	To 7" wide		10.50	.762		62	21		83	103	
	2600	To 9" wide		10.50	.762		67	21		88	109	
	2650	1/4" diameter, up to 3" wide		10.50	.762		85	21		106	129	
	2700	To 5" wide		10.50	.762		94	21		115	138	
	2800	To 7" wide		10.50	.762		98	21		119	143	
	2850	To 9" wide		10.50	.762		107	21		128	153	
	2900	For hot dip galvanized, add					35%					
	4000	Channel slots, 1-3/8" x 1/2" x 8"										
	4100	12 gauge, plain	1 Bric	10.50	.762	C	120	21		141	167	
	4150	16 gauge, galvanized	"	10.50	.762	"	63	21		84	105	
	4200	Channel slot anchors										
	4300	16 gauge, galvanized, 1-1/4" x 3-1/2"				C	28			28	31	
	4350	1-1/4" x 5-1/2"					33			33	36.50	
	4400	1-1/4" x 7-1/2"					38			38	42	
	4500	1/8" plain, 1-1/4" x 3-1/2"					47			47	51.50	
	4550	1-1/4" x 5-1/2"					57.50			57.50	63.50	
	4600	1-1/4" x 7-1/2"					68			68	75	
	4700	For corrugation, add					32			32	35	
	4750	For hot dip galvanized, add					35%					
	5000	Dowels										
	5100	Plain, 1/4" diameter, 3" long				C	17			17	18.70	
	5150	4" long					19.20			19.20	21	
	5200	6" long					23.50			23.50	26	
	5300	3/8" diameter, 3" long					23			23	25.50	
	5350	4" long					28.50			28.50	31.50	
	5400	6" long					39.50			39.50	43.50	
	5500	1/2" diameter, 3" long					34			34	37.50	
	5550	4" long					42			42	46	
	5600	6" long					56			56	61.50	
	5700	5/8" diameter, 3" long					47			47	51.50	
	5750	4" long					59			59	65	
	5800	6" long					83			83	91.50	
	6000	3/4" diameter, 3" long					60			60	66	
	6100	4" long					78			78	86	
	6150	6" long					114			114	125	
	6300	For hot dip galvanized, add					35%					

041 | Mortar & Masonry Accessories

041 500 | Masonry Accessories

			CREW	DAILY OUTPUT	LABOR-HOURS	UNIT	MAT.	LABOR	EQUIP.	TOTAL	TOTAL INCL O&P	
524	0010	**VENT BOX** Extruded aluminum, 4" deep, 2-3/8" x 8-1/8"	1 Bric	30	.267	Ea.	31.50	7.35		38.85	46.50	524
	0050	5" x 8-1/8"		25	.320		43.50	8.85		52.35	62	
	0100	2-1/4" x 25"		25	.320		60	8.85		68.85	80.50	
	0150	5" x 16-1/2"		22	.364		44	10.05		54.05	65	
	0200	6" x 16-1/2"		22	.364		65	10.05		75.05	88	
	0250	7-3/4" x 16-1/2"		20	.400		80	11.05		91.05	106	
	0400	For baked enamel finish, add					35%					
	0500	For cast aluminum, painted, add					60%					
	1000	Stainless steel ventilators, 6" x 6"	1 Bric	25	.320		90	8.85		98.85	114	
	1050	8" x 8"		24	.333		95	9.20		104.20	120	
	1100	12" x 12"		23	.348		110	9.60		119.60	137	
	1150	12" x 6"		24	.333		95	9.20		104.20	120	
	1200	Foundation block vent, galv., 1-1/4" thk, 8" high, 16" long, no damper		30	.267		16	7.35		23.35	30	
	1250	For damper, add					5			5	5.50	

042 | Unit Masonry

042 050 | Chimneys

			CREW	DAILY OUTPUT	LABOR-HOURS	UNIT	MAT.	LABOR	EQUIP.	TOTAL	TOTAL INCL O&P	
054	0010	**CHIMNEY** See Div. 033-130 for foundation, add to prices below										054
	0100	Brick, 16" x 16", 8" flue, scaff. not incl.	D-1	18.20	.879	V.L.F.	13.95	21.50		35.45	51.50	
	0150	16" x 20" with one 8" x 12" flue R042-050		16	1		17.15	24.50		41.65	59.50	
	0200	16" x 24" with two 8" x 8" flues		14	1.143		22.50	28		50.50	71.50	
	0250	20" x 20" with one 12" x 12" flue		13.70	1.168		19.95	28.50		48.45	69.50	
	0300	20" x 24" with two 8" x 12" flues		12	1.333		26.50	33		59.50	83.50	
	0350	20" x 32" with two 12" x 12" flues		10	1.600		33	39.50		72.50	102	

042 100 | Brick Masonry

			CREW	DAILY OUTPUT	LABOR-HOURS	UNIT	MAT.	LABOR	EQUIP.	TOTAL	TOTAL INCL O&P	
108	0010	**COLUMNS** Brick, scaffolding not included										108
	0050	8" x 8", 9 brick	D-1	56	.286	V.L.F.	3.32	7.05		10.37	15.30	
	0100	12" x 8", 13.5 brick		37	.432		4.99	10.65		15.64	23	
	0200	12" x 12", 20 brick		25	.640		7.40	15.75		23.15	34	
	0300	16" x 12", 27 brick		19	.842		9.95	20.50		30.45	45.50	
	0400	16" x 16", 36 brick		14	1.143		13.30	28		41.30	61	
	0500	20" x 16", 45 brick		11	1.455		16.60	36		52.60	77.50	
	0600	20" x 20", 56 brick		9	1.778		20.50	43.50		64	95.50	
	0700	24" x 20", 68 brick		7	2.286		25	56		81	121	
	0800	24" x 24", 81 brick		6	2.667		30	65.50		95.50	142	
	1000	36" x 36", 182 brick		3	5.333		67	131		198	291	
	9000	Minimum labor/equipment charge		2	8	Job		197		197	325	
110	0010	**COMMON BUILDING BRICK** C62, TL lots, material only R042-120										110
	0020	Standard, minimum				M	250			250	275	
	0050	Average (select)				"	310			310	340	
116	0010	**COPING** Stock units										116
	0050	Precast concrete, 10" wide, 4" tapers to 3-1/2", 8" wall	D-1	75	.213	L.F.	9.60	5.25		14.85	19.25	
	0100	12" wide, 3-1/2" tapers to 3", 10" wall		70	.229		10.10	5.60		15.70	20.50	
	0150	16" wide, 4" tapers to 3-1/2", 14" wall		60	.267		13.90	6.55		20.45	26	
	0300	Limestone for 12" wall, 4" thick		90	.178		12.90	4.37		17.27	21.50	
	0350	6" thick		80	.200		15.15	4.92		20.07	25	

For expanded coverage of these items see *Means Concrete & Masonry Cost Data 1999*

042 | Unit Masonry

042 100 | Brick Masonry

			CREW	DAILY OUTPUT	LABOR-HOURS	UNIT	1999 BARE COSTS				TOTAL INCL O&P
							MAT.	LABOR	EQUIP.	TOTAL	
116	0500	Marble, to 4" thick, no wash, 9" wide	D-1	90	.178	L.F.	18.70	4.37		23.07	28
	0550	12" wide		80	.200		27.50	4.92		32.42	38.50
	0700	Terra cotta, 9" wide		90	.178		4.55	4.37		8.92	12.25
	0750	12" wide		80	.200		7.60	4.92		12.52	16.50
	0800	Aluminum, for 12" wall		80	.200		10.75	4.92		15.67	19.95
	9000	Minimum labor/equipment charge		2	8	Job		197		197	325
120	0010	**CORNICES** Brick cornice on existing building									
	0020	Not including scaffolding									
	0110	Face bricks, 12 brick/S.F., minimum	D-1	30	.533	SF Face	4.70	13.10		17.80	26.50
	0150	15 brick/S.F., maximum		23	.696	"	5.60	17.10		22.70	34.50
	9000	Minimum labor/equipment charge		1.50	10.667	Job		262		262	435
124	0010	**FACE BRICK** C216, TL lots, material only									
	0300	Standard modular, 4" x 2-2/3" x 8", minimum				M	330			330	365
	0350	Maximum					450			450	495
	0450	Economy, 4" x 4" x 8", minimum					425			425	470
	0500	Maximum					545			545	600
	0510	Economy, 4" x 4" x 12", minimum					425			425	470
	0520	Maximum					545			545	600
	0550	Jumbo, 6" x 4" x 12", minimum					1,150			1,150	1,250
	0600	Maximum					1,425			1,425	1,575
	0610	Jumbo, 8" x 4" x 12", minimum					1,150			1,150	1,250
	0620	Maximum					1,425			1,425	1,575
	0650	Norwegian, 4" x 3-1/5" x 12", minimum					520			520	570
	0700	Maximum					730			730	805
	0710	Norwegian, 6" x 3-1/5" x 12", minimum					520			520	570
	0720	Maximum					730			730	805
	0850	Standard glazed, plain colors, 4" x 2-2/3" x 8", minimum					985			985	1,075
	0900	Maximum					1,150			1,150	1,275
	1000	Deep trim shades, 4" x 2-2/3" x 8", minimum					1,150			1,150	1,250
	1050	Maximum					1,300			1,300	1,425
	1080	Jumbo utility, 4" x 4" x 12"					750			750	825
	1120	4" x 8" x 8"					1,100			1,100	1,200
	1140	4" x 8" x 16"					2,500			2,500	2,750
	1260	Engineer, 4" x 3-1/5" x 8", minimum					295			295	325
	1270	Maximum					485			485	535
	1350	King, 4" x 2-3/4" x 10", minimum					415			415	455
	1360	Maximum					440			440	485
	1400	Norman, 4" x 2-3/4" x 12"					415			415	455
	1450	Roman, 4" x 2" x 12"					415			415	455
	1500	SCR, 6" x 2-2/3" x 12"					415			415	455
	1550	Double, 4" x 5-1/3" x 8"					415			415	455
	1600	Triple, 4" x 5-1/3" x 12"					415			415	455
	1770	Standard modular, double glazed, 4" x 2-2/3" x 8"					1,000			1,000	1,100
	1850	Jumbo, colored glazed ceramic, 6" x 4" x 12"					1,500			1,500	1,650
	2050	Jumbo utility, glazed, 4" x 4" x 12"					1,075			1,075	1,175
	2100	4" x 8" x 8"					1,500			1,500	1,650
	2150	4" x 16" x 8"					3,000			3,000	3,300
	2160	Fire Brick, 2" x 2-2/3" x 9", minimum									
	2161	Fire Brick, 2" x 2 2/3" x 9", minimum									
	2165	Maximum				M	910			910	1,000
	2170	For less than truck load lots, add					10				
	2180	For buff or gray brick, add					15				
	3050	Used brick, minimum					280			280	310
	3100	Maximum					305			305	335
	3150	Add for brick to match existing work, minimum					5%				

042 | Unit Masonry

042 100 | Brick Masonry

				DAILY	LABOR-			1999 BARE COSTS			TOTAL	
			CREW	OUTPUT	HOURS	UNIT	MAT.	LABOR	EQUIP.	TOTAL	INCL O&P	
124	3200	Maximum R042-120				M	50%					124
134	0010	**LINTELS** See division 051-232										134
162	0010	**SIMULATED BRICK** Aluminum, baked on colors	1 Carp	200	.040	S.F.	2.15	1.09		3.24	4.20	162
	0050	Fiberglass panels		200	.040		2.25	1.09		3.34	4.31	
	0100	Urethane pieces cemented in mastic		150	.053		4.60	1.46		6.06	7.50	
	0150	Vinyl siding panels		200	.040		1.90	1.09		2.99	3.92	
184	0016	**WALLS** R042-120										184
	0800	4" wall, face, 4" x 2-2/3" x 8"	D-8	215	.186	S.F.	2.51	4.69		7.20	10.50	
	0850	4" thick, as back up, 6.75 bricks per S.F. R042-500		240	.167		1.96	4.20		6.16	9.10	
	0900	8" thick wall, 13.50 brick per S.F.		135	.296		4.01	7.45		11.46	16.75	
	1000	12" thick wall, 20.25 bricks per S.F.		95	.421		6.05	10.60		16.65	24	
	1050	16" thick wall, 27.00 bricks per S.F.		75	.533		8.15	13.45		21.60	31.50	
	1200	Reinforced, 4" x 2-2/3" x 8", 4" wall		205	.195		1.97	4.92		6.89	10.30	
	1250	8" thick wall, 13.50 brick per S.F.		130	.308		4.02	7.75		11.77	17.30	
	1300	12" thick wall, 20.25 bricks per S.F.		90	.444		6.05	11.20		17.25	25	
	1350	16" thick wall, 27.00 bricks per S.F.		70	.571		8.15	14.40		22.55	33	
	9000	Minimum labor/ equipment charge	D-1	2	8	Job		197		197	325	
194	0010	**WINDOW SILL** Bluestone, thermal top, 10" wide, 1-1/2" thick	D-1	85	.188	S.F.	12.35	4.63		16.98	21.50	194
	0050	2" thick		75	.213	"	14.25	5.25		19.50	24.50	
	0100	Cut stone, 5" x 8" plain		48	.333	L.F.	10	8.20		18.20	24.50	
	0200	Face brick on edge, brick, 8" wide		80	.200		1.85	4.92		6.77	10.20	
	0400	Marble, 9" wide, 1" thick		85	.188		7	4.63		11.63	15.35	
	0600	Precast concrete, 4" tapers to 3", 9" wide		70	.229		9.05	5.60		14.65	19.25	
	0650	11" wide		60	.267		8.35	6.55		14.90	20	
	0700	13" wide, 3 1/2" tapers to 2 1/2", 12" wall		50	.320		12.15	7.85		20	26.50	
	0900	Slate, colored, unfading, honed, 12" wide, 1" thick		85	.188		14.75	4.63		19.38	24	
	0950	2" thick		70	.229		20.50	5.60		26.10	32	
	9000	Minimum labor/equipment charge	1 Bric	2	4	Job		110		110	183	

042 200 | Concrete Unit Masonry

			CREW	DAILY OUTPUT	LABOR-HOURS	UNIT	MAT.	LABOR	EQUIP.	TOTAL	INCL O&P	
216	0010	**CONCRETE BLOCK, BACK-UP** Scaffolding not included										216
	0020	Sand aggregate, 8" x 16" units, tooled joint 1 side										
	0050	Not-reinforced, 2000 psi, 2" thick	D-8	475	.084	S.F.	.66	2.12		2.78	4.24	
	0200	4" thick		440	.091		.81	2.29		3.10	4.68	
	0300	6" thick		420	.095		1.17	2.40		3.57	5.25	
	0350	8" thick		400	.100		1.29	2.52		3.81	5.60	
	0400	10" thick		390	.103		1.87	2.58		4.45	6.35	
	0450	12" thick	D-9	370	.130		2.04	3.19		5.23	7.55	
	1000	Reinforced, alternate courses, 4" thick	D-8	435	.092		.88	2.32		3.20	4.81	
	1100	6" thick		415	.096		1.24	2.43		3.67	5.40	
	1150	8" thick		395	.101		1.37	2.55		3.92	5.75	
	1200	10" thick		385	.104		1.95	2.62		4.57	6.45	
	1250	12" thick	D-9	365	.132		2.12	3.24		5.36	7.70	
	9000	Minimum labor/equipment charge	D-1	2	8	Job		197		197	325	
220	0010	**CONCRETE BLOCK, DECORATIVE** Scaffolding not included										220
	1000	Fluted high strength										
	1100	Flutes 1 side, 8" x 16" x 4" thick	D-8	345	.116	S.F.	2.59	2.92		5.51	7.70	
	1150	Flutes 2 sides, 8" x 16" x 4" thick		335	.119		3.11	3.01		6.12	8.40	
	1200	8" thick		300	.133		4.01	3.36		7.37	9.95	
	1250	For special colors, add					.23			.23	.25	
	1400	Deep grooved, smooth face										
	1450	8" x 16" x 4" thick	D-8	345	.116	S.F.	1.63	2.92		4.55	6.65	

For expanded coverage of these items see *Means Concrete & Masonry Cost Data 1999*

042 | Unit Masonry

042 200 | Concrete Unit Masonry

			CREW	DAILY OUTPUT	LABOR-HOURS	UNIT	MAT.	LABOR	EQUIP.	TOTAL	TOTAL INCL O&P	
220	1500	8" thick	D-8	300	.133	S.F.	2.80	3.36		6.16	8.65	220
	1600											
	4000	Slump block										
	4100	4" face height x 16" x 4" thick	D-1	165	.097	S.F.	3.72	2.39		6.11	8.05	
	4150	6" thick		160	.100		4.56	2.46		7.02	9.05	
	4200	8" thick		155	.103		6.20	2.54		8.74	11	
	4250	10" thick		140	.114		9.25	2.81		12.06	14.85	
	4300	12" thick		130	.123		9.85	3.03		12.88	15.85	
	5000	Split rib profile units, 1" deep ribs, 8 ribs										
	5100	8" x 16" x 4" thick	D-8	345	.116	S.F.	1.58	2.92		4.50	6.60	
	5150	6" thick		325	.123		1.91	3.10		5.01	7.25	
	5200	8" thick		305	.131		2.35	3.30		5.65	8.05	
	5250	12" thick	D-9	275	.175		3.05	4.29		7.34	10.45	
	9000	Minimum labor/equipment charge	D-1	2	8	Job		197		197	325	
224	0010	**CONCRETE BLOCK, INTERLOCKING** Scaffolding not incl., mortar incl.										224
	0100	Not including grout or reinforcing										
	0200	8" x 16" units, 2,000 psi, 8" thick	D-1	245	.065	S.F.	1.65	1.61		3.26	4.48	
	0300	12" thick	"	220	.073		2.49	1.79		4.28	5.70	
	0400	Including grout & reinforcing, 8" thick	D-4	245	.131		5.20	3.20	.45	8.85	11.45	
	0450	12" thick	"	220	.145		6.15	3.56	.50	10.21	13.15	
	9000	Minimum labor/equipment charge	D-1	2	8	Job		197		197	325	
232	0010	**CONCRETE BLOCK, PARTITIONS** Scaffolding not included										232
	1000	Lightweight block, tooled joints, 2 sides, hollow										
	1100	Not reinforced, 8" x 16" x 4" thick	D-8	440	.091	S.F.	.86	2.29		3.15	4.73	
	1150	6" thick		410	.098		1.22	2.46		3.68	5.40	
	1200	8" thick		385	.104		1.40	2.62		4.02	5.85	
	1250	10" thick		370	.108		1.80	2.72		4.52	6.50	
	1300	12" thick	D-9	350	.137		2.11	3.37		5.48	7.90	
	1500	Reinforced alternate courses, 4" thick	D-8	435	.092		1.16	2.32		3.48	5.10	
	1600	6" thick		405	.099		1.27	2.49		3.76	5.50	
	1650	8" thick		380	.105		1.46	2.65		4.11	6	
	1700	10" thick		365	.110		1.86	2.76		4.62	6.60	
	1750	12" thick	D-9	345	.139		2.21	3.42		5.63	8.10	
	4000	Regular block, tooled joints, 2 sides, hollow										
	4100	Not reinforced, 8" x 16" x 4" thick	D-8	430	.093	S.F.	.77	2.34		3.11	4.73	
	4150	6" thick		400	.100		1.13	2.52		3.65	5.40	
	4200	8" thick		375	.107		1.26	2.69		3.95	5.85	
	4250	10" thick		360	.111		1.83	2.80		4.63	6.65	
	4300	12" thick	D-9	340	.141		2	3.47		5.47	7.95	
	4500	Reinforced alternate courses, 8" x 16" x 4" thick	D-8	425	.094		.84	2.37		3.21	4.86	
	4550	6" thick		395	.101		1.21	2.55		3.76	5.55	
	4600	8" thick		370	.108		1.34	2.72		4.06	6	
	4650	10" thick		355	.113		2.03	2.84		4.87	6.95	
	4700	12" thick	D-9	335	.143		2.09	3.52		5.61	8.15	
	9000	Minimum labor/equipment charge	D-1	2	8	Job		197		197	325	
234	0010	**CONCRETE BRICK** C55, grade N, type I, scaffolding not included										234
	0100	Regular, 4 x 2-1/4 x 8	D-8	220	.182	Ea.	.26	4.58		4.84	7.90	
	0125	Rusticated, 4 x 2-1/4 x 8		220	.182		.29	4.58		4.87	7.90	
	0150	Frog, 4 x 2-1/4 x 8		220	.182		.28	4.58		4.86	7.90	
	0200	Double, 4 x 4-7/8 x 8		180	.222		.46	5.60		6.06	9.75	
248	0010	**GLAZED CONCRETE BLOCK** No scaffolding or reinforcing incl.										248
	0100	Single face, 8" x 16" units, 2" thick	D-8	360	.111	S.F.	5.70	2.80		8.50	10.90	
	0200	4" thick		345	.116		5.45	2.92		8.37	10.85	
	0250	6" thick		330	.121		5.80	3.05		8.85	11.40	

042 | Unit Masonry

042 200 | Concrete Unit Masonry

			CREW	DAILY OUTPUT	LABOR-HOURS	UNIT	1999 BARE COSTS MAT.	LABOR	EQUIP.	TOTAL	TOTAL INCL O&P	
248	0300	8" thick	D-8	310	.129	S.F.	6.20	3.25		9.45	12.20	248
	0350	10" thick	↓	295	.136		6.80	3.42		10.22	13.10	
	0400	12" thick	D-9	280	.171		7.10	4.22		11.32	14.80	
	0700	Double face, 8" x 16" units, 4" thick	D-8	310	.129		8.45	3.25		11.70	14.70	
	0750	6" thick		290	.138		9.25	3.48		12.73	15.95	
	0800	8" thick		270	.148	↓	9.65	3.73		13.38	16.80	
	1500	Cove base, 8" x 16", 2" thick		315	.127	L.F.	6.10	3.20		9.30	12	
	1550	4" thick		285	.140		6.20	3.54		9.74	12.70	
	1600	6" thick		265	.151		6.55	3.80		10.35	13.50	
	1650	8" thick	↓	245	.163	↓	6.95	4.11		11.06	14.45	
	9000	Minimum labor/equipment charge	D-1	2	8	Job		197		197	325	
252	0010	**INSULATION** See also division 072-108										252
	0100	Inserts, styrofoam, plant installed, add to block prices										
	0200	8" x 16" units, 6" thick				S.F.	.74			.74	.81	
	0250	8" thick					.74			.74	.81	
	0300	10" thick					.87			.87	.96	
	0350	12" thick					.91			.91	1	
	0500	8" x 8" units, 8" thick					.60			.60	.66	
	0550	12" thick				↓	.72			.72	.79	
	9000	Minimum labor/equipment charge	D-1	2	8	Job		197		197	325	

042 300 | Reinforced Unit Masonry

			CREW	DAILY OUTPUT	LABOR-HOURS	UNIT	MAT.	LABOR	EQUIP.	TOTAL	INCL O&P	
304	0010	**CONCRETE BLOCK BOND BEAM** Scaffolding not included										304
	0020	Not including grout or reinforcing										
	0100	Regular block, 8" high, 8" thick	D-8	565	.071	L.F.	1.77	1.78		3.55	4.89	
	0150	12" thick	D-9	510	.094	"	2.36	2.32		4.68	6.45	
	2000	Including grout and 2 #5 bars										
	2100	Regular block, 8" high, 8" thick	D-8	300	.133	L.F.	3.12	3.36		6.48	9	
	2150	12" thick	D-9	250	.192	"	4.14	4.72		8.86	12.35	
	9000	Minimum labor/equipment charge	D-1	2	8	Job		197		197	325	
310	0010	**CONCRETE BLOCK, EXTERIOR** Not including scaffolding										310
	0020	Reinforced alt courses, tooled joints 2 sides, foam inserts										
	0100	Regular, 8" x 16" x 6" thick	D-8	390	.103	S.F.	1.27	2.58		3.85	5.70	
	0200	8" thick		365	.110		1.81	2.76		4.57	6.55	
	0250	10" thick	↓	355	.113		2.27	2.84		5.11	7.20	
	0300	12" thick	D-9	330	.145	↓	2.46	3.58		6.04	8.60	
	9000	Minimum labor/equipment charge	D-1	2	8	Job		197		197	325	
320	0010	**CONCRETE BLOCK FOUNDATION WALL** Scaffolding not included										320
	0050	Normal-weight, trowel cut joints, parged 1/2" thick, no reinforcing										
	0200	Hollow, 8" x 16" x 6" thick	D-8	450	.089	S.F.	1.36	2.24		3.60	5.20	
	0250	8" thick		430	.093		1.50	2.34		3.84	5.55	
	0300	10" thick	↓	420	.095		2.08	2.40		4.48	6.25	
	0350	12" thick	D-9	395	.122	↓	2.25	2.99		5.24	7.45	
	1000	Reinforced										
	1100	Hollow, 8" x 16" block, 4" thick	D-8	455	.088	S.F.	1.38	2.22		3.60	5.20	
	1125	6" thick		445	.090		2	2.27		4.27	5.95	
	1150	8" thick		425	.094		2.40	2.37		4.77	6.55	
	1200	10" thick	↓	415	.096		3.26	2.43		5.69	7.60	
	1250	12" thick	D-9	390	.123	↓	3.70	3.03		6.73	9.05	
	9000	Minimum labor/equipment charge	D-1	2	8	Job		197		197	325	
330	0010	**CONCRETE BLOCK, LINTELS** Scaffolding not included										330
	0100	Including grout and horizontal reinforcing										

For expanded coverage of these items see *Means Concrete & Masonry Cost Data 1999*

042 | Unit Masonry

042 300 | Reinforced Unit Masonry

		CREW	DAILY OUTPUT	LABOR-HOURS	UNIT	MAT.	LABOR	EQUIP.	TOTAL	TOTAL INCL O&P	
330	0200	8" x 8" x 8", 1 #4 bar	D-4	300	.107	L.F.	3.31	2.61	.36	6.28	8.30	330
	0250	2 #4 bars		295	.108		3.43	2.66	.37	6.46	8.55	
	1000	12" x 8" x 8", 1 #4 bar		275	.116		4.68	2.85	.40	7.93	10.25	
	1150	2 #5 bars		270	.119		4.92	2.90	.41	8.23	10.60	
	9000	Minimum labor/equipment charge	D-1	2	8	Job		197		197	325	

042 450 | Structural Facing Tile

		CREW	DAILY OUTPUT	LABOR-HOURS	UNIT	MAT.	LABOR	EQUIP.	TOTAL	TOTAL INCL O&P	
454	0010	**STRUCTURAL FACING TILE** Scaffolding not incl, functional colors										454
	0020	6T series, 5-1/3" x 12", 2.3 pieces per S.F., glazed 1 side, 2" thick	D-8	225	.178	S.F.	4.59	4.48		9.07	12.45	
	0100	4" thick		220	.182		5.65	4.58		10.23	13.80	
	0150	Glazed 2 sides		195	.205		9.10	5.15		14.25	18.55	
	0250	6" thick		210	.190		8.40	4.80		13.20	17.20	
	0300	Glazed 2 sides		185	.216		14.45	5.45		19.90	25	
	0400	8" thick		180	.222		10.35	5.60		15.95	20.50	
	9000	Minimum labor/equipment charge	D-1	2	8	Job		197		197	325	

042 500 | Ceramic Veneer

		CREW	DAILY OUTPUT	LABOR-HOURS	UNIT	MAT.	LABOR	EQUIP.	TOTAL	TOTAL INCL O&P	
510	0010	**TERRA COTTA** Coping, split type, not glazed, 9" wide	D-1	90	.178	L.F.	4.78	4.37		9.15	12.50	510
	0100	13" wide		80	.200		7.80	4.92		12.72	16.75	
	0200	Split type, glazed, 9" wide		90	.178		5.55	4.37		9.92	13.40	
	0250	13" wide		80	.200		9.05	4.92		13.97	18.10	
	0500	Partition or back-up blocks, scored, in C.L. lots										
	0700	Non-load bearing 12" x 12", 3" thick, Special Order Only	D-8	550	.073	S.F.	4.45	1.83		6.28	7.95	
	0850	8" thick		400	.100		4.60	2.52		7.12	9.20	
	1000	Load bearing, 12" x 12", 4" thick, in walls		500	.080		3.70	2.02		5.72	7.40	
	1400	8" thick, in walls		400	.100		4.70	2.52		7.22	9.30	
	9000	Minimum labor/equipment charge	D-1	2	8	Job		197		197	325	

042 550 | Masonry Veneer

		CREW	DAILY OUTPUT	LABOR-HOURS	UNIT	MAT.	LABOR	EQUIP.	TOTAL	TOTAL INCL O&P	
554	0010	**BRICK VENEER** Scaffolding not included, truck load lots										554
	0015	Material costs incl. 3% brick and 25% mortar waste										
	2000	Standard, sel. common, 4" x 2-2/3" x 8", (6.75/S.F.)	D-8	230	.174	S.F.	2.55	4.38		6.93	10.05	
	2020	Standard, red, 4" x 2-2/3" x 8", running bond (6.75/SF)		220	.182		2.55	4.58		7.13	10.40	
	2050	Full header every 6th course (7.88/S.F.)		185	.216		2.97	5.45		8.42	12.25	
	2100	English, full header every 2nd course (10.13/S.F.)		140	.286		3.81	7.20		11.01	16.10	
	2150	Flemish, alternate header every course (9.00/S.F.)		150	.267		3.39	6.70		10.09	14.90	
	2200	Flemish, alt. header every 6th course (7.13/S.F.)		205	.195		2.69	4.92		7.61	11.10	
	2250	Full headers throughout (13.50/S.F.)		105	.381		5.05	9.60		14.65	21.50	
	2300	Rowlock course (13.50/S.F.)		100	.400		5.05	10.10		15.15	22.50	
	2350	Rowlock stretcher (4.50/S.F.)		310	.129		1.71	3.25		4.96	7.30	
	2400	Soldier course (6.75/S.F.)		200	.200		2.55	5.05		7.60	11.15	
	2450	Sailor course (4.50/S.F.)		290	.138		1.71	3.48		5.19	7.65	
	2600	Buff or gray face, running bond, (6.75/S.F.)		220	.182		2.70	4.58		7.28	10.55	
	2700	Glazed face brick, running bond		210	.190		7.10	4.80		11.90	15.75	
	2750	Full header every 6th course (7.88/S.F.)		170	.235		8.30	5.95		14.25	18.90	
	3000	Jumbo, 6" x 4" x 12" running bond (3.00/S.F.)		435	.092		3.65	2.32		5.97	7.85	
	3050	Norman, 4" x 2-2/3" x 12" running bond, (4.5/S.F.)		320	.125		3.36	3.15		6.51	8.90	
	3100	Norwegian, 4" x 3-1/5" x 12" (3.75/S.F.)		375	.107		2.15	2.69		4.84	6.80	
	3150	Economy, 4" x 4" x 8" (4.50/S.F.)		310	.129		2.15	3.25		5.40	7.75	
	3200	Engineer, 4" x 3-1/5" x 8" (5.63/S.F.)		260	.154		1.93	3.88		5.81	8.50	
	3250	Roman, 4" x 2" x 12" (6.00/S.F.)		250	.160		4.68	4.03		8.71	11.85	
	3300	SCR, 6" x 2-2/3" x 12" (4.50/S.F.)		310	.129		4.19	3.25		7.44	10	
	3350	Utility, 4" x 4" x 12" (3.00/S.F.)		450	.089		2.45	2.24		4.69	6.40	
	3400	For cavity wall construction, add						15%				
	3450	For stacked bond, add						10%				

042 | Unit Masonry

042 550 | Masonry Veneer

		CREW	DAILY OUTPUT	LABOR-HOURS	UNIT	1999 BARE COSTS				TOTAL INCL O&P
						MAT.	LABOR	EQUIP.	TOTAL	
3500	For interior veneer construction, add						15%			
3550	For curved walls, add						30%			
9000	Minimum labor/equipment charge	D-1	2	8	Job		197		197	325

042 700 | Glass Unit Masonry

		CREW	DAILY OUTPUT	LABOR-HOURS	UNIT	MAT.	LABOR	EQUIP.	TOTAL	TOTAL INCL O&P
0010	**GLASS BLOCK** Scaffolding not included									
0100	Plain, 4" thick, under 1,000 S.F., 6" x 6" block	D-8	115	.348	S.F.	13.85	8.75		22.60	30
0150	8" x 8" block		160	.250		9.40	6.30		15.70	21
0200	12" x 12" block		175	.229		11.20	5.75		16.95	22
0300	1,000 to 5,000 S.F., 6" x 6" block		135	.296		13.40	7.45		20.85	27
0350	8" x 8" block		190	.211		9.05	5.30		14.35	18.80
0400	12" x 12" block		215	.186		10.85	4.69		15.54	19.70
0700	For solar reflective blocks, add					100%				
0800	Under 1,000 S.F., 4" x 8" blocks	D-8	145	.276	S.F.	13.05	6.95		20	26
0850	Over 5,000 S.F.		170	.235		12.15	5.95		18.10	23
1000	Thinline, plain, 3-1/8" thick, under 1,000 S.F., 6" x 6" block		115	.348		11.60	8.75		20.35	27.50
1050	8" x 8" block		160	.250		6.65	6.30		12.95	17.75
1400	For cleaning block after installation (both sides), add		1,000	.040		.10	1.01		1.11	1.78
9000	Minimum labor/equipment charge	D-1	2	8	Job		197		197	325

044 | Stone

044 100 | Rough Stone

		CREW	DAILY OUTPUT	LABOR-HOURS	UNIT	MAT.	LABOR	EQUIP.	TOTAL	TOTAL INCL O&P
0011	**ROUGH STONE WALL**, Dry									
0100	Random fieldstone, under 18" thick	D-12	60	.533	C.F.	9.75	13.40		23.15	33
0150	Over 18" thick	"	63	.508	"	12.50	12.75		25.25	35
9000	Minimum labor/equipment charge	D-1	2	8	Job		197		197	325

044 200 | Cut Stone

		CREW	DAILY OUTPUT	LABOR-HOURS	UNIT	MAT.	LABOR	EQUIP.	TOTAL	TOTAL INCL O&P
0010	**BLUESTONE** Cut to size									
0500	Sills, natural cleft, 10" wide to 6' long, 1-1/2" thick	D-11	70	.343	L.F.	9.05	9		18.05	25
0550	2" thick		63	.381		10.75	10		20.75	28.50
0600	Smooth finish, 1-1/2" thick		70	.343		13.60	9		22.60	30
0650	2" thick		63	.381		15.90	10		25.90	34
0800	Thermal finish, 1-1/2" thick		70	.343		15.25	9		24.25	31.50
0850	2" thick		63	.381		16.10	10		26.10	34.50
1000	Stair treads, natural cleft, 12" wide, 6' long, 1-1/2" thick	D-10	115	.348		13.65	9.05	3.40	26.10	33.50
1050	2" thick		105	.381		15.25	9.90	3.73	28.88	37
1100	Smooth finish, 1-1/2" thick		115	.348		17.85	9.05	3.40	30.30	38
1150	2" thick		105	.381		18.70	9.90	3.73	32.33	41
1300	Thermal finish, 1-1/2" thick		115	.348		19.95	9.05	3.40	32.40	40.50
1350	2" thick		105	.381		22.50	9.90	3.73	36.13	45.50
9000	Minimum labor/equipment charge	D-1	2.50	6.400	Job		157		157	261

044 550 | Marble

		CREW	DAILY OUTPUT	LABOR-HOURS	UNIT	MAT.	LABOR	EQUIP.	TOTAL	TOTAL INCL O&P
0011	**MARBLE** Ashlar, split face, 4" + or - thick, random									
0040	lengths 1' to 4' & heights 2" to 7-1/2", average	D-8	175	.229	S.F.	13.35	5.75		19.10	24
0100	Base, polished, 3/4" or 7/8" thick, polished, 6" high	D-10	65	.615	L.F.	12.10	15.95	6	34.05	46
0260										

For expanded coverage of these items see *Means Concrete & Masonry Cost Data 1999*

044 | Stone

044 550 | Marble

			CREW	DAILY OUTPUT	LABOR-HOURS	UNIT	1999 BARE COSTS MAT.	LABOR	EQUIP.	TOTAL	TOTAL INCL O&P	
554	0300	Carvings or bas relief, from templates, average	D-10	80	.500	S.F.	108	13	4.89	125.89	146	554
	0350	Maximum	"	80	.500	"	252	13	4.89	269.89	305	
	1000	Facing, polished finish, cut to size, 3/4" to 7/8" thick										
	1050	Average	D-10	130	.308	S.F.	17.80	8	3.01	28.81	36	
	1100	Maximum	"	130	.308	"	41	8	3.01	52.01	62	
	2500	Flooring, polished tiles, 12" x 12" x 3/8" thick										
	2510	Thin set, average	D-11	90	.267	S.F.	8.25	7		15.25	20.50	
	2600	Maximum		90	.267		30	7		37	44.50	
	2700	Mortar bed, average		65	.369		8.40	9.70		18.10	25.50	
	2740	Maximum		65	.369		27.50	9.70		37.20	46	
	3500	Thresholds, 3' long, 7/8" thick, 4" to 5" wide, plain	D-12	24	1.333	Ea.	12.85	33.50		46.35	69.50	
	3550	Beveled		24	1.333	"	14.95	33.50		48.45	72	
	3700	Window stools, polished, 7/8" thick, 5" wide		85	.376	L.F.	12	9.45		21.45	29	
	9000	Minimum labor/equipment charge	D-1	2	8	Job		197		197	325	

044 600 | Limestone

			CREW	DAILY OUTPUT	LABOR-HOURS	UNIT	MAT.	LABOR	EQUIP.	TOTAL	TOTAL INCL O&P	
604	0012	LIMESTONE, Cut to size										604
	0020	Veneer facing panels										
	0750	5" thick, 5' x 14' panels	D-10	275	.145	S.F.	22.50	3.77	1.42	27.69	32.50	
	1000	Sugarcube finish, 2" Thick, 3' x 5' panels		275	.145		11.10	3.77	1.42	16.29	19.95	
	1050	3" Thick, 4' x 9' panels		275	.145		11.55	3.77	1.42	16.74	20.50	
	1200	4" Thick, 5' x 11' panels		275	.145		15.40	3.77	1.42	20.59	24.50	
	1400	Sugarcube, textured finish, 4-1/2" thick, 5' x 12'		275	.145		19.90	3.77	1.42	25.09	30	
	1450	5" thick, 5' x 14' panels		275	.145		23	3.77	1.42	28.19	33.50	
	2000	Coping, sugarcube finish, top & 2 sides		30	1.333	C.F.	51	34.50	13.05	98.55	128	
	2100	Sills, lintels, jambs, trim, stops, sugarcube finish, average		20	2		46	52	19.55	117.55	158	
	2150	Detailed		20	2		61	52	19.55	132.55	174	
	2300	Steps, extra hard, 14" wide, 6" rise		50	.800	L.F.	42	21	7.80	70.80	88.50	
	3000	Quoins, plain finish, 6"x12"x12"	D-12	25	1.280	Ea.	101	32		133	164	
	3050	6"x16"x24"	"	25	1.280	"	134	32		166	201	
	9000	Minimum labor/equipment charge	D-1	2	8	Job		197		197	325	

044 650 | Granite

			CREW	DAILY OUTPUT	LABOR-HOURS	UNIT	MAT.	LABOR	EQUIP.	TOTAL	TOTAL INCL O&P	
651	0010	GRANITE Cut to size										651
	0050	Veneer, polished face, 3/4" to 1-1/2" thick										
	0150	Low price, gray, light gray, etc.	D-10	130	.308	S.F.	18.55	8	3.01	29.56	37	
	0180	Medium price, pink, brown, etc.		130	.308		20.50	8	3.01	31.51	39	
	0220	High price, red, black, etc.		130	.308		31.50	8	3.01	42.51	51.50	
	2500	Steps, copings, etc., finished on more than one surface										
	2550	Minimum	D-10	50	.800	C.F.	72	21	7.80	100.80	122	
	2600	Maximum	"	50	.800	"	108	21	7.80	136.80	162	
	3500	Curbing, city street type, See Division 025-254										
	3800	Radius curbs, over 5' radius, add				L.F.	50%					
	3850	Under 5' radius, add				"	100%					
	9000	Minimum labor/equipment charge	D-1	2	8	Job		197		197	325	

044 700 | Sandstone

			CREW	DAILY OUTPUT	LABOR-HOURS	UNIT	MAT.	LABOR	EQUIP.	TOTAL	TOTAL INCL O&P	
704	0011	SANDSTONE OR BROWNSTONE										704
	0100	Sawed face veneer, 2-1/2" thick, to 2' x 4' panels	D-10	130	.308	S.F.	12.45	8	3.01	23.46	30	
	0150	4' thick, to 3'-6" x 8' panels		100	.400		12.45	10.40	3.91	26.76	35	
	0300	Split face, random sizes		100	.400		8.95	10.40	3.91	23.26	31	
	9000	Minimum labor/equipment charge	D-1	2.50	6.400	Job		157		157	261	

044 | Stone

044 750 | Slate

		CREW	DAILY OUTPUT	LABOR-HOURS	UNIT	MAT.	LABOR	EQUIP.	TOTAL	TOTAL INCL O&P
0010	**SLATE** Pennsylvania, blue gray to gray black; Vermont,									
0050	Unfading green, mottled green & purple, gray & purple									
0100	Virginia, blue black									
3100	Stair landings, 1" thick, black, clear	D-1	65	.246	S.F.	11.30	6.05		17.35	22.50
3200	Ribbon	"	65	.246	"	10.90	6.05		16.95	22
3500	Stair treads, sand finish, 1" thick x 12" wide									
3550	Under 3 L.F.	D-10	85	.471	L.F.	13.60	12.20	4.60	30.40	40
3600	3 L.F. to 6 L.F.	"	120	.333	"	14.60	8.65	3.26	26.51	34
3650										
3700	Ribbon, sand finish, 1" thick x 12" wide									
3750	To 6 L.F.	D-10	120	.333	L.F.	9.75	8.65	3.26	21.66	28.50
4000	Stools or sills, sand finish, 1" thick, 6" wide	D-12	160	.200		7.05	5		12.05	16.05
4200	10" wide		90	.356		10.65	8.90		19.55	26.50
4400	2" thick, 6" wide		140	.229		11.35	5.75		17.10	22
4600	10" wide	▼	90	.356	▼	16.95	8.90		25.85	33.50
4800	For lengths over 3', add					25%				
9000	Minimum labor/equipment charge	D-1	2.50	6.400	Job		157		157	261

045 | Masonry Restoration, Cleaning & Refractories

045 100 | Masonry Cleaning

		CREW	DAILY OUTPUT	LABOR-HOURS	UNIT	MAT.	LABOR	EQUIP.	TOTAL	TOTAL INCL O&P
0010	**CLEANING MASONRY** No staging included, unless noted									
0200	Chemical cleaning, brush and wash, minimum	D-1	800	.020	S.F.	.10	.49		.59	.92
0220	Average		400	.040		.15	.98		1.13	1.80
0240	Maximum	▼	330	.048		.20	1.19		1.39	2.19
0400	High pressure water only, minimum	B-9	2,000	.020			.44	.09	.53	.83
0420	Average		1,500	.027			.58	.12	.70	1.11
0440	Maximum		1,000	.040			.87	.18	1.05	1.66
0800	High pressure water and chemical, minimum		1,800	.022		.12	.49	.10	.71	1.05
0820	Average		1,200	.033		.17	.73	.15	1.05	1.58
0840	Maximum		800	.050		.22	1.09	.23	1.54	2.32
1200	Sandblast, wet system, minimum		1,750	.023		.13	.50	.10	.73	1.10
1220	Average		1,100	.036		.20	.79	.16	1.15	1.73
1240	Maximum		700	.057		.27	1.25	.26	1.78	2.67
1400	Dry system, minimum		2,500	.016		.13	.35	.07	.55	.82
1420	Average		1,750	.023		.20	.50	.10	.80	1.17
1440	Maximum	▼	1,000	.040		.27	.87	.18	1.32	1.96
1800	For walnut shells, add					.36			.36	.40
1820	For corn chips, add					.36			.36	.40
2000	Steam cleaning, minimum	B-9	3,000	.013			.29	.06	.35	.56
2020	Average		2,500	.016			.35	.07	.42	.67
2040	Maximum	▼	1,500	.027			.58	.12	.70	1.11
4000	Add for masking doors and windows				▼					.80
4200	Add for pedestrian protection				Job					10%
4400	Add for wire cut face brick				S.F.	.26			.26	.29
9000	Minimum labor/equipment charge	D-4	2	16	Job		390	54.50	444.50	700

For expanded coverage of these items see *Means Concrete & Masonry Cost Data 1999*

045 | Masonry Restoration, Cleaning & Refractories

045 200 | Masonry Restoration

			CREW	DAILY OUTPUT	LABOR-HOURS	UNIT	1999 BARE COSTS MAT.	LABOR	EQUIP.	TOTAL	TOTAL INCL O&P	
210	0010	**CAULKING MASONRY** No staging included, 1/2" x 1/2" joint										210
	0050	Re-caulk only, oil base	1 Bric	225	.036	L.F.	.30	.98		1.28	1.95	
	0100	Butyl		205	.039		.45	1.08		1.53	2.28	
	0200	Polysulfide		200	.040		.65	1.10		1.75	2.54	
	0300	Silicone		195	.041		.80	1.13		1.93	2.75	
	1000	Cut out and re-caulk, oil base		145	.055		.31	1.52		1.83	2.86	
	1050	Butyl		130	.062		.34	1.70		2.04	3.19	
	1100	Polysulfide		125	.064		.57	1.77		2.34	3.54	
	1150	Silicone		120	.067		.66	1.84		2.50	3.77	
	9000	Minimum labor/equipment charge		4	2	Job		55		55	91.50	
240	0010	**NEEDLE BEAM MASONRY** Incl. shoring 10' x 10' opening										240
	0400	Block, concrete, 8" thick	B-9	7.10	5.634	Ea.	28.50	123	25.50	177	265	
	0420	12" thick		6.70	5.970		40.50	130	27	197.50	293	
	0800	Brick, 4" thick with 8" backup block		5.70	7.018		40.50	153	31.50	225	335	
	1000	Brick, solid, 8" thick		6.20	6.452		28.50	141	29	198.50	299	
	1040	12" thick		4.90	8.163		40.50	178	37	255.50	385	
	1080	16" thick		4.50	8.889		65.50	194	40	299.50	440	
	2000	Add for additional floors of shoring	B-1	6	4		28.50	88.50		117	179	
	9000	Minimum labor/equipment charge	"	2	12	Job		265		265	445	
270	0010	**POINTING MASONRY**										270
	0020	Tuck pointing										
	0300	Cut and repoint brick, hard mortar, running bond	1 Bric	60	.133	S.F.	.24	3.68		3.92	6.35	
	0320	Common bond		55	.145		.24	4.01		4.25	6.90	
	0360	Flemish bond		50	.160		.25	4.42		4.67	7.60	
	0400	English bond		45	.178		.25	4.91		5.16	8.40	
	0600	Soft old mortar, running bond		80	.100		.25	2.76		3.01	4.84	
	0620	Common bond		75	.107		.24	2.94		3.18	5.15	
	0640	Flemish bond		70	.114		.25	3.15		3.40	5.50	
	0680	English bond		65	.123		.25	3.40		3.65	5.90	
	0700	Stonework, hard mortar		120	.067	L.F.	.32	1.84		2.16	3.40	
	0720	Soft old mortar		140	.057	"	.32	1.58		1.90	2.96	
	1000	Repoint, mask and grout method, running bond		80	.100	S.F.	.32	2.76		3.08	4.92	
	1020	Common bond		75	.107		.32	2.94		3.26	5.20	
	1040	Flemish bond		70	.114		.32	3.15		3.47	5.55	
	1060	English bond		65	.123		.32	3.40		3.72	5.95	
	2000	Scrub coat, sand grout on walls, minimum		120	.067		3.15	1.84		4.99	6.50	
	2020	Maximum		98	.082		2.25	2.25		4.50	6.20	
	9000	Minimum labor/equipment charge		3	2.667	Job		73.50		73.50	122	
290	0010	**TOOTHING MASONRY**										290
	0500	Brickwork, soft old mortar	1 Clab	40	.200	V.L.F.		4.29		4.29	7.20	
	0520	Hard mortar		30	.267			5.70		5.70	9.55	
	0700	Blockwork, soft old mortar		70	.114			2.45		2.45	4.10	
	0720	Hard mortar		50	.160			3.43		3.43	5.75	
	9000	Minimum labor/equipment charge		4	2	Job		43		43	72	

045 650 | Fire Brick

			CREW	DAILY OUTPUT	LABOR-HOURS	UNIT	MAT.	LABOR	EQUIP.	TOTAL	TOTAL INCL O&P	
654	0010	**FIRE CLAY** Gray, high duty, 100 lb. bag				Bag	39.50			39.50	43.50	654
	0050	100 lb. drum, premixed (400 brick per drum)				Drum	50			50	55	
656	0010	**FIREPLACE** For prefabricated fireplace, see div. 103-054										656
	0100	Brick fireplace, not incl. foundations or chimneys										
	0110	30" x 29" opening, incl. chamber, plain brickwork	D-1	.40	40	Ea.	360	985		1,345	2,025	
	0200	Fireplace box only (110 brick)	"	2	8	"	116	197		313	455	
	0300	For elaborate brickwork and details, add					35%	35%				
	0400	For hearth, brick & stone, add	D-1	2	8	Ea.	132	197		329	470	

Important: See the Reference Section for critical supporting data - Reference Nos., Crews, & City Cost Indexes

045 | Masonry Restoration, Cleaning & Refractories

045 650	Fire Brick	CREW	DAILY OUTPUT	LABOR-HOURS	UNIT	1999 BARE COSTS MAT.	LABOR	EQUIP.	TOTAL	TOTAL INCL O&P
0410	For steel angle, damper, cleanouts, add	D-1	4	4	Ea.	92	98.50		190.50	264
0600	Plain brickwork, incl. metal circulator	↓	.50	32	↓	695	785		1,480	2,075
0800	Face brick only, standard size, 8" x 2-2/3" x 4"		.30	53.333	M	360	1,300		1,660	2,575
0900	Stone fireplace, fieldstone, add				SF Face	9.50			9.50	10.45
1000	Cut stone, add				"	10			10	11
9000	Minimum labor/equipment charge	D-1	2	8	Job		197		197	325

For information about Means Estimating Seminars, see yellow pages 11 and 12 in back of book

For expanded coverage of these items see *Means Concrete & Masonry Cost Data 1999*

Division Notes

		CREW	DAILY OUTPUT	LABOR-HOURS	UNIT	1999 BARE COSTS				TOTAL INCL O&P
						MAT.	LABOR	EQUIP.	TOTAL	

Division 5
Metals

Estimating Tips
050 Materials, Coatings & Fastenings
- Nuts, bolts, washers, connection angles and plates can add a significant amount to both the tonnage of a structural steel job as well as the estimated cost. As a rule of thumb add 10% to the total weight to account for these accessories.
- Type 2 steel construction, commonly referred to as "simple construction," consists generally of field bolted connections with lateral bracing supplied by other elements of the building, such as masonry walls or x-bracing. The estimator should be aware, however, that shop connections may be accomplished by welding or bolting. The method may be particular to the fabrication shop and may have an impact on the estimated cost.

052 Steel Joists
- In any given project the total weight of open web steel joists is determined by the loads to be supported and the design. However, economies can be realized in minimizing the amount of labor used to place the joists. This is done by maximizing the joist spacing and therefore minimizing the number of joists required to be installed on the job. Certain spacings and locations may be required by the design, but in other cases maximizing the spacing and keeping it as uniform as possible will keep the costs down.

053 Metal Decking
- The takeoff and estimating of metal deck involves more than simply the area of the floor or roof and the type of deck specified or shown on the drawings. Many different sizes and types of openings may exist. Small openings for individual pipes or conduits may be drilled after the floor/roof is installed, but larger openings may require special deck lengths as well as reinforcing or structural support. The estimator should determine who will be supplying this reinforcing. Additionally, some deck terminations are part of the deck package, such as screed angles and pour stops, and others will be part of the steel contract, such as angles attached to structural members and cast-in-place angles and plates. The estimator must ensure that all pieces are accounted for in the complete estimate.

055 Metal Fabrications
- The most economical steel stairs are those that use common materials, standard details and most importantly, a uniform and relatively simple method of field assembly. Commonly available A36 channels and plates are very good choices for the main stringers of the stairs, as are angles and tees for the carrier members. Risers and treads are usually made by specialty shops, and it is most economical to use a typical detail in as many places as possible. The stairs should be pre-assembled and shipped directly to the site. The field connections should be simple and straightforward to be accomplished efficiently and with a minimum of equipment and labor.

Reference Numbers
Reference numbers are shown in bold squares at the beginning of some major classifications. These numbers refer to related items in the Reference Section. The reference information may be an estimating procedure, an alternate pricing method or technical information.

Note: Not all subdivisions listed here necessarily appear in this publication.

050 | Metal Materials, Coatings & Fastenings

050 500 | Metal Fastening

			CREW	DAILY OUTPUT	LABOR-HOURS	UNIT	1999 BARE COSTS — MAT.	LABOR	EQUIP.	TOTAL	TOTAL INCL O&P	
510	0005	**CURB EDGING**										510
	0010	Steel angle w/anchors, on forms, 1" x 1", 0.8#/L.F.	E-4	350	.091	L.F.	1.36	2.84	.23	4.43	7.15	
	0300	4" x 4" angles, 8.2#/L.F.	"	275	.116	"	8.15	3.62	.30	12.07	16.25	
	9000	Minimum labor/equipment charge	A-1	4	2	Job		43	17.15	60.15	91	
515	0010	**DRILLING** For anchors, up to 4" deep, incl. bit and layout										515
	0050	in concrete or brick walls and floors, no anchor										
	0100	Holes, 1/4" diameter	1 Carp	75	.107	Ea.	.08	2.91		2.99	4.96	
	0150	For each additional inch of depth, add		430	.019		.02	.51		.53	.87	
	0200	3/8" diameter		63	.127		.07	3.47		3.54	5.90	
	0250	For each additional inch of depth, add		340	.024		.02	.64		.66	1.10	
	0300	1/2" diameter		50	.160		.07	4.37		4.44	7.40	
	0350	For each additional inch of depth, add		250	.032		.02	.87		.89	1.48	
	0400	5/8" diameter		48	.167		.13	4.55		4.68	7.75	
	0450	For each additional inch of depth, add		240	.033		.03	.91		.94	1.56	
	0500	3/4" diameter		45	.178		.14	4.85		4.99	8.25	
	0550	For each additional inch of depth, add		220	.036		.03	.99		1.02	1.70	
	0600	7/8" diameter		43	.186		.17	5.10		5.27	8.70	
	0650	For each additional inch of depth, add		210	.038		.04	1.04		1.08	1.79	
	0700	1" diameter		40	.200		.20	5.45		5.65	9.35	
	0750	For each additional inch of depth, add		190	.042		.05	1.15		1.20	1.98	
	0800	1-1/4" diameter		38	.211		.29	5.75		6.04	9.90	
	0850	For each additional inch of depth, add		180	.044		.07	1.21		1.28	2.11	
	0900	1-1/2" diameter		35	.229		.47	6.25		6.72	10.95	
	0950	For each additional inch of depth, add		165	.048		.12	1.32		1.44	2.35	
	1000	For ceiling installations, add						40%				
	1100	Drilling & layout for drywall or plaster walls, no anchor										
	1200	Holes, 1/4" diameter	1 Carp	150	.053	Ea.	.01	1.46		1.47	2.45	
	1300	3/8" diameter		140	.057		.01	1.56		1.57	2.62	
	1400	1/2" diameter		130	.062		.01	1.68		1.69	2.82	
	1500	3/4" diameter		120	.067		.02	1.82		1.84	3.07	
	1600	1" diameter		110	.073		.03	1.99		2.02	3.35	
	1700	1-1/4" diameter		100	.080		.04	2.18		2.22	3.70	
	1800	1-1/2" diameter		90	.089		.06	2.43		2.49	4.12	
	1900	For ceiling installations, add						40%				
	2000	Minimum labor/equipment charge	1 Carp	4	2	Job		54.50		54.50	91.50	
520	0010	**EXPANSION ANCHORS** & shields										520
	0100	Bolt anchors for concrete, brick or stone, no layout and drilling										
	0200	Expansion shields, zinc, 1/4" diameter, 1" long, single	1 Carp	90	.089	Ea.	.85	2.43		3.28	5	
	0300	1-3/8" long, double		85	.094		.97	2.57		3.54	5.35	
	0400	3/8" diameter, 2" long, single		85	.094		1.45	2.57		4.02	5.90	
	0500	2" long, double		80	.100		1.79	2.73		4.52	6.55	
	0600	1/2" diameter, 2-1/2" long, single		80	.100		2.40	2.73		5.13	7.20	
	0700	2-1/2" long, double		75	.107		2.32	2.91		5.23	7.40	
	0800	5/8" diameter, 2-5/8" long, single		75	.107		3.43	2.91		6.34	8.65	
	0900	3" long, double		70	.114		3.43	3.12		6.55	8.95	
	1000	3/4" diameter, 2-3/4" long, single		70	.114		5.10	3.12		8.22	10.80	
	1100	4" long, double		65	.123		6.80	3.36		10.16	13.10	
	1410	Concrete anchor, w/rod & epoxy cartridge, 1-3/4" diameter x 15" long	E-22	20	1.200		72	34.50		106.50	136	
	1415	18" long		17	1.412		86	40.50		126.50	162	
	1420	2" diameter x 18" long		16	1.500		110	43		153	193	
	1425	24" long		15	1.600		144	46		190	234	
	1430	Chemical anchor, w/rod & epoxy cartridge, 3/4" diam. x 9-1/2" long		27	.889		10.45	25.50		35.95	54	
	1435	1" diameter x 11-3/4" long		24	1		19.80	28.50		48.30	69.50	
	1440	1-1/4" diameter x 14" long		21	1.143		38	33		71	96	
	1500	Self drilling anchor, snap-off, for 1/4" diameter bolt	1 Carp	26	.308		.93	8.40		9.33	15.05	

050 | Metal Materials, Coatings & Fastenings

050 500 | Metal Fastening

			CREW	DAILY OUTPUT	LABOR-HOURS	UNIT	1999 BARE COSTS MAT.	LABOR	EQUIP.	TOTAL	TOTAL INCL O&P	
520	1600	3/8" diameter bolt	1 Carp	23	.348	Ea.	1.40	9.50		10.90	17.45	520
	1700	1/2" diameter bolt		20	.400		2.11	10.90		13.01	20.50	
	1800	5/8" diameter bolt		18	.444		3.57	12.15		15.72	24.50	
	1900	3/4" diameter bolt		16	.500		6.45	13.65		20.10	30	
	2100	Hollow wall anchors for gypsum wall board, plaster or tile										
	2300	1/8" diameter, short				Ea.	.25			.25	.28	
	2400	Long					.28			.28	.31	
	2500	3/16" diameter, short					.59			.59	.65	
	2600	Long					.63			.63	.69	
	2700	1/4" diameter, short					.74			.74	.81	
	2800	Long					.85			.85	.94	
	3000	Toggle bolts, bright steel, 1/8" diameter, 2" long	1 Carp	85	.094		.29	2.57		2.86	4.62	
	3100	4" long		80	.100		.38	2.73		3.11	4.99	
	3200	3/16" diameter, 3" long		80	.100		.36	2.73		3.09	4.97	
	3300	6" long		75	.107		.55	2.91		3.46	5.50	
	3400	1/4" diameter, 3" long		75	.107		.40	2.91		3.31	5.30	
	3500	6" long		70	.114		.60	3.12		3.72	5.85	
	3600	3/8" diameter, 3" long		70	.114		.88	3.12		4	6.15	
	3700	6" long		60	.133		1.30	3.64		4.94	7.55	
	3800	1/2" diameter, 4" long		60	.133		2.79	3.64		6.43	9.15	
	3900	6" long		50	.160		3.71	4.37		8.08	11.40	
	4000	Nailing anchors										
	4100	Nylon nailing anchor, 1/4" diameter, 1" long				C	15.45			15.45	17	
	4200	1-1/2" long					19.90			19.90	22	
	4300	2" long					33			33	36.50	
	4400	Metal nailing anchor, 1/4" diameter, 1" long					21.50			21.50	24	
	4500	1-1/2" long					29.50			29.50	32.50	
	4600	2" long					38			38	41.50	
	8000	Wedge anchors, not including layout or drilling										
	8050	Carbon steel, 1/4" diameter, 1-3/4" long	1 Carp	150	.053	Ea.	.33	1.46		1.79	2.81	
	8100	3 1/4" long		145	.055		.50	1.51		2.01	3.07	
	8150	3/8" diameter, 2-1/4" long		150	.053		.60	1.46		2.06	3.09	
	8200	5" long		145	.055		1.04	1.51		2.55	3.66	
	8250	1/2" diameter, 2-3/4" long		140	.057		.88	1.56		2.44	3.58	
	8300	7" long		130	.062		1.54	1.68		3.22	4.51	
	8350	5/8" diameter, 3-1/2" long		130	.062		1.66	1.68		3.34	4.64	
	8400	8-1/2" long		115	.070		3.24	1.90		5.14	6.75	
	8450	3/4" diameter, 4-1/4" long		115	.070		2.16	1.90		4.06	5.55	
	8500	10" long		100	.080		4.91	2.18		7.09	9.05	
	8550	1" diameter, 6" long		100	.080		7.40	2.18		9.58	11.80	
	8575	9" long		80	.100		9.60	2.73		12.33	15.10	
	8600	12" long		80	.100		10.40	2.73		13.13	15.95	
	8650	1-1/4" diameter, 9" long		70	.114		14.50	3.12		17.62	21	
	8700	12" long		60	.133		14.80	3.64		18.44	22.50	
	8750	For type 303 stainless steel, add					350%					
	8800	For type 316 stainless steel, add					450%					
	9000	Minimum labor/equipment charge	1 Carp	4	2	Job		54.50		54.50	91.50	
530	0005	**LAG SCREWS**										530
	0010	Steel, 1/4" diameter, 2" long	1 Carp	200	.040	Ea.	.05	1.09		1.14	1.89	
	0200	1/2" diameter, 3" long		130	.062		.27	1.68		1.95	3.11	
	0300	5/8" diameter, 3" long		120	.067		.53	1.82		2.35	3.64	
540	0010	**MACHINERY ANCHORS** Standard, flush mounted,										540
	0020	incl. stud w/fiber plug, connecting nut, washer & bolt										
	0200	Material only, 1/2" diameter stud & bolt				Ea.	30.50			30.50	33.50	
	0300	5/8" diameter					34.50			34.50	38	

103

050 | Metal Materials, Coatings & Fastenings

050 500 | Metal Fastening

			CREW	DAILY OUTPUT	LABOR-HOURS	UNIT	MAT.	LABOR	EQUIP.	TOTAL	TOTAL INCL O&P	
540	0500	3/4" diameter				Ea.	37.50			37.50	41.50	540
	0600	7/8" diameter					43.50			43.50	47.50	
	0800	1" diameter					47.50			47.50	52.50	
	0900	1-1/4" diameter					60.50			60.50	66.50	
550	0005	**POWDER ACTUATED** Tools & fasteners										550
	0010	Stud driver, .22 caliber, buy, minimum				Ea.	287			287	315	
	0100	Maximum				"	505			505	555	
	0300	Powder charges for above, low velocity				C	15.05			15.05	16.55	
	0400	Standard velocity					25			25	27.50	
	0600	Drive pins & studs, 1/4" & 3/8" diam., to 3" long, minimum					22			22	24	
	0700	Maximum					57			57	63	
	0800	Pneumatic stud driver for 1/8" diameter studs				Ea.	1,850			1,850	2,025	
	0900	Drive pins for above, 1/2" to 3/4" long				M	400			400	440	
565	0005	**WELDED STUDS**										565
	0010	1/4" diameter, 2-11/16" long	E-10	1,030	.016	Ea.	.16	.49	.49	1.14	1.65	
	0100	4-1/8" long		1,030	.016		.13	.49	.49	1.11	1.61	
	0200	3/8" diameter, 4-1/8" long		1,030	.016		.20	.49	.49	1.18	1.69	
	0300	6-1/8" long		1,030	.016		.25	.49	.49	1.23	1.75	
	9000	Minimum labor/equipment charge	1 Sswk	2	4	Job		122		122	233	
575	0005	**WELDING STRUCTURAL**	R050-520									575
	0010	Field welding, 1/8" E6011, cost per welder, no operating engr.	E-14	8	1	Hr.	2.76	32.50	10.30	45.56	76.50	
	0200	With 1/2 operating engineer	E-13	8	1.500		2.76	46	10.30	59.06	98	
	0300	With 1 operating engineer	E-12	8	2		2.76	60	10.30	73.06	119	
	0500	With no operating engineer, 2# weld rod per ton	E-14	8	1	Ton	2.76	32.50	10.30	45.56	76.50	
	0600	8# E6011 per ton	"	2	4		11	130	41	182	305	
	0800	With one operating engineer per welder, 2# E6011 per ton	E-12	8	2		2.76	60	10.30	73.06	119	
	0900	8# E6011 per ton	"	2	8		11	239	41	291	480	
	1200	Continuous fillet, stick welding, incl. equipment										
	1300	Single pass, 1/8" thick, 0.1#/L.F.	E-14	240	.033	L.F.	.14	1.09	.34	1.57	2.60	
	1400	3/16" thick, 0.2#/L.F.		120	.067		.28	2.17	.69	3.14	5.20	
	1500	1/4" thick, 0.3#/L.F.		80	.100		.41	3.26	1.03	4.70	7.80	
	1610	5/16" thick, 0.4#/L.F.		60	.133		.55	4.35	1.37	6.27	10.35	
	1800	3 passes, 3/8" thick, 0.5#/L.F.		48	.167		.69	5.45	1.72	7.86	13	
	2010	4 passes, 1/2" thick, 0.7#/L.F.		34	.235		.96	7.65	2.42	11.03	18.30	
	2200	5 to 6 passes, 3/4" thick, 1.3#/L.F.		19	.421		1.79	13.75	4.33	19.87	32.50	
	2400	8 to 11 passes, 1" thick, 2.4#/L.F.		10	.800		3.31	26	8.25	37.56	62	
	2600	For all position welding, add, minimum						20%				
	2700	Maximum						300%				
	2900	For semi-automatic welding, deduct, minimum						5%				
	3000	Maximum						15%				
	4000	Cleaning and welding plates, bars, or rods										
	4010	to existing beams, columns, or trusses	E-14	12	.667	L.F.	.69	21.50	6.85	29.04	50	
	9000	Minimum labor/equipment charge	"	4	2	Job		65	20.50	85.50	147	

051 | Structural Metal Framing

051 100 | Bracing

			CREW	DAILY OUTPUT	LABOR-HOURS	UNIT	MAT.	LABOR	EQUIP.	TOTAL	TOTAL INCL O&P	
108	0010	**BRACING**										108
	0300	Let-in, "T" shaped, 22 ga. galv. steel, studs at 16" O.C.	1 Carp	5.80	1.379	C.L.F.	37	37.50		74.50	104	

Important: See the Reference Section for critical supporting data - Reference Nos., Crews, & City Cost Indexes

051 | Structural Metal Framing

051 100 | Bracing

			CREW	DAILY OUTPUT	LABOR-HOURS	UNIT	MAT.	LABOR	EQUIP.	TOTAL	TOTAL INCL O&P	
108	0400	Studs at 24" O.C.	1 Carp	6	1.333	C.L.F.	37	36.50		73.50	102	108
	0500	16 ga. galv. steel straps, studs at 16" O.C.		6	1.333		48	36.50		84.50	114	
	0600	Studs at 24" O.C.	▼	6.20	1.290	▼	48	35		83	112	
110	0005	**PIPE SUPPORT FRAMING**										110
	0010	Under 10#/L.F.	E-4	3,900	.008	Lb.	.90	.26	.02	1.18	1.50	
	0200	10.1 to 15#/L.F.		4,300	.007		.78	.23	.02	1.03	1.32	
	0400	15.1 to 20#/L.F.		4,800	.007		.72	.21	.02	.95	1.20	
	0600	Over 20#/L.F.	▼	5,400	.006	▼	.66	.18	.02	.86	1.10	

051 200 | Structural Steel

			CREW	DAILY OUTPUT	LABOR-HOURS	UNIT	MAT.	LABOR	EQUIP.	TOTAL	TOTAL INCL O&P	
212	0005	**CANOPY FRAMING**										212
	0010	6" and 8" members	E-4	3,000	.011	Lb.	.86	.33	.03	1.22	1.60	
	9000	Minimum labor/equipment charge	1 Sswk	1	8	Job		245		245	465	
215	0010	**CEILING SUPPORTS**										215
	1000	Entrance door/folding partition supports	E-4	60	.533	L.F.	13.20	16.60	1.37	31.17	47.50	
	1100	Linear accelerator door supports		14	2.286		60	71	5.85	136.85	207	
	1200	Lintels or shelf angles, hung, exterior hot dipped galv.		267	.120		9.75	3.73	.31	13.79	18.20	
	1250	Two coats primer paint instead of galv.		267	.120	▼	7.80	3.73	.31	11.84	16.05	
	1400	Monitor support, ceiling hung, expansion bolted		4	8	Ea.	209	249	20.50	478.50	730	
	1450	Hung from pre-set inserts		6	5.333		219	166	13.70	398.70	570	
	1600	Motor supports for overhead doors		4	8	▼	106	249	20.50	375.50	615	
	1700	Partition support for heavy folding partitions, without pocket		24	1.333	L.F.	30	41.50	3.43	74.93	116	
	1750	Supports at pocket only		12	2.667		60	83	6.85	149.85	232	
	2000	Rolling grilles & fire door supports		34	.941	▼	25.50	29.50	2.42	57.42	86.50	
	2100	Spider-leg light supports, expansion bolted to ceiling slab		8	4	Ea.	86	124	10.30	220.30	345	
	2150	Hung from pre-set inserts		12	2.667	"	90	83	6.85	179.85	265	
	2400	Toilet partition support		36	.889	L.F.	30	27.50	2.28	59.78	88	
	2500	X-ray travel gantry support	▼	12	2.667	"	103	83	6.85	192.85	279	
220	0005	**COLUMNS** R051-210										220
	0010	Aluminum, extruded, stock units, 6" diameter	E-4	240	.133	L.F.	8.10	4.15	.34	12.59	17.20	
	0100	8" diameter	"	170	.188		10.80	5.85	.48	17.13	23.50	
	0500	For square columns, add to column prices above					50%					
	0800	Steel, concrete filled, extra strong pipe, 3-1/2" diameter	E-2	660	.085		18.35	2.53	1.53	22.41	26.50	
	0830	4" diameter		780	.072		20	2.14	1.30	23.44	27.50	
	0890	5" diameter		1,020	.055	▼	25.50	1.63	.99	28.12	32	
	1500	Steel pipe, extra strong, no concrete, 3" to 5" diameter		16,000	.004	Lb.	.62	.10	.06	.78	.94	
	3300	Structural tubing, square, A500GrB, 4" to 6" square, light section	▼	11,270	.005	"	.82	.15	.09	1.06	1.27	
	9000	Minimum labor/equipment charge	1 Sswk	1	8	Job		245		245	465	
230	0010	**LIGHTWEIGHT FRAMING** R051-240										230
	0200	For steel studs see division 092-612										
	0400	Angle framing, 4" and larger	E-4	3,000	.011	Lb.	.85	.33	.03	1.21	1.60	
	0450	Less than 4" angles		1,800	.018		.91	.55	.05	1.51	2.10	
	0600	Channel framing, 8" and larger		3,500	.009		.93	.28	.02	1.23	1.59	
	0650	Less than 8" channels	▼	2,000	.016		.94	.50	.04	1.48	2.03	
	1000	Continuous slotted channel framing system, minimum	2 Sswk	2,400	.007		1.20	.20		1.40	1.71	
	1200	Maximum	"	1,600	.010		2.16	.31		2.47	2.96	
	1250	Plate & bar stock for reinforcing beams and trusses					1.02			1.02	1.12	
	1300	Cross bracing, rods, 3/4" diameter	E-3	700	.034		.96	1.07	.12	2.15	3.23	
	1310	7/8" diameter		700	.034		.81	1.07	.12	2	3.06	
	1320	1" diameter		700	.034		.81	1.07	.12	2	3.06	
	1330	Angle, 5" x 5" x 3/8"		2,800	.009		.84	.27	.03	1.14	1.46	
	1350	Hanging lintels, average	▼	850	.028	▼	.90	.88	.10	1.88	2.78	

051 | Structural Metal Framing

051 200 | Structural Steel

			CREW	DAILY OUTPUT	LABOR-HOURS	UNIT	1999 BARE COSTS				TOTAL INCL O&P	
							MAT.	LABOR	EQUIP.	TOTAL		
230	1380	Roof frames, 3'-0" square, 5' span	E-2	4,200	.013	Lb.	.81	.40	.24	1.45	1.88	230
	1400	Tie rod, not upset, 1-1/2" to 4" diameter, with turnbuckle	2 Sswk	800	.020		.90	.61		1.51	2.16	
	1420	No turnbuckle		700	.023		.81	.70		1.51	2.22	
	1500	Upset, 1-3/4" to 4" diameter, with turnbuckle		800	.020		1.02	.61		1.63	2.29	
	1520	No turnbuckle		700	.023		.90	.70		1.60	2.32	
	1600	Tubular aluminum framing for window wall, minimum		600	.027		4.03	.82		4.85	6	
	1800	Maximum		500	.032		11.90	.98		12.88	14.95	
	9000	Minimum labor/equipment charge		2	8	Job		245		245	465	
232	0005	**LINTELS**										232
	0010	Plain steel angles, under 500 lb.	1 Bric	550	.015	Lb.	.60	.40		1	1.32	
	0100	500 to 1000 lb.		640	.013		.57	.35		.92	1.20	
	0200	1,000 to 2,000 lb.		640	.013		.53	.35		.88	1.15	
	0300	2,000 to 4,000 lb.		640	.013		.48	.35		.83	1.10	
	0500	For built-up angles and plates, add to above					.60			.60	.66	
	0700	For engineering, add to above					.15			.15	.16	
	0900	For galvanizing, add to above, under 500 lb.					.42			.42	.46	
	1000	Over 2,000 lb.					.30			.30	.33	
	2000	Steel angles, 3-1/2" x 3", 1/4" thick, 2'-6" long	1 Bric	50	.160	Ea.	8.10	4.42		12.52	16.20	
	2100	4'-6" long		45	.178		14.60	4.91		19.51	24	
	2500	3-1/2" x 3-1/2" x 5/16", 5'-0" long		44	.182		21.50	5		26.50	32.50	
	2600	4" x 3-1/2", 1/4" thick, 5'-0" long		40	.200		18.60	5.50		24.10	29.50	
	2700	9'-0" long		35	.229		33.50	6.30		39.80	47.50	
	2800	4" x 3-1/2" x 5/16", 7'-0" long		38	.211		32.50	5.80		38.30	45	
	2900	5" x 3-1/2" x 5/16", 10'-0" long		35	.229		52	6.30		58.30	68	
	3500	For precast concrete lintels, see div. 034-802										
	9000	Minimum labor/equipment charge	1 Bric	4	2	Job		55		55	91.50	
240	0010	**STEEL CUTTING**										240
	0020	Hand burning, incl. preparation, torch cutting & grinding, no staging										
	0100	Steel to 1/2" thick	E-14	70	.114	L.F.		3.73	1.18	4.91	8.40	
	0150	3/4" thick		50	.160			5.20	1.65	6.85	11.75	
	0200	1" thick		45	.178			5.80	1.83	7.63	13.05	
	9000	Minimum labor/equipment charge	A-1	2	4	Job		86	34.50	120.50	182	
255	0010	**STRUCTURAL STEEL PROJECTS** Bolted, unless noted otherwise										255
	1300	Industrial bldgs., 1 story, beams & girders, steel bearing	E-5	12.90	6.202	Ton	1,200	187	85	1,472	1,775	
	1400	Masonry bearing		10	8		1,200	242	109	1,551	1,900	
	1600	1 story with roof trusses, steel bearing		10.60	7.547		1,425	228	103	1,756	2,075	
	1700	Masonry bearing		8.30	9.639		1,425	291	132	1,848	2,225	
260	0010	**STRUCTURAL STEEL** Bolted, incl. fabrication										260
	0050	Beams, W 6 x 9	E-2	720	.078	L.F.	5.95	2.32	1.41	9.68	12.30	
	0100	W 8 x 10		720	.078		6.60	2.32	1.41	10.33	13	
	0150	W 10 x 15		720	.078		9.90	2.32	1.41	13.63	16.65	
	0200	Columns, W 6 x 15		540	.104		9.90	3.09	1.87	14.86	18.60	
	0250	W 8 x 31		540	.104		20.50	3.09	1.87	25.46	30	
	0500	Girders, W 12 x 22		900	.062		14.50	1.85	1.12	17.47	20.50	
	0550	W 14 x 26		900	.062		17.15	1.85	1.12	20.12	23.50	
	0600	W 16 x 31		900	.062		20.50	1.85	1.12	23.47	27	
	0700	Joists (bar joists, H or K series), span to 30'	E-7	30,000	.003	Lb.	.51	.08	.04	.63	.75	
	0750	Span to 50'	"	20,000	.004	"	.50	.12	.06	.68	.82	
	9000	Minimum labor/equipment charge	E-2	2	28	Job		835	505	1,340	2,075	

052 | Metal Joists

052 100 | Steel Joists

		CREW	DAILY OUTPUT	LABOR-HOURS	UNIT	1999 BARE COSTS MAT.	LABOR	EQUIP.	TOTAL	TOTAL INCL O&P	
108	0005 **COLD-FORMED JOISTS**										108
	0120 Galvanized, 6" deep, 16 gauge	E-4	1,800	.018	L.F.	1.10	.55	.05	1.70	2.31	
	0140 14 gauge		1,800	.018		1.38	.55	.05	1.98	2.62	
	0160 8" deep, 16 gauge		1,550	.021		1.31	.64	.05	2	2.72	
	0180 14 gauge		1,550	.021		1.65	.64	.05	2.34	3.10	
	0200 10" deep, 14 gauge		1,350	.024		1.97	.74	.06	2.77	3.64	
	0220 12 gauge		1,350	.024		2.86	.74	.06	3.66	4.62	
	0240 12" deep, 14 gauge		1,200	.027		2.25	.83	.07	3.15	4.13	
	0260 12 gauge		1,200	.027		3.25	.83	.07	4.15	5.25	
	9000 Minimum labor/equipment charge	1 Sswk	2	4	Job		122		122	233	
110	0010 **OPEN WEB JOISTS**, Truckload lots										110
	0020 K series, horizontal bridging, spans up to 30', minimum	E-7	15	5.333	Ton	990	161	78.50	1,229.50	1,475	
	0050 Average		12	6.667		930	201	98	1,229	1,500	
	0080 Maximum		9	8.889		1,225	269	131	1,625	2,000	
	0410 Span 30' to 50', minimum		17	4.706		875	142	69	1,086	1,300	
	0440 Average		17	4.706		900	142	69	1,111	1,325	
	0460 Maximum		10	8		915	242	118	1,275	1,575	
	1010 CS series, horizontal bridging										
	1020 Spans to 30', minimum	E-7	15	5.333	Ton	815	161	78.50	1,054.50	1,275	
	1040 Average		12	6.667		850	201	98	1,149	1,425	
	1060 Maximum		9	8.889		945	269	131	1,345	1,700	
	2000 LH series, bolted cross bridging										
	2020 Spans to 96', minimum	E-7	16	5	Ton	930	151	73.50	1,154.50	1,375	
	2040 Average		13	6.154		1,025	186	90.50	1,301.50	1,575	
	2080 Maximum		11	7.273		1,325	220	107	1,652	1,975	
	3010 DLH series, bolted cross bridging										
	3020 Spans to 144' (shipped in 2 pieces), minimum	E-7	16	5	Ton	995	151	73.50	1,219.50	1,450	
	3040 Average		13	6.154		885	186	90.50	1,161.50	1,425	
	3100 Maximum		11	7.273		1,050	220	107	1,377	1,675	
	4010 SLH series, bolted cross bridging										
	4020 Spans to 200', minimum	E-7	16	5	Ton	880	151	73.50	1,104.50	1,325	
	4040 Average		13	6.154		950	186	90.50	1,226.50	1,500	
	4060 Maximum		11	7.273		1,200	220	107	1,527	1,825	
	6100 For L.T.L. lots, add					10%	15%				

053 | Metal Decking

053 100 | Steel Deck

		CREW	DAILY OUTPUT	LABOR-HOURS	UNIT	1999 BARE COSTS MAT.	LABOR	EQUIP.	TOTAL	TOTAL INCL O&P	
104	0010 **METAL DECKING** Steel decking										104
	0200 Cellular units, galvanized, 2" deep, 20-20 gauge, over 15 squares	E-4	1,460	.022	S.F.	2.81	.68	.06	3.55	4.45	
	0400 3" deep, galvanized, 20-20 gauge		1,375	.023		2.93	.72	.06	3.71	4.67	
	1000 4-1/2" deep, galvanized, 20-18 gauge		1,100	.029		6.15	.90	.07	7.12	8.55	
	1500 For acoustical deck, add					15%					
	1900 For multi-story or congested site, add						50%				
	2100 Open type, galv., 1-1/2" deep wide rib, 22 gauge, under 50 squares	E-4	4,500	.007	S.F.	.95	.22	.02	1.19	1.48	
	2400 Over 500 squares		5,100	.006		.72	.20	.02	.94	1.18	
	5200 Non-cellular composite deck, galv., 2" deep, 22 gauge		3,860	.008		.96	.26	.02	1.24	1.56	
	5300 20 gauge		3,600	.009		1.08	.28	.02	1.38	1.75	
	5400 18 gauge		3,380	.009		1.49	.29	.02	1.80	2.23	
	5500 16 gauge		3,200	.010		1.75	.31	.03	2.09	2.55	

053 | Metal Decking

053 100 | Steel Deck

		CREW	DAILY OUTPUT	LABOR-HOURS	UNIT	1999 BARE COSTS MAT.	LABOR	EQUIP.	TOTAL	TOTAL INCL O&P	
104	5700	3" deep, galv., 22 gauge	E-4	3,200	.010	S.F.	1.05	.31	.03	1.39	1.78	104
	5800	20 gauge		3,000	.011		1.16	.33	.03	1.52	1.94	
	5900	18 gauge		2,850	.011		1.53	.35	.03	1.91	2.37	
	6000	16 gauge		2,700	.012		2.03	.37	.03	2.43	2.96	
	6100	Slab form, steel, 28 gauge, 9/16" deep, uncoated		4,000	.008		.46	.25	.02	.73	.99	
	6200	Galvanized		4,000	.008		.51	.25	.02	.78	1.05	
	9000	Minimum labor/equipment charge	1 Sswk	1	8	Job		245		245	465	

054 | Cold Formed Metal Framing

054 100 | Load Bearing Metal Studs

		CREW	DAILY OUTPUT	LABOR-HOURS	UNIT	1999 BARE COSTS MAT.	LABOR	EQUIP.	TOTAL	TOTAL INCL O&P	
104	0010	**BRACING**, shear wall X-bracing, per 10' x 10' bay, one face										104
	0120	Metal strap, 20 ga x 4" wide	2 Carp	18	.889	Ea.	14.25	24.50		38.75	56	
	0130	6" wide		18	.889		21	24.50		45.50	63.50	
	0160	18 ga x 4" wide		16	1		22.50	27.50		50	70.50	
	0170	6" wide		16	1		33	27.50		60.50	82	
	0410	Continuous strap bracing, per horizontal row on both faces										
	0420	Metal strap, 20 ga x 2" wide, studs 12" O.C.	1 Carp	7	1.143	C.L.F.	43.50	31		74.50	99.50	
	0430	16" O.C.		8	1		43.50	27.50		71	93	
	0440	24" O.C.		10	.800		43.50	22		65.50	84	
	0450	18 ga x 2" wide, studs 12" O.C.		6	1.333		60.50	36.50		97	128	
	0460	16" O.C.		7	1.143		60.50	31		91.50	119	
	0470	24" O.C.		8	1		60.50	27.50		88	112	
106	0010	**BRIDGING**, solid between studs w/ 1-1/4" leg track, per stud bay										106
	0200	Studs 12" O.C., 18 ga x 2-1/2" wide	1 Carp	125	.064	Ea.	.56	1.75		2.31	3.53	
	0210	3-5/8" wide		120	.067		.65	1.82		2.47	3.77	
	0220	4" wide		120	.067		.67	1.82		2.49	3.79	
	0230	6" wide		115	.070		.89	1.90		2.79	4.16	
	0240	8" wide		110	.073		1.14	1.99		3.13	4.57	
	0300	16 ga x 2-1/2" wide		115	.070		.69	1.90		2.59	3.93	
	0310	3-5/8" wide		110	.073		.80	1.99		2.79	4.20	
	0320	4" wide		110	.073		.84	1.99		2.83	4.24	
	0330	6" wide		105	.076		1.10	2.08		3.18	4.69	
	0340	8" wide		100	.080		1.44	2.18		3.62	5.25	
	1200	Studs 16" O.C., 18 ga x 2-1/2" wide		125	.064		.71	1.75		2.46	3.70	
	1210	3-5/8" wide		120	.067		.84	1.82		2.66	3.97	
	1220	4" wide		120	.067		.86	1.82		2.68	4	
	1230	6" wide		115	.070		1.14	1.90		3.04	4.44	
	1240	8" wide		110	.073		1.46	1.99		3.45	4.93	
	1300	16 ga x 2-1/2" wide		115	.070		.88	1.90		2.78	4.15	
	1310	3-5/8" wide		110	.073		1.03	1.99		3.02	4.45	
	1320	4" wide		110	.073		1.07	1.99		3.06	4.50	
	1330	6" wide		105	.076		1.41	2.08		3.49	5.05	
	1340	8" wide		100	.080		1.84	2.18		4.02	5.70	
	2200	Studs 24" O.C., 18 ga x 2-1/2" wide		125	.064		1.03	1.75		2.78	4.06	
	2210	3-5/8" wide		120	.067		1.21	1.82		3.03	4.38	
	2220	4" wide		120	.067		1.25	1.82		3.07	4.42	
	2230	6" wide		115	.070		1.65	1.90		3.55	5	
	2240	8" wide		110	.073		2.11	1.99		4.10	5.65	

054 | Cold Formed Metal Framing

054 100 | Load Bearing Metal Studs

			CREW	DAILY OUTPUT	LABOR-HOURS	UNIT	1999 BARE COSTS MAT.	LABOR	EQUIP.	TOTAL	TOTAL INCL O&P	
106	2300	16 ga x 2-1/2" wide	1 Carp	115	.070	Ea.	1.27	1.90		3.17	4.58	106
	2310	3-5/8" wide		110	.073		1.49	1.99		3.48	4.95	
	2320	4" wide		110	.073		1.55	1.99		3.54	5.05	
	2330	6" wide		105	.076		2.05	2.08		4.13	5.75	
	2340	8" wide		100	.080		2.66	2.18		4.84	6.60	
	3000	Continuous bridging, per row										
	3100	16 ga x 1-1/2" channel thru studs 12" O.C.	1 Carp	6	1.333	C.L.F.	37	36.50		73.50	102	
	3110	16" O.C.		7	1.143		37	31		68	93	
	3120	24" O.C.		8.80	.909		37	25		62	82.50	
	4100	2" x 2" angle x 18 ga, studs 12" O.C.		7	1.143		66.50	31		97.50	125	
	4110	16" O.C.		9	.889		66.50	24.50		91	114	
	4120	24" O.C.		12	.667		66.50	18.20		84.70	104	
	4200	16 ga, studs 12" O.C.		5	1.600		79	43.50		122.50	160	
	4210	16" O.C.		7	1.143		79	31		110	139	
	4220	24" O.C.		10	.800		79	22		101	124	
110	0010	**FRAMING**, boxed headers/beams										110
	0200	Double, 18 ga x 6" deep	2 Carp	220	.073	L.F.	3.03	1.99		5.02	6.65	
	0210	8" deep		210	.076		3.38	2.08		5.46	7.20	
	0220	10" deep		200	.080		4.05	2.18		6.23	8.10	
	0230	12" deep		190	.084		5.20	2.30		7.50	9.60	
	0300	16 ga x 8" deep		180	.089		3.87	2.43		6.30	8.30	
	0310	10" deep		170	.094		4.71	2.57		7.28	9.50	
	0320	12" deep		160	.100		4.89	2.73		7.62	9.95	
	0400	14 ga x 10" deep		140	.114		5.50	3.12		8.62	11.25	
	0410	12" deep		130	.123		6.05	3.36		9.41	12.25	
	1210	Triple, 18 ga x 8" deep		170	.094		4.50	2.57		7.07	9.25	
	1220	10" deep		165	.097		5.35	2.65		8	10.35	
	1230	12" deep		160	.100		7.10	2.73		9.83	12.40	
	1300	16 ga x 8" deep		145	.110		5.25	3.01		8.26	10.80	
	1310	10" deep		140	.114		6.35	3.12		9.47	12.20	
	1320	12" deep		135	.119		6.60	3.24		9.84	12.70	
	1400	14 ga x 10" deep		115	.139		7.55	3.80		11.35	14.65	
	1410	12" deep		110	.145		8.35	3.97		12.32	15.85	
138	0010	**FRAMING**, stud walls w/ top & bottom track, no openings,										138
	0020	headers, beams, bridging or bracing										
	4100	8' high walls, 18 ga x 2-1/2" wide, studs 12" O.C.	2 Carp	54	.296	L.F.	5.20	8.10		13.30	19.30	
	4110	16" O.C.		77	.208		4.18	5.65		9.83	14.10	
	4120	24" O.C.		107	.150		3.14	4.08		7.22	10.30	
	4130	3-5/8" wide, studs 12" O.C.		53	.302		6	8.25		14.25	20.50	
	4140	16" O.C.		76	.211		4.80	5.75		10.55	14.90	
	4150	24" O.C.		105	.152		3.61	4.16		7.77	10.90	
	4160	4" wide, studs 12" O.C.		52	.308		6.20	8.40		14.60	21	
	4170	16" O.C.		74	.216		4.96	5.90		10.86	15.35	
	4180	24" O.C.		103	.155		3.74	4.24		7.98	11.20	
	4190	6" wide, studs 12" O.C.		51	.314		8	8.55		16.55	23	
	4200	16" O.C.		73	.219		6.40	6		12.40	17.05	
	4210	24" O.C.		101	.158		4.84	4.32		9.16	12.55	
	4220	8" wide, studs 12" O.C.		50	.320		10.15	8.75		18.90	26	
	4230	16" O.C.		72	.222		8.15	6.05		14.20	19.15	
	4240	24" O.C.		100	.160		6.15	4.37		10.52	14.10	
	4300	16 ga x 2-1/2" wide, studs 12" O.C.		47	.340		6.15	9.30		15.45	22.50	
	4310	16" O.C.		68	.235		4.88	6.40		11.28	16.10	
	4320	24" O.C.		94	.170		3.61	4.65		8.26	11.75	
	4330	3-5/8" wide, studs 12" O.C.		46	.348		7.05	9.50		16.55	23.50	
	4340	16" O.C.		66	.242		5.60	6.60		12.20	17.25	

054 | Cold Formed Metal Framing

054 100 | Load Bearing Metal Studs

			CREW	DAILY OUTPUT	LABOR-HOURS	UNIT	1999 BARE COSTS MAT.	LABOR	EQUIP.	TOTAL	TOTAL INCL O&P	
138	4350	24" O.C.	2 Carp	92	.174	L.F.	4.15	4.75		8.90	12.50	138
	4360	4" wide, studs 12" O.C.		45	.356		7.25	9.70		16.95	24.50	
	4370	16" O.C.		65	.246		5.75	6.70		12.45	17.60	
	4380	24" O.C.		90	.178		4.27	4.85		9.12	12.80	
	4390	6" wide, studs 12" O.C.		44	.364		9.30	9.95		19.25	27	
	4400	16" O.C.		64	.250		7.40	6.80		14.20	19.60	
	4410	24" O.C.		88	.182		5.50	4.96		10.46	14.35	
	4420	8" wide, studs 12" O.C.		43	.372		12.10	10.15		22.25	30.50	
	4430	16" O.C.		63	.254		9.60	6.95		16.55	22	
	4440	24" O.C.		86	.186		7.15	5.10		12.25	16.35	
	5100	10' high walls, 18 ga x 2-1/2" wide, studs 12" O.C.		54	.296		6.25	8.10		14.35	20.50	
	5110	16" O.C.		77	.208		4.96	5.65		10.61	14.95	
	5120	24" O.C.		107	.150		3.66	4.08		7.74	10.90	
	5130	3-5/8" wide, studs 12" O.C.		53	.302		7.15	8.25		15.40	21.50	
	5140	16" O.C.		76	.211		5.70	5.75		11.45	15.85	
	5150	24" O.C.		105	.152		4.21	4.16		8.37	11.60	
	5160	4" wide, studs 12" O.C.		52	.308		7.40	8.40		15.80	22	
	5170	16" O.C.		74	.216		5.90	5.90		11.80	16.35	
	5180	24" O.C.		103	.155		4.35	4.24		8.59	11.90	
	5190	6" wide, studs 12" O.C.		51	.314		9.55	8.55		18.10	25	
	5200	16" O.C.		73	.219		7.60	6		13.60	18.35	
	5210	24" O.C.		101	.158		5.60	4.32		9.92	13.45	
	5220	8" wide, studs 12" O.C.		50	.320		12.15	8.75		20.90	28	
	5230	16" O.C.		72	.222		9.65	6.05		15.70	21	
	5240	24" O.C.		100	.160		7.15	4.37		11.52	15.20	
	5300	16 ga x 2-1/2" wide, studs 12" O.C.		47	.340		7.45	9.30		16.75	24	
	5310	16" O.C.		68	.235		5.85	6.40		12.25	17.15	
	5320	24" O.C.		94	.170		4.25	4.65		8.90	12.45	
	5330	3-5/8" wide, studs 12" O.C.		46	.348		8.50	9.50		18	25.50	
	5340	16" O.C.		66	.242		6.70	6.60		13.30	18.45	
	5350	24" O.C.		92	.174		4.88	4.75		9.63	13.30	
	5360	4" wide, studs 12" O.C.		45	.356		8.75	9.70		18.45	26	
	5370	16" O.C.		65	.246		6.90	6.70		13.60	18.80	
	5380	24" O.C.		90	.178		5	4.85		9.85	13.60	
	5390	6" wide, studs 12" O.C.		44	.364		11.20	9.95		21.15	29	
	5400	16" O.C.		64	.250		8.85	6.80		15.65	21	
	5410	24" O.C.		88	.182		6.45	4.96		11.41	15.40	
	5420	8" wide, studs 12" O.C.		43	.372		14.60	10.15		24.75	33	
	5430	16" O.C.		63	.254		11.50	6.95		18.45	24.50	
	5440	24" O.C.		86	.186		8.40	5.10		13.50	17.70	
	6190	12' high walls, 18 ga x 6" wide, studs 12" O.C.		41	.390		11.10	10.65		21.75	30	
	6200	16" O.C.		58	.276		8.75	7.55		16.30	22.50	
	6210	24" O.C.		81	.198		6.40	5.40		11.80	16.10	
	6220	8" wide, studs 12" O.C.		40	.400		14.15	10.90		25.05	34	
	6230	16" O.C.		57	.281		11.15	7.65		18.80	25	
	6240	24" O.C.		80	.200		8.15	5.45		13.60	18.15	
	6390	16 ga x 6" wide, studs 12" O.C.		35	.457		13.15	12.50		25.65	35.50	
	6400	16" O.C.		51	.314		10.25	8.55		18.80	25.50	
	6410	24" O.C.		70	.229		7.40	6.25		13.65	18.60	
	6420	8" wide, studs 12" O.C.		34	.471		17.10	12.85		29.95	40.50	
	6430	16" O.C.		50	.320		13.35	8.75		22.10	29.50	
	6440	24" O.C.		69	.232		9.60	6.35		15.95	21	
	6530	14 ga x 3-5/8" wide, studs 12" O.C.		34	.471		13.05	12.85		25.90	36	
	6540	16" O.C.		48	.333		10.15	9.10		19.25	26.50	
	6550	24" O.C.		65	.246		7.30	6.70		14	19.25	
	6560	4" wide, studs 12" O.C.		33	.485		13.40	13.25		26.65	37	

054 | Cold Formed Metal Framing

054 100 | Load Bearing Metal Studs

				Daily Output	Labor-Hours	Unit	1999 Bare Costs				Total Incl O&P	
			Crew				Mat.	Labor	Equip.	Total		
138	6570	16" O.C.	2 Carp	47	.340	L.F.	10.45	9.30		19.75	27	138
	6580	24" O.C.		64	.250		7.50	6.80		14.30	19.70	
	6730	12 ga x 3-5/8" wide, studs 12" O.C.		31	.516		19.90	14.10		34	45.50	
	6740	16" O.C.		43	.372		15.30	10.15		25.45	34	
	6750	24" O.C.		59	.271		10.70	7.40		18.10	24	
	6760	4" wide, studs 12" O.C.		30	.533		23	14.55		37.55	50	
	6770	16" O.C.		42	.381		17.80	10.40		28.20	37	
	6780	24" O.C.		58	.276		12.40	7.55		19.95	26.50	
	7390	16' high walls, 16 ga x 6" wide, studs 12" O.C.		33	.485		16.95	13.25		30.20	40.50	
	7400	16" O.C.		48	.333		13.15	9.10		22.25	29.50	
	7410	24" O.C.		67	.239		9.30	6.50		15.80	21	
	7420	8" wide, studs 12" O.C.		32	.500		22	13.65		35.65	47.50	
	7430	16" O.C.		47	.340		17.10	9.30		26.40	34.50	
	7440	24" O.C.		66	.242		12.10	6.60		18.70	24.50	
	7560	14 ga x 4" wide, studs 12" O.C.		31	.516		17.35	14.10		31.45	42.50	
	7570	16" O.C.		45	.356		13.40	9.70		23.10	31	
	7580	24" O.C.		61	.262		9.45	7.15		16.60	22.50	
	7590	6" wide, studs 12" O.C.		30	.533		22.50	14.55		37.05	49	
	7600	16" O.C.		44	.364		17.35	9.95		27.30	35.50	
	7610	24" O.C.		60	.267		12.30	7.30		19.60	25.50	
	7760	12 ga x 4" wide, studs 12" O.C.		29	.552		30.50	15.05		45.55	58.50	
	7770	16" O.C.		40	.400		23	10.90		33.90	44	
	7780	24" O.C.		55	.291		16	7.95		23.95	31	
	7790	6" wide, studs 12" O.C.		28	.571		33.50	15.60		49.10	62.50	
	7800	16" O.C.		39	.410		25.50	11.20		36.70	47	
	7810	24" O.C.		54	.296		17.70	8.10		25.80	33	
	8590	20' high walls, 14 ga x 6" wide, studs 12" O.C.		29	.552		27.50	15.05		42.55	55.50	
	8600	16" O.C.		42	.381		21	10.40		31.40	41	
	8610	24" O.C.		57	.281		14.85	7.65		22.50	29	
	8620	8" wide, studs 12" O.C.		28	.571		34.50	15.60		50.10	64	
	8630	16" O.C.		41	.390		26.50	10.65		37.15	47.50	
	8640	24" O.C.		56	.286		18.75	7.80		26.55	33.50	
	8790	12 ga x 6" wide, studs 12" O.C.		27	.593		41	16.20		57.20	72	
	8800	16" O.C.		37	.432		31.50	11.80		43.30	54.50	
	8810	24" O.C.		51	.314		21.50	8.55		30.05	38.50	
	8820	8" wide, studs 12" O.C.		26	.615		50.50	16.80		67.30	83.50	
	8830	16" O.C.		36	.444		38.50	12.15		50.65	63	
	8840	24" O.C.		50	.320		26.50	8.75		35.25	44	

055 | Metal Fabrications

055 100 | Metal Stairs

			Crew	Daily Output	Labor-Hours	Unit	1999 Bare Costs				Total Incl O&P	
							Mat.	Labor	Equip.	Total		
104	0010	**STAIR** Steel, safety nosing, steel stringers										104
	0020	Grating tread and pipe railing, 3'-6" wide	E-4	35	.914	Riser	83.50	28.50	2.35	114.35	148	
	0100	4'-0" wide		30	1.067		92	33	2.74	127.74	167	
	0200	Cement fill metal pan, picket rail, 3'-6" wide		35	.914		71.50	28.50	2.35	102.35	135	
	0300	4'-0" wide		30	1.067		79	33	2.74	114.74	153	
	0350	Wall rail, both sides, 3'-6" wide		53	.604		62	18.80	1.55	82.35	105	
	0500	Checkered plate tread, industrial, 3'-6" wide		28	1.143		101	35.50	2.94	139.44	182	
	0550	Circular, for tanks, 3'-0" wide		33	.970		87.50	30	2.49	119.99	157	

055 | Metal Fabrications

055 100 | Metal Stairs

					1999 BARE COSTS				TOTAL
		CREW	DAILY OUTPUT	LABOR-HOURS	UNIT	MAT.	LABOR	EQUIP.	TOTAL	INCL O&P
0600	For isolated stairs, add				Riser		100%			
0800	Custom steel stairs, 3'-6" wide, minimum	E-4	35	.914		103	28.50	2.35	133.85	170
0810	Average		30	1.067		152	33	2.74	187.74	233
0900	Maximum		20	1.600		222	50	4.11	276.11	345
1100	For 4' wide stairs, add					10%	5%			
1300	For 5' wide stairs, add					20%	10%			
1500	Landing, steel pan, conventional	E-4	160	.200	S.F.	35.50	6.20	.51	42.21	52
1810	Spiral aluminum, 5'-0" diameter, stock units		45	.711	Riser	182	22	1.83	205.83	244
1820	Custom units		45	.711		350	22	1.83	373.83	425
1830	Stock units, 4'-0" diameter, safety treads		50	.640		110	19.90	1.64	131.54	161
1840	Oak treads		50	.640		215	19.90	1.64	236.54	277
1850	5'-0" diameter, safety treads		45	.711		121	22	1.83	144.83	178
1860	Oak treads		45	.711		232	22	1.83	255.83	299
1870	6'-0" diameter, safety treads		40	.800		132	25	2.06	159.06	196
1880	Oak treads		40	.800		254	25	2.06	281.06	330
1900	Spiral, cast iron, 4'-0" diameter, ornamental, minimum		45	.711		166	22	1.83	189.83	226
1920	Maximum		25	1.280		221	40	3.29	264.29	325
2000	Spiral, steel, industrial checkered plate, 4' diameter		45	.711		166	22	1.83	189.83	226
2200	Stock units, 6'-0" diameter		40	.800		199	25	2.06	226.06	269
3900	Industrial ships ladder, 3' W, grating treads, 2 line pipe rail		30	1.067		66	33	2.74	101.74	139
4000	Aluminum		30	1.067		97.50	33	2.74	133.24	173
9000	Minimum labor/equipment charge		2	16	Job		500	41	541	990

055 150 | Ladders

		CREW	DAILY OUTPUT	LABOR-HOURS	UNIT	MAT.	LABOR	EQUIP.	TOTAL	INCL O&P
0010	**FIRE ESCAPE**									
0200	2' wide balcony, 1" x 1/4" bars 1-1/2" O.C.	1 Sswk	5	1.600	L.F.	34	49		83	131
0400	1st story cantilever, standard	"	.09	88.889	Ea.	1,425	2,725		4,150	6,750
0500	Cable counterweight				"	1,325			1,325	1,450
0700	Platform & stair, 36" x 40"	1 Sswk	.17	47.059	Flight	630	1,450		2,080	3,450
0900	For 3'-6" wide escapes, add to above					100%	150%			
0005	**FIRE ESCAPE STAIRS**									
0010	One story, disappearing, stainless steel	2 Sswk	20	.800	V.L.F.	148	24.50		172.50	210
0100	Portable ladder				Ea.	173			173	191
0005	**LADDER**									
0010	Steel, 20" wide, bolted to concrete, with cage	E-4	50	.640	V.L.F.	53	19.90	1.64	74.54	98.50
0100	Without cage		85	.376		24.50	11.70	.97	37.17	50.50
0300	Aluminum, bolted to concrete, with cage		50	.640		100	19.90	1.64	121.54	150
0400	Without cage		85	.376		55.50	11.70	.97	68.17	84.50
1350	Alternating tread stair, 56/68°, steel, standard paint color	2 Sswk	50	.320		132	9.80		141.80	164
1360	Non-standard paint color		50	.320		141	9.80		150.80	174
1370	Galvanized steel		50	.320		149	9.80		158.80	183
1380	Stainless steel		50	.320		226	9.80		235.80	267
1390	68°, aluminum		50	.320		163	9.80		172.80	198
9000	Minimum labor/equipment charge	E-4	2	16	Job		500	41	541	990

055 200 | Handrails & Railings

		CREW	DAILY OUTPUT	LABOR-HOURS	UNIT	MAT.	LABOR	EQUIP.	TOTAL	INCL O&P
0010	**BUMPER RAILS** For garages, 12 ga. rail, 6" wide, with steel									
0020	posts 12'-6" O.C., Minimum	E-4	190	.168	L.F.	8	5.25	.43	13.68	19.25
0030	Average		165	.194		10	6.05	.50	16.55	23
0100	Maximum		140	.229		12	7.10	.59	19.69	27.50
9000	Minimum labor/equipment charge	A-1	1	8	Job		172	68.50	240.50	365
0005	**RAILING, PIPE**									
0010	Aluminum, 2 rail, satin finish, 1-1/4" diameter	E-4	160	.200	L.F.	13	6.20	.51	19.71	26.50

055 | Metal Fabrications

055 200 | Handrails & Railings

			CREW	DAILY OUTPUT	LABOR-HOURS	UNIT	MAT.	LABOR	EQUIP.	TOTAL	TOTAL INCL O&P	
203	0030	Clear anodized	E-4	160	.200	L.F.	16.10	6.20	.51	22.81	30	203
	0040	Dark anodized		160	.200		18.15	6.20	.51	24.86	32.50	
	0080	1-1/2" diameter, satin finish		160	.200		15.55	6.20	.51	22.26	29.50	
	0090	Clear anodized		160	.200		17.35	6.20	.51	24.06	31.50	
	0100	Dark anodized		160	.200		19.25	6.20	.51	25.96	33.50	
	0140	Aluminum, 3 rail, 1-1/4" diam., satin finish		137	.234		19.90	7.25	.60	27.75	36.50	
	0150	Clear anodized		137	.234		25	7.25	.60	32.85	42	
	0160	Dark anodized		137	.234		27.50	7.25	.60	35.35	45	
	0200	1-1/2" diameter, satin finish		137	.234		24	7.25	.60	31.85	41	
	0210	Clear anodized		137	.234		27	7.25	.60	34.85	44.50	
	0220	Dark anodized		137	.234		29.50	7.25	.60	37.35	47	
	0500	Steel, 2 rail, on stairs, primed, 1-1/4" diameter		160	.200		9.35	6.20	.51	16.06	22.50	
	0520	1-1/2" diameter		160	.200		10.30	6.20	.51	17.01	23.50	
	0540	Galvanized, 1-1/4" diameter		160	.200		13	6.20	.51	19.71	26.50	
	0560	1-1/2" diameter		160	.200		14.55	6.20	.51	21.26	28.50	
	0580	Steel, 3 rail, primed, 1-1/4" diameter		137	.234		13.95	7.25	.60	21.80	30	
	0600	1-1/2" diameter		137	.234		14.80	7.25	.60	22.65	31	
	0620	Galvanized, 1-1/4" diameter		137	.234		19.60	7.25	.60	27.45	36	
	0640	1-1/2" diameter		137	.234		21.50	7.25	.60	29.35	38.50	
	0700	Stainless steel, 2 rail, 1-1/4" diam. #4 finish		137	.234		32	7.25	.60	39.85	49.50	
	0720	High polish		137	.234		51.50	7.25	.60	59.35	71	
	0740	Mirror polish		137	.234		64.50	7.25	.60	72.35	85.50	
	0760	Stainless steel, 3 rail, 1-1/2" diam., #4 finish		120	.267		48	8.30	.69	56.99	69.50	
	0770	High polish		120	.267		79.50	8.30	.69	88.49	104	
	0780	Mirror finish		120	.267		97	8.30	.69	105.99	124	
	0900	Wall rail, alum. pipe, 1-1/4" diam., satin finish		213	.150		7.45	4.67	.39	12.51	17.50	
	0905	Clear anodized		213	.150		9.05	4.67	.39	14.11	19.35	
	0910	Dark anodized		213	.150		11	4.67	.39	16.06	21.50	
	0915	1-1/2" diameter, satin finish		213	.150		8.25	4.67	.39	13.31	18.40	
	0920	Clear anodized		213	.150		10.35	4.67	.39	15.41	20.50	
	0925	Dark anodized		213	.150		12.80	4.67	.39	17.86	23.50	
	0930	Steel pipe, 1-1/4" diameter, primed		213	.150		5.70	4.67	.39	10.76	15.60	
	0935	Galvanized		213	.150		8.25	4.67	.39	13.31	18.40	
	0940	1-1/2" diameter		176	.182		5.85	5.65	.47	11.97	17.65	
	0945	Galvanized		213	.150		8.30	4.67	.39	13.36	18.45	
	0955	Stainless steel pipe, 1-1/2" diam., #4 finish		107	.299		25.50	9.30	.77	35.57	46.50	
	0960	High polish		107	.299		52	9.30	.77	62.07	75.50	
	0965	Mirror polish		107	.299		61	9.30	.77	71.07	86	
	9000	Minimum labor/equipment charge	1 Sswk	2	4	Job		122		122	233	
206	0005	**RAILINGS, INDUSTRIAL** Welded										206
	0010	2 rail, 3'-6" high, 1-1/2" pipe	E-4	255	.125	L.F.	13.70	3.90	.32	17.92	23	
	0200	For 4" high kick plate, 10 gauge, add					2.86			2.86	3.15	
	0500	For curved rails, add					30%	30%				
	9000	Minimum labor/equipment charge	1 Sswk	2	4	Job		122		122	233	
208	0005	**RAILINGS, ORNAMENTAL**										208
	0010	Aluminum, bronze or stainless, minimum	1 Sswk	24	.333	L.F.	97	10.20		107.20	126	
	0100	Maximum		9	.889		545	27		572	650	
	0200	Aluminum ornamental rail, minimum		15	.533		44	16.30		60.30	79.50	
	0300	Maximum		8	1		191	30.50		221.50	269	
	0400	Hand-forged wrought iron, minimum		12	.667		95	20.50		115.50	143	
	0500	Maximum		8	1		405	30.50		435.50	505	
	0600	Composite metal and wood or glass, minimum		6	1.333		184	41		225	280	
	0700	Maximum		5	1.600		480	49		529	620	
	9000	Minimum labor/equipment charge		2	4	Job		122		122	233	

055 | Metal Fabrications

055 400 | Castings

			CREW	DAILY OUTPUT	LABOR-HOURS	UNIT	1999 BARE COSTS MAT.	LABOR	EQUIP.	TOTAL	TOTAL INCL O&P	
404	0010	**CONSTRUCTION CASTINGS**										404
	0020	Manhole covers and frames see Division 027-152										
	0100	Column bases, cast iron, 16" x 16", approx. 65 lbs.	E-4	46	.696	Ea.	79	21.50	1.79	102.29	130	
	0200	32" x 32", approx. 256 lbs.		23	1.391	"	295	43.50	3.58	342.08	410	
	0600	Miscellaneous C.I. castings, light sections, less than 150 lbs		3,200	.010	Lb.	1.21	.31	.03	1.55	1.95	
	1300	Special low volume items		3,200	.010	"	2.12	.31	.03	2.46	2.95	

055 500 | Metal Specialties

			CREW	DAILY OUTPUT	LABOR-HOURS	UNIT	MAT.	LABOR	EQUIP.	TOTAL	INCL O&P	
504	0005	**LAMP POSTS**										504
	0010	Aluminum, 7' high, stock units, post only	1 Carp	16	.500	Ea.	65	13.65		78.65	94.50	
	0100	Mild steel, plain		16	.500	"	39	13.65		52.65	66	
	9000	Minimum labor/equipment charge		4	2	Job		54.50		54.50	91.50	
508	0005	**WINDOW GUARDS**										508
	0010	Expanded metal, steel angle frame, permanent	E-4	350	.091	S.F.	14.35	2.84	.23	17.42	21.50	
	0020	Steel bars, 1/2" x 1/2", spaced 5" O.C.	"	290	.110	"	9.90	3.43	.28	13.61	17.75	
	0030	Hinge mounted, add				Opng.	28.50			28.50	31.50	
	0040	Removable type, add				"	18.25			18.25	20	
	0050	For galvanized guards, add				S.F.	35%					
	0070	For pivoted or projected type, add					105%	40%				
	0100	Mild steel, stock units, economy	E-4	405	.079		3.89	2.46	.20	6.55	9.20	
	0200	Deluxe		405	.079		8	2.46	.20	10.66	13.70	
	0400	Woven wire, stock units, 3/8" channel frame, 3' x 5' opening		40	.800	Opng.	105	25	2.06	132.06	166	
	0500	4' x 6' opening		38	.842		168	26	2.16	196.16	237	
	0800	Basket guards for above, add					144			144	158	
	1000	Swinging guards for above, add					49.50			49.50	54.50	
	9000	Minimum labor/equipment charge	1 Sswk	2	4	Job		122		122	233	

057 | Ornamental Metal

057 250 | Ornamental Metal

			CREW	DAILY OUTPUT	LABOR-HOURS	UNIT	1999 BARE COSTS MAT.	LABOR	EQUIP.	TOTAL	TOTAL INCL O&P	
252	0005	**WEATHERVANES**										252
	0010	Residential types, minimum	1 Carp	8	1	Ea.	50.50	27.50		78	102	
	0100	Maximum		2	4	"	765	109		874	1,025	
	9000	Minimum labor/equipment charge		4	2	Job		54.50		54.50	91.50	

058 | Expansion Control

058 100 | Exp. Cover Assemblies

			CREW	DAILY OUTPUT	LABOR-HOURS	UNIT	1999 BARE COSTS MAT.	LABOR	EQUIP.	TOTAL	TOTAL INCL O&P	
104	0010	**EXPANSION JOINT ASSEMBLIES** Custom units										104
	0200	Floor cover assemblies, 1" space, aluminum	1 Sswk	38	.211	L.F.	13.20	6.45		19.65	27	
	0300	Bronze		38	.211		25.50	6.45		31.95	40.50	
	0500	2" space, aluminum		38	.211		15.95	6.45		22.40	30	
	0600	Bronze		38	.211		27.50	6.45		33.95	42.50	
	0800	Wall and ceiling assemblies, 1" space, aluminum		38	.211		7.90	6.45		14.35	21	

058 | Expansion Control

058 100 | Exp. Cover Assemblies

			CREW	DAILY OUTPUT	LABOR-HOURS	UNIT	1999 BARE COSTS MAT.	LABOR	EQUIP.	TOTAL	TOTAL INCL O&P	
104	0900	Bronze	1 Sswk	38	.211	L.F.	27	6.45		33.45	42	104
	1100	2" space, aluminum		38	.211		13.35	6.45		19.80	27	
	1200	Bronze		38	.211		24.50	6.45		30.95	39.50	
	1400	Floor to wall assemblies, 1" space, aluminum		38	.211		12	6.45		18.45	25.50	
	1500	Bronze or stainless		38	.211		29	6.45		35.45	44.50	
	1700	Gym floor angle covers, aluminum, 3" x 3" angle		46	.174		10.40	5.30		15.70	21.50	
	1800	3" x 4" angle		46	.174		12.25	5.30		17.55	23.50	
	2000	Roof closures, aluminum, flat roof, low profile, 1" space		57	.140		24	4.29		28.29	34.50	
	2100	High profile		57	.140		29.50	4.29		33.79	40.50	
	2300	Roof to wall, low profile, 1" space		57	.140		13.30	4.29		17.59	23	
	2400	High profile		57	.140		17.10	4.29		21.39	27	
	9000	Minimum labor/equipment charge		2	4	Job		122		122	233	

For information about Means Estimating Seminars, see yellow pages 11 and 12 in back of book

Division Notes

	CREW	DAILY OUTPUT	LABOR-HOURS	UNIT	1999 BARE COSTS				TOTAL INCL O&P
					MAT.	LABOR	EQUIP.	TOTAL	

Division 6
Wood & Plastics

Estimating Tips
060 Fasteners & Adhesives
- Common to any wood framed structure are the accessory connector items such as screws, nails, adhesives, hangers, connector plates, straps, angles and holdowns. For typical wood framed buildings, such as residential projects, the aggregate total for these items can be significant, especially in areas where seismic loading is a concern. For floor and wall framing, nail quantities can be figured on a "pounds per thousand board feet basis", with 10 to 25 lbs. per MBF the range. Holdowns, hangers and other connectors should be taken off by the piece.

061 Rough Carpentry
- Lumber is a traded commodity and therefore sensitive to supply and demand in the marketplace. Even in "budgetary" estimating of wood framed projects, it is advisable to call local suppliers for the latest market pricing.
- Common quantity units for wood framed projects are "thousand board feet" (MBF). A board foot is a volume of wood, 1" x 1' x 1', or 144 cubic inches. Board foot quantities are generally calculated using nominal material dimensions—dressed sizes are ignored. Board foot per lineal foot of any stick of lumber can be calculated by dividing the nominal cross sectional area by 12. As an example, 2,000 lineal feet of 2 x 12 equates to 4 MBF by dividing the nominal area, 2 x 12, by 12, which equals 2, and multiplying by 2,000 to give 4,000 board feet. This simple rule applies to all nominal dimensioned lumber.
- Waste is an issue of concern at the quantity takeoff for any area of construction. Framing lumber is sold in even foot lengths, i.e., 10', 12', 14', 16', and depending on spans, wall heights and the grade of lumber, waste is inevitable. A rule of thumb for lumber waste is 5% to 10% depending on material quality and the complexity of the framing.
- Wood in various forms and shapes is used in many projects, even where the main structural framing is steel, concrete or masonry. Plywood as a back-up partition material and 2x boards used as blocking and cant strips around roof edges are two common examples. The estimator should ensure that the costs of all wood materials are included in the final estimate.

062 Finish Carpentry
- It is necessary to consider the grade of workmanship when estimating labor costs for erecting millwork and interior finish. In practice, there are three grades: premium, custom and economy. The Means daily output for base and case moldings is in the range of 200 to 250 L.F. per carpenter per day. This is appropriate for most average custom grade projects. For premium projects an adjustment to productivity of 25% to 50% should be made depending on the complexity of the job.

Reference Numbers
Reference numbers are shown in bold squares at the beginning of some major classifications. These numbers refer to related items in the Reference Section. The reference information may be an estimating procedure, an alternate pricing method or technical information.

Note: Not all subdivisions listed here necessarily appear in this publication.

060 | Fasteners & Adhesives

060 500 | Fasteners & Adhesives

			Daily Output	Labor-Hours	Unit	1999 Bare Costs Mat.	Labor	Equip.	Total	Total Incl O&P	
504	0010	**NAILS** Prices of material only, based on 50# box purchase, copper, plain				Lb.	4.10			4.10	4.51	504
	0400	Stainless steel, plain					5.40			5.40	5.95	
	0500	Box, 3d to 20d, bright					1.13			1.13	1.24	
	0520	Galvanized					1.13			1.13	1.24	
	0600	Common, 3d to 60d, plain					.77			.77	.85	
	0700	Galvanized					.99			.99	1.09	
	0800	Aluminum					3.31			3.31	3.64	
	1000	Annular or spiral thread, 4d to 60d, plain					.66			.66	.73	
	1200	Galvanized					.88			.88	.97	
	1400	Drywall nails, plain					.77			.77	.85	
	1600	Galvanized					1.10			1.10	1.21	
	1800	Finish nails, 4d to 10d, plain					.90			.90	.99	
	2000	Galvanized					1.04			1.04	1.14	
	2100	Aluminum					4.84			4.84	5.30	
	2300	Flooring nails, hardened steel, 2d to 10d, plain					1.22			1.22	1.34	
	2400	Galvanized					1.34			1.34	1.47	
	2500	Gypsum lath nails, 1-1/8", 13 ga. flathead, blued					1.33			1.33	1.46	
	2600	Masonry nails, hardened steel, 3/4" to 3" long, plain					1.61			1.61	1.77	
	2700	Galvanized					1.44			1.44	1.58	
	2900	Roofing nails, threaded, galvanized					1.21			1.21	1.34	
	3100	Aluminum					4.70			4.70	5.15	
	3300	Compressed lead head, threaded, galvanized					1.44			1.44	1.58	
	3600	Siding nails, plain shank, galvanized					1.33			1.33	1.46	
	3800	Aluminum					4			4	4.40	
	5000	Add to prices above for cement coating					.07			.07	.08	
	5200	Zinc or tin plating					.12			.12	.13	
	5500	Vinyl coated sinkers, 8d to 16d					.55			.55	.61	
506	0010	**NAILS** mat. only, for pneumatic tools, framing, per carton of 5000, 2"				Ea.	36.50			36.50	40	506
	0100	2-3/8"					41.50			41.50	45.50	
	0200	Per carton of 4000, 3"					37			37	40.50	
	0300	3-1/4"					39			39	43	
	0400	Per carton of 5000, 2-3/8", galv.					56.50			56.50	62	
	0500	Per carton of 4000, 3", galv.					63.50			63.50	70	
	0600	3-1/4", galv.					60			60	66	
	0700	Roofing, per carton of 7200, 1"					36			36	39.50	
	0800	1-1/4"					36.50			36.50	40.50	
	0900	1-1/2"					42			42	46	
	1000	1-3/4"					47			47	51.50	
512	0010	**TIMBER CONNECTORS** Add up cost of each part for total										512
	0020	cost of connection										
	0100	Connector plates, steel, with bolts, straight	2 Carp	75	.213	Ea.	16	5.80		21.80	27.50	
	0110	Tee	"	50	.320		24	8.75		32.75	40.50	
	0200	Bolts, machine, sq. hd. with nut & washer, 1/2" diameter, 4" long	1 Carp	140	.057		.68	1.56		2.24	3.35	
	0300	7-1/2" long		130	.062		.94	1.68		2.62	3.84	
	0500	3/4" diameter, 7-1/2" long		130	.062		1.62	1.68		3.30	4.59	
	0600	15" long		95	.084		2.13	2.30		4.43	6.20	
	0800	Drilling bolt holes in timber, 1/2" diameter		450	.018	Inch		.49		.49	.81	
	0900	1" diameter		350	.023	"		.62		.62	1.04	
	1100	Framing anchors, 2 or 3 dimensional, 10 gauge, no nails incl.		175	.046	Ea.	.39	1.25		1.64	2.52	
	1250	Holdowns, 3 gauge base, 10 gauge body		8	1		13.45	27.50		40.95	60.50	
	1300	Joist and beam hangers, 18 ga. galv., for 2" x 4" joist		175	.046		.48	1.25		1.73	2.61	
	1400	2" x 6" to 2" x 10" joist		165	.048		.56	1.32		1.88	2.84	
	1600	16 ga. galv., 3" x 6" to 3" x 10" joist		160	.050		2.24	1.36		3.60	4.75	
	1700	3" x 10" to 3" x 14" joist		160	.050		2.60	1.36		3.96	5.15	

060 | Fasteners & Adhesives

060 500 | Fasteners & Adhesives

		CREW	DAILY OUTPUT	LABOR-HOURS	UNIT	1999 BARE COSTS MAT.	LABOR	EQUIP.	TOTAL	TOTAL INCL O&P	
512	1800	4" x 6" to 4" x 10" joist	1 Carp	155	.052	Ea.	1.96	1.41		3.37	4.52	512
	1900	4" x 10" to 4" x 14" joist		155	.052		2.67	1.41		4.08	5.30	
	2000	Two-2" x 6" to two-2" x 10" joists		150	.053		2.15	1.46		3.61	4.81	
	2100	Two-2" x 10" to two-2" x 14" joists		150	.053		2.15	1.46		3.61	4.81	
	2300	3/16" thick, 6" x 8" joist		145	.055		4.71	1.51		6.22	7.70	
	2400	6" x 10" joist		140	.057		5.55	1.56		7.11	8.70	
	2500	6" x 12" joist		135	.059		6.70	1.62		8.32	10.05	
	2700	1/4" thick, 6" x 14" joist		130	.062		8.30	1.68		9.98	11.90	
	2800	Joist anchors, 1/4" x 1-1/4" x 18"		140	.057		3.23	1.56		4.79	6.15	
	2900	Plywood clips, extruded aluminum H clip, for 3/4" panels					.11			.11	.12	
	3000	Galvanized 18 ga. back-up clip					.10			.10	.11	
	3200	Post framing, 16 ga. galv. for 4" x 4" base, 2 piece	1 Carp	130	.062		4.65	1.68		6.33	7.90	
	3300	Cap		130	.062		2.29	1.68		3.97	5.30	
	3500	Rafter anchors, 18 ga. galv., 1-1/2" wide, 5-1/4" long		145	.055		.37	1.51		1.88	2.93	
	3600	10-3/4" long		145	.055		.76	1.51		2.27	3.36	
	3800	Shear plates, 2-5/8" diameter		120	.067		1.38	1.82		3.20	4.57	
	3900	4" diameter		115	.070		3.20	1.90		5.10	6.70	
	4000	Sill anchors, embedded in concrete or block, 18-5/8" long		115	.070		.96	1.90		2.86	4.24	
	4100	Spike grids, 4" x 4", flat or curved		120	.067		.40	1.82		2.22	3.48	
	4400	Split rings, 2-1/2" diameter		120	.067		1.15	1.82		2.97	4.32	
	4500	4" diameter		110	.073		1.77	1.99		3.76	5.25	
	4700	Strap ties, 16 ga., 1-3/8" wide, 12" long		180	.044		.91	1.21		2.12	3.03	
	4800	24" long		160	.050		1.42	1.36		2.78	3.85	
	5000	Toothed rings, 2-5/8" or 4" diameter		90	.089		.97	2.43		3.40	5.15	
	5200	Truss plates, nailed, 20 gauge, up to 32' span		17	.471	Truss	7	12.85		19.85	29	
	5400	Washers, 2" x 2" x 1/8"				Ea.	.22			.22	.24	
	5500	3" x 3" x 3/16"				"	.57			.57	.63	
	9000	Minimum labor/equipment charge	1 Carp	4	2	Job		54.50		54.50	91.50	
516	0010	**WOOD SCREWS** #8, 1" long, steel				C	3.46			3.46	3.81	516
	0100	Brass					16.70			16.70	18.35	
	0600	#10, 2" long, steel					7.50			7.50	8.25	
	0700	Brass					39.50			39.50	43.50	
	1500	#12, 3" long, steel					15.90			15.90	17.50	

061 | Rough Carpentry

061 100 | Wood Framing

		CREW	DAILY OUTPUT	LABOR-HOURS	UNIT	1999 BARE COSTS MAT.	LABOR	EQUIP.	TOTAL	TOTAL INCL O&P	
102	0010	**BLOCKING**										102
	2600	Miscellaneous, to wood construction										
	2620	2" x 4"	1 Carp	.17	47.059	M.B.F.	540	1,275		1,815	2,750	
	2625	Pneumatic nailed		.21	38.095		540	1,050		1,590	2,350	
	2660	2" x 8"		.27	29.630		545	810		1,355	1,950	
	2665	Pneumatic nailed		.33	24.242		545	660		1,205	1,700	
	2720	To steel construction										
	2740	2" x 4"	1 Carp	.14	57.143	M.B.F.	540	1,550		2,090	3,200	
	2780	2" x 8"		.21	38.095	"	545	1,050		1,595	2,350	
	9000	Minimum labor/equipment charge		4	2	Job		54.50		54.50	91.50	
104	0012	**BRACING** Let-in, with 1" x 6" boards, studs @ 16" O.C.	1 Carp	150	.053	L.F.	.52	1.46		1.98	3.01	104
	0202	Studs @ 24" O.C.	"	230	.035	"	.52	.95		1.47	2.16	

For expanded coverage of these items see *Means Interior Cost Data 1999*

061 | Rough Carpentry

061 100 | Wood Framing

			CREW	DAILY OUTPUT	LABOR-HOURS	UNIT	1999 BARE COSTS MAT.	LABOR	EQUIP.	TOTAL	TOTAL INCL O&P	
106	0012	**BRIDGING** Wood, for joists 16" O.C., 1" x 3"	1 Carp	130	.062	Pr.	.34	1.68		2.02	3.19	106
	0017	Pneumatic nailed		170	.047		.34	1.28		1.62	2.53	
	0102	2" x 3" bridging		130	.062		.37	1.68		2.05	3.21	
	0107	Pneumatic nailed		170	.047		.37	1.28		1.65	2.55	
	0302	Steel, galvanized, 18 ga., for 2" x 10" joists at 12" O.C.		130	.062		.85	1.68		2.53	3.75	
	0402	24" O.C.		140	.057		1.64	1.56		3.20	4.41	
	0902	Compression type, 16" O.C., 2" x 8" joists		200	.040		1.15	1.09		2.24	3.10	
	1002	2" x 12" joists		200	.040		1.26	1.09		2.35	3.22	
110	0010	**FRAMING, BEAMS & GIRDERS** R061-010										110
	1002	Single, 2" x 6"	2 Carp	700	.023	L.F.	.54	.62		1.16	1.63	
	1007	Pneumatic nailed R061-030		812	.020		.54	.54		1.08	1.49	
	1022	2" x 8"		650	.025		.73	.67		1.40	1.92	
	1027	Pneumatic nailed		754	.021		.73	.58		1.31	1.77	
	1042	2" x 10"		600	.027		1.01	.73		1.74	2.33	
	1047	Pneumatic nailed		696	.023		1.01	.63		1.64	2.16	
	1062	2" x 12"		550	.029		1.29	.79		2.08	2.75	
	1067	Pneumatic nailed		638	.025		1.29	.68		1.97	2.57	
	1082	2" x 14"		500	.032		1.92	.87		2.79	3.57	
	1087	Pneumatic nailed		580	.028		1.92	.75		2.67	3.37	
	1102	3" x 8"		550	.029		2.02	.79		2.81	3.56	
	1122	3" x 10"		500	.032		2.53	.87		3.40	4.24	
	1142	3" x 12"		450	.036		3.04	.97		4.01	4.96	
	1162	3" x 14"		400	.040		3.54	1.09		4.63	5.75	
	1170	4" x 6"	F-3	1,100	.036		2.31	1.01	.40	3.72	4.65	
	1182	4" x 8"		1,000	.040		3.07	1.11	.44	4.62	5.70	
	1202	4" x 10"		950	.042		3.84	1.17	.47	5.48	6.65	
	1222	4" x 12"		900	.044		4.61	1.23	.49	6.33	7.65	
	1242	4" x 14"		850	.047		5.40	1.30	.52	7.22	8.65	
	2002	Double, 2" x 6"	2 Carp	625	.026		1.08	.70		1.78	2.36	
	2007	Pneumatic nailed		725	.022		1.08	.60		1.68	2.20	
	2022	2" x 8"		575	.028		1.46	.76		2.22	2.87	
	2027	Pneumatic nailed		667	.024		1.46	.65		2.11	2.70	
	2042	2" x 10"		550	.029		2.02	.79		2.81	3.56	
	2047	Pneumatic nailed		638	.025		2.02	.68		2.70	3.38	
	2062	2" x 12"		525	.030		2.58	.83		3.41	4.23	
	2067	Pneumatic nailed		610	.026		2.58	.72		3.30	4.04	
	2082	2" x 14"		475	.034		3.83	.92		4.75	5.75	
	2087	Pneumatic nailed		551	.029		3.83	.79		4.62	5.55	
	3002	Triple, 2" x 6"		550	.029		1.62	.79		2.41	3.11	
	3007	Pneumatic nailed		638	.025		1.62	.68		2.30	2.93	
	3022	2" x 8"		525	.030		2.19	.83		3.02	3.80	
	3027	Pneumatic nailed		609	.026		2.19	.72		2.91	3.61	
	3042	2" x 10"		500	.032		3.03	.87		3.90	4.80	
	3047	Pneumatic nailed		580	.028		3.03	.75		3.78	4.60	
	3062	2" x 12"		475	.034		3.87	.92		4.79	5.80	
	3067	Pneumatic nailed		551	.029		3.87	.79		4.66	5.60	
	3082	2" x 14"		450	.036		5.75	.97		6.72	7.90	
	3087	Pneumatic nailed		522	.031		5.75	.84		6.59	7.70	
	9000	Minimum labor/equipment charge	1 Carp	2	4	Job		109		109	183	
112	0010	**FRAMING, CEILINGS**										112
	6002	Suspended, 2" x 3"	2 Carp	1,000	.016	L.F.	.24	.44		.68	1	
	6052	2" x 4"		900	.018		.36	.49		.85	1.21	
	6102	2" x 6"		800	.020		.54	.55		1.09	1.50	
	6152	2" x 8"		650	.025		.73	.67		1.40	1.92	
	9000	Minimum labor/equipment charge	1 Carp	4	2	Job		54.50		54.50	91.50	

061 | Rough Carpentry

061 100 | Wood Framing

			CREW	DAILY OUTPUT	LABOR-HOURS	UNIT	1999 BARE COSTS MAT.	LABOR	EQUIP.	TOTAL	TOTAL INCL O&P	
114	0010	**FRAMING, JOISTS**										114
	2002	Joists, 2" x 4"	2 Carp	1,250	.013	L.F.	.36	.35		.71	.98	
	2007	Pneumatic nailed		1,438	.011		.36	.30		.66	.91	
	2100	2" x 6"		1,250	.013		.54	.35		.89	1.17	
	2105	Pneumatic nailed		1,438	.011		.54	.30		.84	1.10	
	2152	2" x 8"		1,100	.015		.73	.40		1.13	1.46	
	2157	Pneumatic nailed		1,265	.013		.73	.35		1.08	1.38	
	2202	2" x 10"		900	.018		1.01	.49		1.50	1.92	
	2207	Pneumatic nailed		1,035	.015		1.01	.42		1.43	1.82	
	2252	2" x 12"		875	.018		1.29	.50		1.79	2.26	
	2257	Pneumatic nailed		1,006	.016		1.29	.43		1.72	2.15	
	2302	2" x 14"		770	.021		1.92	.57		2.49	3.06	
	2307	Pneumatic nailed		886	.018		1.92	.49		2.41	2.94	
	2352	3" x 6"		925	.017		1.52	.47		1.99	2.46	
	2402	3" x 10"		780	.021		2.53	.56		3.09	3.72	
	2452	3" x 12"		600	.027		3.04	.73		3.77	4.56	
	2502	4" x 6"		800	.020		2.31	.55		2.86	3.45	
	2552	4" x 10"		600	.027		3.84	.73		4.57	5.45	
	2602	4" x 12"		450	.036		4.61	.97		5.58	6.65	
	2607	Sister joist, 2" x 6"		800	.020		.54	.55		1.09	1.50	
	2608	Pneumatic nailed		960	.017		.54	.45		.99	1.35	
	2612	2" x 8"		640	.025		.73	.68		1.41	1.94	
	2613	Pneumatic nailed		768	.021		.73	.57		1.30	1.75	
	2617	2" x 10"		535	.030		1.01	.82		1.83	2.48	
	2618	Pneumatic nailed		642	.025		1.01	.68		1.69	2.25	
	2622	2" x 12"		455	.035		1.29	.96		2.25	3.03	
	2627	Pneumatic nailed		546	.029		1.29	.80		2.09	2.76	
	3000	Composite wood joist 9-1/2" deep		.90	17.778	M.L.F.	1,700	485		2,185	2,650	
	3010	11-1/2" deep		.88	18.182		1,825	495		2,320	2,825	
	3020	14" deep		.82	19.512		1,950	535		2,485	3,050	
	3030	16" deep		.78	20.513		2,600	560		3,160	3,775	
	4000	Open web joist 12" deep		.88	18.182		1,875	495		2,370	2,900	
	4010	14" deep		.82	19.512		2,125	535		2,660	3,225	
	4020	16" deep		.78	20.513		2,200	560		2,760	3,350	
	4030	18" deep		.74	21.622		2,300	590		2,890	3,525	
	6000	Composite rim joist, 1-1/4" x 9-1/2"		90	.178		1,925	4.85		1,929.85	2,125	
	6010	1-1/4" x 11-1/2"		.88	18.182		2,050	495		2,545	3,100	
	6020	1-1/4" x 14-1/2"		.82	19.512		2,525	535		3,060	3,675	
	6030	1-1/4" x 16-1/2"		.78	20.513		2,625	560		3,185	3,800	
	9000	Minimum labor/equipment charge	1 Carp	4	2	Job		54.50		54.50	91.50	
116	0010	**FRAMING, MISCELLANEOUS**										116
	2002	Firestops, 2" x 4"	2 Carp	780	.021	L.F.	.36	.56		.92	1.34	
	2007	Pneumatic nailed		952	.017		.36	.46		.82	1.17	
	2102	2" x 6"		600	.027		.54	.73		1.27	1.81	
	2107	Pneumatic nailed		732	.022		.54	.60		1.14	1.59	
	5002	Nailers, treated, wood construction, 2" x 4"		800	.020		.64	.55		1.19	1.62	
	5007	Pneumatic nailed		960	.017		.64	.45		1.09	1.47	
	5102	2" x 6"		750	.021		.96	.58		1.54	2.03	
	5107	Pneumatic nailed		900	.018		.96	.49		1.45	1.87	
	5122	2" x 8"		700	.023		1.29	.62		1.91	2.46	
	5127	Pneumatic nailed		840	.019		1.29	.52		1.81	2.29	
	5202	Steel construction, 2" x 4"		750	.021		.64	.58		1.22	1.68	
	5222	2" x 6"		700	.023		.96	.62		1.58	2.10	
	5242	2" x 8"		650	.025		1.29	.67		1.96	2.54	
	7002	Rough bucks, treated, for doors or windows, 2" x 6"		400	.040		.96	1.09		2.05	2.89	
	7007	Pneumatic nailed		480	.033		.96	.91		1.87	2.58	

For expanded coverage of these items see *Means Interior Cost Data 1999*

061 | Rough Carpentry

061 100 | Wood Framing

			CREW	DAILY OUTPUT	LABOR-HOURS	UNIT	MAT.	LABOR	EQUIP.	TOTAL	TOTAL INCL O&P	
116	7102	2" x 8"	2 Carp	380	.042	L.F.	1.29	1.15		2.44	3.34	116
	7107	Pneumatic nailed		456	.035		1.29	.96		2.25	3.02	
	8000	Stair stringers, 2" x 10"		130	.123		1.01	3.36		4.37	6.70	
	8100	2" x 12"		130	.123		1.29	3.36		4.65	7	
	8150	3" x 10"		125	.128		2.53	3.49		6.02	8.65	
	8200	3" x 12"		125	.128		3.04	3.49		6.53	9.20	
	8870	Composite LSL, 1-1/4" x 11-1/2"		130	.123		2.06	3.36		5.42	7.85	
	8880	1-1/4" x 14-1/2"		130	.123		2.52	3.36		5.88	8.35	
	9000	Minimum labor/equipment charge	1 Carp	4	2	Job		54.50		54.50	91.50	
118	0010	**FRAMING, COLUMNS**										118
	0100	4" x 4"	2 Carp	390	.041	L.F.	.95	1.12		2.07	2.92	
	0150	4" x 6"		275	.058		2.31	1.59		3.90	5.20	
	0200	4" x 8"		220	.073		3.07	1.99		5.06	6.70	
	0250	6" x 6"		215	.074		5.05	2.03		7.08	8.95	
	0300	6" x 8"		175	.091		4.98	2.50		7.48	9.70	
	0350	6" x 10"		150	.107		7.05	2.91		9.96	12.60	
	9000	Minimum labor/equipment charge	1 Carp	2	4	Job		109		109	183	
120	0010	**FRAMING, ROOFS**										120
	2000	Fascia boards, 2" x 8"	2 Carp	225	.071	L.F.	.73	1.94		2.67	4.05	
	2100	2" x 10"		180	.089		1.01	2.43		3.44	5.15	
	5000	Rafters, to 4 in 12 pitch, 2" x 6", ordinary		1,000	.016		.54	.44		.98	1.32	
	5060	2" x 8", ordinary		950	.017		.73	.46		1.19	1.57	
	5250	Composite rafter, 9-1/2" deep		575	.028		1.93	.76		2.69	3.39	
	5260	11-1/2" deep		575	.028		2.06	.76		2.82	3.54	
	5300	Hip and valley rafters, 2" x 6", ordinary		760	.021		.54	.57		1.11	1.55	
	5360	2" x 8", ordinary		720	.022		.73	.61		1.34	1.82	
	5540	Hip and valley jacks, 2" x 6", ordinary		600	.027		.54	.73		1.27	1.81	
	5600	2" x 8", ordinary		490	.033		.73	.89		1.62	2.29	
	5761	For slopes steeper than 4 in 12, add						30%				
	5770	For dormers or complex roofs, add						50%				
	5780	Rafter tie, 1" x 4", #3	2 Carp	800	.020	L.F.	.37	.55		.92	1.32	
	5800	Ridge board, #2 or better, 1" x 6"		600	.027		.83	.73		1.56	2.14	
	5820	1" x 8"		550	.029		.96	.79		1.75	2.39	
	5840	1" x 10"		500	.032		1.20	.87		2.07	2.78	
	5860	2" x 6"		500	.032		.54	.87		1.41	2.05	
	5880	2" x 8"		450	.036		.73	.97		1.70	2.42	
	5900	2" x 10"		400	.040		1.01	1.09		2.10	2.94	
	5920	Roof cants, split, 4" x 4"		650	.025		.95	.67		1.62	2.17	
	5940	6" x 6"		600	.027		5.05	.73		5.78	6.75	
	5960	Roof curbs, untreated, 2" x 6"		520	.031		.54	.84		1.38	2	
	5980	2" x 12"		400	.040		1.29	1.09		2.38	3.25	
	6000	Sister rafters, 2" x 6"		800	.020		.54	.55		1.09	1.50	
	6020	2" x 8"		640	.025		.73	.68		1.41	1.94	
	6040	2" x 10"		535	.030		1.01	.82		1.83	2.48	
	6060	2" x 12"		455	.035		1.29	.96		2.25	3.03	
	9000	Minimum labor/equipment charge	1 Carp	4	2	Job		54.50		54.50	91.50	
122	0010	**FRAMING, SILLS**										122
	2002	Ledgers, nailed, 2" x 4"	2 Carp	755	.021	L.F.	.36	.58		.94	1.37	
	2052	2" x 6"		600	.027		.54	.73		1.27	1.81	
	2102	Bolted, not including bolts, 3" x 6"		325	.049		1.52	1.34		2.86	3.92	
	2152	3" x 12"		233	.069		3.04	1.87		4.91	6.50	
	2602	Mud sills, redwood, construction grade, 2" x 4"		895	.018		2.67	.49		3.16	3.75	
	2622	2" x 6"		780	.021		4	.56		4.56	5.35	
	4002	Sills, 2" x 4"		600	.027		.36	.73		1.09	1.62	

Reference marker: R061-030 (at row 2000)

Important: See the Reference Section for critical supporting data - Reference Nos., Crews, & City Cost Indexes

061 | Rough Carpentry

061 100 | Wood Framing

			CREW	DAILY OUTPUT	LABOR-HOURS	UNIT	MAT.	LABOR	EQUIP.	TOTAL	TOTAL INCL O&P	
122	4052	2" x 6"	2 Carp	550	.029	L.F.	.54	.79		1.33	1.92	122
	4082	2" x 8"		500	.032		.73	.87		1.60	2.26	
	4202	Treated, 2" x 4"		550	.029		.64	.79		1.43	2.04	
	4222	2" x 6"		500	.032		.96	.87		1.83	2.52	
	4242	2" x 8"		450	.036		1.29	.97		2.26	3.04	
	4402	4" x 4"		450	.036		1.78	.97		2.75	3.58	
	4422	4" x 6"		350	.046		2.67	1.25		3.92	5.05	
	4462	4" x 8"		300	.053		3.56	1.46		5.02	6.35	
	4481	4" x 10"		260	.062		4.21	1.68		5.89	7.45	
	9000	Minimum labor/equipment charge	1 Carp	4	2	Job		54.50		54.50	91.50	
124	0010	**FRAMING, SLEEPERS**										124
	0100	On concrete, treated, 1" x 2"	2 Carp	2,350	.007	L.F.	.17	.19		.36	.49	
	0150	1" x 3"		2,000	.008		.25	.22		.47	.65	
	0200	2" x 4"		1,500	.011		.64	.29		.93	1.20	
	0250	2" x 6"		1,300	.012		.96	.34		1.30	1.62	
	9000	Minimum labor/equipment charge	1 Carp	4	2	Job		54.50		54.50	91.50	
126	0010	**FRAMING, SOFFITS & CANOPIES**										126
	1002	Canopy or soffit framing, 1" x 4"	2 Carp	900	.018	L.F.	.55	.49		1.04	1.42	
	1042	1" x 8"		750	.021		.96	.58		1.54	2.03	
	1102	2" x 4"		620	.026		.36	.70		1.06	1.58	
	1142	2" x 8"		500	.032		.73	.87		1.60	2.26	
	1202	3" x 4"		500	.032		1.01	.87		1.88	2.57	
	1242	3" x 10"		300	.053		2.53	1.46		3.99	5.20	
	9000	Minimum labor/equipment charge	1 Carp	4	2	Job		54.50		54.50	91.50	
127	0010	**FRAMING, TREATED LUMBER**										127
	0020	Water-borne salt, C.C.A., A.C.A., wet, .40 P.C.F. retention										
	0100	2" x 4"				M.B.F.	965			965	1,050	
	0110	2" x 6"					965			965	1,050	
	0120	2" x 8"					965			965	1,050	
	0130	2" x 10"					955			955	1,050	
	0140	2" x 12"					1,100			1,100	1,200	
	0200	4" x 4"					1,325			1,325	1,475	
	0210	4" x 6"					1,325			1,325	1,475	
	0220	4" x 8"					1,325			1,325	1,475	
	0250	Add for .60 P.C.F. retention					40%					
	0260	Add for 2.5 P.C.F. retention					200%					
	0270	Add for K.D.A.T.					20%					
128	0010	**FRAMING, WALLS**	R061-010									128
	2002	Headers over openings, 2" x 6"		2 Carp	360	.044	L.F.	.54	1.21		1.75	2.62	
	2007	2" x 6", pneumatic nailed	R061-030		432	.037		.54	1.01		1.55	2.28	
	2052	2" x 8"			340	.047		.73	1.28		2.01	2.95	
	2057	2" x 8", pneumatic nailed			408	.039		.73	1.07		1.80	2.59	
	2100	2" x 10"			320	.050		1.01	1.36		2.37	3.40	
	2105	2" x 10", pneumatic nailed			384	.042		1.01	1.14		2.15	3.01	
	2152	2" x 12"			300	.053		1.29	1.46		2.75	3.86	
	2157	2" x 12", pneumatic nailed			360	.044		1.29	1.21		2.50	3.45	
	2202	4" x 12"			190	.084		4.61	2.30		6.91	8.90	
	2207	4" x 12", pneumatic nailed			228	.070		4.61	1.92		6.53	8.25	
	2252	6" x 12"			140	.114		8.45	3.12		11.57	14.50	
	5002	Plates, untreated, 2" x 3"			850	.019		.24	.51		.75	1.13	
	5007	2" x 3", pneumatic nailed			1,020	.016		.24	.43		.67	.99	
	5022	2" x 4"			800	.020		.36	.55		.91	1.31	
	5027	2" x 4", pneumatic nailed			960	.017		.36	.45		.81	1.16	
	5041	2" x 6"			750	.021		.54	.58		1.12	1.56	
	5046	2" x 6", pneumatic nailed			900	.018		.54	.49		1.03	1.40	

For expanded coverage of these items see *Means Interior Cost Data 1999*

061 | Rough Carpentry

061 100 | Wood Framing

			CREW	DAILY OUTPUT	LABOR-HOURS	UNIT	MAT.	LABOR	EQUIP.	TOTAL	TOTAL INCL O&P	
128	5122	Studs, 8' high wall, 2" x 3"	2 Carp	1,200	.013	L.F.	.24	.36		.60	.88	128
	5127	2" x 3", pneumatic nailed	R061-010	1,440	.011		.24	.30		.54	.78	
	5142	2" x 4"		1,100	.015		.36	.40		.76	1.06	
	5147	2" x 4", pneumatic nailed	R061-030	1,320	.012		.36	.33		.69	.95	
	5162	2" x 6"		1,000	.016		.54	.44		.98	1.32	
	5167	2" x 6", pneumatic nailed		1,200	.013		.54	.36		.90	1.20	
	5182	3" x 4"		800	.020		1.01	.55		1.56	2.02	
	5187	3" x 4", pneumatic nailed		960	.017		1.01	.45		1.46	1.87	
	8200	For 12' high walls, deduct						5%				
	8220	For stub wall, 6' high, add						20%				
	8240	3' high, add						40%				
	8250	For second story & above, add						5%				
	8300	For dormer & gable, add						15%				
	9000	Minimum labor/equipment charge	1 Carp	4	2	Job		54.50		54.50	91.50	
130	0012	**FURRING** Wood strips, 1" x 2", on walls, on wood		550	.015	L.F.	.18	.40		.58	.86	130
	0017	Pneumatic nailed		710	.011		.18	.31		.49	.71	
	0302	On masonry		495	.016		.18	.44		.62	.94	
	0402	On concrete		260	.031		.18	.84		1.02	1.61	
	0602	1" x 3", on walls, on wood		550	.015		.23	.40		.63	.91	
	0607	Pneumatic nailed		710	.011		.23	.31		.54	.76	
	0702	On masonry		495	.016		.23	.44		.67	.99	
	0802	On concrete		260	.031		.23	.84		1.07	1.66	
	0852	On ceilings, on wood		350	.023		.23	.62		.85	1.29	
	0857	Pneumatic nailed		450	.018		.23	.49		.72	1.06	
	0902	On masonry		320	.025		.23	.68		.91	1.39	
	0952	On concrete		210	.038		.23	1.04		1.27	1.99	
	9000	Minimum labor/equipment charge		4	2	Job		54.50		54.50	91.50	
132	0012	**GROUNDS** For casework, 1" x 2" wood strips, on wood	1 Carp	330	.024	L.F.	.18	.66		.84	1.31	132
	0102	On masonry		285	.028		.18	.77		.95	1.48	
	0202	On concrete		250	.032		.18	.87		1.05	1.66	
	0402	For plaster, 3/4" deep, on wood		450	.018		.18	.49		.67	1.01	
	0502	On masonry		225	.036		.18	.97		1.15	1.82	
	0602	On concrete		175	.046		.18	1.25		1.43	2.29	
	0702	On metal lath		200	.040		.18	1.09		1.27	2.03	
	9000	Minimum labor/equipment charge		4	2	Job		54.50		54.50	91.50	
134	0010	**INSULATION** See division 072										134
136	0010	**LAMINATED** See division 061-804										136
138	0010	**PARTITIONS** Wood stud with single bottom plate and										138
	0020	double top plate, no waste, std. & better lumber										
	0182	2" x 4" studs, 8' high, studs 12" O.C.	2 Carp	80	.200	L.F.	4.36	5.45		9.81	13.95	
	0187	12" O.C., pneumatic nailed		96	.167		4.36	4.55		8.91	12.40	
	0202	16" O.C.		100	.160		3.56	4.37		7.93	11.20	
	0207	16" O.C., pneumatic nailed		120	.133		3.56	3.64		7.20	10	
	0302	24" O.C.		125	.128		2.77	3.49		6.26	8.90	
	0307	24" O.C., pneumatic nailed		150	.107		2.77	2.91		5.68	7.90	
	0382	10' high, studs 12" O.C.		80	.200		5.15	5.45		10.60	14.80	
	0387	12" O.C., pneumatic nailed		96	.167		5.15	4.55		9.70	13.25	
	0402	16" O.C.		100	.160		4.16	4.37		8.53	11.85	
	0407	16" O.C., pneumatic nailed		120	.133		4.16	3.64		7.80	10.65	
	0502	24" O.C.		125	.128		3.17	3.49		6.66	9.35	
	0507	24" O.C., pneumatic nailed		150	.107		3.17	2.91		6.08	8.35	
	0582	12' high, studs 12" O.C.		65	.246		5.95	6.70		12.65	17.80	
	0587	12" O.C., pneumatic nailed		78	.205		5.95	5.60		11.55	15.90	

061 | Rough Carpentry

061 100 | Wood Framing

		CREW	DAILY OUTPUT	LABOR-HOURS	UNIT	MAT.	LABOR	EQUIP.	TOTAL	TOTAL INCL O&P	
138	0602	16" O.C.	2 Carp	80	.200	L.F.	4.75	5.45		10.20	14.40	138
	0607	16" O.C., pneumatic nailed		96	.167		4.75	4.55		9.30	12.85	
	0701	24" O.C.	▼	100	.160	▼	3.56	4.37		7.93	11.20	
	0702											
	0706	24" O.C., pneumatic nailed	2 Carp	120	.133	L.F.	3.56	3.64		7.20	10	
	0782	2" x 6" studs, 8' high, studs 12" O.C.		70	.229		6.50	6.25		12.75	17.60	
	0787	12" O.C., pneumatic nailed		84	.190		6.50	5.20		11.70	15.85	
	0802	16" O.C.		90	.178		5.35	4.85		10.20	13.95	
	0807	16" O.C., pneumatic nailed		108	.148		5.35	4.04		9.39	12.60	
	0902	24" O.C.		115	.139		4.15	3.80		7.95	10.90	
	0907	24" O.C., pneumatic nailed		138	.116		4.15	3.17		7.32	9.85	
	0982	10' high, studs 12" O.C.		70	.229		7.70	6.25		13.95	18.95	
	0987	12" O.C., pneumatic nailed		84	.190		7.70	5.20		12.90	17.20	
	1002	16" O.C.		90	.178		6.25	4.85		11.10	14.95	
	1007	16" O.C., pneumatic nailed		108	.148		6.25	4.04		10.29	13.60	
	1102	24" O.C.		115	.139		4.74	3.80		8.54	11.55	
	1107	24" O.C., pneumatic nailed		138	.116		4.74	3.17		7.91	10.50	
	1182	12' high, studs 12" O.C.		55	.291		8.90	7.95		16.85	23	
	1187	12" O.C., pneumatic nailed		66	.242		8.90	6.60		15.50	21	
	1202	16" O.C.		70	.229		7.10	6.25		13.35	18.30	
	1207	16" O.C., pneumatic nailed		84	.190		7.10	5.20		12.30	16.55	
	1302	24" O.C.		90	.178		5.35	4.85		10.20	13.95	
	1307	24" O.C., pneumatic nailed		108	.148		5.35	4.04		9.39	12.60	
	1402	For horizontal blocking, 2" x 4", add		600	.027		.40	.73		1.13	1.66	
	1502	2" x 6", add		600	.027		.59	.73		1.32	1.87	
	1600	For openings, add		250	.064			1.75		1.75	2.92	
	1702	Headers for above openings, material only, add				B.F.	.60			.60	.66	
	9000	Minimum labor/equipment charge	1 Carp	4	2	Job		54.50		54.50	91.50	
140	0010	**ROUGH HARDWARE** Average % of carpentry material, minimum					.50%					140
	0200	Maximum					1.50%					

061 150 | Sheathing

			CREW	DAILY OUTPUT	LABOR-HOURS	UNIT	MAT.	LABOR	EQUIP.	TOTAL	TOTAL INCL O&P	
154	0010	**SHEATHING** Plywood on roof, CDX	R061-020									154
	0032	5/16" thick		2 Carp	1,600	.010	S.F.	.29	.27		.56	.78	
	0037	Pneumatic nailed	R061-030		1,952	.008		.29	.22		.51	.69	
	0052	3/8" thick			1,525	.010		.32	.29		.61	.83	
	0057	Pneumatic nailed			1,860	.009		.32	.23		.55	.74	
	0102	1/2" thick			1,400	.011		.41	.31		.72	.97	
	0103	Pneumatic nailed			1,708	.009		.41	.26		.67	.88	
	0202	5/8" thick			1,300	.012		.49	.34		.83	1.10	
	0207	Pneumatic nailed			1,586	.010		.49	.28		.77	1	
	0302	3/4" thick			1,200	.013		.58	.36		.94	1.25	
	0307	Pneumatic nailed			1,464	.011		.58	.30		.88	1.14	
	0502	Plywood on walls with exterior CDX, 3/8" thick			1,200	.013		.32	.36		.68	.96	
	0507	Pneumatic nailed			1,488	.011		.32	.29		.61	.84	
	0602	1/2" thick			1,125	.014		.41	.39		.80	1.10	
	0607	Pneumatic nailed			1,395	.011		.41	.31		.72	.97	
	0702	5/8" thick			1,050	.015		.49	.42		.91	1.24	
	0707	Pneumatic nailed			1,302	.012		.49	.34		.83	1.10	
	0802	3/4" thick			975	.016		.58	.45		1.03	1.39	
	0807	Pneumatic nailed			1,209	.013		.58	.36		.94	1.24	
	1000	For shear wall construction, add							20%				
	1200	For structural 1 exterior plywood, add					S.F.	10%					
	1402	With boards, on roof 1" x 6" boards, laid horizontal		2 Carp	725	.022		.99	.60		1.59	2.10	
	1502	Laid diagonal			650	.025		.99	.67		1.66	2.21	
	1702	1" x 8" boards, laid horizontal			875	.018		1.05	.50		1.55	1.99	

For expanded coverage of these items see *Means Interior Cost Data 1999*

061 | Rough Carpentry

061 150 | Sheathing

			CREW	DAILY OUTPUT	LABOR-HOURS	UNIT	MAT.	LABOR	EQUIP.	TOTAL	TOTAL INCL O&P	
154	1802	Laid diagonal	2 Carp	725	.022	S.F.	1.05	.60		1.65	2.16	154
	2000	For steep roofs, add						40%				
	2200	For dormers, hips and valleys, add					5%	50%				
	2402	Boards on walls, 1" x 6" boards, laid regular	2 Carp	650	.025		.99	.67		1.66	2.21	
	2502	Laid diagonal		585	.027		.99	.75		1.74	2.34	
	2702	1" x 8" boards, laid regular		765	.021		1.05	.57		1.62	2.11	
	2802	Laid diagonal		650	.025		1.05	.67		1.72	2.27	
	2852	Gypsum, weatherproof, 1/2" thick		1,050	.015		.21	.42		.63	.93	
	2902	Sealed, 4/10" thick		1,100	.015		.31	.40		.71	1	
	3000	Wood fiber, regular, no vapor barrier, 1/2" thick		1,200	.013		.38	.36		.74	1.03	
	3100	5/8" thick		1,200	.013		.50	.36		.86	1.16	
	3300	No vapor barrier, in colors, 1/2" thick		1,200	.013		.54	.36		.90	1.20	
	3400	5/8" thick		1,200	.013		.67	.36		1.03	1.35	
	3600	With vapor barrier one side, white, 1/2" thick		1,200	.013		.53	.36		.89	1.19	
	3700	Vapor barrier 2 sides, 1/2" thick		1,200	.013		.81	.36		1.17	1.50	
	3800	Asphalt impregnated, 25/32" thick		1,200	.013		.34	.36		.70	.98	
	3850	Intermediate, 1/2" thick		1,200	.013		.28	.36		.64	.92	
	9000	Minimum labor/equipment charge	1 Carp	2	4	Job		109		109	183	

061 160 | Subfloor

			CREW	DAILY OUTPUT	LABOR-HOURS	UNIT	MAT.	LABOR	EQUIP.	TOTAL	TOTAL INCL O&P	
161	0010	FLOORING, WOOD See division 095-604										161
164	0012	SUBFLOOR Plywood, CDX, 1/2" thick	2 Carp	1,500	.011	SF Flr.	.41	.29		.70	.94	164
	0017	Pneumatic nailed		1,860	.009		.41	.23		.64	.84	
	0102	5/8" thick		1,350	.012		.49	.32		.81	1.08	
	0107	Pneumatic nailed		1,674	.010		.49	.26		.75	.98	
	0202	3/4" thick		1,250	.013		.58	.35		.93	1.22	
	0207	Pneumatic nailed		1,550	.010		.58	.28		.86	1.11	
	0302	1-1/8" thick, 2-4-1 including underlayment		1,050	.015		1.18	.42		1.60	2	
	0502	With boards, 1" x 10" S4S, laid regular		1,100	.015		.96	.40		1.36	1.72	
	0602	Laid diagonal		900	.018		.97	.49		1.46	1.88	
	0802	1" x 8" S4S, laid regular		1,000	.016		.86	.44		1.30	1.68	
	0902	Laid diagonal		850	.019		.86	.51		1.37	1.80	
	1100	Wood fiber, T&G, 2' x 8' planks, 1" thick		1,000	.016		1.19	.44		1.63	2.04	
	1200	1-3/8" thick		900	.018		1.46	.49		1.95	2.42	
	9000	Minimum labor/equipment charge	1 Carp	4	2	Job		54.50		54.50	91.50	
168	0010	UNDERLAYMENT Plywood, underlayment grade, 3/8" thick	2 Carp	1,500	.011	SF Flr.	.66	.29		.95	1.22	168
	0016	Pneumatic nailed	"	1,860	.009	"	.66	.23		.89	1.12	
	0102	1/2" thick	2 Carp	1,450	.011	SF Flr.	.75	.30		1.05	1.33	
	0107	Pneumatic nailed		1,798	.009		.75	.24		.99	1.24	
	0202	5/8" thick		1,400	.011		.63	.31		.94	1.21	
	0207	Pneumatic nailed		1,736	.009		.63	.25		.88	1.11	
	0302	3/4" thick		1,300	.012		.86	.34		1.20	1.51	
	0306	Pneumatic nailed		1,612	.010		.86	.27		1.13	1.40	
	0502	Particle board, 3/8" thick		1,500	.011		.38	.29		.67	.91	
	0507	Pneumatic nailed		1,860	.009		.38	.23		.61	.81	
	0602	1/2" thick		1,450	.011		.40	.30		.70	.94	
	0607	Pneumatic nailed		1,798	.009		.40	.24		.64	.85	
	0802	5/8" thick		1,400	.011		.54	.31		.85	1.11	
	0807	Pneumatic nailed		1,736	.009		.54	.25		.79	1.01	
	0902	3/4" thick		1,300	.012		.41	.34		.75	1.01	
	0907	Pneumatic nailed		1,612	.010		.41	.27		.68	.90	
	1102	Hardboard, underlayment grade, 4' x 4', .215" thick		1,500	.011		.41	.29		.70	.94	
	9000	Minimum labor/equipment charge	1 Carp	4	2	Job		54.50		54.50	91.50	

061 | Rough Carpentry

061 200 | Structural Panels

		CREW	DAILY OUTPUT	LABOR-HOURS	UNIT	1999 BARE COSTS MAT.	LABOR	EQUIP.	TOTAL	TOTAL INCL O&P	
208	0010	**STRESSED SKIN PLYWOOD ROOF PANELS** 3/8" group 1 top										208
	0020	skin, 3/8" exterior AD bottom skin										
	0030	1150f stringers, 4' x 8' panels										
	0100	4-1/4" deep	F-3	2,075	.019	SF Roof	3.04	.53	.21	3.78	4.45	
	0200	6-1/8" deep		1,725	.023		3.29	.64	.26	4.19	4.96	
	0300	8-1/8" deep		1,475	.027		3.81	.75	.30	4.86	5.75	
	0500	3/8" top skin, no bottom skin, 5-3/4" deep		1,725	.023		2.88	.64	.26	3.78	4.51	
	0600	7-3/4" deep	↓	1,475	.027		3.29	.75	.30	4.34	5.20	
	0800	For 3-1/2" factory fiberglass insulation, add					.35			.35	.39	
	1000	For 1/2" thick top skin, add				↓	.35			.35	.39	
	1500	Floor panels, substitute 5/8" underlayment as										
	1510	top skin, add to roof panels above				SF Flr.	.41			.41	.45	
	2000	Curved roof panels, 3/8" structural 1 top skin,										
	2010	3/8" exterior AC bottom skin, laminated ribs										
	2200	8' radius, 2-1/4" deep, tie rods not req'd.	F-3	1,150	.035	SF Flr.	5.70	.96	.39	7.05	8.30	
	2400	10' radius, 1-1/2" deep, tie rods are included		950	.042		4.48	1.17	.47	6.12	7.35	
	2600	10' radius, 3-3/8" deep, tie rods not req'd.		1,150	.035		7.80	.96	.39	9.15	10.55	
	2800	12' radius, 2" deep, tie rods are included		950	.042		4.63	1.17	.47	6.27	7.55	
	3000	12' radius, 4-1/2" deep, tie rods not req'd.	↓	1,150	.035	↓	8.10	.96	.39	9.45	10.90	
	4000	Folded plate roofs, structural 1 top skin with intermediate										
	4010	rafters and end chord. Cost of tie rods included										
	4200	Slope 7 in 12, 4' fold, 2" thick, 32' span	F-3	850	.047	SF Flr.	3.71	1.30	.52	5.53	6.80	
	4400	Slope 8-1/2 in 12, 5' fold, 4" thick, 56' span		950	.042		7.40	1.17	.47	9.04	10.60	
	4600	Slope 10 in 12, 8' fold, 4" thick, 52' span		950	.042		4.43	1.17	.47	6.07	7.30	
	4800	Slope 10 in 12, 8' fold, 4" thick, 72' span	↓	1,025	.039	↓	7.80	1.08	.43	9.31	10.80	
	6000	Box beams, structural 1 web										
	6200	24" deep, 2-2" x 4" flanges, 2 webs @ 3/8"	F-3	295	.136	L.F.	8.90	3.76	1.50	14.16	17.65	
	6400	24" deep, 3-2" x 4" flanges, 2 webs @ 1/2"		260	.154		11.05	4.26	1.71	17.02	21	
	6600	48" deep, 3-2" x 6" flanges, 2 webs @ 3/4"	↓	140	.286	↓	19.15	7.90	3.17	30.22	37.50	
	6800	48" deep, 6-2" x 6" flanges, 4 webs @ 3/8",										
	6810	including 2 interior webs	F-3	115	.348	L.F.	39	9.65	3.86	52.51	63	
	7000	For exterior AC outer webs, add					1.03			1.03	1.13	
	7200	For medium density overlaid outer webs, add				↓	1.54			1.54	1.69	

061 250 | Wood Decking

		CREW	DAILY OUTPUT	LABOR-HOURS	UNIT	MAT.	LABOR	EQUIP.	TOTAL	TOTAL INCL O&P	
258	0010	**ROOF DECKS**										258
	0020	For laminated decks, see division 061-808										
	0200	For cementitious decks, see division 035										
	0400	Cedar planks, 3" thick	2 Carp	320	.050	S.F.	5.65	1.36		7.01	8.55	
	0500	4" thick		250	.064		7.65	1.75		9.40	11.30	
	0702	Douglas fir, 3" thick		320	.050		2.12	1.36		3.48	4.62	
	0802	4" thick		250	.064		2.84	1.75		4.59	6.05	
	1002	Hemlock, 3" thick		320	.050		2.12	1.36		3.48	4.62	
	1102	4" thick		250	.064		2.83	1.75		4.58	6.05	
	1302	Western white spruce, 3" thick		320	.050		2.05	1.36		3.41	4.55	
	1402	4" thick	↓	250	.064	↓	2.73	1.75		4.48	5.90	
	9000	Minimum labor/equipment charge	1 Carp	2	4	Job		109		109	183	

061 280 | Mineral Fbr. Cem. Panel

		CREW	DAILY OUTPUT	LABOR-HOURS	UNIT	MAT.	LABOR	EQUIP.	TOTAL	TOTAL INCL O&P	
281	0010	**MINERAL FIBER CEMENT PANELS** Including panels, fasteners,										281
	0100	accessories, trim & sealant										
	0130	Architectural, textured finish, 1/8" thick, minimum	G-3	500	.064	S.F.	5.75	1.70		7.45	9.15	
	0140	Maximum		500	.064		7.25	1.70		8.95	10.80	
	0150	1/4" thick, minimum		500	.064		6.75	1.70		8.45	10.25	
	0200	Maximum	↓	500	.064	↓	8.85	1.70		10.55	12.55	

For expanded coverage of these items see *Means Interior Cost Data 1999*

061 | Rough Carpentry

061 280 | Mineral Fbr. Cem. Panel

		CREW	DAILY OUTPUT	LABOR-HOURS	UNIT	1999 BARE COSTS MAT.	LABOR	EQUIP.	TOTAL	TOTAL INCL O&P	
281	0250	3/8" thick, minimum	G-3	500	.064	S.F.	8.90	1.70		10.60	12.60	281
	0300	Maximum		500	.064		11.75	1.70		13.45	15.75	
	0350	5/8" thick, minimum		300	.107		11.75	2.84		14.59	17.60	
	0400	Maximum		300	.107		17.10	2.84		19.94	23.50	
	2000	Flat sheets, 1/8" thick		1,200	.027		4.05	.71		4.76	5.60	
	2100	1/4" thick		1,020	.031		5.80	.83		6.63	7.75	
	2200	3/8" thick		885	.036		7.30	.96		8.26	9.60	
	2300	5/8" thick		795	.040		9.95	1.07		11.02	12.70	
	3000	Glasweld, mineral enamel coating, 1/8" thick		600	.053		3.50	1.42		4.92	6.15	
	3100	1/4" thick		322	.099		4.45	2.64		7.09	9.20	
	4000	Sandwich panel, Glasweld face and back										
	4100	1" thick, perlite core	G-3	322	.099	S.F.	7.25	2.64		9.89	12.30	
	4200	Polyurethane core		322	.099		7.65	2.64		10.29	12.70	
	4500	2" thick, perlite core		322	.099		7.95	2.64		10.59	13.05	
	4600	Polyurethane core		322	.099		8.35	2.64		10.99	13.50	

061 300 | Heavy Timber Constr.

		CREW	DAILY OUTPUT	LABOR-HOURS	UNIT	MAT.	LABOR	EQUIP.	TOTAL	TOTAL INCL O&P	
304	0010	**FRAMING, HEAVY** Mill timber, beams, single 6" x 10" [R061-010]	2 Carp	1.10	14.545	M.B.F.	1,425	395		1,820	2,250	304
	0100	Single 8" x 16"		1.20	13.333	"	1,625	365		1,990	2,400	
	0202	Built from 2" lumber, multiple 2" x 14"		900	.018	B.F.	.82	.49		1.31	1.71	
	0212	Built from 3" lumber, multiple 3" x 6"		700	.023		1.01	.62		1.63	2.15	
	0222	Multiple 3" x 8"		800	.020		1.01	.55		1.56	2.02	
	0232	Multiple 3" x 10"		900	.018		1.01	.49		1.50	1.92	
	0242	Multiple 3" x 12"		1,000	.016		1.01	.44		1.45	1.84	
	0252	Built from 4" lumber, multiple 4" x 6"		800	.020		1.15	.55		1.70	2.18	
	0262	Multiple 4" x 8"		900	.018		1.15	.49		1.64	2.08	
	0272	Multiple 4" x 10"		1,000	.016		1.15	.44		1.59	2	
	0281											
	0282	Multiple 4" x 12"	2 Carp	1,100	.015	B.F.	1.15	.40		1.55	1.93	
	0292	Columns, structural grade, 1500f, 4" x 4"		450	.036	L.F.	1.67	.97		2.64	3.46	
	0302	6" x 6"		225	.071		5.20	1.94		7.14	9	
	0402	8" x 8"		240	.067		9.95	1.82		11.77	14	
	0502	10" x 10"		90	.178		14.50	4.85		19.35	24	
	0602	12" x 12"		70	.229		21	6.25		27.25	33.50	
	0802	Floor planks, 2" thick, T & G, 2" x 6"		1,050	.015	B.F.	.70	.42		1.12	1.47	
	0902	2" x 10"		1,100	.015		.76	.40		1.16	1.50	
	1102	3" thick, 3" x 6"		1,050	.015		1.15	.42		1.57	1.97	
	1202	3" x 10"		1,100	.015		1.15	.40		1.55	1.93	
	1402	Girders, structural grade, 12" x 12"		800	.020		1.65	.55		2.20	2.72	
	1502	10" x 16"		1,000	.016		1.61	.44		2.05	2.50	
	2050	Roof planks, see division 061-258										
	2302	Roof purlins, 4" thick, structural grade	2 Carp	1,050	.015	B.F.	1.13	.42		1.55	1.94	
	2502	Roof trusses, add timber connectors, division 060-512	"	450	.036	"	1.10	.97		2.07	2.83	
	9000	Minimum labor/equipment charge	1 Carp	2	4	Job		109		109	183	

061 500 | Wood-Metal Systems

		CREW	DAILY OUTPUT	LABOR-HOURS	UNIT	MAT.	LABOR	EQUIP.	TOTAL	TOTAL INCL O&P	
508	0010	**STRUCTURAL JOISTS** Fabricated "I" joists with wood flanges,										508
	0100	Plywood webs, incl. bridging & blocking, panels 24" O.C.										
	1200	15' to 24' span, 50 psf live load	F-5	2,400	.013	SF Flr.	1.44	.37		1.81	2.20	
	1300	55 psf live load		2,250	.014		1.55	.40		1.95	2.36	
	1400	24' to 30' span, 45 psf live load		2,600	.012		1.80	.34		2.14	2.55	
	1500	55 psf live load		2,400	.013		1.80	.37		2.17	2.60	
	1600	Tubular steel open webs, 45 psf, 24" O.C., 40' span	F-3	6,250	.006		1.80	.18	.07	2.05	2.35	
	1700	55' span		7,750	.005		1.75	.14	.06	1.95	2.23	

061 | Rough Carpentry

061 500 | Wood-Metal Systems

		CREW	DAILY OUTPUT	LABOR-HOURS	UNIT	MAT.	LABOR	EQUIP.	TOTAL	TOTAL INCL O&P
1800	70' span	F-3	9,250	.004	SF Flr.	2.27	.12	.05	2.44	2.75
1900	85 psf live load, 26' span	↓	2,300	.017	↓	2.11	.48	.19	2.78	3.33

061 800 | Glued-Laminated Const

		CREW	DAILY OUTPUT	LABOR-HOURS	UNIT	MAT.	LABOR	EQUIP.	TOTAL	TOTAL INCL O&P
0010	**LAMINATED FRAMING** Not including decking									
0020	30 lb., short term live load, 15 lb. dead load									
0200	Straight roof beams, 20' clear span, beams 8' O.C.	F-3	2,560	.016	SF Flr.	1.38	.43	.17	1.98	2.43
0300	Beams 16' O.C.		3,200	.013		1.01	.35	.14	1.50	1.83
0500	40' clear span, beams 8' O.C.		3,200	.013		2.66	.35	.14	3.15	3.65
0600	Beams 16' O.C.	↓	3,840	.010		2.17	.29	.12	2.58	3
0800	60' clear span, beams 8' O.C.	F-4	2,880	.017		4.56	.45	.28	5.29	6.05
0900	Beams 16' O.C.	"	3,840	.013		3.40	.34	.21	3.95	4.53
1100	Tudor arches, 30' to 40' clear span, frames 8' O.C.	F-3	1,680	.024		5.95	.66	.26	6.87	7.95
1200	Frames 16' O.C.	"	2,240	.018		4.66	.49	.20	5.35	6.20
1400	50' to 60' clear span, frames 8' O.C.	F-4	2,200	.022		6.40	.59	.36	7.35	8.40
1500	Frames 16' O.C.		2,640	.018		5.45	.49	.30	6.24	7.15
1700	Radial arches, 60' clear span, frames 8' O.C.		1,920	.025		6	.68	.41	7.09	8.15
1800	Frames 16' O.C.		2,880	.017		4.61	.45	.28	5.34	6.10
2000	100' clear span, frames 8' O.C.		1,600	.030		6.20	.81	.50	7.51	8.75
2100	Frames 16' O.C.		2,400	.020		5.45	.54	.33	6.32	7.25
2300	120' clear span, frames 8' O.C.		1,440	.033		8.25	.90	.55	9.70	11.20
2400	Frames 16' O.C.	↓	1,920	.025		7.55	.68	.41	8.64	9.85
2600	Bowstring trusses, 20' O.C., 40' clear span	F-3	2,400	.017		3.72	.46	.18	4.36	5.05
2700	60' clear span	F-4	3,600	.013		3.34	.36	.22	3.92	4.51
2800	100' clear span		4,000	.012		4.73	.33	.20	5.26	5.95
2900	120' clear span	↓	3,600	.013		5.10	.36	.22	5.68	6.45
3100	For premium appearance, add to S.F. prices					5%				
3300	For industrial type, deduct					15%				
3500	For stain and varnish, add					5%				
3900	For 3/4" laminations, add to straight					25%				
4100	Add to curved				↓	15%				
4300	Alternate pricing method: (use nominal footage of									
4310	components). Straight beams, camber less than 6"	F-3	3.50	11.429	M.B.F.	2,050	315	127	2,492	2,950
4400	Columns, including hardware		2	20		2,225	555	222	3,002	3,600
4600	Curved members, radius over 32'		2.50	16		2,275	445	177	2,897	3,425
4700	Radius 10' to 32'	↓	3	13.333		2,250	370	148	2,768	3,250
4900	For complicated shapes, add maximum					100%				
5100	For pressure treating, add to straight					35%				
5200	Add to curved				↓	45%				
6000	Laminated veneer members, southern pine or western species									
6050	1-3/4" wide x 5-1/2" deep	2 Carp	480	.033	L.F.	3.51	.91		4.42	5.40
6100	9-1/2" deep		480	.033		3.68	.91		4.59	5.55
6150	14" deep		450	.036		5.25	.97		6.22	7.40
6200	18" deep	↓	450	.036	↓	6.80	.97		7.77	9.10
6300	Parallel strand members, southern pine or western species									
6350	1-3/4" wide x 9-1/4" deep	2 Carp	480	.033	L.F.	4.21	.91		5.12	6.15
6400	11-1/4" deep		450	.036		5.15	.97		6.12	7.30
6450	14" deep		400	.040		6.15	1.09		7.24	8.60
6500	3-1/2" wide x 9-1/4" deep		480	.033		8.20	.91		9.11	10.50
6550	11-1/4" deep		450	.036		10.10	.97		11.07	12.70
6600	14" deep		400	.040		12.05	1.09		13.14	15.10
6650	7" wide x 9-1/4" deep		450	.036		16.15	.97		17.12	19.35
6700	11-1/4" deep		420	.038		19.95	1.04		20.99	23.50
6750	14" deep	↓	400	.040	↓	24	1.09		25.09	28
9000	Minimum labor/equipment charge	F-3	2.50	16	Job		445	177	622	930

For expanded coverage of these items see *Means Interior Cost Data 1999*

061 | Rough Carpentry

061 800 | Glued-Laminated Const

			CREW	DAILY OUTPUT	LABOR-HOURS	UNIT	MAT.	LABOR	EQUIP.	TOTAL	TOTAL INCL O&P	
808	0010	**LAMINATED ROOF DECK** Pine or hemlock, 3" thick	2 Carp	425	.038	S.F.	2.84	1.03		3.87	4.84	808
	0100	4" thick		325	.049	"	3.25	1.34		4.59	5.85	
	0300	Cedar, 3" thick		425	.038	S.F.	3.26	1.03		4.29	5.30	
	0400	4" thick		325	.049		3.89	1.34		5.23	6.55	
	0600	Fir, 3" thick		425	.038		2.94	1.03		3.97	4.95	
	0700	4" thick		325	.049		3.47	1.34		4.81	6.05	
	9000	Minimum labor/equipment charge	1 Carp	3	2.667	Job		73		73	122	

061 900 | Wood Trusses

			CREW	DAILY OUTPUT	LABOR-HOURS	UNIT	MAT.	LABOR	EQUIP.	TOTAL	TOTAL INCL O&P	
908	0010	**ROOF TRUSSES**										908
	0020	For timber connectors, see div. 060-512										
	0100	Fink (W) or King post type, 2'-0" O.C.										
	0200	Metal plate connected, 4 in 12 slope										
	0210	24' to 29' span	F-3	3,000	.013	SF Flr.	1.30	.37	.15	1.82	2.20	
	0300	30' to 43' span		3,000	.013		1.45	.37	.15	1.97	2.37	
	0400	44' to 60' span		3,000	.013		1.60	.37	.15	2.12	2.53	
	0600	For change in roof pitch, subtract					.05			.05	.06	
	0700	Glued and nailed, add					50%					

062 | Finish Carpentry

062 200 | Millwork Moldings

			CREW	DAILY OUTPUT	LABOR-HOURS	UNIT	MAT.	LABOR	EQUIP.	TOTAL	TOTAL INCL O&P	
208	0010	**MOLDINGS, BASE**										208
	0500	Base, stock pine, 9/16" x 3-1/2"	1 Carp	240	.033	L.F.	1.16	.91		2.07	2.80	
	0550	9/16" x 4-1/2"		200	.040		1.25	1.09		2.34	3.21	
	0561	Base shoe, oak, 3/4" x 1"		240	.033		.76	.91		1.67	2.36	
	9000	Minimum labor/equipment charge		4	2	Job		54.50		54.50	91.50	
212	0010	**MOLDINGS, CASINGS**										212
	0090	Apron, stock pine, 5/8" x 2"	1 Carp	250	.032	L.F.	.95	.87		1.82	2.51	
	0110	5/8" x 3-1/2"		220	.036		1.40	.99		2.39	3.20	
	0300	Band, stock pine, 11/16" x 1-1/8"		270	.030		.38	.81		1.19	1.77	
	0350	11/16" x 1-3/4"		250	.032		.60	.87		1.47	2.12	
	0700	Casing, stock pine, 11/16" x 2-1/2"		240	.033		.76	.91		1.67	2.36	
	0750	11/16" x 3-1/2"		215	.037		1.46	1.02		2.48	3.31	
	9000	Minimum labor/equipment charge		4	2	Job		54.50		54.50	91.50	
216	0010	**MOLDINGS, CEILINGS**										216
	0600	Bed, stock pine, 9/16" x 1-3/4"	1 Carp	270	.030	L.F.	.60	.81		1.41	2.01	
	0650	9/16" x 2"		240	.033		.72	.91		1.63	2.31	
	1200	Cornice molding, stock pine, 9/16" x 1-3/4"		330	.024		.62	.66		1.28	1.79	
	1300	9/16" x 2-1/4"		300	.027		.83	.73		1.56	2.13	
	2400	Cove scotia, stock pine, 9/16" x 1-3/4"		270	.030		.54	.81		1.35	1.94	
	2500	11/16" x 2-3/4"		255	.031		1.15	.86		2.01	2.70	
	2600	Crown, stock pine, 9/16" x 3-5/8"		250	.032		1.51	.87		2.38	3.12	
	2700	11/16" x 4-5/8"		220	.036		2.17	.99		3.16	4.05	
	9000	Minimum labor/equipment charge		4	2	Job		54.50		54.50	91.50	
220	0010	**MOLDINGS, EXTERIOR**										220
	1500	Cornice, boards, pine, 1" x 2"	1 Carp	330	.024	L.F.	.27	.66		.93	1.40	

Important: See the Reference Section for critical supporting data - Reference Nos., Crews, & City Cost Indexes

062 | Finish Carpentry

062 200 | Millwork Moldings

		CREW	DAILY OUTPUT	LABOR-HOURS	UNIT	MAT.	LABOR	EQUIP.	TOTAL	TOTAL INCL O&P	
220	1700	1" x 6"	1 Carp	250	.032	L.F.	.83	.87		1.70	2.37	220
	2000	1" x 12"		180	.044		1.27	1.21		2.48	3.43	
	2200	Three piece, built-up, pine, minimum		80	.100		1.47	2.73		4.20	6.20	
	2300	Maximum		65	.123		4.62	3.36		7.98	10.70	
	3000	Corner board, sterling pine, 1" x 4"		200	.040		.46	1.09		1.55	2.34	
	3100	1" x 6"		200	.040		.70	1.09		1.79	2.60	
	3350	Fascia, sterling pine, 1" x 6"		250	.032		.70	.87		1.57	2.23	
	3370	1" x 8"		225	.036		.92	.97		1.89	2.63	
	3400	Trim, exterior, sterling pine, back band		250	.032		.55	.87		1.42	2.07	
	3500	Casing		250	.032		.58	.87		1.45	2.10	
	3600	Crown		250	.032		1.18	.87		2.05	2.76	
	3700	Porch rail with balusters		22	.364		8.70	9.95		18.65	26	
	3800	Screen		395	.020		.31	.55		.86	1.27	
	3850											
	4100	Verge board, sterling pine, 1" x 4"	1 Carp	200	.040	L.F.	.32	1.09		1.41	2.18	
	4200	1" x 6"		200	.040		.70	1.09		1.79	2.60	
	4300	2" x 6"		165	.048		1.40	1.32		2.72	3.76	
	4400	2" x 8"		165	.048		1.86	1.32		3.18	4.27	
	4700	For redwood trim, add					200%					
	9000	Minimum labor/equipment charge	1 Carp	4	2	Job		54.50		54.50	91.50	
224	0010	**MOLDINGS, TRIM**										224
	0200	Astragal, stock pine, 11/16" x 1-3/4"	1 Carp	255	.031	L.F.	.78	.86		1.64	2.29	
	0250	1-5/16" x 2-3/16"		240	.033		2.60	.91		3.51	4.37	
	0800	Chair rail, stock pine, 5/8" x 2-1/2"		270	.030		.84	.81		1.65	2.28	
	0900	5/8" x 3-1/2"		240	.033		1.26	.91		2.17	2.91	
	1000	Closet pole, stock pine, 1-1/8" diameter		200	.040		.80	1.09		1.89	2.71	
	1100	Fir, 1-5/8" diameter		200	.040		1.19	1.09		2.28	3.14	
	3300	Half round, stock pine, 1/4" x 1/2"		270	.030		.19	.81		1	1.56	
	3350	1/2" x 1"		255	.031		.34	.86		1.20	1.80	
	3400	Handrail, fir, single piece, stock, hardware not included										
	3450	1-1/2" x 1-3/4"	1 Carp	80	.100	L.F.	1.21	2.73		3.94	5.90	
	3470	Pine, 1-1/2" x 1-3/4"		80	.100		1.05	2.73		3.78	5.70	
	3500	1-1/2" x 2-1/2"		76	.105		1.43	2.87		4.30	6.40	
	3600	Lattice, stock pine, 1/4" x 1-1/8"		270	.030		.32	.81		1.13	1.70	
	3700	1/4" x 1-3/4"		250	.032		.30	.87		1.17	1.79	
	3800	Miscellaneous, custom, pine, 1" x 1"		270	.030		.96	.81		1.77	2.41	
	3900	1" x 3"		240	.033		.77	.91		1.68	2.37	
	4100	Birch or oak, nominal 1" x 1"		240	.033		.46	.91		1.37	2.03	
	4200	Nominal 1" x 3"		215	.037		1.57	1.02		2.59	3.43	
	4400	Walnut, nominal 1" x 1"		215	.037		.70	1.02		1.72	2.47	
	4500	Nominal 1" x 3"		200	.040		2.10	1.09		3.19	4.14	
	4700	Teak, nominal 1" x 1"		215	.037		1.05	1.02		2.07	2.85	
	4800	Nominal 1" x 3"		200	.040		3	1.09		4.09	5.15	
	4900	Quarter round, stock pine, 1/4" x 1/4"		275	.029		.20	.79		.99	1.55	
	4950	3/4" x 3/4"		255	.031		.41	.86		1.27	1.88	
	5600	Wainscot moldings, 1-1/8" x 9/16", 2' high, minimum		76	.105	S.F.	5.60	2.87		8.47	10.95	
	5700	Maximum		65	.123	"	12.35	3.36		15.71	19.20	
	9000	Minimum labor/equipment charge		4	2	Job		54.50		54.50	91.50	
228	0010	**MOLDINGS, WINDOW AND DOOR**										228
	2800	Door moldings, stock, decorative, 1-1/8" wide, plain	1 Carp	17	.471	Set	27	12.85		39.85	51	
	2900	Detailed		17	.471	"	65	12.85		77.85	93	
	3150	Door trim set, 1 head and 2 sides, pine, 2-1/2 wide		5.90	1.356	Opng.	12.45	37		49.45	75.50	
	3170	4-1/2" wide		5.30	1.509	"	22.50	41		63.50	94	
	3200	Glass beads, stock pine, 1/4" x 11/16"		285	.028	L.F.	.29	.77		1.06	1.60	
	3250	3/8" x 1/2"		275	.029		.35	.79		1.14	1.72	
	3270	3/8" x 7/8"		270	.030		.39	.81		1.20	1.78	

For expanded coverage of these items see *Means Interior Cost Data 1999*

062 | Finish Carpentry

062 200 | Millwork Moldings

			CREW	DAILY OUTPUT	LABOR-HOURS	UNIT	MAT.	LABOR	EQUIP.	TOTAL	TOTAL INCL O&P	
228	4850	Parting bead, stock pine, 3/8" x 3/4"	1 Carp	275	.029	L.F.	.28	.79		1.07	1.64	228
	4870	1/2" x 3/4"		255	.031		.35	.86		1.21	1.82	
	5000	Stool caps, stock pine, 11/16" x 3-1/2"		200	.040		1.29	1.09		2.38	3.25	
	5100	1-1/16" x 3-1/4"		150	.053		1.93	1.46		3.39	4.56	
	5300	Threshold, oak, 3' long, inside, 5/8" x 3-5/8"		32	.250	Ea.	6.10	6.80		12.90	18.15	
	5400	Outside, 1-1/2" x 7-5/8"		16	.500	"	24.50	13.65		38.15	50	
	5900	Window trim sets, including casings, header, stops,										
	5910	stool and apron, 2-1/2" wide, minimum	1 Carp	13	.615	Opng.	15	16.80		31.80	44.50	
	5950	Average		10	.800		26	22		48	65	
	6000	Maximum		6	1.333		37	36.50		73.50	102	
	9000	Minimum labor/equipment charge		4	2	Job		54.50		54.50	91.50	

062 300 | Shelving

			CREW	DAILY OUTPUT	LABOR-HOURS	UNIT	MAT.	LABOR	EQUIP.	TOTAL	TOTAL INCL O&P	
304	0010	SHELVING Pine, clear grade, no edge band, 1" x 8"	1 Carp	115	.070	L.F.	1.71	1.90		3.61	5.05	304
	0100	1" x 10"		110	.073		2.31	1.99		4.30	5.85	
	0200	1" x 12"		105	.076		4.18	2.08		6.26	8.05	
	0400	For lumber edge band, by hand, add					1.49			1.49	1.64	
	0420	By machine, add					.95			.95	1.05	
	0600	Plywood, 3/4" thick with lumber edge, 12" wide	1 Carp	75	.107		1.24	2.91		4.15	6.25	
	0700	24" wide		70	.114		2.35	3.12		5.47	7.80	
	0900	Bookcase, clear grade pine, shelves 12" O.C., 8" deep		70	.114	S.F.	4.24	3.12		7.36	9.85	
	1000	12" deep shelves		65	.123	"	4.57	3.36		7.93	10.60	
	1200	Adjustable closet rod and shelf, 12" wide, 3' long		20	.400	Ea.	40.50	10.90		51.40	63	
	1300	8' long		15	.533	"	57	14.55		71.55	87	
	1500	Prefinished shelves with supports, stock, 8" wide		75	.107	L.F.	3.65	2.91		6.56	8.90	
	1600	10" wide		70	.114	"	4.07	3.12		7.19	9.65	
	1800	Custom, high quality dadoed pine shelving units, minimum				S.F.					28	
	1900	Maximum				"					40	
	9000	Minimum labor/equipment charge	1 Carp	4	2	Job		54.50		54.50	91.50	

062 400 | Plastic Laminate

			CREW	DAILY OUTPUT	LABOR-HOURS	UNIT	MAT.	LABOR	EQUIP.	TOTAL	TOTAL INCL O&P	
404	0010	CONVECTOR COVERS Laminated plastic on 3/4"										404
	0020	thick particle board, 12" wide, minimum	1 Carp	16	.500	L.F.	20	13.65		33.65	45	
	0050	Average		13	.615		25.50	16.80		42.30	56	
	0100	Maximum		13	.615		35	16.80		51.80	66.50	
	0300	Add to above for grille, minimum		150	.053	S.F.	1.60	1.46		3.06	4.20	
	0400	Maximum		75	.107	"	4.50	2.91		7.41	9.80	
	9000	Minimum labor/equipment charge		4	2	Job		54.50		54.50	91.50	
408	0010	COUNTER TOP Stock, plastic lam., 24" wide w/backsplash, min.	1 Carp	30	.267	L.F.	4.89	7.30		12.19	17.60	408
	0100	Maximum		25	.320		14.25	8.75		23	30.50	
	0300	Custom plastic, 7/8" thick, aluminum molding, no splash		30	.267		15.70	7.30		23	29.50	
	0400	Cove splash		30	.267		20.50	7.30		27.80	34.50	
	0600	1-1/4" thick, no splash		28	.286		18.50	7.80		26.30	33.50	
	0700	Square splash		28	.286		23	7.80		30.80	38.50	
	0900	Square edge, plastic face, 7/8" thick, no splash		30	.267		19.80	7.30		27.10	34	
	1000	With splash		30	.267		26	7.30		33.30	40.50	
	1200	For stainless channel edge, 7/8" thick, add					2.21			2.21	2.43	
	1300	1-1/4" thick, add					2.58			2.58	2.84	
	1500	For solid color suede finish, add					1.96			1.96	2.16	
	1700	For end splash, add				Ea.	12.35			12.35	13.60	
	1900	For cut outs, standard, add, minimum	1 Carp	32	.250		2.63	6.80		9.43	14.35	
	2000	Maximum		8	1		3.14	27.50		30.64	49	
	2100	Postformed, including backsplash and front edge		30	.267	L.F.	8.55	7.30		15.85	21.50	
	2110	Mitred, add		12	.667	Ea.		18.20		18.20	30.50	

062 | Finish Carpentry

062 400 | Plastic Laminate

		CREW	DAILY OUTPUT	LABOR-HOURS	UNIT	MAT.	LABOR	EQUIP.	TOTAL	TOTAL INCL O&P
2200	Built-in place, 25" wide, plastic laminate	1 Carp	25	.320	L.F.	10.80	8.75		19.55	26.50
2300	Ceramic tile mosaic		25	.320		24.50	8.75		33.25	41.50
2500	Marble, stock, with splash, 1/2" thick, minimum	1 Bric	17	.471		30	13		43	54.50
2700	3/4" thick, maximum	"	13	.615		76	17		93	112
2900	Maple, solid, laminated, 1-1/2" thick, no splash	1 Carp	28	.286		31	7.80		38.80	47
3000	With square splash		28	.286		35	7.80		42.80	51.50
3200	Stainless steel		24	.333	S.F.	73	9.10		82.10	96
3400	Recessed cutting block with trim, 16" x 20" x 1"		8	1	Ea.	41	27.50		68.50	91
3600	Table tops, plastic laminate, square edge, 7/8" thick		45	.178	S.F.	7	4.85		11.85	15.80
3700	1-1/8" thick		40	.200	"	7.20	5.45		12.65	17.10
9000	Minimum labor/equipment charge		3.75	2.133	Job		58		58	97.50

062 500 | Prefin. Wood Paneling

		CREW	DAILY OUTPUT	LABOR-HOURS	UNIT	MAT.	LABOR	EQUIP.	TOTAL	TOTAL INCL O&P
0010	**PANELING, PLYWOOD** R061-020									
2400	Plywood, prefinished, 1/4" thick, 4' x 8' sheets									
2410	with vertical grooves. Birch faced, minimum	2 Carp	500	.032	S.F.	.72	.87		1.59	2.25
2420	Average		420	.038		1.03	1.04		2.07	2.87
2430	Maximum		350	.046		1.49	1.25		2.74	3.73
2600	Mahogany, African		400	.040		1.91	1.09		3	3.93
2700	Philippine (Lauan)		500	.032		.82	.87		1.69	2.36
2900	Oak or Cherry, minimum		500	.032		1.60	.87		2.47	3.22
3000	Maximum		400	.040		2.68	1.09		3.77	4.78
3200	Rosewood		320	.050		3.81	1.36		5.17	6.50
3400	Teak		400	.040		2.68	1.09		3.77	4.78
3600	Chestnut		375	.043		3.97	1.16		5.13	6.30
3800	Pecan		400	.040		1.70	1.09		2.79	3.70
3900	Walnut, minimum		500	.032		2.27	.87		3.14	3.96
3950	Maximum		400	.040		4.33	1.09		5.42	6.60
4000	Plywood, prefinished, 3/4" thick, stock grades, minimum		320	.050		1.03	1.36		2.39	3.42
4100	Maximum		224	.071		4.48	1.95		6.43	8.20
4300	Architectural grade, minimum		224	.071		3.30	1.95		5.25	6.90
4400	Maximum		160	.100		5.05	2.73		7.78	10.10
4600	Plywood, "A" face, birch, V.C., 1/2" thick, natural		450	.036		1.55	.97		2.52	3.32
4700	Select		450	.036		1.70	.97		2.67	3.49
4900	Veneer core, 3/4" thick, natural		320	.050		1.65	1.36		3.01	4.11
5000	Select		320	.050		1.85	1.36		3.21	4.33
5200	Lumber core, 3/4" thick, natural		320	.050		2.47	1.36		3.83	5
5500	Plywood, knotty pine, 1/4" thick, A2 grade		450	.036		1.34	.97		2.31	3.09
5600	A3 grade		450	.036		1.70	.97		2.67	3.49
5800	3/4" thick, veneer core, A2 grade		320	.050		1.75	1.36		3.11	4.22
5900	A3 grade		320	.050		1.96	1.36		3.32	4.45
6100	Aromatic cedar, 1/4" thick, plywood		400	.040		1.70	1.09		2.79	3.70
6200	1/4" thick, particle board		400	.040		.82	1.09		1.91	2.73
9000	Minimum labor/equipment charge	1 Carp	2	4	Job		109		109	183

062 550 | Prefin. Hardboard Panel

		CREW	DAILY OUTPUT	LABOR-HOURS	UNIT	MAT.	LABOR	EQUIP.	TOTAL	TOTAL INCL O&P
0010	**PANELING, HARDBOARD**									
0050	Not incl. furring or trim, hardboard, tempered, 1/8" thick	2 Carp	500	.032	S.F.	.33	.87		1.20	1.82
0100	1/4" thick		500	.032		.37	.87		1.24	1.87
0300	Tempered pegboard, 1/8" thick		500	.032		.33	.87		1.20	1.82
0400	1/4" thick		500	.032		.41	.87		1.28	1.91
0600	Untempered hardboard, natural finish, 1/8" thick		500	.032		.28	.87		1.15	1.77
0700	1/4" thick		500	.032		.31	.87		1.18	1.80
0900	Untempered pegboard, 1/8" thick		500	.032		.32	.87		1.19	1.81

For expanded coverage of these items see *Means Interior Cost Data 1999*

062 | Finish Carpentry

062 550 | Prefin. Hardboard Panel

			CREW	DAILY OUTPUT	LABOR-HOURS	UNIT	MAT.	LABOR	EQUIP.	TOTAL	TOTAL INCL O&P	
554	1000	1/4" thick	2 Carp	500	.032	S.F.	.35	.87		1.22	1.85	554
	1200	Plastic faced hardboard, 1/8" thick		500	.032		.52	.87		1.39	2.03	
	1300	1/4" thick		500	.032		.71	.87		1.58	2.24	
	1500	Plastic faced pegboard, 1/8" thick		500	.032		.50	.87		1.37	2.01	
	1600	1/4" thick		500	.032		.62	.87		1.49	2.14	
	1800	Wood grained, plain or grooved, 1/4" thick, minimum		500	.032		.47	.87		1.34	1.98	
	1900	Maximum		425	.038		.89	1.03		1.92	2.70	
	2100	Moldings for hardboard, wood or aluminum, minimum		500	.032	L.F.	.32	.87		1.19	1.81	
	2200	Maximum		425	.038	"	.90	1.03		1.93	2.71	
	9000	Minimum labor/equipment charge	1 Carp	2	4	Job		109		109	183	

062 600 | Board Paneling

			CREW	DAILY OUTPUT	LABOR-HOURS	UNIT	MAT.	LABOR	EQUIP.	TOTAL	TOTAL INCL O&P	
604	0010	**PANELING, BOARDS**										604
	6400	Wood board paneling, 3/4" thick, knotty pine	2 Carp	300	.053	S.F.	1.24	1.46		2.70	3.80	
	6500	Rough sawn cedar		300	.053		1.60	1.46		3.06	4.20	
	6700	Redwood, clear, 1" x 4" boards		300	.053		3.75	1.46		5.21	6.55	
	6900	Aromatic cedar, closet lining, boards		275	.058		2.83	1.59		4.42	5.75	
	9000	Minimum labor/equipment charge	1 Carp	2	4	Job		109		109	183	

062 700 | Misc. Finish Carpentry

			CREW	DAILY OUTPUT	LABOR-HOURS	UNIT	MAT.	LABOR	EQUIP.	TOTAL	TOTAL INCL O&P	
704	0010	**BEAMS, DECORATIVE** Rough sawn cedar, non-load bearing, 4" x 4"	2 Carp	180	.089	L.F.	1.30	2.43		3.73	5.50	704
	0100	4" x 6"		170	.094		2.50	2.57		5.07	7.05	
	0200	4" x 8"		160	.100		3.21	2.73		5.94	8.10	
	0300	4" x 10"		150	.107		4.46	2.91		7.37	9.80	
	0400	4" x 12"		140	.114		5.40	3.12		8.52	11.15	
	0500	8" x 8"		130	.123		7.55	3.36		10.91	13.90	
	1100	Beam connector plates see div. 060-512										
	9000	Minimum labor/equipment charge	1 Carp	3	2.667	Job		73		73	122	
720	0010	**FIREPLACE MANTEL BEAMS** Rough texture wood, 4" x 8"		36	.222	L.F.	4.24	6.05		10.29	14.80	720
	0100	4" x 10"		35	.229	"	5.30	6.25		11.55	16.30	
	0300	Laminated hardwood, 2-1/4" x 10-1/2" wide, 6' long		5	1.600	Ea.	95.50	43.50		139	178	
	0400	8' long		5	1.600	"	133	43.50		176.50	219	
	0600	Brackets for above, rough sawn		12	.667	Pr.	8.75	18.20		26.95	40	
	0700	Laminated		12	.667	"	13.25	18.20		31.45	45	
	9000	Minimum labor/equipment charge		4	2	Job		54.50		54.50	91.50	
725	0010	**FIREPLACE MANTELS** 6" molding, 6' x 3'-6" opening, minimum	1 Carp	5	1.600	Opng.	127	43.50		170.50	213	725
	0100	Maximum		5	1.600		154	43.50		197.50	242	
	0300	Prefabricated pine, colonial type, stock, deluxe		2	4		745	109		854	1,000	
	0400	Economy		3	2.667		251	73		324	400	
	9000	Minimum labor/equipment charge		3	2.667	Job		73		73	122	
730	0010	**GRILLES** and panels, hardwood, sanded										730
	0020	2' x 4' to 4' x 8', custom designs, unfinished, minimum	1 Carp	38	.211	S.F.	12	5.75		17.75	23	
	0050	Average		30	.267		26	7.30		33.30	40.50	
	0100	Maximum		19	.421		40	11.50		51.50	63.50	
	0300	As above, but prefinished, minimum		38	.211		12	5.75		17.75	23	
	0400	Maximum		19	.421		45	11.50		56.50	69	
	9000	Minimum labor/equipment charge		2	4	Job		109		109	183	
735	0010	**HARDWARE** Finish, see divisions 064-108 & 087										735
	0100	Rough, see division 050										
740	0010	**LOUVERS** Redwood, 2'-0" diameter, full circle	1 Carp	16	.500	Ea.	105	13.65		118.65	139	740
	0100	Half circle		16	.500		104	13.65		117.65	137	
	0200	Octagonal		16	.500		86	13.65		99.65	118	
	0300	Triangular, 5/12 pitch, 5'-0" at base		16	.500		180	13.65		193.65	221	

062 | Finish Carpentry

062 700 | Misc. Finish Carpentry

			CREW	DAILY OUTPUT	LABOR-HOURS	UNIT	MAT.	LABOR	EQUIP.	TOTAL	TOTAL INCL O&P	
740	9000	Minimum labor/equipment charge	1 Carp	3.50	2.286	Job		62.50		62.50	104	740
760	0010	**SHUTTERS, EXTERIOR** Aluminum, louvered, 1'-4" wide, 3'-0" long	1 Carp	10	.800	Pr.	29.50	22		51.50	69	760
	0400	6'-8" long		9	.889		48	24.50		72.50	93	
	1000	Pine, louvered, primed, each 1'-2" wide, 3'-3" long		10	.800		41	22		63	81.50	
	1001	Pine, louvered, primed, each 1'-2" wide, 3'-3" long		20	.400	Ea.	24	10.90		34.90	45	
	1100	4'-7" long		10	.800	Pr.	49	22		71	90.50	
	1101	4'-7" long		20	.400	Ea.	34.50	10.90		45.40	56.50	
	1250	Each 1'-4" wide, 3'-0" long		10	.800	Pr.	37.50	22		59.50	78	
	1251	Each 1'-4" wide, 3'-0" long		20	.400	Ea.	25.50	10.90		36.40	46.50	
	1350	5'-3" long		10	.800	Pr.	53	22		75	95	
	1351	5'-3" long		20	.400	Ea.	31	10.90		41.90	52.50	
	1500	Each 1'-6" wide, 3'-3" long		10	.800	Pr.	45	22		67	86	
	1600	4'-7" long		10	.800	"	61	22		83	104	
	1601	4'-7" long		20	.400	Ea.	38	10.90		48.90	60.50	
	1610	Door blinds, 6'-9" long 1'-3" wide		9	.889	Pr.	118	24.50		142.50	171	
	1615	1'-6" wide		9	.889		127	24.50		151.50	181	
	1620	Hemlock, louvered, 1'-2" wide, 5'-7" long		10	.800		59.50	22		81.50	102	
	1630	Each 1'-4" wide, 2'-2" long		10	.800		37	22		59	77.50	
	1640	3'-0" long		10	.800		39	22		61	79.50	
	1650	3'-3" long		10	.800		42.50	22		64.50	83	
	1660	3'-11" long		10	.800		46.50	22		68.50	88	
	1670	4'-3" long		10	.800		49	22		71	90	
	1680	5'-3" long		10	.800		55	22		77	97	
	1690	5'-11" long		10	.800		60.50	22		82.50	103	
	1700	Door blinds, 6'-9" long, each 1'-3" wide		9	.889		70	24.50		94.50	118	
	1710	1'-6" wide		9	.889		88	24.50		112.50	138	
	1720	Hemlock, solid raised panel, each 1'-4" wide, 3'-3" long		10	.800		60.50	22		82.50	103	
	1730	3'-11" long		10	.800		72	22		94	116	
	1740	4'-3" long		10	.800		76.50	22		98.50	121	
	1750	4'-7" long		10	.800		79.50	22		101.50	124	
	1760	4'-11" long		10	.800		87	22		109	132	
	1770	5'-11" long		10	.800		106	22		128	154	
	1800	Door blinds, 6'-9" long, each 1'-3" wide		9	.889		117	24.50		141.50	169	
	1900	1'-6" wide		9	.889		122	24.50		146.50	175	
	2500	Polystyrene, solid raised panel, each 1'-4" wide, 3'-3" long		10	.800		51	22		73	92.50	
	2700	4'-7" long		10	.800		61.50	22		83.50	104	
	3500	Polystyrene, solid raised panel, each 3'-3" wide, 3'-0" long		10	.800		124	22		146	173	
	3600	3'-11" long		10	.800		154	22		176	206	
	3700	4'-7" long		10	.800		176	22		198	230	
	3800	5'-3" long		10	.800		195	22		217	251	
	3900	6'-8" long		9	.889		219	24.50		243.50	282	
	4500	Polystyrene, louvered, each 1'-2" wide, 3'-3" long		10	.800		39	22		61	79.50	
	4600	4'-7" long		10	.800		49	22		71	90	
	4750	5'-3" long		10	.800		52	22		74	93.50	
	4850	6'-8" long		9	.889		85	24.50		109.50	134	
	6000	Vinyl, louvered, each 1'-2" x 4'-7" long		10	.800		51	22		73	92.50	
	6200	Each 1'-4" x 6'-8" long		9	.889		77.50	24.50		102	126	
	9000	Minimum labor/equipment charge		4	2	Job		54.50		54.50	91.50	
775	0010	**SOFFITS** Wood fiber, no vapor barrier, 15/32" thick	2 Carp	525	.030	S.F.	.73	.83		1.56	2.19	775
	0100	5/8" thick		525	.030	"	.79	.83		1.62	2.26	
	0300	As above, 5/8" thick, with factory finish		525	.030	S.F.	.81	.83		1.64	2.28	
	0500	Hardboard, 3/8" thick, slotted		525	.030		.98	.83		1.81	2.47	
	1000	Exterior AC plywood, 1/4" thick		420	.038		.50	1.04		1.54	2.29	
	1100	1/2" thick		420	.038		.66	1.04		1.70	2.47	

Soffits reference: R061-030

For expanded coverage of these items see *Means Interior Cost Data 1999*

062 | Finish Carpentry

062 700 | Misc. Finish Carpentry

		CREW	DAILY OUTPUT	LABOR-HOURS	UNIT	1999 BARE COSTS				TOTAL INCL O&P	
						MAT.	LABOR	EQUIP.	TOTAL		
775	1150 For aluminum soffit, see division 076-217										775
	9000 Minimum labor/equipment charge	2 Carp	5	3.200	Job		87.50		87.50	146	
778	0010 **DOORS AND FRAMES** See division 081 & 082										778

R061-030

063 | Wood Treatment

063 100 | Preservative Treatment

		CREW	DAILY OUTPUT	LABOR-HOURS	UNIT	1999 BARE COSTS				TOTAL INCL O&P	
						MAT.	LABOR	EQUIP.	TOTAL		
102	0011 **LUMBER TREATMENT**										102
	0402 Fire retardant, wet				M.B.F.	245			245	270	
	0502 KDAT					281			281	310	
	0702 Salt treated, water borne, .40 lb. retention					158			158	174	
	0802 Oil borne, 8 lb. retention					170			170	187	
	1002 Kiln dried lumber, 1" & 2" thick, soft woods					102			102	112	
	1102 Hard woods					107			107	118	
	1500 For small size 1" stock, add					11			11	12.10	
	1700 For full size rough lumber, add					20%					
104	0012 **PLYWOOD TREATMENT** Fire retardant, 1/4" thick				M.S.F.	229			229	252	104
	0032 3/8" thick					245			245	270	
	0052 1/2" thick					260			260	286	
	0072 5/8" thick					275			275	305	
	0102 3/4" thick					305			305	335	
	0200 For KDAT, add					61			61	67	
	0502 Salt treated water borne, .25 lb., wet, 1/4" thick					122			122	134	
	0532 3/8" thick					127			127	140	
	0552 1/2" thick					128			128	140	
	0572 5/8" thick					143			143	157	
	0602 3/4" thick					148			148	163	
	0800 For KDAT add					61			61	67	
	0900 For .40 lb., per C.F. retention, add					51			51	56	
	1000 For certification stamp, add					30			30	33	

064 | Architectural Woodwork

064 100 | Custom Casework

		CREW	DAILY OUTPUT	LABOR-HOURS	UNIT	1999 BARE COSTS				TOTAL INCL O&P	
						MAT.	LABOR	EQUIP.	TOTAL		
102	0010 **CABINETS** Corner china cabinets, stock pine,										102
	0020 80" high, unfinished, minimum	2 Carp	6.60	2.424	Ea.	229	66		295	365	
	0100 Maximum	"	4.40	3.636	"	700	99.50		799.50	935	
	0300 Built-in drawer units, pine, 18" deep, 32" high, unfinished										
	0400 Minimum	2 Carp	53	.302	L.F.	32	8.25		40.25	49	
	0500 Maximum	"	40	.400	"	120	10.90		130.90	150	
	0700 Kitchen base cabinets, hardwood, not incl. counter tops,										
	0710 24" deep, 35" high, prefinished										

Important: See the Reference Section for critical supporting data - Reference Nos., Crews, & City Cost Indexes

064 | Architectural Woodwork

064 100 | Custom Casework

		CREW	DAILY OUTPUT	LABOR-HOURS	UNIT	1999 BARE COSTS MAT.	1999 BARE COSTS LABOR	1999 BARE COSTS EQUIP.	1999 BARE COSTS TOTAL	TOTAL INCL O&P
0800	One top drawer, one door below, 12" wide	2 Carp	24.80	.645	Ea.	114	17.60		131.60	155
0820	15" wide		24	.667		116	18.20		134.20	158
0840	18" wide		23.30	.687		131	18.75		149.75	176
0860	21" wide		22.70	.705		139	19.25		158.25	185
0880	24" wide		22.30	.717		140	19.60		159.60	186
1000	Four drawers, 12" wide		24.80	.645		113	17.60		130.60	154
1020	15" wide		24	.667		146	18.20		164.20	191
1040	18" wide		23.30	.687		158	18.75		176.75	206
1060	24" wide		22.30	.717		178	19.60		197.60	228
1200	Two top drawers, two doors below, 27" wide		22	.727		177	19.85		196.85	228
1220	30" wide		21.40	.748		193	20.50		213.50	247
1240	33" wide		20.90	.766		196	21		217	251
1260	36" wide		20.30	.788		204	21.50		225.50	260
1280	42" wide		19.80	.808		223	22		245	282
1300	48" wide		18.90	.847		242	23		265	305
1500	Range or sink base, two doors below, 30" wide		21.40	.748		148	20.50		168.50	197
1520	33" wide		20.90	.766		154	21		175	204
1540	36" wide		20.30	.788		161	21.50		182.50	213
1560	42" wide		19.80	.808		176	22		198	231
1580	48" wide		18.90	.847		191	23		214	249
1800	For sink front units, deduct					52			52	57
2000	Corner base cabinets, 36" wide, standard	2 Carp	18	.889		163	24.50		187.50	220
2100	Lazy Susan with revolving door	"	16.50	.970		203	26.50		229.50	268
4000	Kitchen wall cabinets, hardwood, 12" deep with two doors									
4050	12" high, 30" wide	2 Carp	24.80	.645	Ea.	87	17.60		104.60	126
4100	36" wide		24	.667		99.50	18.20		117.70	140
4400	15" high, 30" wide		24	.667		93.50	18.20		111.70	134
4420	33" wide		23.30	.687		94	18.75		112.75	135
4440	36" wide		22.70	.705		102	19.25		121.25	144
4450	42" wide		22.70	.705		116	19.25		135.25	160
4700	24" high, 30" wide		23.30	.687		119	18.75		137.75	163
4720	36" wide		22.70	.705		127	19.25		146.25	172
4740	42" wide		22.30	.717		137	19.60		156.60	183
5000	30" high, one door, 12" wide		22	.727		85	19.85		104.85	127
5020	15" wide		21.40	.748		83.50	20.50		104	126
5040	18" wide		20.90	.766		90	21		111	134
5060	24" wide		20.30	.788		110	21.50		131.50	157
5300	Two doors, 27" wide		19.80	.808		121	22		143	170
5320	30" wide		19.30	.829		135	22.50		157.50	186
5340	36" wide		18.80	.851		149	23		172	203
5360	42" wide		18.50	.865		163	23.50		186.50	219
5380	48" wide		18.40	.870		176	23.50		199.50	234
6000	Corner wall, 30" high, 24" wide		18	.889		141	24.50		165.50	196
6050	30" wide		17.20	.930		162	25.50		187.50	221
6100	36" wide		16.50	.970		187	26.50		213.50	251
6500	Revolving Lazy Susan		15.20	1.053		167	28.50		195.50	232
7000	Broom cabinet, 84" high, 24" deep, 18" wide		10	1.600		231	43.50		274.50	325
7500	Oven cabinets, 84" high, 24" deep, 27" wide		8	2		297	54.50		351.50	415
7750	Valance board trim		396	.040	L.F.	7.55	1.10		8.65	10.15
9000	For deluxe models of all cabinets, add					40%				
9500	For custom built in place, add					25%	10%			
9550	Rule of thumb, kitchen cabinets not including									
9560	appliances & counter top, minimum	2 Carp	30	.533	L.F.	79	14.55		93.55	112
9600	Maximum	"	25	.640	"	221	17.45		238.45	273
9700	Minimum labor/equipment charge	1 Carp	3	2.667	Job		73		73	122

For expanded coverage of these items see *Means Interior Cost Data 1999*

064 | Architectural Woodwork

064 100 | Custom Casework

			DAILY	LABOR-		1999 BARE COSTS				TOTAL	
		CREW	OUTPUT	HOURS	UNIT	MAT.	LABOR	EQUIP.	TOTAL	INCL O&P	
104	0010	**CASEWORK, FRAMES**										104
	0050	Base cabinets, counter storage, 36" high, one bay									
	0100	18" wide	1 Carp	2.70	2.963	Ea.	89.50	81		170.50	233
	0400	Two bay, 36" wide		2.20	3.636		137	99.50		236.50	315
	1100	Three bay, 54" wide		1.50	5.333		163	146		309	425
	2800	Book cases, one bay, 7' high, 18" wide		2.40	3.333		105	91		196	268
	3500	Two bay, 36" wide		1.60	5		152	137		289	395
	4100	Three bay, 54" wide		1.20	6.667		252	182		434	580
	5100	Coat racks, one bay, 7' high, 24" wide		4.50	1.778		105	48.50		153.50	197
	5300	Two bay, 48" wide		2.75	2.909		147	79.50		226.50	295
	5800	Three bay, 72" wide		2.10	3.810		215	104		319	410
	6100	Wall mounted cabinet, one bay, 24" high, 18" wide		3.60	2.222		58	60.50		118.50	166
	6800	Two bay, 36" wide		2.20	3.636		84	99.50		183.50	259
	7400	Three bay, 54" wide		1.70	4.706		105	128		233	330
	8400	30" high, one bay, 18" wide		3.60	2.222		63	60.50		123.50	172
	9000	Two bay, 36" wide		2.15	3.721		84	102		186	263
	9400	Three bay, 54" wide		1.60	5		105	137		242	345
	9800	Wardrobe, 7' high, single, 24" wide		2.70	2.963		116	81		197	262
	9880	Partition & adjustable shelves, 48" wide		1.70	4.706		147	128		275	375
	9950	Partition, adjustable shelves & drawers, 48" wide		1.40	5.714		221	156		377	505
	9970	Minimum labor/equipment charge		4	2	Job		54.50		54.50	91.50
106	0010	**CABINET DOORS**										106
	2000	Glass panel, hardwood frame									
	2200	12" wide, 18" high	1 Carp	34	.235	Ea.	14.55	6.40		20.95	27
	2600	30" high		32	.250		24	6.80		30.80	38
	4450	18" wide, 18" high		32	.250		15	6.80		21.80	28
	4550	30" high		29	.276		24	7.55		31.55	39
	5000	Hardwood, raised panel									
	5100	12" wide, 18" high	1 Carp	16	.500	Ea.	20	13.65		33.65	45
	5200	30" high		15	.533		32	14.55		46.55	59.50
	5500	18" wide, 18" high		15	.533		29	14.55		43.55	56.50
	5600	30" high		14	.571		49	15.60		64.60	80
	6000	Plastic laminate on particle board									
	6100	12" wide, 18" high	1 Carp	25	.320	Ea.	13	8.75		21.75	29
	6140	30" high		23	.348		21	9.50		30.50	39
	6500	18" wide, 18" high		24	.333		19	9.10		28.10	36.50
	6600	30" high		22	.364		32	9.95		41.95	51.50
	7000	Plywood, with edge band									
	7010	12" wide, 18" high	1 Carp	27	.296	Ea.	17.15	8.10		25.25	32.50
	7120	30" high		25	.320		29.50	8.75		38.25	47
	7650	18" wide, 18" high		26	.308		25	8.40		33.40	41.50
	7750	30" high		24	.333		43	9.10		52.10	63
	9000	Minimum labor/equipment charge		4	2	Job		54.50		54.50	91.50
108	0010	**CABINET HARDWARE**										108
	1000	Catches, minimum	1 Carp	235	.034	Ea.	.71	.93		1.64	2.34
	1040	Maximum	"	80	.100	"	4.16	2.73		6.89	9.15
	2000	Door/drawer pulls, handles									
	2200	Handles and pulls, projecting, metal, minimum	1 Carp	160	.050	Ea.	1.51	1.36		2.87	3.95
	2240	Maximum		68	.118		7.20	3.21		10.41	13.35
	2300	Wood, minimum		160	.050		1.51	1.36		2.87	3.95
	2340	Maximum		68	.118		4.12	3.21		7.33	9.95
	2600	Flush, metal, minimum		160	.050		1.44	1.36		2.80	3.87
	2640	Maximum		68	.118		10.30	3.21		13.51	16.75
	3000	Drawer tracks/glides, minimum		48	.167	Pr.	5.65	4.55		10.20	13.85
	3040	Maximum		24	.333		16.50	9.10		25.60	33.50

064 | Architectural Woodwork

064 100 | Custom Casework

			CREW	DAILY OUTPUT	LABOR-HOURS	UNIT	1999 BARE COSTS MAT.	LABOR	EQUIP.	TOTAL	TOTAL INCL O&P	
108	4000	Cabinet hinges, minimum	1 Carp	160	.050	Pr.	1.40	1.36		2.76	3.83	108
	4040	Maximum	↓	68	.118	↓	6.20	3.21		9.41	12.20	
110	0010	**DRAWERS**										110
	0100	Solid hardwood front										
	1000	4″ high, 12″ wide	1 Carp	17	.471	Ea.	19.10	12.85		31.95	42.50	
	1200	18″ wide	"	16	.500	"	24.50	13.65		38.15	50	
	2800	Plastic laminate on particle board front										
	3000	4″ high, 12″ wide	1 Carp	17	.471	Ea.	19.55	12.85		32.40	43	
	3200	18″ wide	"	16	.500	"	22.50	13.65		36.15	48	
	5400	Plywood, flush panel front										
	6000	4″ high, 12″ wide	1 Carp	17	.471	Ea.	20	12.85		32.85	43.50	
	6200	18″ wide		16	.500	"	24.50	13.65		38.15	50	
	9000	Minimum labor/equipment charge	↓	4	2	Job		54.50		54.50	91.50	
140	0010	**VANITIES**										140
	8000	Vanity bases, 2 doors, 30″ high, 21″ deep, 24″ wide	2 Carp	20	.800	Ea.	123	22		145	172	
	8050	30″ wide		16	1		129	27.50		156.50	188	
	8100	36″ wide		13.33	1.200		144	33		177	214	
	8150	48″ wide	↓	11.43	1.400	↓	182	38		220	264	
	9000	For deluxe models of all vanities, add to above					40%					
	9500	For custom built in place, add to above					25%	10%				

064 300 | Stairwork & Handrails

			CREW	DAILY OUTPUT	LABOR-HOURS	UNIT	MAT.	LABOR	EQUIP.	TOTAL	INCL O&P	
306	0011	**STAIRS, PREFABRICATED**										306
	0100	Box stairs, prefabricated, 3′-0″ wide										
	0110	Oak treads, no handrails, 2′ high	2 Carp	5	3.200	Flight	216	87.50		303.50	385	
	0200	4′ high		4	4		430	109		539	660	
	0300	6′ high		3.50	4.571		600	125		725	870	
	0400	8′ high		3	5.333		760	146		906	1,075	
	0600	With pine treads for carpet, 2′ high		5	3.200		86	87.50		173.50	241	
	0700	4′ high		4	4		159	109		268	360	
	0800	6′ high		3.50	4.571		233	125		358	465	
	0900	8′ high	↓	3	5.333		266	146		412	535	
	1100	For 4′ wide stairs, add				↓	25%					
	1500	Prefabricated stair rail with balusters, 5 risers	2 Carp	15	1.067	Ea.	223	29		252	294	
	1700	Basement stairs, prefabricated, soft wood,										
	1710	open risers, 3′ wide, 8′ high	2 Carp	4	4	Flight	555	109		664	800	
	1900	Open stairs, prefabricated prefinished poplar, metal stringers,										
	1910	treads 3′-6″ wide, no railings										
	2000	3′ high	2 Carp	5	3.200	Flight	224	87.50		311.50	395	
	2100	4′ high		4	4		485	109		594	720	
	2200	6′ high		3.50	4.571		555	125		680	825	
	2300	8′ high	↓	3	5.333	↓	730	146		876	1,050	
	2500	For prefab. 3 piece wood railings & balusters, add for										
	2600	3′ high stairs	2 Carp	15	1.067	Ea.	30.50	29		59.50	82.50	
	2700	4′ high stairs		14	1.143		49.50	31		80.50	107	
	2800	6′ high stairs		13	1.231		61.50	33.50		95	124	
	2900	8′ high stairs		12	1.333		93.50	36.50		130	164	
	3100	For 3′-6″ x 3′-6″ platform, add	↓	4	4	↓	72.50	109		181.50	263	
	3300	Curved stairways, 3′-3″ wide, prefabricated, oak, unfinished,										
	3310	incl. curved balustrade system, open one side										
	3400	9′ high	2 Carp	.70	22.857	Flight	6,375	625		7,000	8,075	
	3500	10′ high		.70	22.857		7,200	625		7,825	8,975	
	3700	Open two sides, 9′ high		.50	32		10,000	875		10,875	12,500	
	3800	10′ high	↓	.50	32	↓	10,800	875		11,675	13,400	

For expanded coverage of these items see Means Interior Cost Data 1999

064 | Architectural Woodwork

064 300 | Stairwork & Handrails

			CREW	DAILY OUTPUT	LABOR-HOURS	UNIT	MAT.	LABOR	EQUIP.	TOTAL	TOTAL INCL O&P	
306	4000	Residential, wood, oak treads, prefabricated	2 Carp	1.50	10.667	Flight	930	291		1,221	1,500	306
	4200	Built in place	↓	.44	36.364	↓	1,325	995		2,320	3,100	
	4400	Spiral, oak, 4'-6" diameter, unfinished, prefabricated,										
	4500	incl. railing, 9' high	2 Carp	1.50	10.667	Flight	4,000	291		4,291	4,875	
	9000	Minimum labor/equipment charge	"	3	5.333	Job		146		146	244	
308	0010	**STAIR PARTS** Balusters, turned, 30" high, pine, minimum R064-100	1 Carp	28	.286	Ea.	3.50	7.80		11.30	16.90	308
	0100	Maximum		26	.308	"	9	8.40		17.40	24	
	0300	30" high birch balusters, minimum		28	.286	Ea.	6	7.80		13.80	19.65	
	0400	Maximum		26	.308		10	8.40		18.40	25	
	0600	42" high, pine balusters, minimum		27	.296		6	8.10		14.10	20	
	0700	Maximum		25	.320		9.50	8.75		18.25	25	
	0900	42" high birch balusters, minimum		27	.296		7.05	8.10		15.15	21.50	
	1000	Maximum		25	.320	↓	15	8.75		23.75	31	
	1050	Baluster, stock pine, 1-1/16" x 1-1/16"		240	.033	L.F.	1.97	.91		2.88	3.69	
	1100	1-5/8" x 1-5/8"		220	.036	"	1.82	.99		2.81	3.66	
	1200	Newels, 3-1/4" wide, starting, minimum		7	1.143	Ea.	37	31		68	92.50	
	1300	Maximum		6	1.333		120	36.50		156.50	193	
	1500	Landing, minimum		5	1.600		70	43.50		113.50	150	
	1600	Maximum		4	2	↓	170	54.50		224.50	279	
	1800	Railings, oak, built-up, minimum		60	.133	L.F.	5.30	3.64		8.94	11.95	
	1900	Maximum		55	.145		15	3.97		18.97	23	
	2100	Add for sub rail		110	.073		4	1.99		5.99	7.70	
	2300	Risers, beech, 3/4" x 7-1/2" high		64	.125		5.20	3.41		8.61	11.45	
	2400	Fir, 3/4" x 7-1/2" high		64	.125		1.50	3.41		4.91	7.35	
	2600	Oak, 3/4" x 7-1/2" high		64	.125		4.75	3.41		8.16	10.90	
	2800	Pine, 3/4" x 7-1/2" high		66	.121		1.50	3.31		4.81	7.20	
	2850	Skirt board, pine, 1" x 10"		55	.145		1.65	3.97		5.62	8.45	
	2900	1" x 12"		52	.154	↓	2	4.20		6.20	9.25	
	3000	Treads, 1-1/16" x 9-1/2" wide, 3' long, oak		18	.444	Ea.	22	12.15		34.15	44.50	
	3100	4' long, oak		17	.471		29	12.85		41.85	53.50	
	3300	1-1/16" x 11-1/2" wide, 3' long, oak		18	.444		23.50	12.15		35.65	46	
	3400	6' long, oak		14	.571		56	15.60		71.60	87.50	
	3600	Beech treads, add				↓	40%					
	3800	For mitered return nosings, add				L.F.	8.40			8.40	9.25	
	9000	Minimum labor/equipment charge	1 Carp	3	2.667	Job		73		73	122	
310	0010	**RAILING** Custom design, architectural grade, hardwood, minimum		38	.211	L.F.	12	5.75		17.75	23	310
	0100	Maximum		30	.267	"	44	7.30		51.30	60.50	
	0300	Stock interior railing with spindles 6" O.C., 4' long		40	.200	L.F.	28	5.45		33.45	40	
	0400	8' long		48	.167	"	26	4.55		30.55	36	
	9000	Minimum labor/equipment charge	↓	3	2.667	Job		73		73	122	

064 400 | Misc. Ornamental Items

			CREW	DAILY OUTPUT	LABOR-HOURS	UNIT	MAT.	LABOR	EQUIP.	TOTAL	TOTAL INCL O&P	
402	0011	**COLUMNS**										402
	0050	Aluminum, round colonial, 6" diameter	2 Carp	80	.200	V.L.F.	14	5.45		19.45	24.50	
	0100	8" diameter		62.25	.257		17	7		24	30.50	
	0200	10" diameter		55	.291		22	7.95		29.95	37.50	
	0250	Fir, stock units, hollow round, 6" diameter		80	.200		13	5.45		18.45	23.50	
	0300	8" diameter		80	.200		14	5.45		19.45	24.50	
	0350	10" diameter		70	.229		18	6.25		24.25	30.50	
	0400	Solid turned, to 8' high, 3-1/2" diameter		80	.200		7	5.45		12.45	16.85	
	0500	4-1/2" diameter		75	.213		10	5.80		15.80	21	
	0600	5-1/2" diameter		70	.229		13	6.25		19.25	25	
	0800	Square columns, built-up, 5" x 5"		65	.246		11	6.70		17.70	23.50	
	0900	Solid, 3-1/2" x 3-1/2"	↓	130	.123	↓	6	3.36		9.36	12.20	

064 | Architectural Woodwork

064 400 | Misc. Ornamental Items

		CREW	DAILY OUTPUT	LABOR-HOURS	UNIT	MAT.	LABOR	EQUIP.	TOTAL	TOTAL INCL O&P	
402	1600 Hemlock, tapered, T & G, 12" diam, 10' high	2 Carp	100	.160	V.L.F.	30	4.37		34.37	40.50	402
	1700 16' high		65	.246		46	6.70		52.70	62	
	1900 10' high, 14" diameter		100	.160		63	4.37		67.37	77	
	2000 18' high		65	.246		60	6.70		66.70	77.50	
	2200 18" diameter, 12' high		65	.246		76	6.70		82.70	95	
	2300 20' high		50	.320		83	8.75		91.75	106	
	2500 20" diameter, 14' high		40	.400		95	10.90		105.90	123	
	2600 20' high		35	.457		110	12.50		122.50	142	
	2800 For flat pilasters, deduct					33%					
	3000 For splitting into halves, add				Ea.	60			60	66	
	4000 Rough sawn cedar posts, 4" x 4"	2 Carp	250	.064	V.L.F.	2.43	1.75		4.18	5.60	
	4100 4" x 6"		235	.068		3.62	1.86		5.48	7.10	
	4200 6" x 6"		220	.073		5.45	1.99		7.44	9.30	
	4300 8" x 8"		200	.080		5.60	2.18		7.78	9.80	
	9000 Minimum labor/equipment charge	1 Carp	3	2.667	Job		73		73	122	
410	0010 **MILLWORK, HIGH DENSITY POLYMER**										410
	0100 Base, 9/16" x 3-3/16"	1 Carp	230	.035	L.F.	1.20	.95		2.15	2.91	
	0200 Casing, fluted, 5/8" x 3-1/4"		215	.037		1.20	1.02		2.22	3.02	
	0300 Chair rail, 9/16" x 2-1/4"		260	.031		.61	.84		1.45	2.08	
	0400 5/8" x 3-1/8"		230	.035		1.15	.95		2.10	2.86	
	0500 Corner, inside, 1/2" x 1-1/8"		220	.036		.60	.99		1.59	2.32	
	0600 Cove, 13/16" x 3-3/4"		260	.031		1.20	.84		2.04	2.73	
	0700 Crown, 3/4" x 3-13/16"		260	.031		1.20	.84		2.04	2.73	
	0800 Half round, 15/16" x 2"		240	.033		.66	.91		1.57	2.25	

066 | Plastic Fabrications

066 500 | Solid Surfacing Material

		CREW	DAILY OUTPUT	LABOR-HOURS	UNIT	MAT.	LABOR	EQUIP.	TOTAL	TOTAL INCL O&P	
503	0010 **SOLID SURFACE COUNTERTOPS**, Acrylic polymer										503
	0020 Pricing for orders of 100 L.F. or greater										
	0100 25" wide, solid colors	2 Carp	28	.571	L.F.	41	15.60		56.60	71	
	0200 Patterned colors		28	.571		52	15.60		67.60	83	
	0300 Premium patterned colors		28	.571		65	15.60		80.60	97.50	
	0400 With silicone attached 4" backsplash, solid colors		27	.593		45	16.20		61.20	76.50	
	0500 Patterned colors		27	.593		57	16.20		73.20	89.50	
	0600 Premium patterned colors		27	.593		71	16.20		87.20	105	
	0700 With hard seam attached 4" backsplash, solid colors		23	.696		45	19		64	81.50	
	0800 Patterned colors		23	.696		57	19		76	94.50	
	0900 Premium patterned colors		23	.696		71	19		90	110	
	1000 Pricing for order of 51 - 99 L.F.										
	1100 25" wide, solid colors	2 Carp	24	.667	L.F.	47	18.20		65.20	82.50	
	1200 Patterned colors		24	.667		60	18.20		78.20	96.50	
	1300 Premium patterned colors		24	.667		75	18.20		93.20	113	
	1400 With silicone attached 4" backsplash, solid colors		23	.696		52	19		71	89	
	1500 Patterned colors		23	.696		65.50	19		84.50	104	
	1600 Premium patterned colors		23	.696		81.50	19		100.50	122	
	1700 With hard seam attached 4" backsplash, solid colors		20	.800		52	22		74	93.50	
	1800 Patterned colors		20	.800		65.50	22		87.50	109	

For expanded coverage of these items see *Means Interior Cost Data 1999*

066 | Plastic Fabrications

066 500 | Solid Surfacing Material

			CREW	DAILY OUTPUT	LABOR-HOURS	UNIT	MAT.	LABOR	EQUIP.	TOTAL	TOTAL INCL O&P	
503	1900	Premium patterned colors	2 Carp	20	.800	L.F.	81.50	22		103.50	127	503
	2000	Pricing for order of 1 - 50 L.F.										
	2100	25" wide, solid colors	2 Carp	20	.800	L.F.	55.50	22		77.50	97.50	
	2200	Patterned colors		20	.800		70	22		92	114	
	2300	Premium patterned colors		20	.800		88	22		110	133	
	2400	With silicone attached 4" backsplash, solid colors		19	.842		61	23		84	106	
	2500	Patterned colors		19	.842		77	23		100	123	
	2600	Premium patterned colors		19	.842		96	23		119	144	
	2700	With hard seam attached 4" backsplash, solid colors		4	4		61	109		170	250	
	2800	Patterned colors		15	1.067		77	29		106	134	
	2900	Premium patterned colors		15	1.067		96	29		125	154	
	3000	Sinks, pricing for order of 100 or greater units										
	3100	Single bowl, hard seamed, solid colors, 13" x 17"	1 Carp	3	2.667	Ea.	277	73		350	425	
	3200	10" x 15"		7	1.143		128	31		159	193	
	3300	Cutouts for sinks		8	1			27.50		27.50	45.50	
	3400	Sinks, pricing for order of 51 - 99 units										
	3500	Single bowl, hard seamed, solid colors, 13" x 17"	1 Carp	2.55	3.137	Ea.	320	85.50		405.50	495	
	3600	10" x 15"		6	1.333		147	36.50		183.50	223	
	3700	Cutouts for sinks		7	1.143			31		31	52	
	3800	Sinks, pricing for order of 1 - 50 units										
	3900	Single bowl, hard seamed, solid colors, 13" x 17"	1 Carp	2	4	Ea.	375	109		484	595	
	4000	10" x 15"		4.55	1.758		173	48		221	271	
	4100	Cutouts for sinks		5.25	1.524			41.50		41.50	69.50	
	4200	Cooktop cutouts, pricing for 100 or greater units		4	2		20	54.50		74.50	114	
	4300	51 - 99 units		3.40	2.353		23	64		87	134	
	4400	1 - 50 units		3	2.667		27	73		100	152	
505	0010	**VANITY TOPS**										505
	0015	Solid surface, center bowl, 17" x 19"	1 Carp	12	.667	Ea.	163	18.20		181.20	211	
	0020	19" x 25"		12	.667		197	18.20		215.20	248	
	0030	19" x 31"		12	.667		240	18.20		258.20	295	
	0040	19" x 37"		12	.667		279	18.20		297.20	335	
	0050	22" x 25"		10	.800		222	22		244	281	
	0060	22" x 31"		10	.800		259	22		281	320	
	0070	22" x 37"		10	.800		300	22		322	365	
	0080	22" x 43"		10	.800		345	22		367	415	
	0090	22" x 49"		10	.800		380	22		402	455	
	0110	22" x 55"		8	1		430	27.50		457.50	520	
	0120	22" x 61"		8	1		495	27.50		522.50	585	
	0130	22" x 68"		8	1		635	27.50		662.50	740	
	0140	22" x 73"		8	1		715	27.50		742.50	830	
	0150	22" x 85"		8	1		825	27.50		852.50	950	
	0160	Offset bowl, left or right, 22" x 49"		10	.800		455	22		477	535	
	0170	22" x 55"		8	1		520	27.50		547.50	615	
	0180	22" x 61"		8	1		590	27.50		617.50	690	
	0190	22" x 68"		8	1		690	27.50		717.50	805	
	0200	22" x 73"		8	1		850	27.50		877.50	980	
	0210	22" x 85"		8	1		995	27.50		1,022.50	1,150	
	0220	Double bowl, 22" x 61"		8	1		540	27.50		567.50	640	
	0230	Corner top/bowl, 22" x 49"		8	1		420	27.50		447.50	510	
	0240	For aggregate colors, add					35%					
	0250	For faucets and fittings see 151-141										

For information about Means Estimating Seminars, see yellow pages 11 and 12 in back of book

Division 7
Thermal & Moisture Protection

Estimating Tips

071 Waterproofing & Dampproofing
- Be sure of the job specifications before pricing this subdivision. The difference in cost between waterproofing and dampproofing can be great. Waterproofing will hold back standing water. Dampproofing prevents the transmission of water vapor. Also included in this section are vapor retarding membranes.

072 Insulation & Fireproofing
- Insulation and fireproofing products are measured by area, thickness, volume or R value. Specifications may only give what the specific R value should be in a certain situation. The estimator may need to choose the type of insulation to meet that R value.

073 Shingles & Roofing Tiles
074 Preformed Roofing & Siding
- Many roofing and siding products are bought and sold by the square. One square is equal to an area that measures 100 square feet. This simple change in unit of measure could create a large error if the estimator is not observant. Accessories and fasteners necessary for a complete installation must be figured into any calculations for both material and labor.

075 Membrane Roofing
076 Flashing & Sheet Metal
077 Roof Specialties & Accessories
078 Skylights
- The items in these subdivisions compose a roofing system. No one component completes the installation and all must be estimated. Built-up or single ply membrane roofing systems are made up of many products and installation trades. Wood blocking at roof perimeters or penetrations, parapet coverings, reglets, roof drains, gutters, downspouts, sheet metal flashing, skylights, smoke vents or roof hatches all need to be considered along with the roofing material. Several different installation trades will need to work together on the roofing system. Inherent difficulties in the scheduling and coordination of various trades must be accounted for when estimating labor costs.

079 Joint Sealers
- To complete the weather-tight shell the sealants and caulkings must be estimated. Where different materials meet—at expansion joints, at flashing penetrations, and at hundreds of other locations throughout a construction project—they provide another line of defense against water penetration. Often, an entire system is based on the proper location and placement of caulking or sealants. The detail drawings that are included as part of a set of architectural plans, show typical locations for these materials. When caulking or sealants are shown at typical locations, this means the estimator must include them for all the locations where this detail is applicable. Be careful to keep different types of sealants separate, and remember to consider backer rods and primers if necessary.

Reference Numbers
Reference numbers are shown in bold squares at the beginning of some major classifications. These numbers refer to related items in the Reference Section. The reference information may be an estimating procedure, an alternate pricing method or technical information.

Note: Not all subdivisions listed here necessarily appear in this publication.

071 | Waterproofing & Dampproofing

071 100 | Sheet Waterproofing

				DAILY	LABOR-		1999 BARE COSTS				TOTAL	
			CREW	OUTPUT	HOURS	UNIT	MAT.	LABOR	EQUIP.	TOTAL	INCL O&P	
102	0010	**ELASTOMERIC WATERPROOFING**										102
	0050	Acrylic rubber, fluid applied, 20 mils thick	3 Rofc	1,000	.024	S.F.	1.52	.58		2.10	2.72	
	0060	50 mil, reinforced, stucco texture	"	600	.040		2.46	.96		3.42	4.47	
	0090	EPDM, plain, 45 mils thick	2 Rofc	580	.028		.74	.66		1.40	2.02	
	0100	60 mils thick		570	.028		1.08	.68		1.76	2.42	
	0300	Nylon reinforced sheets, 45 mils thick		580	.028		1.04	.66		1.70	2.35	
	0400	60 mils thick		570	.028		1.44	.68		2.12	2.81	
	0600	Vulcanizing splicing tape for above, 2" wide				C.L.F.	33.50			33.50	36.50	
	0700	4" wide				"	67			67	73.50	
	0900	Adhesive, bonding, 60 SF per gal				Gal.	13.60			13.60	14.95	
	1000	Splicing, 75 SF per gal				"	21			21	23	
	1200	Neoprene sheets, plain, 45 mils thick	2 Rofc	580	.028	S.F.	1.09	.66		1.75	2.41	
	1300	60 mils thick		570	.028		1.82	.68		2.50	3.24	
	1500	Nylon reinforced, 45 mils thick		580	.028		1.26	.66		1.92	2.60	
	1600	60 mils thick		570	.028		1.28	.68		1.96	2.64	
	1800	120 mils thick		500	.032		2.54	.77		3.31	4.19	
	1900	Adhesive, splicing, 150 S.F. per gal. per coat				Gal.	18.15			18.15	19.95	
	2100	Fiberglass reinforced, fluid applied, 1/8" thick	2 Rofc	500	.032	S.F.	1.50	.77		2.27	3.05	
	2200	Polyethylene and rubberized asphalt sheets, 1/8" thick		550	.029		.54	.70		1.24	1.87	
	2210	Asphaltic hardboard protection board, 1/8" thick		500	.032		.30	.77		1.07	1.73	
	2220	Asphaltic hardboard protection board, 1/4" thick		450	.036		.52	.86		1.38	2.13	
	2400	Polyvinyl chloride sheets, plain, 10 mils thick		580	.028		.14	.66		.80	1.36	
	2500	20 mils thick		570	.028		.22	.68		.90	1.47	
	2700	30 mils thick		560	.029		.30	.69		.99	1.58	
	3000	Adhesives, trowel grade, 40-100 SF per gal				Gal.	20			20	22	
	3100	Brush grade, 100-250 SF per gal.				"	20			20	22	
	3300	Bitumen modified polyurethane, fluid applied, 55 mils thick	2 Rofc	665	.024	S.F.	.65	.58		1.23	1.77	
	3600	Vinyl plastic, sprayed on, 25 to 40 mils thick		475	.034	"	.98	.81		1.79	2.56	
	9000	Minimum labor/equipment charge		2	8	Job		193		193	350	
104	0010	**MEMBRANE WATERPROOFING** On slabs, 1 ply, felt	G-1	3,000	.019	S.F.	.13	.42	.14	.69	1.06	104
	0100	Glass fiber fabric		2,100	.027		.14	.60	.19	.93	1.46	
	0300	2 ply, felt		2,500	.022		.25	.51	.16	.92	1.38	
	0400	Glass fiber fabric		1,650	.034		.31	.77	.25	1.33	2.02	
	0600	3 ply, felt		2,100	.027		.38	.60	.19	1.17	1.73	
	0700	Glass fiber fabric		1,550	.036		.41	.82	.26	1.49	2.23	
	0900	For installation on walls, add						15%				
	1000	For adhered 1/4" EPS protection board, add	2 Rofc	3,500	.005		.14	.11		.25	.35	
	1050	3/8" thick, add		3,500	.005		.16	.11		.27	.38	
	1060	1/2" thick, add		3,500	.005		.18	.11		.29	.40	
	1070	Fiberglass fabric, black, 20/10 mesh		116	.138	Sq.	9.95	3.32		13.27	17	
	1080	White, 20/10 mesh		116	.138	"	10.25	3.32		13.57	17.35	
	1100	1/16" urethane, troweled		200	.080	S.F.	.69	1.93		2.62	4.27	
	1200	Roller applied, 2 coats		120	.133	"	.60	3.21		3.81	6.50	
	9000	Minimum labor/equipment charge		2	8	Job		193		193	350	

071 450 | Cement. Waterproofing

				DAILY	LABOR-		1999 BARE COSTS				TOTAL	
			CREW	OUTPUT	HOURS	UNIT	MAT.	LABOR	EQUIP.	TOTAL	INCL O&P	
452	0010	**CEMENTITIOUS WATERPROOFING** One coat cement base										452
	0020	1/8" application, sprayed on	G-2	1,000	.024	S.F.	1.50	.55	.24	2.29	2.81	
	0030	2 coat, cementitious/metallic slurry, troweled, 1/4" thick	1 Cefi	2.48	3.226	C.S.F.	35	84.50		119.50	173	
	0040	3 coat, 3/8" thick		1.84	4.348		52.50	114		166.50	239	
	0050	4 coat, 1/2" thick		1.20	6.667		70	174		244	355	

071 | Waterproofing & Dampproofing

071 600 | Bitum. Dampproofing

		CREW	DAILY OUTPUT	LABOR-HOURS	UNIT	MAT.	LABOR	EQUIP.	TOTAL	TOTAL INCL O&P	
602	0010	**BITUMINOUS ASPHALT COATING** For foundation										602
	0030	Brushed on, below grade, 1 coat	1 Rofc	665	.012	S.F.	.06	.29		.35	.60	
	0100	2 coat		500	.016		.10	.39		.49	.81	
	0300	Sprayed on, below grade, 1 coat, 25.6 S.F./gal.		830	.010		.07	.23		.30	.49	
	0400	2 coat, 20.5 S.F./gal.		500	.016		.14	.39		.53	.86	
	0600	Troweled on, asphalt with fibers, 1/16" thick		500	.016		.15	.39		.54	.87	
	0700	1/8" thick		400	.020		.26	.48		.74	1.17	
	1000	1/2" thick		350	.023		.85	.55		1.40	1.94	
	9000	Minimum labor/equipment charge	▼	3	2.667	Job		64.50		64.50	117	

071 750 | Water Repellent Coat

		CREW	DAILY OUTPUT	LABOR-HOURS	UNIT	MAT.	LABOR	EQUIP.	TOTAL	TOTAL INCL O&P	
754	0010	**RUBBER COATING** Water base liquid, roller applied	2 Rofc	7,000	.002	S.F.	.55	.06		.61	.71	754
	0200	Silicone or stearate, sprayed on CMU, 1 coat	1 Rofc	4,000	.002		.26	.05		.31	.37	
	0300	2 coats		3,000	.003	▼	.51	.06		.57	.68	
	9000	Minimum labor/equipment charge	▼	3	2.667	Job		64.50		64.50	117	

071 920 | Vapor Retarders

		CREW	DAILY OUTPUT	LABOR-HOURS	UNIT	MAT.	LABOR	EQUIP.	TOTAL	TOTAL INCL O&P	
922	0010	**BUILDING PAPER** Aluminum and kraft laminated, foil 1 side	1 Carp	37	.216	Sq.	3.55	5.90		9.45	13.80	922
	0100	Foil 2 sides		37	.216		5.70	5.90		11.60	16.15	
	0300	Asphalt, two ply, 30#, for subfloors		19	.421		10.90	11.50		22.40	31.50	
	0400	Asphalt felt sheathing paper, 15#	▼	37	.216	▼	2.68	5.90		8.58	12.85	
	0450	Housewrap, exterior, spun bonded polypropylene										
	0470	Small roll	1 Carp	3,800	.002	S.F.	.10	.06		.16	.21	
	0480	Large roll	"	4,000	.002	"	.09	.05		.14	.19	
	0500	Material only, 3' x 111.1' roll				Ea.	33			33	36	
	0520	9' x 111.1' roll				"	93			93	102	
	0600	Polyethylene vapor barrier, standard, .002" thick	1 Carp	37	.216	Sq.	1.15	5.90		7.05	11.15	
	0700	.004" thick		37	.216		2.32	5.90		8.22	12.45	
	0900	.006" thick		37	.216		2.86	5.90		8.76	13.05	
	1200	.010" thick		37	.216		5.45	5.90		11.35	15.90	
	1300	Clear reinforced, fire retardant, .008" thick		37	.216		8.40	5.90		14.30	19.15	
	1350	Cross laminated type, .003" thick		37	.216		6.50	5.90		12.40	17.05	
	1400	.004" thick		37	.216		7.25	5.90		13.15	17.90	
	1500	Red rosin paper, 5 sq rolls, 4 lb per square		37	.216		1.55	5.90		7.45	11.60	
	1600	5 lbs. per square		37	.216		2	5.90		7.90	12.10	
	1800	Reinf. waterproof, .002" polyethylene backing, 1 side		37	.216		4.92	5.90		10.82	15.30	
	1900	2 sides	▼	37	.216		6.50	5.90		12.40	17.05	
	2100	Roof deck vapor barrier, class 1 metal decks	1 Rofc	37	.216		8.45	5.20		13.65	18.75	
	2200	For all other decks	"	37	.216		5.75	5.20		10.95	15.80	
	2400	Waterproofed kraft with sisal or fiberglass fibers, minimum	1 Carp	37	.216		5.30	5.90		11.20	15.75	
	2500	Maximum		37	.216	▼	13.25	5.90		19.15	24.50	
	9950	Minimum labor/equipment charge	▼	4	2	Job		54.50		54.50	91.50	

072 | Insulation & Fireproofing

072 100 | Building Insulation

		CREW	DAILY OUTPUT	LABOR-HOURS	UNIT	MAT.	LABOR	EQUIP.	TOTAL	TOTAL INCL O&P	
101	0010	**BLOWN-IN INSULATION** Ceilings, with open access										101
	0020	Cellulose, 3-1/2" thick, R13	G-4	5,000	.005	S.F.	.13	.11	.05	.29	.38	

THERMAL & MOISTURE PROTECTION 7

072 | Insulation & Fireproofing

072 100 | Building Insulation

			CREW	DAILY OUTPUT	LABOR-HOURS	UNIT	MAT.	LABOR	EQUIP.	TOTAL	TOTAL INCL O&P	
101	0030	5-3/16" thick, R19	G-4	3,800	.006	S.F.	.19	.14	.07	.40	.52	101
	0050	6-1/2" thick, R22		3,000	.008		.24	.18	.09	.51	.66	
	0100	8-11/16" thick, R30		2,600	.009		.32	.20	.10	.62	.80	
	1000	Fiberglass, 5" thick, R11		3,800	.006		.14	.14	.07	.35	.46	
	1050	6" thick, R13		3,000	.008		.15	.18	.09	.42	.56	
	1100	8-1/2" thick, R19		2,200	.011		.21	.24	.12	.57	.76	
	1200	10" thick, R22		1,800	.013		.24	.29	.15	.68	.91	
	1300	12" thick, R26		1,500	.016		.29	.35	.18	.82	1.11	
	2000	Mineral wool, 4" thick, R12		3,500	.007		.16	.15	.08	.39	.51	
	2050	6" thick, R17		2,500	.010		.18	.21	.11	.50	.68	
	2100	9" thick, R23	▼	1,750	.014	▼	.27	.30	.15	.72	.98	
	2500	Wall installation, incl. drilling & patching from outside, two 1"										
	2510	diam. holes @ 16" O.C., top & mid-point of wall, add to above										
	2700	For masonry	G-4	415	.058	S.F.	.06	1.28	.65	1.99	2.92	
	2800	For wood siding		840	.029		.06	.63	.32	1.01	1.48	
	2900	For stucco/plaster	▼	665	.036	▼	.06	.80	.40	1.26	1.86	
	9000	Minimum labor/equipment charge	A-1	4	2	Job		43	17.15	60.15	91	
106	0010	**FLOOR INSULATION, NONRIGID** Including										106
	0020	spring type wire fasteners										
	2000	Fiberglass, blankets or batts, paper or foil backing										
	2100	1 side, 3-1/2" thick, R11	1 Carp	700	.011	S.F.	.24	.31		.55	.79	
	2150	6" thick, R19		600	.013		.33	.36		.69	.97	
	2200	8-1/2" thick, R30	▼	550	.015	▼	.55	.40		.95	1.27	
	9000	Minimum labor/equipment charge		4	2	Job		54.50		54.50	91.50	
108	0011	**MASONRY INSULATION**										108
	0700	Foamed in place, urethane in 2-5/8" cavity	G-2	1,035	.023	S.F.	.38	.53	.23	1.14	1.54	
	0800	For each 1" added thickness, add	"	2,372	.010	"	.12	.23	.10	.45	.62	
109	0600	**PERIMETER INSULATION**, polystyrene, expanded, 1" thick, R4	1 Carp	680	.012	S.F.	.18	.32		.50	.74	109
	0700	2" thick, R8		675	.012	"	.33	.32		.65	.91	
	9000	Minimum labor/equipment charge		4	2	Job		54.50		54.50	91.50	
110	0010	**POURED INSULATION** Cellulose fiber, R3.8 per inch	1 Carp	200	.040	C.F.	.45	1.09		1.54	2.33	110
	0040	Ceramic type (perlite), R3.2 per inch		200	.040		1.45	1.09		2.54	3.43	
	0080	Fiberglass wool, R4 per inch		200	.040		.29	1.09		1.38	2.15	
	0100	Mineral wool, R3 per inch		200	.040		.30	1.09		1.39	2.16	
	0300	Polystyrene, R4 per inch		200	.040		1.72	1.09		2.81	3.72	
	0400	Vermiculite or perlite, R2.7 per inch		200	.040	▼	1.45	1.09		2.54	3.43	
	9000	Minimum labor/equipment charge		4	2	Job		54.50		54.50	91.50	
111	0012	**REFLECTIVE INSULATION**, aluminum foil on reinforced scrim	1 Carp	1,900	.004	S.F.	.14	.11		.25	.34	111
	0102	Reinforced with woven polyolefin		1,900	.004		.17	.11		.28	.38	
	0502	With single bubble air space, R8.8		1,500	.005		.26	.15		.41	.53	
	0602	With double bubble air space, R9.8		1,500	.005	▼	.28	.15		.43	.55	
	9000	Minimum labor/equipment charge		4	2	Job		54.50		54.50	91.50	
115	0010	**SPRAYED** Fibrous/cementitious, finished wall, 1" thick, R3.7	G-2	2,050	.012	S.F.	.22	.27	.11	.60	.81	115
	0100	Attic, 5.2" thick, R19	"	1,550	.015	"	.36	.35	.15	.86	1.15	
	0300	Foam type, incl. preparation										
	0600	3 #/CF, 1" thick, R3.8	G-2	770	.031	S.F.	.42	.71	.31	1.44	1.98	
	0700	2" thick, R7.5	"	475	.051	"	.84	1.16	.50	2.50	3.36	
	1000	Coating, 50-70 mils, elastomeric aromatic urethane										
	1100	Finish coat, 5 mils, elastomeric aliphatic, 200 S.F./gal.				Gal.	40.50			40.50	44.50	
	9000	Minimum labor/equipment charge	A-1	2	4	Job		86	34.50	120.50	182	

072 | Insulation & Fireproofing

072 100 | Building Insulation

		CREW	DAILY OUTPUT	LABOR-HOURS	UNIT	1999 BARE COSTS MAT.	LABOR	EQUIP.	TOTAL	TOTAL INCL O&P
116	**0010 WALL INSULATION, RIGID**									**116**
0040	Fiberglass, 1.5#/CF, unfaced, 1" thick, R4.1	1 Carp	1,000	.008	S.F.	.23	.22		.45	.62
0060	1-1/2" thick, R6.2		1,000	.008		.30	.22		.52	.70
0080	2" thick, R8.3		1,000	.008		.37	.22		.59	.77
0120	3" thick, R12.4		800	.010		.44	.27		.71	.94
0370	3#/CF, unfaced, 1" thick, R4.3		1,000	.008		.29	.22		.51	.69
0390	1-1/2" thick, R6.5		1,000	.008		.56	.22		.78	.99
0400	2" thick, R8.7		890	.009		.69	.25		.94	1.17
0420	2-1/2" thick, R10.9		800	.010		.86	.27		1.13	1.41
0440	3" thick, R13		800	.010		1.02	.27		1.29	1.58
0520	Foil faced, 1" thick, R4.3		1,000	.008		.68	.22		.90	1.12
0540	1-1/2" thick, R6.5		1,000	.008		.91	.22		1.13	1.37
0560	2" thick, R8.7		890	.009		1.13	.25		1.38	1.65
0580	2-1/2" thick, R10.9		800	.010		1.34	.27		1.61	1.93
0600	3" thick, R13		800	.010		1.46	.27		1.73	2.07
0670	6#/CF, unfaced, 1" thick, R4.3		1,000	.008		.65	.22		.87	1.08
0690	1-1/2" thick, R6.5		890	.009		1.01	.25		1.26	1.52
0700	2" thick, R8.7		800	.010		1.41	.27		1.68	2.01
0721	2-1/2" thick, R10.9		800	.010		1.55	.27		1.82	2.16
0741	3" thick, R13		730	.011		1.86	.30		2.16	2.55
0821	Foil faced, 1" thick, R4.3		1,000	.008		.92	.22		1.14	1.38
0840	1-1/2" thick, R6.5		890	.009		1.32	.25		1.57	1.86
0850	2" thick, R8.7		800	.010		1.72	.27		1.99	2.35
0880	2-1/2" thick, R10.9		800	.010		2.07	.27		2.34	2.74
0900	3" thick, R13		730	.011		2.47	.30		2.77	3.22
1500	Foamglass, 1-1/2" thick, R3.9		800	.010		1.45	.27		1.72	2.06
1550	3" thick, R9		730	.011		2.71	.30		3.01	3.48
1600	Isocyanurate, 4' x 8' sheet, foil faced, both sides									
1610	1/2" thick, R3.9	1 Carp	800	.010	S.F.	.28	.27		.55	.77
1620	5/8" thick, R4.5		800	.010		.29	.27		.56	.78
1630	3/4" thick, R5.4		800	.010		.30	.27		.57	.79
1640	1" thick, R7.2		800	.010		.33	.27		.60	.83
1650	1-1/2" thick, R10.8		730	.011		.37	.30		.67	.91
1660	2" thick, R14.4		730	.011		.47	.30		.77	1.01
1670	3" thick, R21.6		730	.011		1.10	.30		1.40	1.71
1680	4" thick, R28.8		730	.011		1.36	.30		1.66	2
1700	Perlite, 1" thick, R2.77		800	.010		.25	.27		.52	.74
1750	2" thick, R5.55		730	.011		.51	.30		.81	1.06
1900	Extruded polystyrene, 25 PSI compressive strength, 1" thick, R5		800	.010		.31	.27		.58	.80
1940	2" thick R10		730	.011		.61	.30		.91	1.17
1960	3" thick, R15		730	.011		.90	.30		1.20	1.50
2100	Expanded polystyrene, 1" thick, R3.85		800	.010		.15	.27		.42	.62
2120	2" thick, R7.69		730	.011		.32	.30		.62	.85
2140	3" thick, R11.49		730	.011		.52	.30		.82	1.07
9000	Minimum labor/equipment charge		4	2	Job		54.50		54.50	91.50
118	**0010 WALL OR CEILING INSUL., NON-RIGID**									**118**
0040	Fiberglass, kraft faced, batts or blankets									
0060	3-1/2" thick, R11, 11" wide	1 Carp	1,150	.007	S.F.	.19	.19		.38	.53
0080	15" wide		1,600	.005		.19	.14		.33	.44
0100	23" wide		1,600	.005		.19	.14		.33	.44
0140	6" thick, R19, 11" wide		1,000	.008		.28	.22		.50	.68
0160	15" wide		1,350	.006		.28	.16		.44	.58
0180	23" wide		1,600	.005		.28	.14		.42	.54
0200	9" thick, R30, 15" wide		1,150	.007		.50	.19		.69	.87
0220	23" wide		1,350	.006		.50	.16		.66	.82

072 | Insulation & Fireproofing

072 100 | Building Insulation

			CREW	DAILY OUTPUT	LABOR-HOURS	UNIT	MAT.	LABOR	EQUIP.	TOTAL	TOTAL INCL O&P	
118	0240	12" thick, R38, 15" wide	1 Carp	1,000	.008	S.F.	.64	.22		.86	1.07	118
	0260	23" wide	↓	1,350	.006	↓	.64	.16		.80	.97	
	0400	Fiberglass, foil faced, batts or blankets										
	0420	3-1/2" thick, R11, 15" wide	1 Carp	1,600	.005	S.F.	.29	.14		.43	.55	
	0440	23" wide		1,600	.005		.29	.14		.43	.55	
	0460	6" thick, R19, 15" wide		1,350	.006		.35	.16		.51	.66	
	0480	23" wide		1,600	.005		.35	.14		.49	.62	
	0500	9" thick, R30, 15" wide		1,150	.007		.60	.19		.79	.98	
	0550	23" wide	↓	1,350	.006	↓	.60	.16		.76	.93	
	0800	Fiberglass, unfaced, batts or blankets										
	0820	3-1/2" thick, R11, 15" wide	1 Carp	1,350	.006	S.F.	.17	.16		.33	.46	
	0830	23" wide		1,600	.005		.17	.14		.31	.42	
	0860	6" thick, R19, 15" wide		1,150	.007		.29	.19		.48	.64	
	0880	23" wide		1,350	.006		.29	.16		.45	.59	
	0900	9" thick, R30, 15" wide		1,000	.008		.50	.22		.72	.92	
	0920	23" wide		1,150	.007		.50	.19		.69	.87	
	0940	12" thick, R38, 15" wide		1,000	.008		.64	.22		.86	1.07	
	0960	23" wide		1,150	.007		.64	.19		.83	1.02	
	1300	Mineral fiber batts, kraft faced										
	1320	3-1/2" thick, R12	1 Carp	1,600	.005	S.F.	.22	.14		.36	.47	
	1340	6" thick, R19		1,600	.005		.33	.14		.47	.59	
	1380	10" thick, R30		1,350	.006	↓	.53	.16		.69	.85	
	1850	Friction fit wire insulation supports, 16" O.C.	↓	960	.008	Ea.	.05	.23		.28	.44	
	1900	For foil backing, add				S.F.	.04			.04	.04	
	9000	Minimum labor/equipment charge	1 Carp	4	2	Job		54.50		54.50	91.50	

072 200 | Roof & Deck Insulation

			CREW	DAILY OUTPUT	LABOR-HOURS	UNIT	MAT.	LABOR	EQUIP.	TOTAL	TOTAL INCL O&P	
203	0010	**ROOF DECK INSULATION**										203
	0020	Fiberboard low density, 1/2" thick R1.39	1 Rofc	1,000	.008	S.F.	.17	.19		.36	.54	
	0030	1" thick R2.78		800	.010		.32	.24		.56	.79	
	0080	1 1/2" thick R4.17		800	.010		.48	.24		.72	.97	
	0100	2" thick R5.56		800	.010		.64	.24		.88	1.14	
	0110	Fiberboard high density, 1/2" thick R1.3		1,000	.008		.18	.19		.37	.55	
	0120	1" thick R2.5		800	.010		.34	.24		.58	.81	
	0130	1-1/2" thick R3.8		800	.010		.55	.24		.79	1.05	
	0200	Fiberglass, 3/4" thick R2.78		1,000	.008		.39	.19		.58	.78	
	0400	15/16" thick R3.70		1,000	.008		.51	.19		.70	.91	
	0460	1-1/16" thick R4.17		1,000	.008		.64	.19		.83	1.05	
	0600	1-5/16" thick R5.26		1,000	.008		.88	.19		1.07	1.32	
	0650	2-1/16" thick R8.33		800	.010		.95	.24		1.19	1.49	
	0700	2-7/16" thick R10		800	.010		1.07	.24		1.31	1.62	
	1500	Foamglass, 1-3/4" thick R4.5		800	.010		1.41	.24		1.65	1.99	
	1530	3" thick R7.89		700	.011	↓	2.81	.28		3.09	3.59	
	1600	Tapered for drainage		600	.013	B.F.	.91	.32		1.23	1.59	
	1650	Perlite, 1/2" thick R1.32		1,050	.008	S.F.	.25	.18		.43	.61	
	1655	3/4" thick R2.08		800	.010		.30	.24		.54	.77	
	1660	1" thick R2.78		800	.010		.24	.24		.48	.70	
	1670	1-1/2" thick R4.17		800	.010		.36	.24		.60	.84	
	1680	2" thick R5.56		700	.011		.47	.28		.75	1.02	
	1685	2-1/2" thick R6.67		700	.011	↓	.71	.28		.99	1.28	
	1690	Tapered for drainage		800	.010	B.F.	.54	.24		.78	1.03	
	1700	Polyisocyanurate, 2#/CF density, 3/4" thick, R5.1		1,500	.005	S.F.	.30	.13		.43	.56	
	1705	1" thick R7.14		1,400	.006		.32	.14		.46	.60	
	1715	1-1/2" thick R10.87		1,250	.006		.36	.15		.51	.68	
	1725	2" thick R14.29	↓	1,100	.007	↓	.45	.18		.63	.81	

072 | Insulation & Fireproofing

072 200 | Roof & Deck Insulation

		CREW	DAILY OUTPUT	LABOR-HOURS	UNIT	MAT.	LABOR	EQUIP.	TOTAL	TOTAL INCL O&P
1735	2-1/2" thick R16.67	1 Rofc	1,050	.008	S.F.	.51	.18		.69	.89
1745	3" thick R21.74		1,000	.008		.62	.19		.81	1.03
1755	3-1/2" thick R25		1,000	.008		.74	.19		.93	1.16
1765	Tapered for drainage		1,400	.006	B.F.	.38	.14		.52	.67
1900	Extruded Polystyrene									
1910	15 PSI compressive strength, 1" thick, R5	1 Rofc	1,500	.005	S.F.	.22	.13		.35	.47
1920	2" thick, R10		1,250	.006		.35	.15		.50	.66
1930	3" thick R15		1,000	.008		.77	.19		.96	1.20
1932	4" thick R20		1,000	.008		1.06	.19		1.25	1.52
1934	Tapered for drainage		1,500	.005	B.F.	.35	.13		.48	.62
1940	25 PSI compressive strength, 1" thick R5		1,500	.005	S.F.	.33	.13		.46	.59
1942	2" thick R10		1,250	.006		.66	.15		.81	1.01
1944	3" thick R15		1,000	.008		.99	.19		1.18	1.44
1946	4" thick R20		1,000	.008		1.10	.19		1.29	1.56
1948	Tapered for drainage		1,500	.005	B.F.	.40	.13		.53	.67
1950	40 psi compressive strength, 1" thick R5		1,500	.005	S.F.	.35	.13		.48	.62
1952	2" thick R10		1,250	.006		.68	.15		.83	1.03
1954	3" thick R15		1,000	.008		1	.19		1.19	1.45
1956	4" thick R20		1,000	.008		1.34	.19		1.53	1.82
1958	Tapered for drainage		1,400	.006	B.F.	.50	.14		.64	.80
1960	60 PSI compressive strength, 1" thick R5		1,450	.006	S.F.	.42	.13		.55	.70
1962	2" thick R10		1,200	.007		.75	.16		.91	1.12
1964	3" thick R15		975	.008		1.12	.20		1.32	1.59
1966	4" thick R20		950	.008		1.55	.20		1.75	2.07
1968	Tapered for drainage		1,400	.006	B.F.	.60	.14		.74	.91
2010	Expanded polystyrene, 1#/CF density, 3/4" thick R2.89		1,500	.005	S.F.	.18	.13		.31	.43
2020	1" thick R3.85		1,500	.005		.18	.13		.31	.43
2100	2" thick R7.69		1,250	.006		.33	.15		.48	.65
2110	3" thick R11.49		1,250	.006		.50	.15		.65	.83
2120	4" thick R15.38		1,200	.007		.56	.16		.72	.91
2130	5" thick R19.23		1,150	.007		.70	.17		.87	1.08
2140	6" thick R23.26		1,150	.007		.83	.17		1	1.22
2150	Tapered for drainage		1,500	.005	B.F.	.34	.13		.47	.60
2400	Composites with 2" EPS									
2410	1" fiberboard	1 Rofc	950	.008	S.F.	.74	.20		.94	1.18
2420	7/16" oriented strand board		800	.010		.87	.24		1.11	1.40
2430	1/2" plywood		800	.010		.94	.24		1.18	1.47
2440	1" perlite		800	.010		.78	.24		1.02	1.30
2450	Composites with 1 1/2" polyisocyanurate									
2460	1" fiberboard	1 Rofc	800	.010	S.F.	.80	.24		1.04	1.32
2470	1" perlite		850	.009		.83	.23		1.06	1.32
2480	7/16" oriented strand board		800	.010		.95	.24		1.19	1.49
9000	Minimum labor/equipment charge		3.25	2.462	Job		59.50		59.50	108

072 400 | Exterior Insulation

		CREW	DAILY OUTPUT	LABOR-HOURS	UNIT	MAT.	LABOR	EQUIP.	TOTAL	TOTAL INCL O&P
0010	**EXTERIOR INSULATION FINISH SYSTEM**									
0095	Field applied, 1" EPS insulation	J-1	295	.136	S.F.	1.74	3.26	.14	5.14	7.35
0100	With 1/2" cement board sheathing		220	.182		2.77	4.37	.19	7.33	10.40
0105	2" EPS insulation		295	.136		1.91	3.26	.14	5.31	7.55
0110	With 1/2" cement board sheathing		220	.182		2.94	4.37	.19	7.50	10.60
0115	3" EPS insulation		295	.136		2.11	3.26	.14	5.51	7.80
0120	With 1/2" cement board sheathing		220	.182		3.14	4.37	.19	7.70	10.80
0125	4" EPS insulation		295	.136		2.23	3.26	.14	5.63	7.90
0130	With 1/2" cement board sheathing		220	.182		4.28	4.37	.19	8.84	12.05
0140	Premium finish add		1,265	.032		.27	.76	.03	1.06	1.58

072 | Insulation & Fireproofing

072 400 | Exterior Insulation

			CREW	DAILY OUTPUT	LABOR-HOURS	UNIT	1999 BARE COSTS MAT.	LABOR	EQUIP.	TOTAL	TOTAL INCL O&P	
402	0150	Heavy duty reinforcement add	J-1	914	.044	S.F.	1.65	1.05	.05	2.75	3.59	402
	0160	2.5#/S.Y. metal lath substrate add	1 Lath	75	.107	S.Y.	2.12	2.86		4.98	6.90	
	0170	3.4#/S.Y. metal lath substrate add	"	75	.107	"	2.21	2.86		5.07	7	
	0180	Color or texture change,	J-1	1,265	.032	S.F.	.72	.76	.03	1.51	2.07	
	0190	With substrate leveling base coat	1 Plas	530	.015		.72	.39		1.11	1.42	
	0210	With substrate sealing base coat	1 Pord	1,224	.007		.07	.16		.23	.35	
	0220	Prefab. panels, with hat channels 2 1/2" x 3/4", 2" EPS insul.	L-5	1,800	.031		7.70	.96	.31	8.97	10.55	
	0240	3" EPS insulation		1,800	.031		8.55	.96	.31	9.82	11.50	
	0250	4" EPS insulation		1,800	.031		9.55	.96	.31	10.82	12.60	
	0260	1-1/2" profile lightweight metal backing, 1" EPS insulation		1,800	.031		11.75	.96	.31	13.02	15.05	
	0270	2" EPS insulation		1,800	.031		13.10	.96	.31	14.37	16.55	
	0280	3" EPS insulation		1,800	.031		14.65	.96	.31	15.92	18.20	
	0290	4" EPS insulation		1,800	.031		16.35	.96	.31	17.62	20	
	0310	6"-16 Ga. steel stud back-up, 1" EPS insulation		1,800	.031		13.55	.96	.31	14.82	17	
	0320	2" EPS insulation		1,800	.031		15.15	.96	.31	16.42	18.75	
	0330	3" EPS insulation		1,800	.031		16.85	.96	.31	18.12	20.50	
	0340	4" EPS insulation		1,800	.031		18.85	.96	.31	20.12	22.50	
	0350	Premium finish add	J-1	1,265	.032		.27	.76	.03	1.06	1.58	
	0360	Heavy duty reinforcement add	"	914	.044		1.65	1.05	.05	2.75	3.59	
	0370	V groove shape in panel face				L.F.	.52			.52	.57	
	0380	U groove shape in panel face				"	.69			.69	.76	
	0390	Architectural features,										
	0410	Crown moulding 8" high x 4" wide	1 Plas	150	.053	L.F.	1.15	1.37		2.52	3.51	
	0420	Crown moulding 12" high x 6" wide		150	.053		2.15	1.37		3.52	4.61	
	0430	Crown moulding 16" high x 12" wide		150	.053		5.65	1.37		7.02	8.50	
	0433	Crack repair, acrylic rubber, fluid applied, 20 mils thick		350	.023	S.F.	1.32	.59		1.91	2.41	
	0437	50 mils thick, reinforced		200	.040	"	2.46	1.03		3.49	4.39	
	0440	For higher than one story, add						25%				

072 500 | Fireproofing

			CREW	DAILY OUTPUT	LABOR-HOURS	UNIT	MAT.	LABOR	EQUIP.	TOTAL	TOTAL INCL O&P	
554	0010	**SPRAYED** Mineral fiber or cementitious for fireproofing,										554
	0050	not incl tamping or canvas protection										
	0100	1" thick, on flat plate steel	G-2	3,000	.008	S.F.	.42	.18	.08	.68	.85	
	0200	Flat decking		2,400	.010		.42	.23	.10	.75	.95	
	0400	Beams		1,500	.016		.42	.37	.16	.95	1.23	
	0500	Corrugated or fluted decks		1,250	.019		.63	.44	.19	1.26	1.62	
	0700	Columns, 1-1/8" thick		1,100	.022		.47	.50	.21	1.18	1.58	
	0800	2-3/16" thick		700	.034		.88	.79	.34	2.01	2.63	
	0850	For tamping, add						10%				
	0900	For canvas protection, add	G-2	5,000	.005	S.F.	.06	.11	.05	.22	.30	
	9000	Minimum labor/equipment charge	"	3	8	Job		183	78.50	261.50	385	

072 700 | Firestopping

			CREW	DAILY OUTPUT	LABOR-HOURS	UNIT	MAT.	LABOR	EQUIP.	TOTAL	TOTAL INCL O&P	
701	0010	**FIRESTOPPING** R072-030										701
	0100	Metallic piping, non insulated										
	0110	Through walls, 2" diameter	1 Carp	16	.500	Ea.	9.60	13.65		23.25	33.50	
	0120	4" diameter		14	.571		14.65	15.60		30.25	42	
	0130	6" diameter		12	.667		19.70	18.20		37.90	52	
	0140	12" diameter		10	.800		35	22		57	75	
	0150	Through floors, 2" diameter		32	.250		5.80	6.80		12.60	17.85	
	0160	4" diameter		28	.286		8.35	7.80		16.15	22.50	
	0170	6" diameter		24	.333		11	9.10		20.10	27.50	
	0180	12" diameter		20	.400		18.50	10.90		29.40	39	
	0190	Metallic piping, insulated										
	0200	Through walls, 2" diameter	1 Carp	16	.500	Ea.	13.60	13.65		27.25	38	

Important: See the Reference Section for critical supporting data - Reference Nos., Crews, & City Cost Indexes

072 | Insulation & Fireproofing

072 700 | Firestopping

		CREW	DAILY OUTPUT	LABOR-HOURS	UNIT	MAT.	LABOR	EQUIP.	TOTAL	TOTAL INCL O&P
0210	4" diameter	1 Carp	14	.571	Ea.	18.65	15.60		34.25	46.50
0220	6" diameter		12	.667		23.50	18.20		41.70	56.50
0230	12" diameter		10	.800		39	22		61	79
0240	Through floors, 2" diameter		32	.250		9.80	6.80		16.60	22.50
0250	4" diameter		28	.286		12.35	7.80		20.15	26.50
0260	6" diameter		24	.333		15	9.10		24.10	32
0270	12" diameter		20	.400		18.50	10.90		29.40	39
0280	Non metallic piping, non insulated									
0290	Through walls, 2" diameter	1 Carp	12	.667	Ea.	39.50	18.20		57.70	74
0300	4" diameter		10	.800		49.50	22		71.50	91
0310	6" diameter		8	1		69	27.50		96.50	122
0330	Through floors, 2" diameter		16	.500		31	13.65		44.65	57
0340	4" diameter		6	1.333		38.50	36.50		75	103
0350	6" diameter		6	1.333		46	36.50		82.50	112
0370	Ductwork, insulated & non insulated, round									
0380	Through walls, 6" diameter	1 Carp	12	.667	Ea.	20	18.20		38.20	52.50
0390	12" diameter		10	.800		40	22		62	80.50
0400	18" diameter		8	1		65	27.50		92.50	117
0410	Through floors, 6" diameter		16	.500		11	13.65		24.65	35
0420	12" diameter		14	.571		20	15.60		35.60	48
0430	18" diameter		12	.667		35	18.20		53.20	69
0440	Ductwork, insulated & non insulated, rectangular									
0450	With stiffener/closure angle, through walls, 6" x 12"	1 Carp	8	1	Ea.	16.65	27.50		44.15	64
0460	12" x 24"		6	1.333		22	36.50		58.50	85.50
0470	24" x 48"		4	2		63	54.50		117.50	161
0480	With stiffener/closure angle, through floors, 6" x 12"		10	.800		9	22		31	46.50
0490	12" x 24"		8	1		16.20	27.50		43.70	63.50
0500	24" x 48"		6	1.333		32	36.50		68.50	96
0510	Multi trade openings									
0520	Through walls, 6" x 12"	1 Carp	2	4	Ea.	35	109		144	222
0530	12" x 24"	"	1	8		141	218		359	520
0540	24" x 48"	2 Carp	1	16		565	435		1,000	1,350
0550	48" x 96"	"	.75	21.333		2,275	580		2,855	3,475
0560	Through floors, 6" x 12"	1 Carp	2	4		35	109		144	222
0570	12" x 24"	"	1	8		141	218		359	520
0580	24" x 48"	2 Carp	.75	21.333		565	580		1,145	1,600
0590	48" x 96"	"	.50	32		2,275	875		3,150	3,950
0600	Structural penetrations, through walls									
0610	Steel beams, W8 x 10	1 Carp	8	1	Ea.	22	27.50		49.50	69.50
0620	W12 x 14		6	1.333		35	36.50		71.50	99.50
0630	W21 x 44		5	1.600		70	43.50		113.50	150
0640	W36 x 135		3	2.667		170	73		243	310
0650	Bar joists, 18" deep		6	1.333		32	36.50		68.50	96
0660	24" deep		6	1.333		40	36.50		76.50	105
0670	36" deep		5	1.600		60	43.50		103.50	139
0680	48" deep		4	2		70	54.50		124.50	169
0690	Construction joints, floor slab at exterior wall									
0700	Precast, brick, block or drywall exterior									
0710	2" wide joint	1 Carp	125	.064	L.F.	5	1.75		6.75	8.40
0720	4" wide joint	"	75	.107	"	10	2.91		12.91	15.85
0730	Metal panel, glass or curtain wall exterior									
0740	2" wide joint	1 Carp	40	.200	L.F.	11.85	5.45		17.30	22
0750	4" wide joint	"	25	.320	"	16.15	8.75		24.90	32.50
0760	Floor slab to drywall partition									
0770	Flat joint	1 Carp	100	.080	L.F.	4.90	2.18		7.08	9.05
0780	Fluted joint		50	.160		10	4.37		14.37	18.30

072 | Insulation & Fireproofing

072 700 | Firestopping

		CREW	DAILY OUTPUT	LABOR-HOURS	UNIT	MAT.	LABOR	EQUIP.	TOTAL	TOTAL INCL O&P	
701	0790	Etched fluted joint	1 Carp	75	.107	L.F.	6.50	2.91		9.41	12	701
	0800	Floor slab to concrete/masonry partition	R071 -030									
	0810	Flat joint	1 Carp	75	.107	L.F.	11	2.91		13.91	16.95	
	0820	Fluted joint	"	50	.160	"	13	4.37		17.37	21.50	
	0830	Concrete/CMU wall joints										
	0840	1" wide	1 Carp	100	.080	L.F.	6	2.18		8.18	10.25	
	0850	2" wide		75	.107		11	2.91		13.91	16.95	
	0860	4" wide	↓	50	.160	↓	21	4.37		25.37	30.50	
	0870	Concrete/CMU floor joints										
	0880	1" wide	1 Carp	200	.040	L.F.	3	1.09		4.09	5.15	
	0890	2" wide		150	.053		5.50	1.46		6.96	8.50	
	0900	4" wide	↓	100	.080	↓	10.50	2.18		12.68	15.20	

073 | Shingles & Roofing Tiles

073 100 | Shingles

		CREW	DAILY OUTPUT	LABOR-HOURS	UNIT	MAT.	LABOR	EQUIP.	TOTAL	TOTAL INCL O&P	
101	0010	ALUMINUM Shingles, mill finish, .019" thick	1 Carp	5	1.600	Sq.	150	43.50		193.50	238	101
	0100	.020" thick	"	5	1.600		145	43.50		188.50	232	
	0300	For colors, add				↓	15.15			15.15	16.65	
	0600	Ridge cap, .024" thick	1 Carp	170	.047	L.F.	1.85	1.28		3.13	4.19	
	0700	End wall flashing, .024" thick		170	.047		1.26	1.28		2.54	3.54	
	0900	Valley section, .024" thick		170	.047		2.30	1.28		3.58	4.68	
	1000	Starter strip, .024" thick		400	.020		1.20	.55		1.75	2.23	
	1200	Side wall flashing, .024" thick	↓	170	.047	↓	1.25	1.28		2.53	3.53	
	9000	Minimum labor/equipment charge		3	2.667	Job		73		73	122	
103	0010	FIBER CEMENT shingles, 16" x 9.35", 500 lb per square	1 Carp	4	2	Sq.	244	54.50		298.50	360	103
	0200	Shakes, 16" x 9.35", 550 lb per square		2.20	3.636	"	221	99.50		320.50	410	
	0300	Hip & ridge, 4.75 x 14"		1	8	C.L.F.	600	218		818	1,025	
	0400	Hexagonal, 16" x 16"		3	2.667	Sq.	165	73		238	305	
	0500	Square, 16" x 16"	↓	3	2.667		148	73		221	285	
	2000	For steep roofs (7/12 pitch or greater), add				↓		50%				
	9000	Minimum labor/equipment charge	1 Carp	3	2.667	Job		73		73	122	
104	0010	ASPHALT SHINGLES										104
	0100	Standard strip shingles										
	0150	Inorganic, class A, 210-235 lb/sq	1 Rofc	5.50	1.455	Sq.	26	35		61	92.50	
	0155	Pneumatic nailed		7	1.143		26	27.50		53.50	78.50	
	0200	Organic, class C, 235-240 lb/sq		5	1.600		34.50	38.50		73	108	
	0205	Pneumatic nailed	↓	6.25	1.280		34.50	31		65.50	94	
	0250	Standard, laminated multi-layered shingles										
	0300	Class A, 240-260 lb/sq	1 Rofc	4.50	1.778	Sq.	34	43		77	116	
	0305	Pneumatic nailed		5.63	1.422		34	34.50		68.50	100	
	0350	Class C, 260-300 lb/square, 4 bundles/square		4	2		49.50	48		97.50	143	
	0355	Pneumatic nailed	↓	5	1.600	↓	49.50	38.50		88	125	
	0400	Premium, laminated multi-layered shingles										
	0450	Class A, 260-300 lb, 4 bundles/sq	1 Rofc	3.50	2.286	Sq.	43	55		98	148	
	0455	Pneumatic nailed		4.37	1.831		43	44		87	128	
	0500	Class C, 300-385 lb/square, 5 bundles/square		3	2.667		65.50	64.50		130	189	
	0505	Pneumatic nailed		3.75	2.133		65.50	51.50		117	166	

073 | Shingles & Roofing Tiles

073 100 | Shingles

		CREW	DAILY OUTPUT	LABOR-HOURS	UNIT	1999 BARE COSTS MAT.	LABOR	EQUIP.	TOTAL	TOTAL INCL O&P	
104	0800 #15 felt underlayment	1 Rofc	64	.125	Sq.	2.68	3.01		5.69	8.45	104
	0825 #30 felt underlayment		58	.138		5.45	3.32		8.77	12.05	
	0850 Self adhering polyethylene and rubberized asphalt underlayment		22	.364		39.50	8.75		48.25	59.50	
	0900 Ridge shingles		330	.024	L.F.	.72	.58		1.30	1.85	
	0905 Pneumatic nailed		412.50	.019	"	.72	.47		1.19	1.64	
	1000 For steep roofs (7 to 12 pitch or greater), add						50%				
	9000 Minimum labor/equipment charge	1 Rofc	3	2.667	Job		64.50		64.50	117	
106	0010 **SLATE**, Buckingham, Virginia, black										106
	0100 3/16" - 1/4" thick	1 Rots	1.75	4.571	Sq.	540	111		651	795	
	0200 1/4" thick		1.75	4.571		720	111		831	990	
	0900 Pennsylvania black, Bangor, #1 clear		1.75	4.571		435	111		546	680	
	1200 Vermont, unfading, green, mottled green		1.75	4.571		395	111		506	635	
	1300 Semi-weathering green & gray		1.75	4.571		296	111		407	525	
	1400 Purple		1.75	4.571		390	111		501	630	
	1500 Black or gray		1.75	4.571		405	111		516	645	
	2500 Slate roof repair, extensive replacement		1	8		540	194		734	945	
	2600 Repair individual pieces, scattered		19	.421	Ea.	5.40	10.20		15.60	24.50	
	9000 Minimum labor/equipment charge		3	2.667	Job		64.50		64.50	117	
107	0010 **STEEL** Shingles, galvanized, 26 gauge	1 Rots	2.20	3.636	Sq.	149	88		237	325	107
	0200 24 gauge	"	2.20	3.636	"	157	88		245	330	
	0300 For colored galvanized shingles, add				Sq.	41			41	45	
	0500 For 1" factory applied polystyrene insulation, add				"	30			30	33	
	9000 Minimum labor/equipment charge	1 Rots	3	2.667	Job		64.50		64.50	117	
108	0010 **WOOD** 16" No. 1 red cedar shingles, 5" exposure, on roof	1 Carp	2.50	3.200	Sq.	143	87.50		230.50	305	108
	0015 Pneumatic nailed		3.25	2.462		143	67		210	269	
	0200 7-1/2" exposure, on walls		2.05	3.902		95	107		202	283	
	0205 Pneumatic nailed		2.67	2.996		95	82		177	242	
	0300 18" No. 1 red cedar perfections, 5-1/2" exposure, on roof		2.75	2.909		164	79.50		243.50	315	
	0305 Pneumatic nailed		3.57	2.241		164	61		225	283	
	0600 Resquared, and rebutted, 5-1/2" exposure, on roof		3	2.667		199	73		272	340	
	0605 Pneumatic nailed		3.90	2.051		199	56		255	315	
	0900 7-1/2" exposure, on walls		2.45	3.265		146	89		235	310	
	0905 Pneumatic nailed		3.18	2.516		146	68.50		214.50	276	
	1000 Add to above for fire retardant shingles, 16" long					30			30	33	
	1050 18" long					28.50			28.50	31.50	
	1060 Preformed ridge shingles	1 Carp	400	.020	L.F.	1.65	.55		2.20	2.73	
	1100 Hand-split red cedar shakes, 1/2" thick x 24" long, 10" exp. on roof		2.50	3.200	Sq.	138	87.50		225.50	298	
	1105 Pneumatic nailed		3.25	2.462		138	67		205	264	
	1110 3/4" thick x 24" long, 10" exp. on roof		2.25	3.556		138	97		235	315	
	1115 Pneumatic nailed		2.92	2.740		138	75		213	277	
	1200 1/2" thick, 18" long, 8-1/2" exp. on roof		2	4		97.50	109		206.50	290	
	1205 Pneumatic nailed		2.60	3.077		97.50	84		181.50	248	
	1210 3/4" thick x 18" long, 8 1/2" exp. on roof		1.80	4.444		97.50	121		218.50	310	
	1215 Pneumatic nailed		2.34	3.419		97.50	93.50		191	263	
	1255 10" exp. on walls		2	4		110	109		219	305	
	1260 10" exposure on walls, pneumatic nailed		2.60	3.077		110	84		194	262	
	1700 Add to above for fire retardant shakes, 24" long					30			30	33	
	1800 18" long					30			30	33	
	1810 Ridge shakes	1 Carp	350	.023	L.F.	2.35	.62		2.97	3.62	
	2000 White cedar shingles, 16" long, extras, 5" exposure, on roof		2.40	3.333	Sq.	125	91		216	290	
	2005 Pneumatic nailed		3.12	2.564		125	70		195	255	
	2050 5" exposure on walls		2	4		125	109		234	320	
	2055 Pneumatic nailed		2.60	3.077		125	84		209	279	

THERMAL & MOISTURE PROTECTION 7

073 | Shingles & Roofing Tiles

073 100 | Shingles

			CREW	DAILY OUTPUT	LABOR-HOURS	UNIT	MAT.	LABOR	EQUIP.	TOTAL	TOTAL INCL O&P	
108	2100	7-1/2" exposure, on walls	1 Carp	2	4	Sq.	89.50	109		198.50	281	108
	2105	Pneumatic nailed	R061-030	2.60	3.077		89.50	84		173.50	239	
	2150	"B" grade, 5" exposure on walls		2	4		117	109		226	310	
	2155	Pneumatic nailed		2.60	3.077		117	84		201	270	
	2300	For 15# organic felt underlayment on roof, 1 layer, add		64	.125		2.68	3.41		6.09	8.65	
	2400	2 layers, add		32	.250		5.35	6.80		12.15	17.35	
	2600	For steep roofs (7/12 pitch or greater), add to above						50%				
	2700	Panelized systems, No.1 cedar shingles on 5/16" CDX plywood										
	2800	On walls, 8' strips, 7" or 14" exposure	2 Carp	700	.023	S.F.	3.20	.62		3.82	4.56	
	3500	On roofs, 8' strips, 7" or 14" exposure	1 Carp	3	2.667	Sq.	320	73		393	470	
	3505	Pneumatic nailed		4	2	"	320	54.50		374.50	440	
	9000	Minimum labor/equipment charge		3	2.667	Job		73		73	122	

073 200 | Roofing Tile

			CREW	DAILY OUTPUT	LABOR-HOURS	UNIT	MAT.	LABOR	EQUIP.	TOTAL	TOTAL INCL O&P	
201	0010	**ALUMINUM** Tiles with accessories, .032" thick, mission tile	1 Carp	2.50	3.200	Sq.	350	87.50		437.50	530	201
	0200	Spanish tiles		3	2.667	"	350	73		423	505	
	9000	Minimum labor/equipment charge		3	2.667	Job		73		73	122	
202	0010	**CLAY TILE** ASTM C1167, GR 1, severe weathering, acces. incl.										202
	0200	Lanai tile or Classic tile, 158 pc per sq	1 Rots	1.65	4.848	Sq.	490	117		607	755	
	0300	Americana, 158 pc per sq, most colors		1.65	4.848		490	117		607	755	
	0350	Green, gray or brown		1.65	4.848		490	117		607	755	
	0400	Blue		1.65	4.848		490	117		607	755	
	0600	Spanish tile, 171 pc per sq, red		1.80	4.444		305	108		413	535	
	0800	Blend		1.80	4.444		420	108		528	655	
	0900	Glazed white		1.80	4.444		500	108		608	745	
	1100	Mission tile, 192 pc per sq, machine scored finish, red		1.15	6.957		635	168		803	1,000	
	1700	French tile, 133 pc per sq, smooth finish, red		1.35	5.926		575	143		718	890	
	1750	Blue or green		1.35	5.926		685	143		828	1,025	
	1800	Norman black 317 pc per sq		1	8		805	194		999	1,225	
	2200	Williamsburg tile, 158 pc per sq, aged cedar		1.35	5.926		490	143		633	800	
	2250	Gray or green		1.35	5.926		490	143		633	800	
	3000	For steep roofs (7/12 pitch or greater), add to above						50%				
	9000	Minimum labor/equipment charge	1 Rots	3	2.667	Job		64.50		64.50	117	
204	0010	**CONCRETE TILE** Including installation of accessories										204
	0050	Earthtone colors, nailed to wood deck	1 Rots	1.35	5.926	Sq.	103	143		246	375	
	0150	Custom blues		1.35	5.926		114	143		257	385	
	0200	Custom greens		1.35	5.926		114	143		257	385	
	0250	Premium colors		1.35	5.926		153	143		296	430	
	0500	Shakes, 13" x 16-1/2", 90 per sq, 950 lb per sq										
	0600	All colors, nailed to wood deck	1 Rots	1.50	5.333	Sq.	185	129		314	440	
	1500	Accessory pieces, ridge & hip, 10" x 16-1/2", 8 lbs. each				Ea.	2.25			2.25	2.48	
	1700	Rake, 6-1/2" x 16-3/4", 9 lbs. each					2.25			2.25	2.48	
	1800	Mansard hip, 10" x 16-1/2", 9.2 lbs. each					2.25			2.25	2.48	
	1900	Hip starter, 10" x 16-1/2", 10.5 lbs. each					9.50			9.50	10.45	
	2000	3 or 4 way apex, 10" each side, 11.5 lbs. each					10.25			10.25	11.30	
	9000	Minimum labor/equipment charge	1 Rots	3	2.667	Job		64.50		64.50	117	

074 | Preformed Roofing & Siding

074 100 | Preformed Panels

			CREW	DAILY OUTPUT	LABOR-HOURS	UNIT	MAT.	LABOR	EQUIP.	TOTAL	TOTAL INCL O&P	
101	0010	**ALUMINUM ROOFING** Corrugated or ribbed, .0155" thick, natural	G-3	1,200	.027	S.F.	.61	.71		1.32	1.83	101
	0300	Painted		1,200	.027		.87	.71		1.58	2.12	
	0400	Corrugated, .018" thick, on steel frame, natural finish		1,200	.027		.78	.71		1.49	2.02	
	0600	Painted		1,200	.027		.97	.71		1.68	2.23	
	0700	Corrugated, on steel frame, natural, .024" thick		1,200	.027		1.14	.71		1.85	2.41	
	0800	Painted, .024" thick		1,200	.027		1.37	.71		2.08	2.67	
	0900	.032" thick, natural		1,200	.027		1.23	.71		1.94	2.51	
	1200	painted		1,200	.027		1.61	.71		2.32	2.93	
	9000	Minimum labor/equipment charge	1 Rofc	3	2.667	Job		64.50		64.50	117	
104	0010	**FIBERGLASS** Corrugated panels, roofing, 8 oz per SF	G-3	1,000	.032	S.F.	2.17	.85		3.02	3.78	104
	0100	12 oz per SF		1,000	.032		2.87	.85		3.72	4.55	
	0300	Corrugated siding, 6 oz per SF		880	.036		1.88	.97		2.85	3.65	
	0400	8 oz per SF		880	.036		2.17	.97		3.14	3.97	
	0500	Fire retardant		880	.036		3	.97		3.97	4.88	
	0600	12 oz. siding, textured		880	.036		2.70	.97		3.67	4.55	
	0700	Fire retardant		880	.036		4.02	.97		4.99	6	
	0900	Flat panels, 6 oz per SF, clear or colors		880	.036		1.68	.97		2.65	3.43	
	1100	Fire retardant, class A		880	.036		2.91	.97		3.88	4.78	
	1300	8 oz per SF, clear or colors		880	.036		2.17	.97		3.14	3.97	
	9000	Minimum labor/equipment charge	1 Rofc	2	4	Job		96.50		96.50	176	
107	0010	**STEEL ROOFING** on steel frame, corrugated or ribbed, 30 ga galv	G-3	1,100	.029	S.F.	.75	.77		1.52	2.09	107
	0100	28 ga		1,050	.030		.79	.81		1.60	2.19	
	0300	26 ga		1,000	.032		.86	.85		1.71	2.34	
	0400	24 ga		950	.034		1.02	.90		1.92	2.58	
	0600	Colored, 28 ga		1,050	.030		1.05	.81		1.86	2.47	
	0700	26 ga		1,000	.032		1.12	.85		1.97	2.62	
	0710	Flat profile, 1-3/4" standing seams, 10" wide, standard finish, 26 ga		1,000	.032		2.30	.85		3.15	3.92	
	0715	24 ga		950	.034		2.67	.90		3.57	4.40	
	0720	22 ga		900	.036		3.29	.95		4.24	5.15	
	0725	Zinc aluminum alloy finish, 26 ga		1,000	.032		1.80	.85		2.65	3.37	
	0730	24 ga		950	.034		2.15	.90		3.05	3.83	
	0735	22 ga		900	.036		2.47	.95		3.42	4.26	
	0740	12" wide, standard finish, 26 ga		1,000	.032		2.29	.85		3.14	3.91	
	0745	24 ga		950	.034		2.66	.90		3.56	4.39	
	0750	Zinc aluminum alloy finish, 26 ga		1,000	.032		1.70	.85		2.55	3.26	
	0755	24 ga		950	.034		2.03	.90		2.93	3.69	
	0840	Flat profile, 1" x 3/8" batten, 12" wide, standard finish, 26 ga		1,000	.032		1.79	.85		2.64	3.36	
	0845	24 ga		950	.034		2.10	.90		3	3.77	
	0850	22 ga		900	.036		2.52	.95		3.47	4.31	
	0855	Zinc aluminum alloy finish, 26 ga		1,000	.032		1.51	.85		2.36	3.05	
	0860	24 ga		950	.034		1.68	.90		2.58	3.31	
	0865	22 ga		900	.036		1.95	.95		2.90	3.69	
	0870	16-1/2" wide, standard finish, 24 ga		950	.034		2.13	.90		3.03	3.80	
	0875	22 ga		900	.036		2.39	.95		3.34	4.17	
	0880	Zinc aluminum alloy finish, 24 ga		950	.034		1.60	.90		2.50	3.22	
	0885	22 ga		900	.036		1.78	.95		2.73	3.50	
	0890	Flat profile, 2" x 2" batten, 12" wide, standard finish, 26 ga		1,000	.032		2.05	.85		2.90	3.65	
	0895	24 ga		950	.034		2.45	.90		3.35	4.16	
	0900	22 ga		900	.036		3	.95		3.95	4.84	
	0905	Zinc aluminum alloy finish, 26 ga		1,000	.032		1.69	.85		2.54	3.25	
	0910	24 ga		950	.034		1.83	.90		2.73	3.47	
	0915	22 ga		900	.036		2.25	.95		3.20	4.02	
	0920	16-1/2" wide, standard finish, 24 ga		950	.034		2.27	.90		3.17	3.96	
	0925	22 ga		900	.036		2.64	.95		3.59	4.44	

074 | Preformed Roofing & Siding

074 100 | Preformed Panels

			CREW	DAILY OUTPUT	LABOR-HOURS	UNIT	MAT.	LABOR	EQUIP.	TOTAL	TOTAL INCL O&P	
107	0930	Zinc aluminum alloy finish, 24 ga	G-3	950	.034	S.F.	1.80	.90		2.70	3.44	107
	0935	22 ga		900	.036		2.05	.95		3	3.80	
	9000	Minimum labor/equipment charge	1 Rofc	2	4	Job		96.50		96.50	176	

074 600 | Cladding/Siding

			CREW	DAILY OUTPUT	LABOR-HOURS	UNIT	MAT.	LABOR	EQUIP.	TOTAL	TOTAL INCL O&P	
602	0010	ALUMINUM SIDING .019" thick, on steel construction, natural	G-3	775	.041	S.F.	.65	1.10		1.75	2.50	602
	0100	Painted		775	.041		.84	1.10		1.94	2.71	
	0400	Farm type, .021" thick on steel frame, natural		775	.041		.75	1.10		1.85	2.62	
	0600	Painted		775	.041		.92	1.10		2.02	2.80	
	0700	Industrial type, corrugated, on steel, .024" thick, mill		775	.041		.95	1.10		2.05	2.84	
	0900	Painted		775	.041		1.15	1.10		2.25	3.06	
	1000	.032" thick, mill		775	.041		1.30	1.10		2.40	3.22	
	1200	Painted		775	.041		1.65	1.10		2.75	3.60	
	1300	V-Beam, on steel frame, .032" thick, mill		775	.041		1.48	1.10		2.58	3.41	
	1500	Painted		775	.041		1.80	1.10		2.90	3.77	
	1600	.040" thick, mill		775	.041		1.80	1.10		2.90	3.77	
	1800	Painted		775	.041		2.15	1.10		3.25	4.15	
	1910	Minimum labor/equipment charge	1 Carp	3	2.667	Job		73		73	122	
	2000											
	3800	Horizontal, colored clapboard, 8" wide, plain	2 Carp	515	.031	S.F.	1.22	.85		2.07	2.76	
	3810	Insulated		515	.031		1.36	.85		2.21	2.92	
	3830	8" embossed, painted		515	.031		1.40	.85		2.25	2.96	
	3840	Insulated		515	.031		1.54	.85		2.39	3.11	
	3860	12" painted, smooth		600	.027		1.26	.73		1.99	2.61	
	3870	Insulated		600	.027		1.49	.73		2.22	2.86	
	3890	12" embossed, painted		600	.027		1.45	.73		2.18	2.82	
	3900	Insulated		515	.031		1.49	.85		2.34	3.06	
	4000	Vertical board & batten, colored, non-insulated		515	.031		1.06	.85		1.91	2.59	
	4200	For simulated wood design, add					.08			.08	.09	
	4300	Corners for above, outside	2 Carp	515	.031	V.L.F.	1.67	.85		2.52	3.26	
	4500	Inside corners	"	515	.031	"	.94	.85		1.79	2.45	
	4520	For simulated wood design, add				S.F.	.08			.08	.09	
	9000	Minimum labor/equipment charge	1 Carp	3	2.667	Job		73		73	122	
606	0010	STEEL SIDING, Beveled, vinyl coated, 8" wide, including fasteners		265	.030	S.F.	1.12	.82		1.94	2.61	606
	0050	10" wide		275	.029	"	1.19	.79		1.98	2.64	
	0060	Minimum labor/equipment charge		3	2.667	Job		73		73	122	
	0070											
	0080	Galv, corrugated or ribbed, on steel frame, 30 gauge	G-3	800	.040	S.F.	.75	1.06		1.81	2.57	
	0100	28 gauge		795	.040		.79	1.07		1.86	2.62	
	0300	26 gauge		790	.041		.86	1.08		1.94	2.71	
	0400	24 gauge		785	.041		1.03	1.08		2.11	2.90	
	0600	22 gauge		770	.042		1.17	1.11		2.28	3.09	
	0700	Colored, corrugated/ribbed, on steel frame, 10 yr fnsh, 28 ga.		800	.040		1.08	1.06		2.14	2.93	
	0900	26 gauge		795	.040		.95	1.07		2.02	2.80	
	1000	24 gauge		790	.041		1.09	1.08		2.17	2.96	
	1020	20 gauge		785	.041		1.41	1.08		2.49	3.32	
	9000	Minimum labor/equipment charge	1 Carp	3	2.667	Job		73		73	122	
607	0010	VINYL SIDING Solid PVC panels, 8" to 10" wide, plain	"	255	.031	S.F.	.61	.86		1.47	2.10	607
	0100	with 3/8" insulation	1 Carp	255	.031	"	.75	.86		1.61	2.26	
	0200	Soffit and fascia		205	.039	S.F.	1.33	1.07		2.40	3.24	
	0300	Window and door trim moldings		185	.043	L.F.	.31	1.18		1.49	2.32	
	0500	Corner posts, outside corner		205	.039		1.04	1.07		2.11	2.92	
	0600	Inside corner		205	.039		.58	1.07		1.65	2.42	
	9000	Minimum labor/equipment charge		3	2.667	Job		73		73	122	

074 | Preformed Roofing & Siding

074 600 | Cladding/Siding

			CREW	DAILY OUTPUT	LABOR-HOURS	UNIT	1999 BARE COSTS MAT.	LABOR	EQUIP.	TOTAL	TOTAL INCL O&P	
609	0010	**WOOD SIDING, BOARDS**										609
	3200	Wood, cedar bevel, A grade, 1/2" x 6"	1 Carp	250	.032	S.F.	2.02	.87		2.89	3.68	
	3300	1/2" x 8"		275	.029		1.66	.79		2.45	3.16	
	3500	3/4" x 10", clear grade		300	.027		2.16	.73		2.89	3.59	
	3600	"B" grade		300	.027		3.22	.73		3.95	4.76	
	3800	Cedar, rough sawn, 1" x 4", A grade, natural		240	.033		3.01	.91		3.92	4.83	
	3900	Stained		240	.033		3.39	.91		4.30	5.25	
	4100	1" x 12", board & batten, #3 & Btr., natural		260	.031		2.08	.84		2.92	3.70	
	4200	Stained		260	.031		2.42	.84		3.26	4.07	
	4400	1" x 8" channel siding, #3 & Btr., natural		250	.032		2.02	.87		2.89	3.68	
	4500	Stained		250	.032		2.30	.87		3.17	3.99	
	4700	Redwood, clear, beveled, vertical grain, 1/2" x 4"		200	.040		3.22	1.09		4.31	5.35	
	4750	1/2" x 6"		225	.036		2.70	.97		3.67	4.59	
	4800	1/2" x 8"		250	.032		2.19	.87		3.06	3.87	
	5000	3/4" x 10"		300	.027		3.57	.73		4.30	5.15	
	5200	Channel siding, 1" x 10", B grade		285	.028		2.30	.77		3.07	3.81	
	5250	Redwood, T&G boards, B grade, 1" x 4"	2 Carp	300	.053		2.74	1.46		4.20	5.45	
	5270	1" x 8"	"	375	.043		2.36	1.16		3.52	4.55	
	5400	White pine, rough sawn, 1" x 8", natural	1 Carp	275	.029		.69	.79		1.48	2.09	
	5500	Stained		275	.029		1.02	.79		1.81	2.45	
	9000	Minimum labor/equipment charge		2	4	Job		109		109	183	
611	0010	**WOOD PRODUCT SIDING**	R061 -020									611
	0030	Lap siding, hardboard, 7/16" x 8", primed										
	0050	Wood grain texture finish	2 Carp	650	.025	S.F.	.95	.67		1.62	2.17	
	0100	Panels, 7/16" thick, smooth, textured or grooved, primed		700	.023		.81	.62		1.43	1.93	
	0200	Stained		700	.023		.88	.62		1.50	2.01	
	0700	Particle board, overlaid, 3/8" thick		750	.021		.63	.58		1.21	1.66	
	0900	Plywood, medium density overlaid, 3/8" thick		750	.021		1.08	.58		1.66	2.16	
	1000	1/2" thick		700	.023		1.26	.62		1.88	2.43	
	1100	3/4" thick		650	.025		1.47	.67		2.14	2.74	
	1600	Texture 1-11, cedar, 5/8" thick, natural		675	.024		1.50	.65		2.15	2.73	
	1700	Factory stained		675	.024		1.74	.65		2.39	2.99	
	1900	Texture 1-11, fir, 5/8" thick, natural		675	.024		1.01	.65		1.66	2.19	
	2000	Factory stained		675	.024		1.14	.65		1.79	2.33	
	2050	Texture 1-11, S.Y.P., 5/8" thick, natural		675	.024		.83	.65		1.48	1.99	
	2100	Factory stained		675	.024		.93	.65		1.58	2.10	
	2200	Rough sawn cedar, 3/8" thick, natural		675	.024		1.14	.65		1.79	2.33	
	2300	Factory stained		675	.024		1.26	.65		1.91	2.47	
	2500	Rough sawn fir, 3/8" thick, natural		675	.024		.61	.65		1.26	1.75	
	2600	Factory stained		675	.024		.68	.65		1.33	1.83	
	2800	Redwood, textured siding, 5/8" thick		675	.024		1.89	.65		2.54	3.16	
	3000	Polyvinyl chloride coated, 3/8" thick		750	.021		.93	.58		1.51	1.99	
	9000	Minimum labor/equipment charge	1 Carp	2	4	Job		109		109	183	
615	0010	**FIBER CEMENT SIDING**										615
	0020	Lap siding, 5/16" thick, 6" wide, smooth texture	2 Carp	415	.039	S.F.	.93	1.05		1.98	2.79	
	0025	Woodgrain texture		415	.039		.93	1.05		1.98	2.79	
	0030	7-1/2" wide, smooth texture		425	.038		.92	1.03		1.95	2.73	
	0035	Woodgrain texture		425	.038		.92	1.03		1.95	2.73	
	0040	8" wide, smooth texture		425	.038		.92	1.03		1.95	2.74	
	0045	Roughsawn texture		425	.038		.92	1.03		1.95	2.74	
	0050	9-1/2" wide, smooth texture		440	.036		.89	.99		1.88	2.64	
	0055	Woodgrain texture		440	.036		.89	.99		1.88	2.64	
	0060	12" wide, smooth texture		455	.035		.86	.96		1.82	2.56	
	0065	Woodgrain texture		455	.035		.86	.96		1.82	2.56	
	0070	Panel siding, 5/16" thick, smooth texture		750	.021		.77	.58		1.35	1.81	

THERMAL & MOISTURE PROTECTION 7

074 | Preformed Roofing & Siding

074 600 | Cladding/Siding

		CREW	DAILY OUTPUT	LABOR-HOURS	UNIT	1999 BARE COSTS MAT.	LABOR	EQUIP.	TOTAL	TOTAL INCL O&P	
615	0075 Stucco texture	2 Carp	750	.021	S.F.	.77	.58		1.35	1.81	615
	0080 Grooved woodgrain texture		750	.021		.77	.58		1.35	1.81	
	0085 V - grooved woodgrain texture		750	.021		.77	.58		1.35	1.81	
	0090 Wood starter strip		400	.040	L.F.	.25	1.09		1.34	2.11	

075 | Membrane Roofing

075 100 | Built-Up Roofing

		CREW	DAILY OUTPUT	LABOR-HOURS	UNIT	1999 BARE COSTS MAT.	LABOR	EQUIP.	TOTAL	TOTAL INCL O&P	
101	0010 **ASPHALT** Coated felt, #30, 2 sq per roll, not mopped	1 Rofc	58	.138	Sq.	5.45	3.32		8.77	12.05	101
	0200 #15, 4 sq per roll, plain or perforated, not mopped		58	.138		2.68	3.32		6	9	
	0300 Roll roofing, smooth, #65		15	.533		12.10	12.85		24.95	37	
	0500 #90		15	.533		12.65	12.85		25.50	37.50	
	0520 Mineralized		15	.533		15.50	12.85		28.35	40.50	
	0540 D.C. (Double coverage), 19" selvage edge		10	.800		30.50	19.30		49.80	68.50	
	0580 Adhesive (lap cement)				Gal.	3.68			3.68	4.05	
	0600 Steep, flat or dead level asphalt, 10 ton lots, bulk				Ton	230			230	253	
	0800 Packaged				"	255			255	281	
	9000 Minimum labor/equipment charge	1 Rofc	4	2	Job		48		48	88	
102	0010 **BUILT-UP ROOFING**										102
	0120 Asphalt flood coat with gravel/slag surfacing, not including										
	0140 Insulation, flashing or wood nailers										
	0200 Asphalt base sheet, 3 plies #15 asphalt felt, mopped	G-1	22	2.545	Sq.	35.50	57.50	18.60	111.60	165	
	0350 On nailable decks		21	2.667		39.50	60.50	19.45	119.45	175	
	0500 4 plies #15 asphalt felt, mopped		20	2.800		50	63.50	20.50	134	194	
	0550 On nailable decks		19	2.947		46	67	21.50	134.50	196	
	0700 Coated glass base sheet, 2 plies glass (type IV), mopped		22	2.545		38.50	57.50	18.60	114.60	168	
	0850 3 plies glass, mopped		20	2.800		46	63.50	20.50	130	189	
	0950 On nailable decks		19	2.947		44	67	21.50	132.50	194	
	1100 4 plies glass fiber felt (type IV), mopped		20	2.800		55.50	63.50	20.50	139.50	200	
	1150 On nailable decks		19	2.947		51	67	21.50	139.50	202	
	1200 Coated & saturated base sheet, 3 plies #15 asph. felt, mopped		20	2.800		42	63.50	20.50	126	185	
	1250 On nailable decks		19	2.947		40	67	21.50	128.50	190	
	1300 4 plies #15 asphalt felt, mopped		22	2.545		48	57.50	18.60	124.10	179	
	2000 Asphalt flood coat, smooth surface										
	2200 Asphalt base sheet & 3 plies #15 asphalt felt, mopped	G-1	24	2.333	Sq.	36	53	17.05	106.05	155	
	2400 On nailable decks		23	2.435		34	55	17.75	106.75	158	
	2600 4 plies #15 asphalt felt, mopped		24	2.333		42.50	53	17.05	112.55	162	
	2700 On nailable decks		23	2.435		40	55	17.75	112.75	165	
	2900 Coated glass fiber base sheet, mopped, and 2 plies of										
	2910 glass fiber felt (type IV)	G-1	25	2.240	Sq.	33	51	16.35	100.35	147	
	3100 On nailable decks		24	2.333		31.50	53	17.05	101.55	150	
	3200 3 plies, mopped		23	2.435		40.50	55	17.75	113.25	165	
	3300 On nailable decks		22	2.545		38.50	57.50	18.60	114.60	168	
	3800 4 plies glass fiber felt (type IV), mopped		23	2.435		47.50	55	17.75	120.25	173	
	3900 On nailable decks		22	2.545		45.50	57.50	18.60	121.60	176	
	4000 Coated & saturated base sheet, 3 plies #15 asph. felt, mopped		24	2.333		36.50	53	17.05	106.55	155	
	4200 On nailable decks		23	2.435		34	55	17.75	106.75	158	
	4300 4 plies #15 organic felt, mopped		22	2.545		42.50	57.50	18.60	118.60	173	
	4500 Coal tar pitch with gravel/slag surfacing										
	4600 4 plies #15 tarred felt, mopped	G-1	21	2.667	Sq.	97.50	60.50	19.45	177.45	239	

075 | Membrane Roofing

075 100 | Built-Up Roofing

			CREW	DAILY OUTPUT	LABOR-HOURS	UNIT	MAT.	LABOR	EQUIP.	TOTAL	TOTAL INCL O&P	
102	4800	3 plies glass fiber felt (type IV), mopped	G-1	19	2.947	Sq.	80.50	67	21.50	169	234	102
	5000	Coated glass fiber base sheet, and 2 plies of										
	5010	glass fiber felt, (type IV), mopped	G-1	19	2.947	Sq.	80	67	21.50	168.50	234	
	5300	On nailable decks		18	3.111		71	70.50	22.50	164	231	
	5600	4 plies glass fiber felt (type IV), mopped		21	2.667		110	60.50	19.45	189.95	253	
	5800	On nailable decks	▼	20	2.800	▼	101	63.50	20.50	185	250	
103	0010	CANTS 4" x 4", treated timber, cut diagonally	1 Rofc	325	.025	L.F.	.80	.59		1.39	1.96	103
	0100	Foamglass		325	.025		1.92	.59		2.51	3.19	
	0300	Mineral or fiber, trapezoidal, 1"x 4" x 48"		325	.025		.17	.59		.76	1.27	
	0400	1-1/2" x 5-5/8" x 48"		325	.025	▼	.29	.59		.88	1.40	
	9000	Minimum labor/equipment charge	▼	4	2	Job		48		48	88	
104	0010	FELT Glass fibered, #15, no mopping	1 Rofc	58	.138	Sq.	3.70	3.32		7.02	10.10	104
	0300	Base sheet, #45, channel vented		58	.138		16.50	3.32		19.82	24	
	0400	#50, coated		58	.138		7.55	3.32		10.87	14.35	
	0500	Cap, mineral surfaced		58	.138		16.25	3.32		19.57	24	
	0600	Flashing membrane, #65		16	.500		39	12.05		51.05	65	
	0800	Coal tar fibered, #15, no mopping		58	.138		7.90	3.32		11.22	14.75	
	0900	Asphalt felt, #15, 4 sq per roll, no mopping		58	.138		2.68	3.32		6	9	
	1100	#30, 2 sq per roll		58	.138		5.45	3.32		8.77	12.05	
	1200	Double coated, #33		58	.138		5.95	3.32		9.27	12.60	
	1400	#40, base sheet		58	.138		6.30	3.32		9.62	13	
	1450	Coated and saturated		58	.138		6.50	3.32		9.82	13.20	
	1500	Tarred felt, organic, #15, 4 sq rolls		58	.138		7.80	3.32		11.12	14.65	
	1550	#30, 2 sq roll	▼	58	.138		15.60	3.32		18.92	23.50	
	1700	Add for mopping above felts, per ply, asphalt, 24 lb per sq	G-1	192	.292		3.06	6.60	2.13	11.79	17.75	
	1800	Coal tar mopping, 30 lb per sq		186	.301		8.05	6.85	2.20	17.10	24	
	1900	Flood coat, with asphalt, 60 lb per sq		60	.933		7.65	21	6.80	35.45	54.50	
	2000	With coal tar, 75 lb per sq	▼	56	1	▼	20	22.50	7.30	49.80	71.50	
	9000	Minimum labor/equipment charge	1 Rofc	4	2	Job		48		48	88	
105	0010	WALKWAY For built-up roofs, asphalt impregnated, 3' x 6' x 1/2" thk	1 Rofc	400	.020	S.F.	.87	.48		1.35	1.83	105
	0100	3' x 3' x 3/4" thick		400	.020	"	2.07	.48		2.55	3.16	
	9000	Minimum labor/equipment charge	▼	2.75	2.909	Job		70		70	128	

075 150 | Cold Applied Roofing

			CREW	DAILY OUTPUT	LABOR-HOURS	UNIT	MAT.	LABOR	EQUIP.	TOTAL	TOTAL INCL O&P	
152	0010	COLD APPLIED 3-ply system (components listed below)	G-5	50	.800	Sq.		17.70	3.31	21.01	35.50	152
	0100	Spunbond poly. fabric, 1.35 oz/SY, 36"W, 10.8 Sq/roll				Ea.	123			123	135	
	0200	49" wide, 14.6 Sq./roll					169			169	186	
	0300	2.10 oz./S.Y., 36" wide, 10.8 Sq./roll					185			185	203	
	0400	49" wide, 14.6 Sq./roll				▼	250			250	275	
	0500	Base & finish coat, 3 gal./Sq., 5 gal./can				Gal.	3.25			3.25	3.58	
	0600	Coating, ceramic granules, 1/2 Sq./bag				Ea.	11.50			11.50	12.65	
	0700	Aluminum, 2 gal./Sq.				Gal.	9.25			9.25	10.20	
	0800	Emulsion, fibered or non-fibered, 4 gal./Sq.				"	4.25			4.25	4.68	

075 200 | Prepared Roll Roofing

			CREW	DAILY OUTPUT	LABOR-HOURS	UNIT	MAT.	LABOR	EQUIP.	TOTAL	TOTAL INCL O&P	
204	0010	ROLL ROOFING										204
	0100	Asphalt, mineral surface										
	0200	1 ply #15 organic felt, 1 ply mineral surfaced										
	0300	Selvage roofing, lap 19", nailed & mopped	G-1	27	2.074	Sq.	36.50	47	15.15	98.65	142	
	0400	3 plies glass fiber felt (type IV), 1 ply mineral surfaced										
	0500	Selvage roofing, lapped 19", mopped	G-1	25	2.240	Sq.	54	51	16.35	121.35	170	
	0600	Coated glass fiber base sheet, 2 plies of glass fiber										
	0700	Felt (type IV), 1 ply mineral surfaced selvage										

THERMAL & MOISTURE PROTECTION 7

075 | Membrane Roofing

075 200 | Prepared Roll Roofing

			CREW	DAILY OUTPUT	LABOR-HOURS	UNIT	MAT.	LABOR	EQUIP.	TOTAL	TOTAL INCL O&P	
204	0800	Roofing, lapped 19", mopped	G-1	25	2.240	Sq.	57.50	51	16.35	124.85	174	204
	0900	On nailable decks	"	24	2.333	"	54.50	53	17.05	124.55	175	
	1000	3 plies glass fiber felt (type III), 1 ply mineral surfaced										
	1100	Selvage roofing, lapped 19", mopped	G-1	25	2.240	Sq.	54	51	16.35	121.35	170	

075 300 | Elastomeric Roofing

			CREW	DAILY OUTPUT	LABOR-HOURS	UNIT	MAT.	LABOR	EQUIP.	TOTAL	TOTAL INCL O&P	
301	0010	**ELASTOMERIC ROOFING**										301
	0100	For Elastomeric waterproofing, see division 071-102										
	0110	Acrylic rubber, fluid applied, 20 mils thick	G-5	2,000	.020	S.F.	1.80	.44	.08	2.32	2.87	
	0120	50 mils, reinforced		1,200	.033		2.80	.74	.14	3.68	4.57	
	0130	For walking surface, add	↓	900	.044		.85	.98	.18	2.01	2.93	
	0300	Hypalon neoprene, fluid applied, 20 mil thick, not-reinforced	G-1	1,135	.049		2.05	1.12	.36	3.53	4.70	
	0600	Non-woven polyester, reinforced		960	.058		2.07	1.32	.43	3.82	5.15	
	0700	5 coat neoprene deck, 60 mil thick, under 10,000 SF		325	.172		4.56	3.91	1.26	9.73	13.50	
	0900	Over 10,000 SF		625	.090		4.25	2.03	.65	6.93	9.10	
	1300	Vinyl plastic traffic deck, sprayed, 2 to 4 mils thick		625	.090		1.33	2.03	.65	4.01	5.90	
	1500	Vinyl and neoprene membrane traffic deck	↓	1,550	.036	↓	1.41	.82	.26	2.49	3.33	
	9000	Minimum labor/equipment charge	1 Rofc	2	4	Job		96.50		96.50	176	
302	0010	**SINGLE-PLY MEMBRANE**										302
	0800	Chlorosulfonated polyethylene-hypalon (CSPE), 45 mils,										
	0900	0.29 P.S.F., fully adhered	G-5	26	1.538	Sq.	122	34	6.35	162.35	203	
	3500	Ethylene propylene diene monomer (EPDM), 45 mils, 0.28 P.S.F.										
	4810	45 mil, .28 PSF, membrane only				Sq.	34			34	37	
	4820	60 mil, .40 PSF, membrane only				"	44			44	48.50	
	4850	Seam tape for membrane, 4" x 100' roll				Ea.	67			67	73.50	
	4900	Batten strips, 10' sections					2.45			2.45	2.70	
	4910	Cover tape for batten strips, 6" x 100' roll				↓	126			126	139	
	4930	Plate anchors				M	123			123	135	
	4970	Adhesive for fully adhered systems, 60 S.F./gal.				Gal.	13.60			13.60	14.95	
	7500	Polyisobutylene (PIB), 100 mils, 0.57 P.S.F.										
	7600	Loose-laid & ballasted with stone/gravel (10 P.S.F.)	G-5	51	.784	Sq.	123	17.35	3.25	143.60	170	
	7700	Partially adhered with adhesive		35	1.143		154	25.50	4.73	184.23	220	
	7800	Hot asphalt attachment		35	1.143		147	25.50	4.73	177.23	213	
	7900	Fully adhered with contact cement		26	1.538		159	34	6.35	199.35	244	
	8200	Polyvinyl chloride (PVC), heat welded seams										
	8700	Reinforced, 48 mils, 0.33 P.S.F.										
	8750	Loose-laid & ballasted with stone/gravel (12 P.S.F.)	G-5	51	.784	Sq.	85.50	17.35	3.25	106.10	129	
	8800	Partially adhered with mechanical fasteners		35	1.143		76	25.50	4.73	106.23	135	
	8850	Fully adhered with adhesive	↓	26	1.538	↓	108	34	6.35	148.35	187	
	8860	Reinforced, 60 mils, .40 P.S.F.										
	8870	Loose-laid & ballasted with stone/gravel (12 P.S.F.)	G-5	51	.784	Sq.	89.50	17.35	3.25	110.10	134	
	8880	Partially adhered with mechanical fasteners		35	1.143		79.50	25.50	4.73	109.73	139	
	8890	Fully adhered with adhesive		26	1.538		111	34	6.35	151.35	192	

075 350 | Modified Bit. Roofing

				CREW	DAILY OUTPUT	LABOR-HOURS	UNIT	MAT.	LABOR	EQUIP.	TOTAL	TOTAL INCL O&P	
352	0010	**MODIFIED BITUMEN ROOFING**	R075 -030										352
	0020	Base sheet, #15 glass fiber felt, nailed to deck		1 Rofc	58	.138	Sq.	4.38	3.32		7.70	10.85	
	0030	Spot mopped to deck		G-1	295	.190		5.25	4.30	1.39	10.94	15.10	
	0040	Fully mopped to deck		"	192	.292		6.75	6.60	2.13	15.48	22	
	0050	#15 organic felt, nailed to deck		1 Rofc	58	.138		3.37	3.32		6.69	9.75	
	0060	Spot mopped to deck		G-1	295	.190		4.21	4.30	1.39	9.90	14	
	0070	Fully mopped to deck		"	192	.292	↓	5.75	6.60	2.13	14.48	20.50	
	0080	SBS modified, granule surf cap sheet, polyester rein., mopped											
	1500	Glass fiber reinforced, mopped, 160 mils		G-1	2,000	.028	S.F.	.36	.63	.20	1.19	1.78	
	1600	Smooth surface cap sheet, mopped, 145 mils		↓	2,100	.027	↓	.36	.60	.19	1.15	1.71	

075 | Membrane Roofing

075 350 | Modified Bit. Roofing

			CREW	DAILY OUTPUT	LABOR-HOURS	UNIT	1999 BARE COSTS				TOTAL INCL O&P	
							MAT.	LABOR	EQUIP.	TOTAL		
352	1700	Smooth surface flashing, 145 mils	G-1	1,260	.044	S.F.	.36	1.01	.32	1.69	2.60	352
	1800	150 mils		1,260	.044		.35	1.01	.32	1.68	2.59	
	1900	Granular surface flashing, 150 mils		1,260	.044		.38	1.01	.32	1.71	2.62	
	2000	160 mils		1,260	.044		.44	1.01	.32	1.77	2.68	
	2100	APP mod., smooth surf. cap sheet, poly. reinf., torched, 160 mils	G-5	2,100	.019		.35	.42	.08	.85	1.25	
	2150	170 mils		2,100	.019		.39	.42	.08	.89	1.29	
	2200	Granule surface cap sheet, poly. reinf., torched, 180 mils		2,000	.020		.38	.44	.08	.90	1.31	
	2250	Smooth surface flashing, torched, 160 mils		1,260	.032		.35	.70	.13	1.18	1.81	
	2300	170 mils		1,260	.032		.39	.70	.13	1.22	1.85	
	2350	Granule surface flashing, torched, 180 mils		1,260	.032		.38	.70	.13	1.21	1.84	
	2400	Fibrated aluminum coating	1 Rofc	3,800	.002		.08	.05		.13	.17	

075 600 | Roof Maint. & Repairs

						UNIT	MAT.	LABOR	EQUIP.	TOTAL	INCL O&P	
604	0010	**ROOF COATINGS** Asphalt				Gal.	2.71			2.71	2.98	604
	0200	Asphalt base, fibered aluminum coating					7.65			7.65	8.40	
	0300	Asphalt primer, 5 gallon					3.25			3.25	3.58	
	0600	Coal tar pitch, 200 lb. barrels				Ton	540			540	590	
	0700	Tar roof cement, 5 gal. lots				Gal.	5.55			5.55	6.10	
	0800	Glass fibered roof & patching cement, 5 gallon				"	3.45			3.45	3.80	
	0900	Reinforcing glass membrane, 450 S.F./roll				Ea.	45.50			45.50	50	
	1000	Neoprene roof coating, 5 gal, 2 gal/sq				Gal.	20.50			20.50	22.50	
	1100	Roof patch & flashing cement, 5 gallon					18.95			18.95	21	
	1200	Roof restaurant, glass fibered, 3 gal/sq					7.30			7.30	8.05	
	1300	Mineral rubber, 3 gal/sq					4.71			4.71	5.20	

076 | Flashing & Sheet Metal

076 100 | Sheet Metal Roofing

			CREW	DAILY OUTPUT	LABOR-HOURS	UNIT	1999 BARE COSTS				TOTAL INCL O&P	
							MAT.	LABOR	EQUIP.	TOTAL		
101	0010	**COPPER ROOFING** Batten seam, over 10 sq, 16 oz, 130 lb/sq	1 Shee	1.10	7.273	Sq.	395	231		626	805	101
	0200	18 oz, 145 lb per sq		1	8		440	254		694	890	
	0300	20 oz, 160 lb per sq		1	8		490	254		744	940	
	0400	Standing seam, over 10 squares, 16 oz, 125 lb per sq		1.30	6.154		380	195		575	735	
	0600	18 oz, 140 lb per sq		1.20	6.667		425	212		637	810	
	0700	20 oz, 150 lb per sq		1.10	7.273		460	231		691	875	
	0900	Flat seam, over 10 squares, 16 oz, 115 lb per sq		1.20	6.667		350	212		562	725	
	1000	20 oz, 145 lb per sq		1.10	7.273		440	231		671	855	
	1200	For abnormal conditions or small areas, add					25%	100%				
	1300	For lead-coated copper, add					25%					
	9000	Minimum labor/equipment charge	1 Shee	2	4	Job		127		127	204	
102	0010	**LEAD ROOFING** 5 lb. per SF, batten seam	1 Shee	1.20	6.667	Sq.	375	212		587	755	102
	0100	Flat seam		1.30	6.154	"	375	195		570	730	
	9000	Minimum labor/equipment charge		2	4	Job		127		127	204	
104	0010	**STAINLESS STEEL ROOFING** Type 304, batten seam, 28 gauge	1 Shee	1.20	6.667	Sq.	300	212		512	670	104
	0100	26 gauge	"	1.15	6.957		375	221		596	765	
	0200	For standing seam construction, deduct					2%					
	0500	For flat seam construction, deduct					3%					

076 | Flashing & Sheet Metal

076 100 | Sheet Metal Roofing

			CREW	DAILY OUTPUT	LABOR-HOURS	UNIT	1999 BARE COSTS				TOTAL INCL O&P	
							MAT.	LABOR	EQUIP.	TOTAL		
104	0800	For lead or terne coated stainless, 28 gauge, add				Sq.	68.50			68.50	75.50	104
	0900	For 26 gauge, add				↓	91			91	100	
	9000	Minimum labor/equipment charge	1 Shee	2.75	2.909	Job		92.50		92.50	148	
105	0010	**ZINC** Copper alloy roofing, batten seam, .020" thick	1 Shee	1.20	6.667	Sq.	510	212		722	900	105
	0100	.027" thick		1.15	6.957		615	221		836	1,025	
	0300	.032" thick		1.10	7.273		695	231		926	1,125	
	0400	.040" thick	↓	1.05	7.619		820	242		1,062	1,300	
	0600	For standing seam construction, deduct					2%					
	0700	For flat seam construction, deduct				↓	3%					
	9000	Minimum labor/equipment charge	1 Shee	2.75	2.909	Job		92.50		92.50	148	

076 200 | Sheet Mtl Flash & Trim

			CREW	DAILY OUTPUT	LABOR-HOURS	UNIT	MAT.	LABOR	EQUIP.	TOTAL	TOTAL INCL O&P	
201	0010	**DOWNSPOUTS** Aluminum 2" x 3", .020" thick, embossed	1 Shee	190	.042	L.F.	.71	1.34		2.05	2.92	201
	0100	Enameled		190	.042		.68	1.34		2.02	2.89	
	0300	Enameled, .024" thick, 2" x 3"		180	.044		1.09	1.41		2.50	3.46	
	0400	3" x 4"		140	.057		1.41	1.81		3.22	4.46	
	0600	Round, corrugated aluminum, 3" diameter, .020" thick		190	.042		.85	1.34		2.19	3.08	
	0700	4" diameter, .025" thick		140	.057	↓	1.29	1.81		3.10	4.33	
	0900	Wire strainer, round, 2" diameter		155	.052	Ea.	1.75	1.64		3.39	4.56	
	1000	4" diameter		155	.052		1.82	1.64		3.46	4.63	
	1200	Rectangular, perforated, 2" x 3"		145	.055		2.15	1.75		3.90	5.20	
	1300	3" x 4"		145	.055	↓	3.10	1.75		4.85	6.20	
	1500	Copper, round, 16 oz., stock, 2" diameter		190	.042	L.F.	4.88	1.34		6.22	7.50	
	1600	3" diameter		190	.042		3.84	1.34		5.18	6.35	
	1800	4" diameter		145	.055		4.66	1.75		6.41	7.95	
	1900	5" diameter		130	.062		6.70	1.95		8.65	10.55	
	2100	Rectangular, corrugated copper, stock, 2" x 3"		190	.042		3.25	1.34		4.59	5.70	
	2200	3" x 4"		145	.055		4.36	1.75		6.11	7.60	
	2400	Rectangular, plain copper, stock, 2" x 3"		190	.042		4.71	1.34		6.05	7.35	
	2500	3" x 4"		145	.055	↓	6.20	1.75		7.95	9.60	
	2700	Wire strainers, rectangular, 2" x 3"		145	.055	Ea.	2.76	1.75		4.51	5.85	
	2800	3" x 4"		145	.055		4.37	1.75		6.12	7.60	
	3000	Round, 2" diameter		145	.055		2.59	1.75		4.34	5.65	
	3100	3" diameter		145	.055		3.62	1.75		5.37	6.80	
	3300	4" diameter		145	.055		5.60	1.75		7.35	8.95	
	3400	5" diameter		115	.070	↓	8.10	2.21		10.31	12.45	
	3600	Lead-coated copper, round, stock, 2" diameter		190	.042	L.F.	4.88	1.34		6.22	7.50	
	3700	3" diameter		190	.042		4.69	1.34		6.03	7.30	
	3900	4" diameter		145	.055		5.90	1.75		7.65	9.30	
	4000	5" diameter, corrugated		130	.062		5.70	1.95		7.65	9.40	
	4200	6" diameter, corrugated		105	.076		10.40	2.42		12.82	15.30	
	4300	Rectangular, corrugated, stock, 2" x 3"		190	.042		4.08	1.34		5.42	6.65	
	4500	Plain, stock, 2" x 3"		190	.042		6	1.34		7.34	8.75	
	4600	3" x 4"		145	.055		7.55	1.75		9.30	11.10	
	4800	Steel, galvanized, round, corrugated, 2" or 3" diam, 28 ga		190	.042		.68	1.34		2.02	2.89	
	4900	4" diameter, 28 gauge		145	.055		.90	1.75		2.65	3.80	
	5100	5" diameter, 28 gauge		130	.062		1.23	1.95		3.18	4.48	
	5200	26 gauge		130	.062		1.34	1.95		3.29	4.60	
	5400	6" diameter, 28 gauge		105	.076		1.60	2.42		4.02	5.65	
	5500	26 gauge		105	.076		1.40	2.42		3.82	5.40	
	5700	Rectangular, corrugated, 28 gauge, 2" x 3"		190	.042		.53	1.34		1.87	2.72	
	5800	3" x 4"		145	.055		1.48	1.75		3.23	4.44	
	6000	Rectangular, plain, 28 gauge, galvanized, 2" x 3"		190	.042		.79	1.34		2.13	3.01	
	6100	3" x 4"	↓	145	.055	↓	1.21	1.75		2.96	4.14	

076 | Flashing & Sheet Metal

076 200 | Sheet Mtl Flash & Trim

			CREW	DAILY OUTPUT	LABOR-HOURS	UNIT	MAT.	LABOR	EQUIP.	TOTAL	TOTAL INCL O&P	
201	6300	Epoxy painted, 24 gauge, corrugated, 2" x 3"	1 Shee	190	.042	L.F.	1.01	1.34		2.35	3.25	**201**
	6400	3" x 4"		145	.055		1.71	1.75		3.46	4.69	
	6600	Wire strainers, rectangular, 2" x 3"		145	.055	Ea.	1.62	1.75		3.37	4.59	
	6700	3" x 4"		145	.055		2.61	1.75		4.36	5.70	
	6900	Round strainers, 2" or 3" diameter		145	.055		1.20	1.75		2.95	4.13	
	7000	4" diameter		145	.055		1.42	1.75		3.17	4.37	
	7200	5" diameter		145	.055		2.20	1.75		3.95	5.25	
	7300	6" diameter		115	.070		2.63	2.21		4.84	6.45	
	9000	Minimum labor/equipment charge		4	2	Job		63.50		63.50	102	
202	0010	**DRIP EDGE**, aluminum, .016" thick, 5" wide, mill finish	1 Carp	400	.020	L.F.	.20	.55		.75	1.13	**202**
	0100	White finish		400	.020		.22	.55		.77	1.15	
	0200	8" wide, mill finish		400	.020		.30	.55		.85	1.24	
	0300	Ice belt, 28" wide, mill finish		100	.080		3.42	2.18		5.60	7.40	
	0310	Vented, mill finish		400	.020		1.38	.55		1.93	2.43	
	0320	Painted finish		400	.020		1.50	.55		2.05	2.56	
	0400	Galvanized, 5" wide		400	.020		.22	.55		.77	1.15	
	0500	8" wide, mill finish		400	.020		.33	.55		.88	1.27	
	0510	Rake edge, aluminum, 1-1/2" x 1-1/2"		400	.020		.13	.55		.68	1.05	
	0520	3-1/2" x 1-1/2"		400	.020		.19	.55		.74	1.12	
	9000	Minimum labor/equipment charge		4	2	Job		54.50		54.50	91.50	
203	0010	**ELBOWS** Aluminum, 2" x 3", embossed	1 Shee	100	.080	Ea.	.90	2.54		3.44	5.05	**203**
	0100	Enameled		100	.080		1.63	2.54		4.17	5.85	
	0200	3" x 4", .025" thick, embossed		100	.080		3.15	2.54		5.69	7.55	
	0300	Enameled		100	.080		3.15	2.54		5.69	7.55	
	0400	Round corrugated, 3", embossed, .020" thick		100	.080		1.95	2.54		4.49	6.20	
	0500	4", .025" thick		100	.080		2.95	2.54		5.49	7.30	
	0600	Copper, 16 oz. round, 2" diameter		100	.080		11	2.54		13.54	16.15	
	0700	3" diameter		100	.080		5.05	2.54		7.59	9.60	
	0800	4" diameter		100	.080		9.50	2.54		12.04	14.50	
	1000	2" x 3" corrugated		100	.080		5.05	2.54		7.59	9.60	
	1100	3" x 4" corrugated		100	.080		9.75	2.54		12.29	14.75	
	9000	Minimum labor/equipment charge		4	2	Job		63.50		63.50	102	
204	0010	**FLASHING** Aluminum, mill finish, .013" thick	1 Shee	145	.055	S.F.	.34	1.75		2.09	3.18	**204**
	0030	.016" thick		145	.055	"	.50	1.75		2.25	3.36	
	0060	.019" thick		145	.055	S.F.	.79	1.75		2.54	3.68	
	0100	.032" thick		145	.055		.86	1.75		2.61	3.75	
	0200	.040" thick		145	.055		1.44	1.75		3.19	4.39	
	0300	.050" thick		145	.055		1.80	1.75		3.55	4.79	
	0325	Mill finish 5" x 7" step flashing, .016" thick		1,920	.004	Ea.	.10	.13		.23	.32	
	0350	Mill finish 12" x 12" step flashing, .016" thick		1,600	.005	"	.40	.16		.56	.69	
	0400	Painted finish, add				S.F.	.24			.24	.26	
	0500	Fabric-backed 2 sides, .004" thick	1 Shee	330	.024		.93	.77		1.70	2.25	
	0700	.005" thick		330	.024		1.09	.77		1.86	2.43	
	0750	Mastic-backed, self adhesive		460	.017		2.22	.55		2.77	3.33	
	0800	Mastic-coated 2 sides, .004" thick		330	.024		.93	.77		1.70	2.25	
	1000	.005" thick		330	.024		1.09	.77		1.86	2.43	
	1100	.016" thick		330	.024		1.20	.77		1.97	2.55	
	1300	Asphalt flashing cement, 5 gallon				Gal.	3.34			3.34	3.67	
	1600	Copper, 16 oz, sheets, under 1000 lbs.	1 Shee	115	.070	S.F.	3.05	2.21		5.26	6.90	
	1700	Over 4000 lbs.		155	.052		2.85	1.64		4.49	5.75	
	1900	20 oz sheets, under 1000 lbs.		110	.073		3.82	2.31		6.13	7.90	
	2000	Over 4000 lbs.		145	.055		3.55	1.75		5.30	6.70	
	2200	24 oz sheets, under 1000 lbs.		105	.076		4.60	2.42		7.02	8.95	
	2300	Over 4000 lbs.		135	.059		4.25	1.88		6.13	7.70	

THERMAL & MOISTURE PROTECTION 7

076 | Flashing & Sheet Metal

076 200 | Sheet Mtl Flash & Trim

			CREW	DAILY OUTPUT	LABOR-HOURS	UNIT	1999 BARE COSTS MAT.	LABOR	EQUIP.	TOTAL	TOTAL INCL O&P
204	2500	32 oz sheets, under 1000 lbs.	1 Shee	100	.080	S.F.	6.10	2.54		8.64	10.75
	2600	Over 4000 lbs.		130	.062		5.70	1.95		7.65	9.40
	2700	W shape for valleys, 16 oz, 24" wide		100	.080	L.F.	5.90	2.54		8.44	10.55
	2800	Copper, paperbacked 1 side, 2 oz		330	.024	S.F.	.86	.77		1.63	2.18
	2900	3 oz		330	.024		1.12	.77		1.89	2.46
	3100	Paperbacked 2 sides, 2 oz		330	.024		.91	.77		1.68	2.23
	3150	3 oz		330	.024		1.11	.77		1.88	2.45
	3200	5 oz		330	.024		1.74	.77		2.51	3.15
	3250	7 oz		330	.024		2.72	.77		3.49	4.22
	3400	Mastic-backed 2 sides, copper, 2 oz		330	.024		1.02	.77		1.79	2.35
	3500	3 oz		330	.024		1.25	.77		2.02	2.61
	3700	5 oz		330	.024		1.85	.77		2.62	3.27
	3800	Fabric-backed 2 sides, copper, 2 oz		330	.024		1.09	.77		1.86	2.43
	4000	3 oz		330	.024		1.35	.77		2.12	2.72
	4100	5 oz		330	.024		1.90	.77		2.67	3.32
	4300	Copper-clad stainless steel, .015" thick, under 500 lbs.		115	.070		3.10	2.21		5.31	6.95
	4400	Over 2000 lbs.		155	.052		2.99	1.64		4.63	5.90
	4600	.018" thick, under 500 lbs.		100	.080		4.10	2.54		6.64	8.60
	4700	Over 2000 lbs.		145	.055		3	1.75		4.75	6.10
	4900	Fabric, asphalt-saturated cotton, specification grade	1 Rofc	35	.229	S.Y.	1.93	5.50		7.43	12.15
	5000	Utility grade		35	.229		1.22	5.50		6.72	11.40
	5200	Open-mesh fabric, saturated, 40 oz per S.Y.		35	.229		1.35	5.50		6.85	11.55
	5300	Close-mesh fabric, saturated, 17 oz per S.Y.		35	.229		1.42	5.50		6.92	11.60
	5500	Fiberglass, resin-coated		35	.229		1.16	5.50		6.66	11.35
	5600	Asphalt-coated, 40 oz per S.Y.		35	.229		7.90	5.50		13.40	18.75
	5800	Lead, 2.5 lb. per SF, up to 12" wide		135	.059	S.F.	3.25	1.43		4.68	6.20
	5900	Over 12" wide		135	.059		3.25	1.43		4.68	6.20
	6100	Lead-coated copper, fabric-backed, 2 oz	1 Shee	330	.024		1.41	.77		2.18	2.78
	6200	5 oz		330	.024		1.70	.77		2.47	3.10
	6400	Mastic-backed 2 sides, 2 oz		330	.024		1.10	.77		1.87	2.44
	6500	5 oz		330	.024		1.43	.77		2.20	2.80
	6700	Paperbacked 1 side, 2 oz		330	.024		.95	.77		1.72	2.28
	6800	3 oz		330	.024		1.12	.77		1.89	2.46
	7000	Paperbacked 2 sides, 2 oz		330	.024		.98	.77		1.75	2.31
	7100	5 oz		330	.024		1.61	.77		2.38	3
	7300	Polyvinyl chloride, black, .010" thick	1 Rofc	285	.028		.13	.68		.81	1.37
	7400	.020" thick		285	.028		.19	.68		.87	1.44
	7600	.030" thick		285	.028		.29	.68		.97	1.55
	7700	.056" thick		285	.028		.70	.68		1.38	2
	7900	Black or white for exposed roofs, .060" thick		285	.028		1.55	.68		2.23	2.93
	8060	PVC tape, 5" x 45 mils, for joint covers, 100 L.F./roll				Ea.	79.50			79.50	87
	8100	Rubber, butyl, 1/32" thick	1 Rofc	285	.028	S.F.	.70	.68		1.38	2
	8200	1/16" thick		285	.028		1.05	.68		1.73	2.38
	8300	Neoprene, cured, 1/16" thick		285	.028		1.48	.68		2.16	2.86
	8400	1/8" thick		285	.028		2.99	.68		3.67	4.52
	8500	Shower pan, bituminous membrane, 7 oz	1 Shee	155	.052		1.08	1.64		2.72	3.82
	8550	3 ply copper and fabric, 3 oz		155	.052		1.60	1.64		3.24	4.39
	8600	7 oz		155	.052		3.30	1.64		4.94	6.25
	8650	Copper, 16 oz		100	.080		3.05	2.54		5.59	7.40
	8700	Lead on copper and fabric, 5 oz		155	.052		1.70	1.64		3.34	4.50
	8800	7 oz		155	.052		2.87	1.64		4.51	5.80
	8900	Stainless steel sheets, 32 ga, .010" thick		155	.052		2.16	1.64		3.80	5
	9000	28 ga, .015" thick		155	.052		2.55	1.64		4.19	5.45
	9100	26 ga, .018" thick		155	.052		3.16	1.64		4.80	6.10
	9200	24 ga, .025" thick		155	.052		4.10	1.64		5.74	7.15
	9290	For mechanically keyed flashing, add					40%				

076 | Flashing & Sheet Metal

076 200 | Sheet Mtl Flash & Trim

			CREW	DAILY OUTPUT	LABOR-HOURS	UNIT	MAT.	LABOR	EQUIP.	TOTAL	TOTAL INCL O&P	
204	9300	Stainless steel, paperbacked 2 sides, .005" thick	1 Shee	330	.024	S.F.	1.95	.77		2.72	3.37	204
	9320	Steel sheets, galvanized, 20 gauge		130	.062		.72	1.95		2.67	3.92	
	9340	30 gauge		160	.050		.30	1.59		1.89	2.88	
	9400	Terne coated stainless steel, .015" thick, 28 ga		155	.052		3.97	1.64		5.61	7	
	9500	.018" thick, 26 ga		155	.052		4.48	1.64		6.12	7.55	
	9600	Zinc and copper alloy (brass), .020" thick		155	.052		3.20	1.64		4.84	6.15	
	9700	.027" thick		155	.052		4.28	1.64		5.92	7.35	
	9800	.032" thick		155	.052		5	1.64		6.64	8.15	
	9900	.040" thick		155	.052		6.10	1.64		7.74	9.35	
	9950	Minimum labor/equipment charge		3	2.667	Job		84.50		84.50	136	
205	0010	**GUTTERS** Aluminum, stock units, 5" box, .027" thick, plain	1 Shee	120	.067	L.F.	.87	2.12		2.99	4.35	205
	0100	Enameled		120	.067	"	1.07	2.12		3.19	4.57	
	0300	5" box type, .032" thick, plain		120	.067	L.F.	1.08	2.12		3.20	4.58	
	0400	Enameled		120	.067		1.15	2.12		3.27	4.66	
	0600	5" x 6" combination fascia & gutter, .032" thick, enameled		60	.133		3.45	4.23		7.68	10.60	
	0700	Copper, half round, 16 oz, stock units, 4" wide		120	.067		3.23	2.12		5.35	6.95	
	0900	5" wide		120	.067		3.80	2.12		5.92	7.55	
	1000	6" wide		115	.070		4.25	2.21		6.46	8.20	
	1200	K type, 16 oz, stock, 4" wide		120	.067		3.55	2.12		5.67	7.30	
	1300	5" wide		120	.067		3.65	2.12		5.77	7.40	
	1500	Lead coated copper, half round, stock, 4" wide		120	.067		4.87	2.12		6.99	8.75	
	1600	6" wide		115	.070		6.20	2.21		8.41	10.35	
	1800	K type, stock, 4" wide		120	.067		6.95	2.12		9.07	11.05	
	1900	5" wide		120	.067		6.25	2.12		8.37	10.30	
	2100	Stainless steel, half round or box, stock, 4" wide		120	.067		4.65	2.12		6.77	8.50	
	2200	5" wide		120	.067		5	2.12		7.12	8.90	
	2400	Steel, galv, half round or box, 28 ga, 5" wide, plain		120	.067		.90	2.12		3.02	4.39	
	2500	Enameled		120	.067		.94	2.12		3.06	4.43	
	2700	26 ga, stock, 5" wide		120	.067		.95	2.12		3.07	4.44	
	2800	6" wide		120	.067		1.24	2.12		3.36	4.75	
	3000	Vinyl, O.G., 4" wide	1 Carp	110	.073		.85	1.99		2.84	4.26	
	3100	5" wide		110	.073		1	1.99		2.99	4.42	
	3200	4" half round, stock units		110	.073		.68	1.99		2.67	4.07	
	3250	Joint connectors				Ea.	1.36			1.36	1.50	
	3300	Wood, clear treated cedar, fir or hemlock, 3" x 4"	1 Carp	100	.080	L.F.	6.30	2.18		8.48	10.55	
	3400	4" x 5"	"	100	.080	"	7.30	2.18		9.48	11.65	
	9000	Minimum labor/equipment charge	1 Shee	3.75	2.133	Job		67.50		67.50	109	
206	0010	**GUTTER GUARD** 6" wide strip, aluminum mesh	1 Carp	500	.016	L.F.	.37	.44		.81	1.14	206
	0100	Vinyl mesh		500	.016	"	.22	.44		.66	.97	
	9000	Minimum labor/equipment charge		4	2	Job		54.50		54.50	91.50	
207	0010	**MANSARD** Colored aluminum, with battens, .032" thick										207
	0600	Stock units, straight surfaces	1 Shee	115	.070	S.F.	2.13	2.21		4.34	5.90	
	0700	Concave or convex surfaces		75	.107	"	2.35	3.39		5.74	8.05	
	0800	For framing, to 5' high, add		115	.070	L.F.	2.35	2.21		4.56	6.10	
	0900	Soffits, to 1' wide		125	.064	S.F.	1.16	2.03		3.19	4.54	
	9000	Minimum labor/equipment charge		2.50	3.200	Job		102		102	163	
210	0010	**REGLET** Aluminum, .025" thick, in concrete parapet	1 Carp	225	.036	L.F.	.92	.97		1.89	2.63	210
	0100	Copper, 10 oz.		225	.036	"	1.59	.97		2.56	3.37	
	0300	16 oz.		225	.036	L.F.	2.12	.97		3.09	3.95	
	0400	Galvanized steel, 24 gauge		225	.036		.78	.97		1.75	2.48	
	0600	Stainless steel, .020" thick		225	.036		1.57	.97		2.54	3.35	
	0700	Zinc and copper alloy, 20 oz.		225	.036		1.75	.97		2.72	3.55	
	0900	Counter flashing for above, 12" wide, .032" aluminum	1 Shee	150	.053		1.19	1.69		2.88	4.02	
	1000	Copper, 10 oz.		150	.053		3.32	1.69		5.01	6.35	

076 | Flashing & Sheet Metal

076 200 | Sheet Mtl Flash & Trim

			CREW	DAILY OUTPUT	LABOR-HOURS	UNIT	1999 BARE COSTS MAT.	LABOR	EQUIP.	TOTAL	TOTAL INCL O&P	
210	1200	16 oz.	1 Shee	150	.053	L.F.	3.70	1.69		5.39	6.80	210
	1300	Galvanized steel, .020" thick		150	.053		.62	1.69		2.31	3.39	
	1500	Stainless steel, .020" thick		150	.053		2.76	1.69		4.45	5.75	
	1600	Zinc and copper alloy, 20 oz.	↓	150	.053		3.11	1.69		4.80	6.15	
	9000	Minimum labor/equipment charge	1 Carp	3	2.667	Job		73		73	122	
212	0010	**SHEET METAL CLADDING**										212
	0100	Aluminum, up to 6 bends, .032" thick, window casing	1 Carp	180	.044	S.F.	.58	1.21		1.79	2.67	
	0200	Window sill		72	.111	L.F.	.58	3.03		3.61	5.75	
	0300	Door casing		180	.044	S.F.	.58	1.21		1.79	2.67	
	0400	Fascia		250	.032		.58	.87		1.45	2.10	
	0500	Rake trim	↓	225	.036		.58	.97		1.55	2.26	
	0600	Add for colors					.04					
	0700	.024" thick, window casing	1 Carp	180	.044		.90	1.21		2.11	3.02	
	0800	Window sill		72	.111	L.F.	.90	3.03		3.93	6.10	
	0900	Door casing		180	.044	S.F.	.90	1.21		2.11	3.02	
	1000	Fascia		250	.032		.90	.87		1.77	2.45	
	1100	Rake trim		225	.036		.90	.97		1.87	2.61	
	1200	Vinyl coated aluminum, up to 6 bends, window casing		180	.044	↓	.61	1.21		1.82	2.70	
	1300	Window sill		72	.111	L.F.	.61	3.03		3.64	5.75	
	1400	Door casing		180	.044	S.F.	.61	1.21		1.82	2.70	
	1500	Fascia		250	.032		.61	.87		1.48	2.13	
	1600	Rake trim	↓	225	.036	↓	.61	.97		1.58	2.29	
217	0010	**SOFFIT** Aluminum, residential, stock units, .020" thick	1 Carp	210	.038	S.F.	.99	1.04		2.03	2.83	217
	0100	Baked enamel on steel, 16 or 18 gauge		105	.076		3.74	2.08		5.82	7.60	
	0300	Polyvinyl chloride, white, solid		230	.035		.65	.95		1.60	2.30	
	0400	Perforated	↓	230	.035		.65	.95		1.60	2.30	
	0500	For colors, add				↓	.06			.06	.07	
	9000	Minimum labor/equipment charge	1 Carp	3	2.667	Job		73		73	122	

077 | Roof Specialties & Accessories

077 100 | Prefab Roof Specialties

			CREW	DAILY OUTPUT	LABOR-HOURS	UNIT	1999 BARE COSTS MAT.	LABOR	EQUIP.	TOTAL	TOTAL INCL O&P	
103	0010	**EXPANSION JOINT**										103
	0300	Butyl or neoprene center with foam insulation, metal flanges										
	0400	Aluminum, .032" thick for openings to 2-1/2"	1 Rofc	165	.048	L.F.	7.40	1.17		8.57	10.30	
	0600	For joint openings to 3-1/2"		165	.048		8.65	1.17		9.82	11.65	
	0610	For joint openings to 5"		165	.048		10.40	1.17		11.57	13.60	
	0620	For joint openings to 8"		165	.048		16.40	1.17		17.57	20	
	0700	Copper, 16 oz. for openings to 2-1/2"		165	.048		10.40	1.17		11.57	13.60	
	0900	For joint openings to 3-1/2"		165	.048		11.95	1.17		13.12	15.30	
	0910	For joint openings to 5"		165	.048		14	1.17		15.17	17.55	
	0920	For joint openings to 8"		165	.048		21	1.17		22.17	25	
	1000	Galvanized steel, 26 ga. for openings to 2-1/2"		165	.048		6.25	1.17		7.42	9.05	
	1200	For joint openings to 3-1/2"		165	.048		7.40	1.17		8.57	10.30	
	1210	For joint openings to 5"		165	.048		9.25	1.17		10.42	12.35	
	1220	For joint openings to 8"		165	.048		15.75	1.17		16.92	19.50	
	1300	Lead-coated copper, 16 oz. for openings to 2-1/2"		165	.048		18.50	1.17		19.67	22.50	
	1500	For joint openings to 3-1/2"	↓	165	.048	↓	22	1.17		23.17	26	

077 | Roof Specialties & Accessories

077 100 | Prefab Roof Specialties

			CREW	DAILY OUTPUT	LABOR-HOURS	UNIT	MAT.	LABOR	EQUIP.	TOTAL	TOTAL INCL O&P	
103	1600	Stainless steel, .018", for openings to 2-1/2"	1 Rofc	165	.048	L.F.	9.25	1.17		10.42	12.35	103
	1800	For joint openings to 3-1/2"		165	.048		10.55	1.17		11.72	13.75	
	1810	For joint openings to 5"		165	.048		13.05	1.17		14.22	16.50	
	1820	For joint openings to 8"		165	.048		19.85	1.17		21.02	24	
	1900	Neoprene, double-seal type with thick center, 4-1/2" wide		125	.064		8.90	1.54		10.44	12.60	
	1950	Polyethylene bellows, with galv steel flat flanges		100	.080		3.45	1.93		5.38	7.30	
	1960	With galvanized angle flanges	▼	100	.080		3.80	1.93		5.73	7.70	
	2000	Roof joint with extruded aluminum cover, 2"	1 Shee	115	.070		24	2.21		26.21	29.50	
	2100	Roof joint, plastic curbs, foam center, standard	1 Rofc	100	.080		8.70	1.93		10.63	13.05	
	2200	Large		100	.080	▼	11.60	1.93		13.53	16.25	
	2300	Transitions, regular, minimum		10	.800	Ea.	75	19.30		94.30	118	
	2350	Maximum		4	2		95.50	48		143.50	193	
	2400	Large, minimum		9	.889		110	21.50		131.50	160	
	2450	Maximum	▼	3	2.667	▼	115	64.50		179.50	244	
	2500	Roof to wall joint with extruded aluminum cover	1 Shee	115	.070	L.F.	20.50	2.21		22.71	26	
	2650											
	2700	Wall joint, closed cell foam on PVC cover, 9" wide	1 Rofc	125	.064	L.F.	3.10	1.54		4.64	6.20	
	2800	12" wide	"	115	.070	"	3.50	1.68		5.18	6.90	
	9000	Minimum labor/equipment charge	1 Shee	3	2.667	Job		84.50		84.50	136	
104	0010	**FASCIA** Aluminum, reverse board and batten,										104
	0100	.032" thick, colored, no furring included	1 Shee	145	.055	S.F.	2.10	1.75		3.85	5.10	
	0200	Residential type, aluminum	1 Carp	200	.040	L.F.	1.15	1.09		2.24	3.10	
	0220	Vinyl	"	200	.040	"	.80	1.09		1.89	2.71	
	0300	Steel, galv and enameled, stock, no furring, long panels	1 Shee	145	.055	S.F.	2.19	1.75		3.94	5.20	
	0600	Short panels		115	.070	"	3.31	2.21		5.52	7.20	
	9000	Minimum labor/equipment charge	▼	4	2	Job		63.50		63.50	102	
105	0010	**GRAVEL STOP** Aluminum, .050" thick, 4" face height, mill finish	1 Shee	145	.055	L.F.	2.72	1.75		4.47	5.80	105
	0080	Duranodic finish		145	.055		3.69	1.75		5.44	6.85	
	0100	Painted		145	.055		4.26	1.75		6.01	7.50	
	0300	6" face height		135	.059		3.22	1.88		5.10	6.55	
	0350	Duranodic finish		135	.059		4.35	1.88		6.23	7.80	
	0400	Painted		135	.059		5.05	1.88		6.93	8.55	
	0600	8" face height		125	.064		3.98	2.03		6.01	7.65	
	0650	Duranodic finish		125	.064		4.98	2.03		7.01	8.75	
	0700	Painted		125	.064		5.05	2.03		7.08	8.85	
	0900	12" face height, .080 thick, 2 piece		100	.080		6.45	2.54		8.99	11.15	
	0950	Duranodic finish		100	.080		6.30	2.54		8.84	10.95	
	1000	Painted		100	.080		7.40	2.54		9.94	12.20	
	1500	Polyvinyl chloride, 6" face height		135	.059		3.28	1.88		5.16	6.65	
	1600	9" face height		125	.064		3.87	2.03		5.90	7.50	
	1800	Stainless steel, 24 ga., 6" face height		135	.059		7.15	1.88		9.03	10.85	
	1900	12" face height		100	.080		15	2.54		17.54	20.50	
	2100	20 ga., 6" face height		135	.059		8.10	1.88		9.98	11.90	
	2200	12" face height		100	.080	▼	17.10	2.54		19.64	23	
	9000	Minimum labor/equipment charge	▼	3.50	2.286	Job		72.50		72.50	116	

077 200 | Roof Accessories

			CREW	DAILY OUTPUT	LABOR-HOURS	UNIT	MAT.	LABOR	EQUIP.	TOTAL	TOTAL INCL O&P	
205	0010	**ROOF DRAINS**										205
	0020	For roof drains see division 151-125										
206	0010	**ROOF HATCHES** With curb, 1" fiberglass insulation, 2'-6" x 3'-0"										206
	0500	Aluminum curb and cover	G-3	10	3.200	Ea.	405	85		490	585	
	0520	Galvanized steel curb and aluminum cover		10	3.200		340	85		425	515	
	0540	Galvanized steel curb and cover	▼	10	3.200	▼	300	85		385	470	

077 | Roof Specialties & Accessories

077 200 | Roof Accessories

			CREW	DAILY OUTPUT	LABOR-HOURS	UNIT	1999 BARE COSTS MAT.	LABOR	EQUIP.	TOTAL	TOTAL INCL O&P	
206	0600	2'-6" x 4'-6", aluminum curb and cover	G-3	9	3.556	Ea.	560	94.50		654.50	770	206
	0800	Galvanized steel curb and aluminum cover		9	3.556		475	94.50		569.50	680	
	0900	Galvanized steel curb and cover		9	3.556		460	94.50		554.50	660	
	1200	2'-6" x 8'-0", aluminum curb and cover		6.60	4.848		995	129		1,124	1,300	
	1400	Galvanized steel curb and aluminum cover		6.60	4.848		920	129		1,049	1,200	
	1500	Galvanized steel curb and cover		6.60	4.848		905	129		1,034	1,200	
	1800	For plexiglass panels, 2'-6" x 3'-0", add to above					345			345	380	
	9000	Minimum labor/equipment charge	2 Carp	2	8	Job		218		218	365	
207	0010	**SMOKE HATCHES** Unlabeled, not including hand winch operator										207
	0200	For 3'-0" long, add to roof hatches from division 077-206				Ea.	25%	5%				
	0300	For 8'-0" long, add to roof hatches from division 077-206				"	10%	5%				
208	0010	**SMOKE VENT**, insulated, 4' x 4'										208
	0100	Aluminum cover and frame	G-3	13	2.462	Ea.	1,050	65.50		1,115.50	1,250	
	0200	Galvanized steel cover and frame		13	2.462		950	65.50		1,015.50	1,150	
	0300	4' x 8' aluminum cover and frame		8	4		1,425	106		1,531	1,750	
	0400	Galvanized steel cover and frame		8	4		1,250	106		1,356	1,550	
	9000	Minimum labor/equipment charge	2 Carp	2	8	Job		218		218	365	
210	0010	**ROOF VENTS** Mushroom for built-up roofs, aluminum	1 Rofc	30	.267	Ea.	24	6.45		30.45	38	210
	0100	PVC, 6" high		30	.267	"	27.50	6.45		33.95	42	
	9000	Minimum labor/equipment charge		2.75	2.909	Job		70		70	128	
211	0010	**RIDGE VENT**										211
	0100	Aluminum strips, mill finish	1 Rofc	160	.050	L.F.	1.19	1.21		2.40	3.51	
	0150	Painted finish		160	.050	"	2.12	1.21		3.33	4.54	
	0200	Connectors		48	.167	Ea.	1.81	4.02		5.83	9.30	
	0300	End caps		48	.167	"	.76	4.02		4.78	8.15	
	0400	Galvanized strips, with damper and bird screen		160	.050	L.F.	20.50	1.21		21.71	25	
	0430	Molded polyethylene, shingles not included		160	.050	"	2.50	1.21		3.71	4.95	
	0440	End plugs		48	.167	Ea.	.76	4.02		4.78	8.15	
	0450	Flexible roll, shingles not included		160	.050	L.F.	2.24	1.21		3.45	4.66	
212	0010	**VENTS, ONE-WAY** For insul. decks, 1 per M.S.F., plastic, min.	1 Rofc	40	.200	Ea.	12.50	4.82		17.32	22.50	212
	0100	Maximum		20	.400	"	28.50	9.65		38.15	49	
	0300	Aluminum		30	.267	Ea.	12.50	6.45		18.95	25.50	
	0800	Polystyrene baffles, 12" wide for 16" O.C. rafter spacing	1 Carp	90	.089		.45	2.43		2.88	4.56	
	0900	For 24" O.C. rafter spacing		110	.073		1.05	1.99		3.04	4.47	
	9000	Minimum labor/equipment charge		3	2.667	Job		73		73	122	
215	0010	**PITCH POCKETS**										215
	0100	Adjustable, 4" to 7", welded corners, 4" deep	1 Rofc	48	.167	Ea.	10.50	4.02		14.52	18.85	
	0200	Side extenders, 6"	"	240	.033	"	1.70	.80		2.50	3.33	

078 | Skylights

078 100 | Plastic Skylights

			CREW	DAILY OUTPUT	LABOR-HOURS	UNIT	1999 BARE COSTS MAT.	LABOR	EQUIP.	TOTAL	TOTAL INCL O&P	
101	0010	**SKYLIGHT** Plastic domes, flush or curb mounted, ten or										101
	0100	more units, curb not included, "L" frames										
	0300	Nominal size under 10 S.F., double	G-3	130	.246	S.F.	16.65	6.55		23.20	29	
	0400	Single		160	.200		13.25	5.30		18.55	23.50	

078 | Skylights

078 100 | Plastic Skylights

		CREW	DAILY OUTPUT	LABOR-HOURS	UNIT	MAT.	LABOR	EQUIP.	TOTAL	TOTAL INCL O&P	
101	0600	10 S.F. to 20 S.F., double	G-3	315	.102	S.F.	13.55	2.70		16.25	19.30	101
	0700	Single		395	.081		13.50	2.15		15.65	18.35	
	0900	20 S.F. to 30 S.F., double		395	.081		13.90	2.15		16.05	18.80	
	1000	Single		465	.069		11.70	1.83		13.53	15.85	
	1200	30 S.F. to 65 S.F., double		465	.069		14.65	1.83		16.48	19.10	
	1300	Single		610	.052		12.25	1.40		13.65	15.80	
	1500	For insulated 4" curbs, double, add					25%					
	1600	Single, add					30%					
	1800	For integral insulated 9" curbs, double, add					30%					
	1900	Single, add					40%					
	2120	Ventilating insulated plexiglass dome with										
	2130	curb mounting, 36" x 36"	G-3	12	2.667	Ea.	340	71		411	490	
	2150	52" x 52"		12	2.667		510	71		581	680	
	2160	28" x 52"		10	3.200		400	85		485	580	
	2170	36" x 52"		10	3.200		430	85		515	615	
	2180	For electric opening system, add					256			256	281	
	2200	Field fabricated, factory type, aluminum and wire glass	G-3	120	.267	S.F.	13.20	7.10		20.30	26	
	2300	Insulated safety glass with aluminum frame		160	.200		78.50	5.30		83.80	95	
	2400	Sandwich panels, fiberglass, for walls, 1-9/16" thick, to 250 SF		200	.160		13.95	4.26		18.21	22.50	
	2500	250 SF and up		265	.121		12.50	3.21		15.71	19	
	2700	As above, but for roofs, 2-3/4" thick, to 250 SF		295	.108		20	2.89		22.89	26.50	
	2800	250 SF and up		330	.097		16.50	2.58		19.08	22.50	

078 200 | Metal Framed Skylights

		CREW	DAILY OUTPUT	LABOR-HOURS	UNIT	MAT.	LABOR	EQUIP.	TOTAL	TOTAL INCL O&P	
202	0010	**SKYROOFS** Translucent panels, 2-3/4" thick, under 5000 SF	G-3	395	.081	SF Hor.	18.40	2.15		20.55	23.50	202
	0100	Over 5000 SF		465	.069		16.45	1.83		18.28	21	
	0300	Continuous vaulted, semi-circular, to 8' wide, double glazed		145	.221		42	5.85		47.85	56	
	0400	Single glazed		160	.200		27.50	5.30		32.80	39	
	0600	To 20' wide, single glazed		175	.183		30	4.86		34.86	41.50	
	0700	Over 20' wide, single glazed		200	.160		35.50	4.26		39.76	46.50	
	0900	Motorized opening type, single glazed, 1/3 opening		145	.221		38	5.85		43.85	51	
	1000	Full opening		130	.246		43.50	6.55		50.05	58	
	1200	Pyramid type units, self-supporting, to 30' clear opening,										
	1300	square or circular, single glazed, minimum	G-3	200	.160	SF Hor.	20.50	4.26		24.76	29.50	
	1310	Average		165	.194		28.50	5.15		33.65	40	
	1400	Maximum		130	.246		41	6.55		47.55	55.50	
	1500	Grid type, 4' to 10' modules, single glass glazed, minimum		200	.160		26	4.26		30.26	36	
	1550	Maximum		128	.250		43	6.65		49.65	58	
	1600	Preformed acrylic, minimum		300	.107		31	2.84		33.84	39	
	1650	Maximum		175	.183		44	4.86		48.86	56.50	
	9000	Minimum labor/equipment charge	2 Carp	8	2	Job		54.50		54.50	91.50	

079 | Joint Sealers

079 204 | Sealants & Caulkings

		CREW	DAILY OUTPUT	LABOR-HOURS	UNIT	MAT.	LABOR	EQUIP.	TOTAL	TOTAL INCL O&P	
204	0010	**CAULKING AND SEALANTS**										204
	0020	Acoustical sealant, elastomeric, cartridges				Ea.	1.95			1.95	2.15	
	0032	Backer rod, polyethylene, 1/4" diameter	1 Bric	460	.017	L.F.	.01	.48		.49	.80	
	0052	1/2" diameter		460	.017		.03	.48		.51	.82	

079 | Joint Sealers

079 204 | Sealants & Caulkings

		CREW	DAILY OUTPUT	LABOR-HOURS	UNIT	1999 BARE COSTS				TOTAL INCL O&P
						MAT.	LABOR	EQUIP.	TOTAL	
0072	3/4" diameter	1 Bric	460	.017	L.F.	.05	.48		.53	.84
0092	1" diameter	↓	460	.017	↓	.09	.48		.57	.89
0100	Acrylic latex caulk, white									
0200	11 fl. oz cartridge				Ea.	1.96			1.96	2.16
0500	1/4" x 1/2"	1 Bric	248	.032	L.F.	.16	.89		1.05	1.65
0600	1/2" x 1/2"		250	.032		.32	.88		1.20	1.81
0800	3/4" x 3/4"		230	.035		.72	.96		1.68	2.38
0900	3/4" x 1"		200	.040		.96	1.10		2.06	2.89
1000	1" x 1"	↓	180	.044	↓	1.20	1.23		2.43	3.35
1400	Butyl based, bulk				Gal.	22			22	24
1500	Cartridges				"	26.50			26.50	29.50
1700	Bulk, in place 1/4" x 1/2", 154 L.F./gal.	1 Bric	230	.035	L.F.	.14	.96		1.10	1.75
1800	1/2" x 1/2", 77 L.F./gal.	"	180	.044	"	.29	1.23		1.52	2.34
2000	Latex acrylic based, bulk				Gal.	23			23	25.50
2100	Cartridges				"	26			26	28.50
2200	Bulk in place, 1/4" x 1/2", 154 L.F./gal.	1 Bric	230	.035	L.F.	.15	.96		1.11	1.75
2250										
2300	Polysulfide compounds, 1 component, bulk				Gal.	43.50			43.50	47.50
2400	Cartridges				"	46			46	51
2600	1 or 2 component, in place, 1/4" x 1/4", 308 L.F./gal.	1 Bric	145	.055	L.F.	.14	1.52		1.66	2.67
2700	1/2" x 1/4", 154 L.F./gal.		135	.059		.28	1.64		1.92	3.02
2900	3/4" x 3/8", 68 L.F./gal.		130	.062		.64	1.70		2.34	3.51
3000	1" x 1/2", 38 L.F./gal.	↓	130	.062	↓	1.14	1.70		2.84	4.06
3200	Polyurethane, 1 or 2 component				Gal.	48.50			48.50	53
3300	Cartridges				"	46.50			46.50	51
3500	Bulk, in place, 1/4" x 1/4"	1 Bric	150	.053	L.F.	.16	1.47		1.63	2.61
3600	1/2" x 1/4"		145	.055		.31	1.52		1.83	2.87
3800	3/4" x 3/8", 68 L.F./gal.		130	.062		.71	1.70		2.41	3.59
3900	1" x 1/2"	↓	110	.073	↓	1.26	2.01		3.27	4.70
4100	Silicone rubber, bulk				Gal.	34			34	37.50
4200	Cartridges				"	40			40	44
4300	Bulk in place, 1/4" x 1/2", 154 L.F./gal.	1 Bric	235	.034	L.F.	.22	.94		1.16	1.80
4350										
4400	Neoprene gaskets, closed cell, adhesive, 1/8" x 3/8"	1 Bric	240	.033	L.F.	.20	.92		1.12	1.74
4500	1/4" x 3/4"		215	.037		.48	1.03		1.51	2.23
4700	1/2" x 1"		200	.040		1.40	1.10		2.50	3.37
4800	3/4" x 1-1/2"	↓	165	.048	↓	2.91	1.34		4.25	5.40
5500	Resin epoxy coating, 2 component, heavy duty				Gal.	26			26	28.50
5802	Tapes, sealant, P.V.C. foam adhesive, 1/16" x 1/4"				L.F.	.05			.05	.05
5902	1/16" x 1/2"					.07			.07	.08
5952	1/16" x 1"					.11			.11	.12
6002	1/8" x 1/2"				↓	.08			.08	.08
6200	Urethane foam, 2 component, handy pack, 1 C.F.				Ea.	27.50			27.50	30.50
6300	50.0 C.F. pack				C.F.	14.05			14.05	15.45
9000	Minimum labor/equipment charge	1 Bric	4	2	Job		55		55	91.50

For information about Means Estimating Seminars, see yellow pages 11 and 12 in back of book

Division 8
Doors & Windows

Estimating Tips

081 Metal Doors & Frames
- Most metal doors and frames look alike, but there may be significant differences among them. When estimating these items be sure to choose the line item that most closely compares to the specification or door schedule requirements regarding:
  - type of metal
  - metal gauge
  - door core material
  - fire rating
  - finish

082 Wood & Plastic Doors
- Wood and plastic doors vary considerably in price. The primary determinant is the veneer material. Lauan, birch and oak are the most common veneers. Other variables include the following:
  - hollow or solid core
  - fire rating
  - flush or raised panel
  - finish
- Frequently doors, frames, and windows are unique in old buildings. Specified replacement units could be stock, custom (similar to the original) or exact reproduction. The estimator should work closely with a window consultant to determine any extra costs that may be associated with the unusual installation requirements.
- If the specifications require compliance with AWI (Architectural Woodwork Institute) standards or acoustical standards, the cost of the door may increase substantially. All wood doors are priced pre-mortised for hinges and predrilled for cylindrical locksets.

083 Special Doors
- There are many varieties of special doors, and they are usually priced per each. Add frames, hardware or operators required for a complete installation.

085 Metal Windows
- Most metal windows are delivered preglazed. However, some metal windows are priced without glass. Refer to 088 Glazing for glass pricing. The grade C indicates commercial grade windows, usually ASTM C-35.

086 Wood & Plastic Windows
- All wood windows are priced preglazed. The two glazing options priced are single pane float glass and insulating glass 1/2" thick. Add the cost of screens and grills if required.

087 Hardware
- Hardware costs add considerably to the cost of a door. The most efficient method to determine the hardware requirements for a project is to review the door schedule. This schedule, in conjunction with the specifications, is all you should need to take off the door hardware.
- Door hinges are priced by the pair, with most doors requiring 1-1/2 pairs per door. The hinge prices do not include installation labor because it is included in door installation. Hinges are classified according to the frequency of use.

088 Glazing
- Different openings require different types of glass. The three most common types are:
  - float
  - tempered
  - insulating
- Most exterior windows are glazed with insulating glass. Entrance doors and window walls, where the glass is less than 18" from the floor, are generally glazed with tempered glass. Interior windows and some residential windows are glazed with float glass.

089 Glazed Curtain Walls
- Glazed curtain walls consist of the metal tube framing and the glazing material. The cost data in this subdivision is presented for the metal tube framing alone or the composite wall. If your estimate requires a detailed takeoff of the framing, be sure to add the glazing cost.

Reference Numbers
Reference numbers are shown in bold squares at the beginning of some major classifications. These numbers refer to related items in the Reference Section. The reference information may be an estimating procedure, an alternate pricing method or technical information.

Note: Not all subdivisions listed here necessarily appear in this publication.

081 | Metal Doors & Frames

081 100 | Steel Doors & Frames

				DAILY	LABOR-		1999 BARE COSTS				TOTAL	
			CREW	OUTPUT	HOURS	UNIT	MAT.	LABOR	EQUIP.	TOTAL	INCL O&P	
103	0010	**COMMERCIAL STEEL DOORS**										103
	0015	Flush, full panel, hollow core	R081 -010									
	0020	1-3/8" thick, 20 ga., 2'-0" x 6'-8"	2 Carp	20	.800	Ea.	163	22		185	216	
	0040	2'-8" x 6'-8"		18	.889		167	24.50		191.50	225	
	0060	3'-0" x 6'-8"		17	.941		170	25.50		195.50	230	
	0100	3'-0" x 7'-0"		17	.941		178	25.50		203.50	239	
	0120	For vision lite, add					51			51	56	
	0140	For narrow lite, add					60			60	66	
	0160	For bottom louver, add					100			100	110	
	0230	For baked enamel finish, add					30%	15%				
	0260	For galvanizing, add					15%					
	0320	Half glass, 20 ga., 2'-0" x 6'-8"	2 Carp	20	.800	Ea.	208	22		230	266	
	0340	2'-8" x 6'-8"		18	.889		213	24.50		237.50	276	
	0360	3'-0" x 6'-8"		17	.941		218	25.50		243.50	283	
	0400	3'-0" x 7'-0"		17	.941		221	25.50		246.50	287	
	0500	Hollow core, 1-3/4" thick, full panel, 20 ga., 2'-8" x 6'-8"		18	.889		152	24.50		176.50	208	
	0520	3'-0" x 6'-8"		17	.941		173	25.50		198.50	234	
	0640	3'-0" x 7'-0"		17	.941		178	25.50		203.50	239	
	0680	4'-0" x 7'-0"		15	1.067		225	29		254	297	
	0700	4'-0" x 8'-0"		13	1.231		265	33.50		298.50	350	
	1000	18 ga., 2'-8" x 6'-8"		17	.941		182	25.50		207.50	243	
	1020	3'-0" x 6'-8"		16	1		189	27.50		216.50	254	
	1120	3'-0" x 7'-0"		17	.941		210	25.50		235.50	274	
	1180	4'-0" x 7'-0"		14	1.143		230	31		261	305	
	1200	4'-0" x 8'-0"		17	.941		272	25.50		297.50	340	
	1230	Half glass, 20 ga., 2'-8" x 6'-8"		20	.800		246	22		268	310	
	1240	3'-0" x 6'-8"		18	.889		250	24.50		274.50	315	
	1260	3'-0" x 7'-0"		18	.889		268	24.50		292.50	335	
	1280	4'-0" x 7'-0"		16	1		310	27.50		337.50	390	
	1300	4'-0" x 8'-0"		13	1.231		340	33.50		373.50	430	
	1320	18 ga., 2'-8" x 6'-8"		18	.889		279	24.50		303.50	345	
	1340	3'-0" x 6'-8"		17	.941		274	25.50		299.50	345	
	1360	3'-0" x 7'-0"		17	.941		284	25.50		309.50	355	
	1380	4'-0" x 7'-0"		15	1.067		400	29		429	490	
	1400	4'-0" x 8'-0"		14	1.143		465	31		496	560	
	1720	Insulated, 1-3/4" thick, full panel, 18 ga., 3'-0" x 6'-8"		15	1.067		217	29		246	288	
	1740	2'-8" x 7'-0"		16	1		214	27.50		241.50	281	
	1760	3'-0" x 7'-0"		15	1.067		225	29		254	297	
	1800	4'-0" x 8'-0"		13	1.231		315	33.50		348.50	400	
	1820	Half glass, 18 ga., 3'-0" x 6'-8"		16	1		280	27.50		307.50	355	
	1840	2'-8" x 7'-0"		17	.941		277	25.50		302.50	350	
	1860	3'-0" x 7'-0"		16	1		286	27.50		313.50	360	
	1900	4'-0" x 8'-0"		14	1.143		420	31		451	515	
	9000	Minimum labor/equipment charge	1 Carp	4	2	Job		54.50		54.50	91.50	
106	0010	**DOOR FRAMES**										106
	0020	Steel channels with anchors and bar stops										
	0100	6" channel @ 8.2#/L.F., 3' x 7' door, weighs 200#	E-4	13	2.462	Ea.	187	76.50	6.35	269.85	360	
	0200	8" channel @ 11.5#/L.F., 6' x 8' door, weighs 300#		9	3.556		272	111	9.15	392.15	520	
	0300	8' x 12' door, weighs 450#		6.50	4.923		410	153	12.65	575.65	755	
	0800	For frames without bar stops, light sections, deduct					15%					
	0900	Heavy sections, deduct					10%					
	9000	Minimum labor/equipment charge	A-1	4	2	Job		43	17.15	60.15	91	
110	0010	**FIRE DOOR**										110
	0015	Steel, flush, "B" label, 90 minute	R081 -010									
	0020	Full panel, 20 ga., 2'-0" x 6'-8"	2 Carp	20	.800	Ea.	208	22		230	266	
	0040	2'-8" x 6'-8"		18	.889		208	24.50		232.50	270	

Important: See the Reference Section for critical supporting data - Reference Nos., Crews, & City Cost Indexes

081 | Metal Doors & Frames

081 100 | Steel Doors & Frames

			CREW	DAILY OUTPUT	LABOR-HOURS	UNIT	MAT.	LABOR	EQUIP.	TOTAL	TOTAL INCL O&P	
110	0060	3'-0" x 6'-8"	2 Carp	17	.941	Ea.	210	25.50		235.50	274	**110**
	0080	3'-0" x 7'-0"		17	.941		259	25.50		284.50	330	
	0140	18 ga., 3'-0" x 6'-8"		16	1		230	27.50		257.50	299	
	0160	2'-8" x 7'-0"		17	.941		240	25.50		265.50	305	
	0180	3'-0" x 7'-0"		16	1		236	27.50		263.50	305	
	0200	4'-0" x 7'-0"		15	1.067		300	29		329	380	
	0220	For "A" label, 3 hour, 18 ga., use same price as "B" label										
	0240	For vision lite, add				Ea.	56.50			56.50	62.50	
	0520	Flush, "B" label 90 min., composite, 20 ga., 2'-0" x 6'-8"	2 Carp	18	.889		208	24.50		232.50	270	
	0540	2'-8" x 6'-8"		17	.941		208	25.50		233.50	272	
	0560	3'-0" x 6'-8"		16	1		210	27.50		237.50	277	
	0580	3'-0" x 7'-0"		16	1		234	27.50		261.50	305	
	0640	Flush, "A" label 3 hour, composite, 18 ga., 3'-0" x 6'-8"		15	1.067		250	29		279	325	
	0660	2'-8" x 7'-0"		16	1		255	27.50		282.50	325	
	0680	3'-0" x 7'-0"		15	1.067		260	29		289	335	
	0700	4'-0" x 7'-0"		14	1.143		300	31		331	380	
	9000	Minimum labor/equipment charge	1 Carp	4	2	Job		54.50		54.50	91.50	
114	0010	**RESIDENTIAL STEEL DOOR**										**114**
	0020	Prehung, insulated, exterior										
	0030	Embossed, full panel, 2'-8" x 6'-8"	2 Carp	17	.941	Ea.	172	25.50		197.50	232	
	0040	3'-0" x 6'-8"		15	1.067		175	29		204	241	
	0060	3'-0" x 7'-0"		15	1.067		224	29		253	295	
	0070	5'-4" x 6'-8", double		8	2		345	54.50		399.50	470	
	0220	Half glass, 2'-8" x 6'-8"		17	.941		271	25.50		296.50	340	
	0240	3'-0" x 6'-8"		16	1		239	27.50		266.50	310	
	0260	3'-0" x 7'-0"		16	1		292	27.50		319.50	365	
	0270	5'-4" x 6'-8", double		8	2		540	54.50		594.50	685	
	0720	Raised plastic face, full panel, 2'-8" x 6'-8"		16	1		211	27.50		238.50	278	
	0740	3'-0" x 6'-8"		15	1.067		214	29		243	285	
	0760	3'-0" x 7'-0"		15	1.067		227	29		256	299	
	0780	5'-4" x 6'-8", double		8	2		420	54.50		474.50	555	
	0820	Half glass, 2'-8" x 6'-8"		17	.941		250	25.50		275.50	320	
	0840	3'-0" x 6'-8"		16	1		253	27.50		280.50	325	
	0860	3'-0" x 7'-0"		16	1		278	27.50		305.50	350	
	0880	5'-4" x 6'-8", double		8	2		525	54.50		579.50	670	
	1320	Flush face, full panel, 2'-6" x 6'-8"		16	1		190	27.50		217.50	255	
	1340	3'-0" x 6'-8"		15	1.067		193	29		222	261	
	1360	3'-0" x 7'-0"		15	1.067		244	29		273	315	
	1380	5'-4" x 6'-8", double		8	2		380	54.50		434.50	510	
	1420	Half glass, 2'-8" x 6'-8"		17	.941		236	25.50		261.50	300	
	1440	3'-0" x 6'-8"		16	1		238	27.50		265.50	310	
	1460	3'-0" x 7'-0"		16	1		289	27.50		316.50	365	
	1480	5'-4" x 6'-8", double		8	2		470	54.50		524.50	610	
	2300	Interior, residential, closet, bi-fold, 6'-8" x 2'-0" wide		16	1		122	27.50		149.50	180	
	2330	3'-0" wide		16	1		137	27.50		164.50	196	
	2360	4'-0" wide		15	1.067		208	29		237	278	
	2400	5'-0" wide		14	1.143		241	31		272	315	
	2420	6'-0" wide		13	1.231		270	33.50		303.50	355	
	9000	Minimum labor/equipment charge	1 Carp	4	2	Job		54.50		54.50	91.50	
118	0010	**STEEL FRAMES, KNOCK DOWN**										**118**
	0020	18 ga., up to 5-3/4" deep										
	0025	6'-8" high, 3'-0" wide, single	2 Carp	16	1	Ea.	86	27.50		113.50	140	
	0040	6'-0" wide, double		14	1.143		96.50	31		127.50	158	
	0100	7'-0" high, 3'-0" wide, single		16	1		88.50	27.50		116	143	
	0140	6'-0" wide, double		14	1.143		93.50	31		124.50	155	

For expanded coverage of these items see *Means Interior Cost Data 1999*

081 | Metal Doors & Frames

081 100 | Steel Doors & Frames

			Daily Output	Labor-Hours	Unit	1999 Bare Costs Mat.	Labor	Equip.	Total	Total Incl O&P
			Crew							
118	1000	18 ga., up to 4-7/8" deep, 7'-0" H, 3'-0" W, single	2 Carp	16	1	Ea.	70.50	27.50		98	124	118
	1140	6'-0" wide, double		14	1.143		88.50	31		119.50	149
	2800	16 ga., up to 3-7/8" deep, 7'-0" high, 3'-0" wide, single		16	1		70	27.50		97.50	123
	2840	6'-0" wide, double		14	1.143		88	31		119	149
	3600	5-3/4" deep, 7'-0" high, 4'-0" wide, single		15	1.067		75	29		104	132
	3640	8'-0" wide, double		12	1.333		109	36.50		145.50	180
	3700	8'-0" high, 4'-0" wide, single		15	1.067		88.50	29		117.50	147
	3740	8'-0" wide, double		12	1.333		109	36.50		145.50	180
	4000	6-3/4" deep, 7'-0" high, 4'-0" wide, single		15	1.067		81.50	29		110.50	139
	4040	8'-0"		12	1.333		110	36.50		146.50	182
	4100	8'-0" high, 4'-0" wide, single		15	1.067		93	29		122	151
	4140	8'-0" wide, double		12	1.333		119	36.50		155.50	192
	4400	8-3/4" deep, 7'-0" high, 4'-0" wide, single		15	1.067		91	29		120	149
	4440	8'-0" wide, double		12	1.333		124	36.50		160.50	197
	4500	8'-0" high, 4'-0" wide, single		15	1.067		105	29		134	164
	4540	8'-0" wide, double		12	1.333		129	36.50		165.50	203
	4900	For welded frames, add					29.50			29.50	32.50
	5400	16 ga., "B" label, up to 5-3/4" deep, 7'-0" high, 4'-0" wide, single	2 Carp	15	1.067		90	29		119	148
	5440	8'-0" wide, double		12	1.333		116	36.50		152.50	188
	5800	6-3/4" deep, 7'-0" high, 4'-0" wide, single		15	1.067		93	29		122	151
	5840	8'-0" wide, double		12	1.333		114	36.50		150.50	186
	6200	8-3/4" deep, 7'-0" high, 4'-0" wide, single		15	1.067		102	29		131	161
	6240	8'-0" wide, double		12	1.333		125	36.50		161.50	199
	6300	For "A" label use same price as "B" label									
	6400	For baked enamel finish, add					30%	15%			
	6500	For galvanizing, add					15%				
	7900	Transom lite frames, fixed, add	2 Carp	155	.103	S.F.	23	2.82		25.82	30
	8000	Movable, add	"	130	.123	"	27.50	3.36		30.86	36
	9000	Minimum labor/equipment charge	1 Carp	4	2	Job		54.50		54.50	91.50

082 | Wood & Plastic Doors

082 050 | Wood & Plastic Doors

			Crew	Daily Output	Labor-Hours	Unit	1999 Bare Costs Mat.	Labor	Equip.	Total	Total Incl O&P
054	0010	**WOOD FRAMES**										054
	0400	Exterior frame, incl. ext. trim, pine, 5/4 x 4-9/16" deep	2 Carp	375	.043	L.F.	3.70	1.16		4.86	6
	0420	5-3/16" deep		375	.043		3.95	1.16		5.11	6.30
	0440	6-9/16" deep		375	.043		5.40	1.16		6.56	7.90
	0600	Oak, 5/4 x 4-9/16" deep		350	.046		7.95	1.25		9.20	10.85
	0620	5-3/16" deep		350	.046		8.95	1.25		10.20	11.95
	0640	6-9/16" deep		350	.046		9.95	1.25		11.20	13.05
	0800	Walnut, 5/4 x 4-9/16" deep		350	.046		9.35	1.25		10.60	12.40
	0820	5-3/16" deep		350	.046		13.55	1.25		14.80	17
	0840	6-9/16" deep		350	.046		16	1.25		17.25	19.70
	1000	Sills, 8/4 x 8" deep, oak, no horns		100	.160		11.30	4.37		15.67	19.70
	1020	2" horns		100	.160		12.55	4.37		16.92	21
	1040	3" horns		100	.160		14.50	4.37		18.87	23.50
	1100	8/4 x 10" deep, oak, no horns		90	.178		15.15	4.85		20	25
	1120	2" horns		90	.178		16.90	4.85		21.75	26.50
	1140	3" horns		90	.178		18.40	4.85		23.25	28.50

082 | Wood & Plastic Doors

082 050 | Wood & Plastic Doors

			DAILY	LABOR-		1999 BARE COSTS				TOTAL	
		CREW	OUTPUT	HOURS	UNIT	MAT.	LABOR	EQUIP.	TOTAL	INCL O&P	
054	2000	Exterior, colonial, frame & trim, 3' opng., in-swing, minimum	2 Carp	22	.727	Ea.	263	19.85		282.85	320	054
	2010	Average		21	.762		224	21		245	281	
	2020	Maximum		20	.800		885	22		907	1,000	
	2100	5'-4" opening, in-swing, minimum		17	.941		297	25.50		322.50	370	
	2120	Maximum		15	1.067		885	29		914	1,025	
	2140	Out-swing, minimum		17	.941		305	25.50		330.50	380	
	2160	Maximum		15	1.067		920	29		949	1,050	
	2400	6'-0" opening, in-swing, minimum		16	1		285	27.50		312.50	360	
	2420	Maximum		10	1.600		920	43.50		963.50	1,075	
	2460	Out-swing, minimum		16	1		305	27.50		332.50	380	
	2480	Maximum		10	1.600		1,150	43.50		1,193.50	1,325	
	2600	For two sidelights, add, minimum		30	.533	Opng.	294	14.55		308.55	350	
	2620	Maximum		20	.800	"	940	22		962	1,050	
	2700	Custom birch frame, 3'-0" opening		16	1	Ea.	169	27.50		196.50	231	
	2750	6'-0" opening		16	1		240	27.50		267.50	310	
	2900	Exterior, modern, plain trim, 3' opng., in-swing, minimum		26	.615		24.50	16.80		41.30	55	
	2920	Average		24	.667		29.50	18.20		47.70	62.50	
	2940	Maximum		22	.727		36	19.85		55.85	72.50	
	3000	Interior frame, pine, 11/16" x 3-5/8" deep		375	.043	L.F.	3.57	1.16		4.73	5.85	
	3020	4-9/16" deep		375	.043		4.22	1.16		5.38	6.60	
	3200	Oak, 11/16" x 3-5/8" deep		350	.046		4.50	1.25		5.75	7.05	
	3220	4-9/16" deep		350	.046		4.86	1.25		6.11	7.45	
	3240	5-3/16" deep		350	.046		5	1.25		6.25	7.60	
	3400	Walnut, 11/16" x 3-5/8" deep		350	.046		8	1.25		9.25	10.90	
	3420	4-9/16" deep		350	.046		8	1.25		9.25	10.90	
	3440	5-3/16" deep		350	.046		8.30	1.25		9.55	11.25	
	3600	Pocket door frame		16	1	Ea.	67.50	27.50		95	120	
	3800	Threshold, oak, 5/8" x 3-5/8" deep		200	.080	L.F.	2.92	2.18		5.10	6.85	
	3820	4-5/8" deep		190	.084		3.72	2.30		6.02	7.95	
	3840	5-5/8" deep		180	.089		4.47	2.43		6.90	9	
	4000	For casing see division 062-212										
	9000	Minimum labor/equipment charge	1 Carp	4	2	Job		54.50		54.50	91.50	
062	0010	**WOOD DOOR, ARCHITECTURAL**	R082 -120									062
	0015	Flush, int., 1-3/4", 7 ply, hollow core,										
	0020	Lauan face, 2'-0" x 6'-8"	2 Carp	17	.941	Ea.	43	25.50		68.50	90	
	0040	2'-6" x 6'-8"		17	.941		51	25.50		76.50	99	
	0080	3'-0" x 6'-8"		17	.941		46.50	25.50		72	94	
	0100	4'-0" x 6'-8"		16	1		74	27.50		101.50	127	
	0120	Birch face, 2'-0" x 6'-8"		17	.941		46	25.50		71.50	93.50	
	0140	2'-6" x 6'-8"		17	.941		62	25.50		87.50	111	
	0180	3'-0" x 6'-8"		17	.941		65	25.50		90.50	115	
	0200	4'-0" x 6'-8"		16	1		83	27.50		110.50	137	
	0220	Oak face, 2'-0" x 6'-8"		17	.941		63.50	25.50		89	113	
	0240	2'-6" x 6'-8"		17	.941		67.50	25.50		93	118	
	0280	3'-0" x 6'-8"		17	.941		72.50	25.50		98	123	
	0300	4'-0" x 6'-8"		16	1		92	27.50		119.50	147	
	0320	Walnut face, 2'-0" x 6'-8"		17	.941		128	25.50		153.50	184	
	0340	2'-6" x 6'-8"		17	.941		131	25.50		156.50	187	
	0380	3'-0" x 6'-8"		17	.941		136	25.50		161.50	192	
	0400	4'-0" x 6'-8"		16	1		154	27.50		181.50	215	
	0430	For 7'-0" high, add					13			13	14.30	
	0440	For 8'-0" high, add					18.20			18.20	20	
	0460	For 8'-0" high walnut, add					10.90			10.90	12	
	0480	For prefinishing, clear, add					28.50			28.50	31.50	
	0500	For prefinishing, stain, add					39			39	43	
	1320	M.D. overlay on hardboard, 2'-0" x 6'-8"	2 Carp	17	.941		80.50	25.50		106	132	

For expanded coverage of these items see *Means Interior Cost Data 1999*

082 | Wood & Plastic Doors

082 050 | Wood & Plastic Doors

			CREW	DAILY OUTPUT	LABOR-HOURS	UNIT	1999 BARE COSTS MAT.	LABOR	EQUIP.	TOTAL	TOTAL INCL O&P	
062	1340	2'-6" x 6'-8"	2 Carp	17	.941	Ea.	80.50	25.50		106	132	062
	1380	3'-0" x 6'-8"		17	.941		95.50	25.50		121	148	
	1400	4'-0" x 6'-8"		16	1		134	27.50		161.50	193	
	1420	For 7'-0" high, add					7.15			7.15	7.85	
	1440	For 8'-0" high, add					15.80			15.80	17.40	
	1720	H.P. plastic laminate, 2'-0" x 6'-8"	2 Carp	16	1		195	27.50		222.50	261	
	1740	2'-6" x 6'-8"		16	1		195	27.50		222.50	261	
	1780	3'-0" x 6'-8"		15	1.067		222	29		251	293	
	1800	4'-0" x 6'-8"		14	1.143		310	31		341	390	
	1820	For 7'-0" high, add					7.15			7.15	7.85	
	1840	For 8'-0" high, add					18.20			18.20	20	
	2020	5 ply particle core, lauan face, 2'-6" x 6'-8"	2 Carp	15	1.067		65	29		94	121	
	2040	3'-0" x 6'-8"		14	1.143		71	31		102	130	
	2080	3'-0" x 7'-0"		13	1.231		74	33.50		107.50	138	
	2100	4'-0" x 7'-0"		12	1.333		91.50	36.50		128	162	
	2120	Birch face, 2'-6" x 6'-8"		15	1.067		77.50	29		106.50	135	
	2140	3'-0" x 6'-8"		14	1.143		85	31		116	146	
	2180	3'-0" x 7'-0"		13	1.231		87	33.50		120.50	152	
	2200	4'-0" x 7'-0"		12	1.333		106	36.50		142.50	177	
	2220	Oak face, 2'-6" x 6'-8"		15	1.067		85.50	29		114.50	143	
	2240	3'-0" x 6'-8"		14	1.143		94	31		125	156	
	2280	3'-0" x 7'-0"		13	1.231		97	33.50		130.50	163	
	2300	4'-0" x 7'-0"		12	1.333		119	36.50		155.50	191	
	2320	Walnut face, 2'-0" x 6'-8"		15	1.067		95	29		124	153	
	2340	2'-6" x 6'-8"		14	1.143		109	31		140	171	
	2380	3'-0" x 6'-8"		13	1.231		122	33.50		155.50	191	
	2400	4'-0" x 6'-8"		12	1.333		152	36.50		188.50	228	
	2440	For 8'-0" high, add					22			22	24	
	2460	For 8'-0" high walnut, add					12.75			12.75	14.05	
	2480	For solid wood core, add					28.50			28.50	31.50	
	2720	For prefinishing, clear, add					18.60			18.60	20.50	
	2740	For prefinishing, stain, add					39			39	42.50	
	2750											
	3320	M.D. overlay on hardboard, 2'-6" x 6'-8"	2 Carp	14	1.143	Ea.	71.50	31		102.50	131	
	3340	3'-0" x 6'-8"		13	1.231		78.50	33.50		112	143	
	3380	3'-0" x 7'-0"		12	1.333		80	36.50		116.50	149	
	3400	4'-0" x 7'-0"		10	1.600		98	43.50		141.50	181	
	3440	For 8'-0" height, add					22			22	24	
	3460	For solid wood core, add					28.50			28.50	31.50	
	3720	H.P. plastic laminate, 2'-6" x 6'-8"	2 Carp	13	1.231		110	33.50		143.50	178	
	3740	3'-0" x 6'-8"		12	1.333		125	36.50		161.50	198	
	3780	3'-0" x 7'-0"		11	1.455		129	39.50		168.50	209	
	3800	4'-0" x 7'-0"		8	2		157	54.50		211.50	265	
	3840	For 8'-0" height, add					22			22	24	
	3860	For solid wood core, add					27			27	29.50	
	4000	Exterior, flush, solid wood stave core, birch, 1-3/4" x 7'-0" x 2'-6"	2 Carp	15	1.067		138	29		167	200	
	4020	2'-8" wide		15	1.067		144	29		173	207	
	4040	3'-0" wide		14	1.143		152	31		183	220	
	4100	Oak faced 1-3/4" x 7'-0" x 2'-6" wide		15	1.067		151	29		180	215	
	4120	2'-8" wide		15	1.067		162	29		191	227	
	4140	3'-0" wide		14	1.143		173	31		204	242	
	4200	Walnut faced, 1-3/4" x 7'-0" x 2'-6" wide		15	1.067		222	29		251	294	
	4220	2'-8" wide		15	1.067		232	29		261	305	
	4240	3'-0" wide		14	1.143		242	31		273	320	
	4300	For 6'-8" high door, deduct from 7'-0" door					18.20			18.20	20	
	9000	Minimum labor/equipment charge	1 Carp	4	2	Job		54.50		54.50	91.50	

Reference: R082-120

082 | Wood & Plastic Doors

082 050 | Wood & Plastic Doors

		CREW	DAILY OUTPUT	LABOR-HOURS	UNIT	1999 BARE COSTS MAT.	LABOR	EQUIP.	TOTAL	TOTAL INCL O&P	
066	0010 **WOOD DOORS, DECORATOR**										066
	3000 Solid wood, 1-3/4" thick stile and rail										
	3020 Mahogany, 3'-0" x 7'-0", minimum	2 Carp	14	1.143	Ea.	445	31		476	540	
	3030 Maximum		10	1.600		650	43.50		693.50	790	
	3040 3'-6" x 8'-0", minimum		10	1.600		655	43.50		698.50	795	
	3050 Maximum		8	2		755	54.50		809.50	925	
	3100 Pine, 3'-0" x 7'-0", minimum		14	1.143		291	31		322	370	
	3110 Maximum		10	1.600		525	43.50		568.50	650	
	3120 3'-6" x 8'-0", minimum		10	1.600		580	43.50		623.50	710	
	3130 Maximum		8	2		1,575	54.50		1,629.50	1,825	
	3200 Red oak, 3'-0" x 7'-0", minimum		14	1.143		655	31		686	770	
	3210 Maximum		10	1.600		1,175	43.50		1,218.50	1,350	
	3220 3'-6" x 8'-0", minimum		10	1.600		830	43.50		873.50	990	
	3230 Maximum		8	2		1,375	54.50		1,429.50	1,600	
	4000 Hand carved door, mahogany										
	4020 3'-0" x 7'-0", minimum	2 Carp	14	1.143	Ea.	650	31		681	765	
	4030 Maximum		11	1.455		1,550	39.50		1,589.50	1,800	
	4040 3'-6" x 8'-0", minimum		10	1.600		1,050	43.50		1,093.50	1,250	
	4050 Maximum		8	2		2,225	54.50		2,279.50	2,550	
	4200 Red oak, 3'-0" x 7'-0", minimum		14	1.143		1,275	31		1,306	1,450	
	4210 Maximum		11	1.455		3,000	39.50		3,039.50	3,375	
	4220 3'-6" x 8'-0", minimum		10	1.600		2,575	43.50		2,618.50	2,925	
	4280 For 6'-8" high door, deduct from 7'-0" door					23.50			23.50	25.50	
	4400 For custom finish, add					103			103	113	
	4600 Side light, mahogany, 7'-0" x 1'-6" wide, minimum	2 Carp	18	.889		258	24.50		282.50	325	
	4610 Maximum		14	1.143		700	31		731	820	
	4620 8'-0" x 1'-6" wide, minimum		14	1.143		320	31		351	400	
	4630 Maximum		10	1.600		810	43.50		853.50	970	
	4640 Side light, oak, 7'-0" x 1'-6" wide, minimum		18	.889		345	24.50		369.50	420	
	4650 Maximum		14	1.143		805	31		836	935	
	4660 8'-0" x 1-6" wide, minimum		14	1.143		420	31		451	510	
	4670 Maximum		10	1.600		945	43.50		988.50	1,125	
	6520 Interior cafe doors, 2'-6" opening, stock, panel pine		16	1		139	27.50		166.50	199	
	6540 3'-0" opening		16	1		145	27.50		172.50	205	
	6550 Louvered pine										
	6560 2'-6" opening	2 Carp	16	1	Ea.	121	27.50		148.50	179	
	8000 3'-0" opening		16	1		129	27.50		156.50	188	
	8010 2'-6" opening, hardwood		16	1		173	27.50		200.50	236	
	8020 3'-0" opening		16	1		203	27.50		230.50	269	
	8800 Pre-hung doors, see division 082-082										
	9000 Minimum labor/equipment charge	1 Carp	4	2	Job		54.50		54.50	91.50	
070	0010 **WOOD FIRE DOORS** R082-120										070
	0020 Particle core, 7 face plys, "B" label,										
	0040 1 hour, birch face, 1-3/4" x 2'-6" x 6'-8"	2 Carp	14	1.143	Ea.	152	31		183	219	
	0080 3'-0" x 6'-8"		13	1.231		157	33.50		190.50	229	
	0090 3'-0" x 7'-0"		12	1.333		173	36.50		209.50	251	
	0100 4'-0" x 7'-0"		12	1.333		226	36.50		262.50	310	
	0140 Oak face, 2'-6" x 6'-8"		14	1.143		171	31		202	241	
	0180 3'-0" x 6'-8"		13	1.231		178	33.50		211.50	253	
	0190 3'-0" x 7'-0"		12	1.333		185	36.50		221.50	264	
	0200 4'-0" x 7'-0"		12	1.333		244	36.50		280.50	330	
	0240 Walnut face, 2'-6" x 6'-8"		14	1.143		227	31		258	300	
	0280 3'-0" x 6'-8"		13	1.231		243	33.50		276.50	325	
	0290 3'-0" x 7'-0"		12	1.333		261	36.50		297.50	350	
	0300 4'-0" x 7'-0"		12	1.333		355	36.50		391.50	450	

For expanded coverage of these items see Means Interior Cost Data 1999

082 | Wood & Plastic Doors

082 050 | Wood & Plastic Doors

			CREW	DAILY OUTPUT	LABOR-HOURS	UNIT	1999 BARE COSTS MAT.	LABOR	EQUIP.	TOTAL	TOTAL INCL O&P	
070	0440	M.D. overlay on hardboard, 2'-6" x 6'-8"	2 Carp	15	1.067	Ea.	147	29		176	210	070
	0480	3'-0" x 6'-8"		14	1.143		149	31		180	216	
	0490	3'-0" x 7'-0"		13	1.231		159	33.50		192.50	231	
	0500	4'-0" x 7'-0"		12	1.333		202	36.50		238.50	284	
	0540	H.P. plastic laminate, 2'-6" x 6'-8"		13	1.231		233	33.50		266.50	315	
	0590	3'-0" x 7'-0"		11	1.455		253	39.50		292.50	345	
	0600	4'-0" x 7'-0"		10	1.600		335	43.50		378.50	440	
	0740	90 minutes, birch face, 1-3/4" x 2'-6" x 6'-8"		14	1.143		197	31		228	269	
	0780	3'-0" x 6'-8"		13	1.231		204	33.50		237.50	281	
	0790	3'-0" x 7'-0"		12	1.333		211	36.50		247.50	293	
	0800	4'-0" x 7'-0"		12	1.333		294	36.50		330.50	385	
	0840	Oak face, 2'-6" x 6'-8"		14	1.143		187	31		218	258	
	0880	3'-0" x 6'-8"		13	1.231		188	33.50		221.50	264	
	0890	3'-0" x 7'-0"		12	1.333		204	36.50		240.50	285	
	0900	4'-0" x 7'-0"		12	1.333		291	36.50		327.50	380	
	0940	Walnut face, 2'-6" x 6'-8"		14	1.143		284	31		315	360	
	0980	3'-0" x 6'-8"		13	1.231		310	33.50		343.50	395	
	0990	3'-0" x 7'-0"		12	1.333		325	36.50		361.50	415	
	1000	4'-0" x 7'-0"		12	1.333		355	36.50		391.50	450	
	1140	M.D. overlay on hardboard, 2'-6" x 6'-8"		15	1.067		197	29		226	266	
	1180	3'-0" x 6'-8"		14	1.143		204	31		235	276	
	1190	3'-0" x 7'-0"		13	1.231		214	33.50		247.50	292	
	1200	4'-0" x 7'-0"		12	1.333		297	36.50		333.50	385	
	1240	For 8'-0" height, add					52.50			52.50	58	
	1260	For 8'-0" height walnut, add					24			24	26.50	
	1340	H.P. plastic laminate, 2'-6" x 6'-8"	2 Carp	13	1.231		292	33.50		325.50	375	
	1380	3'-0" x 6'-8"		12	1.333		292	36.50		328.50	380	
	1390	3'-0" x 7'-0"		11	1.455		292	39.50		331.50	385	
	1400	4'-0" x 7'-0"		10	1.600		315	43.50		358.50	425	
	2200	Custom architectural "B" label, flush, 1-3/4" thick, birch,										
	2210	Solid core										
	2220	2'-6" x 7'-0"	2 Carp	15	1.067	Ea.	335	29		364	420	
	2260	3'-0" x 7'-0"		14	1.143		340	31		371	425	
	2300	4'-0" x 7'-0"		13	1.231		470	33.50		503.50	570	
	2420	4'-0" x 8'-0"		11	1.455		545	39.50		584.50	665	
	2460	For 6'-8" high door, deduct from 7'-0" door					12.50			12.50	13.75	
	2480	For oak veneer, add					50%					
	2500	For walnut veneer, add					75%					
	9000	Minimum labor/equipment charge	1 Carp	4	2	Job		54.50		54.50	91.50	
074	0010	**WOOD DOORS, PANELED**										074
	0020	Interior, six panel, hollow core, 1-3/8" thick										
	0040	Molded hardboard, 2'-0" x 6'-8"	2 Carp	17	.941	Ea.	40	25.50		65.50	87	
	0060	2'-6" x 6'-8"		17	.941		43	25.50		68.50	90.50	
	0080	3'-0" x 6'-8"		17	.941		47.50	25.50		73	95	
	0140	Embossed print, molded hardboard, 2'-0" x 6'-8"		17	.941		43	25.50		68.50	90.50	
	0160	2'-6" x 6'-8"		17	.941		43	25.50		68.50	90.50	
	0180	3'-0" x 6'-8"		17	.941		47.50	25.50		73	95	
	0540	Six panel, solid, 1-3/8" thick, pine, 2'-0" x 6'-8"		15	1.067		104	29		133	163	
	0560	2'-6" x 6'-8"		14	1.143		117	31		148	181	
	0580	3'-0" x 6'-8"		13	1.231		134	33.50		167.50	205	
	1020	Two panel, bored rail, solid, 1-3/8" thick, pine, 1'-6" x 6'-8"		16	1		190	27.50		217.50	255	
	1040	2'-0" x 6'-8"		15	1.067		249	29		278	325	
	1060	2'-6" x 6'-8"		14	1.143		285	31		316	365	
	1340	Two panel, solid, 1-3/8" thick, fir, 2'-0" x 6'-8"		15	1.067		104	29		133	163	
	1360	2'-6" x 6'-8"		14	1.143		117	31		148	181	

082 | Wood & Plastic Doors

082 050 | Wood & Plastic Doors

		CREW	DAILY OUTPUT	LABOR-HOURS	UNIT	1999 BARE COSTS MAT.	LABOR	EQUIP.	TOTAL	TOTAL INCL O&P	
074	1380	3'-0" x 6'-8"	2 Carp	13	1.231	Ea.	285	33.50		318.50	370	074
	1740	Five panel, solid, 1-3/8" thick, fir, 2'-0" x 6'-8"		15	1.067		186	29		215	254	
	1760	2'-6" x 6'-8"		14	1.143		285	31		316	365	
	1780	3'-0" x 6'-8"		13	1.231		285	33.50		318.50	370	
	9000	Minimum labor/equipment charge	1 Carp	4	2	Job		54.50		54.50	91.50	
078	0010	**WOOD DOORS, RESIDENTIAL**										078
	0200	Exterior, combination storm & screen, pine	R082 -120									
	0260	2'-8" wide	2 Carp	10	1.600	Ea.	191	43.50		234.50	283	
	0280	3'-0" wide		9	1.778		197	48.50		245.50	298	
	0300	7'-1" x 3'-0" wide		9	1.778		198	48.50		246.50	299	
	0400	Full lite, 6'-9" x 2'-6" wide		11	1.455		196	39.50		235.50	282	
	0420	2'-8" wide		10	1.600		201	43.50		244.50	295	
	0440	3'-0" wide		9	1.778		202	48.50		250.50	305	
	0500	7'-1" x 3'-0" wide		9	1.778		221	48.50		269.50	325	
	0700	Dutch door, pine, 1-3/4" x 6'-8" x 2'-8" wide, minimum		12	1.333		525	36.50		561.50	640	
	0720	Maximum		10	1.600		560	43.50		603.50	690	
	0800	3'-0" wide, minimum		12	1.333		550	36.50		586.50	665	
	0820	Maximum		10	1.600		600	43.50		643.50	735	
	1000	Entrance door, colonial, 1-3/4" x 6'-8" x 2'-8" wide		16	1		289	27.50		316.50	365	
	1020	6 panel pine, 3'-0" wide		15	1.067		310	29		339	395	
	1100	8 panel pine, 2'-8" wide		16	1		425	27.50		452.50	515	
	1120	3'-0" wide		15	1.067		460	29		489	555	
	1200	For tempered safety glass lites, add					23			23	25.50	
	1300	Flush, birch, solid core, 1-3/4" x 6'-8" x 2'-8" wide	2 Carp	16	1		66.50	27.50		94	119	
	1320	3'-0" wide		15	1.067		73	29		102	129	
	1350	7'-0" x 2'-8" wide		16	1		74	27.50		101.50	127	
	1360	3'-0" wide		15	1.067		81.50	29		110.50	139	
	1380	For tempered safety glass lites, add					48			48	53	
	1550	For handcarved door, see division 082-066-4000										
	2700	Interior, closet, bi-fold, w/hardware, no frame or trim incl.										
	2720	Flush, birch, 6'-6" or 6'-8" x 2'-6" wide	2 Carp	13	1.231	Ea.	41.50	33.50		75	102	
	2740	3'-0" wide		13	1.231		45	33.50		78.50	106	
	2760	4'-0" wide		12	1.333		75.50	36.50		112	144	
	2780	5'-0" wide		11	1.455		82	39.50		121.50	157	
	2800	6'-0" wide		10	1.600		89	43.50		132.50	171	
	2820	Flush, hardboard, primed, 6'-8" x 2'-6" wide		13	1.231		47.50	33.50		81	109	
	2840	3'-0" wide		13	1.231		48	33.50		81.50	110	
	2860	4'-0" wide		12	1.333		77.50	36.50		114	146	
	2880	5'-0" wide		11	1.455		84.50	39.50		124	160	
	2900	6'-0" wide		10	1.600		91.50	43.50		135	174	
	3000	Raised panel pine, 6'-6" or 6'-8" x 2'-6" wide		13	1.231		114	33.50		147.50	182	
	3020	3'-0" wide		13	1.231		128	33.50		161.50	197	
	3040	4'-0" wide		12	1.333		194	36.50		230.50	275	
	3060	5'-0" wide		11	1.455		225	39.50		264.50	315	
	3080	6'-0" wide		10	1.600		252	43.50		295.50	350	
	3200	Louvered, pine 6'-6" or 6'-8" x 2'-6" wide		13	1.231		89.50	33.50		123	155	
	3220	3'-0" wide		13	1.231		98.50	33.50		132	165	
	3240	4'-0" wide		12	1.333		154	36.50		190.50	230	
	3260	5'-0" wide		11	1.455		139	39.50		178.50	220	
	3280	6'-0" wide		10	1.600		193	43.50		236.50	285	
	4400	Bi-passing closet, incl. hardware and frame, no trim incl.										
	4420	Flush, lauan, 6'-8" x 4'-0" wide	2 Carp	12	1.333	Opng.	137	36.50		173.50	212	
	4440	5'-0" wide		11	1.455		143	39.50		182.50	224	
	4460	6'-0" wide		10	1.600		148	43.50		191.50	236	
	4600	Flush, birch, 6'-8" x 4'-0" wide		12	1.333		158	36.50		194.50	235	

For expanded coverage of these items see Means Interior Cost Data 1999

082 | Wood & Plastic Doors

082 050 | Wood & Plastic Doors

			CREW	DAILY OUTPUT	LABOR-HOURS	UNIT	MAT.	LABOR	EQUIP.	TOTAL	TOTAL INCL O&P	
078	4620	5'-0" wide	2 Carp	11	1.455	Opng.	175	39.50		214.50	260	078
	4640	6'-0" wide		10	1.600		190	43.50		233.50	282	
	4800	Louvered, pine, 6'-8" x 4'-0" wide		12	1.333		315	36.50		351.50	410	
	4820	5'-0" wide		11	1.455		345	39.50		384.50	445	
	4840	6'-0" wide		10	1.600		390	43.50		433.50	500	
	5000	Paneled, pine, 6'-8" x 4'-0" wide		12	1.333		305	36.50		341.50	395	
	5020	5'-0" wide		11	1.455		335	39.50		374.50	430	
	5040	6'-0" wide		10	1.600		375	43.50		418.50	485	
	6100	Folding accordion, closet, including track and frame										
	6120	Vinyl, 2 layer, stock (see also division 106-552)	2 Carp	400	.040	S.F.	2.68	1.09		3.77	4.78	
	6140	Woven mahogany and vinyl, stock		400	.040		1.37	1.09		2.46	3.34	
	6160	Wood slats with vinyl overlay, stock		400	.040		9.35	1.09		10.44	12.15	
	6180	Economy vinyl, stock		400	.040		1.44	1.09		2.53	3.41	
	6200	Rigid PVC		400	.040		4.05	1.09		5.14	6.30	
	6220	For custom partition, add					25%	10%				
	7310	Passage doors, flush, no frame included										
	7320	Hardboard, hollow core, 1-3/8" x 6'-8" x 1'-6" wide	2 Carp	18	.889	Ea.	34	24.50		58.50	78	
	7330	2'-0" wide		18	.889		35.50	24.50		60	79.50	
	7340	2'-6" wide		18	.889		39	24.50		63.50	83.50	
	7350	2'-8" wide		18	.889		40	24.50		64.50	84.50	
	7360	3'-0" wide		17	.941		33	25.50		58.50	79.50	
	7420	Lauan, hollow core, 1-3/8" x 6'-8" x 1'-6" wide		18	.889		19.60	24.50		44.10	62	
	7440	2'-0" wide		18	.889		22.50	24.50		47	65	
	7450	2'-4" wide		18	.889		25.50	24.50		50	68.50	
	7460	2'-6" wide		18	.889		25.50	24.50		50	68.50	
	7480	2'-8" wide		18	.889		26.50	24.50		51	69.50	
	7500	3'-0" wide		17	.941		28	25.50		53.50	74	
	7700	Birch, hollow core, 1-3/8" x 6'-8" x 1'-6" wide		18	.889		27	24.50		51.50	70	
	7720	2'-0" wide		18	.889		32	24.50		56.50	76	
	7740	2'-6" wide		18	.889		37.50	24.50		62	81.50	
	7760	2'-8" wide		18	.889		39	24.50		63.50	83.50	
	7780	3'-0" wide		17	.941		41	25.50		66.50	88	
	8000	Pine louvered, 1-3/8" x 6'-8" x 1'-6" wide		19	.842		95	23		118	144	
	8020	2'-0" wide		18	.889		111	24.50		135.50	163	
	8040	2'-6" wide		18	.889		123	24.50		147.50	177	
	8060	2'-8" wide		18	.889		134	24.50		158.50	188	
	8080	3'-0" wide		17	.941		141	25.50		166.50	199	
	8090											
	8300	Pine paneled, 1-3/8" x 6'-8" x 1'-6" wide	2 Carp	19	.842	Ea.	95	23		118	144	
	8320	2'-0" wide		18	.889		111	24.50		135.50	163	
	8340	2'-6" wide		18	.889		123	24.50		147.50	177	
	8360	2'-8" wide		18	.889		134	24.50		158.50	188	
	8380	3'-0" wide		17	.941		141	25.50		166.50	199	
	9900	Minimum labor/equipment charge	1 Carp	4	2	Job		54.50		54.50	91.50	
082	0010	**PRE-HUNG DOORS**										082
	0300	Exterior, wood, combination storm & screen, 6'-9" x 2'-6" wide	2 Carp	15	1.067	Ea.	200	29		229	269	
	0320	2'-8" wide		15	1.067		200	29		229	269	
	0340	3'-0" wide		15	1.067		209	29		238	279	
	0360	For 7'-0" high door, add					27			27	29.50	
	0370	For aluminum storm doors, see division 083-900										
	1600	Entrance door, flush, birch, solid core										
	1620	4-5/8" solid jamb, 1-3/4" x 6'-8" x 2'-8" wide	2 Carp	16	1	Ea.	172	27.50		199.50	235	
	1640	3'-0" wide	"	16	1		183	27.50		210.50	248	
	1680	For 7'-0" high door, add					17			17	18.70	
	2000	Entrance door, colonial, 6 panel pine										
	2020	4-5/8" solid jamb, 1-3/4" x 6'-8" x 2'-8" wide	2 Carp	16	1	Ea.	405	27.50		432.50	490	

082 | Wood & Plastic Doors

082 050 | Wood & Plastic Doors

		CREW	DAILY OUTPUT	LABOR-HOURS	UNIT	1999 BARE COSTS MAT.	LABOR	EQUIP.	TOTAL	TOTAL INCL O&P
2040	3'-0" wide	2 Carp	16	1	Ea.	430	27.50		457.50	515
2060	For 7'-0" high door, add					17			17	18.70
2200	For 5-5/8" solid jamb, add					17			17	18.70
2990										
4000	Interior, passage door, 4-5/8" solid jamb									
4400	Lauan, flush, solid core, 1-3/8" x 6'-8" x 2'-6" wide	2 Carp	20	.800	Ea.	133	22		155	183
4420	2'-8" wide		20	.800		134	22		156	185
4440	3'-0" wide		19	.842		157	23		180	211
4600	Hollow core, 1-3/8" x 6'-8" x 2'-6" wide		20	.800		99	22		121	146
4620	2'-8" wide		20	.800		99	22		121	146
4640	3'-0" wide		19	.842		101	23		124	150
4700	For 7'-0" high door, add					8.70			8.70	9.55
5000	Birch, flush, solid core, 1-3/8" x 6'-8" x 2'-6" wide	2 Carp	20	.800		138	22		160	189
5020	2'-8" wide		20	.800		141	22		163	192
5040	3'-0" wide		19	.842		147	23		170	200
5200	Hollow core, 1-3/8" x 6'-8" x 2'-6" wide		20	.800		110	22		132	158
5220	2'-8" wide		20	.800		132	22		154	183
5240	3'-0" wide		19	.842		115	23		138	166
5280	For 7'-0" high door, add					8.70			8.70	9.55
5500	Hardboard paneled, 1-3/8" x 6'-8" x 2'-6" wide	2 Carp	20	.800		111	22		133	159
5520	2'-8" wide		20	.800		113	22		135	161
5540	3'-0" wide		19	.842		115	23		138	165
6000	Pine paneled, 1-3/8" x 6'-8" x 2'-6" wide		20	.800		190	22		212	246
6020	2'-8" wide		20	.800		200	22		222	256
6040	3'-0" wide		19	.842		207	23		230	267
6500	For 5-5/8" solid jamb, add					19.60			19.60	21.50
6520	For split jamb, deduct					10.90			10.90	11.95
9000	Minimum labor/equipment charge	1 Carp	4	2	Job		54.50		54.50	91.50

083 | Special Doors

083 050 | Access Doors

		CREW	DAILY OUTPUT	LABOR-HOURS	UNIT	1999 BARE COSTS MAT.	LABOR	EQUIP.	TOTAL	TOTAL INCL O&P
0010	**ACCESS DOORS**									
1000	Fire rated door with lock									
1100	Metal, 12" x 12"	1 Carp	10	.800	Ea.	105	22		127	153
1150	18" x 18"		9	.889		133	24.50		157.50	187
1200	24" x 24"		9	.889		159	24.50		183.50	216
1250	24" x 36"		8	1		210	27.50		237.50	277
1300	24" x 48"		8	1		256	27.50		283.50	325
1350	36" x 36"		7.50	1.067		310	29		339	395
1400	48" x 48"		7.50	1.067		370	29		399	455
1600	Stainless steel, 12" x 12"		10	.800		169	22		191	223
1650	18" x 18"		9	.889		245	24.50		269.50	310
1700	24" x 24"		9	.889		295	24.50		319.50	365
1750	24" x 36"		8	1		360	27.50		387.50	440
2000	Flush door for finishing									
2100	Metal 8" x 8"	1 Carp	10	.800	Ea.	32	22		54	71.50
2150	12" x 12"	"	10	.800	"	34.50	22		56.50	74
3000	Recessed door for acoustic tile									
3100	Metal, 12" x 12"	1 Carp	4.50	1.778	Ea.	40	48.50		88.50	125

For expanded coverage of these items see *Means Interior Cost Data 1999*

083 | Special Doors

083 050 | Access Doors

		Crew	Daily Output	Labor-Hours	Unit	Mat.	Labor	Equip.	Total	Total Incl O&P	
3150	12" x 24"	1 Carp	4.50	1.778	Ea.	55.50	48.50		104	142	054
3200	24" x 24"		4	2		71	54.50		125.50	170	
3250	24" x 36"	↓	4	2	↓	90.50	54.50		145	191	
4000	Recessed door for drywall										
4100	Metal 12" x 12"	1 Carp	6	1.333	Ea.	46	36.50		82.50	112	
4150	12" x 24"		5.50	1.455		65	39.50		104.50	138	
4200	24" x 36"	↓	5	1.600	↓	99.50	43.50		143	182	
6000	Standard door										
6100	Metal, 8" x 8"	1 Carp	10	.800	Ea.	28	22		50	67	
6150	12" x 12"		10	.800		30.50	22		52.50	70	
6200	18" x 18"		9	.889		38	24.50		62.50	82.50	
6250	24" x 24"		9	.889		50	24.50		74.50	95.50	
6300	24" x 36"		8	1		70	27.50		97.50	122	
6350	36" x 36"		8	1		85.50	27.50		113	140	
6500	Stainless steel, 8" x 8"		10	.800		53	22		75	95	
6550	12" x 12"		10	.800		67.50	22		89.50	111	
6600	18" x 18"		9	.889		117	24.50		141.50	170	
6650	24" x 24"	↓	9	.889		153	24.50		177.50	209	
7010	Aluminum cover	G-3	11	2.909	↓	445	77.50		522.50	615	
9000	Minimum labor/equipment charge	1 Carp	4	2	Job		54.50		54.50	91.50	

083 100 | Sliding Doors

		Crew	Daily Output	Labor-Hours	Unit	Mat.	Labor	Equip.	Total	Total Incl O&P	
0010	**GLASS, SLIDING**										102
0012	Vinyl clad, 1" insul. glass, 6'-0" x 6'-10" high	2 Carp	4	4	Opng.	680	109		789	935	
0030	6'-0" x 8'-0" high		4	4	Ea.	1,425	109		1,534	1,750	
0100	8'-0" x 6'-10" high		4	4	Opng.	1,525	109		1,634	1,850	
0500	3 leaf, 9'-0" x 6'-10" high		3	5.333		1,375	146		1,521	1,775	
0600	12'-0" x 6'-10" high	↓	3	5.333	↓	1,725	146		1,871	2,125	
9000	Minimum labor/equipment charge	1 Carp	4	2	Job		54.50		54.50	91.50	
0010	**GLASS, SLIDING**										104
0020	Wood, 5/8" tempered insul. glass, 6' wide, premium	2 Carp	4	4	Ea.	905	109		1,014	1,175	
0100	Economy		4	4		665	109		774	915	
0150	8' wide, wood, premium		3	5.333		1,050	146		1,196	1,400	
0200	Economy		3	5.333		780	146		926	1,100	
0250	12' wide, wood, premium		2.50	6.400		1,675	175		1,850	2,150	
0300	Economy	↓	2.50	6.400	↓	1,100	175		1,275	1,500	
0350	Aluminum, 5/8" tempered insulated glass, 6' wide										
0400	Premium	2 Carp	4	4	Ea.	1,200	109		1,309	1,500	
0450	Economy		4	4		470	109		579	700	
0500	8' wide, premium		3	5.333		1,150	146		1,296	1,500	
0550	Economy		3	5.333		960	146		1,106	1,300	
0600	12' wide, premium		2.50	6.400		1,950	175		2,125	2,425	
0650	Economy	↓	2.50	6.400		1,250	175		1,425	1,675	
1000	Replacement doors, wood										
1050	6' wide, premium	2 Carp	4	4	Ea.	550	109		659	790	
9000	Minimum labor/equipment charge	1 Carp	2	4	Job		109		109	183	

083 200 | Metal-Clad Doors

		Crew	Daily Output	Labor-Hours	Unit	Mat.	Labor	Equip.	Total	Total Incl O&P	
0010	**KALAMEIN**										202
0020	Interior, flush type, 3' x 7'	2 Carp	4.30	3.721	Opng.	165	102		267	350	
9000	Minimum labor/equipment charge	1 Carp	2	4	Job		109		109	183	
0010	**TIN CLAD**										204
0020	3 ply, 6' x 7', double sliding, manual with hardware	2 Carp	1	16	Opng.	1,300	435		1,735	2,150	

Important: See the Reference Section for critical supporting data - Reference Nos., Crews, & City Cost Indexes

083 | Special Doors

083 200 | Metal-Clad Doors

			CREW	DAILY OUTPUT	LABOR-HOURS	UNIT	1999 BARE COSTS MAT.	LABOR	EQUIP.	TOTAL	TOTAL INCL O&P	
204	1000	For electric operator, add	1 Elec	2	4	Opng.	2,300	128		2,428	2,725	204
	9000	Minimum labor/equipment charge	2 Carp	1	16	Job		435		435	730	

083 250 | Cold Storage Doors

			CREW	DAILY OUTPUT	LABOR-HOURS	UNIT	MAT.	LABOR	EQUIP.	TOTAL	TOTAL INCL O&P	
251	0010	**COLD STORAGE**										251
	0020	Single, 20 ga. galvanized steel										
	0300	Horizontal sliding, 5' x 7', manual operation, 2" thick	2 Carp	2	8	Ea.	2,025	218		2,243	2,600	
	0400	4" thick		2	8		2,650	218		2,868	3,300	
	0500	6" thick		2	8		2,575	218		2,793	3,225	
	0800	5' x 7', power operation, 2" thick		1.90	8.421		4,275	230		4,505	5,100	
	0900	4" thick		1.90	8.421		4,350	230		4,580	5,175	
	1000	6" thick		1.90	8.421		4,950	230		5,180	5,825	
	1300	9' x 10', manual operation, 2" insulation		1.70	9.412		3,450	257		3,707	4,225	
	1400	4" insulation		1.70	9.412		3,575	257		3,832	4,350	
	1500	6" insulation		1.70	9.412		4,300	257		4,557	5,150	
	1800	Power operation, 2" insulation		1.60	10		5,950	273		6,223	7,000	
	1900	4" insulation		1.60	10		6,100	273		6,373	7,150	
	2000	6" insulation		1.70	9.412		6,900	257		7,157	8,025	
	2300	For stainless steel face, add					20%					
	3000	Hinged, lightweight, 3' x 7'-0", galvanized 1 face, 2" thick	2 Carp	2	8	Ea.	985	218		1,203	1,450	
	3050	4" thick		1.90	8.421		1,125	230		1,355	1,625	
	3300	Aluminum doors, 3' x 7'-0", 4" thick		1.90	8.421		1,025	230		1,255	1,500	
	3350	6" thick		1.40	11.429		1,825	310		2,135	2,525	
	3600	Stainless steel, 3' x 7'-0", 4" thick		1.90	8.421		1,300	230		1,530	1,825	
	3650	6" thick		1.40	11.429		2,200	310		2,510	2,950	
	3900	Painted, 3' x 7'-0", 4" thick		1.90	8.421		935	230		1,165	1,400	
	3950	6" thick		1.40	11.429		1,800	310		2,110	2,500	
	5000	Bi-parting, electric operated										
	5010	6' x 8' opening, galv. faces, 4" thick for cooler	2 Carp	.80	20	Opng.	5,600	545		6,145	7,075	
	5050	For freezer, 4" thick		.80	20		6,175	545		6,720	7,700	
	5300	For door buck framing and door protection, add		2.50	6.400		460	175		635	795	
	6000	Galvanized batten door, galvanized hinges, 4' x 7'		2	8		1,375	218		1,593	1,900	
	6050	6' x 8'		1.80	8.889		1,875	243		2,118	2,475	
	6500	Fire door, 3 hr., 6' x 8', single slide		.80	20		6,475	545		7,020	8,050	
	6550	Double, bi-parting		.70	22.857		8,400	625		9,025	10,300	
	9000	Minimum labor/equipment charge	1 Carp	2	4	Job		109		109	183	

083 300 | Coiling Doors

			CREW	DAILY OUTPUT	LABOR-HOURS	UNIT	MAT.	LABOR	EQUIP.	TOTAL	TOTAL INCL O&P	
302	0010	**COUNTER DOORS**										302
	0020	Manual, incl. frm and hdwe, galv. stl., 4' roll-up, 6' long	2 Carp	2	8	Opng.	605	218		823	1,025	
	0300	Galvanized steel, UL label		1.80	8.889		760	243		1,003	1,250	
	0600	Stainless steel, 4' high roll-up, 6' long		2	8		1,050	218		1,268	1,525	
	0700	10' long		1.80	8.889		1,525	243		1,768	2,075	
	2000	Aluminum, 4' high, 4' long		2.20	7.273		695	199		894	1,100	
	2020	6' long		2	8		770	218		988	1,200	
	2040	8' long		1.90	8.421		885	230		1,115	1,350	
	2060	10' long		1.80	8.889		1,050	243		1,293	1,575	
	2080	14' long		1.40	11.429		1,550	310		1,860	2,225	
	2100	6' high, 4' long		2	8		770	218		988	1,200	
	2120	6' long		1.60	10		900	273		1,173	1,450	
	2140	10' long		1.40	11.429		1,225	310		1,535	1,875	
	9000	Minimum labor/equipment charge	1 Carp	2	4	Job		109		109	183	

083 400 | Coiling Grilles

			CREW	DAILY OUTPUT	LABOR-HOURS	UNIT	MAT.	LABOR	EQUIP.	TOTAL	TOTAL INCL O&P	
404	0010	**COILING GRILLE**										404
	2020	Aluminum, manual operated, mill finish	2 Sswk	82	.195	S.F.	16.75	5.95		22.70	30	

For expanded coverage of these items see *Means Interior Cost Data 1999*

083 | Special Doors

083 400 | Coiling Grilles

			CREW	DAILY OUTPUT	LABOR-HOURS	UNIT	MAT.	LABOR	EQUIP.	TOTAL	TOTAL INCL O&P	
404	2040	Bronze anodized	2 Sswk	82	.195	S.F.	26.50	5.95		32.45	40.50	404
	2060	Steel, manual operated, 10' x 10' high		1	16	Opng.	1,500	490		1,990	2,575	
	2080	15' x 8' high	↓	.80	20	"	1,750	610		2,360	3,100	
	3000	For safety edge bottom bar, electric, add				L.F.	31			31	34	
	8000	For motor operation, add	2 Sswk	5	3.200	Opng.	755	98		853	1,025	
	9000	Minimum labor/equipment charge	"	1	16	Job		490		490	930	

083 600 | Sectional Overhead Drs

			CREW	DAILY OUTPUT	LABOR-HOURS	UNIT	MAT.	LABOR	EQUIP.	TOTAL	TOTAL INCL O&P	
604	0010	**OVERHEAD, COMMERCIAL** Frames not included										604
	1000	Stock, sectional, heavy duty, wood, 1-3/4" thick, 8' x 8' high	2 Carp	2	8	Ea.	400	218		618	805	
	1200	12' x 12' high		1.50	10.667		850	291		1,141	1,425	
	1300	Chain hoist, 14' x 14' high		1.30	12.308		1,475	335		1,810	2,175	
	1600	20' x 16' high	↓	.65	24.615	↓	3,075	670		3,745	4,500	
	2100	For medium duty custom door, deduct					5%	5%				
	2150	For medium duty stock doors, deduct					10%	5%				
	2300	Fiberglass and aluminum, heavy duty, sectional, 12' x 12' high	2 Carp	1.50	10.667	Ea.	1,250	291		1,541	1,850	
	2450	Chain hoist, 20' x 20' high	"	.50	32		4,275	875		5,150	6,150	
	2900	For electric trolley operator, 1/3 H.P., to 12' x 12', add	1 Carp	2	4		415	109		524	640	
	2950	Over 12' x 12', 1/2 H.P., add	"	1	8	↓	440	218		658	850	
	9000	Minimum labor/equipment charge	2 Carp	1.50	10.667	Job		291		291	485	
606	0010	**RESIDENTIAL GARAGE DOORS** Including hardware, no frame										606
	0050	Hinged, wood, custom, double door, 9' x 7'	2 Carp	4	4	Ea.	300	109		409	515	
	0070	16' x 7'		3	5.333		510	146		656	810	
	0200	Overhead, sectional, incl. hardware, fiberglass, 9' x 7', standard		5.28	3.030		495	82.50		577.50	685	
	0220	Deluxe		5.28	3.030		580	82.50		662.50	775	
	0300	16' x 7', standard		6	2.667		765	73		838	960	
	0320	Deluxe		6	2.667		955	73		1,028	1,175	
	0500	Hardboard, 9' x 7', standard		8	2		315	54.50		369.50	435	
	0520	Deluxe		8	2		380	54.50		434.50	510	
	0600	16' x 7', standard		6	2.667		555	73		628	730	
	0620	Deluxe		6	2.667		650	73		723	830	
	0700	Metal, 9' x 7', standard		5.28	3.030		225	82.50		307.50	385	
	0720	Deluxe		8	2		495	54.50		549.50	635	
	0800	16' x 7', standard		3	5.333		400	146		546	685	
	0820	Deluxe		6	2.667		680	73		753	870	
	0900	Wood, 9' x 7', standard		8	2		350	54.50		404.50	475	
	0920	Deluxe		8	2		1,000	54.50		1,054.50	1,200	
	1000	16' x 7', standard		6	2.667		705	73		778	895	
	1020	Deluxe	↓	6	2.667		1,475	73		1,548	1,750	
	1800	Door hardware, sectional	1 Carp	4	2		154	54.50		208.50	262	
	1810	Door tracks only		4	2		72	54.50		126.50	171	
	1820	One side only	↓	7	1.143		50	31		81	107	
	3000	Swing-up, including hardware, fiberglass, 9' x 7', standard	2 Carp	8	2		485	54.50		539.50	620	
	3020	Deluxe		8	2		575	54.50		629.50	725	
	3100	16' x 7', standard		6	2.667		610	73		683	790	
	3120	Deluxe		6	2.667		710	73		783	905	
	3200	Hardboard, 9' x 7', standard		8	2		251	54.50		305.50	370	
	3220	Deluxe		8	2		330	54.50		384.50	455	
	3300	16' x 7', standard		6	2.667		350	73		423	505	
	3320	Deluxe		6	2.667		520	73		593	690	
	3400	Metal, 9' x 7', standard		8	2		275	54.50		329.50	395	
	3420	Deluxe		8	2		430	54.50		484.50	565	
	3500	16' x 7', standard		6	2.667		430	73		503	595	
	3520	Deluxe		6	2.667		695	73		768	885	
	3600	Wood, 9' x 7', standard		8	2		300	54.50		354.50	420	
	3620	Deluxe	↓	8	2		480	54.50		534.50	620	

083 | Special Doors

083 600 | Sectional Overhead Drs

			CREW	DAILY OUTPUT	LABOR-HOURS	UNIT	MAT.	LABOR	EQUIP.	TOTAL	TOTAL INCL O&P	
606	3700	16' x 7', standard	2 Carp	6	2.667	Ea.	520	73		593	695	606
	3720	Deluxe		6	2.667		735	73		808	930	
	3900	Door hardware only, swing up	1 Carp	4	2		76	54.50		130.50	175	
	3920	One side only		7	1.143		49	31		80	106	
	4000	For electric operator, economy, add		8	1		202	27.50		229.50	268	
	4100	Deluxe, including remote control		8	1		295	27.50		322.50	370	
	4500	For transmitter/receiver control, add to operator				Total	69			69	76	
	4600	Transmitters, additional				"	22.50			22.50	24.50	
	6000	Replace section, on sectional door, fiberglass, 9' x 7'	1 Carp	4	2	Ea.	115	54.50		169.50	219	
	6020	16' x 7'		3.50	2.286		215	62.50		277.50	340	
	6200	Hardboard, 9' x 7'		4	2		121	54.50		175.50	225	
	6220	16' x 7'		3.50	2.286		215	62.50		277.50	340	
	6300	Metal, 9' x 7'		4	2		121	54.50		175.50	225	
	6320	16' x 7'		3.50	2.286		209	62.50		271.50	335	
	6500	Wood, 9' x 7'		4	2		121	54.50		175.50	225	
	6520	16' x 7'		3.50	2.286		234	62.50		296.50	360	
	9000	Minimum labor/equipment charge		2.50	3.200	Job		87.50		87.50	146	
654	0010	**VERTICAL LIFT DOORS**										654
	0020	Motorized, 14 ga. stl, incl., frm and ctrl pnl										
	0050	16' x 16' high	L-10	.50	48	Ea.	14,600	1,475	885	16,960	19,800	
	0100	10' x 20' high		1.30	18.462		16,400	570	340	17,310	19,400	
	0120	15' x 20' high		1.30	18.462		20,200	570	340	21,110	23,700	
	0140	20' x 20' high		1	24		24,500	740	445	25,685	28,700	
	0160	25' x 20' high		1	24		27,600	740	445	28,785	32,200	
	0170	32' x 24' high		.75	32		28,600	985	590	30,175	33,900	
	0180	20' x 25' high		1	24		29,100	740	445	30,285	33,800	
	0200	25' x 25' high		.70	34.286		32,900	1,050	635	34,585	38,800	
	0220	25' x 30' high		.70	34.286		35,400	1,050	635	37,085	41,500	
	0240	30' x 30' high		.70	34.286		40,600	1,050	635	42,285	47,200	
	0260	35' x 30' high		.70	34.286		44,800	1,050	635	46,485	52,000	

083 720 | Special Purpose Doors

			CREW	DAILY OUTPUT	LABOR-HOURS	UNIT	MAT.	LABOR	EQUIP.	TOTAL	TOTAL INCL O&P	
721	0010	**BULKHEAD CELLAR DOORS**										721
	0020	Steel, not incl. sides, 44" x 62"	1 Carp	5.50	1.455	Ea.	180	39.50		219.50	265	
	0100	52" x 73"		5.10	1.569		200	43		243	292	
	0500	With sides and foundation plates, 57" x 45" x 24"		4.70	1.702		235	46.50		281.50	335	
	0600	42" x 49" x 51"		4.30	1.860		283	51		334	395	
	9000	Minimum labor/equipment charge		2	4	Job		109		109	183	
723	0010	**FLOOR, COMMERCIAL**										723
	0020	Aluminum tile, steel frame, one leaf, 2' x 2' opng.	2 Sswk	3.50	4.571	Opng.	340	140		480	640	
	0050	3'-6" x 3'-6" opening		3.50	4.571		615	140		755	940	
	0500	Double leaf, 4' x 4' opening		3	5.333		900	163		1,063	1,300	
	0550	5' x 5' opening		3	5.333		1,325	163		1,488	1,750	
	9000	Minimum labor/equipment charge		2	8	Job		245		245	465	
725	0010	**FLOOR, INDUSTRIAL**										725
	0020	Steel 300 psf L.L., single leaf, 2' x 2', 175#	2 Sswk	6	2.667	Opng.	450	81.50		531.50	650	
	0050	3' x 3' opening, 300#		5.50	2.909		620	89		709	855	
	0300	Double leaf, 4' x 4' opening, 455#		5	3.200		935	98		1,033	1,200	
	0350	5' x 5' opening, 645#		4.50	3.556		1,225	109		1,334	1,550	
	1000	Aluminum, 300 psf L.L., single leaf, 2' x 2', 60#		6	2.667		440	81.50		521.50	640	
	1050	3' x 3' opening, 100#		5.50	2.909		690	89		779	930	
	1500	Double leaf, 4' x 4' opening, 160#		5	3.200		1,075	98		1,173	1,375	
	1550	5' x 5' opening, 235#		4.50	3.556		1,450	109		1,559	1,775	
	9000	Minimum labor/equipment charge		2	8	Job		245		245	465	

For expanded coverage of these items see *Means Interior Cost Data 1999*

083 | Special Doors

083 720 | Special Purpose Doors

		CREW	DAILY OUTPUT	LABOR-HOURS	UNIT	1999 BARE COSTS MAT.	LABOR	EQUIP.	TOTAL	TOTAL INCL O&P	
732	0010	**ROLLING SERVICE DOORS** Steel, manual, 20 ga., incl. hardware									732
	0120	8' x 8' high, class A fire door	2 Sswk	1.40	11.429	Ea.	895	350		1,245	1,650
	0130	12' x 12' high, standard		1.20	13.333		1,125	410		1,535	2,025
	0140	12' x 12' high, class A fire door		1	16		1,575	490		2,065	2,675
	0160	10' x 20' high, standard		.50	32		1,325	980		2,305	3,350
	0180	10' x 20' high, class A fire door		.40	40		2,375	1,225		3,600	4,950
	3000	For 18 ga. doors, add				S.F.	.68			.68	.75
	3300	For enamel finish, add				"	.80			.80	.88
	3600	For safety edge bottom bar, pneumatic, add				L.F.	10.55			10.55	11.60
	4000	For weatherstripping, extruded rubber, jambs, add					6.80			6.80	7.50
	4100	Hood, add					4.34			4.34	4.77
	4200	Sill, add					2.48			2.48	2.73
	4500	Motor operators, to 14' x 14' opening	2 Sswk	5	3.200	Ea.	645	98		743	895
	4700	For fire door, additional fusible link, add				"	12.40			12.40	13.65
	9000	Minimum labor/equipment charge	2 Sswk	1	16	Job		490		490	930
736	0010	**SHOCK ABSORBING DOORS**									736
	0020	Rigid, no frame, 1-1/2" thick, 5' x 7'	2 Sswk	1.90	8.421	Opng.	1,125	258		1,383	1,725
	0100	8' x 8'		1.80	8.889		1,575	272		1,847	2,275
	0500	Flexible, no frame, insulated, .16" thick, economy, 5' x 7'		2	8		1,375	245		1,620	1,975
	0600	Deluxe		1.90	8.421		2,075	258		2,333	2,800
	1000	8' x 8' opening, economy		2	8		2,150	245		2,395	2,825
	1100	Deluxe		1.90	8.421		2,750	258		3,008	3,525
	9000	Minimum labor/equipment charge		2	8	Job		245		245	465

083 750 | Swing Doors

		CREW	DAILY OUTPUT	LABOR-HOURS	UNIT	MAT.	LABOR	EQUIP.	TOTAL	TOTAL INCL O&P	
752	0010	**DOUBLE ACTING**									752
	0020	Including frame, closer, hardware and vision panel									
	1000	.063" aluminum, 7'-0" high, 4'-0" wide	2 Carp	4.20	3.810	Pr.	345	104		449	555
	1050	6'-8" wide	"	4	4	"	480	109		589	710
	2000	Solid core wood, 3/4" thick, metal frame, stainless steel									
	2010	base plate, 7' high opening, 4' wide	2 Carp	4	4	Pr.	705	109		814	960
	2050	7' wide		3.80	4.211	"	1,000	115		1,115	1,300
	9000	Minimum labor/equipment charge		2	8	Job		218		218	365
754	0010	**GLASS DOOR, SWING**									754
	0020	Including hardware, 1/2" thick, tempered, 3' x 7' opening	2 Glaz	2	8	Opng.	1,500	213		1,713	2,000
	0100	6' x 7' opening		1.40	11.429	"	3,000	305		3,305	3,800
	9000	Minimum labor/equipment charge		2	8	Job		213		213	345

083 800 | Sound Retardant Doors

		CREW	DAILY OUTPUT	LABOR-HOURS	UNIT	MAT.	LABOR	EQUIP.	TOTAL	TOTAL INCL O&P	
804	0010	**ACOUSTICAL DOORS**									804
	0020	Including framed seals, 3' x 7', wood, 27 STC rating	2 Carp	1.50	10.667	Ea.	325	291		616	845
	0100	Steel, 40 STC rating		1.50	10.667		1,250	291		1,541	1,850
	0200	45 STC rating		1.50	10.667		1,650	291		1,941	2,300
	0300	48 STC rating		1.50	10.667		2,075	291		2,366	2,775
	0400	52 STC rating		1.50	10.667		2,500	291		2,791	3,225
	9000	Minimum labor/equipment charge	1 Carp	4	2	Job		54.50		54.50	91.50

083 900 | Screen & Storm Doors

		CREW	DAILY OUTPUT	LABOR-HOURS	UNIT	MAT.	LABOR	EQUIP.	TOTAL	TOTAL INCL O&P	
904	0010	**STORM DOORS & FRAMES** Aluminum, residential,									904
	0020	combination storm and screen									
	0400	Clear anodic coating, 6'-8" x 2'-6" wide	2 Carp	15	1.067	Ea.	135	29		164	198
	0420	2'-8" wide		14	1.143		162	31		193	230
	0440	3'-0" wide		14	1.143		162	31		193	230
	0500	For 7' door height, add					5%				

Important: See the Reference Section for critical supporting data - Reference Nos., Crews, & City Cost Indexes

083 | Special Doors

083 900 | Screen & Storm Doors

			CREW	DAILY OUTPUT	LABOR-HOURS	UNIT	MAT.	LABOR	EQUIP.	TOTAL	TOTAL INCL O&P	
904	1000	Mill finish, 6'-8" x 2'-6" wide	2 Carp	15	1.067	Ea.	190	29		219	258	904
	1020	2'-8" wide		14	1.143		190	31		221	261	
	1040	3'-0" wide	↓	14	1.143		206	31		237	279	
	1100	For 7'-0" door, add					5%					
	1500	White painted, 6'-8" x 2'-6" wide	2 Carp	15	1.067		166	29		195	232	
	1520	2'-8" wide		14	1.143		177	31		208	247	
	1540	3'-0" wide	↓	14	1.143		189	31		220	260	
	1600	For 7'-0" door, add				↓	5%					
	2000	Wood door & screen, see division 082-078										
	2020											
	9000	Minimum labor/equipment charge	1 Carp	4	2	Job		54.50		54.50	91.50	

084 | Entrances & Storefronts

084 100 | Aluminum

			CREW	DAILY OUTPUT	LABOR-HOURS	UNIT	MAT.	LABOR	EQUIP.	TOTAL	TOTAL INCL O&P	
101	0010	**ALUMINUM FRAMES**										101
	0020	Entrance, 3' x 7' opening, clear anodized finish	2 Sswk	7	2.286	Opng.	173	70		243	325	
	0100	Bronze finish		7	2.286		295	70		365	460	
	0500	6' x 7' opening, clear finish		6	2.667		270	81.50		351.50	450	
	0520	Bronze finish		6	2.667		305	81.50		386.50	490	
	1000	With 3' high transoms, 3' x 10' opening, clear finish		6.50	2.462		330	75.50		405.50	510	
	1050	Bronze finish		6.50	2.462		365	75.50		440.50	545	
	1100	Black finish		6.50	2.462		430	75.50		505.50	620	
	1500	With 3' high transoms, 6' x 10' opening, clear finish		5.50	2.909		400	89		489	610	
	1550	Bronze finish		5.50	2.909		430	89		519	645	
	1600	Black finish		5.50	2.909	↓	510	89		599	730	
	9000	Minimum labor/equipment charge		4	4	Job		122		122	233	
103	0010	**ALUMINUM DOORS** Commercial entrance										103
	0800	Narrow stile, no glazing, standard hardware, pair of 2'-6" x 7'-0"	2 Carp	1.70	9.412	Pr.	625	257		882	1,125	
	1000	3'-0" x 7'-0", single		3	5.333	Ea.	415	146		561	700	
	1200	Pair of 3'-0" x 7'-0"		1.70	9.412	Pr.	830	257		1,087	1,350	
	1500	3'-6" x 7'-0", single		3	5.333	Ea.	445	146		591	735	
	2000	Medium stile, pair of 2'-6" x 7'-0"		1.70	9.412	Pr.	685	257		942	1,175	
	2100	3'-0" x 7'-0", single		3	5.333	Ea.	545	146		691	840	
	2200	Pair of 3'-0" x 7'-0"		1.70	9.412	Pr.	1,025	257		1,282	1,550	
	2300	3'-6" x 7'-0", single	↓	5.33	3.002	Ea.	640	82		722	840	
	5000	Flush panel doors, pair of 2'-6" x 7'-0"	2 Sswk	2	8	Pr.	835	245		1,080	1,375	
	5050	3'-0" x 7'-0", single		2.50	6.400	Ea.	420	196		616	835	
	5100	Pair of 3'-0" x 7'-0"		2	8	Pr.	865	245		1,110	1,425	
	5150	3'-6" x 7'-0", single	↓	2.50	6.400	Ea.	515	196		711	940	
105	0010	**ALUMINUM DOORS & FRAMES** Entrance, narrow stile, including										105
	0015	hardware & closer, clear finish, not incl. glass, 2'-6" x 7'-0" opng.	2 Sswk	2	8	Ea.	470	245		715	985	
	0020	3'-0" x 7'-0" opening		2	8		410	245		655	920	
	0030	3'-6" x 7'-0" opening		2	8		425	245		670	930	
	0100	3'-0" x 10'-0" opening, 3' high transom		1.80	8.889		675	272		947	1,275	
	0200	3'-6" x 10'-0" opening, 3' high transom		1.80	8.889		665	272		937	1,250	
	0280	5'-0" x 7'-0" opening		2	8	↓	705	245		950	1,250	
	0300	6'-0" x 7'-0" opening	↓	1.30	12.308	Pr.	685	375		1,060	1,475	

For expanded coverage of these items see *Means Interior Cost Data 1999*

084 | Entrances & Storefronts

084 100 | Aluminum

			CREW	DAILY OUTPUT	LABOR-HOURS	UNIT	MAT.	LABOR	EQUIP.	TOTAL	TOTAL INCL O&P	
105	0400	6'-0" x 10'-0" opening, 3' high transom	2 Sswk	1.10	14.545	Pr.	620	445		1,065	1,525	105
	0420	7'-0" x 7'-0" opening		1	16		785	490		1,275	1,800	
	0500	Wide stile, 2'-6" x 7'-0" opening		2	8	Ea.	695	245		940	1,225	
	0520	3'-0" x 7'-0" opening		2	8		615	245		860	1,150	
	0540	3'-6" x 7'-0" opening		2	8		645	245		890	1,175	
	0560	5'-0" x 7'-0" opening		2	8		990	245		1,235	1,575	
	0580	6'-0" x 7'-0" opening		1.30	12.308	Pr.	950	375		1,325	1,775	
	0600	7'-0" x 7'-0" opening		1	16	"	1,075	490		1,565	2,100	
	1100	For full vision doors, with 1/2" glass, add				Leaf	55%					
	1200	For non-standard size, add					67%					
	1300	Light bronze finish, add					36%					
	1400	Dark bronze finish, add					18%					
	1500	For black finish, add					36%					
	1600	Concealed panic device, add					885			885	975	
	1700	Electric striker release, add				Opng.	228			228	251	
	1800	Floor check, add				Leaf	675			675	745	
	1900	Concealed closer, add				"	450			450	495	
	2000	Flush 3' x 7' Insulated, 12"x 12" lite, clear finish	2 Sswk	2	8	Ea.	375	245		620	880	
	9000	Minimum labor/equipment charge	2 Carp	4	4	Job		109		109	183	
109	0010	**BALANCED DOORS**										109
	0020	Hardware & frame, alum. & glass, 3' x 7', econ.	2 Sswk	.90	17.778	Ea.	730	545		1,275	1,825	
	0150	Premium		.70	22.857	"	775	700		1,475	2,175	
	9000	Minimum labor/equipment charge		1	16	Job		490		490	930	
111	0010	**STOREFRONT SYSTEMS** Aluminum frame, clear 3/8" plate glass,										111
	0020	incl. 3' x 7' door with hardware (400 sq. ft. max. wall)										
	0500	Wall height to 12' high, commercial grade	2 Glaz	150	.107	S.F.	11.35	2.84		14.19	17.05	
	0600	Institutional grade		130	.123		15.10	3.27		18.37	22	
	0700	Monumental grade		115	.139		21.50	3.70		25.20	29.50	
	1000	6' x 7' door with hardware, commercial grade		135	.119		11.60	3.15		14.75	17.85	
	1100	Institutional grade		115	.139		15.85	3.70		19.55	23.50	
	1200	Monumental grade		100	.160		29.50	4.26		33.76	39.50	
	1500	For bronze anodized finish, add					15%					
	1600	For black anodized finish, add					30%					
	1700	For stainless steel framing, add to monumental					75%					
	9000	Minimum labor/equipment charge	2 Glaz	1	16	Job		425		425	690	

084 300 | Stainless Steel

			CREW	DAILY OUTPUT	LABOR-HOURS	UNIT	MAT.	LABOR	EQUIP.	TOTAL	TOTAL INCL O&P	
301	0010	**STAINLESS STEEL AND GLASS** Entrance unit, narrow stiles										301
	0020	3' x 7' opening, including hardware, minimum	2 Sswk	1.60	10	Opng.	4,175	305		4,480	5,175	
	0050	Average		1.40	11.429		4,525	350		4,875	5,650	
	0100	Maximum		1.20	13.333		4,850	410		5,260	6,100	
	1000	For solid bronze entrance units, statuary finish, add					60%					
	1100	Without statuary finish, add					45%					
	2000	Balanced doors, 3' x 7', economy	2 Sswk	.90	17.778	Ea.	5,675	545		6,220	7,250	
	2100	Premium		.70	22.857	"	9,750	700		10,450	12,000	
	9000	Minimum labor/equipment charge		2	8	Job		245		245	465	

084 600 | Automatic Doors

			CREW	DAILY OUTPUT	LABOR-HOURS	UNIT	MAT.	LABOR	EQUIP.	TOTAL	TOTAL INCL O&P	
602	0010	**SLIDING ENTRANCE** 12' x 7'-6" opng., 5' x 7' door, 2 way traf.,										602
	0020	mat activated, panic pushout, incl. operator & hardware,										
	0030	not including glass or glazing	2 Glaz	.70	22.857	Opng.	5,575	610		6,185	7,100	
	9000	Minimum labor/equipment charge	"	.70	22.857	Job		610		610	985	
604	0010	**SLIDING PANELS**										604
	0020	Mall fronts, aluminum & glass, 15' x 9' high	2 Glaz	1.30	12.308	Opng.	2,175	325		2,500	2,925	

Important: See the Reference Section for critical supporting data - Reference Nos., Crews, & City Cost Indexes

084 | Entrances & Storefronts

084 600 | Automatic Doors

		CREW	DAILY OUTPUT	LABOR-HOURS	UNIT	1999 BARE COSTS MAT.	LABOR	EQUIP.	TOTAL	TOTAL INCL O&P	
604	0100	24' x 9' high	2 Glaz	.70	22.857	Opng.	3,175	610		3,785	4,450	604
	0200	48' x 9' high, with fixed panels	↓	.90	17.778		5,900	475		6,375	7,250	
	0500	For bronze finish, add				↓	17%					
	9000	Minimum labor/equipment charge	2 Glaz	1	16	Job		425		425	690	

085 | Metal Windows

085 100 | Steel Windows

			CREW	DAILY OUTPUT	LABOR-HOURS	UNIT	1999 BARE COSTS MAT.	LABOR	EQUIP.	TOTAL	TOTAL INCL O&P	
102	0010	**STEEL SASH** Custom units, glazing and trim not included										102
	0100	Casement, 100% vented	2 Sswk	200	.080	S.F.	33.50	2.45		35.95	41.50	
	0200	50% vented		200	.080		28.50	2.45		30.95	36	
	0300	Fixed		200	.080		19.20	2.45		21.65	25.50	
	1000	Projected, commercial, 40% vented		200	.080		30	2.45		32.45	37.50	
	1100	Intermediate, 50% vented		200	.080		33	2.45		35.45	40.50	
	1500	Industrial, horizontally pivoted		200	.080		25	2.45		27.45	32	
	1600	Fixed		200	.080		21.50	2.45		23.95	28	
	2000	Industrial security sash, 50% vented		200	.080		38	2.45		40.45	46	
	2100	Fixed		200	.080		32	2.45		34.45	39.50	
	2500	Picture window		200	.080		13.75	2.45		16.20	19.75	
	3000	Double hung		200	.080	↓	38	2.45		40.45	46	
	5000	Mullions for above, open interior face		240	.067	L.F.	6.85	2.04		8.89	11.45	
	5100	With interior cover		240	.067	"	11.55	2.04		13.59	16.60	
	5200	Single glazing for above, add	2 Glaz	200	.080	S.F.	4.34	2.13		6.47	8.20	
	6000	Double glazing for above, add		200	.080		6.85	2.13		8.98	11	
	6100	Triple glazing for above, add	↓	85	.188	↓	8.35	5		13.35	17.30	
	9000	Minimum labor/equipment charge	1 Sswk	2	4	Job		122		122	233	
104	0010	**STEEL WINDOWS** Stock, including frame, trim and insulating glass	R085-100									104
	1000	Custom units, double hung, 2'-8" x 4'-6" opening	2 Sswk	12	1.333	Ea.	480	41		521	610	
	1100	2'-4" x 3'-9" opening		12	1.333		395	41		436	515	
	1500	Commercial projected, 3'-9" x 5'-5" opening		10	1.600		840	49		889	1,025	
	1600	6'-9" x 4'-1" opening		7	2.286		1,100	70		1,170	1,350	
	2000	Intermediate projected, 2'-9" x 4'-1" opening		12	1.333		470	41		511	600	
	2100	4'-1" x 5'-5" opening	↓	10	1.600	↓	955	49		1,004	1,150	
	9000	Minimum labor/equipment charge	1 Sswk	3	2.667	Job		81.50		81.50	155	

085 200 | Aluminum Windows

			CREW	DAILY OUTPUT	LABOR-HOURS	UNIT	MAT.	LABOR	EQUIP.	TOTAL	TOTAL INCL O&P	
202	0010	**ALUMINUM SASH**										202
	0020	Stock, grade C, glaze & trim not incl., casement	2 Sswk	200	.080	S.F.	26	2.45		28.45	33.50	
	0050	Double hung		200	.080		25	2.45		27.45	32	
	0100	Fixed casement		200	.080		9.55	2.45		12	15.20	
	0150	Picture window		200	.080		11	2.45		13.45	16.75	
	0200	Projected window		200	.080		22	2.45		24.45	29	
	0250	Single hung		200	.080		11.35	2.45		13.80	17.15	
	0300	Sliding		200	.080	↓	14.70	2.45		17.15	21	
	1000	Mullions for above, tubular	↓	240	.067	L.F.	3.90	2.04		5.94	8.15	
	2950	Single glazing for above, add	2 Glaz	200	.080	S.F.	5.30	2.13		7.43	9.30	
	3000	Double glazing for above, add		200	.080		8.55	2.13		10.68	12.90	
	3100	Triple glazing for above, add	↓	85	.188	↓	10.05	5		15.05	19.15	
	9000	Minimum labor/equipment charge	1 Sswk	2	4	Job		122		122	233	

For expanded coverage of these items see Means Interior Cost Data 1999

085 | Metal Windows

085 200 | Aluminum Windows

			CREW	DAILY OUTPUT	LABOR-HOURS	UNIT	MAT.	LABOR	EQUIP.	TOTAL	TOTAL INCL O&P
204	0010	**ALUMINUM WINDOWS** Incl. frame and glazing, grade C									
	1000	Stock units, casement, 3'-1" x 3'-2" opening	2 Sswk	10	1.600	Ea.	255	49		304	375
	1050	Add for storms					51.50			51.50	56.50
	1600	Projected, with screen, 3'-1" x 3'-2" opening	2 Sswk	10	1.600		182	49		231	294
	1700	Add for storms					48.50			48.50	53.50
	2000	4'-5" x 5'-3" opening	2 Sswk	8	2		257	61		318	400
	2100	Add for storms					67			67	74
	2500	Enamel finish windows, 3'-1" x 3'-2"	2 Sswk	10	1.600		164	49		213	273
	2600	4'-5" x 5'-3"		8	2		245	61		306	385
	3000	Single hung, 2' x 3' opening, enameled, standard glazed		10	1.600		123	49		172	228
	3100	Insulating glass		10	1.600		149	49		198	256
	3300	2'-8" x 6'-8" opening, standard glazed		8	2		261	61		322	405
	3400	Insulating glass		8	2		335	61		396	485
	3700	3'-4" x 5'-0" opening, standard glazed		9	1.778		168	54.50		222.50	289
	3800	Insulating glass		9	1.778		236	54.50		290.50	365
	4000	Sliding aluminum, 3' x 2' opening, standard glazed		10	1.600		138	49		187	245
	4100	Insulating glass		10	1.600		153	49		202	261
	4300	5' x 3' opening, standard glazed		9	1.778		175	54.50		229.50	297
	4400	Insulating glass		9	1.778		245	54.50		299.50	375
	4600	8' x 4' opening, standard glazed		6	2.667		252	81.50		333.50	435
	4700	Insulating glass		6	2.667		405	81.50		486.50	600
	5000	9' x 5' opening, standard glazed		4	4		380	122		502	655
	5100	Insulating glass		4	4		610	122		732	905
	5500	Sliding, with thermal barrier and screen, 6' x 4', 2 track		8	2		520	61		581	685
	5700	4 track		8	2		635	61		696	815
	6000	For above units with bronze finish, add					12%				
	6200	For installation in concrete openings, add					5%				
	6400										
	9000	Minimum labor/equipment charge	1 Sswk	3	2.667	Job		81.50		81.50	155

085 500 | Metal Jalousie Windows

			CREW	DAILY OUTPUT	LABOR-HOURS	UNIT	MAT.	LABOR	EQUIP.	TOTAL	TOTAL INCL O&P
502	0010	**JALOUSIES**									
	0020	Aluminum incl. glazing & screens, stock, 1'-7" x 3'-2"	2 Sswk	10	1.600	Ea.	111	49		160	215
	0100	2'-3" x 4'-0"		10	1.600		158	49		207	267
	0200	3'-1" x 2'-0"		10	1.600		109	49		158	213
	0300	3'-1" x 5'-3"		10	1.600		226	49		275	340
	1000	Mullions for above, 2'-0" long		80	.200		8.50	6.10		14.60	21
	1100	5'-3" long		80	.200		14.60	6.10		20.70	27.50
	9000	Minimum labor/equipment charge	1 Sswk	3.50	2.286	Job		70		70	133
504	0013	**LOUVERS** See division 062-740 & 102-104									

085 600 | Metal Storm Windows

			CREW	DAILY OUTPUT	LABOR-HOURS	UNIT	MAT.	LABOR	EQUIP.	TOTAL	TOTAL INCL O&P
601	0010	**STORM WINDOWS** Aluminum, residential									
	0300	Basement, mill finish, incl. fiberglass screen									
	0320	1'-10" x 1'-0" high	2 Carp	30	.533	Ea.	24.50	14.55		39.05	51.50
	0340	2'-9" x 1'-6" high		30	.533		27	14.55		41.55	54
	0360	3'-4" x 2'-0" high		30	.533		32.50	14.55		47.05	60
	1600	Double-hung, combination, storm & screen									
	1700	Custom, clear anodic coating, 2'-0" x 3'-5" high	2 Carp	30	.533	Ea.	63.50	14.55		78.05	94.50
	1720	2'-6" x 5'-0" high		28	.571		85	15.60		100.60	120
	1740	4'-0" x 6'-0" high		25	.640		180	17.45		197.45	228
	1800	White painted, 2'-0" x 3'-5" high		30	.533		75.50	14.55		90.05	108
	1820	2'-6" x 5'-0" high		28	.571		121	15.60		136.60	160
	1840	4'-0" x 6'-0" high		25	.640		218	17.45		235.45	270

085 | Metal Windows

085 600 | Metal Storm Windows

			CREW	DAILY OUTPUT	LABOR-HOURS	UNIT	MAT.	LABOR	EQUIP.	TOTAL	TOTAL INCL O&P	
601	2000	Average quality, clear anodic coating, 2'-0" x 3'-5" high	2 Carp	30	.533	Ea.	64.50	14.55		79.05	95.50	601
	2020	2'-6" x 5'-0" high		28	.571		81.50	15.60		97.10	116	
	2040	4'-0" x 6'-0" high		25	.640		95.50	17.45		112.95	135	
	2400	White painted, 2'-0" x 3'-5" high		30	.533		63.50	14.55		78.05	94.50	
	2420	2'-6" x 5'-0" high		28	.571		70	15.60		85.60	103	
	2440	4'-0" x 6'-0" high		25	.640		77	17.45		94.45	114	
	2600	Mill finish, 2'-0" x 3'-5" high		30	.533		58	14.55		72.55	88	
	2620	2'-6" x 5'-0" high		28	.571		64.50	15.60		80.10	97	
	2640	4'-0" x 6-8" high		25	.640		72.50	17.45		89.95	109	
	4000	Picture window, storm, 1 lite, white or bronze finish										
	4020	4'-6" x 4'-6" high	2 Carp	25	.640	Ea.	97	17.45		114.45	137	
	4040	5'-8" x 4'-6" high		20	.800		110	22		132	158	
	4400	Mill finish, 4'-6" x 4'-6" high		25	.640		97	17.45		114.45	137	
	4420	5'-8" x 4'-6" high		20	.800		110	22		132	158	
	4600	3 lite, white or bronze finish										
	4620	4'-6" x 4'-6" high	2 Carp	25	.640	Ea.	118	17.45		135.45	160	
	4640	5'-8" x 4'-6" high		20	.800		131	22		153	181	
	4800	Mill finish, 4'-6" x 4'-6" high		25	.640		104	17.45		121.45	144	
	4820	5'-8" x 4'-6" high		20	.800		110	22		132	158	
	5001	Sliding glass door, storm window, 6'-0" x 6'-8", fixed	1 Glaz	1.60	5		262	133		395	505	
	5101	Operable	"	2.10	3.810		262	101		363	450	
	6000	Sliding window, storm, 2 lite, white or bronze finish										
	6020	3'-4" x 2'-7" high	2 Carp	28	.571	Ea.	81.50	15.60		97.10	116	
	6040	4'-4" x 3'-3" high		25	.640		111	17.45		128.45	152	
	6060	5'-4" x 6'-0" high		20	.800		178	22		200	233	
	6400	3 lite, white or bronze finish										
	6420	4'-4" x 3'-3" high	2 Carp	25	.640	Ea.	129	17.45		146.45	172	
	6440	5'-4" x 6'-0" high		20	.800		232	22		254	292	
	6460	6'-0" x 6'-0" high		18	.889		233	24.50		257.50	298	
	6800	Mill finish, 4'-4" x 3'-3" high		25	.640		111	17.45		128.45	152	
	6820	5'-4" x 6'-0" high		20	.800		233	22		255	293	
	6840	6'-0" x 6-0" high		18	.889		241	24.50		265.50	305	
	8000	PVC framed										
	8100	Double-hung, combination, storm & screen										
	8120	2'-6" x 3'-5"	2 Carp	15	1.067	Ea.	51	29		80	105	
	8140	4' x 6'	"	12.50	1.280	"	87.50	35		122.50	155	
	8600	Single lite picture storm										
	8620	4'-6" x 4'-6"	2 Carp	12.50	1.280	Ea.	66.50	35		101.50	132	
	8640	5'-8" x 4'-6"	"	10	1.600	"	37.50	43.50		81	114	
	9000	Magnetic interior storm window										
	9100	3/16" plate glass	1 Glaz	107	.075	S.F.	1.95	1.99		3.94	5.40	
	9410	Minimum labor/equipment charge	1 Carp	4	2	Job		54.50		54.50	91.50	

085 700 | Screens

			CREW	DAILY OUTPUT	LABOR-HOURS	UNIT	MAT.	LABOR	EQUIP.	TOTAL	TOTAL INCL O&P	
701	0010	**SCREENS**										701
	0020	For metal sash, aluminum or bronze mesh, flat screen	2 Sswk	1,200	.013	S.F.	2.91	.41		3.32	3.98	
	0500	Wicket screen, inside window		1,000	.016		4.45	.49		4.94	5.85	
	0800	Security screen, aluminum frame with stainless steel cloth		1,200	.013		15.70	.41		16.11	18.05	
	0900	Steel grate, painted, on steel frame		1,600	.010		8.45	.31		8.76	9.85	
	1000	For solar louvers, add		160	.100		16.25	3.06		19.31	24	
	4000	See also division 055-508										

For expanded coverage of these items see *Means Interior Cost Data 1999*

086 | Wood & Plastic Windows

086 100 | Wood Windows

		CREW	DAILY OUTPUT	LABOR-HOURS	UNIT	1999 BARE COSTS				TOTAL INCL O&P
						MAT.	LABOR	EQUIP.	TOTAL	
0010	**AWNING WINDOW** Including frame, screen, and exterior trim									
0100	Average quality, builders model, 34" x 22", standard glazed	1 Carp	10	.800	Ea.	154	22		176	206
0200	Insulating glass		10	.800		221	22		243	280
0300	40" x 28", standard glazed		9	.889		259	24.50		283.50	325
0400	Insulating glass		9	.889		370	24.50		394.50	450
0500	48" x 36", standard glazed		8	1		480	27.50		507.50	575
0600	Insulating glass		8	1		690	27.50		717.50	805
1000	34" x 22"		10	.800		194	22		216	250
1100	40" x 22"		10	.800		214	22		236	272
1200	36" x 28"		9	.889		228	24.50		252.50	292
1300	36" x 36"		9	.889		288	24.50		312.50	355
1400	48" x 28"		8	1		272	27.50		299.50	345
1500	60" x 36"		8	1		380	27.50		407.50	460
2000	Metal clad, deluxe, insulating glass, 34" x 22"		10	.800		153	22		175	206
2100	40" x 22"		10	.800		165	22		187	219
2200	36" x 25"		9	.889		189	24.50		213.50	248
2300	40" x 30"		9	.889		229	24.50		253.50	293
2400	48" x 28"		8	1		221	27.50		248.50	289
2500	60" x 36"		8	1		253	27.50		280.50	325
9000	Minimum labor/equipment charge		4	2	Job		54.50		54.50	91.50
0010	**BOW-BAY WINDOW** Including frame, screen and exterior trim,									
0020	end panels operable									
1000	Fixed type, builders model, 8' x 5' high, std. glazed, 4 panels	2 Carp	10	1.600	Ea.	840	43.50		883.50	995
1050	Insulating glass		10	1.600		1,075	43.50		1,118.50	1,250
1100	10'-0" x 5'-0" high, standard glazed		6	2.667		1,125	73		1,198	1,350
1200	Insulating glass, 6 panels		6	2.667		1,175	73		1,248	1,425
1300	Vinyl clad, premium, insulating glass, 6'-0" x 4'-0"		10	1.600		910	43.50		953.50	1,075
1340	9'-0" x 4'-0"		8	2		1,200	54.50		1,254.50	1,425
1380	10'-0" x 6'-0"		7	2.286		2,050	62.50		2,112.50	2,350
1420	12'-0" x 6'-0"		6	2.667		2,600	73		2,673	2,975
1600	Metal clad, deluxe, insul. glass, 6'-0" x 4'-0" high, 3 panels		10	1.600		760	43.50		803.50	915
1640	9'-0" x 4'-0" high, 4 panels		8	2		1,075	54.50		1,129.50	1,275
1680	10'-0" x 5'-0" high, 5 panels		7	2.286		1,475	62.50		1,537.50	1,725
1720	12'-0" x 6'-0" high, 6 panels		6	2.667		2,050	73		2,123	2,375
2000	Casement, builders model, bow, 8' x 5' high, std. glazed, 4 panels		10	1.600		1,325	43.50		1,368.50	1,525
2050	Insulating glass		10	1.600		1,600	43.50		1,643.50	1,825
2100	12'-0" x 6'-0" high, 6 panels, standard glazed		6	2.667		1,650	73		1,723	1,925
2200	Insulating glass		6	2.667		1,650	73		1,723	1,950
2300	Vinyl clad, premium, insulating glass, 8'-0" x 5'-0"		10	1.600		1,100	43.50		1,143.50	1,300
2340	10'-0" x 5'-0"		8	2		1,575	54.50		1,629.50	1,825
2380	10'-0" x 6'-0"		7	2.286		1,650	62.50		1,712.50	1,900
2420	12'-0" x 6'-0"		6	2.667		1,950	73		2,023	2,275
2600	Metal clad, deluxe, insul. glass, 8'-0" x 5'-0" high, 4 panels		10	1.600		1,150	43.50		1,193.50	1,350
2640	10'-0" x 5'-0" high, 5 panels		8	2		1,250	54.50		1,304.50	1,475
2680	10'-0" x 6'-0" high, 5 panels		7	2.286		1,475	62.50		1,537.50	1,725
2720	12'-0" x 6'-0" high, 6 panels		6	2.667		2,050	73		2,123	2,375
3000	Double hung, bldrs. model, bay, 8' x 4' high, std. glazed		10	1.600		920	43.50		963.50	1,100
3050	Insulating glass		10	1.600		995	43.50		1,038.50	1,175
3100	9'-0" x 5'-0" high, standard glazed		6	2.667		995	73		1,068	1,225
3200	Insulating glass		6	2.667		1,050	73		1,123	1,275
3300	Vinyl clad, premium, insulating glass, 7'-0" x 4'-6"		10	1.600		955	43.50		998.50	1,125
3340	8'-0" x 4'-6"		8	2		975	54.50		1,029.50	1,175
3380	8'-0" x 5'-0"		7	2.286		1,025	62.50		1,087.50	1,225
3420	9'-0" x 5'-0"		6	2.667		1,050	73		1,123	1,275
3600	Metal clad, deluxe, insul. glass, 7'-0" x 4'-0" high		10	1.600		885	43.50		928.50	1,050
3640	8'-0" x 4'-0" high		8	2		915	54.50		969.50	1,100

086 | Wood & Plastic Windows

086 100 | Wood Windows

			CREW	DAILY OUTPUT	LABOR-HOURS	UNIT	MAT.	LABOR	EQUIP.	TOTAL	TOTAL INCL O&P	
108	3680	8'-0" x 5'-0" high	2 Carp	7	2.286	Ea.	950	62.50		1,012.50	1,150	108
	3720	9'-0" x 5'-0" high		6	2.667	↓	1,000	73		1,073	1,225	
	9000	Minimum labor/equipment charge	↓	2.50	6.400	Job		175		175	292	
120	0010	**CASEMENT WINDOW** Including frame, screen, and exterior trim										120
	0100	Avg. quality, bldrs. model, 2'-0" x 3'-0" H, standard glazed	1 Carp	10	.800	Ea.	158	22		180	210	
	0150	Insulating glass		10	.800		190	22		212	246	
	0200	2'-0" x 4'-6" high, standard glazed		9	.889		205	24.50		229.50	266	
	0250	Insulating glass		9	.889		259	24.50		283.50	325	
	0300	2'-3" x 6'-0" high, standard glazed		8	1		220	27.50		247.50	288	
	0350	Insulating glass		8	1		305	27.50		332.50	380	
	0522	Vinyl clad, premium, insulating glass, 2'-0" x 3'-0"		10	.800		192	22		214	248	
	0524	2'-0" x 4'-0"		9	.889		228	24.50		252.50	291	
	0525	2'-0" x 5'-0"		8	1		262	27.50		289.50	335	
	0528	2'-0" x 6'-0"		8	1		310	27.50		337.50	390	
	8000	Solid vinyl, premium, insulating glass, 2'-0" x 3'-0" high		10	.800		161	22		183	214	
	8020	2'-0" x 4'-0" high		9	.889		197	24.50		221.50	258	
	8040	2'-0" x 5'-0" high		8	1		227	27.50		254.50	296	
	8100	Metal clad, deluxe, insulating glass, 2'-0" x 3'-0" high		10	.800		163	22		185	216	
	8120	2'-0" x 4'-0" high		9	.889		196	24.50		220.50	256	
	8140	2'-0" x 5'-0" high		8	1		222	27.50		249.50	291	
	8160	2'-0" x 6'-0" high		8	1		255	27.50		282.50	325	
	8200	For multiple leaf units, deduct for stationary sash										
	8220	2' high				Ea.	16.90			16.90	18.60	
	8240	4'-6" high					19.50			19.50	21.50	
	8260	6' high					26			26	28.50	
	8300	For installation, add per leaf				↓		15%				
	9000	Minimum labor/equipment charge	1 Carp	3	2.667	Job		73		73	122	
124	0010	**DOUBLE HUNG** Including frame, screen, and exterior trim										124
	0100	Avg. quality, bldrs. model, 2'-0" x 3'-0" high, standard glazed	1 Carp	10	.800	Ea.	105	22		127	153	
	0150	Insulating glass		10	.800		149	22		171	201	
	0200	3'-0" x 4'-0" high, standard glazed		9	.889		138	24.50		162.50	193	
	0250	Insulating glass		9	.889		182	24.50		206.50	241	
	0300	4'-0" x 4'-6" high, standard glazed		8	1		169	27.50		196.50	232	
	0350	Insulating glass		8	1		224	27.50		251.50	292	
	1000	Vinyl clad, premium, insulating glass, 2'-6" x 3'-0"		10	.800		237	22		259	298	
	1100	3'-0" x 3'-6"		10	.800		287	22		309	350	
	1200	3'-0" x 4'-0"		9	.889		310	24.50		334.50	380	
	1300	3'-0" x 4'-6"		9	.889		325	24.50		349.50	395	
	1400	3'-0" x 5'-0"		8	1		335	27.50		362.50	415	
	1500	3'-6" x 6'-0"		8	1		560	27.50		587.50	665	
	1540	Solid vinyl, average quality, insulated glass, 2'-0" x 3'-0"		10	.800		120	22		142	168	
	1542	3'-0" x 4'-0"		9	.889		145	24.50		169.50	200	
	1544	4'-0" x 4'-6"		8	1		174	27.50		201.50	237	
	1560	Premium, insulating glass, 2'-6" x 3'-0"		10	.800		136	22		158	186	
	1562	3'-0" x 3'-6"		9	.889		157	24.50		181.50	214	
	1564	3'-0" x 4'-0"		9	.889		167	24.50		191.50	225	
	1566	3'-0" x 4'-6"		9	.889		172	24.50		196.50	230	
	1568	3'-0" x 5'-0"		8	1		176	27.50		203.50	240	
	1570	3'-6" x 6'-0"		8	1		194	27.50		221.50	259	
	2000	Metal clad, deluxe, insulating glass, 2'-6" x 3'-0" high		10	.800		172	22		194	226	
	2100	3'-0" x 3'-6" high		10	.800		204	22		226	262	
	2200	3'-0" x 4'-0" high		9	.889		217	24.50		241.50	280	
	2300	3'-0" x 4'-6" high		9	.889		235	24.50		259.50	299	
	2400	3'-0" x 5'-0" high		8	1		251	27.50		278.50	320	
	2500	3'-6" x 6'-0" high	↓	8	1	↓	305	27.50		332.50	380	

For expanded coverage of these items see *Means Interior Cost Data 1999*

086 | Wood & Plastic Windows

086 100 | Wood Windows

			CREW	DAILY OUTPUT	LABOR-HOURS	UNIT	MAT.	LABOR	EQUIP.	TOTAL	TOTAL INCL O&P	
124	9000	Minimum labor/equipment charge	1 Carp	3	2.667	Job		73		73	122	124
128	0010	**HALF ROUND WINDOW**, Vinyl clad, including grill										128
	0800	8" radius x 1'-4" base	2 Carp	9	1.778	Ea.	350	48.50		398.50	465	
	1040	1'-4" radius x 2'-8" base		8	2		395	54.50		449.50	525	
	1060	1'-6" radius x 3'-0" base		7	2.286		420	62.50		482.50	570	
	1080	1'-8" radius x 3'-4" base		7	2.286		460	62.50		522.50	615	
	2000	2'-0" radius x 4'-0" base	1 Carp	6	1.333		595	36.50		631.50	715	
	2100	2'-4" radius x 4'-8" base		6	1.333		690	36.50		726.50	820	
	2200	2'-6" radius x 5'-0" base		6	1.333		790	36.50		826.50	930	
	2250	2'-8" radius x 5'-4" base	2 Carp	6	2.667		1,100	73		1,173	1,325	
	2300	2'-10" radius x 5'-8" base		6	2.667		1,100	73		1,173	1,350	
	2350	2'-11" radius x 5'-10" base		6	2.667		1,125	73		1,198	1,375	
	3000	3'-0" radius x 6'-0" base	1 Carp	4	2		1,050	54.50		1,104.50	1,275	
	3040	3'-4" radius x 6'-8" base	2 Carp	5	3.200		1,375	87.50		1,462.50	1,675	
	3050	3'-5" radius x 6'-10" base		5	3.200		1,475	87.50		1,562.50	1,775	
	3060	3'-6" radius x 7'-0" base		5	3.200		1,550	87.50		1,637.50	1,850	
	4000	4'-0" radius x 8'-0" base		6	2.667		1,925	73		1,998	2,250	
	5000	Elliptical, 3'-2" x 1'-4"	1 Carp	11	.727		730	19.85		749.85	840	
	5100	5'-0" x 1'-0"		10	.800		730	22		752	840	
	5200	7'-0" x 1'-0"		10	.800		1,050	22		1,072	1,175	
132	0010	**PICTURE WINDOW** Including frame and exterior trim										132
	0100	Average quality, bldrs. model, 3'-6" x 4'-0" high, standard glazed	2 Carp	12	1.333	Ea.	188	36.50		224.50	268	
	0150	Insulating glass		12	1.333		198	36.50		234.50	279	
	0200	4'-0" x 4'-6" high, standard glazed		11	1.455		196	39.50		235.50	283	
	0250	Insulating glass		11	1.455		200	39.50		239.50	286	
	0300	5'-0" x 4'-0" high, standard glazed		11	1.455		198	39.50		237.50	285	
	0350	Insulating glass		11	1.455		248	39.50		287.50	340	
	0400	6'-0" x 4'-6" high, standard glazed		10	1.600		277	43.50		320.50	380	
	0450	Insulating glass		10	1.600		340	43.50		383.50	450	
	1000	Vinyl clad, premium, insulating glass, 4'-0" x 4'-0"		12	1.333		415	36.50		451.50	515	
	1100	4'-0" x 6'-0"		11	1.455		570	39.50		609.50	690	
	1200	5'-0" x 6'-0"		10	1.600		740	43.50		783.50	890	
	1300	6'-0" x 6'-0"		10	1.600		755	43.50		798.50	905	
	2000	Metal clad, deluxe, insulating glass, 4'-0" x 4'-0" high		12	1.333		255	36.50		291.50	340	
	2100	4'-0" x 6'-0" high		11	1.455		375	39.50		414.50	480	
	2200	5'-0" x 6'-0" high		10	1.600		415	43.50		458.50	530	
	2300	6'-0" x 6'-0" high		10	1.600		475	43.50		518.50	600	
	9000	Minimum labor/equipment charge		2.75	5.818	Job		159		159	266	
138	0010	**SOLID VINYL REPLACEMENT WINDOWS** R086-200										138
	0020	White, double hung, up to 83 united inches	2 Carp	8	2	Ea.	144	54.50		198.50	250	
	0040	84 to 93		8	2		144	54.50		198.50	250	
	0060	94 to 101		6	2.667		144	73		217	280	
	0080	102 to 111		6	2.667		165	73		238	305	
	0100	112 to 120		6	2.667		184	73		257	325	
	0120	For each united inch over 120, add		800	.020	Inch	2.15	.55		2.70	3.28	
	0140	Casement windows, one operating sash, 42 to 60 united inches		8	2	Ea.	163	54.50		217.50	272	
	0160	61 to 70		8	2		186	54.50		240.50	297	
	0180	71 to 80		8	2		202	54.50		256.50	315	
	0200	81 to 96		8	2		215	54.50		269.50	330	
	0220	Two operating sash, 58 to 78 united inches		8	2		296	54.50		350.50	415	
	0240	79 to 88		8	2		330	54.50		384.50	455	
	0260	89 to 98		8	2		360	54.50		414.50	490	
	0280	99 to 108		6	2.667		380	73		453	540	
	0300	109 to 121		6	2.667		415	73		488	580	

086 | Wood & Plastic Windows

086 100 | Wood Windows

			Crew	Daily Output	Labor-Hours	Unit	Mat.	Labor	Equip.	Total	Total Incl O&P	
138	0320	Three operating sash, 73 to 108 united inches R086-200	2 Carp	8	2	Ea.	445	54.50		499.50	580	138
	0340	109 to 118		8	2		475	54.50		529.50	615	
	0360	119 to 128		6	2.667		520	73		593	690	
	0380	129 to 138		6	2.667		565	73		638	740	
	0400	139 to 156		6	2.667		600	73		673	780	
	0420	Four operating sash, 89 to 98 united inches		8	2		595	54.50		649.50	745	
	0440	99 to 108		8	2		635	54.50		689.50	790	
	0460	109 to 118		6	2.667		690	73		763	880	
	0480	119 to 128		6	2.667		745	73		818	940	
	0500	129 to 138		6	2.667		800	73		873	1,000	
	0520	139 to 148		6	2.667		860	73		933	1,075	
	0540	149 to 168		4	4		915	109		1,024	1,175	
	0560	Fixed picture window, up to 63 united inches		8	2		124	54.50		178.50	228	
	0580	64 to 83		8	2		166	54.50		220.50	274	
	0600	84 to 101		8	2		211	54.50		265.50	325	
	0620	For each united inch over 101, add		900	.018	Inch	2.30	.49		2.79	3.34	
	0640	Picture window options, low E glazing, up to 101 united inches				Ea.	17.50			17.50	19.25	
	0660	102 to 124					22.50			22.50	25	
	0680	124 and over					34			34	37.50	
	0700	Options, low E glazing, up to 101 united inches					8.75			8.75	9.65	
	0720	102 to 124					22.50			22.50	25	
	0740	124 and over					34			34	37.50	
	0760	Muntins, between glazing, square, per lite					1.65			1.65	1.82	
	0780	Diamond shape, per full or partial diamond					2.75			2.75	3.03	
	0800	Celluose fiber insulation, poured into sash balance cavity	1 Carp	36	.222	C.F.	.45	6.05		6.50	10.65	
	0820	Silicone caulking at perimeter	"	800	.010	L.F.	.13	.27		.40	.60	
140	0010	**SLIDING WINDOW** Including frame, screen, and exterior trim										140
	0100	Average quality, bldrs. model, 3'-0" x 3'-0" high, standard glazed	1 Carp	10	.800	Ea.	126	22		148	176	
	0120	Insulating glass		10	.800		159	22		181	212	
	0200	4'-0" x 3'-6" high, standard glazed		9	.889		150	24.50		174.50	206	
	0220	Insulating glass		9	.889		188	24.50		212.50	248	
	0300	6'-0" x 5'-0" high, standard glazed		8	1		276	27.50		303.50	350	
	0320	Insulating glass		8	1		330	27.50		357.50	410	
	1000	Vinyl clad, premium, insulating glass, 3'-0" x 3'-0"		10	.800		455	22		477	535	
	1050	4'-0" x 3'-6"		9	.889		545	24.50		569.50	635	
	1100	5'-0" x 4'-0"		9	.889		630	24.50		654.50	730	
	1150	6'-0" x 5'-0"		8	1		780	27.50		807.50	905	
	2000	Metal clad, deluxe, insulating glass, 3'-0" x 3'-0" high		10	.800		256	22		278	320	
	2050	4'-0" x 3'-6" high		9	.889		315	24.50		339.50	385	
	2100	5'-0" x 4'-0" high		9	.889		380	24.50		404.50	455	
	2150	6'-0" x 5'-0" high		8	1		460	27.50		487.50	555	
	9000	Minimum labor/equipment charge		3	2.667	Job		73		73	122	
141	0010	**TRANSOM WINDOWS**										141
	0050	Vinyl clad, premium, insulating glass, 32" x 8"	1 Carp	16	.500	Ea.	177	13.65		190.65	217	
	0100	36" x 8"		16	.500		177	13.65		190.65	217	
	0110	36" x 12"		16	.500		215	13.65		228.65	259	
	0150	36" x 48"		12	.667		282	18.20		300.20	340	
	2000	Custom sizes, up to 350 sq. in.		12	.667		197	18.20		215.20	248	
	2100	351 to 750 sq. in.		12	.667		262	18.20		280.20	320	
	2200	751 to 1150 sq. in.		11	.727		325	19.85		344.85	395	
	2300	1151 to 1450 sq. in.		11	.727		375	19.85		394.85	450	
	2400	1451 to 1850 sq. in.	2 Carp	12	1.333		425	36.50		461.50	525	
	2500	1851 to 2250 sq. in.		12	1.333		485	36.50		521.50	595	
	2600	2251 to 2650 sq. in.		11	1.455		545	39.50		584.50	665	
	2700	2651 to 3050 sq. in.		11	1.455		550	39.50		589.50	670	
	2800	3051 to 3450 sq. in.		11	1.455		605	39.50		644.50	730	

For expanded coverage of these items see *Means Interior Cost Data 1999*

086 | Wood & Plastic Windows

086 100 | Wood Windows

			CREW	DAILY OUTPUT	LABOR-HOURS	UNIT	MAT.	LABOR	EQUIP.	TOTAL	TOTAL INCL O&P	
141	2900	3451 to 3850 sq. in.	2 Carp	10	1.600	Ea.	655	43.50		698.50	795	141
	3000	3851 to 4250 sq. in.		10	1.600		710	43.50		753.50	855	
	3100	4251 to 4650 sq. in.		10	1.600		715	43.50		758.50	865	
	3200	4651 to 5050 sq. in.		10	1.600		765	43.50		808.50	920	
	3300	5051 to 5450 sq. in.		9	1.778		815	48.50		863.50	975	
	3400	5451 to 5850 sq. in.		9	1.778		865	48.50		913.50	1,025	
	3600	6251 to 6650 sq. in.		8	2		965	54.50		1,019.50	1,150	
	3700	6651 to 7050 sq. in.		8	2		1,025	54.50		1,079.50	1,225	
	4960	36" x 30", round top		11	1.455		1,025	39.50		1,064.50	1,200	
	5000	36" x 114", round top		10	1.600		1,550	43.50		1,593.50	1,800	
	5200	48" x 72", round top		10	1.600		1,750	43.50		1,793.50	2,000	
	5400	66" x 90", round top		9	1.778		2,500	48.50		2,548.50	2,825	
	5600	70" x 108", round top		8	2		2,650	54.50		2,704.50	3,000	
143	0010	**TRAPEZOID WINDOWS**										143
	0900	20" base x 44" leg x 53" leg	2 Carp	13	1.231	Ea.	335	33.50		368.50	425	
	1000	24" base x 90" leg x 102" leg		8	2		585	54.50		639.50	735	
	3000	36" base x 0" leg x 22" leg		12	1.333		365	36.50		401.50	460	
	3010	36" base x 4" leg x 25" leg		13	1.231		390	33.50		423.50	480	
	3050	36" base x 26" leg x 48" leg		9	1.778		405	48.50		453.50	525	
	3100	36" base x 42" legs, 50" peak		9	1.778		465	48.50		513.50	590	
	3200	36" base x 60" leg x 81" leg		11	1.455		610	39.50		649.50	735	
	4320	44" base x 23" leg x 56" leg		11	1.455		465	39.50		504.50	580	
	4350	44" base x 59" leg x 92" leg		10	1.600		725	43.50		768.50	870	
	4500	46" base x 15" leg x 46" leg		8	2		360	54.50		414.50	490	
	4550	46" base x 16" leg x 48" leg		8	2		375	54.50		429.50	500	
	4600	46" base x 50" leg x 80" leg		7	2.286		595	62.50		657.50	760	
	6600	66" base x 12" leg x 42" leg		8	2		475	54.50		529.50	610	
	6650	66" base x 12" legs, 28" peak		9	1.778		400	48.50		448.50	520	
	6700	68" base x 3" legs, 31" peak		8	2		485	54.50		539.50	625	
144	0010	**WINDOW GRILLE OR MUNTIN** Snap-in type										144
	0020	Colonial or diamond pattern										
	2000	Wood, awning window, glass size 28" x 16" high	1 Carp	30	.267	Ea.	21.50	7.30		28.80	35.50	
	2060	44" x 24" high		32	.250		27.50	6.80		34.30	42	
	2100	Casement, glass size, 20" x 36" high		30	.267		27	7.30		34.30	41.50	
	2180	20" x 56" high		32	.250		36	6.80		42.80	51.50	
	2200	Double hung, glass size, 16" x 24" high		24	.333	Set	57	9.10		66.10	78	
	2280	32" x 32" high		34	.235	"	102	6.40		108.40	124	
	2500	Picture, glass size, 48" x 48" high		30	.267	Ea.	75.50	7.30		82.80	95.50	
	2580	60" x 68" high		28	.286	"	118	7.80		125.80	142	
	2600	Sliding, glass size, 14" x 36" high		24	.333	Set	30.50	9.10		39.60	49	
	2680	36" x 36" high		22	.364	"	48	9.95		57.95	69.50	
	9000	Minimum labor/equipment charge		5	1.600	Job		43.50		43.50	73	
148	0010	**WOOD SASH** Including glazing but not including trim										148
	0050	Custom, 5'-0" x 4'-0", 1" dbl. glazed, 3/16" thick lites	2 Carp	3.20	5	Ea.	185	137		322	435	
	0100	1/4" thick lites		5	3.200		190	87.50		277.50	355	
	0200	1" thick, triple glazed		5	3.200		435	87.50		522.50	625	
	0300	7'-0" x 4'-6" high, 1" double glazed, 3/16" thick lites		4.30	3.721		445	102		547	655	
	0400	1/4" thick lites		4.30	3.721		500	102		602	720	
	0500	1" thick, triple glazed		4.30	3.721		570	102		672	795	
	0600	8'-6" x 5'-0" high, 1" double glazed, 3/16" thick lites		3.50	4.571		595	125		720	865	
	0700	1/4" thick lites		3.50	4.571		655	125		780	930	
	0800	1" thick, triple glazed		3.50	4.571		660	125		785	935	
	0900	Window frames only, based on perimeter length				L.F.	3.65			3.65	4.02	
	1200	Window sill, stock, per lineal foot					8.35			8.35	9.20	

086 | Wood & Plastic Windows

086 100 | Wood Windows

			CREW	DAILY OUTPUT	LABOR-HOURS	UNIT	1999 BARE COSTS MAT.	LABOR	EQUIP.	TOTAL	TOTAL INCL O&P	
148	1250	Casing, stock				L.F.	2.90			2.90	3.19	148
	3000	Replacement sash, double hung, double glazing, to 12 S.F.	1 Carp	64	.125	S.F.	18.30	3.41		21.71	25.50	
	3100	12 S.F. to 20 S.F.		94	.085		15.30	2.32		17.62	20.50	
	3200	20 S.F. and over		106	.075		13.35	2.06		15.41	18.10	
	3800	Triple glazing for above, add					2.68			2.68	2.95	
	7000	Sash, single lite, 2'-0" x 2'-0" high	1 Carp	20	.400	Ea.	34.50	10.90		45.40	56	
	7050	2'-6" x 2'-0" high		19	.421		37	11.50		48.50	60.50	
	7100	2'-6" x 2'-6" high		18	.444		39	12.15		51.15	63.50	
	7150	3'-0" x 2'-0" high		17	.471		49.50	12.85		62.35	76	
	9000	Minimum labor/equipment charge		4	2	Job		54.50		54.50	91.50	
152	0010	**WOOD SCREENS**										152
	0020	Over 3 S.F., 3/4" frames	2 Carp	375	.043	S.F.	3	1.16		4.16	5.25	
	0100	1-1/8" frames		375	.043		2.95	1.16		4.11	5.20	
	0200	Rescreen wood frame		500	.032		.44	.87		1.31	1.94	
	9000	Minimum labor/equipment charge	1 Carp	4	2	Job		54.50		54.50	91.50	

087 | Hardware

087 100 | Finish Hardware

			CREW	DAILY OUTPUT	LABOR-HOURS	UNIT	1999 BARE COSTS MAT.	LABOR	EQUIP.	TOTAL	TOTAL INCL O&P	
101	0010	**AVERAGE** Percentage for hardware, total job cost, minimum									.75%	101
	0050	Maximum									3.50%	
	0500	Total hardware for building, average distribution					85%	15%				
	1000	Door hardware, apartment, interior				Door	104			104	114	
	1500	Hospital bedroom, minimum					236			236	260	
	2000	Maximum					520			520	570	
	2250	School, single exterior, incl. lever, not incl. panic device					350			350	385	
	2500	Single interior, regular use, no lever included					233			233	256	
	2600	Heavy use, incl. lever and closer					410			410	450	
	2850	Stairway, single interior					580			580	640	
	3100	Double exterior, with panic device				Pr.	820			820	905	
	3600	Toilet, public, single interior				Door	128			128	141	
108	0010	**DEADLOCKS** Mortise, heavy duty, outside key	1 Carp	9	.889	Ea.	109	24.50		133.50	161	108
	0020	Double cylinder		9	.889	"	120	24.50		144.50	174	
	0100	Medium duty, outside key		10	.800	Ea.	84.50	22		106.50	130	
	0110	Double cylinder		10	.800		106	22		128	153	
	1000	Tubular, standard duty, outside key		10	.800		45.50	22		67.50	86.50	
	1010	Double cylinder		10	.800		58.50	22		80.50	101	
	1200	Night latch, outside key		10	.800		57.50	22		79.50	99.50	
110	0010	**DOORSTOPS** Holder and bumper, floor or wall	1 Carp	32	.250	Ea.	14	6.80		20.80	27	110
	1300	Wall bumper, 4" diameter, with rubber pad, aluminum		32	.250		6.35	6.80		13.15	18.45	
	1600	Door bumper, floor type, aluminum		32	.250		3.64	6.80		10.44	15.45	
	1900	Plunger type, door mounted		32	.250		22.50	6.80		29.30	36	
	9000	Minimum labor/equipment charge		6	1.333	Job		36.50		36.50	61	
112	0010	**ENTRANCE LOCKS** Cylinder, grip handle, deadlocking latch	1 Carp	9	.889	Ea.	100	24.50		124.50	151	112
	0020	Deadbolt		8	1		121	27.50		148.50	179	
	0100	Push and pull plate, dead bolt		8	1		115	27.50		142.50	173	
	0900	For handicapped lever, add					126			126	139	

For expanded coverage of these items see *Means Interior Cost Data 1999*

087 | Hardware

087 100 | Finish Hardware

		Crew	Daily Output	Labor-Hours	Unit	Mat.	Labor	Equip.	Total	Total Incl O&P	
116	0010 **HINGES** Full mortise, avg. freq., steel base, 4-1/2" x 4-1/2", USP	R087-100			Pr.	17.55			17.55	19.30	116
	0100 5" x 5", USP					28.50			28.50	31	
	0200 6" x 6", USP					59.50			59.50	65.50	
	0400 Brass base, 4-1/2" x 4-1/2", US10					36			36	40	
	0500 5" x 5", US10					51.50			51.50	56.50	
	0600 6" x 6", US10					85.50			85.50	94	
	0800 Stainless steel base, 4-1/2" x 4-1/2", US32					60			60	66	
	0900 For non removable pin, add				Ea.	2.12			2.12	2.33	
	0910 For floating pin, driven tips, add					3.86			3.86	4.25	
	0930 For hospital type tip on pin, add					11.35			11.35	12.45	
	0940 For steeple type tip on pin, add					7.55			7.55	8.35	
	0950 Full mortise, high frequency, steel base, 3-1/2" x 3-1/2", US26D				Pr.	25.50			25.50	28	
	1000 4-1/2" x 4-1/2", USP					43.50			43.50	48	
	1100 5" x 5", USP					49			49	54	
	1200 6" x 6", USP					95			95	105	
	1400 Brass base, 3-1/2" x 3-1/2", US4					38.50			38.50	42.50	
	1430 4-1/2" x 4-1/2", US10					39			39	43	
	1500 5" x 5", US10					95.50			95.50	105	
	1600 6" x 6", US10					121			121	133	
	1800 Stainless steel base, 4-1/2" x 4-1/2", US32					92.50			92.50	102	
	1930 For hospital type tip on pin, add				Ea.	14.90			14.90	16.35	
	1950 Full mortise, low frequency, steel base, 3-1/2" x 3-1/2", US26D				Pr.	12.10			12.10	13.35	
	2000 4-1/2" x 4-1/2", USP					13.35			13.35	14.65	
	2100 5" x 5", USP					21			21	23	
	2200 6" x 6", USP					41.50			41.50	45.50	
	2300 4-1/2" x 4-1/2", US3					9.65			9.65	10.60	
	2310 5" x 5", US3					29.50			29.50	32.50	
	2400 Brass bass, 4-1/2" x 4-1/2", US10					30			30	33	
	2500 5" x 5", US10					45			45	49.50	
	2800 Stainless steel base, 4-1/2" x 4-1/2", US32					50			50	55	
118	0010 **KICK PLATE** 6" high, for 3' door, stainless steel	1 Carp	15	.533	Ea.	15.95	14.55		30.50	42	118
	0500 Bronze		15	.533		19.30	14.55		33.85	45.50	
	2000 Aluminum, .050, with 3 beveled edges, 10" x 28"		15	.533		14.15	14.55		28.70	40	
	2010 10" x 30"		15	.533		15.15	14.55		29.70	41	
	2020 10" x 34"		15	.533		17.20	14.55		31.75	43.50	
	2040 10" x 38"		15	.533		18.95	14.55		33.50	45.50	
	9000 Minimum labor/equipment charge		6	1.333	Job		36.50		36.50	61	
120	0010 **LOCKSET** Standard duty, cylindrical, with sectional trim										120
	0020 Non-keyed, passage	1 Carp	12	.667	Ea.	36	18.20		54.20	70	
	0100 Privacy		12	.667		44	18.20		62.20	79	
	0400 Keyed, single cylinder function		10	.800		64.50	22		86.50	107	
	0420 Hotel		8	1		87	27.50		114.50	142	
	0500 Lever handled, keyed, single cylinder function		10	.800		87	22		109	133	
	1000 Heavy duty with sectional trim, non-keyed, passages		12	.667		102	18.20		120.20	143	
	1100 Privacy		12	.667		129	18.20		147.20	172	
	1400 Keyed, single cylinder function		10	.800		152	22		174	204	
	1420 Hotel		8	1		226	27.50		253.50	295	
	1600 Communicating		10	.800		179	22		201	234	
	1690 For re-core cylinder, add					25.50			25.50	28	
	1700 Residential, interior door, minimum	1 Carp	16	.500		12.25	13.65		25.90	36.50	
	1720 Maximum		8	1		32.50	27.50		60	81.50	
	1800 Exterior, minimum		14	.571		27.50	15.60		43.10	56	
	1810 Average		8	1		58	27.50		85.50	109	
	1820 Maximum		8	1		115	27.50		142.50	172	
	9000 Minimum labor/equipment charge		6	1.333	Job		36.50		36.50	61	

087 | Hardware

087 100 | Finish Hardware

		CREW	DAILY OUTPUT	LABOR-HOURS	UNIT	1999 BARE COSTS MAT.	LABOR	EQUIP.	TOTAL	TOTAL INCL O&P	
125											**125**
0010	**MORTISE LOCKSET** Comm., wrought knobs & full escutcheon trim										
0020	Non-keyed, passage, minimum	1 Carp	9	.889	Ea.	135	24.50		159.50	190	
0030	Maximum		8	1		218	27.50		245.50	286	
0040	Privacy, minimum		9	.889		144	24.50		168.50	199	
0050	Maximum		8	1		236	27.50		263.50	305	
0100	Keyed, office/entrance/apartment, minimum		8	1		165	27.50		192.50	228	
0110	Maximum		7	1.143		283	31		314	360	
0120	Single cylinder, typical, minimum		8	1		142	27.50		169.50	202	
0130	Maximum		7	1.143		262	31		293	340	
0200	Hotel, minimum		7	1.143		170	31		201	239	
0210	Maximum		6	1.333		278	36.50		314.50	365	
0300	Communication, double cylinder, minimum		8	1		170	27.50		197.50	233	
0310	Maximum		7	1.143		221	31		252	295	
1000	Wrought knobs and sectional trim, non-keyed, passage, minimum		10	.800		89.50	22		111.50	135	
1010	Maximum		9	.889		177	24.50		201.50	236	
1040	Privacy, minimum		10	.800		105	22		127	152	
1050	Maximum		9	.889		189	24.50		213.50	249	
1100	Keyed, entrance, office/apartment, minimum		9	.889		156	24.50		180.50	212	
1110	Maximum		8	1		225	27.50		252.50	294	
1120	Single cylinder, typical, minimum		9	.889		150	24.50		174.50	206	
1130	Maximum		8	1		218	27.50		245.50	286	
2000	Cast knobs and full escutcheon trim										
2010	Non-keyed, passage, minimum	1 Carp	9	.889	Ea.	191	24.50		215.50	251	
2020	Maximum		8	1		310	27.50		337.50	385	
2040	Privacy, minimum		9	.889		229	24.50		253.50	293	
2050	Maximum		8	1		335	27.50		362.50	410	
2120	Keyed, single cylinder, typical, minimum		8	1		229	27.50		256.50	298	
2130	Maximum		7	1.143		360	31		391	450	
2200	Hotel, minimum		7	1.143		260	31		291	340	
2210	Maximum		6	1.333		480	36.50		516.50	590	
3000	Cast knob and sectional trim, non-keyed, passage, minimum		10	.800		148	22		170	200	
3010	Maximum		10	.800		295	22		317	360	
3040	Privacy, minimum		10	.800		169	22		191	223	
3050	Maximum		10	.800		295	22		317	360	
3100	Keyed, office/entrance/apartment, minimum		9	.889		191	24.50		215.50	251	
3110	Maximum		9	.889		300	24.50		324.50	370	
3120	Single cylinder, typical, minimum		9	.889		191	24.50		215.50	251	
3130	Maximum		9	.889		370	24.50		394.50	450	
3190	For re-core cylinder, add					26			26	28.50	
3800	Cipher lockset	1 Carp	13	.615		620	16.80		636.80	715	
3900	Keyless, pushbutton type										
4000	Residential/light commercial, deadbolt, standard	1 Carp	9	.889	Ea.	86.50	24.50		111	136	
4010	Heavy duty		9	.889		103	24.50		127.50	154	
4020	Industrial, heavy duty, with deadbolt		9	.889		210	24.50		234.50	272	
4030	Key override		9	.889		233	24.50		257.50	297	
4040	Lever activated handle		9	.889		255	24.50		279.50	320	
4050	Key override		9	.889		283	24.50		307.50	350	
4060	Double sided pushbutton type		8	1		465	27.50		492.50	560	
4070	Key override		8	1		505	27.50		532.50	600	
126											**126**
0010	**HASP** Steel, 3" assembly	1 Carp	26	.308	Ea.	2.32	8.40		10.72	16.60	
0020	4-1/2"		13	.615		2.95	16.80		19.75	31.50	
0040	6"		12.50	.640		4.67	17.45		22.12	34.50	
127											**127**
0010	**PANIC DEVICE** For rim locks, single door, exit only	1 Carp	6	1.333	Ea.	320	36.50		356.50	410	
0020	Outside key and pull		5	1.600		370	43.50		413.50	480	

For expanded coverage of these items see *Means Interior Cost Data 1999*

087 | Hardware

087 100 | Finish Hardware

		CREW	DAILY OUTPUT	LABOR-HOURS	UNIT	MAT.	LABOR	EQUIP.	TOTAL	TOTAL INCL O&P
0200	Bar and vertical rod, exit only	1 Carp	5	1.600	Ea.	475	43.50		518.50	595
0210	Outside key and pull		4	2		565	54.50		619.50	710
0400	Bar and concealed rod		4	2		480	54.50		534.50	615
0600	Touch bar, exit only		6	1.333		380	36.50		416.50	475
0610	Outside key and pull		5	1.600		455	43.50		498.50	575
0700	Touch bar and vertical rod, exit only		5	1.600		515	43.50		558.50	645
0710	Outside key and pull		4	2		600	54.50		654.50	750
1000	Mortise, bar, exit only		4	2		425	54.50		479.50	555
1600	Touch bar, exit only		4	2		485	54.50		539.50	625
2000	Narrow stile, rim mounted, bar, exit only		6	1.333		510	36.50		546.50	620
2010	Outside key and pull		5	1.600		555	43.50		598.50	685
2200	Bar and vertical rod, exit only		5	1.600		525	43.50		568.50	655
2210	Outside key and pull		4	2		525	54.50		579.50	670
2400	Bar and concealed rod, exit only		3	2.667		610	73		683	790
3000	Mortise, bar, exit only		4	2		430	54.50		484.50	560
3600	Touch bar, exit only		4	2		625	54.50		679.50	775
4000	Double doors, exit only		2	4	Pr.	645	109		754	895
4500	Exit & entrance		2	4	"	735	109		844	995
9000	Minimum labor/equipment charge		2.50	3.200	Job		87.50		87.50	146
0010	**PUSH-PULL PLATE**									
0100	Push plate, .050 thick, 4" x 16", aluminum	1 Carp	12	.667	Ea.	4.85	18.20		23.05	36
0500	Bronze		12	.667		10.90	18.20		29.10	42.50
1500	Pull handle and push bar, aluminum		11	.727		105	19.85		124.85	148
2000	Bronze		10	.800		136	22		158	186
3000	Push plate both sides, aluminum		14	.571		12.85	15.60		28.45	40
3500	Bronze		13	.615		32.50	16.80		49.30	63.50
4000	Door pull, designer style, cast aluminum, minimum		12	.667		59	18.20		77.20	95.50
5000	Maximum		8	1		274	27.50		301.50	345
6000	Cast bronze, minimum		12	.667		63.50	18.20		81.70	101
7000	Maximum		8	1		297	27.50		324.50	370
8000	Walnut, minimum		12	.667		49	18.20		67.20	84
9000	Maximum		8	1		272	27.50		299.50	345
9800	Minimum labor/equipment charge		5	1.600	Job		43.50		43.50	73
0010	**SPECIAL HINGES**									
0015	Paumelle, high frequency									
0020	Steel base, 6" x 4-1/2", US10				Pr.	105			105	115
0100	Bronze base, 5" x 4-1/2", US10					141			141	155
0200	Paumelle, average frequency, steel base, 4-1/2" x 3-1/2", US10					71			71	78
0400	Olive knuckle, low frequency, brass base, 6" x 4-1/2", US10					129			129	142
1000	Electric hinge with concealed conductor, average frequency									
1010	Steel base, 4-1/2" x 4-1/2", US26D				Pr.	235			235	259
1100	Bronze base, 4-1/2" x 4-1/2", US26D				"	244			244	268
1200	Electric hinge with concealed conductor, high frequency									
1210	Steel base, 4-1/2" x 4-1/2", US26D				Pr.	175			175	193
1600	Double weight, 800 lb., steel base, removable pin, 5" x 6", USP					111			111	122
1700	Steel base-welded pin, 5" x 6", USP					123			123	135
1800	Triple weight, 2000 lb., steel base, welded pin, 5" x 6", USP					128			128	141
2000	Pivot reinf., high frequency, steel base, 7-3/4" door plate, USP					142			142	156
2200	Bronze base, 7-3/4" door plate, US10					173			173	190
3000	Swing clear, full mortise, full or half surface, high frequency,									
3010	Steel base, 5" high, USP				Pr.	119			119	131
3200	Swing clear, full mortise, average frequency									
3210	Steel base, 4-1/2" high, USP				Pr.	94.50			94.50	104
4000	Wide throw, average frequency, steel base, 4-1/2" x 6", USP					72			72	79.50
4200	High frequency, steel base, 4-1/2" x 6", USP					110			110	121

087 | Hardware

087 100 | Finish Hardware

		Crew	Daily Output	Labor-Hours	Unit	Mat.	Labor	Equip.	Total	Total Incl O&P	
132	4600 Spring hinge, single acting, 6" flange, steel				Ea.	41			41	45.50	132
	4700 Brass					72.50			72.50	79.50	
	4900 Double acting, 6" flange, steel					74.50			74.50	82	
	4950 Brass					122			122	134	
	5000 T-strap, galvanized, 4"				Pr.	14.50			14.50	15.95	
	5010 T-strap, galvanized, 6"					23			23	25	
	5020 T-strap, galvanized, 8"					35			35	38.50	
	9000 Continuous hinge, steel, full mortise, heavy duty 501-85	2 Carp	64	.250	L.F.	10.30	6.80		17.10	23	
134	0010 **WINDOW HARDWARE**										134
	1000 Handles, surface mounted, aluminum	1 Carp	24	.333	Ea.	1.74	9.10		10.84	17.15	
	1020 Brass		24	.333		2.02	9.10		11.12	17.45	
	1040 Chrome		24	.333		1.84	9.10		10.94	17.25	
	1500 Recessed, aluminum		12	.667		1.01	18.20		19.21	31.50	
	1520 Brass		12	.667		1.12	18.20		19.32	31.50	
	1540 Chrome		12	.667		1.06	18.20		19.26	31.50	
	2000 Latches, aluminum		20	.400		1.45	10.90		12.35	19.90	
	2020 Brass		20	.400		1.74	10.90		12.64	20	
	2040 Chrome		20	.400		1.63	10.90		12.53	20	
	9000 Minimum labor/equipment charge		6	1.333	Job		36.50		36.50	61	

087 200 | Operators

		Crew	Daily Output	Labor-Hours	Unit	Mat.	Labor	Equip.	Total	Total Incl O&P	
202	0010 **AUTOMATIC OPENERS** Swing doors, single	2 Skwk	.80	20	Ea.	2,150	560		2,710	3,300	202
	0100 Single operating pair		.50	32	Pr.	4,000	900		4,900	5,900	
	0400 For double simultaneous doors, one way, add		1.20	13.333		335	375		710	990	
	0500 Two way, add		.90	17.778		415	500		915	1,275	
	1000 Sliding doors, 3' wide, including track & hanger, single		.60	26.667	Opng.	3,675	750		4,425	5,300	
	1300 Bi-parting		.50	32		4,425	900		5,325	6,375	
	1450 Activating carpet, single door, one way add		2.20	7.273		680	204		884	1,075	
	1550 Two way, add		1.30	12.308		975	345		1,320	1,650	
	1750 Handicap opener, button operating	1 Carp	1.50	5.333	Ea.	1,250	146		1,396	1,625	
206	0010 **DOOR CLOSER** Rack and pinion	1 Carp	6.50	1.231	Ea.	105	33.50		138.50	173	206
	0020 Adjustable backcheck, 3 way mount, all sizes, regular arm		6	1.333		111	36.50		147.50	183	
	0040 Hold open arm		6	1.333		121	36.50		157.50	194	
	0100 Fusible link		6.50	1.231		94	33.50		127.50	160	
	0200 Non sized, regular arm		6	1.333		105	36.50		141.50	177	
	0240 Hold open arm		6	1.333		131	36.50		167.50	205	
	0400 4 way mount, non sized, regular arm		6	1.333		144	36.50		180.50	219	
	0440 Hold open arm		6	1.333		155	36.50		191.50	232	
	2000 Backcheck and adjustable power, hinge face mount										
	2010 All sizes, regular arm	1 Carp	6.50	1.231	Ea.	133	33.50		166.50	203	
	2040 Hold open arm		6.50	1.231		143	33.50		176.50	214	
	2400 Top jamb mount, all sizes, regular arm		6	1.333		133	36.50		169.50	207	
	2440 Hold open arm		6	1.333		143	36.50		179.50	218	
	2800 Top face mount, all sizes, regular arm		6.50	1.231		132	33.50		165.50	203	
	2840 Hold open arm		6.50	1.231		142	33.50		175.50	214	
	4000 Backcheck, overhead concealed, all sizes, regular arm		5.50	1.455		140	39.50		179.50	221	
	4040 Concealed arm		5	1.600		150	43.50		193.50	237	
	4400 Compact overhead, concealed, all sizes, regular arm		5.50	1.455		255	39.50		294.50	350	
	4440 Concealed arm		5	1.600		266	43.50		309.50	365	
	4800 Concealed in door, all sizes, regular arm		5.50	1.455		94.50	39.50		134	171	
	4840 Concealed arm		5	1.600		102	43.50		145.50	185	
	4900 Floor concealed, all sizes, single acting		2.20	3.636		120	99.50		219.50	298	
	4940 Double acting		2.20	3.636		155	99.50		254.50	335	
	5000 For cast aluminum cylinder, deduct					12.70			12.70	14	

For expanded coverage of these items see *Means Interior Cost Data 1999*

087 | Hardware

087 200 | Operators

		CREW	DAILY OUTPUT	LABOR-HOURS	UNIT	MAT.	LABOR	EQUIP.	TOTAL	TOTAL INCL O&P	
206	5040	For delayed action, add				Ea.	22.50			22.50	24.50	206
	5080	For fusible link arm, add					9.20			9.20	10.15	
	5120	For shock absorbing arm, add					27.50			27.50	30.50	
	5160	For spring power adjustment, add					21			21	23.50	
	6000	Closer-holder, hinge face mount, all sizes, exposed arm	1 Carp	6.50	1.231		97.50	33.50		131	164	
	7000	Electronic closer-holder, hinge facemount, concealed arm		5	1.600		148	43.50		191.50	236	
	7400	With built-in detector		5	1.600		445	43.50		488.50	565	
	9000	Minimum labor/equipment charge		4	2	Job		54.50		54.50	91.50	

087 300 | Weatherstripping/Seals

		CREW	DAILY OUTPUT	LABOR-HOURS	UNIT	MAT.	LABOR	EQUIP.	TOTAL	TOTAL INCL O&P	
302	0010	**ASTRAGALS** One piece overlapping										302
	0400	Cadmium plated steel, flat, 3/16" x 2"	1 Carp	90	.089	L.F.	2.56	2.43		4.99	6.90	
	0600	Prime coated steel, flat, 1/8" x 3"		90	.089		3.56	2.43		5.99	8	
	0800	Stainless steel, flat, 3/32" x 1-5/8"		90	.089		13.35	2.43		15.78	18.75	
	1000	Aluminum, flat, 1/8" x 2"		90	.089		2.57	2.43		5	6.90	
	1200	Nail on, "T" extrusion		120	.067		.56	1.82		2.38	3.67	
	1300	Vinyl bulb insert		105	.076		.92	2.08		3	4.49	
	1600	Screw on, "T" extrusion		90	.089		3.75	2.43		6.18	8.20	
	1700	Vinyl insert		75	.107		2.52	2.91		5.43	7.65	
	2000	"L" extrusion, neoprene bulbs		75	.107		1.47	2.91		4.38	6.50	
	2100	Neoprene sponge insert		75	.107		4.45	2.91		7.36	9.75	
	2200	Magnetic		75	.107		7.35	2.91		10.26	12.90	
	2400	Spring hinged security seal, with cam		75	.107		4.71	2.91		7.62	10.05	
	2600	Spring loaded locking bolt, vinyl insert		45	.178		6.40	4.85		11.25	15.15	
	2800	Neoprene sponge strip, "Z" shaped, aluminum		60	.133		3.05	3.64		6.69	9.45	
	2900	Solid neoprene strip, nail on aluminum strip		90	.089		2.55	2.43		4.98	6.85	
	3000	One piece stile protection										
	3020	Neoprene fabric loop, nail on aluminum strips	1 Carp	60	.133	L.F.	.49	3.64		4.13	6.65	
	3110	Flush mounted aluminum extrusion, 1/2" x 1-1/4"		60	.133		2.44	3.64		6.08	8.80	
	3140	3/4" x 1-3/8"		60	.133		3.08	3.64		6.72	9.50	
	3160	1-1/8" x 1-3/4"		60	.133		4.92	3.64		8.56	11.50	
	3300	Mortise, 9/16" x 3/4"		60	.133		2.61	3.64		6.25	8.95	
	3320	13/16" x 1-3/8"		60	.133		2.83	3.64		6.47	9.20	
	3600	Spring bronze strip, nail on type		105	.076		2.23	2.08		4.31	5.95	
	3620	Screw on, with retainer		75	.107		1.82	2.91		4.73	6.85	
	3800	Flexible stainless steel housing, pile insert, 1/2" door		105	.076		5.05	2.08		7.13	9.05	
	3820	3/4" door		105	.076		5.65	2.08		7.73	9.75	
	4000	Extruded aluminum retainer, flush mount, pile insert		105	.076		1.76	2.08		3.84	5.40	
	4080	Mortise, felt insert		90	.089		3.14	2.43		5.57	7.50	
	4160	Mortise with spring, pile insert		90	.089		2.46	2.43		4.89	6.75	
	4400	Rigid vinyl retainer, mortise, pile insert		105	.076		1.75	2.08		3.83	5.40	
	4600	Wool pile filler strip, aluminum backing		105	.076		1.76	2.08		3.84	5.40	
	5000	Two piece overlapping astragal, extruded aluminum retainer										
	5010	Pile insert	1 Carp	60	.133	L.F.	2.29	3.64		5.93	8.60	
	5020	Vinyl bulb insert		60	.133		1.48	3.64		5.12	7.75	
	5040	Vinyl flap insert		60	.133		4.58	3.64		8.22	11.15	
	5060	Solid neoprene flap insert		60	.133		4.53	3.64		8.17	11.10	
	5080	Hypalon rubber flap insert		60	.133		4.63	3.64		8.27	11.20	
	5090	Snap on cover, pile insert		60	.133		5.30	3.64		8.94	11.95	
	5400	Magnetic aluminum, surface mounted		60	.133		17.90	3.64		21.54	26	
	5500	Interlocking aluminum, 5/8" x 1" neoprene bulb insert		45	.178		2.84	4.85		7.69	11.20	
	5600	Adjustable aluminum, 9/16" x 21/32", pile insert		45	.178		13.50	4.85		18.35	23	
	5790	For vinyl bulb, deduct					.37			.37	.41	
	5800	Magnetic, adjustable, 9/16" x 21/32"	1 Carp	45	.178		17.35	4.85		22.20	27	
	6000	Two piece stile protection										
	6010	Cloth backed rubber loop, 1" gap, nail on aluminum strips	1 Carp	45	.178	L.F.	2.91	4.85		7.76	11.30	

Important: See the Reference Section for critical supporting data - Reference Nos., Crews, & City Cost Indexes

087 | Hardware

087 300 | Weatherstripping/Seals

			CREW	DAILY OUTPUT	LABOR-HOURS	UNIT	1999 BARE COSTS MAT.	LABOR	EQUIP.	TOTAL	TOTAL INCL O&P	
302	6040	Screw on aluminum strips	1 Carp	45	.178	L.F.	4.53	4.85		9.38	13.10	302
	6100	1-1/2" gap, screw on aluminum extrusion		45	.178		4.08	4.85		8.93	12.60	
	6240	Vinyl fabric loop, slotted aluminum extrusion, 1" gap		45	.178		1.45	4.85		6.30	9.70	
	6300	1-1/4" gap		45	.178		4.30	4.85		9.15	12.85	
304	0010	THRESHOLD 3' long door saddles, aluminum	1 Carp	48	.167	L.F.	3.35	4.55		7.90	11.30	304
	0100	Aluminum, 8" wide, 1/2" thick		12	.667	Ea.	28.50	18.20		46.70	62	
	0500	Bronze		60	.133	L.F.	27	3.64		30.64	35.50	
	0600	Bronze, panic threshold, 5" wide, 1/2" thick		12	.667	Ea.	56	18.20		74.20	92	
	0700	Rubber, 1/2" thick, 5-1/2" wide		20	.400		28.50	10.90		39.40	49.50	
	0800	2-3/4" wide		20	.400		13.15	10.90		24.05	33	
	9000	Minimum labor/equipment charge		4	2	Job		54.50		54.50	91.50	
306	0010	WEATHERSTRIPPING Window, double hung, 3' x 5', zinc	1 Carp	7.20	1.111	Opng.	10.60	30.50		41.10	62.50	306
	0100	Bronze		7.20	1.111	"	19.25	30.50		49.75	72	
	0200	Vinyl V strip		7	1.143	Opng.	3.47	31		34.47	56	
	0500	As above but heavy duty, zinc		4.60	1.739		12.85	47.50		60.35	93.50	
	0600	Bronze		4.60	1.739		22.50	47.50		70	104	
	1000	Doors, wood frame, interlocking, for 3' x 7' door, zinc		3	2.667		11.55	73		84.55	135	
	1100	Bronze		3	2.667		18.15	73		91.15	142	
	1300	6' x 7' opening, zinc		2	4		12.60	109		121.60	197	
	1400	Bronze		2	4		24	109		133	209	
	1700	Wood frame, spring type, bronze										
	1800	3' x 7' door	1 Carp	7.60	1.053	Opng.	15.30	28.50		43.80	65	
	1900	6' x 7' door	"	7	1.143	"	16.25	31		47.25	70	
	2200	Metal frame, spring type, bronze										
	2300	3' x 7' door	1 Carp	3	2.667	Opng.	25.50	73		98.50	150	
	2400	6' x 7' door	"	2.50	3.200	"	34.50	87.50		122	184	
	2500	For stainless steel, spring type, add					133%					
	2700	Metal frame, extruded sections, 3' x 7' door, aluminum	1 Carp	2	4	Opng.	33.50	109		142.50	220	
	2800	Bronze		2	4		84.50	109		193.50	276	
	3100	6' x 7' door, aluminum		1.20	6.667		42.50	182		224.50	350	
	3200	Bronze		1.20	6.667		100	182		282	415	
	3500	Threshold weatherstripping										
	3650	Door sweep, flush mounted, aluminum	1 Carp	25	.320	Ea.	9.90	8.75		18.65	25.50	
	3700	Vinyl		25	.320		11.75	8.75		20.50	27.50	
	5000	Garage door bottom weatherstrip, 12' aluminum, clear		14	.571		15.90	15.60		31.50	43.50	
	5010	Bronze		14	.571		60.50	15.60		76.10	92.50	
	5050	Bottom protection, 12' aluminum, clear		14	.571		19.25	15.60		34.85	47	
	5100	Bronze		14	.571		75	15.60		90.60	109	
	9000	Minimum labor/equipment charge		3	2.667	Job		73		73	122	

087 500 | Door/Window Acces.

			CREW	DAILY OUTPUT	LABOR-HOURS	UNIT	MAT.	LABOR	EQUIP.	TOTAL	TOTAL INCL O&P	
506	0010	DOOR ACCESSORIES										506
	1000	Knockers, brass, standard	1 Carp	16	.500	Ea.	34.50	13.65		48.15	61	
	1100	Deluxe		10	.800		107	22		129	155	
	4000	Security chain, standard		18	.444		5.95	12.15		18.10	27	
	4100	Deluxe		18	.444		35.50	12.15		47.65	60	
	9000	Minimum labor/equipment charge		6	1.333	Job		36.50		36.50	61	

For expanded coverage of these items see *Means Interior Cost Data 1999*

088 | Glazing

088 100 | Glass

			CREW	DAILY OUTPUT	LABOR-HOURS	UNIT	MAT.	LABOR	EQUIP.	TOTAL	TOTAL INCL O&P	
112	0010	**CURTAIN WALL** See division 089-200										112
118	0010	**FLOAT GLASS** 3/16" thick, clear, plain	2 Glaz	130	.123	S.F.	3.35	3.27		6.62	9	118
	0200	Tempered, clear		130	.123		4	3.27		7.27	9.70	
	0300	Tinted		130	.123		5	3.27		8.27	10.80	
	0600	1/4" thick, clear, plain		120	.133		4.22	3.55		7.77	10.40	
	0700	Tinted		120	.133		4	3.55		7.55	10.15	
	0800	Tempered, clear		120	.133		5	3.55		8.55	11.25	
	0900	Tinted		120	.133		6.95	3.55		10.50	13.40	
	1600	3/8" thick, clear, plain		75	.213		6.65	5.65		12.30	16.50	
	1700	Tinted		75	.213		8	5.65		13.65	18	
	1800	Tempered, clear		75	.213		10	5.65		15.65	20	
	1900	Tinted		75	.213		12.45	5.65		18.10	23	
	2200	1/2" thick, clear, plain		55	.291		13.05	7.75		20.80	27	
	2300	Tinted		55	.291		14	7.75		21.75	28	
	2400	Tempered, clear		55	.291		15	7.75		22.75	29	
	2500	Tinted		55	.291		18.70	7.75		26.45	33	
	2800	5/8" thick, clear, plain		45	.356		14	9.45		23.45	31	
	2900	Tempered, clear		45	.356		16	9.45		25.45	33	
	3200	3/4" thick, clear, plain		35	.457		18	12.15		30.15	39.50	
	3300	Tempered, clear		35	.457		21	12.15		33.15	43	
	3600	1" thick, clear, plain		30	.533		30	14.20		44.20	56	
	8900	For low emissivity coating for 3/16" and 1/4" only, add to above					3					
	9000	Minimum labor/equipment charge	1 Glaz	2	4	Job		106		106	173	
120	0010	**FULL VISION** Window system with 3/4" glass mullions, 10' high	H-2	130	.185	S.F.	39.50	4.59		44.09	51	120
	0100	10' to 20' high, minimum		110	.218	"	41.50	5.45		46.95	55	
	0150	Average		100	.240	S.F.	45	5.95		50.95	59.50	
	0200	Maximum		80	.300	"	50.50	7.45		57.95	67.50	
	9000	Minimum labor/equipment charge	1 Glaz	2	4	Job		106		106	173	
128	0010	**GLAZING VARIABLES** R088-010										128
	0500	For high rise glazing, from exterior, add per S.F. per story				S.F.					.09	
	0600	For glass replacement, add				"		100%				
	0700	For gasket settings, add				L.F.	3			3	3.30	
	0800	For concrete reglet settings, add				S.F.	20%	25%				
	0900	For sloped glazing, add				"		25%				
	2000	Fabrication, polished edges, 1/4" thick				Inch	.25			.25	.28	
	2100	1/2" thick					.66			.66	.73	
	2500	Mitered edges, 1/4" thick					.66			.66	.73	
	2600	1/2" thick					1.06			1.06	1.17	
132	0010	**INSULATING GLASS** 2 lites 1/8" float, 1/2" thk, under 15 S.F. R088-010										132
	0020	Clear	2 Glaz	95	.168	S.F.	5.80	4.48		10.28	13.65	
	0100	Tinted		95	.168		8.60	4.48		13.08	16.75	
	0200	2 lites 3/16" float, for 5/8" thk unit, 15 to 30 S.F., clear		90	.178		7	4.73		11.73	15.35	
	0400	1" thk, dbl. glazed, 1/4" float, 30-70 S.F., clear		75	.213		9.95	5.65		15.60	20	
	0500	Tinted		75	.213		12	5.65		17.65	22.50	
	2000	Both lites, light & heat reflective		85	.188		16	5		21	25.50	
	2500	Heat reflective, film inside, 1" thick unit, clear		85	.188		14	5		19	23.50	
	2600	Tinted		85	.188		15.10	5		20.10	24.50	
	3000	Film on weatherside, clear, 1/2" thick unit		95	.168		10	4.48		14.48	18.25	
	3100	5/8" thick unit		90	.178		12.65	4.73		17.38	21.50	
	3200	1" thick unit		85	.188		13.80	5		18.80	23.50	
	3350	Minimum	1 Glaz	50	.160		7.80	4.26		12.06	15.50	
	3360	Maximum	"	25	.320		8.45	8.50		16.95	23	
	3370	Reflective or tinted, add					2.15			2.15	2.37	
	9000	Minimum labor/equipment charge	1 Glaz	2	4	Job		106		106	173	

Important: See the Reference Section for critical supporting data - Reference Nos., Crews, & City Cost Indexes

088 | Glazing

088 100 | Glass

			CREW	DAILY OUTPUT	LABOR-HOURS	UNIT	1999 BARE COSTS MAT.	LABOR	EQUIP.	TOTAL	TOTAL INCL O&P	
136	0010	**LAMINATED GLASS** Clear float, .03" vinyl, 1/4" thick	2 Glaz	90	.178	S.F.	6.75	4.73		11.48	15.05	136
	0100	3/8" thick		78	.205		10.95	5.45		16.40	21	
	0200	.06" vinyl, 1/2" thick		65	.246		12.80	6.55		19.35	24.50	
	1000	5/8" thick		90	.178		15	4.73		19.73	24	
	2000	Bullet-resisting, 1-3/16" thick, to 15 S.F.		16	1		33	26.50		59.50	79.50	
	2100	Over 15 S.F.		16	1		29.50	26.50		56	75	
	2500	2-1/4" thick, to 15 S.F.		12	1.333		48.50	35.50		84	111	
	2600	Over 15 S.F.	▼	12	1.333	▼	43	35.50		78.50	105	
144	0010	**MIRRORS** No frames, wall type, 1/4" plate glass, polished edge										144
	0100	Up to 5 S.F.	2 Glaz	125	.128	S.F.	5.50	3.40		8.90	11.55	
	0200	Over 5 S.F.		160	.100		5.35	2.66		8.01	10.15	
	0500	Door type, 1/4" plate glass, up to 12 S.F.		160	.100		5.70	2.66		8.36	10.60	
	1000	Float glass, up to 10 S.F., 1/8" thick		160	.100		3.36	2.66		6.02	8	
	1100	3/16" thick		150	.107		3.91	2.84		6.75	8.90	
	1500	12" x 12" wall tiles, square edge, clear		195	.082		1.43	2.18		3.61	5.10	
	1600	Veined		195	.082		3.65	2.18		5.83	7.55	
	2000	1/4" thick, stock sizes, one way transparent		125	.128		12.45	3.40		15.85	19.20	
	2010	Bathroom, unframed, laminated		160	.100		9.55	2.66		12.21	14.80	
	2500	Tempered	▼	160	.100	▼	10.10	2.66		12.76	15.40	
160	0010	**REFLECTIVE GLASS** 1/4" float with fused metallic oxide, tinted	2 Glaz	115	.139	S.F.	8.30	3.70		12	15.15	160
	0500	1/4" float glass with reflective applied coating		115	.139		6.95	3.70		10.65	13.65	
	2000	Solar film on glass, not including glass, minimum		180	.089		3.35	2.36		5.71	7.50	
	2050	Maximum	▼	225	.071	▼	7.75	1.89		9.64	11.60	
176	0010	**WINDOW GLASS** Clear float, stops, putty bed, 1/8" thick	2 Glaz	480	.033	S.F.	2.75	.89		3.64	4.47	176
	0500	3/16" thick, clear		480	.033		3.40	.89		4.29	5.20	
	0600	Tinted		480	.033		3.85	.89		4.74	5.65	
	0700	Tempered		480	.033		4.66	.89		5.55	6.60	
	2000	Replace broken window lite, 1/8" glass (9 S.F. maximum)	1 Glaz	48	.167		3.22	4.43		7.65	10.75	
	2100	1/4" plate (16 S.F. maximum)	"	48	.167	▼	3.55	4.43		7.98	11.10	
	9000	Minimum labor/equipment charge	2 Glaz	5	3.200	Job		85		85	138	
184	0010	**WIRE GLASS** 1/4" thick, rough obscure (chicken wire)	2 Glaz	135	.119	S.F.	9.40	3.15		12.55	15.45	184
	1000	Polished wire, 1/4" thick, diamond, clear		135	.119		12.15	3.15		15.30	18.45	
	1500	Pinstripe, obscure	▼	135	.119	▼	11.40	3.15		14.55	17.60	

088 400 | Plastic Glazing

			CREW	DAILY OUTPUT	LABOR-HOURS	UNIT	MAT.	LABOR	EQUIP.	TOTAL	INCL O&P	
404	0010	**PLEXIGLASS ACRYLIC** Clear, masked, 1/8" thick, cut sheets	2 Glaz	170	.094	S.F.	2.76	2.50		5.26	7.10	404
	0200	Full sheets		195	.082		1.44	2.18		3.62	5.10	
	0500	1/4" thick, cut sheets		165	.097		4.88	2.58		7.46	9.55	
	0600	Full sheets		185	.086		2.66	2.30		4.96	6.65	
	0900	3/8" thick, cut sheets		155	.103		8.95	2.75		11.70	14.30	
	1000	Full sheets		180	.089		4.82	2.36		7.18	9.15	
	1300	1/2" thick, cut sheets		135	.119		10.30	3.15		13.45	16.45	
	1400	Full sheets		150	.107		10	2.84		12.84	15.60	
	1700	3/4" thick, cut sheets		115	.139		36.50	3.70		40.20	46	
	1800	Full sheets		130	.123		21	3.27		24.27	28.50	
	2100	1" thick, cut sheets		105	.152		41	4.05		45.05	52	
	2200	Full sheets		125	.128		25.50	3.40		28.90	33.50	
	3000	Colored, 1/8" thick, cut sheets		170	.094		8.50	2.50		11	13.40	
	3200	Full sheets		195	.082		5.50	2.18		7.68	9.60	
	3500	1/4" thick, cut sheets		165	.097		9.50	2.58		12.08	14.65	
	3600	Full sheets		185	.086		6.50	2.30		8.80	10.90	
	4000	Mirrors, untinted, cut sheets, 1/8" thick		185	.086		4	2.30		6.30	8.15	
	4200	1/4" thick	▼	180	.089		7.25	2.36		9.61	11.85	

For expanded coverage of these items see *Means Interior Cost Data 1999*

088 | Glazing

088 400 | Plastic Glazing

		CREW	DAILY OUTPUT	LABOR-HOURS	UNIT	1999 BARE COSTS MAT.	LABOR	EQUIP.	TOTAL	TOTAL INCL O&P
0010	**POLYCARBONATE** Clear, masked, cut sheets, 1/8" thick	2 Glaz	170	.094	S.F.	4.75	2.50		7.25	9.25
0500	3/16" thick		165	.097		5.75	2.58		8.33	10.55
1000	1/4" thick		155	.103		6.35	2.75		9.10	11.45
1500	3/8" thick		150	.107		11.70	2.84		14.54	17.50
9000	Minimum labor/equipment charge	1 Glaz	2	4	Job		106		106	173

089 | Glazed Curtain Walls

089 200 | Glazed Curtain Wall

		CREW	DAILY OUTPUT	LABOR-HOURS	UNIT	1999 BARE COSTS MAT.	LABOR	EQUIP.	TOTAL	TOTAL INCL O&P
0010	**TUBE FRAMING** For window walls and store fronts, aluminum, stock									
0050	Plain tube frame, mill finish, 1-3/4" x 1-3/4"	2 Glaz	103	.155	L.F.	6	4.13		10.13	13.30
0150	1-3/4" x 4"		98	.163		7.50	4.34		11.84	15.30
0200	1-3/4" x 4-1/2"		95	.168		8.35	4.48		12.83	16.40
0250	2" x 6"		89	.180		12.60	4.78		17.38	21.50
0350	4" x 4"		87	.184		12.35	4.89		17.24	21.50
0400	4-1/2" x 4-1/2"		85	.188		13.80	5		18.80	23.50
0450	Glass bead		240	.067		1.59	1.77		3.36	4.63
1000	Flush tube frame, mill finish, 1/4" glass, 1-3/4" x 4", open header		80	.200		7.40	5.30		12.70	16.75
1050	Open sill		82	.195		6.40	5.20		11.60	15.45
1100	Closed back header		83	.193		10.35	5.15		15.50	19.65
1150	Closed back sill		85	.188		9.80	5		14.80	18.90
1200	Vertical mullion, one piece		75	.213		10.95	5.65		16.60	21
1250	Two piece		73	.219		11.70	5.85		17.55	22.50
1300	90° or 180° vertical corner post		75	.213		18.40	5.65		24.05	29.50
1400	1-3/4" x 4-1/2", open header		80	.200		9	5.30		14.30	18.55
1450	Open sill		82	.195		7.45	5.20		12.65	16.55
1500	Closed back header		83	.193		11.40	5.15		16.55	21
1550	Closed back sill		85	.188		10.60	5		15.60	19.75
1600	Vertical mullion, one piece		75	.213		11.80	5.65		17.45	22
1650	Two piece		73	.219		12.50	5.85		18.35	23
1700	90° or 180° vertical corner post		75	.213		12.80	5.65		18.45	23.50
2000	Flush tube frame, mill fin. for ins. glass, 2" x 4-1/2", open header		75	.213		10.50	5.65		16.15	21
2050	Open sill		77	.208		9.20	5.55		14.75	19.05
2100	Closed back header		78	.205		11.45	5.45		16.90	21.50
2150	Closed back sill		80	.200		11.30	5.30		16.60	21
2200	Vertical mullion, one piece		70	.229		12.70	6.10		18.80	24
2250	Two piece		68	.235		13.55	6.25		19.80	25
2300	90° or 180° vertical corner post		70	.229		12.80	6.10		18.90	24
5000	Flush tube frame, mill fin., thermal brk., 2-1/4"x 4-1/2", open header		74	.216		11.55	5.75		17.30	22
5050	Open sill		75	.213		10.10	5.65		15.75	20.50
5100	Vertical mullion, one piece		69	.232		13.95	6.15		20.10	25.50
5150	Two piece		67	.239		14.90	6.35		21.25	26.50
5200	90° or 180° vertical corner post		69	.232		13.40	6.15		19.55	25
6980	Door stop (snap in)		380	.042		2.16	1.12		3.28	4.20
7000	For joints, 90°, clip type, add				Ea.	18.45			18.45	20.50
7050	Screw spline joint, add					13.90			13.90	15.30
7100	For joint other than 90°, add					29			29	32
8000	For bronze anodized aluminum, add					15%				
8020	For black finish, add					27%				

089 | Glazed Curtain Walls

089 200 | Glazed Curtain Wall

			CREW	DAILY OUTPUT	LABOR-HOURS	UNIT	1999 BARE COSTS MAT.	LABOR	EQUIP.	TOTAL	TOTAL INCL O&P	
204	8050	For stainless steel materials, add					350%					204
	8100	For monumental grade, add					50%					
	8150	For steel stiffener, add	2 Glaz	200	.080	L.F.	7.10	2.13		9.23	11.25	
	8200	For 2 to 5 stories, add per story				Story		5%				
	9000	Minimum labor/equipment charge	2 Glaz	2	8	Job		213		213	345	
206	0010	**WINDOW WALLS** Aluminum, stock, including glazing, minimum	H-2	160	.150	S.F.	24.50	3.73		28.23	32.50	206
	0050	Average		140	.171	"	29.50	4.27		33.77	39.50	
	0100	Maximum	▼	110	.218	S.F.	93	5.45		98.45	111	
	0500	For translucent sandwich wall systems, see div. 074-104										
	0850	Cost of the above walls depends on material,										
	0860	finish, repetition, and size of units.										
	0870	The larger the opening, the lower the S.F. cost										
	1200	Double glazed acoustical window wall for airports,										
	1220	including 1" thick glass with 2" x 4-1/2" tube frame	H-2	40	.600	S.F.	60.50	14.95		75.45	91	

For information about Means Estimating Seminars, see yellow pages 11 and 12 in back of book

For expanded coverage of these items see *Means Interior Cost Data 1999*

Division Notes

Division 9 Finishes

Estimating Tips
General
- **Room Finish Schedule:** A complete set of plans should contain a room finish schedule. If one is not available, it would be well worth the time and effort to put one together. A room finish schedule should contain the room number, room name (for clarity), floor materials, base materials, wainscot materials, wainscot height, wall materials (for each wall), ceiling materials and special instructions.
- **Surplus Finishes:** Review the specifications to determine if there is any requirement to provide certain amounts of extra materials for the owner's maintenance department. In some cases the owner may require a substantial amount of materials, especially when it is a special order item or long lead time item.

092 Lath, Plaster & Gypsum Board
- Lath is estimated by the square yard for both gypsum and metal lath, plus usually 5% allowance for waste. Furring, channels and accessories are measured by the linear foot. An extra foot should be allowed for each accessory miter or stop.
- Plaster is also estimated by the square yard. Deductions for openings vary by preference, from zero deduction to 50% of all openings over 2 feet in width. Some estimators deduct a percentage of the total yardage for openings. The estimator should allow one extra square foot for each linear foot of horizontal interior or exterior angle located below the ceiling level. Also, double the areas of small radius work.
- Each room should be measured, perimeter times maximum wall height. Ceiling areas are equal to length times width.
- Drywall accessories, studs, track, and acoustical caulking are all measured by the linear foot. Drywall taping is figured by the square foot. Gypsum wallboard is estimated by the square foot. No material deductions should be made for door or window openings under 32 S.F. Coreboard can be obtained in a 1" thickness for solid wall and shaft work. Additions should be made to price out the inside or outside corners.
- Different types of partition construction should be listed separately on the quantity sheets. There may be walls with studs of various widths, double studded, and similar or dissimilar surface materials. Shaft work is usually different construction from surrounding partitions requiring separate quantities and pricing of the work.

093 Tile
094 Terrazzo
- Tile and terrazzo areas are taken off on a square foot basis. Trim and base materials are measured by the linear foot. Accent tiles are listed per each. Two basic methods of installation are used. Mud set is approximately 30% more expensive than the thin set. In terrazzo work, be sure to include the linear footage of embedded decorative strips, grounds, machine rubbing and power cleanup.

095 Acoustical Treatment & Wood Flooring
- Acoustical systems fall into several categories. The takeoff of these materials is by the square foot of area with a 5% allowance for waste. Do not forget about scaffolding, if applicable, when estimating these systems.
- Wood flooring is available in strip, parquet, or block configuration. The latter two types are set in adhesives with quantities estimated by the square foot. The laying pattern will influence labor costs and material waste. In addition to the material and labor for laying wood floors, the estimator must make allowances for sanding and finishing these areas unless the flooring is prefinished.

096 Flooring & Carpet
- Most of the various types of flooring are all measured on a square foot basis. Base is measured by the linear foot. If adhesive materials are to be quantified, they are estimated at a specified coverage rate by the gallon depending upon the specified type and the manufacturer's recommendations.
- Sheet flooring is measured by the square yard. Roll widths vary, so consideration should be given to use the most economical width, as waste must be figured into the total quantity. Consider also the installation methods available, direct glue down or stretched.

099 Painting & Wall Coverings
- Painting is one area where bids vary to a greater extent than almost any other section of a project. This arises from the many methods of measuring surfaces to be painted. The estimator should check the plans and specifications carefully to be sure of the required number of coats.
- Protection of adjacent surfaces is not included in painting costs. When considering the method of paint application, an important factor is the amount of protection and masking required. These must be estimated separately and may be the determining factor in choosing the method of application.
- Wall coverings are estimated by the square foot. The area to be covered is measured, length by height of wall above baseboards, to calculate the square footage of each wall. This figure is divided by the number of square feet in the single roll which is being used. Deduct, in full, the areas of openings such as doors and windows. Where a pattern match is required allow 25%-30% waste. One gallon of paste should be sufficient to hang 12 single rolls of light to medium weight paper.

Reference Numbers
Reference numbers are shown in bold squares at the beginning of some major classifications. These numbers refer to related items in the Reference Section. The reference information may be an estimating procedure, an alternate pricing method or technical information.

Note: Not all subdivisions listed here necessarily appear in this publication.

091 | Metal Support Systems

091 300 | Suspension Systems

		CREW	DAILY OUTPUT	LABOR-HOURS	UNIT	1999 BARE COSTS				TOTAL INCL O&P
						MAT.	LABOR	EQUIP.	TOTAL	
0010	**SUSPENSION SYSTEMS** For boards and tile									
0050	Class A suspension system, 15/16" T bar, 2' x 4' grid	1 Carp	800	.010	S.F.	.31	.27		.58	.80
0300	2' x 2' grid	"	650	.012		.39	.34		.73	.99
0350	For 9/16" grid, add					.13			.13	.14
0360	For fire rated grid, add					.07			.07	.08
0370	For colored grid, add					.15			.15	.17
0400	Concealed Z bar suspension system, 12" module	1 Carp	520	.015		.34	.42		.76	1.07
0600	1-1/2" carrier channels, 4' O.C., add	"	470	.017		.17	.46		.63	.97
0700	Carrier channels for ceilings with									
0900	recessed lighting fixtures, add	1 Carp	460	.017	S.F.	.33	.47		.80	1.15
9000	Minimum labor/equipment charge	"	5	1.600	Job		43.50		43.50	73

092 | Lath, Plaster & Gypsum Board

092 050 | Furring & Lathing

		CREW	DAILY OUTPUT	LABOR-HOURS	UNIT	1999 BARE COSTS				TOTAL INCL O&P
						MAT.	LABOR	EQUIP.	TOTAL	
0010	**FURRING** Beams & columns, 3/4" galvanized channels,									
0030	12" O.C.	1 Lath	155	.052	S.F.	.21	1.38		1.59	2.44
0050	16" O.C.		170	.047		.17	1.26		1.43	2.21
0070	24" O.C.		185	.043		.11	1.16		1.27	1.98
0100	Ceilings, on steel, 3/4" channels, galvanized, 12" O.C.		210	.038		.19	1.02		1.21	1.84
0300	16" O.C.		290	.028		.17	.74		.91	1.37
0400	24" O.C.		420	.019		.11	.51		.62	.95
0600	1-1/2" channels, galvanized, 12" O.C.		190	.042		.26	1.13		1.39	2.09
0700	16" O.C.		260	.031		.23	.82		1.05	1.58
0900	24" O.C.		390	.021		.16	.55		.71	1.05
1000	Walls, 3/4" channels, galvanized, 12" O.C.		235	.034		.19	.91		1.10	1.67
1200	16" O.C.		265	.030		.17	.81		.98	1.48
1300	24" O.C.		350	.023		.11	.61		.72	1.11
1500	1-1/2" channels, galvanized, 12" O.C.		210	.038		.26	1.02		1.28	1.92
1600	16" O.C.		240	.033		.23	.89		1.12	1.69
1800	24" O.C.		305	.026		.16	.70		.86	1.29
8000	Suspended ceilings, including carriers									
8200	1-1/2" carriers, 24" O.C. with:									
8300	3/4" channels, 16" O.C.	1 Lath	165	.048	S.F.	.51	1.30		1.81	2.64
8320	24" O.C.		200	.040		.45	1.07		1.52	2.21
8400	1-1/2" channels, 16" O.C.		155	.052		.57	1.38		1.95	2.84
8420	24" O.C.		190	.042		.50	1.13		1.63	2.35
8600	2" carriers, 24" O.C. with:									
8700	3/4" channels, 16" O.C.	1 Lath	155	.052	S.F.	.17	1.38		1.55	2.40
8720	24" O.C.		190	.042		.12	1.13		1.25	1.93
8800	1-1/2" channels, 16" O.C.		145	.055		.59	1.48		2.07	3.01
8820	24" O.C.		180	.044		.52	1.19		1.71	2.47
9000	Minimum labor/equipment charge		4	2	Job		53.50		53.50	85.50
0010	**GYPSUM LATH** Plain or perforated, nailed, 3/8" thick	1 Lath	85	.094	S.Y.	3.38	2.52		5.90	7.75
0100	1/2" thick, nailed		80	.100		3.96	2.68		6.64	8.65
0300	Clipped to steel studs, 3/8" thick		75	.107		3.78	2.86		6.64	8.75
0400	1/2" thick		70	.114		3.96	3.06		7.02	9.25
0600	Firestop gypsum base, to steel studs, 3/8" thick		70	.114		3.96	3.06		7.02	9.25
0700	1/2" thick		65	.123		4.05	3.30		7.35	9.70

092 | Lath, Plaster & Gypsum Board

092 050 | Furring & Lathing

			CREW	DAILY OUTPUT	LABOR-HOURS	UNIT	1999 BARE COSTS MAT.	LABOR	EQUIP.	TOTAL	TOTAL INCL O&P	
056	0900	Foil back, to steel studs, 3/8" thick	1 Lath	75	.107	S.Y.	3.69	2.86		6.55	8.65	056
	1000	1/2" thick		70	.114		3.78	3.06		6.84	9.05	
	1500	For ceiling installations, add		216	.037			.99		.99	1.59	
	1600	For columns and beams, add		170	.047			1.26		1.26	2.02	
	9000	Minimum labor/equipment charge		4.25	1.882	Job		50.50		50.50	80.50	
058	0010	**METAL LATH** Diamond, expanded, 2.5 lb. per S.Y., painted				S.Y.	1.63			1.63	1.79	058
	0100	Galvanized, 2.5 lb. per S.Y.					1.87			1.87	2.06	
	0300	3.4 lb. per S.Y., painted					1.91			1.91	2.10	
	0400	Galvanized					2.10			2.10	2.31	
	0600	For 15# asphalt sheathing paper, add					.24			.24	.27	
	0900	Flat rib, 1/8" high, 2.75 lb., painted					1.54			1.54	1.69	
	1000	Foil backed					2			2	2.20	
	1200	3.4 lb. per S.Y., painted					1.87			1.87	2.05	
	1300	Galvanized					2.75			2.75	3.03	
	1500	For 15# asphalt sheating paper, add					.24			.24	.27	
	1800	High rib, 3/8" high, 3.4 lb. per S.Y., painted					2.89			2.89	3.18	
	1900	Galvanized					3.73			3.73	4.10	
	2400	High rib, 3/4" high, painted, .60 lb. per S.F.				S.F.	.53			.53	.58	
	2500	.75 lb. per S.F.				"	.66			.66	.73	
	2700	Stucco mesh, painted, 1.8 lb.				S.Y.	3.03			3.03	3.33	
	2800	3.6 lb.					3.36			3.36	3.70	
	3000	K-lath, perforated, absorbent paper, regular					2.33			2.33	2.56	
	3100	Heavy duty					2.75			2.75	3.03	
	3300	Waterproof, heavy duty, grade B backing					2.70			2.70	2.97	
	3400	Fire resistant backing					2.98			2.98	3.28	
	3600	2.5 lb. diamond painted, on wood framing, on walls	1 Lath	85	.094		1.63	2.52		4.15	5.80	
	3700	On ceilings		75	.107		1.63	2.86		4.49	6.35	
	3900	3.4 lb. diamond painted, on wood framing, on walls		80	.100		1.87	2.68		4.55	6.35	
	4000	On ceilings		70	.114		1.87	3.06		4.93	6.95	
	4200	3.4 lb. diamond painted, wired to steel framing		75	.107		1.87	2.86		4.73	6.60	
	4300	On ceilings		60	.133		1.87	3.57		5.44	7.75	
	4600	Cornices, wired to steel		35	.229		1.87	6.15		8.02	11.85	
	4800	Screwed to steel studs, 2.5 lb.		80	.100		1.63	2.68		4.31	6.05	
	4900	3.4 lb.		75	.107		1.91	2.86		4.77	6.65	
	5100	Rib lath, painted, wired to steel, on walls, 2.5 lb.		75	.107		1.54	2.86		4.40	6.25	
	5200	3.4 lb.		70	.114		2.89	3.06		5.95	8.10	
	5400	4.0 lb.		65	.123		2.52	3.30		5.82	8	
	5500	For self-furring lath, add					.06			.06	.07	
	5700	Suspended ceiling system, incl. 3.4 lb. diamond lath, painted	1 Lath	15	.533		8.65	14.30		22.95	32.50	
	5800	Galvanized	"	15	.533		8.90	14.30		23.20	33	
	6000	Hollow metal stud partitions, 3.4 lb. painted lath both sides										
	6010	Non-load bearing, 25 ga., w/rib lath 2-1/2" studs, 12" O.C.	1 Lath	20.30	.394	S.Y.	7.80	10.55		18.35	25.50	
	6300	16" O.C.		21.10	.379		7.30	10.15		17.45	24.50	
	6350	24" O.C.		22.70	.352		6.90	9.45		16.35	22.50	
	6400	3-5/8" studs, 16" O.C.		19.50	.410		7.50	11		18.50	26	
	6600	24" O.C.		20.40	.392		7.05	10.50		17.55	24.50	
	6700	4" studs, 16" O.C.		20.40	.392		8.25	10.50		18.75	26	
	6900	24" O.C.		21.60	.370		7.25	9.95		17.20	24	
	7000	6" studs, 16" O.C.		19.50	.410		8.25	11		19.25	26.50	
	7100	24" O.C.		21.10	.379		7.65	10.15		17.80	24.50	
	7200	L.B. partitions, 16 ga., w/rib lath, 2-1/2" studs, 16" O.C.		20	.400		9.20	10.70		19.90	27.50	
	7300	3-5/8" studs, 16 ga.		19.70	.406		10.55	10.90		21.45	29	
	7500	4" studs, 16 ga.		19.50	.410		11	11		22	29.50	
	7600	6" studs, 16 ga.		18.70	.428		12.65	11.45		24.10	32.50	
	9000	Minimum labor/equipment charge		4.25	1.882	Job		50.50		50.50	80.50	

For expanded coverage of these items see Means Interior Cost Data 1999

092 | Lath, Plaster & Gypsum Board

092 100 | Gypsum Plaster

		CREW	DAILY OUTPUT	LABOR-HOURS	UNIT	MAT.	LABOR	EQUIP.	TOTAL	TOTAL INCL O&P	
108	0010	GYPSUM PLASTER 80# bag, less than 1 ton				Bag	13			13	14.30	108
	0300	2 coats, no lath included, on walls	J-1	105	.381	S.Y.	3.15	9.15	.40	12.70	18.85	
	0400	On ceilings		92	.435		3.15	10.45	.46	14.06	21	
	0900	3 coats, no lath included, on walls		87	.460		4.32	11.05	.49	15.86	23.50	
	1000	On ceilings		78	.513		4.32	12.35	.54	17.21	25.50	
	1600	For irregular or curved surfaces, add						30%				
	1800	For columns & beams, add						50%				
	9000	Minimum labor/equipment charge	1 Plas	1	8	Job		206		206	335	
116	0010	PERLITE OR VERMICULITE PLASTER 100 lb. bags Under 200 bags				Bag	15.20			15.20	16.70	116
	0200											
	0300	2 coats, no lath included, on walls	J-1	92	.435	S.Y.	3.78	10.45	.46	14.69	21.50	
	0400	On ceilings		79	.506		3.78	12.20	.54	16.52	24.50	
	0900	3 coats, no lath included, on walls		74	.541		6.10	13	.57	19.67	28.50	
	1000	On ceilings		63	.635		6.10	15.30	.67	22.07	32.50	
	1700	For irregular or curved surfaces, add to above						30%				
	1800	For columns and beams, add to above						50%				
	1900	For soffits, add to ceiling prices						40%				
	9000	Minimum labor/equipment charge	1 Plas	1	8	Job		206		206	335	

092 150 | Veneer Plaster

		CREW	DAILY OUTPUT	LABOR-HOURS	UNIT	MAT.	LABOR	EQUIP.	TOTAL	TOTAL INCL O&P	
154	0010	THIN COAT Plaster, 1 coat veneer, not incl. lath	J-1	3,600	.011	S.F.	.10	.27	.01	.38	.56	154
	1000	In 50 lb. bags				Bag	7.75			7.75	8.55	

092 300 | Aggregate Coatings

		CREW	DAILY OUTPUT	LABOR-HOURS	UNIT	MAT.	LABOR	EQUIP.	TOTAL	TOTAL INCL O&P	
304	0010	STUCCO, 3 coats 1" thick, float finish, with mesh, on wood frame	J-2	135	.356	S.Y.	5.40	8.70	.31	14.41	20.50	304
	0100	On masonry construction, no mesh incl.	J-1	200	.200		2.04	4.81	.21	7.06	10.30	
	0300	For trowel finish, add	1 Plas	170	.047			1.21		1.21	1.97	
	0400	For 3/4" thick, on masonry, deduct	J-1	880	.045		.56	1.09	.05	1.70	2.46	
	0600	For coloring and special finish, add, minimum		685	.058		.36	1.40	.06	1.82	2.76	
	0700	Maximum		200	.200		1.26	4.81	.21	6.28	9.45	
	0900	For soffits, add	J-2	155	.310		1.94	7.60	.27	9.81	14.80	
	1000	Exterior stucco, with bonding agent, 3 coats, on walls, no mesh incl.	J-1	200	.200		3.25	4.81	.21	8.27	11.65	
	1200	Ceilings		180	.222		3.25	5.35	.24	8.84	12.60	
	1300	Beams		80	.500		3.25	12.05	.53	15.83	24	
	1500	Columns		100	.400		3.25	9.60	.42	13.27	19.75	
	1550	Minimum labor/equipment charge	1 Plas	1	8	Job		206		206	335	
	1600	Mesh, painted, nailed to wood, 1.8 lb.	1 Lath	60	.133	S.Y.	3.03	3.57		6.60	9.05	
	1800	3.6 lb.		55	.145		3.36	3.90		7.26	9.95	
	1900	Wired to steel, painted, 1.8 lb.		53	.151		3.03	4.05		7.08	9.80	
	2100	3.6 lb.		50	.160		3.36	4.29		7.65	10.55	
	9000	Minimum labor/equipment charge		4	2	Job		53.50		53.50	85.50	

092 600 | Gypsum Board Systems

		CREW	DAILY OUTPUT	LABOR-HOURS	UNIT	MAT.	LABOR	EQUIP.	TOTAL	TOTAL INCL O&P	
602	0010	BLUEBOARD For use with thin coat										602
	0100	plaster application (see division 092-154)										
	1000	3/8" thick, on walls or ceilings, standard, no finish included	2 Carp	1,900	.008	S.F.	.19	.23		.42	.59	
	1100	With thin coat plaster finish		875	.018		.29	.50		.79	1.16	
	1400	On beams, columns, or soffits, standard, no finish included		675	.024		.22	.65		.87	1.32	
	1450	With thin coat plaster finish		475	.034		.33	.92		1.25	1.91	
	3000	1/2" thick, on walls or ceilings, standard, no finish included		1,900	.008		.19	.23		.42	.59	
	3100	With thin coat plaster finish		875	.018		.29	.50		.79	1.16	
	3300	Fire resistant, no finish included		1,900	.008		.19	.23		.42	.59	
	3400	With thin coat plaster finish		875	.018		.29	.50		.79	1.16	
	3450	On beams, columns, or soffits, standard, no finish included		675	.024		.22	.65		.87	1.32	
	3500	With thin coat plaster finish		475	.034		.33	.92		1.25	1.91	

092 | Lath, Plaster & Gypsum Board

092 600 | Gypsum Board Systems

			CREW	DAILY OUTPUT	LABOR-HOURS	UNIT	1999 BARE COSTS MAT.	LABOR	EQUIP.	TOTAL	TOTAL INCL O&P	
602	3700	Fire resistant, no finish included	2 Carp	675	.024	S.F.	.22	.65		.87	1.32	602
	3800	With thin coat plaster finish		475	.034		.33	.92		1.25	1.91	
	5000	5/8" thick, on walls or ceilings, fire resistant, no finish included		1,900	.008		.25	.23		.48	.66	
	5100	With thin coat plaster finish		875	.018		.35	.50		.85	1.23	
	5500	On beams, columns, or soffits, no finish included		675	.024		.29	.65		.94	1.40	
	5600	With thin coat plaster finish		475	.034		.40	.92		1.32	1.98	
	6000	For high ceilings, over 8' high, add		3,060	.005		.10	.14		.24	.35	
	6500	For over 3 stories high, add per story		6,100	.003		.05	.07		.12	.18	
	9000	Minimum labor/equipment charge	1 Carp	2	4	Job		109		109	183	
604	0010	**CEILINGS** Gypsum drywall, fire rated, finished										604
	0100	Screwed to grid, channel or joists, 1/2" thick	2 Carp	765	.021	S.F.	.24	.57		.81	1.22	
	0200	5/8" thick		765	.021		.21	.57		.78	1.19	
	0300	Over 8' high, 1/2" thick		615	.026		.24	.71		.95	1.45	
	0400	5/8" thick		615	.026		.21	.71		.92	1.42	
	0600	Grid suspension system, direct hung										
	0700	1-1/2" C.R.C., with 7/8" hi hat furring channel, 16" O.C.	2 Carp	600	.027	S.F.	.73	.73		1.46	2.02	
	0800	24" O.C.		900	.018		.67	.49		1.16	1.55	
	0900	3-5/8" C.R.C., with 7/8" hi hat furring channel, 16" O.C.		600	.027		.77	.73		1.50	2.07	
	1000	24" O.C.		900	.018		.68	.49		1.17	1.56	
608	0010	**DRYWALL** Gypsum plasterboard, nailed or screwed to studs										608
	0100	unless otherwise noted										
	0150	3/8" thick, on walls, standard, no finish included	2 Carp	2,000	.008	S.F.	.16	.22		.38	.55	
	0200	On ceilings, standard, no finish included		1,800	.009		.16	.24		.40	.59	
	0250	On beams, columns, or soffits, no finish included		675	.024		.19	.65		.84	1.29	
	0300	1/2" thick, on walls, standard, no finish included		2,000	.008		.15	.22		.37	.54	
	0350	Taped and finished		965	.017		.24	.45		.69	1.03	
	0400	Fire resistant, no finish included		2,000	.008		.24	.22		.46	.63	
	0450	Taped and finished		965	.017		.33	.45		.78	1.12	
	0500	Water resistant, no finish included		2,000	.008		.23	.22		.45	.62	
	0550	Taped and finished		965	.017		.32	.45		.77	1.11	
	0600	Prefinished, vinyl, clipped to studs		900	.018		.56	.49		1.05	1.43	
	1000	On ceilings, standard, no finish included		1,800	.009		.15	.24		.39	.58	
	1050	Taped and finished		765	.021		.24	.57		.81	1.23	
	1100	Fire resistant, no finish included		1,800	.009		.24	.24		.48	.67	
	1150	Taped and finished		765	.021		.33	.57		.90	1.32	
	1200	Water resistant, no finish included		1,800	.009		.23	.24		.47	.66	
	1250	Taped and finished		765	.021		.32	.57		.89	1.31	
	1500	On beams, columns, or soffits, standard, no finish included		675	.024		.18	.65		.83	1.27	
	1550	Taped and finished		475	.034		.28	.92		1.20	1.85	
	1600	Fire resistant, no finish included		675	.024		.28	.65		.93	1.38	
	1650	Taped and finished		475	.034		.38	.92		1.30	1.96	
	1700	Water resistant, no finish included		675	.024		.26	.65		.91	1.37	
	1750	Taped and finished		475	.034		.37	.92		1.29	1.94	
	2000	5/8" thick, on walls, standard, no finish included		2,000	.008		.24	.22		.46	.63	
	2050	Taped and finished		965	.017		.33	.45		.78	1.12	
	2100	Fire resistant, no finish included		2,000	.008		.21	.22		.43	.60	
	2150	Taped and finished		965	.017		.30	.45		.75	1.09	
	2200	Water resistant, no finish included		2,000	.008		.29	.22		.51	.69	
	2250	Taped and finished		965	.017		.38	.45		.83	1.18	
	2300	Prefinished, vinyl, clipped to studs		900	.018		.65	.49		1.14	1.52	
	3000	On ceilings, standard, no finish included		1,800	.009		.24	.24		.48	.67	
	3050	Taped and finished		765	.021		.33	.57		.90	1.32	
	3100	Fire resistant, no finish included		1,800	.009		.21	.24		.45	.64	
	3150	Taped and finished		765	.021		.30	.57		.87	1.29	
	3200	Water resistant, no finish included		1,800	.009		.29	.24		.53	.73	

For expanded coverage of these items see *Means Interior Cost Data 1999*

092 | Lath, Plaster & Gypsum Board

092 600 | Gypsum Board Systems

							1999 BARE COSTS			TOTAL
			CREW	DAILY OUTPUT	LABOR-HOURS	UNIT	MAT.	LABOR	EQUIP.	TOTAL	INCL O&P
608	3250	Taped and finished	2 Carp	765	.021	S.F.	.38	.57		.95	1.38
	3500	On beams, columns, or soffits, no finish included		675	.024		.27	.65		.92	1.38
	3550	Taped and finished		475	.034		.38	.92		1.30	1.95
	3600	Fire resistant, no finish included		675	.024		.24	.65		.89	1.35
	3650	Taped and finished		475	.034		.35	.92		1.27	1.92
	3700	Water resistant, no finish included		675	.024		.33	.65		.98	1.45
	3750	Taped and finished		475	.034		.44	.92		1.36	2.02
	4000	Fireproofing, beams or columns, 2 layers, 1/2" thick, incl finish		330	.048		.57	1.32		1.89	2.85
	4050	5/8" thick		300	.053		.60	1.46		2.06	3.10
	4100	3 layers, 1/2" thick		225	.071		.99	1.94		2.93	4.34
	4150	5/8" thick		210	.076		.90	2.08		2.98	4.47
	5050	For 1" thick coreboard on columns		480	.033		.53	.91		1.44	2.10
	5100	For foil-backed board, add					.07			.07	.08
	5200	For high ceilings, over 8' high, add	2 Carp	3,060	.005			.14		.14	.24
	5270	For textured spray, add	2 Lath	1,600	.010		.12	.27		.39	.56
	5300	For over 3 stories high, add per story	2 Carp	6,100	.003			.07		.07	.12
	5350	For finishing corners, inside or outside, add	"	1,100	.015	L.F.	.06	.40		.46	.73
	5500	For acoustical sealant, add per bead	1 Carp	500	.016	"	.03	.44		.47	.76
	5550	Sealant, 1 quart tube				Ea.	4.75			4.75	5.20
	5600	Sound deadening board, 1/4" gypsum	2 Carp	1,800	.009	S.F.	.18	.24		.42	.60
	5650	1/2" wood fiber	"	1,800	.009	"	.26	.24		.50	.70
	9000	Minimum labor/equipment charge	1 Carp	2	4	Job		109		109	183
612	0010	**METAL STUDS, DRYWALL** Partitions, 10' high, with runners R092-610									
	2000	Non-load bearing, galvanized, 25 ga. 1-5/8" wide, 16" O.C.	1 Carp	450	.018	S.F.	.15	.49		.64	.97
	2100	24" O.C.		520	.015		.12	.42		.54	.83
	2200	2-1/2" wide, 16" O.C.		440	.018		.17	.50		.67	1.01
	2250	24" O.C.		510	.016		.13	.43		.56	.87
	2300	3-5/8" wide, 16" O.C.		430	.019		.19	.51		.70	1.06
	2350	24" O.C.		500	.016		.16	.44		.60	.91
	2400	4" wide, 16" O.C.		420	.019		.22	.52		.74	1.11
	2450	24" O.C.		490	.016		.18	.45		.63	.94
	2500	6" wide, 16" O.C.		410	.020		.27	.53		.80	1.19
	2550	24" O.C.		480	.017		.22	.45		.67	1
	2600	20 ga. studs, 1-5/8" wide, 16" O.C.		450	.018		.41	.49		.90	1.26
	2650	24" O.C.		520	.015		.33	.42		.75	1.06
	2700	2-1/2" wide, 16" O.C.		440	.018		.44	.50		.94	1.31
	2750	24" O.C.		510	.016		.35	.43		.78	1.11
	2800	3-5/8" wide, 16" O.C.		430	.019		.54	.51		1.05	1.44
	2850	24" O.C.		500	.016		.43	.44		.87	1.21
	2900	4" wide, 16" O.C.		420	.019		.56	.52		1.08	1.49
	2950	24" O.C.		490	.016		.45	.45		.90	1.24
	3000	6" wide, 16" O.C.		410	.020		.72	.53		1.25	1.68
	3050	24" O.C.		480	.017		.58	.45		1.03	1.39
	5000	Load bearing studs, see division 054-138									
	9000	Minimum labor/equipment charge	1 Carp	4	2	Job		54.50		54.50	91.50
620	0010	**PARTITION WALL** Stud wall, 8' to 12' high									
	0050	1/2", interior, gypsum drywall, standard, taped both sides									
	0500	Installed on and incl., 2" x 4" wood studs, 16" O.C.	2 Carp	310	.052	S.F.	.89	1.41		2.30	3.34
	1000	Metal studs, NLB, 25 ga., 16" O.C., 3-5/8" wide		350	.046		.68	1.25		1.93	2.83
	1200	6" wide		330	.048		.76	1.32		2.08	3.06
	1400	Water resistant, on 2" x 4" wood studs, 16" O.C.		310	.052		1.05	1.41		2.46	3.51
	1600	Metal studs, NLB, 25 ga., 16" O.C., 3-5/8" wide		350	.046		.83	1.25		2.08	3
	1800	6" wide		330	.048		.91	1.32		2.23	3.22
	2000	Fire res., 2 layers, 1-1/2 hr., on 2" x 4" wood studs, 16" O.C.		210	.076		1.55	2.08		3.63	5.20
	2200	Metal studs, NLB, 25 ga., 16" O.C., 3-5/8" wide		250	.064		1.33	1.75		3.08	4.38

092 | Lath, Plaster & Gypsum Board

092 600 | Gypsum Board Systems

			DAILY	LABOR-		1999 BARE COSTS				TOTAL
		CREW	OUTPUT	HOURS	UNIT	MAT.	LABOR	EQUIP.	TOTAL	INCL O&P
620	2400	6" wide	2 Carp	230	.070	S.F.	1.41	1.90		3.31	4.73
	2600	Fire & water res., 2 layers, 1-1/2 hr., 2"x4" studs, 16" O.C.		210	.076		1.55	2.08		3.63	5.20
	2800	Metal studs, NLB, 25 ga., 16" O.C., 3-5/8" wide		250	.064		1.33	1.75		3.08	4.38
	3000	6" wide		230	.070		1.41	1.90		3.31	4.73
	3200	5/8", interior, gypsum drywall, standard, taped both sides									
	3400	Installed on and including 2" x 4" wood studs, 16" O.C.	2 Carp	300	.053	S.F.	1.06	1.46		2.52	3.60
	3600	24" O.C.		330	.048		.97	1.32		2.29	3.29
	3800	Metal studs, NLB, 25 ga., 16" O.C., 3-5/8" wide		340	.047		.84	1.28		2.12	3.08
	4000	6" wide		320	.050		.93	1.36		2.29	3.31
	4200	24" O.C., 3-5/8" wide		360	.044		.84	1.21		2.05	2.96
	4400	6" wide		340	.047		.93	1.28		2.21	3.17
	4800	Water resistant, on 2" x 4" wood studs, 16" O.C.		300	.053		1.17	1.46		2.63	3.72
	5000	24" O.C.		330	.048		1.08	1.32		2.40	3.40
	5200	Metal studs, NLB, 25 ga. 16" O.C., 3-5/8" wide		340	.047		.95	1.28		2.23	3.20
	5400	6" wide		320	.050		1.03	1.36		2.39	3.43
	5600	24" O.C., 3-5/8" wide		360	.044		.95	1.21		2.16	3.08
	5800	6" wide		340	.047		1.03	1.28		2.31	3.29
	6000	Fire res., 2 layers, 2 hr., on 2" x 4" wood studs, 16" O.C.		205	.078		1.33	2.13		3.46	5.05
	6200	24" O.C.		235	.068		1.33	1.86		3.19	4.58
	6400	Metal studs, NLB, 25 ga., 16" O.C., 3-5/8" wide		245	.065		1.21	1.78		2.99	4.31
	6600	6" wide		225	.071		1.29	1.94		3.23	4.67
	6800	24" O.C., 3-5/8" wide		265	.060		1.21	1.65		2.86	4.09
	7000	6" wide		245	.065		1.29	1.78		3.07	4.40
	7200	Fire & water res., 2 layers, 2 hr., 2" x 4" studs, 16" O.C.		205	.078		1.43	2.13		3.56	5.15
	7400	24" O.C.		235	.068		1.33	1.86		3.19	4.58
	7600	Metal studs, NLB, 25 ga., 16" O.C., 3-5/8" wide		245	.065		1.21	1.78		2.99	4.31
	7800	6" wide		225	.071		1.29	1.94		3.23	4.67
	8000	24" O.C., 3-5/8" wide		265	.060		1.21	1.65		2.86	4.09
	8200	6" wide		245	.065		1.29	1.78		3.07	4.40
	8600	1/2" blueboard, mesh tape both sides									
	8620	Installed on and including 2" x 4" wood studs, 16" O.C.	2 Carp	300	.053	S.F.	.99	1.46		2.45	3.52
	8640	Metal studs, NLB, 25 ga., 16" O.C., 3-5/8" wide		340	.047		.77	1.28		2.05	3
	8660	6" wide		320	.050		.85	1.36		2.21	3.23
	9000	Exterior, 1/2" gypsum sheathing, 1/2" gypsum finished, interior,									
	9100	including foil faced insulation, metal studs, 20 ga.									
	9200	16" O.C., 3-5/8" wide	2 Carp	290	.055	S.F.	1.28	1.51		2.79	3.93
	9400	6" wide	"	270	.059	"	1.28	1.62		2.90	4.12
624	0010	**SHAFT WALL** Cavity type on 25 ga. J track & C-H studs, 24" O.C.									
	0030	1" thick coreboard wall liner on shaft side									
	0040	2-hour assembly with double layer									
	0060	5/8" fire rated gypsum board on room side	2 Carp	220	.073	S.F.	1	1.99		2.99	4.42
	0100	3-hour assembly with triple layer									
	0300	5/8" fire rated gypsum board on room side	2 Carp	180	.089	S.F.	1.24	2.43		3.67	5.40
	0400	4-hour assembly, 1" coreboard, 5/8" fire rated gypsum board									
	0600	and 3/4" galv. metal furring channels, 24" O.C., with									
	0700	Double layer 5/8" fire rated gypsum board on room side	2 Carp	110	.145	S.F.	1.12	3.97		5.09	7.90
	0900	For taping & finishing, add per side	1 Carp	1,050	.008	"	.09	.21		.30	.45
	1000	For insulation, see div. 072									

092 800 | Drywall Accessories

			CREW	DAILY OUTPUT	LABOR-HOURS	UNIT	MAT.	LABOR	EQUIP.	TOTAL	INCL O&P
804	0010	**ACCESSORIES, DRYWALL** Casing bead, galvanized steel	1 Carp	2.90	2.759	C.L.F.	15.90	75.50		91.40	144
	0100	Vinyl		3	2.667		24	73		97	149
	0300	Corner bead, galvanized steel, 1" x 1"		4	2		10.25	54.50		64.75	103
	0400	1-1/4" x 1-1/4"		3.50	2.286		10.40	62.50		72.90	115

For expanded coverage of these items see *Means Interior Cost Data 1999*

092 | Lath, Plaster & Gypsum Board

092 800 | Drywall Accessories

		CREW	DAILY OUTPUT	LABOR-HOURS	UNIT	1999 BARE COSTS MAT.	LABOR	EQUIP.	TOTAL	TOTAL INCL O&P	
0600	Vinyl corner bead	1 Carp	4	2	C.L.F.	15.75	54.50		70.25	109	804
0700	Door casing, vinyl, for 2" wall systems		2.50	3.200		27.50	87.50		115	177	
0900	Furring channel, galv. steel, 7/8" deep, standard		2.60	3.077		19.25	84		103.25	162	
1000	Resilient		2.55	3.137		19.50	85.50		105	165	
1100	J trim, galvanized steel, 1/2" wide		3	2.667		17.50	73		90.50	141	
1120	5/8" wide		2.95	2.712		17.75	74		91.75	144	
1500	Z stud, galvanized steel, 1-1/2" wide		2.60	3.077		26	84		110	170	
9000	Minimum labor/equipment charge		3	2.667	Job		73		73	122	

093 | Tile

093 100 | Ceramic Tile

		CREW	DAILY OUTPUT	LABOR-HOURS	UNIT	1999 BARE COSTS MAT.	LABOR	EQUIP.	TOTAL	TOTAL INCL O&P
0010	**CERAMIC TILE**									
0600	Cove base, 4-1/4" x 4-1/4" high, mud set	D-7	91	.176	L.F.	3.63	4.23		7.86	10.65
0700	Thin set		128	.125		3.63	3.01		6.64	8.75
0900	6" x 4-1/4" high, mud set		100	.160		2.58	3.85		6.43	8.90
1000	Thin set		137	.117		2.38	2.81		5.19	7.05
1200	Sanitary cove base, 6" x 4-1/4" high, mud set		93	.172		3.49	4.14		7.63	10.40
1300	Thin set		124	.129		3.29	3.10		6.39	8.50
1500	6" x 6" high, mud set		84	.190		4.26	4.58		8.84	11.95
1600	Thin set		117	.137		4.06	3.29		7.35	9.65
2400	Bullnose trim, 4-1/4" x 4-1/4", mud set		82	.195		3.74	4.69		8.43	11.50
2500	Thin set		128	.125		3.54	3.01		6.55	8.65
2700	6" x 4-1/4" bullnose trim, mud set		84	.190		3.68	4.58		8.26	11.30
2800	Thin set		124	.129		3.48	3.10		6.58	8.75
3000	Floors, natural clay, random or uniform, thin set, color group 1		183	.087	S.F.	3.55	2.10		5.65	7.25
3100	Color group 2		183	.087		3.82	2.10		5.92	7.50
3300	Porcelain type, 1 color, color group 2, 1" x 1"		183	.087		4.11	2.10		6.21	7.85
3400	2" x 2" or 2" x 1", thin set		190	.084		4.34	2.03		6.37	7.95
3600	For random blend, 2 colors, add					.75			.75	.83
3700	4 colors, add					1.08			1.08	1.19
4300	Specialty tile, 4-1/4" x 4-1/4" x 1/2", decorator finish	D-7	183	.087		6.95	2.10		9.05	10.95
4500	Add for epoxy grout, 1/16" joint, 1" x 1" tile		800	.020		.53	.48		1.01	1.34
4600	2" x 2" tile		820	.020		.50	.47		.97	1.29
4800	Pregrouted sheets, walls, 4-1/4" x 4-1/4", 6" x 4-1/4"									
4810	and 8-1/2" x 4-1/4", 4 S.F. sheets, silicone grout	D-7	240	.067	S.F.	4.07	1.60		5.67	7
5100	Floors, unglazed, 2 S.F. sheets,									
5110	urethane adhesive	D-7	180	.089	S.F.	4.05	2.14		6.19	7.85
5400	Walls, interior, thin set, 4-1/4" x 4-1/4" tile		190	.084		2.21	2.03		4.24	5.65
5500	6" x 4-1/4" tile		190	.084		2.25	2.03		4.28	5.70
5700	8-1/2" x 4-1/4" tile		190	.084		3.19	2.03		5.22	6.70
5800	6" x 6" tile		200	.080		2.56	1.92		4.48	5.85
5810	8" x 8" tile		225	.071		2.66	1.71		4.37	5.65
5820	12" x 12" tile		300	.053		2.92	1.28		4.20	5.25
5830	16" x 16" tile		500	.032		3.17	.77		3.94	4.70
6000	Decorated wall tile, 4-1/4" x 4-1/4", minimum		270	.059		2.94	1.43		4.37	5.50
6100	Maximum		180	.089		15.25	2.14		17.39	20
6600	Crystalline glazed, 4-1/4" x 4-1/4", mud set, plain		100	.160		3.67	3.85		7.52	10.10
6700	4-1/4" x 4-1/4", scored tile		100	.160		3.97	3.85		7.82	10.40
6900	6" x 6" plain		93	.172		4.43	4.14		8.57	11.40

093 | Tile

093 100 | Ceramic Tile

		CREW	DAILY OUTPUT	LABOR-HOURS	UNIT	1999 BARE COSTS MAT.	LABOR	EQUIP.	TOTAL	TOTAL INCL O&P	
102	7000	For epoxy grout, 1/16" joints, 4-1/4" tile, add	D-7	800	.020	S.F.	.32	.48		.80	1.11	102
	7200	For tile set in dry mortar, add		1,735	.009			.22		.22	.35	
	7300	For tile set in portland cement mortar, add		290	.055			1.33		1.33	2.09	
	9500	Minimum labor/equipment charge		3.25	4.923	Job		118		118	187	

093 300 | Quarry Tile

		CREW	DAILY OUTPUT	LABOR-HOURS	UNIT	MAT.	LABOR	EQUIP.	TOTAL	TOTAL INCL O&P	
304	0010	**QUARRY TILE** Base, cove or sanitary, 2" or 5" high, mud set										304
	0100	1/2" thick	D-7	110	.145	L.F.	3.51	3.50		7.01	9.35	
	0300	Bullnose trim, red, mud set, 6" x 6" x 1/2" thick		120	.133		3.74	3.21		6.95	9.15	
	0400	4" x 4" x 1/2" thick		110	.145		3.75	3.50		7.25	9.65	
	0600	4" x 8" x 1/2" thick, using 8" as edge		130	.123		3.56	2.96		6.52	8.60	
	0700	Floors, mud set, 1,000 S.F. lots, red, 4" x 4" x 1/2" thick		120	.133	S.F.	3.67	3.21		6.88	9.10	
	0900	6" x 6" x 1/2" thick		140	.114		2.65	2.75		5.40	7.25	
	1000	4" x 8" x 1/2" thick		130	.123		3.67	2.96		6.63	8.70	
	1300	For waxed coating, add					.59			.59	.65	
	1500	For colors other than green, add					.34			.34	.37	
	1600	For abrasive surface, add					.41			.41	.45	
	1800	Brown tile, imported, 6" x 6" x 3/4"	D-7	120	.133		4.35	3.21		7.56	9.85	
	1900	8" x 8" x 1"		110	.145		4.93	3.50		8.43	10.90	
	2100	For thin set mortar application, deduct		700	.023			.55		.55	.87	
	2700	Stair tread, 6" x 6" x 3/4", plain		50	.320		3.96	7.70		11.66	16.50	
	2800	Abrasive		47	.340		4.50	8.20		12.70	17.85	
	3000	Wainscot, 6" x 6" x 1/2", thin set, red		105	.152		3.35	3.66		7.01	9.50	
	3100	Colors other than green		105	.152		3.74	3.66		7.40	9.90	
	3300	Window sill, 6" wide, 3/4" thick		90	.178	L.F.	4.32	4.28		8.60	11.50	
	3400	Corners		80	.200	Ea.	4.72	4.81		9.53	12.80	
	9000	Minimum labor/equipment charge		3.25	4.923	Job		118		118	187	

093 700 | Metal Tile

		CREW	DAILY OUTPUT	LABOR-HOURS	UNIT	MAT.	LABOR	EQUIP.	TOTAL	TOTAL INCL O&P	
701	0010	**METAL TILE** 4' x 4' sheet, 24 ga., tile pattern, nailed										701
	0200	Stainless steel	2 Carp	512	.031	S.F.	21.50	.85		22.35	25	
	0400	Aluminized steel	"	512	.031	"	11.45	.85		12.30	14.05	
	9000	Minimum labor/equipment charge	1 Carp	4	2	Job		54.50		54.50	91.50	

093 900 | Tile Setting Materials

		CREW	DAILY OUTPUT	LABOR-HOURS	UNIT	MAT.	LABOR	EQUIP.	TOTAL	TOTAL INCL O&P	
910	0010	**CEMENTITIOUS BACKERBOARD**										910
	0070	Cementitious backerboard, on floor, 3' x 4' x 1/2" sheets	2 Carp	525	.030	S.F.	1.03	.83		1.86	2.53	
	0080	3' x 5' x 1/2" sheets		525	.030		1.03	.83		1.86	2.53	
	0090	3' x 6' x 1/2" sheets		525	.030		1.03	.83		1.86	2.52	
	0100	3' x 4' x 5/8" sheets		525	.030		1.07	.83		1.90	2.56	
	0110	3' x 5' x 5/8" sheets		525	.030		1.05	.83		1.88	2.55	
	0120	3' x 6' x 5/8" sheets		525	.030		1.06	.83		1.89	2.55	
	0150	On wall, 3' x 4' x 1/2" sheets		350	.046		1.03	1.25		2.28	3.23	
	0160	3' x 5' x 1/2" sheets		350	.046		1.03	1.25		2.28	3.23	
	0170	3' x 6' x 1/2" sheets		350	.046		1.03	1.25		2.28	3.22	
	0180	3' x 4' x 5/8" sheets		350	.046		1.07	1.25		2.32	3.26	
	0190	3' x 5' x 5/8" sheets		350	.046		1.05	1.25		2.30	3.25	
	0200	3' x 6' x 5/8" sheets		350	.046		1.06	1.25		2.31	3.25	
	0250	On counter, 3' x 4' x 1/2" sheets		180	.089		1.03	2.43		3.46	5.20	
	0260	3' x 5' x 1/2" sheets		180	.089		1.03	2.43		3.46	5.20	
	0270	3' x 6' x 1/2" sheets		180	.089		1.03	2.43		3.46	5.20	
	0300	3' x 4' x 5/8" sheets		180	.089		1.07	2.43		3.50	5.25	
	0310	3' x 5' x 5/8" sheets		180	.089		1.05	2.43		3.48	5.20	
	0320	3' x 6' x 5/8" sheets		180	.089		1.06	2.43		3.49	5.20	

For expanded coverage of these items see *Means Interior Cost Data 1999*

094 | Terrazzo

094 100 | Portland Cem. Terrazzo

			CREW	DAILY OUTPUT	LABOR-HOURS	UNIT	1999 BARE COSTS MAT.	LABOR	EQUIP.	TOTAL	TOTAL INCL O&P	
104	0010	**TERRAZZO, CAST IN PLACE** Cove base, 6" high, 16ga. zinc	1 Mstz	20	.400	L.F.	2.63	10.60		13.23	19.65	104
	0100	Curb, 6" high and 6" wide		6	1.333		4.33	35.50		39.83	61	
	0300	Divider strip for floors, 14 ga., 1-1/4" deep, zinc		375	.021		.89	.57		1.46	1.87	
	0400	Brass		375	.021		1.65	.57		2.22	2.71	
	0600	Heavy top strip 1/4" thick, 1-1/4" deep, zinc		300	.027		1.50	.71		2.21	2.77	
	1200	For thin set floors, 16 ga., 1/2" x 1/2", zinc		350	.023		.78	.61		1.39	1.82	
	1500	Floor, bonded to concrete, 1-3/4" thick, gray cement	J-3	130	.123	S.F.	2.31	2.97	.76	6.04	8.05	
	1600	White cement, mud set		130	.123		2.63	2.97	.76	6.36	8.40	
	1800	Not bonded, 3" total thickness, gray cement		115	.139		2.89	3.36	.86	7.11	9.40	
	1900	White cement, mud set		115	.139		3.15	3.36	.86	7.37	9.70	
	9000	Minimum labor/equipment charge	1 Mstz	1	8	Job		212		212	335	
108	0010	**TILE OR TERRAZZO BASE** Scratch coat only	1 Mstz	150	.053	S.F.	.30	1.42		1.72	2.56	108
	0500	Scratch and brown coat only		75	.107	"	.55	2.83		3.38	5.10	
	9000	Minimum labor/equipment charge		1	8	Job		212		212	335	

094 200 | Precast Terrazzo

			CREW	DAILY OUTPUT	LABOR-HOURS	UNIT	MAT.	LABOR	EQUIP.	TOTAL	TOTAL INCL O&P	
201	0010	**TERRAZZO, PRECAST** Base, 6" high, straight	1 Mstz	35	.229	L.F.	8.70	6.05		14.75	19.20	201
	0100	Cove		30	.267		10.50	7.10		17.60	22.50	
	0300	8" high base, straight		30	.267		9.50	7.10		16.60	21.50	
	0400	Cove		25	.320		11.55	8.50		20.05	26	
	0600	For white cement, add					.32			.32	.35	
	0700	For 16 ga. zinc toe strip, add					.95			.95	1.05	
	0900	Curbs, 4" x 4" high	1 Mstz	19	.421		22	11.20		33.20	41.50	
	1000	8" x 8" high	"	15	.533		29.50	14.15		43.65	55	
	1200	Floor tiles, non-slip, 1" thick, 12" x 12"	D-1	29	.552	S.F.	14.85	13.55		28.40	39	
	1300	1-1/4" thick, 12" x 12"		29	.552		16.10	13.55		29.65	40	
	1500	16" x 16"		23	.696		17.50	17.10		34.60	48	
	1600	1-1/2" thick, 16" x 16"		21	.762		16	18.75		34.75	48.50	
	1800	For Venetian terrazzo, add					4.75			4.75	5.20	
	1900	For white cement, add					.45			.45	.50	
	2400	Stair treads, 1-1/2" thick, non-slip, three line pattern	2 Mstz	70	.229	L.F.	32	6.05		38.05	44.50	
	2500	Nosing and two lines		70	.229		32	6.05		38.05	44.50	
	2700	2" thick treads, straight		60	.267		34	7.10		41.10	48.50	
	2800	Curved		50	.320		44.50	8.50		53	62.50	
	3000	Stair risers, 1" thick, to 6" high, straight sections		60	.267		9.50	7.10		16.60	21.50	
	3100	Cove		50	.320		11.50	8.50		20	26	
	3300	Curved, 1" thick, to 6" high, vertical		48	.333		20.50	8.85		29.35	36.50	
	3400	Cove		38	.421		27.50	11.20		38.70	47.50	
	3600	Stair tread and riser, single piece, straight, minimum		60	.267		41	7.10		48.10	56	
	3700	Maximum		40	.400		52.50	10.60		63.10	75	
	3900	Curved tread and riser, minimum		40	.400		57	10.60		67.60	79.50	
	4000	Maximum		32	.500		72	13.25		85.25	100	
	4200	Stair stringers, notched, 1" thick		25	.640		23.50	17		40.50	52.50	
	4300	2" thick		22	.727		27.50	19.30		46.80	61	
	4500	Stair landings, structural, non-slip, 1-1/2" thick		85	.188	S.F.	25.50	5		30.50	36	
	4600	3" thick		75	.213		36	5.65		41.65	48.50	
	4800	Wainscot, 12" x 12" x 1" tiles	1 Mstz	12	.667		8.50	17.70		26.20	37.50	
	4900	16" x 16" x 1-1/2" tiles	"	8	1		11.70	26.50		38.20	55	
	9500	Minimum labor/equipment charge	1 Tilf	2	4	Job		107		107	168	

095 | Acoustical Treatment & Wood Flooring

095 100 | Acoustical Ceilings

			CREW	DAILY OUTPUT	LABOR-HOURS	UNIT	1999 BARE COSTS MAT.	LABOR	EQUIP.	TOTAL	TOTAL INCL O&P	
102	0010	**CEILING TILE**, Stapled or cemented										102
	0100	12" x 12" or 12" x 24", not including furring										
	0600	Mineral fiber, vinyl coated, 5/8" thick	1 Carp	1,000	.008	S.F.	.56	.22		.78	.99	
	0700	3/4" thick		1,000	.008		1.23	.22		1.45	1.72	
	0900	Fire rated, 3/4" thick, plain faced		1,000	.008		.82	.22		1.04	1.28	
	1000	Plastic coated face		1,000	.008		.96	.22		1.18	1.42	
	1200	Aluminum faced, 5/8" thick, plain		1,000	.008		1.05	.22		1.27	1.53	
	3000	Wood fiber tile, 1/2" thick		400	.020		.71	.55		1.26	1.69	
	3100	3/4" thick		400	.020		.95	.55		1.50	1.96	
	3300	For flameproofing, add					.09			.09	.10	
	3400	For sculptured 3 dimensional, add					.23			.23	.25	
	3900	For ceiling primer, add					.12			.12	.13	
	4000	For ceiling cement, add					.31			.31	.34	
	9000	Minimum labor/equipment charge	1 Carp	4	2	Job		54.50		54.50	91.50	
104	0010	**SUSPENDED ACOUSTIC CEILING TILES**, Not including										104
	0100	suspension system										
	0300	Fiberglass boards, film faced, 2' x 2' or 2' x 4', 5/8" thick	1 Carp	625	.013	S.F.	.49	.35		.84	1.12	
	0400	3/4" thick		600	.013		1.03	.36		1.39	1.74	
	0500	3" thick, thermal, R11		450	.018		1.21	.49		1.70	2.14	
	0600	Glass cloth faced fiberglass, 3/4" thick		500	.016		1.61	.44		2.05	2.50	
	0700	1" thick		485	.016		1.81	.45		2.26	2.74	
	0820	1-1/2" thick, nubby face		475	.017		2.15	.46		2.61	3.14	
	1110	Mineral fiber tile, lay-in, 2' x 2' or 2' x 4', 5/8" thick, fine texture		625	.013		.40	.35		.75	1.02	
	1115	Rough textured		625	.013		.97	.35		1.32	1.65	
	1125	3/4" thick, fine textured		600	.013		1.09	.36		1.45	1.81	
	1130	Rough textured		600	.013		1.36	.36		1.72	2.11	
	1135	Fissured		600	.013		1.60	.36		1.96	2.37	
	1150	Tegular, 5/8" thick, fine textured		470	.017		.96	.46		1.42	1.84	
	1155	Rough textured		470	.017		1.25	.46		1.71	2.16	
	1165	3/4" thick, fine textured		450	.018		1.36	.49		1.85	2.31	
	1170	Rough textured		450	.018		1.53	.49		2.02	2.49	
	1175	Fissured		450	.018		2.39	.49		2.88	3.44	
	1180	For aluminum face, add					4.36			4.36	4.80	
	1185	For plastic film face, add					.33			.33	.36	
	1190	For fire rating, add					.33			.33	.36	
	1300	Mirror faced panels, 15/16" thick, 2' x 2'	1 Carp	500	.016		5.65	.44		6.09	7	
	1900	Eggcrate, acrylic, 1/2" x 1/2" x 1/2" cubes		500	.016		1.32	.44		1.76	2.18	
	2100	Polystyrene eggcrate, 3/8" x 3/8" x 1/2" cubes		510	.016		1.10	.43		1.53	1.93	
	2200	1/2" x 1/2" x 1/2" cubes		500	.016		1.48	.44		1.92	2.36	
	2210											
	2400	Luminous panels, prismatic, acrylic	1 Carp	400	.020	S.F.	1.59	.55		2.14	2.66	
	2500	Polystyrene		400	.020		.82	.55		1.37	1.81	
	2700	Flat white acrylic		400	.020		2.79	.55		3.34	3.98	
	2800	Polystyrene		400	.020		1.90	.55		2.45	3	
	3000	Drop pan, white, acrylic		400	.020		4.08	.55		4.63	5.40	
	3100	Polystyrene		400	.020		3.41	.55		3.96	4.66	
	3600	Perforated aluminum sheets, .024" thick, corrugated, painted		490	.016		1.62	.45		2.07	2.53	
	3700	Plain		500	.016		1.46	.44		1.90	2.34	
	3720	Mineral fiber, 24" x 24" or 48", reveal edge, painted, 5/8" thick		600	.013		.90	.36		1.26	1.60	
	3740	3/4" thick		575	.014		1.48	.38		1.86	2.27	
	9000	Minimum labor/equipment charge		4	2	Job		54.50		54.50	91.50	
106	0010	**SUSPENDED CEILINGS, COMPLETE** Including standard										106
	0100	suspension system but not incl. 1-1/2" carrier channels										
	0600	Fiberglass ceiling board, 2' x 4' x 5/8", plain faced,	1 Carp	500	.016	S.F.	.99	.44		1.43	1.82	
	0700	Offices, 2' x 4' x 3/4"		380	.021		1.10	.57		1.67	2.17	

For expanded coverage of these items see *Means Interior Cost Data 1999*

095 | Acoustical Treatment & Wood Flooring

095 100 | Acoustical Ceilings

		CREW	DAILY OUTPUT	LABOR-HOURS	UNIT	MAT.	LABOR	EQUIP.	TOTAL	TOTAL INCL O&P
0800	Mineral fiber, on 15/16" T bar susp. 2' x 2' x 3/4" lay-in board	1 Carp	345	.023	S.F.	1.56	.63		2.19	2.78
0810	2' x 4' x 5/8" tile		380	.021		1.37	.57		1.94	2.47
0820	Tegular, 2' x 2' x 5/8" tile on 9/16" grid		250	.032		1.84	.87		2.71	3.48
0830	2' x 4' x 3/4" tile		225	.036		1.92	.97		2.89	3.73
0900	Luminous panels, prismatic, acrylic		255	.031		2.47	.86		3.33	4.15
1200	Metal pan with acoustic pad, steel		75	.107		3.19	2.91		6.10	8.40
1300	Painted aluminum		75	.107		5.65	2.91		8.56	11.10
1500	Aluminum, degreased finish		75	.107		3.68	2.91		6.59	8.90
1600	Stainless steel		75	.107		6.75	2.91		9.66	12.30
1800	Tile, Z bar suspension, 5/8" mineral fiber tile		150	.053		1.43	1.46		2.89	4.01
1900	3/4" mineral fiber tile		150	.053		1.52	1.46		2.98	4.11
2402	For strip lighting, see division 166-130									
2500	For rooms under 500 S.F., add				S.F.		25%			
9000	Minimum labor/equipment charge	1 Carp	2	4	Job		109		109	183

095 250 | Acoustical Space Units

		CREW	DAILY OUTPUT	LABOR-HOURS	UNIT	MAT.	LABOR	EQUIP.	TOTAL	TOTAL INCL O&P
0010	**SOUND ABSORBING PANELS** Perforated steel facing, painted with									
0100	fiberglass or mineral filler, no backs, 2-1/4" thick, modular									
0200	space units, ceiling or wall hung, white or colored	1 Carp	100	.080	S.F.	7.20	2.18		9.38	11.60
0300	Fiberboard sound deadening panels, 1/2" thick	"	600	.013	"	.27	.36		.63	.91
0500	Fiberglass panels, 4' x 8' x 1" thick, with									
0600	glass cloth face for walls, cemented	1 Carp	155	.052	S.F.	4.10	1.41		5.51	6.85
0700	1-1/2" thick, dacron covered, inner aluminum frame,									
0710	wall mounted	1 Carp	300	.027	S.F.	6.95	.73		7.68	8.85
0900	Mineral fiberboard panels, fabric covered, 30"x 108",									
1000	3/4" thick, concealed spline, wall mounted	1 Carp	150	.053	S.F.	5	1.46		6.46	7.95
9000	Minimum labor/equipment charge	"	4	2	Job		54.50		54.50	91.50

095 300 | Acoustical Insulation

		CREW	DAILY OUTPUT	LABOR-HOURS	UNIT	MAT.	LABOR	EQUIP.	TOTAL	TOTAL INCL O&P
0010	**SOUND ATTENUATION** Blanket, 1" thick	1 Carp	925	.009	S.F.	.21	.24		.45	.63
0500	1-1/2" thick		920	.009		.26	.24		.50	.68
1000	2" thick		915	.009		.32	.24		.56	.76
1500	3" thick		910	.009		.44	.24		.68	.88
3400	Urethane plastic foam, open cell, on wall, 2" thick	2 Carp	2,050	.008		2.51	.21		2.72	3.12
3500	3" thick		1,550	.010		3.33	.28		3.61	4.13
3600	4" thick		1,050	.015		4.68	.42		5.10	5.85
3700	On ceiling, 2" thick		1,700	.009		2.50	.26		2.76	3.18
3800	3" thick		1,300	.012		3.33	.34		3.67	4.22
3900	4" thick		900	.018		4.68	.49		5.17	5.95
4000	Nylon matting 0.4" thick, with carbon black spinerette									
4010	plus polyester fabric, on floor	J-4	4,000	.004	S.F.	1.86	.10		1.96	2.20
4200	Fiberglass reinf. backer board underlayment, 7/16" thick, on floor	"	800	.020	"	1.56	.48		2.04	2.48
9000	Minimum labor/equipment charge	1 Carp	5	1.600	Job		43.50		43.50	73

095 600 | Wood Strip Flooring

		CREW	DAILY OUTPUT	LABOR-HOURS	UNIT	MAT.	LABOR	EQUIP.	TOTAL	TOTAL INCL O&P
0010	**WOOD** Fir, vertical grain, 1" x 4", not incl. finish, B & better (R061-030)	1 Carp	255	.031	S.F.	2.30	.86		3.16	3.96
0100	C grade & better		255	.031		2.16	.86		3.02	3.81
0300	Flat grain, 1" x 4", not incl. finish, B & better		255	.031		2.63	.86		3.49	4.32
0400	C & better		255	.031		2.53	.86		3.39	4.21
4000	Maple, strip, 25/32" x 2-1/4", not incl. finish, select		170	.047		2.95	1.28		4.23	5.40
4100	#2 & better		170	.047		2.65	1.28		3.93	5.05
4300	33/32" x 3-1/4", not incl. finish, #1 grade		170	.047		3.25	1.28		4.53	5.75
4400	#2 & better		170	.047		2.90	1.28		4.18	5.35
4600	Oak, white or red, 25/32" x 2-1/4", not incl. finish									
4700	#1 common	1 Carp	170	.047	S.F.	2.70	1.28		3.98	5.10

095 | Acoustical Treatment & Wood Flooring

095 600 | Wood Strip Flooring

			CREW	DAILY OUTPUT	LABOR-HOURS	UNIT	1999 BARE COSTS MAT.	LABOR	EQUIP.	TOTAL	TOTAL INCL O&P	
604	4900	Select quartered, 2-1/4" wide	1 Carp	170	.047	S.F.	3.02	1.28		4.30	5.50	604
	5000	Clear		170	.047		3.25	1.28		4.53	5.75	
	5200	Parquetry, standard, 5/16" thick, not incl. finish, oak, minimum		160	.050		1.54	1.36		2.90	3.98	
	5300	Maximum		100	.080		5.10	2.18		7.28	9.30	
	5500	Teak, minimum		160	.050		4.15	1.36		5.51	6.85	
	5600	Maximum		100	.080		7.25	2.18		9.43	11.65	
	5650	13/16" thick, select grade oak, minimum		160	.050		8	1.36		9.36	11.10	
	5700	Maximum		100	.080		12.15	2.18		14.33	17	
	5800	Custom parquetry, including finish, minimum		100	.080		13.40	2.18		15.58	18.40	
	5900	Maximum		50	.160		17.75	4.37		22.12	27	
	6100	Prefinished, white oak, prime grade, 2-1/4" wide		170	.047		5.85	1.28		7.13	8.60	
	6200	3-1/4" wide		185	.043		7.50	1.18		8.68	10.25	
	6400	Ranch plank		145	.055		7.25	1.51		8.76	10.50	
	6500	Hardwood blocks, 9" x 9", 25/32" thick		160	.050		4.85	1.36		6.21	7.65	
	6700	Parquetry, 5/16" thick, oak, minimum		160	.050		3.30	1.36		4.66	5.90	
	6800	Maximum		100	.080		8.05	2.18		10.23	12.55	
	7000	Walnut or teak, parquetry, minimum		160	.050		4.50	1.36		5.86	7.25	
	7100	Maximum		100	.080		7.85	2.18		10.03	12.30	
	7200	Acrylic wood parquet blocks, 12" x 12" x 5/16",										
	7210	irradiated, set in epoxy	1 Carp	160	.050	S.F.	6.55	1.36		7.91	9.50	
	7400	Yellow pine, 3/4" x 3-1/8", T & G, C & better, not incl. finish	"	200	.040		2.15	1.09		3.24	4.20	
	7500	Refinish wood floor, sand, 2 cts poly, wax, soft wood, min.	1 Clab	400	.020		.65	.43		1.08	1.43	
	7600	Hard wood, max		130	.062		.98	1.32		2.30	3.29	
	7800	Sanding and finishing, 2 coats polyurethane		295	.027		.65	.58		1.23	1.68	
	7900	Subfloor and underlayment, see division 061-164 & 168										
	8015	Transition molding, 2 1/4" wide, 5' long	1 Carp	19.20	.417	Ea.	10.15	11.35		21.50	30.50	
	8300	Floating floor, wood composition strip, complete.	1 Clab	133	.060	S.F.	4.16	1.29		5.45	6.75	
	8310	Floating floor components, T & G wood composite strips					3.87			3.87	4.26	
	8320	Film					.09			.09	.10	
	8330	Foam					.19			.19	.21	
	8340	Adhesive					.06			.06	.07	
	8350	Installation kit					.16			.16	.18	
	8360	Trim, 2" wide x 3' long				L.F.	2.25			2.25	2.48	
	8370	Reducer moulding				"	4.15			4.15	4.57	
	9000	Minimum labor/equipment charge	1 Carp	2	4	Job		109		109	183	

095 650 | Wood Block Flooring

			CREW	DAILY OUTPUT	LABOR-HOURS	UNIT	MAT.	LABOR	EQUIP.	TOTAL	INCL O&P	
651	0010	**WOOD BLOCK FLOORING** End grain flooring, coated, 2" thick	1 Carp	295	.027	S.F.	2.70	.74		3.44	4.21	651
	0400	Natural finish, 1" thick, fir		125	.064		2.80	1.75		4.55	6	
	0600	1-1/2" thick, pine		125	.064		2.75	1.75		4.50	5.95	
	0700	2" thick, pine		125	.064		2.72	1.75		4.47	5.90	
	9000	Minimum labor/equipment charge		2	4	Job		109		109	183	

096 | Flooring & Carpet

096 150 | Marble Flooring

			CREW	DAILY OUTPUT	LABOR-HOURS	UNIT	1999 BARE COSTS MAT.	LABOR	EQUIP.	TOTAL	TOTAL INCL O&P	
151	0010	**MARBLE** Thin gauge tile, 12" x 6", 3/8", White Carara	D-7	60	.267	S.F.	8.60	6.40		15	19.55	151
	0100	Travertine		60	.267		9.45	6.40		15.85	20.50	

For expanded coverage of these items see Means Interior Cost Data 1999

096 | Flooring & Carpet

096 150 | Marble Flooring

		CREW	DAILY OUTPUT	LABOR-HOURS	UNIT	1999 BARE COSTS MAT.	LABOR	EQUIP.	TOTAL	TOTAL INCL O&P	
151	0200	12" x 12" x 3/8", thin set, floors	D-7	60	.267	S.F.	8.60	6.40		15	19.55	151
	0300	On walls		52	.308		8.60	7.40		16	21	
	9000	Minimum labor/equipment charge		3	5.333	Job		128		128	202	

096 250 | Slate Flooring

251	0010	SLATE TILE Vermont, 6" x 6" x 1/4" thick, thin set	D-7	180	.089	S.F.	4.14	2.14		6.28	7.90	251
	9000	Minimum labor/equipment charge	"	3	5.333	Job		128		128	202	

096 350 | Brick Flooring

354	0010	FLOORING										354
	0020	Acid proof shales, red, 8" x 3-3/4" x 1-1/4" thick	D-7	.43	37.209	M	695	895		1,590	2,175	
	0050	2-1/4" thick	D-1	.40	40		755	985		1,740	2,450	
	0200	Acid proof clay brick, 8" x 3-3/4" x 2-1/4" thick	"	.40	40		755	985		1,740	2,450	
	0260	Cast ceramic, pressed, 4" x 8" x 1/2", unglazed	D-7	100	.160	S.F.	4.94	3.85		8.79	11.50	
	0270	Glazed		100	.160		6.60	3.85		10.45	13.30	
	0280	Hand molded flooring, 4" x 8" x 3/4", unglazed		95	.168		6.55	4.05		10.60	13.60	
	0290	Glazed		95	.168		8.20	4.05		12.25	15.40	
	0300	8" hexagonal, 3/4" thick, unglazed		85	.188		7.15	4.53		11.68	15.05	
	0310	Glazed		85	.188		12.95	4.53		17.48	21.50	
	0400	Heavy duty industrial, cement mortar bed, 2" thick, not incl. brick	D-1	80	.200		.71	4.92		5.63	8.95	
	0450	Acid proof joints, 1/4" wide	"	65	.246		1.13	6.05		7.18	11.30	
	0500	Pavers, 8" x 4", 1" to 1-1/4" thick, red	D-7	95	.168		2.88	4.05		6.93	9.55	
	0510	Ironspot	"	95	.168		4.07	4.05		8.12	10.90	
	0540	1-3/8" to 1-3/4" thick, red	D-1	95	.168		2.78	4.14		6.92	9.90	
	0560	Ironspot		95	.168		4.02	4.14		8.16	11.25	
	0580	2-1/4" thick, red		90	.178		2.83	4.37		7.20	10.35	
	0590	Ironspot		90	.178		4.38	4.37		8.75	12.05	
	0800	For sidewalks and patios with pavers, see division 025-158										
	0870	For epoxy joints, add	D-1	600	.027	S.F.	2.15	.66		2.81	3.46	
	0880	For Furan underlayment, add	"	600	.027		1.78	.66		2.44	3.05	
	0890	For waxed surface, steam cleaned, add	D-5	1,000	.008		.15	.22		.37	.54	
	9000	Minimum equipment/labor charge	1 Bric	2	4	Job		110		110	183	

096 600 | Resilient Flooring

601	0010	RESILIENT FLOORING										601
	0800	Base, cove, rubber or vinyl, .080" thick										
	1100	Standard colors, 2-1/2" high	1 Tilf	315	.025	L.F.	.39	.68		1.07	1.50	
	1150	4" high		315	.025		.49	.68		1.17	1.61	
	1200	6" high		315	.025		.73	.68		1.41	1.87	
	1450	1/8" thick, standard colors, 2-1/2" high		315	.025		.40	.68		1.08	1.51	
	1500	4" high		315	.025		.56	.68		1.24	1.69	
	1550	6" high		315	.025		.81	.68		1.49	1.96	
	1600	Corners, 2-1/2" high		315	.025	Ea.	1.02	.68		1.70	2.19	
	1630	4" high		315	.025		1.07	.68		1.75	2.25	
	1660	6" high		315	.025		1.38	.68		2.06	2.59	
	1700	Conductive flooring, rubber tile, 1/8" thick		315	.025	S.F.	2.50	.68		3.18	3.82	
	1800	Homogeneous vinyl tile, 1/8" thick		315	.025		3.42	.68		4.10	4.83	
	2200	Cork tile, standard finish, 1/8" thick		315	.025		2.42	.68		3.10	3.73	
	2250	3/16" thick		315	.025		2.84	.68		3.52	4.19	
	2300	5/16" thick		315	.025		4.26	.68		4.94	5.75	
	2350	1/2" thick		315	.025		4.74	.68		5.42	6.25	
	2500	Urethane finish, 1/8" thick		315	.025		3.65	.68		4.33	5.10	
	2550	3/16" thick		315	.025		4.81	.68		5.49	6.35	
	2600	5/16" thick		315	.025		6.60	.68		7.28	8.30	

096 | Flooring & Carpet

096 600 | Resilient Flooring

		CREW	DAILY OUTPUT	LABOR-HOURS	UNIT	1999 BARE COSTS MAT.	LABOR	EQUIP.	TOTAL	TOTAL INCL O&P	
601	2650	1/2" thick	1 Tilf	315	.025	S.F.	9.20	.68		9.88	11.15	601
	3700	Polyethylene, in rolls, no base incl., landscape surfaces		275	.029		2.19	.78		2.97	3.63	
	3800	Nylon action surface, 1/8" thick		275	.029		2.35	.78		3.13	3.80	
	3900	1/4" thick		275	.029		3.39	.78		4.17	4.95	
	4000	3/8" thick		275	.029		4.25	.78		5.03	5.90	
	5500	Polyvinyl chloride, sheet goods for gyms, 1/4" thick		80	.100		3.43	2.66		6.09	7.95	
	5600	3/8" thick		60	.133		3.87	3.55		7.42	9.85	
	5900	Rubber, sheet goods, 36" wide, 1/8" thick		120	.067		3.01	1.78		4.79	6.10	
	5950	3/16" thick		100	.080		4.28	2.13		6.41	8.05	
	6000	1/4" thick		90	.089		4.95	2.37		7.32	9.20	
	6050	Tile, marbleized colors, 12" x 12", 1/8" thick		400	.020		3.03	.53		3.56	4.17	
	6100	3/16" thick		400	.020		4.34	.53		4.87	5.60	
	6300	Special tile, plain colors, 1/8" thick		400	.020		3.83	.53		4.36	5.05	
	6350	3/16" thick		400	.020		5.15	.53		5.68	6.50	
	7000	Vinyl composition tile, 12" x 12", 1/16" thick		500	.016		.68	.43		1.11	1.42	
	7050	Embossed		500	.016		.86	.43		1.29	1.62	
	7100	Marbleized		500	.016		.86	.43		1.29	1.62	
	7150	Solid		500	.016		.97	.43		1.40	1.74	
	7200	3/32" thick, embossed		500	.016		.87	.43		1.30	1.63	
	7250	Marbleized		500	.016		.98	.43		1.41	1.75	
	7300	Solid		500	.016		1.43	.43		1.86	2.24	
	7350	1/8" thick, marbleized		500	.016		.98	.43		1.41	1.75	
	7400	Solid		500	.016		2.01	.43		2.44	2.88	
	7450	Conductive		500	.016		3.71	.43		4.14	4.75	
	7500	Vinyl tile, 12" x 12", .050" thick, minimum		500	.016		1.54	.43		1.97	2.36	
	7550	Maximum		500	.016		3.01	.43		3.44	3.98	
	7600	1/8" thick, minimum		500	.016		1.94	.43		2.37	2.80	
	7650	Solid colors		500	.016		1.25	.43		1.68	2.05	
	7700	Marbleized or Travertine pattern		500	.016		3.11	.43		3.54	4.09	
	7750	Florentine pattern		500	.016		3.57	.43		4	4.60	
	7800	Maximum		500	.016		7.35	.43		7.78	8.70	
	8000	Vinyl sheet goods, backed, .065" thick, minimum		250	.032		1.25	.85		2.10	2.73	
	8050	Maximum		200	.040		2.30	1.07		3.37	4.21	
	8100	.080" thick, minimum		230	.035		1.48	.93		2.41	3.09	
	8150	Maximum		200	.040		2.61	1.07		3.68	4.55	
	8200	.125" thick, minimum		230	.035		1.63	.93		2.56	3.25	
	8250	Maximum		200	.040		3.57	1.07		4.64	5.60	
	8700	Adhesive cement, 1 gallon does 200 to 300 S.F.				Gal.	13.40			13.40	14.75	
	8800	Asphalt primer, 1 gallon per 300 S.F.					8.40			8.40	9.25	
	8900	Emulsion, 1 gallon per 140 S.F.					8.65			8.65	9.55	
	8950	Latex underlayment, liquid, fortified					27.50			27.50	30	
	9500	Minimum labor/equipment charge	1 Tilf	4	2	Job		53.50		53.50	84	

096 780 | Resilient Accessories

		CREW	DAILY OUTPUT	LABOR-HOURS	UNIT	MAT.	LABOR	EQUIP.	TOTAL	TOTAL INCL O&P	
781	0010	**STAIR TREADS AND RISERS** See index for materials other										781
	0100	than rubber and vinyl										
	0300	Rubber, molded tread, 12" wide, 5/16" thick, black	1 Tilf	115	.070	L.F.	6.55	1.85		8.40	10.20	
	0400	Colors		115	.070		6.75	1.85		8.60	10.40	
	0600	1/4" thick, black		115	.070		6.25	1.85		8.10	9.85	
	0700	Colors		115	.070		6.80	1.85		8.65	10.40	
	0900	Grip strip safety tread, colors, 5/16" thick		115	.070		9.85	1.85		11.70	13.80	
	1000	3/16" thick		120	.067		7.45	1.78		9.23	10.95	
	1200	Landings, smooth sheet rubber, 1/8" thick		120	.067	S.F.	2.47	1.78		4.25	5.50	
	1300	3/16" thick		120	.067	"	3.59	1.78		5.37	6.75	
	1500	Nosings, 3" wide, 3/16" thick, black		140	.057	L.F.	2.41	1.52		3.93	5.05	
	1600	Colors		140	.057		2.53	1.52		4.05	5.20	

For expanded coverage of these items see *Means Interior Cost Data 1999*

096 | Flooring & Carpet

096 780 | Resilient Accessories

		CREW	DAILY OUTPUT	LABOR-HOURS	UNIT	1999 BARE COSTS MAT.	LABOR	EQUIP.	TOTAL	TOTAL INCL O&P	
781	1800 Risers, 7" high, 1/8" thick, flat	1 Tilf	250	.032	L.F.	3.26	.85		4.11	4.94	781
	1900 Coved		250	.032		2.29	.85		3.14	3.87	
	2100 Vinyl, molded tread, 12" wide, colors, 1/8" thick		115	.070		2.63	1.85		4.48	5.80	
	2200 1/4" thick		115	.070		4.33	1.85		6.18	7.70	
	2300 Landing material, 1/8" thick		200	.040	S.F.	2.73	1.07		3.80	4.68	
	2400 Riser, 7" high, 1/8" thick, coved		175	.046	L.F.	1.61	1.22		2.83	3.69	
	2500 Tread and riser combined, 1/8" thick		80	.100	"	4.06	2.66		6.72	8.65	
	9000 Minimum labor/equipment charge		3	2.667	Job		71		71	112	

096 850 | Sheet Carpet

		CREW	DAILY OUTPUT	LABOR-HOURS	UNIT	MAT.	LABOR	EQUIP.	TOTAL	TOTAL INCL O&P	
852	0010 **CARPET** Commercial grades, direct cement										852
	0700 Nylon, level loop, 26 oz., light to medium traffic	1 Tilf	75	.107	S.Y.	12.70	2.84		15.54	18.50	
	0720 28 oz., light to medium traffic		75	.107		13.95	2.84		16.79	19.85	
	0900 32 oz., medium traffic		75	.107		18	2.84		20.84	24.50	
	1100 40 oz., medium to heavy traffic		75	.107		27	2.84		29.84	34	
	2920 Nylon plush, 30 oz., medium traffic		57	.140		13.30	3.74		17.04	20.50	
	3000 36 oz., medium traffic		75	.107		16.75	2.84		19.59	23	
	3100 42 oz., medium to heavy traffic		70	.114		19.30	3.05		22.35	26.50	
	3200 46 oz., medium to heavy traffic		70	.114		23	3.05		26.05	30.50	
	3300 54 oz., heavy traffic		70	.114		26	3.05		29.05	33.50	
	4500 50 oz., medium to heavy traffic		75	.107		59	2.84		61.84	69.50	
	4700 Patterned, 32 oz., medium to heavy traffic		70	.114		58.50	3.05		61.55	69	
	4900 48 oz., heavy traffic		70	.114		59.50	3.05		62.55	70.50	
	5000 For less than full roll, add					25%					
	5100 For small rooms, less than 12' wide, add						25%				
	5200 For large open areas (no cuts), deduct						25%				
	5600 For bound carpet baseboard, add	1 Tilf	300	.027	L.F.	1	.71		1.71	2.22	
	5610 For stairs, not incl. price of carpet, add	"	30	.267	Riser		7.10		7.10	11.20	
	5620 For borders and patterns, add to labor						18%				
	8950 For tackless, stretched installation, add padding to above										
	9000 Sponge rubber pad, minimum	1 Tilf	150	.053	S.Y.	2.55	1.42		3.97	5.05	
	9100 Maximum		150	.053		6.85	1.42		8.27	9.75	
	9200 Felt pad, minimum		150	.053		3.04	1.42		4.46	5.60	
	9300 Maximum		150	.053		5.10	1.42		6.52	7.85	
	9400 Bonded urethane pad, minimum		150	.053		3.10	1.42		4.52	5.65	
	9500 Maximum		150	.053		5.50	1.42		6.92	8.30	
	9600 Prime urethane pad, minimum		150	.053		1.80	1.42		3.22	4.22	
	9700 Maximum		150	.053		3.30	1.42		4.72	5.85	
	9850 For "branded" fiber, add					25%					
	9900 Carpet cleaning machine, rent				Day					35	
	9910 Minimum labor/equipment charge	1 Tilf	3	2.667	Job		71		71	112	

096 900 | Carpet Tile

		CREW	DAILY OUTPUT	LABOR-HOURS	UNIT	MAT.	LABOR	EQUIP.	TOTAL	TOTAL INCL O&P	
901	0010 **CARPET TILE**										901
	0100 Tufted nylon, 18" x 18", hard back, 20 oz.	1 Tilf	150	.053	S.Y.	16.60	1.42		18.02	20.50	
	0110 26 oz.		150	.053		28.50	1.42		29.92	33	
	0200 Cushion back, 20 oz.		150	.053		21	1.42		22.42	25	
	0210 26 oz.		150	.053		32.50	1.42		33.92	38	

097 | Special Flooring & Floor Treatment

097 200 | Epoxy-Marble Flooring

		CREW	DAILY OUTPUT	LABOR-HOURS	UNIT	MAT.	LABOR	EQUIP.	TOTAL	TOTAL INCL O&P	
201	0010	COMPOSITION FLOORING Acrylic, 1/4" thick	C-6	520	.092	S.F.	1.16	2.08	.14	3.38	4.89	201
	0050											
	0600	Epoxy, with colored quartz chips, broadcast, minimum	C-6	675	.071	S.F.	2.04	1.60	.11	3.75	5	
	0700	Maximum		490	.098		2.47	2.21	.15	4.83	6.55	
	0900	Trowelled, minimum		560	.086		2.63	1.93	.13	4.69	6.25	
	1000	Maximum		480	.100		3.83	2.26	.16	6.25	8.10	
	1200	Heavy duty epoxy topping, 1/4" thick,										
	1300	500 to 1,000 S.F.	C-6	420	.114	S.F.	4.02	2.58	.18	6.78	8.90	
	1500	1,000 to 2,000 S.F.		450	.107		2.94	2.41	.17	5.52	7.40	
	1600	Over 10,000 S.F.		480	.100		2.62	2.26	.16	5.04	6.80	
	1800	Epoxy terrazzo, 1/4" thick, chemical resistant, minimum	J-3	200	.080		4.28	1.93	.49	6.70	8.30	
	1900	Maximum	"	150	.107		7	2.58	.66	10.24	12.50	

098 | Special Coatings

098 150 | Glazed Coatings

		CREW	DAILY OUTPUT	LABOR-HOURS	UNIT	MAT.	LABOR	EQUIP.	TOTAL	TOTAL INCL O&P	
150	0010	WALL COATINGS Acrylic glazed coatings, minimum	1 Pord	525	.015	S.F.	.23	.38		.61	.87	150
	0100	Maximum		305	.026		.49	.65		1.14	1.60	
	0300	Epoxy coatings, minimum		525	.015		.30	.38		.68	.95	
	0400	Maximum		170	.047		.93	1.17		2.10	2.93	
	2400	Sprayed perlite or vermiculite, 1/16" thick, minimum		2,935	.003		.19	.07		.26	.32	
	2500	Maximum		640	.013		.56	.31		.87	1.13	
	2700	Vinyl plastic wall coating, minimum		735	.011		.25	.27		.52	.72	
	2800	Maximum		240	.033		.62	.83		1.45	2.03	
	3000	Urethane on smooth surface, 2 coats, minimum		1,135	.007		.18	.18		.36	.49	
	3100	Maximum		665	.012		.43	.30		.73	.96	

099 | Painting & Wall Coverings

099 100 | Exterior Painting

		CREW	DAILY OUTPUT	LABOR-HOURS	UNIT	MAT.	LABOR	EQUIP.	TOTAL	TOTAL INCL O&P	
104	0010	DOORS AND WINDOWS										104
	0100	Door frames & trim, only										
	0110	Brushwork, primer	1 Pord	512	.016	L.F.	.05	.39		.44	.68	
	0120	Finish coat, exterior latex		512	.016		.05	.39		.44	.69	
	0130	Primer & 1 coat, exterior latex		300	.027		.10	.66		.76	1.19	
	0135	2 coats, exterior latex, both sides		15	.533	Ea.	4.62	13.30		17.92	26.50	
	0140	Primer & 2 coats, exterior latex		265	.030	L.F.	.15	.75		.90	1.39	
	0150	Doors, flush, both sides, incl. frame & trim										
	0160	Roll & brush, primer	1 Pord	10	.800	Ea.	3.42	19.90		23.32	36.50	
	0170	Finish coat, exterior latex		10	.800		3.93	19.90		23.83	37	
	0180	Primer & 1 coat, exterior latex		7	1.143		7.35	28.50		35.85	54.50	
	0190	Primer & 2 coats, exterior latex		5	1.600		11.30	40		51.30	77.50	
	0200	Brushwork, stain, sealer & 2 coats polyurethane		4	2		13.10	50		63.10	95.50	
	0210	Doors, French, both sides, 10-15 lite, incl. frame & trim										

For expanded coverage of these items see *Means Interior Cost Data 1999*

099 | Painting & Wall Coverings

099 100 | Exterior Painting

		CREW	DAILY OUTPUT	LABOR-HOURS	UNIT	MAT.	LABOR	EQUIP.	TOTAL	TOTAL INCL O&P	
104	0220 Brushwork, primer	1 Pord	6	1.333	Ea.	1.71	33		34.71	56	104
	0230 Finish coat, exterior latex		6	1.333		1.97	33		34.97	56	
	0240 Primer & 1 coat, exterior latex		3	2.667		3.68	66.50		70.18	112	
	0250 Primer & 2 coats, exterior latex		2	4		5.55	99.50		105.05	168	
	0260 Brushwork, stain, sealer & 2 coats polyurethane	▼	2.50	3.200	▼	4.70	79.50		84.20	135	
	0270 Doors, louvered, both sides, incl. frame & trim										
	0280 Brushwork, primer	1 Pord	7	1.143	Ea.	3.42	28.50		31.92	50.50	
	0290 Finish coat, exterior latex		7	1.143		3.93	28.50		32.43	51	
	0300 Primer & 1 coat, exterior latex		4	2		7.35	50		57.35	89	
	0310 Primer & 2 coats, exterior latex		3	2.667		11.05	66.50		77.55	120	
	0320 Brushwork, stain, sealer & 2 coats polyurethane	▼	4.50	1.778	▼	13.10	44.50		57.60	86.50	
	0330 Doors, panel, both sides, incl. frame & trim										
	0340 Roll & brush, primer	1 Pord	6	1.333	Ea.	3.42	33		36.42	58	
	0350 Finish coat, exterior latex		6	1.333		3.93	33		36.93	58.50	
	0360 Primer & 1 coat, exterior latex		3	2.667		7.35	66.50		73.85	116	
	0370 Primer & 2 coats, exterior latex		2.50	3.200		11.05	79.50		90.55	142	
	0380 Brushwork, stain, sealer & 2 coats polyurethane	▼	3	2.667	▼	13.10	66.50		79.60	122	
	0410 1 to 6 lite										
	0420 Brushwork, primer	1 Pord	13	.615	Ea.	.68	15.30		15.98	25.50	
	0430 Finish coat, exterior latex		13	.615		.78	15.30		16.08	26	
	0440 Primer & 1 coat, exterior latex		8	1		1.45	25		26.45	42	
	0450 Primer & 2 coats, exterior latex		6	1.333		2.18	33		35.18	56.50	
	0460 Stain, sealer & 1 coat varnish	▼	7	1.143	▼	1.86	28.50		30.36	48.50	
	0470 7 to 10 lite										
	0480 Brushwork, primer	1 Pord	11	.727	Ea.	.68	18.10		18.78	30	
	0490 Finish coat, exterior latex		11	.727		.78	18.10		18.88	30.50	
	0500 Primer & 1 coat, exterior latex		7	1.143		1.45	28.50		29.95	48	
	0510 Primer & 2 coats, exterior latex		5	1.600		2.18	40		42.18	67.50	
	0520 Stain, sealer & 1 coat varnish	▼	6	1.333	▼	1.86	33		34.86	56	
	0530 12 lite										
	0540 Brushwork, primer	1 Pord	10	.800	Ea.	.68	19.90		20.58	33	
	0550 Finish coat, exterior latex		10	.800		.78	19.90		20.68	33.50	
	0560 Primer & 1 coat, exterior latex		6	1.333		1.45	33		34.45	55.50	
	0570 Primer & 2 coats, exterior latex		5	1.600		2.18	40		42.18	67.50	
	0580 Stain, sealer & 1 coat varnish	▼	6	1.333	▼	1.84	33		34.84	56	
	0590 For oil base paint, add					10%					
106	0010 **SIDING** Exterior, Alkyd (oil base)										106
	0500 Spray	2 Pord	4,550	.004	S.F.	.07	.09		.16	.22	
	0800 Paint 2 coats, brushwork		1,300	.012		.10	.31		.41	.61	
	1000 Spray		4,550	.004		.14	.09		.23	.29	
	1200 Stucco, rough, oil base, paint 2 coats, brushwork		1,300	.012		.10	.31		.41	.61	
	1400 Roller		1,625	.010		.10	.25		.35	.51	
	1600 Spray		2,925	.005		.11	.14		.25	.34	
	1800 Texture 1-11 or clapboard, oil base, primer coat, brushwork		1,300	.012		.08	.31		.39	.58	
	2000 Spray		4,550	.004		.08	.09		.17	.22	
	2400 Paint 2 coats, brushwork		810	.020		.14	.49		.63	.95	
	2600 Spray		2,600	.006		.16	.15		.31	.42	
	3400 Stain 2 coats, brushwork		950	.017		.08	.42		.50	.77	
	4000 Spray		3,050	.005		.09	.13		.22	.31	
	4200 Wood shingles, oil base primer coat, brushwork		1,300	.012		.07	.31		.38	.58	
	4400 Spray		3,900	.004		.07	.10		.17	.24	
	5000 Paint 2 coats, brushwork		810	.020		.12	.49		.61	.93	
	5200 Spray		2,275	.007		.11	.18		.29	.41	
	6500 Stain 2 coats, brushwork		950	.017		.08	.42		.50	.77	
	7000 Spray	▼	2,660	.006	▼	.11	.15		.26	.36	
	8000 For latex paint, deduct					10%					

Important: See the Reference Section for critical supporting data - Reference Nos., Crews, & City Cost Indexes

099 | Painting & Wall Coverings

099 100 | Exterior Painting

			DAILY	LABOR-		1999 BARE COSTS				TOTAL
		CREW	OUTPUT	HOURS	UNIT	MAT.	LABOR	EQUIP.	TOTAL	INCL O&P
108	0010 **FENCES**									
	0100 Chain link or wire metal, water base									
	0110 Roll & brush, first coat	1 Pord	960	.008	S.F.	.05	.21		.26	.40
	0120 Second coat		1,280	.006	"	.05	.16		.21	.30
	0130 Spray, first coat		2,275	.004	S.F.	.05	.09		.14	.20
	0140 Second coat		2,600	.003	"	.05	.08		.13	.18
	0150 Picket, water base									
	0160 Roll & brush, first coat	1 Pord	865	.009	S.F.	.06	.23		.29	.44
	0170 Second coat		1,050	.008	S.F.	.06	.19		.25	.37
	0180 Spray, first coat		2,275	.004		.06	.09		.15	.20
	0190 Second coat		2,600	.003		.06	.08		.14	.18
	0200 Stockade, water base									
	0210 Roll & brush, first coat	1 Pord	1,040	.008	S.F.	.06	.19		.25	.37
	0220 Second coat		1,200	.007	S.F.	.06	.17		.23	.33
	0230 Spray, first coat		2,275	.004		.06	.09		.15	.20
	0240 Second coat		2,600	.003		.06	.08		.14	.18
112	0010 **MISCELLANEOUS**, for painting metals see Div. 051-255									
	0100 Railing, ext., decorative wood, incl. cap & baluster									
	0110 newels & spindles @ 12" O.C.									
	0120 Brushwork, stain, sand, seal & varnish									
	0130 First coat	1 Pord	90	.089	L.F.	.37	2.21		2.58	4.02
	0140 Second coat	"	120	.067	"	.37	1.66		2.03	3.12
	0150 Rough sawn wood, 42" high, 2"x2" verticals, 6" O.C.									
	0160 Brushwork, stain, each coat	1 Pord	90	.089	L.F.	.12	2.21		2.33	3.74
	0170 Wrought iron, 1" rail, 1/2" sq. verticals									
	0180 Brushwork, zinc chromate, 60" high, bars 6" O.C.									
	0190 Primer	1 Pord	130	.062	L.F.	.24	1.53		1.77	2.76
	0200 Finish coat		130	.062		.15	1.53		1.68	2.66
	0210 Additional coat		190	.042		.17	1.05		1.22	1.90
	0220 Shutters or blinds, single panel, 2'x4', paint all sides									
	0230 Brushwork, primer	1 Pord	20	.400	Ea.	.50	9.95		10.45	16.80
	0240 Finish coat, exterior latex		20	.400		.41	9.95		10.36	16.70
	0250 Primer & 1 coat, exterior latex		13	.615		.80	15.30		16.10	26
	0260 Spray, primer		35	.229		.72	5.70		6.42	10.10
	0270 Finish coat, exterior latex		35	.229		.88	5.70		6.58	10.25
	0280 Primer & 1 coat, exterior latex		20	.400		.78	9.95		10.73	17.10
	0290 For louvered shutters, add				S.F.	10%				
	0300 Stair stringers, exterior, metal									
	0310 Roll & brush, zinc chromate, to 14", each coat	1 Pord	320	.025	L.F.	.05	.62		.67	1.06
	0320 Rough sawn wood, 4" x 12"									
	0330 Roll & brush, exterior latex, each coat	1 Pord	215	.037	L.F.	.06	.93		.99	1.58
	0340 Trellis/lattice, 2"x2" @ 3" O.C. with 2"x8" supports									
	0350 Spray, latex, per side, each coat	1 Pord	475	.017	S.F.	.06	.42		.48	.75
	0450 Decking, Ext., sealer, alkyd, brushwork, sealer coat		1,140	.007		.04	.17		.21	.33
	0460 1st coat		1,140	.007		.05	.17		.22	.33
	0470 2nd coat		1,300	.006		.03	.15		.18	.29
	0500 Paint, alkyd, brushwork, primer coat		1,140	.007		.06	.17		.23	.35
	0510 1st coat		1,140	.007		.06	.17		.23	.35
	0520 2nd coat		1,300	.006	S.F.	.04	.15		.19	.30
	0600 Sand paint, alkyd, brushwork, 1 coat		150	.053	S.F.	.07	1.33		1.40	2.24
116	0010 **SIDING**									
	0100 Aluminum siding									
	0110 Brushwork, primer	2 Pord	2,275	.007	S.F.	.05	.18		.23	.34
	0120 Finish coat, exterior latex		2,275	.007	S.F.	.04	.18		.22	.33
	0130 Primer & 1 coat exterior latex		1,300	.012	S.F.	.09	.31		.40	.60
	0140 Primer & 2 coats exterior latex		975	.016	"	.12	.41		.53	.80

For expanded coverage of these items see *Means Interior Cost Data 1999*

099 | Painting & Wall Coverings

099 100 | Exterior Painting

		CREW	DAILY OUTPUT	LABOR-HOURS	UNIT	MAT.	LABOR	EQUIP.	TOTAL	TOTAL INCL O&P
						\multicolumn{4}{c}{1999 BARE COSTS}	

Line	Description	CREW	DAILY OUTPUT	LABOR-HOURS	UNIT	MAT.	LABOR	EQUIP.	TOTAL	TOTAL INCL O&P
0150	Mineral Fiber shingles									
0160	Brushwork, primer	2 Pord	1,495	.011	S.F.	.08	.27		.35	.51
0170	Finish coat, industrial enamel		1,495	.011	S.F.	.08	.27		.35	.51
0180	Primer & 1 coat enamel		810	.020	S.F.	.15	.49		.64	.97
0190	Primer & 2 coats enamel		540	.030		.23	.74		.97	1.45
0200	Roll, primer		1,625	.010		.09	.25		.34	.49
0210	Finish coat, industrial enamel		1,625	.010		.08	.25		.33	.49
0220	Primer & 1 coat enamel		975	.016		.17	.41		.58	.85
0230	Primer & 2 coats enamel		650	.025		.25	.61		.86	1.27
0240	Spray, primer		3,900	.004		.07	.10		.17	.24
0250	Finish coat, industrial enamel		3,900	.004		.07	.10		.17	.25
0260	Primer & 1 coat enamel		2,275	.007		.13	.18		.31	.44
0270	Primer & 2 coats enamel		1,625	.010		.20	.25		.45	.62
0280	Waterproof sealer, first coat		4,485	.004		.06	.09		.15	.21
0290	Second coat	▼	5,235	.003	▼	.06	.08		.14	.18
0300	Rough wood incl. shingles, shakes or rough sawn siding									
0310	Brushwork, primer	2 Pord	1,280	.013	S.F.	.10	.31		.41	.62
0320	Finish coat, exterior latex		1,280	.013	S.F.	.06	.31		.37	.58
0330	Primer & 1 coat exterior latex		960	.017	S.F.	.16	.41		.57	.86
0340	Primer & 2 coats exterior latex		700	.023	S.F.	.23	.57		.80	1.18
0350	Roll, primer		2,925	.005	S.F.	.13	.14		.27	.37
0360	Finish coat, exterior latex		2,925	.005		.08	.14		.22	.30
0370	Primer & 1 coat exterior latex		1,790	.009		.21	.22		.43	.59
0380	Primer & 2 coats exterior latex		1,300	.012		.28	.31		.59	.81
0390	Spray, primer		3,900	.004		.11	.10		.21	.29
0400	Finish coat, exterior latex		3,900	.004		.06	.10		.16	.23
0410	Primer & 1 coat exterior latex		2,600	.006		.17	.15		.32	.44
0420	Primer & 2 coats exterior latex		2,080	.008		.23	.19		.42	.56
0430	Waterproof sealer, first coat		4,485	.004		.11	.09		.20	.26
0440	Second coat	▼	4,485	.004	▼	.06	.09		.15	.21
0450	Smooth wood incl. butt, T&G, beveled, drop or B&B siding									
0460	Brushwork, primer	2 Pord	2,325	.007	S.F.	.07	.17		.24	.36
0470	Finish coat, exterior latex		1,280	.013	S.F.	.06	.31		.37	.58
0480	Primer & 1 coat exterior latex		800	.020	S.F.	.13	.50		.63	.96
0490	Primer & 2 coats exterior latex		630	.025		.20	.63		.83	1.25
0500	Roll, primer		2,275	.007		.08	.18		.26	.38
0510	Finish coat, exterior latex		2,275	.007		.07	.18		.25	.36
0520	Primer & 1 coat exterior latex		1,300	.012		.15	.31		.46	.66
0530	Primer & 2 coats exterior latex		975	.016		.22	.41		.63	.91
0540	Spray, primer		4,550	.004		.06	.09		.15	.21
0550	Finish coat, exterior latex		4,550	.004		.06	.09		.15	.20
0560	Primer & 1 coat exterior latex		2,600	.006		.12	.15		.27	.38
0570	Primer & 2 coats exterior latex		1,950	.008		.18	.20		.38	.53
0580	Waterproof sealer, first coat		5,230	.003		.06	.08		.14	.19
0590	Second coat	▼	5,980	.003	▼	.06	.07		.13	.18
0600	For oil base paint, add				S.F.	10%				
0010	**TRIM**									
0100	Door frames & trim (see Doors, interior or exterior)									
0110	Fascia, latex paint, one coat coverage									
0120	1" x 4", brushwork	1 Pord	640	.013	L.F.	.02	.31		.33	.53
0130	Roll		1,280	.006		.02	.16		.18	.27
0140	Spray		2,080	.004		.01	.10		.11	.17
0150	1" x 6" to 1" x 10", brushwork		640	.013		.06	.31		.37	.57
0160	Roll		1,230	.007		.06	.16		.22	.32
0170	Spray		2,100	.004		.04	.09		.13	.20
0180	1" x 12", brushwork	▼	640	.013	▼	.06	.31		.37	.57

099 | Painting & Wall Coverings

099 100 | Exterior Painting

			CREW	DAILY OUTPUT	LABOR-HOURS	UNIT	MAT.	LABOR	EQUIP.	TOTAL	TOTAL INCL O&P	
120	0190	Roll	1 Pord	1,050	.008	L.F.	.06	.19		.25	.37	120
	0200	Spray	↓	2,200	.004	↓	.04	.09		.13	.20	
	0210	Gutters & downspouts, metal, zinc chromate paint										
	0220	Brushwork, gutters, 5", first coat	1 Pord	640	.013	L.F.	.05	.31		.36	.57	
	0230	Second coat		960	.008		.05	.21		.26	.39	
	0240	Third coat		1,280	.006		.04	.16		.20	.29	
	0250	Downspouts, 4", first coat		640	.013		.05	.31		.36	.57	
	0260	Second coat		960	.008		.05	.21		.26	.39	
	0270	Third coat	↓	1,280	.006	↓	.04	.16		.20	.29	
	0280	Gutters & downspouts, wood										
	0290	Brushwork, gutters, 5", primer	1 Pord	640	.013	L.F.	.05	.31		.36	.56	
	0300	Finish coat, exterior latex		640	.013		.05	.31		.36	.56	
	0310	Primer & 1 coat exterior latex		400	.020		.10	.50		.60	.92	
	0320	Primer & 2 coats exterior latex		325	.025		.15	.61		.76	1.16	
	0330	Downspouts, 4", primer		640	.013		.05	.31		.36	.56	
	0340	Finish coat, exterior latex		640	.013		.05	.31		.36	.56	
	0350	Primer & 1 coat exterior latex		400	.020		.10	.50		.60	.92	
	0360	Primer & 2 coats exterior latex	↓	325	.025	↓	.07	.61		.68	1.08	
	0370	Molding, exterior, up to 14" wide										
	0380	Brushwork, primer	1 Pord	640	.013	L.F.	.05	.31		.36	.57	
	0390	Finish coat, exterior latex		640	.013		.06	.31		.37	.57	
	0400	Primer & 1 coat exterior latex		400	.020		.12	.50		.62	.94	
	0410	Primer & 2 coats exterior latex		315	.025		.12	.63		.75	1.16	
	0420	Stain & fill		1,050	.008		.05	.19		.24	.36	
	0430	Shellac		1,850	.004		.05	.11		.16	.24	
	0440	Varnish	↓	1,275	.006	↓	.06	.16		.22	.32	
124	0350	**WALLS, MASONRY (CMU)**										124
	0360	Concrete masonry units (CMU), smooth surface										
	0370	Brushwork, latex, first coat	1 Pord	640	.013	S.F.	.03	.31		.34	.55	
	0380	Second coat		960	.008		.03	.21		.24	.37	
	0390	Waterproof sealer, first coat		736	.011		.06	.27		.33	.51	
	0400	Second coat		1,104	.007		.04	.18		.22	.33	
	0410	Roll, latex, paint, first coat		1,465	.005		.04	.14		.18	.26	
	0420	Second coat		1,790	.004		.03	.11		.14	.21	
	0430	Waterproof sealer, first coat		1,680	.005		.06	.12		.18	.26	
	0440	Second coat		2,060	.004		.04	.10		.14	.20	
	0450	Spray, latex, paint, first coat		1,950	.004		.03	.10		.13	.20	
	0460	Second coat		2,600	.003		.02	.08		.10	.15	
	0470	Waterproof sealer, first coat		2,245	.004		.04	.09		.13	.18	
	0480	Second coat	↓	2,990	.003	↓	.03	.07		.10	.14	
	0490	Concrete masonry unit (CMU), porous										
	0500	Brushwork, latex, first coat	1 Pord	640	.013	S.F.	.07	.31		.38	.58	
	0510	Second coat		960	.008		.03	.21		.24	.38	
	0520	Waterproof sealer, first coat		736	.011		.05	.27		.32	.49	
	0530	Second coat		1,104	.007		.04	.18		.22	.33	
	0540	Roll latex, first coat		1,465	.005		.05	.14		.19	.27	
	0550	Second coat		1,790	.004		.03	.11		.14	.21	
	0560	Waterproof sealer, first coat		1,400	.006		.06	.14		.20	.30	
	0570	Second coat		2,200	.004		.04	.09		.13	.20	
	0580	Spray latex, first coat		5,600	.001		.03	.04		.07	.09	
	0590	Second coat		6,400	.001		.02	.03		.05	.08	
	0600	Waterproof sealer, first coat		6,000	.001		.06	.03		.09	.12	
	0610	Second coat	↓	6,400	.001	↓	.03	.03		.06	.09	

For expanded coverage of these items see *Means Interior Cost Data 1999*

099 | Painting & Wall Coverings

099 200 | Interior Painting

		CREW	DAILY OUTPUT	LABOR-HOURS	UNIT	1999 BARE COSTS				TOTAL INCL O&P
						MAT.	LABOR	EQUIP.	TOTAL	
0010	**CABINETS AND CASEWORK**									
1000	Primer coat, oil base, brushwork	1 Pord	650	.012	S.F.	.04	.31		.35	.55
2000	Paint, oil base, brushwork, 1 coat		650	.012		.05	.31		.36	.56
3000	Stain, brushwork, wipe off		650	.012		.04	.31		.35	.54
4000	Shellac, 1 coat, brushwork		650	.012		.05	.31		.36	.55
4500	Varnish, 3 coats, brushwork, sand after 1st coat	↓	325	.025		.16	.61		.77	1.17
5000	For latex paint, deduct				↓	10%				
0010	**DOORS & WINDOWS, LATEX**									
0100	Doors flush, both sides, incl. frame & trim									
0110	Roll & brush, primer	1 Pord	10	.800	Ea.	2.99	19.90		22.89	36
0120	Finish coat, latex		10	.800		3.04	19.90		22.94	36
0130	Primer & 1 coat latex		7	1.143		6.05	28.50		34.55	53
0140	Primer & 2 coats latex		5	1.600		8.90	40		48.90	75
0160	Spray, both sides, primer		20	.400		3.15	9.95		13.10	19.70
0170	Finish coat, latex		20	.400		3.19	9.95		13.14	19.75
0180	Primer & 1 coat latex		11	.727		6.40	18.10		24.50	36.50
0190	Primer & 2 coats latex	↓	8	1		9.40	25		34.40	51
0200	Doors, French, both sides, 10-15 lite, incl. frame & trim									
0210	Roll & brush, primer	1 Pord	6	1.333	Ea.	1.50	33		34.50	55.50
0220	Finish coat, latex		6	1.333		1.52	33		34.52	55.50
0230	Primer & 1 coat latex		3	2.667		3.02	66.50		69.52	111
0240	Primer & 2 coats latex	↓	2	4	↓	4.45	99.50		103.95	167
0260	Doors, louvered, both sides, incl. frame & trim									
0270	Roll & brush, primer	1 Pord	7	1.143	Ea.	2.99	28.50		31.49	50
0280	Finish coat, latex		7	1.143		3.04	28.50		31.54	50
0290	Primer & 1 coat, latex		4	2		5.85	50		55.85	87.50
0300	Primer & 2 coats, latex		3	2.667		9.05	66.50		75.55	118
0320	Spray, both sides, primer		20	.400		3.15	9.95		13.10	19.70
0330	Finish coat, latex		20	.400		3.19	9.95		13.14	19.75
0340	Primer & 1 coat, latex		11	.727		6.40	18.10		24.50	36.50
0350	Primer & 2 coats, latex	↓	8	1		9.60	25		34.60	51
0360	Doors, panel, both sides, incl. frame & trim									
0370	Roll & brush, primer	1 Pord	6	1.333	Ea.	3.15	33		36.15	57.50
0380	Finish coat, latex		6	1.333		3.04	33		36.04	57.50
0390	Primer & 1 coat, latex		3	2.667		6.05	66.50		72.55	115
0400	Primer & 2 coats, latex		2.50	3.200		9.05	79.50		88.55	140
0420	Spray, both sides, primer		10	.800		3.15	19.90		23.05	36
0430	Finish coat, latex		10	.800		3.19	19.90		23.09	36
0440	Primer & 1 coat, latex		5	1.600		6.40	40		46.40	72
0450	Primer & 2 coats, latex	↓	4	2	↓	9.60	50		59.60	91.50
0460	Windows, per interior side, base on 15 SF									
0470	1 to 6 lite									
0480	Brushwork, primer	1 Pord	13	.615	Ea.	.59	15.30		15.89	25.50
0490	Finish coat, enamel		13	.615		.60	15.30		15.90	25.50
0500	Primer & 1 coat enamel		8	1		1.19	25		26.19	42
0510	Primer & 2 coats enamel	↓	6	1.333	↓	1.79	33		34.79	56
0530	7 to 10 lite									
0540	Brushwork, primer	1 Pord	11	.727	Ea.	.59	18.10		18.69	30
0550	Finish coat, enamel		11	.727		.60	18.10		18.70	30
0560	Primer & 1 coat enamel		7	1.143		1.19	28.50		29.69	48
0570	Primer & 2 coats enamel	↓	5	1.600		1.79	40		41.79	67
0590	12 lite									
0600	Brushwork, primer	1 Pord	10	.800	Ea.	.59	19.90		20.49	33
0610	Finish coat, enamel		10	.800		.60	19.90		20.50	33
0620	Primer & 1 coat enamel	↓	6	1.333		1.19	33		34.19	55.50

099 | Painting & Wall Coverings

099 200 | Interior Painting

			CREW	DAILY OUTPUT	LABOR-HOURS	UNIT	MAT.	LABOR	EQUIP.	TOTAL	TOTAL INCL O&P	
214	0630	Primer & 2 coats enamel	1 Pord	5	1.600	Ea.	1.79	40		41.79	67	214
	0650	For oil base paint, add					10%					
216	0010	**DOORS AND WINDOWS, ALKYD (OIL BASE)**										216
	0500	Flush door & frame, 3' x 7', oil, primer, brushwork	1 Pord	10	.800	Ea.	1.71	19.90		21.61	34.50	
	1000	Paint, 1 coat		10	.800		1.79	19.90		21.69	34.50	
	1400	Stain, brushwork, wipe off		18	.444		.84	11.05		11.89	18.95	
	1600	Shellac, 1 coat, brushwork		25	.320		.94	7.95		8.89	14.05	
	1800	Varnish, 3 coats, brushwork, sand after 1st coat		9	.889		3.31	22		25.31	39.50	
	2000	Panel door & frame, 3' x 7', oil, primer, brushwork		6	1.333		1.61	33		34.61	56	
	2200	Paint, 1 coat		6	1.333		1.79	33		34.79	56	
	2600	Stain, brushwork, panel door, 3' x 7', not incl. frame		16	.500		.84	12.45		13.29	21.50	
	2800	Shellac, 1 coat, brushwork		22	.364		.94	9.05		9.99	15.80	
	3000	Varnish, 3 coats, brushwork, sand after 1st coat		7.50	1.067		3.31	26.50		29.81	47	
	4400	Windows, including frame and trim, per side										
	4600	Colonial type, 6/6 lites, 2' x 3', oil, primer, brushwork	1 Pord	14	.571	Ea.	.26	14.25		14.51	23.50	
	5800	Paint, 1 coat		14	.571		.28	14.25		14.53	23.50	
	6200	3' x 5' opening, 6/6 lites, primer coat, brushwork		12	.667		.64	16.60		17.24	27.50	
	6400	Paint, 1 coat		12	.667		.71	16.60		17.31	28	
	6800	4' x 8' opening, 6/6 lites, primer coat, brushwork		8	1		1.36	25		26.36	42	
	7000	Paint, 1 coat		8	1		1.51	25		26.51	42	
	8000	Single lite type, 2' x 3', oil base, primer coat, brushwork		33	.242		.26	6.05		6.31	10.15	
	8200	Paint, 1 coat		33	.242		.28	6.05		6.33	10.15	
	8600	3' x 5' opening, primer coat, brushwork		20	.400		.64	9.95		10.59	16.95	
	8800	Paint, 1 coat		20	.400		.71	9.95		10.66	17.05	
	9200	4' x 8' opening, primer coat, brushwork		14	.571		1.36	14.25		15.61	24.50	
	9400	Paint, 1 coat		14	.571		1.51	14.25		15.76	24.50	
218	0010	**FLOORS**										218
	0100	Concrete										
	0120	1st coat	1 Pord	975	.008	S.F.	.10	.20		.30	.44	
	0130	2nd coat		1,150	.007		.07	.17		.24	.35	
	0140	3rd coat		1,300	.006		.05	.15		.20	.31	
	0150	Roll, latex, block filler										
	0160	1st coat	1 Pord	2,600	.003	S.F.	.13	.08		.21	.26	
	0170	2nd coat		3,250	.002		.08	.06		.14	.19	
	0180	3rd coat		3,900	.002		.06	.05		.11	.14	
	0190	Spray, latex, block filler										
	0200	1st coat	1 Pord	2,600	.003	S.F.	.11	.08		.19	.24	
	0210	2nd coat		3,250	.002		.06	.06		.12	.17	
	0220	3rd coat		3,900	.002		.05	.05		.10	.13	
220	0010	**MISCELLANEOUS PAINTING**										220
	2400	Floors, conc./wood, oil base, primer/sealer coat, brushwork	2 Pord	1,950	.008	S.F.	.05	.20		.25	.38	
	2450	Roller		5,200	.003		.05	.08		.13	.18	
	2600	Spray		6,000	.003		.05	.07		.12	.17	
	2650	Paint 1 coat, brushwork		1,950	.008		.04	.20		.24	.37	
	2800	Roller		5,200	.003		.04	.08		.12	.17	
	2850	Spray		6,000	.003		.04	.07		.11	.16	
	3000	Stain, wood floor, brushwork, 1 coat		4,550	.004		.04	.09		.13	.18	
	3200	Roller		5,200	.003		.04	.08		.12	.17	
	3250	Spray		6,000	.003		.04	.07		.11	.16	
	3400	Varnish, wood floor, brushwork		4,550	.004		.05	.09		.14	.20	
	3450	Roller		5,200	.003		.06	.08		.14	.18	
	3600	Spray		6,000	.003		.06	.07		.13	.17	
	3650	For dust proofing or anti skid, see division 033-454										
	3800	Grilles, per side, oil base, primer coat, brushwork	1 Pord	520	.015	S.F.	.08	.38		.46	.71	
	3850	Spray		1,140	.007		.09	.17		.26	.38	

For expanded coverage of these items see *Means Interior Cost Data 1999*

099 | Painting & Wall Coverings

099 200 | Interior Painting

		CREW	DAILY OUTPUT	LABOR-HOURS	UNIT	1999 BARE COSTS MAT.	LABOR	EQUIP.	TOTAL	TOTAL INCL O&P	
220	3920	Paint 2 coats, brushwork	1 Pord	325	.025	S.F.	.18	.61		.79	1.20	220
	3940	Spray	↓	650	.012	↓	.21	.31		.52	.73	
	5000	Pipe, to 4" diameter, primer or sealer coat, oil base, brushwork	2 Pord	1,250	.013	L.F.	.05	.32		.37	.58	
	5100	Spray		2,165	.007		.05	.18		.23	.35	
	5350	Paint 2 coats, brushwork		775	.021		.09	.51		.60	.94	
	5400	Spray		1,240	.013		.10	.32		.42	.63	
	6300	To 16" diameter, primer or sealer coat, brushwork		310	.052		.20	1.29		1.49	2.32	
	6450	Spray		540	.030		.21	.74		.95	1.44	
	6500	Paint 2 coats, brushwork		195	.082		.37	2.04		2.41	3.74	
	6550	Spray	↓	310	.052	↓	.42	1.29		1.71	2.56	
	7000	Trim, wood, incl. puttying, under 6" wide										
	7200	Primer coat, oil base, brushwork	1 Pord	650	.012	L.F.	.02	.31		.33	.52	
	7250	Paint, 1 coat, brushwork		650	.012		.02	.31		.33	.53	
	7450	3 coats		325	.025		.07	.61		.68	1.07	
	7500	Over 6" wide, primer coat, brushwork		650	.012		.04	.31		.35	.55	
	7550	Paint, 1 coat, brushwork		650	.012		.05	.31		.36	.55	
	7650	3 coats		325	.025	↓	.14	.61		.75	1.15	
	8000	Cornice, simple design, primer coat, oil base, brushwork		650	.012	S.F.	.04	.31		.35	.55	
	8250	Paint, 1 coat		650	.012		.05	.31		.36	.55	
	8350	Ornate design, primer coat		350	.023		.04	.57		.61	.98	
	8400	Paint, 1 coat		350	.023		.05	.57		.62	.98	
	8600	Balustrades, primer coat, oil base, brushwork	↓	520	.015	↓	.04	.38		.42	.67	
	8800											
	8900	Trusses and wood frames, primer coat, oil base, brushwork	1 Pord	800	.010	S.F.	.04	.25		.29	.46	
	8950	Spray		1,200	.007		.04	.17		.21	.32	
	9220	Paint 2 coats, brushwork		500	.016		.09	.40		.49	.75	
	9240	Spray		600	.013		.10	.33		.43	.65	
	9260	Stain, brushwork, wipe off		600	.013		.04	.33		.37	.58	
	9280	Varnish, 3 coats, brushwork	↓	275	.029		.16	.72		.88	1.35	
	9350	For latex paint, deduct				↓	10%					
224	0010	**WALLS AND CEILINGS**										224
	0100	Concrete, dry wall or plaster, oil base, primer or sealer coat										
	0200	Smooth finish, brushwork	1 Pord	1,150	.007	S.F.	.04	.17		.21	.33	
	0240	Roller		2,040	.004		.04	.10		.14	.20	
	0300	Sand finish, brushwork		975	.008		.04	.20		.24	.37	
	0340	Roller		1,150	.007		.04	.17		.21	.33	
	0380	Spray		2,275	.004		.03	.09		.12	.18	
	0800	Paint 2 coats, smooth finish, brushwork		680	.012		.07	.29		.36	.56	
	0840	Roller		800	.010		.07	.25		.32	.49	
	0880	Spray		1,625	.005		.06	.12		.18	.27	
	0900	Sand finish, brushwork		605	.013		.07	.33		.40	.62	
	0940	Roller		1,020	.008		.07	.20		.27	.40	
	0980	Spray		1,700	.005		.06	.12		.18	.26	
	1600	Glaze coating, 5 coats, spray, clear		900	.009		.60	.22		.82	1.02	
	1640	Multicolor	↓	900	.009		.77	.22		.99	1.21	
	1700	For latex paint, deduct					10%					
	1800	For ceiling installations, add				↓		25%				
	2000	Masonry or concrete block, oil base, primer or sealer coat										
	2100	Smooth finish, brushwork	1 Pord	1,224	.007	S.F.	.04	.16		.20	.32	
	2180	Spray		2,400	.003		.06	.08		.14	.21	
	2200	Sand finish, brushwork		1,089	.007		.07	.18		.25	.38	
	2280	Spray		2,400	.003		.06	.08		.14	.21	
	2800	Paint 2 coats, smooth finish, brushwork		756	.011		.14	.26		.40	.58	
	2880	Spray		1,360	.006		.13	.15		.28	.38	
	2900	Sand finish, brushwork		672	.012		.14	.30		.44	.63	
	2980	Spray	↓	1,360	.006	↓	.13	.15		.28	.38	

099 | Painting & Wall Coverings

099 200 | Interior Painting

			CREW	DAILY OUTPUT	LABOR-HOURS	UNIT	1999 BARE COSTS MAT.	LABOR	EQUIP.	TOTAL	TOTAL INCL O&P	
224	3600	Glaze coating, 5 coats, spray, clear	1 Pord	900	.009	S.F.	.60	.22		.82	1.02	224
	3620	Multicolor		900	.009		.77	.22		.99	1.21	
	4000	Block filler, 1 coat, brushwork		425	.019		.11	.47		.58	.89	
	4100	Silicone, water repellent, 2 coats, spray	↓	2,000	.004		.23	.10		.33	.42	
	4120	For latex paint, deduct				↓	10%					
228	0010	**VARNISH** 1 coat + sealer, on wood trim, no sanding included	1 Pord	400	.020	S.F.	.06	.50		.56	.88	228
	0100	Hardwood floors, 2 coats, no sanding included, roller		1,890	.004	"	.11	.11		.22	.29	
	9000	Minimum labor/equipment charge	↓	4	2	Job		50		50	81	

099 700 | Wallpaper

			CREW	DAILY OUTPUT	LABOR-HOURS	UNIT	MAT.	LABOR	EQUIP.	TOTAL	TOTAL INCL O&P	
701	0010	**WALL COVERING** Including sizing, add 10%-30% waste at takeoff										701
	0050	Aluminum foil	1 Pape	275	.029	S.F.	.76	.73		1.49	2.03	
	0100	Copper sheets, .025" thick, vinyl backing		240	.033		4.03	.84		4.87	5.80	
	0300	Phenolic backing		240	.033		5.20	.84		6.04	7.10	
	0600	Cork tiles, light or dark, 12" x 12" x 3/16"		240	.033		2.59	.84		3.43	4.22	
	0700	5/16" thick		235	.034		2.69	.85		3.54	4.35	
	0900	1/4" basketweave		240	.033		4.13	.84		4.97	5.90	
	1000	1/2" natural, non-directional pattern		240	.033		5.95	.84		6.79	7.90	
	1100	3/4" natural, non-directional pattern		240	.033		7.80	.84		8.64	9.95	
	1200	Granular surface, 12" x 36", 1/2" thick		385	.021		.89	.52		1.41	1.83	
	1300	1" thick		370	.022		1.16	.54		1.70	2.17	
	1500	Polyurethane coated, 12" x 12" x 3/16" thick		240	.033		2.79	.84		3.63	4.44	
	1600	5/16" thick		235	.034		3.96	.85		4.81	5.75	
	1800	Cork wallpaper, paperbacked, natural		480	.017		1.58	.42		2	2.42	
	1900	Colors		480	.017		1.96	.42		2.38	2.84	
	2100	Flexible wood veneer, 1/32" thick, plain woods		100	.080		1.59	2.01		3.60	5.05	
	2200	Exotic woods	↓	95	.084	↓	2.42	2.11		4.53	6.10	
	2400	Gypsum-based, fabric-backed, fire										
	2500	resistant for masonry walls, minimum, 21 oz./S.Y.	1 Pape	800	.010	S.F.	.63	.25		.88	1.10	
	2600	Average		720	.011		.87	.28		1.15	1.42	
	2700	Maximum, (small quantities)	↓	640	.013		.97	.31		1.28	1.58	
	2750	Acrylic, modified, semi-rigid PVC, .028" thick	2 Carp	330	.048		.80	1.32		2.12	3.10	
	2800	.040" thick	"	320	.050		1.05	1.36		2.41	3.44	
	3000	Vinyl wall covering, fabric-backed, lightweight, (12-15 oz./S.Y.)	1 Pape	640	.013		.51	.31		.82	1.07	
	3300	Medium weight, type 2, (20-24 oz./S.Y.)		480	.017		.63	.42		1.05	1.38	
	3400	Heavy weight, type 3, (28 oz./S.Y.)	↓	435	.018	↓	1.15	.46		1.61	2.01	
	3600	Adhesive, 5 gal. lots, (18SY/Gal.)				Gal.	8.05			8.05	8.85	
	3700	Wallpaper, average workmanship, solid pattern, low cost paper	1 Pape	640	.013	S.F.	.26	.31		.57	.80	
	3900	basic patterns (matching required), avg. cost paper		535	.015		.47	.38		.85	1.13	
	4000	Paper at $50 per double roll, quality workmanship		435	.018		.89	.46		1.35	1.73	
	4200	Grass cloths with lining paper, minimum		400	.020		.57	.50		1.07	1.45	
	4300	Maximum		350	.023		1.83	.57		2.40	2.95	
	6000	Wallpaper removal, 3 layer, maximum		400	.020	↓	.11	.50		.61	.94	
	9000	Minimum labor/equipment charge	↓	2	4	Job		100		100	164	

099 860 | Special Wall Surfaces

			CREW	DAILY OUTPUT	LABOR-HOURS	UNIT	MAT.	LABOR	EQUIP.	TOTAL	TOTAL INCL O&P	
861	0010	**FIBERGLASS REINFORCED PLASTIC** panels, .090" thick, on walls										861
	0020	Adhesive mounted, embossed surface	2 Carp	640	.025	S.F.	1.09	.68		1.77	2.34	
	0030	Smooth surface		640	.025		1.23	.68		1.91	2.49	
	0040	Fire rated, embossed surface		640	.025		1.57	.68		2.25	2.87	
	0050	Nylon rivet mounted, on drywall, embossed surface		480	.033		1.21	.91		2.12	2.85	
	0060	Smooth surface		480	.033		1.35	.91		2.26	3.01	
	0070	Fire rated, embossed surface		480	.033		1.69	.91		2.60	3.38	
	0080	On masonry, embossed surface	↓	320	.050		1.21	1.36		2.57	3.62	

For expanded coverage of these items see *Means Interior Cost Data 1999*

099 | Painting & Wall Coverings

099 860 | Special Wall Surfaces

			DAILY	LABOR-		\multicolumn{4}{c}{1999 BARE COSTS}	TOTAL
		CREW	OUTPUT	HOURS	UNIT	MAT.	LABOR	EQUIP.	TOTAL	INCL O&P
861	0090	Smooth surface	2 Carp	320	.050	S.F.	1.35	1.36		2.71	3.78	861
	0100	Fire rated, embossed surface		320	.050		1.69	1.36		3.05	4.15
	0110	Nylon rivet and adhesive mounted, on drywall, embossed surface		240	.067		1.30	1.82		3.12	4.48
	0120	Smooth surface		240	.067		1.46	1.82		3.28	4.66
	0130	Fire rated, embossed surface		240	.067		1.79	1.82		3.61	5
	0140	On masonry, embossed surface		190	.084		1.30	2.30		3.60	5.30
	0150	Smooth surface		190	.084		1.46	2.30		3.76	5.45
	0160	Fire rated, embossed surface		190	.084		1.79	2.30		4.09	5.80
	0170	For moldings add	1 Carp	250	.032	L.F.	.22	.87		1.09	1.70
	0180	On ceilings, for lay in grid system, embossed surface		400	.020	S.F.	1.09	.55		1.64	2.11
	0190	Smooth surface		400	.020		1.23	.55		1.78	2.26
	0200	Fire rated, embossed surface		400	.020		1.57	.55		2.12	2.64
863	0010	**RAISED PANEL SYSTEM**, 3/4" MDO										863
	0100	Standard, paint grade	2 Carp	300	.053	S.F.	9.70	1.46		11.16	13.10
	0110	Oak veneer		300	.053		12.15	1.46		13.61	15.80
	0120	Maple veneer		300	.053		14.20	1.46		15.66	18.05
	0130	Cherry veneer		300	.053		17.55	1.46		19.01	21.50
	0300	Class I fire rated, paint grade		300	.053		17.55	1.46		19.01	21.50
	0310	Oak veneer		300	.053		19.80	1.46		21.26	24.50
	0320	Maple veneer		300	.053		21.50	1.46		22.96	26.50
	0330	Cherry veneer		300	.053		25.50	1.46		26.96	30.50
	5000	For prefinished paneling, see division 062-504 and 062-554									
865	0010	**SLATWALL PANELS AND ACCESSORIES**										865
	0100	Slatwall panel, 4' x 8' x 3/4" T, MDF, paint grade	1 Carp	500	.016	S.F.	1.15	.44		1.59	2
	0110	Melamine finish		500	.016		1.65	.44		2.09	2.55
	0120	High pressure plastic laminate finish		500	.016		1.95	.44		2.39	2.88
	0130	Aluminum channel inserts, add					1.40			1.40	1.54
	0200	Accessories, corner forms, 8' L				L.F.	3.10			3.10	3.41
	0210	T-connector, 8' L					4.50			4.50	4.95
	0220	J-mold, 8' L					1.15			1.15	1.27
	0230	Edge cap, 8' L					.75			.75	.83
	0240	Finish end cap, 8' L					2.75			2.75	3.03
	0300	Display hook, 4" L				Ea.	.85			.85	.94
	0310	6" L					.90			.90	.99
	0320	8" L					1			1	1.10
	0330	10" L					1.10			1.10	1.21
	0340	12" L					1.20			1.20	1.32
	0350	Acrylic, 4" L					.70			.70	.77
	0360	6" L					.80			.80	.88
	0370	8" L					.85			.85	.94
	0380	10" L					.95			.95	1.05
	0400	Waterfall hanger, metal, 12" - 16"					5.40			5.40	5.95
	0410	Acrylic					7.70			7.70	8.45
	0500	Shelf bracket, metal, 8"					4.20			4.20	4.62
	0510	10"					4.50			4.50	4.95
	0520	12"					4.80			4.80	5.30
	0530	14"					5.40			5.40	5.95
	0540	16"					6			6	6.60
	0550	Acrylic, 8"					2.50			2.50	2.75
	0560	10"					2.80			2.80	3.08
	0570	12"					3.10			3.10	3.41
	0580	14"					3.50			3.50	3.85
	0600	Shelf, acrylic, 12" x 16" x 1/4"					21			21	23
	0610	12" x 24" x 1/4"					35			35	38.50

099 | Painting & Wall Coverings

099 900 | Surface Preparation

		CREW	DAILY OUTPUT	LABOR-HOURS	UNIT	1999 BARE COSTS MAT.	LABOR	EQUIP.	TOTAL	TOTAL INCL O&P	
902	0010	**REMOVAL** Existing lead paint, by chemicals, per application										902
	0020	See also, Div 020-800, Haz. Mat'l Abatement										
	0050	Baseboard, to 6" wide	1 Pord	64	.125	L.F.	1.35	3.11		4.46	6.55	
	0070	To 12" wide		32	.250	"	2.65	6.20		8.85	13.05	
	0200	Balustrades, one side		28	.286	S.F.	3.01	7.10		10.11	14.90	
	1400	Cabinets, simple design		32	.250		2.63	6.20		8.83	13.05	
	1420	Ornate design		25	.320		3.38	7.95		11.33	16.70	
	1600	Cornice, simple design		60	.133		1.41	3.32		4.73	6.95	
	1620	Ornate design		20	.400		4.16	9.95		14.11	21	
	2800	Doors, one side, flush		84	.095		1.02	2.37		3.39	4.99	
	2820	Two panel		80	.100		1.06	2.49		3.55	5.25	
	2840	Four panel		45	.178		1.87	4.43		6.30	9.25	
	2880	For trim, one side, add		64	.125	L.F.	1.35	3.11		4.46	6.55	
	3000	Fence, picket, one side		30	.267	S.F.	2.83	6.65		9.48	13.95	
	3200	Grilles, one side, simple design		30	.267		2.83	6.65		9.48	13.95	
	3220	Ornate design		25	.320		3.38	7.95		11.33	16.70	
	4400	Pipes, to 4" diameter		90	.089	L.F.	.96	2.21		3.17	4.67	
	4420	To 8" diameter		50	.160		1.68	3.98		5.66	8.35	
	4440	To 12" diameter		36	.222		2.34	5.55		7.89	11.55	
	4460	To 16" diameter		20	.400		4.19	9.95		14.14	21	
	4500	For hangers, add		40	.200	Ea.	2.10	4.98		7.08	10.40	
	4800	Siding		90	.089	S.F.	.96	2.21		3.17	4.67	
	5000	Trusses, open		55	.145	SF Face	1.53	3.62		5.15	7.60	
	6200	Windows, one side only, double hung, 1/1 light, 24" x 48" high		4	2	Ea.	21	50		71	105	
	6220	30" x 60" high		3	2.667		28	66.50		94.50	139	
	6240	36" x 72" high		2.50	3.200		34	79.50		113.50	168	
	6280	40" x 80" high		2	4		42.50	99.50		142	209	
	6400	Colonial window, 6/6 light, 24" x 48" high		2	4		42.50	99.50		142	209	
	6420	30" x 60" high		1.50	5.333		56.50	133		189.50	279	
	6440	36" x 72" high		1	8		84.50	199		283.50	420	
	6480	40" x 80" high		1	8		84.50	199		283.50	420	
	6600	8/8 light, 24" x 48" high		2	4		42.50	99.50		142	209	
	6620	40" x 80" high		1	8		84.50	199		283.50	420	
	6800	12/12 light, 24" x 48" high		1	8		84.50	199		283.50	420	
	6820	40" x 80" high		.75	10.667		113	266		379	560	
	6840	Window frame & trim items, included in pricing above										
	9000	Minimum labor/equipment charge	1 Pord	3	2.667	Job		66.50		66.50	108	
903	0010	**LEAD PAINT ENCAPSULATION**, water based polymer coating, 14 mil DFT										903
	0020	Interior, brushwork, trim, under 6"	1 Pord	240	.033	L.F.	1.99	.83		2.82	3.54	
	0030	6" to 12" wide		180	.044		2.64	1.11		3.75	4.70	
	0040	Balustrades		300	.027		1.59	.66		2.25	2.83	
	0050	Pipe to 4" diameter		500	.016		.95	.40		1.35	1.70	
	0060	To 8" diameter		375	.021		1.27	.53		1.80	2.27	
	0070	To 12" diameter		250	.032		1.90	.80		2.70	3.39	
	0080	To 16" diameter		170	.047		2.80	1.17		3.97	4.99	
	0090	Cabinets, ornate design		200	.040	S.F.	2.38	1		3.38	4.24	
	0100	Simple design		250	.032	"	1.90	.80		2.70	3.39	
	0110	Doors, 3'x 7', both sides, incl. frame & trim										
	0120	Flush	1 Pord	6	1.333	Ea.	24.50	33		57.50	81	
	0130	French, 10-15 lite		3	2.667		4.88	66.50		71.38	113	
	0140	Panel		4	2		29.50	50		79.50	113	
	0150	Louvered		2.75	2.909		27	72.50		99.50	148	
	0160	Windows, per interior side, per 15 S.F.										
	0170	1 to 6 lite	1 Pord	14	.571	Ea.	16.85	14.25		31.10	41.50	
	0180	7 to 10 lite		7.50	1.067		18.60	26.50		45.10	64	

For expanded coverage of these items see *Means Interior Cost Data 1999*

099 | Painting & Wall Coverings

099 900 | Surface Preparation

			CREW	DAILY OUTPUT	LABOR-HOURS	UNIT	MAT.	LABOR	EQUIP.	TOTAL	TOTAL INCL O&P	
903	0190	12 lite	1 Pord	5.75	1.391	Ea.	25	34.50		59.50	84	903
	0200	Radiators		8	1		59.50	25		84.50	106	
	0210	Grilles, vents		275	.029	S.F.	1.73	.72		2.45	3.08	
	0220	Walls, roller, drywall or plaster		1,000	.008		.47	.20		.67	.84	
	0230	With spunbonded reinforcing fabric		720	.011		.53	.28		.81	1.03	
	0240	Wood		800	.010		.59	.25		.84	1.06	
	0250	Ceilings, roller, drywall or plaster		900	.009		.53	.22		.75	.94	
	0260	Wood		700	.011		.68	.28		.96	1.21	
	0270	Exterior, brushwork, gutters and downspouts		300	.027	L.F.	1.59	.66		2.25	2.83	
	0280	Columns		400	.020	S.F.	1.19	.50		1.69	2.12	
	0290	Spray, siding		600	.013	"	.79	.33		1.12	1.41	
	0300	Miscellaneous										
	0310	Electrical conduit, brushwork, to 2" diameter	1 Pord	500	.016	L.F.	.95	.40		1.35	1.70	
	0320	Brick, block or concrete, spray		500	.016	S.F.	.95	.40		1.35	1.70	
	0330	Steel, flat surfaces and tanks to 12"		500	.016		.95	.40		1.35	1.70	
	0340	Beams, brushwork		400	.020		1.19	.50		1.69	2.12	
	0350	Trusses		400	.020		1.19	.50		1.69	2.12	
904	0010	**SANDING** And puttying interior trim, compared to										904
	0100	Painting 1 coat, on quality work				L.F.		100%				
	0300	Medium work						50%				
	0400	Industrial grade						25%				
	0500	Surface protection, placement and removal										
	0510	Basic drop cloths	1 Pord	6,400	.001	S.F.		.03		.03	.05	
	0520	Masking with paper		800	.010		.02	.25		.27	.43	
	0530	Volume cover up (using plastic sheathing, or building paper)		16,000	.001			.01		.01	.02	
906	0010	**SCRAPE AFTER FIRE DAMAGE**										906
	0050	Boards, 1" x 4"	1 Pord	336	.024	L.F.		.59		.59	.97	
	0060	1" x 6"		260	.031			.77		.77	1.25	
	0070	1" x 8"		207	.039			.96		.96	1.57	
	0080	1" x 10"		174	.046			1.14		1.14	1.87	
	0500	Framing, 2" x 4"		265	.030			.75		.75	1.23	
	0510	2" x 6"		221	.036			.90		.90	1.47	
	0520	2" x 8"		190	.042			1.05		1.05	1.71	
	0530	2" x 10"		165	.048			1.21		1.21	1.97	
	0540	2" x 12"		144	.056			1.38		1.38	2.26	
	1000	Heavy framing, 3" x 4"		226	.035			.88		.88	1.44	
	1010	4" x 4"		210	.038			.95		.95	1.55	
	1020	4" x 6"		191	.042			1.04		1.04	1.70	
	1030	4" x 8"		165	.048			1.21		1.21	1.97	
	1040	4" x 10"		144	.056			1.38		1.38	2.26	
	1060	4" x 12"		131	.061			1.52		1.52	2.48	
	2900	For sealing, minimum		825	.010	S.F.	.11	.24		.35	.51	
	2920	Maximum		460	.017	"	.24	.43		.67	.97	
	3000	For sandblasting, see division 045-102										
	3020											
	9000	Minimum labor/equipment charge	1 Pord	3	2.667	Job		66.50		66.50	108	
910	0010	**SURFACE PREPARATION, EXTERIOR**										910
	0015	Doors, per side, not incl. frames or trim										
	0020	Scrape & sand										
	0030	Wood, flush	1 Pord	616	.013	S.F.		.32		.32	.53	
	0040	Wood, detail		496	.016			.40		.40	.65	
	0050	Wood, louvered		280	.029			.71		.71	1.16	
	0060	Wood, overhead		616	.013			.32		.32	.53	
	0070	Wire brush										

099 | Painting & Wall Coverings

099 900 | Surface Preparation

			CREW	DAILY OUTPUT	LABOR-HOURS	UNIT	MAT.	LABOR	EQUIP.	TOTAL	TOTAL INCL O&P	
910	0080	Metal, flush	1 Pord	640	.013	S.F.		.31		.31	.51	910
	0090	Metal, detail		520	.015			.38		.38	.62	
	0100	Metal, louvered		360	.022			.55		.55	.90	
	0110	Metal or fibr., overhead		640	.013			.31		.31	.51	
	0120	Metal, roll up		560	.014			.36		.36	.58	
	0130	Metal, bulkhead		640	.013			.31		.31	.51	
	0140	Power wash, based on 2500 lb. operating pressure										
	0150	Metal, flush	B-9	2,240	.018	S.F.		.39	.08	.47	.74	
	0160	Metal, detail		2,120	.019			.41	.09	.50	.78	
	0170	Metal, louvered		2,000	.020			.44	.09	.53	.83	
	0180	Metal or fibr., overhead		2,400	.017			.36	.08	.44	.69	
	0190	Metal, roll up		2,400	.017			.36	.08	.44	.69	
	0200	Metal, bulkhead		2,200	.018			.40	.08	.48	.75	
	0400	Windows, per side, not incl. trim										
	0410	Scrape & sand										
	0420	Wood, 1-2 lite	1 Pord	320	.025	S.F.		.62		.62	1.01	
	0430	Wood, 3-6 lite		280	.029			.71		.71	1.16	
	0440	Wood, 7-10 lite		240	.033			.83		.83	1.35	
	0450	Wood, 12 lite		200	.040			1		1	1.62	
	0460	Wood, Bay / Bow		320	.025			.62		.62	1.01	
	0470	Wire brush										
	0480	Metal, 1-2 lite	1 Pord	480	.017	S.F.		.41		.41	.68	
	0490	Metal, 3-6 lite		400	.020			.50		.50	.81	
	0500	Metal, Bay / Bow		480	.017			.41		.41	.68	
	0510	Power wash, based on 2500 lb. operating pressure										
	0520	1-2 lite	B-9	4,400	.009	S.F.		.20	.04	.24	.38	
	0530	3-6 lite		4,320	.009			.20	.04	.24	.39	
	0540	7-10 lite		4,240	.009			.21	.04	.25	.40	
	0550	12 lite		4,160	.010			.21	.04	.25	.40	
	0560	Bay / Bow		4,400	.009			.20	.04	.24	.38	
	0600	Siding, scrape and sand, light=10-30%, med.=30-70%										
	0610	Heavy=70-100%, % of surface to sand										
	0620	For Chemical Washing, see Division 045-108										
	0630	For Steam Cleaning, see Division 042-166										
	0640	For Sand Blasting, see Division 042-150										
	0650	Texture 1-11, light	1 Pord	480	.017	S.F.		.41		.41	.68	
	0660	Med.		440	.018			.45		.45	.74	
	0670	Heavy		360	.022			.55		.55	.90	
	0680	Wood shingles, shakes, light		440	.018			.45		.45	.74	
	0690	Med.		360	.022			.55		.55	.90	
	0700	Heavy		280	.029			.71		.71	1.16	
	0710	Clapboard, light		520	.015			.38		.38	.62	
	0720	Med.		480	.017			.41		.41	.68	
	0730	Heavy		400	.020			.50		.50	.81	
	0740	Wire brush										
	0750	Aluminum, light	1 Pord	600	.013	S.F.		.33		.33	.54	
	0760	Med.		520	.015			.38		.38	.62	
	0770	Heavy		440	.018			.45		.45	.74	
	0780	Pressure wash, based on 2500 lb.. operating pressure										
	0790	Stucco	B-9	3,080	.013	S.F.		.28	.06	.34	.53	
	0800	Aluminum or vinyl		3,200	.013			.27	.06	.33	.52	
	0810	Siding, masonry, brick & block		2,400	.017			.36	.08	.44	.69	
	1300	Miscellaneous, wire brush										
	1310	Metal, pedestrian gate	1 Pord	100	.080	S.F.		1.99		1.99	3.25	
920	0010	**SURFACE PREPARATION, INTERIOR**										920
	0020	Doors										

For expanded coverage of these items see Means Interior Cost Data 1999

099 | Painting & Wall Coverings

099 900 | Surface Preparation

			CREW	DAILY OUTPUT	LABOR-HOURS	UNIT	MAT.	LABOR	EQUIP.	TOTAL	TOTAL INCL O&P	
920	0030	Scrape & sand										920
	0040	Wood, flush	1 Pord	616	.013	S.F.		.32		.32	.53	
	0050	Wood, detail		496	.016			.40		.40	.65	
	0060	Wood, louvered	↓	280	.029	↓		.71		.71	1.16	
	0070	Wire brush										
	0080	Metal, flush	1 Pord	640	.013	S.F.		.31		.31	.51	
	0090	Metal, detail		520	.015			.38		.38	.62	
	0100	Metal, louvered	↓	360	.022	↓		.55		.55	.90	
	0110	Hand wash										
	0120	Wood, flush	1 Pord	2,160	.004	S.F.		.09		.09	.15	
	0130	Wood, detailed		2,000	.004			.10		.10	.16	
	0140	Wood, louvered		1,360	.006			.15		.15	.24	
	0150	Metal, flush		2,160	.004			.09		.09	.15	
	0160	Metal, detail		2,000	.004			.10		.10	.16	
	0170	Metal, louvered	↓	1,360	.006	↓		.15		.15	.24	
	0400	Windows, per side, not incl. trim										
	0410	Scrape & sand										
	0420	Wood, 1-2 lite	1 Pord	360	.022	S.F.		.55		.55	.90	
	0430	Wood, 3-6 lite		320	.025			.62		.62	1.01	
	0440	Wood, 7-10 lite		280	.029			.71		.71	1.16	
	0450	Wood, 12 lite		240	.033			.83		.83	1.35	
	0460	Wood, Bay / Bow	↓	360	.022	↓		.55		.55	.90	
	0470	Wire brush										
	0480	Metal, 1-2 lite	1 Pord	520	.015	S.F.		.38		.38	.62	
	0490	Metal, 3-6 lite		440	.018			.45		.45	.74	
	0500	Metal, Bay / Bow	↓	520	.015	↓		.38		.38	.62	
	0600	Walls, sanding, light=10-30%										
	0610	Med.=30-70%, heavy=70-100%, % of surface to sand										
	0620	For Chemical Washing, see Division 045-108										
	0630	For Steam Cleaning, see Division 042-166										
	0640	For Sand Blasting, see Division 042-150										
	0650	Walls, sand										
	0660	Drywall, gypsum, plaster, light	1 Pord	3,077	.003	S.F.		.06		.06	.11	
	0670	Drywall, gypsum, plaster, med.		2,160	.004			.09		.09	.15	
	0680	Drywall, gypsum, plaster, heavy		923	.009			.22		.22	.35	
	0690	Wood, T&G, light		2,400	.003			.08		.08	.14	
	0700	Wood, T&G, med.		1,600	.005			.12		.12	.20	
	0710	Wood, T&G, heavy	↓	800	.010	↓		.25		.25	.41	
	0720	Walls, wash										
	0730	Drywall, gypsum, plaster	1 Pord	3,200	.002	S.F.		.06		.06	.10	
	0740	Wood, T&G		3,200	.002			.06		.06	.10	
	0750	Masonry, brick & block, smooth		2,800	.003			.07		.07	.12	
	0760	Masonry, brick & block, coarse	↓	2,000	.004	↓		.10		.10	.16	

For information about Means Estimating Seminars, see yellow pages 11 and 12 in back of book

Division 10
Specialties

Estimating Tips
General
- The items in this division are usually priced per square foot or each.
- Many items in Division 10 require some type of support system that is not usually furnished with the item. Examples of these systems include blocking for the attachment of grab bars and support angles for ceiling hung toilet partitions. The required blocking or supports must be added to the estimate in the appropriate division.
- Some items in Division 10, such as lockers, may require assembly before installation. Verify the amount of assembly required. Assembly can often exceed installation time.

101 Visual Display Boards, Compartments & Cubicles
- Toilet partitions are priced by the stall. A stall consists of a side wall, pilaster and door with hardware. Toilet tissue holders and grab bars are extra.

106 Partitions & Storage Shelving
- The required acoustical rating of a folding partition can have a significant impact on costs. Verify the sound transmission coefficient rating of the panel priced to the specification requirements.

Reference Numbers
Reference numbers are shown in bold squares at the beginning of some major classifications. These numbers refer to related items in the Reference Section. The reference information may be an estimating procedure, an alternate pricing method or technical information.

Note: Not all subdivisions listed here necessarily appear in this publication.

101 | Visual Display Boards, Compartments & Cubicles

101 100 | Chalkboards

			CREW	DAILY OUTPUT	LABOR-HOURS	UNIT	1999 BARE COSTS MAT.	LABOR	EQUIP.	TOTAL	TOTAL INCL O&P
104	0010	**CHALKBOARDS** Porcelain enamel steel										104
	0100	Freestanding, reversible									
	0120	Economy, wood frame, 4' x 6'									
	0140	Chalkboard both sides				Ea.	460			460	510
	0160	Chalkboard one side, cork other side				"	400			400	440
	0200	Standard, lightweight satin finished aluminum, 4' x 6'									
	0220	Chalkboard both sides				Ea.	475			475	525
	0240	Chalkboard one side, cork other side				"	420			420	460
	0300	Deluxe, heavy duty extruded aluminum, 4' x 6'									
	0320	Chalkboard both sides				Ea.	1,025			1,025	1,150
	0340	Chalkboard one side, cork other side				"	1,200			1,200	1,325
	3900	Wall hung									
	4000	Aluminum frame and chalktrough									
	4300	3' x 5'	2 Carp	15	1.067	Ea.	186	29		215	254
	4600	4' x 12'	"	13	1.231	"	410	33.50		443.50	510
	4700	Wood frame and chalktrough									
	4800	3' x 4'	2 Carp	16	1	Ea.	130	27.50		157.50	189
	5300	4' x 8'	"	13	1.231	"	264	33.50		297.50	345
	5400	Liquid chalk, white porcelain enamel, wall hung									
	5420	Deluxe units, aluminum trim and chalktrough									
	5450	4' x 4'	2 Carp	16	1	Ea.	174	27.50		201.50	238
	5550	4' x 12'	"	12	1.333	"	420	36.50		456.50	520
	5700	Wood trim and chalktrough									
	5900	4' x 4'	2 Carp	16	1	Ea.	360	27.50		387.50	445
	6200	4' x 8'		14	1.143	"	520	31		551	625
	9000	Minimum labor/equipment charge		3	5.333	Job		146		146	244

101 600 | Toilet Compartments

			CREW	DAILY OUTPUT	LABOR-HOURS	UNIT	MAT.	LABOR	EQUIP.	TOTAL	TOTAL INCL O&P
602	0010	**PARTITIONS, TOILET**										602
	0100	Cubicles, ceiling hung, marble	2 Marb	2	8	Ea.	1,300	220		1,520	1,800
	0200	Painted metal	2 Carp	4	4		385	109		494	605
	0250	Phenolic		4	4		730	109		839	985
	0300	Plastic laminate on particle board		4	4		495	109		604	730
	0500	Stainless steel		4	4		965	109		1,074	1,250
	0600	For handicap units, incl. 52" grab bars, add					276			276	305
	0800	Floor & ceiling anchored, marble	2 Marb	2.50	6.400		1,425	176		1,601	1,875
	1000	Painted metal	2 Carp	5	3.200		355	87.50		442.50	535
	1050	Phenolic		5	3.200		785	87.50		872.50	1,000
	1100	Plastic laminate on particle board		5	3.200		470	87.50		557.50	660
	1300	Stainless steel		5	3.200		1,125	87.50		1,212.50	1,375
	1400	For handicap units, incl. 52" grab bars, add					250			250	275
	1600	Floor mounted, marble	2 Marb	3	5.333		840	147		987	1,175
	1700	Painted metal	2 Carp	7	2.286		355	62.50		417.50	495
	1750	Phenolic		7	2.286		730	62.50		792.50	905
	1800	Plastic laminate on particle board		7	2.286		495	62.50		557.50	650
	2000	Stainless steel		7	2.286		1,075	62.50		1,137.50	1,300
	2100	For handicap units, incl. 52" grab bars, add					250			250	275
	2200	For juvenile units, deduct					35			35	38.50
	2400	Floor mounted, headrail braced, marble	2 Marb	3	5.333		980	147		1,127	1,325
	2500	Painted metal	2 Carp	6	2.667		355	73		428	510
	2550	Phenolic		6	2.667		760	73		833	955
	2600	Plastic laminate on particle board		6	2.667		515	73		588	685
	2800	Stainless steel		6	2.667		1,100	73		1,173	1,325
	2900	For handicap units, incl. 52" grab bars, add					250			250	275
	3000	Wall hung partitions, painted metal	2 Carp	7	2.286		450	62.50		512.50	600
	3300	Stainless steel	"	7	2.286		1,075	62.50		1,137.50	1,300

101 | Visual Display Boards, Compartments & Cubicles

101 600 | Toilet Compartments

			DAILY	LABOR-		1999 BARE COSTS				TOTAL
		CREW	OUTPUT	HOURS	UNIT	MAT.	LABOR	EQUIP.	TOTAL	INCL O&P
3400	For handicap units, incl. 52" grab bars, add				Ea.	250			250	275
4000	Screens, entrance, floor mounted, 58" high, 48" wide									
4100	Marble	2 Marb	9	1.778	Ea.	530	49		579	660
4200	Painted metal	2 Carp	15	1.067		166	29		195	231
4300	Plastic laminate on particle board		15	1.067		294	29		323	375
4500	Stainless steel	↓	15	1.067		585	29		614	695
4600	Urinal screen, 18" wide, ceiling braced, marble	D-1	6	2.667		530	65.50		595.50	690
4700	Painted metal	2 Carp	8	2		126	54.50		180.50	231
4800	Plastic laminate on particle board		8	2		235	54.50		289.50	350
5000	Stainless steel	↓	8	2	↓	420	54.50		474.50	550
5100	Floor mounted, head rail braced									
5200	Marble	D-1	6	2.667	Ea.	490	65.50		555.50	650
5300	Painted metal	2 Carp	8	2		166	54.50		220.50	274
5400	Plastic laminate on particle board		8	2		212	54.50		266.50	325
5600	Stainless steel	↓	8	2		500	54.50		554.50	640
5700	Pilaster, flush, marble	D-1	9	1.778		600	43.50		643.50	735
5800	Painted metal	2 Carp	10	1.600		216	43.50		259.50	310
5900	Plastic laminate on particle board		10	1.600		270	43.50		313.50	370
6100	Stainless steel	↓	10	1.600		370	43.50		413.50	480
6200	Post braced, marble	D-1	9	1.778		590	43.50		633.50	720
6300	Painted metal	2 Carp	10	1.600		222	43.50		265.50	320
6400	Plastic laminate on particle board		10	1.600		276	43.50		319.50	380
6600	Stainless steel	↓	10	1.600	↓	365	43.50		408.50	480
6700	Wall hung, bracket supported									
6800	Painted metal	2 Carp	10	1.600	Ea.	225	43.50		268.50	320
6900	Plastic laminate on particle board		10	1.600		108	43.50		151.50	192
7100	Stainless steel		10	1.600		335	43.50		378.50	445
7400	Flange supported, painted metal		10	1.600		165	43.50		208.50	255
7500	Plastic laminate on particle board		10	1.600		160	43.50		203.50	249
7700	Stainless steel		10	1.600		390	43.50		433.50	505
7800	Wedge type, painted metal		10	1.600		195	43.50		238.50	287
8100	Stainless steel	↓	10	1.600	↓	400	43.50		443.50	515
9000	Minimum labor/equipment charge	1 Carp	2.50	3.200	Job		87.50		87.50	146

101 850 | Shower Compartments

		CREW	DAILY OUTPUT	LABOR-HOURS	UNIT	MAT.	LABOR	EQUIP.	TOTAL	INCL O&P
0010	**PARTITIONS, SHOWER** Floor mounted, no plumbing									
0100	Cabinet, incl. base, no door, painted steel, 1" thick walls	2 Shee	5	3.200	Ea.	585	102		687	810
0300	With door, fiberglass		4.50	3.556		480	113		593	705
0600	Galvanized and painted steel, 1" thick walls		5	3.200		620	102		722	850
0800	Stall, 1" thick wall, no base, enameled steel		5	3.200		595	102		697	820
1500	Circular fiberglass, cabinet 36" diameter,		4	4		490	127		617	745
1700	One piece, 36" diameter, less door		4	4		420	127		547	670
1800	With door	↓	3.50	4.571		680	145		825	980
4100	Shower doors, economy plastic, 24" wide	1 Shee	9	.889		88	28		116	142
4200	Tempered glass door, economy		8	1		170	32		202	238
4700	Deluxe, tempered glass, chrome on brass frame, minimum		8	1		215	32		247	288
4800	Maximum		1	8	↓	620	254		874	1,100
9990	Minimum labor/equipment charge	↓	2.50	3.200	Job		102		102	163

102 | Louvers, Corner Protection & Access Flooring

102 100 | Metal Wall Louvers

			CREW	DAILY OUTPUT	LABOR-HOURS	UNIT	MAT.	LABOR	EQUIP.	TOTAL	TOTAL INCL O&P	
104	0010	LOUVERS Aluminum with screen, residential, 8" x 8"	1 Carp	38	.211	Ea.	6.95	5.75		12.70	17.20	104
	0100	12" x 12"		38	.211		8.75	5.75		14.50	19.20	
	0200	12" x 18"		35	.229		12.70	6.25		18.95	24.50	
	0250	14" x 24"		30	.267		16.35	7.30		23.65	30	
	0300	18" x 24"		27	.296		18.85	8.10		26.95	34.50	
	0500	24" x 30"		24	.333		27.50	9.10		36.60	46	
	0700	Triangle, adjustable, small		20	.400		23	10.90		33.90	43.50	
	0800	Large		15	.533		61.50	14.55		76.05	92	
	2100	Midget, aluminum, 3/4" deep, 1" diameter		85	.094		.56	2.57		3.13	4.92	
	2150	3" diameter		60	.133		1.32	3.64		4.96	7.55	
	2200	4" diameter		50	.160		1.66	4.37		6.03	9.15	
	2250	6" diameter		30	.267		2.25	7.30		9.55	14.70	
	2300	Ridge vent strip, mill finish	1 Shee	155	.052	L.F.	1.95	1.64		3.59	4.78	
	2400	Under eaves vent, aluminum, mill finish, 16" x 4"	1 Carp	48	.167	Ea.	1.49	4.55		6.04	9.25	
	2500	16" x 8"		48	.167		1.79	4.55		6.34	9.55	
	7000	Vinyl gable vent, 8" x 8"		38	.211		9.50	5.75		15.25	20	
	7020	12" x 12"		38	.211		17	5.75		22.75	28.50	
	7080	12" x 18"		35	.229		22	6.25		28.25	34.50	
	7200	18" x 24"		30	.267		26	7.30		33.30	40.50	
	9000	Minimum labor/equipment charge		2.50	3.200	Job		87.50		87.50	146	

102 600 | Wall & Corner Guards

			CREW	DAILY OUTPUT	LABOR-HOURS	UNIT	MAT.	LABOR	EQUIP.	TOTAL	TOTAL INCL O&P	
604	0010	CORNER GUARDS Steel angle w/anchors, 1" x 1" x 1/4", 1.5#/L.F.	2 Carp	160	.100	L.F.	2.77	2.73		5.50	7.60	604
	0100	2" x 2" x 1/4" angles, 3.2#/L.F.	"	150	.107	"	6.50	2.91		9.41	12	
	9000	Minimum labor/equipment charge	A-1	2	4	Job		86	34.50	120.50	182	

102 700 | Access Flooring

			CREW	DAILY OUTPUT	LABOR-HOURS	UNIT	MAT.	LABOR	EQUIP.	TOTAL	TOTAL INCL O&P	
705	0010	PEDESTAL ACCESS FLOORS Computer room application, metal										705
	0020	Particle board or steel panels, no covering, under 6,000 S.F.	2 Carp	400	.040	S.F.	5.65	1.09		6.74	8.05	
	0300	Metal covered, over 6,000 S.F.		450	.036		5.75	.97		6.72	7.95	
	0400	Aluminum, 24" panels		500	.032		20.50	.87		21.37	24	
	0600	For carpet covering, add					3.92			3.92	4.32	
	0700	For vinyl floor covering, add					4.18			4.18	4.59	
	0900	For high pressure laminate covering, add					2.59			2.59	2.85	
	0910	For snap on stringer system, add	2 Carp	1,000	.016		1.02	.44		1.46	1.85	
	0950	Office applications, to 8" high, steel panels,										
	0960	no covering, over 6,000 S.F.	2 Carp	500	.032	S.F.	6.65	.87		7.52	8.75	
	1050	Pedestals, 6" to 12"	"	85	.188	Ea.	4.93	5.15		10.08	14.05	

103 | Fireplaces, Exterior Specialties & Flagpoles

103 050 | Prefabricated Fireplaces

			CREW	DAILY OUTPUT	LABOR-HOURS	UNIT	MAT.	LABOR	EQUIP.	TOTAL	TOTAL INCL O&P	
054	0010	FIREPLACE, PREFABRICATED Free standing or wall hung										054
	0100	with hood & screen, minimum	1 Carp	1.30	6.154	Ea.	905	168		1,073	1,275	
	0150	Average		1	8		1,075	218		1,293	1,575	
	0200	Maximum		.90	8.889		2,600	243		2,843	3,275	
	0500	Chimney dbl. wall, all stainless, over 8'-6", 7" diam., add		33	.242	V.L.F.	30.50	6.60		37.10	44.50	
	0600	10" diameter, add		32	.250		43.50	6.80		50.30	59.50	

103 | Fireplaces, Exterior Specialties & Flagpoles

103 050 | Prefabricated Fireplaces

			CREW	DAILY OUTPUT	LABOR-HOURS	UNIT	MAT.	LABOR	EQUIP.	TOTAL	TOTAL INCL O&P	
054	0700	12" diameter, add	1 Carp	31	.258	V.L.F.	57	7.05		64.05	74.50	054
	0800	14" diameter, add		30	.267	↓	72	7.30		79.30	91	
	1000	Simulated brick chimney top, 4' high, 16" x 16"		10	.800	Ea.	155	22		177	208	
	1100	24" x 24"		7	1.143	"	289	31		320	370	
	1500	Simulated logs, gas fired, 40,000 BTU, 2' long, minimum		7	1.143	Set	405	31		436	495	
	1600	Maximum		6	1.333		590	36.50		626.50	710	
	1700	Electric, 1,500 BTU, 1'-6" long, minimum		7	1.143		107	31		138	170	
	1800	11,500 BTU, maximum		6	1.333	↓	232	36.50		268.50	315	
	2000	Fireplace, built-in, 36" hearth, radiant		1.30	6.154	Ea.	465	168		633	790	
	2100	Recirculating, small fan		1	8		665	218		883	1,100	
	2150	Large fan		.90	8.889		1,225	243		1,468	1,750	
	2200	42" hearth, radiant		1.20	6.667		595	182		777	955	
	2300	Recirculating, small fan		.90	8.889		775	243		1,018	1,250	
	2350	Large fan		.80	10		1,475	273		1,748	2,075	
	2400	48" hearth, radiant		1.10	7.273		1,100	199		1,299	1,550	
	2500	Recirculating, small fan		.80	10		1,375	273		1,648	1,950	
	2550	Large fan		.70	11.429		2,125	310		2,435	2,850	
	3000	See through, including doors		.80	10		1,750	273		2,023	2,375	
	3200	Corner (2 wall)	↓	1	8	↓	865	218		1,083	1,325	

103 100 | Fireplace Accessories

			CREW	DAILY OUTPUT	LABOR-HOURS	UNIT	MAT.	LABOR	EQUIP.	TOTAL	TOTAL INCL O&P	
104	0010	**FIREPLACE ACCESSORIES** Chimney screens, galv., 13" x 13" flue	1 Bric	8	1	Ea.	46	27.50		73.50	96.50	104
	0050	Galv., 24" x 24" flue		5	1.600		121	44		165	206	
	0200	Stainless steel, 13" x 13" flue		8	1		256	27.50		283.50	330	
	0250	20" x 20" flue		5	1.600		350	44		394	460	
	0400	Cleanout doors and frames, cast iron, 8" x 8"		12	.667		17	18.40		35.40	49	
	0450	12" x 12"		10	.800		32.50	22		54.50	72	
	0500	18" x 24"		8	1		102	27.50		129.50	158	
	0550	Cast iron frame, steel door, 24" x 30"		5	1.600		220	44		264	315	
	0800	Damper, rotary control, steel, 30" opening		6	1.333		61.50	37		98.50	129	
	0850	Cast iron, 30" opening		6	1.333		69	37		106	137	
	0880	36" opening		6	1.333		74.50	37		111.50	143	
	0900	48" opening		6	1.333		102	37		139	174	
	0920	60" opening		6	1.333		242	37		279	330	
	1000	84" opening, special order		5	1.600		615	44		659	755	
	1050	96" opening, special order	↓	4	2	↓	625	55		680	780	
	1100											
	1200	Steel plate, poker control, 60" opening	1 Bric	8	1	Ea.	218	27.50		245.50	286	
	1250	84" opening, special opening		5	1.600		400	44		444	515	
	1400	"Universal" type, chain operated, 32" x 20" opening		8	1		149	27.50		176.50	210	
	1450	48" x 24" opening		5	1.600		263	44		307	360	
	1600	Dutch Oven door and frame, cast iron, 12" x 15" opening		13	.615		89	17		106	126	
	1650	Copper plated, 12" x 15" opening		13	.615		171	17		188	217	
	1800	Fireplace forms, no accessories, 32" opening		3	2.667		455	73.50		528.50	620	
	1900	36" opening		2.50	3.200		550	88.50		638.50	750	
	2000	40" opening		2	4		660	110		770	910	
	2100	78" opening		1.50	5.333		940	147		1,087	1,275	
	2400	Squirrel and bird screens, galvanized, 8" x 8" flue		16	.500		43	13.80		56.80	70.50	
	2450	13" x 13" flue		12	.667	↓	50.50	18.40		68.90	86	
	9000	Minimum labor/equipment charge	↓	3.50	2.286	Job		63		63	104	

103 200 | Stoves

			CREW	DAILY OUTPUT	LABOR-HOURS	UNIT	MAT.	LABOR	EQUIP.	TOTAL	TOTAL INCL O&P	
201	0010	**WOODBURNING STOVES** Cast iron, minimum	2 Carp	1.30	12.308	Ea.	740	335		1,075	1,375	201
	0020	Average	↓	1	16	↓	1,200	435		1,635	2,025	

103 | Fireplaces, Exterior Specialties & Flagpoles

103 200 | Stoves

		CREW	DAILY OUTPUT	LABOR-HOURS	UNIT	1999 BARE COSTS MAT.	LABOR	EQUIP.	TOTAL	TOTAL INCL O&P	
201	0030	Maximum	2 Carp	.80	20	Ea.	2,000	545		2,545	3,125	201
	0050	For gas log lighter, add				↓	35			35	38.50	

103 460 | Cupolas

			CREW	DAILY OUTPUT	LABOR-HOURS	UNIT	MAT.	LABOR	EQUIP.	TOTAL	INCL O&P	
464	0010	CUPOLA Stock units, pine, painted, 18" sq., 28" high, alum. roof	1 Carp	4.10	1.951	Ea.	94.50	53.50		148	193	464
	0100	Copper roof		3.80	2.105		134	57.50		191.50	243	
	0300	23" square, 33" high, aluminum roof		3.70	2.162		221	59		280	340	
	0400	Copper roof		3.30	2.424		222	66		288	355	
	0600	30" square, 37" high, aluminum roof		3.70	2.162		335	59		394	470	
	0700	Copper roof		3.30	2.424		345	66		411	490	
	0900	Hexagonal, 31" wide, 46" high, copper roof		4	2		460	54.50		514.50	595	
	1000	36" wide, 50" high, copper roof	↓	3.50	2.286		535	62.50		597.50	695	
	1200	For deluxe stock units, add to above					25%					
	1400	For custom built units, add to above					50%	50%				
	1600	Fiberglass, 5'-0" base, 63' high minimum	F-3	6	6.667		2,225	185	74	2,484	2,825	
	1650	Maximum		4	10		2,575	277	111	2,963	3,425	
	1700	6'-0" base, 63' high, minimum		5	8		3,450	222	88.50	3,760.50	4,275	
	1750	Maximum	↓	3	13.333		3,550	370	148	4,068	4,675	
	9000	Minimum labor/equipment charge	1 Carp	2.75	2.909	Job		79.50		79.50	133	

104 | Identifying & Pedestrian Control Devices

104 100 | Directories

			CREW	DAILY OUTPUT	LABOR-HOURS	UNIT	MAT.	LABOR	EQUIP.	TOTAL	INCL O&P	
104	0010	DIRECTORY BOARDS										104
	0050	Plastic, glass covered, 30" x 20"	2 Carp	3	5.333	Ea.	275	146		421	550	
	0100	36" x 48"		2	8		540	218		758	960	
	0900	Outdoor, weatherproof, black plastic, 36" x 24"		2	8		300	218		518	695	
	1000	36" x 36"	↓	1.50	10.667	↓	635	291		926	1,175	
	9000	Minimum labor/equipment charge	1 Carp	1	8	Job		218		218	365	

104 150 | Bulletin Boards

			CREW	DAILY OUTPUT	LABOR-HOURS	UNIT	MAT.	LABOR	EQUIP.	TOTAL	INCL O&P	
151	0011	BULLETIN BOARD										151
	2120	Prefabricated, 1/4" cork, 3' x 5' with aluminum frame	2 Carp	16	1	Ea.	97.50	27.50		125	153	
	2140	Wood frame	"	16	1	"	126	27.50		153.50	184	
	2300	Glass enclosed cabinets, alum., cork panel, hinged doors										
	2600	4' x 7', 3 door	2 Carp	10	1.600	Ea.	1,150	43.50		1,193.50	1,350	
	9000	Minimum labor/equipment charge	"	4	4	Job		109		109	183	

104 300 | Signs

			CREW	DAILY OUTPUT	LABOR-HOURS	UNIT	MAT.	LABOR	EQUIP.	TOTAL	INCL O&P	
304	0012	SIGNS Plaques										304
	3910	20" x 30", up to 450 letters, cast alum.	2 Carp	4	4	Ea.	630	109		739	880	
	4000	Cast bronze		4	4		980	109		1,089	1,250	
	4200	30" x 36", up to 900 letters cast aluminum		3	5.333		1,475	146		1,621	1,875	
	4300	Cast bronze	↓	3	5.333		1,925	146		2,071	2,350	
	5100	Exit signs, 24 ga. alum., 14" x 12" surface mounted	1 Carp	30	.267		12.70	7.30		20	26	
	5200	10" x 7"	"	20	.400		7.75	10.90		18.65	27	
	6400	Replacement sign faces, 6" or 8"	1 Clab	50	.160	↓	21	3.43		24.43	29	
	9000	Minimum labor/equipment charge	1 Carp	4	2	Job		54.50		54.50	91.50	

105 | Lockers, Protective Covers & Postal Specialties

105 050 | Metal Lockers

			CREW	DAILY OUTPUT	LABOR-HOURS	UNIT	1999 BARE COSTS MAT.	LABOR	EQUIP.	TOTAL	TOTAL INCL O&P	
054	0011	**LOCKERS** Steel, baked enamel										054
	0110	Single tier box locker, 12" x 15" x 72"	R105-050	1 Shee	8	1	Ea.	128	32		160	191	
	0120	18" x 15" x 72"			8	1		148	32		180	214	
	0130	12" x 18" x 72"			8	1		132	32		164	197	
	0140	18" x 18" x 72"			8	1		153	32		185	219	
	0410	Double tier, 12" x 15" x 36"			21	.381		110	12.10		122.10	140	
	0420	18" x 15" x 36"			21	.381		116	12.10		128.10	146	
	0430	12" x 18" x 36"			21	.381		94	12.10		106.10	122	
	0440	18" x 18" x 36"			21	.381		95.50	12.10		107.60	124	
	0500	Two person, 18" x 15" x 72"			8	1		173	32		205	241	
	0510	18" x 18" x 72"			8	1		201	32		233	272	
	0520	Duplex, 15" x 15" x 72"			8	1		195	32		227	266	
	0530	15" x 21" x 72"			8	1		222	32		254	295	
	1100	Wire meshed wardrobe, floor. mtd., open front varsity type			7.50	1.067		144	34		178	214	
	2400	16-person locker unit with clothing rack											
	2500	72 wide x 15" deep x 72" high		1 Shee	8	1	Ea.	355	32		387	440	
	2550	18" deep			8	1	"	365	32		397	450	
	3250	Rack w/ 24 wire mesh baskets			1.50	5.333	Set	270	169		439	570	
	3260	30 baskets			1.25	6.400		232	203		435	580	
	3270	36 baskets			.95	8.421		325	267		592	790	
	3280	42 baskets			.80	10		365	320		685	915	
	3600	For hanger rods, add					Ea.	1.65			1.65	1.82	
	9000	Minimum labor/equipment charge		1 Shee	2.50	3.200	Job		102		102	163	

105 200 | Fire Protection Specialties

			CREW	DAILY OUTPUT	LABOR-HOURS	UNIT	MAT.	LABOR	EQUIP.	TOTAL	TOTAL INCL O&P	
220	0010	**FIRE EQUIPMENT CABINETS** Not equipped, 20 ga. steel box,										220
	0040	recessed, D.S. glass in door, box size given											
	1000	Portable extinguisher, single, 8" x 12" x 27", alum. door & frame	Q-12	8	2	Ea.	75.50	58.50		134	175	
	1100	Steel door and frame	"	8	2	"	46	58.50		104.50	143	
	3000	Hose rack assy., 1-1/2" valve & 100' hose, 24" x 40" x 5-1/2"											
	3200	Steel door and frame	Q-12	6	2.667	Ea.	101	78		179	233	
	4000	Hose rack assy., 2-1/2" x 1-1/2" valve, 100' hose, 24" x 40" x 8"											
	4200	Steel door and frame	Q-12	6	2.667	Ea.	108	78		186	241	
	5000	Hose rack assy., 2-1/2" x 1-1/2" valve, 100' hose											
	5010	and extinguisher, 30" x 40" x 8"											
	5200	Steel door and frame	Q-12	5	3.200	Ea.	129	93.50		222.50	289	
225	0010	**FIRE EXTINGUISHERS**										225
	0120	CO2, portable with swivel horn, 5 lb.				Ea.	101			101	111	
	0140	With hose and "H" horn, 10 lb.				"	150			150	165	
	1000	Dry chemical, pressurized											
	1040	Standard type, portable, painted, 2-1/2 lb.				Ea.	25			25	27.50	
	1080	10 lb.					65			65	71.50	
	1100	20 lb.					90			90	99	
	1120	30 lb.					145			145	160	
	2000	ABC all purpose type, portable, 2-1/2 lb.					25			25	27.50	
	2080	9-1/2 lb.					60			60	66	

105 380 | Canopies

			CREW	DAILY OUTPUT	LABOR-HOURS	UNIT	MAT.	LABOR	EQUIP.	TOTAL	TOTAL INCL O&P	
384	0010	**CANOPIES** Wall hung, .032", aluminum, prefinished, 8' x 10'	K-2	1.30	18.462	Ea.	1,250	525	138	1,913	2,475	384
	0300	8' x 20'		1.10	21.818		2,500	620	163	3,283	4,050	
	1000	12' x 20'		1	24		3,200	680	180	4,060	4,975	
	1050											
	2300	Aluminum entrance canopies, flat soffit, .032"											
	2500	3'-6" x 4'-0", clear anodized	2 Carp	4	4	Ea.	525	109		634	765	

105 | Lockers, Protective Covers & Postal Specialties

105 380 | Canopies

			CREW	DAILY OUTPUT	LABOR-HOURS	UNIT	1999 BARE COSTS MAT.	LABOR	EQUIP.	TOTAL	TOTAL INCL O&P	
384	4700	Canvas awnings, including canvas, frame & lettering										384
	5000	Minimum	2 Carp	100	.160	S.F.	36	4.37		40.37	47	
	5300	Average		90	.178		43.50	4.85		48.35	56	
	5500	Maximum		80	.200		88.50	5.45		93.95	106	
	9000	Minimum labor/equipment charge		2	8	Job		218		218	365	
388	0010	**CANOPIES, RESIDENTIAL** Prefabricated										388
	0500	Carport, free standing, baked enamel, alum., .032", 40 psf										
	0520	16' x 8', 4 posts	2 Carp	3	5.333	Ea.	2,250	146		2,396	2,750	
	0600	20' x 10', 6 posts	"	2	8		2,375	218		2,593	2,975	
	1000	Door canopies, extruded alum., .032", 42" projection, 4' wide	1 Carp	8	1		300	27.50		327.50	375	
	1020	6' wide	"	6	1.333		385	36.50		421.50	485	
	1040	8' wide	2 Carp	9	1.778		505	48.50		553.50	635	
	1060	10' wide		7	2.286		600	62.50		662.50	765	
	1080	12' wide		5	3.200		710	87.50		797.50	930	
	1200	54" projection, 4' wide	1 Carp	8	1		385	27.50		412.50	470	
	1220	6' wide	"	6	1.333		510	36.50		546.50	620	
	1240	8' wide	2 Carp	9	1.778		670	48.50		718.50	815	
	1260	10' wide		7	2.286		785	62.50		847.50	965	
	1280	12' wide		5	3.200		905	87.50		992.50	1,150	
	1300	Painted, add					20%					
	1310	Bronze anodized, add					50%					
	3000	Window awnings, aluminum, window 3' high, 4' wide	1 Carp	10	.800		172	22		194	226	
	3020	6' wide	"	8	1		226	27.50		253.50	295	
	3040	9' wide	2 Carp	9	1.778		310	48.50		358.50	420	
	3060	12' wide	"	5	3.200		415	87.50		502.50	600	
	3100	Window, 4' high, 4' wide	1 Carp	10	.800		220	22		242	279	
	3120	6' wide	"	8	1		299	27.50		326.50	375	
	3140	9' wide	2 Carp	9	1.778		410	48.50		458.50	530	
	3160	12' wide	"	5	3.200		555	87.50		642.50	755	
	3200	Window, 6' high, 4' wide	1 Carp	10	.800		310	22		332	375	
	3220	6' wide	"	8	1		425	27.50		452.50	510	
	3240	9' wide	2 Carp	9	1.778		560	48.50		608.50	695	
	3260	12' wide	"	5	3.200		725	87.50		812.50	940	
	3400	Roll-up aluminum, 2'-6" wide	1 Carp	14	.571		83	15.60		98.60	118	
	3420	3' wide		12	.667		100	18.20		118.20	141	
	3440	4' wide		10	.800		129	22		151	179	
	3460	6' wide		8	1		159	27.50		186.50	221	
	3480	9' wide	2 Carp	9	1.778		231	48.50		279.50	335	
	3500	12' wide	"	5	3.200		283	87.50		370.50	455	
	3600	Window awnings, canvas, 24" drop, 3' wide	1 Carp	30	.267	L.F.	53	7.30		60.30	70.50	
	3620	4' wide		40	.200		50	5.45		55.45	64	
	3700	30" drop, 3' wide		30	.267		62.50	7.30		69.80	80.50	
	3720	4' wide		40	.200		55.50	5.45		60.95	70	
	3740	5' wide		45	.178		51	4.85		55.85	64	
	3760	6' wide		48	.167		47.50	4.55		52.05	60	
	3780	8' wide		48	.167		39.50	4.55		44.05	51	
	3800	10' wide		50	.160		36	4.37		40.37	47.50	
	3900	Repair canvas, minimum		8	1	Ea.		27.50		27.50	45.50	
	3920	Maximum		4	2	"		54.50		54.50	91.50	
	9000	Minimum labor/equipment charge		3	2.667	Job		73		73	122	

105 510 | Mail Chutes

			CREW	DAILY OUTPUT	LABOR-HOURS	UNIT	MAT.	LABOR	EQUIP.	TOTAL	TOTAL INCL O&P	
511	0010	**MAIL CHUTES** Aluminum & glass, 14-1/4" wide, 4-5/8" deep	2 Shee	4	4	Floor	630	127		757	900	511
	0100	8-5/8" deep		3.80	4.211	"	700	134		834	985	

105 | Lockers, Protective Covers & Postal Specialties

105 510 | Mail Chutes

			CREW	DAILY OUTPUT	LABOR-HOURS	UNIT	MAT.	LABOR	EQUIP.	TOTAL	TOTAL INCL O&P	
511	0600	Lobby collection boxes, aluminum	2 Shee	5	3.200	Ea.	1,725	102		1,827	2,075	511
	0700	Bronze or stainless	↓	4.50	3.556	"	2,125	113		2,238	2,525	

105 520 | Mail Boxes

			CREW	DAILY OUTPUT	LABOR-HOURS	UNIT	MAT.	LABOR	EQUIP.	TOTAL	TOTAL INCL O&P	
521	0010	**MAIL BOXES** Horiz., key lock, 5"H x 6"W x 15"D, alum., rear load	1 Carp	34	.235	Ea.	34	6.40		40.40	48.50	521
	0100	Front loading		34	.235		38.50	6.40		44.90	53	
	0200	Double, 5"H x 12"W x 15"D, rear loading		26	.308		60.50	8.40		68.90	80.50	
	0300	Front loading		26	.308		65.50	8.40		73.90	86	
	0500	Quadruple, 10"H x 12"W x 15"D, rear loading		20	.400		109	10.90		119.90	138	
	0600	Front loading		20	.400		120	10.90		130.90	150	
	1600	Vault type, horizontal, for apartments, 4" x 5"		34	.235		35.50	6.40		41.90	50	
	1700	Alphabetical directories, 120 names		10	.800		139	22		161	190	
	1900	Letter slot, residential		20	.400		50	10.90		60.90	73.50	
	2000	Post office type		8	1	↓	189	27.50		216.50	254	
	9000	Minimum labor/equipment charge	↓	5	1.600	Job		43.50		43.50	73	

106 | Partitions & Storage Shelving

106 150 | Demountable Partitions

			CREW	DAILY OUTPUT	LABOR-HOURS	UNIT	MAT.	LABOR	EQUIP.	TOTAL	TOTAL INCL O&P	
152	0010	**PARTITIONS, MOVABLE OFFICE** Demountable, add for doors										152
	0100	Do not deduct door openings from total L.F.										
	0900	Demountable gypsum system on 2" to 2-1/2"										
	1000	steel studs, 9' high, 3" to 3-3/4" thick										
	1200	Vinyl clad gypsum	2 Carp	48	.333	L.F.	23	9.10		32.10	40.50	
	1300	Fabric clad gypsum		44	.364		71	9.95		80.95	94.50	
	1500	Steel clad gypsum	↓	40	.400	↓	75.50	10.90		86.40	101	
	1600	1.75 system, aluminum framing, vinyl clad hardboard,										
	1800	paper honeycomb core panel, 1-3/4" to 2-1/2" thick										
	1900	9' high	2 Carp	48	.333	L.F.	48	9.10		57.10	68.50	
	2100	7' high		60	.267		44	7.30		51.30	60	
	2200	5' high	↓	80	.200	↓	38	5.45		43.45	50.50	
	2250	Unitized gypsum system										
	2300	Unitized panel, 9' high, 2" to 2-1/2" thick										
	2350	Vinyl clad gypsum	2 Carp	48	.333	L.F.	64.50	9.10		73.60	86.50	
	2400	Fabric clad gypsum	"	44	.364	"	116	9.95		125.95	145	
	2500	Unitized mineral fiber system										
	2510	Unitized panel, 9' high, 2-1/4" thick, aluminum frame										
	2550	Vinyl clad mineral fiber	2 Carp	48	.333	L.F.	82.50	9.10		91.60	106	
	2600	Fabric clad mineral fiber	"	44	.364	"	105	9.95		114.95	132	
	2800	Movable steel walls, modular system										
	2900	Unitized panels, 9' high, 48" wide										
	3100	Baked enamel, pre-finished	2 Carp	60	.267	L.F.	75.50	7.30		82.80	95	
	3200	Fabric clad steel	"	56	.286	"	115	7.80		122.80	140	
	5500	For acoustical partitions, add, minimum				S.F.	1.33			1.33	1.46	
	5550	Maximum				"	4.87			4.87	5.35	
	5700	For doors, see div. 081 & 082										
	5800	For door hardware, see div. 087										
	6100	In-plant modular office system, w/prehung steel door										
	6200	3" thick honeycomb core panels										

106 | Partitions & Storage Shelving

106 150 | Demountable Partitions

		CREW	DAILY OUTPUT	LABOR-HOURS	UNIT	MAT.	LABOR	EQUIP.	TOTAL	TOTAL INCL O&P	
152	6250	12' x 12', 2 wall	2 Clab	3.80	4.211	Ea.	3,125	90.50		3,215.50	3,575	152
	6300	4 wall		1.90	8.421		4,800	181		4,981	5,600	
	6350	16' x 16', 2 wall		3.60	4.444		4,650	95.50		4,745.50	5,275	
	6400	4 wall		1.80	8.889		6,700	191		6,891	7,675	
	9000	Minimum labor/equipment charge	2 Carp	3	5.333	Job		146		146	244	

106 300 | Portable Partitions

			CREW	DAILY OUTPUT	LABOR-HOURS	UNIT	MAT.	LABOR	EQUIP.	TOTAL	TOTAL INCL O&P	
304	0010	**PARTITIONS, PORTABLE** Divider panels, free standing, fiber core										304
	0020	Fabric face straight										
	0100	3'-0" long, 4'-0" high	2 Carp	100	.160	L.F.	91	4.37		95.37	107	
	0200	5'-0" high		90	.178		92	4.85		96.85	109	
	0500	6'-0" high		75	.213		104	5.80		109.80	124	
	0900	5'-0" long, 4'-0" high		175	.091		68.50	2.50		71	79.50	
	1000	5'-0" high		150	.107		84.50	2.91		87.41	98	
	1500	6'-0" high		125	.128		88	3.49		91.49	103	
	1600	6'-0" long, 5'-0" high		162	.099		67.50	2.70		70.20	78.50	
	3100	Curved, 3'-0" long, 5'-0" high		90	.178		85	4.85		89.85	102	
	3150	6'-0" high		75	.213		98.50	5.80		104.30	118	
	3200	Economical panels, fabric face, 4'-0" long, 5'-0" high		132	.121		123	3.31		126.31	141	
	3250	6'-0" high		112	.143		22	3.90		25.90	30.50	
	3300	5'-0" long, 5'-0" high		150	.107		25	2.91		27.91	32.50	
	3350	6'-0" high		125	.128		31	3.49		34.49	40	
	3380	3'-0" curved, 5'-0" high		90	.178		85	4.85		89.85	102	
	3390	6'-0" high		75	.213		98.50	5.80		104.30	118	
	3450	Acoustical panels, 60 to 90 NRC, 3'-0" long, 5'-0" high		90	.178		77	4.85		81.85	92.50	
	3550	6'-0" high		75	.213		87.50	5.80		93.30	106	
	3600	5'-0" long, 5'-0" high		150	.107		53.50	2.91		56.41	64	
	3650	6'-0" high		125	.128		59.50	3.49		62.99	71.50	
	3700	6'-0" long, 5'-0" high		162	.099		52	2.70		54.70	61.50	
	3750	6'-0" high		138	.116		56.50	3.17		59.67	68	
	3800	Economy acoustical panels, 40 NRC, 4'-0" long, 5'-0" high		132	.121		30.50	3.31		33.81	39.50	
	3850	6'-0" high		112	.143		34.50	3.90		38.40	44.50	
	3900	5'-0" long, 6'-0" high		125	.128		31	3.49		34.49	40	
	3950	6'-0" long, 5'-0" high		162	.099		30.50	2.70		33.20	38.50	
	9000	Minimum labor/equipment charge		3	5.333	Job		146		146	244	

106 520 | Panel Partitions

			CREW	DAILY OUTPUT	LABOR-HOURS	UNIT	MAT.	LABOR	EQUIP.	TOTAL	TOTAL INCL O&P	
522	0010	**PARTITIONS, FOLDING LEAF** Acoustic, wood										522
	0100	Vinyl faced, to 18' high, 6 psf, minimum	2 Carp	60	.267	S.F.	34.50	7.30		41.80	50	
	0150	Average		45	.356		41	9.70		50.70	61.50	
	0200	Maximum		30	.533		53	14.55		67.55	83	
	0400	Formica or hardwood finish, minimum		60	.267		35.50	7.30		42.80	51	
	0500	Maximum		30	.533		38	14.55		52.55	66	
	0600	Wood, low acoustical type, 4.5 psf, to 14' high		50	.320		25.50	8.75		34.25	43	
	9000	Minimum labor/equipment charge		4	4	Job		109		109	183	

106 550 | Accordion Partitions

			CREW	DAILY OUTPUT	LABOR-HOURS	UNIT	MAT.	LABOR	EQUIP.	TOTAL	TOTAL INCL O&P	
552	0010	**PARTITIONS, FOLDING ACCORDION**										552
	0100	Vinyl covered, over 150 S.F., frame not included										
	0300	Residential, 1.25 lb. per S.F., 8' maximum height	2 Carp	300	.053	S.F.	11.60	1.46		13.06	15.20	
	0400	Commercial, 1.75 lb. per S.F., 8' maximum height		225	.071		11.60	1.94		13.54	16	
	0900	Acoustical, 3 lb. per S.F., 17' maximum height		100	.160		17.50	4.37		21.87	26.50	
	1200	5 lb. per S.F., 20' maximum height		95	.168		26	4.60		30.60	36	
	1500	Vinyl clad wood or steel, electric operation, 5.0 psf		160	.100		29	2.73		31.73	36.50	
	1900	Wood, non-acoustic, birch or mahogany, to 10' high		300	.053		15.55	1.46		17.01	19.55	

Important: See the Reference Section for critical supporting data - Reference Nos., Crews, & City Cost Indexes

106 | Partitions & Storage Shelving

106 550 | Accordion Partitions

			CREW	DAILY OUTPUT	LABOR-HOURS	UNIT	1999 BARE COSTS MAT.	LABOR	EQUIP.	TOTAL	TOTAL INCL O&P	
552	9000	Minimum labor/equipment charge	2 Carp	4	4	Job		109		109	183	552

106 750 | Storage & Shelving

			CREW	DAILY OUTPUT	LABOR-HOURS	UNIT	MAT.	LABOR	EQUIP.	TOTAL	INCL O&P	
754	0010	SHELVING Metal, industrial, cross-braced, 3' wide, 12" deep	1 Sswk	175	.046	SF Shlf	10.25	1.40		11.65	13.95	754
	0100	24" deep		330	.024		6.55	.74		7.29	8.65	
	2200	Wide span, 1600 lb. capacity per shelf, 6' wide, 24" deep		380	.021		6.30	.64		6.94	8.15	
	2400	36" deep		440	.018		5.55	.56		6.11	7.15	
	9000	Minimum labor/equipment charge	1 Carp	4	2	Job		54.50		54.50	91.50	

107 | Telephone Specialties

107 550 | Telephone Enclosures

			CREW	DAILY OUTPUT	LABOR-HOURS	UNIT	MAT.	LABOR	EQUIP.	TOTAL	INCL O&P	
551	0010	TELEPHONE ENCLOSURE										551
	0300	Shelf type, wall hung, minimum	2 Carp	5	3.200	Ea.	705	87.50		792.50	925	
	0400	Maximum		5	3.200		2,425	87.50		2,512.50	2,825	
	0600	Booth type, painted steel, indoor or outdoor, minimum		1.50	10.667		2,975	291		3,266	3,750	
	0700	Maximum (stainless steel)		1.50	10.667		9,850	291		10,141	11,300	
	1900	Outdoor, drive-up type, wall mounted		4	4		775	109		884	1,050	
	2000	Post mounted, stainless steel posts		3	5.333		1,200	146		1,346	1,575	
	9000	Minimum labor/equipment charge		4	4	Job		109		109	183	

108 | Toilet & Bath Accessories & Scales

108 200 | Bath Accessories

			CREW	DAILY OUTPUT	LABOR-HOURS	UNIT	MAT.	LABOR	EQUIP.	TOTAL	INCL O&P	
204	0010	BATH ACCESSORIES										204
	0020											
	0200	Curtain rod, stainless steel, 5' long, 1" diameter	1 Carp	13	.615	Ea.	19.60	16.80		36.40	49.50	
	0300	1-1/4" diameter	"	13	.615	"	22.50	16.80		39.30	53	
	0500	Dispenser units, combined soap & towel dispensers,										
	0510	mirror and shelf, flush mounted	1 Carp	10	.800	Ea.	258	22		280	320	
	0600	Towel dispenser and waste receptacle,										
	0610	18 gallon capacity	1 Carp	10	.800	Ea.	271	22		293	335	
	0800	Grab bar, straight, 1-1/4" diameter, stainless steel, 18" long		24	.333		34	9.10		43.10	53	
	0900	24" long		23	.348		37	9.50		46.50	57	
	1000	30" long		22	.364		40	9.95		49.95	60.50	
	1100	36" long		20	.400		42.50	10.90		53.40	65.50	
	1200	1-1/2" diameter, 24" long		23	.348		39.50	9.50		49	59.50	
	1300	36" long		20	.400		46	10.90		56.90	69.50	
	1500	Tub bar, 1-1/4" diameter, 24" x 36"		14	.571		84.50	15.60		100.10	119	
	1600	Plus vertical arm		12	.667		72	18.20		90.20	110	
	1900	End tub bar, 1" diameter, 90° angle, 16" x 32"		12	.667		100	18.20		118.20	141	
	2300	Hand dryer, surface mounted, electric, 115 volt, 20 amp		4	2		485	54.50		539.50	625	

108 | Toilet & Bath Accessories & Scales

108 200 | Bath Accessories

			DAILY	LABOR-			1999 BARE COSTS			TOTAL	
		CREW	OUTPUT	HOURS	UNIT	MAT.	LABOR	EQUIP.	TOTAL	INCL O&P	
204	2400	230 volt, 10 amp	1 Carp	4	2	Ea.	485	54.50		539.50	625	204
	2600	Hat and coat strip, stainless steel, 4 hook, 36" long		24	.333		44	9.10		53.10	64	
	2700	6 hook, 60" long		20	.400		69	10.90		79.90	94.50	
	3000	Mirror, with stainless steel 3/4" square frame, 18" x 24"		20	.400		59.50	10.90		70.40	83.50	
	3100	36" x 24"		15	.533		108	14.55		122.55	144	
	3200	48" x 24"		10	.800		144	22		166	195	
	3300	72" x 24"		6	1.333		196	36.50		232.50	277	
	3500	With 5" stainless steel shelf, 18" x 24"		20	.400		88	10.90		98.90	115	
	3600	36" x 24"		15	.533		132	14.55		146.55	170	
	3700	48" x 24"		10	.800		165	22		187	219	
	3800	72" x 24"		6	1.333		295	36.50		331.50	385	
	4100	Mop holder strip, stainless steel, 5 holders, 48" long		20	.400		60	10.90		70.90	84.50	
	4200	Napkin/tampon dispenser, recessed		15	.533		320	14.55		334.55	375	
	4300	Robe hook, single, regular		36	.222		10.85	6.05		16.90	22	
	4400	Heavy duty, concealed mounting		36	.222		11.40	6.05		17.45	22.50	
	4600	Soap dispenser, chrome, surface mounted, liquid		20	.400		39.50	10.90		50.40	62	
	4700	Powder		20	.400		65.50	10.90		76.40	90.50	
	5000	Recessed stainless steel, liquid		10	.800		65.50	22		87.50	109	
	5100	Powder		10	.800		255	22		277	320	
	5300	Soap tank, stainless steel, 1 gallon		10	.800		153	22		175	205	
	5400	5 gallon		5	1.600		210	43.50		253.50	305	
	5600	Shelf, stainless steel, 5" wide, 18 ga., 24" long		24	.333		34	9.10		43.10	52.50	
	5700	48" long		16	.500		60.50	13.65		74.15	89.50	
	5800	8" wide shelf, 18 ga., 24" long		22	.364		42	9.95		51.95	62.50	
	5900	48" long		14	.571		84	15.60		99.60	119	
	6000	Toilet seat cover dispenser, stainless steel, recessed		20	.400		90	10.90		100.90	117	
	6050	Surface mounted		15	.533		25	14.55		39.55	52	
	6100	Toilet tissue dispenser, surface mounted, SS, single roll		30	.267		10.25	7.30		17.55	23.50	
	6200	Double roll		24	.333		15.20	9.10		24.30	32	
	6290	Toilet seat	1 Plum	40	.200		18.50	6.50		25	30.50	
	6400	Towel bar, stainless steel, 18" long	1 Carp	23	.348		29.50	9.50		39	48	
	6500	30" long		21	.381		33.50	10.40		43.90	54.50	
	6700	Towel dispenser, stainless steel, surface mounted		16	.500		36	13.65		49.65	62.50	
	6800	Flush mounted, recessed		10	.800		134	22		156	185	
	7000	Towel holder, hotel type, 2 guest size		20	.400		11.80	10.90		22.70	31.50	
	7200	Towel shelf, stainless steel, 24" long, 8" wide		20	.400		45	10.90		55.90	68	
	7400	Tumbler holder, tumbler only		30	.267		19.40	7.30		26.70	33.50	
	7500	Soap, tumbler & toothbrush		30	.267		19.40	7.30		26.70	33.50	
	7700	Wall urn ash receiver, surface mount, 11" long		12	.667		98.50	18.20		116.70	139	
	8000	Waste receptacles, stainless steel, with top, 13 gallon		10	.800		180	22		202	234	
	8100	36 gallon		8	1		286	27.50		313.50	360	
	9000	Minimum labor/equipment charge		5	1.600	Job		43.50		43.50	73	
208	0010	**MEDICINE CABINETS** With mirror, st. st. frame, 16" x 22", unlighted	1 Carp	14	.571	Ea.	63.50	15.60		79.10	95.50	208
	0100	Wood frame		14	.571		92.50	15.60		108.10	127	
	0300	Sliding mirror doors, 20" x 16" x 4-3/4", unlighted		7	1.143		82.50	31		113.50	143	
	0400	24" x 19" x 8-1/2", lighted		5	1.600		139	43.50		182.50	226	
	0600	Triple door, 30" x 32", unlighted, plywood body		7	1.143		205	31		236	278	
	0700	Steel body		7	1.143		270	31		301	350	
	0900	Oak door, wood body, beveled mirror, single door		7	1.143		120	31		151	184	
	1000	Double door		6	1.333		305	36.50		341.50	395	
	1200	Hotel cabinets, stainless, with lower shelf, unlighted		10	.800		165	22		187	219	
	1300	Lighted		5	1.600		245	43.50		288.50	345	
	9000	Minimum labor/equipment charge		4	2	Job		54.50		54.50	91.50	

For information about Means Estimating Seminars, see yellow pages 11 and 12 in back of book

Important: See the Reference Section for critical supporting data - Reference Nos., Crews, & City Cost Indexes

Division 11 Equipment

Estimating Tips
General
- The items in this division are usually priced per square foot or each. Many of these items are purchased by the owner for installation by the contractor. Check the specifications for responsibilities, and include time for receiving, storage, installation and mechanical and electrical hook-ups in the appropriate divisions.
- Many items in Division 11 require some type of support system that is not usually furnished with the item. Examples of these systems include blocking for the attachment of casework and support angles for ceiling hung projection screens. The required blocking or supports must be added to the estimate in the appropriate division.
- Some items in Division 11 may require assembly or electrical hook-ups. Verify the amount of assembly required or the need for a hard electrical connection and add the appropriate costs.

Reference Numbers
Reference numbers are shown in bold squares at the beginning of some major classifications. These numbers refer to related items in the Reference Section. The reference information may be an estimating procedure, an alternate pricing method or technical information.

Note: Not all subdivisions listed here necessarily appear in this publication.

110 | Equipment

110 100 | Maintenance Equipment

			DAILY	LABOR-		1999 BARE COSTS				TOTAL
		CREW	OUTPUT	HOURS	UNIT	MAT.	LABOR	EQUIP.	TOTAL	INCL O&P
121	0010 **VACUUM CLEANING**									121
	0020 Central, 3 inlet, residential	1 Skwk	.90	8.889	Total	955	249		1,204	1,475
	0200 Commercial		.70	11.429		1,400	320		1,720	2,075
	0400 5 inlet system, residential		.50	16		1,025	450		1,475	1,875
	0600 7 inlet system, commercial	↓	.40	20		1,100	560		1,660	2,125
	4010 Rule of thumb: First 1200 S.F., installed									1,044
	4020 For each additional S.F., add				S.F.					.17

110 200 | Security/Vault Equip

261	0010 **SAFE**									261
	0015 Office, 4 hr. rating, 30" x 18" x 18" inside				Ea.	3,250			3,250	3,575
	0800 Money, "B" label, 9" x 14" x 14"					445			445	490
	0900 Tool resistive, 24" x 24" x 20"					3,025			3,025	3,325
	1050 Tool and torch resistive, 24" x 24" x 20"					7,675			7,675	8,450

110 300 | Teller & Service Equip

301	0010 **BANK EQUIPMENT**									301
	0020 Alarm system, police	2 Elec	1.60	10	Ea.	3,600	320		3,920	4,450
	0400 Bullet resistant teller window, 44" x 60"	1 Glaz	.60	13.333		2,725	355		3,080	3,575
	0500 48" x 60"	"	.60	13.333		3,975	355		4,330	4,950
	3000 Counters for banks, frontal only	2 Carp	1	16	Station	1,350	435		1,785	2,200
	3100 Complete with steel undercounter		.50	32	"	2,625	875		3,500	4,325
	5400 Partitions, bullet-resistant, 1-3/16" glass, 8' high	↓	10	1.600	L.F.	145	43.50		188.50	233
	5600 Pass thru, bullet-resist. window, painted steel, 24" x 36"	2 Sswk	1.60	10	Ea.	1,400	305		1,705	2,125

110 400 | Ecclesiastical Equip

401	0010 **CHURCH EQUIPMENT**									401
	0020 Altar, wood, custom design, plain	1 Carp	1.40	5.714	Ea.	1,400	156		1,556	1,800
	0050 Deluxe	"	.20	40	"	6,850	1,100		7,950	9,350
	0150 Baptistry, fiberglass, 3'-6" deep, x 13'-7" long,									
	0160 steps at both ends, incl. plumbing, minimum	L-8	1	20	Ea.	2,000	565		2,565	3,125
	0200 Maximum	"	.70	28.571		4,000	810		4,810	5,725
	0250 Add for filter, heater and lights				↓	985			985	1,075
	1500 Pews, bench type, hardwood, minimum	1 Carp	20	.400	L.F.	50.50	10.90		61.40	74
	1550 Maximum	"	15	.533		100	14.55		114.55	135
	1570 For kneeler, add				↓	12.50			12.50	13.75
	4000 Steeples, translucent fiberglass, 30" square, 15' high	F-3	2	20	Ea.	2,000	555	222	2,777	3,375
	4150 25' high	"	1.80	22.222		3,000	615	246	3,861	4,600
	4600 Aluminum, baked finish, 14' high, 16" square					1,550			1,550	1,700
	4640 35' high, 8' base					15,600			15,600	17,100
	4680 152' high, custom				↓	345,500			345,500	380,000
	5000 Wall cross, aluminum, extruded, 2" x 2" section	1 Carp	34	.235	L.F.	28	6.40		34.40	42
	5150 4" x 4" section		29	.276		40	7.55		47.55	56.50
	5300 Bronze, extruded, 1" x 2" section		31	.258		56	7.05		63.05	73.50
	5350 2-1/2" x 2-1/2" section	↓	34	.235	↓	83	6.40		89.40	102

110 500 | Library Equipment

501	0010 **LIBRARY EQUIPMENT**									501
	0020 Bookshelf, mtl, 90" high, 10" shelf, dbl face	1 Carp	11.50	.696	L.F.	89.50	19		108.50	130
	0300 Single face	"	12	.667	"	65	18.20		83.20	102
	0600 For 8" shelving, subtract from above					10%				
	0800 For 42" high with countertop, subtract from above					20%				
	2500 Carrels, hardwood, 36" x 24", minimum	1 Carp	5	1.600	Ea.	560	43.50		603.50	695

110 | Equipment

110 500 | Library Equipment

		CREW	DAILY OUTPUT	LABOR-HOURS	UNIT	1999 BARE COSTS				TOTAL INCL O&P
						MAT.	LABOR	EQUIP.	TOTAL	
501	2650	Maximum	1 Carp	4	2	Ea.	735	54.50		789.50	900
	2850	Metal, minimum		5	1.600		186	43.50		229.50	277
	3000	Maximum	↓	4	2	↓	610	54.50		664.50	760

110 600 | Theater/Stage Equip

601	0010	STAGE EQUIPMENT									
	0050	Control boards with dimmers and breakers, minimum	1 Elec	1	8	Ea.	2,300	255		2,555	2,925
	0150	Maximum	"	.20	40	"	34,500	1,275		35,775	40,000
	0160										
	0500	Curtain track, straight, light duty	2 Carp	20	.800	L.F.	18.25	22		40.25	56.50
	0700	Curved sections		12	1.333	"	110	36.50		146.50	182
	1000	Curtains, velour, medium weight	↓	600	.027	S.F.	12.65	.73		13.38	15.10
	5000	Stages, portable with steps, folding legs, stock, 8" high				SF Stg.	7.50			7.50	8.20
	5100	16" high					15.50			15.50	17.05
	5200	32" high					21			21	23.50
	5300	40" high				↓	16.25			16.25	17.90
604	0011	MOVIE EQUIPMENT									
	0020	Changeover, minimum				Ea.	350			350	385
	3000	Projection screens, rigid, in wall, acrylic, 1/4" thick	2 Glaz	195	.082	S.F.	31.50	2.18		33.68	38.50
	3100	1/2" thick	"	130	.123	"	36.50	3.27		39.77	46
	3700	Sound systems, incl. amplifier, mono, minimum	1 Elec	.90	8.889	Ea.	1,825	284		2,109	2,475
	3800	Dolby/Super Sound, maximum		.40	20		13,700	640		14,340	16,000
	4100	Dual system, 2 channel, front surround, minimum		.70	11.429		3,050	365		3,415	3,950
	4200	Dolby/Super Sound, 4 channel, maximum	↓	.40	20		12,600	640		13,240	14,900
	5700	Seating, painted steel, upholstered, minimum	2 Carp	35	.457		92	12.50		104.50	122
	5800	Maximum	"	28	.571	↓	237	15.60		252.60	286

111 | Mercantile, Commercial & Detention Equipment

111 020 | Barber Shop Equipment

		CREW	DAILY OUTPUT	LABOR-HOURS	UNIT	1999 BARE COSTS				TOTAL INCL O&P
						MAT.	LABOR	EQUIP.	TOTAL	
021	0010	BARBER EQUIPMENT									
	0020	Chair, hydraulic, movable, minimum	1 Carp	24	.333	Ea.	375	9.10		384.10	425
	0050	Maximum	"	16	.500		2,700	13.65		2,713.65	3,000
	0200	Wall hung styling station with mirrors, minimum	L-2	8	2		238	48		286	340
	0300	Maximum	"	4	4		1,500	96.50		1,596.50	1,800
	0500	Sink, hair washing basin, rough plumbing not incl.	1 Plum	8	1		365	32.50		397.50	450
	1000	Sterilizer, liquid solution for tools					125			125	138
	1100	Total equipment, rule of thumb, per chair, minimum	L-8	1	20		1,475	565		2,040	2,550
	1150	Maximum	"	1	20	↓	4,000	565		4,565	5,325

111 040 | Cash Register/Checking

041	0010	CHECKOUT COUNTER									
	0020	Supermarket conveyor, single belt	2 Clab	10	1.600	Ea.	1,925	34.50		1,959.50	2,175
	0100	Double belt, power take-away		9	1.778		3,300	38		3,338	3,700
	0400	Double belt, power take-away, incl. side scanning		7	2.286		4,100	49		4,149	4,575
	0800	Warehouse or bulk type	↓	6	2.667	↓	4,800	57		4,857	5,375
	1000	Scanning system, 2 lanes, w/registers, scan gun & memory				System	12,000			12,000	13,200

111 | Mercantile, Commercial & Detention Equipment

111 040 | Cash Register/Checking

			CREW	DAILY OUTPUT	LABOR-HOURS	UNIT	1999 BARE COSTS MAT.	LABOR	EQUIP.	TOTAL	TOTAL INCL O&P	
041	1100	10 lanes, single processor, full scan, with scales				System	114,000			114,000	125,500	041
	2000	Register, restaurant, minimum				Ea.	500			500	550	
	2100	Maximum					2,200			2,200	2,425	
	2150	Store, minimum					500			500	550	
	2200	Maximum					2,200			2,200	2,425	

111 060 | Display Cases

			CREW	DAILY OUTPUT	LABOR-HOURS	UNIT	MAT.	LABOR	EQUIP.	TOTAL	INCL O&P	
061	0010	**REFRIGERATED FOOD CASES**										061
	0030	Dairy, multi-deck, 12' long	Q-5	3	5.333	Ea.	6,425	157		6,582	7,325	
	0100	For rear sliding doors, add					905			905	1,000	
	0200	Delicatessen case, service deli, 12' long, single deck	Q-5	3.90	4.103		4,350	121		4,471	5,000	
	0300	Multi-deck, 18 S.F. shelf display		3	5.333		6,875	157		7,032	7,825	
	0400	Freezer, self-contained, chest-type, 30 C.F.		3.90	4.103		3,175	121		3,296	3,700	
	0500	Glass door, upright, 78 C.F.		3.30	4.848		6,050	143		6,193	6,875	
	0600	Frozen food, chest type, 12' long		3.30	4.848		4,375	143		4,518	5,025	
	0700	Glass door, reach-in, 5 door		3	5.333		8,400	157		8,557	9,500	
	0800	Island case, 12' long, single deck		3.30	4.848		4,950	143		5,093	5,675	
	0900	Multi-deck		3	5.333		10,400	157		10,557	11,700	
	1000	Meat case, 12' long, single deck		3.30	4.848		3,550	143		3,693	4,125	
	1050	Multi-deck		3.10	5.161		6,175	152		6,327	7,050	
	1100	Produce, 12' long, single deck		3.30	4.848		4,750	143		4,893	5,450	
	1200	Multi-deck		3.10	5.161		5,300	152		5,452	6,075	

111 100 | Laundry/Dry Cleaning

			CREW	DAILY OUTPUT	LABOR-HOURS	UNIT	MAT.	LABOR	EQUIP.	TOTAL	INCL O&P	
101	0010	**LAUNDRY EQUIPMENT** Not incl. rough-in										101
	0500	Dryers, gas fired residential, 16 lb. capacity, average	1 Plum	3	2.667	Ea.	505	87		592	695	
	1000	Commercial, 30 lb. capacity, coin operated, single		3	2.667		2,325	87		2,412	2,675	
	1100	Double stacked		2	4		4,975	130		5,105	5,675	
	1500	Industrial, 30 lb. capacity		2	4		1,975	130		2,105	2,375	
	1600	50 lb. capacity		1.70	4.706		2,450	153		2,603	2,950	
	2000	Dry cleaners, electric, 20 lb. capacity	L-1	.20	80		27,900	2,575		30,475	34,700	
	2050	25 lb. capacity		.17	94.118		36,300	3,025		39,325	44,700	
	2100	30 lb. capacity		.15	106		38,300	3,450		41,750	47,500	
	2150	60 lb. capacity		.09	177		60,000	5,725		65,725	75,000	
	3500	Folders, blankets & sheets, minimum	1 Elec	.17	47.059		22,800	1,500		24,300	27,300	
	3700	King size with automatic stacker		.10	80		43,500	2,550		46,050	52,000	
	3800	For conveyor delivery, add		.45	17.778		5,175	565		5,740	6,575	
	4500	Ironers, institutional, 110", single roll		.20	40		23,800	1,275		25,075	28,200	
	4700	Lint collector, ductwork not included, 8,000 to 10,000 C.F.M.	Q-10	.30	80		6,825	2,375		9,200	11,300	
	5000	Washers, residential, 4 cycle, average	1 Plum	3	2.667		590	87		677	780	
	5300	Commercial, coin operated, average	"	3	2.667		945	87		1,032	1,175	
	6000	Combination washer/extractor, 20 lb. capacity	L-6	1.50	8		3,375	259		3,634	4,100	
	6100	30 lb. capacity		.80	15		7,000	485		7,485	8,450	
	6200	50 lb. capacity		.68	17.647		7,975	570		8,545	9,675	
	6300	75 lb. capacity		.30	40		15,700	1,300		17,000	19,200	
	6350	125 lb. capacity		.16	75		20,000	2,425		22,425	25,800	

111 320 | Projection Screens

			CREW	DAILY OUTPUT	LABOR-HOURS	UNIT	MAT.	LABOR	EQUIP.	TOTAL	INCL O&P	
321	0010	**PROJECTION SCREENS** Wall or ceiling hung, matte white										321
	0100	Manually operated, economy	2 Carp	500	.032	S.F.	4.20	.87		5.07	6.10	
	0300	Intermediate		450	.036		4.90	.97		5.87	7	
	0400	Deluxe		400	.040		6.80	1.09		7.89	9.35	
	9000	Minimum labor/equipment charge		3	5.333	Job		146		146	244	

111 | Mercantile, Commercial & Detention Equipment

111 400 | Service Station Equip

			CREW	DAILY OUTPUT	LABOR-HOURS	UNIT	MAT.	LABOR	EQUIP.	TOTAL	TOTAL INCL O&P
401	0010	**AUTOMOTIVE**									
	0030	Compressors, electric, 1-1/2 H.P., standard controls	L-4	1.50	16	Ea.	320	410		730	1,025
	0550	Dual controls		1.50	16		420	410		830	1,150
	0600	5 H.P., 115/230 volt, standard controls		1	24		1,525	615		2,140	2,725
	0650	Dual controls		1	24		1,625	615		2,240	2,825
	1100	Product dispenser with vapor recovery for 6 nozzles, installed, not									
	1110	including piping to storage tanks				Ea.	15,000			15,000	16,500
	2200	Hoists, single post, 8,000# capacity, swivel arms	L-4	.40	60		3,500	1,550		5,050	6,400
	2400	Two posts, adjustable frames, 11,000# capacity		.25	96		4,500	2,450		6,950	9,050
	2500	24,000# capacity		.15	160		6,000	4,100		10,100	13,400
	2700	7,500# capacity, frame supports		.50	48		5,000	1,225		6,225	7,550
	2800	Four post, roll on ramp		.50	48		4,500	1,225		5,725	7,000
	2810	Hydraulic lifts, above ground, 2 post, clear floor, 6000 lb cap		2.67	8.989		4,700	231		4,931	5,550
	2815	9000 lb capacity		2.29	10.480		11,200	269		11,469	12,700
	2820	15,000 lb capacity		2	12		25,900	310		26,210	29,000
	2825	30,000 lb capacity		1.60	15		27,900	385		28,285	31,200
	2830	4 post, ramp style, 25,000 lb capacity		2	12		10,900	310		11,210	12,500
	2835	35,000 lb capacity		1	24		51,000	615		51,615	57,000
	2840	50,000 lb capacity		1	24		57,000	615		57,615	63,500
	2845	75,000 lb capacity		1	24		66,000	615		66,615	73,500
	2850	For drive thru tracks, add, minimum					700			700	770
	2855	Maximum					1,200			1,200	1,325
	2860	Ramp extensions, 3'(set of 2)					575			575	635
	2865	Rolling jack platform					2,000			2,000	2,200
	2870	Elec/hyd jacking beam					5,350			5,350	5,875
	2880	Scissor lift, portable, 6000 lb capacity					5,250			5,250	5,775
	3000	Lube equipment, 3 reel type, with pumps, not including piping	L-4	.50	48	Set	6,000	1,225		7,225	8,650
	4000	Spray painting booth, 26' long, complete	"	.40	60	Ea.	12,000	1,550		13,550	15,800

111 500 | Parking Control Equip

			CREW	DAILY OUTPUT	LABOR-HOURS	UNIT	MAT.	LABOR	EQUIP.	TOTAL	TOTAL INCL O&P
501	0010	**PARKING EQUIPMENT**									
	5000	Barrier gate with programmable controller	2 Elec	3	5.333	Ea.	2,500	170		2,670	3,025
	5020	Industrial	"	3	5.333		3,500	170		3,670	4,125
	5100	Card reader	1 Elec	2	4		2,000	128		2,128	2,400
	5120	Proximity with customer display	2 Elec	1	16		5,000	510		5,510	6,300
	5200	Cashier booth, average	B-22	1	30		10,000	760	204	10,964	12,500
	5300	Collector station, pay on foot	2 Elec	.20	80		110,000	2,550		112,550	125,000
	5320	Credit card only		.50	32		45,000	1,025		46,025	51,000
	5500	Exit verifier		1	16		22,500	510		23,010	25,600
	5600	Fee computer	1 Elec	1.50	5.333		13,300	170		13,470	15,000
	5700	Full sign, 4" letters	"	2	4		900	128		1,028	1,175
	5800	Inductive loop	2 Elec	4	4		500	128		628	745
	5900	Ticket spitter with time/date stamp, standard		2	8		6,000	255		6,255	7,000
	5920	Mag stripe encoding		2	8		16,000	255		16,255	18,000
	5950	Vehicle detector, microprocessor based	1 Elec	3	2.667		400	85		485	570
	6000	Parking control software, minimum		.50	16		18,000	510		18,510	20,600
	6020	Maximum		.20	40		75,000	1,275		76,275	84,500

111 600 | Loading Dock Equipment

			CREW	DAILY OUTPUT	LABOR-HOURS	UNIT	MAT.	LABOR	EQUIP.	TOTAL	TOTAL INCL O&P
601	0010	**LOADING DOCK**									
	0020	Bumpers, rubber blocks 4-1/2" thk, 10" H, 14" long	1 Carp	26	.308	Ea.	37	8.40		45.40	55
	0200	24" long		22	.364		58	9.95		67.95	80
	0300	36" long		17	.471		68	12.85		80.85	96.50
	0500	12" high, 14" long		25	.320		61	8.75		69.75	81.50
	2200	Dock boards, heavy duty, 60" x 60", aluminum, 5,000 lb. cap.					980			980	1,075

111 | Mercantile, Commercial & Detention Equipment

111 600 | Loading Dock Equipment

			CREW	DAILY OUTPUT	LABOR-HOURS	UNIT	1999 BARE COSTS				TOTAL INCL O&P	
							MAT.	LABOR	EQUIP.	TOTAL		
601	4200	Platform lifter, 6' x 6', portable, 3,000 lb. capacity				Ea.	5,575			5,575	6,125	601
	6200	Shelters, fabric, for truck or train, scissor arms, minimum	1 Carp	1	8		945	218		1,163	1,425	
	6300	Maximum	"	.50	16		1,425	435		1,860	2,275	
603	0012	**DOCK BUMPERS** Bolts not included, 2" x 6" to 4" x 8", average	1 Carp	300	.027	B.F.	.46	.73		1.19	1.73	603

111 700 | Waste Handling Equip

			CREW	DAILY OUTPUT	LABOR-HOURS	UNIT	MAT.	LABOR	EQUIP.	TOTAL	INCL O&P	
701	0010	**WASTE HANDLING**										701
	0020	Compactors, 115 volt, 250#/hr., chute fed	L-4	1	24	Ea.	8,225	615		8,840	10,100	
	0100	Hand fed		2.40	10		5,675	257		5,932	6,675	
	1000	Heavy duty industrial compactor, 0.5 C.Y. capacity		1	24		5,050	615		5,665	6,575	
	1050	1.0 C.Y. capacity		1	24		7,525	615		8,140	9,300	
	1400	For handling hazardous waste materials, 55 gallon drum packer, std.					11,700			11,700	12,900	
	1410	55 gallon drum packer w/HEPA filter					14,900			14,900	16,400	
	1420	55 gallon drum packer w/charcoal & HEPA filter					19,000			19,000	20,900	
	1430	All of the above made explosion proof, add					9,075			9,075	9,975	

111 900 | Detention Equipment

			CREW	DAILY OUTPUT	LABOR-HOURS	UNIT	MAT.	LABOR	EQUIP.	TOTAL	INCL O&P	
901	0011	**DETENTION EQUIPMENT**										901
	0020											
	2000	Cells, prefab., 5' to 6' wide, 7' to 8' high, 7' to 8' deep,										
	2010	bar front, cot, not incl. plumbing	E-4	1.50	21.333	Ea.	6,800	665	55	7,520	8,800	

114 | Food Service, Residential, Darkroom, Athletic Equipment

114 000 | Food Service Equipment

			CREW	DAILY OUTPUT	LABOR-HOURS	UNIT	1999 BARE COSTS				TOTAL INCL O&P	
							MAT.	LABOR	EQUIP.	TOTAL		
002	0010	**RESIDENTIAL APPLIANCES**										002
	0020	Cooking range, 30" free standing, 1 oven, minimum	2 Clab	10	1.600	Ea.	286	34.50		320.50	375	
	0050	Maximum	"	4	4		1,050	86		1,136	1,300	
	0350	Built-in, 30" wide, 1 oven, minimum	1 Elec	6	1.333		405	42.50		447.50	510	
	0400	Maximum	2 Carp	2	8		1,000	218		1,218	1,475	
	0900	Counter top cook tops, 4 burner, standard, minimum	1 Elec	6	1.333		169	42.50		211.50	252	
	0950	Maximum		3	2.667		395	85		480	560	
	1250	Microwave oven, minimum		4	2		92.50	64		156.50	201	
	1300	Maximum		2	4		1,575	128		1,703	1,925	
	1500	Combination range, refrigerator and sink, 30" wide, minimum	L-1	2	8		630	258		888	1,100	
	1550	Maximum	"	1	16		1,250	515		1,765	2,175	
	1640	Combination range, refrigerator, sink, microwave										
	1660	oven and ice maker	L-1	.80	20	Ea.	3,475	645		4,120	4,825	
	1750	Compactor, residential size, 4 to 1 compaction, minimum	1 Carp	5	1.600		330	43.50		373.50	435	
	1800	Maximum	"	3	2.667		360	73		433	515	
	2750	Dishwasher, built-in, 2 cycles, minimum	L-1	4	4		217	129		346	440	
	2800	Maximum		2	8		445	258		703	885	
	3300	Garbage disposer, sink type, minimum		10	1.600		37.50	51.50		89	121	
	3350	Maximum		10	1.600		178	51.50		229.50	276	
	4150	Hood for range, 2 speed, vented, 30" wide, minimum	L-3	5	3.200		37.50	94.50		132	195	
	4200	Maximum	"	3	5.333		278	158		436	560	
	4220	36" wide, minimum	1 Elec	5	1.600		149	51		200	243	

114 | Food Service, Residential, Darkroom, Athletic Equipment

114 000 | Food Service Equipment

		CREW	DAILY OUTPUT	LABOR-HOURS	UNIT	1999 BARE COSTS MAT.	LABOR	EQUIP.	TOTAL	TOTAL INCL O&P
4300	42" wide, minimum	L-3	5	3.200	Ea.	164	94.50		258.50	335
4330	Custom		5	3.200		206	94.50		300.50	380
4350	Maximum	▼	3	5.333		252	158		410	530
4400	Ventless hood, 2 speed, 30" wide, minimum	1 Elec	8	1		41	32		73	94.50
4450	Maximum		7	1.143		196	36.50		232.50	272
4510	36" wide, minimum		7	1.143		155	36.50		191.50	227
4550	Maximum		6	1.333		320	42.50		362.50	415
4580	42" wide, minimum		6	1.333		175	42.50		217.50	259
4600	Maximum	▼	5	1.600		247	51		298	350
4650	For vented 1 speed, deduct from maximum				▼	26			26	28.50
4700										
5380	Oven, built in, standard	1 Elec	4	2	Ea.	350	64		414	485
5390	Deluxe	"	2	4		715	128		843	980
5500	Refrigerator, no frost, 10 C.F. to 12 C.F. minimum	2 Clab	10	1.600		415	34.50		449.50	515
5600	Maximum	"	6	2.667		635	57		692	795
6400	Sump pump cellar drainer, pedestal, 1/3 H.P., molded PVC base	1 Plum	3	2.667		86.50	87		173.50	231
6450	Solid brass	"	2	4	▼	179	130		309	400
6460	Sump pump, see also division 152-480									
7350	Water softener, automatic, to 30 grains per gallon	2 Plum	5	3.200	Ea.	450	104		554	660
7400	To 100 grains per gallon	"	4	4	"	510	130		640	770
0010	**COMMERCIAL KITCHEN EQUIPMENT**									
0020	Bake oven, gas, one section	Q-1	8	2	Ea.	3,450	58.50		3,508.50	3,900
0300	Two sections		7	2.286		6,875	67		6,942	7,675
0600	Three sections	▼	6	2.667		9,825	78.50		9,903.50	10,900
0900	Electric convection, single deck	L-7	4	7		4,675	184		4,859	5,450
1050	Butter pat dispenser	1 Clab	13	.615		395	13.20		408.20	455
1100	Bread dispenser, counter top	"	13	.615		455	13.20		468.20	520
1300	Broiler, without oven, standard	Q-1	8	2		3,325	58.50		3,383.50	3,750
1550	Infra-red	L-7	4	7		4,650	184		4,834	5,400
1650	Cabinet, heated, 1 compartment, reach-in	R-18	5.60	4.643		2,050	117		2,167	2,450
1655	Pass-thru roll-in		5.60	4.643		2,850	117		2,967	3,350
1660	2 compartment, reach-in	▼	4.80	5.417		4,375	136		4,511	5,050
1670	Mobile					2,100			2,100	2,300
1700	Choppers, 5 pounds	R-18	7	3.714		1,475	93.50		1,568.50	1,775
1720	16 pounds		5	5.200		1,850	131		1,981	2,225
1740	35 to 40 pounds	▼	4	6.500		3,575	163		3,738	4,200
1840	Coffee brewer, 5 burners	1 Plum	3	2.667		895	87		982	1,125
1850	Coffee urn, twin 6 gallon urns		2	4		5,675	130		5,805	6,425
1860	Single, 3 gallon	▼	3	2.667		4,125	87		4,212	4,675
1900	Cup and glass dispenser, drop in	1 Clab	4	2		805	43		848	955
1920	Disposable cup, drop in	"	16	.500		226	10.75		236.75	267
2350	Cooler, reach-in, beverage, 6' long	Q-1	6	2.667		2,575	78.50		2,653.50	2,950
2650	Dish dispenser, drop in, 12"	1 Clab	11	.727		945	15.60		960.60	1,050
2660	Mobile	"	10	.800	▼	1,575	17.15		1,592.15	1,775
2700	Dishwasher, commercial, rack type									
2720	10 to 12 racks per hour	Q-1	3.20	5	Ea.	2,350	147		2,497	2,825
2750	Semi-automatic 38 to 50 racks per hour	"	1.30	12.308		4,950	360		5,310	6,025
2800	Automatic, 190 to 230 racks per hour	Q-2	.70	34.286		10,100	1,050		11,150	12,700
2820	235 to 275 racks per hour		.50	48		20,400	1,450		21,850	24,800
2840	8,750 to 12,500 dishes per hour	▼	.20	120	▼	38,400	3,650		42,050	48,000
2950	Dishwasher hood, canopy type	L-3A	10	1.200	L.F.	3,400	36		3,436	3,800
2960	Pant leg type	"	2.50	4.800	Ea.	4,525	145		4,670	5,225
2970	Exhaust hood, sst, gutter on all sides, 4' x 4' x 2'	1 Carp	1.80	4.444		2,500	121		2,621	2,950
2980	4' x 4' x 7'	"	1.60	5		3,900	137		4,037	4,525
3000	Fast food equipment, total package, minimum	6 Skwk	.08	600		103,000	16,800		119,800	141,500
3100	Maximum	"	.07	685	▼	140,500	19,200		159,700	186,500

114 | Food Service, Residential, Darkroom, Athletic Equipment

114 000 | Food Service Equipment

			CREW	DAILY OUTPUT	LABOR-HOURS	UNIT	1999 BARE COSTS				TOTAL INCL O&P	
							MAT.	LABOR	EQUIP.	TOTAL		
004	3300	Food warmer, counter, 1.2 KW				Ea.	615			615	675	004
	3550	1.6 KW					765			765	840	
	3600	Well, hot food, built-in, rectangular, 12" x 20"	R-30	10	2.600		246	66.50		312.50	375	
	3610	Circular, 7 qt		10	2.600		205	66.50		271.50	335	
	3620	Refrigerated, 2 compartments		10	2.600		1,475	66.50		1,541.50	1,725	
	3630	3 compartments		9	2.889		1,500	74		1,574	1,775	
	3640	4 compartments		8	3.250		2,025	83.50		2,108.50	2,350	
	3800	Food mixers, 20 quarts	L-7	7	4		2,975	105		3,080	3,450	
	3850	40 quarts		5.40	5.185		6,900	136		7,036	7,825	
	3900	60 quarts		5	5.600		9,375	147		9,522	10,500	
	4040	80 quarts		3.90	7.179		10,700	189		10,889	12,100	
	4080	130 quarts		2.20	12.727		14,900	335		15,235	17,000	
	4100	Floor type, 20 quarts		15	1.867		3,900	49		3,949	4,375	
	4120	60 quarts		14	2		8,300	52.50		8,352.50	9,200	
	4140	80 quarts		12	2.333		10,400	61.50		10,461.50	11,500	
	4160	140 quarts		8.60	3.256		18,800	85.50		18,885.50	20,800	
	4300	Freezers, reach-in, 44 C.F.	Q-1	4	4		6,800	117		6,917	7,650	
	4500	68 C.F.	"	3	5.333		8,300	157		8,457	9,375	
	4600	Freezer, pre-fab, 8' x 8' w/refrigeration	2 Carp	.45	35.556		6,600	970		7,570	8,875	
	4620	8' x 12'		.35	45.714		8,550	1,250		9,800	11,500	
	4640	8' x 16'		.25	64		11,000	1,750		12,750	15,000	
	4660	8' x 20'		.17	94.118		12,300	2,575		14,875	17,800	
	4680	Reach-in, 1 compartment	Q-1	4	4		1,900	117		2,017	2,250	
	4700	2 compartment	"	3	5.333		3,050	157		3,207	3,600	
	4720	Frost cold plate	R-30	9	2.889		9,975	74		10,049	11,100	
	4750	Fryer, with twin baskets, modular model	Q-1	7	2.286		2,925	67		2,992	3,300	
	5000	Floor model on 6" legs	"	5	3.200		3,675	94		3,769	4,200	
	5100	Extra single basket, large					82.50			82.50	91	
	5300	Griddle, 3' long	Q-1	7	2.286		2,350	67		2,417	2,700	
	5550	4' long	"	6	2.667		3,800	78.50		3,878.50	4,300	
	5700	Hot chocolate dispenser	1 Plum	4	2		700	65		765	870	
	5800	Ice cube maker, 50 pounds per day	Q-1	6	2.667		1,525	78.50		1,603.50	1,800	
	5900	250 pounds per day		1.20	13.333		1,825	390		2,215	2,600	
	6050	500 pounds per day		4	4		2,475	117		2,592	2,875	
	6060	With bin		1.20	13.333		3,325	390		3,715	4,275	
	6090	1000 pounds per day, with bin		1	16		7,200	470		7,670	8,650	
	6100	Ice flakers, 300 pounds per day		1.60	10		3,550	294		3,844	4,350	
	6120	600 pounds per day		.95	16.842		3,675	495		4,170	4,825	
	6130	1000 pounds per day		.75	21.333		5,950	625		6,575	7,525	
	6140	2000 pounds per day		.65	24.615		11,200	720		11,920	13,400	
	6160	Ice storage bin, 500 pound capacity	Q-5	1	16		1,425	470		1,895	2,300	
	6180	1000 pound	"	.56	28.571		2,050	840		2,890	3,600	
	6200	Iced tea brewer	1 Plum	3.44	2.326		615	76		691	800	
	6250	Jet spray dispenser	R-18	4.50	5.778		2,050	145		2,195	2,475	
	6300	Juice dispenser, concentrate	"	4.50	5.778		795	145		940	1,100	
	6350	Kettles, steam-jacketed, 20 gallons	L-7	7	4		4,400	105		4,505	5,025	
	6600	60 gallons	"	6	4.667		5,650	123		5,773	6,400	
	6690	Milk dispenser, bulk, 2 flavor	R-30	8	3.250		880	83.50		963.50	1,100	
	6695	3 flavor	"	8	3.250		1,325	83.50		1,408.50	1,575	
	6700	Peelers, small	R-18	8	3.250		1,675	81.50		1,756.50	1,975	
	6720	Large	"	6	4.333		2,825	109		2,934	3,275	
	6750	Pot sink, 3 compartment	1 Plum	7.25	1.103	L.F.	455	36		491	555	
	6760	Pot washer, small		1.60	5	Ea.	11,900	163		12,063	13,400	
	6770	Large		1.20	6.667		29,700	217		29,917	33,000	
	6800	Pulper/extractor, close coupled, 5 HP		1.90	4.211		2,650	137		2,787	3,150	
	6850	Mobile rack w/pan slide					810			810	895	

114 | Food Service, Residential, Darkroom, Athletic Equipment

114 000 | Food Service Equipment

			CREW	DAILY OUTPUT	LABOR-HOURS	UNIT	MAT.	LABOR	EQUIP.	TOTAL	TOTAL INCL O&P	
004	6900	Range, restaurant type, 6 burners and 1 standard oven, 36" wide	Q-1	7	2.286	Ea.	1,975	67		2,042	2,275	004
	6950	Convection		7	2.286		2,625	67		2,692	3,000	
	7150	2 standard ovens, 24" griddle, 60" wide		6	2.667		4,100	78.50		4,178.50	4,650	
	7200	1 standard, 1 convection oven		6	2.667		5,275	78.50		5,353.50	5,925	
	7450	Heavy duty, single 34" standard oven, open top		5	3.200		3,575	94		3,669	4,075	
	7500	Convection oven		5	3.200		4,750	94		4,844	5,375	
	7700	Griddle top		6	2.667		4,225	78.50		4,303.50	4,775	
	7750	Convection oven		6	2.667		5,175	78.50		5,253.50	5,825	
	7950	Hood fire protection system, minimum		3	5.333		2,675	157		2,832	3,175	
	8050	Maximum		1	16		18,700	470		19,170	21,300	
	8300	Refrigerators, reach-in type, 44 C.F.		5	3.200		4,525	94		4,619	5,125	
	8310	With glass doors, 68 C.F.		4	4		5,950	117		6,067	6,725	
	8320	Refrigerator, reach-in, 1 compartment	R-18	7.80	3.333		1,875	84		1,959	2,175	
	8330	2 compartment		6.20	4.194		2,375	105		2,480	2,775	
	8340	3 compartment		5.60	4.643		3,375	117		3,492	3,925	
	8350	Pre-fab, with refrigeration, 8' x 8'	2 Carp	.45	35.556		5,225	970		6,195	7,375	
	8360	8' x 12'		.35	45.714		6,350	1,250		7,600	9,100	
	8370	8' x 16'		.25	64		7,350	1,750		9,100	11,000	
	8380	8' x 20'		.17	94.118		9,625	2,575		12,200	14,900	
	8390	Pass-thru/roll-in, 1 compartment	R-18	7.80	3.333		2,800	84		2,884	3,200	
	8400	2 compartment		6.24	4.167		3,875	105		3,980	4,450	
	8410	3 compartment		5.60	4.643		5,325	117		5,442	6,050	
	8420	Walk-in, alum, door & floor only, no refrig, 6' x 6' x 7'-6"	2 Carp	1.40	11.429		6,725	310		7,035	7,925	
	8430	10' x 6' x 7'-6"		.55	29.091		9,600	795		10,395	11,900	
	8440	12' x 14' x 7'-6"		.25	64		12,800	1,750		14,550	17,000	
	8450	12' x 20' x 7'-6"		.17	94.118		15,500	2,575		18,075	21,300	
	8460	Refrigerated cabinets, mobile					2,050			2,050	2,250	
	8470	Refrigerator/freezer, reach-in, 1 compartment	R-18	5.60	4.643		4,275	117		4,392	4,900	
	8480	2 compartment		4.80	5.417		5,875	136		6,011	6,675	
	8580	Slicer with table		9	2.889		2,825	72.50		2,897.50	3,225	
	8600	Stainless steel shelving, louvered 4-tier, 20" x 3'	1 Clab	6	1.333		980	28.50		1,008.50	1,125	
	8605	20" x 4'		6	1.333		1,150	28.50		1,178.50	1,325	
	8610	20" x 6'		6	1.333		1,575	28.50		1,603.50	1,800	
	8615	24" x 3'		6	1.333		1,025	28.50		1,053.50	1,175	
	8620	24" x 4'		6	1.333		1,225	28.50		1,253.50	1,375	
	8625	24" x 6'		6	1.333		1,700	28.50		1,728.50	1,900	
	8630	Flat 4-tier, 20" x 3'		6	1.333		900	28.50		928.50	1,050	
	8635	20" x 4'		6	1.333		1,100	28.50		1,128.50	1,250	
	8640	20" x 5'		6	1.333		1,250	28.50		1,278.50	1,425	
	8645	24" x 3'		6	1.333		965	28.50		993.50	1,100	
	8650	24" x 4'		6	1.333		1,200	28.50		1,228.50	1,375	
	8655	24" x 6'		6	1.333		2,300	28.50		2,328.50	2,575	
	8700	Galvanized shelving, louvered 4-tier, 20" x 3'		6	1.333		350	28.50		378.50	435	
	8705	20" x 4'		6	1.333		400	28.50		428.50	490	
	8710	20" x 6'		6	1.333		585	28.50		613.50	695	
	8715	24" x 3'		6	1.333		385	28.50		413.50	475	
	8720	24" x 4'		6	1.333		440	28.50		468.50	530	
	8725	24" x 6'		6	1.333		595	28.50		623.50	705	
	8730	Flat 4-tier, 20" x 3'		6	1.333		355	28.50		383.50	440	
	8735	20" x 4'		6	1.333		410	28.50		438.50	500	
	8740	20" x 6'		6	1.333		550	28.50		578.50	655	
	8745	24" x 3'		6	1.333		380	28.50		408.50	465	
	8750	24" x 4'		6	1.333		440	28.50		468.50	535	
	8755	24" x 6'		6	1.333		595	28.50		623.50	705	
	8760	Stainless steel dunnage rack, 24" x 3'		8	1		525	21.50		546.50	610	
	8765	24" x 4'		8	1		635	21.50		656.50	735	

114 | Food Service, Residential, Darkroom, Athletic Equipment

114 000 | Food Service Equipment

			CREW	DAILY OUTPUT	LABOR-HOURS	UNIT	MAT.	LABOR	EQUIP.	TOTAL	TOTAL INCL O&P	
004	8770	Galvanized dunnage rack, 24" x 3'	1 Clab	8	1	Ea.	124	21.50		145.50	172	004
	8775	24" x 4'	↓	8	1	↓	140	21.50		161.50	190	
	8800	Serving counter, straight	1 Carp	40	.200	L.F.	410	5.45		415.45	460	
	8820	Curved section	"	30	.267	"	575	7.30		582.30	640	
	8825	Solid surface, see section 066-503										
	8830	Soft serve ice cream machine, medium	R-18	11	2.364	Ea.	5,900	59.50		5,959.50	6,575	
	8840	Large	"	9	2.889		8,875	72.50		8,947.50	9,875	
	8850	Steamer, electric 27 KW	L-7	7	4		7,200	105		7,305	8,075	
	9100	Electric, 10 KW or gas 100,000 BTU	"	5	5.600		3,200	147		3,347	3,775	
	9150	Toaster, conveyor type, 16-22 slices per minute					925			925	1,025	
	9160	Pop-up, 2 slot					455			455	500	
	9170	Trash compactor, small, up to 125 lb. compacted weight	L-4	4	6		13,500	154		13,654	15,200	
	9175	Large, up to 175 lb. compacted weight	"	3	8		16,500	205		16,705	18,500	
	9180	Tray and silver dispenser, mobile	1 Clab	16	.500		595	10.75		605.75	675	
	9200	For deluxe models of above equipment, add					75%					
	9400	Rule of thumb: Equipment cost based										
	9410	on kitchen work area										
	9420	Office buildings, minimum	L-7	77	.364	S.F.	45	9.55		54.55	65.50	
	9450	Maximum		58	.483		76	12.70		88.70	105	
	9550	Public eating facilities, minimum		77	.364		59	9.55		68.55	81	
	9600	Maximum		46	.609		96	16		112	132	
	9750	Hospitals, minimum		58	.483		60.50	12.70		73.20	87.50	
	9800	Maximum	↓	39	.718	↓	101	18.85		119.85	143	
008	0010	**WINE CELLAR**, refrigerated, Redwood interior, carpeted, walk-in type										008
	0020	6'-8" high, including racks										
	0200	80"W x 48"D for 900 bottles	2 Carp	1.50	10.667	Ea.	2,975	291		3,266	3,750	
	0250	80" W x 72" D for 1300 bottles		1.33	12.030		3,900	330		4,230	4,825	
	0300	80" W x 94" D for 1900 bottles		1.17	13.675		4,925	375		5,300	6,025	
	0400	80" W x 124" D for 2500 bottles	↓	1	16	↓	6,000	435		6,435	7,325	

114 580 | Disappearing Stairs

			CREW	DAILY OUTPUT	LABOR-HOURS	UNIT	MAT.	LABOR	EQUIP.	TOTAL	TOTAL INCL O&P	
581	0010	**DISAPPEARING STAIRWAY** No trim included										581
	0020	One piece, yellow pine, 8'-0" ceiling	2 Carp	4	4	Ea.	850	109		959	1,125	
	0030	9'-0" ceiling		4	4		875	109		984	1,150	
	0040	10'-0" ceiling		3	5.333		920	146		1,066	1,250	
	0050	11'-0" ceiling		3	5.333		1,075	146		1,221	1,450	
	0060	12'-0" ceiling	↓	3	5.333		1,125	146		1,271	1,500	
	0100	Custom grade, pine, 8'-6" ceiling, minimum	1 Carp	4	2		100	54.50		154.50	202	
	0150	Average		3.50	2.286		105	62.50		167.50	220	
	0200	Maximum	↓	3	2.667	↓	185	73		258	325	
	0250											
	0500	Heavy duty, pivoted, from 7'7" to 12'10" floor to floor	1 Carp	3	2.667	Ea.	315	73		388	470	
	0600	16'-0" ceiling		2	4		1,025	109		1,134	1,325	
	0800	Economy folding, pine, 8'-6" ceiling		4	2		83	54.50		137.50	183	
	0900	9'-6" ceiling	↓	4	2		93.50	54.50		148	195	
	1000	Fire escape, galvanized steel, 8'-0" to 10'-4" ceiling	2 Carp	1	16		1,125	435		1,560	1,950	
	1010	10'-6" to 13'-6" ceiling		1	16		1,400	435		1,835	2,275	
	1100	Automatic electric, aluminum, floor to floor height, 8' to 9'		1	16		5,500	435		5,935	6,800	
	1500	11' to 12'		.90	17.778		5,575	485		6,060	6,925	
	1700	14' to 15'	↓	.70	22.857	↓	6,325	625		6,950	8,000	
	9000	Minimum labor/equipment charge	1 Carp	2	4	Job		109		109	183	
741	0010	**DARKROOM EQUIPMENT**										741
	0020	Developing sink, 5" deep, 24" x 48"	Q-1	2	8	Ea.	3,350	235		3,585	4,050	
	0050	48" x 52"		1.70	9.412		3,600	276		3,876	4,400	
	0200	10" deep, 24" x 48"	↓	1.70	9.412	↓	4,700	276		4,976	5,575	

114 | Food Service, Residential, Darkroom, Athletic Equipment

114 580 | Disappearing Stairs

		CREW	DAILY OUTPUT	LABOR-HOURS	UNIT	1999 BARE COSTS MAT.	LABOR	EQUIP.	TOTAL	TOTAL INCL O&P
0250	24" x 108"	Q-1	1.50	10.667	Ea.	1,700	315		2,015	2,375
0500	Dryers, dehumidified filtered air, 36" x 25" x 68" high	L-7	6	4.667		3,475	123		3,598	4,025
0550	48" x 25" x 68" high		5	5.600		6,575	147		6,722	7,475
2000	Processors, automatic, color print, minimum		4	7		9,500	184		9,684	10,800
2050	Maximum		.60	46.667		70,000	1,225		71,225	79,000
2300	Black and white print, minimum		2	14		7,200	370		7,570	8,525
2350	Maximum		.80	35		47,000	920		47,920	53,000
2600	Manual processor, 16" x 20" maximum print size		2	14		7,250	370		7,620	8,575
2650	20" x 24" maximum print size		1	28		6,825	735		7,560	8,725
3000	Viewing lites, 20" x 24"		6	4.667		300	123		423	535
3100	20" x 24" with color correction		6	4.667		425	123		548	675
3500	Washers, round, minimum sheet 11" x 14"	Q-1	2	8		2,175	235		2,410	2,775
3550	Maximum sheet 20" x 24"		1	16		2,400	470		2,870	3,375
3800	Square, minimum sheet 20" x 24"		1	16		2,150	470		2,620	3,100
3900	Maximum sheet 50" x 56"		.80	20		3,350	585		3,935	4,600
4500	Combination tank sink, tray sink, washers, with									
4510	dry side tables, average	Q-1	.45	35.556	Ea.	7,250	1,050		8,300	9,600

114 760 | Revolving Darkrm Doors

		CREW	DAILY OUTPUT	LABOR-HOURS	UNIT	MAT.	LABOR	EQUIP.	TOTAL	INCL O&P
0010	**DARKROOM DOORS**									
0015	Revolving, standard, 2 way, 36" diameter	2 Carp	3.10	5.161	Opng.	1,525	141		1,666	1,900
0020	41" diameter		3.10	5.161		1,650	141		1,791	2,050
0050	3 way, 51" diameter		1.40	11.429		2,100	310		2,410	2,850
1000	4 way, 49" diameter		1.40	11.429		2,475	310		2,785	3,250
2000	Hinged safety, 2 way, 41" diameter		2.30	6.957		1,950	190		2,140	2,475
2500	3 way, 51" diameter		1.40	11.429		2,500	310		2,810	3,275
3000	Pop out safety, 2 way, 41" diameter		3.10	5.161		2,475	141		2,616	2,950
4000	3 way, 51" diameter		1.40	11.429		2,500	310		2,810	3,275
5000	Wheelchair-type, pop out, 51" diameter		1.40	11.429		2,400	310		2,710	3,175
5020	72" diameter		.90	17.778		5,000	485		5,485	6,300

114 800 | Athletic/Recreational

		CREW	DAILY OUTPUT	LABOR-HOURS	UNIT	MAT.	LABOR	EQUIP.	TOTAL	INCL O&P
0010	**HEALTH CLUB EQUIPMENT**									
0020	Abdominal rack, 2 board capacity				Ea.	370			370	410
0050	Abdominal board, upholstered					415			415	460
0200	Bicycle trainer, minimum					650			650	715
0300	Deluxe, electric					3,300			3,300	3,650
0400	Bar bell set, chrome plated steel, 25 lbs.					195			195	215
0420	100 lbs.					295			295	325
0450	200 lbs.					570			570	625
0500	Weight plates, cast iron, per lb.				Lb.	4			4	4.40
0520	Storage rack, 10 station				Ea.	630			630	695
0600	Circuit training apparatus, 12 machines minimum	2 Clab	1.25	12.800	Set	22,000	275		22,275	24,700
0700	Average		1	16		27,000	345		27,345	30,300
0800	Maximum		.75	21.333		32,000	460		32,460	36,000
0820	Dumbbell set, cast iron, with rack and 5 pair					615			615	675
0900	Squat racks	2 Clab	5	3.200	Ea.	610	68.50		678.50	785
1600	For saunas, see division 130-521									
1640	For steam baths, see division 130-541									
0010	**SCHOOL EQUIPMENT**									
0200	For exterior equipment, see division 028									
0201	For chairs & desks, see division 126-230									
0300	For chalkboards & bulletin boards, see div. 104-151 & 101-104									

114 | Food Service, Residential, Darkroom, Athletic Equipment

114 800 | Athletic/Recreational

		CREW	DAILY OUTPUT	LABOR-HOURS	UNIT	1999 BARE COSTS MAT.	LABOR	EQUIP.	TOTAL	TOTAL INCL O&P	
805	0400	For lockers, see division 105-054										805
	1000	Basketball backstops, wall mtd., 6' extended, fixed, minimum	L-2	1	16	Ea.	525	385		910	1,225	
	1100	Maximum		1	16		685	385		1,070	1,400	
	1200	Swing up, minimum		1	16		1,050	385		1,435	1,800	
	1250	Maximum		1	16		1,875	385		2,260	2,725	
	1300	Portable, manual, heavy duty, spring operated		1.90	8.421		8,825	203		9,028	10,000	
	1400	Ceiling suspended, stationary, minimum		.78	20.513		1,300	495		1,795	2,250	
	1450	Fold up, with accessories, maximum	▼	.40	40		4,725	965		5,690	6,800	
	1600	For electrically operated, add	1 Elec	1	8	▼	1,550	255		1,805	2,100	
	2000	Benches, folding, in wall, 14' table, 2 benches	L-4	2	12	Set	500	310		810	1,050	
	3000	Bleachers, telescoping, manual to 15 tier, minimum	F-5	65	.492	Seat	50	13.70		63.70	78	
	3100	Maximum		60	.533		75	14.85		89.85	108	
	3300	16 to 20 tier, minimum		60	.533		120	14.85		134.85	157	
	3400	Maximum		55	.582		150	16.15		166.15	192	
	3600	21 to 30 tier, minimum		50	.640		125	17.80		142.80	168	
	3700	Maximum	▼	40	.800		150	22		172	202	
	3900	For integral power operation, add, minimum	2 Elec	300	.053		25	1.70		26.70	30	
	4000	Maximum	"	250	.064	▼	40	2.04		42.04	47	
	4100	Boxing ring, elevated, 22' x 22'	L-4	.10	240	Ea.	8,000	6,150		14,150	19,000	
	4110	For cellular plastic foam padding, add		.10	240		3,825	6,150		9,975	14,400	
	4120	Floor level, including posts and ropes only, 20' x 20'		.80	30		1,175	770		1,945	2,575	
	4130	Canvas, 30' x 30'	▼	5	4.800		1,075	123		1,198	1,400	
	4150	Exercise equipment, bicycle trainer					345			345	380	
	4180	Chinning bar, adjustable, wall mounted	1 Carp	5	1.600		245	43.50		288.50	345	
	4200	Exercise ladder, 16' x 1'-7", suspended	L-2	3	5.333		1,050	128		1,178	1,400	
	4210	High bar, floor plate attached	1 Carp	4	2		910	54.50		964.50	1,100	
	4240	Parallel bars, adjustable		4	2		2,000	54.50		2,054.50	2,300	
	4270	Uneven parallel bars, adjustable	▼	4	2		2,375	54.50		2,429.50	2,725	
	4280	Wall mounted, adjustable	L-2	1.50	10.667	Set	750	257		1,007	1,250	
	4300	Rope, ceiling mounted, 18' long	1 Carp	3.66	2.186	Ea.	147	59.50		206.50	261	
	4330	Side horse, vaulting		5	1.600		1,450	43.50		1,493.50	1,675	
	4360	Treadmill, motorized, deluxe, training type	▼	5	1.600		4,650	43.50		4,693.50	5,200	
	4390	Weight lifting multi-station, minimum	2 Clab	1	16	▼	2,775	345		3,120	3,625	
	4500	Gym divider curtain, mesh top, vinyl bottom, manual	L-4	500	.048	S.F.	6	1.23		7.23	8.65	
	4700	Electric roll up	L-7	400	.070		9	1.84		10.84	12.95	
	5500	Gym mats, 2" thick, naugahyde covered					2.64			2.64	2.90	
	5600	Vinyl/nylon covered					5.05			5.05	5.55	
	5800	Wall pads, 1-1/2" thick	2 Carp	640	.025		5.70	.68		6.38	7.40	
	6000	Wrestling mats, 1" thick, heavy duty				▼	5.20			5.20	5.75	
	7000	Scoreboards, baseball, minimum	R-3	1.30	15.385	Ea.	2,300	485	104	2,889	3,425	
	7200	Maximum		.05	400		16,800	12,600	2,725	32,125	41,100	
	7300	Football, minimum		.86	23.256		5,675	735	158	6,568	7,550	
	7400	Maximum		.20	100		52,500	3,150	680	56,330	63,500	
	7500	Basketball (one side), minimum		2.07	9.662		2,425	305	65.50	2,795.50	3,200	
	7600	Maximum		.30	66.667		16,800	2,100	455	19,355	22,300	
	7700	Hockey-basketball (four sides), minimum		.25	80		8,600	2,525	545	11,670	14,000	
	7800	Maximum	▼	.15	133	▼	26,300	4,200	905	31,405	36,400	

115 | Industrial & Process Equipment

115 010 | Specialized Equipment

		CREW	DAILY OUTPUT	LABOR-HOURS	UNIT	1999 BARE COSTS MAT.	LABOR	EQUIP.	TOTAL	TOTAL INCL O&P	
011	0010 **VOCATIONAL SHOP EQUIPMENT**										011
	0020 Benches, work, wood, average	2 Carp	5	3.200	Ea.	400	87.50		487.50	585	
	0100 Metal, average		5	3.200		225	87.50		312.50	395	
	0400 Combination belt & disc sander, 6"		4	4		965	109		1,074	1,225	
	0700 Drill press, floor mounted, 12", 1/2 H.P.		4	4		400	109		509	625	
	0800 Dust collector, not incl. ductwork, 6" diameter	1 Shee	1.10	7.273		2,300	231		2,531	2,925	
	1000 Grinders, double wheel, 1/2 H.P.	2 Carp	5	3.200		254	87.50		341.50	425	
	1300 Jointer, 4", 3/4 H.P.		4	4		1,050	109		1,159	1,325	
	1600 Kilns, 16 C.F., to 2000°		4	4		2,100	109		2,209	2,475	
	1900 Lathe, woodworking, 10", 1/2 H.P.		4	4		550	109		659	790	
	2200 Planer, 13" x 6"		4	4		1,175	109		1,284	1,450	
	2500 Potter's wheel, motorized		4	4		525	109		634	765	
	2800 Saws, band, 14", 3/4 H.P.		4	4		580	109		689	820	
	3100 Metal cutting band saw, 14"		4	4		690	109		799	945	
	3400 Radial arm saw, 10", 2 H.P.		4	4		800	109		909	1,075	
	3700 Scroll saw, 24"		4	4		1,350	109		1,459	1,650	
	4000 Table saw, 10", 3 H.P.		4	4		1,675	109		1,784	2,000	
	4300 Welder AC arc, 30 amp capacity		4	4		425	109		534	655	

116 | Laboratory, Planetarium, Observatory Equipment

116 000 | Laboratory Equipment

		CREW	DAILY OUTPUT	LABOR-HOURS	UNIT	1999 BARE COSTS MAT.	LABOR	EQUIP.	TOTAL	TOTAL INCL O&P	
001	0010 **LABORATORY EQUIPMENT**										001
	0020 Cabinets, base, door units, metal	2 Carp	18	.889	L.F.	115	24.50		139.50	168	
	0300 Drawer units		18	.889		228	24.50		252.50	292	
	0700 Tall storage cabinets, open, 7' high		20	.800		240	22		262	300	
	0900 With glazed doors		20	.800		274	22		296	335	
	1300 Wall cabinets, metal, 12-1/2" deep, open		20	.800		69	22		91	113	
	1500 With doors		20	.800		144	22		166	195	
	1550 Counter tops, not incl. base cabinets, acidproof, minimum		82	.195	S.F.	16	5.35		21.35	26.50	
	1600 Maximum		70	.229		24	6.25		30.25	37	
	1650 Stainless steel		82	.195		61	5.35		66.35	76	
	4200 Alternate pricing method: as percent of lab furniture										
	4400 Installation, not incl. plumbing & duct work				% Furn.					22%	
	4800 Plumbing, final connections, simple system									10%	
	5000 Moderately complex system									15%	
	5200 Complex system									20%	
	5400 Electrical, simple system									10%	
	5600 Moderately complex system									20%	
	5800 Complex system									35%	
	6000 Safety equipment, eye wash, hand held				Ea.	210			210	231	
	6200 Deluge shower				"	500			500	550	

For information about Means Estimating Seminars, see yellow pages 11 and 12 in back of book

Division Notes

	CREW	DAILY OUTPUT	LABOR-HOURS	UNIT	1999 BARE COSTS				TOTAL INCL O&P
					MAT.	LABOR	EQUIP.	TOTAL	

Division 12
Furnishings

Estimating Tips
General
- The items in this division are usually priced per square foot or each. Most of these items are purchased by the owner and placed by the supplier. Do not assume the items in Division 12 will be purchased and installed by the supplier. Check the specifications for responsibilities and include receiving, storage, installation and mechanical and electrical hook-ups in the appropriate divisions.
- Some items in this division require some type of support system that is not usually furnished with the item. Examples of these systems include blocking for the attachment of casework and heavy drapery rods. The required blocking must be added to the estimate in the appropriate division.

Reference Numbers
Reference numbers are shown in bold squares at the beginning of some major classifications. These numbers refer to related items in the Reference Section. The reference information may be an estimating procedure, an alternate pricing method or technical information.

Note: Not all subdivisions listed here necessarily appear in this publication.

125 | Window Treatment

125 100 | Blinds

			DAILY	LABOR-		1999 BARE COSTS				TOTAL
		CREW	OUTPUT	HOURS	UNIT	MAT.	LABOR	EQUIP.	TOTAL	INCL O&P
103	0010 **BLINDS, INTERIOR**									
	0020 Horizontal, 1" aluminum slats, solid color, stock	1 Carp	590	.014	S.F.	2.55	.37		2.92	3.42
	3000 Wood folding panels with movable louvers, 7" x 20" each	↓	17	.471	Pr.	36	12.85		48.85	61
	4000 Fixed louver type, stock units, 8" x 20" each		17	.471		54	12.85		66.85	81
	4450 18" x 40" each	↓	17	.471	↓	112	12.85		124.85	145

125 200 | Shades

			DAILY	LABOR-		1999 BARE COSTS				TOTAL
201	0011 **SHADES** Basswood roll-up, stain finish, 3/8" slats	1 Carp	300	.027	S.F.	10.05	.73		10.78	12.25
	0030 Double layered, heat reflective		685	.012		6.30	.32		6.62	7.50
	0250 7/8" slats		300	.027		8.50	.73		9.23	10.55
	0950 Mylar, single layer, non-heat reflective		685	.012		3.84	.32		4.16	4.75
	1050 Double layered, heat reflective		685	.012		6.50	.32		6.82	7.70
	1150 Triple layered, heat reflective		685	.012		5.95	.32		6.27	7.10
	5000 Thermal, roll up, R-4		44	.182		7.70	4.96		12.66	16.75
	5030 R-10.7	↓	44	.182	↓	8.80	4.96		13.76	18
	5050 Magnetic clips, set of 20				Set	16.45			16.45	18.10

126 | Furniture & Accessories

126 200 | Furniture

			DAILY	LABOR-		1999 BARE COSTS				TOTAL
		CREW	OUTPUT	HOURS	UNIT	MAT.	LABOR	EQUIP.	TOTAL	INCL O&P
205	0010 **DORMITORY FURNITURE** Beds, free standing, minimum				Ea.	202			202	222
	0100 Maximum				"	530			530	580
	2050 Rule of thumb: Total cost for furniture, minimum				Student					1,800
	2150 Maximum				"					3,500
210	0010 **FURNITURE, HOSPITAL**									
	0020 Beds, manual, minimum				Ea.	790			790	865
	0100 Maximum				"	1,375			1,375	1,500
	1100 Patient wall systems, not incl. plumbing, minimum				Room	790			790	870
	1200 Maximum				"	1,450			1,450	1,600
214	0010 **FURNITURE, HOTEL**									
	0020 Standard quality set, minimum				Room	1,475			1,475	1,625
	0200 Maximum				"	7,175			7,175	7,875
222	0010 **FURNITURE, OFFICE**									
	0020 Desks, 29" high, double pedestal, 30" x 60", metal, minimum				Ea.	325			325	360
	0030 Maximum				"	920			920	1,000
226	0010 **FURNITURE, RESTAURANT**									
	0020 Bars, built-in, front bar	1 Carp	5	1.600	L.F.	180	43.50		223.50	271
	0200 Back bar		5	1.600	"	131	43.50		174.50	217
	0500 Booth unit, molded plastic, stub wall and 2 seats, minimum		2	4	Set	310	109		419	525
	0600 Maximum		1.50	5.333	"	1,325	146		1,471	1,700
	0800 Booth seat, upholstered, foursome, single (end) minimum		5	1.600	Ea.	1,025	43.50		1,068.50	1,225
	0900 Maximum		4	2		2,125	54.50		2,179.50	2,450
	1000 Foursome, double, minimum		4	2		1,025	54.50		1,079.50	1,250
	1100 Maximum		3	2.667		2,125	73		2,198	2,475
	1300 Circle booth, upholstered, 1/4 circle, minimum	↓	3	2.667		750	73		823	945

126 | Furniture & Accessories

126 200 | Furniture

			CREW	DAILY OUTPUT	LABOR-HOURS	UNIT	1999 BARE COSTS				TOTAL INCL O&P	
							MAT.	LABOR	EQUIP.	TOTAL		
226	1400	Maximum	1 Carp	2	4	Ea.	1,625	109		1,734	1,975	226
	1500	3/4 circle, minimum	↓	1.50	5.333	↓	2,225	146		2,371	2,700	
	1600	Maximum		1	8		2,900	218		3,118	3,575	

For information about Means Estimating Seminars, see yellow pages 11 and 12 in back of book

For expanded coverage of these items see *Means Interior Cost Data 1999*

Division Notes

	CREW	DAILY OUTPUT	LABOR-HOURS	UNIT	1999 BARE COSTS				TOTAL INCL O&P
					MAT.	LABOR	EQUIP.	TOTAL	

Division 13
Special Construction

Estimating Tips
General
- The items and systems in this division are usually estimated, purchased, supplied and installed as a unit by one or more subcontractors. The estimator must ensure that all parties are operating from the same set of specifications and assumptions and that all necessary items are estimated and will be provided. Many times the complex items and systems are covered but the more common ones such as excavation or a crane are overlooked for the very reason that everyone assumes nobody could miss them. The estimator should be the central focus and be able to ensure that all systems are complete.
- Another area where problems can develop in this division is at the interface between systems. The estimator must ensure, for instance, that anchor bolts, nuts and washers are estimated and included for the air-supported structures and pre-engineered buildings to be bolted to their foundations.

Utility supply is a common area where essential items or pieces of equipment can be missed or overlooked due to the fact that each subcontractor may feel it is the others' responsibility. The estimator should also be aware of certain items which may be supplied as part of a package but installed by others, and ensure that the installing contractor's estimate includes the cost of installation. Conversely, the estimator must also ensure that items are not costed by two different subcontractors, resulting in an inflated overall estimate.

131 Pre-Engineered Structures, Aquatic Facilities & Ice Rinks
- The foundations and floor slab, as well as rough mechanical and electrical, should be estimated, as this work is required for the assembly and erection of the structure. Generally, as noted in the book, the pre-engineered building comes as a shell and additional features must be included by the estimator. Here again, the estimator must have a clear understanding of the scope of each portion of the work and all the necessary interfaces.

132 Tanks, Tank Covers, Filtration Equipment
- The prices in this subdivision for above and below ground storage tanks do not include foundations or hold-down slabs. The estimator should refer to Divisions 2 and 3 for foundation system pricing. In addition to the foundations, required tank accessories such as tank gauges, leak detection devices, and additional manholes and piping must be added to the tank prices.

Reference Numbers
Reference numbers are shown in bold squares at the beginning of some major classifications. These numbers refer to related items in the Reference Section. The reference information may be an estimating procedure, an alternate pricing method or technical information.

Note: Not all subdivisions listed here necessarily appear in this publication.

130 | Special Construction

130 250 | Integrated Ceilings

		CREW	DAILY OUTPUT	LABOR-HOURS	UNIT	MAT.	LABOR	EQUIP.	TOTAL	TOTAL INCL O&P	
251	0010	**INTEGRATED CEILINGS** Lighting, ventilating & acoustical										251
	1800	Radiant hot water system with finished acoustic ceiling,										
	1810	not including supply piping. Heating only (gross S.F.)										
	2000											
	2100	Elementary schools, minimum				S.F.					5.30	
	2200	Maximum									6.65	
	2400	High schools and colleges, minimum									4.75	
	2500	Maximum									6.65	
	2700	Libraries, minimum									4.80	
	2800	Maximum									5.75	
	3000	Hospitals, minimum									6.50	
	3100	Maximum									8.15	
	3300	Office buildings, minimum									4.60	
	3400	Maximum									6.15	
	3600	For combined heating and cooling, add, minimum									30%	
	3700	Maximum				↓					40%	

130 320 | Athletic Rooms

		CREW	DAILY OUTPUT	LABOR-HOURS	UNIT	MAT.	LABOR	EQUIP.	TOTAL	TOTAL INCL O&P	
321	0010	**SPORT COURT** Floors, No. 2 & better maple, 25/32" thick				SF Flr.					6.30	321
	0300	Squash, regulation court in existing building, minimum				Court					14,500	
	0400	Maximum				"					27,100	
	0450	Rule of thumb for components:										
	0470	Walls	3 Carp	.15	160	Court	10,100	4,375		14,475	18,400	
	0500	Floor	"	.25	96		4,525	2,625		7,150	9,350	
	0550	Lighting	2 Elec	.60	26.667	↓	1,425	850		2,275	2,900	

130 380 | Cold Storage Rooms

		CREW	DAILY OUTPUT	LABOR-HOURS	UNIT	MAT.	LABOR	EQUIP.	TOTAL	TOTAL INCL O&P	
381	0010	**REFRIGERATION** Curbs, 12" high, 4" thick, concrete	2 Carp	58	.276	L.F.	3.02	7.55		10.57	15.90	381
	6300	Rule of thumb for complete units, w/o doors & refrigeration, cooler	↓	146	.110	SF Flr.	86	2.99		88.99	99.50	
	6400	Freezer		109.60	.146	"	102	3.99		105.99	119	

130 520 | Saunas

		CREW	DAILY OUTPUT	LABOR-HOURS	UNIT	MAT.	LABOR	EQUIP.	TOTAL	TOTAL INCL O&P	
521	0010	**SAUNA** Prefabricated, incl. heater & controls, 7' high, 6' x 4', C/C	L-7	2.20	12.727	Ea.	3,075	335		3,410	3,925	521
	1700	Door only, cedar, 2'x6', with tempered insulated glass window	2 Carp	3.40	4.706		279	128		407	520	
	1800	Prehung, incl. jambs, pulls & hardware	"	12	1.333		330	36.50		366.50	420	
	2500	Heaters only (incl. above), wall mounted, to 200 C.F.				↓	460			460	510	
	4480	For additional equipment, see div. 114-801										

130 540 | Steam Baths

		CREW	DAILY OUTPUT	LABOR-HOURS	UNIT	MAT.	LABOR	EQUIP.	TOTAL	TOTAL INCL O&P	
541	0010	**STEAM BATH** Heater, timer & head, single, to 140 C.F.	1 Plum	1.20	6.667	Ea.	720	217		937	1,125	541
	0500	To 300 C.F.	"	1.10	7.273		785	237		1,022	1,225	
	2000	Multiple, motels, apts., 2 baths, w/ blow-down assm., 500 C.F.	Q-1	1.30	12.308		2,875	360		3,235	3,750	
	2500	4 baths	"	.70	22.857		3,825	670		4,495	5,250	

130 810 | Acoustical Enclosures

		CREW	DAILY OUTPUT	LABOR-HOURS	UNIT	MAT.	LABOR	EQUIP.	TOTAL	TOTAL INCL O&P	
811	0010	**ACOUSTICAL** Enclosure, 4" thick wall and ceiling panels										811
	0020	8# per S.F., up to 12' span	3 Carp	72	.333	SF Surf	25	9.10		34.10	42.50	
	0300	Better quality panels, 10.5# per S.F.		64	.375		28	10.25		38.25	48	
	0400	Reverb-chamber, 4" thick, parallel walls	↓	60	.400	↓	30	10.90		40.90	51.50	

130 910 | Radiation Protection

		CREW	DAILY OUTPUT	LABOR-HOURS	UNIT	MAT.	LABOR	EQUIP.	TOTAL	TOTAL INCL O&P	
911	0010	**SHIELDING LEAD**										911
	0050											

130 | Special Construction

130 910 | Radiation Protection

		CREW	DAILY OUTPUT	LABOR-HOURS	UNIT	1999 BARE COSTS MAT.	LABOR	EQUIP.	TOTAL	TOTAL INCL O&P
0300	Lead sheets, 1/16" thick	2 Lath	135	.119	S.F.	4.75	3.18		7.93	10.30
0400	1/8" thick		120	.133		10	3.57		13.57	16.70
0500	Lead shielding, 1/4" thick		135	.119		10.60	3.18		13.78	16.75
0550	1/2" thick	↓	120	.133	↓	21.50	3.57		25.07	29
0600	Lead glass, 1/4" thick, 2.0 mm LE, 12" x 16"	2 Glaz	13	1.231	Ea.	256	32.50		288.50	335
0700	24" x 36"	"	8	2	"	915	53		968	1,075
1200	X-ray protection, average radiography or fluoroscopy									
1210	room, up to 300 S.F. floor, 1/16" lead, minimum	2 Lath	.25	64	Total	4,600	1,725		6,325	7,800
1500	Maximum, 7'-0" walls	"	.15	106	"	6,000	2,850		8,850	11,200
1600	Deep therapy X-ray room, 250 KV capacity,									
1800	up to 300 S.F. floor, 1/4" lead, minimum	2 Lath	.08	200	Total	15,500	5,350		20,850	25,700
1900	Maximum, 7'-0" walls	"	.06	266	"	21,000	7,150		28,150	34,500
2000	X-ray viewing panels, clear lead plastic									
2010	7 mm thick, 0.3 mm LE, 2.3 lbs/S.F.	H-3	139	.115	S.F.	122	2.73		124.73	138
2020	12 mm thick, 0.5 mm LE, 3.9 lbs/S.F.		82	.195		165	4.63		169.63	190
2030	18 mm thick, 0.8mm LE, 5.9 lbs/S.F.		54	.296		179	7.05		186.05	209
2040	22 mm thick, 1.0 mm LE, 7.2 lbs/S.F.		44	.364		183	8.65		191.65	215
2050	35 mm thick, 1.5 mm LE, 11.5 lbs/S.F.		28	.571		205	13.55		218.55	249
2060	46 mm thick, 2.0 mm LE, 15.0 lbs/S.F.	↓	21	.762	↓	270	18.10		288.10	325
2090	For panels 12 S.F. to 48 S.F., add crating charge				Ea.					50
4000	X-ray barriers, modular, panels mounted within framework for									
4002	attaching to floor, wall or ceiling, upper portion is clear lead									
4005	plastic window panels 48"H, lower portion is opaque leaded									
4008	steel panels 36"H, structural supports not incl.									
4010	1-section barrier, 36"W x 84"H overall									
4020	0.5 mm LE panels	H-3	6.40	2.500	Ea.	2,750	59.50		2,809.50	3,125
4030	0.8 mm LE panels		6.40	2.500		2,925	59.50		2,984.50	3,325
4040	1.0 mm LE panels		5.33	3.002		3,025	71		3,096	3,450
4050	1.5 mm LE panels	↓	5.33	3.002	↓	3,225	71		3,296	3,675
4060	2-section barrier, 72"W x 84"H overall									
4070	0.5 mm LE panels	H-3	4	4	Ea.	5,700	95		5,795	6,425
4080	0.8 mm LE panels		4	4		6,025	95		6,120	6,775
4090	1.0 mm LE panels		3.56	4.494		6,150	107		6,257	6,950
5000	1.5 mm LE panels	↓	3.20	5		6,650	119		6,769	7,525
5010	3-section barrier, 108"W x 84"H overall									
5020	0.5 mm LE panels	H-3	3.20	5	Ea.	8,150	119		8,269	9,175
5030	0.8 mm LE panels		3.20	5		8,550	119		8,669	9,600
5040	1.0 mm LE panels		2.67	5.993		8,750	142		8,892	9,850
5050	1.5 mm LE panels	↓	2.46	6.504	↓	9,500	154		9,654	10,800
7000	X-ray barriers, mobile, mounted within framework w/casters on									
7005	bottom, clear lead plastic window panels on upper portion,									
7010	opaque on lower, 30"W x 75"H overall, incl. framework									
7020	24"H upper w/0.5 mm LE, 48"H lower w/0.8 mm LE	1 Carp	16	.500	Ea.	1,875	13.65		1,888.65	2,075
7030	48"W x 75"H overall, incl. framework									
7040	36"H upper w/0.5 mm LE, 36"H lower w/0.8 mm LE	1 Carp	16	.500	Ea.	3,300	13.65		3,313.65	3,650
7050	36"H upper w/1.0 mm LE, 36"H lower w/1.5 mm LE	"	16	.500	"	4,000	13.65		4,013.65	4,425
7060	72"W x 75"H overall, incl. framework									
7070	36"H upper w/0.5 mm LE, 36"H lower w/0.8 mm LE	1 Carp	16	.500	Ea.	3,925	13.65		3,938.65	4,325
7080	36"H upper w/1.0 mm LE, 36"H lower w/1.5 mm LE	"	16	.500	"	4,950	13.65		4,963.65	5,475
8900	Minimum labor/equipment charge									
9000	for lines 130-911-0300 to 130-911-1900	2 Lath	4.50	3.556	Job		95.50		95.50	152

131 | Pre-Eng. Structures, Aquatic Facilities and Ice Rinks

131 230 | Greenhouses

			CREW	DAILY OUTPUT	LABOR-HOURS	UNIT	1999 BARE COSTS MAT.	LABOR	EQUIP.	TOTAL	TOTAL INCL O&P	
231	0010	**GREENHOUSE** Shell only, stock units, not incl. 2' stub walls,										231
	0020	foundation, floors, heat or compartments										
	0300	Residential type, free standing, 8'-6" long x 7'-6" wide	2 Carp	59	.271	SF Flr.	35	7.40		42.40	51	
	0400	10'-6" wide		85	.188		27	5.15		32.15	38	
	0600	13'-6" wide		108	.148		24	4.04		28.04	33.50	
	0700	17'-0" wide		160	.100		27	2.73		29.73	34	
	0900	Lean-to type, 3'-10" wide		34	.471		31	12.85		43.85	55.50	
	1000	6'-10" wide		58	.276		24	7.55		31.55	39	
	1050	8'-0" wide	↓	60	.267	↓	22	7.30		29.30	36	
	1060											
	1100	Wall mounted, to existing window, 3' x 3'	1 Carp	4	2	Ea.	335	54.50		389.50	460	
	1120	4' x 5'	"	3	2.667	"	500	73		573	670	
	3900	For cooling, add, minimum				SF Flr.	2.10			2.10	2.31	
	4000	Maximum					5.20			5.20	5.70	
	4200	For heaters, 13.6 MBH, add					4			4	4.40	
	4300	60 MBH, add				↓	1.50			1.50	1.65	
	4500	For benches, 2' x 3'-6", add				SF Hor.	17.90			17.90	19.70	
	4600	3' x 10', add				S.F.	9.70			9.70	10.65	
	4800	For controls, add, minimum				Total	1,800			1,800	1,975	
	4900	Maximum				"	10,700			10,700	11,800	
	5100	For humidification equipment, add				M.C.F.	4.60			4.60	5.05	
	5200	For vinyl shading, add				S.F.	.97			.97	1.07	

131 240 | Portable Buildings

			CREW	DAILY OUTPUT	LABOR-HOURS	UNIT	MAT.	LABOR	EQUIP.	TOTAL	TOTAL INCL O&P	
245	0010	**KIOSKS** Round, 5' diameter, 8' high, 1/4" fiberglass wall				Ea.	5,500			5,500	6,050	245
	0100	1" insulated double wall, fiberglass					6,250			6,250	6,875	
	0500	Rectangular, 5' x 9', 7'-6" high, 1/4" fiberglass wall					8,000			8,000	8,800	
	0600	1" insulated double wall, fiberglass				↓	9,500			9,500	10,500	

131 520 | Swimming Pools

			CREW	DAILY OUTPUT	LABOR-HOURS	UNIT	MAT.	LABOR	EQUIP.	TOTAL	TOTAL INCL O&P	
521	0010	**SWIMMING POOL ENCLOSURE** Translucent, free standing,										521
	0020	not including foundations, heat or light										
	0200	Economy, minimum	2 Carp	200	.080	SF Hor.	10	2.18		12.18	14.65	
	0300	Maximum		100	.160		21	4.37		25.37	30.50	
	0400	Deluxe, minimum		100	.160		23	4.37		27.37	33	
	0600	Maximum	↓	70	.229	↓	250	6.25		256.25	285	
525	0011	**SWIMMING POOLS,** Outdoor, incl. equip. & houses, minimum				SF Surf					36	525
	0300	Maximum									68	
	0400	Residential, incl. equipment, permanent type, minimum									12	
	0700	Maximum									25	
	0900	Municipal, including equipment only, over 5000 S.F., minimum									25	
	1000	Maximum									51	
	1300	Motel or apt., incl. equipment only, under 5000 S.F., minimum									22	
	1400	Maximum				↓					34	

137 | Security Access and Surveillance

137 100 | Security Access

			CREW	DAILY OUTPUT	LABOR-HOURS	UNIT	MAT.	LABOR	EQUIP.	TOTAL	TOTAL INCL O&P	
104	0010	**ACCESS CONTROL**										104
	0020	Card type, 1 time zone, minimum				Ea.	292			292	320	

137 | Security Access and Surveillance

137 100 | Security Access

		CREW	DAILY OUTPUT	LABOR-HOURS	UNIT	1999 BARE COSTS				TOTAL INCL O&P	
						MAT.	LABOR	EQUIP.	TOTAL		
104	0040 Maximum				Ea.	985			985	1,075	104
	0060 3 time zones, minimum					720			720	790	
	0080 Maximum				↓	1,650			1,650	1,825	
	0100 System with printer, and control console, 3 zones				Total	8,075			8,075	8,875	
	0120 6 zones				"	10,600			10,600	11,700	
	0140 For each door, minimum, add				Ea.	1,175			1,175	1,300	
	0160 Maximum, add				"	1,750			1,750	1,925	

For information about Means Estimating Seminars, see yellow pages 11 and 12 in back of book

Division Notes

	CREW	DAILY OUTPUT	LABOR-HOURS	UNIT	1999 BARE COSTS				TOTAL INCL O&P
					MAT.	LABOR	EQUIP.	TOTAL	

Division 14
Conveying Systems

Estimating Tips
General
- Many products in Division 14 will require some type of support or blocking for installation not included with the item itself. Examples are supports for conveyors or tube systems, attachment points for lifts, and footings for hoists or cranes. Add these supports in the appropriate division.

141 Dumbwaiters
142 Elevators
- Dumbwaiters and elevators are estimated and purchased in a method similar to buying a car. The manufacturer has a base unit with standard features. Added to this base unit price will be whatever options the owner or specifications require. Increased load capacity, additional vertical travel, additional stops, higher speed, and cab finish options are items to be considered. When developing an estimate for dumbwaiters and elevators, remember that some items needed by the installers may have to be included as part of the general contract.

Examples are:
- shaftway
- rail support brackets
- machine room
- electrical supply
- sill angles
- electrical connections
- pits
- roof penthouses
- pit ladders

Check the job specifications and drawings before pricing.
- Installation of elevators and handicapped lifts in historic structures can require significant additional costs. The associated structural requirements may involve cutting into and repairing finishes, mouldings, flooring, etc. The estimator must account for these special conditions.

143 Escalators & Moving Walks
- Escalators and moving walks are specialty items installed by specialty contractors. There are numerous options associated with these items. For specific options contact a manufacturer or contractor. In a method similar to estimating dumbwaiters and elevators, you should verify the extent of general contract work and add items as necessary.

144 Lifts
145 Material Handling Systems
146 Hoists & Cranes
- Products such as correspondence lifts, conveyors, chutes, pneumatic tube systems, material handling cranes and hoists as well as other items specified in this subdivision may require trained installers. The general contractor might not have any choice as to who will perform the installation or when it will be performed. Long lead times are often required for these products, making early decisions in scheduling necessary.

Reference Numbers
Reference numbers are shown in bold squares at the beginning of some major classifications. These numbers refer to related items in the Reference Section. The reference information may be an estimating procedure, an alternate pricing method or technical information.

Note: Not all subdivisions listed here necessarily appear in this publication.

141 | Dumbwaiters

141 100 | Manual Dumbwaiters

			CREW	DAILY OUTPUT	LABOR-HOURS	UNIT	1999 BARE COSTS MAT.	LABOR	EQUIP.	TOTAL	TOTAL INCL O&P	
101	0010	DUMBWAITERS 2 stop, hand, minimum	2 Elev	.75	21.333	Ea.	2,225	705		2,930	3,550	101
	0100	Maximum		.50	32	"	5,050	1,050		6,100	7,200	
	0300	For each additional stop, add	↓	.75	21.333	Stop	800	705		1,505	1,975	

141 200 | Electric Dumbwaiters

			CREW	DAILY OUTPUT	LABOR-HOURS	UNIT	MAT.	LABOR	EQUIP.	TOTAL	TOTAL INCL O&P	
201	0010	DUMBWAITERS 2 stop, electric, minimum	2 Elev	.13	123	Ea.	5,600	4,075		9,675	12,500	201
	0100	Maximum		.11	145	"	16,800	4,825		21,625	26,100	
	0600	For each additional stop, add	↓	.54	29.630	Stop	2,475	980		3,455	4,225	

142 | Elevators

142 010 | Elevators

				CREW	DAILY OUTPUT	LABOR-HOURS	UNIT	1999 BARE COSTS MAT.	LABOR	EQUIP.	TOTAL	TOTAL INCL O&P	
011	0012	**ELEVATORS OR LIFTS**											011
	7000	Residential, cab type, 1 floor, 2 stop, minimum		2 Elev	.20	80	Ea.	7,850	2,650		10,500	12,800	
	7100	Maximum			.10	160		13,300	5,300		18,600	22,900	
	7200	2 floor, 3 stop, minimum			.12	133		11,700	4,425		16,125	19,700	
	7300	Maximum			.06	266		19,000	8,850		27,850	34,700	
	7700	Stair climber (chair lift), single seat, minimum			1	16		3,800	530		4,330	5,000	
	7800	Maximum			.20	80		5,225	2,650		7,875	9,900	
	8000	Wheelchair lift, minimum	♿		1	16		5,200	530		5,730	6,550	
	8500	Maximum			.50	32		12,300	1,050		13,350	15,300	
	8700	Stair lift, minimum			1	16		10,300	530		10,830	12,100	
	8900	Maximum		↓	.20	80	↓	16,300	2,650		18,950	22,100	
014	0010	**ELEVATORS**	R142-100										014
	0020	For multi-story buildings, housing project, minimum					% total					2.50%	
	0100	Maximum	R142-200									4.50%	
	0300	Office building, minimum										2.50%	
	0400	Maximum	R142-300				↓					10%	
	0425	Electric freight, base unit, 4000 lb, 200 fpm, 4 stop, std. fin.		2 Elev	.05	320	Ea.	59,000	10,600		69,600	81,500	
	0450	For 5000 lb capacity, add	R142-400					4,250			4,250	4,675	
	0500	For 6000 lb capacity, add						7,475			7,475	8,225	
	0525	For 7000 lb capacity, add						10,000			10,000	11,000	
	0550	For 8000 lb capacity, add						13,900			13,900	15,300	
	0575	For 10000 lb capacity, add						16,500			16,500	18,100	
	0600	For 12000 lb capacity, add						20,000			20,000	22,000	
	0625	For 16000 lb capacity, add						24,000			24,000	26,400	
	0650	For 20000 lb capacity, add						26,400			26,400	29,000	
	0675	For increased speed, 250 fpm, add						8,475			8,475	9,325	
	0700	300 fpm, geared electric, add						10,600			10,600	11,600	
	0725	350 fpm, geared electric, add						12,500			12,500	13,700	
	0750	400 fpm, geared electric, add						13,800			13,800	15,200	
	0775	500 fpm, gearless electric, add						17,300			17,300	19,000	
	0800	600 fpm, gearless electric, add						19,100			19,100	21,000	
	0825	700 fpm, gearless electric, add						22,300			22,300	24,500	
	0850	800 fpm, gearless electric, add						24,800			24,800	27,300	
	0875	For class "B" loading, add						1,475			1,475	1,625	
	0900	For class "C-1" loading, add		↓			↓	3,650			3,650	4,025	

142 | Elevators

142 010 | Elevators

		CREW	DAILY OUTPUT	LABOR-HOURS	UNIT	1999 BARE COSTS				TOTAL INCL O&P
						MAT.	LABOR	EQUIP.	TOTAL	
0925	For class "C-2" loading, add	R142-100			Ea.	4,350			4,350	4,800
0950	For class "C-3" loading, add					5,900			5,900	6,475
0975	For travel over 40 V.L.F., add	R142-200	2 Elev	7.25	2.207	V.L.F.	90	73		163	213
1000	For number of stops over 4, add			.27	59.259	Stop	1,800	1,975		3,775	5,075
1025	Hydraulic freight, base unit, 2000 lb, 50 fpm, 2 stop, std. fin.	R142-300		.10	160	Ea.	30,400	5,300		35,700	41,800
1050	For 2500 lb capacity, add						2,050			2,050	2,250
1075	For 3000 lb capacity, add	R142-400					2,975			2,975	3,275
1100	For 3500 lb capacity, add						5,125			5,125	5,625
1125	For 4000 lb capacity, add						5,475			5,475	6,025
1150	For 4500 lb capacity, add						6,475			6,475	7,125
1175	For 5000 lb capacity, add						8,825			8,825	9,700
1200	For 6000 lb capacity, add						9,075			9,075	10,000
1225	For 7000 lb capacity, add						14,400			14,400	15,800
1250	For 8000 lb capacity, add						15,600			15,600	17,100
1275	For 10000 lb capacity, add						16,400			16,400	18,000
1300	For 12000 lb capacity, add						19,500			19,500	21,400
1325	For 16000 lb capacity, add						25,400			25,400	27,900
1350	For 20000 lb capacity, add						28,200			28,200	31,000
1375	For increased speed, 100 fpm, add						635			635	700
1400	125 fpm, add						1,175			1,175	1,300
1425	150 fpm, add						2,200			2,200	2,425
1450	175 fpm, add						3,450			3,450	3,800
1475	For class "B" loading, add						1,450			1,450	1,600
1500	For class "C-1" loading, add						3,625			3,625	4,000
1525	For class "C-2" loading, add						4,350			4,350	4,775
1550	For class "C-3" loading, add						5,950			5,950	6,550
1575	For travel over 20 V.L.F., add		2 Elev	7.25	2.207	V.L.F.	200	73		273	335
1600	For number of stops over 2, add			.27	59.259	Stop	375	1,975		2,350	3,475
1625	Electric pass., base unit, 2000 lb, 200 fpm, 4 stop, std. fin.			.05	320	Ea.	60,000	10,600		70,600	82,500
1650	For 2500 lb capacity, add						2,425			2,425	2,675
1675	For 3000 lb capacity, add						3,625			3,625	4,000
1700	For 3500 lb capacity, add						5,175			5,175	5,700
1725	For 4000 lb capacity, add						5,250			5,250	5,775
1750	For 4500 lb capacity, add						6,900			6,900	7,600
1775	For 5000 lb capacity, add						8,750			8,750	9,625
1800	For increased speed, 250 fpm, geared electric, add						2,000			2,000	2,200
1825	300 fpm, geared electric, add						4,075			4,075	4,475
1850	350 fpm, geared electric, add						4,800			4,800	5,275
1875	400 fpm, geared electric, add						6,825			6,825	7,525
1900	500 fpm, gearless electric, add						31,600			31,600	34,800
1925	600 fpm, gearless electric, add						33,400			33,400	36,700
1950	700 fpm, gearless electric, add						36,500			36,500	40,200
1975	800 fpm, gearless electric, add						40,300			40,300	44,300
2000	For travel over 40 V.L.F., add		2 Elev	7.25	2.207	V.L.F.	90	73		163	213
2025	For number of stops over 4, add			.27	59.259	Stop	2,125	1,975		4,100	5,425
2050	Hyd. pass., base unit, 1500 lb, 100 fpm, 2 stop, std. fin.			.10	160	Ea.	26,600	5,300		31,900	37,500
2075	For 2000 lb capacity, add						475			475	525
2100	For 2500 lb capacity, add						1,050			1,050	1,150
2125	For 3000 lb capacity, add						2,600			2,600	2,875
2150	For 3500 lb capacity, add						4,450			4,450	4,900
2175	For 4000 lb capacity, add						5,125			5,125	5,650
2200	For 4500 lb capacity, add						6,125			6,125	6,750
2225	For 5000 lb capacity, add						8,525			8,525	9,375
2250	For increased speed, 125 fpm, add						725			725	800
2275	150 fpm, add						1,575			1,575	1,725
2300	175 fpm, add						2,650			2,650	2,900

142 | Elevators

142 010 | Elevators

		CREW	DAILY OUTPUT	LABOR-HOURS	UNIT	1999 BARE COSTS MAT.	LABOR	EQUIP.	TOTAL	TOTAL INCL O&P	
2325	200 fpm, add	R142-100			Ea.	4,275			4,275	4,700	014
2350	For travel over 12 V.L.F., add		2 Elev	7.25	2.207	V.L.F.	200	73		273	335
2375	For number of stops over 2, add	R142-200		.27	59.259	Stop	395	1,975		2,370	3,500
2400	Electric hospital, base unit, 4000 lb, 200 fpm, 4 stop, std fin.			.05	320	Ea.	64,000	10,600		74,600	87,000
2425	For 4500 lb capacity, add	R142-300					4,250			4,250	4,675
2450	For 5000 lb capacity, add						5,550			5,550	6,125
2475	For increased speed, 250 fpm, geared electric, add	R142-400					2,100			2,100	2,300
2500	300 fpm, geared electric, add						4,000			4,000	4,400
2525	350 fpm, geared electric, add						4,900			4,900	5,375
2550	400 fpm, geared electric, add						6,800			6,800	7,500
2575	500 fpm, gearless electric, add						30,200			30,200	33,300
2600	600 fpm, gearless electric, add						33,400			33,400	36,700
2625	700 fpm, gearless electric, add						36,500			36,500	40,100
2650	800 fpm, gearless electric, add						40,300			40,300	44,300
2675	For travel over 40 V.L.F., add		2 Elev	7.25	2.207	V.L.F.	90	73		163	213
2700	For number of stops over 4, add			.27	59.259	Stop	2,525	1,975		4,500	5,850
2725	Hydraulic hospital, base unit, 4000 lb, 100 fpm, 2 stop, std. fin.			.10	160	Ea.	36,400	5,300		41,700	48,300
2750	For 4000 lb capacity, add						4,500			4,500	4,950
2775	For 4500 lb capacity, add						5,125			5,125	5,625
2800	For 5000 lb capacity, add						7,450			7,450	8,200
2825	For increased speed, 125 fpm, add						1,225			1,225	1,350
2850	150 fpm, add						2,050			2,050	2,250
2875	175 fpm, add						3,225			3,225	3,550
2900	200 fpm, add						4,700			4,700	5,175
2925	For travel over 12 V.L.F., add		2 Elev	7.25	2.207	V.L.F.	200	73		273	335
2950	For number of stops over 2, add		"	.27	59.259	Stop	2,675	1,975		4,650	6,000
2975	Passenger elevator options										
3000	2 car group automatic controls		2 Elev	.66	24.242	Ea.	2,125	805		2,930	3,600
3025	3 car group automatic controls			.44	36.364		3,150	1,200		4,350	5,350
3050	4 car group automatic controls			.33	48.485		5,200	1,600		6,800	8,250
3075	5 car group automatic controls			.26	61.538		6,875	2,050		8,925	10,800
3100	6 car group automatic controls			.22	72.727		10,400	2,400		12,800	15,200
3125	Intercom service			3	5.333		310	177		487	615
3150	Duplex car selective collective			.66	24.242		2,375	805		3,180	3,850
3175	Center opening 1 speed doors			2	8		1,200	265		1,465	1,750
3200	Center opening 2 speed doors			2	8		1,550	265		1,815	2,125
3225	Rear opening doors (opposite front)			2	8		3,375	265		3,640	4,125
3250	Side opening 2 speed doors			2	8		5,075	265		5,340	6,000
3275	Automatic emergency power switching			.66	24.242		850	805		1,655	2,175
3300	Manual emergency power switching			8	2		256	66.50		322.50	385
3325	Cab finishes (based on 3500 lb cab size)										
3350	Acrylic panel ceiling					Ea.	355			355	390
3375	Aluminum eggcrate ceiling						430			430	475
3400	Stainless steel doors						725			725	800
3425	Carpet flooring						299			299	330
3450	Epoxy flooring						249			249	274
3475	Quarry tile flooring						375			375	410
3500	Slate flooring						520			520	575
3525	Textured rubber flooring						100			100	110
3550	Stainless steel walls						2,225			2,225	2,450
3575	Stainless steel returns at door						475			475	520
3625	Hall finishes, stainless steel doors						725			725	800
3650	Stainless steel frames						725			725	800
3675	12 month maintenance contract										2,640
3700	Signal devices, hall lanterns		2 Elev	8	2		296	66.50		362.50	430
3725	Position indicators, up to 3			9.40	1.702		206	56.50		262.50	315

142 | Elevators

142 010 | Elevators

		CREW	DAILY OUTPUT	LABOR-HOURS	UNIT	1999 BARE COSTS MAT.	LABOR	EQUIP.	TOTAL	TOTAL INCL O&P
3750	Position indicators, per each over 3	2 Elev	32	.500	Ea.	57	16.60		73.60	88.50
3775	High speed heavy duty door opener	R142-100				1,300			1,300	1,425
3800	Variable voltage, O.H. gearless machine, min.	2 Elev	.16	100		21,000	3,325		24,325	28,300
3815	Maximum	R142-200	.07	228		46,300	7,575		53,875	63,000
3825	Basement installed geared machine		.33	48.485		10,900	1,600		12,500	14,500
3850	Freight elevator options	R142-300								
3875	Doors, bi-parting	2 Elev	.66	24.242	Ea.	3,450	805		4,255	5,025
3900	Power operated door and gate	R142-400	.66	24.242		13,800	805		14,605	16,500
3925	Finishes, steel plate floor					605			605	665
3950	14 ga. 1/4" x 4' steel plate walls					1,450			1,450	1,600
3975	12 month maintenance contract									1,992
4000	Signal devices, hall lanterns	2 Elev	8	2		296	66.50		362.50	430
4025	Position indicators, up to 3		9.40	1.702		206	56.50		262.50	315
4050	Position indicators, per each over 3		32	.500		57	16.60		73.60	88.50
4075	Variable voltage basement installed geared machine		.66	24.242		12,000	805		12,805	14,500
4100	Hospital elevator options									
4125	2 car group automatic controls	2 Elev	.66	24.242	Ea.	2,125	805		2,930	3,600
4150	3 car group automatic controls		.44	36.364		3,125	1,200		4,325	5,325
4175	4 car group automatic controls		.33	48.485		5,150	1,600		6,750	8,175
4200	5 car group automatic controls		.26	61.538		6,825	2,050		8,875	10,700
4225	6 car group automatic controls		.22	72.727		10,300	2,400		12,700	15,100
4250	Intercom service		3	5.333		300	177		477	605
4275	Duplex car selective collective		.66	24.242		2,375	805		3,180	3,850
4300	Center opening 1 speed doors		2	8		1,200	265		1,465	1,750
4325	Center opening 2 speed doors		2	8		1,550	265		1,815	2,125
4350	Rear opening doors (opposite front)		2	8		3,375	265		3,640	4,125
4375	Side opening 2 speed doors		2	8		5,075	265		5,340	6,000
4400	Automatic emergency power switching		.66	24.242		850	805		1,655	2,175
4425	Manual emergency power switching		8	2		256	66.50		322.50	385
4450	Cab finishes (based on 3500# cab size)									
4475	Aluminum eggcrate ceiling				Ea.	430			430	475
4500	Stainless steel doors					725			725	800
4525	Epoxy flooring					249			249	274
4550	Quarry tile flooring					375			375	415
4575	Textured rubber flooring					100			100	110
4600	Stainless steel walls					2,225			2,225	2,450
4625	Stainless steel returns at door					475			475	520
4675	Hall finishes, stainless steel doors					725			725	800
4700	Stainless steel frames					725			725	800
4725	12 month maintenance contract									3,985
4750	Signal devices, hall lanterns	2 Elev	8	2		296	66.50		362.50	430
4775	Position indicators, up to 3		9.40	1.702		206	56.50		262.50	315
4800	Position indicators, per each over 3		32	.500		57	16.60		73.60	88.50
4825	High speed heavy duty door opener					1,300			1,300	1,425
4850	Variable voltage, O.H. gearless machine, min.	2 Elev	.16	100		21,000	3,325		24,325	28,300
4865	Maximum		.07	228		46,300	7,575		53,875	63,000
4875	Basement installed geared machine		.33	48.485		10,900	1,600		12,500	14,500
5000	Drilling for piston, casing included, 18" diameter	B-48	80	.700	V.L.F.	23.50	16.85	24.50	64.85	80.50

144 | Lifts

144 010	Lifts		CREW	DAILY OUTPUT	LABOR-HOURS	UNIT	1999 BARE COSTS				TOTAL INCL O&P	
							MAT.	LABOR	EQUIP.	TOTAL		
011	0010	**CORRESPONDENCE LIFT** 1 floor 2 stop, 25 lb capacity, electric	2 Elev	.20	80	Ea.	4,825	2,650		7,475	9,450	011
	0100	Hand, 5 lb capacity	"	.20	80	"	1,825	2,650		4,475	6,150	

145 | Material Handling Systems

145 600	Chutes		CREW	DAILY OUTPUT	LABOR-HOURS	UNIT	1999 BARE COSTS				TOTAL INCL O&P	
							MAT.	LABOR	EQUIP.	TOTAL		
601	0010	**CHUTES** Linen or refuse, incl. sprinklers, 12' floor height										601
	0020											
	0050	Aluminized steel, 16 ga., 18" diameter	2 Shee	3.50	4.571	Floor	735	145		880	1,050	
	0100	24" diameter		3.20	5		760	159		919	1,100	
	0400	Galvanized steel, 16 ga., 18" diameter		3.50	4.571		700	145		845	1,000	
	0500	24" diameter		3.20	5		790	159		949	1,125	
	0800	Stainless steel, 18" diameter		3.50	4.571		920	145		1,065	1,225	
	0900	24" diameter		3.20	5		970	159		1,129	1,325	
	9000	Minimum labor/equipment charge	1 Shee	1	8	Job		254		254	405	

145 800	Tube Systems											
801	0010	**PNEUMATIC TUBE SYSTEM** Single tube, 2 stations, blower										801
	0020	100' long, stock										
	0100	3" diameter	2 Stpi	.12	133	Total	4,750	4,375		9,125	12,100	
	0300	4" diameter	"	.09	177	"	5,350	5,825		11,175	15,000	
	0400	Twin tube, two stations or more, conventional system										
	0700	3" round	2 Stpi	46	.348	L.F.	11	11.40		22.40	30	
	1050	Add for blower		2	8	System	3,750	262		4,012	4,525	
	1110	Plus for each round station, add		7.50	2.133	Ea.	420	70		490	575	
	1200	Alternate pricing method: base cost, minimum		.75	21.333	Total	4,600	700		5,300	6,150	
	1300	Maximum		.25	64	"	9,125	2,100		11,225	13,300	
	1500	Plus total system length, add, minimum		93.40	.171	L.F.	5.90	5.60		11.50	15.30	
	1600	Maximum		37.60	.426	"	17.45	13.95		31.40	41	

146 | Hoists & Cranes

146 050	Rails		CREW	DAILY OUTPUT	LABOR-HOURS	UNIT	1999 BARE COSTS				TOTAL INCL O&P	
							MAT.	LABOR	EQUIP.	TOTAL		
054	0010	**CRANE RAIL** Box beam bridge, no equipment included	E-4	3,400	.009	Lb.	.87	.29	.02	1.18	1.55	054
	0210	Running track only, 104 lb per yard, 20' piece	"	160	.200	L.F.	15.90	6.20	.51	22.61	30	

146 300	Overhead Bridge Cranes											
301	0010	**OVERHEAD BRIDGE CRANES**										301
	0100	1 girder, 20' span, 3 ton	M-3	1	34	Ea.	14,300	975	111	15,386	17,400	
	0125	5 ton		1	34		15,600	975	111	16,686	18,900	
	0150	7.5 ton		1	34		18,600	975	111	19,686	22,200	
	0175	10 ton		.80	42.500		24,500	1,225	139	25,864	29,000	
	0200	15 ton		.80	42.500		31,400	1,225	139	32,764	36,700	

146 | Hoists & Cranes

146 300 | Overhead Bridge Cranes

		CREW	DAILY OUTPUT	LABOR-HOURS	UNIT	MAT.	LABOR	EQUIP.	TOTAL	TOTAL INCL O&P
0225	30' span, 3 ton	M-3	1	34	Ea.	14,800	975	111	15,886	18,000
0250	5 ton		1	34		16,300	975	111	17,386	19,600
0275	7.5 ton		1	34		19,600	975	111	20,686	23,200
0300	10 ton		.80	42.500		25,300	1,225	139	26,664	30,000
0325	15 ton		.80	42.500		32,800	1,225	139	34,164	38,200
0350	2 girder, 40' span, 3 ton	M-4	.50	72		24,600	2,050	390	27,040	30,800
0375	5 ton		.50	72		25,700	2,050	390	28,140	32,000
0400	7.5 ton		.50	72		28,200	2,050	390	30,640	34,700
0425	10 ton		.40	90		32,900	2,575	490	35,965	40,800
0450	15 ton		.40	90		44,700	2,575	490	47,765	54,000
0475	25 ton		.30	119		53,000	3,425	650	57,075	64,500
0500	50' span, 3 ton		.50	72		28,000	2,050	390	30,440	34,500
0525	5 ton		.50	72		29,000	2,050	390	31,440	35,600
0550	7.5 ton		.50	72		31,100	2,050	390	33,540	37,900
0575	10 ton		.40	90		35,700	2,575	490	38,765	43,900
0600	15 ton		.40	90		46,800	2,575	490	49,865	56,000
0625	25 ton		.30	119		55,500	3,425	650	59,575	67,000

For information about Means Estimating Seminars, see yellow pages 11 and 12 in back of book

Division Notes

	CREW	DAILY OUTPUT	LABOR-HOURS	UNIT	1999 BARE COSTS MAT.	LABOR	EQUIP.	TOTAL	TOTAL INCL O&P

Division 15 Mechanical

Estimating Tips

151 Pipe & Fittings
This subdivision is primarily basic pipe and related materials. The pipe may be used by any of the mechanical disciplines, i.e., plumbing, fire protection, heating, and air conditioning.

- The piping section lists the add to labor for elevated pipe installation. These adds apply to all elevated pipe, fittings, valves, insulation, etc., that are placed above 10' high. CAUTION: the correct percentage may vary for the same pipe. For example, the percentage add for the basic pipe installation should be based on the maximum height that the craftsman must install for that particular section. If the pipe is to be located 14' above the floor but it is suspended on threaded rod from beams, the bottom flange of which is 18' high (4' rods), then the height is actually 18' and the add is 20%. The pipe coverer, however, does not have to go above the 14' and so his add should be 10%.
- Most pipe is priced first as straight pipe with a joint (coupling, weld, etc.) every 10' and a hanger usually every 10'. There are exceptions with hanger spacing such as: for cast iron pipe (5') and plastic pipe (3 per 10'). Following each type of pipe there are several lines listing sizes and the amount to be subtracted to delete couplings and hangers. This is for pipe that is to be buried or supported together on trapeze hangers. The reason that the couplings are deleted is that these runs are usually long and frequently longer lengths of pipe are used. By deleting the couplings the estimator is expected to look up and add back the correct reduced number of couplings.
- When preparing an estimate it may be necessary to approximate the fittings. Fittings usually run between 25% and 50% of the cost of the pipe. The lower percentage is for simpler runs, and the higher number is for complex areas like mechanical rooms.
- For historic restoration projects, the systems must be as invisible as possible, and pathways must be sought for pipes, conduits, and ductwork. While installations in accessible spaces (such as basements and attics) are relatively straightforward to estimate, labor costs may be more difficult to determine when delivery systems must be concealed.

152 Plumbing Fixtures
- Plumbing fixture costs usually require two lines, the fixture itself and its "rough-in, supply and waste".

153 Plumbing Appliances
- Remember that gas and oil fired units need venting.

154 Fire Protection
- Include all valves needed for fire protection system.

155 Heating
- When estimating the cost of an HVAC system, check to see who is responsible for providing and installing the temperature control system. It is possible to overlook controls, assuming that they would be included in the electrical estimate.
- When looking up a boiler be careful on specified capacity. Some manufacturers rate their products on output while others use input.
- Include HVAC insulation for pipe, boiler and duct (wrap and liner).

156 HVAC Piping Specialties
- Be careful when looking up mechanical items to get the correct pressure rating and connection type (thread, weld, flange).

157 Air Conditioning & Ventilation
- Combination heating and cooling units are sized by the air conditioning requirements. (See Reference No. R157-020 for preliminary sizing guide.)
- A ton of air conditioning is nominally 400 CFM.
- Rectangular duct is taken off by the linear foot for each size, but its cost is usually estimated by the pound. Remember that SMACNA standards now base duct on internal pressure.
- Prefabricated duct is estimated and purchased like pipe: straight sections and fittings.
- Note that cranes or other lifting equipment are not included on any lines in Division 15. For example, if a crane is required to lift a heavy piece of pipe into place high above a gym floor, or to put a rooftop unit on the roof of a four-story building, etc., it must be added. Due to the potential for extreme variation—from nothing additional required, to a major crane or helicopter—we feel that including a nominal amount for "lifting contingency" would be useless and detract from the accuracy of the estimate. When using equipment rental from Means do not forget to include the cost of the operator(s).

Reference Numbers
Reference numbers are shown in bold squares at the beginning of some major classifications. These numbers refer to related items in the Reference Section. The reference information may be an estimating procedure, an alternate pricing method or technical information.

Note: Not all subdivisions listed here necessarily appear in this publication.

151 | Pipe & Fittings

151 100 | Miscellaneous Fittings

		CREW	DAILY OUTPUT	LABOR-HOURS	UNIT	1999 BARE COSTS MAT.	LABOR	EQUIP.	TOTAL	TOTAL INCL O&P
105	**0010 BACKFLOW PREVENTER** Includes valves									
	0020 and four test cocks, corrosion resistant, automatic operation									
	1000 Double check principle									
	1080 Threaded, with gate valves									
	1100 3/4" pipe size	1 Plum	16	.500	Ea.	595	16.30		611.30	680
	1120 1" pipe size		14	.571		620	18.65		638.65	710
	1140 1-1/2" pipe size		10	.800		705	26		731	815
	1160 2" pipe size		7	1.143		870	37.50		907.50	1,025
	4000 Reduced pressure principle									
	4100 Threaded, valves are ball									
	4120 3/4" pipe size	1 Plum	16	.500	Ea.	685	16.30		701.30	780
	4140 1" pipe size		14	.571		730	18.65		748.65	830
	4160 1-1/2" pipe size		10	.800		990	26		1,016	1,125
	4180 2" pipe size		7	1.143		1,050	37.50		1,087.50	1,200
	4500 Minimum labor/equipment charge		4	2	Job		65		65	102
	5000 Flanged, bronze, valves are OS&Y									
	5060 2-1/2" pipe size	Q-1	5	3.200	Ea.	2,725	94		2,819	3,150
	5080 3" pipe size		4.50	3.556		3,375	104		3,479	3,900
	5100 4" pipe size		3	5.333		4,800	157		4,957	5,525
	5120 6" pipe size	Q-2	3	8		10,200	243		10,443	11,600
	5600 Flanged, iron, valves are OS&Y									
	5660 2-1/2" pipe size	Q-1	5	3.200	Ea.	1,825	94		1,919	2,150
	5680 3" pipe size		4.50	3.556		1,950	104		2,054	2,300
	5700 4" pipe size		3	5.333		2,575	157		2,732	3,075
	5720 6" pipe size	Q-2	3	8		4,050	243		4,293	4,825
	5800 Rebuild 4" diameter reduced pressure BFP	1 Plum	4	2		206	65		271	330
	5810 6" diameter		2.66	3.008		218	98		316	395
	5820 8" diameter		2	4		270	130		400	500
	5830 10" diameter		1.60	5		315	163		478	600
	9010 Minimum labor/equipment charge		2	4	Job		130		130	204
110	**0010 CLEANOUTS**									
	0060 Floor type									
	0080 Round or square, scoriated nickel bronze top									
	0100 2" pipe size	1 Plum	10	.800	Ea.	84	26		110	134
	0140 4" pipe size	"	6	1.333	"	113	43.50		156.50	193
	0980 Round top, recessed for terrazzo									
	1000 2" pipe size	1 Plum	9	.889	Ea.	84	29		113	138
	1100 4" pipe size	"	4	2		113	65		178	227
	1120 5" pipe size	Q-1	6	2.667		137	78.50		215.50	273
	9000 Minimum labor/equipment charge	1 Plum	3	2.667	Job		87		87	136
115	**0010 CLEANOUT TEE**									
	0100 Cast iron, B&S, with countersunk plug									
	0220 3" pipe size	1 Plum	3.60	2.222	Ea.	87	72.50		159.50	209
	0240 4" pipe size	"	3.30	2.424		108	79		187	243
	0500 For round smooth access cover, same price									
	4000 Plastic, tees and adapters. Add plugs									
	4010 ABS, DWV									
	4020 Cleanout tee, 1-1/2" pipe size	1 Plum	15	.533	Ea.	5.20	17.40		22.60	32.50
	9000 Minimum labor/equipment charge	"	2.75	2.909	Job		95		95	148
120	**0010 CONNECTORS** Flexible, corrugated, 7/8" O.D., 1/2" I.D.									
	0050 Gas, seamless brass, steel fittings									
	0200 12" long	1 Plum	36	.222	Ea.	8.50	7.25		15.75	20.50
	0220 18" long		36	.222		10.55	7.25		17.80	23
	0240 24" long		34	.235		12.50	7.65		20.15	26
	0260 30" long		34	.235		13.50	7.65		21.15	27

Important: See the Reference Section for critical supporting data - Reference Nos., Crews, & City Cost Indexes

151 | Pipe & Fittings

151 100 | Miscellaneous Fittings

			CREW	DAILY OUTPUT	LABOR-HOURS	UNIT	MAT.	LABOR	EQUIP.	TOTAL	TOTAL INCL O&P	
120	9000	Minimum labor/equipment charge	1 Plum	4	2	Job		65		65	102	120
125	0010	**DRAINS**										125
	0020											
	0140	Cornice, C.I., 45° or 90° outlet										
	0200	3" and 4" pipe size	Q-1	12	1.333	Ea.	98	39		137	169	
	0260	For galvanized body, add					19.60			19.60	21.50	
	0280	For polished bronze dome, add					16.65			16.65	18.30	
	0400	Deck, auto park, C.I., 13" top										
	0440	3", 4", 5", and 6" pipe size	Q-1	8	2	Ea.	425	58.50		483.50	560	
	0480	For galvanized body, add				"	202			202	223	
	0500											
	2000	Floor, medium duty, C.I., deep flange, 7" dia top										
	2040	2" and 3" pipe size	Q-1	12	1.333	Ea.	60	39		99	127	
	2080	For galvanized body, add					25			25	27.50	
	2120	For polished bronze top, add					33			33	36.50	
	2500	Heavy duty, cleanout & trap w/bucket, C.I., 15" top										
	2540	2", 3", and 4" pipe size	Q-1	6	2.667	Ea.	1,475	78.50		1,553.50	1,750	
	2560	For galvanized body, add					440			440	485	
	2580	For polished bronze top, add					465			465	510	
	3860	Roof, flat metal deck, C.I. body, 12" C.I. dome										
	3890	3" pipe size	Q-1	14	1.143	Ea.	117	33.50		150.50	182	
	3900	4" pipe size	"	13	1.231	"	117	36		153	186	
	4620	Main, all aluminum, 12" low profile dome										
	4640	2", 3" and 4" pipe size	Q-1	14	1.143	Ea.	130	33.50		163.50	196	
	9200	Minimum labor/equipment charge	"	3.75	4.267	Job		125		125	196	
130	0010	**DIELECTRIC UNIONS** Standard gaskets for water and air										130
	0020	250 psi maximum pressure										
	0280	Female IPT to sweat, straight										
	0340	3/4" pipe size	1 Plum	20	.400	Ea.	3.02	13.05		16.07	24	
	0780	Female IPT to female IPT, straight										
	0800	1/2" pipe size	1 Plum	24	.333	Ea.	4.77	10.85		15.62	22.50	
	0840	3/4" pipe size		20	.400	"	5.35	13.05		18.40	26.50	
	9000	Minimum labor/equipment charge		4	2	Job		65		65	102	
141	0010	**FAUCETS/FITTINGS**										141
	0020											
	0150	Bath, faucets, diverter spout combination, sweat	1 Plum	8	1	Ea.	66	32.50		98.50	124	
	0200	For integral stops, IPS unions, add					31			31	34	
	0500	Drain, central lift, 1-1/2" IPS male	1 Plum	20	.400		37	13.05		50.05	61	
	0600	Trip lever, 1-1/2" IPS male	"	20	.400		37.50	13.05		50.55	62	
	0810	Bidet										
	0812	Fitting, over the rim, swivel spray/pop-up drain	1 Plum	8	1	Ea.	115	32.50		147.50	178	
	0840	Flush valves, with vacuum breaker										
	0850	Water closet										
	0860	Exposed, rear spud	1 Plum	8	1	Ea.	105	32.50		137.50	167	
	0870	Top spud		8	1		96	32.50		128.50	157	
	0880	Concealed, rear spud		8	1		138	32.50		170.50	203	
	0890	Top spud		8	1		138	32.50		170.50	203	
	0900	Wall hung		8	1		121	32.50		153.50	184	
	0920	Urinal										
	0930	Exposed, stall	1 Plum	8	1	Ea.	96	32.50		128.50	157	
	0940	Wall, (washout)		8	1		96	32.50		128.50	157	
	0950	Pedestal, top spud		8	1		98	32.50		130.50	159	
	0960	Concealed, stall		8	1		110	32.50		142.50	172	
	0970	Wall (washout)		8	1		115	32.50		147.50	178	
	0971	Automatic flush sensor and operator for										

For expanded coverage of these items see *Means Mechanical or Plumbing Cost Data 1999*

151 | Pipe & Fittings

151 100 | Miscellaneous Fittings

			CREW	DAILY OUTPUT	LABOR-HOURS	UNIT	MAT.	LABOR	EQUIP.	TOTAL	TOTAL INCL O&P	
141	0972	urinals or water closets	1 Plum	16	.500	Ea.	315	16.30		331.30	370	141
	1000	Kitchen sink faucets, top mount, cast spout		10	.800		46	26		72	91.50	
	1100	For spray, add		24	.333		12	10.85		22.85	30	
	1200	Wall type, swing tube spout		10	.800		57	26		83	104	
	2000	Laundry faucets, shelf type, IPS or copper unions		12	.667		38	21.50		59.50	76	
	2100	Lavatory faucet, centerset, without drain		10	.800		33	26		59	77.50	
	2200	For pop-up drain, add		16	.500		13.70	16.30		30	40.50	
	2800	Self-closing, center set		10	.800		97.50	26		123.50	148	
	2810	Automatic sensor and operator, with faucet head		6.15	1.301		279	42.50		321.50	370	
	2850	Medical, bedpan cleanser, with pedal valve,		12	.667		430	21.50		451.50	510	
	2860	With screwdriver stop valve		12	.667		223	21.50		244.50	279	
	2870	With self-closing spray valve		12	.667		168	21.50		189.50	219	
	2900	Faucet, gooseneck spout, wrist handles, grid drain		10	.800		97	26		123	148	
	2940	Mixing valve, knee action, screwdriver stops		4	2		335	65		400	470	
	3000	Service sink faucet, cast spout, pail hook, hose end		14	.571		68.50	18.65		87.15	105	
	4000	Shower by-pass valve with union		18	.444		46	14.50		60.50	73	
	4100	Shower arm with flange and head		22	.364		18	11.85		29.85	38.50	
	4140	Shower, hand held, pin mount, massage action, chrome		22	.364		66.50	11.85		78.35	91.50	
	4142	Polished brass		22	.364		121	11.85		132.85	152	
	4144	Shower, hand held, wall mtd, adj. spray, 2 wall mounts, chrome		20	.400		128	13.05		141.05	162	
	4146	Polished brass		20	.400		235	13.05		248.05	280	
	4148	Shower, hand held head, bar mounted 24", adj. spray, chrome		20	.400		159	13.05		172.05	196	
	4150	Polished brass		20	.400		350	13.05		363.05	405	
	4200	Shower thermostatic mixing valve, concealed		8	1		222	32.50		254.50	295	
	4300	For inlet strainer, check, and stops, add					66.50			66.50	73	
	5000	Sillcock, compact, brass, IPS or copper to hose	1 Plum	24	.333		4.80	10.85		15.65	22.50	
	6000	Stop and waste valves, bronze										
	6100	Angle, solder end 1/2"	1 Plum	24	.333	Ea.	4.41	10.85		15.26	22	
	6110	3/4"		20	.400		4.85	13.05		17.90	26	
	6300	Straightway, solder end 3/8"		24	.333		4.26	10.85		15.11	21.50	
	6310	1/2"		24	.333		2.45	10.85		13.30	19.70	
	6330	1"		19	.421		4.25	13.75		18	26	
	6400	Straightway, threaded 3/8"		24	.333		4.30	10.85		15.15	21.50	
	6410	1/2"		24	.333		3.31	10.85		14.16	20.50	
	6420	3/4"		20	.400		3.94	13.05		16.99	25	
	6430	1"		19	.421		10.50	13.75		24.25	33	
	7800	Water closet, wax gasket		96	.083		1.29	2.72		4.01	5.65	
	7820	Gasket toilet tank to bowl		32	.250		6.05	8.15		14.20	19.40	
	8000	Water supply stops, polished chrome plate										
	8200	Angle, 3/8"	1 Plum	24	.333	Ea.	4.73	10.85		15.58	22	
	8300	1/2"		22	.364		4.73	11.85		16.58	24	
	8400	Straight, 3/8"		26	.308		7.05	10.05		17.10	23.50	
	8500	1/2"		24	.333		7.05	10.85		17.90	25	
	8600	Water closet, angle, w/flex riser, 3/8"		24	.333		11.05	10.85		21.90	29	
	9000	Minimum labor/equipment charge		4	2	Job		65		65	102	
146	0010	**FLOOR RECEPTORS** For connection to 2", 3" & 4" diameter pipe										146
	0200	12-1/2" square top, 25 sq in open area	Q-1	10	1.600	Ea.	288	47		335	390	
	0300	For grate with 4" diam. x 3-3/4" high funnel, add					51.50			51.50	56.50	
	0400	For grate with 6" diameter x 6" high funnel, add					66.50			66.50	73	
	0700	For acid-resisting bucket, add					81			81	89.50	
	0900	For stainless steel mesh bucket liner, add					64			64	70.50	
	2000	12-5/8" diameter top, 40 sq. in. open area	Q-1	10	1.600		228	47		275	325	
	2100	For options, add same prices as square top										
	3000	8" x 4" rectangular top, 7.5 sq. in. open area	Q-1	14	1.143	Ea.	240	33.50		273.50	315	
	3100	For trap primer connections, add				"	25.50			25.50	28.50	

Important: See the Reference Section for critical supporting data - Reference Nos., Crews, & City Cost Indexes

151 | Pipe & Fittings

151 100 | Miscellaneous Fittings

			CREW	DAILY OUTPUT	LABOR-HOURS	UNIT	MAT.	LABOR	EQUIP.	TOTAL	TOTAL INCL O&P	
146	9000	Minimum labor/equipment charge	Q-1	3	5.333	Job		157		157	245	146
156	0010	**HYDRANTS**										156
	0050	Wall type, moderate climate, bronze, encased										
	0200	3/4" IPS connection	1 Plum	16	.500	Ea.	226	16.30		242.30	275	
	1000	Non-freeze, bronze, exposed										
	1100	3/4" IPS connection, 4" to 9" thick wall	1 Plum	14	.571	Ea.	153	18.65		171.65	198	
	1120	10" to 14" thick wall	"	12	.667		166	21.50		187.50	217	
	1280	For anti-siphon type, add					40.50			40.50	44.50	
	9000	Minimum labor/equipment charge	1 Plum	3	2.667	Job		87		87	136	
165	0010	**SHOCK ABSORBERS**										165
	0490	Copper										
	0500	3/4" male I.P.S. For 1 to 11 fixtures	1 Plum	12	.667	Ea.	15.60	21.50		37.10	51	
	0600	1" male I.P.S., For 12 to 32 fixtures		8	1		40	32.50		72.50	95	
	0700	1-1/4" male I.P.S. For 33 to 60 fixtures		8	1		46	32.50		78.50	102	
	0800	1-1/2" male I.P.S. For 61 to 113 fixtures		8	1		63	32.50		95.50	121	
	0900	2" male I.P.S. For 114 to 154 fixtures		8	1		100	32.50		132.50	161	
	1000	2-1/2" male I.P.S. For 155 to 330 fixtures		4	2		220	65		285	345	
	9000	Minimum labor/equipment charge		3.50	2.286	Job		74.50		74.50	117	
170	0010	**SUPPORTS/CARRIERS** For plumbing fixtures										170
	0020											
	3000	Lavatory, concealed arm										
	3050	Floor mounted, single										
	3100	High back fixture	1 Plum	6	1.333	Ea.	128	43.50		171.50	209	
	3200	Flat slab fixture		6	1.333		149	43.50		192.50	232	
	3220	Paraplegic		6	1.333		136	43.50		179.50	218	
	6980	Water closet, siphon jet										
	7000	Horizontal, adjustable, caulk										
	7040	Single, 4" pipe size	1 Plum	6	1.333	Ea.	205	43.50		248.50	294	
	7060	5" pipe size		6	1.333		271	43.50		314.50	365	
	7100	Double, 4" pipe size		5	1.600		205	52		257	310	
	7120	5" pipe size		5	1.600		271	52		323	380	
	8200	Water closet, residential										
	8220	Vertical centerline, floor mount										
	8240	Single, 3" caulk, 2" or 3" vent	1 Plum	6	1.333	Ea.	147	43.50		190.50	230	
	8260	4" caulk, 2" or 4" vent		6	1.333	"	185	43.50		228.50	272	
	9990	Minimum labor/equipment charge		3.50	2.286	Job		74.50		74.50	117	
181	0010	**TRAPS**										181
	0030	Cast iron, service weight										
	0050	Long P trap, 2" pipe size										
	1100	12" long	Q-1	16	1	Ea.	21.50	29.50		51	69.50	
	3000	P trap, B&S, 2" pipe size		16	1		14.30	29.50		43.80	62	
	3040	3" pipe size		14	1.143		21	33.50		54.50	75.50	
	3800	Drum trap, 4" x 5", 1-1/2" tapping	Q-2	17	1.412		13.50	43		56.50	82	
	3900											
	4700	Copper, drainage, drum trap										
	4840	3" x 6" swivel, 1-1/2" pipe size	1 Plum	16	.500	Ea.	46	16.30		62.30	76	
	5100	P trap, standard pattern										
	5200	1-1/4" pipe size	1 Plum	18	.444	Ea.	25	14.50		39.50	50	
	5240	1-1/2" pipe size		17	.471		25	15.35		40.35	51.50	
	5260	2" pipe size		15	.533		38	17.40		55.40	69	
	5280	3" pipe size		11	.727		92.50	23.50		116	139	
	9000	Minimum labor/equipment charge		3	2.667	Job		87		87	136	
185	0010	**VACUUM BREAKERS** Hot or cold water										185
	1030	Anti-siphon, brass										

For expanded coverage of these items see *Means Mechanical or Plumbing Cost Data 1999*

151 | Pipe & Fittings

151 100 | Miscellaneous Fittings

		CREW	DAILY OUTPUT	LABOR-HOURS	UNIT	MAT.	LABOR	EQUIP.	TOTAL	TOTAL INCL O&P	
185	1060	1/2" size	1 Plum	24	.333	Ea.	20	10.85		30.85	39	185
	1080	3/4" size		20	.400		24	13.05		37.05	47	
	1100	1" size		19	.421		37	13.75		50.75	62	
	1120	1-1/4" size		15	.533		51.50	17.40		68.90	84	
	1140	1-1/2" size		13	.615		76	20		96	115	
	1160	2" size		11	.727		118	23.50		141.50	167	
	9000	Minimum labor/equipment charge		4	2	Job		65		65	102	
195	0010	**VENT FLASHING**										195
	1000	Aluminum with lead ring										
	1050	3" pipe	1 Plum	17	.471	Ea.	7.65	15.35		23	32.50	
	1060	4" pipe	"	16	.500	"	9.25	16.30		25.55	35.50	
	1350	Copper with neoprene ring										
	1440	2" pipe	1 Plum	18	.444	Ea.	14.85	14.50		29.35	39	
	1450	3" pipe		17	.471		17.40	15.35		32.75	43	
	1460	4" pipe		16	.500		19.20	16.30		35.50	46.50	
	9000	Minimum labor/equipment charge		4	2	Job		65		65	102	

151 200 | Pipe, Ident/Test & General

		CREW	DAILY OUTPUT	LABOR-HOURS	UNIT	MAT.	LABOR	EQUIP.	TOTAL	TOTAL INCL O&P	
200	0010	**PIPING** See also divisions 026 & 027 for site work										200
	1000	Add to labor for elevated installation										
	1080	10' to 15' high						10%				
	1100	15' to 20' high						20%				
	1120	20' to 25' high						25%				
	1140	25' to 30' high						35%				
	1160	30' to 35' high						40%				
	1180	35' to 40' high						50%				
	1200	Over 40' high						55%				

151 250 | Brass Pipe

		CREW	DAILY OUTPUT	LABOR-HOURS	UNIT	MAT.	LABOR	EQUIP.	TOTAL	TOTAL INCL O&P	
251	0010	**PIPE, BRASS** Plain end,										251
	0900	Field threaded, coupling & clevis hanger 10' O.C.										
	0920	Regular weight										
	1120	1/2" diameter	1 Plum	48	.167	L.F.	3.99	5.45		9.44	12.90	
	1140	3/4" diameter		46	.174		5.40	5.65		11.05	14.80	
	1160	1" diameter		43	.186		7.80	6.05		13.85	18.05	
	1180	1-1/4" diameter	Q-1	72	.222		11.65	6.50		18.15	23	
	1200	1-1/2" diameter		65	.246		13.80	7.20		21	26.50	
	1220	2" diameter		53	.302		18.75	8.85		27.60	34.50	
	9000	Minimum labor/equipment charge	1 Plum	4	2	Job		65		65	102	
258	0010	**PIPE, BRASS, FITTINGS** Rough bronze, threaded										258
	0020											
	1000	Standard wt., 90° Elbow										
	1100	1/2"	1 Plum	12	.667	Ea.	7.05	21.50		28.55	42	
	1120	3/4"		11	.727		9.50	23.50		33	47.50	
	1140	1"		10	.800		15.40	26		41.40	58	
	1160	1-1/4"	Q-1	17	.941		25	27.50		52.50	70.50	
	1180	1-1/2"	"	16	1		31	29.50		60.50	80	
	1500	45° Elbow, 1/8"	1 Plum	13	.615		8.70	20		28.70	41	
	1580	1/2"		12	.667		8.70	21.50		30.20	43.50	
	1600	3/4"		11	.727		12.35	23.50		35.85	50.50	
	1620	1"		10	.800		21	26		47	64	
	1640	1-1/4"	Q-1	17	.941		33.50	27.50		61	80	
	1660	1-1/2"	"	16	1		42	29.50		71.50	92.50	

151 | Pipe & Fittings

151 250 | Brass Pipe

			CREW	DAILY OUTPUT	LABOR-HOURS	UNIT	MAT.	LABOR	EQUIP.	TOTAL	TOTAL INCL O&P	
258	2000	Tee, 1/8"	1 Plum	9	.889	Ea.	8.30	29		37.30	54.50	258
	2080	1/2"		8	1		8.30	32.50		40.80	60	
	2100	3/4"		7	1.143		11.80	37.50		49.30	71.50	
	2120	1"		6	1.333		21.50	43.50		65	91.50	
	2140	1-1/4"	Q-1	10	1.600		36.50	47		83.50	114	
	2160	1-1/2"	"	9	1.778		41.50	52		93.50	127	
	2500	Coupling, 1/8"	1 Plum	26	.308		5.90	10.05		15.95	22	
	2580	1/2"		15	.533		5.90	17.40		23.30	33.50	
	2600	3/4"		14	.571		8.30	18.65		26.95	38	
	2620	1"		13	.615		14.20	20		34.20	47	
	2640	1-1/4"	Q-1	22	.727		23.50	21.50		45	59.50	
	2660	1-1/2"		20	.800		31	23.50		54.50	70.50	
	2680	2"		18	.889		51	26		77	97	
	9000	Minimum labor/equipment charge	1 Plum	4	2	Job		65		65	102	

151 300 | Cast Iron Pipe

			CREW	DAILY OUTPUT	LABOR-HOURS	UNIT	MAT.	LABOR	EQUIP.	TOTAL	TOTAL INCL O&P	
301	0010	**PIPE, CAST IRON** Soil, on hangers 5' O.C.										301
	0020	Single hub, service wt., lead & oakum joints 10' O.C.										
	2120	2" diameter	Q-1	63	.254	L.F.	4.42	7.45		11.87	16.50	
	2140	3" diameter		60	.267		5.95	7.85		13.80	18.80	
	2160	4" diameter		55	.291		8.25	8.55		16.80	22.50	
	2180	5" diameter	Q-2	76	.316		10.50	9.60		20.10	26.50	
	2200	6" diameter	"	73	.329		12.50	10		22.50	29.50	
	2220	8" diameter	Q-3	59	.542		19.95	16.85		36.80	48.50	
	4000	No hub, couplings 10' O.C.										
	4100	1-1/2" diameter	Q-1	71	.225	L.F.	5.10	6.60		11.70	15.95	
	4120	2" diameter		67	.239		5.20	7		12.20	16.70	
	4140	3" diameter		64	.250		6.80	7.35		14.15	18.95	
	4160	4" diameter		58	.276		8.85	8.10		16.95	22.50	
	4180	5" diameter	Q-2	83	.289		12.55	8.80		21.35	27.50	
	9000	Minimum labor/equipment charge	1 Plum	4	2	Job		65		65	102	
320	0010	**PIPE, CAST IRON, FITTINGS** Soil										320
	0040	Hub and spigot, service weight, lead & oakum joints										
	0080	1/4 bend, 2"	Q-1	16	1	Ea.	6.10	29.50		35.60	52.50	
	0120	3"		14	1.143		10.60	33.50		44.10	64	
	0140	4"		13	1.231		16.55	36		52.55	74.50	
	0160	5"	Q-2	18	1.333		23	40.50		63.50	89	
	0180	6"	"	17	1.412		29	43		72	99	
	0200	8"	Q-3	11	2.909		87	90.50		177.50	238	
	0340	1/8 bend, 2"	Q-1	16	1		4.88	29.50		34.38	51.50	
	0350	3"		14	1.143		8.90	33.50		42.40	62.50	
	0360	4"		13	1.231		12.95	36		48.95	71	
	0380	5"	Q-2	18	1.333		17.85	40.50		58.35	83	
	0400	6"	"	17	1.412		22	43		65	91	
	0420	8"	Q-3	11	2.909		65.50	90.50		156	214	
	0500	Sanitary tee, 2"	Q-1	10	1.600		9.75	47		56.75	84.50	
	0540	3"		9	1.778		17.85	52		69.85	101	
	0620	4"		8	2		22	58.50		80.50	116	
	0700	5"	Q-2	12	2		44	61		105	144	
	0800	6"	"	11	2.182		49.50	66.50		116	159	
	0880	8"	Q-3	7	4.571		144	142		286	380	
	0954	10" x 6"	"	8	4		189	124		313	405	
	5990	No hub										
	6000	Cplg. & labor required at joints not incl. in fitting										
	6010	price. Add 1 coupling per joint for installed price										

For expanded coverage of these items see Means Mechanical or Plumbing Cost Data 1999

151 | Pipe & Fittings

151 300 | Cast Iron Pipe

			CREW	DAILY OUTPUT	LABOR-HOURS	UNIT	1999 BARE COSTS MAT.	LABOR	EQUIP.	TOTAL	TOTAL INCL O&P	
320	6020	1/4 Bend, 1-1/2"	R151 -050			Ea.	4.25			4.25	4.68	320
	6060	2"					4.63			4.63	5.10	
	6080	3"					6.45			6.45	7.10	
	6120	4"					9.25			9.25	10.20	
	6184	1/4 Bend, long sweep, 1-1/2"					11.85			11.85	13.05	
	6186	2"					11.85			11.85	13.05	
	6188	3"					14.10			14.10	15.50	
	6189	4"					22.50			22.50	24.50	
	6190	5"					41.50			41.50	45.50	
	6191	6"					50.50			50.50	55.50	
	6192	8"					135			135	149	
	6193	10"					243			243	267	
	6200	1/8 Bend, 1-1/2"					3.88			3.88	4.27	
	6210	2"					4.26			4.26	4.69	
	6212	3"					5.05			5.05	5.55	
	6214	4"					5.85			5.85	6.40	
	6380	Sanitary Tee, tapped, 1-1/2"					8.40			8.40	9.25	
	6382	2" x 1-1/2"					8.40			8.40	9.25	
	6384	2"					9.30			9.30	10.25	
	6386	3" x 2"					11.90			11.90	13.10	
	6388	3"					22			22	24	
	6390	4" x 1-1/2"					11			11	12.10	
	6392	4" x 2"					11.90			11.90	13.10	
	6394	6" x 1-1/2"					25			25	27.50	
	6396	6" x 2"					25			25	27.50	
	6459	Sanitary Tee, 1-1/2"					5.80			5.80	6.40	
	6460	2"					6.45			6.45	7.10	
	6470	3"					7.80			7.80	8.60	
	6472	4"					12.10			12.10	13.30	
	8000	Coupling, standard (by CISPI Mfrs.)										
	8020	1-1/2"	Q-1	48	.333	Ea.	3.63	9.80		13.43	19.30	
	8040	2"		44	.364		3.63	10.65		14.28	20.50	
	8080	3"		38	.421		4.32	12.35		16.67	24	
	8120	4"		33	.485		5.15	14.25		19.40	28	
	9000	Minimum labor/equipment charge	1 Plum	4	2	Job		65		65	102	

151 400 | Copper Pipe & Tubing

			CREW	DAILY OUTPUT	LABOR-HOURS	UNIT	MAT.	LABOR	EQUIP.	TOTAL	TOTAL INCL O&P	
401	0010	**PIPE, COPPER** Solder joints										401
	1000	Type K tubing, couplings & clevis hangers 10' O.C.										
	1100	1/4" diameter	1 Plum	84	.095	L.F.	1.19	3.10		4.29	6.15	
	1200	1" diameter		66	.121		2.98	3.95		6.93	9.50	
	1260	2" diameter		40	.200		7	6.50		13.50	17.95	
	2000	Type L tubing, couplings & hangers 10' O.C.										
	2100	1/4" diameter	1 Plum	88	.091	L.F.	.87	2.96		3.83	5.60	
	2120	3/8" diameter		84	.095		1.08	3.10		4.18	6.05	
	2140	1/2" diameter		81	.099		1.26	3.22		4.48	6.45	
	2160	5/8" diameter		79	.101		1.72	3.30		5.02	7.05	
	2180	3/4" diameter		76	.105		1.80	3.43		5.23	7.35	
	2200	1" diameter		68	.118		2.46	3.84		6.30	8.70	
	2220	1-1/4" diameter		58	.138		3.11	4.50		7.61	10.45	
	2240	1-1/2" diameter		52	.154		3.94	5		8.94	12.20	
	2260	2" diameter		42	.190		5.95	6.20		12.15	16.25	
	2280	2-1/2" diameter	Q-1	62	.258		8.70	7.55		16.25	21.50	
	2300	3" diameter		56	.286		11.75	8.40		20.15	26	
	2320	3-1/2" diameter		43	.372		15.20	10.90		26.10	34	

151 | Pipe & Fittings

151 400 | Copper Pipe & Tubing

			CREW	DAILY OUTPUT	LABOR-HOURS	UNIT	MAT.	LABOR	EQUIP.	TOTAL	TOTAL INCL O&P	
401	2340	4" diameter	Q-1	39	.410	L.F.	18.65	12.05		30.70	39.50	401
	2360	5" diameter	↓	34	.471		50	13.80		63.80	76.50	
	2380	6" diameter	Q-2	40	.600	↓	59.50	18.25		77.75	94	
	2410	For other than full hard temper, add					21%					
	2590	For silver solder, add						15%				
	3000	Type M tubing, couplings & hangers 10' O.C.										
	3140	1/2" diameter	1 Plum	84	.095	L.F.	1.02	3.10		4.12	6	
	3180	3/4" diameter		78	.103		1.45	3.34		4.79	6.85	
	3200	1" diameter	↓	70	.114	↓	2.01	3.73		5.74	8.05	
	4000	Type DWV tubing, couplings & hangers 10' O.C.										
	4100	1-1/4" diameter	1 Plum	60	.133	L.F.	2.56	4.35		6.91	9.60	
	4120	1-1/2" diameter		54	.148		3.20	4.83		8.03	11.05	
	4140	2" diameter	↓	44	.182		4.18	5.95		10.13	13.85	
	4160	3" diameter	Q-1	58	.276		7	8.10		15.10	20.50	
	4180	4" diameter		40	.400		12.30	11.75		24.05	32	
	4200	5" diameter	↓	36	.444		34.50	13.05		47.55	58.50	
	4220	6" diameter	Q-2	42	.571	↓	45.50	17.40		62.90	77	
	9000	Minimum labor/equipment charge	1 Plum	4	2	Job		65		65	102	
430	0010	**PIPE, COPPER, FITTINGS** Wrought unless otherwise noted										430
	0040	Solder joints, copper x copper										
	0070	90° elbow, 1/4"	1 Plum	22	.364	Ea.	1.09	11.85		12.94	19.75	
	0100	1/2"		20	.400		.38	13.05		13.43	21	
	0120	3/4"		19	.421		.82	13.75		14.57	22.50	
	0130	1"		16	.500		1.84	16.30		18.14	27.50	
	0250	45° elbow, 1/4"		22	.364		2.14	11.85		13.99	21	
	0270	3/8"		22	.364		1.74	11.85		13.59	20.50	
	0280	1/2"		20	.400		.68	13.05		13.73	21.50	
	0290	5/8"		19	.421		3.32	13.75		17.07	25	
	0300	3/4"		19	.421		1.15	13.75		14.90	23	
	0310	1"		16	.500		2.91	16.30		19.21	28.50	
	0320	1-1/4"		15	.533		3.96	17.40		21.36	31.50	
	0330	1-1/2"		13	.615		4.74	20		24.74	36.50	
	0340	2"	↓	11	.727		7.95	23.50		31.45	46	
	0350	2-1/2"	Q-1	13	1.231		16.95	36		52.95	75	
	0360	3"		13	1.231		25	36		61	84	
	0370	3-1/2"		10	1.600		42.50	47		89.50	121	
	0380	4"		9	1.778		49.50	52		101.50	136	
	0390	5"	↓	6	2.667		117	78.50		195.50	250	
	0400	6"	Q-2	9	2.667		187	81		268	335	
	0450	Tee, 1/4"	1 Plum	14	.571		1.83	18.65		20.48	31	
	0470	3/8"		14	.571		.62	18.65		19.27	29.50	
	0480	1/2"		13	.615		.62	20		20.62	32	
	0490	5/8"		12	.667		3.98	21.50		25.48	38.50	
	0500	3/4"		12	.667		1.52	21.50		23.02	35.50	
	0510	1"		10	.800		4.40	26		30.40	46	
	0520	1-1/4"		9	.889		7	29		36	53	
	0530	1-1/2"		8	1		9.70	32.50		42.20	61.50	
	0540	2"	↓	7	1.143		14.35	37.50		51.85	74.50	
	0550	2-1/2"	Q-1	8	2		30.50	58.50		89	126	
	0560	3"		7	2.286		46.50	67		113.50	157	
	0570	3-1/2"		6	2.667		120	78.50		198.50	254	
	0580	4"		5	3.200		95.50	94		189.50	252	
	0590	5"	↓	4	4		298	117		415	510	
	0600	6"	Q-2	6	4		410	122		532	640	
	0612	Tee, reducing on the outlet, 1/4"	1 Plum	15	.533		3.88	17.40		21.28	31.50	
	0613	3/8"	↓	15	.533	↓	3.56	17.40		20.96	31	

For expanded coverage of these items see *Means Mechanical or Plumbing Cost Data 1999*

151 | Pipe & Fittings

151 400 | Copper Pipe & Tubing

		CREW	DAILY OUTPUT	LABOR-HOURS	UNIT	1999 BARE COSTS				TOTAL INCL O&P
						MAT.	LABOR	EQUIP.	TOTAL	
0614	1/2"	1 Plum	14	.571	Ea.	2.96	18.65		21.61	32.50
0615	5/8"		13	.615		5.30	20		25.30	37.50
0616	3/4"		12	.667		1.38	21.50		22.88	35.50
0617	1"		11	.727		4.40	23.50		27.90	42
0618	1-1/4"		10	.800		6.80	26		32.80	48.50
0619	1-1/2"		9	.889		7.25	29		36.25	53.50
0620	2"	▼	8	1		18.30	32.50		50.80	71
0621	2-1/2"	Q-1	9	1.778		35	52		87	120
0622	3"		8	2		38.50	58.50		97	134
0623	4"		6	2.667		68	78.50		146.50	197
0624	5"	▼	5	3.200		315	94		409	490
0625	6"	Q-2	7	3.429		430	104		534	640
0626	8"	"	6	4		1,750	122		1,872	2,125
0630	Tee, reducing on the run, 1/4"	1 Plum	15	.533		4.57	17.40		21.97	32
0631	3/8"		15	.533		6.45	17.40		23.85	34
0632	1/2"		14	.571		4.15	18.65		22.80	33.50
0633	5/8"		13	.615		6.45	20		26.45	38.50
0634	3/4"		12	.667		3	21.50		24.50	37.50
0635	1"		11	.727		5.50	23.50		29	43
0636	1-1/4"		10	.800		8.75	26		34.75	50.50
0637	1-1/2"		9	.889		15.05	29		44.05	62
0638	2"	▼	8	1		19.25	32.50		51.75	72
0639	2-1/2"	Q-1	9	1.778		43.50	52		95.50	130
0640	3"		8	2		64.50	58.50		123	163
0641	4"		6	2.667		143	78.50		221.50	279
0642	5"	▼	5	3.200		315	94		409	490
0643	6"	Q-2	7	3.429		430	104		534	640
0644	8"	"	6	4		1,650	122		1,772	2,025
0650	Coupling, 1/4"	1 Plum	24	.333		.29	10.85		11.14	17.30
0670	3/8"		24	.333		.30	10.85		11.15	17.35
0680	1/2"		22	.364		.33	11.85		12.18	18.90
0690	5/8"		21	.381		1	12.40		13.40	20.50
0700	3/4"		21	.381		.73	12.40		13.13	20.50
0710	1"		18	.444		1.53	14.50		16.03	24
0715	1-1/4"		17	.471		1.96	15.35		17.31	26
0716	1-1/2"		15	.533		3.10	17.40		20.50	30.50
0718	2"	▼	13	.615		5.20	20		25.20	37.50
0721	2-1/2"	Q-1	15	1.067		9.15	31.50		40.65	59
0722	3"		13	1.231		14.05	36		50.05	72
0724	3-1/2"		8	2		25	58.50		83.50	120
0726	4"		7	2.286		25	67		92	133
0728	5"	▼	6	2.667		59.50	78.50		138	188
0731	6"	Q-2	8	3	▼	62.50	91.50		154	212
2000	DWW, solder joints, copper x copper									
2030	90° Elbow, 1-1/4"	1 Plum	13	.615	Ea.	3.52	20		23.52	35.50
2050	1-1/2"		12	.667		4.71	21.50		26.21	39
2070	2"	▼	10	.800		6.85	26		32.85	48.50
2090	3"	Q-1	10	1.600		16.55	47		63.55	91.50
2100	4"	"	9	1.778		77	52		129	167
2250	Tee, Sanitary, 1-1/4"	1 Plum	9	.889		6.75	29		35.75	53
2270	1-1/2"		8	1		8.60	32.50		41.10	60.50
2290	2"	▼	7	1.143		10.05	37.50		47.55	69.50
2310	3"	Q-1	7	2.286		36	67		103	145
2330	4"	"	6	2.667		90.50	78.50		169	222
2400	Coupling, 1-1/4"	1 Plum	14	.571		1.60	18.65		20.25	31
2420	1-1/2"	▼	13	.615	▼	2.05	20		22.05	34

151 | Pipe & Fittings

151 400 | Copper Pipe & Tubing

			CREW	DAILY OUTPUT	LABOR-HOURS	UNIT	1999 BARE COSTS MAT.	LABOR	EQUIP.	TOTAL	TOTAL INCL O&P	
430	2440	2"	1 Plum	11	.727	Ea.	2.82	23.50		26.32	40	430
	2460	3"	Q-1	11	1.455		4.89	42.50		47.39	72.50	
	2480	4"	"	10	1.600	↓	12.45	47		59.45	87	
	9000	Minimum labor/equipment charge	1 Plum	4	2	Job		65		65	102	

151 450 | Corrosion Resistant Pipe

			CREW	DAILY OUTPUT	LABOR-HOURS	UNIT	MAT.	LABOR	EQUIP.	TOTAL	TOTAL INCL O&P	
451	0010	**PIPE, CORROSION RESISTANT** No couplings or hangers										451
	0020	Iron alloy, drain, mechanical joint										
	1000	1-1/2" diameter	Q-1	70	.229	L.F.	22.50	6.70		29.20	35.50	
	1100	2" diameter		66	.242		26	7.10		33.10	39.50	
	1120	3" diameter		60	.267		36	7.85		43.85	52.50	
	1140	4" diameter	↓	52	.308	↓	46.50	9.05		55.55	65	
	2980	Plastic, epoxy, fiberglass filament wound										
	3000	2" diameter	Q-1	62	.258	L.F.	5.85	7.55		13.40	18.30	
	3100	3" diameter		51	.314		9.45	9.20		18.65	25	
	3120	4" diameter	↓	45	.356		11.25	10.45		21.70	29	
	3160	8" diameter	Q-2	38	.632		27	19.20		46.20	59.50	
	3200	12" diameter	"	28	.857	↓	46	26		72	91.50	
	9800	Minimum labor/equipment charge	1 Plum	4	2	Job		65		65	102	

454	0010	**PIPE, CORROSION RESISTANT, FITTINGS**										454
	0030	Iron alloy										
	0050	Mechanical joint										
	0060	1/4 Bend, 1-1/2"	Q-1	12	1.333	Ea.	28	39		67	92	
	0080	2"		10	1.600		36.50	47		83.50	114	
	0090	3"		9	1.778		51	52		103	138	
	0100	4"	↓	8	2	↓	70.50	58.50		129	170	
	0160	Tee and Y, sanitary, straight										
	0170	1-1/2"	Q-1	8	2	Ea.	46	58.50		104.50	143	
	0180	2"		7	2.286		53.50	67		120.50	164	
	0190	3"		6	2.667		66.50	78.50		145	195	
	0200	4"		5	3.200		140	94		234	300	
	0360	Coupling, 1-1/2"		14	1.143		26.50	33.50		60	81.50	
	0380	2"		12	1.333		30.50	39		69.50	94.50	
	0390	3"		11	1.455		32.50	42.50		75	103	
	0400	4"	↓	10	1.600	↓	36.50	47		83.50	114	
	3000	Epoxy, filament wound										
	3030	Quick-lock joint										
	3040	90° Elbow, 2"	Q-1	28	.571	Ea.	43	16.75		59.75	73.50	
	3060	3"		16	1		61	29.50		90.50	114	
	3070	4"		13	1.231		99	36		135	166	
	3190	Tee, 2"		19	.842		101	24.50		125.50	150	
	3200	3"		11	1.455		117	42.50		159.50	196	
	3210	4"	↓	9	1.778		144	52		196	240	
	9000	Minimum labor/equipment charge	1 Plum	4	2	Job		65		65	102	

151 500 | Glass Pipe

501	0010	**PIPE, GLASS** Borosilicate, couplings & hangers 10' O.C.										501
	0020	Drainage										
	1100	1-1/2" diameter	Q-1	52	.308	L.F.	7.90	9.05		16.95	23	
	1120	2" diameter		44	.364		10.45	10.65		21.10	28	
	1140	3" diameter		39	.410		13.90	12.05		25.95	34	
	1160	4" diameter		30	.533		25	15.65		40.65	52	
	1180	6" diameter	↓	26	.615	↓	45	18.05		63.05	78	
	9000	Minimum labor/equipment charge	1 Plum	4	2	Job		65		65	102	

For expanded coverage of these items see *Means Mechanical or Plumbing Cost Data 1999*

151 | Pipe & Fittings

151 500 | Glass Pipe

			CREW	DAILY OUTPUT	LABOR-HOURS	UNIT	1999 BARE COSTS MAT.	LABOR	EQUIP.	TOTAL	TOTAL INCL O&P	
512	0010	**PIPE, GLASS, FITTINGS**										512
	0020	Drainage, beaded ends										
	0040	Coupling & labor required at joints not incl. in fitting										
	0050	price. Add 1 per joint for installed price										
	0070	90° Bend or sweep, 1-1/2"				Ea.	16.25			16.25	17.85	
	0090	2"					20.50			20.50	22.50	
	0100	3"					34			34	37	
	0110	4"					54			54	59.50	
	0120	6" (sweep only)					164			164	181	
	0350	Tee, single sanitary, 1-1/2"					26			26	29	
	0370	2"					26			26	29	
	0380	3"					39			39	43	
	0390	4"					70			70	77	
	0400	6"					188			188	207	
	0500	Coupling, stainless steel, TFE seal ring										
	0520	1-1/2"	Q-1	32	.500	Ea.	11.20	14.70		25.90	35.50	
	0530	2"		30	.533		14.30	15.65		29.95	40.50	
	0540	3"		25	.640		19.30	18.80		38.10	50.50	
	0550	4"		23	.696		33	20.50		53.50	68.50	
	0560	6"		20	.800		74.50	23.50		98	119	
	9000	Minimum labor/equipment charge	1 Plum	4	2	Job		65		65	102	

151 550 | Plastic Pipe

			CREW	DAILY OUTPUT	LABOR-HOURS	UNIT	MAT.	LABOR	EQUIP.	TOTAL	TOTAL INCL O&P	
551	0010	**PIPE, PLASTIC**										551
	0020	Fiberglass reinforced, couplings 10' O.C., hangers 3 per 10'										
	0240	2" diameter	Q-1	58	.276	L.F.	9.55	8.10		17.65	23	
	0280	4" diameter		47	.340		16.40	10		26.40	33.50	
	0300	6" diameter		38	.421		24.50	12.35		36.85	46.50	
	1800	PVC, couplings 10' O.C., hangers 3 per 10'										
	1820	Schedule 40										
	1860	1/2" diameter	1 Plum	54	.148	L.F.	1.37	4.83		6.20	9.05	
	1870	3/4" diameter		51	.157		1.52	5.10		6.62	9.65	
	1880	1" diameter		46	.174		1.82	5.65		7.47	10.85	
	1890	1-1/4" diameter		42	.190		1.86	6.20		8.06	11.75	
	1900	1-1/2" diameter		36	.222		2.06	7.25		9.31	13.60	
	1910	2" diameter	Q-1	59	.271		2.29	7.95		10.24	14.95	
	1920	2-1/2" diameter		56	.286		2.99	8.40		11.39	16.40	
	1930	3" diameter		53	.302		3.51	8.85		12.36	17.70	
	1940	4" diameter		48	.333		4.92	9.80		14.72	20.50	
	1950	5" diameter		43	.372		6.90	10.90		17.80	24.50	
	1960	6" diameter		39	.410		7.75	12.05		19.80	27.50	
	4100	DWV type, schedule 40, couplings 10' O.C., hangers 3 per 10'										
	4120	ABS										
	4140	1-1/4" diameter	1 Plum	42	.190	L.F.	1.88	6.20		8.08	11.75	
	4150	1-1/2" diameter	"	36	.222		1.84	7.25		9.09	13.40	
	4160	2" diameter	Q-1	59	.271		1.96	7.95		9.91	14.60	
	4400	PVC										
	4410	1-1/4" diameter	1 Plum	42	.190	L.F.	1.88	6.20		8.08	11.75	
	4460	2" diameter	Q-1	59	.271		2.16	7.95		10.11	14.80	
	4470	3" diameter		53	.302		3.32	8.85		12.17	17.50	
	4480	4" diameter		48	.333		4.64	9.80		14.44	20.50	
	4490	6" diameter		39	.410		7.75	12.05		19.80	27.50	
	5360	CPVC, couplings 10' O.C., hangers 3 per 10'										
	5380	Schedule 40										
	5460	1/2" diameter	1 Plum	54	.148	L.F.	2.09	4.83		6.92	9.85	

151 | Pipe & Fittings

151 550 | Plastic Pipe

			CREW	DAILY OUTPUT	LABOR-HOURS	UNIT	MAT.	LABOR	EQUIP.	TOTAL	TOTAL INCL O&P	
551	5470	3/4" diameter	1 Plum	51	.157	L.F.	2.47	5.10		7.57	10.70	551
	5480	1" diameter		46	.174		3.18	5.65		8.83	12.35	
	5490	1-1/4" diameter		42	.190		3.76	6.20		9.96	13.85	
	5500	1-1/2" diameter	▼	36	.222		4.37	7.25		11.62	16.15	
	5510	2" diameter	Q-1	59	.271		5.20	7.95		13.15	18.15	
	5520	2-1/2" diameter		56	.286		8.15	8.40		16.55	22	
	5530	3" diameter	▼	53	.302	▼	9.75	8.85		18.60	24.50	
	5560											
	9900	Minimum labor/equipment charge	1 Plum	4	2	Job		65		65	102	
558	0010	**PIPE, PLASTIC, FITTINGS**										558
	2700	PVC (white), schedule 40, socket joints										
	2760	90° elbow, 1/2"	1 Plum	22	.364	Ea.	.23	11.85		12.08	18.80	
	2810	2"	Q-1	28	.571	"	1.34	16.75		18.09	27.50	
	4500	DWV, ABS, non pressure, socket joints										
	4540	1/4 Bend, 1-1/4"	1 Plum	17	.471	Ea.	2.60	15.35		17.95	27	
	4560	1-1/2"	"	16	.500		1.12	16.30		17.42	26.50	
	4570	2"	Q-1	28	.571	▼	1.60	16.75		18.35	28	
	4800	Tee, sanitary										
	4820	1-1/4"	1 Plum	11	.727	Ea.	3.28	23.50		26.78	40.50	
	4830	1-1/2"	"	10	.800		1.91	26		27.91	43	
	4840	2"	Q-1	17	.941	▼	2.87	27.50		30.37	46	
	5000	DWV, PVC, schedule 40, socket joints										
	5040	1/4 bend, 1-1/4"	1 Plum	17	.471	Ea.	1.92	15.35		17.27	26	
	5060	1-1/2"	"	16	.500		.80	16.30		17.10	26.50	
	5070	2"	Q-1	28	.571		1.01	16.75		17.76	27	
	5080	3"		17	.941		3.14	27.50		30.64	46.50	
	5090	4"		14	1.143		6.65	33.50		40.15	60	
	5100	6"	▼	8	2		37.50	58.50		96	133	
	5105	8"	Q-2	10	2.400		39	73		112	157	
	5110	1/4 bend, long sweep, 1-1/2"	1 Plum	16	.500		3.03	16.30		19.33	29	
	5112	2"	Q-1	28	.571		2.29	16.75		19.04	28.50	
	5114	3"		17	.941		6.50	27.50		34	50	
	5116	4"	▼	14	1.143		12.70	33.50		46.20	66.50	
	5215	8"	Q-2	10	2.400		41	73		114	159	
	5250	Tee, sanitary 1-1/4"	1 Plum	11	.727		2.42	23.50		25.92	39.50	
	5254	1-1/2"	"	10	.800		1.43	26		27.43	42.50	
	5255	2"	Q-1	17	.941		2.04	27.50		29.54	45	
	5256	3"		11	1.455		5.40	42.50		47.90	73	
	5257	4"		9	1.778		10.35	52		62.35	93	
	5259	6"	▼	5	3.200		40	94		134	191	
	5261	8"	Q-2	6	4		135	122		257	340	
	5264	2" x 1-1/2"	Q-1	17	.941		4.76	27.50		32.26	48.50	
	5266	3" x 1-1/2"		12	1.333		4.15	39		43.15	65.50	
	5268	4" x 3"		12	1.333		19.05	39		58.05	82	
	5271	6" x 4"	▼	8	2		55.50	58.50		114	153	
	5314	Combination Y & 1/8 bend, 1-1/2"	1 Plum	10	.800		3.42	26		29.42	45	
	5315	2"	Q-1	17	.941		5.90	27.50		33.40	49.50	
	5317	3"		11	1.455		9.75	42.50		52.25	77.50	
	5318	4"	▼	9	1.778	▼	19.10	52		71.10	103	
	5324	Combination Y & 1/8 bend, reducing										
	5325	2" x 2" x 1-1/2"	Q-1	17	.941	Ea.	6.55	27.50		34.05	50	
	5327	3" x 3" x 1-1/2"		13	1.231		19.10	36		55.10	77.50	
	5328	3" x 3" x 2"		12	1.333		20	39		59	83	
	5329	4" x 4" x 2"	▼	11	1.455		58	42.50		100.50	131	
	5331	Wye, 1-1/4"	1 Plum	11	.727	▼	2.21	23.50		25.71	39.50	

For expanded coverage of these items see Means Mechanical or Plumbing Cost Data 1999

151 | Pipe & Fittings

151 550 | Plastic Pipe

		CREW	DAILY OUTPUT	LABOR-HOURS	UNIT	1999 BARE COSTS MAT.	LABOR	EQUIP.	TOTAL	TOTAL INCL O&P
5332	1-1/2"	1 Plum	10	.800	Ea.	2.81	26		28.81	44
5333	2"	Q-1	17	.941		2.72	27.50		30.22	46
5334	3"		11	1.455		6.15	42.50		48.65	74
5335	4"		9	1.778		12.05	52		64.05	95
5336	6"		5	3.200		33	94		127	184
5337	8"	Q-2	5	4.800		59.50	146		205.50	295
5341	2" x 1-1/2"	Q-1	17	.941		5.05	27.50		32.55	48.50
5342	3" x 1-1/2"		12	1.333		6.65	39		45.65	68.50
5343	4" x 3"		10	1.600		11.30	47		58.30	86
5344	6" x 4"		6	2.667		44.50	78.50		123	171
5345	8" x 6"	Q-2	8	3		123	91.50		214.50	279
5347	Double wye, 1-1/2"	1 Plum	8	1		6.05	32.50		38.55	57.50
5348	2"	Q-1	12	1.333		7.80	39		46.80	69.50
5349	3"		8	2		20	58.50		78.50	114
5350	4"		6	2.667		41	78.50		119.50	167
5354	2" x 1-1/2"		11	1.455		7.10	42.50		49.60	75
5355	3" x 2"		8	2		15	58.50		73.50	109
5356	4" x 3"		7	2.286		32.50	67		99.50	141
5357	6" x 4"		5	3.200		67.50	94		161.50	221
5410	Reducer bushing, 2" x 1-1/4"		31	.516		.66	15.15		15.81	24
5412	3" x 1-1/2"		25	.640		4.75	18.80		23.55	34.50
5414	4" x 2"		22	.727		8.30	21.50		29.80	42.50
5416	6" x 4"		14	1.143		24	33.50		57.50	78.50
5418	8" x 6"	Q-2	18	1.333		66.50	40.50		107	137
5500	CPVC, Schedule 80, threaded joints									
5540	90° Elbow, 1/4"	1 Plum	20	.400	Ea.	5.35	13.05		18.40	26.50
5560	1/2"		18	.444		2.09	14.50		16.59	25
5570	3/4"		17	.471		2.67	15.35		18.02	27
5580	1"		15	.533		4.24	17.40		21.64	31.50
5590	1-1/4"		14	.571		9.20	18.65		27.85	39
5600	1-1/2"		13	.615		10.25	20		30.25	43
5610	2"	Q-1	22	.727		12.40	21.50		33.90	47
5620	2-1/2"		18	.889		28.50	26		54.50	72.50
5630	3"		14	1.143		32	33.50		65.50	88
6000	Coupling, 1/4"	1 Plum	20	.400		5.70	13.05		18.75	27
6020	1/2"		18	.444		2.21	14.50		16.71	25
6030	3/4"		17	.471		3.09	15.35		18.44	27.50
6040	1"		15	.533		4.16	17.40		21.56	31.50
6050	1-1/4"		14	.571		6.25	18.65		24.90	36
6060	1-1/2"		13	.615		7.85	20		27.85	40
6070	2"	Q-1	22	.727		9.15	21.50		30.65	43.50
6080	2-1/2"		20	.800		20.50	23.50		44	59
6090	3"		19	.842		22	24.50		46.50	63
9900	Minimum labor/equipment charge	1 Plum	4	2	Job		65		65	102

151 700 | Steel Pipe

0010	**PIPE, STEEL** R151-050									
0020	All pipe sizes are to Spec. A-53 unless noted otherwise									
0050	Schedule 40, threaded, with couplings, and clevis type									
0060	hangers sized for covering, 10' O.C.									
0540	Black, 1/4" diameter	1 Plum	66	.121	L.F.	1.20	3.95		5.15	7.50
0560	1/2" diameter		63	.127		1.15	4.14		5.29	7.75
0570	3/4" diameter		61	.131		1.29	4.28		5.57	8.10
0580	1" diameter		53	.151		1.64	4.92		6.56	9.50
0590	1-1/4" diameter	Q-1	89	.180		1.98	5.30		7.28	10.45
0600	1-1/2" diameter		80	.200		2.26	5.85		8.11	11.70

151 | Pipe & Fittings

151 700 | Steel Pipe

			CREW	DAILY OUTPUT	LABOR-HOURS	UNIT	1999 BARE COSTS MAT.	LABOR	EQUIP.	TOTAL	TOTAL INCL O&P	
701	0610	2" diameter	Q-1	64	.250	L.F.	3.06	7.35		10.41	14.85	701
	0620	2-1/2" diameter		50	.320		4.81	9.40		14.21	20	
	0630	3" diameter		43	.372		6.05	10.90		16.95	24	
	0640	3-1/2" diameter		40	.400		7.90	11.75		19.65	27	
	0650	4" diameter		36	.444		8.75	13.05		21.80	30	
	0670	6" diameter	Q-2	31	.774		22	23.50		45.50	61	
	0680	8" diameter	"	27	.889		31	27		58	76.50	
	1290	Galvanized, 1/4" diameter	1 Plum	66	.121		1.46	3.95		5.41	7.80	
	1310	1/2" diameter		63	.127		1.34	4.14		5.48	7.95	
	1320	3/4" diameter		61	.131		1.53	4.28		5.81	8.40	
	1330	1" diameter		53	.151		1.79	4.92		6.71	9.65	
	1350	1-1/2" diameter	Q-1	80	.200		2.79	5.85		8.64	12.25	
	1360	2" diameter		64	.250		3.36	7.35		10.71	15.20	
	1370	2-1/2" diameter		50	.320		5.35	9.40		14.75	20.50	
	1380	3" diameter		43	.372		6.70	10.90		17.60	24.50	
	1400	4" diameter		36	.444		9.70	13.05		22.75	31	
	1420	6" diameter	Q-2	31	.774		22	23.50		45.50	61	
	1430	8" diameter	"	27	.889		31.50	27		58.50	77	
	2000	Welded, sch. 40, on yoke & roll hangers, sized for covering,										
	2040	Black, 1" diameter	Q-15	93	.172	L.F.	2.12	5.05	.54	7.71	10.80	
	2070	2" diameter		61	.262		3	7.70	.82	11.52	16.25	
	2090	3" diameter		43	.372		4.84	10.90	1.16	16.90	23.50	
	2110	4" diameter		37	.432		6.65	12.70	1.34	20.69	28.50	
	2120	5" diameter		32	.500		10.30	14.70	1.55	26.55	36	
	2130	6" diameter	Q-16	36	.667		16.20	20.50	1.38	38.08	51.50	
	9990	Minimum labor/equipment charge	1 Plum	3	2.667	Job		87		87	136	
716	0010	**PIPE, STEEL, FITTINGS** Threaded										716
	0020	Cast Iron										
	0040	Standard weight, black										
	0060	90° Elbow, straight										
	0070	1/4"	1 Plum	16	.500	Ea.	2.71	16.30		19.01	28.50	
	0080	3/8"		16	.500		3.80	16.30		20.10	29.50	
	0090	1/2"		15	.533		1.73	17.40		19.13	29	
	0100	3/4"		14	.571		1.82	18.65		20.47	31	
	0110	1"		13	.615		2.24	20		22.24	34	
	0130	1-1/2"	Q-1	20	.800		4.37	23.50		27.87	41.50	
	0140	2"		18	.889		6.80	26		32.80	48.50	
	0150	2-1/2"		14	1.143		15.70	33.50		49.20	70	
	0160	3"		10	1.600		25.50	47		72.50	102	
	0180	4"		6	2.667		46	78.50		124.50	173	
	0200	6"	Q-2	7	3.429		115	104		219	289	
	0210	8"	"	6	4		238	122		360	450	
	0500	Tee, straight										
	0510	1/4"	1 Plum	10	.800	Ea.	3.71	26		29.71	45	
	0520	3/8"		10	.800		4	26		30	45.50	
	0540	3/4"		9	.889		3.17	29		32.17	49	
	0550	1"		8	1		2.90	32.50		35.40	54	
	0570	1-1/2"	Q-1	13	1.231		6.95	36		42.95	64	
	0580	2"		11	1.455		9.55	42.50		52.05	77.50	
	0590	2-1/2"		9	1.778		24	52		76	108	
	0600	3"		6	2.667		37	78.50		115.50	163	
	0620	4"		4	4		71	117		188	262	
	0640	6"	Q-2	4	6		160	183		343	460	
	0650	8"	"	3	8		390	243		633	805	
	0700	Standard weight, galvanized cast iron										
	0720	90° Elbow, straight										

For expanded coverage of these items see Means Mechanical or Plumbing Cost Data 1999

151 | Pipe & Fittings

151 700 | Steel Pipe

			CREW	DAILY OUTPUT	LABOR-HOURS	UNIT	1999 BARE COSTS MAT.	LABOR	EQUIP.	TOTAL	TOTAL INCL O&P	
716	0730	1/4"	1 Plum	16	.500	Ea.	5.30	16.30		21.60	31.50	716
	0740	3/8"		16	.500		5.30	16.30		21.60	31.50	
	0750	1/2"		15	.533		5.40	17.40		22.80	33	
	0760	3/4"		14	.571		5.90	18.65		24.55	35.50	
	0770	1"		13	.615		6.80	20		26.80	39	
	0790	1-1/2"	Q-1	20	.800		14.60	23.50		38.10	52.50	
	0800	2"		18	.889		21.50	26		47.50	65	
	0810	2-1/2"		14	1.143		44	33.50		77.50	101	
	0820	3"		10	1.600		67.50	47		114.50	148	
	0840	4"		6	2.667		123	78.50		201.50	258	
	0860	6"	Q-2	7	3.429		365	104		469	565	
	0870	8"	"	6	4		745	122		867	1,000	
	1100	Tee, straight										
	1110	1/4"	1 Plum	10	.800	Ea.	6.75	26		32.75	48.50	
	1120	3/8"		10	.800		6.75	26		32.75	48.50	
	1140	3/4"		9	.889		8.70	29		37.70	55	
	1150	1"		8	1		9.25	32.50		41.75	61	
	1170	1-1/2"	Q-1	13	1.231		21.50	36		57.50	80	
	1180	2"		11	1.455		26.50	42.50		69	96.50	
	1190	2-1/2"		9	1.778		56.50	52		108.50	144	
	1200	3"		6	2.667		148	78.50		226.50	285	
	1220	4"		4	4		171	117		288	370	
	1240	6"	Q-2	4	6		380	183		563	700	
	1250	8"	"	3	8		755	243		998	1,200	
	5000	Malleable iron, 150 lb.										
	5020	Black										
	5040	90° elbow, straight										
	5060	1/4"	1 Plum	16	.500	Ea.	1.46	16.30		17.76	27	
	5070	3/8"		16	.500		1.46	16.30		17.76	27	
	5090	3/4"		14	.571		1.23	18.65		19.88	30.50	
	5100	1"		13	.615		2.14	20		22.14	34	
	5120	1-1/2"	Q-1	20	.800		4.62	23.50		28.12	41.50	
	5130	2"		18	.889		7.95	26		33.95	50	
	5140	2-1/2"		14	1.143		17.40	33.50		50.90	71.50	
	5150	3"		10	1.600		26	47		73	102	
	5170	4"		6	2.667		56	78.50		134.50	184	
	5190	6"	Q-2	7	3.429		168	104		272	350	
	5450	Tee, straight										
	5470	1/4"	1 Plum	10	.800	Ea.	2.09	26		28.09	43.50	
	5480	3/8"		10	.800		2.09	26		28.09	43.50	
	5500	3/4"		9	.889		1.96	29		30.96	47.50	
	5510	1"		8	1		3.33	32.50		35.83	54.50	
	5520	1-1/4"	Q-1	14	1.143		5.40	33.50		38.90	58.50	
	5530	1-1/2"		13	1.231		6.75	36		42.75	64	
	5540	2"		11	1.455		11.45	42.50		53.95	79.50	
	5550	2-1/2"		9	1.778		24	52		76	108	
	5560	3"		6	2.667		35.50	78.50		114	161	
	5570	3-1/2"		5	3.200		86	94		180	242	
	5580	4"		4	4		86	117		203	279	
	5600	6"	Q-2	4	6		249	183		432	560	
	5650	Coupling										
	5670	1/4"	1 Plum	19	.421	Ea.	1.78	13.75		15.53	23.50	
	5680	3/8"		19	.421		1.78	13.75		15.53	23.50	
	5690	1/2"		19	.421		1.38	13.75		15.13	23	
	5700	3/4"		18	.444		1.61	14.50		16.11	24.50	
	5710	1"		15	.533		2.46	17.40		19.86	29.50	

151 | Pipe & Fittings

151 700 | Steel Pipe

			CREW	DAILY OUTPUT	LABOR-HOURS	UNIT	MAT.	LABOR	EQUIP.	TOTAL	TOTAL INCL O&P	
716	5730	1-1/2"	Q-1	24	.667	Ea.	4.23	19.55		23.78	35	716
	5740	2"		21	.762		6.25	22.50		28.75	42	
	5750	2-1/2"		18	.889		17.30	26		43.30	60	
	5760	3"		14	1.143		23.50	33.50		57	78	
	5780	4"		10	1.600		47	47		94	126	
	5800	6"	Q-2	8	3		114	91.50		205.50	268	
	6000	For galvanized elbows, tees, and couplings add					20%					
	9000	Minimum labor/equipment charge	1 Plum	4	2	Job		65		65	102	
720	0010	**PIPE, STEEL, FITTINGS** Flanged, welded and special type										720
	3000	Weld joint, butt, carbon steel, standard weight										
	3040	90° elbow, long radius										
	3050	1/2" pipe size	Q-15	16	1	Ea.	11.85	29.50	3.11	44.46	62.50	
	3060	3/4" pipe size		16	1		11.85	29.50	3.11	44.46	62.50	
	3070	1" pipe size		16	1		6.40	29.50	3.11	39.01	56.50	
	3100	2" pipe size		10	1.600		6.40	47	4.98	58.38	86	
	3120	3" pipe size		7	2.286		9.90	67	7.10	84	124	
	3130	4" pipe size		5	3.200		16.95	94	9.95	120.90	177	
	3136	5" pipe size		4	4		35.50	117	12.45	164.95	237	
	3140	6" pipe size	Q-16	5	4.800		40.50	146	9.95	196.45	284	
	3350	Tee, straight										
	3360	1/2" pipe size	Q-15	10	1.600	Ea.	30.50	47	4.98	82.48	112	
	3370	3/4" pipe size		10	1.600		16.95	47	4.98	68.93	97.50	
	3380	1" pipe size		10	1.600		16.95	47	4.98	68.93	97.50	
	3410	2" pipe size		6	2.667		16.95	78.50	8.30	103.75	150	
	3430	3" pipe size		4	4		23.50	117	12.45	152.95	224	
	3440	4" pipe size		3	5.333		33.50	157	16.60	207.10	300	
	3446	5" pipe size		2.50	6.400		61	188	19.90	268.90	385	
	3450	6" pipe size	Q-16	3	8		61	243	16.55	320.55	465	
	9990	Minimum labor/equipment charge	Q-15	3	5.333	Job		157	16.60	173.60	263	

151 800 | Grooved-Joint Pipe

			CREW	DAILY OUTPUT	LABOR-HOURS	UNIT	MAT.	LABOR	EQUIP.	TOTAL	TOTAL INCL O&P	
801	0010	**PIPE, GROOVED-JOINT STEEL FITTINGS & VALVES**										801
	0020	Pipe includes coupling & clevis type hanger 10' O.C.										
	1000	Schedule 40, black										
	1040	3/4" diameter	1 Plum	71	.113	L.F.	1.76	3.67		5.43	7.70	
	1050	1" diameter		63	.127		1.89	4.14		6.03	8.60	
	1060	1-1/4" diameter		58	.138		2.35	4.50		6.85	9.65	
	1070	1-1/2" diameter		51	.157		2.67	5.10		7.77	10.95	
	1080	2" diameter		40	.200		3.16	6.50		9.66	13.70	
	1090	2-1/2" diameter	Q-1	57	.281		4.43	8.25		12.68	17.80	
	1100	3" diameter		50	.320		5.45	9.40		14.85	20.50	
	1110	4" diameter		45	.356		7.75	10.45		18.20	25	
	1120	5" diameter		37	.432		12	12.70		24.70	33	
	4000	Elbow, 90° or 45°, painted										
	4030	3/4" diameter	1 Plum	50	.160	Ea.	11.45	5.20		16.65	21	
	4040	1" diameter		50	.160		11.45	5.20		16.65	21	
	4050	1-1/4" diameter		40	.200		11.45	6.50		17.95	23	
	4060	1-1/2" diameter		33	.242		11.45	7.90		19.35	25	
	4070	2" diameter		25	.320		11.45	10.45		21.90	29	
	4080	2-1/2" diameter	Q-1	40	.400		11.45	11.75		23.20	31	
	4100	4" diameter		25	.640		22	18.80		40.80	54	
	4110	5" diameter		20	.800		53.50	23.50		77	95.50	
	4250	For galvanized elbows, add					26%					
	4690	Tee, painted										
	4700	3/4" diameter	1 Plum	38	.211	Ea.	17.70	6.85		24.55	30	

For expanded coverage of these items see *Means Mechanical or Plumbing Cost Data 1999*

151 | Pipe & Fittings

151 800 | Grooved-Joint Pipe

		CREW	DAILY OUTPUT	LABOR-HOURS	UNIT	MAT.	LABOR	EQUIP.	TOTAL	TOTAL INCL O&P	
801	4740	1" diameter	1 Plum	33	.242	Ea.	17.70	7.90		25.60	32	801
	4750	1-1/4" diameter		27	.296		17.70	9.65		27.35	34.50	
	4760	1-1/2" diameter		22	.364		17.70	11.85		29.55	38	
	4770	2" diameter		17	.471		17.70	15.35		33.05	43.50	
	4780	2-1/2" diameter	Q-1	27	.593		17.70	17.40		35.10	46.50	
	4800	4" diameter		17	.941		38	27.50		65.50	84.50	
	4810	5" diameter		13	1.231		89	36		125	154	
	4900	For galvanized tees, add					24%					
	9990	Minimum labor/equipment charge	1 Plum	4	2	Job		65		65	102	

151 950 | Valves

			CREW	DAILY OUTPUT	LABOR-HOURS	UNIT	MAT.	LABOR	EQUIP.	TOTAL	TOTAL INCL O&P	
955	0010	**VALVES, BRONZE**										955
	1020	Angle, 150 lb., rising stem, threaded										
	1070	3/4" size	1 Plum	20	.400	Ea.	46	13.05		59.05	71	
	1080	1" size		19	.421		66.50	13.75		80.25	94.50	
	1100	1-1/2" size		13	.615		115	20		135	158	
	1110	2" size		11	.727		180	23.50		203.50	235	
	1380	Ball, 150 psi, threaded										
	1460	3/4" size	1 Plum	20	.400	Ea.	10.55	13.05		23.60	32	
	1750	Check, swing, class 150, regrinding disc, threaded										
	1850	1/2" size	1 Plum	24	.333	Ea.	25	10.85		35.85	44.50	
	1860	3/4" size		20	.400		36	13.05		49.05	60	
	1870	1" size		19	.421		53	13.75		66.75	80	
	1890	1-1/2" size		13	.615		88	20		108	128	
	1900	2" size		11	.727		129	23.50		152.50	179	
	2850	Gate, N.R.S., soldered, 125 psi										
	2920	1/2" size	1 Plum	24	.333	Ea.	13.30	10.85		24.15	31.50	
	2940	3/4" size		20	.400		15.10	13.05		28.15	37	
	2950	1" size		19	.421		21.50	13.75		35.25	45.50	
	2970	1-1/2" size		13	.615		36.50	20		56.50	72	
	2980	2" size		11	.727		52	23.50		75.50	94	
	4850	Globe, class 150, rising stem, threaded										
	4950	1/2" size	1 Plum	24	.333	Ea.	21.50	10.85		32.35	41	
	4960	3/4" size	"	20	.400	"	29.50	13.05		42.55	53	
	5030											
	5600	Relief, pressure & temperature, self-closing, ASME, threaded										
	5640	3/4" size	1 Plum	28	.286	Ea.	61.50	9.30		70.80	82	
	5650	1" size		24	.333		93.50	10.85		104.35	120	
	5660	1-1/4" size		20	.400		178	13.05		191.05	217	
	5670	1-1/2" size		18	.444		340	14.50		354.50	400	
	5680	2" size		16	.500		370	16.30		386.30	435	
	6400	Pressure, water, ASME, threaded										
	6440	3/4" size	1 Plum	28	.286	Ea.	39.50	9.30		48.80	58	
	6450	1" size		24	.333		76.50	10.85		87.35	101	
	6470	1-1/2" size		18	.444		173	14.50		187.50	213	
	6900	Reducing, water pressure										
	6940	1/2" size	1 Plum	24	.333	Ea.	100	10.85		110.85	127	
	6960	1" size	"	19	.421	"	155	13.75		168.75	192	
	8350	Tempering, water, sweat connections										
	8400	1/2" size	1 Plum	24	.333	Ea.	37	10.85		47.85	58	
	8440	3/4" size	"	20	.400	"	45.50	13.05		58.55	70.50	
	8650	Threaded connections										
	8700	1/2" size	1 Plum	24	.333	Ea.	45.50	10.85		56.35	67	
	8740	3/4" size		20	.400	"	177	13.05		190.05	215	
	9000	Minimum labor/equipment charge		4	2	Job		65		65	102	

15 MECHANICAL

Important: See the Reference Section for critical supporting data - Reference Nos., Crews, & City Cost Indexes

151 | Pipe & Fittings

151 950 | Valves

		CREW	DAILY OUTPUT	LABOR-HOURS	UNIT	MAT.	LABOR	EQUIP.	TOTAL	TOTAL INCL O&P
0010	**VALVES, IRON BODY**									
1020	Butterfly, wafer type, gear actuator, 200 lb.									
1030	2" size	1 Plum	14	.571	Ea.	109	18.65		127.65	148
1060	4" size	Q-1	5	3.200	"	145	94		239	305
1650	Gate, 125 lb., N.R.S.									
2150	Flanged									
2240	2-1/2" size	Q-1	5	3.200	Ea.	256	94		350	430
2260	3" size		4.50	3.556		287	104		391	480
2280	4" size	↓	3	5.333	↓	410	157		567	700
3550	OS&Y, 125 lb., flanged									
3680	4" size	Q-1	3	5.333	Ea.	222	157		379	490
3690	5" size	Q-2	3.40	7.059		490	215		705	875
3700	6" size	"	3	8	↓	490	243		733	920
9000	Minimum labor/equipment charge	1 Plum	3	2.667	Job		87		87	136
0010	**VALVES, PLASTIC**									
0020										
1150	Ball, PVC, socket or threaded, single union									
1280	2" size	1 Plum	17	.471	Ea.	67.50	15.35		82.85	98.50
1650	CPVC, socket or threaded, single union									
1770	2" size	1 Plum	17	.471	Ea.	118	15.35		133.35	154
3150	Ball check, PVC, socket or threaded									
3290	2" size	1 Plum	17	.471	Ea.	79	15.35		94.35	111
9000	Minimum labor/equipment charge	"	3.50	2.286	Job		74.50		74.50	117

152 | Plumbing Fixtures

152 100 | Fixtures

		CREW	DAILY OUTPUT	LABOR-HOURS	UNIT	MAT.	LABOR	EQUIP.	TOTAL	TOTAL INCL O&P
0010	**BATHS**									
0100	Tubs, recessed porcelain enamel on cast iron, with trim	R151 -420								
0180	48" x 42"	Q-1	4	4	Ea.	1,050	117		1,167	1,325
0220	72" x 36"		3	5.333		1,100	157		1,257	1,475
0300	Mat bottom, 4' long		5.50	2.909		860	85.50		945.50	1,075
0380	5' long		4.40	3.636		340	107		447	540
0560	Corner 48" x 44"		4.40	3.636		1,200	107		1,307	1,475
2000	Enameled formed steel, 4'-6" long		5.80	2.759		245	81		326	395
2200	5' long	↓	5.50	2.909	↓	229	85.50		314.50	385
4600	Module tub & showerwall surround, molded fiberglass									
4610	5' long x 34" wide x 76" high	Q-1	4	4	Ea.	605	117		722	850
4750	Handicap with 1-1/2" OD grab bar, antiskid bottom									
4760	60" x 32-3/4" x 72" high	Q-1	4	4	Ea.	600	117		717	845
4770	60" x 30" x 71" high with molded seat	"	3.50	4.571	"	755	134		889	1,050
6000	Whirlpool, bath with vented overflow, molded fiberglass									
6100	66" x 48" x 24"	Q-1	1	16	Ea.	1,950	470		2,420	2,875
6400	72" x 36" x 24"		1	16		1,925	470		2,395	2,825
6500	60" x 30" x 21"		1	16		1,675	470		2,145	2,575
6600	72" x 42" x 22"		1	16		2,700	470		3,170	3,700
6700	83" x 65"	↓	.30	53.333		3,700	1,575		5,275	6,525
6710	For color add					10%				
6711	For designer colors and trim add					25%				

For expanded coverage of these items see *Means Mechanical or Plumbing Cost Data 1999*

152 | Plumbing Fixtures

152 100 | Fixtures

			CREW	DAILY OUTPUT	LABOR-HOURS	UNIT	1999 BARE COSTS MAT.	LABOR	EQUIP.	TOTAL	TOTAL INCL O&P
104	7000	Redwood hot tub system	Q-1 R151-420								
	7050	4' diameter x 4' deep	Q-1	1	16	Ea.	925	470		1,395	1,750
	7150	6' diameter x 4' deep		.80	20		1,525	585		2,110	2,600
	7200	8' diameter x 4' deep		.80	20		2,125	585		2,710	3,275
	9000	Minimum labor/equipment charge		3	5.333	Job		157		157	245
	9600	Rough-in, supply, waste and vent, for all above tubs, add		2.07	7.729	Ea.	129	227		356	495
116	0010	**DRINKING FOUNTAIN** For connection to cold water supply									
	1000	Wall mounted, non-recessed									
	2700	Stainless steel, single bubbler, no back	1 Plum	4	2	Ea.	630	65		695	790
	2740	With back		4	2		670	65		735	840
	2780	Dual handle & wheelchair projection type		4	2		465	65		530	610
	2820	Dual level for handicapped type		3.20	2.500		930	81.50		1,011.50	1,150
	3980	For rough-in, supply and waste, add		2.21	3.620		53.50	118		171.50	244
	4000	Wall mounted, semi-recessed									
	4200	Poly-marble, single bubbler	1 Plum	4	2	Ea.	595	65		660	755
	4600	Stainless steel, satin finish, single bubbler	"	4	2	"	430	65		495	570
	6000	Wall mounted, fully recessed									
	6400	Poly-marble, single bubbler	1 Plum	4	2	Ea.	680	65		745	845
	6800	Stainless steel, single bubbler		4	2		550	65		615	705
	7580	For rough-in, supply and waste, add		1.83	4.372		53.50	143		196.50	282
	7590										
	7600	Floor mounted, pedestal type									
	8600	Enameled iron, heavy duty service, 2 bubblers	1 Plum	2	4	Ea.	980	130		1,110	1,275
	8880	For freeze-proof valve system, add		2	4		300	130		430	535
	8900	For rough-in, supply and waste, add		1.83	4.372		53.50	143		196.50	282
	9000	Minimum labor/equipment charge		2	4	Job		130		130	204
124	0010	**INDUSTRIAL SAFETY FIXTURES** Rough-in not included									
	0020										
	1000	Eye wash fountain									
	1400	Plastic bowl, pedestal mounted	Q-1	4	4	Ea.	170	117		287	370
	5000	Shower, single head, drench, ball valve, pull, freestanding		4	4		236	117		353	445
	5200	Horizontal or vertical supply		4	4		221	117		338	425
	6000	Multi-nozzle, eye/face wash combination		4	4		480	117		597	715
	6400	Multi-nozzle, 12 spray, shower only		4	4		1,025	117		1,142	1,300
	6600	For freeze-proof, add		6	2.667		415	78.50		493.50	575
	9000	Minimum labor/equipment charge		3	5.333	Job		157		157	245
128	0010	**INTERCEPTORS**									
	0150	Grease, cast iron, 4 GPM, 8 lb. fat capacity	1 Plum	4	2	Ea.	355	65		420	490
	0200	7 GPM, 14 lb. fat capacity		4	2		490	65		555	640
	1000	10 GPM, 20 lb. fat capacity		4	2		575	65		640	735
	1160	100 GPM, 200 lb. fat capacity	Q-1	2	8		4,125	235		4,360	4,900
	1240	300 GPM, 600 lb. fat capacity	"	1	16		9,125	470		9,595	10,700
	9000	Minimum labor/equipment charge	1 Plum	3	2.667	Job		87		87	136
136	0010	**LAVATORIES** With trim, white unless noted otherwise	R151-420								
	0020										
	0500	Vanity top, porcelain enamel on cast iron									
	0600	20" x 18"	Q-1	6.40	2.500	Ea.	160	73.50		233.50	291
	0640	33" x 19" oval	"	6.40	2.500	"	320	73.50		393.50	470
	0860	For color, add					25%				
	1000	Cultured marble, 19" x 17", single bowl	Q-1	6.40	2.500	Ea.	98.50	73.50		172	223
	1120	25" x 22", single bowl		6.40	2.500		135	73.50		208.50	263
	1900	Stainless steel, self-rimming, 25" x 22", single bowl, ledge		6.40	2.500		149	73.50		222.50	279
	1960	17" x 22", single bowl		6.40	2.500		145	73.50		218.50	274
	2600	Steel, enameled, 20" x 17", single bowl		5.80	2.759		83	81		164	219
	2900	Vitreous china, 20" x 16", single bowl		5.40	2.963		163	87		250	315

Important: See the Reference Section for critical supporting data - Reference Nos., Crews, & City Cost Indexes

152 | Plumbing Fixtures

152 100 | Fixtures

			CREW	DAILY OUTPUT	LABOR-HOURS	UNIT	MAT.	LABOR	EQUIP.	TOTAL	TOTAL INCL O&P	
136	2960	20" x 17", single bowl	Q-1	5.40	2.963	Ea.	157	87		244	310	136
	3580	Rough-in, supply, waste and vent for all above lavatories	R151 -420	2.30	6.957		74	204		278	400	
	4000	Wall hung										
	4040	Porcelain enamel on cast iron, 16" x 14", single bowl	Q-1	8	2	Ea.	330	58.50		388.50	450	
	4180	20" x 18", single bowl	"	8	2	"	185	58.50		243.50	295	
	4580	For color, add					30%					
	6000	Vitreous china, 18" x 15", single bowl with backsplash	Q-1	7	2.286	Ea.	178	67		245	300	
	6960	Rough-in, supply, waste and vent for above lavatories	"	1.66	9.639	"	162	283		445	625	
	9000	Minimum labor/equipment charge	1 Plum	3	2.667	Job		87		87	136	
140	0010	**LAUNDRY SINKS** With trim										140
	0020	Porcelain enamel on cast iron, black iron frame										
	0050	24" x 20", single compartment	Q-1	6	2.667	Ea.	335	78.50		413.50	490	
	0100	24" x 23", single compartment	"	6	2.667	"	365	78.50		443.50	520	
	2000	Molded stone, on wall hanger or legs										
	2020	22" x 23", single compartment	Q-1	6	2.667	Ea.	115	78.50		193.50	248	
	2100	45" x 21", double compartment	"	5	3.200	"	206	94		300	375	
	3000	Plastic, on wall hanger or legs										
	3020	18" x 23", single compartment	Q-1	6.50	2.462	Ea.	80	72.50		152.50	201	
	3100	20" x 24", single compartment		6.50	2.462		106	72.50		178.50	230	
	3200	36" x 23", double compartment		5.50	2.909		124	85.50		209.50	271	
	3300	40" x 24", double compartment		5.50	2.909		184	85.50		269.50	335	
	5000	Stainless steel, counter top, 22" x 17" single compartment		6	2.667		242	78.50		320.50	390	
	5100	22" x 22", single compartment		6	2.667		305	78.50		383.50	455	
	5200	33" x 22", double compartment		5	3.200		281	94		375	455	
	9600	Rough-in, supply, waste and vent, for all laundry sinks		2.14	7.477		85	219		304	440	
	9810	Minimum labor/equipment charge	1 Plum	3	2.667	Job		87		87	136	
148	0011	**SHOWERS**, Stall, with door and trim										148
	0020											
	1520	32" square	Q-1	2	8	Ea.	350	235		585	750	
	1530	36" square		2	8		400	235		635	805	
	1540	Terrazzo receptor, 32" square		2	8		745	235		980	1,175	
	1580	36" corner angle		1.80	8.889		730	261		991	1,225	
	3000	Fiberglass, one piece, with 3 walls, 32" x 32" square		2.40	6.667		297	196		493	630	
	3100	36" x 36" square		2.40	6.667		340	196		536	680	
	4200	Rough-in, supply, waste and vent for above showers		2.05	7.805		80.50	229		309.50	450	
	5500	Head, water economizer, 3.0 GPM	1 Plum	24	.333		57.50	10.85		68.35	80	
	9000	Minimum labor/equipment charge	Q-1	4	4	Job		117		117	184	
152	0010	**SINKS** With faucets and drain										152
	2000	Kitchen, counter top style, P.E. on C.I., 24" x 21" single bowl	Q-1	5.60	2.857	Ea.	195	84		279	345	
	2100	30" x 21" single bowl		5.60	2.857		360	84		444	525	
	2200	32" x 21" double bowl		4.80	3.333		283	98		381	465	
	3000	Stainless steel, self rimming, 19" x 18" single bowl		5.60	2.857		251	84		335	405	
	3100	25" x 22" single bowl		5.60	2.857		276	84		360	435	
	3200	33" x 22" double bowl		4.80	3.333		395	98		493	590	
	3300	43" x 22" double bowl		4.80	3.333		455	98		553	655	
	4000	Steel, enameled, with ledge, 24" x 21" single bowl		5.60	2.857		97.50	84		181.50	238	
	4100	32" x 21" double bowl		4.80	3.333		114	98		212	278	
	4960	For color sinks except stainless steel, add					10%					
	4980	For rough-in, supply, waste and vent, counter top sinks	Q-1	2.14	7.477		85	219		304	440	
	5790	For rough-in, supply, waste & vent, sinks		1.85	8.649		85	254		339	490	
	6650	Service, floor, corner, P.E. on C.I., 28" x 28"		4.40	3.636		495	107		602	705	
	6790	For rough-in, supply, waste & vent, floor service sinks		1.64	9.756		207	286		493	675	
	9000	Minimum labor/equipment charge		4	4	Job		117		117	184	

For expanded coverage of these items see *Means Mechanical or Plumbing Cost Data 1999*

152 | Plumbing Fixtures

152 100 | Fixtures

			CREW	DAILY OUTPUT	LABOR-HOURS	UNIT	1999 BARE COSTS MAT.	LABOR	EQUIP.	TOTAL	TOTAL INCL O&P
168	0010	**URINALS**									
	3000	Wall hung, vitreous china, with hanger & self-closing valve									
	3100	Siphon jet type	Q-1	3	5.333	Ea.	271	157		428	545
	3120	Blowout type		3	5.333		370	157		527	650
	3300	Rough-in, supply, waste & vent		2.83	5.654		87.50	166		253.50	355
	5000	Stall type, vitreous china, includes valve		2.50	6.400		645	188		833	1,000
	6980	Rough-in, supply, waste and vent		1.99	8.040		126	236		362	510
	9000	Minimum labor/equipment charge		4	4	Job		117		117	184
176	0010	**WASH FOUNTAINS** Rigging not included									
	1900	Group, foot control									
	2000	Precast terrazzo, circular, 36" diam., 5 or 6 persons	Q-2	3	8	Ea.	2,600	243		2,843	3,250
	2100	54" diameter for 8 or 10 persons		2.50	9.600		3,250	292		3,542	4,025
	2400	Semi-circular, 36" diam. for 3 persons		3	8		2,400	243		2,643	3,025
	2500	54" diam. for 4 or 5 persons		2.50	9.600		2,900	292		3,192	3,625
	5610	Group, infrared control, barrier free									
	5614	Precast terrazzo									
	5620	Semi-circular 36" diam. for 3 persons	Q-2	3	8	Ea.	3,575	243		3,818	4,300
	5630	46" diam. for 4 persons		2.80	8.571		3,850	261		4,111	4,650
	5640	Circular, 54" diam. for 8 persons, button control		2.50	9.600		6,000	292		6,292	7,050
	5700	Rough-in, supply, waste and vent for above wash fountains	Q-1	1.82	8.791		117	258		375	535
	9000	Minimum labor/equipment charge	Q-2	3	8	Job		243		243	380
180	0010	**WATER CLOSETS**									
	0030	For automatic flush, see 151-141-0972	R151-420								
	0100										
	0150	Tank type, vitreous china, incl. seat, supply pipe w/stop									
	0200	Wall hung, one piece	Q-1	5.30	3.019	Ea.	435	88.50		523.50	620
	0400	Two piece, close coupled		5.30	3.019		380	88.50		468.50	555
	0960	For rough-in, supply, waste, vent and carrier		2.73	5.861		254	172		426	550
	1000	Floor mounted, one piece		5.30	3.019		440	88.50		528.50	620
	1100	Two piece, close coupled, water saver		5.30	3.019		133	88.50		221.50	285
	1960	For color, add					30%				
	1980	For rough-in, supply, waste and vent	Q-1	3.05	5.246	Ea.	116	154		270	370
	3000	Bowl only, with flush valve, seat									
	3100	Wall hung	Q-1	5.80	2.759	Ea.	345	81		426	505
	3200	For rough-in, supply, waste and vent, single WC		2.56	6.250	"	265	183		448	580
	9000	Minimum labor/equipment charge		4	4	Job		117		117	184

152 400 | Pumps

			CREW	DAILY OUTPUT	LABOR-HOURS	UNIT	MAT.	LABOR	EQUIP.	TOTAL	INCL O&P
410	0010	**PUMPS, CIRCULATING** Heated or chilled water application									
	0100										
	0600	Bronze, sweat connections, 1/40 HP, in line									
	0640	3/4" size	Q-1	16	1	Ea.	110	29.50		139.50	167
	1000	Flange connection, 3/4" to 1-1/2" size									
	1040	1/12 HP	Q-1	6	2.667	Ea.	300	78.50		378.50	450
	1060	1/8 HP		6	2.667		520	78.50		598.50	690
	1100	1/3 HP		6	2.667		570	78.50		648.50	745
	1140	2" size, 1/6 HP		5	3.200		740	94		834	960
	1180	2-1/2" size, 1/4 HP		5	3.200		965	94		1,059	1,225
	1220	3" size, 1/4 HP		4	4		1,000	117		1,117	1,275
	9000	Minimum labor/equipment charge		3.25	4.923	Job		144		144	226
450	0010	**PUMPS, PRESSURE BOOSTER SYSTEM**									
	0200	Pump system, with diaphragm tank, control, press. switch									
	0300	1 HP pump	Q-1	1.30	12.308	Ea.	2,950	360		3,310	3,825
	0400	1-1/2 HP pump		1.25	12.800		2,975	375		3,350	3,875

152 | Plumbing Fixtures

152 400 | Pumps

		CREW	DAILY OUTPUT	LABOR-HOURS	UNIT	1999 BARE COSTS MAT.	LABOR	EQUIP.	TOTAL	TOTAL INCL O&P	
450	0420	2 HP pump	Q-1	1.20	13.333	Ea.	3,050	390		3,440	3,950	450
	0440	3 HP pump		1.10	14.545		3,100	425		3,525	4,075	
	0460	5 HP pump	Q-2	1.50	16		3,425	485		3,910	4,525	
	0480	7-1/2 HP pump		1.42	16.901		3,825	515		4,340	5,000	
	0500	10 HP pump		1.34	17.910		4,000	545		4,545	5,250	
	1000	Pump/ energy storage system, diaphragm tank, 3 HP pump										
	1100	motor, PRV, switch, gauge, control center, flow switch										
	1200	125 lb. working pressure	Q-2	.70	34.286	Ea.	8,575	1,050		9,625	11,100	
	1300	250 lb. working pressure		.64	37.500	"	9,375	1,150		10,525	12,100	
	9000	Minimum labor/equipment charge		.30	80	Job		2,425		2,425	3,800	
465	0010	**PUMPS, SEWAGE EJECTOR** With operating and level controls										465
	0100	Simplex system incl. tank, cover, pump 15' head										
	0500	37 gal PE tank, 12 GPM, 1/2 HP, 2" discharge	Q-1	3.20	5	Ea.	360	147		507	625	
	0510	3" discharge		3.10	5.161		385	151		536	660	
	0530	87 GPM, .7 HP, 2" discharge		3.20	5		560	147		707	845	
	0540	3" discharge		3.10	5.161		605	151		756	900	
	0600	45 gal. coated stl tank, 12 GPM, 1/2 HP, 2" discharge		3	5.333		645	157		802	950	
	0610	3" discharge		2.90	5.517		670	162		832	990	
	0630	87 GPM, .7 HP, 2" discharge		3	5.333		825	157		982	1,150	
	0640	3" discharge		2.90	5.517		875	162		1,037	1,225	
	0660	134 GPM, 1 HP, 2" discharge		2.80	5.714		895	168		1,063	1,250	
	0680	3" discharge		2.70	5.926		940	174		1,114	1,300	
	0700	70 gal. PE tank, 12 GPM, 1/2 HP, 2" discharge		2.60	6.154		720	181		901	1,075	
	0710	3" discharge		2.40	6.667		775	196		971	1,150	
	0730	87 GPM, 0.7 HP, 2" discharge		2.50	6.400		935	188		1,123	1,325	
	0740	3" discharge		2.30	6.957		995	204		1,199	1,425	
	0760	134 GPM, 1 HP, 2" discharge		2.20	7.273		1,025	213		1,238	1,450	
	0770	3" discharge		2	8		1,100	235		1,335	1,575	
	9000	Minimum labor/equipment charge		2.50	6.400	Job		188		188	294	
480	0010	**PUMPS, SUBMERSIBLE** Sump										480
	7000	Sump pump, automatic										
	7100	Plastic, 1-1/4" discharge, 1/4 HP	1 Plum	6	1.333	Ea.	117	43.50		160.50	196	
	7140	1/3 HP		5	1.600		142	52		194	238	
	7180	1-1/2" discharge, 1/2 HP		4	2		190	65		255	310	
	7500	Cast iron, 1-1/4" discharge, 1/4 HP		6	1.333		138	43.50		181.50	220	
	7540	1/3 HP		6	1.333		155	43.50		198.50	239	
	7560	1/2 HP		5	1.600		195	52		247	297	
	9000	Minimum labor/equipment charge		4	2	Job		65		65	102	

153 | Plumbing Appliances

153 100 | Water Appliances

		CREW	DAILY OUTPUT	LABOR-HOURS	UNIT	1999 BARE COSTS MAT.	LABOR	EQUIP.	TOTAL	TOTAL INCL O&P	
105	0010	**WATER COOLER**										105
	0100	Wall mounted, non-recessed										
	0140	4 GPH	Q-1	4	4	Ea.	420	117		537	650	
	0160	8 GPH, barrier free, sensor operated		4	4		770	117		887	1,025	
	1000	Dual height, 8.2 GPH		3.80	4.211		690	124		814	950	
	1040	14.3 GPH		3.80	4.211		735	124		859	1,000	

For expanded coverage of these items see *Means Mechanical or Plumbing Cost Data 1999*

153 | Plumbing Appliances

153 100 | Water Appliances

			CREW	DAILY OUTPUT	LABOR-HOURS	UNIT	1999 BARE COSTS MAT.	LABOR	EQUIP.	TOTAL	TOTAL INCL O&P	
105	3300	Semi-recessed, 8.1 GPH	Q-1	4	4	Ea.	690	117		807	940	105
	4600	Floor mounted, flush-to-wall										
	4640	4 GPH	1 Plum	3	2.667	Ea.	480	87		567	665	
	4980	For stainless steel cabinet, add					89.50			89.50	98.50	
	5000	Dual height, 8.2 GPH	1 Plum	2	4		745	130		875	1,025	
	9000	Minimum labor/equipment charge	"	2	4	Job		130		130	204	
110	0010	**WATER HEATERS**										110
	0050											
	1000	Residential, electric, glass lined tank, 5 yr, 10 gal., single element	1 Plum	2.30	3.478	Ea.	202	113		315	400	
	1060	30 gallon, double element		2.20	3.636		259	119		378	470	
	1080	40 gallon, double element		2	4		280	130		410	515	
	1100	52 gallon, double element		2	4		320	130		450	560	
	1120	66 gallon, double element		1.80	4.444		440	145		585	710	
	1140	80 gallon, double element		1.60	5		500	163		663	805	
	2000	Gas fired, glass lined tank, 5 yr, vent not incl., 20 gallon		2.10	3.810		280	124		404	505	
	2040	30 gallon		2	4		287	130		417	520	
	2060	40 gallon		1.90	4.211		310	137		447	555	
	2100	75 gallon		1.50	5.333		630	174		804	965	
	3000	Oil fired, glass lined tank, 5 yr, vent not included, 30 gallon		2	4		775	130		905	1,050	
	3040	50 gallon		1.80	4.444		1,025	145		1,170	1,375	
	4000	Commercial, 100° rise. NOTE: for each size tank, a range of										
	4010	heaters between the ones shown are available										
	4020	Electric										
	4100	5 gal., 3 kW, 12 GPH, 208V	1 Plum	2	4	Ea.	1,200	130		1,330	1,500	
	4160	50 gal., 36 kW, 148 GPH, 208V	"	1.80	4.444		2,775	145		2,920	3,275	
	4480	400 gal., 210 kW, 860 GPH, 480V	Q-1	1	16		16,700	470		17,170	19,100	
	6000	Gas fired, flush jacket, std. controls, vent not incl.										
	6040	75 MBH input, 73 GPH	1 Plum	1.40	5.714	Ea.	1,175	186		1,361	1,575	
	6060	98 MBH input, 95 GPH		1.40	5.714		2,000	186		2,186	2,500	
	6180	200 MBH input, 192 GPH		.60	13.333		3,250	435		3,685	4,250	
	8000	Oil fired, flush jacket, std. controls, vent not incl.										
	8060	103 MBH gross output, 116 GPH	1 Plum	1.10	7.273	Ea.	1,675	237		1,912	2,225	
	8080	122 MBH gross output, 141 GPH	"	1	8		1,850	261		2,111	2,425	
	8160	225 MBH gross output, 256 GPH	Q-1	.80	20		2,675	585		3,260	3,875	
	8280	735 MBH gross output, 880 GPH	"	.40	40		6,075	1,175		7,250	8,500	
	9000	Minimum labor/equipment charge	1 Plum	1.75	4.571	Job		149		149	233	
160	0010	**WATER SUPPLY METERS**										160
	2000	Domestic/commercial, bronze										
	2020	Threaded										
	2060	5/8" diameter, to 20 GPM	1 Plum	16	.500	Ea.	66.50	16.30		82.80	99	
	2080	3/4" diameter, to 30 GPM		14	.571		115	18.65		133.65	156	
	2100	1" diameter, to 50 GPM		12	.667		157	21.50		178.50	206	
	2300	Threaded/flanged										
	2340	1-1/2" diameter, to 100 GPM	1 Plum	8	1	Ea.	485	32.50		517.50	585	
	9000	Minimum labor/equipment charge	"	3.25	2.462	Job		80.50		80.50	126	

Important: See the Reference Section for critical supporting data - Reference Nos., Crews, & City Cost Indexes

154 | Fire Protection

154 100 | Fire Systems

		CREW	DAILY OUTPUT	LABOR-HOURS	UNIT	1999 BARE COSTS MAT.	LABOR	EQUIP.	TOTAL	TOTAL INCL O&P
135	0010 **FIRE HOSE AND EQUIPMENT**									
	2200 Hose, less couplings									
	2260 Synthetic jacket, lined, 300 lb. test, 1-1/2" diameter	Q-12	2,600	.006	L.F.	1.33	.18		1.51	1.74
	2280 2-1/2" diameter	"	2,200	.007	"	2.17	.21		2.38	2.72
	2600 Hose rack, swinging, for 1-1/2" diameter hose,									
	2620 Enameled steel, 50' & 75' lengths of hose	Q-12	20	.800	Ea.	29.50	23.50		53	69
	3750 Hydrants, wall, w/caps, single, flush, polished brass									
	3800 2-1/2" x 2-1/2"	Q-12	5	3.200	Ea.	91.50	93.50		185	247
	4350 Double, projecting, polished brass									
	4400 2-1/2" x 2-1/2" x 4"	Q-12	5	3.200	Ea.	113	93.50		206.50	271
	5600 Nozzles, brass									
	5620 Adjustable fog, 3/4" booster line				Ea.	75.50			75.50	83
	5640 1-1/2" leader line					82			82	90.50
	5660 2-1/2" direct connection					160			160	176
	7140 Standpipe connections, wall, w/plugs & chains									
	7280 Double, flush, polished brass									
	7300 2-1/2" x 2-1/2" x 4"	Q-12	5	3.200	Ea.	219	93.50		312.50	390
	9000 Minimum labor/equipment charge	1 Plum	2	4	Job		130		130	204
160	0010 **FIRE VALVES**									
	3000 Gate, hose, wheel handle, N.R.S., rough brass, 1-1/2"	1 Spri	12	.667	Ea.	58	21.50		79.50	98
	3040 2-1/2", 300 lb.	↓	7	1.143	"	82	37		119	148
	9990 Minimum labor/equipment charge		4	2	Job		65		65	102
170	0010 **SPRINKLER SYSTEM COMPONENTS**									
	0020									
	0800 Air compressor for dry pipe system, automatic, complete									
	0820 280 gal. system capacity, 3/4 HP	1 Spri	1.30	6.154	Ea.	700	200		900	1,075
	1220 Water motor, complete with gong	"	4	2	"	147	65		212	263
	1800 Firecycle system, controls, includes panel,									
	1820 batteries, solenoid valves and pressure switches	Q-13	1	32	Ea.	6,650	990		7,640	8,875
	1980 Detector	1 Spri	16	.500	"	245	16.25		261.25	295
	2600 Sprinkler heads, not including supply piping									
	2640 Dry, pendent, 1/2" orifice, 3/4" or 1" NPT									
	2660 1" to 4-3/4" length	1 Spri	14	.571	Ea.	31	18.55		49.55	63
	2700 11" to 12-3/4" length		14	.571		33.50	18.55		52.05	66
	3600 Foam-water, pendent or upright, 1/2" NPT	↓	12	.667	↓	32	21.50		53.50	69
	3700 Standard spray, pendent or upright, brass, 135° to 286°F									
	3740 1/2" NPT, 1/2" orifice	1 Spri	16	.500	Ea.	3.64	16.25		19.89	29.50
	3790 For riser & feeder piping, see div. 151-701									
	6500 Check, swing, C.I. body, brass fittings, auto. ball drip									
	6520 4" size	Q-12	3	5.333	Ea.	95.50	156		251.50	350
	8200 Dry pipe valve, incl. trim and gauges, 3" size		2	8		950	234		1,184	1,425
	8220 4" size	↓	1	16	↓	1,050	470		1,520	1,875
	9990 Minimum labor/equipment charge	1 Spri	3	2.667	Job		86.50		86.50	136

155 | Heating

155 100 | Boilers

		CREW	DAILY OUTPUT	LABOR-HOURS	UNIT	1999 BARE COSTS MAT.	LABOR	EQUIP.	TOTAL	TOTAL INCL O&P
110	0010 **BOILERS, ELECTRIC, ASME** Standard controls and trim									
	1000 Steam, 6 KW, 20.5 MBH	Q-19	1.20	20	Ea.	7,900	605		8,505	9,650

For expanded coverage of these items see Means Mechanical or Plumbing Cost Data 1999

155 | Heating

155 100 | Boilers

			CREW	DAILY OUTPUT	LABOR-HOURS	UNIT	1999 BARE COSTS				TOTAL INCL O&P	
							MAT.	LABOR	EQUIP.	TOTAL		
110	1160	60 KW, 205 MBH	Q-19	1	24	Ea.	9,575	725		10,300	11,600	110
	1300	240 KW, 819 MBH	↓	.45	53.333		15,100	1,625		16,725	19,100	
	1400	600 KW, 2047 MBH	Q-21	.34	94.118		23,300	2,900		26,200	30,200	
	1540	1800 KW, 6141 MBH	"	.19	168		51,500	5,200		56,700	64,500	
	2000	Hot water, 12 KW, 41 MBH	Q-19	1.30	18.462		3,325	560		3,885	4,525	
	2040	24 KW, 82 MBH		1.20	20		3,550	605		4,155	4,875	
	2060	30 KW, 103 MBH		1.20	20		3,650	605		4,255	4,950	
	2070	36 KW, 123 MBH		1.20	20		3,875	605		4,480	5,200	
	2080	45 KW, 154 MBH		1.10	21.818		3,900	660		4,560	5,325	
	2100	60 KW, 205 MBH	↓	1.10	21.818	↓	4,625	660		5,285	6,125	
	9000	Minimum labor/equipment charge	Q-20	1	20	Job		585		585	930	
115	0010	**BOILERS, GAS FIRED** Natural or propane, standard controls										115
	1000	Cast iron, with insulated jacket										
	2000	Steam, gross output, 81 MBH	Q-7	1.40	22.857	Ea.	1,075	715		1,790	2,300	
	2060	163 MBH		.90	35.556		1,650	1,100		2,750	3,550	
	2200	440 MBH		.55	58.182		3,225	1,825		5,050	6,375	
	2320	1,875 MBH		.28	114		10,400	3,575		13,975	17,000	
	2400	3570 MBH		.18	177		16,400	5,550		21,950	26,800	
	2540	6,970 MBH	↓	.08	400	↓	53,500	12,500		66,000	78,500	
	2800											
	3000	Hot water, gross output, 80 MBH	Q-7	1.46	21.918	Ea.	1,075	685		1,760	2,250	
	3020	100 MBH		1.35	23.704		1,225	740		1,965	2,500	
	3040	122 MBH		1.10	29.091		1,325	910		2,235	2,900	
	3060	163 MBH		1	32		1,650	1,000		2,650	3,375	
	3200	440 MBH		.65	49.231		3,225	1,550		4,775	5,925	
	3320	2,000 MBH		.38	84.211		10,400	2,625		13,025	15,600	
	3540	6,970 MBH	↓	.08	400	↓	53,500	12,500		66,000	78,500	
	4000	Steel, insulating jacket										
	6000	Hot water, including burner & one zone valve, gross output										
	6010	51.2 MBH	Q-6	2	12	Ea.	1,575	365		1,940	2,300	
	6020	72 MBH		2	12		1,750	365		2,115	2,500	
	6040	89 MBH		1.90	12.632		1,775	385		2,160	2,575	
	6060	105 MBH		1.80	13.333		2,000	410		2,410	2,850	
	6080	132 MBH		1.70	14.118		2,275	430		2,705	3,175	
	6100	155 MBH		1.50	16		2,650	490		3,140	3,675	
	6110	186 MBH		1.40	17.143		3,200	525		3,725	4,325	
	6120	227 MBH		1.30	18.462		4,050	565		4,615	5,325	
	6140	292 MBH		1.20	20		4,575	610		5,185	5,975	
	6180	480 MBH		.70	34.286		6,600	1,050		7,650	8,925	
	6200	640 MBH		.60	40		7,850	1,225		9,075	10,600	
	6220	800 MBH		.50	48		9,150	1,475		10,625	12,400	
	6240	960 MBH	↓	.45	53.333	↓	11,400	1,625		13,025	15,100	
	7000	For tankless water heater on smaller gas units, add					10%					
	7050	For additional zone valves up to 312 MBH add				Ea.	101			101	111	
	7060											
	9900	Minimum labor/equipment charge	Q-6	1	24	Job		735		735	1,150	
120	0010	**BOILERS, OIL FIRED** Standard controls, flame retention burner										120
	1000	Cast iron, with insulated flush jacket										
	2000	Steam, gross output, 109 MBH	Q-7	1.20	26.667	Ea.	1,300	835		2,135	2,750	
	2060	207 MBH		.90	35.556		1,800	1,100		2,900	3,725	
	2180	1,084 MBH		.42	76.190		7,400	2,375		9,775	11,900	
	2200	1,360 MBH		.38	84.211		8,650	2,625		11,275	13,600	
	2240	2,175 MBH		.28	114		10,100	3,575		13,675	16,700	
	2340	4,360 MBH	↓	.17	188		18,100	5,875		23,975	29,100	

155 | Heating

155 100 | Boilers

			CREW	DAILY OUTPUT	LABOR-HOURS	UNIT	1999 BARE COSTS MAT.	LABOR	EQUIP.	TOTAL	TOTAL INCL O&P	
120	2460	6,970 MBH	Q-7	.08	400	Ea.	53,000	12,500		65,500	77,500	120
	3000	Hot water, same price as steam										
	5000	Steel, insulated jacket, burner										
	7000	Hot water, gross output, 155 MBH	Q-6	1.90	12.632	Ea.	1,250	385		1,635	1,975	
	7020	122 MBH		1.80	13.333		2,100	410		2,510	2,950	
	7040	137 MBH		1.60	15		2,375	460		2,835	3,350	
	7060	168 MBH		1.50	16		2,625	490		3,115	3,675	
	7080	225 MBH		1.40	17.143		3,125	525		3,650	4,250	
	7100	315 MBH		1.10	21.818		4,675	665		5,340	6,200	
	7120	420 MBH		.80	30		5,175	915		6,090	7,100	
	9000	Minimum labor/equipment charge		1.75	13.714	Job		420		420	655	
125	0010	**BOILERS, GAS/OIL** Combination with burners and controls										125
	1000	Cast iron with insulated jacket										
	2000	Steam, gross output, 720 MBH	Q-7	.40	80	Ea.	6,550	2,500		9,050	11,100	
	2140	2,700 MBH		.19	168		14,200	5,250		19,450	23,800	
	2380	6,970 MBH		.05	640		56,000	20,000		76,000	93,000	
	3000	Hot water, gross output, 584 MBH		.54	59.259		7,350	1,850		9,200	11,000	
	3060	1,460 MBH		.45	71.111		17,800	2,225		20,025	23,100	
	3300	13,500 MBH, 403.3 BHP		.02	1,600		106,500	50,000		156,500	195,500	
	4000	Steel, insulated jacket, skid base, tubeless										
	4500	Steam, 150 psi gross output, 335 MBH, 10 BHP	Q-6	.65	36.923	Ea.	8,875	1,125		10,000	11,600	
	4640	1,339 MBH, 40 BHP		.28	85.714		17,400	2,625		20,025	23,300	
	4720	2,511 MBH, 75 BHP		.17	141		23,800	4,325		28,125	33,000	
130	0010	**BOILERS, SOLID FUEL**										130
	5000	Wood or coal and oil combination, circulator,										
	5050	mixing valve, controls										
	5100	Output (oil),										
	5250	100 MBH, with burner	Q-5	.73	21.918	Ea.	4,300	645		4,945	5,725	
	5300	130 MBH, with burner	"	.69	23.188	"	4,300	685		4,985	5,800	

155 200 | Boiler Accessories

			CREW	DAILY OUTPUT	LABOR-HOURS	UNIT	MAT.	LABOR	EQUIP.	TOTAL	TOTAL INCL O&P	
230	0010	**BURNERS**										230
	0990	Residential, conversion, gas fired, LP or natural										
	1000	Gun type, atmospheric input 72 to 200 MBH	Q-1	2.50	6.400	Ea.	655	188		843	1,025	
	1020	120 to 360 MBH		2	8		725	235		960	1,175	
	1040	280 to 800 MBH		1.70	9.412		1,400	276		1,676	1,975	
	3000	Flame retention oil fired assembly, input										
	3040	2.0 to 5.0 GPH	Q-1	2	8	Ea.	505	235		740	920	
240	0010	**DRAFT CONTROLS**										240
	1000	Barometric, gas fired system only, 6" size for 5" and 6" pipes	1 Shee	20	.400	Ea.	38	12.70		50.70	62	
	1040	8" size, for 7" and 8" pipes	"	18	.444	"	50.50	14.10		64.60	78	
	2000	All fuel, oil, oil/gas, coal										
	2020	10" for 9" and 10" pipes	1 Shee	15	.533	Ea.	82.50	16.95		99.45	118	
	3260	For thermal switch for above, add	"	24	.333		35	10.60		45.60	55.50	
	5000	Vent damper, bi-metal, gas, 3" diameter	Q-9	24	.667		36.50	19.05		55.55	70.50	
	5010	4" diameter		24	.667		41	19.05		60.05	75.50	
	5020	5" diameter		23	.696		49	19.90		68.90	86	
	5030	6" diameter		22	.727		55.50	21		76.50	94.50	
	5040	7" diameter		21	.762		63	22		85	105	
	5050	8" diameter		20	.800		72.50	23		95.50	117	
	5101	Electric, automatic, gas, 4" diameter		24	.667		151	19.05		170.05	197	
	5110	5" diameter		23	.696		154	19.90		173.90	201	
	5121	6" diameter		22	.727		157	21		178	206	
	5130	7" diameter		21	.762		160	22		182	211	

For expanded coverage of these items see *Means Mechanical* or *Plumbing Cost Data 1999*

155 | Heating

155 200 | Boiler Accessories

			CREW	DAILY OUTPUT	LABOR-HOURS	UNIT	MAT.	LABOR	EQUIP.	TOTAL	TOTAL INCL O&P	
240	5140	8" diameter	Q-9	20	.800	Ea.	163	23		186	216	240
	5150	9" diameter		20	.800		197	23		220	253	
	5160	10" diameter		19	.842		200	24		224	259	
	5170	12" diameter		19	.842		440	24		464	525	
	5180	14" diameter		18	.889		430	25.50		455.50	515	
	5190	16" diameter		17	.941		500	27		527	600	
	5200	18" diameter		16	1		560	28.50		588.50	665	
	5250	Automatic, oil, 4" diameter		24	.667		91.50	19.05		110.55	132	
	5260	5" diameter		23	.696		94.50	19.90		114.40	136	
	5270	6" diameter		22	.727		97.50	21		118.50	141	
	5280	7" diameter		21	.762		100	22		122	145	
	5290	8" diameter		20	.800		103	23		126	151	
	5300	9" diameter		20	.800		137	23		160	188	
	5310	10" diameter		19	.842		140	24		164	194	
	5320	12" diameter		19	.842		380	24		404	460	
	5330	14" diameter		18	.889		430	25.50		455.50	515	
	5340	16" diameter		17	.941		500	27		527	600	
	5350	18" diameter		16	1		560	28.50		588.50	665	
	9000	Minimum labor/equipment charge	1 Shee	4	2	Job		63.50		63.50	102	

155 400 | Warm Air Systems

			CREW	DAILY OUTPUT	LABOR-HOURS	UNIT	MAT.	LABOR	EQUIP.	TOTAL	TOTAL INCL O&P	
401	0010	**DUCT FURNACES** Includes burner, controls, stainless steel										401
	0020	heat exchanger. Gas fired, electric ignition										
	1000	Outdoor installation, with vent cap										
	1120	225 MBH output	Q-5	2.50	6.400	Ea.	2,850	189		3,039	3,450	
	1160	375 MBH output		1.60	10		4,050	295		4,345	4,900	
	1180	450 MBH output		1.40	11.429		4,250	335		4,585	5,200	
408	0010	**DUCT HEATERS** Electric, 480 V, 3 Ph										408
	0020	Finned tubular insert, 500°F										
	0100	8" wide x 6" high, 4.0 kW	Q-20	16	1.250	Ea.	510	36.50		546.50	625	
	0120	12" high, 8.0 kW		15	1.333		815	39		854	960	
	0140	18" high, 12.0 kW		14	1.429		1,150	42		1,192	1,325	
	0160	24" high, 16.0 kW		13	1.538		1,475	45		1,520	1,700	
	0180	30" high, 20.0 kW		12	1.667		1,800	48.50		1,848.50	2,050	
	0300	12" wide x 6" high, 6.7 kW		15	1.333		525	39		564	635	
	0320	12" high, 13.3 kW		14	1.429		845	42		887	995	
	0340	18" high, 20.0 kW		13	1.538		1,175	45		1,220	1,375	
	8000	To obtain BTU multiply kW by 3413										
	9900	Minimum labor/equipment charge	1 Shee	4	2	Job		63.50		63.50	102	
420	0010	**FURNACES** Hot air heating, blowers, standard controls										420
	0020	not including gas, oil or flue piping										
	1000	Electric, UL listed										
	1020	10.2 MBH	Q-20	5	4	Ea.	315	117		432	530	
	1100	34.1 MBH	"	4.40	4.545	"	405	133		538	655	
	3000	Gas, AGA certified, direct drive models										
	3020	45 MBH input	Q-9	4	4	Ea.	435	114		549	665	
	3040	60 MBH input		3.80	4.211		580	120		700	835	
	3060	75 MBH input		3.60	4.444		615	127		742	885	
	3100	100 MBH input		3.20	5		655	143		798	950	
	3120	125 MBH input		3	5.333		755	152		907	1,075	
	3130	150 MBH input		2.80	5.714		775	163		938	1,125	
	3140	200 MBH input		2.60	6.154		1,850	176		2,026	2,300	
	6000	Oil, UL listed, atomizing gun type burner										
	6020	56 MBH output	Q-9	3.60	4.444	Ea.	745	127		872	1,025	
	6040	95 MBH output		3.40	4.706		790	134		924	1,075	

Important: See the Reference Section for critical supporting data - Reference Nos., Crews, & City Cost Indexes

155 | Heating

155 400 | Warm Air Systems

			CREW	DAILY OUTPUT	LABOR-HOURS	UNIT	1999 BARE COSTS MAT.	LABOR	EQUIP.	TOTAL	TOTAL INCL O&P	
420	6060	134 MBH output	Q-9	3.20	5	Ea.	1,100	143		1,243	1,425	420
	6080	151 MBH output		3	5.333		1,225	152		1,377	1,575	
	6100	200 MBH input		2.60	6.154		2,050	176		2,226	2,550	
	8500	Wood and coal combination complete										
	8520	95 MBH output	Q-9	3	5.333	Ea.	4,225	152		4,377	4,900	
	8540	140 MBH output (oil)		3	5.333		4,225	152		4,377	4,900	
	8560	163 MBH output (oil)		3	5.333		4,225	152		4,377	4,900	
	9000	Minimum labor/equipment charge		2.75	5.818	Job		166		166	266	
434	0010	**FURNACE COMPONENTS AND COMBINATIONS**										434
	0080	Coils, A/C evaporator, for gas or oil furnaces										
	0090	Add-on, with holding charge										
	0100	Upflow										
	0120	1-1/2 ton cooling	Q-5	4	4	Ea.	108	118		226	305	
	0130	2 ton cooling		3.70	4.324		131	127		258	345	
	0140	3 ton cooling		3.30	4.848		163	143		306	405	
	0150	4 ton cooling		3	5.333		230	157		387	500	
	0160	5 ton cooling		2.70	5.926		295	175		470	600	
	0300	Downflow										
	0330	2-1/2 ton cooling	Q-5	3	5.333	Ea.	151	157		308	415	
	0340	3-1/2 ton cooling		2.60	6.154		204	181		385	510	
	0350	5 ton cooling		2.20	7.273		293	214		507	660	
	0600	Horizontal										
	0630	2 ton cooling	Q-5	3.90	4.103	Ea.	153	121		274	360	
	0640	3 ton cooling		3.50	4.571		176	135		311	405	
	0650	4 ton cooling		3.20	5		221	147		368	475	
	0660	5 ton cooling		2.90	5.517		293	163		456	580	
	2000	Cased evaporator coils for air handlers										
	2100	1-1/2 ton cooling	Q-5	4.40	3.636	Ea.	178	107		285	365	
	2110	2 ton cooling		4.10	3.902		180	115		295	375	
	2120	2-1/2 ton cooling		3.90	4.103		219	121		340	430	
	2130	3 ton cooling		3.70	4.324		219	127		346	440	
	2140	3-1/2 ton cooling		3.50	4.571		267	135		402	505	
	2150	4 ton cooling		3.20	5		268	147		415	525	
	2160	5 ton cooling		2.90	5.517		325	163		488	610	
	3010	Air handler, modular										
	3100	With cased evaporator cooling coil										
	3120	1-1/2 ton cooling	Q-5	3.80	4.211	Ea.	470	124		594	710	
	3130	2 ton cooling		3.50	4.571		470	135		605	730	
	3140	2-1/2 ton cooling		3.30	4.848		495	143		638	765	
	3150	3 ton cooling		3.10	5.161		530	152		682	825	
	3160	3-1/2 ton cooling		2.90	5.517		595	163		758	910	
	3170	4 ton cooling		2.50	6.400		595	189		784	950	
	3180	5 ton cooling		2.10	7.619		715	225		940	1,125	
	3500	With no cooling coil										
	3520	1-1/2 ton coil size	Q-5	12	1.333	Ea.	291	39.50		330.50	380	
	3530	2 ton coil size		10	1.600		335	47		382	445	
	3540	2-1/2 ton coil size		10	1.600		335	47		382	445	
	3554	3 ton coil size		9	1.778		310	52.50		362.50	425	
	3560	3-1/2 ton coil size		9	1.778		355	52.50		407.50	470	
	3570	4 ton coil size		8.50	1.882		325	55.50		380.50	445	
	3580	5 ton coil size		8	2		390	59		449	525	
	4000	Heater for above handlers										
	4120	5 kW, 17.1 MBH	Q-5	16	1	Ea.	230	29.50		259.50	299	
	4130	7.5 kW, 25.6 MBH		15.60	1.026		234	30		264	305	
	4140	10 kW, 34.2 MBH		15.20	1.053		253	31		284	325	
	4150	12.5 KW, 42.7 MBH		14.80	1.081		310	32		342	390	

For expanded coverage of these items see *Means Mechanical or Plumbing Cost Data 1999*

155 | Heating

155 400 | Warm Air Systems

		CREW	DAILY OUTPUT	LABOR-HOURS	UNIT	1999 BARE COSTS MAT.	LABOR	EQUIP.	TOTAL	TOTAL INCL O&P	
461	0010	**MAKE-UP AIR UNIT**									461
	0020	Indoor suspension, natural/LP gas, direct fired,									
	0030	standard control. For flue see division 155-680									
	0040	70°F temperature rise, MBH is input									
	0100	2000 CFM, 168 MBH	Q-6	3	8	Ea.	4,800	245		5,045	5,675
	0220	12,000 CFM, 1005 MBH	"	1	24		7,550	735		8,285	9,450
	0300	24,000 CFM, 2007 MBH	Q-7	1	32		9,825	1,000		10,825	12,400
	0400	50,000 CFM, 4180 MBH	"	.80	40	↓	13,500	1,250		14,750	16,800
	9000	Minimum labor/equipment charge	Q-6	2.75	8.727	Job		267		267	415
471	0010	**SOLAR ENERGY**									471
	0020	System/Package prices, not including connecting									
	0030	pipe, insulation, or special heating/plumbing fixtures									
	0500	Hot water, standard package, low temperature									
	0580	2 collectors, circulator, fittings, 120 gal. tank	Q-1	.40	40	Ea.	2,725	1,175		3,900	4,825
	2250	Controller, liquid temperature	1 Plum	5	1.600	"	92.50	52		144.50	184
	2300	Circulators, air									
	2310	Blowers									
	2520	Space & DHW system, less duct work	Q-9	.50	32	Ea.	1,325	915		2,240	2,950
	2580	8" diameter, 150 CFM		16	1		33.50	28.50		62	83
	2660	Shutter/damper		12	1.333		43	38		81	109
	2670	Shutter motor	↓	16	1		92	28.50		120.50	147
	2800	Circulators, liquid, 1/25 HP, 5.3 GPM	Q-1	14	1.143		139	33.50		172.50	206
	2820	1/20 HP, 17 GPM	"	12	1.333	↓	139	39		178	214
	3000	Collector panels, air with aluminum absorber plate									
	3010	Wall or roof mount									
	3040	Flat black, plastic glazing									
	3080	4' x 8'	Q-9	6	2.667	Ea.	600	76		676	780
	3300	Collector panels, liquid with copper absorber plate									
	3320	Black chrome, tempered glass glazing									
	3330	Alum. frame, 4' x 8', 5/32" single glazing	Q-1	9.50	1.684	Ea.	545	49.50		594.50	680
	3440	Flat black									
	3450	Alum. frame, 3' x 8'	Q-1	9	1.778	Ea.	455	52		507	580
	3500	Alum. frame, 4' x 8.5'		5.50	2.909		520	85.50		605.50	705
	3600	Liquid, full wetted, plastic, alum. frame, 3' x 10'		5	3.200		195	94		289	360
	3650	Collector panel mounting, flat roof or ground rack		7	2.286	↓	64.50	67		131.50	176
	3670	Roof clamps	↓	70	.229	Set	1.61	6.70		8.31	12.25
	3700	Roof strap, teflon	1 Plum	205	.039	L.F.	9.50	1.27		10.77	12.45
	3900	Differential controller with two sensors									
	3930	Thermostat, hard wired	1 Plum	8	1	Ea.	92	32.50		124.50	152
	4050	Pool valve system	"	2.50	3.200	"	199	104		303	380
	4150	Sensors									
	4220	Freeze prevention	1 Plum	32	.250	Ea.	20	8.15		28.15	35
	4260										
	4300	Heat exchanger									
	4315	includes coil, blower, circulator									
	4316	and controller for DHW and space hot air									
	4380	70 MBH	Q-1	3.50	4.571	Ea.	299	134		433	540
	4400	80 MBH	"	3	5.333	"	420	157		577	705
	4580	Fluid to fluid package includes two circulating pumps									
	4590	expansion tank, check valve, relief valve									
	4600	controller, high temperature cutoff and sensors	Q-1	2.50	6.400	Ea.	695	188		883	1,050
	4650	Heat transfer fluid									
	4700	Propylene glycol, inhibited anti-freeze	1 Plum	28	.286	Gal.	8.80	9.30		18.10	24.50
	4800	Solar storage tanks, knocked down									
	5020	7' x 10'-6" = 459 C.F./3000 gallons	Q-10	.80	30	Ea.	10,300	890		11,190	12,700

155 | Heating

155 400 | Warm Air Systems

		CREW	DAILY OUTPUT	LABOR-HOURS	UNIT	MAT.	LABOR	EQUIP.	TOTAL	TOTAL INCL O&P	
471	5210	7' x 14' = 613 C.F./4000 gallons	Q-10	.60	40	Ea.	12,300	1,175		13,475	15,500	471
	5230	10'-6" x 14' = 919 C.F./6000 gallons		.40	60		15,000	1,775		16,775	19,400	
	5250	14' x 17'-6" = 1531 C.F./10,000 gallons	Q-11	.30	106		19,600	3,225		22,825	26,800	
	7000	Solar control valves and vents										
	7070	Air eliminator, automatic 3/4" size	1 Plum	32	.250	Ea.	26	8.15		34.15	41.50	
	7090	Air vent, automatic, 1/8" fitting		32	.250		9.40	8.15		17.55	23	
	7100	Manual, 1/8" NPT		32	.250		2.06	8.15		10.21	15	
	7120	Backflow preventer, 1/2" pipe size		16	.500		56	16.30		72.30	87	
	7130	3/4" pipe size		16	.500		56	16.30		72.30	87	
	7150	Balancing valve, 3/4" pipe size		20	.400		19.50	13.05		32.55	42	
	7180	Draindown valve, 1/2" copper tube		9	.889		187	29		216	252	
	7200	Flow control valve, 1/2" pipe size		22	.364		45.50	11.85		57.35	68.50	
	7220	Expansion tank, up to 5 gal.		32	.250		55.50	8.15		63.65	74	
	7400	Pressure gauge, 2" dial		32	.250		19	8.15		27.15	34	
	7450	Relief valve, temp. and pressure 3/4" pipe size		30	.267		7.40	8.70		16.10	22	
	7500	Solenoid valve, normally closed										
	7750	Vacuum relief valve, 3/4" pipe size	1 Plum	32	.250	Ea.	29.50	8.15		37.65	45.50	
	7800	Thermometers										
	8250	Water storage tank with heat exchanger and electric element										
	8260	66 gal. with 2" x 1/2 lb. density insulation	1 Plum	1.60	5	Ea.	320	163		483	605	
	8270	66 gal. with 2" x 2 lb. density insulation		1.60	5		610	163		773	925	
	8280	80 gal. with 2" x 1/2 lb. density insulation		1.60	5		360	163		523	650	
	8300	80 gal. with 2" x 2 lb. density insulation		1.60	5		700	163		863	1,025	
	8350	120 gal. with 2" x 1/2 lb. density insulation		1.40	5.714		390	186		576	715	
	8500	Water storage module, plastic										
	8600	Tubular, 12" diameter, 4' high	1 Carp	48	.167	Ea.	67	4.55		71.55	81	
	8610	12" diameter, 8' high	"	40	.200		99	5.45		104.45	118	
	8650	Cap, 12" diameter					10			10	11	
	9000	Minimum labor/equipment charge	1 Plum	2	4	Job		130		130	204	
480	0010	**SPACE HEATERS** Cabinet, grilles, fan, controls, burner,										480
	0020	thermostat, no piping. For flue see division 155-680										
	1000	Gas fired, floor mounted										
	1100	60 MBH output	Q-5	10	1.600	Ea.	580	47		627	710	
	1180	180 MBH output		6	2.667		860	78.50		938.50	1,075	
	2000	Suspension mounted, propeller fan, 20 MBH output		8.50	1.882		400	55.50		455.50	525	
	2040	60 MBH output		7	2.286		495	67.50		562.50	645	
	2100	130 MBH output		5	3.200		730	94.50		824.50	955	
	2240	320 MBH output		2	8		1,500	236		1,736	2,025	
	2500	For powered venter and adapter, add					259			259	285	
	5000	Wall furnace, 17.5 MBH output	Q-5	6	2.667		460	78.50		538.50	635	
	5020	24 MBH output		5	3.200		485	94.50		579.50	680	
	5040	35 MBH output		4	4		650	118		768	900	
	9000	Minimum labor/equipment charge		3.50	4.571	Job		135		135	211	

155 600 | Heating System Access.

		CREW	DAILY OUTPUT	LABOR-HOURS	UNIT	MAT.	LABOR	EQUIP.	TOTAL	TOTAL INCL O&P	
620	0010	**HEAT RECOVERY PACKAGES**										620
	0100	Air to air										
	2000	Kitchen exhaust, commercial, heat pipe exchanger										
	2040	Combined supply/exhaust air volume										
	2080	2.5 to 6.0 MCFM	Q-10	2.80	8.571	MCFM	4,400	254		4,654	5,250	
	2120	6 to 16 MCFM		5	4.800		2,700	142		2,842	3,200	
	2160	16 to 22 MCFM		6	4		2,125	119		2,244	2,525	
	9000	Minimum labor/equipment charge	1 Shee	4	2	Job		63.50		63.50	102	
630	0010	**HYDRONIC HEATING** Terminal units, not incl. main supply pipe										630
	1000	Radiation										

For expanded coverage of these items see *Means Mechanical or Plumbing Cost Data 1999*

155 | Heating

155 600 | Heating System Access.

			DAILY OUTPUT	LABOR-HOURS	UNIT	1999 BARE COSTS MAT.	LABOR	EQUIP.	TOTAL	TOTAL INCL O&P
630	1150	Fin tube, wall hung, 14" slope top cover, with damper								
	1200	1-1/4" copper tube, 4-1/4" alum. fin	Q-5	38	.421	L.F.	34.50	12.40		46.90	57.50
	1250	1-1/4" steel tube, 4-1/4" steel fin		36	.444		31	13.10		44.10	54.50
	1255	2" steel tube, 4-1/4" steel fin		32	.500		33.50	14.75		48.25	60
	1310	Baseboard, pkgd, 1/2" copper tube, alum. fin, 7" high		60	.267		6.75	7.85		14.60	19.75
	1320	3/4" copper tube, alum. fin, 7" high		58	.276		8.85	8.15		17	22.50
	1340	1" copper tube, alum. fin, 8-7/8" high		56	.286		14.80	8.40		23.20	29.50
	1360	1-1/4" copper tube, alum. fin, 8-7/8" high		54	.296		22	8.75		30.75	37.50
	1500	Note: fin tube may also require corners, caps, etc.									
	3000	Radiators, cast iron									
	3100	Free standing or wall hung, 6 tube, 25" high	Q-5	96	.167	Section	21	4.91		25.91	30.50
	3950	Unit heaters, propeller, 115 V 2 psi steam, 60°F entering air									
	4000	Horizontal, 12 MBH	Q-5	12	1.333	Ea.	330	39.50		369.50	425
	4060	43.9 MBH		8	2		440	59		499	580
	4240	286.9 MBH		2	8		1,175	236		1,411	1,675
	4250	326.0 MBH		1.90	8.421		1,375	248		1,623	1,925
	4260	364.0 MBH		1.80	8.889		1,525	262		1,787	2,075
	4270	404.0 MBH		1.60	10		1,925	295		2,220	2,575
	4300	For vertical diffuser, add					136			136	149
	4310	Vertical flow, 40.0 MBH	Q-5	11	1.455		465	43		508	575
	4326	131.0 MBH	"	4	4		710	118		828	965
	4354	420 MBH	Q-6	1.80	13.333		2,425	410		2,835	3,300
	4358	500 MBH		1.40	17.143		2,750	525		3,275	3,850
	4362	570 MBH		1.40	17.143		2,850	525		3,375	3,975
	4366	620 MBH		1.30	18.462		3,275	565		3,840	4,475
	4370	960 MBH		1.10	21.818		5,750	665		6,415	7,375
	9000	Minimum labor/equipment charge	Q-5	3.20	5	Job		147		147	231
640	0010	**HUMIDIFIERS**									
	0520	Steam, room or duct, filter, regulators, auto. controls, 220 V									
	0560	22 lb. per hour	Q-5	5	3.200	Ea.	2,200	94.50		2,294.50	2,575
	0580	33 lb. per hour		4	4		2,250	118		2,368	2,650
	0620	100 lb. per hour		3	5.333		3,300	157		3,457	3,900
	9000	Minimum labor/equipment charge		3.50	4.571	Job		135		135	211
651	0010	**INSULATION**									
	0100	Rule of thumb, as a percentage of total mechanical costs				Job				10%	
	0110	Insulation req'd is based on the surface size/area to be covered									
	2900	Domestic water heater wrap kit									
	2920	1-1/2" with vinyl jacket, 20-60 gal.	1 Plum	8	1	Ea.	16.25	32.50		48.75	69
	2925	50 to 80 gallons	"	8	1	"	19.40	32.50		51.90	72.50
	2930	Insulated protectors, (ADA)									
	2935	For exposed piping under sinks or lavatories.									
	2940	Vinyl coated foam, velcro tabs									
	2945	P Trap, 1-1/4" or 1-1/2"	1 Plum	32	.250	Ea.	13.55	8.15		21.70	27.50
	2960	Valve and supply cover									
	2965	1/2", 3/8", and 7/16" pipe size	1 Plum	32	.250	Ea.	12.85	8.15		21	27
	2970	Extension drain cover									
	2975	1-1/4", or 1-1/2" pipe size	1 Plum	32	.250	Ea.	13.20	8.15		21.35	27.50
	2980	Tailpiece offset (wheelchair)									
	2985	1-1/4" pipe size	1 Plum	32	.250	Ea.	14.25	8.15		22.40	28.50
	3000	Ductwork									
	3020	Blanket type, fiberglass, flexible									
	3030	Fire resistant liner, black coating one side									
	3050	1/2" thick, 2 lb. density	Q-14	380	.042	S.F.	.28	1.15		1.43	2.23
	3060	1" thick, 1-1/2 lb. density	"	350	.046	"	.37	1.25		1.62	2.49
	3140	FRK vapor barrier wrap, .75 lb. density									

155 | Heating

155 600 | Heating System Access.

			CREW	DAILY OUTPUT	LABOR-HOURS	UNIT	1999 BARE COSTS MAT.	LABOR	EQUIP.	TOTAL	TOTAL INCL O&P	
651	3160	1" thick	Q-14	350	.046	S.F.	.26	1.25		1.51	2.37	651
	3170	1-1/2" thick		320	.050		.23	1.37		1.60	2.53	
	3180	2" thick		300	.053		.28	1.46		1.74	2.74	
	3190	3" thick		260	.062		.41	1.69		2.10	3.25	
	3200	4" thick		242	.066		.55	1.81		2.36	3.62	
	3490	Board type, fiberglass liner, 3 lb. density										
	3500	Fire resistant, black pigmented, 1 side										
	3520	1" thick	Q-14	150	.107	S.F.	1.10	2.92		4.02	6.05	
	3540	1-1/2" thick	"	130	.123	"	1.36	3.37		4.73	7.10	
	4000	Pipe covering (price copper tube one size less than IPS)										
	6120	2" wall, 1/2" iron pipe size	Q-14	145	.110	L.F.	3.16	3.02		6.18	8.55	
	6210	4" iron pipe size	"	125	.128	"	5.15	3.51		8.66	11.50	
	6600	Fiberglass, with all service jacket										
	6840	1" wall, 1/2" iron pipe size	Q-14	240	.067	L.F.	.92	1.83		2.75	4.05	
	6860	3/4" iron pipe size		230	.070		1.05	1.91		2.96	4.32	
	6870	1" iron pipe size		220	.073		1.07	1.99		3.06	4.49	
	6880	1-1/4" iron pipe size		210	.076		1.22	2.09		3.31	4.81	
	6890	1-1/2" iron pipe size		210	.076		1.30	2.09		3.39	4.90	
	6900	2" iron pipe size		200	.080		1.43	2.19		3.62	5.20	
	7080	1-1/2" wall, 1/2" iron pipe size		230	.070		1.87	1.91		3.78	5.25	
	7140	2" iron pipe size		190	.084		2.53	2.31		4.84	6.60	
	7160	3" iron pipe size		170	.094		2.86	2.58		5.44	7.45	
	7879	Rubber tubing, flexible closed cell foam										
	8100	1/2" wall, 1/4" iron pipe size	1 Asbe	90	.089	L.F.	.56	2.71		3.27	5.10	
	8120	3/8" iron pipe size		90	.089		.61	2.71		3.32	5.15	
	8130	1/2" iron pipe size		89	.090		.68	2.74		3.42	5.30	
	8140	3/4" iron pipe size		89	.090		.75	2.74		3.49	5.40	
	8150	1" iron pipe size		88	.091		.84	2.77		3.61	5.50	
	8170	1-1/2" iron pipe size		87	.092		1.18	2.80		3.98	5.95	
	8180	2" iron pipe size		86	.093		1.19	2.83		4.02	6	
	8200	3" iron pipe size		85	.094		2.65	2.87		5.52	7.70	
	8220	4" iron pipe size		80	.100		3.14	3.05		6.19	8.50	
	8300	3/4" wall, 1/4" iron pipe size		90	.089		.86	2.71		3.57	5.45	
	8330	1/2" iron pipe size		89	.090		1.12	2.74		3.86	5.80	
	8340	3/4" iron pipe size		89	.090		1.38	2.74		4.12	6.05	
	8350	1" iron pipe size		88	.091		1.56	2.77		4.33	6.30	
	8360	1-1/4" iron pipe size		87	.092		2.11	2.80		4.91	7	
	8370	1-1/2" iron pipe size		87	.092		2.39	2.80		5.19	7.30	
	8380	2" iron pipe size		86	.093		2.80	2.83		5.63	7.80	
	8444	1" wall, 1/2" iron pipe size		86	.093		2.18	2.83		5.01	7.10	
	8445	3/4" iron pipe size		84	.095		2.64	2.90		5.54	7.70	
	8446	1" iron pipe size		84	.095		3.07	2.90		5.97	8.20	
	8447	1-1/4" iron pipe size		82	.098		3.47	2.97		6.44	8.75	
	8448	1-1/2" iron pipe size		82	.098		4.03	2.97		7	9.35	
	8449	2" iron pipe size		80	.100		5.40	3.05		8.45	11	
	8450	2-1/2" iron pipe size		80	.100		7	3.05		10.05	12.75	
	8456	Rubber insulation tape, 1/8" x 2" x 30'				Ea.	13.45			13.45	14.80	
	9600	Minimum labor/equipment charge	1 Plum	4	2	Job		65		65	102	
671	0010	**TANKS**										671
	2000	Steel, liquid expansion, ASME, painted, 15 gallon capacity	Q-5	17	.941	Ea.	325	28		353	400	
	2040	30 gallon capacity		12	1.333		360	39.50		399.50	455	
	2080	60 gallon capacity		8	2		490	59		549	635	
	2120	100 gallon capacity		6	2.667		655	78.50		733.50	845	
	3000	Steel ASME expansion, rubber diaphragm, 19 gal. cap. accept.		12	1.333		1,250	39.50		1,289.50	1,425	
	3020	31 gallon capacity		8	2		1,400	59		1,459	1,625	
	3040	61 gallon capacity		6	2.667		1,950	78.50		2,028.50	2,275	

For expanded coverage of these items see *Means Mechanical or Plumbing Cost Data 1999*

155 | Heating

155 600 | Heating System Access.

			CREW	DAILY OUTPUT	LABOR-HOURS	UNIT	1999 BARE COSTS MAT.	LABOR	EQUIP.	TOTAL	TOTAL INCL O&P	
671	3080	119 gallon capacity	Q-5	4	4	Ea.	2,200	118		2,318	2,600	671
	9000	Minimum labor/equipment charge	↓	4	4	Job		118		118	185	
680	0010	**VENT CHIMNEY** Prefab metal, U.L. listed										680
	0020	Gas, double wall, galvanized steel										
	0080	3" diameter	Q-9	72	.222	V.L.F.	3.38	6.35		9.73	13.90	
	0100	4" diameter		68	.235		4.14	6.70		10.84	15.35	
	0120	5" diameter		64	.250		4.91	7.15		12.06	16.85	
	0140	6" diameter		60	.267		5.70	7.60		13.30	18.50	
	0160	7" diameter		56	.286		8.40	8.15		16.55	22.50	
	0180	8" diameter		52	.308		9.35	8.80		18.15	24.50	
	0200	10" diameter		48	.333		19.75	9.55		29.30	37	
	0220	12" diameter		44	.364		26.50	10.40		36.90	45.50	
	0260	16" diameter	↓	40	.400		73.50	11.45		84.95	99	
	0300	20" diameter	Q-10	36	.667		92	19.75		111.75	133	
	0340	24" diameter	"	32	.750	↓	143	22		165	193	
	5000	Vent damper bi-metal 6" flue	Q-9	16	1	Ea.	97.50	28.50		126	153	
	5100	Gas, auto., electric		8	2	"	156	57		213	264	
	7800	All fuel, double wall, stainless steel, 6" diameter		60	.267	V.L.F.	28	7.60		35.60	42.50	
	7802	7" diameter		56	.286		36	8.15		44.15	52.50	
	7804	8" diameter		52	.308		42	8.80		50.80	60	
	7806	10" diameter		48	.333		61	9.55		70.55	83	
	7808	12" diameter		44	.364		82	10.40		92.40	107	
	7810	14" diameter	↓	42	.381	↓	108	10.90		118.90	135	
	8000	All fuel, double wall, stainless steel fittings										
	8010	Roof support 6" diameter	Q-9	30	.533	Ea.	71.50	15.25		86.75	103	
	8020	7" diameter		28	.571		80.50	16.35		96.85	115	
	8030	8" diameter		26	.615		87.50	17.60		105.10	124	
	8040	10" diameter		24	.667		115	19.05		134.05	158	
	8050	12" diameter		22	.727		139	21		160	187	
	8060	14" diameter		21	.762		176	22		198	229	
	8100	Elbow 15°, 6" diameter		30	.533		62.50	15.25		77.75	93	
	8120	7" diameter		28	.571		70	16.35		86.35	103	
	8140	8" diameter		26	.615		80	17.60		97.60	116	
	8160	10" diameter		24	.667		104	19.05		123.05	146	
	8180	12" diameter		22	.727		127	21		148	173	
	8200	14" diameter		21	.762		152	22		174	202	
	8300	Insulated tee with insulated tee cap, 6" diameter		30	.533		118	15.25		133.25	154	
	8340	7" diameter		28	.571		154	16.35		170.35	196	
	8360	8" diameter		26	.615		174	17.60		191.60	219	
	8380	10" diameter		24	.667		245	19.05		264.05	300	
	8400	12" diameter		22	.727		345	21		366	410	
	8420	14" diameter		21	.762		450	22		472	530	
	8500	Joist shield, 6" diameter		30	.533		36	15.25		51.25	64	
	8510	7" diameter		28	.571		39	16.35		55.35	68.50	
	8520	8" diameter		26	.615		48	17.60		65.60	80.50	
	8530	10" diameter		24	.667		64.50	19.05		83.55	102	
	8540	12" diameter		22	.727		80.50	21		101.50	122	
	8550	14" diameter		21	.762		100	22		122	145	
	8600	Round top, 6" diameter		30	.533		40	15.25		55.25	68.50	
	8620	7" diameter		28	.571		54.50	16.35		70.85	86	
	8640	8" diameter		26	.615		73	17.60		90.60	109	
	8660	10" diameter		24	.667		131	19.05		150.05	175	
	8680	12" diameter		22	.727		187	21		208	240	
	8700	14" diameter		21	.762		246	22		268	305	
	8800	Adjustable roof flashing, 6" diameter		30	.533		47.50	15.25		62.75	76.50	
	8820	7" diameter	↓	28	.571	↓	54	16.35		70.35	85.50	

Important: See the Reference Section for critical supporting data - Reference Nos., Crews, & City Cost Indexes

155 | Heating

155 600 | Heating System Access.

			CREW	DAILY OUTPUT	LABOR-HOURS	UNIT	1999 BARE COSTS MAT.	LABOR	EQUIP.	TOTAL	TOTAL INCL O&P	
680	8840	8" diameter	Q-9	26	.615	Ea.	59	17.60		76.60	92.50	680
	8860	10" diameter		24	.667		75.50	19.05		94.55	114	
	8880	12" diameter		22	.727		97.50	21		118.50	141	
	8900	14" diameter		21	.762		122	22		144	169	
	9990	Minimum labor/equipment charge		3	5.333	Job		152		152	244	

156 | HVAC Piping Specialties

156 200 | Heat/Cool Piping Misc.

			CREW	DAILY OUTPUT	LABOR-HOURS	UNIT	1999 BARE COSTS MAT.	LABOR	EQUIP.	TOTAL	TOTAL INCL O&P	
245	0010	**MIXING VALVE** Automatic water tempering										245
	0050	3/4" size	1 Stpi	18	.444	Ea.	335	14.55		349.55	390	
	9000	Minimum labor/equipment charge	"	5	1.600	Job		52.50		52.50	82	
272	0010	**STEAM TRAP**										272
	0020											
	0030	Cast iron body, threaded										
	0040	Inverted bucket										
	0050	1/2" pipe size	1 Stpi	12	.667	Ea.	97	22		119	140	
	0100	1" pipe size		9	.889		256	29		285	330	
	0120	1-1/4" pipe size		8	1		385	33		418	475	
	1000	Float & thermostatic, 15 psi										
	1010	3/4" pipe size	1 Stpi	16	.500	Ea.	93.50	16.40		109.90	129	
	1020	1" pipe size		15	.533		143	17.45		160.45	186	
	1040	1-1/2" pipe size		9	.889		254	29		283	325	
	1060	2" pipe size		6	1.333		460	43.50		503.50	580	
	9000	Minimum labor/equipment charge		4	2	Job		65.50		65.50	103	

156 600 | Strainers

			CREW	DAILY OUTPUT	LABOR-HOURS	UNIT	1999 BARE COSTS MAT.	LABOR	EQUIP.	TOTAL	TOTAL INCL O&P	
608	0010	**STRAINERS, Y TYPE** Bronze body										608
	0020											
	0050	Screwed, 150 lb., 1/4" pipe size	1 Stpi	24	.333	Ea.	15	10.90		25.90	33.50	
	0100	1/2" pipe size		20	.400		15	13.10		28.10	37	
	0120	3/4" pipe size		19	.421		16.35	13.80		30.15	39.50	
	0140	1" pipe size		17	.471		24.50	15.40		39.90	51	
	0160	1-1/2" pipe size		14	.571		53	18.70		71.70	88	
	0180	2" pipe size		13	.615		70.50	20		90.50	109	
	0182	3" pipe size		12	.667		269	22		291	330	
	0220	3" pipe size	Q-5	16	1		535	29.50		564.50	635	
	0240	4" pipe size	"	15	1.067		1,225	31.50		1,256.50	1,400	
	1000	Flanged, 150 lb., 1-1/2" pipe size	1 Stpi	11	.727		320	24		344	390	
	1020	2" pipe size	"	8	1		430	33		463	525	
	1030	2-1/2" pipe size	Q-5	5	3.200		660	94.50		754.50	880	
	1040	3" pipe size		4.50	3.556		815	105		920	1,075	
	1060	4" pipe size		3	5.333		1,250	157		1,407	1,625	
	1100	6" pipe size	Q-6	3	8		2,375	245		2,620	2,975	
	1106	8" pipe size	"	2.60	9.231		3,675	282		3,957	4,500	
	1500	For 300 lb rating, add		40%			40%					
	9000	Minimum labor/equipment charge	1 Stpi	3.75	2.133	Job		70		70	109	

For expanded coverage of these items see *Means Mechanical or Plumbing Cost Data 1999*

157 | Air Conditioning & Ventilation

157 100 | A.C. & Vent. Units

			CREW	DAILY OUTPUT	LABOR-HOURS	UNIT	1999 BARE COSTS MAT.	LABOR	EQUIP.	TOTAL	TOTAL INCL O&P	
110	0010	**ABSORPTION COLD GENERATORS** Water chiller										110
	3000	Gas fired, air cooled										
	3180	3 ton	Q-5	1.30	12.308	Ea.	3,600	365		3,965	4,550	
	9000	Minimum labor/equipment charge	"	1	16	Job		470		470	740	
130	0010	**COMPUTER ROOM UNITS**										130
	1000	Air cooled, includes remote condenser but not										
	1020	interconnecting tubing or refrigerant										
	1160	6 ton	Q-5	.30	53.333	Ea.	15,800	1,575		17,375	19,800	
	1240	10 ton	"	.25	64		18,500	1,875		20,375	23,400	
	1320	20 ton	Q-6	.29	82.759		24,700	2,525		27,225	31,200	
150	0010	**FAN COIL AIR CONDITIONING** Cabinet mounted, filters, controls										150
	0020											
	0100	Chilled water, 1/2 ton cooling	Q-5	8	2	Ea.	730	59		789	900	
	0120	1 ton cooling		6	2.667		830	78.50		908.50	1,050	
	0160	2.5 ton cooling		5	3.200		1,525	94.50		1,619.50	1,825	
	0180	3 ton cooling		4	4		1,675	118		1,793	2,000	
	0200	10 ton cooling	Q-6	2.80	8.571		2,400	262		2,662	3,050	
	0220	15 ton cooling		1.50	16		3,350	490		3,840	4,450	
	0240	20 ton cooling		.80	30		4,300	915		5,215	6,150	
	0260	30 ton cooling		.60	40		6,350	1,225		7,575	8,925	
	0940	Direct expansion, for use w/air cooled condensing, 1.5 ton cooling	Q-5	5	3.200		440	94.50		534.50	635	
	1000	5 ton cooling	"	3	5.333		1,000	157		1,157	1,350	
	1040	10 ton cooling	Q-6	2.60	9.231		2,250	282		2,532	2,925	
	1060	20 ton cooling		.70	34.286		4,175	1,050		5,225	6,250	
	1100	40 ton cooling		.45	53.333		8,775	1,625		10,400	12,200	
	1510	For condensing unit add see division 157-230.										
	3000	Chilled water, horizontal unit, housing, 2 pipe, controls										
	3100	1/2 ton cooling	Q-5	8	2	Ea.	810	59		869	985	
	3110	1 ton cooling		6	2.667		980	78.50		1,058.50	1,200	
	3120	1.5 ton cooling		5.50	2.909		1,175	86		1,261	1,425	
	3130	2 ton cooling		5.25	3.048		1,525	90		1,615	1,825	
	3140	3 ton cooling		4	4		1,625	118		1,743	1,975	
	3150	3.5 ton cooling		3.80	4.211		1,800	124		1,924	2,175	
	3160	4 ton cooling		3.80	4.211		1,800	124		1,924	2,175	
	4000	With electric heat, 2 pipe										
	4100	1/2 ton cooling	Q-5	8	2	Ea.	985	59		1,044	1,175	
	4105	3/4 ton cooling		7	2.286		1,100	67.50		1,167.50	1,300	
	4110	1 ton cooling		6	2.667		1,200	78.50		1,278.50	1,450	
	4120	1.5 ton cooling		5.50	2.909		1,325	86		1,411	1,600	
	4130	2 ton cooling		5.25	3.048		1,675	90		1,765	2,000	
	4135	2.5 ton cooling		4.80	3.333		2,325	98.50		2,423.50	2,700	
	4140	3 ton cooling		4	4		3,100	118		3,218	3,575	
	4150	3.5 ton cooling		3.80	4.211		3,700	124		3,824	4,250	
	4160	4 ton cooling		3.60	4.444		4,250	131		4,381	4,875	
	9000	Minimum labor/equipment charge		3.75	4.267	Job		126		126	197	
160	0010	**HEAT PUMPS** (Not including interconnecting tubing)										160
	1000	Air to air, split system, not including curbs, pads, or ductwork										
	1020	2 ton cooling, 8.5 MBH heat @ 0°F	Q-5	1.20	13.333	Ea.	2,100	395		2,495	2,925	
	1040	3 ton cooling, 13 MBH heat @ 0°F		.80	20		2,700	590		3,290	3,875	
	1080	7.5 ton cooling, 33 MBH heat @ 0°F		.30	53.333		6,575	1,575		8,150	9,675	
	1120	15 ton cooling, 64 MBH heat @ 0°F	Q-6	.26	92.308		11,700	2,825		14,525	17,300	
	1500	Single package, not including curbs, pads, or plenums										
	1520	2 ton cooling, 6.5 MBH heat @ 0°F	Q-5	1.50	10.667	Ea.	2,525	315		2,840	3,275	
	1560	3 ton cooling, 10 MBH heat @ 0°F	"	1.20	13.333		3,025	395		3,420	3,950	
	1660	15 ton cooling, 56 MBH heat @ 0°F	Q-6	.30	80		16,100	2,450		18,550	21,500	

157 | Air Conditioning & Ventilation

157 100 | A.C. & Vent. Units

			DAILY	LABOR-		1999 BARE COSTS				TOTAL	
			CREW	OUTPUT	HOURS	UNIT	MAT.	LABOR	EQUIP.	TOTAL	INCL O&P
160	2000	Water source to air, single package										160
	2100	1 ton cooling, 13 MBH heat @ 75°F	Q-5	2	8	Ea.	965	236		1,201	1,450
	2140	2 ton cooling, 19 MBH heat @ 75°F		1.70	9.412		1,225	277		1,502	1,750
	2220	5 ton cooling, 29 MBH heat @ 75°F		.90	17.778		2,125	525		2,650	3,175
	9000	Minimum labor/equipment charge		1.75	9.143	Job		270		270	420
180	0010	**ROOF TOP AIR CONDITIONERS** Standard controls, curb, economizer										180
	0020										
	1000	Single zone, electric cool, gas heat									
	1090	2 ton cooling, 55 MBH heating	Q-5	1.40	11.429	Ea.	4,050	335		4,385	4,975
	1100	3 ton cooling, 60 MBH heating		1.30	12.308		4,225	365		4,590	5,200
	1120	4 ton cooling, 95 MBH heating		1.10	14.545		4,500	430		4,930	5,625
	1160	10 ton cooling, 200 MBH heating	Q-6	.46	52.174		9,500	1,600		11,100	12,900
	1220	30 ton cooling, 540 MBH heating	Q-7	.22	145		29,100	4,550		33,650	39,100
	1240	40 ton cooling, 675 MBH heating		.16	200		37,900	6,250		44,150	51,500
	1260	50 ton cooling, 810 MBH heating		.13	246		46,000	7,700		53,700	62,500
	1700	Gas cool, gas heat									
	1720	3 ton cooling, 90 MBH heating	Q-5	1.40	11.429	Ea.	5,125	335		5,460	6,150
	2000	Multizone, electric cool, gas heat, economizer									
	2120	20 ton cooling, 360 MBH heating	Q-7	.21	152	Ea.	45,500	4,750		50,250	57,500
	2180	30 ton cooling, 540 MBH heating		.15	213		57,000	6,675		63,675	73,500
	2210	50 ton cooling, 540 MBH heating		.11	290		78,000	9,100		87,100	100,000
	2220	70 ton cooling, 1500 MBH heating		.09	355		109,000	11,100		120,100	137,500
	2240	80 ton cooling, 1500 MBH heating		.08	400		125,000	12,500		137,500	157,000
	2280	105 ton cooling, 1500 MBH heating		.06	533		164,000	16,700		180,700	206,000
	2400	For hot water heat coil, deduct					5%				
	2500	For steam heat coil, deduct					2%				
	2600	For electric heat, deduct					3%	5%			
	9000	Minimum labor/equipment charge	Q-5	1.50	10.667	Job		315		315	490
185	0010	**SELF-CONTAINED SINGLE PACKAGE**										185
	0100	Air cooled, for free blow or duct, including remote condenser									
	0200	3 ton cooling	Q-5	1	16	Ea.	4,300	470		4,770	5,475
	0210	4 ton cooling	"	.80	20		4,675	590		5,265	6,075
	0240	10 ton cooling	Q-7	1	32		9,225	1,000		10,225	11,700
	0280	30 ton cooling	"	.80	40		18,900	1,250		20,150	22,800
	1000	Water cooled for free blow or duct, not including tower									
	1010	Constant volume									
	1100	3 ton cooling	Q-6	1	24	Ea.	3,000	735		3,735	4,450
	1120	5 ton cooling	"	1	24		3,575	735		4,310	5,075
	1140	10 ton cooling	Q-7	.90	35.556		7,275	1,100		8,375	9,750
	1180	30 ton cooling	"	.70	45.714		17,300	1,425		18,725	21,200
	1240	60 ton cooling	Q-8	.30	106		31,800	3,325	165	35,290	40,300
	9000	Minimum labor/equipment charge	Q-5	1	16	Job		470		470	740
187	0010	**SPLIT DUCTLESS SYSTEM**										187
	0100	Cooling only, single zone									
	0110	Wall mount									
	0120	3/4 ton cooling	Q-5	2	8	Ea.	1,375	236		1,611	1,900
	0130	1 ton cooling		1.80	8.889		1,650	262		1,912	2,225
	0140	1-1/2 ton cooling		1.60	10		2,225	295		2,520	2,900
	0150	2 ton cooling		1.40	11.429		2,950	335		3,285	3,775
	1000	Ceiling mount									
	1020	2 ton cooling	Q-5	1.40	11.429	Ea.	3,025	335		3,360	3,850
	1030	3 ton cooling	"	1.20	13.333	"	4,750	395		5,145	5,850
	2000	T-Bar mount									
	2010	2 ton cooling	Q-5	1.40	11.429	Ea.	3,450	335		3,785	4,325

For expanded coverage of these items see *Means Mechanical or Plumbing Cost Data 1999*

157 | Air Conditioning & Ventilation

157 100 | A.C. & Vent. Units

		CREW	DAILY OUTPUT	LABOR-HOURS	UNIT	1999 BARE COSTS MAT.	LABOR	EQUIP.	TOTAL	TOTAL INCL O&P	
187	2020 3 ton cooling	Q-5	1.20	13.333	Ea.	4,250	395		4,645	5,300	187
	2030 3-1/2 ton cooling	↓	1.10	14.545	↓	5,125	430		5,555	6,300	
	3000 Multizone										
	3010 Wall mount										
	3020 2 @ 3/4 ton cooling	Q-5	1.80	8.889	Ea.	4,250	262		4,512	5,075	
	5000 Cooling / Heating										
	5010 Wall mount										
	5110 1 ton cooling	Q-5	1.70	9.412	Ea.	2,075	277		2,352	2,725	
	5120 1-1/2 ton cooling	"	1.50	10.667	"	2,825	315		3,140	3,600	
	5300 Ceiling mount										
	5310 3 ton cooling	Q-5	1	16	Ea.	5,500	470		5,970	6,825	
	7000 Accessories for all split ductless systems										
	7010 Add for ambient frost control	Q-5	8	2	Ea.	234	59		293	350	
	7020 Add for tube / wiring kit										
	7030 15' kit	Q-5	32	.500	Ea.	87	14.75		101.75	119	
	7040 35' kit	"	24	.667	"	173	19.65		192.65	222	
190	0010 **WATER CHILLERS**, With standard controls										190
	0490 Reciprocating, packaged w/integral air cooled condenser, 15 ton cool	Q-7	.37	86.486	Ea.	12,300	2,700		15,000	17,700	
	0500 20 ton cooling		.34	94.955		15,500	2,975		18,475	21,800	
	0520 40 ton cooling	↓	.30	108	↓	24,900	3,375		28,275	32,700	
	0680 Water cooled, single compressor, semi-hermetic, tower not incl.										
	0760 10 ton cooling	Q-6	.36	67.039	Ea.	9,975	2,050		12,025	14,200	
	0840 35 ton cooling	Q-7	.33	97.859	"	16,100	3,050		19,150	22,500	
	0980 Water cooled, multiple compress., semi-hermetic, tower not incl.										
	1100 50 ton cooling	Q-7	.28	113	Ea.	25,100	3,550		28,650	33,200	
	1160 100 ton cooling		.18	179		48,700	5,625		54,325	62,500	
	1200 140 ton cooling	↓	.16	202	↓	56,500	6,325		62,825	72,000	
	9000 Minimum labor/equipment charge	Q-6	1	24	Job		735		735	1,150	
195	0010 **WINDOW UNIT AIR CONDITIONERS**										195
	4500 10,000 BTUH	1 Carp	6	1.333	Ea.	535	36.50		571.50	650	
	4520 12,000 BTUH	L-2	8	2	"	570	48		618	705	
	9000 Minimum labor/equipment charge	1 Carp	2	4	Job		109		109	183	

157 200 | System Components

		CREW	DAILY OUTPUT	LABOR-HOURS	UNIT	MAT.	LABOR	EQUIP.	TOTAL	TOTAL INCL O&P	
201	0010 **COILS, FLANGED**										201
	1500 Hot water heating, 1 row, 24" x 48"	Q-5	3	5.333	Ea.	1,025	157		1,182	1,375	
	9000 Minimum labor/equipment charge	1 Plum	1	8	Job		261		261	410	
210	0010 **COMPRESSORS**										210
	1000 (Ratings are ARI standard 515 group IV using R-22) 2 ton	Q-5	1	16	Ea.	2,650	470		3,120	3,650	
	1100 15 ton	Q-6	.72	33.333		6,275	1,025		7,300	8,500	
	1400 50 ton	"	.20	120		19,200	3,675		22,875	27,000	
	1600 130 ton	Q-7	.21	152	↓	28,100	4,750		32,850	38,400	
230	0010 **CONDENSING UNITS**										230
	0030 Air cooled, compressor, standard controls										
	0050 1.5 ton	Q-5	2.50	6.400	Ea.	800	189		989	1,175	
	0200 2.5 ton		1.70	9.412		1,100	277		1,377	1,650	
	0300 3 ton		1.30	12.308		1,300	365		1,665	2,000	
	0400 4 ton		.90	17.778		1,700	525		2,225	2,700	
	0500 5 ton		.60	26.667	↓	2,075	785		2,860	3,525	
	9000 Minimum labor/equipment charge	↓	1.50	10.667	Job		315		315	490	
240	0010 **COOLING TOWERS** Packaged units										240
	0070 Galvanized steel										
	0080 Draw thru, single flow										
	0100 Belt drive, 60 tons	Q-6	90	.267	TonAC	74	8.15		82.15	94	

157 | Air Conditioning & Ventilation

157 200 | System Components

			CREW	DAILY OUTPUT	LABOR-HOURS	UNIT	MAT.	LABOR	EQUIP.	TOTAL	TOTAL INCL O&P	
240	0150	95 tons	Q-6	100	.240	TonAC	65	7.35		72.35	83	240
	0200	110 tons		109	.220		63.50	6.75		70.25	80.50	
	0250	125 tons		120	.200		62	6.10		68.10	77.50	
	1000	For higher capacities, use multiples										
	1500	Induced air, double flow										
	1900	Gear drive, 150 ton	Q-6	126	.190	TonAC	86	5.80		91.80	104	
	2000	300 ton		129	.186		58.50	5.70		64.20	73	
	2100	600 ton		132	.182		55	5.55		60.55	69	
	2200	Up to 1,000 tons		150	.160		41	4.89		45.89	53	
	3500	For pumps and piping, add		38	.632		37	19.30		56.30	70.50	
	4000	For absorption systems, add					75%	75%				
	5000	Fiberglass										
	5010	Draw thru										
	5100	60 tons	Q-6	1.50	16	Ea.	2,775	490		3,265	3,825	
	5120	125 tons		.99	24.242		5,675	740		6,415	7,400	
	5140	300 tons		.43	55.814		13,300	1,700		15,000	17,300	
	5160	600 tons		.22	109		24,200	3,325		27,525	31,800	
	5180	1000 tons		.15	160		41,500	4,900		46,400	53,500	
	6000	Stainless steel										
	6010	Draw thru										
	6100	60 tons	Q-6	1.50	16	Ea.	7,200	490		7,690	8,700	
	6120	110 tons		.99	24.242		11,500	740		12,240	13,900	
	6140	300 tons		.43	55.814		31,900	1,700		33,600	37,800	
	6160	600 tons		.22	109		49,400	3,325		52,725	59,500	
	6180	1000 tons		.15	160		80,500	4,900		85,400	96,000	
	9000	Minimum labor/equipment charge		1	24	Job		735		735	1,150	
250	0010	**DUCTWORK** R157-050										250
	0020	Fabricated rectangular, includes fittings, joints, supports,										
	0100	Aluminum, alloy 3003-H14, under 100 lb.	Q-10	75	.320	Lb.	3.50	9.50		13	19.05	
	0110	100 to 500 lb.		80	.300		1.44	8.90		10.34	15.85	
	0120	500 to 1,000 lb.		95	.253		1.36	7.50		8.86	13.50	
	0500	Galvanized steel, under 200 lb.		235	.102		3.50	3.03		6.53	8.70	
	0520	200 to 500 lb.		245	.098		.65	2.90		3.55	5.35	
	0540	500 to 1,000 lb.		255	.094		.47	2.79		3.26	4.99	
	0560	1,000 to 2,000 lb.		265	.091		.44	2.68		3.12	4.78	
	0580	Over 5,000 lb.		285	.084		.40	2.50		2.90	4.44	
	0590											
	1000	Stainless steel, type 304, under 100 lb.	Q-10	165	.145	Lb.	3.50	4.31		7.81	10.75	
	1020	100 to 500 lb.		175	.137		1.31	4.06		5.37	7.95	
	1030	500 to 1,000 lb.		190	.126		1.12	3.74		4.86	7.25	
	1300	Flexible, coated fiberglass fabric on corr. resist. metal helix										
	1400	pressure to 12" (WG) UL-181										
	1500	Non-insulated, 3" diameter	Q-9	400	.040	L.F.	.95	1.14		2.09	2.88	
	1540	5" diameter		320	.050		1.11	1.43		2.54	3.51	
	1560	6" diameter		280	.057		1.25	1.63		2.88	4	
	1580	7" diameter		240	.067		1.64	1.91		3.55	4.85	
	1600	8" diameter		200	.080		1.69	2.29		3.98	5.50	
	1640	10" diameter		160	.100		2.17	2.86		5.03	6.95	
	1660	12" diameter		120	.133		2.57	3.81		6.38	8.95	
	1900	Insulated, 1" thick with 3/4 lb., PE jacket, 3" diameter		380	.042		1.64	1.20		2.84	3.73	
	1910	4" diameter		340	.047		1.64	1.34		2.98	3.96	
	1920	5" diameter		300	.053		1.92	1.52		3.44	4.55	
	1940	6" diameter		260	.062		2.15	1.76		3.91	5.20	
	1960	7" diameter		220	.073		2.57	2.08		4.65	6.15	
	1980	8" diameter		180	.089		2.63	2.54		5.17	6.95	
	2020	10" diameter		140	.114		3.42	3.27		6.69	9	

For expanded coverage of these items see *Means Mechanical or Plumbing Cost Data 1999*

157 | Air Conditioning & Ventilation

157 200 | System Components

			CREW	DAILY OUTPUT	LABOR-HOURS	UNIT	MAT.	LABOR	EQUIP.	TOTAL	TOTAL INCL O&P	
250	2040	12" diameter	Q-9	100	.160	L.F.	3.98	4.57		8.55	11.75	250
	2060	14" diameter		80	.200		4.82	5.70		10.52	14.45	
	9990	Minimum labor/equipment charge	1 Shee	3	2.667	Job		84.50		84.50	136	
290	0010	**FANS**										290
	0020	Air conditioning and process air handling										
	0030	Axial flow, compact, low sound, 2.5" S.P.										
	0050	3,800 CFM, 5 HP	Q-20	3.40	5.882	Ea.	3,375	172		3,547	4,000	
	0120	15,600 CFM, 10 HP	"	1.60	12.500	"	5,925	365		6,290	7,100	
	0200	In-line centrifugal, supply/exhaust booster										
	0220	aluminum wheel/hub, disconnect switch, 1/4" S.P.										
	0240	500 CFM, 10" diameter connection	Q-20	3	6.667	Ea.	700	195		895	1,075	
	0280	1,520 CFM, 16" diameter connection		2	10		915	292		1,207	1,475	
	0320	3,480 CFM, 20" diameter connection		.80	25		1,200	730		1,930	2,500	
	0326	5,080 CFM, 20" diameter connection		.75	26.667		1,325	780		2,105	2,725	
	2500	Ceiling fan, right angle, extra quiet, 0.10" S.P.										
	2540	210 CFM	Q-20	19	1.053	Ea.	152	31		183	216	
	2580	885 CFM		16	1.250		365	36.50		401.50	460	
	2620	2,960 CFM		11	1.818		690	53		743	845	
	2640	For wall or roof cap, add	1 Shee	16	.500		100	15.90		115.90	136	
	4500	Corrosive fume resistant, plastic										
	4600	roof ventilators, centrifugal, V belt drive, motor										
	4620	1/4" S.P., 250 CFM, 1/4 HP	Q-20	6	3.333	Ea.	2,125	97.50		2,222.50	2,475	
	4640	895 CFM, 1/3 HP		5	4		2,300	117		2,417	2,725	
	4660	1630 CFM, 1/2 HP		4	5		2,725	146		2,871	3,225	
	4680	2240 CFM, 1 HP		3	6.667		2,850	195		3,045	3,425	
	5000	Utility set, centrifugal, V belt drive, motor										
	5020	1/4" S.P., 1200 CFM, 1/4 HP	Q-20	6	3.333	Ea.	2,925	97.50		3,022.50	3,375	
	5040	1520 CFM, 1/3 HP		5	4		2,925	117		3,042	3,400	
	5060	1850 CFM, 1/2 HP		4	5		2,950	146		3,096	3,450	
	5080	2180 CFM, 3/4 HP		3	6.667		2,950	195		3,145	3,525	
	6650	Residential, bath exhaust, grille, back draft damper										
	6660	50 CFM	Q-20	24	.833	Ea.	13.95	24.50		38.45	54.50	
	6670	110 CFM		22	.909		49.50	26.50		76	97	
	6680	Light combination, squirrel cage, 100 watt, 70 CFM		24	.833		61	24.50		85.50	106	
	6700	Light/heater combination, ceiling mounted										
	6710	70 CFM, 1450 watt	Q-20	24	.833	Ea.	74	24.50		98.50	121	
	6800	Heater combination, recessed, 70 CFM		24	.833		35	24.50		59.50	77.50	
	6820	With 2 infrared bulbs		23	.870		53	25.50		78.50	99	
	6900	Kitchen exhaust, grille, complete, 160 CFM		22	.909		62	26.50		88.50	111	
	6910	180 CFM		20	1		52.50	29		81.50	104	
	6920	270 CFM		18	1.111		94.50	32.50		127	156	
	6940	Residential roof jacks and wall caps										
	6944	Wall cap with back draft damper										
	6946	3" & 4" dia. round duct	1 Shee	11	.727	Ea.	12.70	23		35.70	51	
	6948	6" dia. round duct	"	11	.727	"	30.50	23		53.50	70.50	
	6958	Roof jack with bird screen and back draft damper										
	6960	3" & 4" dia. round duct	1 Shee	11	.727	Ea.	12.20	23		35.20	50.50	
	6962	3-1/4" x 10" rectangular duct	"	10	.800	"	22.50	25.50		48	65	
	6980	Transition										
	6982	3-1/4" x 10" to 6" dia. round	1 Shee	20	.400	Ea.	13.75	12.70		26.45	35.50	
	7100	Direct drive, 320 CFM, 11" sq. damper	Q-20	7	2.857		380	83.50		463.50	555	
	7120	600 CFM, 11" sq. damper	"	6	3.333		390	97.50		487.50	585	
	8000	Ventilation, residential										
	8020	Attic, roof type										
	8030	Aluminum dome, damper & curb										

157 | Air Conditioning & Ventilation

157 200 | System Components

		CREW	DAILY OUTPUT	LABOR-HOURS	UNIT	1999 BARE COSTS MAT.	LABOR	EQUIP.	TOTAL	TOTAL INCL O&P	
290	8040	6" diameter, 300 CFM	1 Elec	16	.500	Ea.	291	15.95		306.95	345	290
	8050	7" diameter, 450 CFM		15	.533		320	17		337	375	
	8060	9" diameter, 900 CFM		14	.571		510	18.25		528.25	590	
	8080	12" diameter, 1000 CFM (gravity)		10	.800		227	25.50		252.50	290	
	8090	16" diameter, 1500 CFM (gravity)		9	.889		274	28.50		302.50	345	
	8100	20" diameter, 2500 CFM (gravity)		8	1		335	32		367	420	
	8110	26" diameter, 4000 CFM (gravity)		7	1.143		405	36.50		441.50	505	
	8120	32" diameter, 6500 CFM (gravity)		6	1.333		560	42.50		602.50	680	
	8130	38" diameter, 8000 CFM (gravity)		5	1.600		830	51		881	990	
	8140	50" diameter, 13,000 CFM (gravity)		4	2		1,200	64		1,264	1,425	
	8160	Plastic, ABS dome										
	8180	1050 CFM	1 Elec	14	.571	Ea.	67	18.25		85.25	102	
	8200	1600 CFM	"	12	.667	"	100	21.50		121.50	143	
	8240	Attic, wall type, with shutter, one speed										
	8250	12" diameter, 1000 CFM	1 Elec	14	.571	Ea.	194	18.25		212.25	241	
	8260	14" diameter, 1500 CFM		12	.667		233	21.50		254.50	289	
	8270	16" diameter, 2000 CFM		9	.889		325	28.50		353.50	405	
	8290	Whole house, wall type, with shutter, one speed										
	8300	30" diameter, 4800 CFM	1 Elec	7	1.143	Ea.	545	36.50		581.50	650	
	8310	36" diameter, 7000 CFM		6	1.333		595	42.50		637.50	720	
	8320	42" diameter, 10,000 CFM		5	1.600		720	51		771	870	
	8330	48" diameter, 16,000 CFM		4	2		945	64		1,009	1,150	
	8340	For two speed, add					60			60	66	
	8350	Whole house, lay-down type, with shutter, one speed										
	8360	30" diameter, 4500 CFM	1 Elec	8	1	Ea.	590	32		622	700	
	8370	36" diameter, 6500 CFM		7	1.143		650	36.50		686.50	770	
	8380	42" diameter, 9000 CFM		6	1.333		765	42.50		807.50	905	
	8390	48" diameter, 12,000 CFM		5	1.600		1,000	51		1,051	1,175	
	8440	For two speed, add					15			15	16.50	
	8450	For 12 hour timer switch, add	1 Elec	32	.250		30	7.95		37.95	45.50	
	9000	Minimum labor/equipment charge	"	4	2	Job		64		64	98.50	

157 400 | Accessories

		CREW	DAILY OUTPUT	LABOR-HOURS	UNIT	MAT.	LABOR	EQUIP.	TOTAL	TOTAL INCL O&P	
401	0010	**AIR FILTERS**										401
	0020											
	0050	Activated charcoal type, full flow				MCFM	600			600	660	
	2000	Electronic air cleaner, duct mounted										
	2150	400 - 1000 CFM	1 Shee	2.30	3.478	Ea.	495	110		605	720	
	2200	1000 - 1400 CFM		2.20	3.636		675	115		790	925	
	2250	1400 - 2000 CFM		2.10	3.810		745	121		866	1,025	
	2950	Mechanical media filtration units										
	3000	High efficiency type, with frame, non-supported				MCFM	45			45	49.50	
	3100	Supported type					55			55	60.50	
	4000	Medium efficiency, extended surface					5			5	5.50	
	4500	Permanent washable					20			20	22	
	5000	Renewable disposable roll					120			120	132	
	5500	Throwaway glass or paper media type				Ea.	3.89			3.89	4.28	
	9000	Minimum labor/equipment charge	1 Shee	2.25	3.556	Job		113		113	181	
420	0010	**CONTROL COMPONENTS**										420
	5000	Thermostats										
	5030	Manual	1 Shee	8	1	Ea.	24	32		56	77.50	
	5040	1 set back, electric, timed		8	1		78.50	32		110.50	137	
	5050	2 set back, electric, timed		8	1		46	32		78	102	
	5200	24 hour, automatic, clock		8	1		90.50	32		122.50	151	

For expanded coverage of these items see *Means Mechanical or Plumbing Cost Data 1999*

157 | Air Conditioning & Ventilation

157 400 | Accessories

			CREW	DAILY OUTPUT	LABOR-HOURS	UNIT	1999 BARE COSTS MAT.	LABOR	EQUIP.	TOTAL	TOTAL INCL O&P	
420	6000	Valves, motorized zone										420
	6100	Sweat connections, 1/2" C x C	1 Stpi	20	.400	Ea.	60	13.10		73.10	86.50	
	6110	3/4" C x C		20	.400		60	13.10		73.10	86.50	
	6120	1" C x C		19	.421		60	13.80		73.80	87.50	
	9000	Minimum labor/equipment charge	1 Plum	4	2	Job		65		65	102	
430	0010	**CONTROL SYSTEMS, ELECTRONIC**										430
	1000	Electronic hydronic controller	1 Plum	8	1	Ea.	31	32.50		63.50	85	
	9000	Minimum labor/equipment charge	"	8	1	Job		32.50		32.50	51	
440	0010	**CURBS/PADS PREFABRICATED**										440
	6000	Pad, fiberglass reinforced concrete with polystyrene foam core										
	6050	Condenser, 2" thick, 20" x 38"	1 Shee	8	1	Ea.	15.85	32		47.85	68.50	
	6090	24" x 36"	"	12	.667		20	21		41	56	
	6280	36" x 36"	Q-9	8	2		31	57		88	126	
	6300	36" x 40"		7	2.286		35	65.50		100.50	143	
	6320	36" x 48"		7	2.286		42	65.50		107.50	152	
450	0010	**DIFFUSERS** Aluminum, opposed blade damper unless noted										450
	0100	Ceiling, linear, also for sidewall										
	0120	2" wide	1 Shee	32	.250	L.F.	24.50	7.95		32.45	40	
	0160	4" wide		26	.308		32.50	9.75		42.25	51.50	
	0180	6" wide		24	.333		40.50	10.60		51.10	61.50	
	0200	8" wide		22	.364		47	11.55		58.55	70.50	
	0500	Perforated, 24" x 24" lay-in panel size, 6" x 6"		16	.500	Ea.	79.50	15.90		95.40	113	
	0520	8" x 8"		15	.533		82	16.95		98.95	117	
	0530	9" x 9"		14	.571		84	18.15		102.15	121	
	0540	10" x 10"		14	.571		86	18.15		104.15	124	
	0560	12" x 12"		12	.667		86	21		107	129	
	0590	16" x 16"		11	.727		107	23		130	155	
	0600	18" x 18"		10	.800		114	25.50		139.50	167	
	0610	20" x 20"		10	.800		130	25.50		155.50	184	
	0620	24" x 24"		9	.889		163	28		191	224	
	1000	Rectangular, 1 to 4 way blow, 6" x 6"		16	.500		46	15.90		61.90	76.50	
	1010	8" x 8"		15	.533		54	16.95		70.95	86.50	
	1014	9" x 9"		15	.533		56	16.95		72.95	88.50	
	1016	10" x 10"		15	.533		67	16.95		83.95	101	
	1020	12" x 6"		15	.533		57	16.95		73.95	89.50	
	1040	12" x 9"		14	.571		69.50	18.15		87.65	106	
	1060	12" x 12"		12	.667		82	21		103	124	
	1070	14" x 6"		13	.615		61	19.55		80.55	99	
	1074	14" x 14"		12	.667		101	21		122	145	
	1150	18" x 18"		9	.889		149	28		177	209	
	1170	24" x 12"		10	.800		134	25.50		159.50	189	
	2000	T bar mounting, 24" x 24" lay-in frame, 6" x 6"		16	.500		75.50	15.90		91.40	109	
	2020	9" x 9"		14	.571		84	18.15		102.15	121	
	2040	12" x 12"		12	.667		111	21		132	156	
	2060	15" x 15"		11	.727		143	23		166	194	
	2080	18" x 18"		10	.800		149	25.50		174.50	205	
	6000	For steel diffusers instead of aluminum, deduct					10%					
	9000	Minimum labor/equipment charge	1 Shee	4	2	Job		63.50		63.50	102	
460	0010	**GRILLES**										460
	0020	Aluminum										
	1000	Air return, 6" x 6"	1 Shee	26	.308	Ea.	12.35	9.75		22.10	29.50	
	1020	10" x 6"		24	.333		14.95	10.60		25.55	33.50	

157 | Air Conditioning & Ventilation

157 400 | Accessories

			CREW	DAILY OUTPUT	LABOR-HOURS	UNIT	1999 BARE COSTS MAT.	LABOR	EQUIP.	TOTAL	TOTAL INCL O&P	
460	1080	16" x 8"	1 Shee	22	.364	Ea.	21.50	11.55		33.05	42	460
	1100	12" x 12"		22	.364		21.50	11.55		33.05	42	
	1120	24" x 12"		18	.444		38.50	14.10		52.60	64.50	
	1300	48" x 24"		12	.667		148	21		169	196	
	9000	Minimum labor/equipment charge		4	2	Job		63.50		63.50	102	
470	0010	**REGISTERS**										470
	0020											
	0980	Air supply										
	1000	Ceiling/wall, O.B. damper, anodized aluminum										
	1010	One or two way deflection, adj. curved face bars										
	1140	14" x 8"	1 Shee	17	.471	Ea.	28	14.95		42.95	54.50	
	3000	Baseboard, hand adj. damper, enameled steel										
	3012	8" x 6"	1 Shee	26	.308	Ea.	8.10	9.75		17.85	24.50	
	3020	10" x 6"		24	.333		8.10	10.60		18.70	26	
	3040	12" x 5"		23	.348		10.35	11.05		21.40	29	
	3060	12" x 6"		23	.348		9.55	11.05		20.60	28	
	3080	12" x 8"		22	.364		13.85	11.55		25.40	33.50	
	3100	14" x 6"		20	.400		10.35	12.70		23.05	32	
	9000	Minimum labor/equipment charge		4	2	Job		63.50		63.50	102	
480	0010	**DUCT ACCESSORIES**										480
	0050	Air extractors, 12" x 4"	1 Shee	24	.333	Ea.	14.45	10.60		25.05	33	
	0100	8" x 6"		22	.364		14.45	11.55		26	34.50	
	0200	20" x 8"		16	.500		32.50	15.90		48.40	61.50	
	0240	18" x 10"		14	.571		32	18.15		50.15	64	
	0280	24" x 12"		10	.800		44.50	25.50		70	89.50	
	3000	Fire damper, curtain type, 1-1/2 hr rated, vertical, 6" x 6"		24	.333		19.70	10.60		30.30	38.50	
	3020	8" x 6"		22	.364		19.70	11.55		31.25	40	
	3240	16" x 14"		18	.444		31.50	14.10		45.60	57	
	3400	24" x 20"		8	1		39.50	32		71.50	94.50	
	5180	Mixing box, includes electric or pneumatic motor										
	5190	Recommend use with attenuator, see 157-480-9000										
	5200	Constant volume, 150 to 270 CFM	Q-9	12	1.333	Ea.	465	38		503	570	
	5210	270 to 600 CFM		11	1.455		475	41.50		516.50	590	
	5500	VAV Cool only, pneum. press indep. 300 to 600 CFM		11	1.455		320	41.50		361.50	415	
	5510	500 to 1000 CFM		9	1.778		325	51		376	440	
	5520	800 to 1600 CFM		9	1.778		335	51		386	450	
	5530	1100 to 2000 CFM		8	2		345	57		402	470	
	5540	1500 to 3000 CFM		7	2.286		370	65.50		435.50	515	
	5550	2000 to 4000 CFM		6	2.667		385	76		461	545	
	5560	For electric, w/thermostat, press. dependent, add					20					
	5990	Multi-blade dampers, opposed blade, 8" x 6"	1 Shee	24	.333		18	10.60		28.60	37	
	5994	8" x 8"		22	.364		18.80	11.55		30.35	39	
	5996	10" x 10"		21	.381		21	12.10		33.10	43	
	6000	12" x 12"		21	.381		24.50	12.10		36.60	46.50	
	6020	12" x 18"		18	.444		32.50	14.10		46.60	58	
	6030	14" x 10"		20	.400		23.50	12.70		36.20	46.50	
	6031	14" x 14"		17	.471		29	14.95		43.95	56	
	6033	16" x 12"		17	.471		29	14.95		43.95	56	
	6035	16" x 16"		16	.500		35.50	15.90		51.40	64.50	
	6037	18" x 14"		16	.500		35.50	15.90		51.40	64.50	
	6038	18" x 18"		15	.533		42	16.95		58.95	73	
	6070	20" x 16"		14	.571		43	18.15		61.15	76	
	6072	20" x 20"		13	.615		51	19.55		70.55	87.50	
	6074	22" x 18"		14	.571		51	18.15		69.15	85	
	6076	24" x 16"		11	.727		50	23		73	92	

For expanded coverage of these items see Means Mechanical or Plumbing Cost Data 1999

157 | Air Conditioning & Ventilation

157 400 | Accessories

		CREW	DAILY OUTPUT	LABOR-HOURS	UNIT	1999 BARE COSTS MAT.	LABOR	EQUIP.	TOTAL	TOTAL INCL O&P	
6078	24" x 20"	1 Shee	8	1	Ea.	59.50	32		91.50	117	480
6080	24" x 24"		8	1		69	32		101	127	
6110	26" x 26"	▼	6	1.333		82.50	42.50		125	159	
6133	30" x 30"	Q-9	6.60	2.424		109	69.50		178.50	231	
6135	32" x 32"		6.40	2.500		124	71.50		195.50	251	
6180	48" x 36"	▼	5.60	2.857	▼	209	81.50		290.50	360	
7500	Variable volume modulating motorized damper, incl. elect. mtr.										
7504	8" x 6"	1 Shee	15	.533	Ea.	119	16.95		135.95	158	
7506	10" x 6"		14	.571		119	18.15		137.15	160	
7510	10" x 10"		13	.615		123	19.55		142.55	167	
7520	12" x 12"		12	.667		126	21		147	173	
7522	12" x 16"		11	.727		132	23		155	182	
7524	16" x 10"		12	.667		127	21		148	174	
7526	16" x 14"		10	.800		133	25.50		158.50	187	
7528	16" x 18"		9	.889		140	28		168	199	
7542	18" x 18"		8	1		146	32		178	212	
7544	20" x 14"		8	1		149	32		181	215	
7546	20" x 18"		7	1.143		158	36.50		194.50	232	
7560	24" x 12"		8	1		151	32		183	217	
7562	24" x 18"		7	1.143		168	36.50		204.50	243	
7568	28" x 10"		7	1.143		250	36.50		286.50	335	
7590	30" x 14"		5	1.600		266	51		317	375	
7600	30" x 18"		4	2		280	63.50		343.50	410	
7610	30" x 24"		3.80	2.105		320	67		387	460	
7700	For thermostat, add	▼	8	1	▼	30	32		62	84	
8000	Multi-blade dampers, parallel blade										
8100	8" x 8"	1 Shee	24	.333	Ea.	52.50	10.60		63.10	75	
8140	16" x 10"		20	.400		55.50	12.70		68.20	81.50	
8160	18" x 12"		18	.444		57	14.10		71.10	85.50	
8220	28" x 16"	▼	10	.800	▼	77	25.50		102.50	126	
9000	Silencers, noise control for air flow, duct				MCFM	41.50			41.50	45.50	
9200	Plenums, measured by panel surface				S.F.	8.25			8.25	9.10	
9900	Minimum labor/equipment charge	1 Shee	4	2	Job		63.50		63.50	102	
0010	**VENTILATORS** Base, damper & bird screen, CFM in 5 MPH wind										490
0520	8" neck diameter, 215 CFM	Q-9	14	1.143	Ea.	55.50	32.50		88	114	
9000	Minimum labor/equipment charge	1 Plum	2	4	Job		130		130	204	

For information about Means Estimating Seminars, see yellow pages 11 and 12 in back of book

Division 16 Electrical

Estimating Tips

160 Raceways
- Conduit should be taken off in three main categories: power distribution, branch power, and branch lighting, so the estimator can concentrate on systems and components, therefore making it easier to ensure all items have been accounted for.
- For cost modifications for elevated conduit installation, add the percentages to labor according to the height of installation and only the quantities exceeding the different height levels, not to the total conduit quantities.

161 Conductors & Grounding
- Remember that aluminum wiring of equal ampacity is larger in diameter than copper and may require larger conduit.
- If more than three wires at a time are being pulled, deduct percentages from the labor hours of that grouping of wires.
- When taking off grounding system, identify separately the type and size of wire and list each unique type of ground connection.

162 Boxes & Wiring Devices
- The estimator should take the weights of materials into consideration when completing a takeoff. Topics to consider include: How will the materials be supported? What methods of support are available? How high will the support structure have to reach? Will the final support structure be able to withstand the total burden? Is the support material included or separate from the fixture, equipment and material specified?

163 Motors, Starters, Boards & Switches
- Supports and concrete pads may be shown on drawings for the larger equipment, or the support system may be just a piece of plywood for the back of a panelboard. In either case, it must be included in the costs.

164 Transformers & Bus Ducts
- Do not overlook the costs for equipment used in the installation. If scaffolding or highlifts are available in the field, contractors may use them in lieu of the proposed ladders and rolling staging.

166 Lighting
- Fixtures should be taken off room by room, using the fixture schedule, specifications, and the ceiling plan. For large concentrations of lighting fixtures in the same area deduct the percentages from labor hours.

168 Special Systems
- When estimating material costs for special systems, it is always prudent to obtain manufacturers' quotations for equipment prices and special installation requirements which will affect the total costs.

Reference Numbers
Reference numbers are shown in bold squares at the beginning of some major classifications. These numbers refer to related items in the Reference Section. The reference information may be an estimating procedure, an alternate pricing method or technical information.

Note: Not all subdivisions listed here necessarily appear in this publication.

160 | Raceways

160 100 | Cable Trays

			CREW	DAILY OUTPUT	LABOR-HOURS	UNIT	1999 BARE COSTS				TOTAL INCL O&P
							MAT.	LABOR	EQUIP.	TOTAL	
150	0010	**WIREWAY** to 15' high										150
	0100	Screw cover, with fittings and supports, 2-1/2" x 2-1/2"	1 Elec	45	.178	L.F.	8.30	5.65		13.95	17.85
	0200	4" x 4"	"	40	.200		9.15	6.40		15.55	19.90
	0400	6" x 6"	2 Elec	60	.267		15.50	8.50		24	30.50
	0600	8" x 8"	"	40	.400		20	12.75		32.75	41.50

160 200 | Conduits

			CREW	DAILY OUTPUT	LABOR-HOURS	UNIT	MAT.	LABOR	EQUIP.	TOTAL	TOTAL INCL O&P
205	0010	**CONDUIT** To 15' high, includes 2 terminations, 2 elbows and	R160-205									205
	0020	11 beam clamps per 100 L.F.									
	2500	Steel, intermediate conduit (IMC), 1/2" diameter	1 Elec	100	.080	L.F.	1.15	2.55		3.70	5.20
	2530	3/4" diameter		90	.089		1.36	2.84		4.20	5.85
	2550	1" diameter		70	.114		1.86	3.65		5.51	7.70
	2570	1-1/4" diameter		65	.123		2.43	3.93		6.36	8.70
	2600	1-1/2" diameter		60	.133		2.79	4.25		7.04	9.60
	2630	2" diameter		50	.160		3.62	5.10		8.72	11.90
	2650	2-1/2" diameter		40	.200		7.05	6.40		13.45	17.60
	2670	3" diameter	2 Elec	60	.267		9.10	8.50		17.60	23
	2700	3-1/2" diameter		54	.296		11.20	9.45		20.65	27
	2730	4" diameter		50	.320		13	10.20		23.20	30
	5000	Electric metallic tubing (EMT), 1/2" diameter	1 Elec	170	.047		.36	1.50		1.86	2.72
	5020	3/4" diameter		130	.062		.53	1.96		2.49	3.61
	5040	1" diameter		115	.070		.86	2.22		3.08	4.37
	5060	1-1/4" diameter		100	.080		1.31	2.55		3.86	5.40
	5080	1-1/2" diameter		90	.089		1.64	2.84		4.48	6.20
	5100	2" diameter		80	.100		2.12	3.19		5.31	7.25
	5120	2-1/2" diameter		60	.133		5.75	4.25		10	12.85
	5140	3" diameter	2 Elec	100	.160		6.30	5.10		11.40	14.85
	5160	3-1/2" diameter		90	.178		8.05	5.65		13.70	17.60
	5180	4" diameter		80	.200		9.15	6.40		15.55	19.90
	5200	Field bends, 45° to 90°, 1/2" diameter	1 Elec	89	.090	Ea.		2.87		2.87	4.43
	5220	3/4" diameter		80	.100			3.19		3.19	4.93
	5240	1" diameter		73	.110			3.50		3.50	5.40
	5260	1-1/4" diameter		38	.211			6.70		6.70	10.40
	5280	1-1/2" diameter		36	.222			7.10		7.10	10.95
	5300	2" diameter		26	.308			9.80		9.80	15.15
	5320	Offsets, 1/2" diameter		65	.123			3.93		3.93	6.05
	5340	3/4" diameter		62	.129			4.12		4.12	6.35
	5360	1" diameter		53	.151			4.82		4.82	7.45
	5380	1-1/4" diameter		30	.267			8.50		8.50	13.15
	5400	1-1/2" diameter		28	.286			9.10		9.10	14.10
	7600	EMT, "T" fittings with covers, 1/2" diameter, set screw		16	.500		9.30	15.95		25.25	35
	9000	Minimum labor/equipment charge		4	2	Job		64		64	98.50
230	0010	**CONDUIT IN CONCRETE SLAB** Including terminations,										230
	0020	fittings and supports									
	3230	PVC, schedule 40, 1/2" diameter	1 Elec	270	.030	L.F.	.35	.95		1.30	1.84
	3250	3/4" diameter		230	.035		.42	1.11		1.53	2.17
	3270	1" diameter		200	.040		.56	1.28		1.84	2.58
	3300	1-1/4" diameter		170	.047		.77	1.50		2.27	3.17
	3330	1-1/2" diameter		140	.057		.96	1.82		2.78	3.87
	3350	2" diameter		120	.067		1.22	2.13		3.35	4.63
	4350	Rigid galvanized steel, 1/2" diameter		200	.040		1.21	1.28		2.49	3.30
	4400	3/4" diameter		170	.047		1.47	1.50		2.97	3.94
	4450	1" diameter		130	.062		2.14	1.96		4.10	5.40
	4500	1-1/4" diameter		110	.073		2.71	2.32		5.03	6.55

160 | Raceways

160 200 | Conduits

			CREW	DAILY OUTPUT	LABOR-HOURS	UNIT	MAT.	LABOR	EQUIP.	TOTAL	TOTAL INCL O&P	
230	4600	1-1/2" diameter	1 Elec	100	.080	L.F.	3.30	2.55		5.85	7.55	230
	4800	2" diameter		90	.089		4.40	2.84		7.24	9.20	
	9000	Minimum labor/equipment charge		4	2	Job		64		64	98.50	
240	0010	**CONDUIT IN TRENCH** Includes terminations and fittings										240
	0020	Does not include excavation or backfill, see div. 022-200										
	0200	Rigid galvanized steel, 2" diameter	1 Elec	150	.053	L.F.	4.24	1.70		5.94	7.30	
	0400	2-1/2" diameter	"	100	.080		7.35	2.55		9.90	12.05	
	0600	3" diameter	2 Elec	160	.100		9.55	3.19		12.74	15.45	
	0800	3-1/2" diameter		140	.114		12.15	3.65		15.80	19	
	1000	4" diameter		100	.160		13.95	5.10		19.05	23.50	
	1200	5" diameter		80	.200		29	6.40		35.40	42	
	1400	6" diameter		60	.267		41.50	8.50		50	58.50	
	9000	Minimum labor/equipment charge	1 Elec	4	2	Job		64		64	98.50	
260	0010	**CUTTING AND DRILLING**										260
	0100	Hole drilling to 10' high, concrete wall										
	0110	8" thick, 1/2" pipe size	1 Elec	12	.667	Ea.		21.50		21.50	33	
	0120	3/4" pipe size		12	.667			21.50		21.50	33	
	0130	1" pipe size		9.50	.842			27		27	41.50	
	0140	1-1/4" pipe size		9.50	.842			27		27	41.50	
	0150	1-1/2" pipe size		9.50	.842			27		27	41.50	
	0160	2" pipe size		4.40	1.818			58		58	89.50	
	0170	2-1/2" pipe size		4.40	1.818			58		58	89.50	
	0180	3" pipe size		4.40	1.818			58		58	89.50	
	0190	3-1/2" pipe size		3.30	2.424			77.50		77.50	120	
	0200	4" pipe size		3.30	2.424			77.50		77.50	120	
	0500	12" thick, 1/2" pipe size		9.40	.851			27		27	42	
	0520	3/4" pipe size		9.40	.851			27		27	42	
	0540	1" pipe size		7.30	1.096			35		35	54	
	0560	1-1/4" pipe size		7.30	1.096			35		35	54	
	0570	1-1/2" pipe size		7.30	1.096			35		35	54	
	0580	2" pipe size		3.60	2.222			71		71	110	
	0590	2-1/2" pipe size		3.60	2.222			71		71	110	
	0600	3" pipe size		3.60	2.222			71		71	110	
	0610	3-1/2" pipe size		2.80	2.857			91		91	141	
	0630	4" pipe size		2.50	3.200			102		102	158	
	0650	16" thick, 1/2" pipe size		7.60	1.053			33.50		33.50	52	
	0670	3/4" pipe size		7	1.143			36.50		36.50	56.50	
	0690	1" pipe size		6	1.333			42.50		42.50	65.50	
	0710	1-1/4" pipe size		5.50	1.455			46.50		46.50	71.50	
	0730	1-1/2" pipe size		5.50	1.455			46.50		46.50	71.50	
	0750	2" pipe size		3	2.667			85		85	131	
	0770	2-1/2" pipe size		2.70	2.963			94.50		94.50	146	
	0790	3" pipe size		2.50	3.200			102		102	158	
	0810	3-1/2" pipe size		2.30	3.478			111		111	171	
	0830	4" pipe size		2	4			128		128	197	
	0850	20" thick, 1/2" pipe size		6.40	1.250			40		40	61.50	
	0870	3/4" pipe size		6	1.333			42.50		42.50	65.50	
	0890	1" pipe size		5	1.600			51		51	79	
	0910	1-1/4" pipe size		4.80	1.667			53		53	82	
	0930	1-1/2" pipe size		4.60	1.739			55.50		55.50	85.50	
	0950	2" pipe size		2.70	2.963			94.50		94.50	146	
	0970	2-1/2" pipe size		2.40	3.333			106		106	164	
	0990	3" pipe size		2.20	3.636			116		116	179	
	1010	3-1/2" pipe size		2	4			128		128	197	
	1030	4" pipe size		1.70	4.706			150		150	232	

For expanded coverage of these items see *Means Electrical Cost Data 1999*

160 | Raceways

	160 200	Conduits	CREW	DAILY OUTPUT	LABOR-HOURS	UNIT	1999 BARE COSTS MAT.	LABOR	EQUIP.	TOTAL	TOTAL INCL O&P
1050		24" thick, 1/2" pipe size	1 Elec	5.50	1.455	Ea.		46.50		46.50	71.50
1070		3/4" pipe size		5.10	1.569			50		50	77.50
1090		1" pipe size		4.30	1.860			59.50		59.50	91.50
1110		1-1/4" pipe size		4	2			64		64	98.50
1130		1-1/2" pipe size		4	2			64		64	98.50
1150		2" pipe size		2.40	3.333			106		106	164
1170		2-1/2" pipe size		2.20	3.636			116		116	179
1190		3" pipe size		2	4			128		128	197
1210		3-1/2" pipe size		1.80	4.444			142		142	219
1230		4" pipe size		1.50	5.333			170		170	263
1500		Brick wall, 8" thick, 1/2" pipe size		18	.444			14.20		14.20	22
1520		3/4" pipe size		18	.444			14.20		14.20	22
1540		1" pipe size		13.30	.602			19.20		19.20	29.50
1560		1-1/4" pipe size		13.30	.602			19.20		19.20	29.50
1580		1-1/2" pipe size		13.30	.602			19.20		19.20	29.50
1600		2" pipe size		5.70	1.404			45		45	69
1620		2-1/2" pipe size		5.70	1.404			45		45	69
1640		3" pipe size		5.70	1.404			45		45	69
1660		3-1/2" pipe size		4.40	1.818			58		58	89.50
1680		4" pipe size		4	2			64		64	98.50
1700		12" thick, 1/2" pipe size		14.50	.552			17.60		17.60	27
1720		3/4" pipe size		14.50	.552			17.60		17.60	27
1740		1" pipe size		11	.727			23		23	36
1760		1-1/4" pipe size		11	.727			23		23	36
1780		1-1/2" pipe size		11	.727			23		23	36
1800		2" pipe size		5	1.600			51		51	79
1820		2-1/2" pipe size		5	1.600			51		51	79
1840		3" pipe size		5	1.600			51		51	79
1860		3-1/2" pipe size		3.80	2.105			67		67	104
1880		4" pipe size		3.30	2.424			77.50		77.50	120
1900		16" thick, 1/2" pipe size		12.30	.650			21		21	32
1920		3/4" pipe size		12.30	.650			21		21	32
1940		1" pipe size		9.30	.860			27.50		27.50	42.50
1960		1-1/4" pipe size		9.30	.860			27.50		27.50	42.50
1980		1-1/2" pipe size		9.30	.860			27.50		27.50	42.50
2000		2" pipe size		4.40	1.818			58		58	89.50
2010		2-1/2" pipe size		4.40	1.818			58		58	89.50
2030		3" pipe size		4.40	1.818			58		58	89.50
2050		3-1/2" pipe size		3.30	2.424			77.50		77.50	120
2070		4" pipe size		3	2.667			85		85	131
2090		20" thick, 1/2" pipe size		10.70	.748			24		24	37
2110		3/4" pipe size		10.70	.748			24		24	37
2130		1" pipe size		8	1			32		32	49.50
2150		1-1/4" pipe size		8	1			32		32	49.50
2170		1-1/2" pipe size		8	1			32		32	49.50
2190		2" pipe size		4	2			64		64	98.50
2210		2-1/2" pipe size		4	2			64		64	98.50
2230		3" pipe size		4	2			64		64	98.50
2250		3-1/2" pipe size		3	2.667			85		85	131
2270		4" pipe size		2.70	2.963			94.50		94.50	146
2290		24" thick, 1/2" pipe size		9.40	.851			27		27	42
2310		3/4" pipe size		9.40	.851			27		27	42
2330		1" pipe size		7.10	1.127			36		36	55.50
2350		1-1/4" pipe size		7.10	1.127			36		36	55.50
2370		1-1/2" pipe size		7.10	1.127			36		36	55.50
2390		2" pipe size		3.60	2.222			71		71	110

Important: See the Reference Section for critical supporting data - Reference Nos., Crews, & City Cost Indexes

160 | Raceways

160 200 | Conduits

			CREW	DAILY OUTPUT	LABOR-HOURS	UNIT	MAT.	LABOR	EQUIP.	TOTAL	TOTAL INCL O&P	
260	2410	2-1/2" pipe size	1 Elec	3.60	2.222	Ea.		71		71	110	260
	2430	3" pipe size		3.60	2.222			71		71	110	
	2450	3-1/2" pipe size		2.80	2.857			91		91	141	
	2470	4" pipe size		2.50	3.200			102		102	158	
	2480											
	3000	Knockouts to 8' high, metal boxes & enclosures										
	3020	With hole saw, 1/2" pipe size	1 Elec	53	.151	Ea.		4.82		4.82	7.45	
	3040	3/4" pipe size		47	.170			5.45		5.45	8.40	
	3050	1" pipe size		40	.200			6.40		6.40	9.85	
	3060	1-1/4" pipe size		36	.222			7.10		7.10	10.95	
	3070	1-1/2" pipe size		32	.250			7.95		7.95	12.30	
	3080	2" pipe size		27	.296			9.45		9.45	14.60	
	3090	2-1/2" pipe size		20	.400			12.75		12.75	19.70	
	4010	3" pipe size		16	.500			15.95		15.95	24.50	
	4030	3-1/2" pipe size		13	.615			19.65		19.65	30.50	
	4050	4" pipe size		11	.727			23		23	36	
	4070	With hand punch set, 1/2" pipe size		40	.200			6.40		6.40	9.85	
	4090	3/4" pipe size		32	.250			7.95		7.95	12.30	
	4110	1" pipe size		30	.267			8.50		8.50	13.15	
	4130	1-1/4" pipe size		28	.286			9.10		9.10	14.10	
	4150	1-1/2" pipe size		26	.308			9.80		9.80	15.15	
	4170	2" pipe size		20	.400			12.75		12.75	19.70	
	4190	2-1/2" pipe size		17	.471			15		15	23	
	4200	3" pipe size		15	.533			17		17	26.50	
	4220	3-1/2" pipe size		12	.667			21.50		21.50	33	
	4240	4" pipe size		10	.800			25.50		25.50	39.50	
	4260	With hydraulic punch, 1/2" pipe size		44	.182			5.80		5.80	8.95	
	4280	3/4" pipe size		38	.211			6.70		6.70	10.40	
	4300	1" pipe size		38	.211			6.70		6.70	10.40	
	4320	1-1/4" pipe size		38	.211			6.70		6.70	10.40	
	4340	1-1/2" pipe size		38	.211			6.70		6.70	10.40	
	4360	2" pipe size		32	.250			7.95		7.95	12.30	
	4380	2-1/2" pipe size		27	.296			9.45		9.45	14.60	
	4400	3" pipe size		23	.348			11.10		11.10	17.15	
	4420	3-1/2" pipe size		20	.400			12.75		12.75	19.70	
275	0010	**MOTOR CONNECTIONS**										275
	0020	Flexible conduit and fittings, 115 volt, 1 phase, up to 1 HP motor	1 Elec	8	1	Ea.	3.95	32		35.95	54	
	9000	Minimum labor/equipment charge	"	4	2	Job		64		64	98.50	
290	0010	**WIREMOLD RACEWAY**										290
	0090	Surface, metal, straight section										
	0100	No. 500	1 Elec	100	.080	L.F.	.63	2.55		3.18	4.63	
	0110	No. 700		100	.080		.71	2.55		3.26	4.72	
	0400	No. 1500, small pancake		90	.089		1.33	2.84		4.17	5.85	
	0600	No. 2000, base & cover, blank		90	.089		1.29	2.84		4.13	5.80	
	0800	No. 3000, base & cover, blank		75	.107		2.53	3.40		5.93	8.05	
	1000	No. 4000, base & cover, blank		65	.123		4.30	3.93		8.23	10.80	
	1200	No. 6000, base & cover, blank		50	.160		7.05	5.10		12.15	15.65	
	2400	Fittings, elbows, No. 500		40	.200	Ea.	1.14	6.40		7.54	11.10	
	2800	Elbow cover, No. 2000		40	.200		2.30	6.40		8.70	12.40	
	2880	Tee, No. 500		42	.190		2.21	6.10		8.31	11.85	
	2900	No. 2000		27	.296		7.05	9.45		16.50	22.50	
	3000	Switch box, No. 500		16	.500		8.10	15.95		24.05	33.50	
	3400	Telephone outlet, No. 1500		16	.500		8.60	15.95		24.55	34	
	3600	Junction box, No. 1500		16	.500		6	15.95		21.95	31	

For expanded coverage of these items see *Means Electrical Cost Data 1999*

160 | Raceways

160 200 | Conduits

			CREW	DAILY OUTPUT	LABOR-HOURS	UNIT	MAT.	LABOR	EQUIP.	TOTAL	TOTAL INCL O&P
290	3800	Plugmold wired sections, No. 2000										290
	4000	1 circuit, 6 outlets, 3 ft. long	1 Elec	8	1	Ea.	21.50	32		53.50	73
	4100	2 circuits, 8 outlets, 6 ft. long		5.30	1.509		36	48		84	114
	4200	Tele-power poles, aluminum, 4 outlets	↓	3.70	2.162	↓	142	69		211	263
	9300	Surface, non-metallic, straight section									
	9310	No. 400, base & cover, blank	1 Elec	160	.050	L.F.	1.03	1.59		2.62	3.59
	9320	Base & cover w/ adhesive		160	.050		1.19	1.59		2.78	3.77
	9340	No. 800, base & cover, blank		145	.055		1.19	1.76		2.95	4.03
	9350	Base & cover w/ adhesive		145	.055		1.38	1.76		3.14	4.24
	9370	No. 2300, base & cover, blank		130	.062		1.72	1.96		3.68	4.92
	9380	Base & cover w/ adhesive		130	.062	↓	1.98	1.96		3.94	5.20
	9400	Fittings, elbows, No. 400		50	.160	Ea.	1.19	5.10		6.29	9.20
	9410	No. 800		45	.178		1.24	5.65		6.89	10.10
	9420	No. 2300		40	.200		1.38	6.40		7.78	11.35
	9430	Tees, No. 400		35	.229		1.57	7.30		8.87	13
	9440	No. 800		32	.250		1.62	7.95		9.57	14.10
	9450	No. 2300		30	.267		1.67	8.50		10.17	15
	9460	Cover clip, No. 400		80	.100		.32	3.19		3.51	5.30
	9470	No. 800		72	.111		.29	3.54		3.83	5.80
	9480	No. 2300		64	.125		.49	3.99		4.48	6.70
	9490	Blank end, No. 400		50	.160		.45	5.10		5.55	8.40
	9510	No. 2300		40	.200		.78	6.40		7.18	10.70
	9520	Round fixture box 5.5" dia x 1"		25	.320		7.80	10.20		18	24.50
	9530	Device box, 1 gang		30	.267		3.44	8.50		11.94	16.95
	9540	2 gang		25	.320	↓	5.10	10.20		15.30	21.50
	9990	Minimum labor/equipment charge	↓	5	1.600	Job		51		51	79

161 | Conductors & Grounding

161 100 | Conductors

			CREW	DAILY OUTPUT	LABOR-HOURS	UNIT	MAT.	LABOR	EQUIP.	TOTAL	TOTAL INCL O&P
105	0010	**ARMORED CABLE**										105
	0020										
	0050	600 volt, copper (BX), #14, 2 conductor, solid	1 Elec	2.40	3.333	C.L.F.	45	106		151	214
	0100	3 conductor, solid		2.20	3.636		57	116		173	242
	0152	#12, 2 conductor, solid		2.10	3.810		45.50	122		167.50	238
	0202	3 conductor, solid		1.80	4.444		66.50	142		208.50	293
	0252	#10, 2 conductor, solid		1.80	4.444		80	142		222	305
	0302	3 conductor, solid		1.50	5.333		105	170		275	380
	0352	#8, 3 conductor, solid		1.20	6.667	↓	172	213		385	520
	9000	Minimum labor/equipment charge		4	2	Job		64		64	98.50
	9010	600 volt, copper (MC) steel clad, #14, 2 wire		2.40	3.333	C.L.F.	43	106		149	212
	9020	3 wire		2.20	3.636		55.50	116		171.50	240
	9040	#12, 2 wire		2.30	3.478		46.50	111		157.50	223
	9050	3 wire		2	4		68.50	128		196.50	273
	9070	#10, 2 wire		2	4		80	128		208	285
	9080	3 wire		1.60	5		120	160		280	380
	9100	#8, 2 wire, stranded		1.80	4.444		152	142		294	385
	9110	3 wire, stranded	↓	1.30	6.154	↓	216	196		412	545
140	0010	**MINERAL INSULATED CABLE** 600 volt										140
	0100	1 conductor, #12	1 Elec	1.60	5	C.L.F.	253	160		413	525

161 | Conductors & Grounding

161 100 | Conductors

		CREW	DAILY OUTPUT	LABOR-HOURS	UNIT	1999 BARE COSTS MAT.	LABOR	EQUIP.	TOTAL	TOTAL INCL O&P
1500	2 conductor, #12	1 Elec	1.40	5.714	C.L.F.	405	182		587	725
1600	#10		1.20	6.667		490	213		703	870
1800	#8		1.10	7.273		610	232		842	1,025
2000	#6		1.05	7.619		775	243		1,018	1,225
2100	#4	2 Elec	2	8		1,025	255		1,280	1,525
2200	3 conductor, #12	1 Elec	1.20	6.667		470	213		683	845
2400	#10		1.10	7.273		585	232		817	1,000
2600	#8		1.05	7.619		710	243		953	1,150
2800	#6		1	8		920	255		1,175	1,400
3000	#4	2 Elec	1.80	8.889		1,200	284		1,484	1,775
3100	4 conductor, #12	1 Elec	1.20	6.667		540	213		753	925
3200	#10		1.10	7.273		640	232		872	1,075
3400	#8		1	8		835	255		1,090	1,325
3600	#6		.90	8.889		1,050	284		1,334	1,600
3620	7 conductor, #12		1.10	7.273		685	232		917	1,125
3640	#10		1	8		855	255		1,110	1,325
3800	M.I. terminations, 600 volt, 1 conductor, #12		8	1	Ea.	8.20	32		40.20	58.50
5500	2 conductor, #12		6.70	1.194		9.10	38		47.10	69
5600	#10		6.40	1.250		11.80	40		51.80	74.50
5800	#8		6.20	1.290		11.80	41		52.80	76.50
6000	#6		5.70	1.404		11.80	45		56.80	82
6200	#4		5.30	1.509		27.50	48		75.50	105
6400	3 conductor, #12		5.70	1.404		10.25	45		55.25	80.50
6500	#10		5.50	1.455		12.75	46.50		59.25	85.50
6600	#8		5.20	1.538		12.75	49		61.75	90
6800	#6		4.80	1.667		12.75	53		65.75	96
7200	#4		4.60	1.739		28	55.50		83.50	117
7400	4 conductor, #12		4.60	1.739		13.70	55.50		69.20	101
7500	#10		4.40	1.818		13.70	58		71.70	105
7600	#8		4.20	1.905		13.70	61		74.70	109
8400	#6		4	2		29	64		93	131
8500	7 conductor, #12		3.50	2.286		17.40	73		90.40	132
8600	#10		3	2.667		32	85		117	166
8800	Crimping tool, plier type					57			57	62.50
9000	Stripping tool					85			85	93.50
9200	Hand vise					37			37	40.50
9500	Minimum labor/equipment charge	1 Elec	4	2	Job		64		64	98.50

161 145

		CREW	DAILY OUTPUT	LABOR-HOURS	UNIT	MAT.	LABOR	EQUIP.	TOTAL	TOTAL INCL O&P
0010	**NON-METALLIC SHEATHED CABLE** 600 volt									
0100	Copper with ground wire, (Romex)									
0152	#14, 2 wire	1 Elec	2.50	3.200	C.L.F.	15.40	102		117.40	175
0202	3 wire		2.30	3.478		25.50	111		136.50	199
0252	#12, 2 wire		2.20	3.636		22.50	116		138.50	204
0302	3 wire		2	4		37	128		165	238
0352	#10, 2 wire		2	4		37	128		165	238
0402	3 wire		1.40	5.714		57.50	182		239.50	345
0452	#8, 3 conductor		1.30	6.154		116	196		312	435
0502	#6, 3 wire		1.20	6.667		179	213		392	525
0550	SE type SER aluminum cable, 3 RHW and									
0602	1 bare neutral, 3 #8 & 1 #8	1 Elec	1.50	5.333	C.L.F.	96	170		266	370
0652	3 #6 & 1 #6	"	1.30	6.154		109	196		305	425
0702	3 #4 & 1 #6	2 Elec	2.20	7.273		122	232		354	495
0752	3 #2 & 1 #4		2	8		179	255		434	590
0802	3 #1/0 & 1 #2		1.80	8.889		271	284		555	740
0852	3 #2/0 & 1 #1		1.60	10		320	320		640	845
0902	3 #4/0 & 1 #2/0		1.40	11.429		455	365		820	1,075

For expanded coverage of these items see Means Electrical Cost Data 1999

161 | Conductors & Grounding

161 100 | Conductors

			CREW	DAILY OUTPUT	LABOR-HOURS	UNIT	1999 BARE COSTS MAT.	LABOR	EQUIP.	TOTAL	TOTAL INCL O&P	
145	6500	Service entrance cap for copper SEU										145
	6700	150 amp	1 Elec	10	.800	Ea.	12.05	25.50		37.55	53	
	6800	200 amp		8	1	"	18.25	32		50.25	69.50	
	9000	Minimum labor/equipment charge	↓	4	2	Job		64		64	98.50	
155	0010	**SPECIAL WIRES & FITTINGS**										155
	1250	Nonshielded, #22-2 conductor	1 Elec	10	.800	C.L.F.	7.50	25.50		33	48	
	9000	Minimum labor/equipment charge	"	4	2	Job		64		64	98.50	
165	0010	**WIRE**										165
	0020	600 volt type THW, copper, solid, #14	1 Elec	13	.615	C.L.F.	4.45	19.65		24.10	35.50	
	0030	#12		11	.727		6.30	23		29.30	43	
	0040	#10	↓	10	.800	↓	9.70	25.50		35.20	50	
	0051	Wire, 600 volt, stranded R160-205										
	0140	#8	1 Elec	8	1	C.L.F.	18.30	32		50.30	69.50	
	0160	#6 R161-100	"	6.50	1.231		29.50	39.50		69	93	
	0180	#4	2 Elec	10.60	1.509		48	48		96	128	
	0200	#3		10	1.600		57	51		108	142	
	0220	#2		9	1.778		71	56.50		127.50	166	
	0240	#1		8	2		89.50	64		153.50	197	
	0260	1/0		6.60	2.424		110	77.50		187.50	241	
	0280	2/0		5.80	2.759		137	88		225	286	
	0300	3/0		5	3.200		172	102		274	345	
	0350	4/0	↓	4.40	3.636		214	116		330	415	
	0400	250 kcmil	3 Elec	6	4		258	128		386	480	
	0420	300 kcmil		5.70	4.211		305	134		439	550	
	0450	350 kcmil		5.40	4.444		355	142		497	610	
	0480	400 kcmil		5.10	4.706		410	150		560	680	
	0490	500 kcmil		4.80	5		500	160		660	795	
	0510	750 kcmil	↓	3.30	7.273		770	232		1,002	1,200	
	0530	Aluminum, stranded, #8	1 Elec	9	.889		12.30	28.50		40.80	57.50	
	0540	#6	"	8	1		15.70	32		47.70	67	
	0560	#4	2 Elec	13	1.231		19.60	39.50		59.10	82	
	0580	#2		10.60	1.509		26.50	48		74.50	104	
	0600	#1		9	1.778		39	56.50		95.50	131	
	0620	1/0		8	2		46	64		110	149	
	0640	2/0		7.20	2.222		55	71		126	171	
	0680	3/0		6.60	2.424		68	77.50		145.50	195	
	0700	4/0	↓	6.20	2.581		76	82.50		158.50	211	
	0720	250 kcmil	3 Elec	8.70	2.759		90.50	88		178.50	236	
	0740	300 kcmil		8.10	2.963		128	94.50		222.50	287	
	0760	350 kcmil		7.50	3.200		130	102		232	300	
	0780	400 kcmil		6.90	3.478		152	111		263	340	
	0800	500 kcmil		6	4		168	128		296	380	
	0850	600 kcmil		5.70	4.211		212	134		346	440	
	0880	700 kcmil	↓	5.10	4.706	↓	245	150		395	500	
	9000	Minimum labor/equipment charge	1 Elec	4	2	Job		64		64	98.50	

161 800 | Grounding

			CREW	DAILY OUTPUT	LABOR-HOURS	UNIT	MAT.	LABOR	EQUIP.	TOTAL	TOTAL INCL O&P	
810	0010	**GROUNDING**										810
	0030	Rod, copper clad, 8' long, 1/2" diameter	1 Elec	5.50	1.455	Ea.	15.65	46.50		62.15	89	
	0040	5/8" diameter		5.50	1.455		16.70	46.50		63.20	90	
	0050	3/4" diameter		5.30	1.509		30	48		78	107	
	0080	10' long, 1/2" diameter		4.80	1.667		17.50	53		70.50	101	
	0090	5/8" diameter		4.60	1.739		18.20	55.50		73.70	106	
	0100	3/4" diameter		4.40	1.818		29.50	58		87.50	122	
	0130	15' long, 3/4" diameter	↓	4	2		79	64		143	186	

161 | Conductors & Grounding

161 800 | Grounding

			CREW	DAILY OUTPUT	LABOR-HOURS	UNIT	MAT.	LABOR	EQUIP.	TOTAL	TOTAL INCL O&P	
810	0260	Wire ground bare armored, #8-1 conductor	1 Elec	2	4	C.L.F.	59.50	128		187.50	263	810
	0280	#4-1 conductor		1.60	5		111	160		271	370	
	0390	Bare copper wire, #8 stranded		11	.727		15.80	23		38.80	53.50	
	0400	#6		10	.800		24	25.50		49.50	65.50	
	0600	#2	2 Elec	10	1.600		58.50	51		109.50	144	
	0800	3/0		6.60	2.424		155	77.50		232.50	291	
	1000	4/0		5.70	2.807		193	89.50		282.50	350	
	1200	250 kcmil	3 Elec	7.20	3.333		229	106		335	415	
	1800	Water pipe ground clamps, heavy duty										
	2000	Bronze, 1/2" to 1" diameter	1 Elec	8	1	Ea.	11.45	32		43.45	62	
	2100	1-1/4" to 2" diameter		8	1		14.90	32		46.90	66	
	2200	2-1/2" to 3" diameter		6	1.333		39.50	42.50		82	109	
	2800	Brazed connections, #6 wire		12	.667		10.45	21.50		31.95	44.50	
	3000	#2 wire		10	.800		14	25.50		39.50	55	
	3100	3/0 wire		8	1		21	32		53	72.50	
	3200	4/0 wire		7	1.143		24	36.50		60.50	83	
	3400	250 kcmil wire		5	1.600		28	51		79	110	
	3600	500 kcmil wire		4	2		34.50	64		98.50	137	
	9000	Minimum labor/equipment charge		4	2	Job		64		64	98.50	

162 | Boxes & Wiring Devices

162 100 | Boxes

			CREW	DAILY OUTPUT	LABOR-HOURS	UNIT	MAT.	LABOR	EQUIP.	TOTAL	TOTAL INCL O&P	
110	0010	**OUTLET BOXES**										110
	0020	Pressed steel, octagon, 4"	1 Elec	20	.400	Ea.	1.44	12.75		14.19	21.50	
	0060	Covers, blank		64	.125		.59	3.99		4.58	6.80	
	0100	Extension		40	.200		2.29	6.40		8.69	12.35	
	0152	Square 4"		18	.444		1.98	14.20		16.18	24	
	0200	Extension		40	.200		2.41	6.40		8.81	12.50	
	0250	Covers, blank		64	.125		.68	3.99		4.67	6.90	
	0300	Plaster rings		64	.125		1.09	3.99		5.08	7.35	
	0652	Switchbox		24	.333		2.21	10.65		12.86	18.90	
	1102	Concrete, floor, 1 gang		4.80	1.667		56	53		109	144	
	9000	Minimum labor/equipment charge		4	2	Job		64		64	98.50	
120	0010	**OUTLET BOXES, PLASTIC**										120
	0050	4" diameter, round with 2 mounting nails	1 Elec	25	.320	Ea.	1.60	10.20		11.80	17.55	
	0102	Bar hanger mounted		23	.348		2.50	11.10		13.60	19.90	
	0202	Square with 2 mounting nails		23	.348		1.99	11.10		13.09	19.35	
	0300	Plaster ring		64	.125		.85	3.99		4.84	7.10	
	0402	Switch box with 2 mounting nails, 1 gang		27	.296		.90	9.45		10.35	15.60	
	0502	2 gang		23	.348		1.94	11.10		13.04	19.30	
	0602	3 gang		18	.444		3.08	14.20		17.28	25.50	
	0702	Old work box		27	.296		1.86	9.45		11.31	16.65	
	9000	Minimum labor/equipment charge		4	2	Job		64		64	98.50	
130	0010	**PULL BOXES & CABINETS**										130
	0100	Sheet metal, pull box, NEMA 1, type SC, 6" W x 6" H x 4" D	1 Elec	8	1	Ea.	8.35	32		40.35	58.50	
	0200	8" W x 8" H x 4" D		8	1		11.45	32		43.45	62	
	0300	10" W x 12" H x 6" D		5.30	1.509		20	48		68	96.50	

For expanded coverage of these items see *Means Electrical Cost Data 1999*

162 | Boxes & Wiring Devices

162 100 | Boxes

			CREW	DAILY OUTPUT	LABOR-HOURS	UNIT	MAT.	LABOR	EQUIP.	TOTAL	TOTAL INCL O&P	
130	0400	16" W x 20" H x 8" D	1 Elec	4	2	Ea.	76	64		140	182	130
	0500	20" W x 24" H x 8" D		3.20	2.500		89	80		169	221	
	0600	24" W x 36" H x 8" D		2.70	2.963		125	94.50		219.50	284	
	0650	Hinged cabinets, NEMA 1, 6" W x 6" H x 4" D		8	1		8.50	32		40.50	59	
	0802	12" W x 16" H x 6" D		4	2		28	64		92	129	
	1000	20" W x 20" H x 6" D		3.60	2.222		56	71		127	172	
	1200	20" W x 20" H x 8" D		3.20	2.500		113	80		193	247	
	1400	24" W x 36" H x 8" D		2.70	2.963		180	94.50		274.50	345	
	1600	24" W x 42" H x 8" D		2	4		273	128		401	495	
	7000	Cabinets, current transformer										
	7050	Single door, 24" H x 24" W x 10" D	1 Elec	1.60	5	Ea.	107	160		267	365	
	7100	30" H x 24" W x 10" D		1.30	6.154		120	196		316	435	
	7150	36" H x 24" W x 10" D		1.10	7.273		134	232		366	505	
	7200	30" H x 30" W x 10" D		1	8		140	255		395	550	
	7250	36" H x 30" W x 10" D		.90	8.889		189	284		473	650	
	7300	36" H x 36" W x 10" D		.80	10		206	320		526	720	
	7500	Double door, 48" H x 36" W x 10" D		.60	13.333		360	425		785	1,050	
	7550	24" H x 24" W x 12" D		1	8		193	255		448	605	
	9990	Minimum labor/ equipment charge		2	4	Job		128		128	197	

162 300 | Wiring Devices

			CREW	DAILY OUTPUT	LABOR-HOURS	UNIT	MAT.	LABOR	EQUIP.	TOTAL	TOTAL INCL O&P	
320	0010	**WIRING DEVICES**										320
	0200	Toggle switch, quiet type, single pole, 15 amp	1 Elec	40	.200	Ea.	4.25	6.40		10.65	14.55	
	0500	20 amp		27	.296		6.30	9.45		15.75	21.50	
	0550	Rocker, 15 amp		40	.200		4.89	6.40		11.29	15.25	
	0560	20 amp		27	.296		11.40	9.45		20.85	27	
	0600	3 way, 15 amp		23	.348		6.50	11.10		17.60	24.50	
	0850	Rocker, 15 amp		23	.348		6.90	11.10		18	25	
	0860	20 amp		18	.444		16.50	14.20		30.70	40	
	0900	4 way, 15 amp		15	.533		18.95	17		35.95	47.50	
	1030	Rocker, 15 amp		15	.533		18.95	17		35.95	47.50	
	1040	20 amp		11	.727		41	23		64	81	
	1650	Dimmer switch, 120 volt, incandescent, 600 watt, 1 pole		16	.500		10.80	15.95		26.75	36.50	
	2460	Receptacle, duplex, 120 volt, grounded, 15 amp		40	.200		1.14	6.40		7.54	11.10	
	2470	20 amp		27	.296		5.95	9.45		15.40	21	
	2490	Dryer, 30 amp		15	.533		11.70	17		28.70	39.50	
	2500	Range, 50 amp		11	.727		16	23		39	53.50	
	2600	Wall plates, stainless steel, 1 gang		80	.100		2.05	3.19		5.24	7.20	
	2800	2 gang		53	.151		4.10	4.82		8.92	11.95	
	3200	Lampholder, keyless		26	.308		5.20	9.80		15	21	
	3400	Pullchain with receptacle		22	.364		8.25	11.60		19.85	27	
	9000	Minimum labor/equipment charge		4	2	Job		64		64	98.50	

163 | Motors, Starters, Boards & Switches

163 100 | Starters & Controls

			CREW	DAILY OUTPUT	LABOR-HOURS	UNIT	MAT.	LABOR	EQUIP.	TOTAL	TOTAL INCL O&P	
140	0010	**VARIABLE FREQUENCY DRIVES/ADJUSTABLE FREQUENCY DRIVES**										140
	0100	Enclosed (NEMA 1), 460 volt, for 3 HP motor size	1 Elec	.80	10	Ea.	1,475	320		1,795	2,125	

163 | Motors, Starters, Boards & Switches

163 100 | Starters & Controls

		Crew	Daily Output	Labor-Hours	Unit	Mat.	Labor	Equip.	Total	Total Incl O&P
140	0110	5 HP motor size	1 Elec	.80	10	Ea.	1,675	320		1,995	2,350
	0120	7.5 HP motor size		.67	11.940		2,375	380		2,755	3,225
	0130	10 HP motor size		.67	11.940		2,375	380		2,755	3,225
	0140	15 HP motor size	2 Elec	.89	17.978		2,575	575		3,150	3,725
	0150	20 HP motor size		.89	17.978		3,800	575		4,375	5,050
	0160	25 HP motor size		.67	23.881		4,200	760		4,960	5,800
	0170	30 HP motor size		.67	23.881		4,825	760		5,585	6,500
	0180	40 HP motor size		.67	23.881		7,100	760		7,860	8,975
	0190	50 HP motor size		.53	30.189		7,725	965		8,690	10,000
	0200	60 HP motor size	R-3	.56	35.714		8,650	1,125	243	10,018	11,500
	0210	75 HP motor size		.56	35.714		11,700	1,125	243	13,068	14,900
	0220	100 HP motor size		.50	40		13,500	1,275	272	15,047	17,100
	0230	125 HP motor size		.50	40		15,900	1,275	272	17,447	19,800
	0240	150 HP motor size		.50	40		18,200	1,275	272	19,747	22,400
	0250	200 HP motor size		.42	47.619		20,500	1,500	325	22,325	25,200
	1100	Custom-engineered, 460 volt, for 3 HP motor size	1 Elec	.56	14.286		2,375	455		2,830	3,300
	1110	5 HP motor size		.56	14.286		2,600	455		3,055	3,550
	1120	7.5 HP motor size		.47	17.021		3,475	545		4,020	4,675
	1130	10 HP motor size		.47	17.021		3,675	545		4,220	4,900
	1140	15 HP motor size	2 Elec	.62	25.806		4,525	825		5,350	6,275
	1150	20 HP motor size		.62	25.806		5,350	825		6,175	7,150
	1160	25 HP motor size		.47	34.043		6,150	1,075		7,225	8,450
	1170	30 HP motor size		.47	34.043		7,375	1,075		8,450	9,800
	1180	40 HP motor size		.47	34.043		7,875	1,075		8,950	10,300
	1190	50 HP motor size		.37	43.243		9,950	1,375		11,325	13,100
	1200	60 HP motor size	R-3	.39	51.282		13,700	1,625	350	15,675	18,000
	1210	75 HP motor size		.39	51.282		14,900	1,625	350	16,875	19,300
	1220	100 HP motor size		.35	57.143		16,200	1,800	390	18,390	21,000
	1230	125 HP motor size		.35	57.143		18,500	1,800	390	20,690	23,600
	1240	150 HP motor size		.35	57.143		20,600	1,800	390	22,790	25,800
	1250	200 HP motor size		.29	68.966		24,000	2,175	470	26,645	30,300
	2000	For complex & special design systems to meet specific									
	2010	requirements, obtain quote from vendor.									

163 200 | Boards

			Crew	Daily Output	Labor-Hours	Unit	Mat.	Labor	Equip.	Total	Total Incl O&P
205	0010	**CIRCUIT BREAKERS** (in enclosure)									
	0100	Enclosed (NEMA 1), 600 volt, 3 pole, 30 amp	1 Elec	3.20	2.500	Ea.	330	80		410	490
	0200	60 amp		2.80	2.857		330	91		421	505
	0400	100 amp		2.30	3.478		380	111		491	585
	0600	225 amp		1.50	5.333		880	170		1,050	1,225
	0700	400 amp	2 Elec	1.60	10		1,500	320		1,820	2,150
	9000	Minimum labor/equipment charge	1 Elec	4	2	Job		64		64	98.50
240	0010	**METER CENTERS AND SOCKETS**									
	0100	Sockets, single position, 4 terminal, 100 amp	1 Elec	3.20	2.500	Ea.	29	80		109	155
	0200	150 amp		2.30	3.478		33.50	111		144.50	208
	0300	200 amp		1.90	4.211		38	134		172	250
	0400	20 amp		3.20	2.500		29	80		109	155
	0500	Double position, 4 terminal, 100 amp		2.80	2.857		122	91		213	275
	0600	150 amp		2.10	3.810		126	122		248	325
	0700	200 amp		1.70	4.706		300	150		450	560
	9000	Minimum labor/equipment charge		3	2.667	Job		85		85	131
245	0010	**PANELBOARDS** (Commercial use)									
	0050	NQOD, w/20 amp 1 pole bolt-on circuit breakers									

For expanded coverage of these items see *Means Electrical Cost Data 1999*

163 | Motors, Starters, Boards & Switches

163 200 | Boards

		CREW	DAILY OUTPUT	LABOR-HOURS	UNIT	1999 BARE COSTS MAT.	LABOR	EQUIP.	TOTAL	TOTAL INCL O&P
0100	3 wire, 120/240 volts, 100 amp main lugs									
0150	10 circuits	1 Elec	1	8	Ea.	390	255		645	820
0200	14 circuits		.88	9.091		455	290		745	950
0250	18 circuits		.75	10.667		500	340		840	1,075
0300	20 circuits		.65	12.308		560	395		955	1,225
0600	4 wire, 120/208 volts, 100 amp main lugs, 12 circuits		1	8		440	255		695	880
0650	16 circuits		.75	10.667		505	340		845	1,075
0700	20 circuits		.65	12.308		590	395		985	1,250
0750	24 circuits		.60	13.333		640	425		1,065	1,350
0800	30 circuits		.53	15.094		740	480		1,220	1,550
0850	225 amp main lugs, 32 circuits	2 Elec	.90	17.778		830	565		1,395	1,800
0900	34 circuits		.84	19.048		850	610		1,460	1,875
0950	36 circuits		.80	20		870	640		1,510	1,950
1000	42 circuits		.68	23.529		975	750		1,725	2,225
1200	NEHB, w/20 amp, 1 pole bolt-on circuit breakers									
1250	4 wire, 277/480 volts, 100 amp main lugs, 12 circuits	1 Elec	.88	9.091	Ea.	840	290		1,130	1,375
1300	20 circuits	"	.60	13.333		1,250	425		1,675	2,025
1350	225 amp main lugs, 24 circuits	2 Elec	.90	17.778		1,425	565		1,990	2,450
1400	30 circuits		.80	20		1,725	640		2,365	2,875
1450	36 circuits		.72	22.222		2,000	710		2,710	3,300
1600	NQOD panel, w/20 amp, 1 pole, circuit breakers									
2000	4 wire, 120/208 volts with main circuit breaker									
2050	100 amp main, 24 circuits	1 Elec	.47	17.021	Ea.	805	545		1,350	1,725
2100	30 circuits	"	.40	20		910	640		1,550	1,975
2200	225 amp main, 32 circuits	2 Elec	.72	22.222		1,550	710		2,260	2,800
2250	42 circuits		.56	28.571		1,675	910		2,585	3,250
2300	400 amp main, 42 circuits		.48	33.333		2,275	1,075		3,350	4,150
2350	600 amp main, 42 circuits		.40	40		3,375	1,275		4,650	5,700
2400	NEHB, with 20 amp, 1 pole circuit breaker									
2450	4 wire, 277/480 volts with main circuit breaker									
2500	100 amp main, 24 circuits	1 Elec	.42	19.048	Ea.	1,650	610		2,260	2,775
2550	30 circuits	"	.38	21.053		1,950	670		2,620	3,175
2600	225 amp main, 30 circuits	2 Elec	.72	22.222		2,450	710		3,160	3,800
2650	42 circuits	"	.56	28.571		3,025	910		3,935	4,725
9000	Minimum labor/equipment charge	1 Elec	1	8	Job		255		255	395
0010	**PANELBOARD & LOAD CENTER CIRCUIT BREAKERS**									
0050	Bolt-on, 10,000 amp IC, 120 volt, 1 pole									
0100	15 to 50 amp	1 Elec	10	.800	Ea.	10	25.50		35.50	50.50
0200	60 amp		8	1		10	32		42	60.50
0300	70 amp		8	1		19	32		51	70.50
0350	240 volt, 2 pole									
0400	15 to 50 amp	1 Elec	8	1	Ea.	22	32		54	73.50
0500	60 amp		7.50	1.067		22	34		56	76.50
0600	80 to 100 amp		5	1.600		85	51		136	173
0700	3 pole, 15 to 60 amp		6.20	1.290		69.50	41		110.50	140
0800	70 amp		5	1.600		87.50	51		138.50	176
0900	80 to 100 amp		3.60	2.222		99.50	71		170.50	219
1000	22,000 amp I.C., 240 volt, 2 pole, 70 - 225 amp		2.70	2.963		430	94.50		524.50	615
1100	3 pole, 70 - 225 amp		2.30	3.478		475	111		586	695
1200	14,000 amp I.C., 277 volts, 1 pole, 15 - 30 amp		8	1		26.50	32		58.50	78.50
1300	22,000 amp I.C., 480 volts, 2 pole, 70 - 225 amp		2.70	2.963		430	94.50		524.50	615
1400	3 pole, 70 - 225 amp		2.30	3.478		475	111		586	695
2060	Plug-in tandem, 120/240 V, 2-15 A, 1 pole		11	.727		17.45	23		40.45	55
2070	1-15 A & 1-20 A		11	.727		17.45	23		40.45	55
2080	2-20 A		11	.727		17.45	23		40.45	55

Important: See the Reference Section for critical supporting data - Reference Nos., Crews, & City Cost Indexes

163 | Motors, Starters, Boards & Switches

163 200 | Boards

			CREW	DAILY OUTPUT	LABOR-HOURS	UNIT	1999 BARE COSTS MAT.	LABOR	EQUIP.	TOTAL	TOTAL INCL O&P	
250	9000	Minimum labor/equipment charge	1 Elec	3	2.667	Job		85		85	131	250

163 300 | Switches

			CREW	DAILY OUTPUT	LABOR-HOURS	UNIT	MAT.	LABOR	EQUIP.	TOTAL	INCL O&P	
350	0010	**RELAYS** Enclosed (NEMA 1)										350
	0100	2 pole, 12 amp	1 Elec	5	1.600	Ea.	81	51		132	168	
	0200	4 pole, 10 amp	"	4.50	1.778	"	108	56.50		164.50	207	
360	0010	**SAFETY SWITCHES**										360
	0100	General duty 240 volt, 3 pole NEMA 1, fusible, 30 amp	1 Elec	3.20	2.500	Ea.	63	80		143	193	
	0200	60 amp		2.30	3.478		107	111		218	289	
	0300	100 amp		1.90	4.211		183	134		317	410	
	0400	200 amp		1.30	6.154		395	196		591	740	
	0500	400 amp	2 Elec	1.80	8.889		995	284		1,279	1,550	
	9990	Minimum labor/equipment charge	1 Elec	3	2.667	Job		85		85	131	
370	0010	**TIME SWITCHES**										370
	0100	Single pole, single throw, 24 hour dial	1 Elec	4	2	Ea.	72	64		136	178	
	0200	24 hour dial with reserve power		3.60	2.222		305	71		376	445	
	0300	Astronomic dial		3.60	2.222		123	71		194	245	
	0400	Astronomic dial with reserve power		3.30	2.424		390	77.50		467.50	550	
	0500	7 day calendar dial		3.30	2.424		111	77.50		188.50	242	
	0600	7 day calendar dial with reserve power		3.20	2.500		335	80		415	495	
	0700	Photo cell 2000 watt		8	1		15.25	32		47.25	66.50	
	1080	Load management device, 2 loads		4	2		530	64		594	685	
	1100	Load management device, 8 loads		1	8		1,550	255		1,805	2,100	
	9000	Minimum labor/equipment charge		3.50	2.286	Job		73		73	113	

164 | Transformers & Bus Ducts

164 100 | Transformers

			CREW	DAILY OUTPUT	LABOR-HOURS	UNIT	1999 BARE COSTS MAT.	LABOR	EQUIP.	TOTAL	TOTAL INCL O&P	
120	0010	**DRY TYPE TRANSFORMER**										120
	0050	Single phase, 240/480 volt primary, 120/240 volt secondary										
	0100	1 kVA	1 Elec	2	4	Ea.	141	128		269	350	
	0300	2 kVA		1.60	5		212	160		372	480	
	0500	3 kVA		1.40	5.714		262	182		444	570	
	0700	5 kVA		1.20	6.667		360	213		573	725	
	0900	7.5 kVA		1.10	7.273		500	232		732	910	
	1100	10 kVA		.80	10		640	320		960	1,200	
	1300	15 kVA	2 Elec	1.20	13.333		875	425		1,300	1,625	
	2300	3 phase, 480 volt primary 120/208 volt secondary										
	2310	Ventilated, 3 kVA	1 Elec	1	8	Ea.	425	255		680	865	
	2700	6 kVA		.80	10		590	320		910	1,150	
	2900	9 kVA		.70	11.429		670	365		1,035	1,300	
	3100	15 kVA	2 Elec	1.10	14.545		875	465		1,340	1,675	
	3300	30 kVA		.90	17.778		1,050	565		1,615	2,025	
	3500	45 kVA		.80	20		1,225	640		1,865	2,325	
	9000	Minimum labor/equipment charge	1 Elec	1	8	Job		255		255	395	

For expanded coverage of these items see *Means Electrical Cost Data 1999*

165 | Power Systems & Capacitors

165 100 | Power Systems

			DAILY	LABOR-		1999 BARE COSTS				TOTAL
		CREW	OUTPUT	HOURS	UNIT	MAT.	LABOR	EQUIP.	TOTAL	INCL O&P
120	0010	**GENERATOR SET**								
	0020	Gas or gasoline operated, includes battery,								
	0050	charger, muffler & transfer switch								
	0200	3 phase 4 wire, 277/480 volt, 7.5 kW	R-3	.83	24.096	Ea.	6,000	760	164	6,924	7,950
	0300	10 kW		.71	28.169		8,200	890	191	9,281	10,600
	0400	20 kW		.63	31.746		10,000	1,000	216	11,216	12,800
	0500	35 kW	↓	.55	36.364	↓	12,000	1,150	247	13,397	15,200

166 | Lighting

166 100 | Lighting

			DAILY	LABOR-		1999 BARE COSTS				TOTAL
		CREW	OUTPUT	HOURS	UNIT	MAT.	LABOR	EQUIP.	TOTAL	INCL O&P
110	0010	**EXIT AND EMERGENCY LIGHTING**								
	0080	Exit light ceiling or wall mount, incandescent, single face	1 Elec	8	1	Ea.	35	32		67	88
	0100	Double face	"	6.70	1.194	"	44	38		82	108
	0300	Emergency light units, battery operated								
	0350	Twin sealed beam light, 25 watt, 6 volt each								
	0500	Lead battery operated	1 Elec	4	2	Ea.	160	64		224	275
	0700	Nickel cadmium battery operated		4	2	"	480	64		544	630
	9000	Minimum labor/equipment charge	↓	4	2	Job		64		64	98.50
115	0010	**EXTERIOR FIXTURES** With lamps								
	0400	Quartz, 500 watt	1 Elec	5.30	1.509	Ea.	51	48		99	131
	0800	Wall pack, mercury vapor, 175 watt		4	2		160	64		224	275
	1000	250 watt		4	2		210	64		274	330
	1100	Low pressure sodium, 35 watt		4	2		208	64		272	330
	1150	55 watt		4	2		280	64		344	410
	1160	High pressure sodium, 70 watt		4	2		195	64		259	315
	1170	150 watt		4	2		230	64		294	350
	1180	Metal Halide, 175 watt		4	2		250	64		314	375
	1190	250 watt		4	2		260	64		324	385
	1200	Floodlights with ballast and lamp,								
	1400	pole mounted, pole not included								
	2250	Low pressure sodium, 55 watt	1 Elec	2.70	2.963	Ea.	485	94.50		579.50	680
	2270	90 watt		2	4	"	535	128		663	785
	9000	Minimum labor/equipment charge	↓	3.75	2.133	Job		68		68	105
130	0010	**INTERIOR LIGHTING FIXTURES** Including lamps, mounting								
	0030	hardware and connections								
	0100	Fluorescent, C.W. lamps, troffer, recess mounted in grid, RS								
	0200	Acrylic lens, 1'W x 4'L, two 40 watt	1 Elec	5.70	1.404	Ea.	46	45		91	120
	0300	2'W x 2'L, two U40 watt		5.70	1.404		50	45		95	124
	0600	2'W x 4'L, four 40 watt		4.70	1.702		56	54.50		110.50	146
	0910	Acrylic lens, 1'W x 4'L, two 32 watt		5.70	1.404		55	45		100	130
	0930	2'W x 2'L, two U32 watt		5.70	1.404		75	45		120	152
	0940	2'W x 4'L, two 32 watt		5.30	1.509		67	48		115	148
	0950	2'W x 4'L, three 32 watt		5	1.600		72	51		123	158
	0960	2'W x 4'L, four 32 watt	↓	4.70	1.702	↓	75	54.50		129.50	167
	1000	Surface mounted, RS								
	1030	Acrylic lens with hinged & latched door frame								
	1100	1'W x 4'L, two 40 watt	1 Elec	7	1.143	Ea.	71	36.50		107.50	135

166 | Lighting

166 100 | Lighting

		CREW	DAILY OUTPUT	LABOR-HOURS	UNIT	1999 BARE COSTS MAT.	LABOR	EQUIP.	TOTAL	TOTAL INCL O&P
1200	2'W x 2'L, two U40 watt	1 Elec	7	1.143	Ea.	85	36.50		121.50	150
1500	2'W x 4'L, four 40 watt		5.30	1.509		91	48		139	175
2100	Strip fixture									
2130	Surface mounted									
2200	4' long, one 40 watt RS	1 Elec	8.50	.941	Ea.	26	30		56	75
2300	4' long, two 40 watt RS	"	8	1		28	32		60	80.50
2600	8' long, one 75 watt, SL	2 Elec	13.40	1.194		39	38		77	102
2700	8' long, two 75 watt, SL	"	12.40	1.290		47	41		88	115
3000	Pendent mounted, industrial, white porcelain enamel									
3030	C.W. lamps									
3100	4' long, two 40 watt, RS	1 Elec	5.70	1.404	Ea.	43	45		88	117
3200	4' long, two 60 watt, HO	"	5	1.600		70	51		121	156
3300	8' long, two 75 watt, SL	2 Elec	8.80	1.818		81	58		139	179
4000	High bay, aluminum reflector									
4030	Single unit, 400 watt DX lamp	2 Elec	4.60	3.478	Ea.	248	111		359	445
4220	Metal halide, integral ballast, ceiling, recess mounted									
4230	prismatic glass lens, floating door									
4240	2'W x 2'L, 250 watt	1 Elec	3.20	2.500	Ea.	245	80		325	395
4250	2'W x 2'L, 400 watt	2 Elec	5.80	2.759		285	88		373	450
4260	Surface mounted, 2'W x 2'L, 250 watt	1 Elec	2.70	2.963		245	94.50		339.50	415
4270	400 watt	2 Elec	4.80	3.333		290	106		396	485
4280	High bay, aluminum reflector,									
4290	Single unit, 400 watt	2 Elec	4.60	3.478	Ea.	340	111		451	545
4300	Single unit, 1000 watt		4	4		485	128		613	730
4310	Twin unit, 400 watt		3.20	5		680	160		840	990
4320	Low bay, aluminum reflector, 250W DX lamp	1 Elec	3.20	2.500		325	80		405	485
4340	High pressure sodium integral ballast ceiling, recess mounted									
4350	prismatic glass lens, floating door									
4360	2'W x 2'L, 150 watt lamp	1 Elec	3.20	2.500	Ea.	300	80		380	455
4370	2'W x 2'L, 400 watt lamp	2 Elec	5.80	2.759		360	88		448	530
4380	Surface mounted, 2'W x 2'L, 150 watt lamp	1 Elec	2.70	2.963		340	94.50		434.50	520
4390	400 watt lamp	2 Elec	4.80	3.333		375	106		481	580
4400	High bay, aluminum reflector,									
4410	Single unit, 400 watt lamp	2 Elec	4.60	3.478	Ea.	310	111		421	510
4430	Single unit, 1000 watt lamp	"	4	4		445	128		573	685
4440	Low bay, aluminum reflector, 150 watt lamp	1 Elec	3.20	2.500		265	80		345	415
4450	Incandescent, high hat can, round alzak reflector, prewired									
4470	100 watt	1 Elec	8	1	Ea.	52	32		84	107
4480	150 watt		8	1		76	32		108	133
4500	300 watt		6.70	1.194		175	38		213	252
4600	Square glass lens with metal trim, prewired									
4630	100 watt	1 Elec	6.70	1.194	Ea.	36	38		74	98.50
4700	200 watt		6.70	1.194		55	38		93	120
6010	Vapor tight, incandescent, ceiling mounted, 200 watt		6.20	1.290		43	41		84	111
6100	Fluorescent, surface mounted, 2 lamps, 4'L, RS, 40 watt		3.20	2.500		86	80		166	218
6850	Vandalproof, surface mounted, fluorescent, two 40 watt		3.20	2.500		171	80		251	310
6860	Incandescent, one 150 watt		8	1		51	32		83	106
6900	Mirror light, fluorescent, RS, acrylic enclosure, two 40 watt		8	1		80	32		112	138
6910	One 40 watt		8	1		62	32		94	118
6920	One 20 watt		12	.667		50	21.50		71.50	88
7500	Ballast replacement, by weight of ballast, to 15' high									
7520	Indoor fluorescent, less than 2 lbs.	1 Elec	10	.800	Ea.		25.50		25.50	39.50
7540	Two 40W, watt reducer, 2 to 5 lbs.		9.40	.851		18	27		45	62
7560	Two F96 slimline, over 5 lbs.		8	1		31	32		63	83.50
7580	Vaportite ballast, less than 2 lbs.		9.40	.851			27		27	42
7600	2 lbs. to 5 lbs.		8.90	.899			28.50		28.50	44.50

For expanded coverage of these items see Means Electrical Cost Data 1999

166 | Lighting

166 100 | Lighting

		CREW	DAILY OUTPUT	LABOR-HOURS	UNIT	1999 BARE COSTS MAT.	LABOR	EQUIP.	TOTAL	TOTAL INCL O&P	
130	7620 Over 5 lbs.	1 Elec	7.60	1.053	Ea.		33.50		33.50	52	130
	7630 Electronic ballast for two tubes		8	1		30	32		62	82.50	
	7640 Dimmable ballast one lamp		8	1		43	32		75	96.50	
	7650 Dimmable ballast two-lamp		7.60	1.053		67	33.50		100.50	126	
	9000 Minimum labor/equipment charge	▼	3	2.667	Job		85		85	131	
140	0010 **LAMPS**										140
	0080 Fluorescent, rapid start, cool white, 2' long, 20 watt	1 Elec	1	8	C	261	255		516	680	
	0100 4' long, 40 watt		.90	8.889		225	284		509	690	
	0170 4' long, 35 watt energy saver		.90	8.889		225	284		509	690	
	0180 4' long, T8, 32 watt energy saver		.90	8.889		325	284		609	795	
	0560 Twin tube compact lamp		.90	8.889		405	284		689	885	
	0570 Double twin tube compact lamp		.80	10		880	320		1,200	1,475	
	0600 Mercury vapor, mogul base, deluxe white, 100 watt		.30	26.667		3,250	850		4,100	4,900	
	0800 400 watt		.30	26.667		3,425	850		4,275	5,100	
	1000 Metal halide, mogul base, 175 watt		.30	26.667		4,100	850		4,950	5,850	
	1100 250 watt		.30	26.667		4,650	850		5,500	6,425	
	1350 High pressure sodium, 70 watt		.30	26.667		4,100	850		4,950	5,850	
	1370 150 watt		.30	26.667		4,425	850		5,275	6,200	
	1500 Low pressure sodium, 35 watt		.30	26.667		5,500	850		6,350	7,375	
	1600 90 watt		.30	26.667		6,975	850		7,825	9,000	
	1800 Incandescent, interior, A21, 100 watt		1.60	5		143	160		303	405	
	1900 A21, 150 watt		1.60	5		150	160		310	410	
	2300 R30, 75 watt		1.30	6.154		575	196		771	940	
	2500 Exterior, PAR 38, 75 watt		1.30	6.154		935	196		1,131	1,325	
	2600 PAR 38, 150 watt		1.30	6.154		1,150	196		1,346	1,550	
	9000 Minimum labor/equipment charge	▼	4	2	Job		64		64	98.50	
145	0010 **RESIDENTIAL FIXTURES**										145
	0400 Fluorescent, interior, surface, circline, 32 watt & 40 watt	1 Elec	20	.400	Ea.	63	12.75		75.75	89	
	0500 2' x 2', two U 40 watt		8	1		77	32		109	134	
	0700 Shallow under cabinet, two 20 watt		16	.500		32	15.95		47.95	59.50	
	0900 Wall mounted, 4'L, one 40 watt, with baffle		10	.800		103	25.50		128.50	153	
	2000 Incandescent, exterior lantern, wall mounted, 60 watt		16	.500		35	15.95		50.95	63	
	2100 Post light, 150W, with 7' post		4	2		116	64		180	227	
	2500 Lamp holder, weatherproof with 150W PAR		16	.500		12	15.95		27.95	37.50	
	2550 With reflector and guard		12	.667		40	21.50		61.50	77	
	2600 Interior pendent, globe with shade, 150 watt		20	.400		110	12.75		122.75	141	
	9000 Minimum labor/equipment charge	▼	4	2	Job		64		64	98.50	
150	0010 **TRACK LIGHTING**										150
	0080 Track, 1 circuit, 4' section	1 Elec	6.70	1.194	Ea.	33	38		71	95.50	
	0100 8' section		5.30	1.509		55	48		103	135	
	0300 3 circuits, 4' section		6.70	1.194		44	38		82	108	
	0400 8' section		5.30	1.509		68	48		116	150	
	9000 Minimum labor/equipment charge	▼	3	2.667	Job		85		85	131	

167 | Electric Utilities

167 100 | Electric Utilities

		CREW	DAILY OUTPUT	LABOR-HOURS	UNIT	1999 BARE COSTS				TOTAL INCL O&P
						MAT.	LABOR	EQUIP.	TOTAL	
110 0010	**ELECTRIC & TELEPHONE SITE WORK** Not including excavation										110
0200	backfill and cast in place concrete									
4200	Underground duct, banks ready for concrete fill, min. of 7.5"									
4400	between conduits, ctr. to ctr.(for wire & cable see div. 161)									
4600	2 @ 2" diameter	2 Elec	240	.067	L.F.	1.12	2.13		3.25	4.52
4800	4 @ 2" diameter		120	.133		2.24	4.25		6.49	9
5600	4 @ 4" diameter		80	.200		4.77	6.40		11.17	15.10
6200	Rigid galvanized steel, 2 @ 2" diameter		180	.089		8.50	2.84		11.34	13.75
6400	4 @ 2" diameter		90	.178		17	5.65		22.65	27.50
7400	4 @ 4" diameter		34	.471		54	15		69	82.50
9990	Minimum labor/equipment charge	1 Elec	3.50	2.286	Job		73		73	113

168 | Special Systems

168 100 | Special Systems

		CREW	DAILY OUTPUT	LABOR-HOURS	UNIT	1999 BARE COSTS				TOTAL INCL O&P
						MAT.	LABOR	EQUIP.	TOTAL	
120 0010	**DETECTION SYSTEMS**, not including wires & conduits										120
0100	Burglar alarm, battery operated, mechanical trigger	1 Elec	4	2	Ea.	249	64		313	375
0200	Electrical trigger		4	2		297	64		361	425
0400	For outside key control, add		8	1		70.50	32		102.50	127
0600	For remote signaling circuitry, add		8	1		112	32		144	173
0800	Card reader, flush type, standard		2.70	2.963		835	94.50		929.50	1,075
1000	Multi-code		2.70	2.963		1,075	94.50		1,169.50	1,325
1200	Door switches, hinge switch		5.30	1.509		52.50	48		100.50	133
1400	Magnetic switch		5.30	1.509		62	48		110	143
1600	Exit control locks, horn alarm		4	2		310	64		374	440
1800	Flashing light alarm		4	2		350	64		414	485
2000	Indicating panels, 1 channel		2.70	2.963		330	94.50		424.50	510
2200	10 channel	2 Elec	3.20	5		1,125	160		1,285	1,500
2400	20 channel		2	8		2,200	255		2,455	2,825
2600	40 channel		1.14	14.035		4,000	450		4,450	5,100
2800	Ultrasonic motion detector, 12 volt	1 Elec	2.30	3.478		206	111		317	400
3000	Infrared photoelectric detector		2.30	3.478		170	111		281	360
3200	Passive infrared detector		2.30	3.478		254	111		365	450
3400	Glass break alarm switch		8	1		42.50	32		74.50	96.50
3420	Switchmats, 30" x 5'		5.30	1.509		76	48		124	158
3440	30" x 25'		4	2		182	64		246	299
3460	Police connect panel		4	2		219	64		283	340
3480	Telephone dialer		5.30	1.509		345	48		393	455
3500	Alarm bell		4	2		69.50	64		133.50	175
3520	Siren		4	2		131	64		195	243
3540	Microwave detector, 10' to 200'		2	4		600	128		728	855
3560	10' to 350'		2	4		1,750	128		1,878	2,125
3594	Fire, alarm control panel									
3600	4 zone	2 Elec	2	8	Ea.	920	255		1,175	1,400
3800	8 zone		1	16		1,400	510		1,910	2,350
4000	12 zone		.67	23.988		1,825	765		2,590	3,175
4200	Battery and rack	1 Elec	4	2		690	64		754	860
4400	Automatic charger		8	1		445	32		477	540
4600	Signal bell		8	1		49.50	32		81.50	104

For expanded coverage of these items see *Means Electrical Cost Data 1999*

168 | Special Systems

168 100 | Special Systems

			CREW	DAILY OUTPUT	LABOR-HOURS	UNIT	MAT.	LABOR	EQUIP.	TOTAL	TOTAL INCL O&P	
120	4800	Trouble buzzer or manual station	1 Elec	8	1	Ea.	37	32		69	90	120
	5000	Detector, rate of rise		8	1		33.50	32		65.50	86.50	
	5100	Fixed temperature		8	1		28	32		60	80.50	
	5200	Smoke detector, ceiling type		6.20	1.290		75	41		116	146	
	5400	Duct type		3.20	2.500		250	80		330	400	
	5600	Strobe and horn		5.30	1.509		95	48		143	180	
	5800	Fire alarm horn		6.70	1.194		36.50	38		74.50	99	
	6000	Door holder, electro-magnetic		4	2		77.50	64		141.50	184	
	6200	Combination holder and closer		3.20	2.500		430	80		510	600	
	6400	Code transmitter		4	2		690	64		754	860	
	6600	Drill switch		8	1		86.50	32		118.50	145	
	6800	Master box		2.70	2.963		3,100	94.50		3,194.50	3,550	
	7000	Break glass station		8	1		50	32		82	105	
	7800	Remote annunciator, 8 zone lamp		1.80	4.444		175	142		317	410	
	8000	12 zone lamp	2 Elec	2.60	6.154		300	196		496	635	
	8200	16 zone lamp	"	2.20	7.273		300	232		532	690	
	8400	Standpipe or sprinkler alarm, alarm device	1 Elec	8	1		125	32		157	188	
	8600	Actuating device		8	1		290	32		322	370	
	9410	Minimum labor/equipment charge		4	2	Job		64		64	98.50	
125	0010	**DOORBELL SYSTEM** Incl. transformer, button & signal										125
	0020											
	1000	Door chimes, 2 notes, minimum	1 Elec	16	.500	Ea.	22	15.95		37.95	48.50	
	1020	Maximum		12	.667		112	21.50		133.50	156	
	1100	Tube type, 3 tube system		12	.667		101	21.50		122.50	144	
	1180	4 tube system		10	.800		264	25.50		289.50	330	
	1900	For transformer & button, minimum add		5	1.600		12.50	51		63.50	93	
	1960	Maximum, add		4.50	1.778		37	56.50		93.50	128	
	3000	For push button only, minimum		24	.333		2.43	10.65		13.08	19.10	
	3100	Maximum		20	.400		19.45	12.75		32.20	41	
	9000	Minimum labor/equipment charge		4	2	Job		64		64	98.50	
130	0010	**ELECTRIC HEATING**										130
	1300	Baseboard heaters, 2' long, 375 watt	1 Elec	8	1	Ea.	36	32		68	89	
	1400	3' long, 500 watt		8	1		40	32		72	93.50	
	1600	4' long, 750 watt		6.70	1.194		48	38		86	112	
	1800	5' long, 935 watt		5.70	1.404		59	45		104	134	
	2000	6' long, 1125 watt		5	1.600		65	51		116	151	
	2400	8' long, 1500 watt		4	2		81	64		145	188	
	2600	9' long, 1680 watt		3.60	2.222		134	71		205	257	
	2800	10' long, 1875 watt		3.30	2.424		134	77.50		211.50	267	
	2950	Wall heaters with fan, 120 to 277 volt										
	3002	1500 watt	1 Elec	4	2	Ea.	118	64		182	229	
	3040	2250 watt		4	2		235	64		299	360	
	3070	4000 watt		3.50	2.286		240	73		313	375	
	3600	Thermostats, integral		16	.500		23	15.95		38.95	50	
	3800	Line voltage, 1 pole		8	1		23	32		55	75	
	3810	2 pole		8	1		23	32		55	75	
	9990	Minimum labor/equipment charge		4	2	Job		64		64	98.50	
150	0010	**PUBLIC ADDRESS SYSTEM**										150
	0100	Conventional, office	1 Elec	5.33	1.501	Speaker	91	48		139	174	
	0200	Industrial		2.70	2.963	"	176	94.50		270.50	340	
	9000	Minimum labor/equipment charge		3.50	2.286	Job		73		73	113	
155	0010	**SOUND SYSTEM** not including rough-in wires, cables & conduits										155
	2020	11 station capacity	2 Elec	4	4	Ea.	645	128		773	905	

168 | Special Systems

168 100 | Special Systems

			CREW	DAILY OUTPUT	LABOR-HOURS	UNIT	1999 BARE COSTS MAT.	LABOR	EQUIP.	TOTAL	TOTAL INCL O&P	
155	3600	House telephone, talking station	1 Elec	1.60	5	Ea.	300	160		460	575	155
	3800	Press to talk, release to listen	"	5.30	1.509		70	48		118	152	
	4000	System-on button					42			42	46	
	4200	Door release	1 Elec	4	2		74	64		138	180	
	4400	Combination speaker and microphone		8	1		128	32		160	191	
	4600	Termination box		3.20	2.500		40	80		120	167	
	4800	Amplifier or power supply		5.30	1.509		460	48		508	580	
	5000	Vestibule door unit		16	.500	Name	84.50	15.95		100.45	118	
	5200	Strip cabinet		27	.296	Ea.	160	9.45		169.45	191	
	5400	Directory		16	.500	"	75	15.95		90.95	107	
	9000	Minimum labor/equipment charge		3.50	2.286	Job		73		73	113	
160	0010	**T.V. SYSTEMS** not including rough-in wires, cables & conduits										160
	5000	T.V. Antenna only, minimum	1 Elec	6	1.333	Ea.	33	42.50		75.50	102	
	5100	Maximum		4	2	"	140	64		204	253	
	9000	Minimum labor/equipment charge		3.75	2.133	Job		68		68	105	
170	0010	**RESIDENTIAL WIRING**										170
	0020	20' avg. runs and #14/2 wiring incl. unless otherwise noted										
	1000	Service & panel, includes 24' SE-AL cable, service eye, meter,										
	1010	Socket, panel board, main bkr., ground rod, 15 or 20 amp										
	1020	1-pole circuit breakers, and misc. hardware										
	1100	100 amp, with 10 branch breakers	1 Elec	1.19	6.723	Ea.	400	214		614	770	
	1110	With PVC conduit and wire		.92	8.696		425	277		702	900	
	1120	With RGS conduit and wire		.73	10.959		540	350		890	1,125	
	1150	150 amp, with 14 branch breakers		1.03	7.767		620	248		868	1,075	
	1170	With PVC conduit and wire		.82	9.756		680	310		990	1,225	
	1180	With RGS conduit and wire		.67	11.940		875	380		1,255	1,550	
	1200	200 amp, with 18 branch breakers	2 Elec	1.80	8.889		810	284		1,094	1,325	
	1220	With PVC conduit and wire		1.46	10.959		870	350		1,220	1,500	
	1230	With RGS conduit and wire		1.24	12.903		1,125	410		1,535	1,875	
	1800	Lightning surge suppressor for above services, add	1 Elec	32	.250		39.50	7.95		47.45	56	
	2000	Switch devices										
	2100	Single pole, 15 amp, Ivory, with a 1-gang box, cover plate,										
	2110	Type NM (Romex) cable	1 Elec	17.10	.468	Ea.	6.80	14.90		21.70	30.50	
	2120	Type MC (BX) cable		14.30	.559		16.30	17.85		34.15	45.50	
	2130	EMT & wire		5.71	1.401		17.05	44.50		61.55	88	
	2150	3-way, #14/3, type NM cable		14.55	.550		10.30	17.55		27.85	38.50	
	2170	Type MC cable		12.31	.650		20	20.50		40.50	54	
	2180	EMT & wire		5	1.600		19.40	51		70.40	101	
	2200	4-way, #14/3, type NM cable		14.55	.550		22.50	17.55		40.05	52	
	2220	Type MC cable		12.31	.650		32.50	20.50		53	67.50	
	2230	EMT & wire		5	1.600		31.50	51		82.50	114	
	2250	S.P., 20 amp, #12/2, type NM cable		13.33	.600		12	19.15		31.15	42.50	
	2270	Type MC cable		11.43	.700		20	22.50		42.50	56.50	
	2280	EMT & wire		4.85	1.649		23	52.50		75.50	107	
	2290	S.P. rotary dimmer, 600W, no wiring		17	.471		15.15	15		30.15	39.50	
	2300	S.P. rotary dimmer, 600W, type NM cable		14.55	.550		18.25	17.55		35.80	47	
	2320	Type MC cable		12.31	.650		27.50	20.50		48	62.50	
	2330	EMT & wire		5	1.600		29.50	51		80.50	112	
	2350	3-way rotary dimmer, type NM cable		13.33	.600		21	19.15		40.15	52.50	
	2370	Type MC cable		11.43	.700		30.50	22.50		53	68	
	2380	EMT & wire		4.85	1.649		32	52.50		84.50	117	
	2400	Interval timer wall switch, 20 amp, 1-30 min., #12/2										
	2410	Type NM cable	1 Elec	14.55	.550	Ea.	29	17.55		46.55	59	
	2420	Type MC cable		12.31	.650		34.50	20.50		55	70	
	2430	EMT & wire		5	1.600		39.50	51		90.50	123	

For expanded coverage of these items see *Means Electrical Cost Data 1999*

168 | Special Systems

168 100 | Special Systems

		CREW	DAILY OUTPUT	LABOR-HOURS	UNIT	MAT.	LABOR	EQUIP.	TOTAL	TOTAL INCL O&P
2500	Decorator style									
2510	S.P., 15 amp, type NM cable	1 Elec	17.10	.468	Ea.	9.95	14.90		24.85	34
2520	Type MC cable		14.30	.559		19.45	17.85		37.30	49
2530	EMT & wire		5.71	1.401		20	44.50		64.50	91
2550	3-way, #14/3, type NM cable		14.55	.550		13.45	17.55		31	42
2570	Type MC cable		12.31	.650		23.50	20.50		44	57.50
2580	EMT & wire		5	1.600		22.50	51		73.50	104
2600	4-way, #14/3, type NM cable		14.55	.550		26	17.55		43.55	55.50
2620	Type MC cable		12.31	.650		35.50	20.50		56	71
2630	EMT & wire		5	1.600		35	51		86	118
2650	S.P., 20 amp, #12/2, type NM cable		13.33	.600		15.15	19.15		34.30	46
2670	Type MC cable		11.43	.700		23.50	22.50		46	60
2680	EMT & wire		4.85	1.649		26	52.50		78.50	110
2700	S.P., slide dimmer, type NM cable		17.10	.468		25.50	14.90		40.40	51.50
2720	Type MC cable		14.30	.559		35	17.85		52.85	66
2730	EMT & wire		5.71	1.401		37	44.50		81.50	110
2770	Type MC cable		14.30	.559		34.50	17.85		52.35	65.50
2780	EMT & wire		5.71	1.401		36.50	44.50		81	109
2800	3-way touch dimmer, type NM cable		13.33	.600		39	19.15		58.15	72.50
2820	Type MC cable		11.43	.700		48.50	22.50		71	88
2830	EMT & wire		4.85	1.649		50	52.50		102.50	137
3100	S.P. switch/15 amp recpt., Ivory, 1-gang box, plate									
3110	Type NM cable	1 Elec	11.43	.700	Ea.	14.70	22.50		37.20	50.50
3120	Type MC cable		10	.800		24	25.50		49.50	66
3130	EMT & wire		4.40	1.818		26	58		84	118
3150	S.P. switch/pilot light, type NM cable		11.43	.700		15.30	22.50		37.80	51.50
3170	Type MC cable		10	.800		25	25.50		50.50	66.50
3180	EMT & wire		4.43	1.806		26.50	57.50		84	118
3190	2-S.P. switches, 2-#14/2, no wiring		14	.571		5.20	18.25		23.45	34
3200	2-S.P. switches, 2-#14/2, type NM cables		10	.800		17.05	25.50		42.55	58.50
3220	Type MC cable		8.89	.900		32.50	28.50		61	80
3230	EMT & wire		4.10	1.951		28	62		90	127
3250	3-way switch/15 amp recpt., #14/3, type NM cable		10	.800		21	25.50		46.50	62.50
3270	Type MC cable		8.89	.900		31	28.50		59.50	78.50
3280	EMT & wire		4.10	1.951		30	62		92	129
3300	2-3 way switches, 2-#14/3, type NM cables		8.89	.900		28	28.50		56.50	75.50
3320	Type MC cable		8	1		44	32		76	98
3330	EMT & wire		4	2		35	64		99	137
3350	S.P. switch/20 amp recpt., #12/2, type NM cable		10	.800		24.50	25.50		50	66.50
3370	Type MC cable		8.89	.900		30	28.50		58.50	77.50
3380	EMT & wire		4.10	1.951		35	62		97	135
3400	Decorator style									
3410	S.P. switch/15 amp recpt., type NM cable	1 Elec	11.43	.700	Ea.	17.85	22.50		40.35	54
3420	Type MC cable		10	.800		27.50	25.50		53	69.50
3430	EMT & wire		4.40	1.818		29	58		87	122
3450	S.P. switch/pilot light, type NM cable		11.43	.700		18.45	22.50		40.95	55
3470	Type MC cable		10	.800		28	25.50		53.50	70
3480	EMT & wire		4.40	1.818		29.50	58		87.50	122
3500	2-S.P. switches, 2-#14/2, type NM cables		10	.800		20	25.50		45.50	61.50
3520	Type MC cable		8.89	.900		35.50	28.50		64	83.50
3530	EMT & wire		4.10	1.951		31	62		93	130
3550	3-way/15 amp recpt., #14/3, type NM cable		10	.800		24	25.50		49.50	66
3580	EMT & wire		4.10	1.951		33	62		95	133
3650	2-3 way switches, 2-#14/3, type NM cables		8.89	.900		31.50	28.50		60	79
3670	Type MC cable		8	1		47.50	32		79.50	102
3680	EMT & wire		4	2		38	64		102	140

168 | Special Systems

168 100 | Special Systems

		CREW	DAILY OUTPUT	LABOR-HOURS	UNIT	1999 BARE COSTS MAT.	LABOR	EQUIP.	TOTAL	TOTAL INCL O&P
3700	S.P. switch/20 amp recpt., #12/2, type NM cable	1 Elec	10	.800	Ea.	27.50	25.50		53	70
3720	Type MC cable		8.89	.900		33	28.50		61.50	81
3730	EMT & wire		4.10	1.951		38.50	62		100.50	138
4000	Receptacle devices									
4010	Duplex outlet, 15 amp recpt., Ivory, 1-gang box, plate									
4015	Type NM cable	1 Elec	14.55	.550	Ea.	5.40	17.55		22.95	33
4020	Type MC cable		12.31	.650		14.90	20.50		35.40	48.50
4030	EMT & wire		5.33	1.501		15.65	48		63.65	91
4050	With #12/2, type NM cable		12.31	.650		6.85	20.50		27.35	39.50
4070	Type MC cable		10.67	.750		15	24		39	53.50
4080	EMT & wire		4.71	1.699		17.65	54		71.65	103
4100	20 amp recpt., #12/2, type NM cable		12.31	.650		11.70	20.50		32.20	45
4120	Type MC cable		10.67	.750		19.80	24		43.80	59
4130	EMT & wire		4.71	1.699		22.50	54		76.50	108
4140	For GFI see line 4300 below									
4150	Decorator style, 15 amp recpt., type NM cable	1 Elec	14.55	.550	Ea.	8.55	17.55		26.10	36.50
4170	Type MC cable		12.31	.650		18.05	20.50		38.55	52
4180	EMT & wire		5.33	1.501		18.80	48		66.80	94.50
4200	With #12/2, type NM cable		12.31	.650		10	20.50		30.50	43
4220	Type MC cable		10.67	.750		18.15	24		42.15	57
4230	EMT & wire		4.71	1.699		21	54		75	107
4250	20 amp recpt. #12/2, type NM cable		12.31	.650		14.85	20.50		35.35	48.50
4270	Type MC cable		10.67	.750		23	24		47	62.50
4280	EMT & wire		4.71	1.699		25.50	54		79.50	112
4300	GFI, 15 amp recpt., type NM cable		12.31	.650		33	20.50		53.50	68.50
4320	Type MC cable		10.67	.750		42.50	24		66.50	84
4330	EMT & wire		4.71	1.699		43.50	54		97.50	131
4350	GFI with #12/2, type NM cable		10.67	.750		34.50	24		58.50	75
4370	Type MC cable		9.20	.870		42.50	27.50		70	90
4380	EMT & wire		4.21	1.900		45.50	60.50		106	144
4400	20 amp recpt., #12/2 type NM cable		10.67	.750		36	24		60	76.50
4420	Type MC cable		9.20	.870		44	27.50		71.50	91.50
4430	EMT & wire		4.21	1.900		47	60.50		107.50	145
4500	Weather-proof cover for above receptacles, add		32	.250		4.40	7.95		12.35	17.15
4550	Air conditioner outlet, 20 amp-240 volt recpt.									
4560	30' of #12/2, 2 pole circuit breaker									
4570	Type NM cable	1 Elec	10	.800	Ea.	40	25.50		65.50	83.50
4580	Type MC cable		9	.889		50	28.50		78.50	99.50
4590	EMT & wire		4	2		50	64		114	154
4600	Decorator style, type NM cable		10	.800		43.50	25.50		69	87.50
4620	Type MC cable		9	.889		54	28.50		82.50	104
4630	EMT & wire		4	2		54	64		118	158
4650	Dryer outlet, 30 amp-240 volt recpt., 20' of #10/3									
4660	2 pole circuit breaker									
4670	Type NM cable	1 Elec	6.41	1.248	Ea.	50.50	40		90.50	117
4680	Type MC cable		5.71	1.401		54	44.50		98.50	129
4690	EMT & wire		3.48	2.299		53.50	73.50		127	172
4700	Range outlet, 50 amp-240 volt recpt., 30' of #8/3									
4710	Type NM cable	1 Elec	4.21	1.900	Ea.	80	60.50		140.50	182
4720	Type MC cable		4	2		100	64		164	209
4730	EMT & wire		2.96	2.703		74.50	86		160.50	215
4750	Central vacuum outlet, Type NM cable		6.40	1.250		43	40		83	109
4770	Type MC cable		5.71	1.401		56	44.50		100.50	131
4780	EMT & wire		3.48	2.299		53	73.50		126.50	171
4800	30 amp-110 volt locking recpt., #10/2 circ. bkr.									
4810	Type NM cable	1 Elec	6.20	1.290	Ea.	50	41		91	119

For expanded coverage of these items see *Means Electrical Cost Data 1999*

168 | Special Systems

168 100	Special Systems	CREW	DAILY OUTPUT	LABOR-HOURS	UNIT	1999 BARE COSTS MAT.	LABOR	EQUIP.	TOTAL	TOTAL INCL O&P
4820	Type MC cable	1 Elec	5.40	1.481	Ea.	68	47.50		115.50	148
4830	EMT & wire	↓	3.20	2.500	↓	61.50	80		141.50	191
4900	Low voltage outlets									
4910	Telephone recpt., 20' of 4/C phone wire	1 Elec	26	.308	Ea.	6.70	9.80		16.50	22.50
4920	TV recpt., 20' of RG59U coax wire, F type connector	"	16	.500	"	11.40	15.95		27.35	37
4950	Door bell chime, transformer, 2 buttons, 60' of bellwire									
4970	Economy model	1 Elec	11.50	.696	Ea.	48.50	22		70.50	88
4980	Custom model		11.50	.696		83.50	22		105.50	127
4990	Luxury model, 3 buttons	↓	9.50	.842	↓	228	27		255	293
6000	Lighting outlets									
6050	Wire only (for fixture), type NM cable	1 Elec	32	.250	Ea.	3.95	7.95		11.90	16.65
6070	Type MC cable		24	.333		11.05	10.65		21.70	28.50
6080	EMT & wire		10	.800		10.90	25.50		36.40	51.50
6100	Box (4"), and wire (for fixture), type NM cable		25	.320		7.85	10.20		18.05	24.50
6120	Type MC cable		20	.400		14.95	12.75		27.70	36
6130	EMT & wire	↓	11	.727	↓	14.80	23		37.80	52.50
6200	Fixtures (use with lines 6050 or 6100 above)									
6210	Canopy style, economy grade	1 Elec	40	.200	Ea.	25.50	6.40		31.90	38
6220	Custom grade		40	.200		46	6.40		52.40	60.50
6250	Dining room chandelier, economy grade		19	.421		76	13.45		89.45	105
6270	Luxury grade		15	.533		495	17		512	570
6310	Kitchen fixture (fluorescent), economy grade		30	.267		51.50	8.50		60	69.50
6320	Custom grade		25	.320		161	10.20		171.20	193
6350	Outdoor, wall mounted, economy grade		30	.267		27	8.50		35.50	42.50
6360	Custom grade		30	.267		101	8.50		109.50	124
6370	Luxury grade		25	.320		227	10.20		237.20	266
6410	Outdoor PAR floodlights, 1 lamp, 150 watt		20	.400		20	12.75		32.75	41.50
6420	2 lamp, 150 watt each		20	.400		33.50	12.75		46.25	56.50
6430	For infrared security sensor, add		32	.250		87	7.95		94.95	108
6450	Outdoor, quartz-halogen, 300 watt flood		20	.400		38	12.75		50.75	61.50
6600	Recessed downlight, round, pre-wired, 50 or 75 watt trim		30	.267		35	8.50		43.50	51.50
6610	With shower light trim		30	.267		42	8.50		50.50	59
6620	With wall washer trim		28	.286		52.50	9.10		61.60	72
6630	With eye-ball trim	↓	28	.286		49	9.10		58.10	68
6640	For direct contact with insulation, add					1.60			1.60	1.76
6700	Porcelain lamp holder	1 Elec	40	.200		3.50	6.40		9.90	13.70
6710	With pull switch		40	.200		3.75	6.40		10.15	14
6750	Fluorescent strip, 1-20 watt tube, wrap around diffuser, 24"		24	.333		51.50	10.65		62.15	73
6760	1-40 watt tube, 48"		24	.333		65	10.65		75.65	88
6770	2-40 watt tubes, 48"		20	.400		78	12.75		90.75	106
6780	With residential ballast		20	.400		89.50	12.75		102.25	118
6800	Bathroom heat lamp, 1-250 watt		28	.286		30.50	9.10		39.60	47.50
6810	2-250 watt lamps	↓	28	.286	↓	51	9.10		60.10	70
6820	For timer switch, see line 2400									
6900	Outdoor post lamp, incl. post, fixture, 35' of #14/2									
6910	Type NMC cable	1 Elec	3.50	2.286	Ea.	166	73		239	296
6920	Photo-eye, add		27	.296		29	9.45		38.45	46.50
6950	Clock dial time switch, 24 hr., w/enclosure, type NM cable		11.43	.700		51	22.50		73.50	90.50
6970	Type MC cable		11	.727		60	23		83	103
6980	EMT & wire	↓	4.85	1.649	↓	61	52.50		113.50	149
7000	Alarm systems									
7050	Smoke detectors, box, #14/3, type NM cable	1 Elec	14.55	.550	Ea.	28.50	17.55		46.05	58.50
7070	Type MC cable		12.31	.650		36	20.50		56.50	71.50
7080	EMT & wire	↓	5	1.600		35	51		86	118
7090	For relay output to security system, add				↓	11.75			11.75	12.95
8000	Residential equipment									

168 | Special Systems

168 100 | Special Systems

		CREW	DAILY OUTPUT	LABOR-HOURS	UNIT	1999 BARE COSTS MAT.	LABOR	EQUIP.	TOTAL	TOTAL INCL O&P
8050	Disposal hook-up, incl. switch, outlet box, 3' of flex									
8060	20 amp-1 pole circ. bkr., and 25' of #12/2									
8070	Type NM cable	1 Elec	10	.800	Ea.	19.80	25.50		45.30	61.50
8080	Type MC cable		8	1		29	32		61	81.50
8090	EMT & wire	↓	5	1.600	↓	32	51		83	114
8100	Trash compactor or dishwasher hook-up, incl. outlet box,									
8110	3' of flex, 15 amp-1 pole circ. bkr., and 25' of #14/2									
8120	Type NM cable	1 Elec	10	.800	Ea.	13.75	25.50		39.25	54.50
8130	Type MC cable		8	1		25	32		57	77
8140	EMT & wire	↓	5	1.600	↓	26	51		77	108
8150	Hot water sink dispensor hook-up, use line 8100									
8200	Vent/exhaust fan hook-up, type NM cable	1 Elec	32	.250	Ea.	3.95	7.95		11.90	16.65
8220	Type MC cable		24	.333		11.05	10.65		21.70	28.50
8230	EMT & wire	↓	10	.800	↓	10.90	25.50		36.40	51.50
8250	Bathroom vent fan, 50 CFM (use with above hook-up)									
8260	Economy model	1 Elec	15	.533	Ea.	21.50	17		38.50	50
8270	Low noise model		15	.533		30	17		47	59.50
8280	Custom model	↓	12	.667	↓	111	21.50		132.50	155
8300	Bathroom or kitchen vent fan, 110 CFM									
8310	Economy model	1 Elec	15	.533	Ea.	53	17		70	85
8320	Low noise model	"	15	.533	"	72	17		89	106
8350	Paddle fan, variable speed (w/o lights)									
8360	Economy model (AC motor)	1 Elec	10	.800	Ea.	94.50	25.50		120	144
8370	Custom model (AC motor)		10	.800		165	25.50		190.50	222
8380	Luxury model (DC motor)		8	1		325	32		357	410
8390	Remote speed switch for above, add	↓	12	.667	↓	21	21.50		42.50	56
8500	Whole house exhaust fan, ceiling mount, 36", variable speed									
8510	Remote switch, incl. shutters, 20 amp-1 pole circ. bkr.									
8520	30' of #12/2, type NM cable	1 Elec	4	2	Ea.	680	64		744	845
8530	Type MC cable		3.50	2.286		690	73		763	875
8540	EMT & wire	↓	3	2.667	↓	695	85		780	890
8600	Whirlpool tub hook-up, incl. timer switch, outlet box									
8610	3' of flex, 20 amp-1 pole GFI circ. bkr.									
8620	30' of #12/2, type NM cable	1 Elec	5	1.600	Ea.	75.50	51		126.50	162
8630	Type MC cable		4.20	1.905		81.50	61		142.50	184
8640	EMT & wire	↓	3.40	2.353	↓	84	75		159	209
8650	Hot water heater hook-up, incl. 1-2 pole circ. bkr., box;									
8660	3' of flex, 20' of #10/2, type NM cable	1 Elec	5	1.600	Ea.	20	51		71	101
8670	Type MC cable		4.20	1.905		32	61		93	130
8680	EMT & wire	↓	3.40	2.353	↓	28	75		103	147
9000	Heating/air conditioning									
9050	Furnace/boiler hook-up, incl. firestat, local on-off switch									
9060	Emergency switch, and 40' of type NM cable	1 Elec	4	2	Ea.	42	64		106	145
9070	Type MC cable		3.50	2.286		57.50	73		130.50	176
9080	EMT & wire	↓	1.50	5.333	↓	58.50	170		228.50	330
9100	Air conditioner hook-up, incl. local 60 amp disc. switch									
9110	3' sealtite, 40 amp, 2 pole circuit breaker									
9130	40' of #8/2, type NM cable	1 Elec	3.50	2.286	Ea.	133	73		206	259
9140	Type MC cable		3	2.667		171	85		256	320
9150	EMT & wire	↓	1.30	6.154	↓	141	196		337	460
9200	Heat pump hook-up, 1-40 & 1-100 amp 2 pole circ. bkr.									
9210	Local disconnect switch, 3' sealtite									
9220	40' of #8/2 & 30' of #3/2									
9230	Type NM cable	1 Elec	1.30	6.154	Ea.	340	196		536	680
9240	Type MC cable		1.08	7.407		425	236		661	830
9250	EMT & wire	↓	.94	8.511	↓	340	271		611	795

For expanded coverage of these items see Means Electrical Cost Data 1999

168 | Special Systems

168 100	Special Systems	CREW	DAILY OUTPUT	LABOR-HOURS	UNIT	1999 BARE COSTS MAT.	LABOR	EQUIP.	TOTAL	TOTAL INCL O&P
9500	Thermostat hook-up, using low voltage wire									
9520	Heating only	1 Elec	24	.333	Ea.	6.40	10.65		17.05	23.50
9530	Heating/cooling	"	20	.400	"	8	12.75		20.75	28.50

For information about Means Estimating Seminars, see yellow pages 11 and 12 in back of book

Assemblies Section

Table of Contents

Foundations — 355
Table No.		Page
A1.1-124	Spread Footing	356
A1.1-144	Strip Footing	357
A1.1-214	Concrete Wall	358
A1.1-242	Concrete Block Wall	359
A1.1-294	Foundation Underdrain	360

Substructures — 363
Table No.		Page
A2.1-104	Interior Slab on Grade	364

Superstructures — 365
Table No.		Page
A3.5-154	Floor–Ceiling, Concrete Slab	366
A3.5-212	Floor–Ceiling, Conc. Panel	367
A3.5-214	Floor–Ceiling, Conc. Plank	368
A3.5-314	Floor–Ceiling, Struc. Steel	369
A3.5-414	Floor–Ceiling, Steel Joists	370
A3.5-711	Manufactured, Wood Joists	371
A3.5-714	Floor–Ceiling, Wood Joists	372
A3.7-511	Roof Truss, Wood	373
A3.9-104	Stairs	374
A3.9-900	Selective Price Sheet	375

Exterior Closure — 377
Table No.		Page
A4.1-208	Masonry Wall, Concrete Block	378
A4.1-258	Masonry Wall, Brick–Stone	379
A4.1-288	Parapet Wall	380
A4.1-289	Masonry Restoration–Cleaning	381
A4.1-416	Wood Frame Exterior Wall	382
A4.6-142	Doors, Metal–Commercial	383
A4.6-144	Doors, Residential–Exterior	384
A4.6-152	Doors, Sliding-Patio	385
A4.6-702	Doors, Overhead	386
A4.7-142	Windows–Aluminum	387
A4.7-144	Windows–Wood	388
A4.7-145	Windows–Wood	389
A4.7-152	Storm Windows & Doors	390
A4.7-700	Aluminum Frame, Window Wall	391
A4.9-200	Selective Price Sheet	392
A4.9-500	Selective Price Sheet	394

Roofing — 397
Table No.		Page
A5.1-192	Steel Joist Roof & Ceiling	398
A5.1-492	Wood Frame Roof & Ceiling	399
A5.8-104	Roof Hatches, Skylights	400
A5.9-300	Selective Price Sheet	401
A5.9-500	Selective Price Sheet	403

Interior Construction — 405
Table No.		Page
A6.1-222	Partitions, Concrete Block	406
A6.1-592	Partitions, Wood Stud	407
A6.1-594	Partitions, Metal Stud, NLB	408
A6.1-595	Partitions, Drywall	409
A6.1-596	Partitions, Metal Stud, LB	410
A6.1-692	Partitions, Plaster & Lath	411
A6.1-842	Partitions, Movable Office	412
A6.4-142	Doors, Interior Flush, Wood	413
A6.4-144	Doors, Interior Solid & Louvered	414
A6.4-146	Doors, Interior Flush, Metal	415
A6.4-148	Doors, Closet	416
A6.7-242	Ceiling, Suspended Plaster	417
A6.7-342	Ceiling, Suspended Acoustical	418
A6.7-442	Ceilings, Suspended Gypsum Board	419
A6.9-100	Selective Price Sheet	420
A6.9-300	Selective Price Sheet	422
A6.9-500	Selective Price Sheet	423
A6.9-600	Selective Price Sheet	425
A6.9-700	Selective Price Sheet	427
A6.9-800	Selective Price Sheet	429

Conveying Systems — 431
Table No.		Page
A7.1-142	Oil Hydraulic Elevators	432

Mechanical — 433
Table No.		Page
A8.1-710	Plumbing–Public Restroom	434
A8.1-720	Plumbing–Public Restroom	435
A8.1-920	Plumbing–Two Fixture Bathroom	436
A8.1-931	Plumbing–Three Fixture Bathroom	437
A8.1-932	Plumbing–Three Fixture Bathroom	438
A8.1-933	Plumbing–Three Fixture Bathroom	439
A8.1-940	Plumbing–Four Fixture Bathroom	440
A8.1-950	Plumbing–Five Fixture Bathroom	441
A8.2-910	Fire Sprinkler Systems, Wet	442
A8.2-920	Fire Sprinkler Systems, Dry	443
A8.3-270	Heating–Oil Fired Hot Water	444
A8.3-280	Heating–Gas Fired Hot Water	445
A8.3-310	Heating–Cooling, Oil, Forced Air	446
A8.3-320	Heating–Cooling, Gas, Forced Air	447
A8.5-400	Circulating Pumps	448
A8.7-100	Unit Heaters	449
A8.7-220	Boilers, Gas or Gas/Oil	451
A8.8-200	Heat Exchanger	453
A8.8-400	AC Unit, Package, Water Cooled	455
A8.8-500	AC Unit, Package, DX, Air Cooled	457
A8.8-600	Fan Coil Air Conditioner	459
A8.8-800	Thru-Wall Units	461

Electrical — 463
Table No.		Page
A9.1-220	Commercial Service–3 Phase	464
A9.1-230	Residential Service–Single Phase	465
A9.2-252	Light Pole	466
A9.2-900	Lighting, Fluorescent	468
A9.2-910	Lighting, Incandescent	469
A9.2-920	Lighting, High Intensity	470
A9.4-910	Heat, Baseboard	471
A9.9-500	Selective Price Sheet	472

Special Construction — 475
Table No.		Page
A11.1-242	Kitchens	476
A11.1-742	Wood Burning Stoves	477
A11.1-744	Masonry Fireplace	478
A11.2-100	Tanks, Fiberglass	479
A11.2-200	Tanks, Steel	481
A11.9-100	Selective Price Sheet	483

Site Work — 485
Table No.		Page
A12.1-116	Excavation, Utility Trench	486
A12.1-462	Excavation, Footings or Trench	487
A12.1-464	Excavation, Foundation	488
A12.3-940	Septic Systems	489
A12.5-404	Driveways	490
A12.5-514	Parking Lots, Asphalt	491
A12.5-524	Parking Lots, Concrete	492
A12.7-104	Sidewalks	493
A12.7-604	Landscaping–Lawn Establishment	494
A12.9-300	Selective Price Sheet	495
A12.9-700	Selective Price Sheet	497

How to Use the Assemblies Cost Tables

The following is a detailed explanation of a sample Assemblies Cost Table. Most Assembly Tables are separated into three parts: 1) an illustration of the system to be estimated; 2) the components and related costs of a typical system; and 3) the costs for similar systems with dimensional and/or size variations. For costs of the components that comprise these systems or "assemblies," refer to the Unit Price Section. Next to each bold number below is the item being described with the appropriate component of the sample entry following in parenthesis. In most cases, if the work is to be subcontracted, the general contractor will need to add an additional markup (R.S. Means suggests using 10%) to the "Total" figures.

1 System/Line Numbers (A3.5-714-1700)

Each Assemblies Cost Line has been assigned a unique identification number based on the UniFormat classification system.

UniFormat Division

3.5 714 1700

Means Subdivision
Means Major Classification
Means Individual Line Number

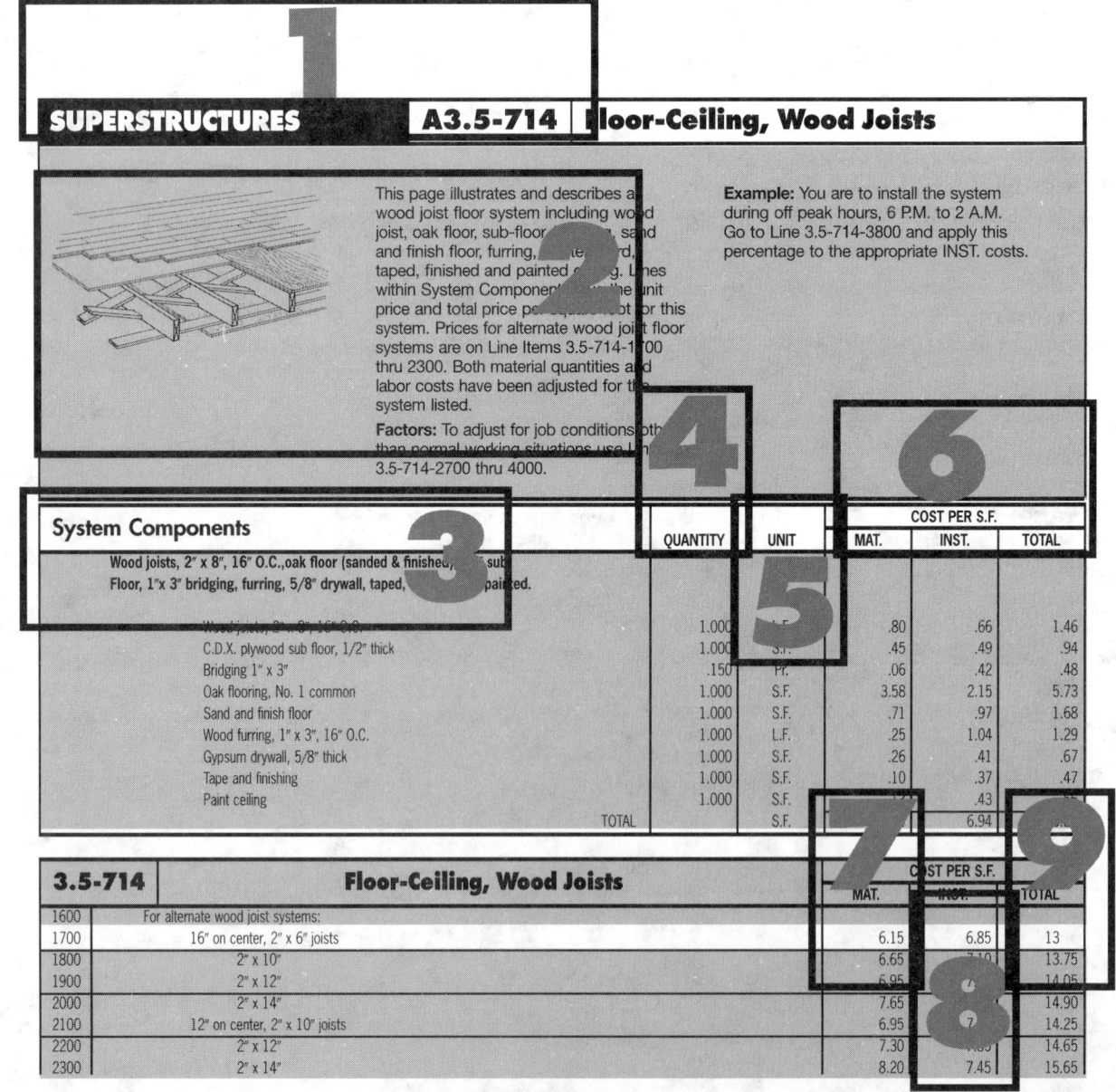

SUPERSTRUCTURES — A3.5-714 Floor-Ceiling, Wood Joists

This page illustrates and describes a wood joist floor system including wood joist, oak floor, sub-floor, furring, sand and finish floor, furring, insulation board, taped, finished and painted ceiling. Lines within System Components give the unit price and total price per square foot for this system. Prices for alternate wood joist floor systems are on Line Items 3.5-714-1700 thru 2300. Both material quantities and labor costs have been adjusted for the system listed.

Factors: To adjust for job conditions other than normal working situations use Lines 3.5-714-2700 thru 4000.

Example: You are to install the system during off peak hours, 6 P.M. to 2 A.M. Go to Line 3.5-714-3800 and apply this percentage to the appropriate INST. costs.

System Components

Wood joists, 2" x 8", 16" O.C., oak floor (sanded & finished), sub-Floor, 1" x 3" bridging, furring, 5/8" drywall, taped, finished, painted.

	QUANTITY	UNIT	MAT.	INST.	TOTAL
Wood joists, 2" x 8", 16" O.C.	1.000	S.F.	.80	.66	1.46
C.D.X. plywood sub floor, 1/2" thick	1.000	S.F.	.45	.49	.94
Bridging 1" x 3"	.150	Pr.	.06	.42	.48
Oak flooring, No. 1 common	1.000	S.F.	3.58	2.15	5.73
Sand and finish floor	1.000	S.F.	.71	.97	1.68
Wood furring, 1" x 3", 16" O.C.	1.000	L.F.	.25	1.04	1.29
Gypsum drywall, 5/8" thick	1.000	S.F.	.26	.41	.67
Tape and finishing	1.000	S.F.	.10	.37	.47
Paint ceiling	1.000	S.F.		.43	
TOTAL		S.F.		6.94	

3.5-714	Floor-Ceiling, Wood Joists	MAT.	INST.	TOTAL
1600	For alternate wood joist systems:			
1700	16" on center, 2" x 6" joists	6.15	6.85	13
1800	2" x 10"	6.65	7.10	13.75
1900	2" x 12"	6.95	7.10	14.05
2000	2" x 14"	7.65	7.25	14.90
2100	12" on center, 2" x 10" joists	6.95	7.30	14.25
2200	2" x 12"	7.30	7.35	14.65
2300	2" x 14"	8.20	7.45	15.65

2 Illustration
At the top of most assembly tables is an illustration, a brief description, and the design criteria used to develop the cost.

3 System Components
The components of a typical system are listed separately to show what has been included in the development of the total system price. The table below contains prices for other similar systems with dimensional and/or size variations.

4 Quantity
This is the number of line item units required for one system unit. For example, we assume that it will take .15 pair of 1" × 3" bridging on a square foot basis.

5 Unit of Measure for Each Item
The abbreviated designation indicates the unit of measure, as defined by industry standards, upon which the price of the component is based. For example, wood joists are priced by the L.F. (linear foot) while plywood is priced by S.F. (square foot).

6 Unit of Measure for Each System (Cost per S.F.)
Costs shown in the three right hand columns have been adjusted by the component quantity and unit of measure for the entire system. In this example, "Cost per S.F." is the unit of measure for this system or "assembly."

7 Materials (6.15)
This column contains the Materials Cost of each component. These cost figures are bare costs plus 10% for profit.

8 Installation (6.85)
Installation includes labor and equipment plus the installing contractor's overhead and profit. Equipment costs are the bare rental costs plus 10% for profit. The labor overhead and profit is defined on the inside back cover of this book.

9 Total (13.00)
The figure in this column is the sum of the material and installation costs.

Material Cost	+	Installation Cost	=	Total
$6.15	+	$6.85	=	$13.00

353

Division 1
Foundations

FOUNDATIONS — A1.1-124 Spread Footing

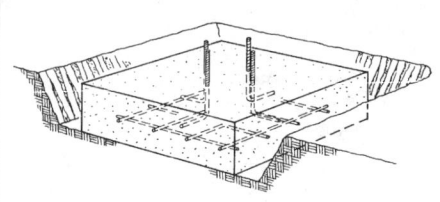

This page illustrates and describes a spread footing system including concrete, forms, reinforcing and anchor bolts. Lines within System Components give the unit price and total price on a cost each basis for this system. Prices for alternate spread footing systems are on Line Items 1.1-124-1300 thru 2300. Both material quantities and labor costs have been adjusted for the system listed.

Factors: To adjust for job conditions other than normal working situations use Lines 1.1-124-2900 thru 4000.

Example: You are to install the system in an existing occupied building. Access to the site and protection to the building are mandatory. Go to Lines 1.1-124-3600 and 3800 and apply these percentages to the appropriate MAT. and INST. costs.

System Components	QUANTITY	UNIT	COST EACH		
			MAT.	INST.	TOTAL
Interior column footing, 3' square 1' thick, 2000 psi concrete, Including forms, reinforcing, and anchor bolts.					
Concrete, 2000 psi	.330	C.Y.	20.46		20.46
Placing concrete	.330	C.Y.		11.23	11.23
Forms, footing, 4 uses	12.000	SFCA	6.48	40.08	46.56
Reinforcing	11.000	Lb.	3.41	4.62	8.03
Anchor bolts, 3/4" diameter	2.000	Ea.	1.14	3.66	4.80
TOTAL			31.49	59.59	91.08

1.1-124	Spread Footing	COST EACH		
		MAT.	INST.	TOTAL
1200	Above system with the following:			
1300	3' square x 1' thick, 3000 psi concrete	33	59.50	92.50
1400	4000 psi concrete	33.50	59.50	93
1600	For alternate footing systems:			
1700	4' square x 1' thick, 2000 psi concrete	52.50	85.50	138
1800	3000 psi concrete	55.50	85.50	141
1900	4000 psi concrete	56.50	85.50	142
2100	5' square x 1'-3" thick, 2000 psi concrete	98.50	143	241.50
2200	3000 psi concrete	104	143	247
2300	4000 psi concrete	106	143	249
2600				
2700				
2900	Cut & patch to match existing construction, add, minimum	2%	3%	
3000	Maximum	5%	9%	
3100	Dust protection, add, minimum	1%	2%	
3200	Maximum	4%	11%	
3300	Equipment usage curtailment, add, minimum	1%	1%	
3400	Maximum	3%	10%	
3500	Material handling & storage limitation, add, minimum	1%	1%	
3600	Maximum	6%	7%	
3700	Protection of existing work, add, minimum	2%	2%	
3800	Maximum	5%	7%	
3900	Shift work requirements, add, minimum		5%	
4000	Maximum		30%	

FOUNDATIONS — A1.1-144 | Strip Footing

This page illustrates and describes a strip footing system including concrete, forms, reinforcing, keyway and dowels. Lines within System Components give the unit price and total price per linear foot for this system. Prices for alternate strip footing systems are on Line Items 1.1-144-1500 thru 2500. Both material quantities and labor costs have been adjusted for the system listed.

Factors: To adjust for job conditions other than normal working situations use Lines 1.1-144-2900 thru 4000.

Example: You are to install this footing, and due to a lack of accessibility, only hand tools can be used. Material handling is also a problem. Go to Lines 1.1-144-3400 and 3600 and apply these percentages to the appropriate MAT. and INST. costs.

System Components	QUANTITY	UNIT	COST PER L.F. MAT.	INST.	TOTAL
Strip footing, 2'-0" wide x 1'-0" thick, 2000 psi concrete including forms Reinforcing, keyway, and dowels.					
Concrete, 2000 psi	.074	C.Y.	4.59		4.59
Placing concrete	.074	C.Y.		1.16	1.16
Forms, footing, 4 uses	2.000	S.F.	1.38	5.70	7.08
Reinforcing	3.170	Lb.	.98	1.33	2.31
Keyway, 2" x 4", 4 uses	1.000	L.F.	.21	.69	.90
Dowels, #4 bars, 2' long, 24" O.C.	.500	Ea.	.22	.92	1.14
TOTAL		L.F.	7.38	9.80	17.18

1.1-144	Strip Footing	MAT.	INST.	TOTAL
1400	Above system with the following:			
1500	2'-0" wide x 1' thick, 3000 psi concrete	7.75	9.80	17.55
1600	4000 psi concrete	7.85	9.80	17.65
1800	For alternate footing systems:			
1900	2'-6" wide x 1' thick, 2000 psi concrete	8.80	10.45	19.25
2000	3000 psi concrete	9.30	10.45	19.75
2100	4000 psi concrete	9.40	10.45	19.85
2300	3'-0" wide x 1' thick, 2000 psi concrete	10.10	11.05	21.15
2400	3000 psi concrete	10.65	11.05	21.70
2500	4000 psi concrete	10.85	11.05	21.90
2700				
2800				
2900	Cut & patch to match existing construction, add, minimum	2%	3%	
3000	Maximum	5%	9%	
3100	Dust protection, add, minimum	1%	2%	
3200	Maximum	4%	11%	
3300	Equipment usage curtailment, add, minimum	1%	1%	
3400	Maximum	3%	10%	
3500	Material handling & storage limitation, add, minimum	1%	1%	
3600	Maximum	6%	7%	
3700	Protection of existing work, add, minimum	2%	2%	
3800	Maximum	5%	7%	
3900	Shift work requirements, add, minimum		5%	
4000	Maximum		30%	

FOUNDATIONS — A1.1-214 | Concrete Wall

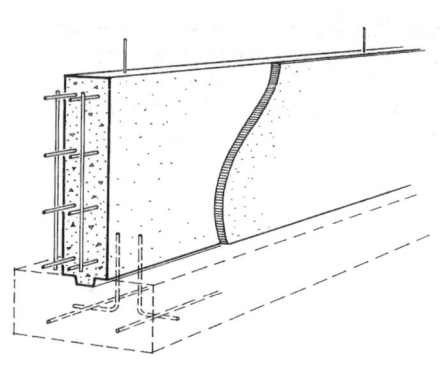

This page illustrates and describes a concrete wall system including concrete, placing concrete, forms, reinforcing, insulation, waterproofing and anchor bolts. Lines within System Components give the unit price and total price per linear foot for this system. Prices for alternate concrete wall systems are on Line Items 1.1-214-1500 thru 2600. Both material quantities and labor costs have been adjusted for the system listed.

Factors: To adjust for job conditions other than normal working situations use Lines 1.1-214-2900 thru 4000.

Example: You are to install this wall system where delivery of material is difficult. Go to Line 1.1-214-3600 and apply these percentages to the appropriate MAT. and INST. costs.

System Components	QUANTITY	UNIT	COST PER L.F.		
			MAT.	INST.	TOTAL
Cast in place concrete foundation wall, 8" thick, 3' high, 2500 psi Concrete including forms, reinforcing, waterproofing, and anchor bolts.					
Concrete, 2500 psi, 8" thick, 3' high	.070	C.Y.	4.41		4.41
Forms, wall, 4 uses	6.000	S.F.	4.08	29.52	33.60
Reinforcing	6.000	Lb.	1.86	1.74	3.60
Placing concrete	.070	C.Y.		2.27	2.27
Waterproofing	3.000	S.F.	.33	2.10	2.43
Rigid insulaton, 1" polystyrene	3.000	S.F.	.60	1.62	2.22
Anchor bolts, 1/2" diameter, 4' O.C.	.250	Ea.	.34	.48	.82
TOTAL		L.F.	11.62	37.73	49.35

1.1-214	Concrete Wall	COST PER L.F.		
		MAT.	INST.	TOTAL
1400	For alternate wall systems:			
1500	8" thick, 2500 psi concrete, 4' high	15.80	50.50	66.30
1600	6' high	23.50	75	98.50
1700	8' high	31.50	100	131.50
1800	3500 psi concrete, 4' high	16.20	50.50	66.70
1900	6' high	24	75	99
2000	8' high	32	100	132
2100	12" thick, 2500 psi concrete, 4' high	20	53	73
2200	6' high	29	78.50	107.50
2300	8' high	39	104	143
2400	3500 psi concrete, 4' high	21	53	74
2500	8' high	40	104	144
2600	10' high	49.50	131	180.50
2700				
2900	Cut & patch to match existing construction, add, minimum	2%	3%	
3000	Maximum	5%	9%	
3100	Dust protection, add, minimum	1%	2%	
3200	Maximum	4%	11%	
3300	Equipment usage curtailment, add, minimum	1%	1%	
3400	Maximum	3%	10%	
3500	Material handling & storage limitation, add, minimum	1%	1%	
3600	Maximum	6%	7%	
3700	Protection of existing work, add, minimum	2%	2%	
3800	Maximum	5%	7%	
3900	Shift work requirements, add, minimum		5%	
4000	Maximum		30%	
4100				

FOUNDATIONS — A1.1-242 | Concrete Block Wall

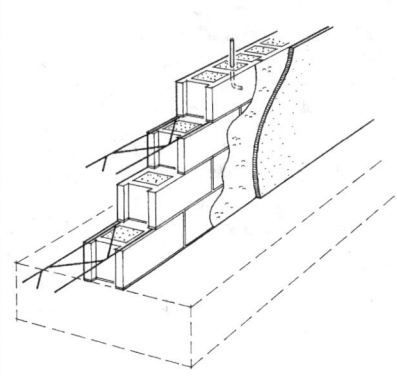

This page illustrates and describes a concrete block wall system including concrete block, masonry reinforcing, parging, waterproofing insulation and anchor bolts. Lines within System Components give the unit price and total price per linear foot for this system. Prices for alternate concrete block wall systems are on Line Items 1.1-242-1300 thru 2600. Both material quantities and labor costs have been adjusted for the system listed.

Factors: To adjust for job conditions other than normal working situations use Lines 1.1-242-2900 thru 4000.

Example: You are to install the system to match an existing foundation wall. Go to Line 1.1-242-3000 and apply these percentages to the appropriate MAT. and INST. costs.

System Components	QUANTITY	UNIT	COST PER L.F.		
			MAT.	INST.	TOTAL
Concrete block, 8" thick, masonry reinforcing, parged and Waterproofed, insulation and anchor bolts, wall 2'-8" high.					
Concrete block, 8" x 8" x 16"	2.670	S.F.	4.41	10.36	14.77
Masonry reinforcing	2.000	L.F.	.22	.24	.46
Parging	.193	S.Y.	.69	1.56	2.25
Waterproofing	2.670	S.F.	.29	1.87	2.16
Insulation, 1" rigid polystyrene	2.670	S.F.	.53	1.44	1.97
Anchor bolts, 1/2" diameter, 4' O.C.	.250	Ea.	.34	.48	.82
TOTAL			6.48	15.95	22.43

1.1-242	Concrete Block Wall	COST PER L.F.		
		MAT.	INST.	TOTAL
1200	For alternate wall systems:			
1300	8" thick block, 4' high	9.55	23.50	33.05
1400	6' high	14.10	35	49.10
1500	8' high	18.80	47	65.80
1600	Grouted solid, 4' high	13.30	32	45.30
1700	6' high	19.75	47.50	67.25
1800	8' high	26.50	63.50	90
2100	12" thick block, 4' high	12.95	28	40.95
2200	6' high	19.15	42	61.15
2300	8' high	25.50	55.50	81
2400	Grouted solid, 4' high	19.10	37	56.10
2500	6' high	28.50	55	83.50
2600	8' high	38	73.50	111.50
2700				
2900	Cut & patch to match existing construction, add, minimum	2%	3%	
3000	Maximum	5%	9%	
3100	Dust protection, add, minimum	1%	2%	
3200	Maximum	4%	11%	
3300	Equipment usage curtailment, add, minimum	1%	1%	
3400	Maximum	3%	10%	
3500	Material handling & storage limitation, add, minimum	1%	1%	
3600	Maximum	6%	7%	
3700	Protection of existing work, add, minimum	2%	2%	
3800	Maximum	5%	7%	
3900	Shift work requirements, add, minimum		5%	
4000	Maximum		30%	

FOUNDATIONS — A1.1-294 Foundation Underdrain

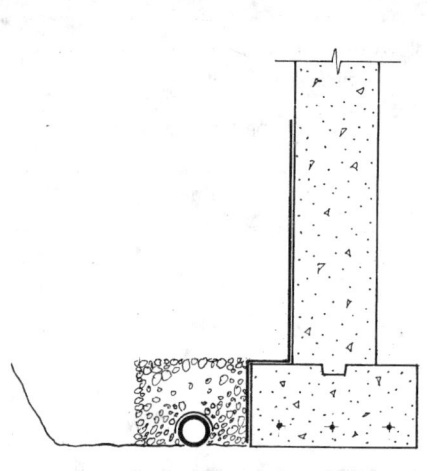

General: Footing drains can be placed either inside or outside of foundation walls depending upon the source of water to be intercepted. If the source of subsurface water is principally from grade or a subsurface stream above the bottom of the footing, outside drains should be used. For high water tables, use inside drains or both inside and outside.

The effectiveness of underdrains depends on good waterproofing. This must be carefully installed and protected during construction.

Costs below include the labor and materials for the pipe and 6" only of gravel or crushed stone around pipe. Excavation and backfill are not included.

System Components	QUANTITY	UNIT	COST PER L.F. MAT.	COST PER L.F. INST.	COST PER L.F. TOTAL
Foundation underdrain, outside, PVC 4" diameter.					
PVC pipe 4" diam. S.D.R. 35	1.000	L.F.	2.39	2.60	4.99
Pipe bedding, graded gravel 3/4" to 1/2"	.070	C.Y.	1.37	.54	1.91
Total			3.76	3.14	6.90

1.1-294	Foundation Underdrain	MAT.	INST.	TOTAL
0900	For alternate drain systems:			
1000	Foundation underdrain, outside only, PVC, 4" diameter	3.76	3.14	6.90
1100	6" diameter	6.10	3.47	9.57
1200	Bituminous fiber, 4" diameter	3.76	3.14	6.90
1300	6" diameter	6.10	3.47	9.57
1400	Porous concrete, 6" diameter	4.31	3.78	8.09
1450	8" diameter	5.30	5.10	10.40
1500	12" diameter	9.75	5.85	15.60
1600	Corrugated metal, 16 ga. asphalt coated, 6" diameter	4.59	6.05	10.64
1650	8" diameter	6.25	6.40	12.65
1700	10" diameter	7.70	6.75	14.45
2000	Vitrified clay, C-211, 4" diameter	3.49	5.65	9.14
2050	6" diameter	5.05	7.20	12.25
2100	12" diameter	12.05	8.75	20.80
3000	Outside and inside, PVC, 4" diameter	7.50	6.25	13.75
3100	6" diameter	12.20	6.95	19.15
3200	Bituminous fiber, 4" diameter	7.50	6.25	13.75
3300	6" diameter	12.20	6.95	19.15
3400	Porous concrete, 6" diameter	8.60	7.60	16.20
3450	8" diameter	10.60	10.15	20.75
3500	12" diameter	19.55	11.65	31.20
3600	Corrugated metal, 16 ga., asphalt coated, 6" diameter	9.15	12.20	21.35
3650	8" diameter	12.50	12.80	25.30
3700	10" diameter	15.35	13.45	28.80
4000	Vitrified clay, C-211, 4" diameter	6.95	11.30	18.25
4050	6" diameter	10.10	14.40	24.50
4100	12" diameter	24	17.40	41.40
4700	Cut & patch to match existing construction, add, minimum	2%	3%	
4800	Maximum	5%	9%	
4900	Dust protection, add, minimum	1%	2%	
5000	Maximum	4%	11%	
5100	Equipment usage curtailment, add, minimum	1%	1%	
5200	Maximum	3%	10%	
5300	Material handling & storage limitation, add, minimum	1%	1%	

FOUNDATIONS

A1.1-294 Foundation Underdrain

1.1-294	Foundation Underdrain	COST PER L.F.		
		MAT.	INST.	TOTAL
5400	Maximum	6%	7%	
5500	Protection of existing work, add, minimum	2%	2%	
5600	Maximum	5%	7%	
5700	Shift work requirements, add, minimum		5%	
5800	Maximum		30%	
5900	Temporary shoring and bracing, add, minimum	2%	5%	
6000	Maximum	5%	12%	

For information about Means Estimating Seminars, see yellow pages 11 and 12 in back of book

Division 2
Substructures

SUBSTRUCTURES A2.1-104 Interior Slab on Grade

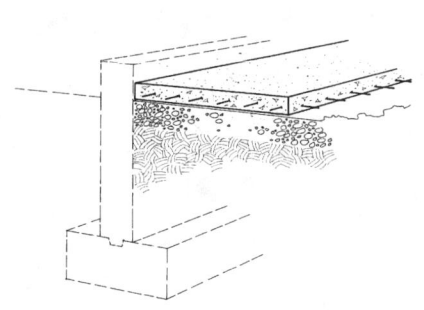

This page illustrates and describes a slab on grade system including slab, bank run gravel, bulkhead forms, placing concrete, welded wire fabric, vapor barrier, steel trowel finish and curing paper. Lines within System Components give the unit price and total price per square foot for this system. Prices for alternate slab on grade systems are on Line Items 2.1-104-1500 thru 2600. Both material quantities and labor costs have been adjusted for the system listed.

Factors: To adjust for job conditions other than normal working situations use Lines 2.1-104-2900 thru 4000.

Example: You are to install the system at a site where protection of the existing building is required. Go to Line 2.1-104-3800 and apply these percentages to the appropriate MAT. and INST. costs.

System Components	QUANTITY	UNIT	COST PER S.F. MAT.	INST.	TOTAL
Ground slab, 4" thick, 3000 psi concrete, 4" granular base, vapor barrier Welded wire fabric, screed and steel trowel finish.					
Concrete, 4" thick, 3000 psi concrete	.012	C.Y.	.80		.80
Bank run gravel, 4" deep	.074	C.Y.	.07	.06	.13
Polyethylene vapor barrier, 10 mil.	.011	C.S.F.	.07	.11	.18
Bulkhead forms, expansion material	.100	L.F.	.03	.23	.26
Welded wire fabric, 6 x 6 - #10/10	.011	C.S.F.	.08	.28	.36
Place concrete	.012	C.Y.		.21	.21
Screed & steel trowel finish	1.000	S.F.		.61	.61
TOTAL			1.05	1.50	2.55

2.1-104	Interior Slab on Grade	COST PER S.F. MAT.	INST.	TOTAL
1400	Above system with the following:			
1500	4" thick slab, 3000 psi concrete, 6" deep bank run gravel	1.26	1.50	2.76
1600	12" deep bank run gravel	1.55	1.53	3.08
1700				
1800				
1900				
2000	For alternate slab systems:			
2100	5" thick slab, 3000 psi concrete, 6" deep bank run gravel	1.47	1.55	3.02
2200	12" deep bank run gravel	1.76	1.58	3.34
2300				
2400				
2500	6" thick slab, 3000 psi concrete, 6" deep bank run gravel	1.73	1.61	3.34
2600	12" deep bank run gravel	2.02	1.64	3.66
2700				
2900	Cut & patch to match existing construction, add, minimum	2%	3%	
3000	Maximum	5%	9%	
3100	Dust protection, add, minimum	1%	2%	
3200	Maximum	4%	11%	
3300	Equipment usage curtailment, add, minimum	1%	1%	
3400	Maximum	3%	10%	
3500	Material handling & storage limitation, add, minimum	1%	1%	
3600	Maximum	6%	7%	
3700	Protection of existing work, add, minimum	2%	2%	
3800	Maximum	5%	7%	
3900	Shift work requirements, add, minimum		5%	
4000	Maximum		30%	

For information about Means Estimating Seminars, see yellow pages 11 and 12 in back of book

Division 3
Superstructures

SUPERSTRUCTURES A3.5-154 | Floor - Ceiling, Concrete Slab

This page illustrates and describes a reinforced concrete slab system including concrete, placing concrete, formwork, reinforcing, steel trowel finish, V.A. floor tile and acoustical spray ceiling finish. Lines within System Components give the unit price per square foot for this system. Prices for alternate reinforced concrete slab systems are on Line Items 3.5-154-1500 thru 1800. Both material quantities and labor costs have been adjusted for the system listed.

Factors: To adjust for job conditions other than normal working situations use Lines 3.5-154-2700 thru 4000.

Example: You are to install the system to match an existing floor system. Go to Line 3.5-154-2800 and apply these percentages to the appropriate MAT. and INST. costs.

System Components	QUANTITY	UNIT	COST PER S.F.		
			MAT.	INST.	TOTAL
Flat slab system, reinforced concrete with vinyl tile floor, sprayed Acoustical ceiling finish, not including columns.					
Concrete, 4000 psi, 6" thick	.020	C.Y.	1.37		1.37
Placing concrete	.020	C.Y.		.46	.46
Formwork, 4 use	1.000	S.F.	.89	3.83	4.72
Edge form	.120	S.F.	.09	.74	.83
Reinforcing steel	3.000	Lb.	.93	1.26	2.19
Steel trowel finish	1.000	S.F.		.56	.56
Vinyl asbestos floor tile	1.000	S.F.	2.13	.67	2.80
Acoustical spray ceiling finish	1.000	S.F.	.21	.11	.32
TOTAL		S.F.	5.62	7.63	13.25

3.5-154	Floor - Ceiling, Concrete Slab	COST PER S.F.		
		MAT.	INST.	TOTAL
1400	For alternate slab systems:			
1500	Concrete, 4000 psi, 7" thick	5.90	7.95	13.85
1600	8" thick	6.30	8.40	14.70
1700	9" thick	6.65	8.75	15.40
1800	10" thick	7.05	9.25	16.30
1900				
2000				
2100				
2200				
2300				
2400				
2500				
2700	Cut & patch to match existing construction, add, minimum	2%	3%	
2800	Maximum	5%	9%	
2900	Dust protection, add, minimum	1%	2%	
3000	Maximum	4%	11%	
3100	Equipment usage curtailment, add, minimum	1%	1%	
3200	Maximum	3%	10%	
3300	Material handling & storage limitation, add, minimum	1%	1%	
3400	Maximum	6%	7%	
3500	Protection of existing work, add, minimum	2%	2%	
3600	Maximum	5%	7%	
3700	Shift work requirements, add, minimum		5%	
3800	Maximum		30%	
3900	Temporary shoring and bracing, add, minimum	2%	5%	
4000	Maximum	5%	12%	

SUPERSTRUCTURES   A3.5-212 | Floor - Ceiling, Conc. Panel

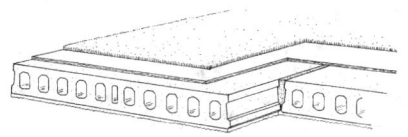

This page illustrates and describes a hollow core prestressed concrete panel system including hollow core slab, grout, carpet, carpet padding, and sprayed ceiling. Lines within System Components give the unit price and total price per square foot for this system. Prices for alternate hollow core prestressed concrete panel systems are on Line Items 3.5-212-1300 thru 1600. Both material and labor costs have been adjusted for the system listed.

Factors: To adjust for job conditions other than normal working situations use Lines 3.5-212-2700 thru 3800.

Example: You are to install the system where dust control is a major concern. Go to Line 3.5-212-2800 and apply these percentages to the appropriate MAT. and INST. costs.

System Components	QUANTITY	UNIT	COST PER S.F. MAT.	INST.	TOTAL
Precast hollow core plank with carpeted floors, padding And sprayed textured ceiling.					
Hollow core plank, 4" thick with grout topping	1.000	S.F.	5.10	1.57	6.67
Nylon carpet, 26 oz. medium traffic	.110	S.Y.	2.18	.49	2.67
Carpet padding, minimum quality	.110	S.Y.	.31	.25	.56
Sprayed texture ceiling	1.000	S.F.	.13	.43	.56
TOTAL		S.F.	7.72	2.74	10.46

3.5-212	Floor - Ceiling, Conc. Panel	COST PER S.F. MAT.	INST.	TOTAL
1200	For alternate floor systems:			
1300	Hollow core concrete plank, with grout, 6" thick	7.55	2.43	9.98
1400	8" thick	7.90	2.19	10.09
1500	10" thick	8.85	1.81	10.66
1600	12" thick	7.85	1.88	9.73
1700				
1800				
1900				
2000				
2100				
2200				
2300				
2400				
2500				
2700	Dust protection, add, minimum	1%	2%	
2800	Maximum	4%	11%	
2900	Equipment usage curtailment, add, minimum	1%	1%	
3000	Maximum	3%	10%	
3100	Material handling & storage limitation, add, minimum	1%	1%	
3200	Maximum	6%	7%	
3300	Protection of existing work, add, minimum	2%	2%	
3400	Maximum	5%	7%	
3500	Shift work requirements, add, minimum		5%	
3600	Maximum		30%	
3700	Temporary shoring and bracing, add, minimum	2%	5%	
3800	Maximum	5%	12%	

SUPERSTRUCTURES | A3.5-214 | Floor - Ceiling, Conc. Plank

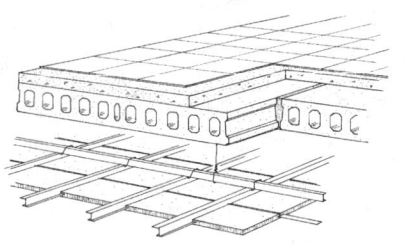

This page illustrates and describes a hollow core plank system including precast hollow core plank, concrete topping, V.A. tile, concealed suspension system and ceiling tile. Lines within System Components give the unit price and total price per square foot for this system. Prices for alternate hollow core plank systems are on Line Items 3.5-214-1500 thru 1800. Both material quantities and labor costs have been adjusted for the system listed.

Factors: To adjust for job conditions other than normal working situations use Lines 3.5-214-2900 thru 4000.

Example: You are to install the system where equipment usage is a problem. Go to Line 3.5-214-3200 and apply these percentages to the appropriate MAT. and INST. costs.

System Components

System Components	QUANTITY	UNIT	MAT.	INST.	TOTAL
Precast hollow core plank with 2" topping, vinyl composition floor tile And suspended acoustical tile ceiling.					
Hollow core concrete plank, 4" thick	1.000	S.F.	5.10	1.57	6.67
Concrete topping, 2" thick	1.000	S.F.	.71	1.91	2.62
Vinyl composition tile, .08" thick	1.000	S.F.	.96	.67	1.63
Concealed Z bar suspension system, 12" module	1.000	S.F.	.37	.70	1.07
Ceiling tile, mineral fiber, 3/4" thick	1.000	S.F.	1.35	.37	1.72
TOTAL		S.F.	8.49	5.22	13.71

3.5-214		Floor - Ceiling, Conc. Plank	MAT.	INST.	TOTAL
1400	For alternate floor systems:				
1500		Hollow core concrete plank, 6" thick	8.30	4.91	13.21
1600		8" thick	8.70	4.67	13.37
1700		10" thick	9.65	4.29	13.94
1800		12" thick	8.65	4.36	13.01
1900					
2000					
2100					
2200					
2300					
2400					
2500					
2600					
2700					
2900	Dust protection, add, minimum		1%	2%	
3000		Maximum	4%	11%	
3100	Equipment usage curtailment, add, minimum		1%	1%	
3200		Maximum	3%	10%	
3300	Material handling & storage limitation, add, minimum		1%	1%	
3400		Maximum	6%	7%	
3500	Protection of existing work, add, minimum		2%	2%	
3600		Maximum	5%	7%	
3700	Shift work requirements, add, minimum			5%	
3800		Maximum		30%	
3900	Temporary shoring and bracing, add, minimum		2%	5%	
4000		Maximum	5%	12%	

SUPERSTRUCTURES | A3.5-314 | Floor - Ceiling, Struc. Steel

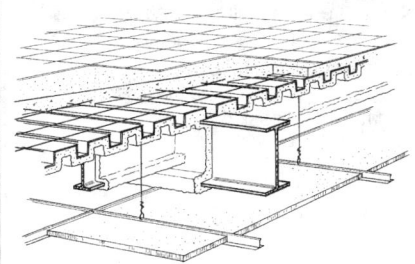

This page illustrates and describes a structural steel w/metal decking and concrete system including steel beams, steel decking, shear studs, concrete, placing concrete, edge form, steel trowel finish, curing, wire fabric, fireproofing, beams and decking, tile floor, and suspended ceiling. Lines within System Components give the unit price and total price per square foot for this system. Prices for alternate structural steel w/metal decking and concrete systems are on Line Items 3.5-314-1900 thru 2400. Both material quantities and labor costs have been adjusted for the system listed.

Factors: To adjust for job conditions other than normal working situations use Lines 3.5-314-2900 thru 4000.

Example: You are to install the system where material handling and storage are a problem. Go to Line 3.5-314-3400 and apply these percentages to the appropriate MAT. and INST. costs.

System Components	QUANTITY	UNIT	COST PER S.F.		
			MAT.	INST.	TOTAL
Composite structural beams, 20 ga. 3" deep steel decking, shear studs, 3000 psi, concrete, placing concrete, edge forms, steel trowel finish, Welded wire fabric fireproofing, tile floor and suspended ceiling.					
Steel deck, 20 gage, 3" deep, galvanized	1.000	S.F.	1.28	.66	1.94
Structural steel framing	.004	Ton	5.30	1.75	7.05
Shear studs, 3/4"	.250	Ea.	.07	.37	.44
Concrete, 3000 psi, 5" thick	.015	C.Y.	1.01		1.01
Place concrete	.015	C.Y.		.34	.34
Edge form	.140	L.F.	.06	.39	.45
Steel trowel finish	1.000	S.F.		.56	.56
Welded wire fabric 6 x 6 - #10/10	.011	C.S.F.	.08	.28	.36
Fireproofing, sprayed	1.880	S.F.	.86	1.45	2.31
Vinyl composition floor tile	1.000	S.F.	.75	.67	1.42
Suspended acoustical ceiling	1.000	S.F.	1.21	.96	2.17
TOTAL		S.F.	10.62	7.43	18.05

3.5-314	Floor - Ceiling, Struc. Steel	COST PER S.F.		
		MAT.	INST.	TOTAL
1800	For alternate floor systems:			
1900	Composite deck, galvanized, 3" deep, 22 ga.	10.50	7.40	17.90
2000	18 ga.	11	7.45	18.45
2100	16 ga.	11.55	7.50	19.05
2200	Composite deck, galvanized, 2" deep, 22 ga.	10.40	7.30	17.70
2300	20 ga.	10.55	7.35	17.90
2400	16 ga.	11.25	7.40	18.65
2500				
2900	Dust protection, add, minimum	1%	2%	
3000	Maximum	4%	11%	
3100	Equipment usage curtailment, add, minimum	1%	1%	
3200	Maximum	3%	10%	
3300	Material handling & storage limitation, add, minimum	1%	1%	
3400	Maximum	6%	7%	
3500	Protection of existing work, add, minimum	2%	2%	
3600	Maximum	5%	7%	
3700	Shift work requirements, add, minimum		5%	
3800	Maximum		30%	
3900	Temporary shoring and bracing, add, minimum	2%	5%	
4000	Maximum	5%	12%	

For expanded coverage of these items see *Means Concrete & Masonry Cost Data 1999*

SUPERSTRUCTURES — A3.5-414 Floor - Ceiling, Steel Joists

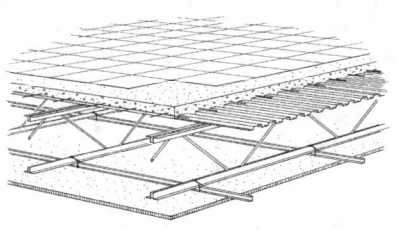

This page illustrates and describes an open web joist and steel slab-form system including open web steel joist, slab form, concrete, placing concrete, wire fabric, steel trowel finish, tile floor and plasterboard. Lines within System Components give the unit price and total price per square foot for this system. Prices for alternate open web joists and steel slab-form systems are on Line Items 3.5-414-1900 thru 2200. Both material quantities and labor costs have been adjusted for the systems listed.

Factors: To adjust for job conditions other than normal working situations use Lines 3.5-414-2900 thru 4000.

Example: You are to install the system in a congested commercial area and most work will be done at night. Go to Line 3.5-414-3800 and apply this percentage to the appropriate INST. cost.

System Components	QUANTITY	UNIT	MAT.	INST.	TOTAL
Open web steel joists, 24" O.C., slab form, 3000 psi concrete, welded Wire fabric, steel trowel finish, floor tile, 5/8" drywall ceiling.					
Open web steel joists, 12" deep, 5.2#/L.F., 24" O.C.	2.630	Lb.	1.42	.74	2.16
Slab form, 28 gage, 9/16" deep, galvanized	1.000	S.F.	.56	.49	1.05
Concrete, 3000 psi, 2-1/2" thick	.008	C.Y.	.54		.54
Placing concrete	.008	C.Y.		.19	.19
Welded wire fabric 6 x 6 - #10/10	.011	C.S.F.	.08	.28	.36
Steel trowel finish	1.000	S.F.		.56	.56
Vinyl composition floor tile	1.000	S.F.	.75	.67	1.42
Ceiling furring, 3/4" channels, 24" O.C.	1.000	S.F.	.13	.82	.95
Gypsum drywall, 5/8" thick, finished	1.000	S.F.	.36	.96	1.32
Paint ceiling	1.000	S.F.	.13	.43	.56
TOTAL		S.F.	3.97	5.14	9.11

3.5-414	Floor - Ceiling, Steel Joists	MAT.	INST.	TOTAL
1800	For alternate floor systems:			
1900	Open web joists, 16" deep, 6.6#/L.F.	4.33	5.30	9.63
2000	20" deep, 8.4# L.F.	4.82	5.55	10.37
2100	24" deep, 11.5# L.F.	5.65	6	11.65
2200	26" deep, 12.8# L.F.	6	6.20	12.20
2300				
2400				
2500				
2600				
2700				
2900	Dust protection, add, minimum	1%	2%	
3000	Maximum	4%	11%	
3100	Equipment usage curtailment, add, minimum	1%	1%	
3200	Maximum	3%	10%	
3300	Material handling & storage limitation, add, minimum	1%	1%	
3400	Maximum	6%	7%	
3500	Protection of existing work, add, minimum	2%	2%	
3600	Maximum	5%	7%	
3700	Shift work requirements, add, minimum		5%	
3800	Maximum		30%	
3900	Temporary shoring and bracing, add, minimum	2%	5%	
4000	Maximum	5%	12%	

SUPERSTRUCTURES A3.5-711 Manufactured Wood Joists

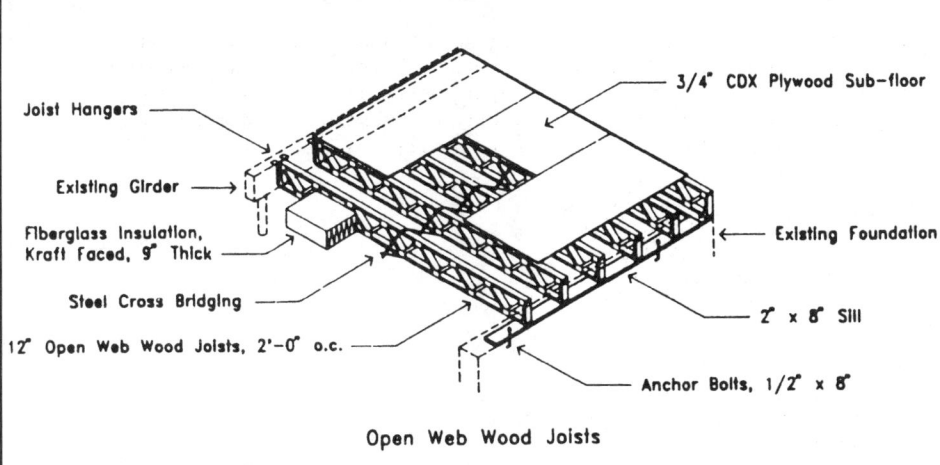

Open Web Wood Joists

This page illustrates and describes floor framing systems including sills, joist hangers, joists, bridging, subfloor and insulation. Lines within systems components give the unit price and total price per square foot for this system. Prices for alternate joist types are on line items 3.5-711-0100 through 0700. Both material quantities and labor costs have been adjusted for the system listed.

Factors: To adjust for job conditions other than normal working situations use lines 3.5-711-2700 through 4000.

Example: You are to install the system where delivery of material is difficult. Go to line 3.5-711-3400 and apply these percentages to the appropriate MAT. and INST. costs.

System Components	QUANTITY	UNIT	COST PER S.F.		
			MAT.	INST.	TOTAL
Open web wood joists, sill, butt to girder, 5/8" subfloor, insul.					
Anchor bolt, hook type, with nut and washer, 1/2" x 8" long	.250	Ea.	.01	.05	.06
Joist & beam hanger, 18 ga. galvanized	.750	Ea.	.05	.17	.22
Bridging, steel, compression, for 2" x 12" joists	.001	C.Pr.	.14	.18	.32
Framing, open web wood joists, 12" deep	.001	M.L.F.	2.08	.83	2.91
Framing, sills, 2" x 8"	.001	M.B.F.	.60	1.10	1.70
Sub-floor, plywood, CDX, 3/4" thick	1.000	S.F.	.54	.54	1.08
Insulation, fiberglass, kraft face, 9" thick x 23" wide	1.000	S.F.	.55	.27	.82
TOTAL			3.97	3.14	7.11

3.5-711	Open Web Wood Joists	COST PER S.F.		
		MAT.	INST.	TOTAL
0080	For alternate floor systems:			
0100	12" open web joists, sill, butt to girder, 5/8"subflr	3.97	3.14	7.11
0200	14" joists	4.22	3.20	7.42
0300	16" joists	4.32	3.25	7.57
0400	18" joists	4.42	3.30	7.72
0450	Wood struc."I"joists,24"O.C.,to 24'span,50 PSF LL, butt to girder	3.47	2.93	6.40
0500	55 PSF LL	3.59	2.97	6.56
0600	to 30'span, 45 PSF LL	3.87	2.88	6.75
0700	55 PSF LL	3.87	2.93	6.80
2700	Cut & patch to match existing construction, add, minimum	2%	3%	
2800	Maximum	5%	9%	
2900	Dust protection, add, minimum	1%	2%	
3000	Maximum	4%	11%	
3100	Equipment usage curtailment, add, minimum	1%	1%	
3200	Maximum	3%	10%	
3300	Material handling & storage limitation, add, minimum	1%	1%	
3400	Maximum	6%	7%	
3500	Protection of existing work, add, minimum	2%	2%	
3600	Maximum	5%	7%	
3700	Shift work requirements, add, minimum		5%	
3800	Maximum		30%	
3900	Temporary shoring and bracing, add, minimum	2%	5%	
4000	Maximum	5%	12%	

SUPERSTRUCTURES — A3.5-714 | Floor-Ceiling, Wood Joists

This page illustrates and describes a wood joist floor system including wood joist, oak floor, sub-floor, bridging, sand and finish floor, furring, plasterboard, taped, finished and painted ceiling. Lines within System Components give the unit price and total price per square foot for this system. Prices for alternate wood joist floor systems are on Line Items 3.5-714-1700 thru 2300. Both material quantities and labor costs have been adjusted for the system listed.

Factors: To adjust for job conditions other than normal working situations use Lines 3.5-714-2700 thru 4000.

Example: You are to install the system during off peak hours, 6 P.M. to 2 A.M. Go to Line 3.5-714-3800 and apply this percentage to the appropriate INST. costs.

System Components

System Components	QUANTITY	UNIT	COST PER S.F. MAT.	INST.	TOTAL
Wood joists, 2" x 8", 16" O.C., oak floor (sanded & finished), 1/2" sub Floor, 1"x 3" bridging, furring, 5/8" drywall, taped, finished and painted.					
Wood joists, 2" x 8", 16" O.C.	1.000	L.F.	.80	.66	1.46
C.D.X. plywood sub floor, 1/2" thick	1.000	S.F.	.45	.49	.94
Bridging 1" x 3"	.150	Pr.	.06	.42	.48
Oak flooring, No. 1 common	1.000	S.F.	3.58	2.15	5.73
Sand and finish floor	1.000	S.F.	.71	.97	1.68
Wood furring, 1" x 3", 16" O.C.	1.000	L.F.	.25	1.04	1.29
Gypsum drywall, 5/8" thick	1.000	S.F.	.26	.41	.67
Tape and finishing	1.000	S.F.	.10	.37	.47
Paint ceiling	1.000	S.F.	.13	.43	.56
TOTAL		S.F.	6.34	6.94	13.28

3.5-714 Floor-Ceiling, Wood Joists

		MAT.	INST.	TOTAL
1600	For alternate wood joist systems:			
1700	16" on center, 2" x 6" joists	6.15	6.85	13
1800	2" x 10"	6.65	7.10	13.75
1900	2" x 12"	6.95	7.10	14.05
2000	2" x 14"	7.65	7.25	14.90
2100	12" on center, 2" x 10" joists	6.95	7.30	14.25
2200	2" x 12"	7.30	7.35	14.65
2300	2" x 14"	8.20	7.45	15.65
2400				
2500				
2700	Cut & patch to match existing construction, add, minimum	2%	3%	
2800	Maximum	5%	9%	
2900	Dust protection, add, minimum	1%	2%	
3000	Maximum	4%	11%	
3100	Equipment usage curtailment, add, minimum	1%	1%	
3200	Maximum	3%	10%	
3300	Material handling & storage limitation, add, minimum	1%	1%	
3400	Maximum	6%	7%	
3500	Protection of existing work, add, minimum	2%	2%	
3600	Maximum	5%	7%	
3700	Shift work requirements, add, minimum		5%	
3800	Maximum		30%	
3900	Temporary shoring and bracing, add, minimum	2%	5%	
4000	Maximum	5%	12%	

SUPERSTRUCTURES — A3.7-511 | Roof Truss, Wood

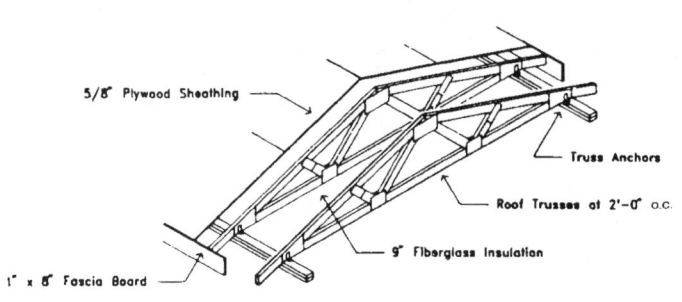

Wood Fabricated Roof Truss System

This page illustrates and describes a sloped roof truss framing system including trusses, truss anchors, sheathing, fascia and insulation. Lines 3.7-511-1500 through 1800 are for a flat roof framing system including flat roof trusses, truss anchors, sheathing, fascia and insulation. Lines within system components give the unit price and total price per square foot for this system. Prices for alternate sizes and systems are given in line items 3.7-511-0100 through 1800. Both material quantities and labor costs have been adjusted for the system listed.

Factors: To adjust for job conditions other than normal working situations use lines 3.7-511-2700 through 4000.

Example: You are to install the system where crane placement and movement will be difficult. Go to line 3.7-511-3200 and apply these percentages to the appropriate MAT. and INST. costs.

System Components	QUANTITY	UNIT	COST PER S.F.		
			MAT.	INST.	TOTAL
Roof truss, 2' O.C., 4/12 slope, 12' span, 5/8 sheath., fascia, insul.					
Timber connectors, rafter anchors, galv., 1 1/2" x 5 1/4"	.084	Ea.	.03	.21	.24
Plywood sheathing, CDX, 5/8" thick	1.054	S.F.	.57	.59	1.16
Truss, 2' O.C., metal plate connectors, 12' span	.042	Ea.	1.28	1.13	2.41
Molding, fascia trim, 1" x 8"	.167	L.F.	.17	.27	.44
Insulation, fiberglass, kraft face, 9" thick x 23" wide	1.000	S.F.	.55	.27	.82
TOTAL			2.60	2.47	5.07

3.7-511	Roof Truss, Wood	MAT.	INST.	TOTAL
0090	For alternate roof systems:			
0100	Roof truss, 2'O.C., 4/12p, 1'ovhg, 12'span, 5/8"sheath, fascia, insul.	2.60	2.47	5.07
0200	20' span	2.24	2.11	4.35
0300	24' span	2.22	1.97	4.19
0400	26' span	3.95	2.63	6.58
0500	28' span	2.22	1.93	4.15
0600	30' span	2.64	1.90	4.54
0700	32' span	2.47	1.87	4.34
0800	34' span	2.67	1.85	4.52
0900	8/12 pitch, 20' span	2.98	2.26	5.24
1000	24' span	2.95	2.12	5.07
1100	26' span	4.52	2.87	7.39
1200	28' span	2.95	2.07	5.02
1300	32' span	2.92	2.02	4.94
1400	36' span	2.91	1.98	4.89
1500	Flat roof frame, fab.strl.joists, 2' O.C., 15'-24' span, 50 PSF LL	2.78	1.67	4.45
1600	55 PSF LL	2.90	1.71	4.61
1700	24'-30'span, 45 PSF LL	3.17	1.60	4.77
1800	55 PSF LL	3.17	1.65	4.82
2700	Cut & patch to match existing construction, add, minimum	2%	3%	
2800	Maximum	5%	9%	
2900	Dust protection, add, minimum	1%	2%	
3000	Maximum	4%	11%	
3100	Equipment usage curtailment, add, minimum	1%	1%	
3200	Maximum	3%	10%	
3300	Material handling & storage limitation, add, minimum	1%	1%	
3400	Maximum	6%	7%	
3500	Protection of existing work, add, minimum	2%	2%	
3600	Maximum	5%	7%	
3700	Shift work requirements, add, minimum		5%	
3800	Maximum		30%	
3900	Temporary shoring and bracing, add, minimum	2%	5%	
4000	Maximum	5%	12%	

For expanded coverage of these items see *Means Concrete & Masonry Cost Data 1999*

SUPERSTRUCTURES A3.9-104 | Stairs

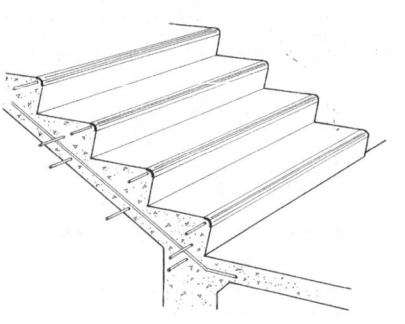

This page illustrates and describes a stair system based on a cost per flight price. Prices for various stair systems are on Line Items 3.9-104-0700 thru 3200. Both material quantities and labor costs have been adjusted for the system listed.

Factors: To adjust for job conditions other than normal working situations use Lines 3.9-104-3500 thru 4200.

Example: You are to install the system during evenings only. Go to Line 3.9-104-4200 and apply this percentage to the appropriate MAT. and INST. costs.

System Components	QUANTITY	UNIT	COST PER FLIGHT		
			MAT.	INST.	TOTAL
Below are various stair systems based on cost per flight of stairs, no side Walls. Stairs are 4'-0" wide, railings are included unless otherwise noted					

3.9-104	Stairs	COST PER FLIGHT		
		MAT.	INST.	TOTAL
0700	Concrete, cast in place, no nosings, no railings, 12 risers	305	1,300	1,605
0800	24 risers	610	2,600	3,210
0900	Add for 1 intermediate landing	79.50	355	434.50
1000	Concrete, cast in place, with nosings, no railings, 12 risers	665	1,525	2,190
1100	24 risers	1,325	3,025	4,350
1200	Add for 1 intermediate landing	109	370	479
1300	Steel, grating tread, safety nosing, 12 risers	1,200	750	1,950
1400	24 risers	2,425	1,500	3,925
1500	Add for intermediate landing	630	199	829
1600	Steel, cement fill pan tread, 12 risers	1,025	750	1,775
1700	24 risers	2,075	1,500	3,575
1800	Add for intermediate landing	630	199	829
1900	Spiral, industrial, 4' - 6" diameter, 12 risers	2,175	530	2,705
2000	24 risers	4,375	1,050	5,425
2100	Wood, box stairs, oak treads, 12 risers	2,400	560	2,960
2200	24 risers	4,775	1,125	5,900
2300	Add for 1 intermediate landing	146	93.50	239.50
2400	Wood, basement stairs, no risers, 12 steps	675	201	876
2500	24 steps	1,350	405	1,755
2600	Add for 1 intermediate landing	29	17.70	46.70
2700	Wood, open, rough sawn cedar, 12 steps	995	335	1,330
2800	24 steps	1,975	670	2,645
2900	Add for 1 intermediate landing	14.65	18.30	32.95
3000	Wood, residential, oak treads, 12 risers	1,600	1,825	3,425
3100	24 risers	3,200	3,625	6,825
3200	Add for 1 intermediate landing	132	84.50	216.50
3500	Dust protection, add, minimum	1%	2%	
3600	Maximum	4%	11%	
3700	Material handling & storage limitation, add, minimum	1%	1%	
3800	Maximum	6%	7%	
3900	Protection of existing work, add, minimum	2%	2%	
4000	Maximum	5%	7%	
4100	Shift work requirements, add, minimum		5%	
4200	Maximum		30%	

SUPERSTRUCTURES — A3.9-900 Floor & Ceiling

3.9-900	Selective Price Sheet	MAT.	INST.	TOTAL
0100	Flooring, carpet, nylon, level loop, 26 oz. light traffic	1.55	.50	2.05
0200	40 oz. heavy traffic	3.27	.50	3.77
0300	Nylon, plush, 20 oz. light traffic	1.03	.65	1.68
0400	24 oz. medium traffic	2.05	.50	2.55
0500	26 oz. heavy traffic	2.83	.53	3.36
0600	28 oz. heavy traffic	3.16	.53	3.69
0700	Tile, foamed back, needle punch	2.42	.59	3.01
0800	Tufted loop	1.02	.59	1.61
0900	Wool, 36 oz. medium traffic, level loop	7.10	.53	7.63
1000	48 oz. heavy traffic, patterned	7.25	.53	7.78
1100	Composition, epoxy, with colored chips, minimum	2.24	2.78	5.02
1200	Maximum	2.72	3.84	6.56
1300	Trowelled, minimum	2.89	3.36	6.25
1400	Maximum	4.21	3.91	8.12
1500	Terrazzo, 1/4" thick, chemical resistant, minimum	4.70	3.59	8.29
1600	Maximum	7.70	4.78	12.48
1700	Resilient, asphalt tile, 1/8" thick	1.03	.84	1.87
1800	Conductive flrg, rubber, 1/8" thick	2.75	1.07	3.82
1900	Cork tile, 1/8" thick, standard finish	2.66	1.07	3.73
2000	Urethane finish	4.02	1.07	5.09
2100	PVC sheet goods for gyms, 1/4" thick	3.77	4.20	7.97
2200	3/8" thick	4.26	5.60	9.86
2300	Vinyl composition 12" x 12" tile, plain, 1/16" thick	.75	.67	1.42
2400	1/8" thick	2.21	.67	2.88
2500	Vinyl tile, 12" x 12" x 1/8" thick, minimum	2.13	.67	2.80
2600	Maximum	8.05	.67	8.72
2700	Vinyl sheet goods, backed, .093" thick	1.63	1.46	3.09
2800	.250" thick			
2900	Wood, maple strip 25/32" x 2-1/4", finished, select	3.96	3.12	7.08
3000	2nd and better	3.63	3.12	6.75
3100	Oak, 25/32" x 2-1/4" finished, clear	4.04	3.12	7.16
3200	No. 1 common	4.29	3.12	7.41
3300	Parquet, standard 5/16" thick finished, minimum	2.40	3.26	5.66
3400	Maximum	6.35	4.63	10.98
3500	Custom finished, minimum	14.75	3.66	18.41
3600	Maximum	19.50	7.30	26.80
3700	Prefinished, oak, 2-1/4" wide	6.45	2.15	8.60
3800	Ranch plank	8	2.52	10.52
3900	Sleepers on concrete, treated, 24" O.C., 1" x 2"	.15	.25	.40
4000	1" x 3"	.22	.29	.51
4100	2" x 4"	.57	.39	.96
4200	2" x 6"	.84	.45	1.29
4300	Ceiling, plaster, gypsum, 2 coats	.38	1.95	2.33
4400	3 coats	.53	2.29	2.82
4500	Perlite or vermiculite, 2 coats	.46	2.28	2.74
4600	3 coats	.75	2.86	3.61
4700	Gypsum lath, plain, 3/8" thick	.41	.45	.86
4800	1/2" thick	.48	.48	.96
4900	Firestop, 3/8" thick	.48	.54	1.02
5000	1/2" thick	.49	.58	1.07
5100	Metal lath, rib, 2.75 lb.	.19	.51	.70
5200	3.40 lb.	.35	.54	.89
5300	Diamond, 2.50 lb.	.20	.51	.71
5400	3.40 lb.	.23	.63	.86
5500	Drywall, taped and finished, standard, 1/2" thick	.27	.96	1.23
5600	5/8" thick	.36	.96	1.32
5700	Fire resistant, 1/2" thick	.36	.96	1.32
5800	5/8" thick	.33	.96	1.29
5900	Water resistant, 1/2" thick	.35	.96	1.31
6000	5/8" thick	.42	.76	1.18

For expanded coverage of these items see Means Concrete & Masonry Cost Data 1999

SUPERSTRUCTURES

A3.9-900 Floor & Ceiling

3.9-900 Selective Price Sheet

		COST PER S.F.		
		MAT.	INST.	TOTAL
6100	Finish, instead of taping			
6200	For thin coat plaster, add	.11	.45	.56
6300	Finish, textured spray, add			
6400	Drywall, no finish included, see system 069-700	.13	.43	.56
6500	Tile, stapled or glued, plastic coated min. fiber, 5/8" thick	.62	.37	.99
6600	3/4" thick	1.35	.37	1.72
6700	Wood fiber, 1/2" thick	.78	.91	1.69
6800	3/4" thick	1.05	.91	1.96
6900	Suspended, film faced fiberglass boards, 5/8" thick	.54	.58	1.12
7000	3" thick	1.33	.81	2.14
7100	5/8" thick min. fiber boards, standard face	.63	.54	1.17
7200	Aluminum faced	5.80	.61	6.41
7500	Ceiling suspension systems, for tile, class "A", "T" bar, 2' x 4' grid	.34	.46	.80
7600	2' x 2' grid	.43	.56	.99
7700	Concealed "Z" bar, 12" module	.37	.70	1.07
7800				
7900	For plaster or drywall, 3/4" channels, steel furring 16" O.C.	.19	1.18	1.37
8000	24" O.C.	.13	.82	.95
8100	1-1/2" channels, 16" O.C.	.26	1.32	1.58
8200	24" O.C.	.17	.88	1.05
8300	Ceiling framing, 2" x 4" studs, 16" O.C.	.30	.61	.91
8400	24" O.C.	.20	.41	.61

For information about Means Estimating Seminars, see yellow pages 11 and 12 in back of book

Division 4
Exterior Closure

EXTERIOR CLOSURE — A4.1-208 — Masonry Wall, Concrete Block

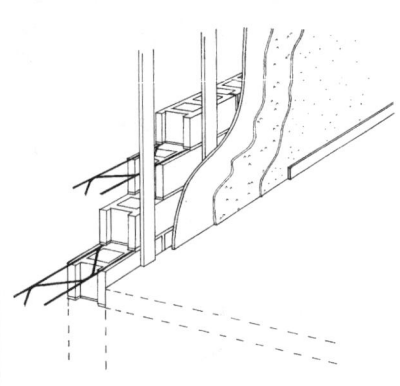

This page illustrates and describes a masonry concrete block system including concrete block wall, pointed, reinforcing, waterproofing, gypsum plaster on gypsum lath, and furring. Lines within System Components give the unit price and total price per square foot for this system. Prices for alternate masonry concrete block wall systems are on Line Items 04.1-208-1500 thru 2200. Both material quantities and labor costs have been adjusted for the system listed.

Factors: To adjust for job conditions other than normal working situations use Lines 04.1-208-2700 thru 4000.

Example: You are to install the system and match existing construction at several locations. Go to Line 04.1-208-2800 and apply these percentages to the appropriate MAT. and INST. costs.

System Components	QUANTITY	UNIT	COST PER S.F. MAT.	COST PER S.F. INST.	COST PER S.F. TOTAL
Concrete block, 8" thick, reinforced every 2 courses, waterproofing gypsum Plaster over gypsum lath on 1" x 3" furring, interior painting & baseboard.					
Concrete block, 8" x 8" x 16", reinforced	1.000	S.F.	2.64	3.93	6.57
Silicone waterproofing, 2 coats	1.000	S.F.	.56	.12	.68
Bituminous coating, 1/16" thick	1.000	S.F.	.17	.70	.87
Furring, 1" x 3", 16" O.C.	1.000	L.F.	.25	1.41	1.66
Gypsum lath, 3/8" thick	.110	S.Y.	.41	.44	.85
Gypsum plaster, 2 coats	.110	S.Y.	.38	1.69	2.07
Painting, 2 coats	1.000	S.F.	.09	.33	.42
Baseboard wood, 9/16" x 2-5/8"	.100	L.F.	.14	.19	.33
TOTAL		S.F.	4.64	8.81	13.45

4.1-208	Masonry Wall, Concrete Block	MAT.	INST.	TOTAL
1400	For alternate exterior wall systems:			
1500	8" thick block, fluted 2 sides	6.40	10.45	16.85
1600	Deep grooved	5.10	10.45	15.55
1700	Slump block	8.80	9.10	17.90
1800	Split rib	4.58	10.35	14.93
1900				
2000	12" thick block, regular	4.20	10.65	14.85
2100	Slump block	12.85	9.90	22.75
2200	Split rib	5.35	12	17.35
2300				
2400				
2500				
2700	Cut & patch to match existing construction, add, minimum	2%	3%	
2800	Maximum	5%	9%	
2900	Dust protection, add, minimum	1%	2%	
3000	Maximum	4%	11%	
3100	Equipment usage curtailment, add, minimum	1%	1%	
3200	Maximum	3%	10%	
3300	Material handling & storage limitation, add, minimum	1%	1%	
3400	Maximum	6%	7%	
3500	Protection of existing work, add, minimum	2%	2%	
3600	Maximum	5%	7%	
3700	Shift work requirements, add, minimum		5%	
3800	Maximum		30%	
3900	Temporary shoring and bracing, add, minimum	2%	5%	
4000	Maximum	5%	12%	

EXTERIOR CLOSURE — A4.1-258 Masonry Wall, Brick - Stone

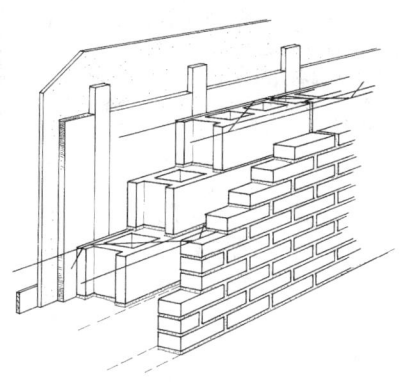

This page illustrates and describes a masonry wall, brick-stone system including brick, concrete block, durawall, insulation, plasterboard, taped and finished, furring, baseboard and painting interior. Lines within System Components give the unit price and total price per square foot for this system. Prices for alternate masonry wall, brick-stone systems are on Line Item 4.1-258-1500 thru 2500. Both material quantities and labor costs have been adjusted for the system listed.

Factors: To adjust for job conditions other than normal working situations use Lines 4.1-258-3100 thru 4200.

Example: You are to install the system without damaging the existing work. Go to Line 4.1-258-3900 and apply these percentages to the appropriate MAT. and INST. costs.

System Components	QUANTITY	UNIT	COST PER S.F.		
			MAT.	INST.	TOTAL
Face brick, 4"thick, concrete block back-up, reinforce every second course, 3/4"insulation, furring, 1/2"drywall, taped, finish, and painted, baseboard					
Face brick, 4" brick	1.000	S.F.	2.80	7.60	10.40
Concrete back-up block, reinforced 8" thick	1.000	S.F.	1.51	4.22	5.73
3/4" rigid polystyrene insulation	1.000	S.F.	.34	.46	.80
Furring, 1" x 3", wood, 16" O.C.	1.000	L.F.	.25	.74	.99
Drywall, 1/2" thick	1.000	S.F.	.17	.37	.54
Taping & finishing	1.000	S.F.	.10	.37	.47
Painting, 2 coats	1.000	S.F.	.13	.43	.56
Baseboard, wood, 9/16" x 2-5/8"	.100	L.F.	.14	.19	.33
TOTAL		S.F.	5.44	14.38	19.82

4.1-258	Masonry Wall, Brick - Stone	COST PER S.F.		
		MAT.	INST.	TOTAL
1400	For alternate exterior wall systems:			
1500	Face brick, Norman, 4" x 2-2/3" x 12" (4.5 per S.F.)	6.35	12	18.35
1600	Roman, 4" x 2" x 12" (6.0 per S.F.)	7.80	13.50	21.30
1700	Engineer, 4" x 3-1/5" x 8" (5.63 per S.F.)	4.76	13.20	17.96
1800	S.C.R., 6" x 2-2/3" x 12" (4.5 per S.F.)	7.25	12.20	19.45
1900	Jumbo, 6" x 4" x 12" (3.0 per S.F.)	6.65	10.60	17.25
2000	Norwegian, 6" x 3-1/5" x 12" (3.75 per S.F.)	5	11.25	16.25
2100				
2200				
2300	Stone, veneer, fieldstone, 6" thick	8	12.20	20.20
2400	Marble, 2" thick	37	21.50	58.50
2500	Limestone, 2" thick	14.85	14.55	29.40
2600				
2700				
3100	Cut & patch to match existing construction, add, minimum	2%	3%	
3200	Maximum	5%	9%	
3300	Dust protection, add, minimum	1%	2%	
3400	Maximum	4%	11%	
3500	Equipment usage curtailment, add, minimum	1%	1%	
3600	Maximum	3%	10%	
3700	Material handling & storage limitation, add, minimum	1%	1%	
3800	Maximum	6%	7%	
3900	Protection of existing work, add, minimum	2%	2%	
4000	Maximum	5%	7%	
4100	Shift work requirements, add, minimum		5%	
4200	Maximum		30%	

EXTERIOR CLOSURE — A4.1-288 Parapet Wall

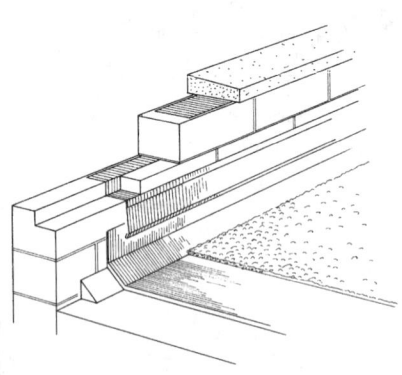

This page illustrates and describes a parapet wall system including wall, coping, flashing and cant strip. Lines within System Components give the unit price and cost per lineal foot for this system. Prices for alternate parapet wall systems are on Lines 4.1-288-1300 thru 2400. Both material quantities and labor costs have been adjusted for the system listed.

Factors: To adjust for job conditions other than normal working situations, use Lines 4.1-288-2900 thru 4000.

Example: You are to install the system without damaging the adjacent property. Go to Line 4.1-288-3600 and apply these percentages to the appropriate MAT. and INST. costs.

System Components	QUANTITY	UNIT	COST PER L.F. MAT.	INST.	TOTAL
Concrete block parapet, incl. reinf., coping, flashing & cant strip, 2' high					
8" concrete block	2.000	S.F.	5.28	7.86	13.14
Masonry reinforcing	1.000	L.F.	.11	.12	.23
Coping, precast	1.000	L.F.	11.10	9.30	20.40
Roof cant	1.000	L.F.	2.11	1.08	3.19
Through wall flashing	1.000	L.F.	1.75	1.62	3.37
Cap flashing	1.000	L.F.	3.35	3.54	6.89
TOTAL		L.F.	23.70	23.52	47.22

4.1-288	Parapet Wall		COST PER L.F. MAT.	INST.	TOTAL
1200	For alternate systems:				
1300	Concrete block				
1400	12" thick		31	27.50	58.50
1500	Split rib block, 8" thick		23.50	26.50	50
1600	12" thick		29.50	31.50	61
1700	Brick, common brick, 8" wall		27	40	67
1800	12" wall		31.50	50.50	82
1900	4" brick, 4" backup block		26	39	65
2000	8" backup block		27	39.50	66.50
2100	Stucco on masonry		24	24.50	48.50
2200	On wood frame		10.80	14.10	24.90
2300	Wood, T 1-11 siding		20	26	46
2400	Boards, 1" x 6" cedar		22.50	29	51.50
2500					
2600					
2700					
2900	Dust protection, add, minimum		1%	2%	
3000	Maximum		4%	11%	
3100	Equipment usage curtailment, add, minimum		1%	1%	
3200	Maximum		3%	10%	
3300	Material handling & storage limitation, add, minimum		1%	1%	
3400	Maximum		6%	7%	
3500	Protection of existing work, add, minimum		2%	2%	
3600	Maximum		5%	7%	
3700	Shift work requirements, add, minimum			5%	
3800	Maximum			30%	
3900	Temporary shoring and bracing, add, minimum		2%	5%	
4000	Maximum		5%	12%	

EXTERIOR CLOSURE — A4.1-289 — Masonry Restoration - Cleaning

This page illustrates and describes a masonry cleaning and restoration system, including staging, cleaning, repointing. Lines within System Components give the unit price and cost per square foot for this system. Prices for alternate systems are on Lines 3.1-289-1300 thru 2500. Both material quantities and labor costs have been adjusted for the system listed.

Factors: To adjust for conditions other than normal working situations, use Lines 4.1-289-2900 thru 4200.

Example: You are to clean a wall and be concerned about dust control. Go to line 4.1-289-3100 and apply these percentages to the appropriate MAT. and INST. costs.

System Components	QUANTITY	UNIT	COST PER S.F. MAT.	INST.	TOTAL
Repoint existing building, brick, running bond, high pressure cleaning, Water only, soft old mortar.					
Scaffold, building exterior	.010	C.S.F.	.27	.46	.73
Cleaning, high pressure water only	1.000	S.F.		1.22	1.22
Repoint, brick running bond	1.000	S.F.	.27	4.57	4.84
TOTAL		S.F.	.54	6.25	6.79

4.1-289	Masonry Restoration - Cleaning	MAT.	INST.	TOTAL
1200	For alternate masonry surfaces:			
1300	Brick, common bond	.54	6.55	7.09
1400	Flemish bond	.55	6.90	7.45
1500	English bond	.55	7.30	7.85
1600	Add for wire cut face brick	.29		.29
1700	Stone, 2' x 2' blocks	.62	4.29	4.91
1800	2' x 4' blocks	.53	3.64	4.17
2000	Add to above prices for alternate cleaning systems:			
2100	Chemical brush and wash	.09	.82	.91
2200	High pressure chemical and water	.06	.42	.48
2300	Sandblasting, wet system	.17	1.14	1.31
2400	Dry system	.15	.67	.82
2500	Steam cleaning		.34	.34
2600				
2900	Cut & patch to match existing construction, add, minimum	2%	3%	
3000	Maximum	5%	9%	
3100	Dust protection, add, minimum	1%	2%	
3200	Maximum	4%	11%	
3300	Equipment usage curtailment, add, minimum	1%	1%	
3400	Maximum	3%	10%	
3500	Material handling & storage limitation, add, minimum	1%	1%	
3600	Maximum	6%	7%	
3700	Pedestrian protection, add			
3800				
3900	Protection of existing work, add, minimum	2%	2%	
4000	Maximum	5%	7%	
4100	Shift work requirements, add, minimum		5%	
4200	Maximum		30%	

EXTERIOR CLOSURE — A4.1-416 Wood Frame Exterior Wall

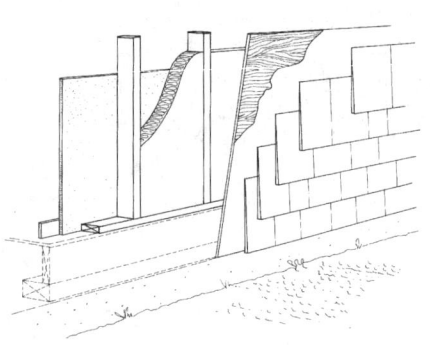

This page illustrates and describes a wood frame exterior wall system including wood studs, sheathing, felt, insulation, plasterboard, taped and finished, baseboard and painted interior. Lines within System Components give the unit price and total price per square foot for this system. Prices for alternate wood frame exterior wall systems are on Line Items 4.1-416-1700 thru 2700. Both material quantities and labor costs have been adjusted for the system listed.

Factors: To adjust for job conditions other than normal working situations use Lines 4.1-416-3100 thru 4200.

Example: You are to install the system with need for complete temporary bracing. Go to Line 4.1-416-4200 and apply these percentages to the appropriate MAT. and INST. costs.

System Components	QUANTITY	UNIT	COST PER S.F. MAT.	INST.	TOTAL
Wood stud wall, cedar shingle siding, building paper, plywood sheathing, Insulation, 5/8" drywall, taped, finished and painted, baseboard.					
2" x 4" wood studs, 16" O.C.	.100	L.F.	.46	.73	1.19
1/2" CDX sheathing	1.000	S.F.	.45	.52	.97
18" No. 1 red cedar shingles, 7-1/2" exposure	.008	C.S.F.	1.06	1.30	2.36
15# felt paper	.010	C.S.F.	.03	.10	.13
3-1/2" fiberglass insulation	1.000	S.F.	.32	.23	.55
5/8" drywall, taped and finished	1.000	S.F.	.36	.74	1.10
Baseboard trim, stock pine, 9/16" x 3-1/2", painted	.100	L.F.	.14	.19	.33
Paint, 2 coats, interior	1.000	S.F.	.13	.43	.56
TOTAL		S.F.	2.95	4.24	7.19

4.1-416	Wood Frame Exterior Wall	MAT.	INST.	TOTAL
1600	For alternate exterior wall systems:			
1700	Aluminum siding, horizontal clapboard	3.23	4.36	7.59
1800	Cedar bevel siding, 1/2" x 6", vertical, painted	4.11	4.40	8.51
1900	Redwood siding 1" x 4" to 1" x 6" vertical, T & G	5.45	4.77	10.22
2000	Board and batten	4.18	4.35	8.53
2100	Ship lap siding	4.11	4.40	8.51
2200	Plywood, grooved (T1-11) fir	3	4.02	7.02
2300	Redwood	3.54	4.02	7.56
2400	Southern yellow pine	2.80	4.02	6.82
2500	Masonry on stud wall, stucco, wire and plaster	2.54	4.54	7.08
2600	Stone veneer	7.25	8.35	15.60
2700	Brick veneer, brick $275 per M	4.69	10.55	15.24
2800				
2900				
3100	Cut & patch to match existing construction, add, minimum	2%	3%	
3200	Maximum	5%	9%	
3300	Dust protection, add, minimum	1%	2%	
3400	Maximum	4%	11%	
3500	Material handling & storage limitation, add, minimum	1%	1%	
3600	Maximum	6%	7%	
3700	Protection of existing work, add, minimum	2%	2%	
3800	Maximum	5%	7%	
3900	Shift work requirements, add, minimum		5%	
4000	Maximum		30%	
4100	Temporary shoring and bracing, add, minimum	2%	5%	
4200	Maximum	5%	12%	

Important: See the Reference Section for critical supporting data - Reference Nos., Crews, & City Cost Indexes

EXTERIOR CLOSURE — A4.6-142 | Doors, Metal - Commercial

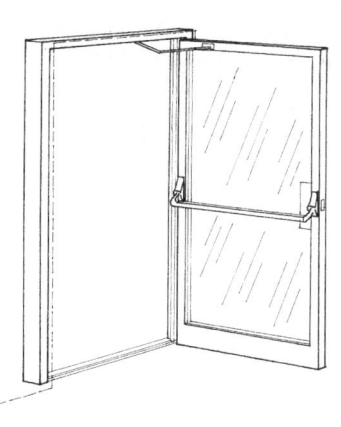

This page illustrates and describes a commercial metal door system, including a single aluminum and glass door, narrow stiles, jamb, hardware weatherstripping, panic hardware and closer. Lines within System Components give the unit price and total price on a cost each basis for this system. Prices for alternate commercial metal door systems are on Line Items 4.6-142-1300 thru 2500. Both material quantities and labor costs have been adjusted for the system listed.

Factors: To adjust for job conditions other than normal working situations, use Lines 4.6-142-3100 thru 4000.

Example: You are to install the system and cut and patch to match existing construction. Go to Line 4.6-142-3200 and apply these percentages to the appropriate MAT. and INST. costs.

System Components	QUANTITY	UNIT	COST EACH		
			MAT.	INST.	TOTAL
Single aluminum and glass door, 3'-0"x7'-0", with narrow stiles, ext. jamb. Weatherstripping, 1/2" tempered insul. glass, panic hardware, and closer.					
Aluminum door, 3'-0" x 7'-0" x 1-3/4", narrow stiles	1.000	Ea.	455	465	920
Tempered insulating glass, 1/2" thick	20.000	S.F.	330	251	581
Panic hardware	1.000	Set	350	61	411
Automatic closer	1.000	Ea.	78	56.50	134.50
TOTAL		Ea.	1,213	833.50	2,046.50

4.6-142		Doors, Metal - Commercial	COST EACH		
			MAT.	INST.	TOTAL
1200		For alternate door systems:			
1300		Single aluminum and glass with transom, 3'-0" x 10'-0"	1,625	990	2,615
1400		Anodized aluminum and glass, 3'-0" x 7'-0"	1,375	995	2,370
1500		With transom, 3'-0" x 10'-0"	1,900	1,175	3,075
1600		Steel, deluxe, hollow metal 3'-0" x 7'-0"	845	315	1,160
1700		With transom 3'-0" x 10'-0"	1,075	360	1,435
1800		Fire door, "A" label, 3'-0" x 7'-0"	865	315	1,180
1900		Double, aluminum and glass, 6'-0" x 7'-0"	2,025	1,425	3,450
2000		With transom, 6'-0" x 10'-0"	2,225	1,750	3,975
2100		Anodized aluminum and glass 6'-0" x 7'-0"	2,300	1,675	3,975
2200		With transom, 6'-0" x 10'-0"	2,475	2,050	4,525
2300		Steel, deluxe, hollow metal, 6'-0" x 7'-0"	1,400	550	1,950
2400		With transom, 6'-0" x 10'-0"	1,850	635	2,485
2500		Fire door, "A" label, 6'-0" x 7'-0"	1,400	545	1,945
2800					
2900					
3100		Cut & patch to match existing construction, add, minimum	2%	3%	
3200		Maximum	5%	9%	
3300		Dust protection, add, minimum	1%	2%	
3400		Maximum	4%	11%	
3500		Material handling & storage limitation, add, minimum	1%	1%	
3600		Maximum	6%	7%	
3700		Protection of existing work, add, minimum	2%	2%	
3800		Maximum	5%	7%	
3900		Shift work requirements, add, minimum		5%	
4000		Maximum		30%	

EXTERIOR CLOSURE — A4.6-144 — Doors, Residential - Exterior

This page illustrates and describes residential door systems including a door, frame, trim, hardware, weatherstripping, stained and finished. Lines within System Components give the unit price and total price on a cost each basis for this system. Prices for alternate residential door systems are on Line Items 4.6-144-1500 thru 2200. Both material quantities and labor costs have been adjusted for the system listed.

Factors: To adjust for job conditions other than normal working situations use Lines 4.6-144-3100 thru 4000.

Example: You are to install the system with a material handling and storage limitation. Go to Line 4.6-144-3600 and apply these percentages to the appropriate MAT. and INST. costs.

System Components	QUANTITY	UNIT	COST EACH MAT.	COST EACH INST.	COST EACH TOTAL
Single solid wood colonial door, 3' x 6'-8" with wood frame and trim, Stained and finished, including hardware and weatherstripping.					
Solid wood colonial door, fir 3' x 6'-8" x 1-3/4", hinges	1.000	Ea.	364.45	49	413.45
Exterior frame, with trim	1.000	Set	101.15	33.15	134.30
Interior trim	1.000	Set	13.70	62	75.70
Lockset	1.000	Set	30	26	56
Sill, oak 8" deep	3.500	Ea.	48.30	25.55	73.85
Weatherstripping	1.000	Set	16.85	48	64.85
Stained and finished	1.000	Ea.	3.58	40.50	44.08
TOTAL		Ea.	578.03	284.20	862.23

4.6-144	Doors, Residential - Exterior	MAT.	INST.	TOTAL
1400	For alternate exterior door system:			
1500	Single doors			
1600	Hollow metal exterior door, plain	430	273	703
1700	Solid core wood door, plain	315	273	588
1800				
1900	Double doors, 6' x 6'-8"			
2000	Solid colonial double doors, fir	985	375	1,360
2100	Hollow metal exterior doors, plain	690	360	1,050
2200	Hollow core wood doors, plain	455	360	815
2300				
2800				
2900				
3100	Cut & patch to match existing construction, add, minimum	2%	3%	
3200	Maximum	5%	9%	
3300	Dust protection, add, minimum	1%	2%	
3400	Maximum	4%	11%	
3500	Material handling & storage limitation, add, minimum	1%	1%	
3600	Maximum	6%	7%	
3700	Protection of existing work, add, minimum	2%	2%	
3800	Maximum	5%	7%	
3900	Shift work requirements, add, minimum		5%	
4000	Maximum		30%	

EXTERIOR CLOSURE — A4.6-152 | Doors, Sliding - Patio

This page illustrates and describes sliding door systems including a sliding door, frame, interior and exterior trim with exterior staining. Lines within System Components give the unit price and total price on a cost each basis for this system. Prices for alternate sliding door systems are on Line Items 4.6-152-1100 thru 2400. Both material quantities and labor costs have been adjusted for the system listed.

Factors: To adjust for job conditions other than normal working situations use Lines 4.6-152-2700 thru 4000.

Example: You are to install the system with temporary shoring and bracing. Go to Line 4.6-152-3900 and apply these percentages to the appropriate MAT. and INST. costs.

System Components	QUANTITY	UNIT	COST EACH MAT.	COST EACH INST.	COST EACH TOTAL
Sliding wood door, 6'-0" x 6'-8", with wood frame, interior and exterior Trim and exterior staining.					
Sliding wood door, standard, 6'-0" x 6'-8", insulated glass	1.000	Ea.	730	183	913
Interior & exterior trim	1.000	Set	17	30.40	47.40
Stain door & trim	1.000	Ea.	3.47	27.30	30.77
TOTAL		Ea.	750.47	240.70	991.17

4.6-152	Doors, Sliding - Patio	MAT.	INST.	TOTAL
1000	For alternate sliding door systems:			
1100	Wood, standard, 8'-0" x 6'-8", insulated glass	880	305	1,185
1200	12'-0" x 6'-8"	1,225	370	1,595
1300	Vinyl coated, 6'-0" x 6'-8"	1,025	241	1,266
1400	8'-0" x 6'-8"	1,175	305	1,480
1500	12'-0" x 6'-8"	1,875	370	2,245
1700	Aluminum, standard, 6'-0" x 6'-8", insulated glass	550	258	808
1800	8'-0" x 6'-8"	1,100	325	1,425
1900	12'-0" x 6'-8"	1,425	390	1,815
2000	Anodized, 6'-0" x 6'-8"	1,350	258	1,608
2100	8'-0" x 6'-8"	1,300	325	1,625
2200	12'-0" x 6'-8"	2,175	390	2,565
2300				
2400	Deduct for single glazing	48		48
2500				
2700	Cut & patch to match existing construction, add, minimum	2%	3%	
2800	Maximum	5%	9%	
2900	Dust protection, add, minimum	1%	2%	
3000	Maximum	4%	11%	
3100	Equipment usage curtailment, add, minimum	1%	1%	
3200	Maximum	3%	10%	
3300	Material handling & storage limitation, add, minimum	1%	1%	
3400	Maximum	6%	7%	
3500	Protection of existing, work, add, minimum	2%	2%	
3600	Maximum	5%	7%	
3700	Shift work requirements, add, minimum		5%	
3800	Maximum		30%	
3900	Temporary shoring and bracing, add, minimum	2%	5%	
4000	Maximum	5%	12%	

For expanded coverage of these items see *Means Building Construction Cost Data 1999*

EXTERIOR CLOSURE — A4.6-702 — Doors, Overhead

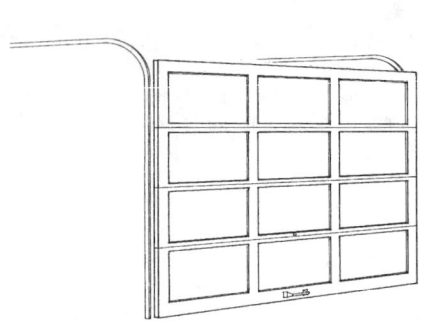

This page illustrates and describes overhead door systems including an overhead door, track, hardware, trim, and electric door opener. Lines within System Components give the unit price and total price on a cost each basis for this system. Prices for alternate overhead door systems are on Line Items 4.6-702-1300 thru 2300. Both material quantities and labor costs have been adjusted for the system listed.

Factors: To adjust for job conditions other than normal working situations use Lines 4.6-702-3100 thru 4000.

Example: You are to install the system and match existing construction. Go to Line 4.6-702-3200 and apply these percentages to the appropriate MAT. and INST. costs.

System Components	QUANTITY	UNIT	COST EACH MAT.	INST.	TOTAL
Wood overhead door, commercial sectional, including track, door, hardware And trim, electrically operated.					
Commercial, heavy duty wood door, 8' x 8' x 1-3/4" thick	1.000	Ea.	440	365	805
Wood frames and trim	1.000	Set	64.80	82.56	147.36
Painting, two coats	1.000	Ea.	15.84	129.60	145.44
Electric trolley operator	1.000	Ea.	455	183	638
TOTAL		Ea.	975.64	760.16	1,735.80

4.6-702	Doors, Overhead	MAT.	INST.	TOTAL
1200	For alternate sectional overhead door systems:			
1300	Commercial, wood, 1-3/4" thick, 12' x 12'	1,525	1,075	2,600
1400	14' x 14'	2,250	1,275	3,525
1500	Fiberglass & aluminum 12' x 12'	1,975	1,100	3,075
1600	20' x 20'	5,425	2,775	8,200
1700	Residential, wood, 9' x 7'	455	293	748
1800	16' x 7'	870	440	1,310
1900	Hardboard faced, 9' x 7'	415	293	708
2000	16' x 7'	705	440	1,145
2100	Fiberglass & aluminum, 9' x 7'	615	340	955
2200	16' x 7'	935	440	1,375
2300	For residential electric opener, add	325	45.50	370.50
2400				
2500				
2600				
2700				
2800				
2900				
3100	Cut & patch to match existing construction, add, minumum	2%	3%	
3200	Maximum	5%	9%	
3300	Dust protection, add, minimum	1%	2%	
3400	Maximum	4%	11%	
3500	Material handling & storage limitation, add, minimum	1%	1%	
3600	Maximum	6%	7%	
3700	Protection of existing work, add, minimum	2%	2%	
3800	Maximum	5%	7%	
3900	Shift work requirements, add, minimum		5%	
4000	Maximum		30%	

EXTERIOR CLOSURE — A4.7-142 — Windows - Aluminum

This page illustrates and describes an aluminum window system including double hung aluminum window, exterior and interior trim, hardware and insulating glass. Lines within System Components give the unit price and total price on a cost each basis for this system. Prices for alternate aluminum window systems are on Line Items 4.7-142-1100 thru 2400. Both material quantities and labor costs have been adjusted for the system listed.

Factors: To adjust for job conditions other than normal working situations use Lines 4.7-142-3100 thru 4000.

Example: You are to install the system and cut and patch to match existing construction. Go to Line 4.7-142-3200 and apply these percentages to the appropriate MAT. and INST. costs.

System Components	QUANTITY	UNIT	MAT.	INST.	TOTAL
Double hung aluminum window, 2'-4" x 2'-6" exterior and interior trim, Hardware glazed with insulating glass.					
Double hung aluminum window, 2'-4" x 2'-6"	1.000	Ea.	160.33	27.17	187.50
Exterior and interior trim	1.000	Set	16.50	28	44.50
Hardware	1.000	Set	1.91	15.25	17.16
Insulating glass	5.830	S.F.	55.09	20.11	75.20
TOTAL		Ea.	233.83	90.53	324.36

4.7-142	Windows - Aluminum	MAT.	INST.	TOTAL
1000	For alternate window systems:			
1100	Aluminum, double hung, 2'-8" x 4'-6"	475	149	624
1200	3'-4" x 5'-6"	720	225	945
1300	Casement, 3'-6" x 2'-4"	330	109	439
1400	4'-6" x 2'-4"	435	137	572
1500	5'-6" x 2'-4"	535	180	715
1600	Projected window, 2'-1" x 3'-0"	231	94	325
1700	3'-5" x 3'-0"	380	135	515
1800	4'-0" x 4'-0"	585	206	791
1900	Horizontal sliding 3'-0" x 3'-0"	249	116	365
2000	3'-6" x 4'-0"	390	165	555
2100	5'-0" x 6'-0"	810	320	1,130
2200	Picture window, 3'-8" x 3'-1"	262	135	397
2300	4'-4" x 4'-5"	440	207	647
2400	5'-8" x 4'-9"	620	294	914
2500				
2600				
2700				
2800				
2900				
3100	Cut & patch to match existing construction, add, minimum	2%	3%	
3200	Maximum	5%	9%	
3300	Dust protection, add, minimum	1%	2%	
3400	Maximum	4%	11%	
3500	Material handling & storage limitation, add, minimum	1%	1%	
3600	Maximum	6%	7%	
3700	Protection of existing work, add, minimum	2%	2%	
3800	Maximum	5%	7%	
3900	Shift work requirements, add, minimum		5%	
4000	Maximum		30%	

For expanded coverage of these items see *Means Building Construction Cost Data 1999*

EXTERIOR CLOSURE — A4.7-144 Windows - Wood

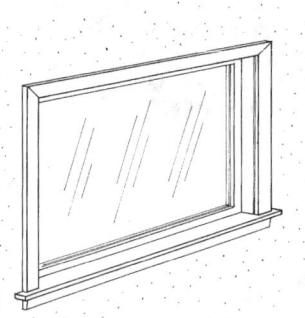

This page illustrates and describes a wood window system including wood picture window, exterior and interior trim, hardware and insulating glass. Lines within System Components give the unit price and total price on a cost each basis for this system. Prices for alternate wood window systems are on Line Items 4.7-144-1300 thru 1800. Both material quantities and labor costs have been adjusted for the system listed.

Factors: To adjust for job conditions other than normal working situations use Lines 4.7-144-3100 thru 4000.

Example: You are to install the above system where dust control is vital. Go to Line 4.7-144-3400 and apply these percentages to the appropriate MAT. and INST. costs.

System Components	QUANTITY	UNIT	COST EACH		
			MAT.	INST.	TOTAL
Wood picture window 4'-0" x 4'-6", exterior and interior trim, hardware, Glazed with insulating glass.					
4'-0" x 4'-6" wood picture window with insulating glass	1.000	Ea.	219	66.50	285.50
Exterior and interior trim	1.000	Set	40.50	61	101.50
Hardware	1.000	Set	1.91	15.25	17.16
TOTAL		Ea.	261.41	142.75	404.16

4.7-144	Windows - Wood	COST EACH		
		MAT.	INST.	TOTAL
1200	For alternate window systems:			
1300	Picture window 5'-0" x 4'-0"	315	143	458
1400	6'-0" x 4'-6"	415	149	564
1500	Bow, bay window, 8'-0" x 5'-0", standard	1,800	149	1,949
1600	Deluxe	1,325	149	1,474
1700	Bow, bay window, 12'-0" x 6'-0" standard	2,300	198	2,498
1800	Deluxe	1,850	198	2,048
1900				
2000				
2100				
2200				
2300				
2400				
2500				
2600				
2700				
2800				
2900				
3100	Cut & patch to match existing construction, add, minimum	2%	3%	
3200	Maximum	5%	9%	
3300	Dust protection, add, minimum	1%	2%	
3400	Maximum	4%	11%	
3500	Material handling & storage limitation, add, minimum	1%	1%	
3600	Maximum	6%	7%	
3700	Protection of existing work, add, minimum	2%	2%	
3800	Maximum	5%	7%	
3900	Shift work requirements, add, minimum		5%	
4000	Maximum		30%	

EXTERIOR CLOSURE — A4.7-145 | Windows - Wood

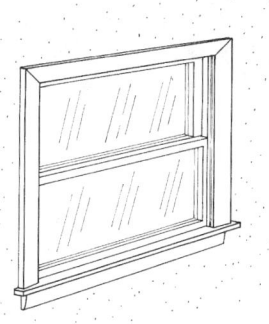

This page illustrates and describes a wood window system including double hung wood window, exterior and interior trim, hardware and insulating glass. Lines within System Components give the unit price and total price on a cost each basis for this system. Prices for alternate wood window systems are on Line Items 4.7-145-1300 thru 2300. Both material quantities and labor costs have been adjusted for the system listed.

Factors: To adjust for job conditions other than normal working situations use Lines 4.7-145-3100 thru 4000.

Example: You are to install the system during evening hours only. Go to Line 4.7-145-4000 and apply this percentage to the appropriate INST. cost.

System Components

System Components	QUANTITY	UNIT	MAT.	INST.	TOTAL
Double hung wood window 2'-0" x 3'-0", exterior and interior trim, Hardware, glazed with insulating glass.					
2'-0" x 3'-0" double hung wood window, with insulating glass	1.000	Ea.	164	36.50	200.50
Exterior and interior trim	1.000	Set	16.50	28	44.50
Hardware	1.000	Set	1.91	15.25	17.16
TOTAL		Ea.	182.41	79.75	262.16

4.7-145 Windows - Wood

Line	Description	MAT.	INST.	TOTAL
1200	For alternate window systems:			
1300	Double hung, 3'-0" x 4'-0"	230	92.50	322.50
1400	4'-0" x 4'-6"	288	122	410
1500	Casement 2'-0" x 3'-0"	227	80	307
1600	2 leaf, 4'-0" x 4'-0"	600	133	733
1700	3 leaf, 6'-0" x 6'-0"	1,050	213	1,263
1800	Awning, 2'-10" x 1'-10"	261	80	341
1900	3'-6" x 2'-4"	440	92.50	532.50
2000	4'-0" x 3'-0"	800	122	922
2100	Horizontal sliding 3'-0" x 2'-0"	193	80	273
2200	4'-0" x 3'-6"	237	92.50	329.50
2300	6'-0" x 5'-0"	405	122	527
2400				
2500				
2600				
2700				
2800				
2900				
3100	Cut & patch to match existing construction, add, minimum	2%	3%	
3200	Maximum	5%	9%	
3300	Dust protection, add, minimum	1%	2%	
3400	Maximum	4%	11%	
3500	Material handling & storage limitation, add, minimum	1%	1%	
3600	Maximum	6%	7%	
3700	Protection of existing work, add, minimum	2%	2%	
3800	Maximum	5%	7%	
3900	Shift work requirements, add, minimum		5%	
4000	Maximum		30%	

EXTERIOR CLOSURE — A4.7-152 — Storm Windows & Doors

This page illustrates and describes storm window and door systems based on a cost each price. Prices for alternate storm window and door systems are on Line Items 4.7-152-0400 thru 2400. Both material quantities and labor costs have been adjusted for the system listed.

Factors: To adjust for job conditions other than normal working situations use Lines 4.7-152-3100 thru 4000 and apply these percentages to the appropriate MAT and INST. costs.

Example: You are to install the system and protect all existing construction. Go to Line 4.7-152-3800 and apply these percentages to the appropriate MAT. and INST. costs.

4.7-152	Storm Windows & Doors	MAT.	INST.	TOTAL
0350	Storm Window and door systems, single glazed			
0400	Window, custom aluminum anodized, 2'-0" x 3'-5"	70	24.50	94.50
0500	2'-6" x 5'-0"	93.50	26	119.50
0600	4'-0" x 6'-0"	198	29.50	227.50
0700	White painted aluminum, 2'-0" x 3'-5"	83.50	24.50	108
0800	2'-6" x 5'-0"	134	26	160
0900	4'-0" x 6'-0"	240	29.50	269.50
1000	Average quality aluminum, anodized, 2'-0" x 3'-5"	71	24.50	95.50
1100	2'-6" x 5'-0"	89.50	26	115.50
1200	4'-0" x 6'-0"	105	29.50	134.50
1300	White painted aluminum, 2'-0" x 3'-5"	70	24.50	94.50
1400	2'-6" x 5'-0"	77	26	103
1500	4'-0" x 6'-0"	84.50	29.50	114
1600	Mill finish, 2'-0" x 3'-5"	63.50	24.50	88
1700	2'-6" x 5'-0"	71	26	97
1800	4'-0" x 6'-0"	79.50	29.50	109
1900				
2000	Door, aluminum anodized 3'-0" x 6'-8"	178	52	230
2100	White painted aluminum, 3'-0" x 6'-8"	208	52	260
2200	Mill finish, 3'-0" x 6'-8"	227	52	279
2300				
2400	Wood, storm and screen, painted	217	81	298
2500				
2600				
2700				
2800				
3100	Cut & patch to match existing construction, add, minimum	2%	3%	
3200	Maximum	5%	9%	
3300	Dust protection, add, minimum	1%	2%	
3400	Maximum	4%	11%	
3500	Material handling & storage limitation, add, minimum	1%	1%	
3600	Maximum	6%	7%	
3700	Protection of existing work, add, minimum	2%	2%	
3800	Maximum	5%	7%	
3900	Shift work requirements, add, minimum		5%	
4000	Maximum		30%	

EXTERIOR CLOSURE — A4.7-700 Aluminum Frame, Window Wall

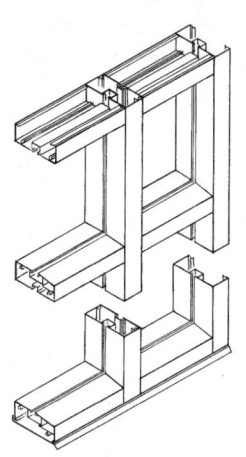

This page illustrates and describes a window wall system including aluminum tube framing, caulking, and glass. Lines within System Components give the unit price and total price per square foot for this system. Prices for alternate window wall systems are on Line Items 4.7-700-1400 thru 2600. Both material quantities and labor costs have been adjusted for the system listed.

Factors: To adjust for job conditions other than normal working situations use Lines 4.7-700-3100 thru 4000.

Example: You are to install the system with need for complete dust protection. Go to Line 4.7-700-3400 and apply these percentages to the appropriate MAT. and INST. costs.

System Components			COST PER S.F.		
	QUANTITY	UNIT	MAT.	INST.	TOTAL
Window wall, including aluminum header, sill, mullions, caulking And glass					
Header, mill finish, 1-3/4" x 4-1/2" deep	.167	L.F.	2.09	1.39	3.48
Sill, mill finish, 1-3/4" x 4-1/2" deep	.167	L.F.	1.95	1.35	3.30
Vertical mullion, 1-3/4" x 4-1/2" deep, 6' O.C.	.191	L.F.	4.92	3.38	8.30
Caulking	.381	L.F.	.07	.56	.63
Glass, 1/4" plate	1.000	S.F.	4.64	5.75	10.39
TOTAL		S.F.	13.67	12.43	26.10

4.7-700	Aluminum Frame, Window Wall	COST PER S.F.		
		MAT.	INST.	TOTAL
1200	For alternate systems:			
1300				
1400	Mill finish, 2" x 4-1/2" deep, insulating glass	15.95	14.35	30.30
1500	Thermo-break, 2-1/4" x 4-1/2" deep, insulating glass	16.30	14.60	30.90
1600	Bronze finish, 1-3/4" x 4-1/2" deep, 1/4" plate glass	15.25	13.55	28.80
1700	2" x 4-1/2" deep, insulating glass	17.70	15.55	33.25
1800	Thermo-break, 2-1/4" x 4-1/2" deep, insulating glass	18.10	15.80	33.90
1900				
2000	Black finish, 1-3/4" x 4-1/2" deep, 1/4" plate glass	16.05	14.10	30.15
2100	2" x 4-1/2" deep, insulating glass	18.55	16.15	34.70
2200	Thermo-break, 2-1/4" x 4-1/2" deep, insulating glass	18.95	16.40	35.35
2300				
2400	Stainless steel, 1-3/4" x 4-1/2" deep, 1/4" plate glass	20.50	17	37.50
2500	2" x 4-1/2" deep, insulating glass	23	19.25	42.25
2600	Thermo-break, 2-1/4" x 4-1/2" deep, insulating glass	23.50	19.70	43.20
2700				
3100	Cut & patch to match existing construction, add, minimum	2%	3%	
3200	Maximum	5%	9%	
3300	Dust protection, add, minimum	1%	2%	
3400	Maximum	4%	11%	
3500	Material handling, & storage limitation, add, minimum	1%	1%	
3600	Maximum	6%	7%	
3700	Protection of existing work, add, minimum	2%	2%	
3800	Maximum	5%	7%	
3900	Shift work requirements, add, minimum		5%	
4000	Maximum		30%	

For expanded coverage of these items see *Means Building Construction Cost Data 1999*

EXTERIOR CLOSURE — A4.9-200 Exterior Wall

4.9-200 Selective Price Sheet

		COST PER S.F.		
		MAT.	INST.	TOTAL
0100	Exterior surface, masonry, concrete block, standard 4" thick	.85	3.88	4.73
0200	6" thick	1.24	4.17	5.41
0300	8" thick	1.38	4.45	5.83
0400	12" thick	2.20	5.75	7.95
0500	Split rib, 4" thick	1.74	4.84	6.58
0600	8" thick	2.58	5.45	8.03
0700	Brick running bond, standard size, 6.75/S.F.	2.80	7.60	10.40
0800	Buff, 6.75/S.F.	2.97	7.60	10.57
0900	Stucco, on frame	.66	1.62	2.28
1000	On masonry	.25	.90	1.15
1100	Metal, aluminum, horizontal, plain	1.34	1.42	2.76
1200	Insulated	1.50	1.42	2.92
1300	Vertical, plain	1.17	1.42	2.59
1400	Insulated	1.22	1.48	2.70
1500	Wood, beveled siding, "A" grade cedar, 1/2" x 6"	2.22	1.46	3.68
1600	1/2" x 8"	1.83	1.33	3.16
1700	Shingles, 16" #1 red, 7-1/2" exposure	1.05	1.78	2.83
1800	18" perfections, 7-1/2" exposure	1.61	1.49	3.10
1900	Handsplit, 10" exposure	1.52	1.46	2.98
2000	White cedar, 7-1/2" exposure	.98	1.83	2.81
2100	Vertical, board & batten, redwood	3.54	1.83	5.37
2200	White pine	.76	1.33	2.09
2300	T. & G. boards, redwood, 1" x 4"	3.01	2.44	5.45
2400	1' x 8"	2.60	1.95	4.55
2500				
2600	Interior surface, drywall, taped & finished, standard, 1/2"	.27	.76	1.03
2700	5/8" thick	.36	.76	1.12
2800	Fire resistant, 1/2" thick	.36	.76	1.12
2900	5/8" thick	.33	.76	1.09
3000	Moisture resistant, 1/2" thick	.35	.76	1.11
3100	5/8" thick	.42	.76	1.18
3200	Core board, 1" thick	.58	1.52	2.10
3300	Plaster, gypsum, 2 coats	.38	1.71	2.09
3400	3 coats	.53	2.06	2.59
3500	Perlite or vermiculite, 2 coats	.46	1.95	2.41
3600	3 coats	.75	2.40	3.15
3700	Gypsum lath, standard, 3/8" thick	.41	.45	.86
3800	1/2" thick	.48	.48	.96
3900	Fire resistant, 3/8" thick	.48	.54	1.02
4000	1/2" thick	.49	.58	1.07
4100	Metal lath, diamond, 2.5 lb.	.20	.45	.65
4200	Rib, 3.4 lb.	.35	.54	.89
4300	Framing metal studs including top and bottom			
4400	Runners, walls 10' high			
4500	24" O.C., non load bearing 20 gauge, 2-1/2" wide	.39	.72	1.11
4600	3-5/8" wide	.48	.73	1.21
4700	4" wide	.49	.75	1.24
4800	6" wide	.63	.76	1.39
4900	Load bearing 18 gauge, 2-1/2" wide	.40	.69	1.09
5000	3-5/8" wide	.46	.70	1.16
5100	4" wide	4.11	7.10	11.21
5200	6" wide	.62	.73	1.35
5300	16" O.C., non load bearing 20 gauge, 2-1/2" wide	.48	.83	1.31
5400	3-5/8" wide	.59	.85	1.44
5500	4" wide	.62	.87	1.49
5600	6" wide	.79	.89	1.68
5700	Load bearing 18 gauge, 2-1/2" wide	.55	.95	1.50
5800	3-5/8" wide	.63	.96	1.59
5900	4" wide	.65	.99	1.64
6000	6" wide	.84	1	1.84

EXTERIOR CLOSURE

A4.9-200 Exterior Wall

4.9-200 Selective Price Sheet

		COST PER S.F.		
		MAT.	INST.	TOTAL
6100	Framing wood studs incl. double top plate and			
6200	Single bottom plate, walls 10' high			
6300	24" O.C., 2" x 4"	.35	.59	.94
6400	2" x 6"	.52	.64	1.16
6500	16" O.C., 2" x 4"	.46	.73	1.19
6600	2" x 6"	.69	.81	1.50
6700	Sheathing, boards, 1" x 6"	1.09	1.12	2.21
6800	1" x 8"	1.15	.96	2.11
6900	Plywood, 3/8" thick	.35	.61	.96
7000	1/2" thick	.45	.65	1.10
7100	5/8" thick	.54	.70	1.24
7200	3/4" thick	.64	.75	1.39
7300	Wood fiber, 5/8" thick	.55	.61	1.16
7400	Gypsum weatherproof, 1/2" thick	.23	.70	.93
7500	Insulation, fiberglass batts, 3-1/2" thick, R11	.27	.52	.79
7600	6" thick, R19	.36	.61	.97
7700	Poured 4" thick, fiberglass wool, R4/inch	.32	1.83	2.15
7800	Mineral wool, R3/inch	.33	1.83	2.16
7900	Polystyrene, R4/inch	1.89	1.83	3.72
8000	Perlite or vermiculite, R2.7/inch	1.60	1.83	3.43
8100	Rigid, fiberglass, R4.3/inch, 1" thick	.32	.37	.69
8200	R8.7/inch, 2" thick	.76	.41	1.17

EXTERIOR CLOSURE | A4.9-500 | Hardware

4.9-500 Selective Price Sheet

		COST EACH		
		MAT.	INST.	TOTAL
0100	Door closer, rack and pinion	116	56.50	172.50
0200	Backcheck and adjustable power	122	61	183
0300	Regular, hinge face mount, all sizes, regular arm	146	56.50	202.50
0400	Hold open arm	157	56.50	213.50
0500	Top jamb mount, all sizes, regular arm	146	61	207
0600	Hold open arm	157	61	218
0700	Stop face mount, all sizes, regular arm	146	56.50	202.50
0800	Hold open arm	157	56.50	213.50
0900	Fusible link, hinge face mount, all sizes, regular arm	156	56.50	212.50
1000	Hold open arm	167	56.50	223.50
1100	Top jamb mount, all sizes, regular arm	156	61	217
1200	Hold open arm	167	61	228
1300	Stop face mount, all sizes, regular arm	156	56.50	212.50
1400	Hold open arm	167	56.50	223.50
1500				
1600				
1700	Door stops			
1800				
1900	Holder & bumper, floor or wall	15.40	11.45	26.85
2000	Wall bumper	7	11.45	18.45
2100	Floor bumper	4	11.45	15.45
2200	Plunger type, door mounted	24.50	11.45	35.95
2300	Hinges, full mortise, material only, per pair			
2400	Low frequency, 4-1/2" x 4-1/2", steel base, USP	14.65		14.65
2500	Brass base, US10	33		33
2600	Stainless steel base, US32	55		55
2700	Average frequency, 4-1/2" x 4-1/2", steel base, USP	19.30		19.30
2800	Brass base, US10	40		40
2900	Stainless steel base, US32	66		66
3000	High frequency, 4-1/2" x 4-1/2", steel base, USP	48		48
3100	Brass base, US10	43		43
3200	Stainless steel base, US32	102		102
3300	Kick plate			
3400				
3500	6" high, for 3'-0" door, aluminum	17.55	24.50	42.05
3600	Bronze	21	24.50	45.50
3700	Panic device			
3800				
3900	For rim locks, single door, exit	350	61	411
4000	Outside key and pull	405	73	478
4100	Bar and vertical rod, exit only	520	73	593
4200	Outside key and pull	620	91.50	711.50
4300	Lockset			
4400				
4500	Heavy duty, cylindrical, passage doors	112	30.50	142.50
4600	Classroom	249	45.50	294.50
4700	Bedroom, bathroom, and inner office doors	141	30.50	171.50
4800	Apartment, office, and corridor doors	197	36.50	233.50
4900	Standard duty, cylindrical, exit doors	70.50	36.50	107
5100	Passage doors	48.50	30.50	79
5200	Public restroom, classroom, & office doors	96	45.50	141.50
5300	Deadlock, mortise, heavy duty	120	40.50	160.50
5400	Double cylinder	133	40.50	173.50
5500	Entrance lock, cylinder, deadlocking latch	110	40.50	150.50
5600	Deadbolt	133	45.50	178.50
5700	Commercial, mortise, wrought knob, keyed, minimum	156	45.50	201.50
5800	Maximum	288	52	340
5900	Cast knob, keyed, minimum	210	40.50	250.50
6000	Maximum	410	40.50	450.50
6100	Push-pull			

Important: See the Reference Section for critical supporting data - Reference Nos., Crews, & City Cost Indexes

EXTERIOR CLOSURE — A4.9-500 Hardware

4.9-500 Selective Price Sheet

		COST EACH		
		MAT.	INST.	TOTAL
6200				
6300	Aluminum	5.35	30.50	35.85
6400	Bronze	12	30.50	42.50
6500	Door pull, designer style, minimum	65	30.50	95.50
6600	Maximum	300	45.50	345.50
6700	Threshold			
6800				
6900	3'-0" long door saddles, aluminum, minimum	3.68	7.60	11.28
7000	Maximum	31.50	30.50	62
7100	Bronze, minimum	29.50	6.10	35.60
7200	Maximum	61.50	30.50	92
7300	Rubber, 1/2" thick, 5-1/2" wide	31	18.30	49.30
7400	2-3/4" wide	14.45	18.30	32.75
7500	Weatherstripping, per set			
7600				
7700	Doors, wood frame, interlocking for 3' x 7' door, zinc	12.70	122	134.70
7800	Bronze	19.95	122	141.95
7900	Wood frame, spring type for 3' x 7' door, bronze	16.85	48	64.85
8000	Metal frame, spring type for 3' x 7' door, bronze	28	122	150
8100	For stainless steel, spring type, add	133%		
8200				
8300	Metal frame, extruded sections, 3' x 7' door, aluminum	37	183	220
8400	Bronze	93	183	276

For information about Means Estimating Seminars, see yellow pages 11 and 12 in back of book

For expanded coverage of these items see *Means Building Construction Cost Data 1999*

Division 5
Roofing

ROOFING

A5.1-192 Steel Joist Roof & Ceiling

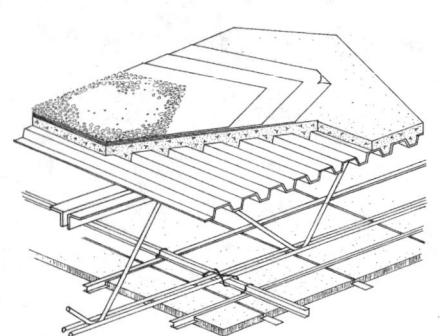

This page illustrates and describes a flat roof bar joist system including asphalt and gravel roof, lightweight concrete, metal decking, open web joists, and suspended acoustic ceiling. Lines within System Components give the unit price and total price per square foot for this system. Prices for alternate flat roof bar joist systems are on Line Items 5.1-192-1300 thru 1600. Both material quantities and labor costs have been adjusted for the system listed.

Factors: To adjust for job conditions other than normal working situations use Lines 5.1-192-2700 thru 4000.

Example: You are to install the system where material handling and storage present some problem. Go to Line 5.1-192-3300 and apply these percentages to the appropriate MAT. and INST. costs.

System Components	QUANTITY	UNIT	COST PER S.F.		
			MAT.	INST.	TOTAL
Three ply asphalt and gravel roof on lightweight concrete, metal decking on Web joist 4' O.C., with suspended acoustic ceiling.					
Open web joist, 10" deep, 4' O.C.	1.250	Lb.	.68	.36	1.04
Metal decking, 1-1/2" deep, 22 Ga., galvanized	1.000	S.F.	1.04	.44	1.48
Gravel roofing, 3 ply asphalt	.010	C.S.F.	.53	1.26	1.79
Perlite roof fill, 3" thick	1.000	S.F.	.92	.38	1.30
Suspended ceiling, 3/4" mineral fiber on "Z" bar suspension	1.000	S.F.	1.67	2.44	4.11
TOTAL		S.F.	4.84	4.88	9.72

5.1-192	Steel Joist Roof & Ceiling	COST PER S.F.		
		MAT.	INST.	TOTAL
1200	For alternate roof systems:			
1300	Open web bar joist, 16" deep, 5#/L.F.	5.05	4.98	10.03
1400	18" deep, 6.6#/L.F.	5.25	5.10	10.35
1500	20" deep, 9.6#/L.F.	5.45	5.20	10.65
1600	24" deep, 11.52#/L.F.	5.70	5.30	11
1700				
1800				
1900				
2000				
2100				
2200				
2300				
2400				
2500				
2700	Cut & patch to match existing construction, add, minimum	2%	3%	
2800	Maximum	5%	9%	
2900	Dust protection, add, minimum	1%	2%	
3000	Maximum	4%	11%	
3100	Equipment usage curtailment, add, minimum	1%	1%	
3200	Maximum	3%	10%	
3300	Material handling & storage limitation, add, minimum	1%	1%	
3400	Maximum	6%	7%	
3500	Protection of existing work, add, minimum	2%	2%	
3600	Maximum	5%	7%	
3700	Shift work requirements, add, minimum		5%	
3800	Maximum		30%	
3900	Temporary shoring and bracing, add, minimum	2%	5%	
4000	Maximum	5%	12%	

ROOFING | A5.1-492 | Wood Frame Roof & Ceiling

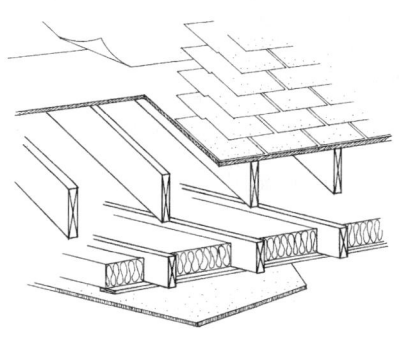

This page illustrates and describes a wood frame roof system including rafters, ceiling joists, sheathing, building paper, asphalt shingles, roof trim, furring, insulation, plaster and paint. Lines within System Components give the unit price and total price per square foot for this system. Prices for alternate wood frame roof systems are on Line Items 5.1-492-1900 thru 2700. Both material quantities and labor costs have been adjusted for the system listed.

Factors: To adjust for job conditions other than normal working situations use Lines 5.1-492-3300 thru 4000.

Example: You are to install the system while protecting existing work. Go to Line 5.1-492-3800 and apply these percentages to the appropriate MAT. and INST. costs.

System Components

System Components	QUANTITY	UNIT	COST PER S.F. MAT.	INST.	TOTAL
Wood frame roof system, 4 in 12 pitch, including rafters, sheathing, Shingles, insulation, drywall, thin coat plaster, and painting.					
Rafters, 2" x 6", 16" O.C., 4 in 12 pitch	1.080	L.F.	.64	.79	1.43
Ceiling joists, 2" x 6", 16 O.C.	1.000	L.F.	.59	.58	1.17
Sheathing, 1/2" CDX	1.080	S.F.	.49	.56	1.05
Building paper, 15# felt	.011	C.S.F.	.03	.11	.14
Asphalt shingles, 240#	.011	C.S.F.	.42	.77	1.19
Roof trim	.100	L.F.	.10	.16	.26
Furring, 1" x 3", 16" O.C.	1.000	L.F.	.25	1.04	1.29
Fiberglass insulation, 6" batts	1.000	S.F.	.39	.27	.66
Gypsum board, 1/2" thick	1.000	S.F.	.17	.41	.58
Thin coat plaster	1.000	S.F.	.11	.45	.56
Paint, roller, 2 coats	1.000	S.F.	.13	.43	.56
TOTAL		S.F.	3.32	5.57	8.89

5.1-492	Wood Frame Roof & Ceiling	MAT.	INST.	TOTAL
1800	For alternate roof systems:			
1900	Rafters 16" O.C., 2" x 8"	3.54	5.60	9.14
2000	2" x 10"	3.88	6	9.88
2100	2" x 12"	4.21	6.15	10.36
2200	Rafters 24" O.C., 2" x 6"	3	5.20	8.20
2300	2" x 8"	3.17	5.25	8.42
2400	2" x 10"	3.42	5.55	8.97
2500	2" x 12"	3.67	5.65	9.32
2600	Roof pitch, 6 in 12, add	3%	10%	
2700	8 in 12, add	5%	12%	
2800				
2900				
3000				
3100				
3300	Cut & patch to match existing construction, add, minimum	2%	3%	
3400	Maximum	5%	9%	
3500	Material handling & storage limitation, add, minimum	1%	1%	
3600	Maximum	6%	7%	
3700	Protection of existing work, add, minimum	2%	2%	
3800	Maximum	5%	7%	
3900	Shift work requirements, add, minimum		5%	
4000	Maximum		30%	

ROOFING — A5.8-104 Roof Hatches, Skylights

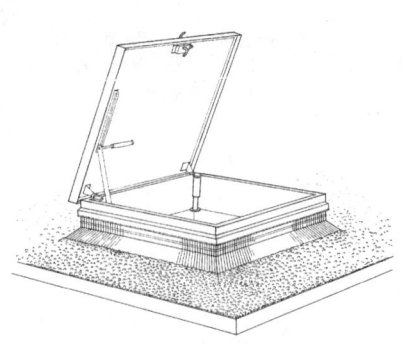

This page illustrates and describes a roof hatch system. Lines within System Components give the unit price and total cost each for this system. Prices for alternate systems are on Lines 5.8-104-1500 thru 2400. Both material quantities and labor costs have been adjusted for the system listed.

Factors: To adjust for job conditions other than normal working situations use Lines 5.8-104-2900 thru 4000.

Example: You are to install the system and cut and patch to match existing construction. Use line 5.8-104-3000 and apply these percentages to the appropriate MAT. and INST. costs.

System Components	QUANTITY	UNIT	COST EACH MAT.	COST EACH INST.	COST EACH TOTAL
Roof hatch, 2'-6" x 3'-0", aluminum, curb and cover included. Through steel construction.					
Roof hatch, 2'-6" x 3'-0", aluminum	1.000	Ea.	445	139	584
Cutout decking	11.000	L.F.		92.29	92.29
Frame opening	44.000	L.F.	44	48.40	92.40
Flashing, 16 oz. copper	16.000	S.F.	53.60	56.64	110.24
Cant strip, 4 x 4, foamglass	12.000	L.F.	25.32	12.96	38.28
TOTAL		Ea.	567.92	349.29	917.21

5.8-104	Roof Hatches, Skylights	MAT.	INST.	TOTAL
1400	For alternate systems:			
1500	Roof hatch, aluminum, curb and cover, 2'-6" x 4'-6"	770	420	1,190
1600	2'-6" x 8'-0"	1,325	595	1,920
1700	Skylight, plexiglass dome, with curb mounting, 30" x 32"	500	325	825
1800	30" x 45"	595	405	1,000
1900	40" x 45"	695	525	1,220
2000	Smoke hatch, unlabeled, 2'-6" x 3'-0"	680	385	1,065
2100	2'-6" x 4'-6"	925	460	1,385
2200	2'-6" x 8'-0"	1,425	620	2,045
2300				
2400	For steel ladder, add per vertical linear foot	27	23.50	50.50
2500				
2600				
2700				
2900	Cut & patch to match existing construction, add, minimum	2%	3%	
3000	Maximum	5%	9%	
3100	Dust protection, add, minimum	1%	2%	
3200	Maximum	4%	11%	
3300	Equipment usage curtailment, add, minimum	1%	1%	
3400	Maximum	3%	10%	
3500	Material handling & storage limitation, add, minimum	1%	1%	
3600	Maximum	6%	7%	
3700	Protection of existing work, add, minimum	2%	2%	
3800	Maximum	5%	7%	
3900	Shift work requirements, add, minimum		5%	
4000	Maximum		30%	

ROOFING — A5.9-300 Roofing & Ceiling Finish

5.9-300 Selective Price Sheet

Line	Description	MAT.	INST.	TOTAL
0100	Roofing, built-up, asphalt roll roof, 3 ply organic/mineral surface	.40	1.03	1.43
0200	3 plies glass fiber felt type iv, 1 ply mineral surface	.59	1.11	1.70
0300	Cold applied, 3 ply		.36	.36
0400	Coal tar pitch, 4 ply tarred felt	1.07	1.32	2.39
0500	Mopped, 3 ply glass fiber	.89	1.46	2.35
0600	4 ply organic felt	1.07	1.32	2.39
0700	Elastomeric, hypalon, neoprene unreinforced	2.26	2.44	4.70
0800	Polyester reinforced	2.28	2.88	5.16
0900	Neoprene, 5 coats 60 mils	5	8.50	13.50
1000	Over 10,000 S.F.	4.68	4.42	9.10
1100	PVC, traffic deck sprayed	1.46	4.42	5.88
1200	With neoprene	1.55	1.78	3.33
1300	Shingles, fiber cement, strip, 14" x 30", 325#/sq.	2.68	.92	3.60
1500	Shake, 9.35" x 16" 500#/sq.	2.43	1.66	4.09
1600				
1700	Asphalt, strip, 210-235#/sq.	.29	.64	.93
1800	235-240#/sq.	.38	.70	1.08
1900	Class A laminated	.38	.78	1.16
2000	Class C laminated	.55	.88	1.43
2100	Slate, buckingham, 3/16" thick	5.95	2.01	7.96
2200	Black, 1/4" thick	7.90	2.01	9.91
2300	Wood, shingles, 16" no. 1, 5" exp.	1.57	1.46	3.03
2400	Red cedar, 18" perfections	1.81	1.33	3.14
2500	Shakes, 24", 10" exposure	1.52	1.46	2.98
2600	18", 8-1/2" exposure	1.07	1.83	2.90
2700	Insulation, ceiling batts, fiberglass, 3-1/2" thick, R11	.21	.23	.44
2800	6" thick, R19	.31	.27	.58
2900	9" thick, R30	.55	.32	.87
3000	12" thick, R38	.70	.37	1.07
3100	Mineral, 3-1/2" thick, R13	.24	.23	.47
3200	Fiber, 6" thick, R19	.36	.23	.59
3300	Roof deck, fiberboard, 1" thick, R2.78	.35	.44	.79
3400	Mineral, 2" thick, R5.26	.70	.44	1.14
3500	Perlite boards, 3/4" thick, R2.08	.33	.44	.77
3600	2" thick, R5.26	.52	.50	1.02
3700	Polystyrene extruded, R5.26, 1" thick,	.24	.23	.47
3800	2" thick R10	.38	.28	.66
3900	40 PSI compressive strength, 1" thick R5	.39	.23	.62
4000	Tapered for drainage	.55	.25	.80
4100	Foamglass, 1 1/2" thick R4.55	1.55	.44	1.99
4200	3" thick R9.00	3.09	.50	3.59
4300	Ceiling, plaster, gypsum, 2 coats	.38	1.95	2.33
4400	3 coats	.53	2.29	2.82
4500	Perlite or vermiculite, 2 coats	.46	2.28	2.74
4600	3 coats	.75	2.86	3.61
4700	Gypsum lath, plain 3/8" thick	.41	.45	.86
4800	1/2" thick	.48	.48	.96
4900	Firestop, 3/8" thick	.48	.54	1.02
5000	1/2" thick	.49	.58	1.07
5100	Metal lath, rib, 2.75 lb.	.19	.51	.70
5200	3.40 lb.	.35	.54	.89
5300	Diamond, 2.50 lb.	.20	.51	.71
5400	3.40 lb.	.23	.63	.86
5500	Drywall, taped and finished standard, 1/2" thick	.27	.96	1.23
5600	5/8" thick	.36	.96	1.32
5700	Fire resistant, 1/2" thick	.36	.96	1.32
5800	5/8" thick	.33	.96	1.29
5900	Water resist., 1/2" thick	.35	.96	1.31
6000	5/8" thick	.42	.96	1.38
6100	Finish, instead of taping			

For expanded coverage of these items see Means Building Construction Cost Data 1999

ROOFING

A5.9-300 Roofing & Ceiling Finish

5.9-300 Selective Price Sheet

		COST PER S.F.		
		MAT.	INST.	TOTAL
6200	For thin coat plaster, add	.11	.45	.56
6300	Finish textured spray, add	.13	.43	.56
6400	Drywall, no finish included, see system A6.9-700			
6500	Tile, stapled glued, mineral fiber plastic coated, 5/8" thick	.62	.37	.99
6600	3/4" thick	1.35	.37	1.72
6700	Wood fiber, 1/2" thick	.78	.91	1.69
6800	3/4" thick	1.05	.91	1.96
6900	Suspended, fiberglass film faced, 5/8" thick	.54	.58	1.12
7000	3" thick	1.33	.81	2.14
7100	Mineral fiber 5/8" thick, standard face	.63	.54	1.17
7200	Aluminum faced	5.80	.61	6.41
7300	Wood fiber reveal edge, 1" thick			
7400	3" thick			
7500	Ceiling suspension systems, for tile, "T" bar, class "A", 2' x 4' grid	.34	.46	.80
7600	2' x 2' grid	.43	.56	.99
7700	Concealed "Z" bar, 12" module	.37	.70	1.07
7800				
7900	Plaster/drywall, 3/4" channels, steel furring, 16" O.C.	.19	1.18	1.37
8000	24" O.C.	.13	.82	.95
8100	1-1/2" channels, 16" O.C.	.26	1.32	1.58
8200	24" O.C.	.17	.88	1.05
8300	Ceiling framing, 2" x 4" studs, 16" O.C.	.30	.61	.91
8400	24" O.C.	.20	.41	.61

ROOFING — A5.9-500 | Roof Accessory

5.9-500 Selective Price Sheet

		COST PER L.F.		
		MAT.	INST.	TOTAL
0100	Downspouts per L.F., aluminum, enameled .024" thick, 2" x 3"	1.20	2.26	3.46
0200	3" x 4"	1.55	2.91	4.46
0300	Round .025" thick, 3" diam.	.94	2.14	3.08
0400	4" diam.	1.42	2.91	4.33
0500	Copper, round 16 oz. stock, 2" diam.	5.35	2.14	7.49
0600	3" diam.	4.22	2.14	6.36
0700	4" diam.	5.15	2.81	7.96
0800	5" diam.	7.40	3.13	10.53
0900	Rectangular, 2" x 3"	5.20	2.14	7.34
1000	3" x 4"	6.80	2.81	9.61
1100	Lead coated copper, round, 2" diam.	5.35	2.14	7.49
1200	3" diam.	5.15	2.14	7.29
1300	4" diam.	6.50	2.81	9.31
1400	5" diam.	6.25	3.13	9.38
1500	Rectangular, 2" x 3"	6.60	2.14	8.74
1600	3" x 4"	8.30	2.81	11.11
1700	Steel galvanized, round 28 gauge, 3" diam.	.75	2.14	2.89
1800	4" diam.	.99	2.81	3.80
1900	5" diam.	1.35	3.13	4.48
2000	6" diam.	1.76	3.88	5.64
2100	Rectangular, 2" x 3"	.87	2.14	3.01
2200	3" x 4"	1.33	2.81	4.14
2300	Elbows, aluminum, round, 3" diam.	2.15	4.07	6.22
2400	4" diam.	3.25	4.07	7.32
2500	Rectangular, 2" x 3"	.99	4.07	5.06
2600	3" x 4"	3.47	4.07	7.54
2700	Copper, round 16 oz., 2" diam.	12.10	4.07	16.17
2800	3" diam.	5.55	4.07	9.62
2900	4" diam.	10.45	4.07	14.52
3100	Rectangular, 2" x 3"	5.55	4.07	9.62
3200	3" x 4"	10.70	4.07	14.77
3300	Drip edge per L.F., aluminum, 5" wide	.22	.91	1.13
3400	8" wide	.33	.91	1.24
3500	28" wide	3.76	3.66	7.42
3600				
3700	Steel galvanized, 5" wide	.24	.91	1.15
3800	8" wide	.36	.91	1.27
3900				
4000				
4100				
4200				
4300	Flashing 12" wide per S.F., aluminum, mill finish, .013" thick	.37	2.81	3.18
4400	.019" thick	.87	2.81	3.68
4500	.040" thick	1.58	2.81	4.39
4600	.050" thick	1.98	2.81	4.79
4700	Copper, mill finish, 16 oz.	3.35	3.54	6.89
4800	20 oz.	4.20	3.70	7.90
4900	24 oz.	5.05	3.88	8.93
5000	32 oz.	6.70	4.07	10.77
5100	Lead, 2.5 lb./S.F., 12" wide	3.58	2.60	6.18
5200	Over 12" wide	3.58	2.60	6.18
5300	Lead-coated copper, fabric backed, 2 oz.	1.55	1.23	2.78
5400	5 oz.	1.87	1.23	3.10
5500	Mastic backed, 2 oz.	1.21	1.23	2.44
5600	5 oz.	1.57	1.23	2.80
5700	Paper backed, 2 oz.	1.05	1.23	2.28
5800	3 oz.	1.23	1.23	2.46
5900	Polyvinyl chloride, black, .010" thick	.14	1.23	1.37
6000	.020" thick	.21	1.23	1.44
6100	.030" thick	.32	1.23	1.55

For expanded coverage of these items see Means Building Construction Cost Data 1999

ROOFING | A5.9-500 | Roof Accessory

5.9-500 Selective Price Sheet

		COST PER L.F.		
		MAT.	INST.	TOTAL
6200	.056" thick	.77	1.23	2
6300	Steel, galvanized, 20 gauge	.79	3.13	3.92
6400	30 gauge	.33	2.55	2.88
6500	Stainless, 32 gauge, .010" thick	2.38	2.63	5.01
6600	28 gauge, .015" thick	2.80	2.63	5.43
6700	26 gauge, .018" thick	3.48	2.63	6.11
6800	24 gauge, .025" thick	4.51	2.63	7.14
6900	Gutters per L.F., aluminum, 5" box, .027" thick	.96	3.39	4.35
7000	.032" thick	1.19	3.39	4.58
7100	Copper, half round, 4" wide	3.55	3.39	6.94
7200	6" wide	4.68	3.54	8.22
7300	Steel, 26 gauge galvanized, 5" wide	1.05	3.39	4.44
7400	6" wide	1.36	3.39	4.75
7500	Wood, treated hem-fir, 3" x 4"	6.90	3.66	10.56
7600	4" x 5"	8	3.66	11.66
7700	Reglet per L.F., aluminum, .025" thick	1.01	1.62	2.63
7800	Copper, 10 oz.	1.75	1.62	3.37
7900	Steel, galvanized, 24 gauge	.86	1.62	2.48
8000	Stainless, .020" thick	1.73	1.62	3.35
8100	Counter flashing 12" wide per L.F., aluminum, .032" thick	1.31	2.71	4.02
8200	Copper, 10 oz.	3.65	2.71	6.36
8300	Steel, galvanized, 24 gauge	.68	2.71	3.39
8400	Stainless, .020" thick	3.04	2.71	5.75

For information about Means Estimating Seminars, see yellow pages 11 and 12 in back of book

Division 6
Interior Construction

INTERIOR CONSTR. | A6.1-222 | Partitions, Concrete Block

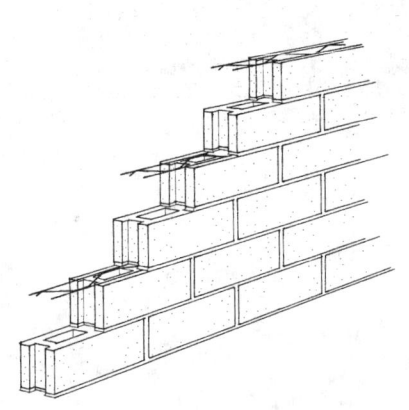

This page illustrates and describes a concrete block wall system including concrete block, horizontal reinforcing alternate courses, mortar, and tooled joints both sides. Lines within System Components give the unit price and total price per square foot for this system. Prices for alternate concrete block wall systems are on Line Items 6.1-222-0900 thru 2100. Both material quantities and labor costs have been adjusted for the system listed.

Factors: To adjust for job conditions other than normal working situations use Lines 6.1-222-2900 thru 4000.

Example: You are to install the system and protect all existing work. Go to Line 6.1-222-3600 and apply these percentages to the appropriate MAT. and INST. costs.

System Components	QUANTITY	UNIT	COST PER S.F. MAT.	INST.	TOTAL
Concrete block partition, including horizontal reinforcing every second Course, mortar, tooled joints both sides.					
8" x 16" concrete block, normal weight, 4" thick	1.000	S.F.	.85	3.88	4.73
Horizontal reinforcing every second course	.750	L.F.	.08	.09	.17
TOTAL		S.F.	.93	3.97	4.90

6.1-222	Partitions, Concrete Block	MAT.	INST.	TOTAL
0800	For alternate block partition systems:			
0900	8" x 16" concrete block, normal weight, 6" thick	1.32	4.26	5.58
1000	8" thick	1.46	4.54	6
1100	10" thick	2.10	4.73	6.83
1200	12" thick	2.28	5.85	8.13
1300	8" x 16" concrete block, lightweight, 4" thick	1.02	3.88	4.90
1400	6" thick	1.42	4.16	5.58
1500	8" thick	1.62	4.42	6.04
1600	10" thick	2.06	4.60	6.66
1700	12" thick	2.40	5.70	8.10
1800	8" x 16" glazed concrete block, 4" thick	6.10	4.93	11.03
1900	8" thick	6.90	5.50	12.40
2000	Structural facing tile, 6T series, glazed 2 sides, 4" thick	10.10	8.65	18.75
2100	6" thick	16	9.10	25.10
2200				
2300				
2400				
2500				
2600				
2900	Cut & patch to match existing construction, add, minimum	2%	3%	
3000	Maximum	5%	9%	
3100	Dust protection, add, minimum	1%	2%	
3200	Maximum	4%	11%	
3300	Material handling & storage limitation, add, minimum	1%	1%	
3400	Maximum	6%	7%	
3500	Protection of existing work, add, minimum	2%	2%	
3600	Maximum	5%	7%	
3700	Shift work requirements, add, minimum		5%	
3800	Maximum		30%	
3900	Temporary shoring and bracing, add, minimum	2%	5%	
4000	Maximum	5%	12%	

INTERIOR CONSTR. — A6.1-592 | Partitions, Wood Stud

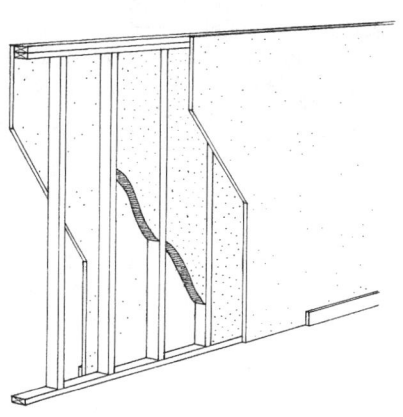

This page illustrates and describes a wood stud partition system including wood studs with plates, gypsum plasterboard – taped and finished, insulation, baseboard and painting. Lines within System Components give the unit price and total price per square foot for this system. Prices for alternate wood stud partition systems are on Line Items 6.1-592-1300 thru 2700. Both material quantities and labor costs have been adjusted for the system listed.

Factors: To adjust for job conditions other than normal working situations use Lines 6.1-592-2900 thru 4000.

Example: You are to install the system where material handling and storage present a serious problem. Go to Line 6.1-592-3400 and apply these percentages to the appropriate MAT. and INST. costs.

System Components

System Components	QUANTITY	UNIT	MAT.	INST.	TOTAL
Wood stud wall, 2"x4", 16" O.C., dbl. top plate, sngl bot. plate, 5/8" dwl. Taped, finished and painted on 2 faces, insulation, baseboard, wall 8' high					
Wood studs, 2" x 4", 16" O.C., 8' high	1.000	S.F.	.49	.91	1.40
Gypsum drywall, 5/8" thick	2.000	S.F.	.52	.74	1.26
Taping and finishing	2.000	S.F.	.20	.74	.94
Insulation, 3-1/2" fiberglass batts	1.000	S.F.	.32	.23	.55
Baseboard, painted	.200	L.F.	.35	.62	.97
Painting, roller, 2 coats	2.000	S.F.	.26	.86	1.12
TOTAL		S.F.	2.14	4.10	6.24

6.1-592	Partitions, Wood Stud	MAT.	INST.	TOTAL
1200	For alternate wood stud systems:			
1300	2" x 3" studs, 8' high, 16" O.C.	2.11	4.05	6.16
1400	24" O.C.	2.01	3.88	5.89
1500	10' high, 16" O.C.	2.08	3.88	5.96
1600	24" O.C.	1.98	3.75	5.73
1700	2" x 4" studs, 8' high, 24" O.C.	2.03	3.92	5.95
1800	10' high, 16" O.C.	2.11	3.92	6.03
1900	24" O.C.	2	3.78	5.78
2000	12' high, 16" O.C.	2.07	3.92	5.99
2100	24" O.C.	1.93	3.77	5.70
2200	2" x 6" studs, 8' high, 16" O.C.	2.38	4.20	6.58
2300	24" O.C.	2.22	3.98	6.20
2400	10' high, 16" O.C.	2.34	4	6.34
2500	24" O.C.	2.17	3.83	6
2600	12' high, 16" O.C.	2.28	4.03	6.31
2700	24" O.C.	2.12	3.84	5.96
2900	Cut & patch to match existing construction, add, minimum	2%	3%	
3000	Maximum	5%	9%	
3100	Dust protection, add, minimum	1%	2%	
3200	Maximum	4%	11%	
3300	Material handling & storage limitation, add, minimum	1%	1%	
3400	Maximum	6%	7%	
3500	Protection of existing work, add, minimum	2%	2%	
3600	Maximum	5%	7%	
3700	Shift work requirements, add, minimum		5%	
3800	Maximum		30%	
3900	Temporary shoring and bracing, add, minimum	2%	5%	
4000	Maximum	5%	12%	

For expanded coverage of these items see *Means Interior Cost Data 1999*

INTERIOR CONSTR. — A6.1-594 — Partitions, Metal Stud, NLB

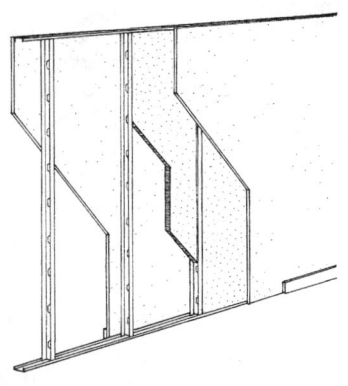

This page illustrates and describes a non-load bearing metal stud partition system including metal studs with runners, gypsum plasterboard, taped and finished, insulation, baseboard and painting. Lines within System Components give the unit price and total price per square foot for this system. Prices for alternate non-load bearing metal stud partition systems are on Line Items 6.1-594-1300 thru 2300. Both material quantities and labor costs have been adjusted for the system listed.

Factors: To adjust for job conditions other than normal working situations use Lines 6.1-594-2900 thru 4000.

Example: You are to install the system and cut and patch to match existing construction. Go to Line 6.1-594-3000 and apply these percentages to the appropriate MAT. and INST. costs.

System Components	QUANTITY	UNIT	COST PER S.F.		
			MAT.	INST.	TOTAL
Non-load bearing metal studs, including top & bottom runners, 5/8" drywall, Taped, finished and painted 2 faces, insulation, painted baseboard.					
Metal studs, 25 ga., 3-5/8" wide, 24" O.C.	1.000	S.F.	.18	.73	.91
Gypsum drywall, 5/8" thick	2.000	S.F.	.52	.74	1.26
Taping & finishing	2.000	S.F.	.20	.74	.94
Insulation, 3-1/2" fiberglass batts	1.000	S.F.	.32	.23	.55
Baseboard, painted	.200	L.F.	.29	.49	.78
Painting, roller work, 2 coats	2.000	S.F.	.26	.86	1.12
TOTAL		S.F.	1.77	3.79	5.56

6.1-594	Partitions, Metal Stud, NLB	COST PER S.F.		
		MAT.	INST.	TOTAL
1200	For alternate metal stud systems:			
1300	Non-load bearing, 25 ga., 24" O.C., 2-1/2" wide	1.74	3.78	5.52
1400	6" wide	1.83	3.82	5.65
1500	16" O.C., 2-1/2" wide	1.78	3.96	5.74
1600	3-5/8" wide	1.82	3.97	5.79
1700	6" wide	1.89	4.01	5.90
1800	20 ga., 24" O.C., 2-1/2" wide	1.98	3.78	5.76
1900	3-5/8" wide	2.08	3.81	5.89
2000	6" wide	2.22	3.82	6.04
2100	16" O.C., 2-1/2" wide	2.08	3.96	6.04
2200	3-5/8" wide	2.20	4	6.20
2300	6" wide	2.38	4.01	6.39
2400				
2500				
2600				
2700				
2900	Cut & patch to match existing construction, add, minimum	2%	3%	
3000	Maximum	5%	9%	
3100	Dust protection, add, minimum	1%	2%	
3200	Maximum	4%	11%	
3300	Material handling & storage limitation, add, minimum	1%	1%	
3400	Maximum	6%	7%	
3500	Protection of existing work, add, minimum	2%	2%	
3600	Maximum	5%	7%	
3700	Shift work requirements, add, minimum		5%	
3800	Maximum		30%	
3900	Temporary shoring and bracing, add, minimum	2%	5%	
4000	Maximum	5%	12%	

INTERIOR CONSTR. | A6.1-595 | Partitions, Drywall

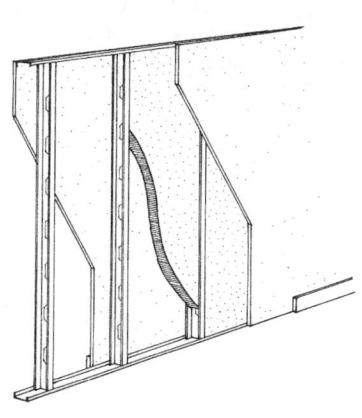

This page illustrates and describes a drywall system including gypsum plasterboard, taped and finished, metal studs with runners, insulation, baseboard and painting. Lines within System Components give the unit price and total price per square foot for this system. Prices for alternate drywall systems are on Line Items 6.1-595-1300 thru 1900. Both material quantities and labor costs have been adjusted for the system listed.

Factors: To adjust for job conditions other than normal working situations use Lines 6.1-595-2900 thru 4000.

Example: You are to install the system and control dust in the work area. Go to Line 6.1-595-3100 and apply these percentages to the appropriate MAT. and INST. costs.

System Components	QUANTITY	UNIT	COST PER S.F.		
			MAT.	INST.	TOTAL
Gypsum drywall, taped, finished and painted 2 faces, galvanized metal studs Including top & bottom runners, insulation, painted baseboard, wall 10' high					
Gypsum drywall, 5/8" thick, standard	2.000	S.F.	.52	.74	1.26
Taping and finishing	2.000	S.F.	.20	.74	.94
Metal studs, 20 ga., 3-5/8" wide, 24" O.C.	1.000	S.F.	.18	.73	.91
Insulation, 3-1/2" fiberglass batts	1.000	S.F.	.32	.23	.55
Baseboard, painted	.200	L.F.	.28	.38	.66
Painting, roller 2 coats	2.000	S.F.	.16	.82	.98
TOTAL		S.F.	1.66	3.64	5.30

6.1-595	Partitions, Drywall	COST PER S.F.		
		MAT.	INST.	TOTAL
1200	For alternate drywall systems:			
1300	Gypsum drywall, 5/8" thick, fire resistant	1.60	3.64	5.24
1400	Water resistant	1.78	3.64	5.42
1500	1/2" thick, standard	1.48	3.64	5.12
1600	Fire resistant	1.66	3.64	5.30
1700	Water resistant	1.64	3.64	5.28
1800	3/8" thick, vinyl faced, standard	2.38	4.52	6.90
1900	5/8" thick, vinyl faced, fire resistant	2.56	4.52	7.08
2000				
2100				
2200				
2300				
2400				
2500				
2600				
2700				
2900	Cut & patch to match existing construction, add, minimum	2%	3%	
3000	Maximum	5%	9%	
3100	Dust protection, add, minimum	1%	2%	
3200	Maximum	4%	11%	
3300	Material handling & storage limitation, add, minimum	1%	1%	
3400	Maximum	6%	7%	
3500	Protection of existing work, add, minimum	2%	2%	
3600	Maximum	5%	7%	
3700	Shift work requirements, add, minimum		5%	
3800	Maximum		30%	
3900	Temporary shoring and bracing, add, minimum	2%	5%	
4000	Maximum	5%	12%	

For expanded coverage of these items see *Means Interior Cost Data 1999*

INTERIOR CONSTR. | A6.1-596 | Partitions, Metal Stud, LB

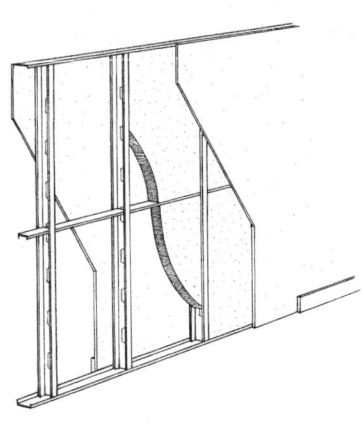

This page illustrates and describes a load bearing metal stud wall system including metal studs, sheetrock–taped and finished, insulation, baseboard and painting. Lines within System Components give the unit price and total price per square foot for this system. Prices for alternate load bearing metal stud wall systems are on Line Items 6.1-596-1500 thru 2500. Both material quantities and labor costs have been adjusted for the system listed.

Factors: To adjust for job conditions other than normal working situations use Lines 6.1-596-2900 thru 4000.

Example: You are to install the system using temporary shoring and bracing. Go to Line 6.1-596-3900 and apply these percentages to the appropriate MAT. and INST. costs.

System Components	QUANTITY	UNIT	COST PER S.F.		
			MAT.	INST.	TOTAL
Load bearing, 18 ga., 3-5/8", galvanized metal studs, 24" O.C., including Top and bottom runners, 1/2" drywall, taped, finished and painted 2 Faces, 3" insulation, and painted baseboard, wall 10' high.					
Metal studs, 24" O.C., 18 ga., 3-5/8" wide, galvanized	1.000	S.F.	.46	.70	1.16
Gypsum drywall 1/2" thick	2.000	S.F.	.34	.74	1.08
Taping and finishing	2.000	S.F.	.20	.74	.94
Insulation, 3-1/2" fiberglass batts	1.000	S.F.	.32	.23	.55
Baseboard, painted	.200	L.F.	.29	.49	.78
Painting, roller 2 coats	2.000	S.F.	.26	.86	1.12
TOTAL		S.F.	1.87	3.76	5.63

6.1-596	Partitions, Metal Stud, LB	COST PER S.F.		
		MAT.	INST.	TOTAL
1400	For alternate metal stud systems:			
1500	Load bearing, 18 ga., 24" O.C., 2-1/2" wide	1.81	3.75	5.56
1600	6" wide	2.03	3.79	5.82
1700	16" O.C. 2-1/2" wide	1.91	3.92	5.83
1800	3-5/8" wide	1.99	3.93	5.92
1900	6" wide	2.19	3.97	6.16
2000	16 ga., 24" O.C., 2-1/2" wide	1.88	3.84	5.72
2100	3-5/8" wide	1.95	3.86	5.81
2200	6" wide	2.12	3.89	6.01
2300	16" O.C., 2-1/2" wide	1.99	4.04	6.03
2400	3-5/8" wide	2.08	4.05	6.13
2500	6" wide	2.30	4.10	6.40
2600				
2700				
2900	Cut & patch to match existing construction, add, minimum	2%	3%	
3000	Maximum	5%	9%	
3100	Dust protection, add, minumum	1%	2%	
3200	Maximum	4%	11%	
3300	Material handling & storage limitation, add, minimum	1%	1%	
3400	Maximum	6%	7%	
3500	Protection of existing work, add, minimum	2%	2%	
3600	Maximum	5%	7%	
3700	Shift work requirements, add, minimum		5%	
3800	Maximum		30%	
3900	Temporary shoring and bracing, add, minimum	2%	5%	
4000	Maximum	5%	12%	

INTERIOR CONSTR. | A6.1-692 | Partitions, Plaster & Lath

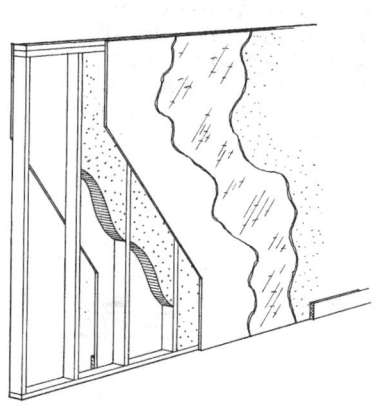

This page illustrates and describes a plaster and lath system including gypsum plaster, gypsum lath, wood studs with plates, insulation, baseboard and painting. Lines within System Components give the unit price and price per square foot for this system. Prices for alternate plaster and lath systems are on Line Items 6.1-692-1500 thru 2500. Both material quantities and labor costs have been adjusted for the system listed.

Factors: To adjust for job conditions other than normal working situations use Lines 6.1-692-2900 thru 4000.

Example: You are to install the system during evening hours only. Go to Line 6.1-692-3800 and apply this percentage to the appropriate INST. costs.

System Components

Gypsum plaster, 2 coats, over 3/8" lath, 2 faces, 2" x 4" wood Stud partition, 24"O.C. incl. double top plate, single bottom plate, 3-1/2" Insulation, baseboard and painting.

System Components	QUANTITY	UNIT	COST PER S.F.		
			MAT.	INST.	TOTAL
Gypsum plaster, 2 coats	.220	S.Y.	.76	3.39	4.15
Lath, gypsum, 3/8" thick	.220	S.Y.	.82	.89	1.71
Wood studs, 2" x 4", 24" O.C.	1.000	S.F.	.35	.59	.94
Insulation, 3-1/2" fiberglass batts	1.000	S.F.	.32	.23	.55
Baseboard, 9/16" x 3-1/2", painted	.200	L.F.	.28	.38	.66
Paint, 2 coats	2.000	S.F.	.26	.86	1.12
TOTAL		S.F.	2.79	6.34	9.13

6.1-692 Partitions, Plaster & Lath

Line	Description	MAT.	INST.	TOTAL
1400	For alternate plaster systems:			
1500	Gypsum plaster, 3 coats	3.08	7	10.08
1600	Perlite plaster, 2 coats	2.95	6.80	9.75
1700	3 coats	3.52	7.70	11.22
1800				
1900				
2000	For alternate lath systems:			
2100	Gypsum lath, 1/2" thick	3.09	6.85	9.94
2200	Foil back, 3/8" thick	3.02	6.90	9.92
2300	1/2" thick	3.05	7	10.05
2400	Metal lath, 2.5 Lb. diamond	2.52	6.80	9.32
2500	3.4 Lb. diamond	2.58	6.90	9.48
2600				
2700				
2900	Cut & patch to match existing construction, add, minimum	2%	3%	
3000	Maximum	5%	9%	
3100	Dust protection, add, minimum	1%	2%	
3200	Maximum	4%	11%	
3300	Material handling & storage limitation, add, minimum	1%	1%	
3400	Maximum	6%	7%	
3500	Protection of existing work, add, minimum	2%	2%	
3600	Maximum	5%	7%	
3700	Shift work requirements, add, minimum		5%	
3800	Maximum		30%	
3900	Temporary shoring and bracing, add, minimum	2%	5%	
4000	Maximum	5%	12%	

For expanded coverage of these items see *Means Interior Cost Data 1999*

INTERIOR CONSTR. — A6.1-842 Partitions, Movable Office

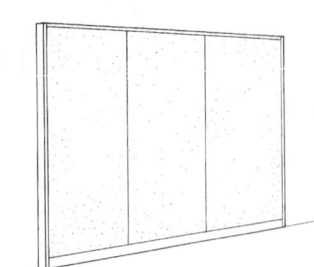

This page illustrates and describes a movable office partition system including demountable office partitions of various styles and sizes based on a cost per square foot basis. Prices for alternate movable office partition systems are on Line Items 6.1-842-0300 thru 3700.

6.1-842	Partitions, Movable Office	MAT.	INST.	TOTAL
0250	Office partition, demountable, no deduction for door opening, add for doors			
0300	Air wall, cork finish, semi acoustic, 1-5/8" thick, minimum	20	2.25	22.25
0400	Maximum	24	3.85	27.85
0500	Acoustic, 2" thick, minimum	21	2.40	23.40
0600	Maximum	31	3.25	34.25
0700				
0800				
0900	In-plant modular office system, w/prehung steel door			
1000	3" thick honeycomb core panels			
1100	12' x 12', 2 wall	6.85	.30	7.15
1200	4 wall	15.90	.90	16.80
1300				
1400				
1500	Gypsum, demountable, 3" to 3-3/4" thick x 9' high, vinyl clad	2.78	1.69	4.47
1600	Fabric clad	8.65	1.84	10.49
1700	1.75 system, vinyl clad hardboard, paper honeycomb core panel			
1800	1-3/4" to 2-1/2" thick x 9' high	5.90	1.69	7.59
1900	Unitized gypsum panel, 2" to 2-1/2" thick x 9' high, vinyl clad	7.90	1.69	9.59
2000	Fabric clad	14.20	1.84	16.04
2100				
2200				
2300	Unitized mineral fiber panel system, 2-1/4" thick x 9' high			
2400	Vinyl clad mineral fiber	10.05	1.69	11.74
2500	Fabric clad mineral fiber	12.75	1.84	14.59
2600				
2700	Movable steel walls, modular system			
2800	Unitized panels, 48" wide x 9' high			
2900	Baked enamel, pre-finished	9.20	1.35	10.55
3000	Fabric clad	14.10	1.45	15.55
3100	For acoustical partitions, add, minimum	1.46		1.46
3200	Maximum	5.35		5.35
3300				
3400				
3500	Note: For door prices, see divisions 081 & 082			
3600	For door hardware prices, see division 087			
3700				
3800				
3900				
4000				

INTERIOR CONSTR. — A6.4-142 — Doors, Interior Flush, Wood

This page illustrates and describes flush interior door systems including hollow core door, jamb, header and trim with hardware. Lines within System Components give the unit price and total price on a cost each basis for this system. Prices for alternate flush interior door systems are on Line items 6.4-142-1100 thru 2400. Both material quantities and labor costs have been adjusted for the system listed.

Factors: To adjust for job conditions other than normal working situations use Lines 6.1-142-2700 thru 3800.

Example: You are to install the system in an area where dust protection is vital. Go to Line 6.4-142-3000 and apply these percentages to the appropriate MAT. and INST. costs.

System Components	QUANTITY	UNIT	COST EACH		
			MAT.	INST.	TOTAL
Single hollow core door, include jamb, header, trim and hardware, painted.					
Hollow core Lauan, 1-3/8" thick, 2'-0" x 6'-8", painted	1.000	Ea.	26.17	59.60	85.77
Wood jamb, 4-9/16" deep	1.000	Set	74.24	31.20	105.44
Trim, casing	1.000	Set	27.20	48.64	75.84
Hardware, hinges, lockset	1.000	Set	28.10	23	51.10
TOTAL		Ea.	155.71	162.44	318.15

6.4-142	Doors, Interior Flush, Wood	COST EACH		
		MAT.	INST.	TOTAL
1000	For alternate door systems:			
1100	Lauan (Mahogany) hollow core, 1-3/8" x 2'-6" x 6'-8"	162	165	327
1200	2'-8" x 6'-8"	165	167	332
1300	3'-0" x 6'-8"	170	173	343
1500	Birch, hollow core, 1-3/8" x 2'-0" x 6'-8"	167	162	329
1600	2'-6" x 6'-8"	175	165	340
1700	2'-8" x 6'-8"	179	167	346
1800	3'-0" x 6'-8"	184	173	357
1900	Solid core, pre-hung, 1-3/8" x 2'-6" x 6'-8"	286	161	447
2000	2'-8" x 6'-8"	291	163	454
2100	3'-0" x 6'-8"	300	168	468
2200				
2400	For metal frame instead of wood, add	50%	20%	
2600				
2700	Cut & patch to match existing construction, add, minimum	2%	3%	
2800	Maximum	5%	9%	
2900	Dust protection, add, minimum	1%	2%	
3000	Maximum	4%	11%	
3100	Equipment usage curtailment, add, minimum	1%	1%	
3200	Maximum	3%	10%	
3300	Material handling & storage limitation, add, minimum	1%	1%	
3400	Maximum	6%	7%	
3500	Protection of existing work, add, minimum	2%	2%	
3600	Maximum	5%	7%	
3700	Shift work requirements, add, minimum		5%	
3800	Maximum		30%	
3900				

For expanded coverage of these items see *Means Interior Cost Data 1999*

INTERIOR CONSTR.   A6.4-144 Doors, Interior Solid & Louvered

This page illustrates and describes interior, solid and louvered door systems including a pine panel door, wood jambs, header, and trim with hardware. Lines within System Components give the unit price and total price on a cost each basis for this system. Prices for alternate interior, solid and louvered systems are on Line Items 6.4-144-1200 thru 2400. Both material quantities and labor costs have been adjusted for the system listed.

Factors: To adjust for job conditions other than normal working situations use Lines 6.4-144-2900 thru 4000.

Example: You are to install the system during night hours only. Go to Line 6.4-144-4000 and apply these percentages to the appropriate INST. costs.

System Components	QUANTITY	UNIT	COST EACH		
			MAT.	INST.	TOTAL
Single interior door, including jamb, header, trim and hardware, painted.					
Solid pine panel door, painted 1-3/8" thick, 2'-0" x 6'-8"	1.000	Ea.	123.67	59.60	183.27
Wooden jamb, 4-5/8" deep	1.000	Set	74.24	31.20	105.44
Trim, casing	1.000	Set	27.20	48.64	75.84
Hardware, hinges, lockset	1.000	Set	28.10	23	51.10
TOTAL		Ea.	253.21	162.44	415.65

6.4-144	Doors, Interior Solid & Louvered	COST EACH		
		MAT.	INST.	TOTAL
1000				
1100	For alternate door systems:			
1200	Solid pine, painted raised panel, 1-3/8" x 2'-6" x 6'-8"	270	165	435
1300	2'-8" x 6'-8"	283	167	450
1400	3'-0" x 6'-8"	295	173	468
1500				
1600	Louvered pine, painted 1'-6" x 6'-8"	236	160	396
1700	2'-0" x 6'-8"	256	165	421
1800	2'-6" x 6'-8"	272	167	439
1900	3'-0" x 6'-8"	295	173	468
2200	For prehung door, deduct	5%	30%	
2300				
2400	For metal frame instead of wood, add	50%	20%	
2500				
2900	Cut & patch to match existing construction, add, minimum	2%	3%	
3000	Maximum	5%	9%	
3100	Dust protection, add, minimum	1%	2%	
3200	Maximum	4%	11%	
3300	Equipment usage curtailment, add, minimum	1%	1%	
3400	Maximum	3%	10%	
3500	Material handling & storage limitation, add, minimum	1%	1%	
3600	Maximum	6%	7%	
3700	Protection of existing work, add, minimum	2%	2%	
3800	Maximum	5%	7%	
3900	Shift work requirements, add, minimum		5%	
4000	Maximum		30%	

INTERIOR CONSTR. — A6.4-146 — Doors, Interior Flush, Metal

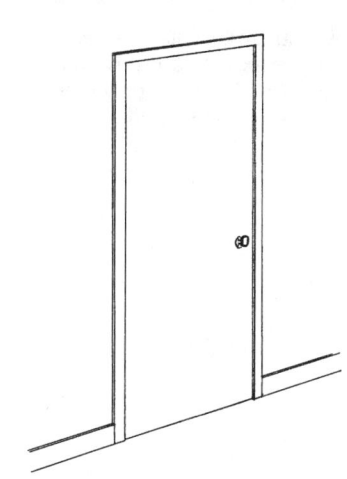

This page illustrates and describes interior metal door systems including a metal door, metal frame and hardware. Lines within System Components give the unit price and total price on a cost each for this system. Prices for alternate interior metal door systems are on Line Items 6.4-146-1100 thru 2100. Both material quantities and labor costs have been adjusted for the system listed.

Factors: To adjust for job conditions other than normal working situations use Lines 6.4-146-2900 thru 4000.

Example: You are to install the system while protecting existing construction. Go to Line 6.4-146-3700 and apply these percentages to the appropriate MAT. and INST. costs.

System Components	QUANTITY	UNIT	COST EACH		
			MAT.	INST.	TOTAL
Single metal door, including frame and hardware.					
Hollow metal door, 1-3/8" thick, 2'-6" x 6'-8", painted	1.000	Ea.	195.67	68.10	263.77
Metal frame, 5-3/4" deep	1.000	Set	78	45.50	123.50
Hinges and passage lockset	1.000	Set	69.95	23	92.95
TOTAL		Ea.	343.62	136.60	480.22

6.4-146	Doors, Interior Flush, Metal	COST EACH		
		MAT.	INST.	TOTAL
1000	For alternate systems:			
1100	Hollow metal doors, 1-3/8" thick, 2'-8" x 6'-8"	355	137	492
1200	3'-0" x 7'-0"	365	143	508
1300				
1400	Interior fire door, 1-3/8" thick, 2'-6" x 6'-8"	405	137	542
1500	2'-8" x 6'-8"	410	137	547
1600	3'-0" x 7'-0"	410	143	553
1700				
1800	Add to fire doors:			
1900	Baked enamel finish	30%	15%	
2000	Galvanizing	15%		
2200				
2300				
2400				
2900	Cut & patch to match existing construction, add, minimum	2%	3%	
3000	Maximum	5%	9%	
3100	Dust protection, add, minimum	1%	2%	
3200	Maximum	4%	11%	
3300	Equipment usage curtailment, add, minimum	1%	1%	
3400	Maximum	3%	10%	
3500	Material handling & storage limitation, add, minimum	1%	1%	
3600	Maximum	6%	7%	
3700	Protection of existing work, add, minimum	2%	2%	
3800	Maximum	5%	7%	
3900	Shift work requirements, add, minimum		5%	
4000	Maximum		30%	

INTERIOR CONSTR. | A6.4-148 | Doors, Closet

This page illustrates and describes an interior closet door system including an interior closet door, painted, with trim and hardware. Prices for alternate interior closet door systems are on Line Items 6.4-148-0500 thru 2200. Both material quantities and labor costs have been adjusted for the system listed.

Factors: To adjust for job conditions other than normal working situations use Lines 6.4-148-2900 thru 4000.

Example: You are to install the system and match the existing construction. Go to Line 6.4-148-2900 and apply these percentages to the appropriate MAT. and INST. costs.

6.4-148	Doors, Closet	COST PER SET		
		MAT.	INST.	TOTAL
0350	Interior closet door painted, including frame, trim and hardware, prehung.			
0400	Bi-fold doors			
0500	Pine paneled, 3'-0" x 6'-8"	223	135	358
0600	6'-0" x 6'-8"	375	181	556
0700	Birch, hollow core, 3'-0" x 6'-8"	142	146	288
0800	6'-0" x 6'-8"	216	195	411
0900	Lauan, hollow core, 3'-0" x 6'-8"	132	135	267
1000	6'-0" x 6'-8"	197	181	378
1100	Louvered pine, 3'-0" x 6'-8"	191	135	326
1200	6'-0" x 6'-8"	310	181	491
1300				
1400	Sliding, bi-passing closet doors			
1500	Pine paneled, 4'-0" x 6'-8"	425	143	568
1600	6'-0" x 6'-8"	510	181	691
1700	Birch, hollow core, 4'-0" x 6'-8"	262	143	405
1800	6'-0" x 6'-8"	310	181	491
1900	Lauan, hollow core, 4'-0" x 6'-8"	239	143	382
2000	6'-0" x 6'-8"	262	181	443
2100	Louvered pine, 4'-0" x 6'-8"	440	143	583
2200	6'-0" x 6'-8"	525	181	706
2300				
2400				
2500				
2600				
2700				
2800				
2900	Cut & patch to match existing construction, add, minimum	2%	3%	
3000	Maximum	5%	9%	
3100	Dust protection, add, minimum	1%	2%	
3200	Maximum	4%	11%	
3300	Equipment usage curtailment, add, minimum	1%	1%	
3400	Maximum	3%	10%	
3500	Material handling & storage limitation, add, minimum	1%	1%	
3600	Maximum	6%	7%	
3700	Protection of existing work, add, minimum	2%	2%	
3800	Maximum	5%	7%	
3900	Shift work requirements, add, minimum		5%	
4000	Maximum		30%	

INTERIOR CONSTR. — A6.7-242 | Ceiling, Suspended Plaster

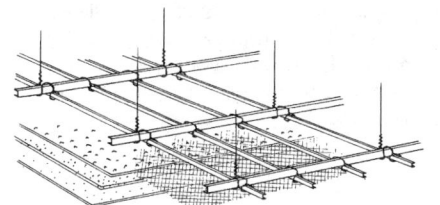

This page illustrates and describes suspended plaster and lath systems including gypsum plaster, lath, furring and runners with ceiling painted. Lines within System Components give the unit price and total price per square foot for this system. Prices for alternate suspended plaster and lath systems are on Line Items 6.7-242-1300 thru 2300. Both material quantities and labor costs have been adjusted for the system listed.

Factors: To adjust for job conditions other than normal working situations use Lines 6.7-242-2900 thru 4000.

Example: You are to install the system to match existing construction. Go to Line 6.7-242-2900 and apply these percentages to the appropriate MAT. and INST. costs.

System Components

System Components	QUANTITY	UNIT	MAT.	INST.	TOTAL
Gypsum plaster, 3 coats, on 3.4# rib lath, on 3/4" C.R.C. furring on 1-1/2" main runners, ceiling painted.					
Gypsum plaster, 3 coats	.110	S.Y.	.52	2.27	2.79
3.4# rib lath	.110	S.Y.	.35	.54	.89
Main runners, 1-1/2" C.R.C. 24" O.C.	.333	S.F.	.17	.88	1.05
Furring 3/4" C.R.C. 16" O.C.	1.000	S.F.	.19	1.18	1.37
Painting, 2 coats, roller work	1.000	S.F.	.13	.43	.56
TOTAL		S.F.	1.36	5.30	6.66

6.7-242	Ceiling, Suspended Plaster	MAT.	INST.	TOTAL
1200	For alternate plaster ceiling systems:			
1300	Gypsum plaster, 3 coats, on 2.5# diamond lath	1.21	5.25	6.46
1400	On 3/8" gypsum lath	1.47	5.25	6.72
1500	2 coats, on 3.4# rib lath	1.49	5.30	6.79
1600	On 2.5# diamond lath	1.07	4.93	6
1700	On 3/8" gypsum lath	1.33	4.93	6.26
1800	Perlite plaster, 3 coats, on 3.4# rib lath	1.58	5.90	7.48
1900	On 2.5# diamond lath	1.43	5.85	7.28
2000	On 3/8" gypsum lath	1.69	5.85	7.54
2100	2 coats, on 3.4# rib lath	1.30	5.25	6.55
2200	On 2.5# diamond lath	1.15	5.25	6.40
2300	On 3/8" gypsum lath	1.41	5.25	6.66
2400				
2500				
2600				
2700				
2900	Cut & patch to match existing construction, add, minimum	2%	3%	
3000	Maximum	5%	9%	
3100	Dust protection, add, minimum	1%	2%	
3200	Maximum	4%	11%	
3300	Equipment usage curtailment, add, minimum	1%	1%	
3400	Maximum	3%	10%	
3500	Material handling & storage limitation, add, minimum	1%	1%	
3600	Maximum	6%	7%	
3700	Protection of existing work, add, minimum	2%	2%	
3800	Maximum	5%	7%	
3900	Shift work requirements, add, minimum		5%	
4000	Maximum		30%	

INTERIOR CONSTR. | A6.7-342 | Ceiling, Suspended Acoustical

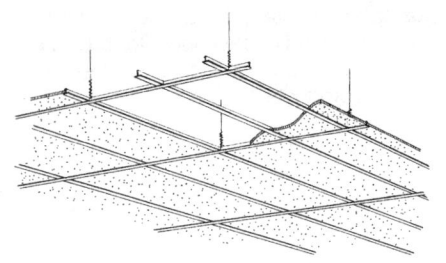

This page illustrates suspended acoustical board systems including acoustic ceiling board, hangers, and T bar suspension. Lines within System Components give the unit price and total price per square foot for this system. Prices for alternate suspended acoustical board systems are on Line Items 6.7-342-1100 thru 2400. Both material quantities and labor costs have been adjusted for the system listed.

Factors: To adjust for job conditions other than normal working situations use Lines 6.7-342-2900 thru 4000.

Example: You are to install the system and protect existing construction. Go to Line 6.7-342-3800 and apply these percentages to the appropriate MAT. and INST. costs.

System Components	QUANTITY	UNIT	COST PER S.F.		
			MAT.	INST.	TOTAL
Suspended acoustical ceiling board installed on exposed grid system.					
Fiberglass boards, film faced, 2' x 4', 5/8" thick	1.000	S.F.	.54	.58	1.12
Hangers, #12 wire	1.000	S.F.	.02	.06	.08
T bar suspension system, 2' x 4' grid	1.000	S.F.	.34	.46	.80
TOTAL		S.F.	.90	1.10	2

6.7-342		Ceiling, Suspended Acoustical	COST PER S.F.		
			MAT.	INST.	TOTAL
1000		For alternate suspended ceiling systems:			
1100		2' x 4' grid, mineral fiber board, aluminum faced, 5/8" thick	6.60	1.08	7.68
1200		Standard faced	.99	1.06	2.05
1300		Plastic faced	1.33	1.43	2.76
1400		Fiberglass, film faced, 3" thick, R11	1.69	1.33	3.02
1500		Grass cloth faced, 3/4" thick	2.13	1.25	3.38
1600		1" thick	2.35	1.27	3.62
1700		1-1/2" thick, nubby face	2.73	1.29	4.02
2200					
2300					
2400		Add for 2' x 2' grid system	.09	.11	.20
2500					
2600					
2700					
2900		Cut & patch to match existing construction, add, minimum	2%	3%	
3000		Maximum	5%	9%	
3100		Dust protection, add, minimum	1%	2%	
3200		Maximum	4%	11%	
3300		Equipment usage curtailment, add, minimum	1%	1%	
3400		Maximum	3%	10%	
3500		Material handling & storage limitation, add, minimum	1%	1%	
3600		Maximum	6%	7%	
3700		Protection of existing work, add, minimum	2%	2%	
3800		Maximum	5%	7%	
3900		Shift work requirements, add, minimum		5%	
4000		Maximum		30%	

INTERIOR CONSTR. — A6.7-442 — Ceilings Suspended Gypsum Board

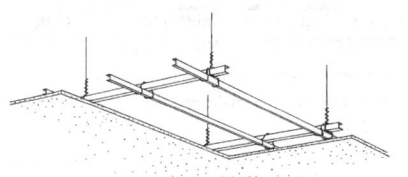

This page illustrates and describes suspended gypsum board systems including gypsum board, metal furring, taping, finished and painted. Lines within System Components give the unit price and total price per square foot for this system. Prices for alternate suspended gypsum board systems are on Line Items 6.7-442-1500 thru 1700. Both material quantities and labor costs have been adjusted for the system listed.

Factors: To adjust for job conditions other than normal working situations use Lines 6.7-442-2900 thru 4000.

Example: You are to install the system and control dust in the working area. Go to Line 6.7-442-3200 and apply these percentages to the appropriate MAT. and INST. costs.

System Components	QUANTITY	UNIT	COST PER S.F. MAT.	INST.	TOTAL
Suspended ceiling gypsum board, 4' x 8' x 5/8" thick, On metal furring, taped, finished and painted.					
Gypsum drywall, 4' x 8', 5/8" thick, screwed	1.000	S.F.	.26	.41	.67
Main runners, 1-1/2" C.R.C., 4' O.C.	.500	S.F.	.09	.44	.53
25 ga., channels, 2' O.C.	1.000	S.F.	.13	.82	.95
Taped and finished	1.000	S.F.	.10	.37	.47
Paint, 2 coats, roller work	1.000	S.F.	.13	.43	.56
TOTAL		S.F.	.71	2.47	3.18

6.7-442	Ceilings, Suspended Gypsum Board	MAT.	INST.	TOTAL
1400	For alternate drywall ceiling systems:			
1500	Thin coat plaster, 2 coats paint	.59	2.12	2.71
1600	Spray-on sand finish, no paint	.61	2.10	2.71
1700	12" x 12" x 3/4" acoustical wood fiber tile	1.53	2.58	4.11
1800				
1900				
2000				
2100				
2200				
2300				
2400				
2500				
2600				
2700				
2900	Cut & patch to match existing construction, add, minimum	2%	3%	
3000	Maximum	5%	9%	
3100	Dust protection, add, minimum	1%	2%	
3200	Maximum	4%	11%	
3300	Equipment usage curtailment, add, minimum	1%	1%	
3400	Maximum	3%	10%	
3500	Material handling & storage limitation, add, minimum	1%	1%	
3600	Maximum	6%	7%	
3700	Protection of existing work, add, minimum	2%	2%	
3800	Maximum	5%	7%	
3900	Shift work requirements, add, minimum		5%	
4000	Maximum		30%	

For expanded coverage of these items see *Means Interior Cost Data 1999*

INTERIOR CONSTR. | A6.9-100 | Stud & Furring

6.9-100 Selective Price Sheet

			COST PER S.F.		
			MAT.	INST.	TOTAL
0100	Studs				
0200					
0300		24" O.C. metal, 10' high wall, including			
0400		Top and bottom runners			
0500		Non load bearing, galvanized 25 Ga., 1-5/8" wide	.13	.70	.83
0600		2-1/2" wide	.15	.72	.87
0700		3-5/8" wide	.18	.73	.91
0800		4" wide	.19	.75	.94
0900		6" wide	.24	.76	1
1000					
1100		Galvanized 20 Ga., 2-1/2" wide	.39	.72	1.11
1200		3-5/8" wide	.48	.73	1.21
1300		4" wide	.49	.75	1.24
1400		6" wide	.63	.76	1.39
1500		Load bearing, painted 18 Ga., 2-1/2" wide	.40	.69	1.09
1600		3-5/8" wide	.46	.70	1.16
1700		4" wide	4.11	7.10	11.21
1800		6" wide	.62	.73	1.35
1900		Galvanized 18 Ga., 2-1/2" wide	.40	.69	1.09
2000		3-5/8" wide	.46	.70	1.16
2100		4" wide	4.11	7.10	11.21
2200		6" wide	.62	.73	1.35
2300		Galvanized 16 Ga., 2-1/2" wide	.47	.78	1.25
2400		3-5/8" wide	.54	.80	1.34
2500		4" wide	.55	.81	1.36
2600		6" wide	.71	.83	1.54
2700					
2800					
2900		24" O.C. wood, 10' high wall, including			
3000		Double top plate and shoe			
3100		2" x 4"	.41	.69	1.10
3200		2" x 6"	.60	.74	1.34
3300					
3400					
3500	Furring, 24" O.C. 10' high wall, metal, 3/4" channels		.13	.82	.95
3600		1-1/2" channels	.17	.88	1.05
3700		Wood, on wood, 1" x 2" strips	.10	.33	.43
3800		1" x 3" strips	.13	.33	.46
3900		On masonry, 1" x 2" strips	.10	.37	.47
4000		1" x 3" strips	.13	.37	.50
4100		On concrete, 1" x 2" strips	.10	.71	.81
4200		1" x 3" strips	.13	.71	.84
4300	Studs				
4400					
4500		16" O.C., metal, 10' high wall, including			
4600		Top and bottom runners			
4700		Non load bearing, galvanized 25 Ga., 1-5/8" wide	.16	.81	.97
4800		2-1/2" wide	.18	.83	1.01
4900		3-5/8" wide	.21	.85	1.06
5000		4" wide	.24	.87	1.11
5100		6" wide	.30	.89	1.19
5200					
5300		Galvanized 20 Ga., 2-1/2" wide	.48	.83	1.31
5400		3-5/8" wide	.59	.85	1.44
5500		4" wide	.62	.87	1.49
5600		6" wide	.79	.89	1.68
5700		Load bearing, painted 18 Ga., 2-1/2" wide	.55	.95	1.50
5800		3-5/8" wide	.63	.96	1.59
5900		4" wide	.65	.99	1.64
6000		6" wide	.84	1	1.84

INTERIOR CONSTR. | A6.9-100 | Stud & Furring

6.9-100 Selective Price Sheet

		COST PER S.F.		
		MAT.	INST.	TOTAL
6100	Galvanized 18 Ga., 2-1/2" wide	.55	.95	1.50
6200	3-5/8" wide	.63	.96	1.59
6300	4" wide	.65	.99	1.64
6400	6" wide	.84	1	1.84
6500	Galvanized 16 Ga., 2-1/2" wide	.64	1.08	1.72
6600	3-5/8" wide	.74	1.11	1.85
6700	4" wide	.76	1.13	1.89
6800	6" wide	.97	1.15	2.12
6900				
7000				
7100	16" O.C., wood, 10' high wall, including			
7200	Double top plate and shoe			
7300	2" x 4"	.50	.80	1.30
7400	2" x 6"	.60	.71	1.31
7500				
7600				
7700	Furring, 16" O.C. 10' high wall, metal, 3/4" channels	.19	1.18	1.37
7800	1-1/2" channels	.26	1.32	1.58
7900	Wood, on wood, 1" x 2" strips	.15	.50	.65
8000	1" x 3" strips	.19	.50	.69
8100	On masonry, 1" x 2" strips	.15	.56	.71
8200	1" x 3" strips	.19	.56	.75
8300	On concrete, 1" x 2" strips	.15	1.06	1.21
8400	1" x 3" strips	.19	1.06	1.25

For expanded coverage of these items see *Means Interior Cost Data 1999*

INTERIOR CONSTR. | A6.9-300 | Plaster & Drywall

6.9-300 Selective Price Sheet

		COST PER S.F.		
		MAT.	INST.	TOTAL
0100	Lath, gypsum perforated			
0200				
0300	Regular, 3/8" thick	.41	.45	.86
0400	1/2" thick	.48	.54	1.02
0500	Fire resistant, 3/8" thick	.48	.54	1.02
0600	1/2" thick	.49	.58	1.07
0700	Foil back, 3/8" thick	.45	.51	.96
0800	1/2" thick	.46	.54	1
0900				
1000	Metal lath			
1100	Diamond painted, 2.5 lb.	.20	.45	.65
1200	3.4 lb.	.23	.51	.74
1300	Rib painted, 2.75 lb	.19	.51	.70
1400	3.40 lb	.35	.54	.89
1500				
1600				
1700	Plaster, gypsum, 2 coats	.38	1.71	2.09
1800	3 coats	.53	2.06	2.59
1900	Perlite/vermiculite, 2 coats	.46	1.95	2.41
2000	3 coats	.75	2.40	3.15
2100	Bondcrete, 1 coat	.40	.90	1.30
2200				
2500				
2600				
2700	Drywall, standard, 3/8" thick, no finish included	.18	.37	.55
2800	1/2" thick, no finish included	.17	.37	.54
2900	Taped and finished	.27	.76	1.03
3000	5/8" thick, no finish included	.26	.37	.63
3100	Taped and finished	.36	.76	1.12
3200	Fire resistant, 1/2" thick, no finish included	.26	.37	.63
3300	Taped and finished	.36	.76	1.12
3400	5/8" thick, no finish included	.23	.37	.60
3500	Taped and finished	.33	.76	1.09
3600	Water resistant, 1/2" thick, no finish included	.25	.37	.62
3700	Taped and finished	.35	.76	1.11
3800	5/8" thick, no finish included	.32	.37	.69
3900	Taped and finished	.42	.76	1.18
4000	Finish, instead of taping			
4100	For thin coat plaster, add	.11	.45	.56
4200	Finish, textured spray, add	.13	.43	.56

INTERIOR CONSTR. | A6.9-500 | Hardware

6.9-500 Selective Price Sheet

		COST EACH		
		MAT.	INST.	TOTAL
0100	Door closer, rack and pinion	116	56.50	172.50
0200	Backcheck and adjustable power	122	61	183
0300	Regular, hinge face mount, all sizes, regular arm	146	56.50	202.50
0400	Hold open arm	157	56.50	213.50
0500	Top jamb mount, all sizes, regular arm	146	61	207
0600	Hold open arm	157	61	218
0700	Stop face mount, all sizes, regular arm	146	56.50	202.50
0800	Hold open arm	157	56.50	213.50
0900	Fusible link, hinge face mount, all sizes, regular arm	156	56.50	212.50
1000	Hold open arm	167	56.50	223.50
1100	Top jamb mount, all sizes, regular arm	156	61	217
1200	Hold open arm	167	61	228
1300	Stop face mount, all sizes, regular arm	156	56.50	212.50
1400	Hold open arm	167	56.50	223.50
1500				
1600				
1700	Door stops			
1800				
1900	Holder & bumper, floor or wall	15.40	11.45	26.85
2000	Wall bumper	7	11.45	18.45
2100	Floor bumper	4	11.45	15.45
2200	Plunger type, door mounted	24.50	11.45	35.95
2300	Hinges, full mortise, material only, per pair			
2400	Low frequency, 4-1/2" x 4-1/2", steel base, USP	14.65		14.65
2500	Brass base. US10	33		33
2600	Stainless steel base, US32	55		55
2700	Average frequency, 4-1/2" x 4-1/2", steel base, USP	19.30		19.30
2800	Brass base, US10	40		40
2900	Stainless steel base, US32	66		66
3000	High frequency, 4-1/2" x 4-1/2", steel base, USP	48		48
3100	Brass base, US10	43		43
3200	Stainless steel base, US32	102		102
3300	Kick plate			
3400				
3500	6" high, for 3'-0" door, aluminum	17.55	24.50	42.05
3600	Bronze	21	24.50	45.50
3700	Panic device			
3800				
3900	For rim locks, single door, exit	350	61	411
4000	Outside key and pull	405	73	478
4100	Bar and vertical rod, exit only	520	73	593
4200	For touch bar	620	91.50	711.50
4300	Lockset			
4400				
4500	Heavy duty, cylindrical, passage doors	112	30.50	142.50
4600	Classroom	249	45.50	294.50
4700	Bedroom, bathroom, and inner office doors	141	30.50	171.50
4800	Apartment, office, and corridor doors	197	36.50	233.50
4900	Standard duty, cylindrical, exit doors	70.50	36.50	107
5000	Inner office doors			
5100	Passage doors	48.50	30.50	79
5200	Public restroom, classroom, & office doors	96	45.50	141.50
5300	Deadlock, mortise, heavy duty	120	40.50	160.50
5400	Double cylinder	133	40.50	173.50
5500	Entrance lock, cylinder, deadlocking latch	110	40.50	150.50
5600	Deadbolt	133	45.50	178.50
5700	Commercial, mortise, wrought knob, keyed, minimum	156	45.50	201.50
5800	Maximum	288	52	340
5900	Cast knob, keyed, minimum	210	40.50	250.50
6000	Maximum	410	40.50	450.50

For expanded coverage of these items see *Means Interior Cost Data 1999*

INTERIOR CONSTR. | A6.9-500 | Hardware

6.9-500 Selective Price Sheet

		COST EACH		
		MAT.	INST.	TOTAL
6100	Push-pull			
6200				
6300	Aluminum	5.35	30.50	35.85
6400	Bronze	12	30.50	42.50
6500	Door pull, designer style, minimum	65	30.50	95.50
6600	Maximum	300	45.50	345.50
6700	Threshold			
6800				
6900	3'-0" long door saddles, aluminum, minimum	3.68	7.60	11.28
7000	Maximum	31.50	30.50	62
7100	Bronze, minimum	29.50	6.10	35.60
7200	Maximum	61.50	30.50	92
7300	Rubber, 1/2" thick, 5-1/2" wide	31	18.30	49.30
7400	2-3/4" wide	14.45	18.30	32.75
7500	Weatherstripping, per set			
7600				
7700	Doors, wood frame, interlocking for 3' x 7' door, zinc	12.70	122	134.70
7800	Bronze	19.95	122	141.95
7900	Wood frame, spring type for 3' x 7' door, bronze	16.85	48	64.85
8000	Metal frame, spring type for 3' x 7' door, bronze	28	122	150
8100	For stainless steel, spring type, add	133%		
8200				
8300	Metal frame, extruded sections, 3' x 7' door, aluminum	37	183	220
8400	Bronze	93	183	276

INTERIOR CONSTR. | A6.9-600 | Interior Wall Finish

6.9-600 Selective Price Sheet

		COST PER S.F.		
		MAT.	INST.	TOTAL
0100	Painting, on plaster or drywall, brushwork, primer and 1 ct.	.08	.48	.56
0200	Primer and 2 ct.	.13	.76	.89
0300	Rollerwork, primer and 1 ct.	.08	.41	.49
0400	Primer and 2 ct.	.12	.57	.69
0500	Woodwork incl. puttying, brushwork, primer and 1 ct.	.09	.72	.81
0600	Primer and 2 ct.	.13	.96	1.09
0700	Wood trim to 6" wide, enamel, primer and 1 ct.	.09	.41	.50
0800	Primer and 2 ct.	.13	.52	.65
0900	Cabinets and casework, enamel, primer and 1 ct.	.09	.81	.90
1000	Primer and 2 ct.	.13	1	1.13
1100	On masonry or concrete, latex, brushwork, primer and 1 ct.	.16	.68	.84
1200	Primer and 2 ct.	.22	.97	1.19
1300	For block filler, add	.11	.83	.94
1400				
1500	Varnish, wood trim, sealer 1 ct., sanding, puttying, quality work	.13	1.46	1.59
1600	Medium work	.10	1.13	1.23
1700	Without sanding	.12	.17	.29
1800				
1900	Wall coverings, wall paper, at $9.70 per double roll, average workmanship	.29	.51	.80
2000	At $20.00 per double roll, average workmanship	.52	.61	1.13
2100	At $44.00 per double roll, quality workmanship	.98	.75	1.73
2200				
2300	Grass cloths with lining paper, minimum	.63	.82	1.45
2400	Maximum	2.01	.94	2.95
2500	Vinyl, fabric backed, light weight	.56	.51	1.07
2600	Medium weight	.70	.68	1.38
2700	Heavy weight	1.26	.75	2.01
2800				
2900	Cork tiles, 12" x 12", 3/16" thick	2.85	1.37	4.22
3000	5/16" thick	2.96	1.39	4.35
3100	Granular surface, 12" x 36", 1/2" thick	.98	.85	1.83
3200	1" thick	1.28	.89	2.17
3300	Aluminum foil	.84	1.19	2.03
3400				
3500	Tile, ceramic, adhesive set, 4-1/4" x 4-1/4"	2.43	3.20	5.63
3600	6" x 6"	2.82	3.04	5.86
3700	Decorated, 4-1/4" x 4-1/4", minimum	3.23	2.25	5.48
3800	Maximum	16.80	3.37	20.17
3900	For epoxy grout, add	.35	.76	1.11
4000	Pregrouted sheets	4.48	2.53	7.01
4100	Glass mosaics, 3/4" tile on 12" sheets, minimum	16.15	8.30	24.45
4200	Color group 8	53	9.50	62.50
4300	Metal, tile pattern, 4' x 4' sheet, 24 ga., nailed			
4400	Stainless steel	23.50	1.43	24.93
4500	Aluminized steel	12.60	1.43	14.03
4600				
4700	Brick, interior veneer, 4" face brick, running bond, minimum	2.77	7.75	10.52
4800	Maximum	2.77	7.75	10.52
4900	Simulated, urethane pieces, set in mastic	5.05	2.44	7.49
5000	Fiberglass panels	2.48	1.83	4.31
5100	Wall coating, on drywall, thin coat, plain	.11	.45	.56
5200	Stipple	.11	.45	.56
5300	Textured spray	.13	.43	.56
5400				
5500	Paneling not incl. furring or trim, hardboard, tempered, 1/8" thick	.36	1.46	1.82
5600	1/4" thick	.41	1.46	1.87
5700	Plastic faced, 1/8" thick	.57	1.46	2.03
5800	1/4" thick	.78	1.46	2.24
5900	Woodgrained, 1/4" thick, minimum	.52	1.46	1.98
6000	Maximum	.98	1.72	2.70

For expanded coverage of these items see *Means Interior Cost Data 1999*

INTERIOR CONSTR. | A6.9-600 | Interior Wall Finish

6.9-600	Selective Price Sheet	COST PER S.F.		
		MAT.	INST.	TOTAL
6100	Plywood, 4' x 8' shts. 1/4" thick, prefin., birch faced, min.	.79	1.46	2.25
6200	Maximum	1.64	2.09	3.73
6300	Walnut, minimum	2.50	1.46	3.96
6400	Maximum	4.76	1.83	6.59
6500	Mahogany, african	2.10	1.83	3.93
6600	Philippine	.90	1.46	2.36
6700	Chestnut	4.37	1.95	6.32
6800	Pecan	1.87	1.83	3.70
6900	Rosewood	4.19	2.29	6.48
7000	Teak	2.95	1.83	4.78
7100	Aromatic cedar, plywood	1.87	1.83	3.70
7200	Particle board	.90	1.83	2.73
7300	Wood board, 3/4" thick, knotty pine	1.36	2.44	3.80
7400	Rough sawn cedar	1.76	2.44	4.20
7500	Redwood, clear	4.13	2.44	6.57
7600	Aromatic cedar	3.11	2.66	5.77

INTERIOR CONSTR. — A6.9-700 Ceiling Finish

6.9-700 Selective Price Sheet

		COST PER S.F.		
		MAT.	INST.	TOTAL
0100	Ceiling, plaster, gypsum, 2 coats	.38	1.95	2.33
0200	3 coats	.53	2.29	2.82
0300	Perlite or vermiculite, 2 coats	.46	2.28	2.74
0400	3 coats	.75	2.86	3.61
0500	Gypsum lath, plain, 3/8" thick	.41	.45	.86
0600	1/2" thick	.48	.48	.96
0700	Firestop, 3/8" thick	.48	.54	1.02
0800	1/2" thick	.49	.58	1.07
0900	Metal lath, rib, 2.75 lb.	.19	.51	.70
1000	3.40 lb.	.35	.54	.89
1100	Diamond, 2.50 lb.	.20	.51	.71
1200	3.40 lb.	.23	.63	.86
1300				
1400				
1500	Drywall, standard, 1/2" thick, no finish included	.17	.41	.58
1600	Taped and finished	.27	.96	1.23
1700	5/8" thick, no finish included	.26	.41	.67
1800	Taped and finished	.36	.96	1.32
1900	Fire resistant, 1/2" thick, no finish included	.26	.41	.67
2000	Taped and finished	.36	.96	1.32
2100	5/8" thick, no finish included	.23	.41	.64
2200	Taped and finished	.33	.96	1.29
2300	Water resistant, 1/2" thick, no finish included	.25	.41	.66
2400	Taped and finished	.35	.96	1.31
2500	5/8" thick, no finish included	.32	.41	.73
2600	Taped and finished	.42	.96	1.38
2700	Finish, instead of taping			
2800	For thin coat plaster, add	.11	.45	.56
2900	Finish, textured spray, add	.13	.43	.56
3000				
3100				
3200				
3300	Tile, stapled or glued, mineral fiber plastic coated, 5/8" thick	.62	.37	.99
3400	3/4" thick	1.35	.37	1.72
3500	Wood fiber, 1/2" thick	.78	.91	1.69
3600	3/4" thick	1.05	.91	1.96
3700	Suspended, fiberglass, film faced, 5/8" thick	.54	.58	1.12
3800	3" thick	1.33	.81	2.14
3900	Mineral fiber, 5/8" thick, standard	.63	.54	1.17
4000	Aluminum	5.80	.61	6.41
4100	Wood fiber, reveal edge, 1" thick			
4200	3" thick			
4300	Framing, metal furring, 3/4" channels, 12" O.C.	.21	1.63	1.84
4400	16" O.C.	.19	1.18	1.37
4500	24" O.C.	.13	.82	.95
4600				
4700	1-1/2" channels, 12" O.C.	.29	1.80	2.09
4800	16" O.C.	.26	1.32	1.58
4900	24" O.C.	.17	.88	1.05
5000				
5100				
5200				
5300	Ceiling suspension systems, for tile,			
5400	Concealed "Z" bar, 12" module	.37	.70	1.07
5500	Class A, "T" bar 2'-0" x 4'-0" grid	.34	.46	.80
5600	2'-0" x 2'-0" grid	.43	.56	.99
5700	Carrier channels for lighting fixtures, add	.36	.79	1.15
5800				
5900				
6000				

For expanded coverage of these items see Means Interior Cost Data 1999

INTERIOR CONSTR. — A6.9-700 Ceiling Finish

6.9-700 Selective Price Sheet

		COST PER S.F.		
		MAT.	INST.	TOTAL
6100	Wood, furring 1" x 3", on wood, 12" O.C.	.25	1.04	1.29
6200	16" O.C.	.19	.78	.97
6300	24" O.C.	.13	.52	.65
6400				
6500	On concrete, 12" O.C.	.25	1.74	1.99
6600	16" O.C.	.19	1.31	1.50
6700	24" O.C.	.13	.87	1
6800				
6900	Joists, 2" x 4", 12" O.C.	.52	.75	1.27
7000	16" O.C.	.43	.63	1.06
7100	24" O.C.	.35	.51	.86
7200	32" O.C.	.27	.39	.66
7300	2" x 6", 12" O.C.	.77	.76	1.53
7400	16" O.C.	.64	.63	1.27
7500	24" O.C.	.51	.50	1.01
7600	32" O.C.	.38	.37	.75

INTERIOR CONSTR. — A6.9-800 Floor Finish

6.9-800 Selective Price Sheet

		\multicolumn{3}{c}{COST PER S.F.}		
		MAT.	INST.	TOTAL
0100	Flooring, carpet, acrylic, 26 oz. light traffic	1.55	.50	2.05
0200	35 oz. heavy traffic	3.27	.50	3.77
0300	Nylon anti-static, 15 oz. light traffic	1.03	.65	1.68
0400	22 oz. medium traffic	2.05	.50	2.55
0500	26 oz. heavy traffic	2.83	.53	3.36
0600	28 oz. heavy traffic	3.16	.53	3.69
0700	Tile, foamed back, needle punch	2.42	.59	3.01
0800	Tufted loop	1.02	.59	1.61
0900	Wool, 36 oz. medium traffic	7.10	.53	7.63
1000	42 oz. heavy traffic	7.25	.53	7.78
1100	Composition, epoxy, with colored chips, minimum	2.24	2.78	5.02
1200	Maximum	2.72	3.84	6.56
1300	Trowelled, minimum	2.89	3.36	6.25
1400	Maximum	4.21	3.91	8.12
1500	Terrazzo, 1/4" thick, chemical resistant, minimum	4.70	3.59	8.29
1600	Maximum	7.70	4.78	12.48
1700	Resilient, asphalt tile, 1/8" thick	1.03	.84	1.87
1800	Conductive flooring, rubber, 1/8" thick	2.75	1.07	3.82
1900	Cork tile 1/8" thick, standard finish	2.66	1.07	3.73
2000	Urethane finish	4.02	1.07	5.09
2100	PVC sheet goods for gyms, 1/4" thick	3.77	4.20	7.97
2200	3/8" thick	4.26	5.60	9.86
2300	Vinyl composition 12" x 12" tile, plain, 1/16" thick	.75	.67	1.42
2400	1/8" thick	2.21	.67	2.88
2500	Vinyl tile, 12" x 12" x 1/8" thick, minimum	2.13	.67	2.80
2600	Maximum	8.05	.67	8.72
2700	Vinyl sheet goods, backed, .093" thick	1.63	1.46	3.09
2800	.250" thick			
2900	Slate, random rectangular, 1/4" thick	4.61	4.34	8.95
3000	1/2" thick	4.29	6.20	10.49
3100	Natural cleft, irregular, 3/4" thick	1.98	7.10	9.08
3200	For sand rubbed finish, add	2.75		2.75
3300	Terrazzo, cast in place, bonded 1-3/4" thick, gray cement	2.54	5.50	8.04
3400	White cement	2.89	5.50	8.39
3500	Not bonded 3" thick, gray cement	3.17	6.25	9.42
3600	White cement	3.47	6.25	9.72
3700	Precast, 12" x 12" x 1" thick	16.35	22.50	38.85
3800	1-1/4" thick	17.70	22.50	40.20
3900	16" x 16" x 1-1/4" thick	19.25	28.50	47.75
4000	1-1/2" thick	17.60	31	48.60
4100	Marble travertine, standard, 12" x 12" x 3/4" thick	10.40	10.10	20.50
4200				
4300	Tile, ceramic, natural clay, thin set	3.91	3.32	7.23
4400	Porcelain, thin set	4.77	3.20	7.97
4500	Specialty, decorator finish	7.65	3.32	10.97
4600				
4700	Quarry, red, mud set, 4" x 4" x 1/2" thick	4.04	5.05	9.09
4800	6" x 6" x 1/2" thick	2.92	4.34	7.26
4900	Brown, imported, 6" x 6" x 3/4" thick	4.79	5.05	9.84
5000	8" x 8" x 1" thick	5.40	5.50	10.90
5100	Slate, vermont, thin set, 6" x 6" x 1/4" thick	4.55	3.37	7.92
5200				
5300	Wood, maple strip, 25/32" x 2-1/4", finished, select	3.37	2.32	5.69
5400	2nd and better	3.04	2.32	5.36
5500	Oak, 25/32" x 2-1/4" finished, clear	3.09	2.32	5.41
5600	No. 1 common	3.70	2.32	6.02
5700	Parquet, standard, 5/16", finished, minimum	1.81	2.46	4.27
5800	Maximum	5.75	3.83	9.58
5900	Custom, finished, minimum	14.75	3.66	18.41
6000	Maximum	19.50	7.30	26.80

For expanded coverage of these items see *Means Interior Cost Data 1999*

INTERIOR CONSTR. — A6.9-800 Floor Finish

6.9-800 Selective Price Sheet

		COST PER S.F.		
		MAT.	INST.	TOTAL
6100	Prefinished, oak, 2-1/4" wide	6.45	2.15	8.60
6200	Ranch plank	8	2.52	10.52
6300	Sleepers on concrete, treated, 24" O.C., 1" x 2"	.14	.24	.38
6400	1" x 3"	.24	.31	.55
6500	2" x 4"	.63	.43	1.06
6600	2" x 6"	.93	.49	1.42
6700	Refinish old floors, minimum	.71	.72	1.43
6800	Maximum	1.08	2.21	3.29
6900	Subflooring, plywood, CDX, 1/2" thick	.45	.49	.94
7000	5/8" thick	.54	.54	1.08
7100	3/4" thick	.64	.58	1.22
7200				
7300	1" x 10" boards, S4S, laid regular	1.06	.66	1.72
7400	Laid diagonal	1.07	.81	1.88
7500	1" x 8" boards, S4S, laid regular	.95	.73	1.68
7600	Laid diagonal	.94	.86	1.80
7700	Underlayment, plywood, underlayment grade, 3/8" thick	.73	.49	1.22
7800	1/2" thick	.83	.50	1.33
7900	5/8" thick	.69	.52	1.21
8000	3/4" thick	.95	.56	1.51
8100	Particle board, 3/8" thick	.42	.49	.91
8200	1/2" thick	.44	.50	.94
8300	5/8" thick	.59	.52	1.11
8400	3/4" thick	.45	.56	1.01

For information about Means Estimating Seminars, see yellow pages 11 and 12 in back of book

Division 7
Conveying Systems

CONVEYING — A7.1-142 | Oil Hydraulic Elevators

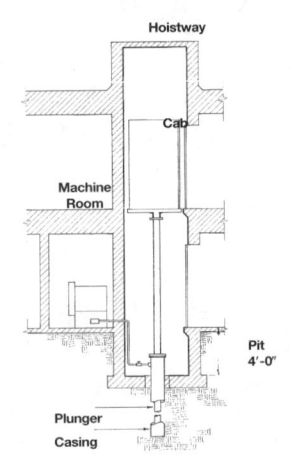

This page illustrates and describes oil hydraulic elevator systems. Prices for various oil hydraulic elevator systems are on Line Items 7.1-142-0400 thru 2000. Both material quantities and labor costs have been adjusted for the system listed.

Factors: To adjust for job conditions other than normal working situations use Lines 7.1-142-3100 thru 4000.

Example: You are to install the system with limited equipment usage. Go to Line 7.1-142-3400 and apply this percentage to the appropriate TOTAL costs.

7.1-142	Oil Hydraulic Elevators	MAT.	INST.	TOTAL
0310	Oil-hydraulic elevator systems			
0320	Including piston and piston shaft			
0330				
0400	1500 Lb. passenger, 2 floors	29,200	8,300	37,500
0500	3 floors	32,800	12,800	45,600
0600	4 floors	44,000	18,000	62,000
0700	5 floors	47,200	22,500	69,700
0800	6 floors	50,000	26,800	76,800
0900				
1000	2500 Lb. passenger, 2 floors	30,400	8,300	38,700
1100	3 floors	34,000	12,800	46,800
1200	4 floors	42,300	18,000	60,300
1300	5 floors	45,500	22,500	68,000
1400	6 floors	51,500	26,800	78,300
1500				
1600	4000 Lb. passenger, 2 floors	34,900	8,300	43,200
1700	3 floors	39,300	12,800	52,100
1800	4 floors	49,600	18,000	67,600
1900	5 floors	53,000	22,500	75,500
2000	6 floors	56,000	26,800	82,800
2100				
2200				
2300				
2400				
2500				
2600				
2700				
2800				
2900				
3000				
3100	Dust protection, add, minimum	1%	2%	
3200	Maximum	4%	11%	
3300	Equipment usage curtailment, add, minimum	1%	1%	
3400	Maximum	3%	10%	
3500	Material handling & storage limitation, add, minimum	1%	1%	
3600	Maximum	6%	7%	
3700	Protection of existing work, add, minimum	2%	2%	
3800	Maximum	5%	7%	
3900	Shift work requirements, add, minimum		5%	
4000	Maximum		30%	

Division 8
Mechanical

MECHANICAL | A8.1-710 | Plumbing - Public Restroom

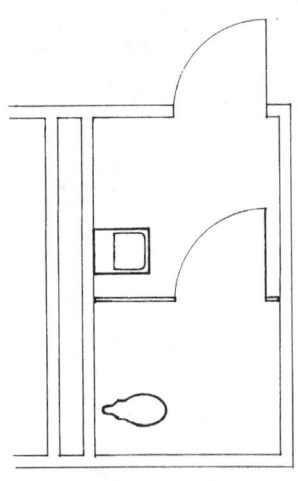

This page illustrates and describes a women's public restroom system including a water closet, lavatory, accessories, and service piping. Lines within System Components give the unit price and total price on a cost each basis for this system. Prices for alternate women's public restroom systems are on Line Items 8.1-710-1400 thru 1700. Both material quantities and labor costs have been adjusted for the system listed.

Factors: To adjust for job conditions other than normal working situations use Lines 8.1-710-2900 thru 4000.

Example: You are to install the system and protect surrounding area from dust. Go to Line 8.1-710-3100 and apply these percentages to the MAT. and INST. costs.

System Components	QUANTITY	UNIT	COST EACH		
			MAT.	INST.	TOTAL
Public women's restroom incl. water closet, lavatory, accessories and Necessary service piping to install this system in one wall.					
Water closet, wall mounted, one piece	1.000	Ea.	380	127	507
Rough-in waste and vent for water closet	1.000	Set	292	287	579
Lavatory, 20" x 18" P.E. cast iron with accessories	1.000	Ea.	203	92	295
Rough-in waste and vent for lavatory	1.000	Set	178	445	623
Partition, painted metal between walls, floor mounted, access.	1.000	Ea.	759	158.60	917.60
Accessories	1.000	Set	541.30	96.30	637.60
TOTAL		System	2,353.30	1,205.90	3,559.20

8.1-710	Plumbing - Public Restroom	COST EACH		
		MAT.	INST.	TOTAL
1200				
1300	For alternate size restrooms:			
1400	Two water closets, two lavatories	3,950	2,300	6,250
1500				
1600	For each additional water closet over 2, add	1,075	530	1,605
1700	For each additional lavatory over 2, add	520	575	1,095
1800				
1900				
2400	NOTE: PLUMBING APPROXIMATIONS			
2500	WATER CONTROL: water meter, backflow preventer,			
2600	Shock absorbers, vacuum breakers, mixer....10 to 15% of fixtures			
2700	PIPE AND FITTINGS: .... 30 to 60% of fixtures			
2800				
2900	Cut & patch to match existing construction, add, minimum	2%	3%	
3000	Maximum	5%	9%	
3100	Dust protection, add, minimum	1%	2%	
3200	Maximum	4%	11%	
3300	Equipment usage curtailment, add, minimum	1%	1%	
3400	Maximum	3%	10%	
3500	Material handling & storage limitation, add, minimum	1%	1%	
3600	Maximum	6%	7%	
3700	Protection of existing work, add, minimum	2%	2%	
3800	Maximum	5%	7%	
3900	Shift work requirements, add, minimum		5%	
4000	Maximum		30%	

MECHANICAL | A8.1-720 | Plumbing - Public Restroom

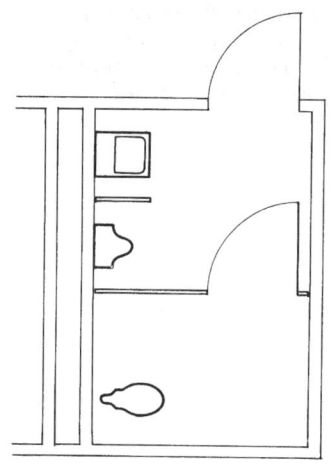

This page illustrates and describes a men's public restroom system including a water closet, urinal, lavatory, accessories and service piping. Lines within System Components give the unit price and total price on a cost each basis for this system. Prices for alternate men's public restroom systems are on Line Items 8.1-720-1800 thru 2200. Both material quantities and labor costs have been adjusted for the system listed.

Factors: To adjust for job conditions other than normal working situations use Lines 8.1-720-2900 thru 4000.

Example: You are to install the system and match existing construction. Go to Line 8.1-720-3000 and apply these percentages to the appropriate MAT. and INST. costs.

System Components	QUANTITY	UNIT	COST EACH MAT.	INST.	TOTAL
Public men's restroom incl. water closet, urinal, lavatory, accessories, And necessary service piping to install this system in one wall.					
Water closet, wall mounted, one piece	1.000	Ea.	380	127	507
Rough-in waste & vent for water closet	1.000	Set	292	287	579
Urinal, wall hung	1.000	Ea.	298	245	543
Rough-in waste & vent for urinal	1.000	Set	96.50	260	356.50
Lavatory, 20" x 18", P.E. cast iron with accessories	1.000	Ea.	203	92	295
Rough-in waste & vent for lavatory	1.000	Set	178	445	623
Partition, painted mtl., between walls, floor mntd., accessories	1.000	Ea.	759	158.60	917.60
Urinal screen, painted metal, wall mounted	1.000	Ea.	247	73	320
Accessories	1.000	Set	191.30	71.80	263.10
TOTAL		System	2,644.80	1,759.40	4,404.20

8.1-720	Plumbing - Public Restroom	COST EACH MAT.	INST.	TOTAL
1600				
1700	For alternate size restrooms:			
1800	Two water closets, two urinals, two lavatories	4,875	3,425	8,300
1900				
2000	For each additional water closet over 2, add	1,075	530	1,605
2100	For each additional urinal over 2, add	640	580	1,220
2200	For each additional lavatory over 2, add	520	575	1,095
2300				
2400	NOTE: PLUMBING APPROXIMATIONS			
2500	WATER CONTROL: water meter, backflow preventer,			
2600	Shock absorbers, vacuum breakers, mixer....10 to 15% of fixtures			
2700	PIPE AND FITTINGS: .... 30 to 60% of fixtures			
2800				
2900	Cut & patch to match existing construction, add, minimum	2%	3%	
3000	Maximum	5%	9%	
3100	Dust protection, add, minimum	1%	2%	
3200	Maximum	4%	11%	
3300	Equipment usage curtailment, add, minimum	1%	1%	
3400	Maximum	3%	10%	
3500	Material handling, & storage limitation, add, minimum	1%	1%	
3600	Maximum	6%	7%	
3700	Protection of existing work, add, minimum	2%	2%	
3800	Maximum	5%	7%	
3900	Shift work requirements, add, minimum		5%	
4000	Maximum		30%	

MECHANICAL | A8.1-920 | Plumbing - Two Fixture Bathroom

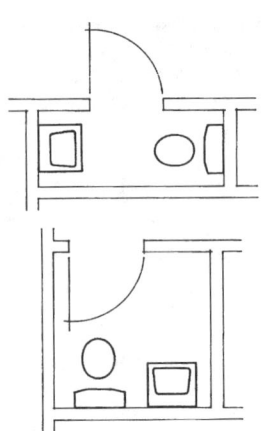

This page illustrates and describes a two fixture lavatory system including a water closet, lavatory, accessories and all service piping. Lines within System Components give the unit price and total price on a cost each basis for this system. Prices for an alternate two fixture lavatory system are on Line Item 8.1-920-1900. Both material quantities and labor costs have been adjusted for the system listed.

Factors: To adjust for job conditions other than normal working situations use Lines 8.1-920-2900 thru 4000.

Example: You are to install the system while controlling dust in the work area. Go to Line 8.1-920-3200 and apply these percentages to the appropriate MAT. and INST. costs.

System Components	QUANTITY	UNIT	COST EACH		
			MAT.	INST.	TOTAL
Two fixture bathroom incl. water closet, lavatory, accessories and Necessary service piping to install this system in 2 walls.					
Water closet, floor mounted, 2 piece, close coupled	1.000	Ea.	146	139	285
Rough in waste & vent for water closet	1.000	Set	128	241	369
Lavatory, 20" x 18", P.E. cast iron with accessories	1.000	Ea.	203	92	295
Rough in waste & vent for lavatory	1.000	Set	178	445	623
Additional service piping					
1/2" copper pipe with sweat solder joints	10.000	L.F.	13.90	50.50	64.40
2" black schedule 40 steel pipe with threaded couplings	12.000	L.F.	40.44	138	178.44
4" cast iron soil pipe with lead and oakum joints	7.000	L.F.	63.70	93.45	157.15
Accessories					
Toilet tissue dispenser, chrome, single roll	1.000	Ea.	11.30	12.20	23.50
18" long stainless steel towel bar	1.000	Ea.	32	15.90	47.90
Medicine cabinet with mirror, 20" x 16", unlighted	1.000	Ea.	69.50	26	95.50
TOTAL		System	885.84	1,253.05	2,138.89

8.1-920	Plumbing - Two Fixture Bathroom	COST EACH		
		MAT.	INST.	TOTAL
1800				
1900	Above system installed in 1 wall with all necessary service piping	840	1,100	1,940
2000				
2400	NOTE: PLUMBING APPROXIMATIONS			
2500	WATER CONTROL: water meter, backflow preventer,			
2600	Shock absorbers, vacuum breakers, mixer....10 to 15% of fixtures			
2700	PIPE AND FITTINGS: .... 30 to 60% of fixtures			
2800				
2900	Cut & patch to match existing construction, add, minimum	2%	3%	
3000	Maximum	5%	9%	
3100	Dust protection, add, minimum	1%	2%	
3200	Maximum	4%	11%	
3300	Equipment usage curtailment, add, minimum	1%	1%	
3400	Maximum	3%	10%	
3500	Material handling & storage limitation, add, minimum	1%	1%	
3600	Maximum	6%	7%	
3700	Protection of existing work, add, minimum	2%	2%	
3800	Maximum	5%	7%	
3900	Shift work requirements, add, minimum		5%	
4000	Maximum		30%	

MECHANICAL — A8.1-931 | Plumbing - Three Fixture Bathroom

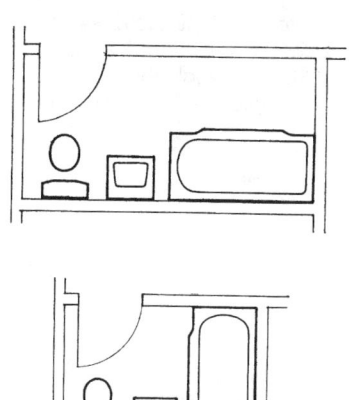

This page illustrates and describes a three fixture bathroom system including a water closet, tub, lavatory, accessories and service piping. Lines within System Components give the unit price and total price on a cost each basis for this system. Prices for an alternate three fixture bathroom system are on Line Item 8.1-931-1700. Both material quantities and labor costs have been adjusted for the system listed.

Factors: To adjust for job conditions other than normal working situations use Lines 8.1-931-2900 thru 4000.

Example: You are to install the system and protect all existing work. Go to Line 8.1-931-3800 and apply these percentages to the appropriate MAT. and INST. costs.

System Components

	QUANTITY	UNIT	MAT.	INST.	TOTAL
Three fixture bathroom incl. water closet, bathtub, lavatory, accessories, And necessary service piping to install this system in 2 walls.					
Water closet, floor mounted, 2 piece, close coupled	1.000	Ea.	146	139	285
Rough-in waste & vent for water closet	1.000	Set	119.04	224.13	343.17
Bathtub, P.E. cast iron 5' long with accessories	1.000	Ea.	375	167	542
Rough-in waste & vent for bathtub	1.000	Set	134.90	337.25	472.15
Lavatory, 20" x 18" P.E. cast iron with accessories	1.000	Ea.	203	92	295
Rough-in waste & vent for lavatory	1.000	Set	178	445	623
Accessories					
Toilet tissue dispenser, chrome, single roll	1.000	Ea.	11.30	12.20	23.50
18" long stainless steel towel bar	2.000	Ea.	64	31.80	95.80
Medicine cabinet with mirror, 20" x 16", unlighted	1.000	Ea.	69.50	26	95.50
TOTAL		System	1,300.74	1,474.38	2,775.12

8.1-931 Plumbing - Three Fixture Bathroom

		MAT.	INST.	TOTAL
1600				
1700	Above system installed in one wall with all necessary service piping	1,275	1,450	2,725
2400	NOTE: PLUMBING APPROXIMATIONS			
2500	WATER CONTROL: water meter, backflow preventer,			
2600	Shock absorbers, vacuum breakers, mixer....10 to 15% of fixtures			
2700	PIPE AND FITTINGS: .... 30 to 60% of fixtures			
2800				
2900	Cut & patch to match existing construction, add, minimum	2%	3%	
3000	Maximum	5%	9%	
3100	Dust protection, add, minimum	1%	2%	
3200	Maximum	4%	11%	
3300	Equipment usage curtailment, add, minimum	1%	1%	
3400	Maximum	3%	10%	
3500	Material handling & storage limitation, add, minimum	1%	1%	
3600	Maximum	6%	7%	
3700	Protection of existing work, add, minimum	2%	2%	
3800	Maximum	5%	7%	
3900	Shift work requirements, add, minimum		5%	
4000	Maximum		30%	

MECHANICAL — A8.1-932 Plumbing - Three Fixture Bathroom

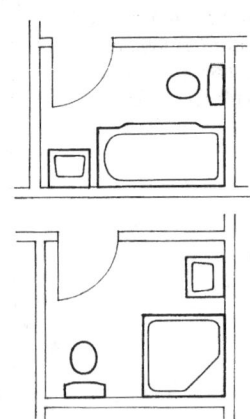

This page illustrates and describes a three fixture bathroom system including a water closet, tub, lavatory, accessories, and service piping. Lines within System Components give the unit price and total price on a cost each basis for this system. Prices for an alternate three fixture bathroom system are on Line Item 8.1-932-2000. Both material quantities and labor costs have been adjusted for the system listed.

Factors: To adjust for job conditions other than normal working situations use Lines 8.1-932-2900 thru 4000.

Example: You are to install the system and protect the surrounding area from dust. Go to Line 8.1-932-3100 and apply these percentages to the appropriate MAT. and INST. costs.

System Components	QUANTITY	UNIT	COST EACH MAT.	INST.	TOTAL
Three fixture bathroom incl. water closet, bathtub, lavatory, accessories,					
And necessary service piping to install this system in 2 walls.					
Water closet, floor mounted, 2 piece, close coupled	1.000	Ea.	146	139	285
Rough-in waste & vent for water closet	1.000	Set	128	241	369
Bathtub, P.E. cast iron, 5' long with accessories	1.000	Ea.	375	167	542
Rough-in waste & vent for bathtub	1.000	Set	142	355	497
Lavatory, 20" x 18" P.E. cast iron with accessories	1.000	Ea.	203	92	295
Rough-in waste & vent for lavatory	1.000	Set	178	445	623
Additional service piping					
1-1/4" copper DWV type tubing, sweat solder joints	6.000	L.F.	16.86	40.80	57.66
2" black schedule 40 steel pipe with threaded couplings	12.000	L.F.	40.44	138	178.44
Accessories					
Toilet tissue dispenser, chrome, single roll	1.000	Ea.	11.30	12.20	23.50
18" long stainless steel towel bar	2.000	Ea.	64	31.80	95.80
Medicine cabinet with mirror, 20" x 16", unlighted	1.000	Ea.	69.50	26	95.50
TOTAL		System	1,374.10	1,687.80	3,061.90

8.1-932	Plumbing - Three Fixture Bathroom	COST EACH MAT.	INST.	TOTAL
2000	Above system with corner contour tub, P.E. cast iron	2,300	1,700	4,000
2300				
2400	NOTE: PLUMBING APPROXIMATIONS			
2500	WATER CONTROL: water meter, backflow preventer,			
2600	Shock absorbers, vacuum breakers, mixer....10 to 15% of fixtures			
2700	PIPE AND FITTINGS: .... 30 to 60% of fixtures			
2800				
2900	Cut & patch to match existing construction, add, minimum	2%	3%	
3000	Maximum	5%	9%	
3100	Dust protection, add, minimum	1%	2%	
3200	Maximum	4%	11%	
3300	Equipment usage curtailment, add, minimum	1%	1%	
3400	Maximum	3%	10%	
3500	Material handling & storage limitation, add, minimum	1%	1%	
3600	Maximum	6%	7%	
3700	Protection of existing work, add, minimum	2%	2%	
3800	Maximum	5%	7%	
3900	Shift work requirements, add, minimum		5%	
4000	Maximum		30%	

MECHANICAL | A8.1-933 | Plumbing - Three Fixture Bathroom

This page illustrates and describes a three fixture bathroom system including a water closet, shower, lavatory, accessories, and service piping, Lines within System Components give the unit price and total price on a cost each basis for this system. Prices for an alternate three fixture bathroom system are on Line Item 8.1-933-2200. Both material quantities and labor costs have been adjusted for the system listed.

Factors: To adjust for job conditions other than normal working situations use Lines 8.1-933-2900 thru 4000.

Example: You are to install the system and protect existing construction. Go to Line 8.1-933-3700 and apply these percentages to the appropriate MAT. and INST. costs.

System Components

	QUANTITY	UNIT	COST EACH		
			MAT.	INST.	TOTAL
Three fixture bathroom incl. water closet, shower, lavatory, accessories, And necessary service piping to install this system in 2 walls.					
Water closet, floor mounted, 2 piece, close coupled	1.000	Ea.	146	139	285
Rough-in waste & vent for water closet	1.000	Set	128	241	369
32" shower, enameled stall, molded stone receptor	1.000	Ea.	385	365	750
Rough-in waste & vent for shower	1.000	Set	88.50	360	448.50
Lavatory, 20" x 18" P.E. cast iron with accessories	1.000	Ea.	203	92	295
Rough-in waste & vent for lavatory	1.000	Set	178	445	623
Additional service piping					
1-1/4" Copper DWV type tubing, sweat solder joints	4.000	L.F.	11.24	27.20	38.44
2" black schedule 40 steel pipe with threaded couplings	6.000	L.F.	20.22	69	89.22
4" cast iron soil with lead and oakum joints	7.000	L.F.	63.70	93.45	157.15
Accessories					
Toilet tissue dispenser, chrome, single roll	1.000	Ea.	11.30	12.20	23.50
18" long stainless steel towel bar	2.000	Ea.	64	31.80	95.80
Medicine cabinet with mirror, 20" x 16", unlighted	1.000	Ea.	69.50	26	95.50
TOTAL		System	1,368.46	1,901.65	3,270.11

8.1-933	Plumbing - Three Fixture Bathroom	COST EACH		
		MAT.	INST.	TOTAL
2100	Above system installed with 36" corner angle shower, enameled steel,			
2200	Molded stone receptor	1,800	1,950	3,750
2300				
2400	NOTE: PLUMBING APPROXIMATIONS			
2500	WATER CONTROL: water meter, backflow preventer,			
2600	Shock absorbers, vacuum breakers, mixer....10 to 15% of fixtures			
2700	PIPE AND FITTINGS: .... 30 to 60% of fixtures			
2800				
2900	Cut & patch to match existing construction, add, minimum	2%	3%	
3000	Maximum	5%	9%	
3100	Dust protection, add, minimum	1%	2%	
3200	Maximum	4%	11%	
3300	Equipment usage curtailment, add, minimum	1%	1%	
3400	Maximum	3%	10%	
3500	Material handling & storage limitation, add, minimum	1%	1%	
3600	Maximum	6%	7%	
3700	Protection of existing work, add, minimum	2%	2%	
3800	Maximum	5%	7%	
3900	Shift work requirements, add, minimum		5%	
4000	Maximum		30%	

For expanded coverage of these items see *Means Mechanical or Plumbing Cost Data 1999*

MECHANICAL | A8.1-940 | Plumbing - Four Fixture Bathroom

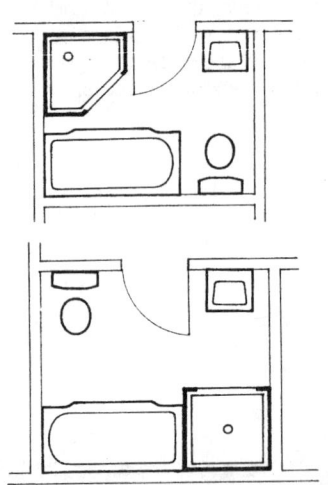

This page illustrates and describes a four fixture bathroom system including a water closet, shower, bathtub, lavatory, accessories, and service piping. Lines within System Components give the unit price and total price on a cost each basis for this system. Prices for an alternate four fixture bathroom system are on Line Item 8.1-940-1900. Both material quantities and labor costs have been adjusted for the system listed.

Factors: To adjust for job conditions other than normal working situations use Lines 8.1-940-2900 thru 4000.

Example: You are to install the system during weekends and evenings. Go to Line 8.1-940-4000 and apply these percentages to the appropriate MAT. and INST. costs.

System Components	QUANTITY	UNIT	COST EACH		
			MAT.	INST.	TOTAL
Four fixture bathroom incl. water closet, shower, bathtub, lavatory Accessories and necessary service piping to install this system in 2 walls.					
Water closet, floor mounted, 2 piece, close coupled	1.000	Ea.	146	139	285
Rough-in waste & vent for water closet	1.000	Set	128	241	369
32" shower, enameled steel stall, molded stone receptor	1.000	Ea.	385	365	750
Rough-in waste & vent for shower	1.000	Set	88.50	360	448.50
Bathtub, P.E. cast iron, 5' long with accessories	1.000	Ea.	375	167	542
Rough-in waste & vent for bathtub	1.000	Set	142	355	497
Lavatory, 20" x 18" P.E. cast iron with accessories	1.000	Ea.	203	92	295
Rough-in waste & vent for lavatory	1.000	Set	178	445	623
Accessories					
Toilet tissue dispenser, chrome, single roll	1.000	Ea.	11.30	12.20	23.50
18" long stainless steel towel bar	2.000	Ea.	64	31.80	95.80
Medicine cabinet with mirror, 20" x 16" unlighted	1.000	Ea.	69.50	26	95.50
TOTAL		System	1,790.30	2,234	4,024.30

8.1-940	Plumbing - Four Fixture Bathroom	COST EACH		
		MAT.	INST.	TOTAL
1900	Above system with 36" corner angle shower, plumbing in 3 walls	2,275	2,475	4,750
2000				
2300				
2400	NOTE: PLUMBING APPROXIMATIONS			
2500	WATER CONTROL: water meter, backflow preventer,			
2600	Shock absorbers, vacuum breakers, mixer....10 to 15% of fixtures			
2700	PIPE AND FITTINGS: .... 30 to 60% of fixtures			
2800				
2900	Cut & patch to match existing construction, add, minimum	2%	3%	
3000	Maximum	5%	9%	
3100	Dust protection, add, minimum	1%	2%	
3200	Maximum	4%	11%	
3300	Equipment usage curtailment, add, minimum	1%	1%	
3400	Maximum	3%	10%	
3500	Material handling & storage limitation, add, minimum	1%	1%	
3600	Maximum	6%	7%	
3700	Protection of existing work, add, minimum	2%	2%	
3800	Maximum	5%	7%	
3900	Shift work requirements, add, minimum		5%	
4000	Maximum		30%	

MECHANICAL — A8.1-950 Plumbing - Five Fixture Bathroom

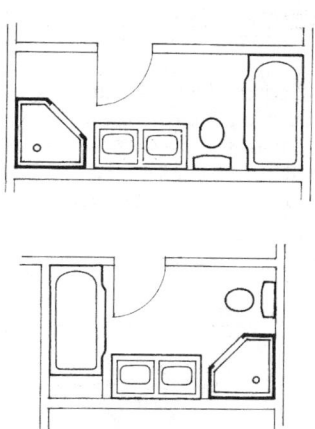

This page illustrates and describes a five fixture bathroom system including a water closet, shower, bathtub, lavatories, accessories, and service piping. Lines within System Components give the unit price and total price on a cost each basis for this system. Prices for an alternate five fixture bathroom system are on Line Item 8.1-950-1900. Both material quantities and labor costs have been adjusted for the system listed.

Factors: To adjust for job conditions other than normal working situations use Lines 8.1-950-2900 thru 4000.

Example: You are to install and match any existing construction. Go to Line 8.1-950-2900 and apply these percentages to the appropriate MAT. and INST. costs.

System Components

System Components	QUANTITY	UNIT	MAT.	INST.	TOTAL
Five fixture bathroom incl. water closet, shower, bathtub, 2 lavatories, Accessories and necessary service piping to install this system in 1 wall.					
Water closet, floor mounted, 2 piece, close coupled	1.000	Ea.	146	139	285
Rough-in waste & vent for water closet	1.000	Set	128	241	369
36" corner angle shower, enameled steel stall, molded stone receptor	1.000	Ea.	805	410	1,215
Rough-in waste & vent for shower	1.000	Set	88.50	360	448.50
Bathtub, P.E. cast iron, 5' long with accessories	1.000	Ea.	375	167	542
Rough-in waste & vent for bathtub	1.000	Set	142	355	497
Lavatories, 20" x 18" cabinet mntd, PECI with access. & cabinet	2.000	Ea.	642	345.30	987.30
Rough-in waste & vent for lavatories	1.600	Set	130.40	512	642.40
Accessories					
Toilet tissue dispenser, chrome, single roll	1.000	Ea.	11.30	12.20	23.50
18" long stainless steel towel bars	2.000	Ea.	64	31.80	95.80
Medicine cabinet with mirror, 20" x 16", unlighted	2.000	Ea.	139	52	191
TOTAL		System	2,671.20	2,625.30	5,296.50

8.1-950	Plumbing - Five Fixture Bathroom	MAT.	INST.	TOTAL
1900	Above system installed in 2 walls with all necessary service piping	2,700	2,700	5,400
2000				
2100				
2200				
2300				
2400	NOTE: PLUMBING APPROXIMATIONS			
2500	WATER CONTROL: water meter, backflow preventer,			
2600	Shock absorbers, vacuum breakers, mixer....10 to 15% of fixtures			
2700	PIPE AND FITTINGS: .... 30 to 60% of fixtures			
2800				
2900	Cut & patch to match existing construction, add, minimum	2%	3%	
3000	Maximum	5%	9%	
3100	Dust protection, add, minimum	1%	2%	
3200	Maximum	4%	11%	
3300	Equipment usage curtailment, add, minimum	1%	1%	
3400	Maximum	3%	10%	
3500	Material handling & storage limitation, add, minimum	1%	1%	
3600	Maximum	6%	7%	
3700	Protection of existing work, add, minimum	2%	2%	
3800	Maximum	5%	7%	
3900	Shift work requirements, add, minimum		5%	
4000	Maximum		30%	

For expanded coverage of these items see *Means Mechanical or Plumbing Cost Data 1999*

MECHANICAL — A8.2-910 Fire Sprinkler Systems, Wet

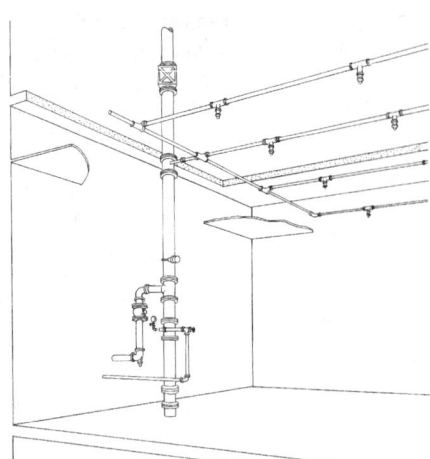

This page illustrates and describes a wet type fire sprinkler system. Lines within System Components give the unit cost of a system for a 2,000 square foot building. Lines 8.2-910-1900 thru 2600 give the square foot costs for alternate systems. Both material quantities and labor costs have been adjusted for the system listed.

Factors: To adjust for conditions other than normal working conditions, use Lines 8.2-910-2900 thru 4000.

System Components	QUANTITY	UNIT	MAT.	INST.	TOTAL
Wet pipe fire sprinkler system, ordinary hazard, open area to 2000 S.F. On one floor.					
4" OS & Y valve	1.000	Ea.	244	245	489
Wet pipe alarm valve	1.000	Ea.	775	365	1,140
Water motor alarm	1.000	Ea.	161	102	263
3" check valve	1.000	Ea.	105	244	349
Pipe riser, 4" diameter	10.000	L.F.	73	213.30	286.30
Water gauges and trim	1.000	Set	1,150	735	1,885
Electric fire horn	1.000	Ea.	40	59	99
Sprinkler head supply piping	168.000	L.F.	473.55	1,642.10	2,115.65
Pipe fittings	1.000	Set	384.48	1,554	1,938.48
Sprinkler heads	16.000	Ea.	64	408	472
Fire department connection	1.000	Ea.	241	147	388
TOTAL		System	3,711.03	5,714.40	9,425.43

8.2-910	Fire Sprinkler Systems, Wet	MAT.	INST.	TOTAL
1900	Ordinary hazard, one floor, area to 2000 S.F./floor	1.86	2.84	4.70
2000	For each additional floor, add per floor	.50	1.90	2.40
2100	Area to 3200 S.F./floor	1.34	2.59	3.93
2200	For each additional floor, add per floor	.49	1.99	2.48
2300	Area to 5000 S.F./floor	1.18	2.47	3.65
2400	For each additional floor, add per floor	.63	2.09	2.72
2500	Area to 8000 S.F./floor	.85	2.04	2.89
2600	For each additional floor, add per floor	.51	1.80	2.31
2700				
2900	Cut & patch to match existing construction, add, minimum	2%	3%	
3000	Maximum	5%	9%	
3100	Dust protection, add, minimum	1%	2%	
3200	Maximum	4%	11%	
3300	Equipment usage curtailment, add, minimum	1%	1%	
3400	Maximum	3%	10%	
3500	Material handling & storage limitation, add, minimum	1%	1%	
3600	Maximum	6%	7%	
3700	Protection of existing work, add, minimum	2%	2%	
3800	Maximum	5%	7%	
3900	Shift work requirements, add, minimum		5%	
4000	Maximum		30%	

MECHANICAL | A8.2-920 | Fire Sprinkler Systems, Dry

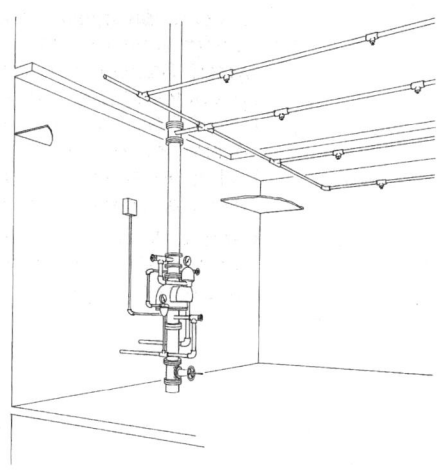

This page illustrates and describes a dry type fire sprinkler system. Lines within System Components give the unit cost of a system for a 2,000 square foot building. Lines 8.2-920-1700 thru 2400 give the square foot costs for alternate systems. Both material quantities and labor costs have been adjusted for the system listed.

Factors: To adjust for conditions other than normal working conditions, use Lines 8.2-920-2900 thru 4000.

System Components	QUANTITY	UNIT	COST EACH		
			MAT.	INST.	TOTAL
Pre-action fire sprinkler system, ordinary hazard, open area to 2000 S.F. On one floor.					
Air compressor	1.000	Ea.	770	315	1,085
4" OS & Y valve	1.000	Ea.	244	245	489
Pipe riser 4" diameter	10.000	L.F.	73	213.30	286.30
Sprinkler head supply piping	163.000	L.F.	457.05	1,589.85	2,046.90
Pipe fittings	1.000	Set	372.88	1,522	1,894.88
Detectors	2.000	Ea.	538	51	589
Sprinkler heads	16.000	Ea.	64	408	472
Fire department connection	1.000	Ea.	241	147	388
TOTAL		System	2,759.93	4,491.15	7,251.08

8.2-920	Fire Sprinkler Systems, Dry	COST PER S.F.		
		MAT.	INST.	TOTAL
1700	Ordinary hazard, one floor, area to 2000 S.F./floor	1.38	2.24	3.62
1800	For each additional floor, add per floor	.48	1.86	2.34
1900	Area to 3200 S.F./ floor	1.06	2.24	3.30
2000	For each additional floor, add per floor	.49	1.99	2.48
2100	Area to 5000 S.F./ floor	1.10	2.25	3.35
2200	For each additional floor, add per floor	.63	2.09	2.72
2300	Area to 8000 S.F./ floor	.84	1.91	2.75
2400	For each additional floor, add per floor	.51	1.80	2.31
2500				
2600				
2700				
2800				
2900	Cut & patch to match existing construction, add, minimum	2%	3%	
3000	Maximum	5%	9%	
3100	Dust protection, add, minimum	1%	2%	
3200	Maximum	4%	11%	
3300	Equipment usage curtailment, add, minimum	1%	1%	
3400	Maximum	3%	10%	
3500	Material handling & storage limitation, add, minimum	1%	1%	
3600	Maximum	6%	7%	
3700	Protection of existing work, add, minimum	2%	2%	
3800	Maximum	5%	7%	
3900	Shift work requirements, add, minimum		5%	
4000	Maximum		30%	

For expanded coverage of these items see Means Mechanical or Plumbing Cost Data 1999

MECHANICAL | A8.3-270 | Heating - Oil Fired Hot Water

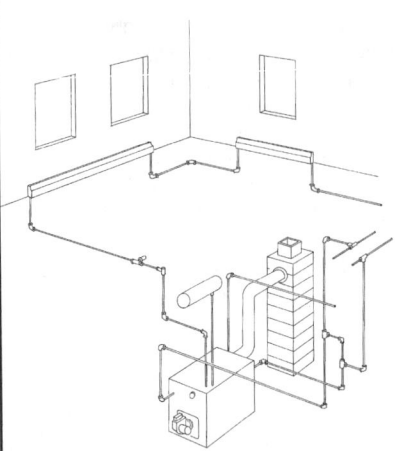

This page illustrates and describes an oil fired hot water baseboard system including an oil fired boiler, fin tube radiation and all fittings and piping. Lines within System Components give the unit price and total price per square foot for this system. Prices for alternate oil fired hot water baseboard systems are on Line Items 8.3-270-1700 thru 2100. Both material quantities and labor costs have been adjusted for the system listed.

Factors: To adjust for job conditions other than normal working situations use Lines 8.3-270-2900 thru 4000.

Example: You are to install the system while protecting all existing work. Go to Line 8.3-270-3700 and apply these percentages to the appropriate MAT. and INST. costs.

System Components	QUANTITY	UNIT	COST PER S.F.		
			MAT.	INST.	TOTAL
Oil fired hot water baseboard system including boiler, fin tube radiation And all necessary fittings and piping.					
Area to 800 S.F.					
Boiler, cast iron, w/oil piping, 97 MBH	1.000	Ea.	1,718.75	756.25	2,475
Copper piping	130.000	L.F.	444.60	916.50	1,361.10
Fin tube radiation	68.000	L.F.	659.60	867	1,526.60
Circulator	1.000	Ea.	330	122	452
Oil tank	1.000	Ea.	251	148	399
Expansion tank, ASME	1.000	Ea.	360	52.50	412.50
TOTAL		System	3,763.95	2,862.25	6,626.20
COST PER S.F.		S.F.	4.70	3.58	8.28

8.3-270	Heating - Oil Fired Hot Water	COST PER S.F.		
		MAT.	INST.	TOTAL
1600	For alternate hot water systems:			
1700	Cast iron boiler, area to 1000 S.F.	4.09	3.09	7.18
1800	To 1200 S.F.	3.57	2.81	6.38
1900	To 1600 S.F.	3.95	2.83	6.78
2000	To 2000 S.F.	3.34	2.54	5.88
2100	To 3000 S.F.	2.54	2.14	4.68
2200				
2300				
2700				
2800				
2900	Cut & patch to match existing construction, add, minimum	2%	3%	
3000	Maximum	5%	9%	
3100	Dust protection, add, minimum	1%	2%	
3200	Maximum	4%	11%	
3300	Equipment usage curtailment, add, minimum	1%	1%	
3400	Maximum	3%	10%	
3500	Material handling & storage limitation, add, minimum	1%	1%	
3600	Maximum	6%	7%	
3700	Protection of existing work, add, minimum	2%	2%	
3800	Maximum	5%	7%	
3900	Shift work requirements, add, minimum		5%	
4000	Maximum		30%	

MECHANICAL | A8.3-280 | Heating - Gas Fired Hot Water

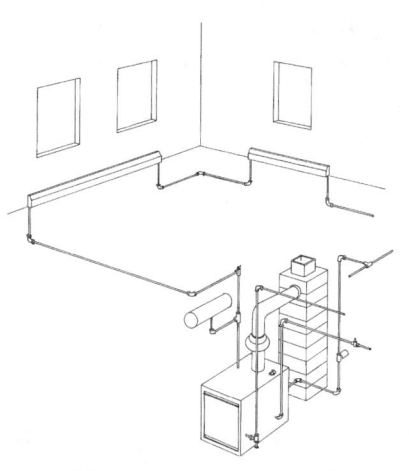

This page illustrates and describes a gas fired hot water baseboard system including a gas fired boiler, fin tube radiation, fittings and piping. Lines within System Components give the unit price and total price per square foot for this system. Prices for alternate gas fired hot water baseboard systems are on Line Items 8.3-280-1500 thru 1900. Both material quantities and labor costs have been adjusted for the system listed.

Factors: To adjust for job conditions other than normal working situations use Lines 8.3-280-2900 thru 4000.

Example: You are to install the system with minimal equipment usage. Go to Line 8.3-280-3400 and apply these percentages to the appropriate MAT. and INST. costs.

System Components	QUANTITY	UNIT	COST PER S.F.		
			MAT.	INST.	TOTAL
Gas fired hot water baseboard system including boiler, fin tube radiation, All necessary fittings and piping.					
Area to 800 S.F.					
Cast iron boiler, insulating jacket, gas piping, 80 MBH	1.000	Ea.	1,468.75	1,343.75	2,812.50
Copper piping	130.000	L.F.	444.60	916.50	1,361.10
Fin tube radiation	68.000	L.F.	659.60	867	1,526.60
Circulator, flange connection	1.000	Ea.	330	122	452
Expansion tank, ASME	1.000	Ea.	360	52.50	412.50
TOTAL		System	3,262.95	3,301.75	6,564.70
COST PER S.F.		S.F.	4.08	4.13	8.21

8.3-280	Heating - Gas Fired Hot Water	COST PER S.F.		
		MAT.	INST.	TOTAL
1400	For alternate hot water systems:			
1500	Cast iron boiler, area to 1000 S.F.	3.48	3.61	7.09
1600	To 1200 S.F.	3.06	3.25	6.31
1700	To 1600 S.F.	3.57	3.17	6.74
1800	To 2000 S.F.	3.13	2.84	5.97
1900	To 3000 S.F.	2.55	2.49	5.04
2000				
2100				
2900	Cut & patch to match existing construction, add, minimum	2%	3%	
3000	Maximum	5%	9%	
3100	Dust protection, add, minimum	1%	2%	
3200	Maximum	4%	11%	
3300	Equipment usage curtailment, add, minimum	1%	1%	
3400	Maximum	3%	10%	
3500	Material handling & storage limitation, add, minimum	1%	1%	
3600	Maximum	6%	7%	
3700	Protection of existing work, add, minimum	2%	2%	
3800	Maximum	5%	7%	
3900	Shift work requirements, add, minimum		5%	
4000	Maximum		30%	

MECHANICAL — A8.3-310 Heating-Cooling, Oil, Forced Air

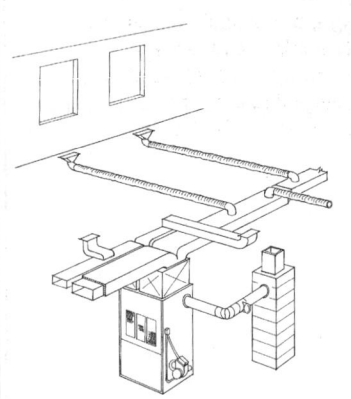

This page illustrates and describes an oil fired forced air system including an oil fired furnace, ductwork, registers and hookups. Lines within System Components give the unit price and total price per square foot for this system. Prices for alternate oil fired forced air systems are on Line Items 8.3-310-1700 thru 2800. Both material quantities and labor costs have been adjusted for the system listed.

Factors: To adjust for job conditions other than normal working situations use Lines 8.3-310-3100 thru 4200.

Example: You are to install the system during evenings and weekends. Go to Line 8.3-310-4200 and apply this percentage to the appropriate INST. cost.

System Components	QUANTITY	UNIT	COST PER S.F.		
			MAT.	INST.	TOTAL
Oil fired hot air heating system including furnace, ductwork, registers And all necessary hookups.					
Area to 800 S.F., heat only					
Furnace, oil, atomizing gun type burner, w/oil piping	1.000	Ea.	1,025	255	1,280
Oil tank, steel, 275 gallon	1.000	Ea.	251	148	399
Duct, galvanized, steel	312.000	Lb.	1,201.20	1,513.20	2,714.40
Insulation, blanket type, duct work	270.000	S.F.	110.70	561.60	672.30
Flexible duct, 6" diameter, insulated	100.000	L.F.	237	282	519
Registers, baseboard, gravity, 12" x 6"	8.000	Ea.	84	141.60	225.60
Return, damper, 36" x 18"	1.000	Ea.	137	40.50	177.50
TOTAL		System	3,045.90	2,941.90	5,987.80
COST PER S.F.		S.F.	3.81	3.68	7.49

8.3-310	Heating-Cooling, Oil, Forced Air	COST PER S.F.		
		MAT.	INST.	TOTAL
1600	For alternate heating systems:			
1700	Oil fired, area to 1000 S.F.	3.08	2.98	6.06
1800	To 1200 S.F.	2.67	2.62	5.29
1900	To 1600 S.F.	2.19	2.20	4.39
2000	To 2000 S.F.	1.68	2.83	4.51
2100	To 3000 S.F.	1.41	2.24	3.65
2200	For combined heating and cooling systems:			
2300	Oil fired, heating and cooling, area to 800 S.F.	5.60	4.37	9.97
2400	To 1000 S.F.	5	3.56	8.56
2500	To 1200 S.F.	4.27	3.10	7.37
2600	To 1600 S.F.	3.47	2.58	6.05
2700	To 2000 S.F.	2.76	3.17	5.93
2800	To 3000 S.F.	2.24	2.48	4.72
3100	Cut & patch to match existing construction, add, minimum	2%	3%	
3200	Maximum	5%	9%	
3300	Dust protection, add, minimum	1%	2%	
3400	Maximum	4%	11%	
3500	Equipment usage curtailment, add, minimum	1%	1%	
3600	Maximum	3%	10%	
3700	Material handling & storage limitation, add, minimum	1%	1%	
3800	Maximum	6%	7%	
3900	Protection of existing work, add, minimum	2%	2%	
4000	Maximum	5%	7%	
4100	Shift work requirements, add, minimum		5%	
4200	Maximum		30%	

MECHANICAL — A8.3-320 Heating-Cooling, Gas, Forced Air

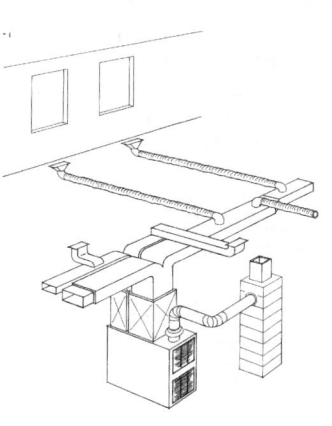

This page illustrates and describes a gas fired forced air system including a gas fired furnace, ductwork, registers and hookups. Lines within System Components give the unit price and total price per square foot for this system. Prices for alternate gas fired forced air systems are on Line Items 8.3-320-1500 thru 2600. Both material quantities and labor costs have been adjusted for the system listed.

Factors: To adjust for job conditions other than normal working situations use Lines 8.3-320-2900 thru 4000.

Example: You are to install the system with material handling and storage limitations. Go to Line 8.3-320-3500 and apply these percentages to the appropriate MAT. and INST. costs.

System Components

System Components	QUANTITY	UNIT	COST PER S.F. MAT.	COST PER S.F. INST.	COST PER S.F. TOTAL
Gas fired hot air heating system including furnace, ductwork, registers And all necessary hookups.					
Area to 800 S.F., heat only					
Furnace, gas, AGA certified, direct drive, w/gas piping, 44 MBH	1.000	Ea.	600	228.75	828.75
Duct, galvanized steel	312.000	Lb.	1,201.20	1,513.20	2,714.40
Insulation, blanket type, ductwork	270.000	S.F.	110.70	561.60	672.30
Flexible duct, 6" diameter, insulated	100.000	L.F.	237	282	519
Registers, baseboard, gravity, 12" x 6"	8.000	Ea.	84	141.60	225.60
Return, damper, 36" x 18"	1.000	Ea.	137	40.50	177.50
TOTAL		System	2,369.90	2,767.65	5,137.55
COST PER S.F.		S.F.	2.96	3.46	6.42

8.3-320	Heating-Cooling, Gas, Forced Air	MAT.	INST.	TOTAL
1400	For alternate heating systems:			
1500	Gas fired, area to 1000 S.F.	2.56	2.81	5.37
1600	To 1200 S.F.	2.24	2.49	4.73
1700	To 1600 S.F.	2.11	2.34	4.45
1800	To 2000 S.F.	1.43	2.75	4.18
1900	To 3000 S.F.	1.14	2.19	3.33
2000	For combined heating and cooling systems:			
2100	Gas fired, heating and cooling, area to 800 S.F.	4.77	4.14	8.91
2200	To 1000 S.F.	4.48	3.39	7.87
2300	To 1200 S.F.	3.84	2.97	6.81
2400	To 1600 S.F.	3.38	2.72	6.10
2500	To 2000 S.F.	2.51	3.10	5.61
2600	To 3000 S.F.	1.97	2.44	4.41
2900	Cut & patch to match existing construction, add, minimum	2%	3%	
3000	Maximum	5%	9%	
3100	Dust protection, add, minimum	1%	2%	
3200	Maximum	4%	11%	
3300	Equipment usage curtailment, add, minimum	1%	1%	
3400	Maximum	3%	10%	
3500	Material handling & storage limitation, add, minimum	1%	1%	
3600	Maximum	6%	7%	
3700	Protection of existing work, add, minimum	2%	2%	
3800	Maximum	5%	7%	
3900	Shift work requirements, add, minimum		5%	
4000	Maximum		30%	

For expanded coverage of these items see *Means Mechanical or Plumbing Cost Data 1999*

MECHANICAL | A8.5-400 | Circulating Pumps

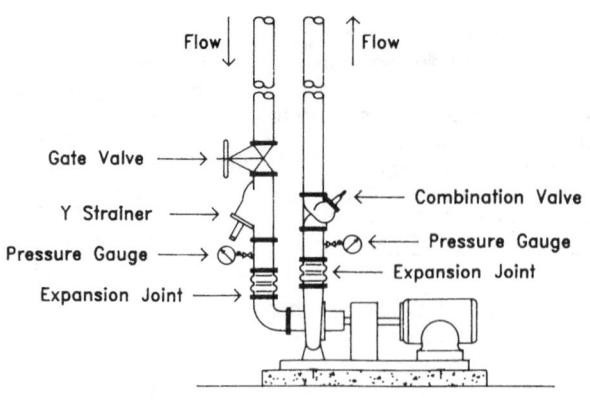

Base Mounted End-Suction Pump

This page illustrates and describes end suction base mounted circulating pumps, including strainer and piping. Lines within system components give the material and installation price on a cost each basis for the components. Prices for alternate circulating pumps are on Line items 8.5-414-1010 thru 1050. Material quantities and labor costs have been adjusted for the system listed.

Factors: To adjust for job conditions other than normal working situations uses Lines 8.5-414-2700 thru 4000.

System Components	QUANTITY	UNIT	COST EACH		
			MAT.	INST.	TOTAL
Circulator pump, end suction, including pipe, Valves, fittings and guages.					
Pump, circulating, CI, base mounted, 2-1/2" size, 3 HP, to 150 GPM	1.000	Ea.	1,925	410	2,335
Pipe, black steel, Sch. 40, on yoke & roll hangers, 10' O.C., 2-1/2" dia	12.000	L.F.	52.80	201.72	254.52
Elbow, 90°, weld joint, steel, 2-1/2" pipe size	1.000	Ea.	9.50	98.85	108.35
Flange, weld neck, 150 LB, 2-1/2" pipe size	8.000	Ea.	180	395.36	575.36
Valve, iron body, gate, 125 lb., N.R.S., flanged, 2-1/2" size	1.000	Ea.	282	147	429
Strainer, Y type, iron body, flanged, 125 lb., 2-1/2" pipe size	1.000	Ea.	105	148	253
Multipurpose valve, CI body, 2" size	1.000	Ea.	365	51.50	416.50
Expansion joint, flanged spool, 6" F to F, 2-1/2" dia	2.000	Ea.	336	119	455
T-O-L, weld joint, socket, 1/4" pipe size, nozzle	2.000	Ea.	9.48	68.76	78.24
T-O-L, weld joint, socket, 1/2" pipe size, nozzle	2.000	Ea.	9.48	71.98	81.46
Control gauges, pressure or vacuum, 3-1/2" diameter dial	2.000	Ea.	29.70	25.60	55.30
Pressure/temperature relief plug, 316 SS, 3/4" OD, 7-1/2" insertion	2.000	Ea.	79	25.60	104.60
Insulation, fiberglass pipe covering, 1-1/2" wall, 2-1/2" IPS	12.000	L.F.	36.72	48.60	85.32
Pump control system	1.000	Ea.	880	375	1,255
Pump balancing	1.000	Ea.		170	170
TOTAL			4,299.68	2,356.97	6,656.65

8.5-414	Circulating Pump Systems, End Suction	COST EACH		
		MAT.	INST.	TOTAL
1000	For alternate pump sizes:			
1010	Pump, base mtd with motor, end-suction, 2-1/2" size, 3 HP, to 150 GPM	4,300	2,350	6,650
1020	3" size, 5 HP, to 225 GPM	4,800	2,700	7,500
1030	4" size, 7-1/2 HP, to 350 GPM	5,775	3,250	9,025
1040	5" size, 15 HP, to 1000 GPM	8,325	4,925	13,250
1050	6" size, 25 HP, to 1550 GPM	11,200	5,975	17,175
2700	Cut & patch to match existing construction, add, minimum	2%	3%	
2800	Maximum	5%	9%	
2900	Dust protection, add, minimum	1%	2%	
3000	Maximum	4%	11%	
3100	Equipment usage curtailment, add, minimum	1%	1%	
3200	Maximum	3%	10%	
3300	Material handling & storage limitation, add, minimum	1%	1%	
3400	Maximum	6%	7%	
3500	Protection of existing work, add, minimum	2%	2%	
3600	Maximum	5%	7%	
3700	Shift work requirements, add, minimum		5%	
3800	Maximum		30%	
3900	Temporary shoring and bracing, add, minimum	2%	5%	
4000	Maximum	5%	12%	

MECHANICAL — A8.7-100 Unit Heaters

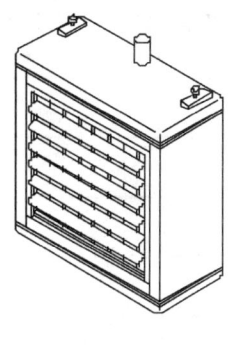

Gas Unit Heater

Hydronic Unit Heater

This page illustrates and describes unit heaters including piping and vents. Lines within Systems Components give the material and installation price on a cost each basis for this system. Prices for alternate unit heater systems are on Line Items 8.7-110-1010 thru 8.7-130-1040. Material quantities and labor costs have been adjusted for the system listed.

Factors: To adjust for job conditions other than normal working situations use Lines 8.7-130-2700 thru 4000.

System Components	QUANTITY	UNIT	COST EACH MAT.	COST EACH INST.	COST EACH TOTAL
Unit heaters complete with piping, thermostats and chimney as required					
Space heater, propeller fan, 20 MBH output	1.000	Ea.	440	87	527
Pipe, black steel, Sch 40, threaded, W/coupling & hangers, 10' OC, 3/4" dia	20.000	L.F.	29.82	140.70	170.52
Elbow, 90°, black steel, straight, 1/2" dia.	3.000	Ea.	3.36	81	84.36
Elbow, 90°, black steel, straight, 3/4" dia.	3.000	Ea.	4.05	87	91.05
Tee, black steel, reducing, 3/4" dia.	1.000	Ea.	3.26	45.50	48.76
Union, black with brass seat, 3/4" dia.	1.000	Ea.	5.70	31.50	37.20
Pipe nipples, black, 1/2" dia	2.000	Ea.	2.52	13	15.52
Pipe nipples, black, 3/4" dia	2.000	Ea.			
Pipe cap, black, 3/4" dia.	1.000	Ea.	1.51	12.75	14.26
Gas cock, brass, 3/4" size	1.000	Ea.	11.35	18.55	29.90
Thermostat, 1 set back, electric, timed	1.000	Ea.	86	51	137
Wiring, thermostat hook-up	1.000	Ea.	7	16.45	23.45
Vent chimney, prefab metal, U.L. listed, gas, double wall, galv. st, 4" dia	12.000	L.F.	54.60	129.60	184.20
Vent chimney, gas, double wall, galv. steel, elbow 90°, 4" dia.	2.000	Ea.	37.40	43	80.40
Vent chimney, gas, double wall, galv. steel, Tee, 4" dia.	1.000	Ea.	23.50	28	51.50
Vent chimney, gas, double wall, galv. steel, T cap, 4" dia.	1.000	Ea.	2.22	17.45	19.67
Vent chimney, gas, double wall, galv. steel, roof flashing, 4" dia.	1.000	Ea.	8.10	21.50	29.60
Vent chimney, gas, double wall, galv. steel, top, 4" dia.	1.000	Ea.	8.95	16.65	25.60
TOTAL			729.34	840.65	1,569.99

8.7-110	Unit Heaters, Gas	COST EACH MAT.	COST EACH INST.	COST EACH TOTAL
1000	For alternate unit heaters:			
1010	Space heater, suspended, gas fired, propeller fan, 20 MBH	730	840	1,570
1020	60 MBH	855	880	1,735
1030	100 MBH	1,075	935	2,010
1040	160 MBH	1,250	1,025	2,275
1050	200 MBH	1,525	1,125	2,650
1060	280 MBH	1,925	1,200	3,125
1070	320 MBH	2,625	1,375	4,000

8.7-120	Unit Heaters, Hydronic	COST EACH MAT.	COST EACH INST.	COST EACH TOTAL
1010	Space heater, suspended, horiz. mount, HW, prop. fan, 20 MBH	1,475	900	2,375
1020	60 MBH	1,925	1,025	2,950
1030	100 MBH	2,200	1,100	3,300
1040	150 MBH	2,575	1,225	3,800
1050	200 MBH	2,750	1,375	4,125
1060	300 MBH	3,075	1,600	4,675

For expanded coverage of these items see *Means Mechanical or Plumbing Cost Data 1999*

MECHANICAL — A8.7-100 Unit Heaters

8.7-130 Cabinet Unit Heaters, Hydronic

		COST EACH		
		MAT.	INST.	TOTAL
1010	Unit heater, cabinet type, horizontal blower, hot water, 20 MBH	1,600	885	2,485
1020	60 MBH	2,250	970	3,220
1030	100 MBH	2,400	1,075	3,475
1040	120 MBH	2,500	1,100	3,600
2700	Cut & patch to match existing construction, add, minimum	2%	3%	
2800	Maximum	5%	9%	
2900	Dust protection, add, minimum	1%	2%	
3000	Maximum	4%	11%	
3100	Equipment usage curtailment, add, minimum	1%	1%	
3200	Maximum	3%	10%	
3300	Material handling & storage limitation, add, minimum	1%	1%	
3400	Maximum	6%	7%	
3500	Protection of existing work, add, minimum	2%	2%	
3600	Maximum	5%	7%	
3700	Shift work requirements, add, minimum		5%	
3800	Maximum		30%	
3900	Temporary shoring and bracing, add, minimum	2%	5%	
4000	Maximum	5%	12%	

MECHANICAL — A8.7-220 | Boilers

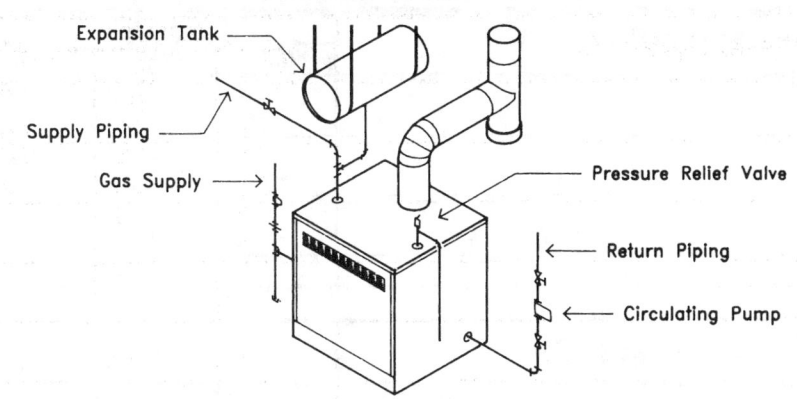

Cast Iron Boiler, Hot Water, Gas Fired

This page illustrates and describes boilers including expansion tank, circulating pump and all service piping. Lines within Systems Components give the material and installation price on a cost each basis for the components. Prices for alternate boiler systems are on Line Items 8.7-220-1010 thru 8.7-235-1040. Material quantities and labor costs have been adjusted for the system listed.

Factors: To adjust for job conditions other than normal working situations use Line 8.7235-2700 thru 4000.

System Components	QUANTITY	UNIT	MAT.	INST.	TOTAL
Cast iron boiler, including piping, chimney and accessories					
Boilers, gas fired, std controls, CI, insulated, HW, gross output 100 MBH	1.000	Ea.	1,350	1,150	2,500
Pipe, black steel, Sch 40, threaded, W/coupling & hangers, 10' OC, 3/4" dia	20.000	L.F.	31.95	150.75	182.70
Pipe, black steel, Sch 40, threaded, W/coupling & hangers, 10' OC, 1" dia.	20.000	L.F.	38.92	165.55	204.47
Elbow, 90°, black, straight, 3/4" dia.	9.000	Ea.	12.15	261	273.15
Elbow, 90°, black, straight, 1" dia.	6.000	Ea.	14.10	189	203.10
Tee, black, straight, 3/4" dia.	2.000	Ea.	4.32	91	95.32
Tee, black, straight, 1" dia.	2.000	Ea.	7.32	102	109.32
Tee, black, reducing, 1" dia.	2.000	Ea.	8.20	102	110.20
Pipe cap, black, 3/4" dia.	1.000	Ea.	1.51	12.75	14.26
Union, black with brass seat, 3/4" dia.	2.000	Ea.	11.40	63	74.40
Union, black with brass seat, 1" dia.	2.000	Ea.	14.70	68	82.70
Pipe nipples, black, 3/4" dia	5.000	Ea.			
Pipe nipples, black, 1" dia	3.000	Ea.			
Valves, bronze, gate, N.R.S., threaded, class 150, 3/4" size	2.000	Ea.	51	41	92
Valves, bronze, gate, N.R.S., threaded, class 150, 1" size	2.000	Ea.	66	43	109
Gas cock, brass, 3/4" size	1.000	Ea.	11.35	18.55	29.90
Thermometer, stem type, 9" case, 8" stem, 3/4" NPT	2.000	Ea.	108	29.30	137.30
Tank, steel, liquid expansion, ASME, painted, 15 gallon capacity	1.000	Ea.	355	43.50	398.50
Pump, circulating, bronze, flange connection, 3/4" to 1-1/2" size, 1/8 HP	1.000	Ea.	570	122	692
Vent chimney, all fuel, pressure tight, double wall, SS, 6" dia	20.000	L.F.	750	244	994
Vent chimney, elbow, 90° fixed, 6" dia	2.000	Ea.	426	49	475
Vent chimney, Tee, 6" dia	2.000	Ea.	280	61	341
Vent chimney, ventilated roof thimble, 6" dia	1.000	Ea.	187	28	215
Vent chimney, adjustable roof flashing, 6" dia	1.000	Ea.	52	24.50	76.50
Vent chimney, stack cap, 6" diameter	1.000	Ea.	148	15.95	163.95
Insulation, fiberglass pipe covering, 1" wall, 1" IPS	20.000	L.F.	23.60	66.20	89.80
TOTAL			4,522.52	3,141.05	7,663.57

8.7-220	Boiler, Cast Iron, Hot Water, Gas	MAT.	INST.	TOTAL
1000	For alternate boilers:			
1010	Boiler, cast iron, gas, hot water, 100 MBH	4,525	3,150	7,675
1020	200 MBH	5,250	3,650	8,900
1030	320 MBH	5,625	3,950	9,575
1040	440 MBH	7,475	4,800	12,275
1050	544 MBH	11,100	7,550	18,650
1060	765 MBH	13,900	8,050	21,950
1070	1088 MBH	15,500	8,400	23,900
1080	1530 MBH	19,100	10,800	29,900
1090	2312 MBH	23,100	11,400	34,500

For expanded coverage of these items see *Means Mechanical or Plumbing Cost Data 1999*

MECHANICAL — A8.7-220 Boilers

8.7-225 Boiler, Cast Iron, Steam, Gas

		\multicolumn{3}{c}{COST EACH}
		MAT.	INST.	TOTAL
1010	Boiler, cast iron, gas, steam, 100 MBH	3,625	3,075	6,700
1020	200 MBH	7,925	5,800	13,725
1030	320 MBH	9,050	6,500	15,550
1040	544 MBH	12,300	9,850	22,150
1050	765 MBH	14,100	10,500	24,600
1060	1275 MBH	16,900	11,500	28,400
1070	2675 MBH	25,100	15,600	40,700

8.7-230 Boiler, Cast Iron, Hot Water, Gas/Oil

		COST EACH		
		MAT.	INST.	TOTAL
1010	Boiler, cast iron, gas & oil, hot water, 584 MBH	15,300	8,275	23,575
1020	876 MBH	19,500	8,800	28,300
1030	1168 MBH	24,800	8,925	33,725
1040	1460 MBH	29,400	10,900	40,300
1050	2044 MBH	37,100	11,800	48,900
1060	2628 MBH	48,300	13,800	62,100

8.7-235 Boiler, Cast Iron, Steam, Gas/Oil

		COST EACH		
		MAT.	INST.	TOTAL
1010	Boiler, cast iron, gas & oil, steam, 810 MBH	16,100	11,700	27,800
1020	1360 MBH	18,700	12,800	31,500
1030	2040 MBH	23,900	16,300	40,200
1040	2700 MBH	25,900	17,700	43,600
2700	Cut & patch to match existing construction, add, minimum	2%	3%	
2800	Maximum	5%	9%	
2900	Dust protection, add, minimum	1%	2%	
3000	Maximum	4%	11%	
3100	Equipment usage curtailment, add, minimum	1%	1%	
3200	Maximum	3%	10%	
3300	Material handling & storage limitation, add, minimum	1%	1%	
3400	Maximum	6%	7%	
3500	Protection of existing work, add, minimum	2%	2%	
3600	Maximum	5%	7%	
3700	Shift work requirements, add, minimum		5%	
3800	Maximum		30%	
3900	Temporary shoring and bracing, add, minimum	2%	5%	
4000	Maximum	5%	12%	

MECHANICAL — A8.8-200 | Heat Exchanger

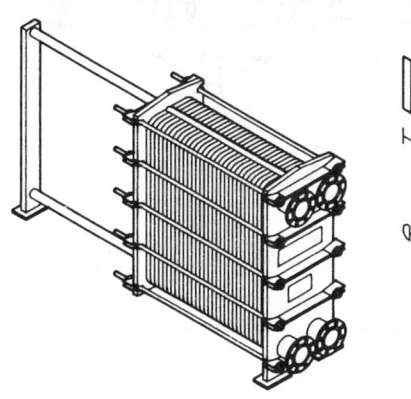
Plate Heat Exchanger

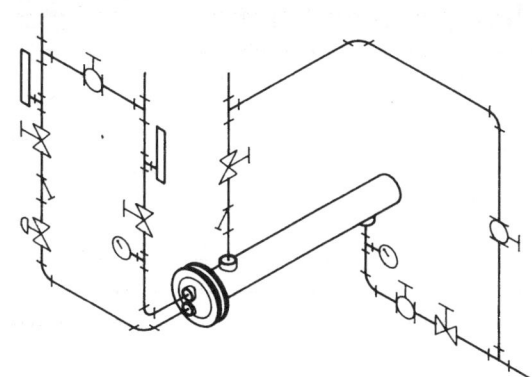
Shell and Tube Heat Exchanger

This page illustrates and describes plate and shell and tube type heat exchangers including pressure gauge and exchanger control system. Lines within Systems Components give the material and installation price on a cost each basis for the components. Prices for alternate heat exchanger systems are on Line Items 8.8-210-1010 thru 8.8-220-1040. Material quantities and labor costs have been adjusted for the system listed.

Factors: To adjust for job conditions other than normal working situations use Lines 8.8-220-2700 thru 4000.

System Components

System Components	QUANTITY	UNIT	MAT.	INST.	TOTAL
Shell and tube type heat exchanger with related valves and piping.					
Heat exchanger, 4 pass, 3/4" O.D. copper tubes, by steam at 10 psi, 40 GPM	1.000	Ea.	2,250	185	2,435
Pipe, black steel, Sch 40, threaded, W/couplings & hangers, 10' OC, 2" dia.	40.000	L.F.	170.19	580.75	750.94
Elbow, 90°, straight, 2" dia.	16.000	Ea.	140	656	796
Reducer, black steel, concentric, 2" dia.	2.000	Ea.	19.40	70	89.40
Valves, bronze, gate, rising stem, threaded, class 150, 2" size	6.000	Ea.	438	222	660
Valves, bronze, globe, class 150, rising stem, threaded, 2" size	2.000	Ea.	290	74	364
Strainers, Y type, bronze body, screwed, 150 lb., 2" pipe size	2.000	Ea.	155	63	218
Valve, electric motor actuated, brass, 2 way, screwed, 1-1/2" pipe size	1.000	Ea.	365	32	397
Union, black with brass seat, 2" dia.	8.000	Ea.	123.20	344	467.20
Tee, black, straight, 2" dia.	9.000	Ea.	94.50	603	697.50
Tee, black, reducing run and outlet, 2" dia.	4.000	Ea.	62.80	268	330.80
Pipe nipple, black, 2" dia.	21.000	Ea.			
Thermometers, stem type, 9" case, 8" stem, 3/4" NPT	2.000	Ea.	108	29.30	137.30
Gauges, pressure or vacuum, 3-1/2" diameter dial	2.000	Ea.	29.70	25.60	55.30
Insulation, fiberglass pipe covering, 1" wall, 2" IPS	40.000	L.F.	62.80	146	208.80
Heat exchanger control system	1.000	Ea.	1,850	1,325	3,175
Coil balancing	1.000	Ea.		71.50	71.50
TOTAL			6,158.59	4,695.15	10,853.74

8.8-210	Heat Exchanger, Plate Type	MAT.	INST.	TOTAL
1000	For alternate heat exchangers:			
1010	Plate heat exchanger, 400 GPM	27,200	9,550	36,750
1020	800 GPM	44,900	12,100	57,000
1030	1200 GPM	87,000	16,300	103,300
1040	1800 GPM	129,000	20,400	149,400

8.8-220	Heat Exchanger, Shell & Tube	MAT.	INST.	TOTAL
1010	Shell & tube heat exchanger, 40 GPM	6,150	4,700	10,850
1020	96 GPM	11,400	8,425	19,825
1030	240 GPM	20,000	11,400	31,400
1040	600 GPM	38,300	16,000	54,300
2700	Cut & patch to match existing construction, add, minimum	2%	3%	
2800	Maximum	5%	9%	
2900	Dust protection, add, minimum	1%	2%	
3000	Maximum	4%	11%	
3100	Equipment usage curtailment, add, minimum	1%	1%	

For expanded coverage of these items see *Means Mechanical or Plumbing Cost Data 1999*

MECHANICAL | A8.8-200 Heat Exchanger

8.8-220 Heat Exchanger, Shell & Tube

		COST EACH		
		MAT.	INST.	TOTAL
3200	Maximum	3%	10%	
3300	Material handling & storage limitation, add, minimum	1%	1%	
3400	Maximum	6%	7%	
3500	Protection of existing work, add, minimum	2%	2%	
3600	Maximum	5%	7%	
3700	Shift work requirements, add, minimum		5%	
3800	Maximum		30%	
3900	Temporary shoring and bracing, add, minimum	2%	5%	
4000	Maximum	5%	12%	

MECHANICAL — A8.8-400 AC Unit, Package, Water Cooled

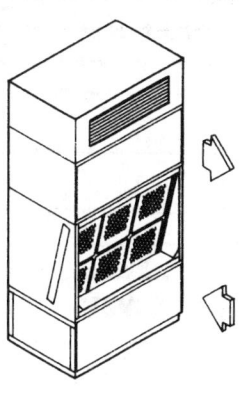
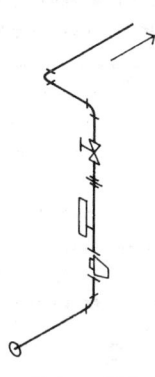

Condenser Supply Water Piping

Condenser Return Water Piping

Self–Contained Air Conditioner Unit, Water Cooled

This page illustrates and describes packaged electrical air conditioning units including multizone control and related piping. Lines within Systems Components give the material and installation price on a cost each basis for the components. Prices for alternate packaged electrical A/C unit systems are on Line Items 8.8-410-1010 thru 8.8-422-1060. Material quantities and labor costs have been adjusted for the system listed.

Factors: To adjust for job conditions other than normal working situations use Lines 8.8-422-2700 thru 4000.

System Components	QUANTITY	UNIT	COST EACH MAT.	COST EACH INST.	COST EACH TOTAL
Packaged water cooled electric air conditioning unit with related piping and valves.					
Self-contained, water cooled, elect. heat, not inc tower, 5 ton, const vol	1.000	Ea.	6,400	955	7,355
Pipe, black steel, Sch 40, threaded, W/cplg & hangers, 10' OC, 1-1/4" dia.	20.000	L.F.	46.87	177.38	224.25
Elbow, 90°, black, straight, 1-1/4" dia.	6.000	Ea.	23.16	201	224.16
Tee, black, straight, 1-1/4" dia.	2.000	Ea.	11.90	105	116.90
Tee, black, reducing, 1-1/4" dia.	2.000	Ea.	14.20	105	119.20
Thermometers, stem type, 9" case, 8" stem, 3/4" NPT	2.000	Ea.	108	29.30	137.30
Union, black with brass seat, 1-1/4" dia.	2.000	Ea.	21.20	70	91.20
Pipe nipple, black, 1-1/4" dia	3.000	Ea.			
Valves, bronze, gate, N.R.S., threaded, class 150, 1-1/4" size	2.000	Ea.	89	54	143
Circuit setter, bal valve, bronze body, threaded, 1-1/4" pipe size	1.000	Ea.	94.50	27.50	122
Insulation, fiberglass pipe covering, 1" wall, 1-1/4" IPS	20.000	L.F.	26.80	69.40	96.20
Control system, pneumatic, A/C Unit with heat	1.000	Ea.	1,850	1,450	3,300
Re-heat coil balancing	1.000	Ea.		76	76
Rooftop unit heat/cool balancing	1.000	Ea.		265	265
TOTAL			8,685.63	3,584.58	12,270.21

8.8-410	AC Unit, Package, Elec. Ht., Water Cooled	MAT.	INST.	TOTAL
1000	For alternate A/C systems:			
1010	A/C, Self contained, single pkg., water cooled, elect. heat, 5 Ton	8,675	3,575	12,250
1020	10 Ton	14,300	4,450	18,750
1030	20 Ton	22,500	5,700	28,200
1040	30 Ton	31,000	6,175	37,175
1050	40 Ton	36,800	6,825	43,625
1060	50 Ton	46,700	8,200	54,900

8.8-412	AC Unit, Package, Elec. Ht., Water Cooled, VAV	MAT.	INST.	TOTAL
1010	A/C, Self contained, single pkg., water cooled, elect. ht, VAV, 10 Ton	16,900	4,450	21,350
1020	20 Ton	26,700	5,700	32,400
1030	30 Ton	36,300	6,175	42,475
1040	40 Ton	44,600	6,825	51,425
1050	50 Ton	55,000	8,200	63,200
1060	60 Ton	63,500	9,975	73,475

MECHANICAL | A8.8-400 | AC Unit, Package, Water Cooled

8.8-420	AC Unit, Package, Hot Water Coil, Water Cooled	COST EACH		
		MAT.	INST.	TOTAL
1010	A/C, Self contn'd, single pkg., water cool, H/W ht, const. vol, 5 Ton	7,350	5,000	12,350
1020	10 Ton	12,000	5,975	17,975
1030	20 Ton	20,200	7,500	27,700
1040	30 Ton	26,600	9,550	36,150
1050	40 Ton	32,600	11,600	44,200
1060	50 Ton	40,000	14,300	54,300

8.8-422	AC Unit, Package, HW Coil, Water Cooled, VAV	COST EACH		
		MAT.	INST.	TOTAL
1010	A/C, Self contn'd, single pkg., water cool, H/W ht, VAV, 10 Ton	14,600	5,625	20,225
1020	20 Ton	24,400	7,300	31,700
1030	30 Ton	31,900	9,325	41,225
1040	40 Ton	40,400	11,200	51,600
1050	50 Ton	48,500	13,800	62,300
1060	60 Ton	58,500	13,900	72,400
2700	Cut & patch to match existing construction, add, minimum	2%	3%	
2800	Maximum	5%	9%	
2900	Dust protection, add, minimum	1%	2%	
3000	Maximum	4%	11%	
3100	Equipment usage curtailment, add, minimum	1%	1%	
3200	Maximum	3%	10%	
3300	Material handling & storage limitation, add, minimum	1%	1%	
3400	Maximum	6%	7%	
3500	Protection of existing work, add, minimum	2%	2%	
3600	Maximum	5%	7%	
3700	Shift work requirements, add, minimum		5%	
3800	Maximum		30%	
3900	Temporary shoring and bracing, add, minimum	2%	5%	
4000	Maximum	5%	12%	

MECHANICAL — A8.8-500 — AC Unit, Package, DX, Air Cooled

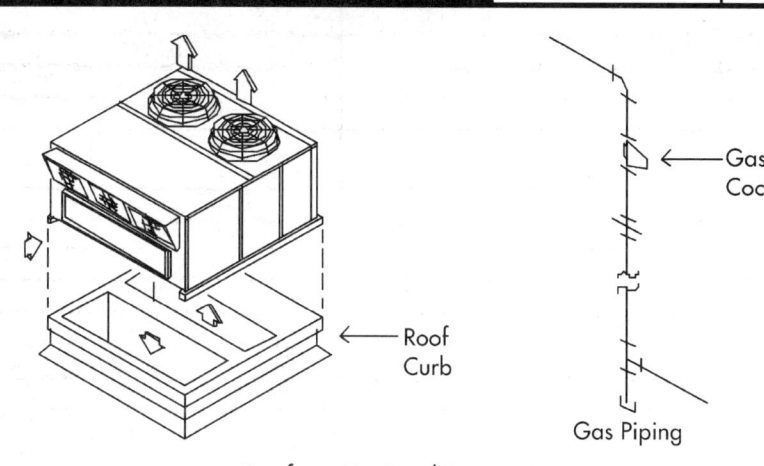

Rooftop Air Conditioner Unit

This page illustrates and describes packaged air conditioners including rooftop DX unit, pipes and fittings. Lines with Systems Components give the material and installation price on a cost each basis for the components. Prices for alternate A/C systems are on Line Items 8.8-510-1010 thru 1060. Material quantities and labor costs have been adjusted for the system listed.

Factors: To adjust for job conditions other than normal working situations use Lines 8.8-510-2700 thru 4000.

System Components

System Components	QUANTITY	UNIT	COST EACH MAT.	COST EACH INST.	COST EACH TOTAL
Packaged rooftop DX unit, gas, with related piping and valves.					
Roof top A/C, curb, economizer, sgl zone, elec cool, gas ht, 5 ton, 112 MBH	1.000	Ea.	5,150	1,325	6,475
Pipe, black steel, Sch 40, threaded, W/cplgs & hangers, 10' OC, 1" dia	20.000	L.F.	38.01	161.70	199.71
Elbow, 90°, black, straight, 3/4" dia.	3.000	Ea.	4.05	87	91.05
Elbow, 90°, black, straight, 1" dia.	3.000	Ea.	7.05	94.50	101.55
Tee, black, reducing, 1" dia.	1.000	Ea.	4.10	51	55.10
Union, black with brass seat, 1" dia.	1.000	Ea.	7.35	34	41.35
Pipe nipple, black, 3/4" dia	2.000	Ea.	2.84	13.40	16.24
Pipe nipple, black, 1" dia	2.000	Ea.			
Cap, black, 1" dia.	1.000	Ea.	1.86	13.60	15.46
Gas cock, brass, 1" size	1.000	Ea.	13.85	21.50	35.35
Control system, pneumatic, Rooftop A/C unit	1.000	Ea.	1,850	1,450	3,300
Rooftop unit heat/cool balancing	1.000	Ea.		265	265
TOTAL			7,079.11	3,516.70	10,595.81

8.8-510 Rooftop Air Conditioner, Const. Volume

		COST EACH MAT.	COST EACH INST.	COST EACH TOTAL
1000	For alternate A/C systems:			
1010	A/C, Rooftop, DX cool, gas heat, curb, economizer, fltrs, 5 Ton	7,075	3,525	10,600
1020	7-1/2 Ton	9,975	4,025	14,000
1030	12-1/2 Ton	13,900	5,225	19,125
1040	18 Ton	18,600	6,300	24,900
1050	25 Ton	29,100	8,000	37,100
1060	40 Ton	43,700	12,000	55,700
1010	A/C, Rooftop, DX cool, gas heat, curb, ecmizr, fltrs, VAV, 12-1/2 Ton	16,500	5,300	21,800
1020	18 Ton	21,400	6,450	27,850
1030	25 Ton	33,300	8,225	41,525
1040	40 Ton	51,500	12,600	64,100
1050	60 Ton	72,000	17,900	89,900
1060	80 Ton	112,000	21,900	133,900
2700	Cut & patch to match existing construction, add, minimum	2%	3%	
2800	Maximum	5%	9%	
2900	Dust protection, add, minimum	1%	2%	
3000	Maximum	4%	11%	
3100	Equipment usage curtailment, add, minimum	1%	1%	
3200	Maximum	3%	10%	
3300	Material handling & storage limitation, add, minimum	1%	1%	
3400	Maximum	6%	7%	
3500	Protection of existing work, add, minimum	2%	2%	

For expanded coverage of these items see *Means Mechanical or Plumbing Cost Data 1999*

MECHANICAL | A8.8-500 | AC Unit, Package, DX, Air Cooled

8.8-510	Rooftop Air Conditioner, Const. Volume	COST EACH		
		MAT.	INST.	TOTAL
3600	Maximum	5%	7%	
3700	Shift work requirements, add, minimum		5%	
3800	Maximum		30%	
3900	Temporary shoring and bracing, add, minimum	2%	5%	
4000	Maximum	5%	12%	

MECHANICAL — A8.8-600 — Fan Coil Air Conditioner

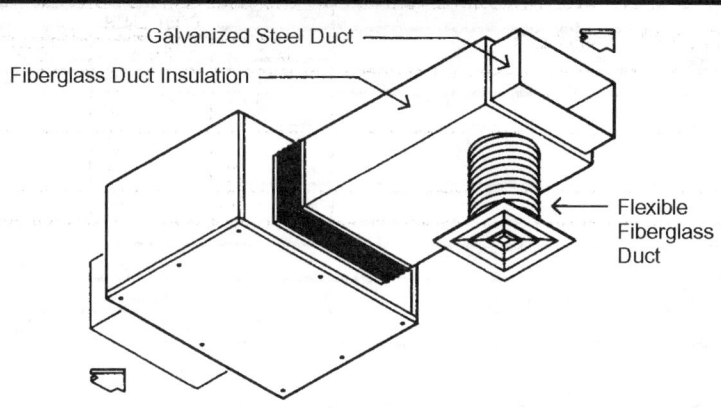

Horizontal Fan Coil Air Conditioning System

This page illustrates and describes fan coil air conditioners including duct work, duct installation, piping and diffusers. Lines within Systems Components give the material and installation price on a cost each basis for the components. Prices for alternate fan coil A/C unit systems are on Line Items 8.8-610-1010 thru 8.8-630-1120. Material quantities and labor costs have been adjusted for the system listed.

Factors: To adjust for job conditions other than normal working situations use Lines 8.8-630-2700 thru 4000.

System Components

System Components	QUANTITY	UNIT	MAT.	INST.	TOTAL
Fan coil A/C system, horizontal, with housing, controls, 2 pipe, 1/2 ton					
Fan coil A/C, horizontal housing, filters, chilled water, 1/2 ton cooling	1.000	Ea.	890	92.50	982.50
Pipe, black steel, Sch 40, threaded, W/cplgs & hangers, 10' OC, 3/4" dia.	20.000	L.F.	30.53	144.05	174.58
Elbow, 90°, black, straight, 3/4" dia.	6.000	Ea.	8.10	174	182.10
Tee, black, straight, 3/4" dia.	2.000	Ea.	4.32	91	95.32
Union, black with brass seat, 3/4" dia.	2.000	Ea.	11.40	63	74.40
Pipe nipples, 3/4" diam	3.000	Ea.			
Valves, bronze, gate, N.R.S., threaded, class 150, 3/4" size	2.000	Ea.	51	41	92
Circuit setter, balance valve, bronze body, threaded, 3/4" pipe size	1.000	Ea.	49.50	20.50	70
Insulation, fiberglass pipe covering, 1" wall, 3/4" IPS	20.000	L.F.	23	63.40	86.40
Ductwork, 12" x 8" fabricated, galvanized steel, 12 LF	55.000	Lb.	211.75	266.75	478.50
Insulation, ductwork, blanket type, fiberglass, 1" thk, 1-1/2 LB density	40.000	S.F.	16.40	83.20	99.60
Diffusers, aluminum, OB damper, ceiling, perf, 24"x24" panel size, 6"x6"	2.000	Ea.	174	51	225
Ductwork, flexible, fiberglass fabric, insulated, 1"thk, PE jacket, 6" dia	16.000	L.F.	37.92	45.12	83.04
Round volume control damper 6" dia.	2.000	Ea.	55	37	92
Fan coil unit balancing	1.000	Ea.		49.25	49.25
Re-heat coil balancing	1.000	Ea.		76	76
Diffuser/register, high, balancing	2.000	Ea.		136.40	136.40
TOTAL			1,562.92	1,434.17	2,997.09

8.8-610	Fan Coil A/C Unit, Two Pipe	MAT.	INST.	TOTAL
1000	For alternate A/C units:			
1010	Fan coil A/C system, cabinet mounted, controls, 2 pipe, 1/2 Ton	985	770	1,755
1020	1 Ton	1,150	860	2,010
1030	1-1/2 Ton	1,225	870	2,095
1040	2 Ton	1,725	1,050	2,775
1050	3 Ton	2,275	1,100	3,375

8.8-615	Fan Coil A/C Unit, Two Pipe, Electric Heat	MAT.	INST.	TOTAL
1010	Fan coil A/C system, cabinet mntd, elect. ht, controls, 2 pipe, 1/2 Ton	1,100	770	1,870
1020	1 Ton	1,325	860	2,185
1030	1-1/2 Ton	1,575	870	2,445
1040	2 Ton	2,250	1,075	3,325
1050	3 Ton	3,950	1,100	5,050

For expanded coverage of these items see *Means Mechanical or Plumbing Cost Data 1999*

MECHANICAL — A8.8-600 Fan Coil Air Conditioner

8.8-620	Fan Coil A/C Unit, Four Pipe	COST EACH		
		MAT.	INST.	TOTAL
1010	Fan coil A/C system, cabinet mounted, controls, 4 pipe, 1/2 Ton	1,500	1,500	3,000
1020	1 Ton	1,700	1,575	3,275
1030	1-1/2 Ton	1,800	1,600	3,400
1040	2 Ton	2,275	1,650	3,925
1050	3 Ton	3,100	1,775	4,875

8.8-625	Fan Coil A/C, Horizontal, Duct Mount, 2 Pipe	COST EACH		
		MAT.	INST.	TOTAL
1010	Fan coil A/C system, horizontal w/housing, controls, 2 pipe, 1/2 Ton	1,575	1,425	3,000
1020	1 Ton	2,200	2,100	4,300
1030	1-1/2 Ton	2,900	2,750	5,650
1040	2 Ton	2,950	3,300	6,250
1050	3 Ton	3,500	4,400	7,900
1060	3-1/2 Ton	3,675	4,525	8,200
1070	4 Ton	3,775	5,150	8,925
1080	5 Ton	4,425	6,550	10,975
1090	6 Ton	4,475	7,025	11,500
1100	7 Ton	4,650	7,275	11,925
1110	8 Ton	4,650	7,425	12,075
1120	10 Ton	5,225	7,700	12,925

8.8-630	Fan Coil A/C, Horiz., Duct Mount, 2 Pipe, Elec. Ht.	COST EACH		
		MAT.	INST.	TOTAL
1010	Fan coil A/C system, horiz. hsng, elect. ht, ctrls, 2 pipe, 1/2 Ton	1,750	1,450	3,200
1020	1 Ton	2,450	2,100	4,550
1030	1-1/2 Ton	3,075	2,750	5,825
1040	2 Ton	3,125	3,300	6,425
1050	3 Ton	5,100	4,525	9,625
1060	3-1/2 Ton	5,750	4,525	10,275
1070	4 Ton	6,475	5,175	11,650
1080	5 Ton	7,400	6,550	13,950
1090	6 Ton	7,450	7,050	14,500
1100	7 Ton	7,800	7,000	14,800
1110	8 Ton	8,375	7,075	15,450
1120	10 Ton	8,900	7,300	16,200
2700	Cut & patch to match existing construction, add, minimum	2%	3%	
2800	Maximum	5%	9%	
2900	Dust protection, add, minimum	1%	2%	
3000	Maximum	4%	11%	
3100	Equipment usage curtailment, add, minimum	1%	1%	
3200	Maximum	3%	10%	
3300	Material handling & storage limitation, add, minimum	1%	1%	
3400	Maximum	6%	7%	
3500	Protection of existing work, add, minimum	2%	2%	
3600	Maximum	5%	7%	
3700	Shift work requirements, add, minimum		5%	
3800	Maximum		30%	
3900	Temporary shoring and bracing, add, minimum	2%	5%	
4000	Maximum	5%	12%	

MECHANICAL — A8.8-800 Thru-Wall Units

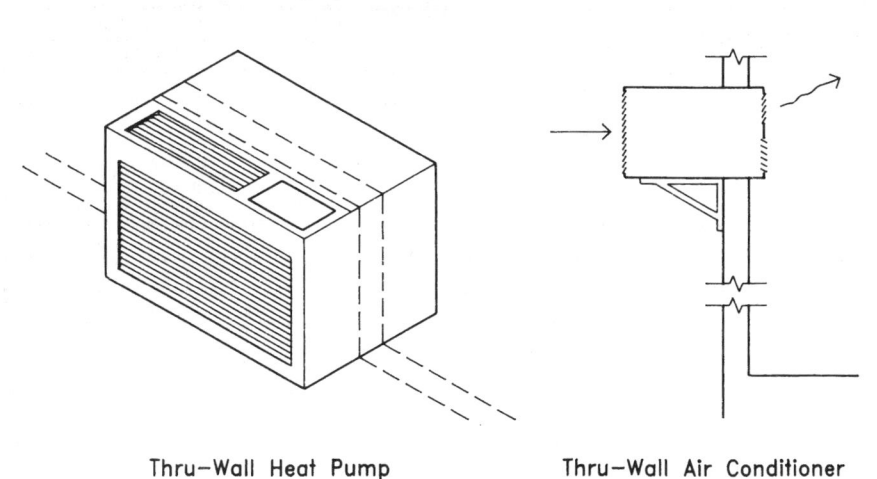

Thru-Wall Heat Pump   Thru-Wall Air Conditioner

This page illustrates and describes thru-wall air conditioning and heat pump units. Lines within Systems Components give the material and installation price on a cost each basis for the components. Prices for alternate thru-wall unit systems are on Line Items 8.8-810-1010 thru 1050. Material quantities and labor costs have been adjusted for the system listed.

Factors: To adjust for job conditions other than normal working conditions use Lines 8.8-810-2700 thru 4000.

System Components	QUANTITY	UNIT	COST EACH MAT.	COST EACH INST.	COST EACH TOTAL
Electric thru-wall air conditioning unit.					
A/C unit, thru-wall, electric heat., cabinet, louver, 1/2 ton	1.000	Ea.	980	123	1,103
TOTAL			980	123	1,103

8.8-810	Thru-Wall A/C Unit	MAT.	INST.	TOTAL
1000	For alternate A/C units:			
1010	A/C Unit, thru-the-wall, sup. elect. heat, cabinet, louver, 1/2 Ton	980	123	1,103
1020	3/4 Ton	1,000	148	1,148
1030	1 Ton	1,050	185	1,235
1040	1-1/2 Ton	1,500	310	1,810
1050	2 Ton	1,500	390	1,890
1010	Heat pump, thru-the-wall, cabinet, louver, 1/2 Ton	1,250	92.50	1,342.50
1020	3/4 Ton	1,325	123	1,448
1030	1 Ton	1,375	185	1,560
1040	Sup. elect. heat, 1-1/2 Ton	2,525	475	3,000
1050	2 Ton	2,775	490	3,265
2700	Cut & patch to match existing construction, add, minimum	2%	3%	
2800	Maximum	5%	9%	
2900	Dust protection, add, minimum	1%	2%	
3000	Maximum	4%	11%	
3100	Equipment usage curtailment, add, minimum	1%	1%	
3200	Maximum	3%	10%	
3300	Material handling & storage limitation, add, minimum	1%	1%	
3400	Maximum	6%	7%	
3500	Protection of existing work, add, minimum	2%	2%	
3600	Maximum	5%	7%	
3700	Shift work requirements, add, minimum		5%	
3800	Maximum		30%	
3900	Temporary shoring and bracing, add, minimum	2%	5%	
4000	Maximum	5%	12%	

For information about Means Estimating Seminars, see yellow pages 11 and 12 in back of book

Division 9
Electrical

SERVICE & DISTRIB.   A9.1-220   Commercial Service - 3 Phase

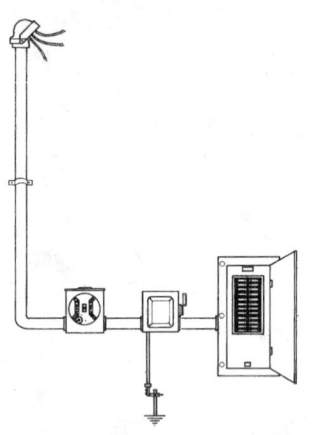

This page illustrates and describes commercial service systems including a meter socket, service head and cable, entrance switch, steel conduit, copper wire, panel board, ground rod, wire, and conduit. Lines within System Components give the unit price and total price on a cost each basis for this system. Prices for alternate commercial service systems are on Line Items 9.1-220-1500 thru 1700. Both material quantities and labor costs have been adjusted for the system listed.

Factors: To adjust for job conditions other than normal working situations use Lines 9.1-220-2900 thru 4000.

Example: You are to install the system with maximum equipment usage curtailment. Go to Line 9.1-220-3400 and apply these percentages to the appropriate MAT. and INST. costs.

System Components	QUANTITY	UNIT	COST EACH		
			MAT.	INST.	TOTAL
Commercial electric service including service breakers, metering 120/208 Volt, 3 phase, 4 wire, feeder, and panel board.					
100 Amp Service					
Meter socket	1.000	Ea.	32	123	155
Service head and cable	1.000	Ea.	46.45	112	158.45
Service entrance switch	1.000	Ea.	201	208	409
Rigid steel conduit	20.000	L.F.	53.40	121	174.40
600 volt copper wire #3	1.000	C.L.F.	62.50	79	141.50
Panel board, 24 circuits, 20 Amp breakers	1.000	Ea.	705	655	1,360
Ground rod plus wire and conduit	1.000	Ea.	29.45	96.20	125.65
TOTAL		Ea.	1,129.80	1,394.20	2,524

9.1-220	Commercial Service - 3 Phase	COST EACH		
		MAT.	INST.	TOTAL
1400	For alternate size services:			
1500	120/208 Volt, 3 phase, 4 wire service, 60 Amp	760	1,050	1,810
1600	200 Amp	2,125	2,350	4,475
1700	400 Amp	4,400	2,950	7,350
1800				
1900				
2000				
2100				
2200				
2300				
2400				
2500				
2900	Cut & patch to match existing construction, add, minimum	2%	3%	
3000	Maximum	5%	9%	
3100	Dust protection, add, minimum	1%	2%	
3200	Maximum	4%	11%	
3300	Equipment usage curtailment, add, minimum	1%	1%	
3400	Maximum	3%	10%	
3500	Material handling & storage limitation, add, minimum	1%	1%	
3600	Maximum	6%	7%	
3700	Protection of existing work, add, minimum	2%	2%	
3800	Maximum	5%	7%	
3900	Shift work requirements, add, minimum		5%	
4000	Maximum		30%	

SERVICE & DISTRIB. | A9.1-230 | Residential Service - Single Phase

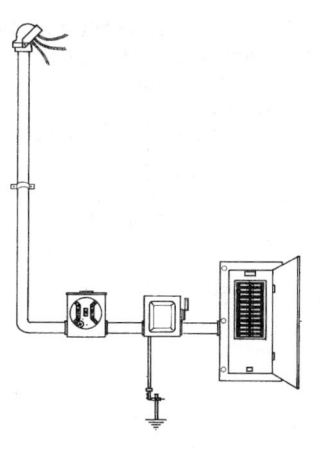

This page illustrates and describes a residential, single phase system including a weather cap, service entrance cable, meter socket, entrance switch, ground rod, ground cable, EMT, and panelboard. Lines with System Components give the unit price and total price on a cost each basis for this system. Prices for an alternate residential, single phase system are also given. Both material quantities and labor costs have been adjusted for the system listed.

Factors: To adjust for job conditions other than normal working situations use Lines 9.1-230-2900 thru 4000.

Example: You are to install the system with a minimum equipment usage curtailment. Go to Line 9.1-230-3300 and apply these percentages to the appropriate MAT. and INST. costs.

System Components	QUANTITY	UNIT	COST EACH		
			MAT.	INST.	TOTAL
100 Amp Service, single phase					
Weathercap	1.000	Ea.	7.05	33	40.05
Service entrance cable	.200	C.L.F.	39.40	79	118.40
Meter socket	1.000	Ea.	32	123	155
Entrance disconnect switch	1.000	Ea.	201	208	409
Ground rod, with clamp	1.000	Ea.	19.25	82	101.25
Ground cable	.100	C.L.F.	12.20	24.70	36.90
Panelboard, 12 circuit	1.000	Ea.	173	330	503
TOTAL		Ea.	483.90	879.70	1,363.60
200 Amp Service, single phase					
Weathercap	1.000	Ea.	20	49.50	69.50
Service entrance cable	.200	C.L.F.	100	113	213
Meter socket	1.000	Ea.	42	208	250
Entrance disconnect switch	1.000	Ea.	435	305	740
Ground rod, with clamp	1.000	Ea.	32.50	89.50	122
Ground cable	.100	C.L.F.	15	13.60	28.60
3/4" EMT	10.000	L.F.	5.80	30.30	36.10
Panelboard, 24 circuit	1.000	Ea.	475	520	995
TOTAL		Ea.	1,125.30	1,328.90	2,454.20

9.1-230	Residential Service - Single Phase	COST EACH		
		MAT.	INST.	TOTAL
2800				
2900	Cut & patch to match existing construction, add, minimum	2%	3%	
3000	Maximum	5%	9%	
3100	Dust protection, add, minimum	1%	2%	
3200	Maximum	4%	11%	
3300	Equipment usage curtailment, add, minimum	1%	1%	
3400	Maximum	3%	10%	
3500	Material handling & storage limitation, add, minimum	1%	1%	
3600	Maximum	6%	7%	
3700	Protection of existing work, add, minimum	2%	2%	
3800	Maximum	5%	7%	
3900	Shift work requirements, add, minimum		5%	
4000	Maximum		30%	

ELECTRICAL | A9.2-252 | Light Pole

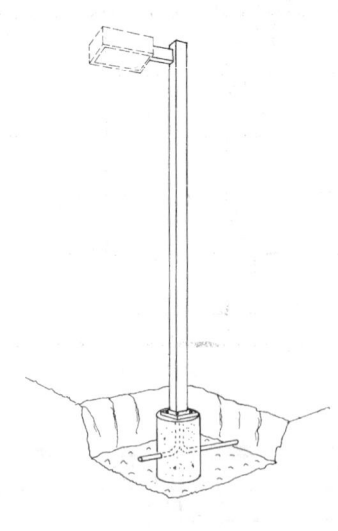

This page illustrates and describes light poles for parking or walkway area lighting. Included are aluminum or steel light poles, single or multiple fixture bracket arms, excavation, concrete footing, backfill and compaction. Lines within system components give the unit price and total price on a cost per each basis. Prices for alternate systems are shown on lines 9.2-252-0200 through 1440. Both material quantities and labor costs have been adjusted for the system listed.

Factors: To adjust for job conditions other than normal working situations use lines 9.2-252-2700 through 3600.

Example: You are to install the system where you must be careful not to damage existing walks or parking areas. Go to line 9.2-252-3400 and apply these percentages to the appropriate MAT. and INST. costs.

System Components			COST EACH		
	QUANTITY	UNIT	MAT.	INST.	TOTAL
Light poles, aluminum, 20' high, 1 arm bracket					
Aluminum light pole, 20', no concrete base	1.000	Ea.	655	391.50	1,046.50
Bracket arm for Aluminum light pole	1.000	Ea.	82.50	49.50	132
Excavation by hand, pits to 6' deep, heavy soil or clay	2.368	C.Y.		170.50	170.50
Footing, concrete incl forms, reinforcing, spread, under 1 C.Y.	.465	C.Y.	45.08	60.01	105.09
Backfill by hand	1.903	C.Y.		49.48	49.48
Compaction vibrating plate	1.903	C.Y.		7.67	7.67
TOTAL			782.58	728.66	1,511.24

9.2-252	Light Pole (Installed)	COST EACH		
		MAT.	INST.	TOTAL
0195	For alternate light pole systems:			
0200	Light pole, aluminum, 20' high, 1 arm bracket	785	730	1,515
0240	2 arm brackets	865	730	1,595
0280	3 arm brackets	950	755	1,705
0320	4 arm brackets	1,025	755	1,780
0360	30' high, 1 arm bracket	1,375	920	2,295
0400	2 arm brackets	1,450	920	2,370
0440	3 arm brackets	1,525	945	2,470
0480	4 arm brackets	1,600	945	2,545
0680	40' high, 1 arm bracket	1,650	1,225	2,875
0720	2 arm brackets	1,725	1,225	2,950
0760	3 arm brackets	1,825	1,250	3,075
0800	4 arm brackets	1,900	1,250	3,150
0840	Steel, 20' high, 1 arm bracket	980	775	1,755
0880	2 arm brackets	1,050	775	1,825
0920	3 arm brackets	1,075	800	1,875
0960	4 arm brackets	1,150	800	1,950
1000	30' high, 1 arm bracket	1,125	975	2,100
1040	2 arm brackets	1,200	975	2,175
1080	3 arm brackets	1,225	1,000	2,225
1120	4 arm brackets	1,300	1,000	2,300
1320	40' high, 1 arm bracket	1,475	1,325	2,800
1360	2 arm brackets	1,550	1,325	2,875
1400	3 arm brackets	1,575	1,350	2,925

ELECTRICAL — A9.2-252 Light Pole

9.2-252	Light Pole (Installed)	COST EACH		
		MAT.	INST.	TOTAL
1440	4 arm brackets	1,650	1,350	3,000
2700	Cut & patch to match existing construction, add, minimum	2%	3%	
2800	Maximum	5%	9%	
2900	Equipment usage curtailment, add, minimum	1%	1%	
3000	Maximum	3%	10%	
3100	Material handling & storage limitation, add, minimum	1%	1%	
3200	Maximum	6%	7%	
3300	Protection of existing work, add, minimum	2%	2%	
3400	Maximum	5%	7%	
3500	Shift work requirements, add, minimum		5%	
3600	Maximum		30%	

For expanded coverage of these items see *Means Electrical Cost Data 1999*

LIGHTING & POWER A9.2-900 | Lighting, Fluorescent

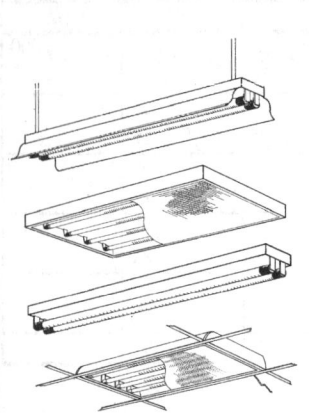

This page illustrates and describes fluorescent lighting systems including a fixture, lamp, outlet box and wiring. Lines within System Components give the unit price and total price on a cost each basis for this system. Prices for alternate fluorescent lighting systems are on Line Items 9.2-900-1300 thru 1500. Both material quantities and labor costs have been adjusted for the system listed.

Factors: To adjust for job conditions other than normal working situations use Lines 9.2-900-2900 thru 4000.

Example: You are to install the system during evening hours. Go to Line 9.2-900-3900 and apply this percentage to the appropriate INST. cost.

System Components	QUANTITY	UNIT	COST EACH		
			MAT.	INST.	TOTAL
Fluorescent lighting, including fixture, lamp, outlet box and wiring.					
Recessed lighting fixture, on suspended system	1.000	Ea.	61.50	84	145.50
Outlet box	1.000	Ea.	2.93	28.15	31.08
#12 wire	.660	C.L.F.	4.59	23.76	28.35
Conduit, EMT, 1/2" conduit	20.000	L.F.	8	46.40	54.40
TOTAL		Ea.	77.02	182.31	259.33

9.2-900	Lighting, Fluorescent	COST EACH		
		MAT.	INST.	TOTAL
1200	For alternate lighting fixtures:			
1300	Surface mounted, 2' x 4', acrylic prismatic diffuser	116	185	301
1400	Strip fixture, 8' long, two 8' lamps	67.50	174	241.50
1500	Pendant mounted, industrial, 8' long, with reflectors	105	200	305
1600				
1700				
1800				
1900				
2000				
2100				
2200				
2300				
2900	Cut & patch to match existing construction, add, minimum	2%	3%	
3000	Maximum	5%	9%	
3100	Dust protection, add, minimum	1%	2%	
3200	Maximum	4%	11%	
3300	Equipment usage curtailment, add, minimum	1%	1%	
3400	Maximum	3%	10%	
3500	Material handling & storage limitation, add, minimum	1%	1%	
3600	Maximum	6%	7%	
3700	Protection of existing work, add, minimum	2%	2%	
3800	Maximum	5%	7%	
3900	Shift work requirements, add, minimum		5%	
4000	Maximum		30%	

LIGHTING & POWER — A9.2-910 | Lighting, Incandescent

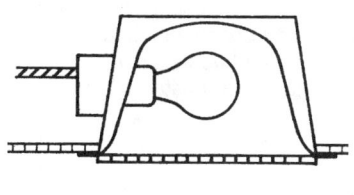
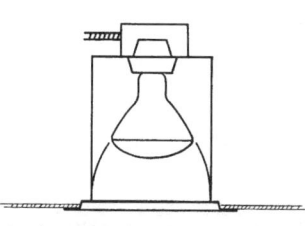

This page illustrates and describes incandescent lighting systems including a fixture, lamp, outlet box, conduit and wiring. Lines within System Components give the unit price and total price on a cost each basis for this system. Prices for an alternate incandescent lighting system are also given. Both material quantities and labor costs have been adjusted for the system listed.

Factors: To adjust for conditions other than normal working situations use Lines 9.2-910-2900 thru 4000.

Example: You are to install the system and cut and match existing construction. Go to Line 9.2-910-3000 and apply this percentage to the appropriate INST. costs.

System Components

System Components	QUANTITY	UNIT	COST EACH MAT.	COST EACH INST.	COST EACH TOTAL
Incandescent light fixture, including lamp, outlet box, conduit and wiring.					
Recessed wide reflector with flat glass lens	1.000	Ea.	60.50	59	119.50
Outlet box	1.000	Ea.	2.93	28.15	31.08
Armored cable, 3 wire	.200	C.L.F.	12.50	35.80	48.30
TOTAL		Ea.	75.93	122.95	198.88
Recessed, R-40 flood lamp with reflector skirt	1.000	Ea.	83.50	49.50	133
150 watt R-40 flood lamp	.010	Ea.	6.10	3.05	9.15
Outlet box	1.000	Ea.	2.93	28.15	31.08
Romex, 12-2 with ground	.200	C.L.F.	5	35.80	40.80
Conduit, 1/2" EMT	20.000	L.F.	8	46.40	54.40
TOTAL		Ea.	22.03	113.40	135.43

9.2-910	Lighting, Incandescent	MAT.	INST.	TOTAL
2900	Cut & patch to match existing construction, add, minimum	2%	3%	
3000	Maximum	5%	9%	
3100	Dust protection, add, minimum	1%	2%	
3200	Maximum	4%	11%	
3300	Equipment usage curtailment, add, minimum	1%	1%	
3400	Maximum	3%	10%	
3500	Material handling & storage limitation, add, minimum	1%	1%	
3600	Maximum	6%	7%	
3700	Protection of existing work, add, minimum	2%	2%	
3800	Maximum	5%	7%	
3900	Shift work requirements, add, minimum		5%	
4000	Maximum		30%	

For expanded coverage of these items see *Means Electrical Cost Data 1999*

LIGHTING & POWER — A9.2-920 Lighting, High Intensity

 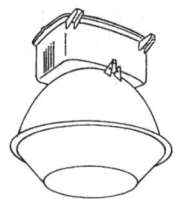

This page illustrates and describes high intensity lighting systems including a lamp, EMT conduit, EMT "T" fitting with cover, and wire. Lines within System Components give the unit price and total price on a cost each basis for this system. Prices for alternate high intensity lighting systems are on Line Items 9.2-920-1100 thru 1800. Both material quantities and labor costs have been adjusted for the system listed.

Factors: To adjust for job conditions other than normal working situations use Lines 9.2-920-2900 thru 4000.

Example: You are to install the system and protect existing construction. Go to Line 9.2-920-3700 and apply these percentages to the appropriate MAT. and INST. costs.

System Components	QUANTITY	UNIT	COST EACH MAT.	COST EACH INST.	COST EACH TOTAL
High intensity lighting system consisting of 400 watt mercury vapor fixture And lamp with 1/2" EMT conduit and fittings using #12 wire, high bay.					
400 watt mercury vapor fixture and lamp, high bay	1.000	Ea.	273	171	444
1/2" EMT conduit	30.000	L.F.	12	69.60	81.60
1/2" EMT "T" fitting with cover	1.000	Ea.	10.25	24.50	34.75
#12 wire	.600	L.F.	4.17	21.60	25.77
TOTAL		Ea.	299.42	286.70	586.12

9.2-920	Lighting, High Intensity	MAT.	INST.	TOTAL
1000	For alternate high intensity systems:			
1100	High bay: 400 watt, metal halide fixture and lamp	400	287	687
1200	High pressure sodium	365	287	652
1300	1000 watt, mercury vapor	455	315	770
1400	Metal halide	560	315	875
1500	High pressure sodium	515	315	830
1600	Low bay: 250 watt, mercury vapor	299	287	586
1700	Metal halide	385	239	624
1800	150 watt, high pressure sodium	320	239	559
1900				
2000				
2100				
2200				
2300				
2400				
2500				
2600				
2700				
2900	Cut & patch to match existing construction, add, minimum	2%	3%	
3000	Maximum	5%	9%	
3100	Dust protection, add, minimum	1%	2%	
3200	Maximum	4%	11%	
3300	Equipment usage curtailment, add, minimum	1%	1%	
3400	Maximum	3%	10%	
3500	Material handling & storage limitation, add, minimum	1%	1%	
3600	Maximum	6%	7%	
3700	Protection of existing work, add, minimum	2%	2%	
3800	Maximum	5%	7%	
3900	Shift work requirements, add, minimum		5%	
4000	Maximum		30%	

SPECIAL | A9.4-910 | Heat, Baseboard

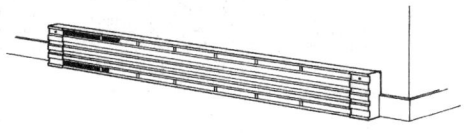

This page illustrates and describes baseboard heat systems including a thermostat, outlet box, breaker, and feed. Lines within System Components give the unit price and total price on a cost each basis for this system. Prices for alternate baseboard heat systems are on Line Items 9.4-910-1500 thru 1800. Both material quantities and labor costs have been adjusted for the system listed.

Factors: To adjust for job conditions other than normal working situations use Lines 9.4-910-2900 thru 4000.

Example: You are to install the system during evenings and weekends only. Go to Line 9.4-910-4000 and apply this percentage to the appropriate INST. cost.

System Components	QUANTITY	UNIT	COST EACH		
			MAT.	INST.	TOTAL
Baseboard heat including thermostat, outlet box, breaker and feed.					
Electric baseboard heater, 4' long	1.000	Ea.	53	59	112
Thermostat, integral	1.000	Ea.	25.50	24.50	50
Romex, 12-3 with ground	.400	C.L.F.	16.20	78.80	95
Panel board breaker, 20 Amp	1.000	Ea.	24	49.50	73.50
Outlet box	1.000	Ea.	2.18	22	24.18
TOTAL		Ea.	120.88	233.80	354.68

9.4-910	Heat, Baseboard	COST EACH		
		MAT.	INST.	TOTAL
1400	For alternate baseboard heating systems:			
1500	Electric baseboard, 2' long	107	224	331
1600	6' long	139	254	393
1700	8' long	157	273	430
1800	10' long	215	295	510
1900				
2000				
2100				
2200				
2300				
2400				
2500				
2600				
2700				
2900	Cut & patch to match existing construction, add, minimum	2%	3%	
3000	Maximum	5%	9%	
3100	Dust protection, add, minimum	1%	2%	
3200	Maximum	4%	11%	
3300	Equipment usage curtailment, add, minimum	1%	1%	
3400	Maximum	3%	10%	
3500	Material handling & storage limitation, add, minimum	1%	1%	
3600	Maximum	6%	7%	
3700	Protection of existing work, add, minimum	2%	2%	
3800	Maximum	5%	7%	
3900	Shift work requirements, add, minimum		5%	
4000	Maximum		30%	

ELECTRICAL — A9.9-500 Wiring Devices

9.9-500	Selective Price Sheet	COST EACH		
		MAT.	INST.	TOTAL
0100	Using non-metallic sheathed, cable, air conditioning receptacle	12.85	39.50	52.35
0200	Disposal wiring	11.05	44	55.05
0300	Dryer circuit	34.50	71.50	106
0400	Duplex receptacle	12.85	30.50	43.35
0500	Fire alarm or smoke detector	62.50	39.50	102
0600	Furnace circuit & switch	17.75	65.50	83.25
0700	Ground fault receptacle	56	49.50	105.50
0800	Heater circuit	12.30	49.50	61.80
0900	Lighting wiring	12.30	24.50	36.80
1000	Range circuit	49.50	98.50	148
1100	Switches single pole	12.65	24.50	37.15
1200	3-way	15	33	48
1300	Water heater circuit	15.40	79	94.40
1400	Weatherproof receptacle	93.50	65.50	159
1500	Using BX cable, air conditioning receptacle	21.50	47.50	69
1600	Disposal wiring	17.60	52.50	70.10
1700	Dryer circuit	40.50	85.50	126
1800	Duplex receptacle	21.50	36.50	58
1900	Fire alarm or smoke detector	62.50	39.50	102
2000	Furnace circuit & switch	22.50	79	101.50
2100	Ground fault receptacle	64.50	60	124.50
2200	Heater circuit	18.15	60	78.15
2300	Lighting wiring	21	29.50	50.50
2400	Range circuit	67	120	187
2500	Switches, single pole	19.45	29.50	48.95
2600	3-way	23.50	39.50	63
2700	Water heater circuit	23.50	94	117.50
2800	Weatherproof receptacle	102	79	181
2900	Using EMT conduit, air conditioning receptacle	24.50	59	83.50
3000	Disposal wiring	20.50	65.50	86
3100	Dryer circuit	44	107	151
3200	Duplex receptacle	24.50	45.50	70
3300	Fire alarm or smoke detector	70	59	129
3400	Furnace circuit & switch	29.50	98.50	128
3500	Ground fault receptacle	69.50	73	142.50
3600	Heater circuit	23	73	96
3700	Lighting wiring	24	37	61
3800	Range circuit	75	146	221
3900	Switches, single pole	22.50	37	59.50
4000	3-way	26.50	49.50	76
4100	Water heater circuit	26.50	116	142.50
4200	Weatherproof receptacle	108	98.50	206.50
4300	Using aluminum conduit, air conditioning receptacle	28	79	107
4400	Disposal wiring	26	87.50	113.50
4500	Dryer circuit	48.50	141	189.50
4600	Duplex receptacle	28	60.50	88.50
4700	Fire alarm or smoke detector	82.50	79	161.50
4800	Furnace circuit & switch	37.50	131	168.50
4900	Ground fault receptacle	75	98.50	173.50
5000	Heater circuit	28	98.50	126.50
5100	Lighting wiring	29.50	49.50	79
5200	Range circuit	86.50	197	283.50
5300	Switches, single pole	35	49.50	84.50
5400	3-way	38.50	65.50	104
5500	Water heater circuit	38.50	158	196.50
5600	Weatherproof receptacle	120	131	251
5700	Using galvanized steel conduit	26.50	84	110.50
5800	Disposal wiring	25	94	119
5900	Dryer circuit	45.50	152	197.50
6000	Duplex receptacle	26.50	64.50	91

ELECTRICAL | A9.9-500 | Wiring Devices

9.9-500 Selective Price Sheet

		\multicolumn{3}{c}{COST EACH}		
		MAT.	INST.	TOTAL
6100	Fire alarm or smoke detector	78	84	162
6200	Furnace circuit & switch	36.50	141	177.50
6300	Ground fault receptacle	72.50	104	176.50
6400	Heater circuit	27	104	131
6500	Lighting wiring	28.50	52.50	81
6600	Range circuit	81	208	289
6700	Switches, single pole	31	52.50	83.50
6800	3-way	34	68	102
6900	Water heater circuit	34	164	198
7000	Weatherproof receptacle	114	141	255
7100				
7200				
7300				
7400				
7500				
7600				
7700				
7800				
7900				
8000				
8100				
8200				
8300				
8400				

For information about Means Estimating Seminars, see yellow pages 11 and 12 in back of book

For expanded coverage of these items see *Means Electrical Cost Data 1999*

Division 11
Special Construction

SPECIAL CONSTR. A11.1-242 Kitchens

This page illustrates and describes kitchen systems including top and bottom cabinets, custom laminated plastic top, single bowl sink, and appliances. Lines within System Components give the unit price and total price on a cost each basis for this system. Prices for alternate kitchen systems are on Line Items 11.1-242-1500 and 1600. Both material quantities and labor costs have been adjusted for the system listed.

Factors: To adjust for job conditions other than normal working situations use Lines 11.1-242-2900 thru 4000.

Example: You are to install the system and protect the work area from dust. Go to Line 11.1-242-3200 and apply these percentages to the appropriate MAT. and INST. costs.

System Components	QUANTITY	UNIT	COST EACH		
			MAT.	INST.	TOTAL
Kitchen cabinets including wall and base cabinets, custom laminated Plastic top, sink & appliances, no plumbing or electrical rough-in included.					
Prefinished wood cabinets, average quality, wall and base	20.000	L.F.	1,740	490	2,230
Custom laminated plastic counter top	20.000	L.F.	108	244	352
Stainless steel sink, 22" x 25"	1.000	Ea.	305	131	436
Faucet, top mount	1.000	Ea.	50.50	41	91.50
Dishwasher, built-in	1.000	Ea.	239	201	440
Compactor, built-in	1.000	Ea.	360	73	433
Range hood, 30", ductless	1.000	Ea.	86.50	202.50	289
TOTAL		Ea.	2,889	1,382.50	4,271.50

11.1-242	Kitchens	COST EACH		
		MAT.	INST.	TOTAL
1400	For alternate kitchen systems:			
1500	Prefinished wood cabinets, high quality	6,225	1,525	7,750
1600	Custom cabinets, built in place, high quality	8,075	1,775	9,850
1700				
1800				
1900				
2000				
2100				
2200	NOTE: No plumbing or electric rough-ins are included in the above			
2300	Prices, for plumbing see Division 15, for electric see Division 16.			
2400				
2500				
2600				
2700				
2900	Cut & patch to match existing construction, add, minimum	2%	3%	
3000	Maximum	5%	9%	
3100	Dust protection, add, minimum	1%	2%	
3200	Maximum	4%	11%	
3300	Equipment usage curtailment, add, minimum	1%	1%	
3400	Maximum	3%	10%	
3500	Material handling & storage limitation, add, minimum	1%	1%	
3600	Maximum	6%	7%	
3700	Protection of existing work, add, minimum	2%	2%	
3800	Maximum	5%	7%	
3900	Shift work requirements, add, minimum		5%	
4000	Maximum		30%	

Important: See the Reference Section for critical supporting data - Reference Nos., Crews, & City Cost Indexes

SPECIAL CONSTR. | A11.1-742 | Wood Burning Stoves

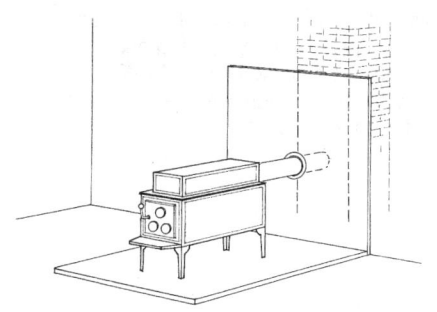

This page illustrates and describes a wood burning stove system including a free standing stove, preformed hearth, masonry chimney, and necessary piping and fittings. Lines within System Components give the unit price and total price on a cost each basis for this system. Prices for alternate wood burning stove systems are on Line Items 11.1-742-1600 thru 2000. Both material quantities and labor costs have been adjusted for the system listed.

Factors: To adjust for job conditions other than normal working situations use Lines 11.1-742-2900 thru 4000.

Example: You are to install the system and protect existing construction. Go to Line 11.1-742-3500 and apply these percentages to the appropriate MAT., and INST. costs.

System Components	QUANTITY	UNIT	COST EACH		
			MAT.	INST.	TOTAL
Cast iron, free standing, wood burning stove with preformed hearth, masonry Chimney, and all necessary piping and fittings to install in chimney.					
Cast iron wood burning stove, stove pipe	1.000	Ea.	815	560	1,375
Wall panel or hearth, non-combustible	1.000	Ea.	383.80	103.55	487.35
16" x 16" brick chimney, 8" x 8" flue	20.000	V.L.F.	383.75	900	1,283.75
Foundation	.500	C.Y.	69.50	77.15	146.65
TOTAL		Ea.	1,652.05	1,640.70	3,292.75

11.1-742	Wood Burning Stoves	COST EACH		
		MAT.	INST.	TOTAL
1400	For alternate wood burning systems:			
1500				
1600	Installed in existing fireplace	1,025	615	1,640
1700				
1800	Installed with insulated metal chimney			
1900	System including ceiling package,			
2000	Metal chimney to 10 L.F.	1,700	865	2,565
2100				
2200				
2300				
2400				
2500				
2600				
2700				
2900	Dust protection, add, minimum	1%	2%	
3000	Maximum	4%	11%	
3100	Equipment usage curtailment, add, minimum	1%	1%	
3200	Maximum	3%	10%	
3300	Material handling & storage limitation, add, minimum	1%	1%	
3400	Maximum	6%	7%	
3500	Protection of existing work, add, minimum	2%	2%	
3600	Maximum	5%	7%	
3700	Shift work requirements, add, minimum		5%	
3800	Maximum		30%	
3900	Temporary shoring and bracing, add, minimum	2%	5%	
4000	Maximum	5%	12%	

For expanded coverage of these items see *Means Interior Cost Data 1999*

SPECIAL CONSTR. | A11.1-744 | Masonry Fireplace

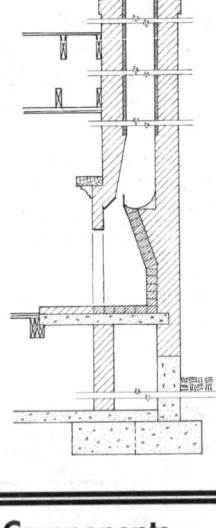

This page illustrates and describes masonry fireplace systems including a brick fireplace, footing, foundation, hearth, firebox, chimney and flue. Lines within System Components give the unit price and total price on a cost each basis for this system. Prices for alternate masonry fireplace systems are on Line Items 11.1-744-1300 thru 1500. Both material quantities and labor costs have been adjusted for the system listed.

Factors: To adjust for job conditions other than normal working situations use Lines 11.1-744-2700 thru 4000.

Example: You are to install the system with some temporary shoring and bracing. Go to Line 11.1-744-3900 and apply these percentages to the appropriate MAT. and INST. costs.

System Components	QUANTITY	UNIT	COST EACH		
			MAT.	INST.	TOTAL
Brick masonry fireplace, including footing, foundation, hearth, firebox, Chimney and flue, chimney 12' above firebox.					
Footing, 4' x 7' x 12" thick, 3000 psi concrete	1.040	C.Y.	100.83	134.22	235.05
Foundation, 12" concrete block	180.000	S.F.	446.40	891	1,337.40
Fireplace, brick faced, 6'-0" wide x 5'-0" high	1.000	Ea.	395	1,625	2,020
Hearth	1.000	Ea.	145	325	470
Chimney, 20" x 20", one 12" x 12" flue, 12 V.L.F.	12.000	V.L.F.	264	570	834
Mantle, wood	7.000	L.F.	32.62	71.05	103.67
TOTAL		Ea.	1,383.85	3,616.27	5,000.12

11.1-744	Masonry Fireplace	COST EACH		
		MAT.	INST.	TOTAL
1200	Above system with the following:			
1300	Chimney, 20" x 20", one 12" x 12" flue, 18 V.L.F.	1,525	3,900	5,425
1400	24 V.L.F.	1,650	4,175	5,825
1500	Fieldstone face instead of brick	1,700	3,625	5,325
1600				
1700				
1800				
1900				
2000				
2100				
2200				
2300				
2700	Cut & patch to match existing construction, add, minimum	2%	3%	
2800	Maximum	5%	9%	
2900	Dust protection, add, minimum	1%	2%	
3000	Maximum	4%	11%	
3100	Equipment usage curtailment, add, minimum	1%	1%	
3200	Maximum	3%	10%	
3300	Material handling & storage limitation, add, minimum	1%	1%	
3400	Maximum	6%	7%	
3500	Protection of existing work, add, minimum	2%	2%	
3600	Maximum	5%	7%	
3700	Shift work requirements, add, minimum		5%	
3800	Maximum		30%	
3900	Temporary shoring and bracing, add, minimum	2%	5%	
4000	Maximum	5%	12%	

SPECIAL CONSTR. | A11.2-100 | Tanks, Fiberglass

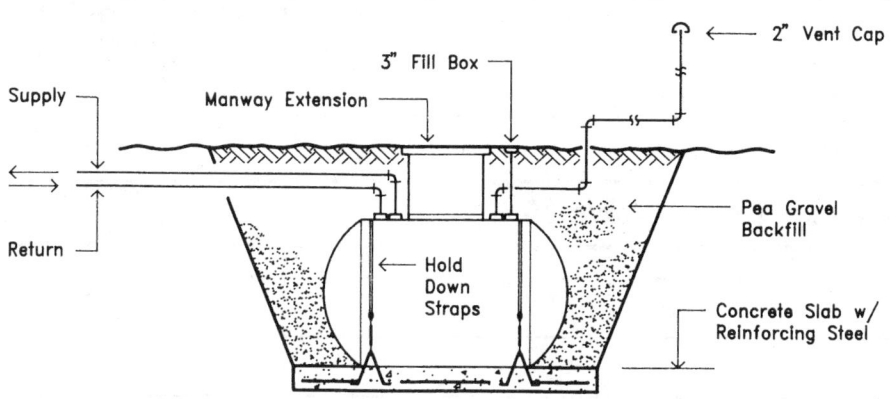

Fiberglass Underground Fuel Storage Tank, Single Wall

This page illustrates and describes fiberglass tanks including hold down slab, reinforcing steel and peastone gravel. Lines within Systems Components give the material and installation price on a cost each basis for the components. Prices for alternate fiberglass tank systems are on Line items 11.2-105-1010 thru 11.2-110-1100. Material quantities and labor costs have been adjusted for the system listed.

Factors To adjust for job conditions other than normal working situations use Lines 11.2-110-2700 thru 4000.

System Components	QUANTITY	UNIT	COST EACH MAT.	COST EACH INST.	COST EACH TOTAL
Single wall underground fiberglass storage tanks including, excavation, hold down slab, backfill, manway extension and related piping.					
Tank, fiberglass, underground, single wall, U.L. listed, 550 gal	1.000	Ea.	1,525	276	1,801
Tank, fiberglass, manways, add	1.000	Ea.	920		920
Tank, for hold-downs 500-4000 gal, add	1.000	Ea.	176	98	274
Foot valve, single poppet, 3/4" dia	1.000	Ea.	41.50	23	64.50
Tubing, copper, Type L, 3/4" dia	120.000	L.F.	237.60	642	879.60
Elbow 90°, copper, wrought, cu x cu, 3/4" dia.	8.000	Ea.	7.20	172	179.20
Fuel oil specialties, valve, ball chk, globe type, fusible, 3/4" dia	2.000	Ea.	52	41	93
Elbow 90°, black steel, straight, 2" dia.	3.000	Ea.	26.25	123	149.25
Union, black steel, with brass seat, 2" dia.	1.000	Ea.	15.40	43	58.40
Pipe and nipples, steel, Sch. 40, threaded, black, 2" dia	2.000	Ea.	128.06	437	565.06
Vent protector / breather, 2" dia.	1.000	Ea.	14.10	12.80	26.90
Pipe, black steel, welded, Sch. 40, 3" dia.	30.000	L.F.	159	551.10	710.10
Elbow 90°, steel, weld joint, butt, 3" dia.	3.000	Ea.	32.70	338.40	371.10
Flange, weld neck, 150 lb., 3" pipe size	1.000	Ea.	23.50	56.41	79.91
Fuel fill box, locking inner cover, 3" dia.	1.000	Ea.	100	82	182
Remote tank gauging system, 30', 5" pointer travel	1.000	Ea.	1,300	164	1,464
Tank leak detector system, 8 channel, external monitoring	1.000	Ea.	1,700		1,700
Tank leak detection system, probes, well monitoring, liquid phase detection	2.000	Ea.	1,530		1,530
Excavating, trench, NO sheeting or dewatering, 6'-10' D,3/4 CY hyd backhoe	18.000	C.Y.		93.96	93.96
Concrete hold down pad, 6' x 5' x 8" thick	30.000	C.Y.	53.40	29.40	82.80
Reinforcing in hold down pad, #3 to #7	120.000	Lb.	34.80	50.40	85.20
Stone back-fill, hand spread, pea gravel	9.000	C.Y.	400.50	283.50	684
Corrosion resistance, wrap & coat, small diam pipe, 1" diam, add	120.000	L.F.	130.80		130.80
Corrosion resistance, wrap & coat, small diameter pipe, 2" diam, add	36.000	L.F.	43.20		43.20
Corrosion resistance wrap & coat, 4" diam, add	30.000	L.F.	43.20		43.20
TOTAL			8,694.21	3,516.97	12,211.18

11.2-105	Fiberglass Fuel Tank, Single Wall	COST EACH MAT.	COST EACH INST.	COST EACH TOTAL
1000	For alternate storage tanks:			
1010	Storage tank, fuel, underground, single wall fiberglass, 550 Gal.	8,700	3,500	12,200
1020	2000 Gal.	11,200	4,850	16,050
1030	4000 Gal.	15,500	6,675	22,175
1040	6000 Gal.	16,600	7,475	24,075
1050	8000 Gal.	20,800	9,200	30,000
1060	10,000 Gal.	25,000	10,000	35,000
1070	15,000 Gal.	29,000	12,500	41,500

For expanded coverage of these items see Means Interior Cost Data 1999

SPECIAL CONSTR. | A11.2-100 Tanks, Fiberglass

11.2-105 Fiberglass Fuel Tank, Single Wall

		COST EACH		
		MAT.	INST.	TOTAL
1080	20,000 Gal.	37,000	15,200	52,200
1090	25,000 Gal.	45,800	17,800	63,600
1100	30,000 Gal.	52,500	19,200	71,700
1110	40,000 Gal.	66,500	24,200	90,700
1120	48,000 Gal.	93,000	27,900	120,900

11.2-110 Fiberglass Fuel Tank, Double Wall

		COST EACH		
		MAT.	INST.	TOTAL
1010	Storage tank, fuel, underground, double wall fiberglass, 550 Gal.	10,800	4,025	14,825
1020	2500 Gal.	15,800	5,675	21,475
1030	4000 Gal.	20,000	7,075	27,075
1040	6000 Gal.	21,700	7,975	29,675
1050	8000 Gal.	27,100	9,700	36,800
1060	10,000 Gal.	31,700	11,300	43,000
1070	15,000 Gal.	41,400	13,000	54,400
1080	20,000 Gal.	50,500	15,900	66,400
1090	25,000 Gal.	60,500	18,400	78,900
1100	30,000 Gal.	68,500	19,500	88,000
2700	Cut & patch to match existing construction, add, minimum	2%	3%	
2800	Maximum	5%	9%	
2900	Dust protection, add, minimum	1%	2%	
3000	Maximum	4%	11%	
3100	Equipment usage curtailment, add, minimum	1%	1%	
3200	Maximum	3%	10%	
3300	Material handling & storage limitation, add, minimum	1%	1%	
3400	Maximum	6%	7%	
3500	Protection of existing work, add, minimum	2%	2%	
3600	Maximum	5%	7%	
3700	Shift work requirements, add, minimum		5%	
3800	Maximum		30%	
3900	Temporary shoring and bracing, add, minimum	2%	5%	
4000	Maximum	5%	12%	

SPECIAL CONSTR. | A11.2-200 Tanks, Steel

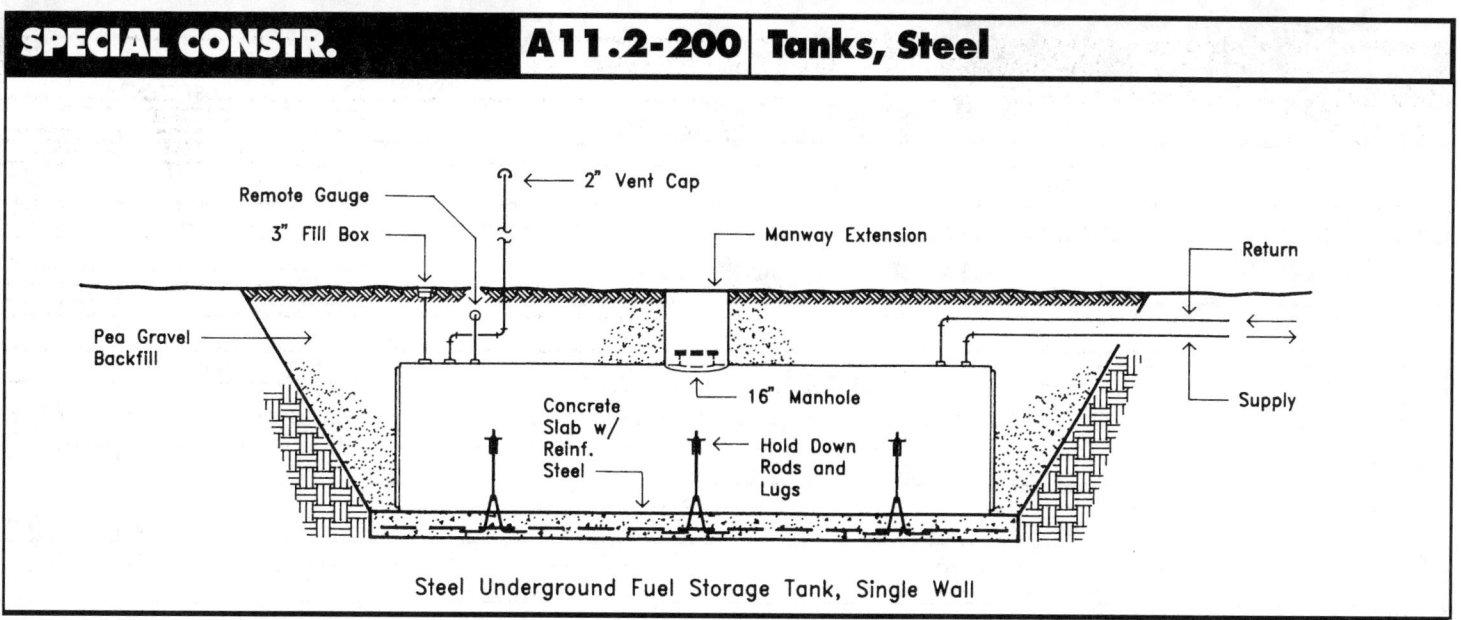

Steel Underground Fuel Storage Tank, Single Wall

System Components

System Components	QUANTITY	UNIT	MAT.	INST.	TOTAL
Single wall underground steel storage tank including, excavation, hold down slab, backfill, manway extension and related piping.					
Tank, steel, underground, sti-P3, set in place, 500 gal, 7 Ga. shell	1.000	Ea.	905	273	1,178
Tank, for manways, add	1.000	Ea.	505		505
Tanks, for hold-downs, 500-2000 gal, add	1.000	Ea.	288	98	386
Foot valve, single poppet, 3/4" dia	1.000	Ea.	41.50	23	64.50
Tubing, copper, Type L, 3/4" dia.	120.000	L.F.	237.60	642	879.60
Elbow 90°, copper, wrought, cu x cu, 3/4" dia.	8.000	Ea.	7.20	172	179.20
Fuel oil valve, ball chk, globe type, fusible, 3/4" dia.	2.000	Ea.	52	41	93
Elbow 90°, black steel, straight, 2" dia.	3.000	Ea.	26.25	123	149.25
Union, black steel, with brass seat, 3/4" dia.	1.000	Ea.	5.70	31.50	37.20
Pipe and nipples, steel, Sch. 40, threaded, black, 2" dia	2.000	Ea.	128.06	437	565.06
Vent protector / breather, 2" dia.	1.000	Ea.	14.10	12.80	26.90
Pipe, black steel, welded, Sch. 40, 3" dia.	30.000	L.F.	159	551.10	710.10
Elbow 90°, steel, weld joint, butt, 90° elbow, 3" dia.	3.000	Ea.	32.70	338.40	371.10
Flange, steel, weld neck, 150 lb., 3" pipe size	1.000	Ea.	23.50	56.41	79.91
Fuel fill box, locking inner cover, 3" dia.	1.000	Ea.	100	82	182
Remote tank gauging system, 30', 5" pointer travel	1.000	Ea.	1,300	164	1,464
Tank leak detector system, 8 channel, external monitoring	1.000	Ea.	1,700		1,700
Tank leak detection system, probes, well monitoring, liquid phase detection	2.000	Ea.	1,530		1,530
Excavation, NO sheeting or dewatering, 6'-10' D, 3/4 CY hyd backhoe	18.000	C.Y.		93.96	93.96
Concrete hold down pad, 6' x 5' x 8" thick	30.000	C.Y.	53.40	29.40	82.80
Reinforcing in hold down pad, #3 to #7	120.000	Lb.	34.80	50.40	85.20
Stone back-fill, hand spread, pea gravel	9.000	C.Y.	400.50	283.50	684
Corrosion resistance, wrap & coat, small diam pipe, 1" dia., add	120.000	L.F.	130.80		130.80
Corrosion resistance, wrap & coat, small diameter pipe, 2" dia., add	36.000	L.F.	43.20		43.20
Corrosion resistance wrap & coat, 4" dia., add	30.000	L.F.	43.20		43.20
TOTAL			7,761.51	3,502.47	11,263.98

11.2-205	Steel Fuel Tank, Single Wall	MAT.	INST.	TOTAL
1000	For alternate storage tanks:			
1010	Storage tank, fuel, underground, single wall steel, 550 Gal.	7,750	3,500	11,250
1020	2000 Gal.	11,000	4,850	15,850
1030	5000 Gal.	16,800	6,925	23,725
1040	10,000 Gal.	25,800	10,700	36,500
1050	15,000 Gal.	32,700	12,500	45,200
1060	20,000 Gal.	41,000	15,100	56,100
1070	25,000 Gal.	48,700	17,700	66,400

For expanded coverage of these items see *Means Interior Cost Data 1999*

SPECIAL CONSTR. | A11.2-200 Tanks, Steel

11.2-205 Steel Fuel Tank, Single Wall

		MAT.	INST.	TOTAL
1080	30,000 Gal.	57,500	18,900	76,400
1090	40,000 Gal.	70,000	23,900	93,900

11.2-210 Steel Fuel Tank, Double Wall

		MAT.	INST.	TOTAL
1010	Storage tank, fuel, underground, double wall steel, 500 Gal.	10,200	4,100	14,300
1020	2000 Gal.	13,800	5,450	19,250
1030	4000 Gal.	19,600	7,175	26,775
1040	6000 Gal.	23,200	7,925	31,125
1050	8000 Gal.	27,700	9,825	37,525
1060	10,000 Gal.	32,600	11,400	44,000
1070	15,000 Gal.	41,100	13,300	54,400
1080	20,000 Gal.	49,800	16,100	65,900
1090	25,000 Gal.	61,500	18,400	79,900
1100	30,000 Gal.	70,000	19,600	89,600
1110	40,000 Gal.	86,000	24,700	110,700
1120	50,000 Gal.	102,500	29,700	132,200

11.2-220 Steel Tank, Above Ground, Single Wall

		MAT.	INST.	TOTAL
1010	Storage tank, fuel, above ground, single wall steel, 550 Gal.	5,275	2,875	8,150
1020	2000 Gal.	6,025	2,950	8,975
1030	5000 Gal.	9,600	4,550	14,150
1040	10,000 Gal.	12,600	4,825	17,425
1050	15,000 Gal.	15,600	4,975	20,575
1060	20,000 Gal.	17,400	5,125	22,525
1070	25,000 Gal.	20,500	5,250	25,750
1080	30,000 Gal.	23,700	5,475	29,175

11.2-230 Steel Tank, Above Ground, Double Wall

		MAT.	INST.	TOTAL
1010	Storage tank, fuel, above ground, double wall steel, 500 Gal.	9,200	2,925	12,125
1020	2000 Gal.	10,900	2,975	13,875
1030	4000 Gal.	15,000	3,050	18,050
1040	6000 Gal.	17,700	4,700	22,400
1050	8000 Gal.	19,500	4,825	24,325
1060	10,000 Gal.	20,700	4,925	25,625
1070	15,000 Gal.	27,100	5,100	32,200
1080	20,000 Gal.	29,800	5,250	35,050
1090	25,000 Gal.	34,600	5,400	40,000
1100	30,000 Gal.	37,200	5,625	42,825
2700	Cut & patch to match existing construction, add, minimum	2%	3%	
2800	Maximum	5%	9%	
2900	Dust protection, add, minimum	1%	2%	
3000	Maximum	4%	11%	
3100	Equipment usage curtailment, add, minimum	1%	1%	
3200	Maximum	3%	10%	
3300	Material handling & storage limitation, add, minimum	1%	1%	
3400	Maximum	6%	7%	
3500	Protection of existing work, add, minimum	2%	2%	
3600	Maximum	5%	7%	
3700	Shift work requirements, add, minimum		5%	
3800	Maximum		30%	
3900	Temporary shoring and bracing, add, minimum	2%	5%	
4000	Maximum	5%	12%	

SPECIAL — A11.9-100 Kitchen

11.9-100 Selective Price Sheet

		COST EACH		
		MAT.	INST.	TOTAL
0100	Cabinets standard wood, base, one drawer one door, 12" wide	125	29.50	154.50
0200	15" wide	127	30.50	157.50
0300	18" wide	144	31.50	175.50
0400	21" wide	153	32	185
0500	24" wide	153	33	186
0600				
0700	Two drawers two doors, 27" wide	195	33	228
0800	30" wide	213	34	247
0900	33" wide	216	35	251
1000	36" wide	224	36	260
1100	42" wide	245	37	282
1200	48" wide	266	38.50	304.50
1300	Drawer base (4 drawers), 12" wide	124	29.50	153.50
1400	15" wide	160	30.50	190.50
1500	18" wide	174	31.50	205.50
1600	24" wide	195	33	228
1700	Sink or range base, 30" wide	163	34	197
1800	33" wide	169	35	204
1900	36" wide	177	36	213
2000	42" wide	194	37	231
2100	Corner base, 36" wide	179	40.50	219.50
2200	Lazy susan with revolving door	223	44.50	267.50
2300	Cabinets standard wood, wall two doors, 12" high, 30" wide	96	29.50	125.50
2400	36" wide	109	30.50	139.50
2500	15" high, 30" high	103	30.50	133.50
2600	36" wide	112	32	144
2700	24" high, 30" wide	131	31.50	162.50
2800	36" wide	140	32	172
2900	30" high, 30" wide	148	38	186
3000	36" wide	164	39	203
3100	42" wide	179	39.50	218.50
3200	48" wide	194	39.50	233.50
3300	One door, 30" high, 12" wide	93.50	33	126.50
3400	15" wide	91.50	34	125.50
3500	18" wide	99	35	134
3600	24" wide	121	36	157
3700	Corner, 30" high, 24" wide	155	40.50	195.50
3800	36" wide	206	44.50	250.50
3900	Broom, 84" high, 24" deep, 18" wide	254	73	327
4000	Oven, 84" high, 24" deep, 27" wide	325	91.50	416.50
4100	Valance board, 4' long	33	7.40	40.40
4200	6' long	50	11.10	61.10
4300	Counter tops, laminated plastic, stock 25" wide w/backsplash, min.	5.40	12.20	17.60
4400	Maximum	15.65	14.60	30.25
4500	Custom, 7/8" thick, no splash	17.30	12.20	29.50
4600	Cove splash	22.50	12.20	34.70
4700	1-1/4" thick, no splash	20.50	13.05	33.55
4800	Square splash	25.50	13.05	38.55
4900	Post formed	9.40	12.20	21.60
5000				
5100	Maple laminated 1-1/2" thick, no splash	34	13.05	47.05
5200	Square splash	38.50	13.05	51.55
5300				
5400				
5500	Appliances, range, free standing, minimum	315	57.50	372.50
5600	Maximum	1,150	144	1,294
5700	Built-in, minimum	445	65.50	510.50
5800	Maximum	1,100	365	1,465
5900	Counter top range 4 burner, maximum	186	65.50	251.50
6000	Maximum	430	131	561

For expanded coverage of these items see *Means Interior Cost Data 1999*

SPECIAL 11.9-100 | A11.9-100 Kitchen

Selective Price Sheet

		COST EACH		
		MAT.	INST.	TOTAL
6100	Compactor, built-in, minimum	360	73	433
6200	Maximum	395	122	517
6300	Dishwasher, built-in, minimum	239	201	440
6400	Maximum	485	400	885
6500	Garbage disposer, sink-pipe, minimum	41	80	121
6600	Maximum	196	80	276
6700	Range hood, 30" wide, 2 speed, minimum	41.50	153	194.50
6800	Maximum	305	255	560
6900	Refrigerator, no frost, 12 cu. ft.	455	57.50	512.50
7000	20 cu. ft.	700	95.50	795.50
7100	Plumb. not incl. rough-ins, sinks porc. C.I., single bowl, 21" x 24"	214	131	345
7200	21" x 30"	395	131	526
7300	Double bowl, 20" x 32"	310	153	463
7400				
7500	Stainless steel, single bowl, 19" x 18"	276	131	407
7600	22" x 25"	305	131	436
7700				
7800				
7900				
8000				
8100				
8200				
8300				
8400				

For information about Means Estimating Seminars, see yellow pages 11 and 12 in back of book

Division 12
Site Work

SITE WORK — A12.1-116 Excavation, Utility Trench

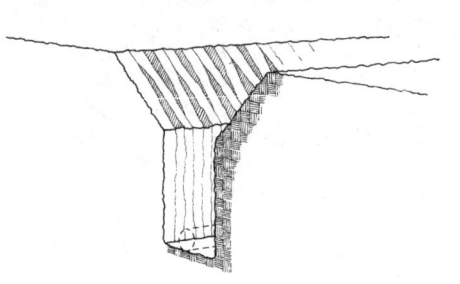

This page illustrates and describes utility trench excavation with backfill systems including a trench, backfill, excavated material, utility pipe or ductwork not included. Lines within System Components give the unit price and total price on a linear foot basis for this system. Prices for alternate utility trench excavation with backfill systems are on Line Items 12.1-116-1100 thru 2500. Both material quantities and labor costs have been adjusted for the system listed.

Factors: To adjust for job conditions other than normal working situations use Lines 12.1-116-3100 thru 4000.

Example: You are to install the system and protect existing construction. Go to Line 12.1-116-3600 and apply these percentages to the appropriate TOTAL cost.

System Components	QUANTITY	UNIT	COST PER L.F.		
			EQUIP.	LABOR	TOTAL
Cont. utility trench excav. with 3/8 C.Y. wheel mtd. backhoe, Backfilling with excav. mat. and comp. in 12" lifts. Trench is 2' wide by 4' dp. Cost of utility piping or ductwork is not incl. Cost based on an Excavation production rate of 150 C.Y. daily no hauling included.					
Machine excavate trench, 2' wide by 4' deep	.296	C.Y.	.47	1.28	1.75
Dozer backfill with excavated material	.296	C.Y.	.24	.35	.59
Compact in 12" lifts, vibrating plate	.296	C.Y.	.07	1.14	1.21
TOTAL			.78	2.77	3.55

12.1-116	Excavation, Utility Trench	COST PER L.F.		
		EQUIP.	LABOR	TOTAL
1000	Alternate size trenches:			
1100	2' wide x 2' deep	.40	1.39	1.79
1200	3' deep	.60	2.08	2.68
1300	With sloping sides, 2' wide x 5' deep	2.21	7.80	10.01
1400	6' deep	2.95	10.40	13.35
1500	7' deep	3.78	13.35	17.13
1600	8' deep	4.70	16.70	21.40
1700	9' deep	5.75	20.50	26.25
1800	10' deep	6.85	24.50	31.35

12.1-116	Excavation, Utility Trench	COST PER L.F.		
		MAT.	INST.	TOTAL
2000	For hauling excavated material up to 2 miles & backfilling w/ gravel			
2100	Gravel, 2' wide by 2' deep, add	1.12	2.60	3.72
2200	4' deep, add	2.25	5.20	7.45
2300	6' deep, add	8.45	19.50	27.95
2400	8' deep, add	13.50	31	44.50
2500	10' deep, add	19.70	45.50	65.20
2600				
2700				
2800	For shallow, hand excavated trenches, no backfill, to 6' dp, light soil		36	36
2900	Heavy soil		72	72
3000				
3100	Equipment usage curtailment, add, minimum	1%	1%	
3200	Maximum	3%	10%	
3300	Material handling & storage limitation, add, minimum	1%	1%	
3400	Maximum	6%	7%	
3500	Protection of existing work, add, minimum	2%	2%	
3600	Maximum	5%	7%	
3700	Shift work requirements, add, minimum		5%	
3800	Maximum		30%	
3900	Temporary shoring and bracing, add, minimum	2%	5%	
4000	Maximum	5%	12%	

SITE WORK | A12.1-462 | Excavation, Footings or Trench

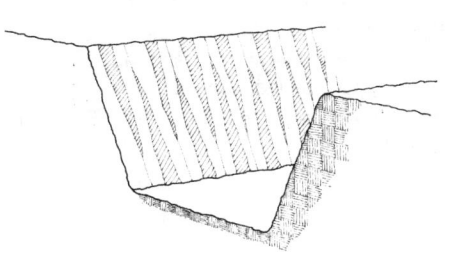

This page illustrates and describes continuous footing and trench excavation systems including a wheel mounted backhoe, operator, equipment rental, fuel, oil, mobilization, no hauling or backfill. Lines within System Components give the unit price and total price per linear foot for this system. Prices for alternate continuous footing and trench excavation systems are on Line Items 12.1-462-1300 thru 2700. Both material quantities and labor costs have been adjusted for the system listed.

Factors: To adjust for job conditions other than normal working situations use Lines 12.1-462-2900 thru 4000.

Example: You are to install the system and supply dust protection. Go to Line 12.1-462-3000 and apply this percentage to the appropriate TOTAL costs.

System Components

System Components	QUANTITY	UNIT	COST PER L.F.		
			EQUIP.	LABOR	TOTAL
Continuous footing or trench excav. w/ 3/4 C.Y. wheel mntd backhoe					
Including operator, equipment rental, fuel, oil and mobilization. Trench					
Is 4' wide at bottom, 3' deep w/sides sloped 1 to 2 and 200' long. Costs					
Are based on a production rate of 240 C.Y./day. No hauling/backfill incl.					
Equipment operator	4.000	Hr.		180	180
3/4 C.Y. backhoe, wheel mounted	.500	Day	82.50		82.50
Operating expense (fuel, oil)	4.000	Hr.	37.80		37.80
Mobilization	1.000	Ea.		359	359
TOTAL	120.000	C.Y.	120.30	539	659.30
COST PER L.F.		L.F.	.60	2.70	3.30

12.1-462 Excavation, Footings or Trench

		COST PER L.F.		
		EQUIP.	LABOR	TOTAL
1200	For alternate trench sizes, 4' bottom with sloped sides:			
1300	2' deep, 50' long	1.79	10.80	12.59
1400	100' long	.97	5.40	6.37
1500	300' long	.40	1.80	2.20
1600	4' deep, 50' long	1.93	10.80	12.73
1700	100' long	1.11	5.40	6.51
1800	300' long	.84	2.48	3.32
1900	6' deep, 50' long	2.15	10.80	12.95
2000	100' long	1.32	6.05	7.37
2100	300' long	1.60	3.60	5.20
2200	8' deep, 50' long	2.41	10.80	13.21
2300	100' long	2.41	7.20	9.61
2400	300' long	2.41	3.60	6.01
2500	10' deep, 50' long	3.61	12.60	16.21
2600	100' long	3.47	8.75	12.22
2700	300' long	3.37	6.25	9.62
2800				
2900	Dust protection, add, minimum	1%	2%	
3000	Maximum	4%	11%	
3100	Equipment usage curtailment, add, minimum	1%	1%	
3200	Maximum	3%	10%	
3300	Material handling & storage limitation, add, minimum	1%	1%	
3400	Maximum	6%	7%	
3500	Protection of existing work, add, minimum	2%	2%	
3600	Maximum	5%	7%	
3700	Shift work requirements, add, minimum		5%	
3800	Maximum		30%	
3900	Temporary shoring and bracing, add, minimum	2%	5%	
4000	Maximum	5%	12%	

For expanded coverage of these items see *Means Site Work & Landscape Cost Data 1999*

SITE WORK — A12.1-464 Excavation, Foundation

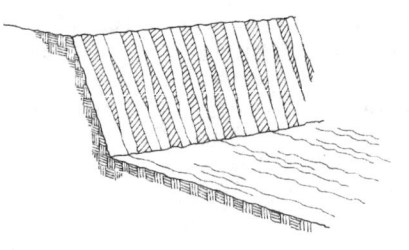

This page illustrates and describes foundation excavation systems including a backhoe-loader, operator, equipment rental, fuel, oil, mobilization, hauling material, no backfilling. Lines within System Components give the unit price and total price per cubic yard for this system. Prices for alternate foundation excavation systems are on Line Items 12.1-464-1600 thru 2200. Both material quantities and labor costs have been adjusted for the system listed.

Factors: To adjust for job conditions other than normal working situations use Lines 12.1-464-2900 thru 4000.

Example: You are to install the system with the use of temporary shoring and bracing. Go to Line 12.1-464-3900 and apply these percentages to the appropriate TOTAL costs.

System Components			COST PER C.Y.		
	QUANTITY	UNIT	EQUIP.	LABOR	TOTAL
Foundation excav w/ 3/4 C.Y. backhoe-loader, incl. operator, equip Rental, fuel, oil, and mobilization. Hauling of excavated material is Included. Prices based on one day production of 360 C.Y. in medium soil Without backfilling.					
Equipment operator	8.000	Hr.		360	360
Backhoe-loader, 3/4 C.Y.	1.000	Day	165		165
Operating expense (fuel, oil)	8.000	Hr.	75.60		75.60
Hauling, 12 C.Y. trucks, 1 mile round trip	360.000	C.Y.		1,072.80	1,072.80
Mobilization	1.000	Ea.		359	359
TOTAL	360.000	C.Y.	240.60	1,791.80	2,032.40
COST PER C.Y.		C.Y.	.67	4.98	5.65

12.1-464	Excavation, Foundation	COST PER C.Y.		
		EQUIP.	LABOR	TOTAL
1400	For alternate size excavations:			
1500				
1600	100 C.Y.	.22	8.60	8.82
1700	200 C.Y.	.67	5.80	6.47
1800	300 C.Y.	.69	5.20	5.89
1900	400 C.Y.	.66	4.87	5.53
2000	500 C.Y.	.67	4.71	5.38
2100	600 C.Y.	.65	4.58	5.23
2200	700 C.Y.	.66	4.47	5.13
2300				
2400				
2500				
2900	Dust protection, add, minimum	1%	2%	
3000	Maximum	4%	11%	
3100	Equipment usage curtailment, add, minimum	1%	1%	
3200	Maximum	3%	10%	
3300	Material handling & storage limitation, add, minimum	1%	1%	
3400	Maximum	6%	7%	
3500	Protection of existing work, add, minimum	2%	2%	
3600	Maximum	5%	7%	
3700	Shift work requirements, add, minimum		5%	
3800	Maximum		30%	
3900	Temporary shoring and bracing, add, minimum	2%	5%	
4000	Maximum	5%	12%	

SITE WORK — A12.3-940 Septic Systems

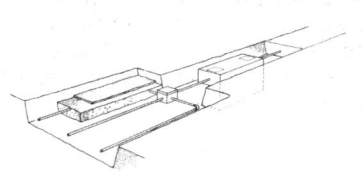

This page illustrates and describes drainage and utilities – septic system including a tank, distribution box, excavation, piping, crushed stone and backfill. Lines within System Components give the unit price and total price on a cost each basis for this system. Prices for alternate drainage and utilities – septic systems are on Line Items 12.4-940-1700 thru 2000. Both material quantities and labor costs have been adjusted for the system listed.

Factors: To adjust for job conditions other than normal working situations use Lines 12.3-940-3100 thru 4000.

Example: You are to install the system with a material handling limitation. Go to Line 12.3-940-3500 and apply these percentages to the appropriate MAT. and INST. costs.

System Components	QUANTITY	UNIT	COST EACH MAT.	COST EACH INST.	COST EACH TOTAL
Septic system including tank, distribution box, excavation, piping, crushed Stone and backfill for a 1000 S.F. leaching field.					
Precast concrete septic tank, 1000 gal. capacity	1.000	Ea.	495	163.65	658.65
Concrete distribution box	1.000	Ea.	82.50	36	118.50
Sch. 40 sewer pipe, PVC, 4" diameter	25.000	L.F.	406.30	442	848.30
Sch. 40 sewer pipe fittings, PVC, 4" diameter	8.000	Ea.	29.84	648	677.84
Trench and tank excavation	120.000	C.Y.		499.30	499.30
Crushed stone backfill	76.000	C.Y.	459.80	589	1,048.80
Backfill with excavated material	26.000	C.Y.		30.94	30.94
Building paper	6.000	C.S.F.	13.20	59.40	72.60
TOTAL		System	1,486.64	2,468.29	3,954.93

12.3-940	Septic Systems	MAT.	INST.	TOTAL
1600	For alternate septic systems:			
1700	1000 gal. tank with 2000 S.F. field	2,100	3,500	5,600
1800	With leaching pits	1,850	760	2,610
1900	2000 gal. tank with 2000 S.F. field	2,575	3,600	6,175
2000	With leaching pits	2,425	1,125	3,550
2100				
2200				
2300				
2400				
2500				
2600				
2700				
2800				
2900				
3100	Dust protection, add, minimum	1%	2%	
3200	Maximum	4%	11%	
3300	Equipment usage curtailment, add, minimum	1%	1%	
3400	Maximum	3%	10%	
3500	Material handling & storage limitation, add, minimum	1%	1%	
3600	Maximum	6%	7%	
3700	Protection of existing work, add, minimum	2%	2%	
3800	Maximum	5%	7%	
3900	Shift work requirements, add, minimum		5%	
4000	Maximum		30%	

For expanded coverage of these items see *Means Site Work & Landscape Cost Data 1999*

SITE WORK — A12.5-404 Driveways

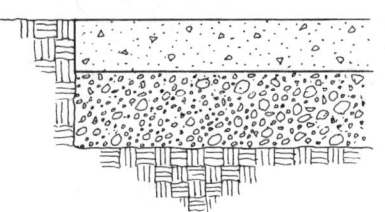

This page illustrates and describes driveway systems including concrete slab, gravel base, broom finish, compaction, and joists. Lines within System Components give the unit price and total price on a cost each basis for this system. Prices for alternate driveway systems are on Line Items 12.5-404-1300 thru 2700. Both material quantities and labor costs have been adjusted for the system listed.

Factors: To adjust for job conditions other than normal working situations use Lines 12.5-404-2900 thru 4000.

Example: You are to install the system and match existing construction. Go to Line 12.5-404-3000 and apply these percentages to the appropriate MAT. and INST. costs.

System Components	QUANTITY	UNIT	COST EACH		
			MAT.	INST.	TOTAL
Complete driveway, 10' x 30', 4" concrete slab, 3000 psi, on 6" compacted Gravel base, concrete broom finished and cured with 10' x 10' joints.					
Grade and compact subgrade	33.000	S.Y.		46.20	46.20
Place and compact 6" crushed stone base	33.000	S.Y.	224.40	40.92	265.32
Place and remove edgeforms (4 use)	80.000	L.F.	20.80	184.80	205.60
Place and broom finish 4" concrete slab, 3000 psi	4.000	C.Y.	268	227.40	495.40
Spray on membrane curing compound	3.000	S.F.	7.98	18.15	26.13
Saw cut 3" deep joints	60.000	L.F.	22.20	58.80	81
TOTAL		Ea.	543.38	576.27	1,119.65

12.5-404	Driveways	COST EACH		
		MAT.	INST.	TOTAL
1200	For alternate driveway systems:			
1300	Concrete: 10' x 30' with 6" concrete on 6" crushed stone	675	615	1,290
1400	20' x 30' with 4" concrete	1,100	1,100	2,200
1500	With 6" concrete	1,375	1,175	2,550
1600	10' wide, for each additional 10' length over 30', 4" thick, add	178	185	363
1700	6" thick, add	228	198	426
1800	20' wide, for each additional 10' length over 30', 4" thick, add	360	355	715
1900	6" thick, add	445	375	820
2000	Asphalt: 10' x 30' with 2" binder, 1" topping on 6" cr. st., sealed	390	530	920
2100	3" binder, 1" topping	440	540	980
2200	20' x 30' with 2" binder, 1" topping	780	700	1,480
2300	3" binding, 1" topping	875	715	1,590
2400	10' wide for each add'l. 10' length over 30', 2" b + 1" t, add	130	57	187
2500	3" binder, 1" topping	146	59.50	205.50
2600	20' wide for each add'l. 10' length over 30', 2" b + 1" t, add	260	114	374
2700	3" binder, 1" topping	292	119	411
2800				
2900	Cut & patch to match existing construction, add, minimum	2%	3%	
3000	Maximum	5%	9%	
3100	Dust protection, add, minimum	1%	2%	
3200	Maximum	4%	11%	
3300	Equipment usage curtailment, add, minimum	1%	1%	
3400	Maximum	3%	10%	
3500	Material handling & storage limitation, add, minimum	1%	1%	
3600	Maximum	6%	7%	
3700	Protection of existing work, add, minimum	2%	2%	
3800	Maximum	5%	7%	
3900	Shift work requirements, add, minimum		5%	
4000	Maximum		30%	

SITE WORK — A12.5-514 Parking Lots, Asphalt

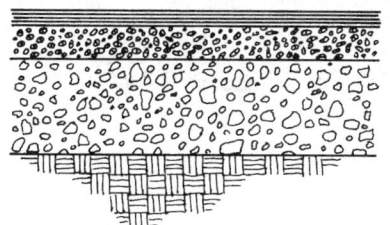

This page illustrates and describes asphalt parking lot systems including asphalt binder, topping, crushed stone base, painted parking stripes and concrete parking blocks. Lines within System Components give the unit price and total price per square yard for this system. Prices for alternate asphalt parking lot systems are on Line Items 12.5-514-1500 thru 2500. Both material quantities and labor costs have been adjusted for the system listed.

Factors: To adjust for job conditions other than normal working situations use Lines 12.5-514-2900 thru 4000.

Example: You are to install the system and match existing construction. Go to Line 12.5-514-2900 and apply these percentages to the appropriate MAT. and INST. costs.

System Components	QUANTITY	UNIT	COST PER S.Y. MAT.	INST.	TOTAL
Parking lot consisting of 2" asphalt binder and 1" topping on 6" Crushed stone base with painted parking stripes and concrete parking blocks					
Fine grade and compact subgrade	1.000	S.Y.		1.40	1.40
6" crushed stone base, stone	.320	Ton	6.80	1.24	8.04
2" asphalt binder	1.000	S.Y.	2.98	.85	3.83
1" asphalt topping	1.000	S.Y.	1.72	.57	2.29
Paint parking stripes	.500	L.F.	.05	.07	.12
6" x 10" x 6' precast concrete parking blocks	.020	Ea.	.57	.24	.81
Mobilization of equipment	.005	Ea.		1.80	1.80
TOTAL		S.Y.	12.12	6.17	18.29

12.5-514	Parking Lots, Asphalt	MAT.	INST.	TOTAL
1400	For alternate parking lot systems:			
1500	Above system on 9" crushed stone	15.45	6.30	21.75
1600	12" crushed stone	19.15	6.40	25.55
1700	On bank run gravel, 6" deep	7.90	5.45	13.35
1800	9" deep	9.10	5.60	14.70
1900	12" deep	10.45	5.70	16.15
2000	3" binder plus 1" topping on 6" crushed stone	13.55	6.40	19.95
2100	9" deep crushed stone	16.90	6.55	23.45
2200	12" deep crushed stone	20.50	6.65	27.15
2300	On bank run gravel, 6" deep	9.35	5.70	15.05
2400	9" deep	10.55	5.85	16.40
2500	12" deep	11.90	5.95	17.85
2600				
2700				
2900	Cut & patch to match existing construction, add, minimum	2%	3%	
3000	Maximum	5%	9%	
3100	Dust protection, add, minimum	1%	2%	
3200	Maximum	4%	11%	
3300	Equipment usage curtailment, add, minimum	1%	1%	
3400	Maximum	3%	10%	
3500	Material handling & storage limitation, add, minimum	1%	1%	
3600	Maximum	6%	7%	
3700	Protection of existing work, add, minimum	2%	2%	
3800	Maximum	5%	7%	
3900	Shift work requirements, add, minimum		5%	
4000	Maximum		30%	

For expanded coverage of these items see *Means Site Work & Landscape Cost Data 1999*

SITE WORK — A12.5-524 | Parking Lots, Concrete

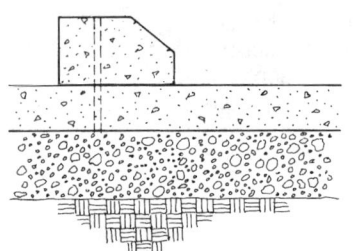

This page illustrates and describes concrete parking lot systems including a concrete slab, unreinforced, compacted gravel base, broom finished, cured, joints, painted parking stripes, and parking blocks. Lines within System Components give the unit price and total price per square yard for this system. Prices for alternate concrete parking lot systems are on Line Items 12.5-524-1500 thru 2500. All materials have been adjusted according to the system listed.

Factors: To adjust for job conditions other than normal working situations use Lines 12.5-524-2900 thru 4000.

Example: You are to install the system and protect existing construction. Go to Line 12.5-524-3800 and apply these percentages to the appropriate MAT. and INST. costs.

System Components	QUANTITY	UNIT	COST PER S.Y. MAT.	INST.	TOTAL
Parking lot, 4" slab, 3000 psi concrete on 6" compacted gravel base With 12' x 12' joints, painted parking strips, conc. parking blocks.					
Grade and compact subgrade	1.000	S.Y.		1.40	1.40
6" crushed stone base, stone	.320	Ton	6.80	1.24	8.04
Place and remove edge forms, 4 use	.250	L.F.	.07	.58	.65
Place and broom finish 4" slab, 3000 psi concrete	1.000	S.F.	7.37	1.88	9.25
Spray on membrane curing compound	1.000	S.F.	.24	.38	.62
Saw cut 3" deep joints	2.250	L.F.	.83	2.21	3.04
Paint parking stripes	.500	L.F.	.05	.07	.12
6" x 10" x 6' precast concrete parking blocks	.020	Ea.	.57	.24	.81
TOTAL		S.Y.	15.93	8	23.93

12.5-524	Parking Lots, Concrete	MAT.	INST.	TOTAL
1400	For alternate parking lot systems:			
1500	Above system on 3" crushed stone	15.95	8	23.95
1600	9" crushed stone	19.30	8.15	27.45
1700	On bank run gravel, 6" deep	11.70	7.30	19
1800	9" deep	12.90	7.40	20.30
1900	On compacted subgrade only	9.15	6.75	15.90
2000	6" concrete slab, 3000 psi on 3" crushed stone	19.50	8.90	28.40
2100	6" crushed stone	19.50	8.90	28.40
2200	9" crushed stone	23	9	32
2300	On bank run gravel, 6" deep	15.25	8.20	23.45
2400	9" deep	16.45	8.30	24.75
2500	On compacted subgrade only	19.50	8.90	28.40
2600				
2700				
2900	Cut & patch to match existing construction, add, minimum	2%	3%	
3000	Maximum	5%	9%	
3100	Dust protection, add, minimum	1%	2%	
3200	Maximum	4%	11%	
3300	Equipment usage curtailment, add, minimum	1%	1%	
3400	Maximum	3%	10%	
3500	Material handling & storage limitation, add, minimum	1%	1%	
3600	Maximum	6%	7%	
3700	Protection of existing work, add, minimum	2%	2%	
3800	Maximum	5%	7%	
3900	Shift work requirements, add, minimum		5%	
4000	Maximum		30%	

SITE WORK — A12.7-104 Sidewalks

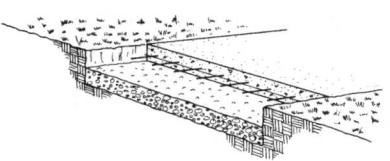

This page illustrates and describes sidewalk systems including concrete, welded wire and broom finish. Lines within System Components give unit price and total price per square foot for this system. Prices for alternate sidewalk systems are on Line Items 12.7-104-1700 thru 1900. Both material quantities and labor costs have been adjusted for the system listed.

Factors: To adjust for job conditions other than normal working situations use Lines 12.7-104-2900 thru 4000.

Example: You are to install the system and match existing construction. Go to Line 12.7-104-2900 and apply these percentages to the appropriate MAT. and INST. costs.

System Components

4" thick concrete sidewalk with welded wire fabric
3000 psi air entrained concrete, broom finish.

System Components	QUANTITY	UNIT	MAT.	INST.	TOTAL
Gravel fill, 4" deep	.012	C.Y.	.07	.06	.13
Compact fill	.012	C.Y.		.02	.02
Hand grade	1.000	S.F.		1.35	1.35
Edge form	.250	L.F.	.07	.58	.65
Welded wire fabric	.011	S.F.	.08	.28	.36
Concrete, 3000 psi air entrained	.012	C.Y.	.80		.80
Place concrete	.012	C.Y.		.21	.21
Broom finish	1.000	S.F.		.53	.53
TOTAL		S.F.	1.02	3.03	4.05

12.7-104	Sidewalks	MAT.	INST.	TOTAL
1600	For alternate sidewalk systems:			
1700	Asphalt (bituminous), 2" thick	.40	1.74	2.14
1800	Brick, on sand, bed, 4.5 brick per S.F.	3.26	6.50	9.76
1900	Flagstone, slate, 1" thick, rectangular	3.08	7.10	10.18
2000				
2100				
2200				
2300				
2400				
2500				
2600				
2700				
2900	Cut & patch to match existing construction, add, minimum	2%	3%	
3000	Maximum	5%	9%	
3100	Dust protection, add, minimum	1%	2%	
3200	Maximum	4%	11%	
3300	Equipment usage curtailment, add, minimum	1%	1%	
3400	Maximum	3%	10%	
3500	Material handling & storage limitation, add, minimum	1%	1%	
3600	Maximum	6%	7%	
3700	Protection of existing work, add, minimum	2%	2%	
3800	Maximum	5%	7%	
3900	Shift work requirements, add, minimum		5%	
4000	Maximum		30%	

For expanded coverage of these items see *Means Site Work & Landscape Cost Data 1999*

SITE WORK

A12.7-604 Landscaping - Lawn Establishment

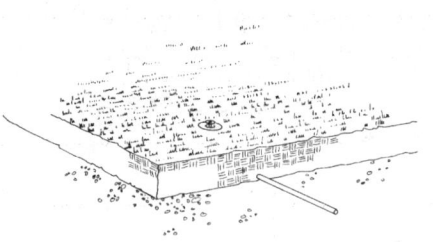

This page describes landscaping—lawn establishment systems including loam, lime, fertilizer, side and top mulching. Lines within system components give the unit price and total price per square yard for this system. Prices for alternate landscaping—lawn establishment systems are on Line Items 12.7-604-1100 and 1200. Both material quantities and labor costs have been adjusted for the system listed.

Factors: To adjust for job conditions other than normal working situations use Lines 12.7-604-2900 thru 4000.

Example: You are to install the system and provide dust protection. Go to Line 12.7-604-3200 and apply these percentages to the appropriate MAT. and INST. costs.

System Components	QUANTITY	UNIT	COST PER S.Y.		
			MAT.	INST.	TOTAL
Establishing lawns with loam, lime, fertilizer, seed and top mulching On rough graded areas.					
Furnish and place loam 4" deep	.110	C.Y.	2.51	.66	3.17
Fine grade, lime, fertilize and seed	1.000	S.Y.	.33	2.05	2.38
Hay mulch, 1 bale/M.S.F.	1.000	S.Y.	.08	.36	.44
Rolling with hand roller	1.000	S.Y.		.61	.61
TOTAL		S.Y.	2.92	3.68	6.60

12.7-604		Landscaping - Lawn Establishment	COST PER S.Y.		
			MAT.	INST.	TOTAL
1000		For alternate lawn systems:			
1100		Above system with jute mesh in place of hay mulch	3.63	3.76	7.39
1200		Above system with sod in place of seed	4.57	1.34	5.91
1300					
1400					
1500					
1600					
1700					
1800					
1900					
2000					
2100					
2200					
2300					
2400					
2500					
2600					
2700					
2900		Cut & patch to match existing construction, add, minimum	2%	3%	
3000		Maximum	5%	9%	
3100		Dust protection, add, minimum	1%	2%	
3200		Maximum	4%	11%	
3300		Equipment usage curtailment, add, minimum	1%	1%	
3400		Maximum	3%	10%	
3500		Material handling & storage limitation, add, minimum	1%	1%	
3600		Maximum	6%	7%	
3700		Protection of existing work, add, minimum	2%	2%	
3800		Maximum	5%	7%	
3900		Shift work requirements, add, minimum		5%	
4000		Maximum		30%	

SITE WORK — A12.9-300 Demolition

12.9-300 Selective Price Sheet

		UNIT	TOTAL COST
0100	Cabinets, base	L.F.	7.20
0200	Wall	L.F.	7.20
0300	Carpet, bonded	S.F.	.29
0400	Tackless	S.F.	.06
0500	Ceiling, tile, adhesive bonded	S.F.	.64
0600	On suspension system	S.F.	.76
0700	Sheetrock, on furring	S.F.	.72
0800	On suspension system	S.F.	.80
0900	Plaster, on wire lath	S.F.	1.01
1000	On suspension system	S.F.	1.01
1100	Chimney, brick, 16" x 16"	V.L.F.	20
1200	20" x 20"	V.L.F.	36
1300	Concrete, footing, 1' thick, 2' wide	L.F.	11.15
1400	2' thick, 3' wide	L.F.	19.05
1500	Slab, 6" thick, plain	S.F.	4.43
1600	Mesh reinforced	S.F.	4.88
1700	Wall, interior, 6" thick	S.F.	10.40
1800	12" thick	S.F.	16.65
1900	Door and frame, wood	Ea.	41
2000	Hollow metal	Ea.	63.50
2100	Ducts, small size, 4" x 8"	L.F.	1.44
2200	Large size, 30" x 72"	L.F.	5.75
2300	Fascia, to 6" wide	L.F.	.57
2400	To 10" wide	L.F.	.72
2500	Flooring, brick	S.F.	1.21
2600	Ceramic	S.F.	.92
2700	Linoleum	S.F.	.41
2800	Resilient tile	S.F.	.57
2900	Terrazzo, cast in place	S.F.	1.91
3000			
3100	Wood, strip	S.F.	1.12
3200	Block	S.F.	.91
3300	Subflooring, tongue and groove boards	S.F.	1.12
3400	Plywood	S.F.	.61
3500	Framing, steel girders, 10" x 12"	L.F.	12.20
3600			
3700	Wood, studs, 2" x 4"	L.F.	.29
3800	Rafters, 2" x 8"	L.F.	.69
3900			
4000			
4100			
4200			
4300	Gutters, attached	L.F.	1.20
4400	Built in	L.F.	2.87
4500	Masonry, veneer, by hand, brick to 4" thick	S.F.	2.59
4600	Marble to 2" thick	S.F.	2.02
4700	Granite to 4" thick	S.F.	2.13
4800	Stone to 8" thick	S.F.	2.07
4900	Walls, brick, 4" thick	S.F.	4.68
5000	8" thick	S.F.	6.20
5100	12" thick	S.F.	7.55
5200	16" thick	S.F.	9.20
5300	Block, 4" thick	S.F.	1.03
5400	6" thick	S.F.	1.36
5500	8" thick	S.F.	2.05
5600	12" thick	S.F.	2.50
5700	Paneling, plywood	S.F.	.29
5800	Woodboards, tongue and groove	S.F.	.82

For expanded coverage of these items see Means Site Work & Landscape Cost Data 1999

SITE WORK | A12.9-300 Demolition

12.9-300 Demolition Selective Price Sheet

			UNIT	TOTAL COST
5900	Piping, to 2" diameter		L.F.	2.04
6000		To 4" diameter	L.F.	2.72
6100		To 8" diameter	L.F.	8.15
6200		To 16" diameter	L.F.	13.60
6300				
6400				
6500	Roofing, built up, 5 ply		S.F.	.91
6600		Shingles, asphalt strip	S.F.	.42
6700	Stairs, wood, minimum		Riser	14.35
6800		Maximum	Riser	22
6900	Toilet fixtures, bathtub		Ea.	102
7000		Sink	Ea.	51
7100		Shower	Ea.	81.50
7200		Toilet	Ea.	58.50
7300		Urinal	Ea.	58.50
7400		Vanity	Ea.	41
7500	Walls, partitions, studs and sheet rock		S.F.	1.71
7600		Studs and plaster	S.F.	3.42
7700	Windows, wood, to 12 S.F.		Ea.	13.05
7800		To 50 S.F.	Ea.	22
7900		Metal, to 12 S.F.	Ea.	22
8000		To 50 S.F.	Ea.	72

Important: See the Reference Section for critical supporting data - Reference Nos., Crews, & City Cost Indexes

SITE WORK — A12.9-700 Planting & Ground Cover

12.9-700 Selective Price Sheet

Line	Description	MAT.	INST.	TOTAL
0100	Shrubs and trees, Evergreen, in prepared beds			
0200				
0300	Arborvitae pyramidal, 4'-5'	38.50	62	100.50
0400	Globe, 12"-15"	11	9.25	20.25
0500	Cedar, blue, 8'-10'	122	103	225
0600	Hemlock, Canadian, 2-1/2'-3'	15.70	24.50	40.20
0700	Juniper, andora, 18"-24"	15.40	11.10	26.50
0800	Wiltoni, 15"-18"	15.95	11.10	27.05
0900	Skyrocket, 4-1/2'-5'	42.50	33.50	76
1000	Blue pfitzer, 2'-2-1/2'	17.60	20	37.60
1100	Ketleerie, 2-1/2'-3'	31	17.75	48.75
1200	Pine, black, 2-1/2'-3'	32.50	17.75	50.25
1300	Mugo, 18"-24"	33	14.80	47.80
1400	White, 4'-5'	48.50	24.50	73
1500	Spruce, blue, 18"-24"	31	14.80	45.80
1600	Norway, 4'-5'	61.50	24.50	86
1700	Yew, denisforma, 12"-15"	25	14.80	39.80
1800	Capitata, 18"-24"	23	29.50	52.50
1900	Hicksi, 2'-2-1/2'	28.50	29.50	58
2000				
2100	Trees, Deciduous, in prepared beds			
2200				
2300	Beech, 5'-6'	220	37	257
2400	Dogwood, 4'-5'	67	46	113
2500	Elm, 8'-10'	77	92.50	169.50
2600	Magnolia, 4'-5'	60	92.50	152.50
2700	Maple, red, 8'-10', 1-1/2" caliper	138	185	323
2800	Oak, 2-1/2"-3" caliper	175	620	795
2900	Willow, 6'-8', 1" caliper	69	92.50	161.50
3000				
3100	Shrubs, Broadleaf Evergreen, in prepared beds			
3200				
3300	Andromeda, 15"-18", container	15.40	9.25	24.65
3400	Azalea, 15"-18", container	21	9.25	30.25
3500	Barberry, 9"-12", container	12.60	6.85	19.45
3600	Boxwood, 15"-18", B & B	17.90	9.25	27.15
3700	Euonymus, emerald gaiety, 12"-15", container	13.50	7.75	21.25
3800	Holly, 15"-18", B & B	18.45	9.25	27.70
3900	Mount laurel, 18"-24", B & B	53	11.10	64.10
4000	Privet, 18"-24", B & B	9.90	6.85	16.75
4100	Rhodendron, 18"-24", container	27.50	18.50	46
4200	Rosemary, 1 gal. container	38.50	1.48	39.98
4300	Deciduous, amalanchier, 2'-3', B & B	60.50	15.60	76.10
4400	Azalea, 15"-18", B & B	20	9.25	29.25
4500	Bayberry, 2'-3', B & B	24.50	15.60	40.10
4600	Cotoneaster, 15"-18", B & B	15.40	11.10	26.50
4700	Dogwood, 3'-4', B & B	23	46	69
4800	Euonymus, alatus compacta, 15"-18", container	22	11.10	33.10
4900	Forsythia, 2'-3', container	17.60	14.80	32.40
5000	Honeysuckle, 3'-4', B & B	18.70	14.80	33.50
5100	Hydrangea, 2'-3', B & B	22	15.60	37.60
5200	Lilac, 3'-4', B & B	42	46	88
5300	Quince, 2'-3', B & B	9.90	15.60	25.50
5400				
5500	Ground Cover			
5600				
5700	Plants, Pachysandra, prepared beds, per hundred	37.50	59	96.50
5800	Vinca minor or English ivy, per hundred	44	74	118
5900	Plant bed prep. 18" dp., mach., per square foot	1.52	.26	1.78
6000	By hand, per square foot	1.52	1.85	3.37

For expanded coverage of these items see Means Site Work & Landscape Cost Data 1999

SITE WORK

A12.9-700 Planting & Ground Cover

12.9-700 Selective Price Sheet

		\multicolumn{3}{c}{COST PER UNIT}		
		MAT.	INST.	TOTAL
6100	Stone chips, Georgia marble, 50# bags, per bag	3.70	1.71	5.41
6200	Onyx gemstone, per bag	14.45	3.42	17.87
6300	Quartz, per bag	6.05	3.42	9.47
6400	Pea gravel, truck load lots, per cubic yard	27	31.50	58.50
6500	Mulch, polyethylene mulch, per square yard	.17	.29	.46
6600	Wood chips, 2" deep, per square yard	1.82	1.31	3.13
6700	Peat moss, 1" deep, per square yard	1.70	.32	2.02
6800	Erosion control per square yard, Jute mesh stapled	.79	.44	1.23
6900	Plastic netting, stapled	.44	.36	.80
7000	Polypropylene mesh, stapled	1.10	.36	1.46
7100	Tobacco netting, stapled	.08	.36	.44
7200	Lawns per square yard, seeding incl. fine grade, limestone, fert. and seed	.33	2.05	2.38
7300	Sodding, incl. fine grade, level ground	220	73.50	293.50
7400	On slope			
7500	Edging, per linear foot, Redwood, untreated, 1" x 4"	1.47	1.46	2.93
7600	2" x 4"	2.93	2.22	5.15
7700	Stl. edge strips, 1/4" x 5" inc. stakes	3.03	2.22	5.25
7800	3/16" x 4"	2.42	2.22	4.64
7900	Brick edging, set on edge	1.98	4.83	6.81
8000	Set flat	.99	1.76	2.75
8100				
8200				
8300				
8400				

For information about Means Estimating Seminars, see yellow pages 11 and 12 in back of book

Reference Section

We've put all the reference information into one section, making it easy to find what you need to know... and easy to use the book on a daily basis. This section is visually identified by a vertical gray bar on the edge of pages.

In the reference number information that follows, you'll see the background that relates to the "reference numbers" that appeared in the Unit Price Section. You'll find reference tables, explanations and estimating information that support how we arrived at the unit price data. Also included are alternate pricing methods, technical data and estimating procedures along with information on design and economy in construction.

Also in this Reference Section, we've included Change Orders, information on pricing changes to contract documents; Crew Listings, a full listing of all the crews, equipment and their costs; Historical Cost Indexes for cost comparisons over time; City Cost Indexes and Location Factors for adjusting costs to the region you are in; and an explanation of all abbreviations used in the book.

Table of Contents

Reference Numbers
010	Overhead & Misc. Data	500
011	Special Project Procedures	508
015	Construction Aids	509
016	Material & Equipment	511
020	Subsurface Investigation & Demolition	512
021	Site Preparation & Excavation Support	514
022	Earthwork	515
023	Tunneling, Piles & Caissons	518
025	Paving & Surfacing	519
027	Sewerage & Drainage	520
029	Landscaping	520
031	Concrete Formwork	521
033	Cast-in-Place Concrete	526
034	Precast Concrete	534
035	Cementitious Decks & Toppings	535
042	Unit Masonry	535
061	Rough Carpentry	540
064	Architectural Woodwork	543
072	Fire & Smoke Protection	544
075	Membrane Roofing	544
081	Metal Doors & Frames	545

Reference Numbers (cont.)
082	Wood & Plastic Doors	545
085	Metal Windows	545
086	Wood & Plastic Windows	546
087	Hardware	546
088	Glazing	546
092	Lath, Plaster & Gypsum Board	547
105	Lockers	548
142	Elevators	548
151	Plumbing	551
155	Heating	552
157	Air Conditioning & Ventilation	553
160	Design & Cost Tables	553

Change Orders 554
Crew Listings 558
Historical Cost Indexes 582
City Cost Indexes 583
Location Factors 602
Abbreviations 607

General Requirements | R010 | Overhead & Miscellaneous Data

R010-005 Tips for Accurate Estimating

1. Use pre-printed or columnar forms for orderly sequence of dimensions and locations and for recording telephone quotations.
2. Use only the front side of each paper or form except for certain pre-printed summary forms.
3. Be consistent in listing dimensions: For example, length x width x height. This helps in rechecking to ensure that, the total length of partitions is appropriate for the building area.
4. Use printed (rather than measured) dimensions where given.
5. Add up multiple printed dimensions for a single entry where possible.
6. Measure all other dimensions carefully.
7. Use each set of dimensions to calculate multiple related quantities.
8. Convert foot and inch measurements to decimal feet when listing. Memorize decimal equivalents to .01 parts of a foot (1/8" equals approximately .01').
9. Do not "round off" quantities until the final summary.
10. Mark drawings with different colors as items are taken off.
11. Keep similar items together, different items separate.
12. Identify location and drawing numbers to aid in future checking for completeness.
13. Measure or list everything on the drawings or mentioned in the specifications.
14. It may be necessary to list items not called for to make the job complete.
15. Be alert for: Notes on plans such as N.T.S. (not to scale); changes in scale throughout the drawings; reduced size drawings; discrepancies between the specifications and the drawings.
16. Develop a consistent pattern of performing an estimate. For example:
    a. Start the quantity takeoff at the lower floor and move to the next higher floor.
    b. Proceed from the main section of the building to the wings.
    c. Proceed from south to north or vice versa, clockwise or counterclockwise.
    d. Take off floor plan quantities first, elevations next, then detail drawings.
17. List all gross dimensions that can be either used again for different quantities, or used as a rough check of other quantities for verification (exterior perimeter, gross floor area, individual floor areas, etc.).
18. Utilize design symmetry or repetition (repetitive floors, repetitive wings, symmetrical design around a center line, similar room layouts, etc.). Note: Extreme caution is needed here so as not to omit or duplicate an area.
19. Do not convert units until the final total is obtained. For instance, when estimating concrete work, keep all units to the nearest cubic foot, then summarize and convert to cubic yards.
20. When figuring alternatives, it is best to total all items involved in the basic system, then total all items involved in the alternates. Therefore you work with positive numbers in all cases. When adds and deducts are used, it is often confusing whether to add or subtract a portion of an item; especially on a complicated or involved alternate.

R010-010 Architectural Fees

Tabulated below are typical percentage fees by project size, for good professional architectural service. Fees may vary from those listed depending upon degree of design difficulty and economic conditions in any particular area.

Rates can be interpolated horizontally and vertically. Various portions of the same project requiring different rates should be adjusted proportionately.

For alterations, add 50% to the fee for the first $500,000 of project cost and add 25% to the fee for project cost over $500,000.

Architectural fees tabulated below include Engineering Fees.

Building Types	Total Project Size in Thousands of Dollars						
	100	250	500	1,000	5,000	10,000	50,000
Factories, garages, warehouses, repetitive housing	9.0%	8.0%	7.0%	6.2%	5.3%	4.9%	4.5%
Apartments, banks, schools, libraries, offices, municipal buildings	11.7	10.8	8.5	7.3	6.4	6.0	5.6
Churches, hospitals, homes, laboratories, museums, research	14.0	12.8	11.9	10.9	8.5	7.8	7.2
Memorials, monumental work, decorative furnishings	—	16.0	14.5	13.1	10.0	9.0	8.3

General Requirements — R010 Overhead & Miscellaneous Data

R010-030 Engineering Fees

Typical **Structural Engineering Fees** based on type of construction and total project size. These fees are included in Architectural Fees.

Type of Construction	Total Project Size (in thousands of dollars)			
	$500	$500-$1,000	$1,000-$5,000	Over $5000
Industrial buildings, factories & warehouses	Technical payroll times 2.0 to 2.5	1.60%	1.25%	1.00%
Hotels, apartments, offices, dormitories, hospitals, public buildings, food stores		2.00%	1.70%	1.20%
Museums, banks, churches and cathedrals		2.00%	1.75%	1.25%
Thin shells, prestressed concrete, earthquake resistive		2.00%	1.75%	1.50%
Parking ramps, auditoriums, stadiums, convention halls, hangars & boiler houses		2.50%	2.00%	1.75%
Special buildings, major alterations, underpinning & future expansion		Add to above 0.5%	Add to above 0.5%	Add to above 0.5%

For complex reinforced concrete or unusually complicated structures, add 20% to 50%.

Typical **Mechanical and Electrical Engineering Fees** based on the size of the subcontract. These fees are included in Architectural Fees.

Type of Construction	Subcontract Size							
	$25,000	$50,000	$100,000	$225,000	$350,000	$500,000	$750,000	$1,000,000
Simple structures	6.4%	5.7%	4.8%	4.5%	4.4%	4.3%	4.2%	4.1%
Intermediate structures	8.0	7.3	6.5	5.6	5.1	5.0	4.9	4.8
Complex structures	12.0	9.0	9.0	8.0	7.5	7.5	7.0	7.0

For renovations, add 15% to 25% to applicable fee.

R010-040 Builder's Risk Insurance

Builder's Risk Insurance is insurance on a building during construction. Premiums are paid by the owner or the contractor. Blasting, collapse and underground insurance would raise total insurance costs above those listed. Floater policy for materials delivered to the job runs $.75 to $1.25 per $100 value. Contractor equipment insurance runs $.50 to $1.50 per $100 value. Insurance for miscellaneous tools to $1,500 value runs from $3.00 to $7.50 per $100 value.

Tabulated below are New England Builder's Risk insurance rates in dollars per $100 value for $1,000 deductible. For $25,000 deductible, rates can be reduced 13% to 34%. On contracts over $1,000,000, rates may be lower than those tabulated. Policies are written annually for the total completed value in place. For "all risk" insurance (excluding flood, earthquake and certain other perils) add $.025 to total rates below.

Coverage	Frame Construction (Class 1)		Brick Construction (Class 4)		Fire Resistive (Class 6)	
	Range	Average	Range	Average	Range	Average
Fire Insurance	$.300 to $.420	$.394	$.132 to $.189	$.174	$.052 to $.080	$.070
Extended Coverage	.115 to .150	.144	.080 to .105	.101	.081 to .105	.100
Vandalism	.012 to .016	.015	.008 to .011	.011	.008 to .011	.010
Total Annual Rate	$.427 to $.586	$.553	$.220 to $.305	$.286	$.141 to $.196	$.180

General Requirements — R010 Overhead & Miscellaneous Data

R010-050 General Contractor's Overhead

The table below shows a contractor's overhead as a percentage of direct cost in two ways. The figures on the right are for the overhead, markup based on both material and labor. The figures on the left are based on the entire overhead applied only to the labor. This figure would be used if the owner supplied the materials or if a contract is for labor only. Note: Some of these markups are included in the labor rates shown on Reference Table R010-070.

Items of General Contractor's Indirect Costs	% of Direct Costs	
	As a Markup of Labor Only	As a Markup of Both Material and Labor
Field Supervision	6.0%	2.9%
Main Office Expense (see details below)	16.2	7.7
Tools and Minor Equipment	1.0	0.5
Workers' Compensation & Employers' Liability. See R010-060	18.3	8.7
Field Office, Sheds, Photos, Etc.	1.5	0.7
Performance and Payment Bond, 0.7% to 1.5%. See R010-080	2.3	1.1
Unemployment Tax See R010-100 (Combined Federal and State)	7.0	3.3
Social Security and Medicare, See R010-100	7.7	3.7
Sales Tax — add if applicable 42/80 x % as markup of total direct costs including both material and labor. See R010-090		
Sub Total	60.0%	28.5%
*Builder's Risk Insurance ranges from .141% to .586%. See R010-040	0.6	0.3
*Public Liability Insurance	3.2	1.5
Grand Total	63.8%	30.3%

*Paid by Owner or Contractor

Main Office Expense

A General Contractor's main office expense consists of many items not detailed in the front portion of the book. The percentage of main office expense declines with increased annual volume of the contractor. Typical main office expense ranges from 2% to 20% with the median about 7.2% of total volume. This equals about 7.7% of direct costs. The following are approximate percentages of total overhead for different items usually included in a General Contractor's main office overhead. With different accounting procedures, these percentages may vary.

Item	Typical Range	Average
Managers', clerical and estimators' salaries	40% to 55%	48%
Profit sharing, pension and bonus plans	2 to 20	12
Insurance	5 to 8	6
Estimating and project management (not including salaries)	5 to 9	7
Legal, accounting and data processing	0.5 to 5	3
Automobile and light truck expense	2 to 8	5
Depreciation of overhead capital expenditures	2 to 6	4
Maintenance of office equipment	0.1 to 1.5	1
Office rental	3 to 5	4
Utilities including phone and light	1 to 3	2
Miscellaneous	5 to 15	8
Total		100%

General Requirements — R010 Overhead & Miscellaneous Data

R010-060 Workers' Compensation Insurance Rates by Trade

The table below tabulates the national averages for Workers' Compensation insurance rates by trade and type of building. The average "Insurance Rate" is multiplied by the "% of Building Cost" for each trade. This produces the "Workers' Compensation Cost" by % of total labor cost, to be added for each trade by building type to determine the weighted average Workers' Compensation rate for the building types analyzed.

Trade	Insurance Rate (% Labor Cost) Range	Insurance Rate (% Labor Cost) Average	% of Building Cost Office Bldgs.	% of Building Cost Schools & Apts.	% of Building Cost Mfg.	Workers' Compensation Office Bldgs.	Workers' Compensation Schools & Apts.	Workers' Compensation Mfg.
Excavation, Grading, etc.	4.0 % to 26.6%	11.6%	4.8%	4.9%	4.5%	0.56%	0.57%	0.52%
Piles & Foundations	8.1 to 80.1	30.3	7.1	5.2	8.7	2.15	1.58	2.64
Concrete	7.2 to 39.4	19.1	5.0	14.8	3.7	0.96	2.83	0.71
Masonry	5.3 to 48.6	18.0	6.9	7.5	1.9	1.24	1.35	0.34
Structural Steel	8.1 to 132.9	42.8	10.7	3.9	17.6	4.58	1.67	7.53
Miscellaneous & Ornamental Metals	5.4 to 34.0	14.1	2.8	4.0	3.6	0.39	0.56	0.51
Carpentry & Millwork	7.0 to 49.9	19.9	3.7	4.0	0.5	0.74	0.80	0.10
Metal or Composition Siding	7.3 to 36.7	18.3	2.3	0.3	4.3	0.42	0.05	0.79
Roofing	8.1 to 88.8	34.6	2.3	2.6	3.1	0.80	0.90	1.07
Doors & Hardware	3.6 to 28.8	11.8	0.9	1.4	0.4	0.11	0.17	0.05
Sash & Glazing	5.3 to 30.0	14.7	3.5	4.0	1.0	0.51	0.59	0.15
Lath & Plaster	5.5 to 37.4	15.8	3.3	6.9	0.8	0.52	1.09	0.13
Tile, Marble & Floors	3.3 to 29.5	10.3	2.6	3.0	0.5	0.27	0.31	0.05
Acoustical Ceilings	4.2 to 26.7	12.4	2.4	0.2	0.3	0.30	0.02	0.04
Painting	5.6 to 41.1	15.6	1.5	1.6	1.6	0.23	0.25	0.25
Interior Partitions	7.0 to 49.9	19.9	3.9	4.3	4.4	0.78	0.86	0.88
Miscellaneous Items	2.8 to 112.5	19.3	5.2	3.7	9.7	1.00	0.71	1.87
Elevators	2.0 to 20.0	8.9	2.1	1.1	2.2	0.19	0.10	0.20
Sprinklers	2.7 to 20.6	9.1	0.5	—	2.0	0.05	—	0.18
Plumbing	3.0 to 15.9	9.0	4.9	7.2	5.2	0.44	0.65	0.47
Heat., Vent., Air Conditioning	3.9 to 29.2	12.8	13.5	11.0	12.9	1.73	1.41	1.65
Electrical	3.2 to 11.6	7.0	10.1	8.4	11.1	0.71	0.59	0.78
Total	2.0 % to 132.9%	—	100.0%	100.0%	100.0%	18.68%	17.06%	20.91%
		Overall Weighted Average	18.88%					

Workers' Compensation Insurance Rates by States

The table below lists the weighted average Workers' Compensation base rate for each state with a factor comparing this with the national average of 18.3%.

State	Weighted Average	Factor	State	Weighted Average	Factor	State	Weighted Average	Factor
Alabama	30.4%	166	Kentucky	19.8%	108	North Dakota	16.7%	91
Alaska	12.8	70	Louisiana	27.2	149	Ohio	16.1	88
Arizona	17.6	96	Maine	21.8	119	Oklahoma	21.9	120
Arkansas	13.0	71	Maryland	11.9	65	Oregon	19.2	105
California	18.6	102	Massachusetts	26.5	145	Pennsylvania	22.9	125
Colorado	26.4	144	Michigan	21.7	119	Rhode Island	22.3	122
Connecticut	21.1	115	Minnesota	37.6	205	South Carolina	13.9	76
Delaware	12.3	67	Mississippi	23.8	130	South Dakota	17.9	98
District of Columbia	25.2	138	Missouri	15.8	86	Tennessee	14.4	79
Florida	28.0	153	Montana	37.3	204	Texas	24.7	135
Georgia	24.9	136	Nebraska	15.7	86	Utah	12.9	70
Hawaii	16.7	91	Nevada	17.8	97	Vermont	14.9	81
Idaho	11.8	64	New Hampshire	23.5	128	Virginia	11.8	64
Illinois	27.5	150	New Jersey	11.0	60	Washington	12.0	66
Indiana	7.1	39	New Mexico	23.1	126	West Virginia	14.0	77
Iowa	14.6	80	New York	17.0	93	Wisconsin	13.9	76
Kansas	11.0	60	North Carolina	14.0	77	Wyoming	8.9	49
			Weighted Average for U.S. is	18.9% of payroll = 100%				

Rates in the following table are the base or manual costs per $100 of payroll for Workers' Compensation in each state. Rates are usually applied to straight time wages only and not to premium time wages and bonuses.

The weighted average skilled worker rate for 35 trades is 18.3%. For bidding purposes, apply the full value of Workers' Compensation directly to total labor costs, or if labor is 38%, materials 42% and overhead and profit 20% of total cost, carry 38/80 x 18.3% = 8.7% of cost (before overhead and profit) into overhead. Rates vary not only from state to state but also with the experience rating of the contractor.

Rates are the most current available at the time of publication.

General Requirements

R010 Overhead & Miscellaneous Data

R010-060 Workers' Compensation Insurance Rates by Trade and State (cont.)

State	Carpentry — 3 stories or less	Carpentry — interior cab. work	Carpentry — general	Concrete Work — NOC	Concrete Work — flat (flr., sdwk.)	Electrical Wiring — inside	Excavation — earth NOC	Excavation — rock	Glaziers	Insulation Work	Lathing	Masonry	Painting & Decorating	Pile Driving	Plastering	Plumbing	Roofing	Sheet Metal Work (HVAC)	Steel Erection — door & sash	Steel Erection — inter., ornam.	Steel Erection — structure	Steel Erection — NOC	Tile Work — (interior ceramic)	Waterproofing	Wrecking
	5651	5437	5403	5213	5221	5190	6217	6217	5462	5479	5443	5022	5474	6003	5480	5183	5551	5538	5102	5102	5040	5057	5348	9014	5701
AL	36.41	14.51	34.52	32.46	16.19	9.57	20.98	20.98	24.55	20.09	15.28	29.78	21.80	64.38	33.79	11.96	57.62	25.78	16.41	16.41	54.68	66.67	16.19	6.92	54.68
AK	11.88	6.71	10.26	10.24	6.88	5.18	8.62	8.62	11.65	9.76	7.11	8.12	10.50	38.68	11.01	4.79	14.75	7.23	13.03	13.03	25.07	25.07	7.20	5.45	25.07
AZ	21.46	9.11	26.40	16.82	9.92	8.14	9.97	9.97	14.03	24.32	8.83	17.04	12.65	23.74	13.75	9.23	20.48	11.54	14.38	14.38	50.31	27.82	7.33	6.15	50.31
AR	15.17	10.19	14.14	13.26	7.02	6.32	9.49	9.49	10.53	11.82	9.78	11.16	12.11	19.97	10.44	7.22	24.38	9.62	8.74	8.74	21.42	23.91	7.25	4.95	21.42
CA	28.28	9.07	28.28	13.18	13.18	9.93	7.88	7.88	16.37	23.34	10.90	14.55	19.45	21.18	18.12	11.59	39.79	15.33	13.55	13.55	23.93	21.91	7.74	19.45	21.91
CO	32.22	13.54	20.95	20.96	15.13	9.20	15.99	15.99	15.98	21.31	14.68	31.06	21.85	41.53	37.40	14.50	59.10	12.54	11.83	11.83	73.46	43.49	15.04	12.26	73.46
CT	19.25	13.14	24.07	20.48	14.17	6.68	8.42	8.42	21.25	34.89	13.64	25.45	18.84	24.54	17.60	12.25	33.98	13.93	13.67	13.67	50.86	35.83	13.94	5.02	50.86
DE	13.83	13.83	11.56	9.28	6.29	5.82	8.54	8.54	11.18	11.56	10.51	9.85	13.41	11.64	10.51	5.41	22.89	10.29	10.21	10.21	26.69	10.21	7.54	9.85	25.69
DC	17.51	10.80	18.88	29.27	16.85	8.76	17.96	17.96	28.00	22.14	12.07	29.67	16.85	42.12	17.06	12.83	22.39	15.78	33.66	33.66	66.43	42.52	16.42	4.66	66.43
FL	36.73	23.28	29.09	29.92	16.15	10.51	15.27	15.27	17.81	25.18	24.27	28.72	28.92	49.35	28.79	13.37	53.20	17.12	18.67	18.67	43.71	50.61	12.56	7.89	43.71
GA	31.04	16.02	32.71	20.67	15.12	9.82	19.55	19.55	21.97	19.15	26.66	23.03	21.20	40.88	19.50	11.14	40.72	18.65	13.74	13.74	36.03	53.09	13.08	10.16	36.03
HI	17.38	11.62	28.20	13.74	12.27	7.10	7.73	7.73	20.55	21.19	10.94	17.87	11.33	20.15	15.61	6.06	33.24	8.02	11.11	11.11	31.71	21.70	9.78	11.54	31.71
ID	12.68	6.50	16.29	9.46	9.04	5.37	6.87	6.87	8.58	11.01	8.97	9.38	8.83	18.27	8.94	5.04	21.34	7.76	7.51	7.51	26.68	24.89	5.35	7.44	26.68
IL	18.94	12.54	23.02	36.76	13.56	9.82	10.43	10.43	27.14	25.52	17.50	23.22	14.93	52.40	15.82	14.48	37.32	17.03	25.56	25.56	78.98	70.79	15.71	7.31	78.98
IN	7.26	3.59	6.96	7.15	3.63	3.16	3.96	3.96	5.31	7.74	4.20	5.31	5.56	12.13	5.48	3.02	12.13	4.44	5.63	5.63	21.36	12.17	3.33	4.00	21.36
IA	10.26	6.79	14.54	12.94	6.78	4.20	5.47	5.47	13.54	18.19	5.82	12.97	7.52	19.90	13.44	6.97	21.56	7.44	12.92	12.92	53.87	36.20	7.13	5.05	17.98
KS	9.56	7.37	9.65	11.58	7.05	4.20	4.33	4.33	6.34	14.80	8.60	11.77	8.23	16.03	12.20	5.20	26.06	6.39	5.35	5.35	17.84	32.15	4.14	4.04	17.84
KY	16.47	15.26	24.34	22.12	9.53	8.95	13.67	13.67	15.96	14.68	10.62	22.00	19.83	30.44	13.94	10.38	32.83	15.92	13.21	13.21	45.21	33.73	10.60	8.85	45.21
LA	29.63	22.95	26.01	20.86	14.80	10.48	24.73	24.73	23.88	20.82	14.00	21.27	27.63	54.39	21.42	13.78	49.11	21.35	15.51	15.51	66.41	36.94	12.82	10.26	66.41
ME	13.43	10.42	43.59	24.29	11.12	10.02	14.75	14.75	13.35	15.39	14.03	17.26	16.07	31.44	17.95	11.12	32.07	17.70	15.08	15.08	37.84	61.81	11.66	9.37	37.84
MD	10.55	5.95	10.55	11.35	5.05	5.15	9.25	9.25	13.20	13.05	6.45	11.35	6.75	27.45	6.65	5.55	22.80	7.00	9.15	9.15	26.80	18.50	6.35	3.50	26.80
MA	15.25	11.38	22.82	39.38	16.79	6.14	10.72	10.72	16.78	27.76	14.02	29.03	14.95	29.58	13.75	8.49	67.48	13.20	16.07	16.07	80.76	79.51	16.46	6.62	62.87
MI	15.62	10.60	17.70	31.29	11.92	5.77	12.80	12.80	11.11	25.59	11.14	18.30	17.86	64.20	20.11	8.04	38.89	11.27	14.73	14.73	41.58	39.66	10.84	10.42	41.58
MN	27.66	28.76	49.94	30.20	22.59	8.28	19.73	19.73	30.01	37.20	23.93	29.89	19.91	80.08	23.93	15.88	88.83	13.91	27.21	27.21	132.92	31.83	29.54	8.71	132.92
MS	21.77	16.71	28.09	17.88	11.02	10.84	13.03	13.03	18.18	21.21	14.41	22.67	17.90	77.98	20.06	10.84	36.25	20.16	14.52	14.52	37.42	42.77	12.76	8.68	37.42
MO	18.72	7.52	11.84	13.28	10.66	5.79	11.05	11.05	8.97	19.99	9.67	13.57	11.77	16.88	14.22	7.10	25.74	9.76	13.82	13.82	47.98	31.96	5.83	5.71	47.98
MT	30.63	15.19	47.53	32.78	24.74	11.01	26.63	26.63	25.04	38.54	19.54	48.55	41.06	53.68	27.00	15.03	85.06	16.93	33.95	33.95	86.98	55.25	13.30	12.10	86.98
NE	16.19	9.23	15.94	17.31	12.73	5.43	10.19	10.19	12.36	16.79	9.34	18.07	11.58	22.01	14.62	9.06	33.91	13.86	10.75	10.75	25.03	26.96	7.88	5.47	25.03
NV	15.42	15.42	15.42	12.86	12.86	8.82	10.62	10.62	12.65	17.78	20.58	14.66	27.12	10.39	20.58	11.30	25.86	29.24	12.56	12.56	27.12	27.12	10.61	10.39	27.12
NH	21.36	9.69	18.75	35.09	10.57	6.26	13.35	13.35	12.80	48.52	10.92	30.06	16.38	29.92	13.78	7.97	66.23	15.20	13.84	13.84	50.50	39.47	11.61	7.64	50.50
NJ	10.40	8.85	10.40	10.83	8.37	4.23	7.95	7.95	7.36	12.78	7.88	10.77	11.49	11.32	7.88	5.48	29.41	6.20	8.03	8.03	22.52	12.96	5.74	5.37	29.92
NM	25.35	13.09	20.45	19.66	13.39	6.34	10.95	10.95	14.58	31.49	16.25	26.97	16.87	33.27	15.64	12.10	43.41	16.46	21.26	21.26	67.82	29.91	9.67	10.65	67.82
NY	15.39	6.82	14.50	24.92	15.16	6.89	9.69	9.69	16.92	15.82	13.00	18.61	12.55	27.49	13.03	9.03	32.78	14.13	14.12	14.12	27.11	24.09	10.56	7.48	32.53
NC	14.43	9.91	15.37	16.82	6.37	7.64	7.73	7.73	9.52	12.92	8.00	12.94	10.40	17.95	14.47	6.93	25.39	10.26	13.32	13.32	39.03	16.68	7.68	3.86	39.03
ND	13.89	13.89	13.89	12.17	12.17	6.16	9.91	9.91	9.85	9.38	13.16	12.20	11.42	29.82	13.16	8.05	31.37	8.05	13.89	13.89	29.82	29.82	9.63	31.37	29.82
OH	13.27	13.27	13.27	13.45	13.45	6.02	13.45	13.45	18.28	16.31	16.31	15.62	18.28	13.45	16.31	7.96	28.62	24.12	13.45	13.45	13.45	13.45	13.08	13.45	13.45
OK	26.16	11.79	19.33	15.51	11.50	7.41	18.45	18.45	13.55	18.00	12.05	16.80	17.10	36.26	18.29	8.72	42.26	12.45	11.17	11.17	69.45	46.76	11.42	8.20	69.45
OR	29.51	9.28	20.03	16.50	10.61	6.63	12.94	12.94	14.95	19.68	12.27	12.43	19.83	22.05	13.85	8.38	38.11	11.85	11.01	11.01	61.69	25.54	9.92	12.10	61.69
PA	15.80	15.80	19.85	28.18	11.84	7.80	12.74	12.74	15.69	19.85	18.94	18.96	22.05	32.12	18.94	11.57	43.30	12.58	24.71	24.71	59.05	24.71	11.83	18.96	81.34
RI	21.32	11.02	18.77	22.11	15.55	5.86	12.16	12.16	17.02	20.95	11.89	20.66	19.86	41.76	14.19	7.25	29.48	10.52	13.18	13.18	78.79	49.67	14.34	9.90	78.79
SC	20.63	13.45	18.64	10.77	8.42	7.13	8.76	8.76	14.61	12.03	7.43	10.83	10.94	19.82	17.30	7.52	26.81	11.23	9.33	9.33	17.82	23.27	6.07	4.47	17.82
SD	14.61	9.94	20.92	21.64	9.04	5.72	11.73	11.73	14.77	17.73	10.89	13.30	13.25	32.14	16.96	9.50	29.39	11.35	11.51	11.51	46.57	33.20	9.85	5.59	46.57
TN	15.36	9.54	13.55	13.95	8.57	5.37	9.59	9.59	10.44	18.17	9.13	15.12	12.87	19.05	12.54	6.76	26.46	12.10	9.44	9.44	42.77	16.07	6.12	5.79	42.77
TX	28.29	18.95	28.29	25.59	19.49	11.60	18.16	18.16	14.17	25.84	13.47	23.12	18.29	43.91	20.99	12.88	47.24	22.92	14.29	14.29	50.47	31.01	9.94	11.38	54.81
UT	11.17	11.17	11.17	17.68	7.99	7.05	6.38	6.38	9.55	10.95	12.32	13.75	15.29	17.24	10.60	6.41	26.27	6.30	8.99	8.99	23.51	23.51	6.06	5.83	26.53
VT	9.68	7.02	14.48	29.73	11.12	4.56	9.17	9.17	12.21	11.43	8.08	10.80	7.69	18.34	10.19	7.90	26.72	10.85	10.23	10.23	25.83	48.65	6.67	7.28	25.83
VA	10.97	7.45	8.50	12.32	5.85	3.48	6.44	6.44	13.64	9.75	7.10	9.11	8.54	27.35	7.24	5.56	19.12	7.55	11.52	11.52	21.92	30.41	5.83	2.78	21.92
WA	8.78	8.78	8.78	8.53	8.53	3.68	8.82	8.82	8.71	9.93	8.78	11.54	10.23	20.99	11.78	5.41	23.39	3.94	16.21	16.21	16.21	16.21	9.81	10.23	16.21
WV	15.43	15.43	15.43	20.87	20.87	5.01	9.14	9.14	7.33	7.33	16.88	16.02	16.88	10.56	16.88	7.40	12.04	7.33	14.98	14.98	13.27	14.98	16.02	4.87	13.27
WI	10.47	10.13	19.98	8.91	8.50	5.73	7.00	7.00	9.67	13.88	13.48	15.43	12.10	17.04	11.81	5.95	29.35	8.64	11.52	11.52	36.51	18.72	8.45	3.92	36.51
WY	8.13	8.13	8.13	8.13	8.13	8.13	8.13	8.13	8.13	8.13	8.13	8.13	8.13	8.13	8.13	8.13	8.13	8.13	8.13	8.13	8.13	8.13	8.13	8.13	8.13
AVG.	18.27	11.79	19.92	19.12	11.74	7.04	11.59	11.59	14.71	18.86	12.43	18.01	15.62	30.30	15.84	8.99	34.61	12.77	14.05	14.05	42.77	32.59	10.33	8.46	42.49

General Requirements — R010 Overhead & Miscellaneous Data

R010-060 Workers' Compensation (cont.) (Canada in Canadian dollars)

Province		Alberta	British Columbia	Manitoba	Ontario	New Brunswick	Newfndld. & Labrador	Northwest Territories	Nova Scotia	Prince Edward Island	Quebec	Saskatchewan	Yukon
Carpentry—3 stories or less	Rate	3.10	6.74	9.10	9.63	3.62	5.11	5.25	5.99	5.68	14.46	5.21	2.35
	Code	25401	70600	40102	723	422	403	4-41	4013	401	80110	B12-02	4-042
Carpentry—interior cab. work	Rate	2.34	3.30	9.10	9.63	4.57	5.11	5.25	5.99	5.68	14.46	4.38	2.35
	Code	42133	60412	40102	723	427	403	4-41	4013	401	80110	B11-25	4-042
CARPENTRY—general	Rate	3.10	6.74	9.10	9.63	3.62	5.11	5.25	5.99	5.68	14.46	5.21	2.35
	Code	25401	70600	40102	723	422	403	4-41	4013	401	80110	B12-02	4-042
CONCRETE WORK—NOC	Rate	4.43	6.74	9.16	13.06	3.62	5.11	5.25	7.87	5.68	17.01	8.20	3.25
	Code	42104	70604	40110	745	422	403	4-41	4222	401	80100	B14-04	2-032
CONCRETE WORK—flat (flr. sidewalk)	Rate	4.43	6.74	9.16	13.06	3.62	5.11	5.25	7.87	5.68	17.01	8.20	3.25
	Code	42104	70604	40110	745	422	403	4-41	4222	401	80100	B14-04	2-032
ELECTRICAL Wiring—inside	Rate	2.03	4.18	5.37	4.39	1.36	4.14	3.50	3.30	3.40	7.75	4.38	2.35
	Code	42124	71100	40203	704	426	400	4-46	4261	402	80170	B11-05	4-041
EXCAVATION—earth NOC	Rate	2.65	4.05	9.10	5.03	2.73	5.11	4.50	3.96	5.68	8.23	5.89	3.25
	Code	40604	72607	40706	711	421	403	4-43	4214	401	80030	R11-06	2-016
EXCAVATION—rock	Rate	2.65	4.05	9.10	5.03	2.73	5.11	4.50	3.96	5.68	8.23	5.89	3.25
	Code	40604	72607	40706	711	421	403	4-43	4214	401	80030	R11-06	2-016
GLAZIERS	Rate	2.62	2.47	5.37	9.81	4.57	3.90	5.25	7.75	3.40	15.13	8.20	2.35
	Code	42121	60236	40109	751	423	402	4-41	4233	402	80150	B13-04	4-042
INSULATION WORK	Rate	3.09	6.29	9.10	9.81	4.57	3.90	5.25	7.75	5.68	15.72	5.21	3.25
	Code	42184	70504	40102	751	423	402	4-41	4234	401	80120	B12-07	2-035
LATHING	Rate	6.13	6.29	9.10	9.63	4.57	3.90	5.25	6.14	3.40	15.72	8.20	3.25
	Code	42135	70500	40102	723	427	402	4-41	4271	402	80120	B13-02	2-036
MASONRY	Rate	4.43	6.74	9.10	11.87	4.57	5.11	5.25	7.75	5.68	17.01	8.20	3.25
	Code	42102	70602	40102	741	423	403	4-41	4231	401	80100	B15-01	2-032
PAINTING & DECORATING	Rate	3.65	6.29	9.16	11.60	4.57	3.90	5.25	6.14	3.40	15.72	5.21	3.25
	Code	42111	70501	40105	719	427	402	4-41	4275	402	80120	B12-01	2-036
PILE DRIVING	Rate	4.43	17.50	9.10	8.64	3.62	9.15	4.50	7.87	5.68	8.23	5.21	3.25
	Code	42159	72502	40706	732	422	404	4-43	4221	401	80030	B12-10	2-030
PLASTERING	Rate	6.13	6.29	9.16	11.60	4.57	3.90	5.25	6.14	3.40	15.72	8.20	3.25
	Code	42135	70502	40108	719	427	402	4-41	4271	402	80120	B13-02	2-036
PLUMBING	Rate	2.03	3.89	5.37	4.93	1.95	3.70	3.50	3.70	3.40	8.39	4.38	2.35
	Code	42122	70712	40204	707	424	401	4-46	4241	402	80160	B11-01	4-039
ROOFING	Rate	8.56	6.74	9.16	11.87	7.36	5.11	5.25	7.75	5.68	23.51	8.20	3.25
	Code	42118	70600	40403	728	430	403	4-41	4235	401	80130	B15-02	2-031
SHEET METAL WORK (HVAC)	Rate	2.03	3.89	9.10	4.93	1.95	3.70	3.50	7.75	3.40	8.39	4.38	2.35
	Code	42117	70714	40402	707	424	401	4-46	4236	402	80160	B11-07	4-040
STEEL ERECTION—door & sash	Rate	3.09	17.50	9.10	18.50	3.62	9.15	5.25	7.87	5.68	30.18	8.20	3.25
	Code	42106	72509	40502	748	422	404	4-41	4223	401	80080	B15-03	2-012
STEEL ERECTION—inter., ornam.	Rate	3.09	17.50	9.10	18.50	3.62	5.11	5.25	7.87	5.68	30.18	8.20	3.25
	Code	42106	72509	40502	748	422	403	4-41	4223	401	80080	B15-03	2-012
STEEL ERECTION—structure	Rate	3.09	17.50	9.10	18.50	3.62	9.15	5.25	10.71	5.68	30.18	8.20	3.25
	Code	42106	72509	40502	748	422	404	4-41	4227	401	80080	B15-04	2-012
STEEL ERECTION—NOC	Rate	3.09	17.50	9.10	18.50	3.62	9.15	5.25	10.71	5.68	30.18	8.20	3.25
	Code	42106	72509	40502	748	422	404	4-41	4227	401	80080	B15-03	2-012
TILE WORK—inter. (ceramic)	Rate	3.13	6.29	3.72	11.60	4.57	3.90	5.25	6.14	3.40	15.72	8.20	3.25
	Code	42113	70506	40103	719	427	402	4-41	4276	402	80120	B13-01	2-034
WATERPROOFING	Rate	3.65	6.74	9.10	9.63	4.57	5.11	5.25	7.75	3.40	23.51	4.38	3.25
	Code	42139	70620	40102	723	423	403	4-41	4239	402	80130	B11-17	2-030
WRECKING	Rate	12.86	6.74	9.16	18.50	2.73	5.11	4.50	3.96	5.68	36.09	8.20	3.25
	Code	42108	70600	40106	748	421	403	4-43	4211	401	80220	B14-07	2-030

General Requirements — R010 Overhead & Miscellaneous Data

R010-070 Contractor's Overhead & Profit

Below are the **average** installing contractor's percentage mark-ups applied to base labor rates to arrive at typical billing rates.

Column A: Labor rates are based on union wages averaged for 30 major U.S. cities. Base rates including fringe benefits are listed hourly and daily. These figures are the sum of the wage rate and employer-paid fringe benefits such as vacation pay, employer-paid health and welfare costs, pension costs, plus appropriate training and industry advancement funds costs.

Column B: Workers' Compensation rates are the national average of state rates established for each trade.

Column C: Column C lists average fixed overhead figures for all trades. Included are Federal and State Unemployment costs set at 7.0%; Social Security Taxes (FICA) set at 7.65%; Builder's Risk Insurance costs set at 0.34%; and Public Liability costs set at 1.55%. All the percentages except those for Social Security Taxes vary from state to state as well as from company to company.

Columns D and E: Percentages in Columns D and E are based on the presumption that the installing contractor has annual billing of $1,500,000 and up. Overhead percentages may increase with smaller annual billing. The overhead percentages for any given contractor may vary greatly and depend on a number of factors, such as the contractor's annual volume, engineering and logistical support costs, and staff requirements. The figures for overhead and profit will also vary depending on the type of job, the job location, and the prevailing economic conditions. All factors should be examined very carefully for each job.

Column F: Column F lists the total of Columns B, C, D, and E.

Column G: Column G is Column A (hourly base labor rate) multiplied by the percentage in Column F (O&P percentage).

Column H: Column H is the total of Column A (hourly base labor rate) plus Column G (Total O&P).

Column I: Column I is Column H multiplied by eight hours.

		A		B	C	D	E	F	G	H	I
		Base Rate Incl. Fringes		Workers' Comp. Ins.	Average Fixed Overhead	Overhead	Profit	Total Overhead & Profit		Rate with O & P	
Abbr.	Trade	Hourly	Daily					%	Amount	Hourly	Daily
Skwk	Skilled Workers Average (35 trades)	$28.05	$224.40	18.3%	16.5%	16.0%	15.0%	65.8%	$18.45	$46.50	$372.00
	Helpers Average (5 trades)	20.85	166.80	19.7				67.2	14.00	34.85	278.80
	Foreman Average, Inside ($.50 over trade)	28.55	228.40	18.3				65.8	18.80	47.35	378.80
	Foreman Average, Outside ($2.00 over trade)	30.05	240.40	18.3				65.8	19.75	49.80	398.40
Clab	Common Building Laborers	21.45	171.60	19.9				67.4	14.45	35.90	287.20
Asbe	Asbestos/Insulation Workers/Pipe Coverers	30.45	243.60	18.9				66.4	20.20	50.65	405.20
Boil	Boilermakers	32.85	262.80	16.6				64.1	21.05	53.90	431.20
Bric	Bricklayers	27.60	220.80	18.0				65.5	18.10	45.70	365.60
Brhe	Bricklayer Helpers	21.60	172.80	18.0				65.5	14.15	35.75	286.00
Carp	Carpenters	27.30	218.40	19.9				67.4	18.40	45.70	365.60
Cefi	Cement Finishers	26.15	209.20	11.7				59.2	15.50	41.65	333.20
Elec	Electricians	31.90	255.20	7.0				54.5	17.40	49.30	394.40
Elev	Elevator Constructors	33.15	265.20	8.9				56.4	18.70	51.85	414.80
Eqhv	Equipment Operators, Crane or Shovel	29.35	234.80	11.6				59.1	17.35	46.70	373.60
Eqmd	Equipment Operators, Medium Equipment	28.40	227.20	11.6				59.1	16.80	45.20	361.60
Eqlt	Equipment Operators, Light Equipment	27.20	217.60	11.6				59.1	16.10	43.30	346.40
Eqol	Equipment Operators, Oilers	24.05	192.40	11.6				59.1	14.20	38.25	306.00
Eqmm	Equipment Operators, Master Mechanics	30.05	240.40	11.6				59.1	17.75	47.80	382.40
Glaz	Glaziers	26.60	212.80	14.7				62.2	16.55	43.15	345.20
Lath	Lathers	26.80	214.40	12.4				59.9	16.05	42.85	342.80
Marb	Marble Setters	27.50	220.00	18.0				65.5	18.00	45.50	364.00
Mill	Millwrights	28.75	230.00	11.9				59.4	17.10	45.85	366.80
Mstz	Mosaic and Terrazzo Workers	26.55	212.40	10.3				57.8	15.35	41.90	335.20
Pord	Painters, Ordinary	24.90	199.20	15.6				63.1	15.70	40.60	324.80
Psst	Painters, Structural Steel	26.00	208.00	51.6				99.1	25.75	51.75	414.00
Pape	Paper Hangers	25.10	200.80	15.6				63.1	15.85	40.95	327.60
Pile	Pile Drivers	27.20	217.60	30.3				77.8	21.15	48.35	386.80
Plas	Plasterers	25.70	205.60	15.8				63.3	16.25	41.95	335.60
Plah	Plasterer Helpers	21.60	172.80	15.8				63.3	13.65	35.25	282.00
Plum	Plumbers	32.60	260.80	9.0				56.5	18.40	51.00	408.00
Rodm	Rodmen (Reinforcing)	30.40	243.20	32.6				80.1	24.35	54.75	438.00
Rofc	Roofers, Composition	24.10	192.80	34.6				82.1	19.80	43.90	351.20
Rots	Roofers, Tile and Slate	24.20	193.60	34.6				82.1	19.85	44.05	352.40
Rohe	Roofer Helpers (Composition)	18.10	144.80	34.6				82.1	14.85	32.95	263.60
Shee	Sheet Metal Workers	31.75	254.00	12.8				60.3	19.15	50.90	407.20
Spri	Sprinkler Installers	32.50	260.00	9.1				56.6	18.40	50.90	407.20
Stpi	Steamfitters or Pipefitters	32.75	262.00	9.0				56.5	18.50	51.25	410.00
Ston	Stone Masons	27.70	221.60	18.0				65.5	18.15	45.85	366.80
Sswk	Structural Steel Workers	30.60	244.80	42.8				90.3	27.65	58.25	466.00
Tilf	Tile Layers (Floor)	26.65	213.20	10.3				57.8	15.40	42.05	336.40
Tilh	Tile Layer Helpers	21.45	171.60	10.3				57.8	12.40	33.85	270.80
Trlt	Truck Drivers, Light	21.75	174.00	15.6				63.1	13.70	35.45	283.60
Trhv	Truck Drivers, Heavy	22.10	176.80	15.6				63.1	13.95	36.05	288.40
Sswl	Welders, Structural Steel	30.60	244.80	42.8				90.3	27.65	58.25	466.00
Wrck	*Wrecking	21.45	171.60	42.5				90.0	19.30	40.75	326.00

*Not included in Averages.

General Requirements | R010 | Overhead & Miscellaneous Data

R010-080 Performance Bond

This table shows the cost of a Performance Bond for a construction job scheduled to be completed in 12 months. Add 1% of the premium cost per month for jobs requiring more than 12 months to complete. The rates are "standard" rates offered to contractors that the bonding company considers financially sound and capable of doing the work. Preferred rates are offered by some bonding companies based upon financial strength of the contractor. Actual rates vary from contractor to contractor and from bonding company to bonding company. Contractors should prequalify through a bonding agency before submitting a bid on a contract that requires a bond.

Contract Amount	Building Construction Class B Projects			Highways & Bridges Class A New Construction			Class A-1 Highway Resurfacing		
First $ 100,000 bid	$25.00 per M			$15.00 per M			$9.40 per M		
Next 400,000 bid	$ 2,500	plus	$15.00 per M	$ 1,500	plus	$10.00 per M	$ 940	plus	$7.20 per M
Next 2,000,000 bid	8,500	plus	10.00 per M	5,500	plus	7.00 per M	3,820	plus	5.00 per M
Next 2,500,000 bid	28,500	plus	7.50 per M	19,500	plus	5.50 per M	15,820	plus	4.50 per M
Next 2,500,000 bid	47,250	plus	7.00 per M	33,250	plus	5.00 per M	28,320	plus	4.50 per M
Over 7,500,000 bid	64,750	plus	6.00 per M	45,750	plus	4.50 per M	39,570	plus	4.00 per M

R010-090 Sales Tax by State

State sales tax on materials is tabulated below (5 states have no sales tax). Many states allow local jurisdictions, such as a county or city, to levy additional sales tax.

Some projects may be sales tax exempt, particularly those constructed with public funds.

State	Tax (%)	State	Tax (%)	State	Tax (%)	State	Tax (%)
Alabama	4	Illinois	6.25	Montana	0	Rhode Island	7
Alaska	0	Indiana	5	Nebraska	4.5	South Carolina	5
Arizona	5	Iowa	5	Nevada	6.75	South Dakota	4
Arkansas	4.625	Kansas	4.9	New Hampshire	0	Tennessee	6
California	7.25	Kentucky	6	New Jersey	6	Texas	6.25
Colorado	3	Louisiana	4	New Mexico	5	Utah	4.75
Connecticut	6	Maine	6	New York	4	Vermont	5
Delaware	0	Maryland	5	North Carolina	4	Virginia	4.5
District of Columbia	5.75	Massachusetts	5	North Dakota	5	Washington	6.5
Florida	6	Michigan	6	Ohio	5	West Virginia	6
Georgia	4	Minnesota	6.5	Oklahoma	4.5	Wisconsin	5
Hawaii	4	Mississippi	7	Oregon	0	Wyoming	4
Idaho	5	Missouri	4.225	Pennsylvania	6	Average	4.71 %

R010-100 Unemployment Taxes and Social Security Taxes

Mass. State Unemployment tax ranges from 1.8% to 7.7% plus an experience rating assessment the following year, on the first $10,800 of wages. Federal Unemployment tax is 6.2% of the first $7,000 of wages. This is reduced by a credit for payment to the state. The minimum Federal Unemployment tax is .8% after all credits.

Combined rates in Mass. thus vary from 2.6% to 8.5% of the first $10,800 of wages. Combined average U.S. rate is about 7.0% of the first $7,000. Contractors with permanent workers will pay less since the average annual wages for skilled workers is $28.05 x 2,000 hours or about $56,100 per year. The average combined rate for U.S. would thus be 7.0% x $7,000 ÷ $56,100 = 0.9% of total wages for permanent employees.

Rates vary not only from state to state but also with the experience rating of the contractor.

Social Security (FICA) for 1999 is estimated at time of publication to be 7.65% of wages up to $68,400.

General Requirements — R011 Special Project Procedures

R011-010 Repair and Remodeling

Cost figures are based on new construction utilizing the most cost-effective combination of labor, equipment and material with the work scheduled in proper sequence to allow the various trades to accomplish their work in an efficient manner.

The costs for repair and remodeling work must be modified due to the following factors that may be present in any given repair and remodeling project.

1. Equipment usage curtailment due to the physical limitations of the project, with only hand-operated equipment being used.
2. Increased requirement for shoring and bracing to hold up the building while structural changes are being made and to allow for temporary storage of construction materials on above-grade floors.
3. Material handling becomes more costly due to having to move within the confines of an enclosed building. For multi-story construction, low capacity elevators and stairwells may be the only access to the upper floors.
4. Large amount of cutting and patching and attempting to match the existing construction is required. It is often more economical to remove entire walls rather than create many new door and window openings. This sort of trade-off has to be carefully analyzed.
5. Cost of protection of completed work is increased since the usual sequence of construction usually cannot be accomplished.
6. Economies of scale usually associated with new construction may not be present. If small quantities of components must be custom fabricated due to job requirements, unit costs will naturally increase. Also, if only small work areas are available at a given time, job scheduling between trades becomes difficult and subcontractor quotations may reflect the excessive start-up and shut-down phases of the job.
7. Work may have to be done on other than normal shifts and may have to be done around an existing production facility which has to stay in production during the course of the repair and remodeling.
8. Dust and noise protection of adjoining non-construction areas can involve substantial special protection and alter usual construction methods.
9. Job may be delayed due to unexpected conditions discovered during demolition or removal. These delays ultimately increase construction costs.
10. Piping and ductwork runs may not be as simple as for new construction. Wiring may have to be snaked through walls and floors.
11. Matching "existing construction" may be impossible because materials may no longer be manufactured. Substitutions may be expensive.
12. Weather protection of existing structure requires additional temporary structures to protect building at openings.
13. On small projects, because of local conditions, it may be necessary to pay a tradesman for a minimum of four hours for a task that is completed in one hour.

All of the above areas can contribute to increased costs for a repair and remodeling project. Each of the above factors should be considered in the planning, bidding and construction stage in order to minimize the increased costs associated with repair and remodeling jobs.

General Requirements — R015 Construction Aids

R015-100 Steel Tubular Scaffolding

On new construction, tubular scaffolding is efficient up to 60' high or five stories. Above this it is usually better to use a hung scaffolding if construction permits. Swing scaffolding operations may interfere with tenants. In this case, the tubular is more practical at all heights.

In repairing or cleaning the front of an existing building the cost of tubular scaffolding per S.F. of building front increases as the height increases above the first tier. The first tier cost is relatively high due to leveling and alignment.

The minimum efficient crew for erection is three workers. For heights over 50', a crew of four is more efficient. Use two or more on top and two at the bottom for handing up or hoisting. Four workers can erect and dismantle about nine frames per hour up to five stories. From five to eight stories they will average six frames per hour. With 7' horizontal spacing this will run about 400 S.F. and 265 S.F. of wall surface, respectively. Time for placing planks must be added to the above. On heights above 50', five planks can be placed per labor-hour.

The cost per 1,000 S.F. of building front in the table below was developed by pricing the materials required for a typical tubular scaffolding system eleven frames long and two frames high. Planks were figured five wide for standing plus two wide for materials.

Frames are 5' wide and usually spaced 7' O.C. horizontally. Sidewalk frames are 6' wide. Rental rates will be lower for jobs over three months duration.

For jobs under twenty-five frames, add 50% to rental cost. These figures do not include accessories which are listed separately below. Large quantities for long periods can reduce rental rates by 20%.

Item	Unit	Monthly Rent	Per 1,000 S.F. of Building Front — No. of Pieces	Per 1,000 S.F. of Building Front — Rental per Month
5' Wide Standard Frame, 6'-4" High	Ea.	$ 3.75	24	$ 90.00
Leveling Jack & Plate		1.50	24	36.00
Cross Brace		.60	44	26.40
Side Arm Bracket, 21"		1.50	12	18.00
Guardrail Post		1.00	12	12.00
Guardrail, 7' Section		.75	22	16.50
Stairway Section		10.00	2	20.00
Stairway Starter Bar		.10	1	.10
Stairway Inside Handrail		5.00	2	10.00
Stairway Outside Handrail		5.00	2	10.00
Walk-Thru Frame Guardrail		2.00	2	4.00
			Total	$243.00
			Per C.S.F., 1 Use/Mo.	$ 24.30

Scaffolding is often used as falsework over 15' high during construction of cast-in-place concrete beams and slabs. Two foot wide scaffolding is generally used for heavy beam construction. The span between frames depends upon the load to be carried with a maximum span of 5'.

Heavy duty shoring frames with a capacity of 10,000#/leg can be spaced up to 10' O. C. depending upon form support design and loading.

Scaffolding used as horizontal shoring requires less than half the material required with conventional shoring.

On new construction, erection is done by carpenters.

Rolling towers supporting horizontal shores can reduce labor and speed the job. For maintenance work, catwalks with spans up to 70' can be supported by the rolling towers.

General Requirements | R015 | Construction Aids

R015-200 Pump Staging

Pump staging is generally not available for rent. Purchase prices for individual items are shown in the chart below.

Item	Unit	Purchase, Each	Per 2,400 S.F. of Building Front	
			No. of Pieces	Cost to Buy
Aluminum pole section, 24' long	Ea.	$335.00	6	$2,010.00
Aluminum splice joint, 6' long		68.00	3	204.00
Aluminum foldable brace		48.50	3	145.50
Aluminum pump jack		111.00	3	333.00
Aluminum support for workbench/back safety rail		59.00	3	177.00
Aluminum scaffold plank/workbench, 14" wide x 24' long		545.00	4	2,180.00
Safety net, 22' long		267.00	2	534.00
Aluminum plank end safety rail		183.00	2	366.00
			Total System	$5,949.50
			Per C.S.F., 1 Use	$247.90

This system in place will cover up to 2,400 square feet of wall area. The cost in place will depend on how many uses are realized during the life of the equipment. Several options are given in Division 015-257. The above prices are bare costs.

General Requirements — R016 Material & Equipment

R016-410 Contractor Equipment

Rental Rates shown in the front of the book pertain to late model high quality machines in excellent working condition, rented from equipment dealers. Rental rates from contractors may be substantially lower than the rental rates from equipment dealers depending upon economic conditions. For older, less productive machines, reduce rates by a maximum of 15%. Any overtime must be added to the base rates. For shift work, rates are lower. Usual rule of thumb is 150% of one shift rate for two shifts; 200% for three shifts.

For periods of less than one week, operated equipment is usually more economical to rent than renting bare equipment and hiring an operator.

Equipment moving and mobilization costs must be added to rental rates where applicable. A large crane, for instance, may take two days to erect and two days to dismantle.

Rental rates vary throughout the country with larger cities generally having lower rates. Lease plans for new equipment are available for periods in excess of six months with a percentage of payments applying toward purchase.

Monthly rental rates vary from 2% to 5% of the cost of the equipment depending on the anticipated life of the equipment and its wearing parts. Weekly rates are about 1/3 the monthly rates and daily rental rates about 1/3 the weekly rate.

The hourly operating costs for each piece of equipment include costs to the user such as fuel, oil, lubrication, normal expendables for the equipment, and a percentage of mechanic's wages chargeable to maintenance. The hourly operating costs listed do not include the operator's wages.

The daily cost for equipment used in the standard crews is figured by dividing the weekly rate by five, then adding eight times the hourly operating cost to give the total daily equipment cost, not including the operator. This figure is in the right hand column of Division 016 under Crew Equip. Cost./Day

Pile Driving rates shown for pile hammer and extractor do not include leads, crane, boiler or compressor. Vibratory pile driving requires an added field specialist during set-up and pile driving operation for the electric model. The hydraulic model requires a field specialist for set-up only. Up to 125 reuses of sheet piling are possible using vibratory drivers. For normal conditions, crane capacity for hammer type and size are as follows.

Crane Capacity	Hammer Type and Size		
	Air or Steam	Diesel	Vibratory
25 ton	to 8,750 ft.-lb.		70 H.P.
40 ton	15,000 ft.-lb.	to 32,000 ft.-lb.	170 H.P.
60 ton	25,000 ft.-lb.		300 H.P.
100 ton		112,000 ft.-lb.	

Cranes should be specified for the job by size, building and site characteristics, availability, performance characteristics, and duration of time required.

Backhoes & Shovels rent for about the same as equivalent size cranes but maintenance and operating expense is higher. Crane operators rate must be adjusted for high boom heights. Average adjustments: for 150' boom add $.75 per hour; over 185', add $1.25 per hour; over 210', add $1.75 per hour; over 250', add $2.50 per hour and over 295', add $4.00 per hour.

Tower Cranes

Capacity In Kip-Feet	Typical Jib Length in Feet	Speed at Maximum Reach and Load	Purchase Price (New)		Monthly Rental, to 6 mo.	
			Crane & 80' Mast	Mast Sections	Crane & 80' Mast	Mast Sections
725	100	350 FPM	$245,800	$650 /L.F.	$ 8,170	$17.30 /L.F.
900	100	500	291,800	750	7,010	18.60
*1100	130	1000	404,500	880	10,130	23.50
1450	150	1000	563,200	1,240	14,480	27.70
2150	200	1000	691,200	1,420	18,200	32.10
3000	200	1000	983,000	1,450	23,780	38.10

*Most widely used.

Tower Cranes of the climbing or static type have jibs from 50' to 200' and capacities at maximum reach range from 4,000 to 14,000 pounds. Lifting capacities increase up to maximum load as the hook radius decreases.

Typical rental rates, based on purchase price are about 2% to 3% per month.

Erection and dismantling runs between $12,500 and $80,000. Climbing operation takes ten labor hours per 20' climb. Crane dead time is about five hours per 40' climb. If crane is bolted to side of the building add cost of ties and extra mast sections. Mast sections cost $500 to $1,500 per vertical foot or can be rented at 2% to 3% of purchase price per month. Contractors using climbers claim savings of $1.50 per C.Y. of concrete placed, plus $.15 per S.F. of formwork. Climbing cranes have from 80' to 180' of mast while static cranes have 80' to 800' of mast.

Truck Cranes can be converted to tower cranes by using tower attachments. Mast heights over 400' have been used. See Division 016-460 for rental rates of high boom cranes.

A single 100' high material **Hoist and Tower** can be erected and dismantled for about $15,000; a double 100' high hoist and tower for about $20,000. Erection costs for additional heights are $100 and $125 per vertical foot respectively up to 150' and $100 to $150 per vertical foot over 150' high. A 40' high portable Buck hoist costs about $5,000 to erect and dismantle. Additional heights run $80 per vertical foot to 80' and $100 per vertical foot for the next 100'. Most material hoists do not meet local code requirements for carrying personnel.

A 150' high **Personnel Hoist** requires about 500 to 800 labor hours to erect and dismantle with costs ranging from $12,000 to $28,000. Budget erection cost is $150 per vertical foot for all trades. Local code requirements or labor scarcity requiring overtime can add up to 50% to any of the above erection costs.

Earthmoving Equipment: The selection of earthmoving equipment depends upon the type and quantity of material, moisture content, haul distance, haul road, time available, and equipment available. Short haul cut and fill operations may require dozers only, while another operation may require excavators, a fleet of trucks, and spreading and compaction equipment. Stockpiled material and granular material are easily excavated with front end loaders. Scrapers are most economically used with hauls between 300' and 1-1/2 miles if adequate haul roads can be maintained. Shovels are often used for blasted rock and any material where a vertical face of 8' or more can be excavated. Special conditions may dictate the use of draglines, clamshells, or backhoes. Spreading and compaction equipment must be matched to the soil characteristics, the compaction required and the rate the fill is being supplied.

Site Work — R020 Subsurface Invest. & Demol.

R020-510 General Demolition

When estimating demolition the authors recommend getting a bid from a local contractor, if possible. Variables including disposal sites, protection of adjacent structures, salvage, and economic conditions can affect costs by 100%.

In calculating the line item costs of this major classification, three preliminary qualifications are assumed:

1. The tools used for demolition are generally of the hand or pneumatic hand type (note crew size).
2. The cost of rubbish handling (removing rubbish to on-site containers or trucks) is not included.
3. The cost of hauling rubbish to an approved dumpsite is not included.

For total general demolition cost, add rubbish handling and hauling. (See Division 020-620).

R020-708 Electrical Demolition (Removal for Replacement)

The purpose of this reference number is to provide a guide to users for electrical "removal for replacement" by applying the rule of thumb: 1/3 of new installation time (typical range from 20% to 50%) for removal. Remember to use reasonable judgment when applying the suggested percentage factor. For example:

Contractors have been requested to remove an existing fluorescent lighting fixture and replace with a new fixture utilizing energy saver lamps and electronic ballast:

In order to fully understand the extent of the project, contractors should visit the job site and estimate the time to perform the renovation work in accordance with applicable national, state and local regulation and codes.

The contractor may need to add extra labor hours to his estimate if he discovers unknown concealed conditions such as: contaminated asbestos ceiling, broken acoustical ceiling tile and need to repair, patch and touch-up paint all the damaged or disturbed areas, tasks normally assigned to general contractors. In addition, the owner could request that the contractors salvage the materials removed and turn over the the materials to the owner or dispose of the materials to a reclamation station. The normal removal item is 0.5 labor-hour for a lighting fixture and 1.5 labor-hours for new installation time. Revise the estimate times from 2 labor-hours work up to a minimum 4 labor-hours work for just fluorescent lighting fixture.

For removal of large concentrations of lighting fixtures in the same area, apply an "economy of scale" to reduce estimating labor hours.

R020-820 Asbestos Removal Process

Asbestos removal is accomplished by a specialty contractor who understands the federal and state regulations regarding the handling and disposal of the material. The process of asbestos removal is divided into many individual steps. An accurate estimate can be calculated only after all the steps have been priced.

The steps are generally as follows:

1. Obtain an asbestos abatement plan from an industrial hygienist.
2. Monitor the air quality in and around the removal area and along the path of travel between the removal area and transport area. This establishes the background contamination.
3. Construct a two part decontamination chamber at entrance to removal area.
4. Install a HEPA filter to create a negative pressure in the removal area.
5. Install wall, floor and ceiling protection as required by the plan, usually 2 layers of fireproof 6 mil polyethylene.
6. Industrial hygienist visually inspects work area to verify compliance with plan.
7. Provide temporary supports for conduit and piping affected by the removal process.
8. Proceed with asbestos removal and bagging process. Monitor air quality as described in Step #2. Discontinue operations when contaminate levels exceed applicable standards.
9. Document the legal disposal of materials in accordance with EPA standards.
10. Thoroughly clean removal area including all ledges, crevices and surfaces.
11. Post abatement inspection by industrial hygienist to verify plan compliance.
12. Provide a certificate from a licensed industrial hygienist attesting that contaminate levels are within acceptable standards before returning area to regular use.

R020-880 Underground Storage Tank Removal

Underground Storage Tank Removal can be divided into two categories: Non-Leaking and Leaking. Prior to removing an underground storage tank, tests should be made, with the proper authorities present, to determine whether a tank has been leaking or the surrounding soil has been contaminated.

To safely remove Liquid Underground Storage Tanks:

1. Excavate to the top of the tank.
2. Disconnect all piping.
3. Open all tank vents and access ports.
4. Remove all liquids and/or sludge.
5. Purge the tank with an inert gas.
6. Provide access to the inside of the tank and clean out the interior using proper personal protective equipment (PPE).
7. Excavate soil surrounding the tank using proper PPE for on-site personnel.
8. Pull and properly dispose of the tank.
9. Clean up the site of all contaminated material.
10. Install new tanks or close the excavation.

Site Work | R020 | Subsurface Invest. & Demol.

R020-890 Lead Paint Remediation Methods

Lead paint remediation can be accomplished by the following methods.
1. Abrasive blast
2. Chemical stripping
3. Power tool cleaning with vacuum collection system
4. Encapsulation
5. Remove and replace
6. Enclosure

Each of these methods has strengths and weakness depending on the specific circumstances of the project. The following is an overview of each method.

1. **Abrasive blasting** is usually accomplished with sand or recyclable metallic blast. Before work can begin, the area must be contained to ensure the blast material with lead does not escape to the atmosphere. The use of vacuum blast greatly reduces the containment requirements. Lead abatement equipment that may be associated with this work includes a negative air machine. In addition, it is necessary to have an industrial hygienist monitor the project on a continual basis. When the work is complete, the spent blast sand with lead must be disposed of as a hazardous material. If metallic shot was used, the lead is separated from the shot and disposed of as hazardous material. Worker protection includes disposable clothing and respiratory protection.

2. **Chemical stripping** requires strong chemicals be applied to the surface to remove the lead paint. Before the work can begin, the area under/adjacent to the work area must be covered to catch the chemical and removed lead. After the chemical is applied to the painted surface it is usually covered with paper. The chemical is left in place for the specified period, then the paper with lead paint is pulled or scraped off. The process may require several chemical applications. The paper with chemicals and lead paint adhered to it, plus the containment and loose scrapings collected by a HEPA (High Efficiency Particulate Air Filter) vac, must be disposed of as a hazardous material. The chemical stripping process usually requires a neutralizing agent and several wash downs after the paint is removed. Worker protection includes a neoprene or other compatible protective clothing and respiratory protection with face shield. An industrial hygienist is required intermittently during the process.

3. **Power tool cleaning** is accomplished using shrouded needle blasting guns. The shrouding with different end configurations is held up against the surface to be cleaned. The area is blasted with hardened needles and the shroud captures the lead with a HEPA vac and deposits it in a holding tank. An industrial hygienist monitors the project, protective clothing and a respirator is required until air samples prove otherwise. When the work is complete the lead must be disposed of as a hazardous material.

4. **Encapsulation** is a method that leaves the well bonded lead paint in place after the peeling paint has been removed. Before the work can begin, the area under/adjacent to the work must be covered to catch the scrapings. The scraped surface is then washed with a detergent and rinsed. The prepared surface is covered with approximately 10 mils of paint. A reinforcing fabric can also be embedded in the paint covering. The scraped paint and containment must be disposed of as a hazardous material. Workers must wear protective clothing and respirators.

5. **Remove and replace** is an effective way to remove lead paint from windows, gypsum walls and concrete masonry surfaces. The painted materials are removed and new materials are installed. Workers should wear a respirator and tyvek suit. The demolished materials must be disposed of as hazardous waste if it fails the TCLP (Toxicity Characteristic Leachate Process) test.

6. **Enclosure** is the process that permanently seals lead painted materials in place. This process has many applications such as covering lead painted drywall with new dry wall, covering exterior construction with tyvek paper then residing, or covering lead painted structural members with aluminum or plastic. The seams on all enclosing materials must be securely sealed. An industrial hygienist monitors the project, and protective clothing and a respirator is required until air samples prove otherwise.

All the processes require clearance monitoring and wipe testing as required by the hygienist.

Site Work | R021 | Site Prep. & Excav. Support

R021-620 Wood Sheet Piling

Wood sheet piling may be used for depths to 20' where there is no ground water. If moderate ground water is encountered Tongue & Groove sheeting will help to keep it out. When considerable ground water is present, steel sheeting must be used.

For estimating purposes on trench excavation, sizes are as follows:

Depth	Sheeting	Wales	Braces	B.F. per S.F.
To 8'	3 x 12's	6 x 8's, 2 line	6 x 8's, @ 10'	4.0 @ 8'
8' x 12'	3 x 12's	10 x 10's, 2 line	10 x 10's, @ 9'	5.0 average
12' to 20'	3 x 12's	12 x 12's, 3 line	12 x 12's, @ 8'	7.0 average

Sheeting to be toed in at least 2' depending upon soil conditions. A five person crew with an air compressor and sheeting driver can drive and brace 440 SF/day at 8' deep, 360 SF/day at 12' deep, and 320 SF/day at 16' deep. For normal soils, piling can be pulled in 1/3 the time to install. Pulling difficulty increases with the time in the ground. Production can be increased by high pressure jetting. Figures below assume 50% of lumber is salvaged and includes pulling costs. Some jurisdictions require an equipment operator in addition to Crew B-31.

Sheeting Pulled

Daily Cost Crew B-31	L.H./Day	Hourly Cost	Daily Cost	8' Depth, 440 S.F./Day To Drive (1 Day)	8' Depth, 440 S.F./Day To Pull (1/3 Day)	16' Depth, 320 S.F./Day To Drive (1 Day)	16' Depth, 320 S.F./Day To Pull (1/3 Day)
1 Foreman	8	$23.45	$ 187.60	$ 187.60	$ 62.47	$ 187.60	$ 62.47
3 Laborers	24	21.45	514.80	514.80	171.43	514.80	171.43
1 Carpenter	8	27.30	218.40	218.40	72.73	218.40	72.73
1 Air Compressor			116.80	116.80	38.89	116.80	38.89
1 Sheeting Driver			5.95	5.95	1.98	5.95	1.98
2 -50 Ft. Air Hoses, 1-1/2" Diam.			12.80	12.80	4.26	12.80	4.26
Lumber (50% salvage)				1.76 MBF 576.40		2.24 MBF 733.60	
Total			$1,056.35	$1,632.75	$351.76	$1,789.95	$351.76
Total/S.F.				$ 3.71	$ .80	$ 5.59	$ 1.10
Total (Drive and Pull)/S.F.				$ 4.51		$ 6.69	

Sheeting Left in Place

Daily Cost	8' Depth 440 S.F./Day		10' Depth 400 S.F./Day		12' Depth 360 S.F./Day		16' Depth 320 S.F./Day		18' Depth 305 S.F./Day		20' Depth 280 S.F./Day	
Crew B-31		$1,073.30		$1,073.30		$1,073.30		$1,073.30		$1,073.30		$1,073.30
Lumber	1.76 M	1,152.80	1.8 M	1,179.00	1.8 M	1,179.00	2.24 M	1,467.20	2.1 M	1,375.50	1.9 M	1,244.50
Total in Place		$2,226.10		$2,252.30		$2,252.30		$2,540.50		$2,448.80		$2,317.80
Total/S.F.		$ 5.06		$ 5.63		$ 6.26		$ 7.94		$ 8.03		$ 8.28
Total/M.B.F.		$1,264.83		$1,251.28		$1,251.28		$1,134.15		$1,166.10		$1,219.89

Site Work — R022 Earthwork

R022-220 Compacting Backfill

Compaction of fill in embankments, around structures, in trenches, and under slabs is important to control settlement. Factors affecting compaction are:
1. Soil gradation
2. Moisture content
3. Equipment used
4. Depth of fill per lift
5. Density required

The costs for testing and soil analyses are listed in Division 014-108. Also, see Division 022 for further backfill, borrow, and compaction costs.

Example:

Compact granular fill around a building foundation using a 21" wide x 24" vibratory plate in 8" lifts. Operator moves at 50 FPM working a 50 minute hour to develop 95% Modified Proctor Density with 4 passes.

Production Rate:

$$\frac{1.75' \text{ plate width} \times 50 \text{ F.P.M.} \times 50 \text{ min./hr.} \times .67' \text{ lift}}{27 \text{ C.F. per C.Y.}} = 108.5 \text{ C.Y./hr.}$$

Production Rate for 4 Passes:

$$\frac{108.5 \text{ C.Y.}}{4 \text{ passes}} = 27.125 \text{ C.Y./hr.} \times 8 \text{ hrs.} = 217 \text{ C.Y./day}$$

	Compacting 217 C.Y. with 21" Wide Vibratory Plate	L.H./Day	Hourly Cost	Daily Cost	C.Y. Cost
1	Laborer	8	$21.45	$171.60	$ .79
1	Vibratory Plate Compactor			52.00	.24
Total for 217 C.Y./day				$223.60	$1.03

Site Work — R022 Earthwork

R022-240 Excavating

The selection of equipment used for structural excavation and bulk excavation or for grading is determined by the following factors.
1. Quantity of material.
2. Type of material.
3. Depth or height of cut.
4. Length of haul.
5. Condition of haul road.
6. Accessibility of site.
7. Moisture content and dewatering requirements.
8. Availability of excavating and hauling equipment.

Some additional costs must be allowed for hand trimming the sides and bottom of concrete pours and other excavation below the general excavation.

Number of B.C.Y. per truck = 1.5 C.Y. bucket × 8 passes = 12 loose C.Y.

$$= 12 \times \frac{100}{118} = 10.2 \text{ B.C.Y. per truck}$$

Truck Haul Cycle:

Load truck 8 passes	=	4 minutes
Haul distance 1 mile	=	9 minutes
Dump time	=	2 minutes
Return 1 mile	=	7 minutes
Spot under machine	=	1 minute
		23 minute cycle

When planning excavation and fill, the following should also be considered.
1. Swell factor.
2. Compaction factor.
3. Moisture content.
4. Density requirements.

A typical example for scheduling and estimating the cost of excavation of a 15' deep basement on a dry site when the material must be hauled off the site, is outlined below.

Assumptions:
1. Swell factor, 18%.
2. No mobilization or demobilization.
3. Allowance included for idle time and moving on job.
4. No dewatering, sheeting, or bracing.
5. No truck spotter or hand trimming.

Fleet Haul Production per day in B.C.Y.

$$4 \text{ trucks} \times \frac{50 \text{ min. hour}}{23 \text{ min. haul cycle}} \times 8 \text{ hrs.} \times 10.2 \text{ B.C.Y.}$$

$$= 4 \times 2.2 \times 8 \times 10.2 = 718 \text{ B.C.Y./day}$$

	Excavating Cost with a 1-1/2 C.Y. Hydraulic Excavator 15' Deep, 2 Mile Round Trip Haul	L.H./Day	Hourly Cost	Daily Cost	Subtotal	Unit Price
1	Equipment Operator	8	$29.35	$ 234.80		
1	Oiler	8	24.05	192.40		
4	Truck Drivers	32	22.10	707.20	$1,134.40	$1.58
1	Hydraulic Excavator			712.70		
4	Dump Trucks			1,769.00	2,481.70	3.45
Total for 720 B.C.Y.					$3,616.10	$5.02

Description		1-1/2 C.Y. Hyd. Backhoe 15' Deep		1-1/2 C.Y. Power Shovel 7' Bank		1-1/2 C.Y. Dragline 7' Deep		2-1/2 C.Y. Trackloader Stockpile
Operator (and Oiler, if required)		$ 427.20		$ 427.20		$ 427.20		$ 427.20
Truck Drivers	3 Ea.	530.40	4 Ea.	707.20	3 Ea.	530.40	4 Ea.	707.20
Equipment Rental		712.70		864.00		892.85		865.10
20 C.Y. Trailer Dump Trucks	3 Ea.	1,326.75	4 Ea.	1,769.00	3 Ea.	1,326.75	4 Ea.	1,769.00
Total Cost per Day		$2,997.05		$3,767.40		$3,177.20		$3,768.50
Daily Production, C.Y. Bank Measure		720.00		960.00		640.00		1000.00
Cost per C.Y.		$ 4.16		$ 3.92		$ 4.96		$ 3.77

Add the mobilization and demobilization costs to the total excavation costs. When equipment is rented for more than three days, there is often no mobilization charge by the equipment dealer. On larger jobs outside of urban areas, scrapers can move earth economically provided a dump site or fill area and adequate haul roads are available. Excavation within sheeting bracing or cofferdam bracing is usually done with a clamshell and production is low, since the clamshell may have to be guided by hand between the bracing. When excavating or filling an area enclosed with a wellpoint system, add 10% to 15% to the cost to allow for restricted access. When estimating earth excavation quantities for structures, allow work space outside the building footprint for construction of the foundation, and a slope of 1:1 unless sheeting is used.

Site Work — R022 Earthwork

R022-250 Excavating Equipment

The table below lists THEORETICAL hourly production in C.Y./hr. bank measure for some typical excavation equipment. Figures assume 50 minute hours, 83% job efficiency, 100% operator efficiency, 90° swing and properly sized hauling units, which must be modified for adverse digging and loading conditions. Actual production costs in the front of the book average about 50% of the theoretical values listed here.

Equipment	Soil Type	B.C.Y. Weight	% Swell	1 C.Y.	1-1/2 C.Y	2 C.Y.	2-1/2 C.Y.	3 C.Y.	3-1/2 C.Y.	4 C.Y.
Hydraulic Excavator "Backhoe" 15' Deep Cut	Moist loam, sandy clay	3400 lb.	40%	85	125	175	220	275	330	380
	Sand and gravel	3100	18	80	120	160	205	260	310	365
	Common earth	2800	30	70	105	150	190	240	280	330
	Clay, hard, dense	3000	33	65	100	130	170	210	255	300
Power Shovel Optimum Cut (Ft.)	Moist loam, sandy clay	3400	40	170 (6.0)	245 (7.0)	295 (7.8)	335 (8.4)	385 (8.8)	435 (9.1)	475 (9.4)
	Sand and gravel	3100	18	165 (6.0)	225 (7.0)	275 (7.8)	325 (8.4)	375 (8.8)	420 (9.1)	460 (9.4)
	Common earth	2800	30	145 (7.8)	200 (9.2)	250 (10.2)	295 (11.2)	335 (12.1)	375 (13.0)	425 (13.8)
	Clay, hard, dense	3000	33	120 (9.0)	175 (10.7)	220 (12.2)	255 (13.3)	300 (14.2)	335 (15.1)	375 (16.0)
Drag Line Optimum Cut (Ft.)	Moist loam, sandy clay	3400	40	130 (6.6)	180 (7.4)	220 (8.0)	250 (8.5)	290 (9.0)	325 (9.5)	385 (10.0)
	Sand and gravel	3100	18	130 (6.6)	175 (7.4)	210 (8.0)	245 (8.5)	280 (9.0)	315 (9.5)	375 (10.0)
	Common earth	2800	30	110 (8.0)	160 (9.0)	190 (9.9)	220 (10.5)	250 (11.0)	280 (11.5)	310 (12.0)
	Clay, hard, dense	3000	33	90 (9.3)	130 (10.7)	160 (11.8)	190 (12.3)	225 (12.8)	250 (13.3)	280 (12.0)

Equipment	Soil Type	B.C.Y. Weight	% Swell	Wheel Loaders				Track Loaders		
				3 C.Y.	4 C.Y.	6 C.Y.	8 C.Y.	2-1/4 C.Y.	3 C.Y.	4 C.Y.
Loading Tractors	Moist loam, sandy clay	3400	40	260	340	510	690	135	180	250
	Sand and gravel	3100	18	245	320	480	650	130	170	235
	Common earth	2800	30	230	300	460	620	120	155	220
	Clay, hard, dense	3000	33	200	270	415	560	110	145	200
	Rock, well-blasted	4000	50	180	245	380	520	100	130	180

Site Work | R023 | Tunneling, Piles & Caissons

R023-620 Wood Bearing Piles

Untreated Southern Yellow Pine is most generally used for pile foundations cut off below the low water line. These are driven with the bark on. All piles cut off above the low water line should be treated with a preservative or encased in concrete for the section above water.

Item	Unit Cost	Units	Quantity	Total Cost	Cost/Pile	Cost/L.F.
50' Treated Piles, 13" Butt, 7" Tip	$ 10.91	L.F.	200	$109,100.00	$545.50	$10.91
Installation, Crew B-19	3,203.65	Day	13	41,647.45	208.24	4.16
Mobilization & Demobilization, Crew B-19	3,203.65	Day	3	9,610.95	48.05	.96
Transportation of Equip. One Way	1,090.75	Day	1	1,090.75	5.45	.11
Totals				$161,449.15	$807.24	$16.14

The above figures are based on driving 800 L.F. daily which can be considered average. Time is included for moving rig, cutoff & ordinary delays. A general observation is that the cost of a pile in place complete is about two times the cost of pile only. See also equipment rental division 016-408 and R016-410 for equipment capacities.

R023-810 Caissons

The three principal types of cassions are:

(1) **Belled Caissons,** which except for shallow depths and poor soil conditions, are generally recommended. They provide more bearing than shaft area. Because of its conical shape, no horizontal reinforcement of the bell is required.

(2) **Straight Shaft Caissons** are used where relatively light loads are to be supported by caissons that rest on high value bearing strata. While the shaft is larger in diameter than for belled types this is more than offset by the saving in time and labor.

(3) **Keyed Caissons** are used when extremely heavy loads are to be carried. A keyed or socketed caisson transfers its load into rock by a combination of end-bearing and shear reinforcing of the shaft. The most economical shaft often consists of a steel casing, a steel wide flange core and concrete. Allowable compressive stresses of $0.225\, f'c$ for concrete, 16,000 psi for the wide flange core, and 9,000 psi for the steel casing are commonly used. The usual range of shaft diameter is 18" to 84". The number of sizes specified for any one project should be limited due to the problems of casing and auger storage. When hand work is to be performed, shaft diameters should not be less than 32". When inspection of borings is required a minimum shaft diameter of 30" is recommended. Concrete caissons are intended to be poured against earth excavation so permanent forms which add to cost should not be used if the excavation is clean and the earth sufficiently impervious to prevent excessive loss of concrete.

Soil Conditions for Belling		
Good	Requires Handwork	Not Recommended
Clay	Hard Shale	Silt
Sandy Clay	Limestone	Sand
Silty Clay	Sandstone	Gravel
Clayey Silt	Weathered Mica	Igneous Rock
Hard-pan		
Soft Shale		
Decomposed Rock		

Site Work — R025 Paving & Surfacing

R025-110 Bituminous Paving

| City | Bituminous Asphalt per Ton* | Pavement (3") 6.13 S.Y./ton | | | | Sidewalks (2") 9.2 S.Y./ton | | | |
| | | Cost per S.Y. | | | Per Ton | Cost per S.Y. | | | Per Ton |
		Material*	Installation	Total	Total	Material*	Installation	Total	Total
Atlanta	$24.65	$4.02	$ .71	$4.73	$28.99	$2.68	$1.12	$3.80	$34.96
Baltimore	30.75	5.02	.77	5.79	35.47	3.34	1.31	4.65	42.78
Boston	35.00	5.71	1.02	6.73	41.27	3.80	2.16	5.96	54.83
Buffalo	32.00	5.22	.99	6.21	38.05	3.48	2.03	5.51	50.69
Chicago	33.00	5.38	1.02	6.40	39.24	3.59	2.16	5.75	52.90
Cincinnati	33.50	5.46	.87	6.33	38.82	3.64	1.71	5.35	49.22
Cleveland	29.80	4.86	.96	5.82	35.70	3.24	2.05	5.29	48.67
Columbus	26.75	4.36	.86	5.22	32.00	2.91	1.65	4.56	41.95
Dallas	23.95	3.91	.70	4.61	28.24	2.60	1.09	3.69	33.95
Denver	24.50	4.00	.74	4.74	29.04	2.66	1.24	3.90	35.88
Detroit	28.25	4.61	.96	5.57	34.15	3.07	2.02	5.09	46.83
Houston	29.55	4.82	.74	5.56	34.10	3.21	1.24	4.45	40.94
Indianapolis	26.50	4.32	.87	5.19	31.83	2.88	1.68	4.56	41.95
Kansas City	23.50	3.83	.89	4.72	28.92	2.55	1.76	4.31	39.65
Los Angeles	30.00	4.89	1.01	5.90	36.20	3.26	2.16	5.42	49.86
Memphis	28.20	4.60	.69	5.29	32.44	3.07	1.09	4.16	38.27
Milwaukee	26.40	4.31	.99	5.30	32.47	2.87	2.05	4.92	45.26
Minneapolis	27.75	4.53	.94	5.47	33.53	3.02	1.95	4.97	45.72
Nashville	27.75	4.53	.73	5.26	32.24	3.02	1.21	4.23	38.92
New Orleans	37.00	6.04	.69	6.73	41.27	4.02	1.09	5.11	47.01
New York City	43.05	7.02	1.24	8.26	50.65	4.68	2.93	7.61	70.01
Philadelphia	26.50	4.32	1.00	5.32	32.58	2.88	2.17	5.05	46.46
Phoenix	23.25	3.79	.77	4.56	27.93	2.53	1.35	3.88	35.70
Pittsburgh	31.30	5.11	.90	6.01	36.86	3.40	1.80	5.20	47.84
St. Louis	24.50	4.00	.97	4.97	30.48	2.66	2.06	4.72	43.42
San Antonio	27.10	4.42	.67	5.09	31.22	2.95	1.00	3.95	36.34
San Diego	27.50	4.49	1.01	5.50	33.74	2.99	2.16	5.15	47.38
San Francisco	32.00	5.22	1.03	6.25	38.30	3.48	2.17	5.65	51.98
Seattle	33.25	5.42	.96	6.38	39.12	3.61	2.01	5.62	51.70
Washington, D.C.	35.00	5.71	.77	6.48	39.73	3.80	1.34	5.14	47.29
Average	$29.40	$4.80	$ .88	$5.68	$34.82	$3.20	$1.73	$4.92	$45.28

Assumed density is 145 lb. per C.F.
*Includes delivery within 20 miles

Table below shows quantities and bare costs for 1000 S.Y. of Bituminous Paving.

| Item | Roads and Parking Areas, 3" Thick (025-104-0460) | | Sidewalks, 2" Thick (025-128-0010) | |
	Quantities	Cost	Quantities	Cost
Bituminous asphalt	163 tons @ $29.40 per ton	$4,792.20	109 tons @ $29.40 per ton	$3,204.60
Installation using	Crew B-25B @ $4,331.00 /4900SY/ day x 1000	883.88	Crew B-37 @ $1,244.45 /720 SY/day x 1000	1,728.40
Total per 1000 S.Y.		$5,676.08		$4,933.00
Total per S.Y.		$ 5.68		$ 4.93
Total per Ton		$ 34.82		$ 45.26

Site Work | R027 | Sewerage & Drainage

R027-110   Concrete Pipe

Prices given are for inside 20 mile delivery zone. Add $1.70 per ton of pipe for each additional 10 miles. Minimum truckload is 10 tons. The non-reinforced pipe listed in the front of the book is designation ASTM C14-59 extra strength. The reinforced pipe listed is ASTM C76-65T class 3, no gaskets. The installation cost given includes shaping bottom of the trench, placing the pipe, and backfilling and tamping to the top of the pipe only.

Site Work | R029 | Landscaping

R029-310   Seeding

The type of grass is determined by light, shade and moisture content of soil plus intended use. Fertilizer should be disked 4" before seeding. For steep slopes disk five tons of mulch and lay two tons of hay or straw on surface per acre after seeding. Surface mulch can be staked, lightly disked or tar emulsion sprayed. Material for mulch can be wood chips, peat moss, partially rotted hay or straw, wood fibers and sprayed emulsions. Hemp seed blankets with fertilizer are also available. For spring seeding, watering is necessary. Late fall seeding may have to be reseeded in the spring. Hydraulic seeding, power mulching, and aerial seeding can be used on large areas.

R029-545   Cost of Trees: Based on Pin Oak (Quercus palustris)

Tree Diameter	Normal Height	Catalog List Price of Tree	Guying Material	Equipment Charge	Installation Labor	Total
2 to 3 inch	14 feet	$ 130	$ 15.00	$ 58.31	$ 73.76	$ 277.07
3 to 4 inch	16 feet	248	18.00	97.18	122.93	486.11
4 to 5 inch	18 feet	390	65.00	116.62	147.52	719.14
6 to 7 inch	22 feet	790	80.00	145.78	184.40	1,200.18
8 to 9 inch	26 feet	1,300	100.00	194.37	245.87	1,840.23

Installation Time & Cost for Planting Trees, Bare Costs												
Ball Size Diam. X Depth	Soil in Ball	Weight of Ball	Hole Diam. Req'd	Hole Excavation	Amount of Soil Displ.	Topsoil Handled	Time Required in Labor-Hours					Cost	
							Dig & Lace	Handle Ball	Dig Hole	Plant & Prune	Water & Guy	Total L.H.	Crew	Total per Tree
Inches	C.F.	Lbs.	Feet	C.F.	C.F.	C.F.								
12 x 12	0.70	56.00	2.00	4.00	3.00	11.00	.25	.17	.33	.25	.07	1.10	1 Clab	$ 23.60
18 x 16	2.00	160.00	2.50	8.00	6.00	21.00	.50	.33	.47	.35	.08	1.70	2 Clab	36.47
24 x 18	4.00	320.00	3.00	13.00	9.00	38.00	1.00	.67	1.08	.82	.20	3.80	3 Clab	81.51
30 x 21	7.50	600.00	4.00	27.00	19.50	76.00	.82	.71	.79	1.22	.26	3.80		123.46
36 x 24	12.50	980.00	4.50	38.00	25.50	114.00	1.08	.95	1.11	1.32	.30	4.76		154.65
42 x 27	19.00	1,520.00	5.50	64.00	45.00	185.00	1.90	1.27	1.87	1.43	.34	6.80	B-6	220.93
48 x 30	28.00	2,040.00	6.00	85.00	57.00	254.00	2.41	1.60	2.06	1.55	.39	8.00	@	259.92
54 x 33	38.50	3,060.00	7.00	127.00	88.50	370.00	2.86	1.90	2.39	1.76	.45	9.40	$32.49	305.41
60 x 36	52.00	4,160.00	7.50	159.00	107.00	474.00	3.26	2.17	2.73	2.00	.51	10.70	per	347.64
66 x 39	68.00	5,440.00	8.00	196.00	128.00	596.00	3.61	2.41	3.07	2.26	.58	11.90	Labor-	386.63
72 x 42	87.00	7,160.00	9.00	267.00	180.00	785.00	3.90	2.60	3.71	2.78	.70	13.70	hour	445.11

Concrete | R031 | Concrete Formwork

R031-010 Wall Form Materials

Aluminum Forms

Approximate weight is 3 lbs. per S.F.C.A. Standard widths are available from 4" to 36" with 36" most common. Standard lengths of 2', 4', 6' to 8' are available. Forms are lightweight and fewer ties are needed with the wider widths. The form face is either smooth or textured.

Cost of bare forms per S.F.C.A. with different facing surface is listed below. Typical material cost including usual accessories but not including form ties is $18.05 per S.F.C.A.

Forms may also be rented.

	Purchase Cost Per S.F.							
Finish	3' x 8'	2' x 8'	12" x 8'	6" x 8'	3' x 4'	2' x 4'	12" x 4'	6" x 4'
Smooth Aluminum (.096" Face Sheet)	$12.47	$15.40	$20.86	$34.55	$13.36	$18.38	$24.12	$37.69
Textured Brick Aluminum	$14.51	$18.49	$24.95	$39.68	$16.67	$22.02	$28.26	$44.98

Metal Framed Plywood Forms

Manufacturers claim over 75 reuses of plywood and over 300 reuses of steel frames. Sale price for steel framed forms is $8.50 per S.F. for 2' x 8' to $12.15 per S.F. for 2' x 3'. Narrower forms range between $11.75 per S.F. to $21.60 per S.F. for 1' x 3'. Many specials such as corners, fillers, pilasters, etc. are available. Monthly rental is generally about 15% of purchase price for first month and 9% per month thereafter with 90% of rental applied to purchase for the first month and decreasing percentages thereafter. Aluminum framed forms cost 25% to 30% more than steel framed.

Rule of thumb purchase price including corners, specials, etc.; steel framed $12.20 per S.F.; aluminum framed $17.30 per S.F.

Reconditioned steel framed forms are rented for an average of $1.30 per S.F per month. Aluminum framed forms are rented for $2.25 per S.F. for the first month and $1.50 per S.F. per month thereafter.

After the first month, extra days may be prorated from the monthly charge. Rental rates do not include ties, accessories, cleaning, loss of hardware or freight in and out. Approximate weight is 5 lbs. per S.F. for steel; 3 lbs. per S.F. for aluminum.

Forms can be rented with option to buy.

Plywood Forms, Job Fabricated

There are two types of plywood used for concrete forms.

1. Exterior plyform which is completely waterproof. This is face oiled to facilitate stripping. Ten reuses can be expected with this type with 25 reuses possible.
2. An overlaid type consists of a resin fiber fused to exterior plyform. No oiling is required except to facilitate cleaning. This is available in both high density (HDO) and medium density overlaid (MDO). Using HDO, 50 reuses can be expected with 200 possible.

Plyform is available in 5/8" and 3/4" thickness. High density overlaid is available in 3/8", 1/2", 5/8" and 3/4" thickness.

5/8" thick is sufficient for most building forms, while 3/4" is best on heavy construction.

For prices on plywood and framing lumber see R061-010 and R061-020.

Plywood Forms, Modular, Prefabricated

There are many plywood forming systems without frames. Most of these are manufactured from 1-1/8" (HDO) plywood and have some hardware attached. These are used principally for foundation walls 8' or less high. With care and maintenance, 100 reuses can be attained with decreasing quality of surface finish. Sale price of 2' x 8' panels is $6.20 per S.F. with 4' x 8' fillers costing $24.40 per S.F. Typical forms and accessories for 1000 S.F. of form area cost $6,970 not including form ties.

Steel Forms

Approximate weight is 6-1/2 lbs. per S.F.C.A. including accessories. Standard widths are available from 2" to 24", with 24" most common. Standard lengths are from 2' to 8', with 4' the most common. Forms are easily ganged into modular units.

Sale price for typical hand set job is $12.15 per S.F.C.A. including all usual accessories, specials, corners, etc., but not including ties or freight. Cost of bare forms runs from $9.75 for wide forms to over $21.60 per S.F.C.A. for narrow widths and/or short lengths. Forms are usually leased for 15% of the purchase price per month prorated daily over 30 days. Standard 6000 lb. wall ties for 12" walls cost $84 per hundred and 24" long ties cost $121 per hundred.

Rental may be applied to sale price and usually rental forms are bought. With careful handling and cleaning 200 to 400 reuses are possible.

Straight wall gang forms up to 12' x 20' or 8' x 30' can be fabricated. These crane handled forms usually cost from $20.50 to $28.20 per S.F.C.A. or can be leased for 8.7% per month. Straight wall gang forms utilizing 40,000 lb. and 60,000 lb. ties with sizes from 24' x 10' to 24' x 24' cost from $21.50 to $29.75 per S.F. including all accessories and taper ties. Rental rates on these gang forms run from $.30 to $.65 per week per S.F.C.A.

Individual job analysis is available from the manufacturer at no charge.

Concrete — R031 Concrete Formwork

R031-020 Floor Pans and Domes

For 8' to 15' Ceiling Heights Using Crew C-2 at $26.66 per Labor-Hour	20" Pans (031-150)				19" Domes (031-150)			
	(Line 3500)	1 Use	(Line 3650)	4 Use	(Line 4000)	1 Use	(Line 4150)	4 Use
Rent 20" pans or 19" domes		$ 82.00		$ 25.00		$ 82.00		$ 25.00
Adjustable shores and accessories		46.00		25.25		46.00		25.25
110 S.F. 3/4" plyform at $880 per M.S.F.		96.80		31.46		96.80		31.46
210 B.F. supporting joists, girts and braces at $540 per MBF		113.40		36.86		113.40		36.86
Labor handle, place, strip, oil and clean pans and domes	1.5 L.H.	39.99	1.0 L.H.	26.66	1.8 L.H.	47.99	1.2 L.H.	31.99
Make up, erect, remove wood decking	10 L.H.	266.60	8.5 L.H.	226.61	10.0 L.H.	266.60	8.5 L.H.	226.61
Total per 100 S.F. of floor area		$644.79		$371.84		$652.79		$377.17

The figures above are for closed deck forming. For open deck forming deduct $25 per 100 S.F. for four uses. For pan rental, figure $.82 per S.F. of total area for one use; $.41 for two uses; $.30 for three uses; and $.25 for four uses, which is about the most that can be expected for any one project. The purchase price of fiberglass long pans is $5.75 per S.F.C.A. or an average $11.50 per S.F. of floor area.*

For two-way grid system, 19" steel domes are leased for $.25 to $.75 and 30" fiberglass domes are leased for $.50 to $2.25 per S.F. of floor area.

The purchase price of custom size fiberglass forms runs from $6.00 to $17.00 per S.F.C.A.*

For slab height from 15' to 20' add $55 per 100 S.F. and for 20' to 35' add $75 per 100 S.F., both for four uses.

*It is necessary to divide the purchase cost by the number of expected uses to determine the cost per use.

R031-040 Forms for Reinforced Concrete

Design Economy

Avoid many sizes in proportioning beams and columns.

From story to story avoid changing column dimensions. Gain strength by adding steel or using a richer mix. If a change in size of column is necessary, vary one dimension only to minimize form alterations. Keep beams and columns the same width.

From floor to floor in a multi-story building vary beam depth, not width, as that will leave slab panel form unchanged. It is cheaper to vary the strength of a beam from floor to floor by means of steel area than by 2" changes in either width or depth.

Cost Factors

Material includes the cost of lumber, cost of rent for metal pans or forms if used, nails, form ties, form oil, bolts and accessories.

Labor includes the cost of carpenters to make up, erect, remove and repair, plus common labor to clean and move. Having carpenters remove forms minimizes repairs.

Improper alignment and condition of forms will increase finishing cost. When forms are heavily oiled, concrete surfaces must be neutralized before finishing. Special curing compounds will cause spillages to spall off in first frost. Gang forming methods will reduce costs on large projects.

Materials Used

Boards are seldom used unless their architectural finish is required. Generally, steel, fiberglass and plywood are used for contact surfaces. Labor on plywood is 10% less than with boards. The plywood is backed up with 2 x 4's at 12" to 32" O.C. Walers are generally 2 - 2 x 4's. Column forms are held together with steel yokes or bands. Shoring is with adjustable shoring or scaffolding for high ceilings.

Reuse

Floor and column forms can be reused four or possibly five times without excessive repair. Remember to allow for 10% waste on each reuse.

When modular sized wall forms are made, up to twenty uses can be expected with exterior plyform.

When forms are reused, the cost to erect, strip, clean and move will not be affected. 10% replacement of lumber should be included and about one hour of carpenter time for repairs on each reuse per 100 S.F.

The reuse cost for certain accessory items normally rented on a monthly basis will be lower than the cost for the first use.

After fifth use, new material required plus time needed for repair prevent form cost from dropping further and it may go up. Much depends on care in stripping, the number of special bays, changes in beam or column sizes and other factors.

Costs for multiple use of formwork may be developed as follows:

2 Uses
$$\frac{(1\text{st Use} + \text{Reuse})}{2} = \text{avg. cost}/2 \text{ uses}$$

3 Uses
$$\frac{(1\text{st Use} + 2 \text{ Reuse})}{3} = \text{avg. cost}/3 \text{ uses}$$

4 Uses
$$\frac{(1\text{st use} + 3 \text{ Reuse})}{4} = \text{avg. cost}/4 \text{ uses}$$

Concrete — R031 Concrete Formwork

R031-050 Forms In Place

This section assumes that all cuts are made with power saws, that adjustable shores are employed and that maximum use is made of commercial form ties and accessories. Bare costs are used in the table below.

BEAM AND GIRDER, INTERIOR, 12" Wide (Line 031-138-2000)			First Use			Reuse		
Item	Cost	Unit	Quantity	Material	Installation	Quantity	Material	Installation
5/8" exterior plyform	$760.00	M.S.F.	115 S.F.	$ 87.40		11.5 S.F.	$ 8.75	
Lumber	540.00	M.B.F.	200 B.F.	108.00		20.0 B.F.	10.80	
Accessories, incl. adjustable shores			Allow	24.00		Allow	24.00	
Make up, crew C-2	26.66	L.H.	6.4 L.H.		$170.60	1.0 L.H.		$ 26.65
Erect and strip			8.3 L.H.		221.30	8.3 L.H.		221.30
Clean and move			1.3 L.H.		34.65	1.3 L.H.		34.65
Total per 100 S.F.C.A.			16.0 L.H.	$219.40	$426.55	10.6 L.H.	$43.55	$282.60

For structural steel frame with beams encased, subtract 1.2 labor-hours, and 50 B.F. lumber or about $55.00 per 100 S.F.C.A. for the first use and $32 for each reuse.

BOX CULVERT, 5' to 8' Square or Rectangular (Line 031-146-0010)			First Use			Reuse		
Item	Cost	Unit	Quantity	Material	Installation	Quantity	Material	Installation
3/4" exterior plyform	$880.00	M.S.F.	110 S.F.	$ 96.80		11.0 S.F.	$ 9.70	
Lumber	540.00	M.B.F.	170 B.F.	91.80		17.0 B.F.	9.20	
Accessories			Allow	19.00		Allow	19.00	
Build in place, crew C-1	25.84	L.H.	14.5 L.H.		$374.70	14.5 L.H.		$374.70
Strip and salvage			4.3 L.H.		111.10	4.3 L.H.		111.10
Total per 100 S.F.C.A.			18.8 L.H.	$207.60	$485.80	18.8 L.H.	$37.90	$485.80

COLUMNS, 24" x 24" (Line 031-142-6500)			First Use			Reuse		
Item	Cost	Unit	Quantity	Material	Installation	Quantity	Material	Installation
5/8" exterior plyform	$760.00	M.S.F.	120 S.F.	$ 91.20		12.0 S.F.	$ 9.10	
Lumber	540.00	M.B.F.	125 B.F.	67.50		12.5 B.F.	6.75	
Clamps, chamfer strips and accessories			Allow	24.00		Allow	24.00	
Make up, crew C-1	25.84	L.H.	5.8 L.H.		$149.85	1.0 L.H.		$ 25.85
Erect and strip			9.8 L.H.		253.25	9.8 L.H.		253.25
Clean and move			1.2 L.H.		31.00	1.2 L.H.		31.00
Total per 100 S.F.C.A.			16.8 L.H.	$182.70	$434.10	12.0 L.H.	$39.85	$310.10

FLAT SLAB WITH DROP PANELS (Line 031-150-2000)			First Use			Reuse		
Item	Cost	Unit	Quantity	Material	Installation	Quantity	Material	Installation
5/8" exterior plyform	$760.00	M.S.F.	115 S.F.	$ 87.40		11.5 S.F.	$ 8.75	
Lumber	540.00	M.B.F.	210 B.F.	113.40		21.0 B.F.	11.35	
Accessories, incl. adjustable shores			Allow	24.00		Allow	24.00	
Make up, crew C-2	26.66	L.H.	3.5 L.H.		$ 93.30	1.0 L.H.		$ 26.65
Erect and strip			6.0 L.H.		159.95	6.0 L.H.		159.95
Clean and move			1.2 L.H.		32.00	1.2 L.H.		32.00
Total per 100 S.F.C.A.			10.7 L.H.	$224.80	$285.25	8.2 L.H.	$44.10	$218.60

Drop panels included but column caps figure with columns.

FOOTINGS, SPREAD (Line 031-158-5000)			First Use			Reuse		
Item	Cost	Unit	Quantity	Materials	Installation	Quantity	Material	Installation
Lumber	$540.00	M.B.F.	260 B.F.	$140.40		26 B.F.	$14.05	
Accessories			Allow	7.65		Allow	7.65	
Make up, crew C-1	25.84	L.H.	4.7 L.H.		$121.45	1.0 L.H.		$ 25.85
Erect and strip			4.2 L.H.		108.55	4.2 L.H.		108.55
Clean and move			1.6 L.H.		41.35	1.6 L.H.		41.35
Total per 100 S.F.C.A.			10.5 L.H.	$148.05	$271.35	6.8 L.H.	$21.70	$175.75

Concrete | R031 | Concrete Formwork

R031-050 Forms In Place (cont.)

FOUNDATION WALL, 8' High (Line 031-182-2000)

Item	Cost	Unit	First Use Quantity	First Use Material	First Use Installation	Reuse Quantity	Reuse Material	Reuse Installation
5/8" exterior plyform	$760.00	M.S.F.	110 S.F.	$ 83.60		11.0 S.F.	$ 8.35	
Lumber	540.00	M.B.F.	140 B.F.	75.60		14.0 B.F.	7.55	
Accessories			Allow	24.00		Allow	24.00	
Make up, crew C-2	26.66	L.H.	5.0 L.H.		$133.30	1.0 L.H.		$ 26.65
Erect and strip			6.5 L.H.		173.30	6.5 L.H.		173.30
Clean and move			1.5 L.H.		40.00	1.5 L.H.		40.00
Total per 100 S.F.C.A.			13.0 L.H.	$183.20	$346.60	9.0 L.H.	$39.90	$239.95

PILE CAPS, Square or Rectangular (Line 031-158-3000)

Item	Cost	Unit	First Use Quantity	First Use Material	First Use Installation	Reuse Quantity	Reuse Material	Reuse Installation
5/8" exterior plyform	$760.00	M.S.F.	110 S.F.	$ 83.60		11.0 S.F.	$ 8.35	
Lumber	540.00	M.B.F.	160 B.F.	86.40		16.0 B.F.	8.65	
Accessories			Allow	7.28		Allow	7.28	
Make up, crew C-1	25.84	L.H.	4.5 L.H.		$116.30	1.0 L.H.		$ 25.85
Erect and strip			5.0 L.H.		129.20	5.0 L.H.		129.20
Clean and move			1.5 L.H.		38.75	1.5 L.H.		38.75
Total per 100 S.F.C.A.			11.0 L.H.	$177.28	$284.25	7.5 L.H.	$24.28	$193.80

STAIRS, Average Run (Inclined Length x Width) (Line 031-174-0010)

Item	Cost	Unit	First Use Quantity	First Use Materials	First Use Installation	Reuse Quantity	Reuse Material	Reuse Installation
5/8" exterior plyform	$760.00	M.S.F.	110 S.F.	$ 83.60		11.0 S.F.	$ 8.35	
Lumber	540.00	M.B.F.	425 B.F.	229.50		42.5 B.F.	22.95	
Accessories			Allow	19.00		Allow	19.00	
Build in place, crew C-2	26.66	L.H.	25.0 L.H.		$666.50	25.0 L.H.		$666.50
Strip and salvage			4.0 L.H.		106.65	4.0 L.H.		106.65
Total per 100 S.F.			29.0 L.H.	$332.10	$773.15	29.0 L.H.	$50.30	$773.15

Concrete — R031 Concrete Formwork

R031-060 Formwork Labor Hours

Item	Unit	Fabricate	Erect & Strip	Clean & Move	Total Hours 1 Use	2 Use	3 Use	4 Use
Beam and Girder, interior beams, 12" wide	100 S.F.	6.4	8.3	1.3	16.0	13.3	12.4	12.0
Hung from steel beams		5.8	7.7	1.3	14.8	12.4	11.6	11.2
Beam sides only, 36" high		5.8	7.2	1.3	14.3	11.9	11.1	10.7
Beam bottoms only, 24" wide		6.6	13.0	1.3	20.9	18.1	17.2	16.7
Box out for openings		9.9	10.0	1.1	21.0	16.6	15.1	14.3
Buttress forms, to 8' high		6.0	6.5	1.2	13.7	11.2	10.4	10.0
Centering, steel, 3/4" rib lath			1.0		1.0			
3/8" rib lath or slab form			0.9		0.9			
Chamfer strip or keyway	100 L.F.		1.5		1.5	1.5	1.5	1.5
Columns, fiber tube 8" diameter			20.6		20.6			
12"			21.3		21.3			
16"			22.9		22.9			
20"			23.7		23.7			
24"			24.6		24.6			
30"			25.6		25.6			
Round Steel, 12" diameter			22.0		22.0	22.0	22.0	22.0
16"			25.6		25.6	25.6	25.6	25.6
20"			30.5		30.5	30.5	30.5	30.5
24"			37.7		37.7	37.7	37.7	37.7
Plywood 8" x 8"	100 S.F.	7.0	11.0	1.2	19.2	16.2	15.2	14.7
12" x 12"		6.0	10.5	1.2	17.7	15.2	14.4	14.0
16" x 16"		5.9	10.0	1.2	17.1	14.7	13.8	13.4
24" x 24"		5.8	9.8	1.2	16.8	14.4	13.6	13.2
Steel framed plywood 8" x 8"			10.0	1.0	11.0	11.0	11.0	11.0
12" x 12"			9.3	1.0	10.3	10.3	10.3	10.3
16" x 16"			8.5	1.0	9.5	9.5	9.5	9.5
24" x 24"			7.8	1.0	8.8	8.8	8.8	8.8
Drop head forms, plywood		9.0	12.5	1.5	23.0	19.0	17.7	17.0
Coping forms		8.5	15.0	1.5	25.0	21.3	20.0	19.4
Culvert, box			14.5	4.3	18.8	18.8	18.8	18.8
Curb forms, 6" to 12" high, on grade		5.0	8.5	1.2	14.7	12.7	12.1	11.7
On elevated slabs		6.0	10.8	1.2	18.0	15.5	14.7	14.3
Edge forms to 6" high, on grade	100 L.F.	2.0	3.5	0.6	6.1	5.6	5.4	5.3
7" to 12" high	100 S.F.	2.5	5.0	1.0	8.5	7.8	7.5	7.4
Equipment foundations		10.0	18.0	2.0	30.0	25.5	24.0	23.3
Flat slabs, including drops		3.5	6.0	1.2	10.7	9.5	9.0	8.8
Hung from steel		3.0	5.5	1.2	9.7	8.7	8.4	8.2
Closed deck for domes		3.0	5.8	1.2	10.0	9.0	8.7	8.5
Open deck for pans		2.2	5.3	1.0	8.5	7.9	7.7	7.6
Footings, continuous, 12" high		3.5	3.5	1.5	8.5	7.3	6.8	6.6
Spread, 12" high		4.7	4.2	1.6	10.5	8.7	8.0	7.7
Pile caps, square or rectangular		4.5	5.0	1.5	11.0	9.3	8.7	8.4
Grade beams, 24" deep		2.5	5.3	1.2	9.0	8.3	8.0	7.9
Lintel or Sill forms		8.0	17.0	2.0	27.0	23.5	22.3	21.8
Spandrel beams, 12" wide		9.0	11.2	1.3	21.5	17.5	16.2	15.5
Stairs			25.0	4.0	29.0	29.0	29.0	29.0
Trench forms in floor		4.5	14.0	1.5	20.0	18.3	17.7	17.4
Walls, Plywood, at grade, to 8' high		5.0	6.5	1.5	13.0	11.0	9.7	9.5
8' to 16'		7.5	8.0	1.5	17.0	13.8	12.7	12.1
16' to 20'		9.0	10.0	1.5	20.5	16.5	15.2	14.5
Foundation walls, to 8' high		4.5	6.5	1.0	12.0	10.3	9.7	9.4
8' to 16' high		5.5	7.5	1.0	14.0	11.8	11.0	10.6
Retaining wall to 12' high, battered		6.0	8.5	1.5	16.0	13.5	12.7	12.3
Radial walls to 12' high, smooth		8.0	9.5	2.0	19.5	16.0	14.8	14.3
But in 2' chords		7.0	8.0	1.5	16.5	13.5	12.5	12.0
Prefabricated modular, to 8' high		—	4.3	1.0	5.3	5.3	5.3	5.3
Steel, to 8' high		—	6.8	1.2	8.0	8.0	8.0	8.0
8' to 16' high		—	9.1	1.5	10.6	10.3	10.2	10.2
Steel framed plywood to 8' high		—	6.8	1.2	8.0	7.5	7.3	7.2
8' to 16' high		—	9.3	1.2	10.5	9.5	9.2	9.0

Concrete — R033 Cast-In-Place Concrete

R033-010 Proportionate Quantities

The tables below show both quantities per S.F. of floor areas as well as form and reinforcing quantities per C.Y. Unusual structural requirements would increase the ratios below. High strength reinforcing would reduce the steel weights. Figures are for 3000 psi concrete and 60,000 psi reinforcing unless specified otherwise.

Type of Construction	Live Load	Span	Per S.F. of Floor Area				Per C.Y. of Concrete		
			Concrete	Forms	Reinf.	Pans	Forms	Reinf.	Pans
Flat Plate	50 psf	15 Ft.	.46 C.F.	1.06 S.F.	1.71 lb.		62 S.F.	101 lb.	
		20	.63	1.02	2.40		44	104	
		25	.79	1.02	3.03		35	104	
	100	15	.46	1.04	2.14		61	126	
		20	.71	1.02	2.72		39	104	
		25	.83	1.01	3.47		33	113	
Flat Plate (waffle construction) 20" domes	50	20	.43	1.00	2.10	.84 S.F.	63	135	53 S.F.
		25	.52	1.00	2.90	.89	52	150	46
		30	.64	1.00	3.70	.87	42	155	37
	100	20	.51	1.00	2.30	.84	53	125	45
		25	.64	1.00	3.20	.83	42	135	35
		30	.76	1.00	4.40	.81	36	160	29
Waffle Construction 30" domes	50	25	.69	1.06	1.83	.68	42	72	40
		30	.74	1.06	2.39	.69	39	87	39
		35	.86	1.05	2.71	.69	33	85	39
		40	.78	1.00	4.80	.68	35	165	40
Flat Slab (two way with drop panels)	50	20	.62	1.03	2.34		45	102	
		25	.77	1.03	2.99		36	105	
		30	.95	1.03	4.09		29	116	
	100	20	.64	1.03	2.83		43	119	
		25	.79	1.03	3.88		35	133	
		30	.96	1.03	4.66		29	131	
	200	20	.73	1.03	3.03		38	112	
		25	.86	1.03	4.23		32	133	
		30	1.06	1.03	5.30		26	135	
One Way Joists 20" Pans	50	15	.36	1.04	1.40	.93	78	105	70
		20	.42	1.05	1.80	.94	67	120	60
		25	.47	1.05	2.60	.94	60	150	54
	100	15	.38	1.07	1.90	.93	77	140	66
		20	.44	1.08	2.40	.94	67	150	58
		25	.52	1.07	3.50	.94	55	185	49
One Way Joists 8" x 16" filler blocks	50	15	.34	1.06	1.80	.81 Ea.	84	145	64 Ea.
		20	.40	1.08	2.20	.82	73	145	55
		25	.46	1.07	3.20	.83	63	190	49
	100	15	.39	1.07	1.90	.81	74	130	56
		20	.46	1.09	2.80	.82	64	160	48
		25	.53	1.10	3.60	.83	56	190	42
One Way Beam & Slab	50	15	.42	1.30	1.73		84	111	
		20	.51	1.28	2.61		68	138	
		25	.64	1.25	2.78		53	117	
	100	15	.42	1.30	1.90		84	122	
		20	.54	1.35	2.69		68	154	
		25	.69	1.37	3.93		54	145	
	200	15	.44	1.31	2.24		80	137	
		20	.58	1.40	3.30		65	163	
		25	.69	1.42	4.89		53	183	
Two Way Beam & Slab	100	15	.47	1.20	2.26		69	130	
		20	.63	1.29	3.06		55	131	
		25	.83	1.33	3.79		43	123	
	200	15	.49	1.25	2.70		41	149	
		20	.66	1.32	4.04		54	165	
		25	.88	1.32	6.08		41	187	

Concrete | R033 | Cast-In-Place Concrete

R033-010 Proportionate Quantities (cont.)

4000 psi Concrete and 60,000 psi Reinforcing—Form and Reinforcing Quantities per C.Y.					
Item	Size	Forms	Reinforcing	Minimum	Maximum
Columns (square tied)	10" x 10"	130 S.F.C.A.	#5 to #11	220 lbs.	875 lbs.
	12" x 12"	108	#6 to #14	200	955
	14" x 14"	92	#7 to #14	190	900
	16" x 16"	81	#6 to #14	187	1082
	18" x 18"	72	#6 to #14	170	906
	20" x 20"	65	#7 to #18	150	1080
	22" x 22"	59	#8 to #18	153	902
	24" x 24"	54	#8 to #18	164	884
	26" x 26"	50	#9 to #18	169	994
	28" x 28"	46	#9 to #18	147	864
	30" x 30"	43	#10 to #18	146	983
	32" x 32"	40	#10 to #18	175	866
	34" x 34"	38	#10 to #18	157	772
	36" x 36"	36	#10 to #18	175	852
	38" x 38"	34	#10 to #18	158	765
	40" x 40"	32	#10 to #18	143	692

Item	Size	Form	Spiral	Reinforcing	Minimum	Maximum
Columns (spirally reinforced)	12" diameter	34.5 L.F.	190 lbs.	#4 to #11	165 lbs.	1505 lbs.
		34.5	190	#14 & #18	—	1100
	14"	25	170	#4 to #11	150	970
		25	170	#14 & #18	800	1000
	16"	19	160	#4 to #11	160	950
		19	160	#14 & #18	605	1080
	18"	15	150	#4 to #11	160	915
		15	150	#14 & #18	480	1075
	20"	12	130	#4 to #11	155	865
		12	130	#14 & #18	385	1020
	22"	10	125	#4 to #11	165	775
		10	125	#14 & #18	320	995
	24"	9	120	#4 to #11	195	800
		9	120	#14 & #18	290	1150
	26"	7.3	100	#4 to #11	200	729
		7.3	100	#14 & #18	235	1035
	28"	6.3	95	#4 to #11	175	700
		6.3	95	#14 & #18	200	1075
	30"	5.5	90	#4 to #11	180	670
		5.5	90	#14 & #18	175	1015
	32"	4.8	85	#4 to #11	185	615
		4.8	85	#14 & #18	155	955
	34"	4.3	80	#4 to #11	180	600
		4.3	80	#14 & #18	170	855
	36"	3.8	75	#4 to #11	165	570
		3.8	75	#14 & #18	155	865
	40"	3.0	70	#4 to #11	165	500
		3.0	70	#14 & #18	145	765

Concrete

R033 Cast-In-Place Concrete

R033-010 Proportionate Quantities (cont.)

		3000 psi Concrete and 60,000 psi Reinforcing—Form and Reinforcing Quantities per C.Y.				
Item	Type	Loading	Height	C.Y./L.F.	Forms/C.Y.	Reinf./C.Y.
Retaining Walls	Cantilever	Level Backfill	4 Ft.	.2 C.Y.	49 S.F.	35 lbs.
			8	.5	42	45
			12	.8	35	70
			16	1.1	32	85
			20	1.6	28	105
		Highway Surcharge	4	.3	41	35
			8	.5	36	55
			12	.8	33	90
			16	1.2	30	120
			20	1.7	27	155
		Railroad Surcharge	4	.4	28	45
			8	.8	25	65
			12	1.3	22	90
			16	1.9	20	100
			20	2.6	18	120
	Gravity, with Vertical Face	Level Backfill	4	.4	37	None
			7	.6	27	↓
			10	1.2	20	
		Sloping Surcharge	4	.3	31	
			7	.8	21	
			10	1.6	15	↓

		Live Load in Kips per Linear Foot							
	Span	Under 1 Kip		2 to 3 Kips		4 to 5 Kips		6 to 7 Kips	
		Forms	Reinf.	Forms	Reinf.	Forms	Reinf.	Forms	Reinf.
Beams	10 Ft.	—	—	90 S.F.	170 #	85 S.F.	175 #	75 S.F.	185 #
	16	130 S.F.	165 #	85	180	75	180	65	225
	20	110	170	75	185	62	200	51	200
	26	90	170	65	215	62	215	—	—
	30	85	175	60	200	—	—	—	—

Item	Size	Type	Forms per C.Y.	Reinforcing per C.Y.
Spread Footings	Under 1 C.Y.	1,000 psf soil	24 S.F.	44 lbs.
		5,000	24	42
		10,000	24	52
	1 C.Y. to 5 C.Y.	1,000	14	49
		5,000	14	50
		10,000	14	50
	Over 5 C.Y.	1,000	9	54
		5,000	9	52
		10,000	9	56
Pile Caps (30 Ton Concrete Piles)	Under 5 C.Y.	shallow caps	20	65
		medium	20	50
		deep	20	40
	5 C.Y. to 10 C.Y.	shallow	14	55
		medium	15	45
		deep	15	40
	10 C.Y. to 20 C.Y.	shallow	11	60
		medium	11	45
		deep	12	35
	Over 20 C.Y.	shallow	9	60
		medium	9	45
		deep	10	40

Concrete | R033 | Cast-In-Place Concrete

R033-010 Proportionate Quantities (cont.)

	3000 psi Concrete and 60,000 psi Reinforcing — Form and Reinforcing Quantities per C.Y.					
Item	Size	Pile Spacing	50 T Pile	100 T Pile	50 T Pile	100 T Pile
Pile Caps (Steel H Piles)	Under 5 C.Y.	24" O.C.	24 S.F.	24 S.F.	75 lbs.	90 lbs.
		30"	25	25	80	100
		36"	24	24	80	110
	5 C.Y. to 10 C.Y.	24"	15	15	80	110
		30"	15	15	85	110
		36"	15	15	75	90
	Over 10 C.Y.	24"	13	13	85	90
		30"	11	11	85	95
		36"	10	10	85	90

		8" Thick		10" Thick		12" Thick		15" Thick	
	Height	Forms	Reinf.	Forms	Reinf.	Forms	Reinf.	Forms	Reinf.
Basement Walls	7 Ft.	81 S.F.	44 lbs.	65 S.F.	45 lbs.	54 S.F.	44 lbs.	41 S.F.	43 lbs.
	8		44		45		44		43
	9		46		45		44		43
	10		57		45		44		43
	12		83		50		52		43
	14		116		65		64		51
	16				86		90		65
	18						106		70

R033-020 Materials for One C.Y. of Concrete

This is an approximate method of figuring quantities of cement, sand and coarse aggregate for a field mix with waste allowance included.

With crushed gravel as coarse aggregate, to determine barrels of cement required, divide 10 by total mix; that is, for 1:2:4 mix, 10 divided by 7 = 1-3/7 barrels.

If the coarse aggregate is crushed stone, use 10-1/2 instead of 10 as given for gravel.

To determine tons of sand required, multiply barrels of cement by parts of sand and then by 0.2; that is, for the 1:2:4 mix, as above, 1-3/7 x 2 x .2 = .57 tons.

Tons of crushed gravel are in the same ratio to tons of sand as parts in the mix, or 4/2 x .57 = 1.14 tons.

1 bag cement = 94#
4 bags = 1 barrel
1 C.Y. sand or crushed gravel = 2700#
1 ton sand or crushed gravel = 20 C.F.
1 C.Y. crushed stone = 2575#
1 ton crushed stone = 21 C.F.

Average carload of cement is 692 bags; of sand or gravel is 56 tons.

Do not stack stored cement over 10 bags high.

Concrete — R033 Cast-In-Place Concrete

R033-060 Concrete Material Net Prices

Costs below are C.Y. of concrete delivered; per ton of bulk cement; per bag cement delivered T.L.L.; per ton for stone and sand aggregates loaded at plant (no trucking included) and per 4 C.F. bag for perlite or vermiculite aggregate delivered T.L.L.

City	Ready Mix Concrete Regular Weight 3000 psi	Ready Mix Concrete Regular Weight 5000 psi	Cement T.L. Lots Bulk per Ton	Cement T.L. Lots Bags per Bag	Aggregates per Ton Crushed Stone 1-1/2"	Aggregates per Ton Crushed Stone 3/4"	Sand	Vermiculite or Perlite 4 C.F. Bag
Atlanta	$58.00	$63.00	$72.25	$6.35	$13.70	$14.00	$13.45	$10.35
Baltimore	62.00	67.00	77.00	6.75	9.25	9.80	9.50	8.85
Boston	66.00	72.00	84.00	7.40	11.45	12.65	10.50	9.75
Buffalo	67.00	73.00	89.20	7.65	11.65	12.10	12.30	10.10
Chicago	58.00	64.00	83.35	7.10	9.25	9.55	8.00	8.70
Cincinnati	55.00	60.00	78.35	6.65	8.30	10.30	7.00	10.15
Cleveland	60.00	66.00	84.55	7.20	13.40	13.95	9.90	9.95
Columbus	59.00	63.00	82.05	7.30	12.10	12.35	6.75	10.10
Dallas	65.00	70.00	77.15	6.50	16.10	16.35	7.05	9.80
Denver	59.00	67.00	82.05	8.00	10.10	10.30	8.00	10.20
Detroit	63.00	68.00	80.85	7.10	8.80	9.00	8.70	10.00
Houston	64.00	70.00	84.85	7.25	18.30	18.50	10.50	8.95
Indianapolis	60.00	68.00	79.60	6.85	7.85	8.40	9.90	9.95
Kansas City	56.00	61.00	74.65	6.35	7.80	8.15	7.00	10.20
Los Angeles	54.00	62.00	87.05	7.75	12.95	13.55	12.50	10.40
Memphis	60.00	64.00	77.15	6.65	11.75	12.10	9.35	9.60
Milwaukee	62.00	67.00	87.20	7.45	8.75	9.15	8.55	9.40
Minneapolis	63.00	68.00	84.30	7.20	14.65	14.90	9.85	9.55
Nashville	55.00	60.00	74.65	6.40	9.25	9.45	11.60	9.10
New Orleans	58.00	66.00	78.05	6.60	15.15	15.75	13.05	9.80
New York City	70.00	78.00	88.35	7.60	24.25	25.85	14.50	10.35
Philadelphia	56.00	64.00	80.85	7.05	10.90	11.50	7.50	9.15
Phoenix	65.00	70.00	78.90	7.15	11.20	11.70	11.50	9.70
Pittsburgh	61.00	65.00	75.90	6.55	14.85	15.00	10.50	9.55
St. Louis	53.00	59.00	77.15	6.55	9.70	10.60	9.55	9.80
San Antonio	53.00	57.00	74.65	6.35	7.85	8.05	5.90	8.90
San Diego	57.00	63.00	84.55	7.20	9.20	9.40	8.10	8.95
San Francisco	78.00	83.00	88.00	7.55	18.50	20.55	12.50	9.55
Seattle	60.00	66.00	82.05	7.05	14.80	15.25	11.90	9.95
Washington, D.C.	73.00	83.00	80.85	6.95	13.80	14.80	11.25	10.20
Average	$61.00	$66.90	$81.00	$7.00	$12.20	$12.75	$9.90	$9.70

R033-070 Ready Mix Material Prices

Table below lists national average prices per C.Y. of concrete. Prices in the key cities for different strengths can be closely estimated by factoring against the 3000 psi or 5000 psi price from R033-060 above or from the City Cost Indexes, cast-in-place concrete material factor.

Strength in psi	Design Mix Nominal Mix	Bags per C.Y.	Heavy Weight Regular	Heavy Weight High Early	Light Weight 110# per C.F.	Light Weight All Light Weight	Admixtures and Special Items — Add to Each C.Y. of Concrete for the Following Items:		
2,000	1:3:5	4.5	$57.95	$63.60	$72.45	$86.95	Calcium chloride, 1%	$1.75	per C.Y.
2,500	1:2-½:4-½	5	59.15	65.40	73.95	88.75	" 2%	3.00	per C.Y.
3,000	1:2:4	5.5	61.00	67.90	76.25	91.50	Water reducing agent	.25	per bag
3,500	1:2:3½	6	62.55	70.05	78.20	93.85	Set retarder	.62	per bag
3,750	1:2:3¼	6.3	63.45	71.35	79.30	95.20	High early cement	1.25	per bag
4,000	1:2:3	6.5	64.05	72.20	80.05	96.10	White cement	9.55	per bag
4,500	1:2:2½	7	65.90	74.65	82.40	98.85	Pump aid	2.12	per C.Y.
5,000	1:1-½:2-½	7.5	65.90	75.30	82.40	98.85	Winter concrete	4.50	per C.Y.
	1:1:2	8	70.50	77.55	—	Perlite 1:6=	Synthetic Fiber Reinforcing	8.50	per C.Y.
	1:4 topping	7.5	67.00	73.70	—	$89.10			
	1:3 topping	8.5	71.90	79.10	—				
	1:2 topping	11	78.25	86.10	—				

Concrete | R033 | Cast-In-Place Concrete

R033-090 Placing Ready Mixed Concrete

For ground pours allow for 5% waste when figuring quantities.

Prices in the front of the book assume normal deliveries. If deliveries are made before 8 A.M. or after 5 P.M. or on Saturday afternoons add $25 per C.Y. Large volume discounts are not included in prices in front of book.

For the lower floors without truck access, concrete may be wheeled in rubber tired buggies, conveyer handled, crane handled or pumped. Pumping is economical if there is top steel. Conveyers are more efficient for thick slabs. Concrete pump with an operator can be rented from $620 per day for up to 25 C.Y. to $1,495 per day for a 400 C.Y. pour. Figures include travel time if done at straight time. Pumping lightweight concrete costs an extra $2.35 per C.Y.

At higher floors the rubber tired buggies may be hoisted by a hoisting tower then wheeled to location. Placement by a conveyer is limited to three floors and is best for high volume pours. Pumped concrete is best when building has no crane access. Concrete may be pumped directly as high as thirty-six stories using special pumping techniques. Normal maximum height is about fifteen stories.

Best pumping aggregate is screened and graded bank gravel rather than crushed stone.

Pumping downward is more difficult than pumping upwards. Horizontal distance from pump to pour may increase preparation time prior to pour. Placing by cranes, either mobile, climbing or tower types continues as the most efficient method for high rise concrete buildings.

	Cost per C.Y. for Wheeled Concrete, Dumped Only (Add to appropriate placing cost)							
	10 C.F. Walking Cart				18 C.F. Riding Cart			
Item	Hourly Cost	Wheeled up to 50 ft.	Wheeled up to 150 ft.	Wheeled up to 250 ft.	Hourly Cost	Wheeled up to 50 ft.	Wheeled up to 150 ft.	Wheeled up to 250 ft.
Laborer	$21.45	$5.36	$ 7.16	$ 9.55	$21.45	$2.15	$2.79	$3.65
.125 Labor foreman	2.93	.73	.98	1.30	2.93	.29	.38	.50
Concrete cart	6.24	1.56	2.08	2.78	10.42	1.04	1.35	1.77
Total Cost/C.Y.		$7.65	$10.22	$13.63		$3.48	$4.52	$5.92
Hourly production		4 C.Y.				10 C.Y.		

Concrete | R033 | Cast-In-Place Concrete

R033-100 Average C.Y. of Concrete

Rubbing and floor finish not included — 4 uses of forms assumed, 5 story building.

Item	Description	Strength in psi	Ready Mix	Place	Forms	Reinforcing	Total
Beams	10' span	4000	$64.00	$55.06	$280.83	$ 99.75	$499.64
5 kip/L.F.	25'		64.00	36.71	256.41	122.55	479.67
Beam & Slab, 1 way	15'	4000	64.00	16.94	365.40	53.68	500.02
125 psf Sup. L.	25'		64.00	14.68	234.90	67.76	381.34
Beam & Slab, 2 way	15'	4000	64.00	16.94	306.36	57.20	444.50
125 psf Sup. L.	25'		64.00	14.68	190.92	54.12	323.72
Columns,	16" x 16"	4000	64.00	36.71	346.68	310.66	758.05
square tied	24" x 24"		64.00	23.94	230.04	256.76	574.74
Columns, Tied	16" diameter	4000	64.00	36.71	214.89	296.94	612.54
reinforced	24" diameter		64.00	23.94	145.62	294.00	527.56
Flat Plate,	15' span	4000	64.00	20.02	181.78	55.44	321.24
125 psf Sup. L.	25'		64.00	16.94	98.34	49.72	229.00
Flat Slab with drops,	20'	4000	64.00	20.02	138.03	52.36	274.41
125 psf Sup. L.	30'		64.00	16.94	93.09	57.64	231.67
Grade Wall,	8" thick	3000	61.00	12.87	277.02	18.92	369.81
8' high	15" thick		61.00	11.03	140.22	18.49	230.74
Metal Pan Joists,	15" span	4000	64.00	16.94	247.41	20.21	348.56
125 psf Sup. L.	25' span		64.00	14.68	203.99	34.83	317.50
Pile Caps	under 5 C.Y.	3000	61.00	12.87	55.80	21.32	150.99
"	over 10 C.Y.		61.00	5.39	27.90	19.68	113.97
Slab	4" thick	3500	62.50	10.53	15.28	15.39	103.70
on Grade	6" thick		62.50	7.02	9.96	10.26	89.74
Spread	under 1 C.Y.	3000	61.00	21.06	60.72	23.00	165.78
Footings	over 5 C.Y.		61.00	10.53	22.77	27.00	121.30
Strip	9" x 18" plain	3000	61.00	10.53	75.60	—	147.13
Footings	12" x 36" reinforced		61.00	7.47	37.80	20.00	126.27
Waffle 30" Domes	20' span	4000	64.00	16.94	207.09	62.06	350.09
125 psf Sup. L.	30' span		64.00	14.68	164.61	59.16	302.45

*Placement by direct chute assumed. All others, placement by pump assumed.

Concrete | R033 | Cast-In-Place Concrete

R033-120 Lift Slabs

The cost advantage of the lift slab method is due to placing all concrete, reinforcing steel, inserts and electrical conduit at ground level and in reduction of formwork. Minimum economical project size is about 30,000 S.F. Slabs may be tilted for parking garage ramps.

It is now used in all types of buildings and has gone up to 22 stories high in apartment buildings. Current trend is to use post-tensioned flat plate slabs with spans from 22′ to 35′. Cylindrical void forms are used when deep slabs are required. One pound of prestressing steel is about equal to seven pounds of conventional reinforcing.

To be considered cured for stressing and lifting, a slab must have attained 75% of design strength. Seven days are usually sufficient with four to five days possible if high early strength cement is used. Slabs can be stacked using two coats of a non-bonding agent to insure that slabs do not stick to each other. Lifting is done by companies specializing in this work. Lift rate is 5′ to 15′ per hour with an average of 10′ per hour. Total areas up to 33,000 S.F. have been lifted at one time. 24 to 36 jacking columns are common. Most economical bay sizes are 24′ to 28′ with four to fourteen stories most efficient. Continuous design reduces reinforcing steel cost. Use of post-tensioned slabs allows larger bay sizes. Supplementary reinforcing, post-tensioned tendons, accessories and field labor cost about $2.47 per pound of tendon.

Table below shows the usual range and average S.F. cost of a typical lift slab project that has been designed to take advantage of lift slab techniques. Figures include Subs Overhead and Profit.

Item	Description	Typical Range	Average	Sub Total
Concrete Slabs	Edge and bulkhead forms	$ .05 to $ .39	$ .22	
	Reinforcing and post-tensioning steel	$1.51 to $ 2.70	2.11	
	Reinforcing and accessories	$ .06 to $ .15	.11	$4.99
	Concrete cast at ground level	$1.45 to $ 2.45	1.95	
	Float or trowel finish	$ .49 to $ .70	.60	
Lifting Slabs	Separating and curing compound	$ .03 to $ .08	.06	
	Lifting collars	$ .25 to $ .52	.39	2.63
	Lifting and welding	$1.27 to $ 3.08	2.18	
Columns	Fabricated columns & accessories	$ .70 to $ 2.05	1.38	
	Set initial stage	$ .05 to $ .22	.14	1.78
	Column splicing	$ .13 to $ .38	.26	
Miscellaneous	Grout plates, patching, bolts, etc.	$ .05 to $ .23	.14	.14
Total in place per S.F.		$6.04 to $12.95	$9.54	$9.54

Typical Cost per S.F. for Lift Slabs Project Incl. Subs O & P

R033-130 Granolithic Finish and Base

Description	(Line 033-454-0850)	1″ Topping	(Line 033-454-0950)	2″ Topping	(Line 033-130-0200)	1″ x 5″ Straight
Cement @ $7.00 per bag	3.60 bags	$ 25.20	7.20 bags	50.40	1.70 bags	$ 11.90
Sand @ $14.35 per C.Y.	3.60 C.F.	1.91	7.20 C.F.	3.83	1.70 C.F.	.90
Peastone @ $20.00 Per C.Y.	5.40 C.F.	4.00	10.80 C.F.	8.00	1.85 C.F.	1.37
Clean, Mix, Place forms, and finish: Crew C-10 @ $24.58 per L.H.	4.07 L.H.	$100.04	4.80 L.H.	$117.98	13.70 L.H.	$336.75
TOTALS	100 S.F.	$131.15	100 S.F.	$180.21	100 L.F.	$350.92

Granolithic Topping, Mix 1:1:1-1/2

R033-140 Integral Floor Finish

Mix 1:1:2		(Line 033-454-0450)	1/2″ Thick	(Line 033-454-0600)	1″ Thick
Cement @	$ 7.00 per bag	1.7 bag	$11.90	3.4 bag	$ 23.80
Sand @	$14.35 per C.Y.	0.8 C.F.	.43	1.6 C.F.	.85
Gravel @	$18.25 per C.Y.	3.2 C.F.	2.16	6.4 C.F.	4.33
Mix, place and finish using Crew C-10 @	$24.58 per L.H.	2.52 L.H.	61.94	3.21 L.H.	78.90
Total for 100 S.F.			$76.43		$107.88

Concrete | R034 | Precast Concrete

R034-030 Prestressed Precast Concrete Structural Units

See also R032-090 for post-tensioned prestressed concrete.

Type	Location	Depth	Span in Ft.	Live Load Lb. per S.F.	Cost per S.F. Incl. Subs O & P Delivered	Cost per S.F. Incl. Subs O & P Erected
Double Tee	Floor	28" to 34"	60 to 80	50 to 80	$ 5.85 to 8.15	$ 7.00 to 9.80
	Roof	12" to 24"	30 to 50	40	$ 3.90 to 6.20	$ 4.70 to 7.45
	Wall	Width 8'	Up to 55' high	Wind	$4.10 to $ 8.25	$4.90 to $ 9.90
Multiple Tee	Roof	8" to 12"	15 to 40	40	$ 4.10	$ 4.90
	Floor	8" to 12"	15 to 30	100	$ 4.30	$ 4.95
Plank	Roof or Floor	4"	Roof 13 / Floor 12	40 for Roof	$ 3.75	$ 4.70
		6"	22 / 18		4.00	5.20
		8"	26 / 25		4.25	5.30
		10"	33 / 29	100 for Floor	4.75	5.95
		12"	42 / 32		5.00	6.25
Single Tee	Roof	28"	40	40	$ 6.75 *	$ 7.75 *
		32"	80		8.00	9.20 *
		36"	100		10.70 *	12.30 *
		48"	120		11.25 *	12.95 *
AASHO Girder	Bridges	Type 4	100	Highway	$107/L.F.	$161/L.F.
		5	110		142	178
		6	125		178	214
Box Beam	Bridges	15"	40 to 100	Highway	$115/L.F.	$173/L.F.
		27"			153	191
		33"			176	211

*Costs are for 10' wide members; for 8' wide members add $.55 per S.F.

The costs above are based on a project of 10,000 to 20,000 S.F. with a haul distance of 25 to 50 miles.

The majority of precast projects today utilize double tees rather than single tees because of speed and ease of installation. As a result casting beds at manufacturing plants are normally formed for double tees. Single tee projects will therefore require an initial set up charge of approximately $7,000 to be spread over the individual single tee costs. The prices above for single tees includes this cost based on a project size of 15,000 square feet.

For floors, a 2" to 3" topping is field cast over the shapes. For roofs, insulating concrete or rigid insulation is placed over the shapes. Topping is not included in the above costs.

Hauling costs (incl. above) run from $.50 per S.F. for short haul to $.90 for 50 mile haul. Member lengths up to 40' are standard haul, 40' to 60' require special permits and lengths over 60' must be escorted. Over width and/or over length can add up to 100% on hauling costs.

Multiple tee erection runs between $.55 to $1.50 per S.F. and single tee erection runs between $.70 to $1.70 per S.F. Large heavy members may require two cranes for lifting which would increase these erection costs by about 45%. An eight man erection crew and crane will run about $3,000 to $5,500 per day depending on location and size of crane. The crew can install 12 to 20 double tees, or 45 to 70 quad tees or planks per day.

The cost of supporting beams must be added to the above costs. Simple support beams run from $42 to $110 per L.F. delivered. Inverted tee beams run from $72 to $260 per L.F. delivered. Standard sized columns run $40 to $160 per L.F. delivered.

Grouting of connections must be added to the above. Typical costs are about $20 per connection but can go as high as $50 per connection.

Grouting planks run between $.40 to $.60 per S.F.

Single story buildings, including double tee roof members, supporting columns and girders, but no foundations, cost from $8.75 to $30.00 per S.F. of floor area. Parking garages run from $11.00 to $22.00 per S.F. above the foundations. Optimum parking garage design runs .02 C.Y. per S.F with overall costs for concrete in place running between $540 to $750 per C.Y.

Several system buildings utilizing precast members are available. Heights can go to 22 stories for apartment buildings with costs ranging from $11.00 to $40.00 per S.F. depending on the system, its components, its location and the degree of interior finish supplied. Optimum design ratio is 3 S.F. of surface to 1 S.F. of floor area.

Concrete — R035 Cementitious Decks & Toppings

R035-010 Lightweight Concrete

Vermiculite or Perlite come in bags of 4 C.F. under various trade names. Weight is about 8 lbs. per C.F. For insulating roof fill use 1:6 mix. For structural deck use 1:4 mix over gypsum boards, steeltex, steel centering, etc. supported by closely spaced joists or bulb trees. For structural slabs use 1:3:2 vermiculite sand concrete over steeltex, metal lath, steel centering, etc. on joists spaced 2'-0" O.C. for maximum L.L. of 80#/S.F. Use same mix for slab base fill over steel flooring or regular reinforced concrete slab when tile, terrazzo or other finish is to be laid over.

For slabs on grade use 1:3:2 mix when tile, etc. finish is to be laid over. If radiant heating units are installed use a 1:6 mix for a base. After coils are in place, cover with a regular granolithic finish (mix 1:3:2) to a minimum depth of 1-1/2" over top of units.

Reinforce all slabs with 6 x 6 or 10 x 10 welded wire mesh.

Vermiculite concrete can be purchased ready mixed but the following breakdown is included for field mix. Prices given below are for a one story building and assume 50 C.Y. or more. For less than 50 C.Y. add 10%. For over one story add $3.35 per C.Y. Screed finish cost is included below. Ready mix 1:6 costs $86.20 per C.Y. delivered in truckload lots.

See R033-070 for prices of ready mix lightweight concrete.

Quantities per C.Y., Field Mix			(Line 0110) 1:6 Mix Insulating Roof Fill		1:3:2 Mix Lightweight Structural Concrete	
Portland cement @	$ 7.00	per bag	5.0 bags	$ 35.00	6.2 bags	$ 43.40
Vermiculite or Perlite @	$ 9.70	per bag	7.5 bags	72.75		
treated type @	$11.30	per bag			4.7 bags	53.11
Sand @	$14.35	per C.Y.			12.5 C.F.	6.64
Plant and Water				6.37		6.37
Labor, machine mix, hoist and place, Crew C-8 @	$35.60	per L.H.	1.12 L.H.	39.87	.91 L.H.	32.40
Total in place, per C.Y.				$153.99		$141.92

Masonry — R042 Unit Masonry

R042-050 Brick Chimneys

Quantities	16" x 16"		20" x 20"		20" x 24"		20" x 32"	
Brick at $300 per M	28 brick	$ 8.40	37 brick	$11.10	42 brick	$12.60	51 brick	$15.30
Type M mortar at $3.82 per C.F.	.5 C.F.	1.91	.6 C.F.	2.29	1.0 C.F.	3.82	1.3 C.F.	4.97
Flue tile (per foot)	8" x 8"	3.35	12" x 12"	5.70	2 @ 8" x 12"	9.60	2 @ 12" x 12"	11.40
Install tile & brick, crew D-1	.055 day	21.65	.073 day	28.73	.083 day	32.67	.10 day	39.36
Total per V.L.F.		$35.31		$47.82		$58.69		$71.03

Material costs include 3% waste for brick and 25% waste for mortar.

Labor costs are bare costs and do not include contractor's O&P.

Labor for chimney brick using D-1 crew is 31 hours per thousand brick or about $750 per thousand brick. An 8" x 12" flue takes 33 brick and two 8" x 8" flues take 37 brick.

For information about Means Estimating Seminars, see yellow pages 11 and 12 in back of book

Masonry — R042 Unit Masonry

R042-120 Common and Face Brick Prices

Prices are based on truckload lot purchases for Common Building Brick and Facing Brick. Prices are per M, (thousand), brick.

City	Material — Brick per M Delivered — Common	Material — Face	Mortar 3/8" Joint	Installation — Common in 8" Wall — Bare Costs	Installation — Common in 8" Wall — Incl. O & P	Installation — Face Brick, 4" Veneer — Bare Costs	Installation — Face Brick, 4" Veneer — Incl. O & P	Total — Common in 8" Wall — Bare Costs	Total — Common in 8" Wall — Incl. O & P	Total — Face Brick, 4" Veneer — Bare Costs	Total — Face Brick, 4" Veneer — Incl. O & P
Atlanta	$190	$235	$38.90 for 8" Wall and $32.05 for 4" Wall	$363	$ 600	$ 435	$ 720	$ 597	$ 858	$ 709	$1,022
Baltimore	235	305		444	734	532	881	725	1,043	879	1,262
Boston	305	430		768	1,271	922	1,526	1,121	1,660	1,397	2,048
Buffalo	260	325		671	1,110	805	1,332	978	1,448	1,172	1,736
Chicago	260	350		709	1,174	851	1,409	1,016	1,511	1,244	1,841
Cincinnati	230	305		536	886	643	1,064	811	1,190	989	1,444
Cleveland	235	325		646	1,069	775	1,283	927	1,379	1,142	1,687
Columbus	235	300		537	890	645	1,067	818	1,199	986	1,443
Dallas	200	350		362	599	434	718	607	868	827	1,150
Denver	210	285		429	710	515	852	684	990	840	1,210
Detroit	235	335		679	1,123	814	1,348	959	1,432	1,191	1,762
Houston	250	370		406	672	487	807	703	998	901	1,261
Indianapolis	255	280		554	917	665	1,101	856	1,249	986	1,453
Kansas City	260	285		545	902	654	1,083	852	1,240	980	1,441
Los Angeles	250	275		687	1,136	824	1,364	983	1,462	1,139	1,710
Memphis	190	220		391	646	469	776	625	904	727	1,060
Milwaukee	280	360		655	1,084	786	1,301	982	1,444	1,189	1,744
Minneapolis	255	375		620	1,027	744	1,232	922	1,358	1,163	1,692
Nashville	185	215		382	632	458	758	611	884	711	1,037
New Orleans	210	285		337	558	405	670	592	839	730	1,028
New York City	300	380		918	1,520	1,102	1,824	1,266	1,902	1,525	2,290
Philadelphia	245	340		713	1,180	856	1,417	1,004	1,501	1,238	1,837
Phoenix	340	375		416	688	499	826	805	1,116	917	1,286
Pittsburgh	210	290		596	986	715	1,183	851	1,267	1,046	1,547
St. Louis	235	240		641	1,061	769	1,273	922	1,370	1,048	1,580
San Antonio	260	410		343	567	411	680	649	904	865	1,180
San Diego	285	460		602	996	722	1,195	934	1,361	1,228	1,751
San Francisco	350	480		783	1,296	940	1,556	1,183	1,736	1,467	2,135
Seattle	340	425		619	1,024	742	1,229	1,008	1,452	1,212	1,745
Washington, D.C.	210	275		454	751	544	901	709	1,031	860	1,248
Average	$250	$330		$560	$ 930	$ 670	$1,112	$ 860	$1,250	$1,040	$1,520

Common building brick manufactured according to ASTM C62 and facing brick manufactured according to ASTM C216 are the two standard bricks available for general building use.

Building brick is made in three grades; SW, where high resistance to damage caused by cyclic freezing is required; MW, where moderate resistance to cyclic freezing is needed; and NW, where little resistance to cyclic freezing is needed. Facing brick is made in only the two grades SW and MW. Additionally, facing brick is available in three types; FBS, for general use; FBX, for general use where a higher degree of precision and lower permissible variation in size than FBS is needed; and FBA, for general use to produce characteristic architectural effects resulting from non-uniformity in size and texture of the units.

In figuring above installation costs, a D-8 Crew (with a daily output of 1.5 M) was used for the 4" veneer. A D-8 Crew (with a daily output of 1.8 M) was used for the 8" solid wall.

In figuring the total cost including overhead and profit, an allowance of 10% was added to the sum of the cost of the brick and mortar. Also, 3% breakage was included for both the bare costs and the costs with overhead and profit. If bricks are delivered palletized with 280 to 300 per pallet, or packaged, allow only 1-1/2% for breakage. Then add $10 per M to the cost of brick and deduct two hours helper time. The net result is a savings of $30 to $40 per M in place. Packaged or palletized delivery is practical when a job is big enough to have a crane or other equipment available to handle a package of brick. This is so on all industrial work but not always true on small commercial buildings.

The prices above are for bricks used in commercial, apartment house or industial construction. If it is possible to obtain the price of the actual brick to be used, it should be done and substituted in the table. The use of buff and gray face is increasing, and there is a continuing trend to the Norman, Roman, Jumbo and SCR brick.

See R042-500 for brick quantities per S.F. and mortar quantities per M brick. (Average prices for the various sizes are listed in Division 4)

Common red clay brick for backup is not used that often. Concrete block is the most usual backup material with occasional use of sand lime or cement brick. Sand lime cost about $15 per M less than red clay and cement brick are about $5 per M less than red clay. These figures may be substituted in the common brick breakdown for the cost of these items in place, as labor is about the same. Building brick is commonly used in solid walls for strength and as a fire stop.

Brick panels built on the ground and then crane erected to the upper floors have proven to be economical. This allows the work to be done under cover and without scaffolding.

Masonry — R042 Unit Masonry

R042-220 Interlocking Grout Block Walls

Cost per 100 S.F. of 8" x 16" Interlocking Grout Block, "Open End" Type							
8" x 16" Sand Aggregate		8" Thick Block		12" Thick Block		16" Thick Block	
113 block delivered		$1.50 ea.	$169.50	$2.30 ea.	$259.90	$3.55 ea.	$ 401.15
Type M mortar @ $3.82 per C.F.		7.0 C.F.	26.74	10.4 C.F.	39.73	13.8 C.F.	52.72
Minimum reinf. req.@ $ .27 per lb.							
8" block #4 @ 24" horiz.		33.4 lb.	9.02				
32" vert.		40.0 lb.	10.80				
12" & 16" block #5 @ 8" horiz.				99.7 lb.	26.92	99.7 lb.	26.92
16" vert.				50.2 lb.	13.55	50.2 lb.	13.55
Type PM mortar @ $3.17 C.F.		25.8 C.F.	81.79	42.2 C.F.	133.77	56.1 C.F.	177.84
Installation Crew D-4 @ $893.35 per day		.408 days	364.49	.455 days	406.47	.541 days	483.30
Total per 100 S.F.			$662.34		$880.34		$1,155.48
1 S.F.			6.62		8.80		11.55

R042-500 Brick, Block & Mortar Quantities

Running Bond						For Other Bonds Standard Size Add to S.F. Quantities in Table to Left		
Number of Brick per S.F. of Wall - Single Wythe with 3/8" Joints				C.F. of Mortar per M Bricks, Waste Included				
Type Brick	Nominal Size (incl. mortar) L H W	Modular Coursing	Number of Brick per S.F.	3/8" Joint	1/2" Joint	Bond Type	Description	Factor
Standard	8 x 2-2/3 x 4	3C=8"	6.75	10.3	12.9	Common	full header every fifth course	+20%
Economy	8 x 4 x 4	1C=4"	4.50	11.4	14.6		full header every sixth course	+16.7%
Engineer	8 x 3-1/5 x 4	5C=16"	5.63	10.6	13.6	English	full header every second course	+50%
Fire	9 x 2-1/2 x 4-1/2	2C=5"	6.40	550 # Fireclay	—	Flemish	alternate headers every course	+33.3%
Jumbo	12 x 4 x 6 or 8	1C=4"	3.00	23.8	30.8		every sixth course	+5.6%
Norman	12 x 2-2/3 x 4	3C=8"	4.50	14.0	17.9	Header = W x H exposed		+100%
Norwegian	12 x 3-1/5 x 4	5C=16"	3.75	14.6	18.6	Rowlock = H x W exposed		+100%
Roman	12 x 2 x 4	2C=4"	6.00	13.4	17.0	Rowlock stretcher = L x W exposed		+33.3%
SCR	12 x 2-2/3 x 6	3C=8"	4.50	21.8	28.0	Soldier = H x L exposed		—
Utility	12 x 4 x 4	1C=4"	3.00	15.4	19.6	Sailor = W x L exposed		-33.3%

Concrete Blocks Nominal Size	Approximate Weight per S.F.		Blocks per 100 S.F.	Mortar per M block	
	Standard	Lightweight		Partitions	Back up
2" x 8" x 16"	20 PSF	15 PSF	113	16 C.F.	36 C.F.
4"	30	20		31	51
6"	42	30		46	66
8"	55	38		62	82
10"	70	47		77	97
12"	85	55		92	112

For information about Means Estimating Seminars, see yellow pages 11 and 12 in back of book

Metals — R050 — Materials, Coatings, & Fastenings

R050-520 Welded Structural Steel

Usual weight reductions with welded design run 10% to 20% compared with bolted or riveted connections. This amounts to about the same total cost compared with bolted structures since field welding is more expensive than bolts. For normal spans of 18' to 24' figure 6 to 7 connections per ton.

Trusses — For welded trusses add 4% to weight of main members for connections. Up to 15% less steel can be expected in a welded truss compared to one that is shop bolted. Cost of erection is the same whether shop bolted or welded.

General — Typical electrodes for structural steel welding are E6010, E6011, E60T and E70T. Typical buildings vary between 2# to 8# of weld rod per ton of steel. Buildings utilizing continuous design require about three times as much welding as conventional welded structures. In estimating field erection by welding, it is best to use the average linear feet of weld per ton to arrive at the welding cost per ton. The type, size and position of the weld will have a direct bearing on the cost per linear foot. A typical field welder will deposit 1.8# to 2# of weld rod per hour manually. Using semiautomatic methods can increase production by as much as 50% to 75%. Below is the cost per hour for manual welding.

Welded Structural Steel in Field, per Hour

Item			No Operating Engr.	1/2 Operating Engr.	1 Operating Engr.
2 lb. weld rod	$1.30	per lb.	$ 2.60	$ 2.60	$ 2.60
Equipment (for welding only)	$205	/40 hrs.	5.13	5.13	5.13
Operating cost @	$5.17	per hour	5.17	5.17	5.17
Welder Foreman 1 hr. @	$32.60	per hour	32.60	32.60	32.60
Operating engineer @	$27.20	per hour	—	13.60	27.20
Total per Welder Hour (Bare Costs)			$45.50	$59.10	$72.70

The welding costs per ton of structural steel will vary from $45 to $290 per ton depending on Union requirements, crew size, design and inspection required.

Metals — R051 — Structural Metal Framing

R051-215 Structural Steel Estimating for Repair and Remodeling Projects

The correct approach to estimating structural steel is dependent upon the amount of steel required for the particular project. If the project is a sizable addition to a building, the data can be used directly from the cost data book. This is not the case however if the project requires a small amount of steel, for instance to reinforce existing roof or floor structural systems. To better understand this please refer to Line No. 051-260-0600. This line provides pricing for a W16x31 beam with bolted connections. The bare material cost is $20.50 per L.F., labor is $1.85 per L.F., equipment is $1.12 per L.F., and the bare cost total is $23.47 per L.F. The total including overhead and profit, is $27.00 per L.F. Assume your project requires the reinforcement of roof system structural members of a 3 story building required for the installation a new piece of HVAC equipment, including 4 members 30 feet long. The total cost, including overhead and profit, per Line No. 051-260-0600 to install these members would be: 30 feet x 4 beams x $27.00 per foot = $3,240. An analysis of this cost will reveal that the price is wholly inadequate.

The first problem is apparent if you examine the amount of steel that can be installed per day. Line 051-260-0600 indicates 900 linear feet can be installed by a 5 man crew with an 80 ton crane. This productivity is correct for new construction but certainly is not for repair and remodeling work. Installation of new structural steel considers that each member is installed from the foundation to the roof of the structure in a planned and systematic manner with a crane having unrestricted access to all parts of the project. Additionally each connection is planned and detailed with full field access for fit-up and final bolting. The erection is planned and progresses such that interferences and conflicts with other structural members are minimized, if not completely eliminated. All of these assumptions are clearly not the case with a repair and remodeling job and a significant decrease in the stated productivity will be observed.

A crane will certainly be needed to lift the members into the general area of the project but in most cases will not be able to place the beams into their final position. An opening in the existing roof may not be large enough to permit the beams to pass through and it may be necessary to bring them into the building through existing windows or doors. Moving the beams to the actual area where they will be installed may involve hand labor and the use of dollies. Finally, hoists and/or jacks may be needed for final positioning.

The connection of new members to existing can often be accomplished by field bolting with accurate field measurements and good planning but in many cases access to both sides of existing members is not possible and field welding becomes the only alternative. In addition to the cost of the actual welding, protection of existing finishes, systems and structure and fire protection must be considered.

New beams can never be installed tight to the existing decks or floors which they must support and the use of shims and tack welding becomes necessary. Additionally, further planning and cost is involved in assuring that existing loads are minimized during the installation and shimming process.

It is apparent that installation of structural steel as part of a repair and remodeling project involves more than simply installing the members and estimating the cost in the same manner as new construction. The best procedure for estimating the total cost is adequate planning and coordination of each process and activity that will be needed. Unit costs for the materials, labor and equipment can then be attached to each needed activity and a final, complete price can be determined.

Metals   R051   Structural Metal Framing

R051-240   Structural Steel Extras

Principal Extras in Dollars Per Ton

Item quantity — using 5 tons per size as base price. Under 5 tons to 3 tons inclusive add $6 per ton. Under 3 tons to 2 tons inclusive add $11 per ton. Under 2 tons to 1 ton inclusive add $16 per ton. Under 1 ton to 1/2 ton add $55 per ton. Under 1/2 ton add $100 per ton.

Size Extras:

W Shapes: W36 x 393-135, W33 x 354-118, W30 x 326-90, W27 x 217-84, W24 x 176; W21 x 166, W18 x 311-130, W14 x 426-145, W12 x 336-136, add $20; W24 x 162-55, W21 x 147-44, W18 x 119-35, W16 x 100-26, W14 x 132-22, W12 x 120-14, W10 x 112-12, W8 x 67-10, W6 x 25-9, W5 x 19-16, and W4 x 13, no add; W14 x 808-455 add $124. For specification extras see R051-230.

Miscellaneous Shapes: M14 x 18 to M5 x 18.9 no add. Standard Beams: S24 x 121-80, S20 x 96-66 add $140; S18 x 70 & 54.7, S15 x 50 & 42.9, S12 x 50-31.8, S10 x 35 & 25.4, S8 x 23 & 18.4, S7 x 20 & 15.3 and S6 x 17.25 & 12.5 add $80.

Standard Channels: C15 x 50-33.9, C12 x 30-20.7, C10 x 30-15.3, C9 x 20-13.4, C8 x 18.75-11.5, C7 x 14.75-9.8 add $60.

Miscellaneous Channels: MC18 x 58 to MC13 x 31.8 add $80; MC12 x 50 to MC6 x 18 add $80. Car Building Sections: add $120. Bulb Angles: add $140. Angles Equal & Unequal Leg: add $80.

Cambering: Channels, standard beams, tees & wide flange shapes to 300 lbs./ft. add $60.

Galvanizing under 1 ton, $600; over 20 tons, $500 per ton. For color coating of galvanizing add 40% to prices.

Government Specifications: MIL-S-20166 B, class U, type 1, Grade M-medium add $20; Grade HT-high tensile add $15. American Association of State Highway & Transportation Officials (AASHTO): Without Charpy Impacts, Grade M 188 no add; Grade M 222 add $65; M 223, Gr. 50 add $15.

Cut Lengths: 10' to 20' add $20; 20' to 25' add $20; 25' to 65' no add; over 65' to 90' no add; over 90' add $5.

Milling One or Two Ends: 10 lbs./ft. to 100 lbs./ft., over 10' add $70; over 100 lbs./ft., over 10' add $60.

Handling & Loading: Under 5 tons add $10. Banding or Wiring: add $10. Special loading: add $10. Special marking: add $10.

Special Testing: Bend Tests, $10, Charpy Impact Testing: one set of tests — impact strength values only, $5; one set of tests — impact strength values, lateral expansion, percent shear fracture, $7.

Special Straightening: For tolerances not more restrictive than 50% of standard camber or sweep, $7.

Splitting Beams to Produce Tees: over 15 lbs./ft.-30 lbs./ft., $60, over 30 lbs./ft.-150 lbs./ft. $40, over 150 lbs./ft., $35.

Chemistry: Ladle analysis limits for carbon, manganese, silicon & copper tests run from $10 to $30 per ton.

R051-250   Subpurlins

Bulb tee and truss tee subpurlins are structural members designed to support and reinforce a variety of roof deck systems such as precast cement fiber roof deck tiles, monolithic roof deck systems, and gypsum or lightweight concrete over formboard. Other uses include interstitial service ceiling systems, wall panel systems, and joist anchoring in bond beams.

The table below shows bare costs for material only for subpurlins spaced at 32-5/8" O.C., purchased in lots of 6,000 to 16,000 L.F. (see Division 051-210 for pricing on a square foot basis). Maximum span is based on a 3-span condition with a total allowable vertical load of 55 psf.

	Bulb Tees, Painted			Truss Tees, Painted							
Type	Wt. per L.F.	Cost per L.F.	Max. Span	Size	Wt. per L.F.	Cost per L.F.	Max. Span	Size	Wt. per L.F.	Cost per L.F.	Max. Span
112	1.48 #	$ .85	5'-6"	2"	1.10 #	$ .74	5'-9"	2-1/2"	1.39 #	$ .84	7'-0"
158	1.68	.86	6'-4"		1.27	.79	6'-0"		1.85	1.15	8'-9"
168	1.87	.91	7'-8"		1.33	.80	6'-0"	3"	1.14	.74	7'-3"
178	2.15	1.00	8'-9"		1.78	1.08	7'-6"		1.88	1.15	9'-0"
218	3.19	1.26	10'-2"	2-1/2"	1.12	.74	6'-9"	3-1/2"	1.17	.75	7'-9"
228	3.87	1.60	12'-0"		1.34	.80	6'-9"		1.90	1.17	10'-9"

Wood & Plastics — R061 Rough Carpentry

R061-010 Thirty City Lumber Prices

Prices for boards are for #2 or better or sterling, whichever is in best supply. Dimension lumber is "Standard or Better" either Southern Yellow Pine (S.Y.P.), Spruce-Pine-Fir (S.P.F.), Hem-Fir (H.F.) or Douglas Fir (D.F.). The species of lumber used in a geographic area is listed by city. Plyform is 3/4" BB oil sealed fir or S.Y.P. whichever prevails locally, 3/4" CDX is S.Y.P. or Fir.

These are prices at the time of publication and should be checked against the current market price. Relative differences between cities will stay approximately constant.

City	Species	Contractor Purchases per M.B.F. S4S								Contractor Purchases per M.S.F.	
		Dimensions						Boards		3/4" Ext. Plyform	3/4" Thick CDX T&G
		2"x4"	2"x6"	2"x8"	2"x10"	2"x12"	4"x4"	1"x6"	1"x12"		
Atlanta	S.P.F.	$549	$525	$586	$683	$832	$687	$832	$1,417	$750	$600
Baltimore	S.P.F.	630	558	526	566	619	786	1,300	1,800	922	765
Boston	S.P.F.	455	415	420	515	569	1,203	1,120	1,360	860	610
Buffalo	H.F.	535	576	515	531	556	855	1,400	1,660	796	662
Chicago	S.P.F.	486	468	501	561	603	575	1,061	1,350	665	578
Cincinnati	S.P.F.	599	683	691	795	883	863	1,200	1,460	936	686
Cleveland	S.P.F.	612	574	591	744	812	656	1,082	2,099	859	625
Columbus	S.P.F.	515	657	633	745	826	620	1,560	2,140	989	579
Dallas	S.P.F.	575	489	525	640	550	557	800	1,131	797	589
Denver	H.F.	574	574	588	639	599	799	848	1,243	997	672
Detroit	S.P.F.	645	690	600	859	895	495	1,240	2,050	860	593
Houston	S.Y.P.	480	488	488	494	583	669	777	940	821	525
Indianapolis	S.Y.F.	510	495	620	620	670	740	665	890	785	590
Kansas City	D.F.	570	550	540	570	600	720	1,050	1,300	800	600
Los Angeles	D.F.	500	510	515	510	530	580	1,063	1,231	950	565
Memphis	S.P.F.	635	595	630	695	700	890	999	1,445	795	780
Milwaukee	S.P.F.	640	612	612	743	806	702	850	1,280	847	688
Minneapolis	S.P.F.	509	496	488	563	686	562	1,316	1,549	948	562
Nashville	S.P.F.	527	540	523	567	564	720	1,100	1,500	758	563
New Orleans	S.Y.P.	525	525	510	510	519	610	650	1,700	725	535
New York City	S.P.F.	490	475	550	555	525	870	880	1,210	887	594
Philadelphia	H.F.	555	540	540	565	615	670	1,325	1,600	1,204	650
Phoenix	D.F.	559	599	650	699	699	945	1,295	1,599	1,090	690
Pittsburgh	H.F.	554	591	648	681	714	666	1,260	1,590	1,030	624
St. Louis	S.P.F.	444	428	375	365	460	715	1,000	719	516	516
San Antonio	S.Y.P.	440	443	443	475	535	514	677	1,345	825	583
San Diego	D.F.	475	475	500	515	535	640	1,164	1,295	1,070	675
San Francisco	D.F.	490	490	471	484	484	700	1,100	1,490	1,159	644
Seattle	S.P.F.	577	567	599	693	720	681	720	1,188	811	591
Washington, DC	S.P.F.	516	499	533	627	651	757	900	1,330	938	612
Average		$539	$538	$547	$607	$645	$715	$1,041	$1,430	$880	$618

To convert square feet of surface to board feet, 4% waste included.

S4S Size	Multiply S.F. by	T & G Size	Multiply S.F. by	Flooring Size	Multiply S.F. by
1 x 4	1.18	1 x 4	1.27	25/32" x 2-1/4"	1.37
1 x 6	1.13	1 x 6	1.18	25/32" x 3-1/4"	1.29
1 x 8	1.11	1 x 8	1.14	15/32" x 1-1/2"	1.54
1 x 10	1.09	2 x 6	2.36	1" x 3"	1.28
				1" x 4"	1.24

Wood & Plastics — R061 Rough Carpentry

R061-020 Plywood

There are two types of plywood used in construction: interior, which is moisture resistant but not waterproofed, and exterior, which is waterproofed.

The grade of the exterior surface of the plywood sheets is designated by the first letter: A, for smooth surface with patches allowed; B, for solid surface with patches and plugs allowed; C, which may be surface plugged or may have knot holes up to 1″ wide; and D, which is used only for interior type plywood and may have knot holes up to 2-1/2″ wide. "Structural Grade" is specifically designed for engineered applications such as box beams. All CC & DD grades have roof and floor spans marked on them.

Underlayment grade plywood runs from 1/4″ to 1-1/4″ thick. Thicknesses 5/8″ and over have optional tongue and groove joints which eliminates the need for blocking the edges. Underlayment 19/32″ and over may be referred to as Sturd-i-Floor.

The price of plywood can fluctuate widely due to geographic and economic conditions. When one or two local prices are known, the relative prices for other types and sizes may be found by direct factoring of the prices in the table below.

Typical uses for various plywood grades are as follows:

AA-AD Interior — cupboards, shelving, paneling, furniture
BB Plyform — concrete form plywood
CDX — wall and roof sheathing
Structural — box beams, girders, stressed skin panels
AA-AC Exterior — fences, signs, siding, soffits, etc.
Underlayment — base for resilient floor coverings
Overlaid HDO — high density for concrete forms & highway signs
Overlaid MDO — medium density for painting, siding, soffits & signs
303 Siding — exterior siding, textured, striated, embossed, etc.

Grade	Type	4'x8'	Type	4'x8'	4'x10'
	National Average Price in Lots of 10 MSF, per MSF-January 1999				
Sanded Grade	1/4″ Interior AD	$ 449	1/4″ Exterior AC	$ 496	$ 520
	3/8″	500	3/8″	556	572
	1/2″	598	1/2″	662	704
	5/8″	708	5/8″	774	864
	3/4″	748	3/4″	840	978
	1″	870	1″	1,090	1,127
	1-1/4″	1,043	Exterior AA, add	150	155
	Interior AA, add	150	Exterior AB, add	145	140
			CD Structural 1	Underlayment	
Unsanded Grade 4' x 8' Sheets	5/16″ CDX	$ 318	5/16″, 4'x8' sheets $378	3/8″, 4'x8' sheets	$ 453
	3/8″	320	3/8″ 475	1/2″	526
	1/2″	410	1/2″ 545	5/8″T&G	627
	5/8″	493	5/8″ 648	3/4″T&G	810
	3/4″	582	3/4″ 724	1-1/8″ 2-4-1 T&G	1,269
	3/4″ T&G	618			
Form Plywood	5/8″ Exterior, oiled BB, plyform	$ 865	5/8″ HDO (overlay 2 sides)		$2,148
	3/4″ Exterior, oiled BB, plyform	975	3/4″ HDO (overlay 2 sides)		2,214
Overlaid 4'x8' Sheets	Overlay 2 Sides MDO 3/8″ thick	$1,025	Overlay 1 Side MDO 3/8″ thick		$ 918
	1/2″	1,199	1/2″		1,058
	5/8″	1,299	5/8″		1,188
	3/4″	1,399	3/4″		1,393
303 Siding	Fir, rough sawn, natural finish, 3/8″ thick	$ 682	Texture 1-11	5/8″ thick, Fir	$1,037
	Redwood	1,890		Redwood	1,890
	Cedar	1,890		Cedar	1,537
	Southern Yellow Pine	693		Southern Yellow	832
Waferboard/O.S.B.	1/4″ sheathing	$ 150	19/32″ T&G		$ 270
	7/16″ sheathing	174	23/32″ T&G		298

For 2 MSF to 10 MSF, add 10%. For less than 2 MSF, add 15%.

Wood & Plastics — R061 Rough Carpentry

R061-030 Lumber Product Material Prices

The price of forest products fluctuates widely from location to location and from season to season depending upon economic conditions. The table below indicates National Average material prices in effect Jan. 1, 1999. The table shows relative differences between various sizes, grades and species. These percentage differentials remain fairly constant even though lumber prices in general may change significantly during the year.

Availability of certain items depends upon geographic location and must be checked prior to firm price bidding.

National Average Contractor Price, Quantity Purchase

Dimension Lumber, S4S, #2 & Better, KD

	Species	2"x4"	2"x6"	2"x8"	2"x10"	2"x12"
Framing Lumber per MBF	Douglas Fir	$530	$537	$544	$566	$578
	Spruce	507	492	515	560	589
	Southern Yellow Pine	487	485	512	523	568
	Hem-Fir	555	570	573	604	621

Heavy Timbers, Fir

3" x 4" thru 3" x 12"	$1,012
4" x 4" thru 4" x 12"	1,153
6" x 6" thru 6" x 12"	1,739
8" x 8" thru 8" x 12"	1,868
10" x 10" and 10" x 12"	1,739

S4S "D" Quality or Clear, KD

	Species	1"x4"	1"x6"	1"x8"	1"x10"	1"x12"
Boards per MBF *See also Cedar Siding	Sugar Pine	$980	$1,400	$1,400	$1,505	$2,226
	Idaho Pine	1,288	1,631	1,645	1,764	2,240
	Engleman Spruce	1,288	1,778	1,778	1,848	2,198
	So. Yellow Pine	1,190	1,351	1,358	1,400	1,526
	Ponderosa Pine	1,064	1,456	1,526	1,631	2,198
	Redwood, CVG	3,940	3,800	3,750	3,770	5,940

S4S #2 & Better or Sterling, KD

Species	1"x4"	1"x6"	1"x8"	1"x10"	1"x12"
Sugar Pine	$630	$658	$686	$875	$1,022
Idaho Pine	826	826	812	826	945
Engleman Spruce	546	588	560	805	889
So. Yellow Pine	546	574	700	840	973
Ponderosa Pine	560	651	609	749	861

Flooring per MSF

1" x 4" Vertical grain, Fir "B" & better	$2,300
2-1/4" x 25/32", Oak, clear	3,200
Select	3,050
#1 common	2,700
Oak, prefinished, standard & better	3,750
Standard	3,200
2-1/4" x 25/32" Maple, select	$2,970
#2 & better	2,700
2-1/4" x 33/32" Maple, #2 & better	3,132
3-1/4" x 33/32" Maple, #2 & better	2,916
Parquet, unfinished, 5/16", minimum	1,539
Maximum	4,800

Siding per MBF

Clapboard, Cedar, beveled	
1/2" x 6" thru 1/2" x 8", clear	$1,404
"A" grade	1,377
"B" grade	972
3/4" x 10" "clear"	2,700
"A" grade	2,430
Redwood, beveled	
1/2" x 6" thru 1/2" x 8", vertical grain, clear	1,907
3/4" x 10" vertical grain, clear	2,889
*Rough sawn, Cedar, T&G, "A" grade 1" x 4"	$2,434
1" x 6"	3,201
"STK" grade, 1" x 6"	1,614
Board, "STK" grade, 1" x 8"	1,561
Board & Batten 1" x 12"	1,561
Cedar channel siding 1" x 8", #3 & better	$1,513
Factory stained	1,693
White Pine siding, T&G, rough sawn	$507
Factory stained	556

Shingles per CSF

Red Cedar	
5X—16" long #1 regular	$157
#2	177
18" long perfections #1	202
#2	133
Resquared & Rebutted #1	118
Handsplit shakes, resawn	
24" long, 1/2" to 3/4"	182
18" long, 1/2" to 3/4"	162
White Cedar shingles	
16" long, extra grade (East Coast)	$144
Clear, 1st grade (East Coast)	120
Fire retardant Red Cedar	
5X — 16" long	$257
18" long perfections	275
Handsplit & resawn	
24" long, 1/2" to 3/4"	275
18" long, 1/2" to 3/4"	290

Wood & Plastics — R061 Rough Carpentry

R061-100 Wood Roof Trusses

Loading figures represent live load. An additional load of 10 psf on the top chord and 10 psf on the bottom chord is included in the truss design. Spacing is 24" O.C.

Span in Feet	Cost per Truss for Different Live Loads and Roof Pitches					
	Flat	4 in 12 Pitch		5 in 12 Pitch		8 in 12 Pitch
	40 psf	30 psf	40 psf	30 psf	40 psf	30 psf
20	$ 70.00	$39.00	$41.00	$42.00	$46.00	$ 54.00
22	77.00	43.00	45.00	46.00	50.00	58.00
24	84.00	47.00	49.00	50.00	54.00	62.00
26	91.00	50.00	52.00	53.00	57.00	65.00
28	98.00	52.00	54.00	55.00	59.00	67.00
30	105.00	63.00	65.00	66.00	70.00	78.00
32	112.00	65.00	67.00	68.00	72.00	80.00
34	119.00	76.00	78.00	79.00	83.00	91.00
36	126.00	80.00	82.00	83.00	87.00	95.00
38	133.00	83.00	85.00	86.00	90.00	98.00
40	140.00	90.00	92.00	93.00	97.00	105.00

Wood & Plastics — R064 Architectural Woodwork

R064-100 Wood Stair, Residential

One Flight with 8'-6" Story Height, 3'-6" Wide Oak Treads Open One Side, Built in Place				
Item	Quantity	Unit Cost	Bare Costs	Costs Incl. Subs O & P
Treads 10-1/2" x 1-1/16" thick	11 Ea.	$ 26.00	$ 286.00	$ 314.60
Landing tread nosing, rabbeted	1 Ea.	7.80	7.80	8.60
Risers 3/4" thick	12 Ea.	11.50	138.00	151.80
Single end starting step (range $175 to $210)	1 Ea.	193.00	193.00	212.40
Balusters (range $4.50 to $25.00)	22 Ea.	7.75	170.50	187.60
Newels, starting & landing (range $40 to $120)	2 Ea.	73.00	146.00	160.60
Rail starter (range $39 to $190)	1 Ea.	67.00	67.00	73.80
Handrail (range $4.50 to $10.30)	26 L.F.	7.00	182.00	200.20
Cove trim	50 L.F.	.55	27.50	30.20
Rough stringers three - 2 x 12's, 14' long	84 B.F.	.65	54.60	60.00
Carpenter's installation: Bare Cost	36 Hrs.	$ 27.30	$ 982.80	
Incl. Subs O & P		$ 45.70		$1,645.20
	Total per Flight		$2,255.20	$3,045.00

Add for rail return on second floor and for varnishing or other finish. Adjoining walls or landings must be figured separately.

Thermal & Moist. Protection | R072 | Fire & Smoke Protection

R072-030 Firestopping

Firestopping is the sealing of structural, mechanical, electrical and other penetrations through fire-rated assemblies. The basic components of firestop systems are safing insulation and firestop sealant on both sides of wall penetrations and the top side of floor penetrations.

Pipe penetrations are assumed to be through concrete, grout, or joint compound and can be sleeved or unsleeved. Costs for the penetrations and sleeves are not included. An annular space of 1" is assumed. Escutcheons are not included.

Metallic pipe is assumed to be copper, aluminum, cast iron or similar metallic material. Insulated metallic pipe is assumed to be covered with a thermal insulating jacket of varying thickness and materials.

Non-metallic pipe is assumed to be PVC, CPVC, FR Polypropylene or similar plastic piping material. Intumescent firestop sealant or wrap strips are included. Collars on both sides of wall penetrations and a sheet metal plate on the underside of floor penetrations are included.

Ductwork is assumed to be sheet metal, stainless steel or similar metallic material. Duct penetrations are assumed to be through concrete, grout or joint compound. Costs for penetrations and sleeves are not included. An annular space of 1/2" is assumed.

Multi-trade openings include costs for sheet metal forms, firestop mortar, wrap strips, collars and sealants as necessary.

Structural penetrations joints are assumed to be 1/2" or less. CMU walls are assumed to be within 1-1/2" of metal deck. Drywall walls are assumed to be tight to the underside of metal decking.

Metal panel, glass or curtain wall systems include a spandrel area of 5' filled with mineral wool foil-faced insulation. Fasteners and stiffeners are included.

Thermal & Moist. Protection | R075 | Membrane Roofing

R075-030 Modified Bitumen Roofing

The cost of modified bitumen roofing is highly dependent on the type of installation that is planned. Installation is based on the type of modifier used in the bitumen. The two most popular modifiers are atactic polypropylene (APP) and styrene butadiene styrene (SBS). The modifiers are added to heated bitumen during the manufacturing process to change its characteristics. A polyethylene, polyester or fiberglass reinforcing sheet is then sandwiched between layers of this bitumen. When completed, the result is a pre-assembled, built-up roof that has increased elasticity and weatherablility. Some manufacturers include a surfacing material such as ceramic or mineral granules, metal particles or sand.

The preferred method of adhering SBS-modified bitumen roofing to the substrate is with hot-mopped asphalt (much the same as built-up roofing). This installation method requires a tar kettle/pot to heat the asphalt, as well as the labor, tools and equipment necessary to distribute and spread the hot asphalt.

The alternative method for applying APP and SBS modified bitumen is as follows. A skilled installer uses a torch to melt a small pool of bitumen off the membrane. This pool must form across the entire roll for proper adhesion. The installer must unroll the roofing at a pace slow enough to melt the bitumen, but fast enough to prevent damage to the rest of the membrane.

Modified bitumen roofing provides the advantages of both built-up and single-ply roofing. Labor costs are reduced over those of built-up roofing because only a single ply is necessary. The elasticity of single-ply roofing is attained with the reinforcing sheet and polymer modifiers. Modifieds have some self-healing characteristics and because of their multi-layer construction, they offer the reliability and safety of built-up roofing.

Doors & Windows — R081 — Metal Doors & Frames

R081-010 Hollow Metal Doors

Table below lists material prices only, not including hardware or labor.

Door Thickness and Size		Full Flush Doors, 18 Ga.				Flush Fire Doors			
		Hollow Metal		Composite Core		Hollow Metal "B"		Hollow Metal Class "A"	
		Plain	Glazed	Plain	Glazed	20 Ga.	18 Ga.	16 Ga.	18 Ga.
1-3/4"	3'-0" x 6'-8"	$195	$245	$218	$270	$185	$215	$260	$227
	3'-0" x 7'-0"	205	255	225	275	195	221	275	232
	3'-6" x 7'-0"	230	280	265	315	230	270	305	284
	3'-0" x 8'-0"	260	315	285	340	240	280	322	294
	4'-0" x 8'-0"	300	350	320	385	305	342	355	347
1-3/8"	2'-0" x 6'-8"	145	190	—	—	165	—	—	—
	2'-6" x 6'-8"	155	205	—	—	180	—	—	—
	3'-0" x 7'-0"	165	215	—	—	190	—	—	—

*Indicates 20 gauge doors.

Doors & Windows — R082 — Wood & Plastic Doors

R082-120 Wood Doors

Table below lists price per door only, not including frame, hardware or labor. For pre-hung exterior door units up to 3' x 7', add $162 per door for wood frame and hardware for types not listed under pre-hung. Pricing is for ten or more doors. Doors are factory trimmed for butts and locksets.

Door Thickness and Size		Flush Type Doors (Interior)					Architectural (1-3/4" Ext., 1-3/8" Int.)				Pre-hung	
		Hollow Core		Solid Particle Core			Pine		Fir			
		Lauan	Birch	Lauan	Birch	Oak	Panel	Glazed	Panel	Glazed	Pine Panel	Flush Birch S. C.
1-3/4"	2'-6" x 6'-8"	$47	$48	$70	$78 *	$ 88	$330	$365	$200	$215	$455	$210
	3'-0" x 6'-8"	48	55	75	82 *	91	345	380	205	221	475	225
	3'-0" x 7'-0"	54	60	85	89 *	99	385	410	225	234	480	235
	3'-6" x 7'-0"	69	69	90	93 *	108	—	—	—	—	—	—
	4'-0" x 7'-0"	72	73	93	96 *	115	—	—	—	—	—	—
1-3/8"	2'-0" x 6'-8"	30	44	68	74 *	84	104	—	121	—	177	160
	2'-6" x 6'-8"	33	42	66	80 *	88	125	159	135	—	260	165
	3'-0" x 6'-8"	37	47	74	87 *	94	148	175	155	—	285	170
	3'-0" x 7'-0"	46	55	86	92 *	98	190	—	175	—	—	—

*Add to the above for the following birch face door types:

Solid wood stave core, add $31
3/4 hour label door, add $61
1 hour label door, add $72
1-1/2 hour label door, add $82
8' high door, add 31%

Doors & Windows — R085 — Metal Windows

R085-100 Steel Sash

Ironworker crew will erect 25 S.F. or 1.3 sash unit per hour, whichever is less.

Mechanic will point 30 L.F. per hour.

Painter will paint 90 S.F. per coat per hour.

Glazier production depends on light size.

Allow 1 lb. special steel sash putty per 16" x 20" light.

Doors & Windows | R086 | Wood & Plastic Windows

R086-200 Replacement Windows

Replacement windows are typically measured per United Inch. United Inches are calculated by rounding the width and height of the window opening up to the nearest inch, then adding the two figures.

The labor cost for replacement windows includes removal of sash, existing sash balance or weights, parting bead where necessary and installation of new window.

Debris hauling and dump fees are not included.

Doors & Windows | R087 | Hardware

R087-100 Hinges

All closer equipped doors should have ball bearing hinges. Lead lined or extremely heavy doors require special strength hinges. Usually 1-1/2 pair of hinges are used per door up to 7'-6" high openings. Table below shows typical hinge requirements.

Use Frequency	Type Hinge Required	Type of Opening	Type of Structure
High	Heavy weight ball bearing	Entrances	Banks, Office buildings, Schools, Stores & Theaters
		Toilet Rooms	Office buildings and Schools
Average	Standard weight ball bearing	Entrances	Dwellings
		Corridors	Office buildings and Schools
		Toilet Rooms	Stores
Low	Plain bearing	Interior	Dwellings

Door Thickness	Weight of Doors in Pounds per Square Foot					
	White Pine	Oak	Hollow Core	Solid Core	Hollow Metal
1-3/8"	3 psf	6 psf	1-1/2 psf	3-1/2 — 4 psf	6-1/2 psf
1-3/4"	3-1/2	7	2-1/2	4-1/2 — 5-1/4	6-1/2
2-1/4"	4-1/2	9	—	5-1/2 — 6-3/4	6-1/2

Doors & Windows | R088 | Glazing

R088-010 Glazing Labor

Glass sizes are estimated by the "united inch" (height + width). Table below shows the number of lights glazed in an eight hour period by the crew size indicated, for glass up to 1/4" thick. Square or nearly square lights are more economical on a S.F. basis. Long slender lights will have a high S.F. installation cost. For insulated glass reduce production by 33%. For 1/2" float glass reduce production by 50%. Production time for glazing with two glaziers per day averages: 1/4" float glass 120 S.F.; 1/2" float glass 55 S.F.; 1/2" insulated glass 95 S.F.; 3/4" insulated glass 75 S.F.

Glazing Method	United Inches per Light							
	40"	60"	80"	100"	135"	165"	200"	240"
Number of Men in Crew	1	1	1	1	2	3	3	4
Industrial sash, putty	60	45	24	15	18	—	—	—
With stops, putty bed	50	36	21	12	16	8	4	3
Wood stops, rubber	40	27	15	9	11	6	3	2
Metal stops, rubber	30	24	14	9	9	6	3	2
Structural glass	10	7	4	3	—	—	—	—
Corrugated glass	12	9	7	4	4	4	3	—
Storefronts	16	15	13	11	7	6	4	4
Skylights, putty glass	60	36	21	12	16	—	—	—
Thiokol set	15	15	11	9	9	6	3	2
Vinyl set, snap on	18	18	13	12	12	7	5	4
Maximum area per light	2.8 S.F.	6.3 S.F.	11.1 S.F.	17.4 S.F.	31.6 S.F.	47 S.F.	69 S.F.	100 S.F.
Daily Bare Crew Cost	$212.80	$212.80	$212.80	$212.80	$425.60	$638.40	$638.40	$851.20

Finishes | R092 | Lath, Plaster & Gypsum Board

R092-105 Gypsum Plaster

Quantities for 100 S.Y.	2 Coat, 5/8" Thick		3 Coat, 3/4" Thick		
	Base	Finish	Scratch	Brown	Finish
	1:3 Mix	2:1 Mix	1:2 Mix	1:3 Mix	2:1 Mix
Gypsum plaster	1300 lb.		1350 lb.	650 lb.	
Sand	1.75 C.Y.		1.85 C.Y.	1.35 C.Y.	
Finish hydrated lime		340 lb.			340 lb.
Gauging plaster		170 lb.			170 lb.

Total, in Place for 100 S.Y. on Walls	2 Coat, 5/8" Thick			3 Coat, 3/4" Thick		
	Quantities	Bare Cost	Incl. O & P	Quantities	Bare Cost	Incl. O & P
Gypsum plaster @ $ 13.00 per 80 lb. bag	1300 lb.	$ 211.25	$ 232.38	2000 lb.	$ 325.00	$ 357.50
Finish hydrated lime @ $ 5.42 per 50 lb. bag	340 lb.	36.86	40.55	340 lb.	36.86	40.55
Gauging plaster @ $ 14.75 per 100 lb. bag	170 lb.	25.08	27.59	170 lb.	25.08	27.59
Sand @ $ 21.85 per C.Y.	1.7 C.Y.	37.15	40.87	2.0 C.Y.	43.70	48.07
J-1 crew @ $1,004.85 & $1,617.50 per day	.87 days	874.22	1,407.23	1.05 days	1055.09	1,698.38
Cleaning, staging, handling, patching	.09 days	87.77	142.64	.10 days	97.52	158.49
Total per 100 S.Y. in place		$1,272.33	$1,891.26		$1,583.25	$2,330.58

R092-610 Studs, Joists and Track

Material prices per 1000 L.F., for galvanized studs, joists and tracks. Panhead, framing screws, 7/16" long are $9.30 per thousand; 1-5/8" long are $14.50 per thousand.

Non-load bearing, 20 ga. stud and track are primarily used for curtain wall. (C.W.)

	Non-Load Bearing				Load Bearing 1-5/8" Flange—Light Gauge Structural					
	25 Ga.		20 Ga. (C.W.)		18 Ga.		16 Ga.		14 Ga.	
Size	Stud	Track	Stud	Track	Stud	Track	Stud	Track	Stud	Track
1-5/8"	$140	$137	$240	$230						
2-1/2"	165	162	280	270	$500	$450	$ 610	$ 560	$ 760	$ 710
3-5/8"	195	192	325	315	560	510	690	640	850	800
4"	220	217	360	350	590	540	730	680	900	850
6"	310	305	460	448	750	700	920	870	1,130	980
8"					895	845	1,125	1,075	1,400	1,350

	Non-Load Bearing				Load Bearing—Extra Wide Flange — 2" Flange					
	25 Ga.		22 Ga.		18 Ga.		16 Ga.		14 Ga.	12 Ga.
Size	C-H Stud	J-Track	C-H Stud	J-Track	Joist	Track	Joist	Track	Joist	Track	Joist	Track
2-1/2"	$480	$380	$780	$510	—	$620	—	$ 880	—	$1,025		—
4"	576	540	990	750	$ 800	790	$1,020	990	$1,170	1,110	$1,900	$1,860
6"					840	810	1,050	1,000	1,280	1,200	2,000	1,910
8"					1,020	980	1,240	1,170	1,550	1,500	2,440	2,200
10"							1,520	1,420	1,880	1,780	2,900	2,700
12"							1,390	1,290	2,140	2,040	3,320	3,120

Specialties — R105 Lockers

R105-050 Steel Lockers

Price per Opening, Material Only, Based on 100 Openings, Not Including Locks

Single Tier	1-Wide	3-Wide	Double Tier	1-Wide	3-Wide
12" x 12" x 60"	$121.50	$101.50	12" x 12" x 30"	$72.00	$61.50
12" x 15" x 60"	128.00	106.00	12" x 12" x 36"	76.00	63.50
12" x 18" x 60"	136.00	111.50	12" x 15" x 36"	78.00	66.50
12" x 12" x 72"	134.00	113.00	12" x 18" x 36"	84.00	69.00
12" x 15" x 72"	141.00	117.00	15" x 15" x 36"	84.00	74.00
12" x 18" x 72"	147.00	121.00	**Multiple Tier**	**1-Wide**	**3-Wide**
15" x 18" x 72"	159.00	135.50	5-High 12" x 12" x 12"	$33.00	$28.00
18" x 18" x 72"	164.50	140.50	12" x 15" x 12"	34.50	29.00
18" x 21" x 72"	175.00	147.50	15" x 15" x 12"	38.00	33.00
			6-High 12" x 12" x 12"	31.00	27.00
			12" x 15" x 12"	34.00	28.00

Conveying Systems — R142 Elevators

R142-100 Freight Elevators

Capacities run from 2,000 lbs. to over 100,000 lbs. with 3,000 lbs. to 10,000 lbs. most common. Travel speeds are generally lower and control less intricate than on passenger elevators. Unit prices in division 142-010 are for hydraulic and geared elevators.

Conveying Systems — R142 Elevators

R142-200 Elevator Selective Costs
See R142-400 for cost development.

		Passenger		Freight		Hospital	
A. Base Unit		Hydraulic	Electric	Hydraulic	Electric	Hydraulic	Electric
	Capacity	1,500 Lb.	2,000 Lb.	2,000 Lb.	4,000 Lb.	4,000 lb.	4,000 lb.
	Speed	100 F.P.M.	200 F.P.M.	50 F.P.M.	200 F.P.M.	100 F.P.M.	200 F.P.M.
	#Stops/Travel Ft.	2/12	4/40	2/20	4/40	2/20	4/40
	Push Button Oper.	Yes	Yes	Yes	Yes	Yes	Yes
	Telephone Box & Wire	"	"	"	"	"	"
	Emergency Lighting	"	"	No	No	"	"
	Cab	Plastic Lam. Walls	Plastic Lam. Walls	Painted Steel	Painted Steel	Plastic Lam. Walls	Plastic Lam. Walls
	Cove Lighting	Yes	Yes	No	No	Yes	Yes
	Floor	V.C.T.	V.C.T.	Wood w/Safety Treads	Wood w/Safety Treads	V.C.T.	V.C.T.
	Doors, & Speedside Slide	Yes	Yes	Yes	Yes	Yes	Yes
	Gates, Manual	No	No	No	No	No	No
	Signals, Lighted Buttons	Car and Hall	Car and Hall	Car and Hall	Car and Hall	Car and Hall	Car and Hall
	O.H. Geared Machine	N.A.	Yes	N.A.	Yes	N.A.	Yes
	Variable Voltage Contr.	"	"	N.A.	"	"	"
	Emergency Alarm	Yes	"	Yes	"	Yes	"
	Class "A" Loading	N.A.	N.A.	"	"	N.A.	N.A.
	Base Cost	$37,250	$82,150	$41,500	$81,070	$48,005	$86,500
B. Capacity Adjustment							
	2,000 Lb.	$ 525					
	2,500	1,150	$ 2,675	$ 2,242			
	3,000	2,865	4,000	3,271			
	3,500	4,890	5,700	5,628			
	4,000	5,640	5,780	6,022			
	4,500	6,750	7,600	7,115		$ 5,628	$ 4,685
	5,000	9,380	9,620	9,700	$ 4,682	8,198	6,118
	6,000			9,990	8,216		
	7,000			15,786	11,000		
	8,000			17,120	15,333		
	10,000			18,008	18,106		
	12,000			21,435	22,000		
	16,000			27,950	26,422		
	20,000			31,016	29,008		
C. Travel Over Base		$ 331 V.L.F.	$ 207 V.L.F.	$ 331 V.L.F.	$ 207 V.L.F.	$ 331 V.L.F.	$ 207 V.L.F.
D. Additional Stops		$ 3,410 Ea.	$ 5,319 Ea.	$ 3,385 Ea.	$ 4,963 Ea.	$ 5,904 Ea.	$ 5,752 Ea.
E. Speed Adjustment							
	100 F.P.M.			$ 700			
	125	$ 800		1,296		$ 1,341	
	150	1,725		2,418		2,259	
	175	2,910		3,792		3,546	
	200	4,695				5,174	
Geared 4 Flrs. Min.	250		$ 2,200		$ 9,318		$ 2,366
	300		4,485		11,625		4,410
	350		5,270		13,720		5,380
	400		7,518		15,210		7,493
Gearless 4 Flrs. Min.	500		34,780		19,050		33,255
	600		36,729		21,050		36,730
	700		40,202		24,522		40,098
	800		44,300		27,258		44,305
	1,000		Spec. Applic.		Spec. Applic.		Spec. Applic.
	1,200		"		"		"
F. Other Than Class "A" Loading							
	"B"			$ 1,600	$ 1,625		
	"C-1"			3,994	4,018		
	"C-2"			4,782	4,796		
	"C-3"			6,542	6,585		

Conveying Systems — R142 Elevators

R142-200 Elevator Selective Costs (cont.)

	Passenger	Freight	Hospital
G. Options			
1. Controls			
Automatic, 2 car group	$3,564		$3,557
3 car group	5,304		5,269
4 car group	8,156		8,087
5 car group	10,663		10,588
6 car group	15,097		14,990
Emergency, fireman service	Yes		Yes
Intercom service	600		600
Selective collective, single car	—		—
Duplex car	3,816		3,816
2. Doors			
Center opening, 1 speed	$1,720		$1,720
2 speed	2,100		2,100
Rear opening-opposite front	4,012		4,012
Side opening, 2 speed	5,980		5,980
Freight, bi-parting	—	$ 5,000	—
Power operated door and gate	—	16,500	—
3. Emergency power switching, automatic	$2,150		$2,150
Manual	382		382
4. Finishes based on 3500# cab			
Ceilings, acrylic panel	$390		
Aluminum egg crate	475		$475
Doors, stainless steel	800 Ea.		800 Ea.
Floors, carpet, class "A" — (Finish flooring by others)	329		—
Epoxy	274		274
Quarry tile	410		412
Slate	573		—
Steel plate	—	$ 665	
Textured rubber	110		110
Walls, plastic laminate	Std.		Std.
Stainless steel	2,445		2,445
Return at door	520		520
Steel plate, 1/4" x 4' high, 14 ga. above	—	$ 1,601	—
Entrance, doors, baked enamel	Std.		Std.
Stainless steel	800 Ea.		800 Ea.
Frames, baked enamel	Std.		Std.
Stainless steel	800 Ea.		800 Ea.
5. Maintenance contract - 12 months	$2,840	$ 2,122	$4,125
6. Signal devices			
Hall lantern, each	$426	$ 426	$426
Position indicator, car or lobby	312	312	312
Add for over three each, per floor	88	88	88
7. Specialties			
High speed, heavy duty door opener	$1,420		$1,420
Variable voltage, O.H. gearless machine	28,100-62,400		28,100-62,400
Basement installed geared machine	$14,400	$14,450	$14,400

Conveying Systems — R142 Elevators

R142-300 Passenger Elevators

Electric elevators are used generally but hydraulic elevators can be used for lifts up to 70′ and where large capacities are required. Hydraulic speeds are limited to 200 F.P.M. but cars are self leveling at the stops. On low rises, hydraulic installation runs about 15% less than standard electric types but on higher rises this installation cost advantage is reduced. Maintenance of hydraulic elevators is about the same as electric type but underground portion is not included in the maintenance contract.

In electric elevators there are several control systems available, the choice of which will be based upon elevator use, size, speed and cost criteria. The two types of drives are geared for low speeds and gearless for 450 F.P.M. and over.

The tables on the preceding pages illustrate typical installed costs of the various types of elevators available.

R142-400 Elevator Cost Development

Requirement: One passenger elevator, five story hydraulic, 2,500 lb. capacity, 12′ floor to floor, speed 150 F.P.M., emergency power switching and maintenance contract.

Description	Total Cost
A. Base Elevator, (Hydraulic Passenger)	$37,250
B. Capacity Adjustment (2,500 lb.)	1,150
C. Excess Travel Over Base (4 x 12′) = 48′ — (12′ for Base Unit) = 36′ x $331 per V.L.F.	11,916
D. Stops Over Base 5 — (2 for base unit) = 3 x $3,410 Ea.	10,230
E. Speed Adjustment (150 F.P.M.)	1,725
F. Options:	
1. Intercom Service	600
2. Emergency power switching, automatic	2,150
3. Stainless steel entrance doors 5 x $800 Ea.	4,000
4. Maintenance Contract (12 months)	2,840
5. Position indicators 2 x $312	624
Total Cost	$72,485

Mechanical — R151 Plumbing

R151-050 Pipe Material Considerations

1. Malleable fittings should be used for gas service.
2. Malleable fittings are used where there are stresses/strains due to expansion and vibration.
3. Cast fittings may be broken as an aid to disassembling of heating lines frozen by long use, temperature and minerals.
4. Cast iron pipe is extensively used for underground and submerged service.
5. Type M (light wall) copper tubing is available in hard temper only and is used for nonpressure and less severe applications than K and L.
6. Type L (medium wall) copper tubing, available hard or soft for interior service.
7. Type K (heavy wall) copper tubing, available in hard or soft temper for use where conditions are severe. For underground and interior service.
8. Hard drawn tubing requires fewer hangers or supports but should not be bent. Silver brazed fittings are recommended, however soft solder is normally used.
9. Type DMV (very light wall) copper tubing designed for drainage, waste and vent plus other non-critical pressure services.

Domestic/Imported Pipe and Fittings Cost

The prices shown in this publication for steel/cast iron pipe and steel, cast iron, malleable iron fittings are based on domestic production sold at the normal trade discounts. The above listed items of foreign manufacture may be available at prices of 1/3 to 1/2 those shown. Some imported items after minor machining or finishing operations are being sold as domestic to further complicate the system.

Caution: Most pipe prices in this book also include a coupling and pipe hangers which for the larger sizes can add significantly to the per foot cost and should be taken into account when comparing "book cost" with quoted supplier's cost.

Mechanical — R151 Plumbing

R151-420 Plumbing Fixture Installation Time

Item	Rough-In	Set	Total Hours	Item	Rough-In	Set	Total Hours
Bathtub	5	5	10	Shower head only	2	1	3
Bathtub and shower, cast iron	6	6	12	Shower drain	3	1	4
Fire hose reel and cabinet	4	2	6	Shower stall, slate		15	15
Floor drain to 4 inch diameter	3	1	4	Slop sink	5	3	8
Grease trap, single, cast iron	5	3	8	Test 6 fixtures			14
Kitchen gas range		4	4	Urinal, wall	6	2	8
Kitchen sink, single	4	4	8	Urinal, pedestal or floor	6	4	10
Kitchen sink, double	6	6	12	Water closet and tank	4	3	7
Laundry tubs	4	2	6	Water closet and tank, wall hung	5	3	8
Lavatory wall hung	5	3	8	Water heater, 45 gals. gas, automatic	5	2	7
Lavatory pedestal	5	3	8	Water heaters, 65 gals. gas, automatic	5	2	7
Shower and stall	6	4	10	Water heaters, electric, plumbing only	4	2	6

Fixture prices in front of book are based on the cost per fixture set in place. The rough-in cost, which must be added for each fixture, includes carrier, if required, some supply, waste and vent pipe connecting fittings and stops. The lengths of rough-in pipe are nominal runs which would connect to the larger runs and stacks. The supply runs and DWV runs and stacks must be accounted for in separate entries. In the eastern half of the United States it is common for the plumber to carry these to a point 5' outside the building.

Mechanical — R155 Heating

R155-720 Demolition (Selective vs. Removal for Replacement)

Demolition can be divided into two basic categories.

One type of demolition involves the removal of material with no concern for its replacement. The labor-hours to estimate this work are found in Div. 020-700 under "Selective Demolition". It is selective in that individual items or all the material installed as a system or trade grouping such as plumbing or heating systems are removed. This may be accomplished by the easiest way possible, such as sawing, torch cutting, or sledge hammer as well as simple unbolting.

The second type of demolition is the removal of some item for repair or replacement. This removal may involve careful draining, opening of unions, disconnecting and tagging of electrical connections, capping of pipes/ducts to prevent entry of debris or leakage of the material contained as well as transport of the item away from its in-place location to a truck/dumpster. An approximation of the time required to accomplish this type of demolition is to use half of the time indicated as necessary to install a new unit. For example; installation of a new pump might be listed as requiring 6 labor-hours so if we had to estimate the removal of the old pump we would allow an additional 3 hours for a total of 9 hours. That is, the complete replacement of a defective pump with a new pump would be estimated to take 9 labor-hours.

Mechanical | R157 | Air Conditioning & Ventilation

R157-050 Ductwork

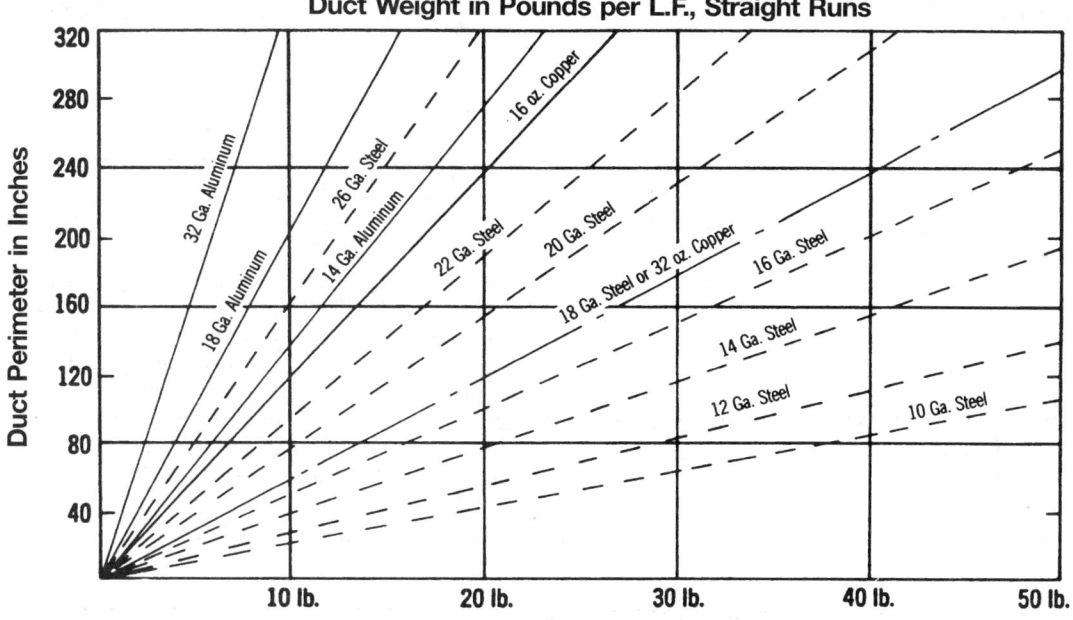

Duct Weight in Pounds per L.F., Straight Runs

Add to the above for fittings; 90° elbow is 3 L.F.; 45° elbow is 2.5 L.F.; offset is 4 L.F.; transition offset is 6 L.F.; square-to-round transition is 4 L.F.; 90° reducing elbow is 5 L.F. For bracing and waste, add 20% to aluminum and copper, 15% to steel.

Electrical | R160 | Design & Cost Tables

R160-205 Conductors in Conduit

Table below lists maximum number of conductors for various sized conduit using THW, TW or THWN insulations.

Copper Wire Size	1/2"			3/4"			1"			1-1/4"			1-1/2"			2"			2-1/2"			3"			3-1/2"		4"	
	TW	THW	THWN	TW	THW	THWN	TW	THW	THWN	TW	THW	THWN	TW	THW	THWN	TW	THW	THWN	TW	THW	THWN	THW	THWN	THW	THWN	THW	THWN
#14	9	6	13	15	10	24	25	16	39	44	29	69	60	40	94	99	65	154	142	93		143		192			
#12	7	4	10	12	8	18	19	13	29	35	24	51	47	32	70	78	53	114	111	76	164	117		157			
#10	5	4	6	9	6	11	15	11	18	26	19	32	36	26	44	60	43	73	85	61	104	95	160	127		163	
#8	2	1	3	4	3	5	7	5	9	12	10	16	17	13	22	28	22	36	40	32	51	49	79	66	106	85	136
#6		1	1	2	2	4	4	4	6	7	7	11	10	10	15	16	16	26	23	23	37	36	57	48	76	62	98
#4		1	1	1	1	2	3	3	4	5	5	7	7	7	9	12	12	16	17	17	22	27	35	36	47	47	60
#3		1	1	1	1	1	2	2	3	4	4	6	6	6	8	10	10	13	15	15	19	23	29	31	39	40	51
#2		1	1	1	1	1	2	2	3	4	4	5	5	5	7	9	9	11	13	13	16	20	25	27	33	34	43
#1				1	1	1	1	1	1	3	3	3	4	4	5	6	6	8	9	9	12	14	18	19	25	25	32
1/0				1	1	1	1	1	1	2	2	3	3	3	4	5	5	7	8	8	10	12	15	16	21	21	27
2/0					1	1	1	1	1	1	1	2	3	3	3	5	5	6	7	7	8	10	13	14	17	18	22
3/0					1	1	1	1	1	1	1	1	2	2	3	4	4	5	6	6	7	9	11	12	14	15	18
4/0						1	1	1	1	1	1	1	1	1	2	3	3	4	5	5	6	7	9	10	12	13	15
250 kcmil										1	1	1	1	1	1	2	2	3	4	4	4	6	7	8	10	10	12
300										1	1	1	1	1	1	2	2	3	3	3	4	5	6	7	8	9	11
350												1	1	1	1	1	1	2	3	3	3	4	5	6	7	8	9
400													1	1	1	1	1	1	2	2	3	4	5	5	6	7	8
500													1	1	1	1	1	1	1	1	2	3	4	4	5	6	7
600															1	1	1	1	1	1	1	3	3	4	4	5	5
700																1	1	1	1	1	1	2	3	3	4	4	5
750																1	1	1	1	1	1	2	2	3	3	4	4

Change Orders

Change Order Considerations

A Change Order is a written document, usually prepared by the design professional, and signed by the owner, the architect/engineer and the contractor. A change order states the agreement of the parties to: an addition, deletion, or revision in the work; an adjustment in the contract sum, if any; or an adjustment in the contract time, if any. Change orders, or "extras" in the construction process occur after execution of the construction contract and impact architects/engineers, contractors and owners.

Change orders that are properly recognized and managed can ensure orderly, professional and profitable progress for all who are involved in the project. There are many causes for change orders and change order requests. In all cases, change orders or change order requests should be addressed promptly and in a precise and prescribed manner. The following paragraphs include information regarding change order pricing and procedures.

The Causes of Change Orders

Reasons for issuing change orders include:

- Unforeseen field conditions that require a change in the work
- Correction of design discrepancies, errors or omissions in the contract documents
- Owner-requested changes, either by design criteria, scope of work, or project objectives
- Completion date changes for reasons unrelated to the construction process
- Changes in building code interpretations, or other public authority requirements that require a change in the work
- Changes in availability of existing or new materials and products

Procedures

Properly written contract documents must include the correct change order procedures for all parties—owners, design professionals and contractors—to follow in order to avoid costly delays and litigation.

Being "in the right" is not always a sufficient or acceptable defense. The contract provisions requiring notification and documentation must be adhered to within a defined or reasonable time frame.

The appropriate method of handling change orders is by a written proposal and acceptance by all parties involved. Prior to starting work on a project, all parties should identify their authorized agents who may sign and accept change orders, as well as any limits placed on their authority.

Time may be a critical factor when the need for a change arises. For such cases, the contractor might be directed to proceed on a "time and materials" basis, rather than wait for all paperwork to be processed—a delay that could impede progress. In this situation, the contractor must still follow the prescribed change order procedures, including but not limited to, notification and documentation.

All forms used for change orders should be dated and signed by the proper authority. Lack of documentation can be very costly, especially if legal judgments are to be made and if certain field personnel are no longer available. For time and material change orders, the contractor should keep accurate daily records of all labor and material allocated to the change. Forms that can be used to document change order work are available in *Means Forms for Building Construction Professionals*.

Owners or awarding authorities who do considerable and continual building construction (such as the federal government) realize the inevitability of change orders for numerous reasons, both predictable and unpredictable. As a result, the federal government, the American Institute of Architects (AIA), the Engineers Joint Contract Documents Committee (EJCDC) and other contractor, legal and technical organizations have developed standards and procedures to be followed by all parties to achieve contract continuance and timely completion, while being financially fair to all concerned.

In addition to the change order standards put forth by industry associations, there are also many books available on the subject.

Pricing Change Orders

When pricing change orders, regardless of their cause, the most significant factor is *when* the change occurs. The need for a change may be perceived in the field or requested by the architect/engineer *before* any of the actual installation has begun, or may evolve or appear *during* construction when the item of work in question is partially installed. In the latter cases, the original sequence of construction is disrupted, along with all contiguous and supporting systems. Change orders cause the greatest impact when they occur *after* the installation has been completed and must be uncovered, or even replaced. Post-completion changes may be caused by necessary design changes, product failure, or changes in the owner's requirements that are not discovered until the building or the systems begin to function.

Specified procedures of notification and record keeping must be adhered to and enforced regardless of the stage of construction: *before, during,* or *after* installation. Some bidding documents anticipate change orders by requiring that unit prices including overhead and profit percentages—for additional as well as deductible changes—be listed. Generally these unit prices do not fully take into account the ripple effect, or impact on other trades, and should be used for general guidance only.

When pricing change orders, it is important to classify the time frame in which the change occurs. There are two basic time frames for change orders: *pre-installation change orders*, which occur before the start of construction, and *post-installation change orders*, which involve reworking after the original installation. Change orders that occur between these stages may be priced according to the extent of work completed using a combination of techniques developed for pricing *pre-* and *post-installation* changes.

The following factors are the basis for a check list to use when preparing a change order estimate.

Factors To Consider When Pricing Change Orders

As an estimator begins to prepare a change order, the following questions should be reviewed to determine their impact on the final price.

General

- Is the change order work *pre-installation* or *post-installation*?

Change order work costs vary according to how much of the installation has been completed. Once workers have the project scoped in their mind, even though they have not started, it can be difficult to refocus. Consequently they may spend more than the normal amount of time understanding the change. Also, modifications to work in place such as trimming or refitting usually take more time than was initially estimated. The greater the amount of work in place, the more reluctant workers are to change it. Psychologically they may resent the change and as a result the rework takes longer than normal. Post-installation change order estimates must include demolition of existing work as required to accomplish the change. If the work is performed at a later time, additional obstacles such as building finishes may be present which must be protected. Regardless of whether the change occurs pre-installation or post-installation, attempt to isolate the identifiable factors and price them separately. For example, add shipping costs that may be required pre-installation or any demolition required post-installation. Then analyze the potential impact on productivity of psychological and/or learning curve factors and adjust the output rates accordingly. One approach is to break down the typical workday into segments and quantify the impact on each segment. The following chart may be useful as a guide:

	Activities (Productivity) Expressed as Percentages of a Workday		
Task	Means Mechanical Cost Data (for New Construction)	Pre-Installation Change Orders	Post-Installation Change Orders
1. Study plans	3%	6%	6%
2. Material procurement	3%	3%	3%
3. Receiving and storing	3%	3%	3%
4. Mobilization	5%	5%	5%
5. Site movement	5%	5%	8%
6. Layout and marking	8%	10%	12%
7. Actual installation	64%	59%	54%
8. Clean-up	3%	3%	3%
9. Breaks—non-productive	6%	6%	6%
Total	100%	100%	100%

Change Order Installation Efficiency

The labor-hours expressed (for new construction) are based on average installation time, using an efficiency level of approximately 60-65%. For change order situations, adjustments to this efficiency level should reflect the daily labor-hour allocation for that particular occurrence.

If any of the specific percentages expressed in the above chart do not apply to a particular project situation, then those percentage points should be reallocated to the appropriate task(s). Example: Using data for new construction, assume there is no new material being utilized. The percentages for Tasks 2 and 3 would therefore be reallocated to other tasks. If the time required for Tasks 2 and 3 can now be applied to installation, we can add the time allocated for *Material Procurement* and *Receiving and Storing* to the *Actual Installation* time for new construction, thereby increasing the Actual Installation percentage.

This chart shows that, due to reduced productivity, labor costs will be higher than those for new construction by 5% to 15% for pre-installation change orders and by 15% to 25% for post-installation change orders. Each job and change order is unique and must be examined individually. Many factors, covered elsewhere in this section, can each have a significant impact on productivity and change order costs. All such factors should be considered in every case.

- Will the change substantially delay the original completion date?

  A significant change in the project may cause the original completion date to be extended. The extended schedule may subject the contractor to new wage rates dictated by relevant labor contracts. Project supervision and other project overhead must also be extended beyond the original completion date. The schedule extension may also put installation into a new weather season. For example, underground piping scheduled for October installation was delayed until January. As a result, frost penetrated the trench area, thereby changing the degree of difficulty of the task. Changes and delays may have a ripple effect throughout the project. This effect must be analyzed and negotiated with the owner.

- What is the net effect of a deduct change order?

  In most cases, change orders resulting in a deduction or credit reflect only bare costs. The contractor may retain the overhead and profit based on the original bid.

Materials

- Will you have to pay more or less for the new material, required by the change order, than you paid for the original purchase?

  The same material prices or discounts will usually apply to materials purchased for change orders as new construction. In some instances, however, the contractor may forfeit the advantages of competitive pricing for change orders. Consider the following example:

  A contractor purchased over $20,000 worth of fan coil units for an installation, and obtained the maximum discount. Some time later it was determined the project required an additional matching unit. The contractor has to purchase this unit from the original supplier to ensure a match. The supplier at this time may not discount the unit because of the small quantity, and the fact that he is no longer in a competitive situation. The impact of quantity on purchase can add between 0% and 25% to material prices and/or subcontractor quotes.

- If materials have been ordered or delivered to the job site, will they be subject to a cancellation charge or restocking fee?

  Check with the supplier to determine if ordered materials are subject to a cancellation charge. Delivered materials not used as result of a change order may be subject to a restocking fee if returned to the supplier. Common restocking charges run between 20% and 40%. Also, delivery charges to return the goods to the supplier must be added.

Labor

- How efficient is the existing crew at the actual installation?

  Is the same crew that performed the initial work going to do the change order? Possibly the change consists of the installation of a unit identical to one already installed; therefore the change should take less time. Be sure to consider this potential productivity increase and modify the productivity rates accordingly.

- If the crew size is increased, what impact will that have on supervision requirements?

  Under most bargaining agreements or management practices, there is a point at which a working foreman is replaced by a nonworking foreman. This replacement increases project overhead by adding a nonproductive worker. If additional workers are added to accelerate the project or to perform changes while maintaining the schedule, be sure to add additional supervision time if warranted. Calculate the hours involved and the additional cost directly if possible.

- What are the other impacts of increased crew size?

  The larger the crew, the greater the potential for productivity to decrease. Some of the factors that cause this productivity loss are: overcrowding (producing restrictive conditions in the working space), and possibly a shortage of any special tools and equipment required. Such factors affect not only the crew working on the elements directly involved in the change order, but other crews whose movement may also be hampered.

  As the crew increases, check its basic composition for changes by the addition or deletion of apprentices or nonworking foreman and quantify the potential effects of equipment shortages or other logistical factors.

- As new crews, unfamiliar with the project, are brought onto the site, how long will it take them to become oriented to the project requirements?

  The orientation time for a new crew to become 100% effective varies with the site and type of project. Orientation is easiest at a new construction site, and most difficult at existing, very restrictive renovation sites. The type of work also affects orientation time. When all elements of the work are exposed, such as concrete or masonry work, orientation is decreased. When the work is concealed or less visible, such as existing electrical systems, orientation takes longer. Usually orientation can be accomplished in one day or less. Costs for added orientation should be itemized and added to the total estimated cost.

- How much actual production can be gained by working overtime?

  Short term overtime can be used effectively to accomplish more work in a day. However, as overtime is scheduled to run beyond several weeks, studies have shown marked decreases in output. The following chart shows the effect of long term overtime on worker efficiency. If the anticipated change requires extended overtime to keep the job on schedule, these factors can be used as a guide to predict the impact on time and cost. Add project overhead, particularly supervision, that may also be incurred.

Days per Week	Hours per Day	Production Efficiency					Payroll Cost Factors	
		1 Week	2 Weeks	3 Weeks	4 Weeks	Average 4 Weeks	@ 1-1/2 Times	@ 2 Times
5	8	100%	100%	100%	100%	100%	100%	100%
	9	100	100	95	90	96.25	105.6	111.1
	10	100	95	90	85	91.25	110.0	120.0
	11	95	90	75	65	81.25	113.6	127.3
	12	90	85	70	60	76.25	116.7	133.3
6	8	100	100	95	90	96.25	108.3	116.7
	9	100	95	90	85	92.50	113.0	125.9
	10	95	90	85	80	87.50	116.7	133.3
	11	95	85	70	65	78.75	119.7	139.4
	12	90	80	65	60	73.75	122.2	144.4
7	8	100	95	85	75	88.75	114.3	128.6
	9	95	90	80	70	83.75	118.3	136.5
	10	90	85	75	65	78.75	121.4	142.9
	11	85	80	65	60	72.50	124.0	148.1
	12	85	75	60	55	68.75	126.2	152.4

Effects of Overtime

Caution: Under many labor agreements, Sundays and holidays are paid at a higher premium than the normal overtime rate.

The use of long-term overtime is counterproductive on almost any construction job; that is, the longer the period of overtime, the lower the actual production rate. Numerous studies have been conducted, and while they have resulted in slightly different numbers, all reach the same conclusion. The figure above tabulates the effects of overtime work on efficiency.

As illustrated, there can be a difference between the *actual* payroll cost per hour and the *effective* cost per hour for overtime work. This is due to the reduced production efficiency with the increase in weekly hours beyond 40. This difference between actual and effective cost results from overtime work over a prolonged period. Short-term overtime work does not result in as great a reduction in efficiency, and in such cases, effective cost may not vary significantly from the actual payroll cost. As the total hours per week are increased on a regular basis, more time is lost because of fatigue, lowered morale, and an increased accident rate.

As an example, assume a project where workers are working 6 days a week, 10 hours per day. From the figure above (based on productivity studies), the average effective productive hours over a four-week period are:

$$0.875 \times 60 = 52.5$$

Depending upon the locale and day of week, overtime hours may be paid at time and a half or double time. For time and a half, the overall (average) *actual* payroll cost (including regular and overtime hours) is determined as follows:

$$\frac{40 \text{ reg. hrs.} + (20 \text{ overtime hrs.} \times 1.5)}{60 \text{ hrs.}} = 1.167$$

Based on 60 hours, the payroll cost per hour will be 116.7% of the normal rate at 40 hours per week. However, because the effective production (efficiency) for 60 hours is reduced to the equivalent of 52.5 hours, the effective cost of overtime is calculated as follows:

For time and a half:

$$\frac{40 \text{ reg. hrs.} + (20 \text{ overtime hrs.} \times 1.5)}{52.5 \text{ hrs.}} = 1.33$$

Installed cost will be 133% of the normal rate (for labor).

Thus, when figuring overtime, the actual cost per unit of work will be higher than the apparent overtime payroll dollar increase, due to the reduced productivity of the longer workweek. These efficiency calculations are true only for those cost factors determined by hours worked. Costs that are applied weekly or monthly, such as equipment rentals, will not be similarly affected.

Equipment

- What equipment is required to complete the change order?

Change orders may require extending the rental period of equipment already on the job site, or the addition of special equipment brought in to accomplish the change work. In either case, the additional rental charges and operator labor charges must be added.

Summary

The preceding considerations and others you deem appropriate should be analyzed and applied to a change order estimate. The impact of each should be quantified and listed on the estimate to form an audit trail.

Change orders that are properly identified, documented, and managed help to ensure the orderly, professional and profitable progress of the work. They also minimize potential claims or disputes at the end of the project.

Crews

Crew No.	Bare Costs		Incl. Subs O & P		Cost Per Labor-Hour	
Crew A-1	Hr.	Daily	Hr.	Daily	Bare Costs	Incl. O&P
1 Building Laborer	$21.45	$171.60	$35.90	$287.20	$21.45	$35.90
1 Gas Eng. Power Tool		68.65		75.50	8.58	9.44
8 L.H., Daily Totals		$240.25		$362.70	$30.03	$45.34
Crew A-1A	Hr.	Daily	Hr.	Daily	Bare Costs	Incl. O&P
1 Skilled Worker	$28.05	$224.40	$46.50	$372.00	$28.05	$46.50
1 Shot Blaster, 20"		131.90		145.10	16.49	18.14
8 L.H., Daily Totals		$356.30		$517.10	$44.54	$64.64
Crew A-2	Hr.	Daily	Hr.	Daily	Bare Costs	Incl. O&P
2 Laborers	$21.45	$343.20	$35.90	$574.40	$21.55	$35.75
1 Truck Driver (light)	21.75	174.00	35.45	283.60		
1 Light Truck, 1.5 Ton		171.95		189.15	7.16	7.88
24 L.H., Daily Totals		$689.15		$1047.15	$28.71	$43.63
Crew A-2A	Hr.	Daily	Hr.	Daily	Bare Costs	Incl. O&P
2 Laborers	$21.45	$343.20	$35.90	$574.40	$21.55	$35.75
1 Truck Driver (light)	21.75	174.00	35.45	283.60		
1 Light Truck, 1.5 ton		171.95		189.15		
1 Concrete Saw		110.65		121.70	11.78	12.95
24 L.H., Daily Totals		$799.80		$1168.85	$33.33	$48.70
Crew A-3	Hr.	Daily	Hr.	Daily	Bare Costs	Incl. O&P
1 Truck Driver (heavy)	$22.10	$176.80	$36.05	$288.40	$22.10	$36.05
1 Dump Truck, 12 Ton		364.30		400.75	45.54	50.09
8 L.H., Daily Totals		$541.10		$689.15	$67.64	$86.14
Crew A-3A	Hr.	Daily	Hr.	Daily	Bare Costs	Incl. O&P
1 Truck Driver (light)	$21.75	$174.00	$35.45	$283.60	$21.75	$35.45
1 Pickup truck (4x4)		145.50		160.05	18.19	20.01
8 L.H., Daily Totals		$319.50		$443.65	$39.94	$55.46
Crew A-3B	Hr.	Daily	Hr.	Daily	Bare Costs	Incl. O&P
1 Equip. Oper. (medium)	$28.40	$227.20	$45.20	$361.60	$25.25	$40.63
1 Truck Driver (heavy)	22.10	176.80	36.05	288.40		
1 Dump Truck, 16 Ton		442.25		486.50	27.64	30.40
16 L.H., Daily Totals		$846.25		$1136.50	$52.89	$71.03
Crew A-3C	Hr.	Daily	Hr.	Daily	Bare Costs	Incl. O&P
1 Equip. Oper. (light)	$27.20	$217.60	$43.30	$346.40	$27.20	$43.30
1 Wheeled Skid Steer Loader		230.25		253.30	28.78	31.66
8 L.H., Daily Totals		$447.85		$599.70	$55.98	$74.96
Crew A-4	Hr.	Daily	Hr.	Daily	Bare Costs	Incl. O&P
2 Carpenters	$27.30	$436.80	$45.70	$731.20	$26.50	$44.00
1 Painter, Ordinary	24.90	199.20	40.60	324.80		
24 L.H., Daily Totals		$636.00		$1056.00	$26.50	$44.00
Crew A-5	Hr.	Daily	Hr.	Daily	Bare Costs	Incl. O&P
2 Laborers	$21.45	$343.20	$35.90	$574.40	$21.48	$35.85
.25 Truck Driver (light)	21.75	43.50	35.45	70.90		
.25 Light Truck, 1.5 Ton		42.99		47.30	2.39	2.63
18 L.H., Daily Totals		$429.69		$692.60	$23.87	$38.48
Crew A-6	Hr.	Daily	Hr.	Daily	Bare Costs	Incl. O&P
1 Chief Of Party	$27.20	$217.60	$43.30	$346.40	$25.63	$40.78
1 Instrument Man	24.05	192.40	38.25	306.00		
16 L.H., Daily Totals		$410.00		$652.40	$25.63	$40.78

Crew No.	Bare Costs		Incl. Subs O & P		Cost Per Labor-Hour	
Crew A-7	Hr.	Daily	Hr.	Daily	Bare Costs	Incl. O&P
1 Chief Of Party	$27.20	$217.60	$43.30	$346.40	$24.03	$38.80
1 Instrument Man	24.05	192.40	38.25	306.00		
1 Rodman/Chainman	20.85	166.80	34.85	278.80		
24 L.H., Daily Totals		$576.80		$931.20	$24.03	$38.80
Crew A-8	Hr.	Daily	Hr.	Daily	Bare Costs	Incl. O&P
1 Chief Of Party	$27.20	$217.60	$43.30	$346.40	$23.24	$37.81
1 Instrument Man	24.05	192.40	38.25	306.00		
2 Rodmen/Chainmen	20.85	333.60	34.85	557.60		
32 L.H., Daily Totals		$743.60		$1210.00	$23.24	$37.81
Crew A-9	Hr.	Daily	Hr.	Daily	Bare Costs	Incl. O&P
1 Asbestos Foreman	$30.95	$247.60	$51.50	$412.00	$30.51	$50.76
7 Asbestos Workers	30.45	1705.20	50.65	2836.40		
64 L.H., Daily Totals		$1952.80		$3248.40	$30.51	$50.76
Crew A-10	Hr.	Daily	Hr.	Daily	Bare Costs	Incl. O&P
1 Asbestos Foreman	$30.95	$247.60	$51.50	$412.00	$30.51	$50.76
7 Asbestos Workers	30.45	1705.20	50.65	2836.40		
64 L.H., Daily Totals		$1952.80		$3248.40	$30.51	$50.76
Crew A-10A	Hr.	Daily	Hr.	Daily	Bare Costs	Incl. O&P
1 Asbestos Foreman	$30.95	$247.60	$51.50	$412.00	$30.62	$50.93
2 Asbestos Workers	30.45	487.20	50.65	810.40		
24 L.H., Daily Totals		$734.80		$1222.40	$30.62	$50.93
Crew A-10B	Hr.	Daily	Hr.	Daily	Bare Costs	Incl. O&P
1 Asbestos Foreman	$30.95	$247.60	$51.50	$412.00	$30.58	$50.86
3 Asbestos Workers	30.45	730.80	50.65	1215.60		
32 L.H., Daily Totals		$978.40		$1627.60	$30.58	$50.86
Crew A-10C	Hr.	Daily	Hr.	Daily	Bare Costs	Incl. O&P
3 Asbestos Workers	$30.45	$730.80	$50.65	$1215.60	$30.45	$50.65
1 Flatbed truck		171.95		189.15	7.16	7.88
24 L.H., Daily Totals		$902.75		$1404.75	$37.61	$58.53
Crew A-10D	Hr.	Daily	Hr.	Daily	Bare Costs	Incl. O&P
2 Asbestos Workers	$30.45	$487.20	$50.65	$810.40	$28.58	$46.56
1 Equip. Oper. (crane)	29.35	234.80	46.70	373.60		
1 Equip. Oper. Oiler	24.05	192.40	38.25	306.00		
1 Hydraulic crane, 33 ton		694.95		764.45	21.72	23.89
32 L.H., Daily Totals		$1609.35		$2254.45	$50.30	$70.45
Crew A-11	Hr.	Daily	Hr.	Daily	Bare Costs	Incl. O&P
1 Asbestos Foreman	$30.95	$247.60	$51.50	$412.00	$30.51	$50.76
7 Asbestos Workers	30.45	1705.20	50.65	2836.40		
2 Chipping Hammers		25.90		28.50	.40	.45
64 L.H., Daily Totals		$1978.70		$3276.90	$30.91	$51.21
Crew A-12	Hr.	Daily	Hr.	Daily	Bare Costs	Incl. O&P
1 Asbestos Foreman	$30.95	$247.60	$51.50	$412.00	$30.51	$50.76
7 Asbestos Workers	30.45	1705.20	50.65	2836.40		
1 Large Prod. Vac. Loader		524.90		577.40	8.20	9.02
64 L.H., Daily Totals		$2477.70		$3825.80	$38.71	$59.78
Crew A-13	Hr.	Daily	Hr.	Daily	Bare Costs	Incl. O&P
1 Equip. Oper. (light)	$27.20	$217.60	$43.30	$346.40	$27.20	$43.30
1 Large Prod. Vac. Loader		524.90		577.40	65.61	72.17
8 L.H., Daily Totals		$742.50		$923.80	$92.81	$115.47

Crews

Crew No.	Bare Costs		Incl. Subs O & P		Cost Per Labor-Hour	
Crew B-1	Hr.	Daily	Hr.	Daily	Bare Costs	Incl. O&P
1 Labor Foreman (outside)	$23.45	$187.60	$39.25	$314.00	$22.12	$37.02
2 Laborers	21.45	343.20	35.90	574.40		
24 L.H., Daily Totals		$530.80		$888.40	$22.12	$37.02
Crew B-2	Hr.	Daily	Hr.	Daily	Bare Costs	Incl. O&P
1 Labor Foreman (outside)	$23.45	$187.60	$39.25	$314.00	$21.85	$36.57
4 Laborers	21.45	686.40	35.90	1148.80		
40 L.H., Daily Totals		$874.00		$1462.80	$21.85	$36.57
Crew B-3	Hr.	Daily	Hr.	Daily	Bare Costs	Incl. O&P
1 Labor Foreman (outside)	$23.45	$187.60	$39.25	$314.00	$23.16	$38.06
2 Laborers	21.45	343.20	35.90	574.40		
1 Equip. Oper. (med.)	28.40	227.20	45.20	361.60		
2 Truck Drivers (heavy)	22.10	353.60	36.05	576.80		
1 F.E. Loader, T.M., 2.5 C.Y.		865.10		951.60		
2 Dump Trucks, 16 Ton		884.50		972.95	36.45	40.10
48 L.H., Daily Totals		$2861.20		$3751.35	$59.61	$78.16
Crew B-3A	Hr.	Daily	Hr.	Daily	Bare Costs	Incl. O&P
4 Laborers	$21.45	$686.40	$35.90	$1148.80	$22.84	$37.76
1 Equip. Oper. (med.)	28.40	227.20	45.20	361.60		
1 Hyd. Excavator, 1.5 C.Y.		712.70		783.95	17.82	19.60
40 L.H., Daily Totals		$1626.30		$2294.35	$40.66	$57.36
Crew B-3B	Hr.	Daily	Hr.	Daily	Bare Costs	Incl. O&P
2 Laborers	$21.45	$343.20	$35.90	$574.40	$23.35	$38.26
1 Equip. Oper. (med.)	28.40	227.20	45.20	361.60		
1 Truck Drivers (heavy)	22.10	176.80	36.05	288.40		
1 Backhoe Loader, 80 H.P.		290.10		319.10		
1 Dump Trucks, 16 Ton		442.25		486.50	22.89	25.17
32 L.H., Daily Totals		$1479.55		$2030.00	$46.24	$63.43
Crew B-3C	Hr.	Daily	Hr.	Daily	Bare Costs	Incl. O&P
3 Laborers	$21.45	$514.80	$35.90	$861.60	$23.19	$38.23
1 Equip. Oper. (med.)	28.40	227.20	45.20	361.60		
1 F.E. Loader, 3.75 C.Y.		576.90		634.60	18.03	19.83
32 L.H., Daily Totals		$1318.90		$1857.80	$41.22	$58.06
Crew B-4	Hr.	Daily	Hr.	Daily	Bare Costs	Incl. O&P
1 Labor Foreman (outside)	$23.45	$187.60	$39.25	$314.00	$21.89	$36.48
4 Laborers	21.45	686.40	35.90	1148.80		
1 Truck Driver (heavy)	22.10	176.80	36.05	288.40		
1 Tractor, 4 x 2, 195 H.P.		324.05		356.45		
1 Platform Trailer		150.70		165.75	9.89	10.88
48 L.H., Daily Totals		$1525.55		$2273.40	$31.78	$47.36
Crew B-5	Hr.	Daily	Hr.	Daily	Bare Costs	Incl. O&P
1 Labor Foreman (outside)	$23.45	$187.60	$39.25	$314.00	$23.72	$39.04
4 Laborers	21.45	686.40	35.90	1148.80		
2 Equip. Oper. (med.)	28.40	454.40	45.20	723.20		
1 Air Compr., 250 C.F.M.		124.90		137.40		
2 Air Tools & Accessories		39.00		42.90		
2-50 Ft. Air Hoses, 1.5" Dia.		16.40		18.05		
1 F.E. Loader, T.M., 2.5 C.Y.		865.10		951.60	18.67	20.53
56 L.H., Daily Totals		$2373.80		$3335.95	$42.39	$59.57

Crew No.	Bare Costs		Incl. Subs O & P		Cost Per Labor-Hour	
Crew B-6	Hr.	Daily	Hr.	Daily	Bare Costs	Incl. O&P
2 Laborers	$21.45	$343.20	$35.90	$574.40	$23.37	$38.37
1 Equip. Oper. (light)	27.20	217.60	43.30	346.40		
1 Backhoe Loader, 48 H.P.		218.80		240.70	9.12	10.03
24 L.H., Daily Totals		$779.60		$1161.50	$32.49	$48.40
Crew B-7	Hr.	Daily	Hr.	Daily	Bare Costs	Incl. O&P
1 Labor Foreman (outside)	$23.45	$187.60	$39.25	$314.00	$22.94	$38.01
4 Laborers	21.45	686.40	35.90	1148.80		
1 Equip. Oper. (med.)	28.40	227.20	45.20	361.60		
1 Chipping Machine		214.10		235.50		
1 F.E. Loader, T.M., 2.5 C.Y.		865.10		951.60		
2 Chain Saws, 36"		106.10		116.70	24.69	27.16
48 L.H., Daily Totals		$2286.50		$3128.20	$47.63	$65.17
Crew B-7A	Hr.	Daily	Hr.	Daily	Bare Costs	Incl. O&P
2 Laborers	$21.45	$343.20	$35.90	$574.40	$23.37	$38.37
1 Equip. Oper. (light)	27.20	217.60	43.30	346.40		
1 Rake w/Tractor		218.90		240.80		
2 Chain Saws, 18"		54.60		60.05	11.40	12.54
24 L.H., Daily Totals		$834.30		$1221.65	$34.77	$50.91
Crew B-8	Hr.	Daily	Hr.	Daily	Bare Costs	Incl. O&P
1 Labor Foreman (outside)	$23.45	$187.60	$39.25	$314.00	$23.93	$38.98
2 Laborers	21.45	343.20	35.90	574.40		
2 Equip. Oper. (med.)	28.40	454.40	45.20	723.20		
1 Equip. Oper. Oiler	24.05	192.40	38.25	306.00		
2 Truck Drivers (heavy)	22.10	353.60	36.05	576.80		
1 Hyd. Crane, 25 Ton		549.35		604.30		
1 F.E. Loader, T.M., 2.5 C.Y.		865.10		951.60		
2 Dump Trucks, 16 Ton		884.50		972.95	35.92	39.51
64 L.H., Daily Totals		$3830.15		$5023.25	$59.85	$78.49
Crew B-9	Hr.	Daily	Hr.	Daily	Bare Costs	Incl. O&P
1 Labor Foreman (outside)	$23.45	$187.60	$39.25	$314.00	$21.85	$36.57
4 Laborers	21.45	686.40	35.90	1148.80		
1 Air Compr., 250 C.F.M.		124.90		137.40		
2 Air Tools & Accessories		39.00		42.90		
2-50 Ft. Air Hoses, 1.5" Dia.		16.40		18.05	4.51	4.96
40 L.H., Daily Totals		$1054.30		$1661.15	$26.36	$41.53
Crew B-9A	Hr.	Daily	Hr.	Daily	Bare Costs	Incl. O&P
2 Laborers	$21.45	$343.20	$35.90	$574.40	$21.67	$35.95
1 Truck Driver (heavy)	22.10	176.80	36.05	288.40		
1 Water Tanker		205.10		225.60		
1 Tractor		324.05		356.45		
2-50 Ft. Disch. Hoses		10.80		11.90	22.50	24.75
24 L.H., Daily Totals		$1059.95		$1456.75	$44.17	$60.70
Crew B-9B	Hr.	Daily	Hr.	Daily	Bare Costs	Incl. O&P
2 Laborers	$21.45	$343.20	$35.90	$574.40	$21.67	$35.95
1 Truck Driver (heavy)	22.10	176.80	36.05	288.40		
2-50 Ft. Disch. Hoses		10.80		11.90		
1 Water Tanker		205.10		225.60		
1 Tractor		324.05		356.45		
1 Pressure Washer		55.40		60.95	24.81	27.29
24 L.H., Daily Totals		$1115.35		$1517.70	$46.48	$63.24

Crews

Crew No.	Bare Costs		Incl. Subs O & P		Cost Per Labor-Hour	
Crew B-9C	Hr.	Daily	Hr.	Daily	Bare Costs	Incl. O&P
1 Labor Foreman (outside)	$23.45	$187.60	$39.25	$314.00	$21.85	$36.57
4 Laborers	21.45	686.40	35.90	1148.80		
1 Air Compr., 250 C.F.M.		124.90		137.40		
2-50 Ft. Air Hoses, 1.5" Dia.		16.40		18.05		
2 Breaker, Pavement, 60 lb.		39.00		42.90	4.51	4.96
40 L.H., Daily Totals		$1054.30		$1661.15	$26.36	$41.53
Crew B-10	Hr.	Daily	Hr.	Daily	Bare Costs	Incl. O&P
1 Equip. Oper. (med.)	$28.40	$227.20	$45.20	$361.60	$26.08	$42.10
.5 Laborer	21.45	85.80	35.90	143.60		
12 L.H., Daily Totals		$313.00		$505.20	$26.08	$42.10
Crew B-10A	Hr.	Daily	Hr.	Daily	Bare Costs	Incl. O&P
1 Equip. Oper. (med.)	$28.40	$227.20	$45.20	$361.60	$26.08	$42.10
.5 Laborer	21.45	85.80	35.90	143.60		
1 Roll. Compact., 2K Lbs.		93.05		102.35	7.75	8.53
12 L.H., Daily Totals		$406.05		$607.55	$33.83	$50.63
Crew B-10B	Hr.	Daily	Hr.	Daily	Bare Costs	Incl. O&P
1 Equip. Oper. (med.)	$28.40	$227.20	$45.20	$361.60	$26.08	$42.10
.5 Laborer	21.45	85.80	35.90	143.60		
1 Dozer, 200 H.P.		838.95		922.85	69.91	76.90
12 L.H., Daily Totals		$1151.95		$1428.05	$95.99	$119.00
Crew B-10C	Hr.	Daily	Hr.	Daily	Bare Costs	Incl. O&P
1 Equip. Oper. (med.)	$28.40	$227.20	$45.20	$361.60	$26.08	$42.10
.5 Laborer	21.45	85.80	35.90	143.60		
1 Dozer, 200 H.P.		838.95		922.85		
1 Vibratory Roller, Towed		112.90		124.20	79.32	87.25
12 L.H., Daily Totals		$1264.85		$1552.25	$105.40	$129.35
Crew B-10D	Hr.	Daily	Hr.	Daily	Bare Costs	Incl. O&P
1 Equip. Oper. (med.)	$28.40	$227.20	$45.20	$361.60	$26.08	$42.10
.5 Laborer	21.45	85.80	35.90	143.60		
1 Dozer, 200 H.P		838.95		922.85		
1 Sheepsft. Roller, Towed		124.90		137.40	80.32	88.35
12 L.H., Daily Totals		$1276.85		$1565.45	$106.40	$130.45
Crew B-10E	Hr.	Daily	Hr.	Daily	Bare Costs	Incl. O&P
1 Equip. Oper. (med.)	$28.40	$227.20	$45.20	$361.60	$26.08	$42.10
.5 Laborer	21.45	85.80	35.90	143.60		
1 Tandem Roller, 5 Ton		152.85		168.15	12.74	14.01
12 L.H., Daily Totals		$465.85		$673.35	$38.82	$56.11
Crew B-10F	Hr.	Daily	Hr.	Daily	Bare Costs	Incl. O&P
1 Equip. Oper. (med.)	$28.40	$227.20	$45.20	$361.60	$26.08	$42.10
.5 Laborer	21.45	85.80	35.90	143.60		
1 Tandem Roller, 10 Ton		245.10		269.60	20.43	22.47
12 L.H., Daily Totals		$558.10		$774.80	$46.51	$64.57
Crew B-10G	Hr.	Daily	Hr.	Daily	Bare Costs	Incl. O&P
1 Equip. Oper. (med.)	$28.40	$227.20	$45.20	$361.60	$26.08	$42.10
.5 Laborer	21.45	85.80	35.90	143.60		
1 Sheepsft. Roll., 130 H.P.		558.70		614.55	46.56	51.21
12 L.H., Daily Totals		$871.70		$1119.75	$72.64	$93.31

Crew No.	Bare Costs		Incl. Subs O & P		Cost Per Labor-Hour	
Crew B-10H	Hr.	Daily	Hr.	Daily	Bare Costs	Incl. O&P
1 Equip. Oper. (med.)	$28.40	$227.20	$45.20	$361.60	$26.08	$42.10
.5 Laborer	21.45	85.80	35.90	143.60		
1 Diaphr. Water Pump, 2"		29.15		32.05		
1-20 Ft. Suction Hose, 2"		6.50		7.15		
2-50 Ft. Disch. Hoses, 2"		8.80		9.70	3.70	4.07
12 L.H., Daily Totals		$357.45		$554.10	$29.78	$46.17
Crew B-10I	Hr.	Daily	Hr.	Daily	Bare Costs	Incl. O&P
1 Equip. Oper. (med.)	$28.40	$227.20	$45.20	$361.60	$26.08	$42.10
.5 Laborer	21.45	85.80	35.90	143.60		
1 Diaphr. Water Pump, 4"		64.40		70.85		
1-20 Ft. Suction Hose, 4"		12.50		13.75		
2-50 Ft. Disch. Hoses, 4"		17.00		18.70	7.83	8.61
12 L.H., Daily Totals		$406.90		$608.50	$33.91	$50.71
Crew B-10J	Hr.	Daily	Hr.	Daily	Bare Costs	Incl. O&P
1 Equip. Oper. (med.)	$28.40	$227.20	$45.20	$361.60	$26.08	$42.10
.5 Laborer	21.45	85.80	35.90	143.60		
1 Centr. Water Pump, 3"		37.90		41.70		
1-20 Ft. Suction Hose, 3"		9.50		10.45		
2-50 Ft. Disch. Hoses, 3"		10.80		11.90	4.85	5.34
12 L.H., Daily Totals		$371.20		$569.25	$30.93	$47.44
Crew B-10K	Hr.	Daily	Hr.	Daily	Bare Costs	Incl. O&P
1 Equip. Oper. (med.)	$28.40	$227.20	$45.20	$361.60	$26.08	$42.10
.5 Laborer	21.45	85.80	35.90	143.60		
1 Centr. Water Pump, 6"		159.45		175.40		
1-20 Ft. Suction Hose, 6"		21.50		23.65		
2-50 Ft. Disch. Hoses, 6"		39.00		42.90	18.33	20.16
12 L.H., Daily Totals		$532.95		$747.15	$44.41	$62.26
Crew B-10L	Hr.	Daily	Hr.	Daily	Bare Costs	Incl. O&P
1 Equip. Oper. (med.)	$28.40	$227.20	$45.20	$361.60	$26.08	$42.10
.5 Laborer	21.45	85.80	35.90	143.60		
1 Dozer, 75 H.P.		307.75		338.50	25.65	28.21
12 L.H., Daily Totals		$620.75		$843.70	$51.73	$70.31
Crew B-10M	Hr.	Daily	Hr.	Daily	Bare Costs	Incl. O&P
1 Equip. Oper. (med.)	$28.40	$227.20	$45.20	$361.60	$26.08	$42.10
.5 Laborer	21.45	85.80	35.90	143.60		
1 Dozer, 300 H.P.		1131.00		1244.10	94.25	103.68
12 L.H., Daily Totals		$1444.00		$1749.30	$120.33	$145.78
Crew B-10N	Hr.	Daily	Hr.	Daily	Bare Costs	Incl. O&P
1 Equip. Oper. (med.)	$28.40	$227.20	$45.20	$361.60	$26.08	$42.10
.5 Laborer	21.45	85.80	35.90	143.60		
1 F.E. Loader, T.M., 1.5 C.Y.		350.10		385.10	29.18	32.09
12 L.H., Daily Totals		$663.10		$890.30	$55.26	$74.19
Crew B-10O	Hr.	Daily	Hr.	Daily	Bare Costs	Incl. O&P
1 Equip. Oper. (med.)	$28.40	$227.20	$45.20	$361.60	$26.08	$42.10
.5 Laborer	21.45	85.80	35.90	143.60		
1 F.E. Loader, T.M., 2.25 C.Y.		510.40		561.45	42.53	46.79
12 L.H., Daily Totals		$823.40		$1066.65	$68.61	$88.89
Crew B-10P	Hr.	Daily	Hr.	Daily	Bare Costs	Incl. O&P
1 Equip. Oper. (med.)	$28.40	$227.20	$45.20	$361.60	$26.08	$42.10
.5 Laborer	21.45	85.80	35.90	143.60		
1 F.E. Loader, T.M., 2.5 C.Y.		865.10		951.60	72.09	79.30
12 L.H., Daily Totals		$1178.10		$1456.80	$98.17	$121.40

Crews

Crew No.	Bare Costs		Incl. Subs O & P		Cost Per Labor-Hour	
Crew B-10Q	Hr.	Daily	Hr.	Daily	Bare Costs	Incl. O&P
1 Equip. Oper. (med.)	$28.40	$227.20	$45.20	$361.60	$26.08	$42.10
.5 Laborer	21.45	85.80	35.90	143.60		
1 F.E. Loader, T.M., 5 C.Y.		1142.00		1256.20	95.17	104.68
12 L.H., Daily Totals		$1455.00		$1761.40	$121.25	$146.78
Crew B-10R	Hr.	Daily	Hr.	Daily	Bare Costs	Incl. O&P
1 Equip. Oper. (med.)	$28.40	$227.20	$45.20	$361.60	$26.08	$42.10
.5 Laborer	21.45	85.80	35.90	143.60		
1 F.E. Loader, W.M., 1 C.Y.		244.65		269.10	20.39	22.43
12 L.H., Daily Totals		$557.65		$774.30	$46.47	$64.53
Crew B-10S	Hr.	Daily	Hr.	Daily	Bare Costs	Incl. O&P
1 Equip. Oper. (med.)	$28.40	$227.20	$45.20	$361.60	$26.08	$42.10
.5 Laborer	21.45	85.80	35.90	143.60		
1 F.E. Loader, W.M., 1.5 C.Y.		320.10		352.10	26.68	29.34
12 L.H., Daily Totals		$633.10		$857.30	$52.76	$71.44
Crew B-10T	Hr.	Daily	Hr.	Daily	Bare Costs	Incl. O&P
1 Equip. Oper. (med.)	$28.40	$227.20	$45.20	$361.60	$26.08	$42.10
.5 Laborer	21.45	85.80	35.90	143.60		
1 F.E. Ldr, W.M., 2.5CY		450.50		495.55	37.54	41.30
12 L.H., Daily Totals		$763.50		$1000.75	$63.62	$83.40
Crew B-10U	Hr.	Daily	Hr.	Daily	Bare Costs	Incl. O&P
1 Equip. Oper. (med.)	$28.40	$227.20	$45.20	$361.60	$26.08	$42.10
.5 Laborer	21.45	85.80	35.90	143.60		
1 F.E. Loader, W.M., 5.5 C.Y.		926.50		1019.15	77.21	84.93
12 L.H., Daily Totals		$1239.50		$1524.35	$103.29	$127.03
Crew B-10V	Hr.	Daily	Hr.	Daily	Bare Costs	Incl. O&P
1 Equip. Oper. (med.)	$28.40	$227.20	$45.20	$361.60	$26.08	$42.10
.5 Laborer	21.45	85.80	35.90	143.60		
1 Dozer, 700 H.P.		2765.00		3041.50	230.42	253.46
12 L.H., Daily Totals		$3078.00		$3546.70	$256.50	$295.56
Crew B-10W	Hr.	Daily	Hr.	Daily	Bare Costs	Incl. O&P
1 Equip. Oper. (med.)	$28.40	$227.20	$45.20	$361.60	$26.08	$42.10
.5 Laborer	21.45	85.80	35.90	143.60		
1 Dozer, 105 H.P.		417.45		459.20	34.79	38.27
12 L.H., Daily Totals		$730.45		$964.40	$60.87	$80.37
Crew B-10X	Hr.	Daily	Hr.	Daily	Bare Costs	Incl. O&P
1 Equip. Oper. (med.)	$28.40	$227.20	$45.20	$361.60	$26.08	$42.10
.5 Laborer	21.45	85.80	35.90	143.60		
1 Dozer, 410 H.P.		1380.00		1518.00	115.00	126.50
12 L.H., Daily Totals		$1693.00		$2023.20	$141.08	$168.60
Crew B-10Y	Hr.	Daily	Hr.	Daily	Bare Costs	Incl. O&P
1 Equip. Oper. (med.)	$28.40	$227.20	$45.20	$361.60	$26.08	$42.10
.5 Laborer	21.45	85.80	35.90	143.60		
1 Vibratory Drum Roller		351.85		387.05	29.32	32.25
12 L.H., Daily Totals		$664.85		$892.25	$55.40	$74.35
Crew B-11	Hr.	Daily	Hr.	Daily	Bare Costs	Incl. O&P
1 Equipment Oper. (med.)	$28.40	$227.20	$45.20	$361.60	$24.93	$40.55
1 Laborer	21.45	171.60	35.90	287.20		
16 L.H., Daily Totals		$398.80		$648.80	$24.93	$40.55

Crew No.	Bare Costs		Incl. Subs O & P		Cost Per Labor-Hour	
Crew B-11A	Hr.	Daily	Hr.	Daily	Bare Costs	Incl. O&P
1 Equipment Oper. (med.)	$28.40	$227.20	$45.20	$361.60	$24.93	$40.55
1 Laborer	21.45	171.60	35.90	287.20		
1 Dozer, 200 H.P.		838.95		922.85	52.43	57.68
16 L.H., Daily Totals		$1237.75		$1571.65	$77.36	$98.23
Crew B-11B	Hr.	Daily	Hr.	Daily	Bare Costs	Incl. O&P
1 Equipment Oper. (med.)	$28.40	$227.20	$45.20	$361.60	$24.93	$40.55
1 Laborer	21.45	171.60	35.90	287.20		
1 Dozer, 200 H.P.		838.95		922.85		
1 Air Powered Tamper		14.80		16.30		
1 Air Compr. 365 C.F.M.		174.30		191.75		
2-50 Ft. Air Hoses, 1.5" Dia.		16.40		18.05	65.28	71.81
16 L.H., Daily Totals		$1443.25		$1797.75	$90.21	$112.36
Crew B-11C	Hr.	Daily	Hr.	Daily	Bare Costs	Incl. O&P
1 Equipment Oper. (med.)	$28.40	$227.20	$45.20	$361.60	$24.93	$40.55
1 Laborer	21.45	171.60	35.90	287.20		
1 Backhoe Loader, 48 H.P.		218.80		240.70	13.68	15.04
16 L.H., Daily Totals		$617.60		$889.50	$38.61	$55.59
Crew B-11K	Hr.	Daily	Hr.	Daily	Bare Costs	Incl. O&P
1 Equipment Oper. (med.)	$28.40	$227.20	$45.20	$361.60	$24.93	$40.55
1 Laborer	21.45	171.60	35.90	287.20		
1 Trencher, 8' D., 16" W.		535.90		589.50	33.49	36.84
16 L.H., Daily Totals		$934.70		$1238.30	$58.42	$77.39
Crew B-11L	Hr.	Daily	Hr.	Daily	Bare Costs	Incl. O&P
1 Equipment Oper. (med.)	$28.40	$227.20	$45.20	$361.60	$24.93	$40.55
1 Laborer	21.45	171.60	35.90	287.20		
1 Grader, 30,000 Lbs.		575.55		633.10	35.97	39.57
16 L.H., Daily Totals		$974.35		$1281.90	$60.90	$80.12
Crew B-11M	Hr.	Daily	Hr.	Daily	Bare Costs	Incl. O&P
1 Equipment Oper. (med.)	$28.40	$227.20	$45.20	$361.60	$24.93	$40.55
1 Laborer	21.45	171.60	35.90	287.20		
1 Backhoe Loader, 80 H.P.		290.10		319.10	18.13	19.94
16 L.H., Daily Totals		$688.90		$967.90	$43.06	$60.49
Crew B-12	Hr.	Daily	Hr.	Daily	Bare Costs	Incl. O&P
1 Equip. Oper. (crane)	$29.35	$234.80	$46.70	$373.60	$26.70	$42.48
1 Equip. Oper. Oiler	24.05	192.40	38.25	306.00		
16 L.H., Daily Totals		$427.20		$679.60	$26.70	$42.48
Crew B-12A	Hr.	Daily	Hr.	Daily	Bare Costs	Incl. O&P
1 Equip. Oper. (crane)	$29.35	$234.80	$46.70	$373.60	$26.70	$42.48
1 Equip. Oper. Oiler	24.05	192.40	38.25	306.00		
1 Hyd. Excavator, 1 C.Y.		547.60		602.35	34.23	37.65
16 L.H., Daily Totals		$974.80		$1281.95	$60.93	$80.13
Crew B-12B	Hr.	Daily	Hr.	Daily	Bare Costs	Incl. O&P
1 Equip. Oper. (crane)	$29.35	$234.80	$46.70	$373.60	$26.70	$42.48
1 Equip. Oper. Oiler	24.05	192.40	38.25	306.00		
1 Hyd. Excavator, 1.5 C.Y.		712.70		783.95	44.54	49.00
16 L.H., Daily Totals		$1139.90		$1463.55	$71.24	$91.48
Crew B-12C	Hr.	Daily	Hr.	Daily	Bare Costs	Incl. O&P
1 Equip. Oper. (crane)	$29.35	$234.80	$46.70	$373.60	$26.70	$42.48
1 Equip. Oper. Oiler	24.05	192.40	38.25	306.00		
1 Hyd. Excavator, 2 C.Y.		1023.00		1125.30	63.94	70.33
16 L.H., Daily Totals		$1450.20		$1804.90	$90.64	$112.81

Crews

Crew No.	Bare Costs		Incl. Subs O & P		Cost Per Labor-Hour	
Crew B-12D	Hr.	Daily	Hr.	Daily	Bare Costs	Incl. O&P
1 Equip. Oper. (crane)	$29.35	$234.80	$46.70	$373.60	$26.70	$42.48
1 Equip. Oper. Oiler	24.05	192.40	38.25	306.00		
1 Hyd. Excavator, 3.5 C.Y.		2156.00		2371.60	134.75	148.23
16 L.H., Daily Totals		$2583.20		$3051.20	$161.45	$190.71
Crew B-12E	Hr.	Daily	Hr.	Daily	Bare Costs	Incl. O&P
1 Equip. Oper. (crane)	$29.35	$234.80	$46.70	$373.60	$26.70	$42.48
1 Equip. Oper. Oiler	24.05	192.40	38.25	306.00		
1 Hyd. Excavator, .5 C.Y.		336.45		370.10	21.03	23.13
16 L.H., Daily Totals		$763.65		$1049.70	$47.73	$65.61
Crew B-12F	Hr.	Daily	Hr.	Daily	Bare Costs	Incl. O&P
1 Equip. Oper. (crane)	$29.35	$234.80	$46.70	$373.60	$26.70	$42.48
1 Equip. Oper. Oiler	24.05	192.40	38.25	306.00		
1 Hyd. Excavator, .75 C.Y.		449.10		494.00	28.07	30.88
16 L.H., Daily Totals		$876.30		$1173.60	$54.77	$73.36
Crew B-12G	Hr.	Daily	Hr.	Daily	Bare Costs	Incl. O&P
1 Equip. Oper. (crane)	$29.35	$234.80	$46.70	$373.60	$26.70	$42.48
1 Equip. Oper. Oiler	24.05	192.40	38.25	306.00		
1 Power Shovel, .5 C.Y.		472.00		519.20		
1 Clamshell Bucket, .5 C.Y		49.90		54.90	32.62	35.88
16 L.H., Daily Totals		$949.10		$1253.70	$59.32	$78.36
Crew B-12H	Hr.	Daily	Hr.	Daily	Bare Costs	Incl. O&P
1 Equip. Oper. (crane)	$29.35	$234.80	$46.70	$373.60	$26.70	$42.48
1 Equip. Oper. Oiler	24.05	192.40	38.25	306.00		
1 Power Shovel, 1 C.Y.		506.80		557.50		
1 Clamshell Bucket, 1 C.Y.		67.10		73.80	35.87	39.46
16 L.H., Daily Totals		$1001.10		$1310.90	$62.57	$81.94
Crew B-12I	Hr.	Daily	Hr.	Daily	Bare Costs	Incl. O&P
1 Equip. Oper. (crane)	$29.35	$234.80	$46.70	$373.60	$26.70	$42.48
1 Equip. Oper. Oiler	24.05	192.40	38.25	306.00		
1 Power Shovel, .75 C.Y.		491.60		540.75		
1 Dragline Bucket, .75 C.Y.		33.55		36.90	32.82	36.10
16 L.H., Daily Totals		$952.35		$1257.25	$59.52	$78.58
Crew B-12J	Hr.	Daily	Hr.	Daily	Bare Costs	Incl. O&P
1 Equip. Oper. (crane)	$29.35	$234.80	$46.70	$373.60	$26.70	$42.48
1 Equip. Oper. Oiler	24.05	192.40	38.25	306.00		
1 Gradall, 3 Ton, .5 C.Y.		636.75		700.40	39.80	43.78
16 L.H., Daily Totals		$1063.95		$1380.00	$66.50	$86.26
Crew B-12K	Hr.	Daily	Hr.	Daily	Bare Costs	Incl. O&P
1 Equip. Oper. (crane)	$29.35	$234.80	$46.70	$373.60	$26.70	$42.48
1 Equip. Oper. Oiler	24.05	192.40	38.25	306.00		
1 Gradall, 3 Ton, 1 C.Y.		805.75		886.35	50.36	55.40
16 L.H., Daily Totals		$1232.95		$1565.95	$77.06	$97.88
Crew B-12L	Hr.	Daily	Hr.	Daily	Bare Costs	Incl. O&P
1 Equip. Oper. (crane)	$29.35	$234.80	$46.70	$373.60	$26.70	$42.48
1 Equip. Oper. Oiler	24.05	192.40	38.25	306.00		
1 Power Shovel, .5 C.Y.		472.00		519.20		
1 F.E. Attachment, .5 C.Y.		55.05		60.55	32.94	36.23
16 L.H., Daily Totals		$954.25		$1259.35	$59.64	$78.71
Crew B-12M	Hr.	Daily	Hr.	Daily	Bare Costs	Incl. O&P
1 Equip. Oper. (crane)	$29.35	$234.80	$46.70	$373.60	$26.70	$42.48
1 Equip. Oper. Oiler	24.05	192.40	38.25	306.00		
1 Power Shovel, .75 C.Y.		491.60		540.75		
1 F.E. Attachment, .75 C.Y.		102.50		112.75	37.13	40.84
16 L.H., Daily Totals		$1021.30		$1333.10	$63.83	$83.32
Crew B-12N	Hr.	Daily	Hr.	Daily	Bare Costs	Incl. O&P
1 Equip. Oper. (crane)	$29.35	$234.80	$46.70	$373.60	$26.70	$42.48
1 Equip. Oper. Oiler	24.05	192.40	38.25	306.00		
1 Power Shovel, 1 C.Y.		506.80		557.50		
1 F.E. Attachment, 1 C.Y.		131.00		144.10	39.86	43.85
16 L.H., Daily Totals		$1065.00		$1381.20	$66.56	$86.33
Crew B-12O	Hr.	Daily	Hr.	Daily	Bare Costs	Incl. O&P
1 Equip. Oper. (crane)	$29.35	$234.80	$46.70	$373.60	$26.70	$42.48
1 Equip. Oper. Oiler	24.05	192.40	38.25	306.00		
1 Power Shovel, 1.5 C.Y.		704.30		774.75		
1 F.E. Attachment, 1.5 C.Y.		159.70		175.65	54.00	59.40
16 L.H., Daily Totals		$1291.20		$1630.00	$80.70	$101.88
Crew B-12P	Hr.	Daily	Hr.	Daily	Bare Costs	Incl. O&P
1 Equip. Oper. (crane)	$29.35	$234.80	$46.70	$373.60	$26.70	$42.48
1 Equip. Oper. Oiler	24.05	192.40	38.25	306.00		
1 Crawler Crane, 40 Ton		704.30		774.75		
1 Dragline Bucket, 1.5 C.Y.		48.15		52.95	47.03	51.73
16 L.H., Daily Totals		$1179.65		$1507.30	$73.73	$94.21
Crew B-12Q	Hr.	Daily	Hr.	Daily	Bare Costs	Incl. O&P
1 Equip. Oper. (crane)	$29.35	$234.80	$46.70	$373.60	$26.70	$42.48
1 Equip. Oper. Oiler	24.05	192.40	38.25	306.00		
1 Hyd. Excavator, 5/8 C.Y.		394.25		433.70	24.64	27.10
16 L.H., Daily Totals		$821.45		$1113.30	$51.34	$69.58
Crew B-12R	Hr.	Daily	Hr.	Daily	Bare Costs	Incl. O&P
1 Equip. Oper. (crane)	$29.35	$234.80	$46.70	$373.60	$26.70	$42.48
1 Equip. Oper. Oiler	24.05	192.40	38.25	306.00		
1 Hyd. Excavator, 1.5 C.Y.		712.70		783.95	44.54	49.00
16 L.H., Daily Totals		$1139.90		$1463.55	$71.24	$91.48
Crew B-12S	Hr.	Daily	Hr.	Daily	Bare Costs	Incl. O&P
1 Equip. Oper. (crane)	$29.35	$234.80	$46.70	$373.60	$26.70	$42.48
1 Equip. Oper. Oiler	24.05	192.40	38.25	306.00		
1 Hyd. Excavator, 2.5 C.Y.		1695.00		1864.50	105.94	116.53
16 L.H., Daily Totals		$2122.20		$2544.10	$132.64	$159.01
Crew B-12T	Hr.	Daily	Hr.	Daily	Bare Costs	Incl. O&P
1 Equip. Oper. (crane)	$29.35	$234.80	$46.70	$373.60	$26.70	$42.48
1 Equip. Oper. Oiler	24.05	192.40	38.25	306.00		
1 Crawler Crane, 75 Ton		929.30		1022.25		
1 F.E. Attachment, 3 C.Y.		300.15		330.15	76.84	84.52
16 L.H., Daily Totals		$1656.65		$2032.00	$103.54	$127.00
Crew B-12V	Hr.	Daily	Hr.	Daily	Bare Costs	Incl. O&P
1 Equip. Oper. (crane)	$29.35	$234.80	$46.70	$373.60	$26.70	$42.48
1 Equip. Oper. Oiler	24.05	192.40	38.25	306.00		
1 Crawler Crane, 75 Ton		929.30		1022.25		
1 Dragline Bucket, 3 C.Y.		82.70		90.95	63.25	69.58
16 L.H., Daily Totals		$1439.20		$1792.80	$89.95	$112.06

Crews

Crew No.	Bare Costs		Incl. Subs O & P		Cost Per Labor-Hour	
Crew B-13	Hr.	Daily	Hr.	Daily	Bare Costs	Incl. O&P
1 Labor Foreman (outside)	$23.45	$187.60	$39.25	$314.00	$23.24	$38.26
4 Laborers	21.45	686.40	35.90	1148.80		
1 Equip. Oper. (crane)	29.35	234.80	46.70	373.60		
1 Equip. Oper. Oiler	24.05	192.40	38.25	306.00		
1 Hyd. Crane, 25 Ton		549.35		604.30	9.81	10.79
56 L.H., Daily Totals		$1850.55		$2746.70	$33.05	$49.05
Crew B-13A	Hr.	Daily	Hr.	Daily	Bare Costs	Incl. O&P
1 Foreman	$23.45	$187.60	$39.25	$314.00	$23.91	$39.08
2 Laborers	21.45	343.20	35.90	574.40		
2 Equipment Operator	28.40	454.40	45.20	723.20		
2 Truck Drivers (heavy)	22.10	353.60	36.05	576.80		
1 Crane, 75 Ton		929.30		1022.25		
1 F.E. Ldr, 3.75 C.Y.		1142.00		1256.20		
2 Dump Trucks, 12 Ton		728.60		801.45	50.00	55.00
56 L.H., Daily Totals		$4138.70		$5268.30	$73.91	$94.08
Crew B-13B	Hr.	Daily	Hr.	Daily	Bare Costs	Incl. O&P
1 Labor Foreman (outside)	$23.45	$187.60	$39.25	$314.00	$23.24	$38.26
4 Laborers	21.45	686.40	35.90	1148.80		
1 Equip. Oper. (crane)	29.35	234.80	46.70	373.60		
1 Equip. Oper. Oiler	24.05	192.40	38.25	306.00		
1 Hyd. Crane, 55 Ton		793.10		872.40	14.16	15.58
56 L.H., Daily Totals		$2094.30		$3014.80	$37.40	$53.84
Crew B-13C	Hr.	Daily	Hr.	Daily	Bare Costs	Incl. O&P
1 Labor Foreman (outside)	$23.45	$187.60	$39.25	$314.00	$23.24	$38.26
4 Laborers	21.45	686.40	35.90	1148.80		
1 Equip. Oper. (crane)	29.35	234.80	46.70	373.60		
1 Equip. Oper. Oiler	24.05	192.40	38.25	306.00		
1 Crawler Crane, 100 Ton		1131.00		1244.10	20.20	22.22
56 L.H., Daily Totals		$2432.20		$3386.50	$43.44	$60.48
Crew B-14	Hr.	Daily	Hr.	Daily	Bare Costs	Incl. O&P
1 Labor Foreman (outside)	$23.45	$187.60	$39.25	$314.00	$22.74	$37.69
4 Laborers	21.45	686.40	35.90	1148.80		
1 Equip. Oper. (light)	27.20	217.60	43.30	346.40		
1 Backhoe Loader, 48 H.P.		218.80		240.70	4.56	5.01
48 L.H., Daily Totals		$1310.40		$2049.90	$27.30	$42.70
Crew B-15	Hr.	Daily	Hr.	Daily	Bare Costs	Incl. O&P
1 Equipment Oper. (med)	$28.40	$227.20	$45.20	$361.60	$23.81	$38.64
.5 Laborer	21.45	85.80	35.90	143.60		
2 Truck Drivers (heavy)	22.10	353.60	36.05	576.80		
2 Dump Trucks, 16 Ton		884.50		972.95		
1 Dozer, 200 H.P.		838.95		922.85	61.55	67.71
28 L.H., Daily Totals		$2390.05		$2977.80	$85.36	$106.35
Crew B-16	Hr.	Daily	Hr.	Daily	Bare Costs	Incl. O&P
1 Labor Foreman (outside)	$23.45	$187.60	$39.25	$314.00	$22.11	$36.78
2 Laborers	21.45	343.20	35.90	574.40		
1 Truck Driver (heavy)	22.10	176.80	36.05	288.40		
1 Dump Truck, 16 Ton		442.25		486.50	13.82	15.20
32 L.H., Daily Totals		$1149.85		$1663.30	$35.93	$51.98

Crew No.	Bare Costs		Incl. Subs O & P		Cost Per Labor-Hour	
Crew B-17	Hr.	Daily	Hr.	Daily	Bare Costs	Incl. O&P
2 Laborers	$21.45	$343.20	$35.90	$574.40	$23.05	$37.79
1 Equip. Oper. (light)	27.20	217.60	43.30	346.40		
1 Truck Driver (heavy)	22.10	176.80	36.05	288.40		
1 Backhoe Loader, 48 H.P.		218.80		240.70		
1 Dump Truck, 12 Ton		364.30		400.75	18.22	20.04
32 L.H., Daily Totals		$1320.70		$1850.65	$41.27	$57.83
Crew B-18	Hr.	Daily	Hr.	Daily	Bare Costs	Incl. O&P
1 Labor Foreman (outside)	$23.45	$187.60	$39.25	$314.00	$22.12	$37.02
2 Laborers	21.45	343.20	35.90	574.40		
1 Vibrating Compactor		52.00		57.20	2.17	2.38
24 L.H., Daily Totals		$582.80		$945.60	$24.29	$39.40
Crew B-19	Hr.	Daily	Hr.	Daily	Bare Costs	Incl. O&P
1 Pile Driver Foreman	$29.20	$233.60	$51.90	$415.20	$27.59	$47.12
4 Pile Drivers	27.20	870.40	48.35	1547.20		
2 Equip. Oper. (crane)	29.35	469.60	46.70	747.20		
1 Equip. Oper. Oiler	24.05	192.40	38.25	306.00		
1 Crane, 40 Ton & Access.		704.30		774.75		
60 L.F. Leads, 15K Ft. Lbs.		105.00		115.50		
1 Hammer, 15K Ft. Lbs.		321.75		353.95		
1 Air Compr., 600 C.F.M.		272.90		300.20		
2-50 Ft. Air Hoses, 3" Dia.		33.70		37.05	22.46	24.71
64 L.H., Daily Totals		$3203.65		$4597.05	$50.05	$71.83
Crew B-19A	Hr.	Daily	Hr.	Daily	Bare Costs	Incl. O&P
1 Pile Driver Foreman	$29.20	$233.60	$51.90	$415.20	$27.59	$47.12
4 Pile Drivers	27.20	870.40	48.35	1547.20		
2 Equip. Oper. (crane)	29.35	469.60	46.70	747.20		
1 Equip. Oper. Oiler	24.05	192.40	38.25	306.00		
1 Crawler Crane, 75 Ton		929.30		1022.25		
60 Leads, 25K ft.lbs		126.00		138.60		
1 Air Compressor, 750 CFM		288.55		317.40		
4-50 Ft. Air Hose, 3" Dia.		67.40		74.15	22.05	24.26
64 L.H., Daily Totals		$3177.25		$4568.00	$49.64	$71.38
Crew B-20	Hr.	Daily	Hr.	Daily	Bare Costs	Incl. O&P
1 Labor Foreman (out)	$23.45	$187.60	$39.25	$314.00	$24.32	$40.55
1 Skilled Worker	28.05	224.40	46.50	372.00		
1 Laborer	21.45	171.60	35.90	287.20		
24 L.H., Daily Totals		$583.60		$973.20	$24.32	$40.55
Crew B-20A	Hr.	Daily	Hr.	Daily	Bare Costs	Incl. O&P
1 Labor Foreman	$23.45	$187.60	$39.25	$314.00	$25.90	$41.75
1 Laborer	21.45	171.60	35.90	287.20		
1 Plumber	32.60	260.80	51.00	408.00		
1 Plumber Apprentice	26.10	208.80	40.85	326.80		
32 L.H., Daily Totals		$828.80		$1336.00	$25.90	$41.75
Crew B-21	Hr.	Daily	Hr.	Daily	Bare Costs	Incl. O&P
1 Labor Foreman (out)	$23.45	$187.60	$39.25	$314.00	$25.04	$41.43
1 Skilled Worker	28.05	224.40	46.50	372.00		
1 Laborer	21.45	171.60	35.90	287.20		
.5 Equip. Oper. (crane)	29.35	117.40	46.70	186.80		
.5 S.P. Crane, 5 Ton		135.73		149.30	4.85	5.33
28 L.H., Daily Totals		$836.73		$1309.30	$29.89	$46.76

Crews

Crew No.	Bare Costs		Incl. Subs O & P		Cost Per Labor-Hour	
Crew B-21A	Hr.	Daily	Hr.	Daily	Bare Costs	Incl. O&P
1 Labor Foreman	$23.45	$187.60	$39.25	$314.00	$26.59	$42.74
1 Laborer	21.45	171.60	35.90	287.20		
1 Plumber	32.60	260.80	51.00	408.00		
1 Plumber Apprentice	26.10	208.80	40.85	326.80		
1 Equip. Oper. (crane)	29.35	234.80	46.70	373.60		
1 S.P. Crane, 12 Ton		391.35		430.50	9.78	10.76
40 L.H., Daily Totals		$1454.95		$2140.10	$36.37	$53.50
Crew B-22	Hr.	Daily	Hr.	Daily	Bare Costs	Incl. O&P
1 Labor Foreman (out)	$23.45	$187.60	$39.25	$314.00	$25.32	$41.78
1 Skilled Worker	28.05	224.40	46.50	372.00		
1 Laborer	21.45	171.60	35.90	287.20		
.75 Equip. Oper. (crane)	29.35	176.10	46.70	280.20		
.75 S.P. Crane, 5 Ton		203.59		223.95	6.79	7.46
30 L.H., Daily Totals		$963.29		$1477.35	$32.11	$49.24
Crew B-22A	Hr.	Daily	Hr.	Daily	Bare Costs	Incl. O&P
1 Labor Foreman (out)	$23.45	$187.60	$39.25	$314.00	$24.51	$40.54
1 Skilled Worker	28.05	224.40	46.50	372.00		
2 Laborers	21.45	343.20	35.90	574.40		
.75 Equipment Oper. (crane)	29.35	176.10	46.70	280.20		
.75 Crane, 5 Ton		203.59		223.95		
1 Generator, 5 KW		45.90		50.50		
1 Butt Fusion Machine		.45		.50	6.58	7.24
38 L.H., Daily Totals		$1181.24		$1815.55	$31.09	$47.78
Crew B-22B	Hr.	Daily	Hr.	Daily	Bare Costs	Incl. O&P
1 Skilled Worker	$28.05	$224.40	$46.50	$372.00	$24.75	$41.20
1 Laborer	21.45	171.60	35.90	287.20		
1 Electro Fusion Machine		.45		.50	.03	.03
16 L.H., Daily Totals		$396.45		$659.70	$24.78	$41.23
Crew B-23	Hr.	Daily	Hr.	Daily	Bare Costs	Incl. O&P
1 Labor Foreman (outside)	$23.45	$187.60	$39.25	$314.00	$21.85	$36.57
4 Laborers	21.45	686.40	35.90	1148.80		
1 Drill Rig, Wells		1776.00		1953.60		
1 Light Truck, 3 Ton		179.45		197.40	48.89	53.77
40 L.H., Daily Totals		$2829.45		$3613.80	$70.74	$90.34
Crew B-23A	Hr.	Daily	Hr.	Daily	Bare Costs	Incl. O&P
1 Labor Foreman (outside)	$23.45	$187.60	$39.25	$314.00	$24.43	$40.12
1 Laborers	21.45	171.60	35.90	287.20		
1 Equip. Operator, medium	28.40	227.20	45.20	361.60		
1 Drill Rig, Wells		1776.00		1953.60		
1 Pickup Truck, 3/4 Ton		128.95		141.85	79.37	87.31
24 L.H., Daily Totals		$2491.35		$3058.25	$103.80	$127.43
Crew B-23B	Hr.	Daily	Hr.	Daily	Bare Costs	Incl. O&P
1 Labor Foreman (outside)	$23.45	$187.60	$39.25	$314.00	$24.43	$40.12
1 Laborers	21.45	171.60	35.90	287.20		
1 Equip. Operator, medium	28.40	227.20	45.20	361.60		
1 Drill Rig, Wells		1776.00		1953.60		
1 Pickup Truck, 3/4 Ton		128.95		141.85		
1 Pump, Cntfgl, 6"		159.45		175.40	86.02	94.62
24 L.H., Daily Totals		$2650.80		$3233.65	$110.45	$134.74
Crew B-24	Hr.	Daily	Hr.	Daily	Bare Costs	Incl. O&P
1 Cement Finisher	$26.15	$209.20	$41.65	$333.20	$24.97	$41.08
1 Laborer	21.45	171.60	35.90	287.20		
1 Carpenter	27.30	218.40	45.70	365.60		
24 L.H., Daily Totals		$599.20		$986.00	$24.97	$41.08

Crew No.	Bare Costs		Incl. Subs O & P		Cost Per Labor-Hour	
Crew B-25	Hr.	Daily	Hr.	Daily	Bare Costs	Incl. O&P
1 Labor Foreman	$23.45	$187.60	$39.25	$314.00	$23.53	$38.74
7 Laborers	21.45	1201.20	35.90	2010.40		
3 Equip. Oper. (med.)	28.40	681.60	45.20	1084.80		
1 Asphalt Paver, 130 H.P.		1299.00		1428.90		
1 Tandem Roller, 10 Ton		245.10		269.60		
1 Roller, Pneumatic Wheel		244.20		268.60	20.32	22.35
88 L.H., Daily Totals		$3858.70		$5376.30	$43.85	$61.09
Crew B-25B	Hr.	Daily	Hr.	Daily	Bare Costs	Incl. O&P
1 Labor Foreman	$23.45	$187.60	$39.25	$314.00	$23.93	$39.28
7 Laborers	21.45	1201.20	35.90	2010.40		
4 Equip. Oper. (medium)	28.40	908.80	45.20	1446.40		
1 Asphalt Paver, 130 H.P.		1299.00		1428.90		
2 Rollers, Steel Wheel		490.20		539.20		
1 Roller, Pneumatic Wheel		244.20		268.60	21.18	23.30
96 L.H., Daily Totals		$4331.00		$6007.50	$45.11	$62.58
Crew B-26	Hr.	Daily	Hr.	Daily	Bare Costs	Incl. O&P
1 Labor Foreman (outside)	$23.45	$187.60	$39.25	$314.00	$24.14	$40.13
6 Laborers	21.45	1029.60	35.90	1723.20		
2 Equip. Oper. (med.)	28.40	454.40	45.20	723.20		
1 Rodman (reinf.)	30.40	243.20	54.75	438.00		
1 Cement Finisher	26.15	209.20	41.65	333.20		
1 Grader, 30,000 Lbs.		575.55		633.10		
1 Paving Mach. & Equip.		1321.00		1453.10	21.55	23.71
88 L.H., Daily Totals		$4020.55		$5617.80	$45.69	$63.84
Crew B-27	Hr.	Daily	Hr.	Daily	Bare Costs	Incl. O&P
1 Labor Foreman (outside)	$23.45	$187.60	$39.25	$314.00	$21.95	$36.74
3 Laborers	21.45	514.80	35.90	861.60		
1 Berm Machine		70.30		77.35	2.20	2.42
32 L.H., Daily Totals		$772.70		$1252.95	$24.15	$39.16
Crew B-28	Hr.	Daily	Hr.	Daily	Bare Costs	Incl. O&P
2 Carpenters	$27.30	$436.80	$45.70	$731.20	$25.35	$42.43
1 Laborer	21.45	171.60	35.90	287.20		
24 L.H., Daily Totals		$608.40		$1018.40	$25.35	$42.43
Crew B-29	Hr.	Daily	Hr.	Daily	Bare Costs	Incl. O&P
1 Labor Foreman (outside)	$23.45	$187.60	$39.25	$314.00	$23.24	$38.26
4 Laborers	21.45	686.40	35.90	1148.80		
1 Equip. Oper. (crane)	29.35	234.80	46.70	373.60		
1 Equip. Oper. Oiler	24.05	192.40	38.25	306.00		
1 Gradall, 3 Ton, 1/2 C.Y.		636.75		700.40	11.37	12.51
56 L.H., Daily Totals		$1937.95		$2842.80	$34.61	$50.77
Crew B-30	Hr.	Daily	Hr.	Daily	Bare Costs	Incl. O&P
1 Equip. Oper. (med.)	$28.40	$227.20	$45.20	$361.60	$24.20	$39.10
2 Truck Drivers (heavy)	22.10	353.60	36.05	576.80		
1 Hyd. Excavator, 1.5 C.Y.		712.70		783.95		
2 Dump Trucks, 16 Ton		884.50		972.95	66.55	73.21
24 L.H., Daily Totals		$2178.00		$2695.30	$90.75	$112.31
Crew B-31	Hr.	Daily	Hr.	Daily	Bare Costs	Incl. O&P
1 Labor Foreman (outside)	$23.45	$187.60	$39.25	$314.00	$23.02	$38.53
3 Laborers	21.45	514.80	35.90	861.60		
1 Carpenter	27.30	218.40	45.70	365.60		
1 Air Compr., 250 C.F.M.		124.90		137.40		
1 Sheeting Driver		11.20		12.30		
2-50 Ft. Air Hoses, 1.5" Dia.		16.40		18.05	3.81	4.19
40 L.H., Daily Totals		$1073.30		$1708.95	$26.83	$42.72

Crews

Crew No.	Bare Costs		Incl. Subs O & P		Cost Per Labor-Hour	
Crew B-32	Hr.	Daily	Hr.	Daily	Bare Costs	Incl. O&P
1 Laborer	$21.45	$171.60	$35.90	$287.20	$26.66	$42.88
3 Equip. Oper. (med.)	28.40	681.60	45.20	1084.80		
1 Grader, 30,000 Lbs.		575.55		633.10		
1 Tandem Roller, 10 Ton		245.10		269.60		
1 Dozer, 200 H.P.		838.95		922.85	51.86	57.05
32 L.H., Daily Totals		$2512.80		$3197.55	$78.52	$99.93
Crew B-32A	Hr.	Daily	Hr.	Daily	Bare Costs	Incl. O&P
1 Laborer	$21.45	$171.60	$35.90	$287.20	$26.08	$42.10
2 Equip. Oper. (medium)	28.40	454.40	45.20	723.20		
1 Grader, 30,000 Lbs.		575.55		633.10		
1 Roller, Vibratory, 29,000 Lbs.		421.75		463.95	41.55	45.71
24 L.H., Daily Totals		$1623.30		$2107.45	$67.63	$87.81
Crew B-32B	Hr.	Daily	Hr.	Daily	Bare Costs	Incl. O&P
1 Laborer	$21.45	$171.60	$35.90	$287.20	$26.08	$42.10
2 Equip. Oper. (medium)	28.40	454.40	45.20	723.20		
1 Dozer, 200 H.P.		838.95		922.85		
1 Roller, Vibratory, 29,000 Lbs.		421.75		463.95	52.53	57.78
24 L.H., Daily Totals		$1886.70		$2397.20	$78.61	$99.88
Crew B-32C	Hr.	Daily	Hr.	Daily	Bare Costs	Incl. O&P
1 Labor Foreman	$23.45	$187.60	$39.25	$314.00	$25.26	$41.11
2 Laborers	21.45	343.20	35.90	574.40		
3 Equip. Oper. (medium)	28.40	681.60	45.20	1084.80		
1 Grader, 30,000 Lbs.		575.55		633.10		
1 Roller, Steel Wheel		245.10		269.60		
1 Dozer, 200 H.P.		838.95		922.85	34.58	38.03
48 L.H., Daily Totals		$2872.00		$3798.75	$59.84	$79.14
Crew B-33	Hr.	Daily	Hr.	Daily	Bare Costs	Incl. O&P
1 Equip. Oper. (med.)	$28.40	$227.20	$45.20	$361.60	$26.41	$42.54
.5 Laborer	21.45	85.80	35.90	143.60		
.25 Equip. Oper. (med.)	28.40	56.80	45.20	90.40		
14 L.H., Daily Totals		$369.80		$595.60	$26.41	$42.54
Crew B-33A	Hr.	Daily	Hr.	Daily	Bare Costs	Incl. O&P
1 Equip. Oper. (med.)	$28.40	$227.20	$45.20	$361.60	$26.41	$42.54
.5 Laborer	21.45	85.80	35.90	143.60		
.25 Equip. Oper. (med.)	28.40	56.80	45.20	90.40		
1 Scraper, Towed, 7 C.Y.		77.50		85.25		
1 Dozer, 300 H.P.		1131.00		1244.10		
.25 Dozer, 300 H.P.		282.75		311.00	106.52	117.17
14 L.H., Daily Totals		$1861.05		$2235.95	$132.93	$159.71
Crew B-33B	Hr.	Daily	Hr.	Daily	Bare Costs	Incl. O&P
1 Equip. Oper. (med.)	$28.40	$227.20	$45.20	$361.60	$26.41	$42.54
.5 Laborer	21.45	85.80	35.90	143.60		
.25 Equip. Oper. (med.)	28.40	56.80	45.20	90.40		
1 Scraper, Towed, 10 C.Y.		202.45		222.70		
1 Dozer, 300 H.P.		1131.00		1244.10		
.25 Dozer, 300 H.P.		282.75		311.00	115.44	126.99
14 L.H., Daily Totals		$1986.00		$2373.40	$141.85	$169.53

Crew No.	Bare Costs		Incl. Subs O & P		Cost Per Labor-Hour	
Crew B-33C	Hr.	Daily	Hr.	Daily	Bare Costs	Incl. O&P
1 Equip. Oper. (med.)	$28.40	$227.20	$45.20	$361.60	$26.41	$42.54
.5 Laborer	21.45	85.80	35.90	143.60		
.25 Equip. Oper. (med.)	28.40	56.80	45.20	90.40		
1 Scraper, Towed, 12 C.Y.		202.45		222.70		
1 Dozer, 300 H.P.		1131.00		1244.10		
.25 Dozer, 300 H.P.		282.75		311.00	115.44	126.99
14 L.H., Daily Totals		$1986.00		$2373.40	$141.85	$169.53
Crew B-33D	Hr.	Daily	Hr.	Daily	Bare Costs	Incl. O&P
1 Equip. Oper. (med.)	$28.40	$227.20	$45.20	$361.60	$26.41	$42.54
.5 Laborer	21.45	85.80	35.90	143.60		
.25 Equip. Oper. (med.)	28.40	56.80	45.20	90.40		
1 S.P. Scraper, 14 C.Y.		1617.00		1778.70		
.25 Dozer, 300 H.P.		282.75		311.00	135.70	149.27
14 L.H., Daily Totals		$2269.55		$2685.30	$162.11	$191.81
Crew B-33E	Hr.	Daily	Hr.	Daily	Bare Costs	Incl. O&P
1 Equip. Oper. (med.)	$28.40	$227.20	$45.20	$361.60	$26.41	$42.54
.5 Laborer	21.45	85.80	35.90	143.60		
.25 Equip. Oper. (med.)	28.40	56.80	45.20	90.40		
1 S.P. Scraper, 24 C.Y.		1912.00		2103.20		
.25 Dozer, 300 H.P.		282.75		311.00	156.77	172.44
14 L.H., Daily Totals		$2564.55		$3009.80	$183.18	$214.98
Crew B-33F	Hr.	Daily	Hr.	Daily	Bare Costs	Incl. O&P
1 Equip. Oper. (med.)	$28.40	$227.20	$45.20	$361.60	$26.41	$42.54
.5 Laborer	21.45	85.80	35.90	143.60		
.25 Equip. Oper. (med.)	28.40	56.80	45.20	90.40		
1 Elev. Scraper, 11 C.Y.		688.55		757.40		
.25 Dozer, 300 H.P.		282.75		311.00	69.38	76.32
14 L.H., Daily Totals		$1341.10		$1664.00	$95.79	$118.86
Crew B-33G	Hr.	Daily	Hr.	Daily	Bare Costs	Incl. O&P
1 Equip. Oper. (med.)	$28.40	$227.20	$45.20	$361.60	$26.41	$42.54
.5 Laborer	21.45	85.80	35.90	143.60		
.25 Equip. Oper. (med.)	28.40	56.80	45.20	90.40		
1 Elev. Scraper, 20 C.Y.		984.55		1083.00		
.25 Dozer, 300 H.P.		282.75		311.00	90.52	99.57
14 L.H., Daily Totals		$1637.10		$1989.60	$116.93	$142.11
Crew B-34A	Hr.	Daily	Hr.	Daily	Bare Costs	Incl. O&P
1 Truck Driver (heavy)	$22.10	$176.80	$36.05	$288.40	$22.10	$36.05
1 Dump Truck, 12 Ton		364.30		400.75	45.54	50.09
8 L.H., Daily Totals		$541.10		$689.15	$67.64	$86.14
Crew B-34B	Hr.	Daily	Hr.	Daily	Bare Costs	Incl. O&P
1 Truck Driver (heavy)	$22.10	$176.80	$36.05	$288.40	$22.10	$36.05
1 Dump Truck, 16 Ton		442.25		486.50	55.28	60.81
8 L.H., Daily Totals		$619.05		$774.90	$77.38	$96.86
Crew B-34C	Hr.	Daily	Hr.	Daily	Bare Costs	Incl. O&P
1 Truck Driver (heavy)	$22.10	$176.80	$36.05	$288.40	$22.10	$36.05
1 Truck Tractor, 40 Ton		426.30		468.95		
1 Dump Trailer, 16.5 C.Y.		132.60		145.85	69.86	76.85
8 L.H., Daily Totals		$735.70		$903.20	$91.96	$112.90

Crews

Crew No.	Bare Costs		Incl. Subs O & P		Cost Per Labor-Hour	
Crew B-34D	Hr.	Daily	Hr.	Daily	Bare Costs	Incl. O&P
1 Truck Driver (heavy)	$22.10	$176.80	$36.05	$288.40	$22.10	$36.05
1 Truck Tractor, 40 Ton		426.30		468.95		
1 Dump Trailer, 20 C.Y.		135.10		148.60	70.18	77.19
8 L.H., Daily Totals		$738.20		$905.95	$92.28	$113.24
Crew B-34E	Hr.	Daily	Hr.	Daily	Bare Costs	Incl. O&P
1 Truck Driver (heavy)	$22.10	$176.80	$36.05	$288.40	$22.10	$36.05
1 Truck, Off Hwy., 25 Ton		699.00		768.90	87.38	96.11
8 L.H., Daily Totals		$875.80		$1057.30	$109.48	$132.16
Crew B-34F	Hr.	Daily	Hr.	Daily	Bare Costs	Incl. O&P
1 Truck Driver (heavy)	$22.10	$176.80	$36.05	$288.40	$22.10	$36.05
1 Truck, Off Hwy., 22 C.Y.		1038.00		1141.80	129.75	142.73
8 L.H., Daily Totals		$1214.80		$1430.20	$151.85	$178.78
Crew B-34G	Hr.	Daily	Hr.	Daily	Bare Costs	Incl. O&P
1 Truck Driver (heavy)	$22.10	$176.80	$36.05	$288.40	$22.10	$36.05
1 Truck, Off Hwy., 34 C.Y.		1400.00		1540.00	175.00	192.50
8 L.H., Daily Totals		$1576.80		$1828.40	$197.10	$228.55
Crew B-34H	Hr.	Daily	Hr.	Daily	Bare Costs	Incl. O&P
1 Truck Driver (heavy)	$22.10	$176.80	$36.05	$288.40	$22.10	$36.05
1 Truck, Off Hwy., 42 C.Y.		1598.00		1757.80	199.75	219.73
8 L.H., Daily Totals		$1774.80		$2046.20	$221.85	$255.78
Crew B-34J	Hr.	Daily	Hr.	Daily	Bare Costs	Incl. O&P
1 Truck Driver (heavy)	$22.10	$176.80	$36.05	$288.40	$22.10	$36.05
1 Truck, Off Hwy., 60 C.Y.		2238.00		2461.80	279.75	307.73
8 L.H., Daily Totals		$2414.80		$2750.20	$301.85	$343.78
Crew B-34K	Hr.	Daily	Hr.	Daily	Bare Costs	Incl. O&P
1 Truck Driver (heavy)	$22.10	$176.80	$36.05	$288.40	$22.10	$36.05
1 Truck Tractor, 240 H.P.		530.20		583.20		
1 Low Bed Trailer		383.75		422.15	114.24	125.67
8 L.H., Daily Totals		$1090.75		$1293.75	$136.34	$161.72
Crew B-35	Hr.	Daily	Hr.	Daily	Bare Costs	Incl. O&P
1 Laborer Foreman (out)	$23.45	$187.60	$39.25	$314.00	$26.49	$42.93
1 Skilled Worker	28.05	224.40	46.50	372.00		
1 Welder (plumber)	32.60	260.80	51.00	408.00		
1 Laborer	21.45	171.60	35.90	287.20		
1 Equip. Oper. (crane)	29.35	234.80	46.70	373.60		
1 Equip. Oper. Oiler	24.05	192.40	38.25	306.00		
1 Electric Welding Mach.		49.70		54.65		
1 Hyd. Excavator, .75 C.Y.		449.10		494.00	10.39	11.43
48 L.H., Daily Totals		$1770.40		$2609.45	$36.88	$54.36
Crew B-35A	Hr.	Daily	Hr.	Daily	Bare Costs	Incl. O&P
1 Laborer Foreman (out)	$23.45	$187.60	$39.25	$314.00	$25.77	$41.93
2 Laborers	21.45	343.20	35.90	574.40		
1 Skilled Worker	28.05	224.40	46.50	372.00		
1 Welder (plumber)	32.60	260.80	51.00	408.00		
1 Equip. Oper. (crane)	29.35	234.80	46.70	373.60		
1 Equip. Oper. Oiler	24.05	192.40	38.25	306.00		
1 Welder, 300 amp		82.35		90.60		
1 Crane, 75 Ton		929.30		1022.25	18.07	19.87
56 L.H., Daily Totals		$2454.85		$3460.85	$43.84	$61.80

Crew No.	Bare Costs		Incl. Subs O & P		Cost Per Labor-Hour	
Crew B-36	Hr.	Daily	Hr.	Daily	Bare Costs	Incl. O&P
1 Labor Foreman (outside)	$23.45	$187.60	$39.25	$314.00	$24.63	$40.29
2 Laborers	21.45	343.20	35.90	574.40		
2 Equip. Oper. (med.)	28.40	454.40	45.20	723.20		
1 Dozer, 200 H.P.		838.95		922.85		
1 Aggregate Spreader		71.05		78.15		
1 Tandem Roller, 10 Ton		245.10		269.60	28.88	31.77
40 L.H., Daily Totals		$2140.30		$2882.20	$53.51	$72.06
Crew B-36A	Hr.	Daily	Hr.	Daily	Bare Costs	Incl. O&P
1 Labor Foreman	$23.45	$187.60	$39.25	$314.00	$25.71	$41.69
2 Laborers	21.45	343.20	35.90	574.40		
4 Equip. Oper. (med.)	28.40	908.80	45.20	1446.40		
1 Dozer, 200 H.P.		838.95		922.85		
1 Aggregate Spreader		71.05		78.15		
1 Roller, Steel Wheel		245.10		269.60		
1 Roller, Pneumatic Wheel		244.20		268.60	24.99	27.49
56 L.H., Daily Totals		$2838.90		$3874.00	$50.70	$69.18
Crew B-36B	Hr.	Daily	Hr.	Daily	Bare Costs	Incl. O&P
1 Labor Foreman	$23.45	$187.60	$39.25	$314.00	$25.26	$40.99
2 Laborers	21.45	343.20	35.90	574.40		
4 Equip. Oper. (medium)	28.40	908.80	45.20	1446.40		
1 Truck Driver, Heavy	22.10	176.80	36.05	288.40		
1 Grader, 30,000 Lbs.		575.55		633.10		
1 F.E. Loader, crl, 1.5 C.Y.		399.70		439.65		
1 Dozer, 300 H.P.		1131.00		1244.10		
1 Roller, vibratory		421.75		463.95		
1 Truck, Tractor, 240 H.P.		530.20		583.20		
1 Water Tanker, 5000 Gal.		205.10		225.60	50.99	56.09
64 L.H., Daily Totals		$4879.70		$6212.80	$76.25	$97.08
Crew B-37	Hr.	Daily	Hr.	Daily	Bare Costs	Incl. O&P
1 Labor Foreman (outside)	$23.45	$187.60	$39.25	$314.00	$22.74	$37.69
4 Laborers	21.45	686.40	35.90	1148.80		
1 Equip. Oper. (light)	27.20	217.60	43.30	346.40		
1 Tandem Roller, 5 Ton		152.85		168.15	3.18	3.50
48 L.H., Daily Totals		$1244.45		$1977.35	$25.92	$41.19
Crew B-38	Hr.	Daily	Hr.	Daily	Bare Costs	Incl. O&P
1 Labor Foreman (outside)	$23.45	$187.60	$39.25	$314.00	$24.39	$39.91
2 Laborers	21.45	343.20	35.90	574.40		
1 Equip. Oper. (light)	27.20	217.60	43.30	346.40		
1 Equip. Oper. (medium)	28.40	227.20	45.20	361.60		
1 Backhoe Loader, 48 H.P.		218.80		240.70		
1 Demol.Hammer,(1200 l		180.15		198.15		
1 F.E. Loader (170 H.P.)		576.90		634.60		
1 Pavt. Rem. Bucket		44.45		48.90	25.51	28.06
40 L.H., Daily Totals		$1995.90		$2718.75	$49.90	$67.97
Crew B-39	Hr.	Daily	Hr.	Daily	Bare Costs	Incl. O&P
1 Labor Foreman (outside)	$23.45	$187.60	$39.25	$314.00	$22.74	$37.69
4 Laborers	21.45	686.40	35.90	1148.80		
1 Equip. Oper. (light)	27.20	217.60	43.30	346.40		
1 Air Compr., 250 C.F.M.		124.90		137.40		
2 Air Tools & Accessories		39.00		42.90		
2-50 Ft. Air Hoses, 1.5" Dia.		16.40		18.05	3.76	4.13
48 L.H., Daily Totals		$1271.90		$2007.55	$26.50	$41.82

Crews

Crew No.	Bare Costs		Incl. Subs O & P		Cost Per Labor-Hour	
Crew B-40	Hr.	Daily	Hr.	Daily	Bare Costs	Incl. O&P
1 Pile Driver Foreman	$29.20	$233.60	$51.90	$415.20	$27.59	$47.12
4 Pile Drivers	27.20	870.40	48.35	1547.20		
2 Equip. Oper. (crane)	29.35	469.60	46.70	747.20		
1 Equip. Oper. Oiler	24.05	192.40	38.25	306.00		
1 Crane, 40 Ton		704.30		774.75		
1 Vibratory Hammer & Gen.		1219.00		1340.90	30.05	33.06
64 L.H., Daily Totals		$3689.30		$5131.25	$57.64	$80.18
Crew B-41	Hr.	Daily	Hr.	Daily	Bare Costs	Incl. O&P
1 Labor Foreman (outside)	$23.45	$187.60	$39.25	$314.00	$22.29	$37.11
4 Laborers	21.45	686.40	35.90	1148.80		
.25 Equip. Oper. (crane)	29.35	58.70	46.70	93.40		
.25 Equip. Oper. Oiler	24.05	48.10	38.25	76.50		
.25 Crawler Crane, 40 Ton		176.07		193.70	4.00	4.40
44 L.H., Daily Totals		$1156.87		$1826.40	$26.29	$41.51
Crew B-42	Hr.	Daily	Hr.	Daily	Bare Costs	Incl. O&P
1 Labor Foreman (outside)	$23.45	$187.60	$39.25	$314.00	$24.16	$40.76
4 Laborers	21.45	686.40	35.90	1148.80		
1 Equip. Oper. (crane)	29.35	234.80	46.70	373.60		
1 Equip. Oper. Oiler	24.05	192.40	38.25	306.00		
1 Welder	30.60	244.80	58.25	466.00		
1 Hyd. Crane, 25 Ton		549.35		604.30		
1 Gas Welding Machine		82.35		90.60		
1 Horz. Boring Csg. Mch.		490.70		539.75	17.54	19.29
64 L.H., Daily Totals		$2668.40		$3843.05	$41.70	$60.05
Crew B-43	Hr.	Daily	Hr.	Daily	Bare Costs	Incl. O&P
1 Labor Foreman (outside)	$23.45	$187.60	$39.25	$314.00	$23.53	$38.65
3 Laborers	21.45	514.80	35.90	861.60		
1 Equip. Oper. (crane)	29.35	234.80	46.70	373.60		
1 Equip. Oper. Oiler	24.05	192.40	38.25	306.00		
1 Drill Rig & Augers		1776.00		1953.60	37.00	40.70
48 L.H., Daily Totals		$2905.60		$3808.80	$60.53	$79.35
Crew B-44	Hr.	Daily	Hr.	Daily	Bare Costs	Incl. O&P
1 Pile Driver Foreman	$29.20	$233.60	$51.90	$415.20	$27.27	$46.83
4 Pile Drivers	27.20	870.40	48.35	1547.20		
2 Equip. Oper. (crane)	29.35	469.60	46.70	747.20		
1 Laborer	21.45	171.60	35.90	287.20		
1 Crane, 40 Ton, & Access.		704.30		774.75		
45 L.F. Leads, 15K Ft. Lbs.		78.75		86.65	12.24	13.46
64 L.H., Daily Totals		$2528.25		$3858.20	$39.51	$60.29
Crew B-45	Hr.	Daily	Hr.	Daily	Bare Costs	Incl. O&P
1 Equip. Oper. (med.)	$28.40	$227.20	$45.20	$361.60	$25.25	$40.63
1 Truck Driver (heavy)	22.10	176.80	36.05	288.40		
1 Dist. Tank Truck, 3K Gal.		364.95		401.45		
1 Tractor, 4 x 2, 250 H.P.		380.00		418.00	46.56	51.22
16 L.H., Daily Totals		$1148.95		$1469.45	$71.81	$91.85
Crew B-46	Hr.	Daily	Hr.	Daily	Bare Costs	Incl. O&P
1 Pile Driver Foreman	$29.20	$233.60	$51.90	$415.20	$24.66	$42.72
2 Pile Drivers	27.20	435.20	48.35	773.60		
3 Laborers	21.45	514.80	35.90	861.60		
1 Chain Saw, 36" Long		53.05		58.35	1.11	1.22
48 L.H., Daily Totals		$1236.65		$2108.75	$25.77	$43.94

Crew No.	Bare Costs		Incl. Subs O & P		Cost Per Labor-Hour	
Crew B-47	Hr.	Daily	Hr.	Daily	Bare Costs	Incl. O&P
1 Blast Foreman	$23.45	$187.60	$39.25	$314.00	$24.03	$39.48
1 Driller	21.45	171.60	35.90	287.20		
1 Equip. Oper. (light)	27.20	217.60	43.30	346.40		
1 Crawler Type Drill, 4"		311.55		342.70		
1 Air Compr., 600 C.F.M.		272.90		300.20		
2-50 Ft. Air Hoses, 3" Dia.		33.70		37.05	25.76	28.33
24 L.H., Daily Totals		$1194.95		$1627.55	$49.79	$67.81
Crew B-47A	Hr.	Daily	Hr.	Daily	Bare Costs	Incl. O&P
1 Drilling Foreman	$23.45	$187.60	$39.25	$314.00	$25.62	$41.40
1 Equip. Oper. (heavy)	29.35	234.80	46.70	373.60		
1 Oiler	24.05	192.40	38.25	306.00		
1 Quarry Drill		482.05		530.25	20.09	22.09
24 L.H., Daily Totals		$1096.85		$1523.85	$45.71	$63.49
Crew B-47C	Hr.	Daily	Hr.	Daily	Bare Costs	Incl. O&P
1 Laborer	$21.45	$171.60	$35.90	$287.20	$24.33	$39.60
1 Equip. Oper. (light)	27.20	217.60	43.30	346.40		
1 Air Compressor, 750 CFM		288.55		317.40		
2-50' Air Hose, 3"		33.70		37.05		
1 Air Track Drill, 4"		311.55		342.70	39.61	43.57
16 L.H., Daily Totals		$1023.00		$1330.75	$63.94	$83.17
Crew B-47E	Hr.	Daily	Hr.	Daily	Bare Costs	Incl. O&P
1 Laborer Forman	$23.45	$187.60	$39.25	$314.00	$21.95	$36.74
3 Laborers	21.45	514.80	35.90	861.60		
1 Truck, Flatbed, 3 ton		179.45		197.40	5.61	6.17
32 L.H., Daily Totals		$881.85		$1373.00	$27.56	$42.91
Crew B-48	Hr.	Daily	Hr.	Daily	Bare Costs	Incl. O&P
1 Labor Foreman (outside)	$23.45	$187.60	$39.25	$314.00	$24.06	$39.31
3 Laborers	21.45	514.80	35.90	861.60		
1 Equip. Oper. (crane)	29.35	234.80	46.70	373.60		
1 Equip. Oper. Oiler	24.05	192.40	38.25	306.00		
1 Equip. Oper. (light)	27.20	217.60	43.30	346.40		
1 Centr. Water Pump, 6"		159.45		175.40		
1-20 Ft. Suction Hose, 6"		21.50		23.65		
1-50 Ft. Disch. Hose, 6"		19.50		21.45		
1 Drill Rig & Augers		1776.00		1953.60	35.29	38.82
56 L.H., Daily Totals		$3323.65		$4375.70	$59.35	$78.13
Crew B-49	Hr.	Daily	Hr.	Daily	Bare Costs	Incl. O&P
1 Labor Foreman (outside)	$23.45	$187.60	$39.25	$314.00	$25.11	$41.53
3 Laborers	21.45	514.80	35.90	861.60		
2 Equip. Oper. (crane)	29.35	469.60	46.70	747.20		
2 Equip. Oper. Oilers	24.05	384.80	38.25	612.00		
1 Equip. Oper. (light)	27.20	217.60	43.30	346.40		
2 Pile Drivers	27.20	435.20	48.35	773.60		
1 Hyd. Crane, 25 Ton		549.35		604.30		
1 Centr. Water Pump, 6"		159.45		175.40		
1-20 Ft. Suction Hose, 6"		21.50		23.65		
1-50 Ft. Disch. Hose, 6"		19.50		21.45		
1 Drill Rig & Augers		1776.00		1953.60	28.70	31.57
88 L.H., Daily Totals		$4735.40		$6433.20	$53.81	$73.10

Crews

Crew No.	Bare Costs		Incl. Subs O & P		Cost Per Labor-Hour	
Crew B-50	Hr.	Daily	Hr.	Daily	Bare Costs	Incl. O&P
2 Pile Driver Foremen	$29.20	$467.20	$51.90	$830.40	$26.34	$45.23
6 Pile Drivers	27.20	1305.60	48.35	2320.80		
2 Equip. Oper. (crane)	29.35	469.60	46.70	747.20		
1 Equip. Oper. Oiler	24.05	192.40	38.25	306.00		
3 Laborers	21.45	514.80	35.90	861.60		
1 Crane, 40 Ton		704.30		774.75		
60 L.F. Leads, 15K Ft. Lbs.		105.00		115.50		
1 Hammer, 15K Ft. Lbs.		321.75		353.95		
1 Air Compr., 600 C.F.M.		272.90		300.20		
2-50 Ft. Air Hoses, 3" Dia.		33.70		37.05		
1 Chain Saw, 36" Long		53.05		58.35	13.31	14.64
112 L.H., Daily Totals		$4440.30		$6705.80	$39.65	$59.87
Crew B-51	Hr.	Daily	Hr.	Daily	Bare Costs	Incl. O&P
1 Labor Foreman (outside)	$23.45	$187.60	$39.25	$314.00	$21.83	$36.38
4 Laborers	21.45	686.40	35.90	1148.80		
1 Truck Driver (light)	21.75	174.00	35.45	283.60		
1 Light Truck, 1.5 Ton		171.95		189.15	3.58	3.94
48 L.H., Daily Totals		$1219.95		$1935.55	$25.41	$40.32
Crew B-52	Hr.	Daily	Hr.	Daily	Bare Costs	Incl. O&P
1 Carpenter Foreman	$29.30	$234.40	$49.05	$392.40	$25.21	$42.01
1 Carpenter	27.30	218.40	45.70	365.60		
3 Laborers	21.45	514.80	35.90	861.60		
1 Cement Finisher	26.15	209.20	41.65	333.20		
.5 Rodman (reinf.)	30.40	121.60	54.75	219.00		
.5 Equip. Oper. (med.)	28.40	113.60	45.20	180.80		
.5 F.E. Ldr., T.M., 2.5 C.Y.		432.55		475.80	7.72	8.50
56 L.H., Daily Totals		$1844.55		$2828.40	$32.93	$50.51
Crew B-53	Hr.	Daily	Hr.	Daily	Bare Costs	Incl. O&P
1 Equip. Oper. (light)	$27.20	$217.60	$43.30	$346.40	$27.20	$43.30
1 Trencher, Chain, 12 H.P.		97.30		107.05	12.16	13.38
8 L.H., Daily Totals		$314.90		$453.45	$39.36	$56.68
Crew B-54	Hr.	Daily	Hr.	Daily	Bare Costs	Incl. O&P
1 Equip. Oper. (light)	$27.20	$217.60	$43.30	$346.40	$27.20	$43.30
1 Trencher, Chain, 40 H.P.		210.90		232.00	26.36	29.00
8 L.H., Daily Totals		$428.50		$578.40	$53.56	$72.30
Crew B-54A	Hr.	Daily	Hr.	Daily	Bare Costs	Incl. O&P
.17 Labor Forman	$23.45	$31.89	$39.25	$53.38	$27.68	$44.34
1 Equipment Operator (med.)	28.40	227.20	45.20	361.60		
1 Wheel Trencher, 67HP		399.35		439.30	42.67	46.93
9.36 L.H., Daily Totals		$658.44		$854.28	$70.35	$91.27
Crew B-54B	Hr.	Daily	Hr.	Daily	Bare Costs	Incl. O&P
.25 Labor Foreman	$23.45	$46.90	$39.25	$78.50	$27.41	$44.01
1 Equipment Operator (med.)	28.40	227.20	45.20	361.60		
1 Wheel Trencher, 150HP		565.20		621.70	56.52	62.17
10 L.H., Daily Totals		$839.30		$1061.80	$83.93	$106.18
Crew B-55	Hr.	Daily	Hr.	Daily	Bare Costs	Incl. O&P
2 Laborers	$21.45	$343.20	$35.90	$574.40	$21.55	$35.75
1 Truck Driver (light)	21.75	174.00	35.45	283.60		
1 Auger, 4" to 36" Dia		459.30		505.25		
1 Flatbed 3 Ton Truck		179.45		197.40	26.61	29.28
24 L.H., Daily Totals		$1155.95		$1560.65	$48.16	$65.03

Crew No.	Bare Costs		Incl. Subs O & P		Cost Per Labor-Hour	
Crew B-56	Hr.	Daily	Hr.	Daily	Bare Costs	Incl. O&P
1 Laborer	$21.45	$171.60	$35.90	$287.20	$24.33	$39.60
1 Equip. Oper. (light)	27.20	217.60	43.30	346.40		
1 Crawler Type Drill, 4"		311.55		342.70		
1 Air Compr., 600 C.F.M.		272.90		300.20		
1-50 Ft. Air Hose, 3" Dia.		16.85		18.55	37.58	41.34
16 L.H., Daily Totals		$990.50		$1295.05	$61.91	$80.94
Crew B-57	Hr.	Daily	Hr.	Daily	Bare Costs	Incl. O&P
1 Labor Foreman (outside)	$23.45	$187.60	$39.25	$314.00	$24.49	$39.88
2 Laborers	21.45	343.20	35.90	574.40		
1 Equip. Oper. (crane)	29.35	234.80	46.70	373.60		
1 Equip. Oper. (light)	27.20	217.60	43.30	346.40		
1 Equip. Oper. Oiler	24.05	192.40	38.25	306.00		
1 Power Shovel, 1 C.Y.		506.80		557.50		
1 Clamshell Bucket, 1 C.Y.		67.10		73.80		
1 Centr. Water Pump, 6"		159.45		175.40		
1-20 Ft. Suction Hose, 6"		21.50		23.65		
20-50 Ft. Disch. Hoses, 6"		390.00		429.00	23.85	26.24
48 L.H., Daily Totals		$2320.45		$3173.75	$48.34	$66.12
Crew B-58	Hr.	Daily	Hr.	Daily	Bare Costs	Incl. O&P
2 Laborers	$21.45	$343.20	$35.90	$574.40	$23.37	$38.37
1 Equip. Oper. (light)	27.20	217.60	43.30	346.40		
1 Backhoe Loader, 48 H.P.		218.80		240.70		
1 Small Helicopter		3510.00		3861.00	155.37	170.90
24 L.H., Daily Totals		$4289.60		$5022.50	$178.74	$209.27
Crew B-59	Hr.	Daily	Hr.	Daily	Bare Costs	Incl. O&P
1 Truck Driver (heavy)	$22.10	$176.80	$36.05	$288.40	$22.10	$36.05
1 Truck, 30 Ton		324.05		356.45		
1 Water tank, 5000 Gal.		205.10		225.60	66.14	72.76
8 L.H., Daily Totals		$705.95		$870.45	$88.24	$108.81
Crew B-60	Hr.	Daily	Hr.	Daily	Bare Costs	Incl. O&P
1 Labor Foreman (outside)	$23.45	$187.60	$39.25	$314.00	$24.88	$40.37
2 Laborers	21.45	343.20	35.90	574.40		
1 Equip. Oper. (crane)	29.35	234.80	46.70	373.60		
2 Equip. Oper. (light)	27.20	435.20	43.30	692.80		
1 Equip. Oper. Oiler	24.05	192.40	38.25	306.00		
1 Crawler Crane, 40 Ton		704.30		774.75		
45 L.F. Leads, 15K Ft. Lbs.		78.75		86.65		
1 Backhoe Loader, 48 H.P.		218.80		240.70	17.89	19.68
56 L.H., Daily Totals		$2395.05		$3362.90	$42.77	$60.05
Crew B-61	Hr.	Daily	Hr.	Daily	Bare Costs	Incl. O&P
1 Labor Foreman (outside)	$23.45	$187.60	$39.25	$314.00	$23.00	$38.05
3 Laborers	21.45	514.80	35.90	861.60		
1 Equip. Oper. (light)	27.20	217.60	43.30	346.40		
1 Cement Mixer, 2 C.Y.		259.45		285.40		
1 Air Compr., 160 C.F.M.		97.40		107.15	8.92	9.81
40 L.H., Daily Totals		$1276.85		$1914.55	$31.92	$47.86
Crew B-62	Hr.	Daily	Hr.	Daily	Bare Costs	Incl. O&P
2 Laborers	$21.45	$343.20	$35.90	$574.40	$23.37	$38.37
1 Equip. Oper. (light)	27.20	217.60	43.30	346.40		
1 Loader, Skid Steer		111.25		122.40	4.64	5.10
24 L.H., Daily Totals		$672.05		$1043.20	$28.01	$43.47

Crews

Crew No.	Bare Costs		Incl. Subs O & P		Cost Per Labor-Hour	
Crew B-63	Hr.	Daily	Hr.	Daily	Bare Costs	Incl. O&P
4 Laborers	$21.45	$686.40	$35.90	$1148.80	$22.60	$37.38
1 Equip. Oper. (light)	27.20	217.60	43.30	346.40		
1 Loader, Skid Steer		111.25		122.40	2.78	3.06
40 L.H., Daily Totals		$1015.25		$1617.60	$25.38	$40.44
Crew B-64	Hr.	Daily	Hr.	Daily	Bare Costs	Incl. O&P
1 Laborer	$21.45	$171.60	$35.90	$287.20	$21.60	$35.68
1 Truck Driver (light)	21.75	174.00	35.45	283.60		
1 Power Mulcher (small)		114.95		126.45		
1 Light Truck, 1.5 Ton		171.95		189.15	17.93	19.72
16 L.H., Daily Totals		$632.50		$886.40	$39.53	$55.40
Crew B-65	Hr.	Daily	Hr.	Daily	Bare Costs	Incl. O&P
1 Laborer	$21.45	$171.60	$35.90	$287.20	$21.60	$35.68
1 Truck Driver (light)	21.75	174.00	35.45	283.60		
1 Power Mulcher (large)		282.35		310.60		
1 Light Truck, 1.5 Ton		171.95		189.15	28.39	31.23
16 L.H., Daily Totals		$799.90		$1070.55	$49.99	$66.91
Crew B-66	Hr.	Daily	Hr.	Daily	Bare Costs	Incl. O&P
1 Equip. Oper. (light)	$27.20	$217.60	$43.30	$346.40	$27.20	$43.30
1 Backhoe Ldr. w/Attchmt.		200.50		220.55	25.06	27.57
8 L.H., Daily Totals		$418.10		$566.95	$52.26	$70.87
Crew B-67	Hr.	Daily	Hr.	Daily	Bare Costs	Incl. O&P
1 Millwright	$28.75	$230.00	$45.85	$366.80	$27.98	$44.58
1 Equip. Oper. (light)	27.20	217.60	43.30	346.40		
1 Forklift		171.10		188.20	10.69	11.76
16 L.H., Daily Totals		$618.70		$901.40	$38.67	$56.34
Crew B-68	Hr.	Daily	Hr.	Daily	Bare Costs	Incl. O&P
2 Millwrights	$28.75	$460.00	$45.85	$733.60	$28.23	$45.00
1 Equip. Oper. (light)	27.20	217.60	43.30	346.40		
1 Forklift		171.10		188.20	7.13	7.84
24 L.H., Daily Totals		$848.70		$1268.20	$35.36	$52.84
Crew B-69	Hr.	Daily	Hr.	Daily	Bare Costs	Incl. O&P
1 Labor Foreman (outside)	$23.45	$187.60	$39.25	$314.00	$23.53	$38.65
3 Laborers	21.45	514.80	35.90	861.60		
1 Equip Oper. (crane)	29.35	234.80	46.70	373.60		
1 Equip Oper. Oiler	24.05	192.40	38.25	306.00		
1 Truck Crane, 80 Ton		1098.00		1207.80	22.88	25.16
48 L.H., Daily Totals		$2227.60		$3063.00	$46.41	$63.81
Crew B-69A	Hr.	Daily	Hr.	Daily	Bare Costs	Incl. O&P
1 Labor Foreman	$23.45	$187.60	$39.25	$314.00	$23.73	$38.97
3 Laborers	21.45	514.80	35.90	861.60		
1 Equip. Oper. (medium)	28.40	227.20	45.20	361.60		
1 Concrete Finisher	26.15	209.20	41.65	333.20		
1 Curb Paver		453.90		499.30	9.46	10.40
48 L.H., Daily Totals		$1592.70		$2369.70	$33.19	$49.37
Crew B-69B	Hr.	Daily	Hr.	Daily	Bare Costs	Incl. O&P
1 Labor Foreman	$23.45	$187.60	$39.25	$314.00	$23.73	$38.97
3 Laborers	21.45	514.80	35.90	861.60		
1 Equip. Oper. (medium)	28.40	227.20	45.20	361.60		
1 Cement Finisher	26.15	209.20	41.65	333.20		
1 Curb/Gutter Paver		905.75		996.35	18.87	20.76
48 L.H., Daily Totals		$2044.55		$2866.75	$42.60	$59.73

Crew No.	Bare Costs		Incl. Subs O & P		Cost Per Labor-Hour	
Crew B-70	Hr.	Daily	Hr.	Daily	Bare Costs	Incl. O&P
1 Labor Foreman (outside)	$23.45	$187.60	$39.25	$314.00	$24.71	$40.36
3 Laborers	21.45	514.80	35.90	861.60		
3 Equip. Oper. (med.)	28.40	681.60	45.20	1084.80		
1 Motor Grader, 30,000 Lb.		575.55		633.10		
1 Grader Attach., Ripper		62.90		69.20		
1 Road Sweeper, S.P.		194.30		213.75		
1 F.E. Loader, 1-3/4 C.Y.		320.10		352.10	20.59	22.65
56 L.H., Daily Totals		$2536.85		$3528.55	$45.30	$63.01
Crew B-71	Hr.	Daily	Hr.	Daily	Bare Costs	Incl. O&P
1 Labor Foreman (outside)	$23.45	$187.60	$39.25	$314.00	$24.71	$40.36
3 Laborers	21.45	514.80	35.90	861.60		
3 Equip. Oper. (med.)	28.40	681.60	45.20	1084.80		
1 Pvmt. Profiler, 450 H.P.		3431.00		3774.10		
1 Road Sweeper, S.P.		194.30		213.75		
1 F.E. Loader, 1-3/4 C.Y.		320.10		352.10	70.45	77.50
56 L.H., Daily Totals		$5329.40		$6600.35	$95.16	$117.86
Crew B-72	Hr.	Daily	Hr.	Daily	Bare Costs	Incl. O&P
1 Labor Foreman (outside)	$23.45	$187.60	$39.25	$314.00	$25.18	$40.97
3 Laborers	21.45	514.80	35.90	861.60		
4 Equip. Oper. (med.)	28.40	908.80	45.20	1446.40		
1 Pvmt. Profiler, 450 H.P.		3431.00		3774.10		
1 Hammermill, 250 H.P.		1176.00		1293.60		
1 Windrow Loader		919.85		1011.85		
1 Mix Paver 165 H.P.		1435.00		1578.50		
1 Roller, Pneu. Tire, 12 T.		244.20		268.60	112.59	123.85
64 L.H., Daily Totals		$8817.25		$10548.65	$137.77	$164.82
Crew B-73	Hr.	Daily	Hr.	Daily	Bare Costs	Incl. O&P
1 Labor Foreman (outside)	$23.45	$187.60	$39.25	$314.00	$26.04	$42.13
2 Laborers	21.45	343.20	35.90	574.40		
5 Equip. Oper. (med.)	28.40	1136.00	45.20	1808.00		
1 Road Mixer, 310 H.P.		993.15		1092.45		
1 Roller, Tandem, 12 Ton		245.10		269.60		
1 Hammermill, 250 H.P.		1176.00		1293.60		
1 Motor Grader, 30,000 Lb.		575.55		633.10		
.5 F.E. Loader, 1-3/4 C.Y.		160.05		176.05		
.5 Truck, 30 Ton		162.02		178.25		
.5 Water Tank 5000 Gal.		102.55		112.80	53.35	58.69
64 L.H., Daily Totals		$5081.22		$6452.25	$79.39	$100.82
Crew B-74	Hr.	Daily	Hr.	Daily	Bare Costs	Incl. O&P
1 Labor Foreman (outside)	$23.45	$187.60	$39.25	$314.00	$25.34	$41.01
1 Laborer	21.45	171.60	35.90	287.20		
4 Equip. Oper. (med.)	28.40	908.80	45.20	1446.40		
2 Truck Drivers (heavy)	22.10	353.60	36.05	576.80		
1 Motor Grader, 30,000 Lb.		575.55		633.10		
1 Grader Attach., Ripper		62.90		69.20		
2 Stabilizers, 310 H.P.		1394.10		1533.50		
1 Flatbed Truck, 3 Ton		179.45		197.40		
1 Chem. Spreader, Towed		99.30		109.25		
1 Vibr. Roller, 29,000 Lb.		421.75		463.95		
1 Water Tank 5000 Gal.		205.10		225.60		
1 Truck, 30 Ton		324.05		356.45	50.97	56.07
64 L.H., Daily Totals		$4883.80		$6212.85	$76.31	$97.08

Crews

Crew No.	Bare Costs		Incl. Subs O & P		Cost Per Labor-Hour	
Crew B-75	Hr.	Daily	Hr.	Daily	Bare Costs	Incl. O&P
1 Labor Foreman (outside)	$23.45	$187.60	$39.25	$314.00	$25.80	$41.71
1 Laborer	21.45	171.60	35.90	287.20		
4 Equip. Oper. (med.)	28.40	908.80	45.20	1446.40		
1 Truck Driver (heavy)	22.10	176.80	36.05	288.40		
1 Motor Grader, 30,000 Lb.		575.55		633.10		
1 Grader Attach., Ripper		62.90		69.20		
2 Stabilizers, 310 H.P.		1394.10		1533.50		
1 Dist. Truck, 3000 Gal.		364.95		401.45		
1 Vibr. Roller, 29,000 Lb.		421.75		463.95	50.34	55.38
56 L.H., Daily Totals		$4264.05		$5437.20	$76.14	$97.09
Crew B-76	Hr.	Daily	Hr.	Daily	Bare Costs	Incl. O&P
1 Dock Builder Foreman	$29.20	$233.60	$51.90	$415.20	$27.55	$47.26
5 Dock Builders	27.20	1088.00	48.35	1934.00		
2 Equip. Oper. (crane)	29.35	469.60	46.70	747.20		
1 Equip. Oper. Oiler	24.05	192.40	38.25	306.00		
1 Crawler Crane, 50 Ton		844.70		929.15		
1 Barge, 400 Ton		452.65		497.90		
1 Hammer, 15K Ft. Lbs.		321.75		353.95		
60 L.F. Leads, 15K Ft. Lbs.		105.00		115.50		
1 Air Compr., 600 C.F.M.		272.90		300.20		
2-50 Ft. Air Hoses, 3" Dia.		33.70		37.05	28.20	31.02
72 L.H., Daily Totals		$4014.30		$5636.15	$55.75	$78.28
Crew B-77	Hr.	Daily	Hr.	Daily	Bare Costs	Incl. O&P
1 Labor Foreman	$23.45	$187.60	$39.25	$314.00	$21.91	$36.48
3 Laborers	21.45	514.80	35.90	861.60		
1 Truck Driver (light)	21.75	174.00	35.45	283.60		
1 Crack Cleaner, 25 H.P.		76.90		84.60		
1 Crack Filler, Trailer Mtd.		144.35		158.80		
1 Flatbed Truck, 3 Ton		179.45		197.40	10.02	11.02
40 L.H., Daily Totals		$1277.10		$1900.00	$31.93	$47.50
Crew B-78	Hr.	Daily	Hr.	Daily	Bare Costs	Incl. O&P
1 Labor Foreman	$23.45	$187.60	$39.25	$314.00	$21.83	$36.38
4 Laborers	21.45	686.40	35.90	1148.80		
1 Truck Driver (light)	21.75	174.00	35.45	283.60		
1 Paint Striper, S.P.		203.75		224.15		
1 Flatbed Truck, 3 Ton		179.45		197.40		
1 Pickup Truck, 3/4 Ton		128.95		141.85	10.67	11.74
48 L.H., Daily Totals		$1560.15		$2309.80	$32.50	$48.12
Crew B-79	Hr.	Daily	Hr.	Daily	Bare Costs	Incl. O&P
1 Labor Foreman	$23.45	$187.60	$39.25	$314.00	$21.91	$36.48
3 Laborers	21.45	514.80	35.90	861.60		
1 Truck Driver (light)	21.75	174.00	35.45	283.60		
1 Thermo. Striper, T.M.		243.70		268.05		
1 Flatbed Truck, 3 Ton		179.45		197.40		
2 Pickup Truck, 3/4 Ton		257.90		283.70	17.03	18.73
40 L.H., Daily Totals		$1557.45		$2208.35	$38.94	$55.21
Crew B-80	Hr.	Daily	Hr.	Daily	Bare Costs	Incl. O&P
1 Labor Foreman	$23.45	$187.60	$39.25	$314.00	$23.46	$38.48
1 Laborer	21.45	171.60	35.90	287.20		
1 Truck Driver (light)	21.75	174.00	35.45	283.60		
1 Equip. Oper. (light)	27.20	217.60	43.30	346.40		
1 Flatbed Truck, 3 Ton		179.45		197.40		
1 Fence Post Auger, TM		360.00		396.00	16.86	18.54
32 L.H., Daily Totals		$1290.25		$1824.60	$40.32	$57.02

Crew No.	Bare Costs		Incl. Subs O & P		Cost Per Labor-Hour	
Crew B-80A	Hr.	Daily	Hr.	Daily	Bare Costs	Incl. O&P
3 Laborer	$21.45	$514.80	$35.90	$861.60	$21.45	$35.90
1 Flatbed Truck, 3 Ton		179.45		197.40	7.48	8.22
24 L.H., Daily Totals		$694.25		$1059.00	$28.93	$44.12
Crew B-80B	Hr.	Daily	Hr.	Daily	Bare Costs	Incl. O&P
3 Laborer	$21.45	$514.80	$35.90	$861.60	$22.89	$37.75
1 Equip. Oper. (light)	27.20	217.60	43.30	346.40		
1 Crane, flatbed mnt		282.80		311.10	8.84	9.72
32 L.H., Daily Totals		$1015.20		$1519.10	$31.73	$47.47
Crew B-81	Hr.	Daily	Hr.	Daily	Bare Costs	Incl. O&P
1 Laborer	$21.45	$171.60	$35.90	$287.20	$23.98	$39.05
1 Equip. Oper. (med.)	28.40	227.20	45.20	361.60		
1 Truck Driver (heavy)	22.10	176.80	36.05	288.40		
1 Hydromulcher, T.M.		281.75		309.95		
1 Tractor Truck, 4x2		324.05		356.45	25.24	27.77
24 L.H., Daily Totals		$1181.40		$1603.60	$49.22	$66.82
Crew B-82	Hr.	Daily	Hr.	Daily	Bare Costs	Incl. O&P
1 Laborer	$21.45	$171.60	$35.90	$287.20	$24.33	$39.60
1 Equip. Oper. (light)	27.20	217.60	43.30	346.40		
1 Horiz. Borer, 6 H.P.		47.80		52.60	2.99	3.29
16 L.H., Daily Totals		$437.00		$686.20	$27.32	$42.89
Crew B-83	Hr.	Daily	Hr.	Daily	Bare Costs	Incl. O&P
1 Tugboat Captain	$28.40	$227.20	$45.20	$361.60	$24.93	$40.55
1 Tugboat Hand	21.45	171.60	35.90	287.20		
1 Tugboat, 250 H.P.		438.50		482.35	27.41	30.15
16 L.H., Daily Totals		$837.30		$1131.15	$52.34	$70.70
Crew B-84	Hr.	Daily	Hr.	Daily	Bare Costs	Incl. O&P
1 Equip. Oper. (med.)	$28.40	$227.20	$45.20	$361.60	$28.40	$45.20
1 Rotary Mower/Tractor		208.50		229.35	26.06	28.67
8 L.H., Daily Totals		$435.70		$590.95	$54.46	$73.87
Crew B-85	Hr.	Daily	Hr.	Daily	Bare Costs	Incl. O&P
3 Laborers	$21.45	$514.80	$35.90	$861.60	$22.97	$37.79
1 Equip. Oper. (med.)	28.40	227.20	45.20	361.60		
1 Truck Driver (heavy)	22.10	176.80	36.05	288.40		
1 Aerial Lift Truck		569.50		626.45		
1 Brush Chipper, 130 H.P.		214.10		235.50		
1 Pruning Saw, Rotary		24.15		26.55	20.19	22.21
40 L.H., Daily Totals		$1726.55		$2400.10	$43.16	$60.00
Crew B-86	Hr.	Daily	Hr.	Daily	Bare Costs	Incl. O&P
1 Equip. Oper. (med.)	$28.40	$227.20	$45.20	$361.60	$28.40	$45.20
1 Stump Chipper, S.P.		162.40		178.65	20.30	22.33
8 L.H., Daily Totals		$389.60		$540.25	$48.70	$67.53
Crew B-86A	Hr.	Daily	Hr.	Daily	Bare Costs	Incl. O&P
1 Equip. Oper. (medium)	$28.40	$227.20	$45.20	$361.60	$28.40	$45.20
1 Grader, 30,000 Lbs.		575.55		633.10	71.94	79.14
8 L.H., Daily Totals		$802.75		$994.70	$100.34	$124.34
Crew B-86B	Hr.	Daily	Hr.	Daily	Bare Costs	Incl. O&P
1 Equip. Oper. (medium)	$28.40	$227.20	$45.20	$361.60	$28.40	$45.20
1 Dozer, 200 H.P.		838.95		922.85	104.87	115.36
8 L.H., Daily Totals		$1066.15		$1284.45	$133.27	$160.56

Crews

Crew No.	Bare Costs		Incl. Subs O & P		Cost Per Labor-Hour	

Crew B-87	Hr.	Daily	Hr.	Daily	Bare Costs	Incl. O&P
1 Laborer	$21.45	$171.60	$35.90	$287.20	$27.01	$43.34
4 Equip. Oper. (med.)	28.40	908.80	45.20	1446.40		
2 Feller Bunchers, 50 H.P.		779.80		857.80		
1 Log Chipper, 22" Tree		2042.00		2246.20		
1 Dozer, 105 H.P.		307.75		338.50		
1 Chainsaw, Gas, 36" Long		53.05		58.35	79.57	87.52
40 L.H., Daily Totals		$4263.00		$5234.45	$106.58	$130.86

Crew B-88	Hr.	Daily	Hr.	Daily	Bare Costs	Incl. O&P
1 Laborer	$21.45	$171.60	$35.90	$287.20	$27.41	$43.87
6 Equip. Oper. (med.)	28.40	1363.20	45.20	2169.60		
2 Feller Bunchers, 50 H.P.		779.80		857.80		
1 Log Chipper, 22" Tree		2042.00		2246.20		
2 Log Skidders, 50 H.P.		744.30		818.75		
1 Dozer, 105 H.P.		307.75		338.50		
1 Chainsaw, Gas, 36" Long		53.05		58.35	70.12	77.14
56 L.H., Daily Totals		$5461.70		$6776.40	$97.53	$121.01

Crew B-89	Hr.	Daily	Hr.	Daily	Bare Costs	Incl. O&P
1 Equip. Oper. (light)	$27.20	$217.60	$43.30	$346.40	$24.48	$39.38
1 Truck Driver (light)	21.75	174.00	35.45	283.60		
1 Truck, Stake Body, 3 Ton		179.45		197.40		
1 Concrete Saw		110.65		121.70		
1 Water Tank, 65 Gal.		12.00		13.20	18.88	20.77
16 L.H., Daily Totals		$693.70		$962.30	$43.36	$60.15

Crew B-89A	Hr.	Daily	Hr.	Daily	Bare Costs	Incl. O&P
1 Skilled Worker	$28.05	$224.40	$46.50	$372.00	$24.75	$41.20
1 Laborer	21.45	171.60	35.90	287.20		
1 Core Drill (large)		61.35		67.50	3.83	4.22
16 L.H., Daily Totals		$457.35		$726.70	$28.58	$45.42

Crew B-89B	Hr.	Daily	Hr.	Daily	Bare Costs	Incl. O&P
1 Equip. Oper. (light)	$27.20	$217.60	$43.30	$346.40	$24.48	$39.38
1 Truck Driver, Light	21.75	174.00	35.45	283.60		
1 Wall Saw, Hydraulic, 10 H.P.		133.05		146.35		
1 Generator, Diesel, 100 KW		203.70		224.05		
1 Water Tank, 65 Gal.		12.00		13.20		
1 Flatbed Truck, 3 Ton		179.45		197.40	33.01	36.31
16 L.H., Daily Totals		$919.80		$1211.00	$57.49	$75.69

Crew B-90	Hr.	Daily	Hr.	Daily	Bare Costs	Incl. O&P
1 Labor Foreman (outside)	$23.45	$187.60	$39.25	$314.00	$23.30	$38.21
3 Laborers	21.45	514.80	35.90	861.60		
2 Equip. Oper. (light)	27.20	435.20	43.30	692.80		
2 Truck Drivers (heavy)	22.10	353.60	36.05	576.80		
1 Road Mixer, 310 H.P.		993.15		1092.45		
1 Dist. Truck, 2000 Gal.		340.30		374.35	20.84	22.92
64 L.H., Daily Totals		$2824.65		$3912.00	$44.14	$61.13

Crew B-90A	Hr.	Daily	Hr.	Daily	Bare Costs	Incl. O&P
1 Labor Foreman	$23.45	$187.60	$39.25	$314.00	$25.71	$41.69
2 Laborers	21.45	343.20	35.90	574.40		
4 Equip. Oper. (medium)	28.40	908.80	45.20	1446.40		
2 Graders, 30,000 Lbs.		1151.10		1266.20		
1 Roller, Steel Wheel		245.10		269.60		
1 Roller, Pneumatic Wheel		244.20		268.60	29.29	32.22
56 L.H., Daily Totals		$3080.00		$4139.20	$55.00	$73.91

Crew B-90B	Hr.	Daily	Hr.	Daily	Bare Costs	Incl. O&P
1 Labor Foreman	$23.45	$187.60	$39.25	$314.00	$25.26	$41.11
2 Laborers	21.45	343.20	35.90	574.40		
3 Equip. Oper. (medium)	28.40	681.60	45.20	1084.80		
1 Roller, Steel Wheel		245.10		269.60		
1 Roller, Pneumatic Wheel		244.20		268.60		
1 Road Mixer, 310 H.P.		993.15		1092.45	30.88	33.97
48 L.H., Daily Totals		$2694.85		$3603.85	$56.14	$75.08

Crew B-91	Hr.	Daily	Hr.	Daily	Bare Costs	Incl. O&P
1 Labor Foreman (outside)	$23.45	$187.60	$39.25	$314.00	$25.26	$40.99
2 Laborers	21.45	343.20	35.90	574.40		
4 Equip. Oper. (med.)	28.40	908.80	45.20	1446.40		
1 Truck Driver (heavy)	22.10	176.80	36.05	288.40		
1 Dist. Truck, 3000 Gal.		364.95		401.45		
1 Aggreg. Spreader, S.P.		635.50		699.05		
1 Roller, Pneu. Tire, 12 Ton		244.20		268.60		
1 Roller, Steel, 10 Ton		245.10		269.60	23.28	25.61
64 L.H., Daily Totals		$3106.15		$4261.90	$48.54	$66.60

Crew B-92	Hr.	Daily	Hr.	Daily	Bare Costs	Incl. O&P
1 Labor Foreman (outside)	$23.45	$187.60	$39.25	$314.00	$21.95	$36.74
3 Laborers	21.45	514.80	35.90	861.60		
1 Crack Cleaner, 25 H.P.		76.90		84.60		
1 Air Compressor		76.30		83.95		
1 Tar Kettle, T.M.		22.95		25.25		
1 Flatbed Truck, 3 Ton		179.45		197.40	11.11	12.22
32 L.H., Daily Totals		$1058.00		$1566.80	$33.06	$48.96

Crew B-93	Hr.	Daily	Hr.	Daily	Bare Costs	Incl. O&P
1 Equip. Oper. (med.)	$28.40	$227.20	$45.20	$361.60	$28.40	$45.20
1 Feller Buncher, 50 H.P.		389.90		428.90	48.74	53.61
8 L.H., Daily Totals		$617.10		$790.50	$77.14	$98.81

Crew B-94A	Hr.	Daily	Hr.	Daily	Bare Costs	Incl. O&P
1 Laborer	$21.45	$171.60	$35.90	$287.20	$21.45	$35.90
1 Diaph. Water Pump, 2"		29.15		32.05		
1-20 Ft. Suction Hose, 2"		6.50		7.15		
2-50 Ft. Disch. Hoses, 2"		8.80		9.70	5.56	6.11
8 L.H., Daily Totals		$216.05		$336.10	$27.01	$42.01

Crew B-94B	Hr.	Daily	Hr.	Daily	Bare Costs	Incl. O&P
1 Laborer	$21.45	$171.60	$35.90	$287.20	$21.45	$35.90
1 Diaph. Water Pump, 4"		64.40		70.85		
1-20 Ft. Suction Hose, 4"		12.50		13.75		
2-50 Ft. Disch. Hoses, 4"		17.00		18.70	11.74	12.91
8 L.H., Daily Totals		$265.50		$390.50	$33.19	$48.81

Crew B-94C	Hr.	Daily	Hr.	Daily	Bare Costs	Incl. O&P
1 Laborer	$21.45	$171.60	$35.90	$287.20	$21.45	$35.90
1 Centr. Water Pump, 3"		37.90		41.70		
1-20 Ft. Suction Hose, 3"		9.50		10.45		
2-50 Ft. Disch. Hoses, 3"		10.80		11.90	7.28	8.00
8 L.H., Daily Totals		$229.80		$351.25	$28.73	$43.90

Crew B-94D	Hr.	Daily	Hr.	Daily	Bare Costs	Incl. O&P
1 Laborer	$21.45	$171.60	$35.90	$287.20	$21.45	$35.90
1 Centr. Water Pump, 6"		159.45		175.40		
1-20 Ft. Suction Hose, 6"		21.50		23.65		
2-50 Ft. Disch. Hoses, 6"		39.00		42.90	27.49	30.24
8 L.H., Daily Totals		$391.55		$529.15	$48.94	$66.14

Crews

Crew No.	Bare Costs		Incl. Subs O & P		Cost Per Labor-Hour	
Crew B-95	Hr.	Daily	Hr.	Daily	Bare Costs	Incl. O&P
1 Equip. Oper. (crane)	$29.35	$234.80	$46.70	$373.60	$25.40	$41.30
1 Laborer	21.45	171.60	35.90	287.20		
16 L.H., Daily Totals		$406.40		$660.80	$25.40	$41.30

Crew No.	Bare Costs		Incl. Subs O & P		Cost Per Labor-Hour	
Crew B-95A	Hr.	Daily	Hr.	Daily	Bare Costs	Incl. O&P
1 Equip. Oper. (crane)	$29.35	$234.80	$46.70	$373.60	$25.40	$41.30
1 Laborer	21.45	171.60	35.90	287.20		
1 Hyd. Excavator, 5/8 C.Y.		394.25		433.70	24.64	27.10
16 L.H., Daily Totals		$800.65		$1094.50	$50.04	$68.40

Crew B-95B	Hr.	Daily	Hr.	Daily	Bare Costs	Incl. O&P
1 Equip. Oper. (crane)	$29.35	$234.80	$46.70	$373.60	$25.40	$41.30
1 Laborer	21.45	171.60	35.90	287.20		
1 Hyd. Excavator, 1.5 C.Y.		712.70		783.95	44.54	49.00
16 L.H., Daily Totals		$1119.10		$1444.75	$69.94	$90.30

Crew B-95C	Hr.	Daily	Hr.	Daily	Bare Costs	Incl. O&P
1 Equip. Oper. (crane)	$29.35	$234.80	$46.70	$373.60	$25.40	$41.30
1 Laborer	21.45	171.60	35.90	287.20		
1 Hyd. Excavator, 2.5 C.Y.		1695.00		1864.50	105.94	116.53
16 L.H., Daily Totals		$2101.40		$2525.30	$131.34	$157.83

Crew C-1	Hr.	Daily	Hr.	Daily	Bare Costs	Incl. O&P
3 Carpenters	$27.30	$655.20	$45.70	$1096.80	$25.84	$43.25
1 Laborer	21.45	171.60	35.90	287.20		
32 L.H., Daily Totals		$826.80		$1384.00	$25.84	$43.25

Crew C-2	Hr.	Daily	Hr.	Daily	Bare Costs	Incl. O&P
1 Carpenter Foreman (out)	$29.30	$234.40	$49.05	$392.40	$26.66	$44.63
4 Carpenters	27.30	873.60	45.70	1462.40		
1 Laborer	21.45	171.60	35.90	287.20		
48 L.H., Daily Totals		$1279.60		$2142.00	$26.66	$44.63

Crew C-2A	Hr.	Daily	Hr.	Daily	Bare Costs	Incl. O&P
1 Carpenter Foreman	$29.30	$234.40	$49.05	$392.40	$26.47	$43.95
3 Carpenters	27.30	655.20	45.70	1096.80		
1 Cement Finisher	26.15	209.20	41.65	333.20		
1 Laborer	21.45	171.60	35.90	287.20		
48 L.H., Daily Totals		$1270.40		$2109.60	$26.47	$43.95

Crew C-3	Hr.	Daily	Hr.	Daily	Bare Costs	Incl. O&P
1 Rodman Foreman	$32.40	$259.20	$58.35	$466.80	$28.01	$49.06
4 Rodmen (reinf.)	30.40	972.80	54.75	1752.00		
1 Equip. Oper. (light)	27.20	217.60	43.30	346.40		
2 Laborers	21.45	343.20	35.90	574.40		
3 Stressing Equipment		40.50		44.55		
.5 Grouting Equipment		117.63		129.40	2.47	2.72
64 L.H., Daily Totals		$1950.93		$3313.55	$30.48	$51.78

Crew C-4	Hr.	Daily	Hr.	Daily	Bare Costs	Incl. O&P
1 Rodman Foreman	$32.40	$259.20	$58.35	$466.80	$30.90	$55.65
3 Rodmen (reinf.)	30.40	729.60	54.75	1314.00		
3 Stressing Equipment		40.50		44.55	1.27	1.39
32 L.H., Daily Totals		$1029.30		$1825.35	$32.17	$57.04

Crew C-5	Hr.	Daily	Hr.	Daily	Bare Costs	Incl. O&P
1 Rodman Foreman	$32.40	$259.20	$58.35	$466.80	$29.63	$51.76
4 Rodmen (reinf.)	30.40	972.80	54.75	1752.00		
1 Equip. Oper. (crane)	29.35	234.80	46.70	373.60		
1 Equip. Oper. Oiler	24.05	192.40	38.25	306.00		
1 Hyd. Crane, 25 Ton		549.35		604.30	9.81	10.79
56 L.H., Daily Totals		$2208.55		$3502.70	$39.44	$62.55

Crew C-6	Hr.	Daily	Hr.	Daily	Bare Costs	Incl. O&P
1 Labor Foreman (outside)	$23.45	$187.60	$39.25	$314.00	$22.57	$37.42
4 Laborers	21.45	686.40	35.90	1148.80		
1 Cement Finisher	26.15	209.20	41.65	333.20		
2 Gas Engine Vibrators		74.90		82.40	1.56	1.72
48 L.H., Daily Totals		$1158.10		$1878.40	$24.13	$39.14

Crew C-7	Hr.	Daily	Hr.	Daily	Bare Costs	Incl. O&P
1 Labor Foreman (outside)	$23.45	$187.60	$39.25	$314.00	$23.26	$38.21
5 Laborers	21.45	858.00	35.90	1436.00		
1 Cement Finisher	26.15	209.20	41.65	333.20		
1 Equip. Oper. (med.)	28.40	227.20	45.20	361.60		
1 Equip. Oper. (oiler)	24.05	192.40	38.25	306.00		
2 Gas Engine Vibrators		74.90		82.40		
1 Concrete Bucket, 1 C.Y.		24.45		26.90		
1 Hyd. Crane, 55 Ton		793.10		872.40	12.40	13.63
72 L.H., Daily Totals		$2566.85		$3732.50	$35.66	$51.84

Crew C-8	Hr.	Daily	Hr.	Daily	Bare Costs	Incl. O&P
1 Labor Foreman (outside)	$23.45	$187.60	$39.25	$314.00	$24.07	$39.35
3 Laborers	21.45	514.80	35.90	861.60		
2 Cement Finishers	26.15	418.40	41.65	666.40		
1 Equip. Oper. (med.)	28.40	227.20	45.20	361.60		
1 Concrete Pump (small)		645.60		710.15	11.53	12.68
56 L.H., Daily Totals		$1993.60		$2913.75	$35.60	$52.03

Crew C-8A	Hr.	Daily	Hr.	Daily	Bare Costs	Incl. O&P
1 Labor Foreman (outside)	$23.45	$187.60	$39.25	$314.00	$23.35	$38.38
3 Laborers	21.45	514.80	35.90	861.60		
2 Cement Finishers	26.15	418.40	41.65	666.40		
48 L.H., Daily Totals		$1120.80		$1842.00	$23.35	$38.38

Crew C-8B	Hr.	Daily	Hr.	Daily	Bare Costs	Incl. O&P
1 Labor Foreman (outside)	$23.45	$187.60	$39.25	$314.00	$23.24	$38.43
3 Laborers	21.45	514.80	35.90	861.60		
1 Equipment Operator	28.40	227.20	45.20	361.60		
1 Vibrating Screed		47.40		52.15		
1 Vibratory Roller		421.75		463.95		
1 Dozer, 200 HP		838.95		922.85	32.70	35.97
40 L.H., Daily Totals		$2237.70		$2976.15	$55.94	$74.40

Crew C-8C	Hr.	Daily	Hr.	Daily	Bare Costs	Incl. O&P
1 Labor Forman	$23.45	$187.60	$39.25	$314.00	$23.73	$38.97
3 Laborers	21.45	514.80	35.90	861.60		
1 Cement Finisher	26.15	209.20	41.65	333.20		
1 Equipment Operator (med.)	28.40	227.20	45.20	361.60		
1 Shotcrete Rig, 12 CY/hr		376.00		413.60	7.83	8.62
48 L.H., Daily Totals		$1514.80		$2284.00	$31.56	$47.59

Crews

Crew No.	Bare Costs		Incl. Subs O & P		Cost Per Labor-Hour	
Crew C-8D	Hr.	Daily	Hr.	Daily	Bare Costs	Incl. O&P
1 Labor Foreman	$23.45	$187.60	$39.25	$314.00	$24.56	$40.03
1 Laborers	21.45	171.60	35.90	287.20		
1 Cement Finisher	26.15	209.20	41.65	333.20		
1 Equipment Operator (light)	27.20	217.60	43.30	346.40		
1 Compressor, 250 CFM		124.90		137.40		
2 Hoses, 1", 50'		10.40		11.45	4.23	4.65
32 L.H., Daily Totals		$921.30		$1429.65	$28.79	$44.68
Crew C-8E	Hr.	Daily	Hr.	Daily	Bare Costs	Incl. O&P
1 Labor Foreman	$23.45	$187.60	$39.25	$314.00	$24.56	$40.03
1 Laborers	21.45	171.60	35.90	287.20		
1 Cement Finisher	26.15	209.20	41.65	333.20		
1 Equipment Operator (light)	27.20	217.60	43.30	346.40		
1 Compressor, 250 CFM		124.90		137.40		
2 Hoses, 1", 50'		10.40		11.45		
1 Concrete Pump (small)		645.60		710.15	24.40	26.84
32 L.H., Daily Totals		$1566.90		$2139.80	$48.96	$66.87
Crew C-10	Hr.	Daily	Hr.	Daily	Bare Costs	Incl. O&P
1 Laborer	$21.45	$171.60	$35.90	$287.20	$24.58	$39.73
2 Cement Finishers	26.15	418.40	41.65	666.40		
24 L.H., Daily Totals		$590.00		$953.60	$24.58	$39.73
Crew C-11	Hr.	Daily	Hr.	Daily	Bare Costs	Incl. O&P
1 Struc. Steel Foreman	$32.60	$260.80	$62.05	$496.40	$29.96	$55.17
6 Struc. Steel Workers	30.60	1468.80	58.25	2796.00		
1 Equip. Oper. (crane)	29.35	234.80	46.70	373.60		
1 Equip. Oper. Oiler	24.05	192.40	38.25	306.00		
1 Truck Crane, 150 Ton		1553.00		1708.30	21.57	23.73
72 L.H., Daily Totals		$3709.80		$5680.30	$51.53	$78.90
Crew C-12	Hr.	Daily	Hr.	Daily	Bare Costs	Incl. O&P
1 Carpenter Foreman (out)	$29.30	$234.40	$49.05	$392.40	$27.00	$44.79
3 Carpenters	27.30	655.20	45.70	1096.80		
1 Laborer	21.45	171.60	35.90	287.20		
1 Equip. Oper. (crane)	29.35	234.80	46.70	373.60		
1 Hyd. Crane, 12 Ton		443.45		487.80	9.24	10.16
48 L.H., Daily Totals		$1739.45		$2637.80	$36.24	$54.95
Crew C-13	Hr.	Daily	Hr.	Daily	Bare Costs	Incl. O&P
1 Struc. Steel Worker	$30.60	$244.80	$58.25	$466.00	$29.50	$54.07
1 Welder	30.60	244.80	58.25	466.00		
1 Carpenter	27.30	218.40	45.70	365.60		
1 Gas Welding Machine		82.35		90.60	3.43	3.77
24 L.H., Daily Totals		$790.35		$1388.20	$32.93	$57.84
Crew C-14	Hr.	Daily	Hr.	Daily	Bare Costs	Incl. O&P
1 Carpenter Foreman (out)	$29.30	$234.40	$49.05	$392.40	$26.61	$44.91
5 Carpenters	27.30	1092.00	45.70	1828.00		
4 Laborers	21.45	686.40	35.90	1148.80		
4 Rodmen (reinf.)	30.40	972.80	54.75	1752.00		
2 Cement Finishers	26.15	418.40	41.65	666.40		
1 Equip. Oper. (crane)	29.35	234.80	46.70	373.60		
1 Equip. Oper. Oiler	24.05	192.40	38.25	306.00		
1 Crane, 80 Ton, & Tools		1098.00		1207.80	7.63	8.39
144 L.H., Daily Totals		$4929.20		$7675.00	$34.24	$53.30

Crew No.	Bare Costs		Incl. Subs O & P		Cost Per Labor-Hour	
Crew C-14A	Hr.	Daily	Hr.	Daily	Bare Costs	Incl. O&P
1 Carpenter Foreman (out)	$29.30	$234.40	$49.05	$392.40	$27.41	$46.32
16 Carpenters	27.30	3494.40	45.70	5849.60		
4 Rodmen (reinf.)	30.40	972.80	54.75	1752.00		
2 Laborers	21.45	343.20	35.90	574.40		
1 Cement Finisher	26.15	209.20	41.65	333.20		
1 Equip. Oper. (med)	28.40	227.20	45.20	361.60		
1 Gas Engine Vibrator		37.45		41.20		
1 Concrete Pump (small)		645.60		710.15	3.42	3.76
200 L.H., Daily Totals		$6164.25		$10014.55	$30.83	$50.08
Crew C-14B	Hr.	Daily	Hr.	Daily	Bare Costs	Incl. O&P
1 Carpenter Foreman (out)	$29.30	$234.40	$49.05	$392.40	$27.36	$46.14
16 Carpenters	27.30	3494.40	45.70	5849.60		
4 Rodmen (reinf.)	30.40	972.80	54.75	1752.00		
2 Laborers	21.45	343.20	35.90	574.40		
2 Cement Finishers	26.15	418.40	41.65	666.40		
1 Equip. Oper. (med)	28.40	227.20	45.20	361.60		
1 Gas Engine Vibrator		37.45		41.20		
1 Concrete Pump (small)		645.60		710.15	3.28	3.61
208 L.H., Daily Totals		$6373.45		$10347.75	$30.64	$49.75
Crew C-14C	Hr.	Daily	Hr.	Daily	Bare Costs	Incl. O&P
1 Carpenter Foreman (out)	$29.30	$234.40	$49.05	$392.40	$26.13	$44.14
6 Carpenters	27.30	1310.40	45.70	2193.60		
2 Rodmen (reinf)	30.40	486.40	54.75	876.00		
4 Laborers	21.45	686.40	35.90	1148.80		
1 Cement Finisher	26.15	209.20	41.65	333.20		
1 Gas Engine Vibrator		37.45		41.20	.33	.37
112 L.H., Daily Totals		$2964.25		$4985.20	$26.46	$44.51
Crew C-14D	Hr.	Daily	Hr.	Daily	Bare Costs	Incl. O&P
1 Carpenter Foreman (out)	$29.30	$234.40	$49.05	$392.40	$27.16	$45.59
18 Carpenters	27.30	3931.20	45.70	6580.80		
2 Rodmen (reinf.)	30.40	486.40	54.75	876.00		
2 Laborers	21.45	343.20	35.90	574.40		
1 Cement Finisher	26.15	209.20	41.65	333.20		
1 Equip. Oper. (med.)	28.40	227.20	45.20	361.60		
1 Gas Engine Vibrator		37.45		41.20		
1 Concrete Pump (small)		645.60		710.15	3.42	3.76
200 L.H., Daily Totals		$6114.65		$9869.75	$30.58	$49.35
Crew C-14E	Hr.	Daily	Hr.	Daily	Bare Costs	Incl. O&P
1 Carpenter Foreman (out)	$29.30	$234.40	$49.05	$392.40	$26.91	$46.25
2 Carpenters	27.30	436.80	45.70	731.20		
4 Rodmen (reinf.)	30.40	972.80	54.75	1752.00		
3 Laborers	21.45	514.80	35.90	861.60		
1 Cement Finisher	26.15	209.20	41.65	333.20		
1 Gas Engine Vibrator		37.45		41.20	.43	.47
88 L.H., Daily Totals		$2405.45		$4111.60	$27.34	$46.72
Crew C-14F	Hr.	Daily	Hr.	Daily	Bare Costs	Incl. O&P
1 Laborer Foreman (out)	$23.45	$187.60	$39.25	$314.00	$24.81	$40.11
2 Laborers	21.45	343.20	35.90	574.40		
6 Cement Finishers	26.15	1255.20	41.65	1999.20		
1 Gas Engine Vibrator		37.45		41.20	.52	.57
72 L.H., Daily Totals		$1823.45		$2928.80	$25.33	$40.68

Crews

Crew No.	Bare Costs		Incl. Subs O & P		Cost Per Labor-Hour	
Crew C-14G	Hr.	Daily	Hr.	Daily	Bare Costs	Incl. O&P
1 Laborer Foreman	$23.45	$187.60	$39.25	$314.00	$24.42	$39.66
2 Laborers	21.45	343.20	35.90	574.40		
4 Cement Finishers	26.15	836.80	41.65	1332.80		
1 Gas Engine Vibrator		37.45		41.20	.67	.74
56 L.H., Daily Totals		$1405.05		$2262.40	$25.09	$40.40
Crew C-14H	Hr.	Daily	Hr.	Daily	Bare Costs	Incl. O&P
1 Carpenter Foreman (out)	$29.30	$234.40	$49.05	$392.40	$26.98	$45.46
2 Carpenters	27.30	436.80	45.70	731.20		
1 Rodman (reinf.)	30.40	243.20	54.75	438.00		
1 Laborer	21.45	171.60	35.90	287.20		
1 Cement Finisher	26.15	209.20	41.65	333.20		
1 Gas Engine Vibrator		37.45		41.20	.78	.86
48 L.H., Daily Totals		$1332.65		$2223.20	$27.76	$46.32
Crew C-15	Hr.	Daily	Hr.	Daily	Bare Costs	Incl. O&P
1 Carpenter Foreman (out)	$29.30	$234.40	$49.05	$392.40	$25.66	$42.91
2 Carpenters	27.30	436.80	45.70	731.20		
3 Laborers	21.45	514.80	35.90	861.60		
2 Cement Finishers	26.15	418.40	41.65	666.40		
1 Rodman (reinf.)	30.40	243.20	54.75	438.00		
72 L.H., Daily Totals		$1847.60		$3089.60	$25.66	$42.91
Crew C-16	Hr.	Daily	Hr.	Daily	Bare Costs	Incl. O&P
1 Labor Foreman (outside)	$23.45	$187.60	$39.25	$314.00	$25.48	$42.77
3 Laborers	21.45	514.80	35.90	861.60		
2 Cement Finishers	26.15	418.40	41.65	666.40		
1 Equip. Oper. (med.)	28.40	227.20	45.20	361.60		
2 Rodmen (reinf.)	30.40	486.40	54.75	876.00		
1 Concrete Pump (small)		645.60		710.15	8.97	9.86
72 L.H., Daily Totals		$2480.00		$3789.75	$34.45	$52.63
Crew C-17	Hr.	Daily	Hr.	Daily	Bare Costs	Incl. O&P
2 Skilled Worker Foremen	$30.05	$480.80	$49.80	$796.80	$28.45	$47.16
8 Skilled Workers	28.05	1795.20	46.50	2976.00		
80 L.H., Daily Totals		$2276.00		$3772.80	$28.45	$47.16
Crew C-17A	Hr.	Daily	Hr.	Daily	Bare Costs	Incl. O&P
2 Skilled Worker Foremen	$30.05	$480.80	$49.80	$796.80	$28.46	$47.15
8 Skilled Workers	28.05	1795.20	46.50	2976.00		
.125 Equip. Oper. (crane)	29.35	29.35	46.70	46.70		
.125 Crane, 80 Ton, & Tools		137.25		151.00	1.69	1.86
81 L.H., Daily Totals		$2442.60		$3970.50	$30.15	$49.01
Crew C-17B	Hr.	Daily	Hr.	Daily	Bare Costs	Incl. O&P
2 Skilled Worker Foremen	$30.05	$480.80	$49.80	$796.80	$28.47	$47.15
8 Skilled Workers	28.05	1795.20	46.50	2976.00		
.25 Equip. Oper. (crane)	29.35	58.70	46.70	93.40		
.25 Crane, 80 Ton, & Tools		274.50		301.95		
.25 Walk Behind Power Tools		12.24		13.45	3.50	3.85
82 L.H., Daily Totals		$2621.44		$4181.60	$31.97	$51.00
Crew C-17C	Hr.	Daily	Hr.	Daily	Bare Costs	Incl. O&P
2 Skilled Worker Foremen	$30.05	$480.80	$49.80	$796.80	$28.48	$47.14
8 Skilled Workers	28.05	1795.20	46.50	2976.00		
.375 Equip. Oper. (crane)	29.35	88.05	46.70	140.10		
.375 Crane, 80 Ton & Tools		411.75		452.95	4.96	5.46
83 L.H., Daily Totals		$2775.80		$4365.85	$33.44	$52.60

Crew No.	Bare Costs		Incl. Subs O & P		Cost Per Labor-Hour	
Crew C-17D	Hr.	Daily	Hr.	Daily	Bare Costs	Incl. O&P
2 Skilled Worker Foremen	$30.05	$480.80	$49.80	$796.80	$28.49	$47.14
8 Skilled Workers	28.05	1795.20	46.50	2976.00		
.5 Equip. Oper. (crane)	29.35	117.40	46.70	186.80		
.5 Crane, 80 Ton & Tools		549.00		603.90	6.54	7.19
84 L.H., Daily Totals		$2942.40		$4563.50	$35.03	$54.33
Crew C-17E	Hr.	Daily	Hr.	Daily	Bare Costs	Incl. O&P
2 Skilled Worker Foremen	$30.05	$480.80	$49.80	$796.80	$28.45	$47.16
8 Skilled Workers	28.05	1795.20	46.50	2976.00		
1 Hyd. Jack with Rods		60.50		66.55	.76	.83
80 L.H., Daily Totals		$2336.50		$3839.35	$29.21	$47.99
Crew C-18	Hr.	Daily	Hr.	Daily	Bare Costs	Incl. O&P
.125 Labor Foreman (out)	$23.45	$23.45	$39.25	$39.25	$21.67	$36.27
1 Laborer	21.45	171.60	35.90	287.20		
1 Concrete Cart, 10 C.F.		49.90		54.90	5.54	6.10
9 L.H., Daily Totals		$244.95		$381.35	$27.21	$42.37
Crew C-19	Hr.	Daily	Hr.	Daily	Bare Costs	Incl. O&P
.125 Labor Foreman (out)	$23.45	$23.45	$39.25	$39.25	$21.67	$36.27
1 Laborer	21.45	171.60	35.90	287.20		
1 Concrete Cart, 18 C.F.		83.35		91.70	9.26	10.19
9 L.H., Daily Totals		$278.40		$418.15	$30.93	$46.46
Crew C-20	Hr.	Daily	Hr.	Daily	Bare Costs	Incl. O&P
1 Labor Foreman (outside)	$23.45	$187.60	$39.25	$314.00	$23.16	$38.20
5 Laborers	21.45	858.00	35.90	1436.00		
1 Cement Finisher	26.15	209.20	41.65	333.20		
1 Equip. Oper. (med.)	28.40	227.20	45.20	361.60		
2 Gas Engine Vibrators		74.90		82.40		
1 Concrete Pump (small)		645.60		710.15	11.26	12.38
64 L.H., Daily Totals		$2202.50		$3237.35	$34.42	$50.58
Crew C-21	Hr.	Daily	Hr.	Daily	Bare Costs	Incl. O&P
1 Labor Foreman (outside)	$23.45	$187.60	$39.25	$314.00	$23.16	$38.20
5 Laborers	21.45	858.00	35.90	1436.00		
1 Cement Finisher	26.15	209.20	41.65	333.20		
1 Equip. Oper. (med.)	28.40	227.20	45.20	361.60		
2 Gas Engine Vibrators		74.90		82.40		
1 Concrete Conveyer		180.90		199.00	4.00	4.40
64 L.H., Daily Totals		$1737.80		$2726.20	$27.16	$42.60
Crew C-22	Hr.	Daily	Hr.	Daily	Bare Costs	Incl. O&P
1 Rodman Foreman	$32.40	$259.20	$58.35	$466.80	$30.60	$54.85
4 Rodmen (reinf.)	30.40	972.80	54.75	1752.00		
.125 Equip. Oper. (crane)	29.35	29.35	46.70	46.70		
.125 Equip. Oper. Oiler	24.05	24.05	38.25	38.25		
.125 Hyd. Crane, 25 Ton		68.67		75.55	1.63	1.80
42 L.H., Daily Totals		$1354.07		$2379.30	$32.23	$56.65
Crew C-23	Hr.	Daily	Hr.	Daily	Bare Costs	Incl. O&P
2 Skilled Worker Foremen	$30.05	$480.80	$49.80	$796.80	$28.18	$46.35
6 Skilled Workers	28.05	1346.40	46.50	2232.00		
1 Equip. Oper. (crane)	29.35	234.80	46.70	373.60		
1 Equip. Oper. Oiler	24.05	192.40	38.25	306.00		
1 Crane, 90 Ton		1012.00		1113.20	12.65	13.92
80 L.H., Daily Totals		$3266.40		$4821.60	$40.83	$60.27

Crews

Crew No.	Bare Costs Hr.	Daily	Incl. Subs O & P Hr.	Daily	Cost Per Labor-Hour Bare Costs	Incl. O&P
Crew C-24						
2 Skilled Worker Foremen	$30.05	$480.80	$49.80	$796.80	$28.18	$46.35
6 Skilled Workers	28.05	1346.40	46.50	2232.00		
1 Equip. Oper. (crane)	29.35	234.80	46.70	373.60		
1 Equip. Oper. Oiler	24.05	192.40	38.25	306.00		
1 Truck Crane, 150 Ton		1553.00		1708.30	19.41	21.35
80 L.H., Daily Totals		$3807.40		$5416.70	$47.59	$67.70
Crew C-25						
2 Rodmen (reinf.)	$30.40	$486.40	$54.75	$876.00	$24.25	$43.85
2 Rodmen Helpers	18.10	289.60	32.95	527.20		
32 L.H., Daily Totals		$776.00		$1403.20	$24.25	$43.85
Crew D-1						
1 Bricklayer	$27.60	$220.80	$45.70	$365.60	$24.60	$40.73
1 Bricklayer Helper	21.60	172.80	35.75	286.00		
16 L.H., Daily Totals		$393.60		$651.60	$24.60	$40.73
Crew D-2						
3 Bricklayers	$27.60	$662.40	$45.70	$1096.80	$25.39	$42.08
2 Bricklayer Helpers	21.60	345.60	35.75	572.00		
.5 Carpenter	27.30	109.20	45.70	182.80		
44 L.H., Daily Totals		$1117.20		$1851.60	$25.39	$42.08
Crew D-3						
3 Bricklayers	$27.60	$662.40	$45.70	$1096.80	$25.30	$41.91
2 Bricklayer Helpers	21.60	345.60	35.75	572.00		
.25 Carpenter	27.30	54.60	45.70	91.40		
42 L.H., Daily Totals		$1062.60		$1760.20	$25.30	$41.91
Crew D-4						
1 Bricklayer	$27.60	$220.80	$45.70	$365.60	$24.50	$40.13
2 Bricklayer Helpers	21.60	345.60	35.75	572.00		
1 Equip. Oper. (light)	27.20	217.60	43.30	346.40		
1 Grout Pump, 50 C.F./hr		67.35		74.10		
1 Hoses & Hopper		31.50		34.65		
1 Accessories		10.50		11.55	3.42	3.76
32 L.H., Daily Totals		$893.35		$1404.30	$27.92	$43.89
Crew D-5						
1 Bricklayer	$27.60	$220.80	$45.70	$365.60	$27.60	$45.70
8 L.H., Daily Totals		$220.80		$365.60	$27.60	$45.70
Crew D-6						
3 Bricklayers	$27.60	$662.40	$45.70	$1096.80	$24.71	$40.92
3 Bricklayer Helpers	21.60	518.40	35.75	858.00		
.25 Carpenter	27.30	54.60	45.70	91.40		
50 L.H., Daily Totals		$1235.40		$2046.20	$24.71	$40.92
Crew D-7						
1 Tile Layer	$26.65	$213.20	$42.05	$336.40	$24.05	$37.95
1 Tile Layer Helper	21.45	171.60	33.85	270.80		
16 L.H., Daily Totals		$384.80		$607.20	$24.05	$37.95
Crew D-8						
3 Bricklayers	$27.60	$662.40	$45.70	$1096.80	$25.20	$41.72
2 Bricklayer Helpers	21.60	345.60	35.75	572.00		
40 L.H., Daily Totals		$1008.00		$1668.80	$25.20	$41.72

Crew No.	Bare Costs Hr.	Daily	Incl. Subs O & P Hr.	Daily	Cost Per Labor-Hour Bare Costs	Incl. O&P
Crew D-9						
3 Bricklayers	$27.60	$662.40	$45.70	$1096.80	$24.60	$40.73
3 Bricklayer Helpers	21.60	518.40	35.75	858.00		
48 L.H., Daily Totals		$1180.80		$1954.80	$24.60	$40.73
Crew D-10						
1 Bricklayer Foreman	$29.60	$236.80	$49.00	$392.00	$25.95	$42.58
1 Bricklayer	27.60	220.80	45.70	365.60		
2 Bricklayer Helpers	21.60	345.60	35.75	572.00		
1 Equip. Oper. (crane)	29.35	234.80	46.70	373.60		
1 Truck Crane, 12.5 Ton		391.35		430.50	9.78	10.76
40 L.H., Daily Totals		$1429.35		$2133.70	$35.73	$53.34
Crew D-11						
1 Bricklayer Foreman	$29.60	$236.80	$49.00	$392.00	$26.27	$43.48
1 Bricklayer	27.60	220.80	45.70	365.60		
1 Bricklayer Helper	21.60	172.80	35.75	286.00		
24 L.H., Daily Totals		$630.40		$1043.60	$26.27	$43.48
Crew D-12						
1 Bricklayer Foreman	$29.60	$236.80	$49.00	$392.00	$25.10	$41.55
1 Bricklayer	27.60	220.80	45.70	365.60		
2 Bricklayer Helpers	21.60	345.60	35.75	572.00		
32 L.H., Daily Totals		$803.20		$1329.60	$25.10	$41.55
Crew D-13						
1 Bricklayer Foreman	$29.60	$236.80	$49.00	$392.00	$26.18	$43.10
1 Bricklayer	27.60	220.80	45.70	365.60		
2 Bricklayer Helpers	21.60	345.60	35.75	572.00		
1 Carpenter	27.30	218.40	45.70	365.60		
1 Equip. Oper. (crane)	29.35	234.80	46.70	373.60		
1 Truck Crane, 12.5 Ton		391.35		430.50	8.15	8.97
48 L.H., Daily Totals		$1647.75		$2499.30	$34.33	$52.07
Crew E-1						
1 Welder Foreman	$32.60	$260.80	$62.05	$496.40	$30.13	$54.53
1 Welder	30.60	244.80	58.25	466.00		
1 Equip. Oper. (light)	27.20	217.60	43.30	346.40		
1 Gas Welding Machine		82.35		90.60	3.43	3.77
24 L.H., Daily Totals		$805.55		$1399.40	$33.56	$58.30
Crew E-2						
1 Struc. Steel Foreman	$32.60	$260.80	$62.05	$496.40	$29.77	$54.29
4 Struc. Steel Workers	30.60	979.20	58.25	1864.00		
1 Equip. Oper. (crane)	29.35	234.80	46.70	373.60		
1 Equip. Oper. Oiler	24.05	192.40	38.25	306.00		
1 Crane, 90 Ton		1012.00		1113.20	18.07	19.88
56 L.H., Daily Totals		$2679.20		$4153.20	$47.84	$74.17
Crew E-3						
1 Struc. Steel Foreman	$32.60	$260.80	$62.05	$496.40	$31.27	$59.52
1 Struc. Steel Worker	30.60	244.80	58.25	466.00		
1 Welder	30.60	244.80	58.25	466.00		
1 Gas Welding Machine		82.35		90.60	3.43	3.77
24 L.H., Daily Totals		$832.75		$1519.00	$34.70	$63.29
Crew E-4						
1 Struc. Steel Foreman	$32.60	$260.80	$62.05	$496.40	$31.10	$59.20
3 Struc. Steel Workers	30.60	734.40	58.25	1398.00		
1 Gas Welding Machine		82.35		90.60	2.57	2.83
32 L.H., Daily Totals		$1077.55		$1985.00	$33.67	$62.03

Crews

Crew No.	Bare Costs		Incl. Subs O & P		Cost Per Labor-Hour	
Crew E-5	Hr.	Daily	Hr.	Daily	Bare Costs	Incl. O&P
2 Struc. Steel Foremen	$32.60	$521.60	$62.05	$992.80	$30.22	$55.85
5 Struc. Steel Workers	30.60	1224.00	58.25	2330.00		
1 Equip. Oper. (crane)	29.35	234.80	46.70	373.60		
1 Welder	30.60	244.80	58.25	466.00		
1 Equip. Oper. Oiler	24.05	192.40	38.25	306.00		
1 Crane, 90 Ton		1012.00		1113.20		
1 Gas Welding Machine		82.35		90.60	13.68	15.05
80 L.H., Daily Totals		$3511.95		$5672.20	$43.90	$70.90
Crew E-6	Hr.	Daily	Hr.	Daily	Bare Costs	Incl. O&P
3 Struc. Steel Foremen	$32.60	$782.40	$62.05	$1489.20	$30.27	$56.06
9 Struc. Steel Workers	30.60	2203.20	58.25	4194.00		
1 Equip. Oper. (crane)	29.35	234.80	46.70	373.60		
1 Welder	30.60	244.80	58.25	466.00		
1 Equip. Oper. Oiler	24.05	192.40	38.25	306.00		
1 Equip. Oper. (light)	27.20	217.60	43.30	346.40		
1 Crane, 90 Ton		1012.00		1113.20		
1 Gas Welding Machine		82.35		90.60		
1 Air Compr., 160 C.F.M.		97.40		107.15		
2 Impact Wrenches		57.60		63.35	9.76	10.74
128 L.H., Daily Totals		$5124.55		$8549.50	$40.03	$66.80
Crew E-7	Hr.	Daily	Hr.	Daily	Bare Costs	Incl. O&P
1 Struc. Steel Foreman	$32.60	$260.80	$62.05	$496.40	$30.22	$55.85
4 Struc. Steel Workers	30.60	979.20	58.25	1864.00		
1 Equip. Oper. (crane)	29.35	234.80	46.70	373.60		
1 Equip. Oper. Oiler	24.05	192.40	38.25	306.00		
1 Welder Foreman	32.60	260.80	62.05	496.40		
2 Welders	30.60	489.60	58.25	932.00		
1 Crane, 90 Ton		1012.00		1113.20		
2 Gas Welding Machines		164.70		181.15	14.71	16.18
80 L.H., Daily Totals		$3594.30		$5762.75	$44.93	$72.03
Crew E-8	Hr.	Daily	Hr.	Daily	Bare Costs	Incl. O&P
1 Struc. Steel Foreman	$32.60	$260.80	$62.05	$496.40	$30.05	$55.26
4 Struc. Steel Workers	30.60	979.20	58.25	1864.00		
1 Welder Foreman	32.60	260.80	62.05	496.40		
4 Welders	30.60	979.20	58.25	1864.00		
1 Equip. Oper. (crane)	29.35	234.80	46.70	373.60		
1 Equip. Oper. Oiler	24.05	192.40	38.25	306.00		
1 Equip. Oper. (light)	27.20	217.60	43.30	346.40		
1 Crane, 90 Ton		1012.00		1113.20		
4 Gas Welding Machines		329.40		362.35	12.90	14.19
104 L.H., Daily Totals		$4466.20		$7222.35	$42.95	$69.45
Crew E-9	Hr.	Daily	Hr.	Daily	Bare Costs	Incl. O&P
2 Struc. Steel Foremen	$32.60	$521.60	$62.05	$992.80	$30.27	$56.06
5 Struc. Steel Workers	30.60	1224.00	58.25	2330.00		
1 Welder Foreman	32.60	260.80	62.05	496.40		
5 Welders	30.60	1224.00	58.25	2330.00		
1 Equip. Oper. (crane)	29.35	234.80	46.70	373.60		
1 Equip. Oper. Oiler	24.05	192.40	38.25	306.00		
1 Equip. Oper. (light)	27.20	217.60	43.30	346.40		
1 Crane, 90 Ton		1012.00		1113.20		
5 Gas Welding Machines		411.75		452.95	11.12	12.24
128 L.H., Daily Totals		$5298.95		$8741.35	$41.39	$68.30

Crew No.	Bare Costs		Incl. Subs O & P		Cost Per Labor-Hour	
Crew E-10	Hr.	Daily	Hr.	Daily	Bare Costs	Incl. O&P
1 Welder Foreman	$32.60	$260.80	$62.05	$496.40	$31.60	$60.15
1 Welder	30.60	244.80	58.25	466.00		
4 Gas Welding Machines		329.40		362.35		
1 Truck, 3 Ton		179.45		197.40	31.80	34.98
16 L.H., Daily Totals		$1014.45		$1522.15	$63.40	$95.13
Crew E-11	Hr.	Daily	Hr.	Daily	Bare Costs	Incl. O&P
2 Painters, Struc. Steel	$26.00	$416.00	$51.75	$828.00	$25.16	$45.67
1 Building Laborer	21.45	171.60	35.90	287.20		
1 Equip. Oper. (light)	27.20	217.60	43.30	346.40		
1 Air Compressor 250 C.F.M.		124.90		137.40		
1 Sand Blaster		31.50		34.65		
1 Sand Blasting Accessories		10.50		11.55	5.22	5.74
32 L.H., Daily Totals		$972.10		$1645.20	$30.38	$51.41
Crew E-12	Hr.	Daily	Hr.	Daily	Bare Costs	Incl. O&P
1 Welder Foreman	$32.60	$260.80	$62.05	$496.40	$29.90	$52.67
1 Equip. Oper. (light)	27.20	217.60	43.30	346.40		
1 Gas Welding Machine		82.35		90.60	5.15	5.66
16 L.H., Daily Totals		$560.75		$933.40	$35.05	$58.33
Crew E-13	Hr.	Daily	Hr.	Daily	Bare Costs	Incl. O&P
1 Welder Foreman	$32.60	$260.80	$62.05	$496.40	$30.80	$55.80
.5 Equip. Oper. (light)	27.20	108.80	43.30	173.20		
1 Gas Welding Machine		82.35		90.60	6.86	7.55
12 L.H., Daily Totals		$451.95		$760.20	$37.66	$63.35
Crew E-14	Hr.	Daily	Hr.	Daily	Bare Costs	Incl. O&P
1 Welder Foreman	$32.60	$260.80	$62.05	$496.40	$32.60	$62.05
1 Gas Welding Machine		82.35		90.60	10.29	11.32
8 L.H., Daily Totals		$343.15		$587.00	$42.89	$73.37
Crew E-16	Hr.	Daily	Hr.	Daily	Bare Costs	Incl. O&P
1 Welder Foreman	$32.60	$260.80	$62.05	$496.40	$31.60	$60.15
1 Welder	30.60	244.80	58.25	466.00		
1 Gas Welding Machine		82.35		90.60	5.15	5.66
16 L.H., Daily Totals		$587.95		$1053.00	$36.75	$65.81
Crew E-17	Hr.	Daily	Hr.	Daily	Bare Costs	Incl. O&P
1 Structural Steel Foreman	$32.60	$260.80	$62.05	$496.40	$31.60	$60.15
1 Structural Steel Worker	30.60	244.80	58.25	466.00		
1 Power Tool		2.00		2.20	.13	.14
16 L.H., Daily Totals		$507.60		$964.60	$31.73	$60.29
Crew E-18	Hr.	Daily	Hr.	Daily	Bare Costs	Incl. O&P
1 Structural Steel Foreman	$32.60	$260.80	$62.05	$496.40	$30.56	$56.40
3 Structural Steel Workers	30.60	734.40	58.25	1398.00		
1 Equipment Operator (med.)	28.40	227.20	45.20	361.60		
1 Crane, 20 Ton		512.55		563.80	12.81	14.10
40 L.H., Daily Totals		$1734.95		$2819.80	$43.37	$70.50
Crew E-19	Hr.	Daily	Hr.	Daily	Bare Costs	Incl. O&P
1 Structural Steel Worker	$30.60	$244.80	$58.25	$466.00	$30.13	$54.53
1 Structural Steel Foreman	32.60	260.80	62.05	496.40		
1 Equip. Oper. (light)	27.20	217.60	43.30	346.40		
1 Power Tool		2.00		2.20		
1 Crane, 20 ton		512.55		563.80	21.44	23.58
24 L.H., Daily Totals		$1237.75		$1874.80	$51.57	$78.11

Crews

Crew No.	Bare Costs		Incl. Subs O & P		Cost Per Labor-Hour	
Crew E-20	Hr.	Daily	Hr.	Daily	Bare Costs	Incl. O&P
1 Structural Steel Foreman	$32.60	$260.80	$62.05	$496.40	$29.88	$54.78
5 Structural Steel Workers	30.60	1224.00	58.25	2330.00		
1 Equip. Oper. (crane)	29.35	234.80	46.70	373.60		
1 Oiler	24.05	192.40	38.25	306.00		
1 Power Tool		2.00		2.20		
1 Crane, 40 ton		694.70		764.15	10.89	11.97
64 L.H., Daily Totals		$2608.70		$4272.35	$40.77	$66.75
Crew E-22	Hr.	Daily	Hr.	Daily	Bare Costs	Incl. O&P
1 Skilled Worker Foreman	$30.05	$240.40	$49.80	$398.40	$28.72	$47.60
2 Skilled Worker	28.05	448.80	46.50	744.00		
24 L.H., Daily Totals		$689.20		$1142.40	$28.72	$47.60
Crew E-24	Hr.	Daily	Hr.	Daily	Bare Costs	Incl. O&P
3 Structural Steel Worker	$30.60	$734.40	$58.25	$1398.00	$30.05	$54.99
1 Equipment Operator (medium)	28.40	227.20	45.20	361.60		
1-25 ton crane		549.35		604.30	17.17	18.88
32 L.H., Daily Totals		$1510.95		$2363.90	$47.22	$73.87
Crew F-2A	Hr.	Daily	Hr.	Daily	Bare Costs	Incl. O&P
2 Carpenters	$27.30	$436.80	$45.70	$731.20	$27.30	$45.70
16 L.H., Daily Totals		$436.80		$731.20	$27.30	$45.70
Crew F-3	Hr.	Daily	Hr.	Daily	Bare Costs	Incl. O&P
4 Carpenters	$27.30	$873.60	$45.70	$1462.40	$27.71	$45.90
1 Equip. Oper. (crane)	29.35	234.80	46.70	373.60		
1 Hyd. Crane, 12 Ton		443.45		487.80	11.09	12.19
40 L.H., Daily Totals		$1551.85		$2323.80	$38.80	$58.09
Crew F-4	Hr.	Daily	Hr.	Daily	Bare Costs	Incl. O&P
4 Carpenters	$27.30	$873.60	$45.70	$1462.40	$27.10	$44.63
1 Equip. Oper. (crane)	29.35	234.80	46.70	373.60		
1 Equip. Oper. Oiler	24.05	192.40	38.25	306.00		
1 Hyd. Crane, 55 Ton		793.10		872.40	16.52	18.18
48 L.H., Daily Totals		$2093.90		$3014.40	$43.62	$62.81
Crew F-5	Hr.	Daily	Hr.	Daily	Bare Costs	Incl. O&P
1 Carpenter Foreman	$29.30	$234.40	$49.05	$392.40	$27.80	$46.54
3 Carpenters	27.30	655.20	45.70	1096.80		
32 L.H., Daily Totals		$889.60		$1489.20	$27.80	$46.54
Crew F-6	Hr.	Daily	Hr.	Daily	Bare Costs	Incl. O&P
2 Carpenters	$27.30	$436.80	$45.70	$731.20	$25.37	$41.98
2 Building Laborers	21.45	343.20	35.90	574.40		
1 Equip. Oper. (crane)	29.35	234.80	46.70	373.60		
1 Hyd. Crane, 12 Ton		443.45		487.80	11.09	12.19
40 L.H., Daily Totals		$1458.25		$2167.00	$36.46	$54.17
Crew F-7	Hr.	Daily	Hr.	Daily	Bare Costs	Incl. O&P
2 Carpenters	$27.30	$436.80	$45.70	$731.20	$24.38	$40.80
2 Building Laborers	21.45	343.20	35.90	574.40		
32 L.H., Daily Totals		$780.00		$1305.60	$24.38	$40.80

Crew No.	Bare Costs		Incl. Subs O & P		Cost Per Labor-Hour	
Crew G-1	Hr.	Daily	Hr.	Daily	Bare Costs	Incl. O&P
1 Roofer Foreman	$26.10	$208.80	$47.55	$380.40	$22.67	$41.29
4 Roofers, Composition	24.10	771.20	43.90	1404.80		
2 Roofer Helpers	18.10	289.60	32.95	527.20		
1 Application Equipment		165.70		182.35		
1 Tar Kettle/Pot		45.90		50.50		
1 Crew Truck		197.30		217.05	7.30	8.03
56 L.H., Daily Totals		$1678.50		$2762.20	$29.97	$49.32
Crew G-2	Hr.	Daily	Hr.	Daily	Bare Costs	Incl. O&P
1 Plasterer	$25.70	$205.60	$41.95	$335.60	$22.92	$37.70
1 Plasterer Helper	21.60	172.80	35.25	282.00		
1 Building Laborer	21.45	171.60	35.90	287.20		
1 Grouting Equipment		235.25		258.75	9.80	10.78
24 L.H., Daily Totals		$785.25		$1163.55	$32.72	$48.48
Crew G-3	Hr.	Daily	Hr.	Daily	Bare Costs	Incl. O&P
2 Sheet Metal Workers	$31.75	$508.00	$50.90	$814.40	$26.60	$43.40
2 Building Laborers	21.45	343.20	35.90	574.40		
32 L.H., Daily Totals		$851.20		$1388.80	$26.60	$43.40
Crew G-4	Hr.	Daily	Hr.	Daily	Bare Costs	Incl. O&P
1 Labor Foreman (outside)	$23.45	$187.60	$39.25	$314.00	$22.12	$37.02
2 Building Laborers	21.45	343.20	35.90	574.40		
1 Light Truck, 1.5 Ton		171.95		189.15		
1 Air Compr., 160 C.F.M.		97.40		107.15	11.22	12.35
24 L.H., Daily Totals		$800.15		$1184.70	$33.34	$49.37
Crew G-5	Hr.	Daily	Hr.	Daily	Bare Costs	Incl. O&P
1 Roofer Foreman	$26.10	$208.80	$47.55	$380.40	$22.10	$40.25
2 Roofers, Composition	24.10	385.60	43.90	702.40		
2 Roofer Helpers	18.10	289.60	32.95	527.20		
1 Application Equipment		165.70		182.25	4.14	4.56
40 L.H., Daily Totals		$1049.70		$1792.25	$26.24	$44.81
Crew G-6A	Hr.	Daily	Hr.	Daily	Bare Costs	Incl. O&P
2 Roofers Composition	$24.10	$385.60	$43.90	$702.40	$24.10	$43.90
1 Small Compressor		20.95		23.05		
2 Pneumatic Nailers		39.90		43.90	3.80	4.18
16 L.H., Daily Totals		$446.45		$769.35	$27.90	$48.08
Crew G-7	Hr.	Daily	Hr.	Daily	Bare Costs	Incl. O&P
1 Carpenter	$27.30	$218.40	$45.70	$365.60	$27.30	$45.70
1 Small Compressor		20.95		23.05		
1 Pneumatic Nailer		19.95		21.95	5.11	5.62
8 L.H., Daily Totals		$259.30		$410.60	$32.41	$51.32
Crew H-1	Hr.	Daily	Hr.	Daily	Bare Costs	Incl. O&P
2 Glaziers	$26.60	$425.60	$43.15	$690.40	$28.60	$50.70
2 Struc. Steel Workers	30.60	489.60	58.25	932.00		
32 L.H., Daily Totals		$915.20		$1622.40	$28.60	$50.70
Crew H-2	Hr.	Daily	Hr.	Daily	Bare Costs	Incl. O&P
2 Glaziers	$26.60	$425.60	$43.15	$690.40	$24.88	$40.73
1 Building Laborer	21.45	171.60	35.90	287.20		
24 L.H., Daily Totals		$597.20		$977.60	$24.88	$40.73
Crew H-3	Hr.	Daily	Hr.	Daily	Bare Costs	Incl. O&P
1 Glazier	$26.60	$212.80	$43.15	$345.20	$23.73	$39.00
1 Helper	20.85	166.80	34.85	278.80		
16 L.H., Daily Totals		$379.60		$624.00	$23.73	$39.00

Crews

Crew No.	Bare Costs Hr.	Bare Costs Daily	Incl. Subs O & P Hr.	Incl. Subs O & P Daily	Cost Per Labor-Hour Bare Costs	Cost Per Labor-Hour Incl. O&P
Crew J-1						
3 Plasterers	$25.70	$616.80	$41.95	$1006.80	$24.06	$39.27
2 Plasterer Helpers	21.60	345.60	35.25	564.00		
1 Mixing Machine, 6 C.F.		42.45		46.70	1.06	1.17
40 L.H., Daily Totals		$1004.85		$1617.50	$25.12	$40.44
Crew J-2						
3 Plasterers	$25.70	$616.80	$41.95	$1006.80	$24.52	$39.87
2 Plasterer Helpers	21.60	345.60	35.25	564.00		
1 Lather	26.80	214.40	42.85	342.80		
1 Mixing Machine, 6 C.F.		42.45		46.70	.88	.97
48 L.H., Daily Totals		$1219.25		$1960.30	$25.40	$40.84
Crew J-3						
1 Terrazzo Worker	$26.55	$212.40	$41.90	$335.20	$24.15	$38.10
1 Terrazzo Helper	21.75	174.00	34.30	274.40		
1 Terrazzo Grinder, Electric		45.70		50.25		
1 Terrazzo Mixer		52.80		58.10	6.16	6.77
16 L.H., Daily Totals		$484.90		$717.95	$30.31	$44.87
Crew J-4						
1 Tile Layer	$26.65	$213.20	$42.05	$336.40	$24.05	$37.95
1 Tile Layer Helper	21.45	171.60	33.85	270.80		
16 L.H., Daily Totals		$384.80		$607.20	$24.05	$37.95
Crew K-1						
1 Carpenter	$27.30	$218.40	$45.70	$365.60	$24.52	$40.58
1 Truck Driver (light)	21.75	174.00	35.45	283.60		
1 Truck w/Power Equip.		179.45		197.40	11.22	12.34
16 L.H., Daily Totals		$571.85		$846.60	$35.74	$52.92
Crew K-2						
1 Struc. Steel Foreman	$32.60	$260.80	$62.05	$496.40	$28.32	$51.92
1 Struc. Steel Worker	30.60	244.80	58.25	466.00		
1 Truck Driver (light)	21.75	174.00	35.45	283.60		
1 Truck w/Power Equip.		179.45		197.40	7.48	8.22
24 L.H., Daily Totals		$859.05		$1443.40	$35.80	$60.14
Crew L-1						
1 Electrician	$31.90	$255.20	$49.30	$394.40	$32.25	$50.15
1 Plumber	32.60	260.80	51.00	408.00		
16 L.H., Daily Totals		$516.00		$802.40	$32.25	$50.15
Crew L-2						
1 Carpenter	$27.30	$218.40	$45.70	$365.60	$24.08	$40.28
1 Carpenter Helper	20.85	166.80	34.85	278.80		
16 L.H., Daily Totals		$385.20		$644.40	$24.08	$40.28
Crew L-3						
1 Carpenter	$27.30	$218.40	$45.70	$365.60	$29.56	$47.90
.5 Electrician	31.90	127.60	49.30	197.20		
.5 Sheet Metal Worker	31.75	127.00	50.90	203.60		
16 L.H., Daily Totals		$473.00		$766.40	$29.56	$47.90
Crew L-3A						
1 Carpenter Foreman (outside)	$29.30	$234.40	$49.05	$392.40	$30.12	$49.67
.5 Sheet Metal Worker	31.75	127.00	50.90	203.60		
12 L.H., Daily Totals		$361.40		$596.00	$30.12	$49.67

Crew No.	Bare Costs Hr.	Bare Costs Daily	Incl. Subs O & P Hr.	Incl. Subs O & P Daily	Cost Per Labor-Hour Bare Costs	Cost Per Labor-Hour Incl. O&P
Crew L-4						
2 Skilled Workers	$28.05	$448.80	$46.50	$744.00	$25.65	$42.62
1 Helper	20.85	166.80	34.85	278.80		
24 L.H., Daily Totals		$615.60		$1022.80	$25.65	$42.62
Crew L-5						
1 Struc. Steel Foreman	$32.60	$260.80	$62.05	$496.40	$30.71	$57.14
5 Struc. Steel Workers	30.60	1224.00	58.25	2330.00		
1 Equip. Oper. (crane)	29.35	234.80	46.70	373.60		
1 Hyd. Crane, 25 Ton		549.35		604.30	9.81	10.79
56 L.H., Daily Totals		$2268.95		$3804.30	$40.52	$67.93
Crew L-5A						
1 Structural Steel Foreman	$32.60	$260.80	$62.05	$496.40	$30.79	$56.31
2 Structural Steel Worker	30.60	489.60	58.25	932.00		
1 Equip. Oper. (crane)	29.35	234.80	46.70	373.60		
1 Crane, SP, 25 Ton		547.90		602.70	17.12	18.83
32 L.H., Daily Totals		$1533.10		$2404.70	$47.91	$75.14
Crew L-6						
1 Plumber	$32.60	$260.80	$51.00	$408.00	$32.37	$50.43
.5 Electrician	31.90	127.60	49.30	197.20		
12 L.H., Daily Totals		$388.40		$605.20	$32.37	$50.43
Crew L-7						
2 Carpenters	$27.30	$436.80	$45.70	$731.20	$26.29	$43.41
1 Building Laborer	21.45	171.60	35.90	287.20		
.5 Electrician	31.90	127.60	49.30	197.20		
28 L.H., Daily Totals		$736.00		$1215.60	$26.29	$43.41
Crew L-8						
2 Carpenters	$27.30	$436.80	$45.70	$731.20	$28.36	$46.76
.5 Plumber	32.60	130.40	51.00	204.00		
20 L.H., Daily Totals		$567.20		$935.20	$28.36	$46.76
Crew L-9						
1 Labor Foreman (inside)	$21.95	$175.60	$36.75	$294.00	$24.76	$42.54
2 Building Laborers	21.45	343.20	35.90	574.40		
1 Struc. Steel Worker	30.60	244.80	58.25	466.00		
.5 Electrician	31.90	127.60	49.30	197.20		
36 L.H., Daily Totals		$891.20		$1531.60	$24.76	$42.54
Crew L-10						
1 Structural Steel Foreman	$32.60	$260.80	$62.05	$496.40	$30.85	$55.67
1 Structural Steel Worker	30.60	244.80	58.25	466.00		
1 Equip. Oper. (crane)	29.35	234.80	46.70	373.60		
1 Hyd. Crane, 12 Ton		443.45		487.80	18.48	20.32
24 L.H., Daily Totals		$1183.85		$1823.80	$49.33	$75.99
Crew M-1						
3 Elevator Constructors	$33.15	$795.60	$51.85	$1244.40	$31.49	$49.25
1 Elevator Apprentice	26.50	212.00	41.45	331.60		
5 Hand Tools		85.00		93.50	2.66	2.92
32 L.H., Daily Totals		$1092.60		$1669.50	$34.15	$52.17
Crew Q-1						
1 Plumber	$32.60	$260.80	$51.00	$408.00	$29.35	$45.92
1 Plumber Apprentice	26.10	208.80	40.85	326.80		
16 L.H., Daily Totals		$469.60		$734.80	$29.35	$45.92

Crews

Crew No.	Bare Costs		Incl. Subs O & P		Cost Per Labor-Hour	
Crew Q-1C	Hr.	Daily	Hr.	Daily	Bare Costs	Incl. O&P
1 Plumber	$32.60	$260.80	$51.00	$408.00	$29.03	$45.68
1 Plumber Apprentice	26.10	208.80	40.85	326.80		
1 Equip. Oper. (medium)	28.40	227.20	45.20	361.60		
1 Trencher, Chain		535.90		589.50	22.33	24.56
24 L.H., Daily Totals		$1232.70		$1685.90	$51.36	$70.24
Crew Q-2	Hr.	Daily	Hr.	Daily	Bare Costs	Incl. O&P
2 Plumbers	$32.60	$521.60	$51.00	$816.00	$30.43	$47.62
1 Plumber Apprentice	26.10	208.80	40.85	326.80		
24 L.H., Daily Totals		$730.40		$1142.80	$30.43	$47.62
Crew Q-3	Hr.	Daily	Hr.	Daily	Bare Costs	Incl. O&P
1 Plumber Foreman (ins)	$33.10	$264.80	$51.80	$414.40	$31.10	$48.66
2 Plumbers	32.60	521.60	51.00	816.00		
1 Plumber Apprentice	26.10	208.80	40.85	326.80		
32 L.H., Daily Totals		$995.20		$1557.20	$31.10	$48.66
Crew Q-4	Hr.	Daily	Hr.	Daily	Bare Costs	Incl. O&P
1 Plumber Foreman (ins)	$33.10	$264.80	$51.80	$414.40	$31.10	$48.66
1 Plumber	32.60	260.80	51.00	408.00		
1 Welder (plumber)	32.60	260.80	51.00	408.00		
1 Plumber Apprentice	26.10	208.80	40.85	326.80		
1 Electric Welding Mach.		49.70		54.65	1.55	1.71
32 L.H., Daily Totals		$1044.90		$1611.85	$32.65	$50.37
Crew Q-5	Hr.	Daily	Hr.	Daily	Bare Costs	Incl. O&P
1 Steamfitter	$32.75	$262.00	$51.25	$410.00	$29.48	$46.13
1 Steamfitter Apprentice	26.20	209.60	41.00	328.00		
16 L.H., Daily Totals		$471.60		$738.00	$29.48	$46.13
Crew Q-6	Hr.	Daily	Hr.	Daily	Bare Costs	Incl. O&P
2 Steamfitters	$32.75	$524.00	$51.25	$820.00	$30.57	$47.83
1 Steamfitter Apprentice	26.20	209.60	41.00	328.00		
24 L.H., Daily Totals		$733.60		$1148.00	$30.57	$47.83
Crew Q-7	Hr.	Daily	Hr.	Daily	Bare Costs	Incl. O&P
1 Steamfitter Foreman (ins)	$33.25	$266.00	$52.05	$416.40	$31.24	$48.89
2 Steamfitters	32.75	524.00	51.25	820.00		
1 Steamfitter Apprentice	26.20	209.60	41.00	328.00		
32 L.H., Daily Totals		$999.60		$1564.40	$31.24	$48.89
Crew Q-8	Hr.	Daily	Hr.	Daily	Bare Costs	Incl. O&P
1 Steamfitter Foreman (ins)	$33.25	$266.00	$52.05	$416.40	$31.24	$48.89
1 Steamfitter	32.75	262.00	51.25	410.00		
1 Welder (steamfitter)	32.75	262.00	51.25	410.00		
1 Steamfitter Apprentice	26.20	209.60	41.00	328.00		
1 Electric Welding Mach.		49.70		54.65	1.55	1.71
32 L.H., Daily Totals		$1049.30		$1619.05	$32.79	$50.60
Crew Q-9	Hr.	Daily	Hr.	Daily	Bare Costs	Incl. O&P
1 Sheet Metal Worker	$31.75	$254.00	$50.90	$407.20	$28.58	$45.80
1 Sheet Metal Apprentice	25.40	203.20	40.70	325.60		
16 L.H., Daily Totals		$457.20		$732.80	$28.58	$45.80
Crew Q-10	Hr.	Daily	Hr.	Daily	Bare Costs	Incl. O&P
2 Sheet Metal Workers	$31.75	$508.00	$50.90	$814.40	$29.63	$47.50
1 Sheet Metal Apprentice	25.40	203.20	40.70	325.60		
24 L.H., Daily Totals		$711.20		$1140.00	$29.63	$47.50
Crew Q-11	Hr.	Daily	Hr.	Daily	Bare Costs	Incl. O&P
1 Sheet Metal Foreman (ins)	$32.25	$258.00	$51.70	$413.60	$30.29	$48.55
2 Sheet Metal Workers	31.75	508.00	50.90	814.40		
1 Sheet Metal Apprentice	25.40	203.20	40.70	325.60		
32 L.H., Daily Totals		$969.20		$1553.60	$30.29	$48.55
Crew Q-12	Hr.	Daily	Hr.	Daily	Bare Costs	Incl. O&P
1 Sprinkler Installer	$32.50	$260.00	$50.90	$407.20	$29.25	$45.80
1 Sprinkler Apprentice	26.00	208.00	40.70	325.60		
16 L.H., Daily Totals		$468.00		$732.80	$29.25	$45.80
Crew Q-13	Hr.	Daily	Hr.	Daily	Bare Costs	Incl. O&P
1 Sprinkler Foreman (ins)	$33.00	$264.00	$51.70	$413.60	$31.00	$48.55
2 Sprinkler Installers	32.50	520.00	50.90	814.40		
1 Sprinkler Apprentice	26.00	208.00	40.70	325.60		
32 L.H., Daily Totals		$992.00		$1553.60	$31.00	$48.55
Crew Q-14	Hr.	Daily	Hr.	Daily	Bare Costs	Incl. O&P
1 Asbestos Worker	$30.45	$243.60	$50.65	$405.20	$27.40	$45.58
1 Asbestos Apprentice	24.35	194.80	40.50	324.00		
16 L.H., Daily Totals		$438.40		$729.20	$27.40	$45.58
Crew Q-15	Hr.	Daily	Hr.	Daily	Bare Costs	Incl. O&P
1 Plumber	$32.60	$260.80	$51.00	$408.00	$29.35	$45.92
1 Plumber Apprentice	26.10	208.80	40.85	326.80		
1 Electric Welding Mach.		49.70		54.65	3.11	3.42
16 L.H., Daily Totals		$519.30		$789.45	$32.46	$49.34
Crew Q-16	Hr.	Daily	Hr.	Daily	Bare Costs	Incl. O&P
2 Plumbers	$32.60	$521.60	$51.00	$816.00	$30.43	$47.62
1 Plumber Apprentice	26.10	208.80	40.85	326.80		
1 Electric Welding Mach.		49.70		54.65	2.07	2.28
24 L.H., Daily Totals		$780.10		$1197.45	$32.50	$49.90
Crew Q-17	Hr.	Daily	Hr.	Daily	Bare Costs	Incl. O&P
1 Steamfitter	$32.75	$262.00	$51.25	$410.00	$29.48	$46.13
1 Steamfitter Apprentice	26.20	209.60	41.00	328.00		
1 Electric Welding Mach.		49.70		54.65	3.11	3.42
16 L.H., Daily Totals		$521.30		$792.65	$32.59	$49.55
Crew Q-17A	Hr.	Daily	Hr.	Daily	Bare Costs	Incl. O&P
1 Steamfitter	$32.75	$262.00	$51.25	$410.00	$29.43	$46.32
1 Steamfitter Apprentice	26.20	209.60	41.00	328.00		
1 Equip. Oper. (crane)	29.35	234.80	46.70	373.60		
1 Truck Crane, 12 Ton		443.45		487.80		
1 Electric Welding Mach.		49.70		54.65	20.55	22.60
24 L.H., Daily Totals		$1199.55		$1654.05	$49.98	$68.92
Crew Q-18	Hr.	Daily	Hr.	Daily	Bare Costs	Incl. O&P
2 Steamfitters	$32.75	$524.00	$51.25	$820.00	$30.57	$47.83
1 Steamfitter Apprentice	26.20	209.60	41.00	328.00		
1 Electric Welding Mach.		49.70		54.65	2.07	2.28
24 L.H., Daily Totals		$783.30		$1202.65	$32.64	$50.11
Crew Q-19	Hr.	Daily	Hr.	Daily	Bare Costs	Incl. O&P
1 Steamfitter	$32.75	$262.00	$51.25	$410.00	$30.28	$47.18
1 Steamfitter Apprentice	26.20	209.60	41.00	328.00		
1 Electrician	31.90	255.20	49.30	394.40		
24 L.H., Daily Totals		$726.80		$1132.40	$30.28	$47.18

Crews

Crew No.	Bare Costs		Incl. Subs O & P		Cost Per Labor-Hour	
	Hr.	Daily	Hr.	Daily	Bare Costs	Incl. O&P
Crew Q-20						
1 Sheet Metal Worker	$31.75	$254.00	$50.90	$407.20	$29.24	$46.50
1 Sheet Metal Apprentice	25.40	203.20	40.70	325.60		
.5 Electrician	31.90	127.60	49.30	197.20		
20 L.H., Daily Totals		$584.80		$930.00	$29.24	$46.50
Crew Q-21	Hr.	Daily	Hr.	Daily	Bare Costs	Incl. O&P
2 Steamfitters	$32.75	$524.00	$51.25	$820.00	$30.90	$48.20
1 Steamfitter Apprentice	26.20	209.60	41.00	328.00		
1 Electrician	31.90	255.20	49.30	394.40		
32 L.H., Daily Totals		$988.80		$1542.40	$30.90	$48.20
Crew Q-22	Hr.	Daily	Hr.	Daily	Bare Costs	Incl. O&P
1 Plumber	$32.60	$260.80	$51.00	$408.00	$29.35	$45.92
1 Plumber Apprentice	26.10	208.80	40.85	326.80		
1 Truck Crane, 12 Ton		443.45		487.80	27.72	30.49
16 L.H., Daily Totals		$913.05		$1222.60	$57.07	$76.41
Crew Q-22A	Hr.	Daily	Hr.	Daily	Bare Costs	Incl. O&P
1 Plumber	$32.60	$260.80	$51.00	$408.00	$27.38	$43.61
1 Plumber Apprentice	26.10	208.80	40.85	326.80		
1 Laborer	21.45	171.60	35.90	287.20		
1 Equip. Oper. (crane)	29.35	234.80	46.70	373.60		
1 Truck Crane, 12 Ton		443.45		487.80	13.86	15.24
32 L.H., Daily Totals		$1319.45		$1883.40	$41.24	$58.85
Crew Q-23	Hr.	Daily	Hr.	Daily	Bare Costs	Incl. O&P
1 Plumber Foreman	$34.60	$276.80	$54.15	$433.20	$31.87	$50.12
1 Plumber	32.60	260.80	51.00	408.00		
1 Equip. Oper. (medium)	28.40	227.20	45.20	361.60		
1 Power Tools		2.00		2.20		
1 Crane, 20 Ton		512.55		563.80	21.44	23.58
24 L.H., Daily Totals		$1279.35		$1768.80	$53.31	$73.70
Crew R-1	Hr.	Daily	Hr.	Daily	Bare Costs	Incl. O&P
1 Electrician Foreman	$32.40	$259.20	$50.05	$400.40	$28.30	$44.61
3 Electricians	31.90	765.60	49.30	1183.20		
2 Helpers	20.85	333.60	34.85	557.60		
48 L.H., Daily Totals		$1358.40		$2141.20	$28.30	$44.61
Crew R-1A	Hr.	Daily	Hr.	Daily	Bare Costs	Incl. O&P
1 Electrician	$31.90	$255.20	$49.30	$394.40	$26.38	$42.08
1 Helper	20.85	166.80	34.85	278.80		
16 L.H., Daily Totals		$422.00		$673.20	$26.38	$42.08
Crew R-2	Hr.	Daily	Hr.	Daily	Bare Costs	Incl. O&P
1 Electrician Foreman	$32.40	$259.20	$50.05	$400.40	$28.45	$44.91
3 Electricians	31.90	765.60	49.30	1183.20		
2 Helpers	20.85	333.60	34.85	557.60		
1 Equip. Oper. (crane)	29.35	234.80	46.70	373.60		
1 S.P. Crane, 5 Ton		271.45		298.60	4.85	5.33
56 L.H., Daily Totals		$1864.65		$2813.40	$33.30	$50.24
Crew R-3	Hr.	Daily	Hr.	Daily	Bare Costs	Incl. O&P
1 Electrician Foreman	$32.40	$259.20	$50.05	$400.40	$31.59	$49.08
1 Electrician	31.90	255.20	49.30	394.40		
.5 Equip. Oper. (crane)	29.35	117.40	46.70	186.80		
.5 S.P. Crane, 5 Ton		135.73		149.30	6.79	7.46
20 L.H., Daily Totals		$767.53		$1130.90	$38.38	$56.54

Crew No.	Bare Costs		Incl. Subs O & P		Cost Per Labor-Hour	
Crew R-4	Hr.	Daily	Hr.	Daily	Bare Costs	Incl. O&P
1 Struc. Steel Foreman	$32.60	$260.80	$62.05	$496.40	$31.26	$57.22
3 Struc. Steel Workers	30.60	734.40	58.25	1398.00		
1 Electrician	31.90	255.20	49.30	394.40		
1 Gas Welding Machine		82.35		90.60	2.06	2.26
40 L.H., Daily Totals		$1332.75		$2379.40	$33.32	$59.48
Crew R-5	Hr.	Daily	Hr.	Daily	Bare Costs	Incl. O&P
1 Electrician Foreman	$32.40	$259.20	$50.05	$400.40	$27.93	$44.11
4 Electrician Linemen	31.90	1020.80	49.30	1577.60		
2 Electrician Operators	31.90	510.40	49.30	788.80		
4 Electrician Groundmen	20.85	667.20	34.85	1115.20		
1 Crew Truck		197.30		217.05		
1 Tool Van		212.10		233.30		
1 Pickup Truck, 3/4 Ton		128.95		141.85		
.2 Crane, 55 Ton		158.62		174.50		
.2 Crane, 12 Ton		88.69		97.55		
.2 Auger, Truck Mtd.		355.20		390.70		
1 Tractor w/Winch		296.95		326.65	16.34	17.97
88 L.H., Daily Totals		$3895.41		$5463.60	$44.27	$62.08
Crew R-6	Hr.	Daily	Hr.	Daily	Bare Costs	Incl. O&P
1 Electrician Foreman	$32.40	$259.20	$50.05	$400.40	$27.93	$44.11
4 Electrician Linemen	31.90	1020.80	49.30	1577.60		
2 Electrician Operators	31.90	510.40	49.30	788.80		
4 Electrician Groundmen	20.85	667.20	34.85	1115.20		
1 Crew Truck		197.30		217.05		
1 Tool Van		212.10		233.30		
1 Pickup Truck, 3/4 Ton		128.95		141.85		
.2 Crane, 55 Ton		158.62		174.50		
.2 Crane, 12 Ton		88.69		97.55		
.2 Auger, Truck Mtd.		355.20		390.70		
1 Tractor w/Winch		296.95		326.65		
3 Cable Trailers		419.70		461.65		
.5 Tensioning Rig		135.95		149.55		
.5 Cable Pulling Rig		813.50		894.85	31.90	35.09
88 L.H., Daily Totals		$5264.56		$6969.65	$59.83	$79.20
Crew R-7	Hr.	Daily	Hr.	Daily	Bare Costs	Incl. O&P
1 Electrician Foreman	$32.40	$259.20	$50.05	$400.40	$22.78	$37.38
5 Electrician Groundmen	20.85	834.00	34.85	1394.00		
1 Crew Truck		197.30		217.05	4.11	4.52
48 L.H., Daily Totals		$1290.50		$2011.45	$26.89	$41.90
Crew R-8	Hr.	Daily	Hr.	Daily	Bare Costs	Incl. O&P
1 Electrician Foreman	$32.40	$259.20	$50.05	$400.40	$28.30	$44.61
3 Electrician Linemen	31.90	765.60	49.30	1183.20		
2 Electrician Groundmen	20.85	333.60	34.85	557.60		
1 Pickup Truck, 3/4 Ton		128.95		141.85		
1 Crew Truck		197.30		217.05	6.80	7.48
48 L.H., Daily Totals		$1684.65		$2500.10	$35.10	$52.09
Crew R-9	Hr.	Daily	Hr.	Daily	Bare Costs	Incl. O&P
1 Electrician Foreman	$32.40	$259.20	$50.05	$400.40	$26.44	$42.17
1 Electrician Lineman	31.90	255.20	49.30	394.40		
2 Electrician Operators	31.90	510.40	49.30	788.80		
4 Electrician Groundmen	20.85	667.20	34.85	1115.20		
1 Pickup Truck, 3/4 Ton		128.95		141.85		
1 Crew Truck		197.30		217.05	5.10	5.61
64 L.H., Daily Totals		$2018.25		$3057.70	$31.54	$47.78

Crews

Crew No.	Bare Costs		Incl. Subs O & P		Cost Per Labor-Hour	
Crew R-10	Hr.	Daily	Hr.	Daily	Bare Costs	Incl. O&P
1 Electrician Foreman	$32.40	$259.20	$50.05	$400.40	$30.14	$47.02
4 Electrician Linemen	31.90	1020.80	49.30	1577.60		
1 Electrician Groundman	20.85	166.80	34.85	278.80		
1 Crew Truck		197.30		217.05		
3 Tram Cars		528.75		581.65	15.13	16.64
48 L.H., Daily Totals		$2172.85		$3055.50	$45.27	$63.66
Crew R-11	Hr.	Daily	Hr.	Daily	Bare Costs	Incl. O&P
1 Electrician Foreman	$32.40	$259.20	$50.05	$400.40	$28.90	$45.43
4 Electricians	31.90	1020.80	49.30	1577.60		
1 Helper	20.85	166.80	34.85	278.80		
1 Common Laborer	21.45	171.60	35.90	287.20		
1 Crew Truck		197.30		217.05		
1 Crane, 12 Ton		443.45		487.80	11.44	12.59
56 L.H., Daily Totals		$2259.15		$3248.85	$40.34	$58.02
Crew R-12	Hr.	Daily	Hr.	Daily	Bare Costs	Incl. O&P
1 Carpenter Foreman	$27.80	$222.40	$46.55	$372.40	$25.62	$43.31
4 Carpenters	27.30	873.60	45.70	1462.40		
4 Common Laborers	21.45	686.40	35.90	1148.80		
1 Equip. Oper. (med.)	28.40	227.20	45.20	361.60		
1 Steel Worker	30.60	244.80	58.25	466.00		
1 Dozer, 200 H.P.		838.95		922.85		
1 Pickup Truck, 3/4 Ton		128.95		141.85	11.00	12.10
88 L.H., Daily Totals		$3222.30		$4875.90	$36.62	$55.41
Crew R-13	Hr.	Daily	Hr.	Daily	Bare Costs	Incl. O&P
1 Electrician Foreman	$32.40	$259.20	$50.05	$400.40	$30.25	$47.15
3 Electricians	31.90	765.60	49.30	1183.20		
1 Equipment Operator	29.35	234.80	46.70	373.60		
1 Equipment Oiler	24.05	192.40	38.25	306.00		
.25-1 Hyd Crane, 33 Ton		173.74		191.10	3.62	3.98
48 L.H., Daily Totals		$1625.74		$2454.30	$33.87	$51.13
Crew R-15	Hr.	Daily	Hr.	Daily	Bare Costs	Incl. O&P
1 Electrician Foreman	$32.40	$259.20	$50.05	$400.40	$31.20	$48.42
4 Electricians	31.90	1020.80	49.30	1577.60		
1 Equipment Operator	27.20	217.60	43.30	346.40		
1 Aerial Lift Truck		281.35		309.50	5.86	6.45
48 L.H., Daily Totals		$1778.95		$2633.90	$37.06	$54.87
Crew R-18	Hr.	Daily	Hr.	Daily	Bare Costs	Incl. O&P
.25 Electrician Foreman	$32.40	$64.80	$50.05	$100.10	$25.14	$40.47
1 Electrician	31.90	255.20	49.30	394.40		
2 Helpers	20.85	333.60	34.85	557.60		
26 L.H., Daily Totals		$653.60		$1052.10	$25.14	$40.47
Crew R-19	Hr.	Daily	Hr.	Daily	Bare Costs	Incl. O&P
.5 Electrician Foreman	$32.40	$129.60	$50.05	$200.20	$32.00	$49.45
2 Electricians	31.90	510.40	49.30	788.80		
20 L.H., Daily Totals		$640.00		$989.00	$32.00	$49.45
Crew R-21	Hr.	Daily	Hr.	Daily	Bare Costs	Incl. O&P
1 Electrician Foreman	$32.40	$259.20	$50.05	$400.40	$31.94	$49.38
3 Electricians	31.90	765.60	49.30	1183.20		
.1 Equip. Oper. (med.)	28.40	22.72	45.20	36.16		
.1 Hyd. Crane 25 Ton		54.79		60.25	1.67	1.84
32. L.H., Daily Totals		$1102.31		$1680.01	$33.61	$51.22

Crew No.	Bare Costs		Incl. Subs O & P		Cost Per Labor-Hour	
Crew R-22	Hr.	Daily	Hr.	Daily	Bare Costs	Incl. O&P
.66 Electrician Foreman	$32.40	$171.07	$50.05	$264.26	$27.23	$43.20
2 Helpers	20.85	333.60	34.85	557.60		
2 Electricians	31.90	510.40	49.30	788.80		
37.28 L.H., Daily Totals		$1015.07		$1610.66	$27.23	$43.20

Historical Cost Indexes

The table below lists both the Means Historical Cost Index based on Jan. 1, 1993 = 100 as well as the computed value of an index based on Jan. 1, 1999 costs. Since the Jan. 1, 1999 figure is estimated, space is left to write in the actual index figures as they become available through either the quarterly "Means Construction Cost Indexes" or as printed in the "Engineering News-Record." To compute the actual index based on Jan. 1, 1999 = 100, divide the Historical Cost Index for a particular year by the actual Jan. 1, 1999 Construction Cost Index. Space has been left to advance the index figures as the year progresses.

Year	Historical Cost Index Jan. 1, 1993 = 100		Current Index Based on Jan. 1, 1999 = 100		Year	Historical Cost Index Jan. 1, 1993 = 100	Current Index Based on Jan. 1, 1999 = 100		Year	Historical Cost Index Jan. 1, 1993 = 100	Current Index Based on Jan. 1, 1999 = 100	
	Est.	Actual	Est.	Actual		Actual	Est.	Actual		Actual	Est.	Actual
Oct 1999					July 1984	82.0	70.4		July 1966	22.7	19.5	
July 1999					1983	80.2	68.9		1965	21.7	18.6	
April 1999					1982	76.1	65.4		1964	21.2	18.2	
Jan 1999	116.4		100.0	100.0	1981	70.0	60.1		1963	20.7	17.8	
July 1998		115.1	98.9		1980	62.9	54.0		1962	20.2	17.4	
1997		112.8	96.9		1979	57.8	49.7		1961	19.8	17.0	
1996		110.2	94.7		1978	53.5	46.0		1960	19.7	16.9	
1995		107.6	92.4		1977	49.5	42.5		1959	19.3	16.6	
1994		104.4	89.7		1976	46.9	40.3		1958	18.8	16.2	
1993		101.7	87.4		1975	44.8	38.5		1957	18.4	15.8	
1992		99.4	85.4		1974	41.4	35.6		1956	17.6	15.1	
1991		96.8	83.2		1973	37.7	32.4		1955	16.6	14.3	
1990		94.3	81.0		1972	34.8	29.9		1954	16.0	13.7	
1989		92.1	79.2		1971	32.1	27.6		1953	15.8	13.6	
1988		89.9	77.2		1970	28.7	24.7		1952	15.4	13.2	
1987		87.7	75.3		1969	26.9	23.1		1951	15.0	12.9	
1986		84.2	72.4		1968	24.9	21.4		1950	13.7	11.8	
1985		82.6	71.0		1967	23.5	20.2		1949	13.3	11.4	

Adjustments to Costs

The Historical Cost Index can be used to convert National Average building costs at a particular time to the approximate building costs for some other time.

Example:

Estimate and compare construction costs for different years in the same city.

To estimate the National Average construction cost of a building in 1970, knowing that it cost $900,000 in 1999:

INDEX in 1970 = 28.7

INDEX in 1999 = 116.4

Note: The City Cost Indexes for Canada can be used to convert U.S. National averages to local costs in Canadian dollars.

Time Adjustment using the Historical Cost Indexes:

$$\frac{\text{Index for Year A}}{\text{Index for Year B}} \times \text{Cost in Year B} = \text{Cost in Year A}$$

$$\frac{\text{INDEX 1970}}{\text{INDEX 1999}} \times \text{Cost 1999} = \text{Cost 1970}$$

$$\frac{28.7}{116.4} \times \$900{,}000 = .247 \times \$900{,}000 = \$222{,}300$$

The construction cost of the building in 1970 is $222,300.

How to Use the City Cost Indexes

What you should know before you begin

Means City Cost Indexes (CCI) are an extremely useful tool to use when you want to compare costs from city to city and region to region.

This publication contains average construction cost indexes for 305 major U.S. and Canadian cities and Location Factors covering over 930 three-digit zip code locations.

Keep in mind that a City Cost Index number is a *percentage ratio* of a specific city's cost to the national average cost of the same item at a stated time period.

In other words, these index figures represent relative construction *factors* (or, if you prefer, multipliers) for Material and Installation costs, as well as the weighted average for Total In Place costs for each CSI MasterFormat division. Installation costs include both labor and equipment rental costs.

The 30 City Average Index is the average of 30 major U.S. cities and serves as a National Average.

Index figures for both material and installation are based on the 30 major city average of 100 and represent the cost relationship as of July 1, 1998. The index for each division is computed from representative material and labor quantities for that division. The weighted average for each city is a weighted total of the components listed above it, but does not include relative productivity between trades or cities.

As changes occur in local material prices, labor rates and equipment rental rates, the impact of these changes should be accurately measured by the change in the City Cost Index for each particular city (as compared to the 30 City Average).

> *Therefore, if you know (or have estimated) building costs in one city today, you can easily convert those costs to expected building costs in another city.*
>
> *In addition, by using the Historical Cost Index, you can easily convert National Average building costs at a particular time to the approximate building costs for some other time. The City Cost Indexes can then be applied to calculate the costs for a particular city.*

Quick Calculations

Location Adjustment Using the City Cost Indexes:

$$\frac{\text{Index for City A}}{\text{Index for City B}} \times \text{Cost in City B} = \text{Cost in City A}$$

Time Adjustment for the National Average Using the Historical Cost Index:

$$\frac{\text{Index for Year A}}{\text{Index for Year B}} \times \text{Cost in Year B} = \text{Cost in Year A}$$

Adjustment from the National Average:

$$\frac{\text{Index for City A}}{100} \times \text{National Average Cost} = \text{Cost in City A}$$

Since each of the other R.S. Means publications contains many different items, any *one* item multiplied by the particular city index may give incorrect results. However, the larger the number of items compiled, the closer the results should be to actual costs for that particular city.

The City Cost Indexes for Canadian cities are calculated using Canadian material and equipment prices and labor rates, in Canadian dollars. Therefore, indexes for Canadian cities can be used to convert U.S. National Average prices to local costs in Canadian dollars.

How to use this section

1. Compare costs from city to city.

In using the Means Indexes, remember that an index number is not a fixed number but a *ratio:* It's a percentage ratio of a building component's cost at any stated time to the National Average cost of that same component at the same time period. Put in the form of an equation:

$$\frac{\text{Specific City Cost}}{\text{National Average Cost}} \times 100 = \text{City Index Number}$$

Therefore, when making cost comparisons between cities, do not subtract one city's index number from the index number of another city and read the result as a percentage difference. Instead, divide one city's index number by that of the other city. The resulting number may then be used as a multiplier to calculate cost differences from city to city.

The formula used to find cost differences between cities for the purpose of comparison is as follows:

$$\frac{\text{City A Index}}{\text{City B Index}} \times \text{City B Cost (Known)} = \text{City A Cost (Unknown)}$$

In addition, you can use *Means CCI* to calculate and compare costs division by division between cities using the same basic formula. (Just be sure that you're comparing similar divisions.)

2. Compare a specific city's construction costs with the National Average.

When you're studying construction location feasibility, it's advisable to compare a prospective project's cost index with an index of the National Average cost.

For example, divide the weighted average index of construction costs of a specific city by that of the 30 City Average, which = 100.

$$\frac{\text{City Index}}{100} = \% \text{ of National Average}$$

As a result, you get a ratio that indicates the relative cost of construction in that city in comparison with the National Average.

3. Convert U.S. National Average to actual costs in Canadian City

$$\frac{\text{Index for Canadian City}}{100} \times \text{National Average Cost} = \text{Cost in Canadian City in \$ CAN}$$

4. Adjust construction cost data based on a National Average.

When you use a source of construction cost data which is based on a National Average (such as *Means cost data publications*), it is necessary to adjust those costs to a specific location.

$$\frac{\text{City Index}}{100} \times \text{"Book" Cost Based on National Average Costs} = \text{City Cost (Unknown)}$$

5. When applying the City Cost Indexes to demolition projects, use the appropriate division index. For example, for removal of existing doors and windows, use the Division 8 index.

What you might like to know about how we developed the Indexes

To create a reliable index, R.S. Means researched the building type most often constructed in the United States and Canada. Because it was concluded that no one type of building completely represented the building construction industry, nine different types of buildings were combined to create a composite model.

The exact material, labor and equipment quantities are based on detailed analysis of these nine building types, then each quantity is weighted in proportion to expected usage. These various material items, labor hours, and equipment rental rates are thus combined to form a composite building representing as closely as possible the actual usage of materials, labor and equipment used in the North American Building Construction Industry.

The following structures were chosen to make up that composite model:

1. Factory, 1 story
2. Office, 2–4 story
3. Store, Retail
4. Town Hall, 2–3 story
5. High School, 2–3 story
6. Hospital, 4–8 story
7. Garage, Parking
8. Apartment, 1–3 story
9. Hotel/Motel, 2–3 story

For the purposes of ensuring the timeliness of the data, the components of the index for the composite model have been streamlined. They currently consist of:

- specific quantities of 66 commonly used construction materials;
- specific labor-hours for 21 building construction trades; and
- specific days of equipment rental for 6 types of construction equipment (normally used to install the 66 material items by the 21 trades.)

A sophisticated computer program handles the updating of all costs for each city on a quarterly basis. Material and equipment price quotations are gathered quarterly from over 305 cities in the United States and Canada. These prices and the latest negotiated labor wage rates for 21 different building trades are used to compile the quarterly update of the City Cost Index.

The 30 major U.S. cities used to calculate the National Average are:

Atlanta, GA
Baltimore, MD
Boston, MA
Buffalo, NY
Chicago, IL
Cincinnati, OH
Cleveland, OH
Columbus, OH
Dallas, TX
Denver, CO
Detroit, MI
Houston, TX
Indianapolis, IN
Kansas City, MO
Los Angeles, CA
Memphis, TN
Milwaukee, WI
Minneapolis, MN
Nashville, TN
New Orleans, LA
New York, NY
Philadelphia, PA
Phoenix, AZ
Pittsburgh, PA
St. Louis, MO
San Antonio, TX
San Diego, CA
San Francisco, CA
Seattle, WA
Washington, DC

F.Y.I.: The CSI MasterFormat Divisions

1. General Requirements
2. Site Work
3. Concrete
4. Masonry
5. Metals
6. Wood & Plastics
7. Thermal & Moisture Protection
8. Doors & Windows
9. Finishes
10. Specialties
11. Equipment
12. Furnishings
13. Special Construction
14. Conveying Systems
15. Mechanical
16. Electrical

The information presented in the CCI is organized according to the Construction Specifications Institute (CSI) MasterFormat.

What the CCI does not indicate

The weighted average for each city is a total of the components listed above weighted to reflect typical usage, but it does *not* include the productivity variations between trades or cities.

In addition, the CCI does not take into consideration factors such as the following:

- managerial efficiency
- competitive conditions
- automation
- restrictive union practices
- Unique local requirements
- regional variations due to specific building codes

City Cost Indexes

DIVISION		UNITED STATES 30 CITY AVERAGE			ALABAMA												
					BIRMINGHAM			HUNTSVILLE			MOBILE			MONTGOMERY			TUSCALOOSA		
		MAT.	INST.	TOTAL	MAT.	INST.	TOTAL	MAT.	INST.	TOTAL	MAT.	INST.	TOTAL	MAT.	INST.	TOTAL	MAT.	INST.	TOTAL
2	SITE WORK	100.0	100.0	100.0	89.7	93.7	92.8	88.8	93.1	92.1	100.3	87.3	90.3	100.8	87.1	90.3	89.2	92.6	91.9
031	CONCRETE FORMWORK	100.0	100.0	100.0	95.4	78.5	81.0	97.0	61.5	66.6	97.0	65.4	69.9	95.1	58.7	63.9	97.0	48.1	55.1
032	CONCRETE REINFORCEMENT	100.0	100.0	100.0	92.7	82.1	86.7	92.7	70.7	80.3	95.7	64.2	77.9	95.7	81.1	87.5	92.7	81.5	86.4
033	CAST IN PLACE CONCRETE	100.0	100.0	100.0	96.2	69.2	84.9	91.0	65.0	80.1	96.1	65.5	83.3	97.8	58.7	81.4	94.8	56.0	78.5
3	CONCRETE	100.0	100.0	100.0	89.6	77.1	83.3	87.2	66.0	76.5	90.1	66.7	78.3	90.8	64.6	77.6	89.0	59.1	73.9
4	MASONRY	100.0	100.0	100.0	84.1	74.0	77.8	84.0	60.8	69.6	84.7	64.3	72.1	85.1	44.7	60.0	84.3	47.2	61.2
5	METALS	100.0	100.0	100.0	98.8	93.6	96.9	98.4	88.9	95.0	97.0	86.4	93.2	97.1	91.6	95.1	97.5	92.3	95.6
6	WOOD & PLASTICS	100.0	100.0	100.0	95.4	79.7	87.3	94.4	61.1	77.2	94.4	66.7	80.1	92.0	61.1	76.0	94.4	48.4	70.7
7	THERMAL & MOISTURE PROTECTION	100.0	100.0	100.0	97.6	68.8	84.2	97.3	62.3	81.0	97.2	64.2	81.9	97.1	56.7	78.4	97.3	55.2	77.8
8	DOORS & WINDOWS	100.0	100.0	100.0	97.0	76.2	91.9	97.0	59.4	87.9	97.0	62.9	88.7	97.0	63.1	88.8	97.0	59.3	87.9
092	LATH, PLASTER & GYPSUM BOARD	100.0	100.0	100.0	113.3	79.6	91.6	109.8	60.4	77.9	109.8	66.2	81.6	109.8	60.4	77.9	109.8	47.3	69.5
095	ACOUSTICAL TREATMENT & WOOD FLOORING	100.0	100.0	100.0	100.2	79.6	86.8	100.2	60.4	74.4	100.2	66.2	78.1	100.2	60.4	74.4	100.2	47.3	65.9
096	FLOORING & CARPET	100.0	100.0	100.0	99.0	60.9	89.7	99.0	52.7	87.7	107.3	66.1	97.2	107.3	34.1	89.5	99.0	50.1	87.1
099	PAINTING & WALL COVERINGS	100.0	100.0	100.0	90.8	57.5	71.2	90.8	56.3	70.6	90.8	65.2	75.8	90.8	64.1	75.1	90.8	55.2	69.9
9	FINISHES	100.0	100.0	100.0	99.2	73.3	85.9	98.7	58.9	78.3	102.5	65.7	83.6	102.6	54.3	77.9	98.7	48.4	72.9
10-14	TOTAL DIV. 10 - 14	100.0	100.0	100.0	100.0	83.2	96.4	100.0	77.9	95.3	100.0	77.8	95.3	100.0	75.1	94.7	100.0	71.9	94.1
15	MECHANICAL	100.0	100.0	100.0	100.0	70.7	86.9	100.0	56.6	80.6	100.0	60.2	82.2	100.0	50.9	78.1	100.0	44.7	75.3
16	ELECTRICAL	100.0	100.0	100.0	95.5	69.4	77.9	95.9	70.8	79.0	95.9	65.8	75.6	95.5	48.1	63.5	95.8	69.4	78.0
1-16	WEIGHTED AVERAGE	100.0	100.0	100.0	96.5	77.0	87.1	96.1	68.4	82.7	97.0	68.9	83.4	97.1	60.8	79.6	96.2	62.2	79.8

DIVISION		ALASKA									ARIZONA								
		ANCHORAGE			FAIRBANKS			JUNEAU			FLAGSTAFF			MESA/TEMPE			PHOENIX		
		MAT.	INST.	TOTAL	MAT.	INST.	TOTAL	MAT.	INST.	TOTAL	MAT.	INST.	TOTAL	MAT.	INST.	TOTAL	MAT.	INST.	TOTAL
2	SITE WORK	127.1	136.7	134.5	113.1	136.7	131.3	124.2	136.7	133.9	89.4	100.4	97.8	77.4	99.8	94.7	77.1	100.7	95.2
031	CONCRETE FORMWORK	129.9	120.0	121.4	131.4	126.1	126.9	131.2	120.0	121.6	106.6	79.6	83.5	99.6	71.9	75.8	100.9	79.4	82.5
032	CONCRETE REINFORCEMENT	143.8	115.1	127.7	120.9	115.2	117.7	107.0	115.1	111.6	104.4	82.9	92.3	107.0	79.4	91.4	105.1	83.2	92.8
033	CAST IN PLACE CONCRETE	178.7	119.1	153.8	151.3	119.7	138.0	179.4	119.1	154.2	95.7	80.4	89.3	95.7	71.5	85.6	95.8	79.9	89.2
3	CONCRETE	152.2	117.8	134.9	130.2	120.7	125.4	147.8	117.9	132.7	122.1	80.2	100.9	100.5	73.1	86.7	100.1	80.0	90.0
4	MASONRY	174.8	124.1	143.3	167.6	124.1	140.6	155.1	124.1	135.8	101.6	71.2	82.7	111.0	58.2	78.2	97.6	75.6	84.0
5	METALS	129.8	102.6	120.0	129.9	102.9	120.2	130.2	102.6	120.2	98.6	76.1	90.5	100.6	76.1	91.8	102.0	78.0	93.3
6	WOOD & PLASTICS	123.4	118.5	120.8	123.7	126.4	125.1	123.4	118.5	120.8	110.8	80.4	95.1	102.3	78.0	89.8	103.6	79.9	91.4
7	THERMAL & MOISTURE PROTECTION	198.8	112.6	158.8	195.0	114.5	157.7	195.5	112.6	157.1	110.3	78.2	95.4	105.6	70.4	89.3	105.6	78.3	92.9
8	DOORS & WINDOWS	132.1	112.3	127.3	129.1	116.6	126.1	129.1	112.3	125.0	102.6	79.4	97.0	102.0	77.5	96.0	101.1	79.1	95.8
092	LATH, PLASTER & GYPSUM BOARD	126.5	119.0	121.7	126.5	127.2	127.0	126.5	119.0	121.7	95.4	79.8	85.3	96.5	77.3	84.1	97.0	79.3	85.6
095	ACOUSTICAL TREATMENT & WOOD FLOORING	133.0	119.0	123.9	133.0	127.2	129.3	133.0	119.0	123.9	98.3	79.8	86.3	102.7	77.3	86.3	102.7	79.3	87.5
096	FLOORING & CARPET	130.2	130.9	130.4	130.4	130.9	130.5	130.2	130.9	130.4	99.7	65.8	91.5	104.3	74.4	97.0	104.6	74.6	97.3
099	PAINTING & WALL COVERINGS	122.9	117.8	119.9	122.9	122.6	122.7	122.9	117.8	119.9	103.7	63.2	79.9	115.0	67.9	87.4	115.0	64.3	85.3
9	FINISHES	143.9	122.2	132.8	141.9	127.4	134.5	142.6	122.2	132.1	98.2	75.3	86.4	100.0	72.0	85.6	100.1	76.9	88.2
10-14	TOTAL DIV. 10 - 14	100.0	116.7	103.5	100.0	117.7	103.7	100.0	116.7	103.5	100.0	84.0	96.6	100.0	77.6	95.3	100.0	84.0	96.6
15	MECHANICAL	106.9	109.9	108.2	106.9	118.3	112.0	106.9	111.9	109.1	99.9	83.2	92.4	99.8	71.7	87.3	99.8	83.2	92.4
16	ELECTRICAL	158.6	118.6	131.6	161.4	118.6	132.5	161.4	118.6	132.5	101.8	63.5	75.9	101.0	42.9	61.8	110.5	63.5	78.8
1-16	WEIGHTED AVERAGE	133.1	117.7	125.7	129.3	120.7	125.1	131.2	118.0	124.8	102.8	78.2	91.0	100.6	69.5	85.6	100.6	79.0	90.2

DIVISION		ARIZONA						ARKANSAS											
		PRESCOTT			TUCSON			FORT SMITH			JONESBORO			LITTLE ROCK			PINE BLUFF		
		MAT.	INST.	TOTAL	MAT.	INST.	TOTAL	MAT.	INST.	TOTAL	MAT.	INST.	TOTAL	MAT.	INST.	TOTAL	MAT.	INST.	TOTAL
2	SITE WORK	75.6	100.1	94.5	73.6	100.4	94.2	76.1	82.4	80.9	101.1	96.9	97.9	76.1	82.4	80.9	79.1	82.4	81.6
031	CONCRETE FORMWORK	101.1	73.5	77.4	100.4	79.1	82.2	98.8	50.0	57.0	82.9	58.1	61.6	92.9	54.8	60.2	74.8	54.7	57.6
032	CONCRETE REINFORCEMENT	104.4	73.2	86.8	104.0	82.9	92.1	96.6	71.4	82.4	92.5	56.4	72.2	96.9	61.4	76.9	96.8	61.4	76.9
033	CAST IN PLACE CONCRETE	95.6	77.9	88.2	88.7	79.8	85.0	82.3	53.8	70.4	86.7	66.3	78.2	83.3	53.8	70.9	83.5	53.8	71.1
3	CONCRETE	106.7	74.7	90.6	96.5	79.8	88.0	82.6	56.1	69.2	83.2	62.3	72.7	82.7	56.4	69.4	84.0	56.4	70.0
4	MASONRY	102.1	70.1	82.2	97.8	71.1	81.2	94.6	58.1	71.9	87.1	58.8	69.5	92.5	58.1	71.1	108.7	58.1	77.3
5	METALS	98.6	70.9	88.6	101.3	76.7	92.4	97.4	71.2	88.0	91.7	82.5	88.4	97.0	67.8	86.5	96.1	67.8	85.9
6	WOOD & PLASTICS	105.0	72.9	88.4	103.7	79.9	91.4	99.4	49.5	73.6	80.7	59.5	69.8	95.6	56.0	75.2	72.7	56.0	64.1
7	THERMAL & MOISTURE PROTECTION	108.7	75.1	93.1	106.3	74.3	91.5	96.1	55.1	77.1	105.7	61.1	85.0	94.7	55.8	76.6	94.6	55.8	76.6
8	DOORS & WINDOWS	102.6	72.5	95.3	99.7	79.1	94.7	97.6	50.8	86.3	98.9	56.9	88.7	97.6	53.0	86.8	93.1	53.0	83.3
092	LATH, PLASTER & GYPSUM BOARD	93.2	72.1	79.6	97.3	79.3	85.7	94.8	48.9	65.2	99.8	58.8	73.3	94.8	55.6	69.5	86.5	55.6	66.5
095	ACOUSTICAL TREATMENT & WOOD FLOORING	98.3	72.1	81.4	104.1	79.3	88.0	101.7	48.9	67.5	102.3	58.8	74.1	101.7	55.6	71.8	97.6	55.6	70.4
096	FLOORING & CARPET	98.0	65.5	90.1	103.7	65.8	94.5	119.3	70.4	107.4	79.2	56.0	73.6	120.7	70.4	108.5	108.3	70.4	99.1
099	PAINTING & WALL COVERINGS	103.7	63.2	79.9	112.3	63.2	83.5	97.1	71.4	82.0	85.1	64.2	72.9	97.1	54.6	72.2	97.1	54.6	72.2
9	FINISHES	96.2	70.9	83.2	99.9	75.0	87.1	102.1	56.0	78.4	92.1	58.4	74.9	102.5	57.8	79.6	96.8	57.8	76.8
10-14	TOTAL DIV. 10 - 14	100.0	83.0	96.4	100.0	84.1	96.6	100.0	67.8	93.2	100.0	69.2	93.5	100.0	68.7	93.4	100.0	68.7	93.4
15	MECHANICAL	99.9	73.1	87.9	99.7	77.7	89.9	100.0	53.4	79.2	100.1	53.6	79.4	100.0	58.0	81.3	100.0	56.4	80.5
16	ELECTRICAL	101.3	61.1	74.2	104.6	67.3	79.4	96.0	61.7	72.9	101.2	60.7	73.9	97.0	65.4	75.7	94.9	65.4	75.0
1-16	WEIGHTED AVERAGE	100.3	73.6	87.4	99.4	77.6	88.9	96.1	60.7	79.0	95.2	64.8	80.5	95.9	62.3	79.7	95.4	62.0	79.3

COST INDEXES

585

City Cost Indexes

DIVISION		ARKANSAS TEXARKANA			CALIFORNIA ANAHEIM			CALIFORNIA BAKERSFIELD			CALIFORNIA FRESNO			CALIFORNIA LOS ANGELES			CALIFORNIA OAKLAND		
		MAT.	INST.	TOTAL	MAT.	INST.	TOTAL	MAT.	INST.	TOTAL	MAT.	INST.	TOTAL	MAT.	INST.	TOTAL	MAT.	INST.	TOTAL
2	SITE WORK	95.7	83.0	86.0	88.7	111.5	106.2	94.4	108.3	105.1	95.8	108.3	105.5	87.0	110.6	105.1	127.5	105.1	110.3
031	CONCRETE FORMWORK	83.9	48.1	53.2	103.3	120.1	117.7	94.0	119.2	115.6	100.0	123.7	120.3	106.4	119.7	117.8	107.7	138.5	134.0
032	CONCRETE REINFORCEMENT	96.2	54.6	72.8	108.5	115.3	112.3	108.1	114.7	111.9	108.6	115.0	112.2	111.9	115.2	113.8	99.5	115.6	108.6
033	CAST IN PLACE CONCRETE	83.4	51.7	70.1	97.2	121.2	107.2	92.8	119.7	104.1	101.6	117.7	108.3	90.7	118.4	102.3	118.9	121.4	120.0
3	CONCRETE	79.6	51.5	65.4	114.2	118.6	116.4	111.4	117.5	114.5	116.2	118.9	117.5	113.1	117.3	115.2	125.3	126.9	126.1
4	MASONRY	94.7	41.3	61.5	87.4	122.9	109.4	106.4	115.3	111.9	109.0	116.8	113.8	100.6	122.9	114.4	139.6	124.9	130.5
5	METALS	88.5	64.4	79.8	110.5	101.4	107.2	105.0	99.6	103.1	106.9	100.8	104.7	109.3	99.5	105.8	102.5	105.4	103.5
6	WOOD & PLASTICS	83.5	51.6	67.0	99.6	117.5	108.9	87.9	117.6	103.3	101.1	123.5	112.7	99.4	117.1	108.5	107.8	140.7	124.8
7	THERMAL & MOISTURE PROTECTION	95.6	50.0	74.4	120.9	120.7	120.8	104.3	110.1	107.0	101.0	112.2	106.2	113.8	119.4	116.3	111.8	131.2	120.8
8	DOORS & WINDOWS	98.1	48.7	86.1	105.7	114.2	107.7	104.5	113.8	106.8	104.5	116.6	107.4	100.5	114.0	103.7	105.3	128.5	110.9
092	LATH, PLASTER & GYPSUM BOARD	90.1	51.1	64.9	91.1	118.2	108.6	91.1	118.2	108.6	90.0	124.2	112.1	87.0	118.2	107.1	86.8	141.7	122.3
095	ACOUSTICAL TREATMENT & WOOD FLOORING	104.4	51.1	69.9	122.0	118.2	119.5	122.0	118.2	119.5	122.0	124.2	123.4	120.8	118.2	119.1	116.9	141.7	133.0
096	FLOORING & CARPET	111.3	53.4	97.2	127.1	116.8	124.6	122.7	77.5	111.7	123.4	116.8	121.8	117.2	116.8	117.1	113.0	116.8	113.9
099	PAINTING & WALL COVERINGS	97.1	45.0	66.5	116.7	118.8	117.9	119.9	110.8	114.5	119.3	99.4	107.6	116.6	120.0	118.6	121.5	123.9	123.0
9	FINISHES	99.9	48.9	73.8	116.4	119.1	117.8	118.0	111.5	114.7	118.1	120.0	119.1	112.8	118.9	115.9	115.7	134.0	125.1
10 - 14	TOTAL DIV. 10 - 14	100.0	49.3	89.3	100.0	117.1	103.6	100.0	117.4	103.7	100.0	135.6	107.5	100.0	115.9	103.4	100.0	139.5	108.3
15	MECHANICAL	100.0	47.4	76.5	100.2	118.7	108.4	100.2	102.2	101.1	100.2	112.6	105.7	100.1	118.6	108.3	100.1	137.5	116.8
16	ELECTRICAL	98.1	50.5	66.0	93.4	109.6	104.3	93.8	95.1	94.7	92.6	102.3	99.2	106.8	121.4	116.6	111.4	129.6	123.7
1 - 16	WEIGHTED AVERAGE	94.7	53.4	74.8	104.9	115.1	109.8	104.3	107.0	105.6	105.3	112.3	108.7	105.0	116.5	110.6	109.9	126.5	117.9

DIVISION		CALIFORNIA OXNARD			CALIFORNIA REDDING			CALIFORNIA RIVERSIDE			CALIFORNIA SACRAMENTO			CALIFORNIA SAN DIEGO			CALIFORNIA SAN FRANCISCO		
		MAT.	INST.	TOTAL	MAT.	INST.	TOTAL	MAT.	INST.	TOTAL	MAT.	INST.	TOTAL	MAT.	INST.	TOTAL	MAT.	INST.	TOTAL
2	SITE WORK	95.4	105.9	103.5	100.4	107.3	105.7	87.6	109.1	104.1	93.2	111.9	107.6	87.3	102.6	99.1	128.3	112.0	115.8
031	CONCRETE FORMWORK	101.1	120.1	117.4	100.7	123.2	120.0	104.4	119.9	117.7	106.2	123.9	121.3	103.9	119.4	117.2	107.9	139.9	135.2
032	CONCRETE REINFORCEMENT	108.1	114.8	111.9	104.8	114.8	110.4	107.1	114.9	111.5	100.6	115.2	108.7	110.9	114.7	113.1	113.3	116.3	115.0
033	CAST IN PLACE CONCRETE	98.5	120.2	107.6	111.5	117.1	113.9	96.3	121.1	106.7	103.2	117.6	109.2	92.4	109.1	99.4	118.8	123.4	120.7
3	CONCRETE	114.7	118.1	116.4	125.0	118.4	121.7	113.7	118.4	116.1	117.7	118.9	118.3	113.6	114.0	113.8	127.1	128.4	127.8
4	MASONRY	112.0	114.4	113.5	113.0	112.2	112.5	85.2	115.9	104.2	112.1	116.1	114.6	102.3	114.9	110.1	139.9	135.4	137.1
5	METALS	104.5	100.4	103.0	108.9	99.8	105.6	110.5	100.7	107.0	98.6	100.2	99.2	108.5	99.9	105.4	107.1	108.5	107.6
6	WOOD & PLASTICS	97.6	117.6	107.9	98.7	123.5	111.5	99.6	117.5	108.9	103.0	123.6	113.6	99.1	117.5	108.6	107.8	141.0	124.9
7	THERMAL & MOISTURE PROTECTION	109.9	115.5	112.5	110.6	113.8	112.1	120.0	116.5	118.4	121.0	115.1	118.3	113.5	109.2	111.5	111.8	135.3	122.7
8	DOORS & WINDOWS	103.2	114.3	105.9	106.0	115.0	108.2	105.7	114.2	107.7	116.6	115.0	116.2	104.4	114.3	106.8	107.3	131.3	113.1
092	LATH, PLASTER & GYPSUM BOARD	91.1	118.2	108.6	91.1	124.2	112.5	90.8	118.2	108.4	85.2	124.2	110.4	90.0	118.2	108.1	89.0	141.7	123.0
095	ACOUSTICAL TREATMENT & WOOD FLOORING	122.0	118.2	119.5	128.9	124.2	125.9	120.7	118.2	119.0	125.1	124.2	124.5	123.6	118.1	120.0	126.5	141.7	136.4
096	FLOORING & CARPET	122.7	116.8	121.3	121.9	116.8	120.7	127.0	116.8	124.5	115.4	116.8	115.7	123.5	116.1	121.7	113.0	116.8	113.9
099	PAINTING & WALL COVERINGS	119.3	114.3	116.4	119.3	104.4	110.6	116.7	118.8	117.9	119.7	106.5	111.9	116.7	116.5	116.5	121.5	140.2	132.5
9	FINISHES	117.8	118.7	118.3	119.3	120.2	119.8	116.0	119.1	117.6	116.2	120.6	118.5	115.9	118.8	117.4	117.8	136.2	127.2
10 - 14	TOTAL DIV. 10 - 14	100.0	117.5	103.7	100.0	135.3	107.4	100.0	117.1	103.6	100.0	135.7	107.5	100.0	117.3	103.7	100.0	140.2	108.5
15	MECHANICAL	100.2	118.7	108.5	100.2	112.1	105.5	100.1	118.6	108.4	100.0	116.9	107.6	100.1	116.7	107.5	100.1	167.5	130.2
16	ELECTRICAL	97.6	111.8	107.1	102.7	86.5	91.8	93.6	102.3	99.5	102.1	108.2	106.2	93.8	94.3	94.1	107.3	149.4	135.7
1 - 16	WEIGHTED AVERAGE	105.4	113.8	109.4	108.4	108.9	108.6	104.6	112.8	108.6	106.9	114.5	110.5	104.9	109.5	107.1	111.0	138.2	124.2

DIVISION		CALIFORNIA SAN JOSE			CALIFORNIA SANTA BARBARA			CALIFORNIA STOCKTON			CALIFORNIA VALLEJO			COLORADO COLORADO SPRINGS			COLORADO DENVER		
		MAT.	INST.	TOTAL	MAT.	INST.	TOTAL	MAT.	INST.	TOTAL	MAT.	INST.	TOTAL	MAT.	INST.	TOTAL	MAT.	INST.	TOTAL
2	SITE WORK	130.8	101.6	108.3	95.8	108.3	105.4	93.7	107.6	104.4	89.2	112.1	106.8	120.7	99.2	104.1	119.9	108.6	111.2
031	CONCRETE FORMWORK	103.4	138.9	133.8	101.6	119.9	117.3	95.4	123.6	119.6	108.2	137.8	133.5	92.4	76.4	78.7	102.9	78.1	81.7
032	CONCRETE REINFORCEMENT	105.1	116.2	111.4	108.1	114.9	111.9	108.6	115.2	112.3	99.2	116.1	108.8	97.5	79.7	87.5	97.0	80.2	87.5
033	CAST IN PLACE CONCRETE	117.1	121.9	119.1	98.1	119.9	107.3	98.1	117.6	106.3	106.6	119.4	112.0	109.4	81.4	97.7	102.3	81.0	93.4
3	CONCRETE	123.5	127.5	125.5	114.5	117.9	116.2	114.1	118.8	116.5	119.3	125.8	122.6	102.5	79.2	90.7	107.0	79.8	93.3
4	MASONRY	147.6	136.1	140.5	106.8	115.8	112.4	111.6	120.1	116.9	79.9	133.5	113.2	105.1	71.3	84.1	104.1	79.5	88.8
5	METALS	111.0	108.5	110.1	104.3	100.3	102.9	106.5	101.1	104.6	101.9	102.9	102.2	100.2	85.3	94.9	103.5	86.0	97.2
6	WOOD & PLASTICS	105.0	140.6	123.4	97.6	117.6	107.9	92.5	123.5	108.5	102.1	140.4	121.9	90.9	77.7	84.1	101.9	79.3	90.2
7	THERMAL & MOISTURE PROTECTION	106.6	134.7	119.6	105.3	113.0	108.9	110.0	111.0	110.5	126.3	131.3	128.6	105.5	80.8	94.1	104.9	83.1	94.8
8	DOORS & WINDOWS	95.3	129.5	103.6	104.5	114.3	106.9	103.7	115.0	106.4	117.9	131.0	121.1	96.3	79.4	92.2	95.5	80.9	92.0
092	LATH, PLASTER & GYPSUM BOARD	91.6	141.7	124.0	91.1	118.2	108.6	92.2	124.2	112.8	85.7	141.7	121.9	91.0	76.9	81.9	100.5	78.8	86.5
095	ACOUSTICAL TREATMENT & WOOD FLOORING	113.8	141.7	131.9	122.0	118.2	119.5	122.0	124.2	123.4	125.1	141.7	135.9	96.6	76.9	83.8	95.2	78.8	84.6
096	FLOORING & CARPET	119.7	116.8	119.0	122.7	104.8	118.4	122.7	116.8	121.3	119.7	116.8	119.0	111.5	71.2	101.7	112.5	91.6	107.4
099	PAINTING & WALL COVERINGS	121.3	127.4	124.9	119.3	114.3	116.4	119.3	103.4	110.0	117.7	120.1	119.1	116.1	65.2	86.2	116.0	78.1	93.8
9	FINISHES	117.0	134.4	125.9	118.1	116.6	117.3	118.0	119.3	119.0	114.7	133.0	124.1	102.4	73.9	87.8	103.6	80.4	91.7
10 - 14	TOTAL DIV. 10 - 14	100.0	139.3	108.3	100.0	117.5	103.7	100.0	135.6	107.5	100.0	137.8	108.0	100.0	84.6	96.7	100.0	84.2	96.7
15	MECHANICAL	100.2	145.9	120.6	100.2	118.7	108.4	100.2	112.6	105.7	100.2	136.6	116.4	100.0	73.9	88.3	99.9	81.6	91.7
16	ELECTRICAL	108.0	131.8	124.1	90.4	106.4	101.2	101.7	106.7	105.1	98.1	127.1	117.6	94.7	83.6	87.2	96.7	85.2	89.0
1 - 16	WEIGHTED AVERAGE	110.1	129.7	119.6	104.6	112.9	108.6	105.9	113.2	109.4	105.5	127.0	115.9	100.7	80.3	90.8	101.9	84.8	93.6

City Cost Indexes

		COLORADO													CONNECTICUT					
	DIVISION	FORT COLLINS			GRAND JUNCTION			GREELEY			PUEBLO			BRIDGEPORT			BRISTOL		
		MAT.	INST.	TOTAL	MAT.	INST.	TOTAL	MAT.	INST.	TOTAL	MAT.	INST.	TOTAL	MAT.	INST.	TOTAL	MAT.	INST.	TOTAL
2	SITE WORK	132.6	102.5	109.4	136.5	101.1	109.3	116.7	101.4	104.9	127.5	95.7	103.1	113.0	99.6	102.7	112.1	99.6	102.5
031	CONCRETE FORMWORK	102.3	71.7	76.1	110.3	54.1	62.2	99.2	58.7	64.6	104.4	76.9	80.8	97.6	94.3	94.8	97.6	104.5	103.5
032	CONCRETE REINFORCEMENT	101.6	71.0	84.4	109.8	76.9	91.3	101.2	60.7	78.4	102.4	79.6	89.6	116.7	124.1	120.9	116.7	124.0	120.8
033	CAST IN PLACE CONCRETE	118.8	75.3	100.6	118.0	52.9	90.7	99.3	71.7	87.7	105.8	81.8	95.8	112.2	112.6	112.4	105.1	112.6	108.3
3	CONCRETE	121.2	73.3	97.0	119.5	58.8	88.9	104.4	64.1	84.1	108.2	79.5	93.7	117.4	105.8	111.6	114.0	110.3	112.1
4	MASONRY	115.4	70.8	87.7	145.5	60.0	92.4	109.3	50.6	72.8	106.5	69.0	83.2	106.2	111.7	109.6	95.9	111.7	105.7
5	METALS	99.5	81.1	92.9	101.8	79.2	93.7	99.5	68.4	88.3	103.4	86.4	97.3	101.9	103.8	102.6	101.9	103.8	102.6
6	WOOD & PLASTICS	101.6	72.3	86.5	109.4	56.0	81.8	98.3	60.0	78.5	103.6	77.9	90.4	100.2	88.4	94.1	100.2	102.3	101.3
7	THERMAL & MOISTURE PROTECTION	105.5	76.2	91.9	103.6	63.4	85.0	104.7	67.4	87.4	103.0	79.3	92.0	101.2	107.8	104.3	101.4	105.7	103.4
8	DOORS & WINDOWS	93.8	71.0	88.3	101.1	58.3	90.7	93.8	52.5	83.8	95.5	79.5	91.6	109.1	103.7	107.8	109.1	106.2	108.4
092	LATH, PLASTER & GYPSUM BOARD	99.3	71.5	81.4	106.4	54.7	73.0	98.2	58.9	72.9	91.2	76.9	82.0	98.0	87.0	90.9	98.0	101.4	100.2
095	ACOUSTICAL TREATMENT & WOOD FLOORING	89.7	71.5	77.9	92.8	54.7	68.1	89.7	58.9	69.8	101.0	76.9	85.4	101.7	87.0	92.2	101.7	101.4	101.5
096	FLOORING & CARPET	112.3	87.8	106.4	122.2	87.8	113.8	111.0	87.8	105.4	118.8	91.6	112.2	96.9	113.7	101.0	96.9	113.7	101.0
099	PAINTING & WALL COVERINGS	116.0	64.7	85.9	127.4	38.0	74.9	116.0	40.3	71.6	127.5	60.4	88.1	89.3	103.1	97.4	89.3	113.3	103.4
9	FINISHES	102.9	73.9	88.1	108.5	58.8	83.0	101.6	62.0	81.3	106.6	77.7	91.8	98.5	97.5	98.0	98.5	106.8	102.8
10 - 14	TOTAL DIV. 10 - 14	100.0	74.2	94.6	100.0	67.9	93.2	100.0	69.4	93.5	100.0	85.2	96.9	100.0	110.8	102.3	100.0	112.6	102.7
15	MECHANICAL	99.9	76.6	89.5	99.8	42.2	74.1	99.9	68.0	85.7	99.8	78.5	90.3	100.0	102.2	101.0	100.0	104.0	101.8
16	ELECTRICAL	89.6	75.9	80.4	95.2	67.8	76.7	89.6	75.9	80.4	96.6	71.8	79.9	104.7	98.1	100.2	104.7	94.6	97.9
1 - 16	WEIGHTED AVERAGE	103.2	77.9	91.0	106.9	63.7	86.0	100.2	69.1	85.2	102.6	79.2	91.3	104.4	102.5	103.5	103.4	104.2	103.8

		CONNECTICUT																	
	DIVISION	HARTFORD			NEW BRITAIN			NEW HAVEN			NORWALK			STAMFORD			WATERBURY		
		MAT.	INST.	TOTAL	MAT.	INST.	TOTAL	MAT.	INST.	TOTAL	MAT.	INST.	TOTAL	MAT.	INST.	TOTAL	MAT.	INST.	TOTAL
2	SITE WORK	112.3	99.6	102.5	112.3	99.6	102.5	112.0	100.4	103.1	112.8	99.6	102.6	113.5	99.6	102.8	112.5	99.6	102.6
031	CONCRETE FORMWORK	96.7	104.5	103.4	98.0	104.5	103.6	97.4	104.7	103.6	97.6	94.4	94.9	97.6	94.6	95.0	97.6	104.7	103.7
032	CONCRETE REINFORCEMENT	116.7	124.0	120.9	116.7	124.0	120.8	116.7	124.1	120.9	116.7	124.4	121.0	116.7	124.4	121.0	116.7	124.1	120.9
033	CAST IN PLACE CONCRETE	104.9	112.6	108.1	106.9	112.6	109.3	108.7	112.6	110.4	110.5	115.4	112.5	112.3	115.4	113.6	112.3	112.7	112.4
3	CONCRETE	113.8	110.3	112.0	114.9	110.3	112.5	116.7	110.4	113.5	116.6	106.9	111.7	117.4	107.0	112.2	117.4	110.4	113.9
4	MASONRY	95.8	111.7	105.7	96.0	111.7	105.7	96.1	111.7	105.8	96.3	116.9	109.1	96.4	116.9	109.1	96.4	111.7	105.9
5	METALS	102.3	103.8	102.8	98.5	103.8	100.4	98.5	103.9	100.5	101.9	104.4	102.8	101.9	104.5	102.8	101.9	103.9	102.6
6	WOOD & PLASTICS	100.2	102.3	101.3	100.2	102.3	101.3	100.2	102.3	101.3	100.2	88.4	94.1	100.2	88.4	94.1	100.2	102.3	101.3
7	THERMAL & MOISTURE PROTECTION	100.2	105.7	102.8	101.4	105.7	103.4	101.5	108.6	104.8	101.4	109.5	105.1	101.4	109.5	105.1	101.4	107.9	104.4
8	DOORS & WINDOWS	109.1	106.2	108.4	109.1	106.2	108.4	109.1	111.3	109.6	109.1	103.7	107.8	109.1	103.7	107.8	109.1	111.3	109.6
092	LATH, PLASTER & GYPSUM BOARD	98.0	101.4	100.2	98.0	101.4	100.2	98.0	101.4	100.2	98.0	87.0	90.9	98.0	87.0	90.9	98.0	101.4	100.2
095	ACOUSTICAL TREATMENT & WOOD FLOORING	101.7	101.4	101.5	101.7	101.4	101.5	101.7	101.4	101.5	101.7	87.0	92.2	101.7	87.0	92.2	101.7	101.4	101.5
096	FLOORING & CARPET	96.9	113.7	101.0	96.9	113.7	101.0	96.9	113.7	101.0	96.9	119.6	102.4	96.9	119.6	102.4	96.9	113.7	101.0
099	PAINTING & WALL COVERINGS	89.3	113.3	103.4	89.3	113.3	103.4	89.3	106.8	99.6	89.3	110.9	102.0	89.3	110.9	102.0	89.3	111.5	102.3
9	FINISHES	98.5	106.8	102.7	98.5	106.8	102.8	98.5	106.0	102.4	98.5	99.6	99.1	98.5	99.6	99.1	98.4	106.6	102.6
10 - 14	TOTAL DIV. 10 - 14	100.0	112.6	102.7	100.0	112.6	102.7	100.0	112.6	102.7	100.0	110.7	102.3	100.0	110.8	102.3	100.0	112.6	102.7
15	MECHANICAL	100.0	104.1	101.8	100.0	104.1	101.8	100.0	104.1	101.8	100.0	102.2	101.0	100.0	102.3	101.0	100.0	104.1	101.8
16	ELECTRICAL	103.9	101.2	102.1	104.7	99.5	101.2	104.7	99.5	101.1	104.7	93.7	97.2	104.7	114.0	111.0	103.8	98.1	100.0
1 - 16	WEIGHTED AVERAGE	103.3	105.3	104.3	103.0	105.0	104.0	103.2	105.3	104.2	103.7	102.7	103.2	103.9	106.1	105.0	103.7	105.0	104.4

		D.C.			DELAWARE			FLORIDA										
	DIVISION	WASHINGTON			WILMINGTON			DAYTONA BEACH			FORT LAUDERDALE			JACKSONVILLE			MELBOURNE		
		MAT.	INST.	TOTAL	MAT.	INST.	TOTAL	MAT.	INST.	TOTAL	MAT.	INST.	TOTAL	MAT.	INST.	TOTAL	MAT.	INST.	TOTAL
2	SITE WORK	105.3	92.0	95.1	94.2	114.4	109.8	123.7	87.6	95.9	108.7	74.0	82.0	123.8	88.0	96.2	132.0	87.5	97.8
031	CONCRETE FORMWORK	97.2	81.3	83.6	102.3	92.9	94.2	97.5	69.7	73.7	94.6	66.2	70.3	97.2	62.5	67.5	91.0	69.3	72.4
032	CONCRETE REINFORCEMENT	102.0	98.0	99.7	96.3	90.3	92.9	95.7	79.8	86.7	95.7	84.3	89.3	95.7	65.3	78.6	96.7	79.8	87.2
033	CAST IN PLACE CONCRETE	117.0	86.7	104.3	80.3	90.1	84.4	93.3	73.6	85.0	97.8	72.7	87.3	94.2	61.1	80.3	108.3	73.1	93.5
3	CONCRETE	108.3	87.9	98.0	98.2	92.8	95.5	88.8	74.3	81.5	90.8	73.3	82.0	89.2	64.1	76.6	98.2	73.9	86.0
4	MASONRY	93.4	82.9	86.9	105.8	88.2	94.8	85.1	70.5	76.1	85.3	67.4	74.2	84.3	60.2	69.3	79.8	69.6	73.5
5	METALS	97.6	113.1	103.2	96.8	113.3	102.8	99.3	93.1	97.1	98.7	95.6	97.6	98.9	87.3	94.7	107.2	93.1	102.1
6	WOOD & PLASTICS	96.3	81.2	88.5	106.2	93.1	99.4	95.1	70.0	82.2	89.7	67.6	78.3	95.1	63.2	78.7	88.1	70.0	78.7
7	THERMAL & MOISTURE PROTECTION	95.1	84.0	90.0	99.3	101.4	100.3	97.4	72.2	85.7	97.4	70.4	84.9	97.7	67.1	83.5	97.6	71.8	85.6
8	DOORS & WINDOWS	100.4	90.1	97.9	99.2	97.0	98.6	99.3	67.2	91.5	97.0	67.1	89.7	99.3	59.5	89.6	98.5	67.2	90.9
092	LATH, PLASTER & GYPSUM BOARD	100.7	80.4	87.6	103.1	92.6	96.3	109.8	69.7	83.8	109.3	67.1	82.1	109.8	62.6	79.3	106.2	69.6	82.6
095	ACOUSTICAL TREATMENT & WOOD FLOORING	97.1	80.4	86.3	98.8	92.6	94.8	100.2	69.6	80.3	100.2	67.1	78.7	100.2	62.6	75.8	96.0	69.6	78.9
096	FLOORING & CARPET	92.4	91.2	92.1	77.0	91.4	80.5	112.8	72.0	102.8	112.8	74.9	103.6	112.8	61.5	100.3	109.6	72.0	100.4
099	PAINTING & WALL COVERINGS	101.0	96.9	98.6	87.4	95.2	92.0	106.6	91.5	97.7	103.1	63.3	79.7	106.6	61.0	79.9	106.6	90.4	97.1
9	FINISHES	94.0	84.3	89.1	93.3	92.6	93.0	107.3	72.4	89.4	105.2	67.1	85.7	107.3	61.9	84.0	105.4	72.0	88.3
10 - 14	TOTAL DIV. 10 - 14	100.0	94.5	98.8	100.0	103.1	100.6	100.0	79.5	95.7	100.0	80.0	95.8	100.0	73.7	94.5	100.0	79.1	95.6
15	MECHANICAL	100.0	90.6	95.9	100.2	89.6	95.5	100.0	74.2	88.5	100.0	69.6	86.4	100.0	62.6	83.3	100.0	73.7	88.3
16	ELECTRICAL	99.7	98.1	98.6	100.7	97.4	98.5	95.9	70.7	78.9	95.9	84.6	88.2	95.4	68.8	77.5	95.6	67.4	76.6
1 - 16	WEIGHTED AVERAGE	99.6	92.0	96.0	98.8	97.2	98.0	98.7	75.9	87.7	97.9	75.1	86.9	98.6	68.6	84.1	100.6	75.1	88.3

City Cost Indexes

		FLORIDA																	
	DIVISION	MIAMI			ORLANDO			PANAMA CITY			PENSACOLA			ST. PETERSBURG			TALLAHASSEE		
		MAT.	INST.	TOTAL	MAT.	INST.	TOTAL	MAT.	INST.	TOTAL	MAT.	INST.	TOTAL	MAT.	INST.	TOTAL	MAT.	INST.	TOTAL
2	SITE WORK	108.0	73.9	81.8	124.3	87.2	95.8	139.5	85.0	97.6	136.9	87.3	98.7	124.6	87.0	95.7	125.2	86.7	95.5
031	CONCRETE FORMWORK	94.4	66.2	70.2	97.3	64.9	69.5	96.1	34.4	43.2	85.3	63.2	66.3	94.5	58.7	63.8	97.3	48.1	55.2
032	CONCRETE REINFORCEMENT	95.7	84.2	89.3	95.7	79.7	86.7	99.9	64.0	79.7	102.4	64.3	80.9	99.1	73.6	84.8	95.7	64.6	78.2
033	CAST IN PLACE CONCRETE	95.3	71.2	85.2	101.4	73.4	89.7	98.9	41.1	74.7	98.9	65.2	84.8	105.4	66.2	89.0	97.6	55.4	79.9
3	CONCRETE	89.6	72.8	81.1	92.8	72.1	82.3	97.1	44.1	70.4	95.9	65.7	80.6	95.0	65.8	80.3	90.7	55.8	73.2
4	MASONRY	81.1	67.3	72.5	82.2	70.5	75.0	88.7	35.0	55.4	86.4	63.2	72.0	124.4	62.6	86.0	87.1	49.1	63.5
5	METALS	99.2	95.2	97.8	108.4	92.7	102.8	97.6	72.9	88.7	97.5	86.9	93.7	101.3	89.6	97.1	99.2	85.6	94.3
6	WOOD & PLASTICS	89.7	67.6	78.3	95.1	64.0	79.1	93.7	34.6	63.2	81.9	64.1	72.7	91.9	58.8	74.8	95.1	46.5	70.1
7	THERMAL & MOISTURE PROTECTION	100.5	71.6	87.1	97.7	71.6	85.6	97.9	36.6	69.5	97.6	63.5	81.8	97.3	59.8	79.9	97.8	55.6	78.1
8	DOORS & WINDOWS	97.0	67.8	89.9	99.3	63.1	90.5	97.0	32.4	81.4	97.0	61.0	88.3	98.0	56.4	87.9	99.3	49.7	87.2
092	LATH, PLASTER & GYPSUM BOARD	109.3	67.1	82.1	109.8	63.4	79.9	108.0	33.1	59.6	103.8	63.5	77.8	107.5	58.0	75.6	109.8	45.4	68.2
095	ACOUSTICAL TREATMENT & WOOD FLOORING	100.2	67.1	78.7	100.2	63.4	76.4	94.7	33.1	54.8	94.7	63.5	74.5	94.7	58.0	70.9	100.2	45.4	64.7
096	FLOORING & CARPET	121.5	74.8	110.2	112.8	72.0	102.8	112.1	23.6	90.6	106.6	65.4	96.6	111.3	65.2	100.1	112.8	47.8	97.0
099	PAINTING & WALL COVERINGS	103.1	63.3	79.7	106.6	70.1	85.2	106.6	31.2	62.4	106.6	70.9	85.7	106.6	59.0	78.7	106.6	50.2	73.5
9	FINISHES	108.1	67.1	87.1	107.3	66.5	86.3	106.9	31.5	68.2	104.3	64.4	83.9	105.4	59.7	82.0	107.4	47.5	76.7
10 - 14	TOTAL DIV. 10 - 14	100.0	80.0	95.8	100.0	78.7	95.5	100.0	59.3	91.4	100.0	66.3	92.9	100.0	69.5	93.6	100.0	71.3	94.0
15	MECHANICAL	100.0	68.9	86.1	100.0	65.4	84.5	100.0	32.0	69.7	100.0	63.6	83.8	100.0	63.5	83.7	100.0	50.6	78.0
16	ELECTRICAL	96.4	81.5	86.3	96.5	57.2	70.0	94.1	42.8	59.5	99.5	64.1	75.6	96.3	61.8	73.1	96.5	53.0	67.1
1 - 16	WEIGHTED AVERAGE	98.0	74.3	86.6	100.4	70.6	86.1	99.6	45.6	73.5	99.2	68.5	84.4	101.5	67.5	85.1	99.1	58.6	79.6

		FLORIDA			GEORGIA														
	DIVISION	TAMPA			ALBANY			ATLANTA			AUGUSTA			COLUMBUS			MACON		
		MAT.	INST.	TOTAL	MAT.	INST.	TOTAL	MAT.	INST.	TOTAL	MAT.	INST.	TOTAL	MAT.	INST.	TOTAL	MAT.	INST.	TOTAL
2	SITE WORK	124.9	87.0	95.8	108.9	75.9	83.5	113.8	93.3	98.0	109.6	91.8	95.9	108.9	76.0	83.6	109.7	94.1	97.7
031	CONCRETE FORMWORK	98.9	58.8	64.6	96.9	52.3	58.7	98.3	75.5	78.8	94.9	63.3	67.8	98.5	66.9	71.5	95.9	67.8	71.8
032	CONCRETE REINFORCEMENT	95.7	73.7	83.3	95.7	88.4	91.6	102.0	89.7	95.1	107.8	73.3	88.3	95.7	88.4	91.6	98.1	88.7	92.8
033	CAST IN PLACE CONCRETE	103.2	66.3	87.7	99.6	49.2	78.5	103.8	71.6	90.3	98.1	57.7	81.2	99.2	49.8	78.5	97.9	53.7	79.4
3	CONCRETE	93.8	65.8	79.7	91.8	59.8	75.6	98.4	76.9	87.6	94.6	63.6	79.0	91.7	66.4	78.9	91.2	68.1	79.6
4	MASONRY	86.0	62.6	71.4	87.2	39.9	57.8	89.5	68.5	76.4	89.6	50.4	65.2	87.2	40.3	58.1	102.5	48.0	68.7
5	METALS	102.2	89.7	97.7	96.6	92.3	95.1	93.6	80.0	88.7	92.3	71.9	84.9	97.0	92.6	95.4	91.9	93.4	92.5
6	WOOD & PLASTICS	96.9	58.8	77.2	94.4	52.9	73.0	98.6	77.7	87.8	95.0	66.3	80.2	96.4	72.9	84.3	99.5	71.6	85.1
7	THERMAL & MOISTURE PROTECTION	97.6	60.9	80.6	97.5	57.8	79.1	94.5	74.4	85.2	93.9	60.1	78.2	97.2	60.0	79.9	96.0	65.3	81.7
8	DOORS & WINDOWS	99.3	55.7	88.7	97.0	57.0	87.3	95.8	75.5	90.9	92.4	61.2	84.8	97.0	68.1	90.0	95.4	68.4	88.9
092	LATH, PLASTER & GYPSUM BOARD	109.8	58.0	76.4	109.8	52.0	72.5	119.5	77.4	92.4	118.4	65.7	84.4	109.8	72.6	85.8	116.0	71.2	87.1
095	ACOUSTICAL TREATMENT & WOOD FLOORING	100.2	58.0	72.9	100.2	52.0	68.9	106.1	77.4	87.5	106.1	65.7	79.9	100.2	72.6	82.3	92.5	71.2	78.7
096	FLOORING & CARPET	112.8	65.2	101.2	112.8	39.9	95.0	85.9	76.1	83.6	84.8	50.8	76.6	112.8	40.5	95.2	88.0	46.9	78.0
099	PAINTING & WALL COVERINGS	106.6	59.0	78.7	103.1	50.3	72.1	93.9	78.2	84.7	93.9	47.8	66.8	103.1	48.2	70.9	104.8	58.9	77.9
9	FINISHES	107.3	59.7	82.9	105.3	48.8	76.4	93.8	76.0	84.7	93.1	59.5	75.9	105.2	60.4	82.2	91.3	63.1	76.8
10 - 14	TOTAL DIV. 10 - 14	100.0	73.9	94.5	100.0	74.8	94.7	100.0	81.7	96.1	100.0	74.0	94.5	100.0	77.3	95.2	100.0	78.9	95.6
15	MECHANICAL	100.0	63.5	83.7	100.0	56.1	80.4	100.1	77.9	90.2	100.1	53.3	79.2	100.0	45.9	75.8	100.0	51.7	78.4
16	ELECTRICAL	95.4	61.8	72.8	90.0	65.9	73.7	93.6	84.2	87.3	95.7	58.3	70.5	91.3	46.9	61.4	89.4	67.8	74.8
1 - 16	WEIGHTED AVERAGE	99.8	67.6	84.2	97.4	61.6	80.1	96.9	79.3	88.4	95.7	62.7	79.8	97.5	59.7	79.2	95.7	67.6	82.2

		GEORGIA			HAWAII			IDAHO										
	DIVISION	SAVANNAH			VALDOSTA			HONOLULU			BOISE			LEWISTON			POCATELLO		
		MAT.	INST.	TOTAL	MAT.	INST.	TOTAL	MAT.	INST.	TOTAL	MAT.	INST.	TOTAL	MAT.	INST.	TOTAL	MAT.	INST.	TOTAL
2	SITE WORK	109.5	77.8	85.1	120.2	76.3	86.4	119.3	109.3	111.6	84.4	102.5	98.3	89.0	95.6	94.0	86.8	102.5	98.9
031	CONCRETE FORMWORK	96.7	62.4	67.3	81.8	53.6	57.6	104.9	152.3	145.5	99.1	88.5	90.0	109.6	81.7	85.7	99.0	88.3	89.8
032	CONCRETE REINFORCEMENT	101.4	73.6	85.7	101.6	53.3	74.3	108.1	125.8	118.1	101.1	80.1	89.3	114.1	99.5	105.8	101.4	80.0	89.3
033	CAST IN PLACE CONCRETE	96.1	57.4	79.9	97.5	58.1	81.0	180.8	132.4	160.5	100.0	93.1	97.1	108.4	95.3	102.9	99.2	93.0	96.6
3	CONCRETE	90.8	64.3	77.4	95.4	56.9	76.0	155.2	138.6	146.8	103.8	88.3	96.0	115.7	89.7	102.6	103.5	88.1	95.7
4	MASONRY	91.0	60.1	71.8	93.9	52.9	68.4	131.0	139.0	136.0	136.3	79.5	101.1	136.4	95.1	110.7	130.7	77.3	97.6
5	METALS	97.3	88.3	94.1	96.8	81.0	91.1	116.2	109.7	113.9	113.5	80.1	101.4	97.2	89.0	94.3	113.8	79.7	101.5
6	WOOD & PLASTICS	94.5	62.5	77.9	78.0	51.6	64.3	101.9	155.6	129.6	97.1	88.4	92.6	91.0	76.3	88.7	97.1	88.4	92.6
7	THERMAL & MOISTURE PROTECTION	97.5	60.9	80.6	97.2	62.7	81.2	111.9	135.0	122.6	96.2	83.6	90.3	165.1	87.1	128.9	96.4	79.7	88.6
8	DOORS & WINDOWS	97.0	58.5	87.6	92.7	47.8	81.8	108.8	145.9	117.8	95.2	80.7	91.7	116.0	78.6	106.9	95.2	76.3	90.6
092	LATH, PLASTER & GYPSUM BOARD	109.8	61.8	78.8	102.7	50.6	69.1	108.5	157.3	140.0	89.6	87.8	88.5	150.6	75.6	102.2	89.6	87.8	88.5
095	ACOUSTICAL TREATMENT & WOOD FLOORING	100.2	61.8	75.3	94.7	50.6	66.1	122.0	157.3	144.9	101.0	87.8	92.5	149.4	75.6	101.6	101.0	87.8	92.5
096	FLOORING & CARPET	112.8	59.9	99.9	104.9	47.8	91.0	123.7	135.6	126.6	104.6	69.4	96.0	146.2	96.5	134.1	104.9	69.4	96.3
099	PAINTING & WALL COVERINGS	103.1	59.8	77.7	103.1	43.6	68.2	119.3	153.2	139.2	113.2	63.8	84.2	141.6	79.9	105.4	113.2	66.9	86.0
9	FINISHES	105.5	61.6	83.0	101.4	50.9	75.5	121.8	150.7	136.6	99.5	82.7	90.9	170.5	83.5	125.9	99.6	83.1	91.1
10 - 14	TOTAL DIV. 10 - 14	100.0	75.1	94.8	100.0	73.6	94.4	100.0	132.1	106.8	100.0	85.9	97.0	100.0	99.8	100.0	100.0	85.9	97.0
15	MECHANICAL	100.0	55.7	80.2	100.0	48.7	77.1	100.2	126.5	111.9	99.8	85.7	93.5	100.6	94.4	97.9	99.8	85.7	93.5
16	ELECTRICAL	92.7	65.4	74.3	88.2	38.8	54.9	112.4	128.7	123.4	82.5	79.9	80.8	84.7	90.3	88.5	85.6	79.0	81.2
1 - 16	WEIGHTED AVERAGE	97.8	65.6	82.3	97.3	55.6	77.1	116.0	130.7	123.1	101.9	85.1	93.8	113.5	90.6	102.4	101.9	84.4	93.5

City Cost Indexes

DIVISION		IDAHO TWIN FALLS			ILLINOIS CHICAGO			ILLINOIS DECATUR			ILLINOIS EAST ST. LOUIS			ILLINOIS JOLIET			ILLINOIS PEORIA		
		MAT.	INST.	TOTAL	MAT.	INST.	TOTAL	MAT.	INST.	TOTAL	MAT.	INST.	TOTAL	MAT.	INST.	TOTAL	MAT.	INST.	TOTAL
2	SITE WORK	94.4	100.6	99.2	84.2	94.0	91.7	82.6	96.7	93.5	101.6	97.2	98.2	84.9	93.3	91.4	90.9	95.8	94.7
031	CONCRETE FORMWORK	102.5	44.1	52.5	105.1	126.4	123.3	100.9	94.4	95.4	92.8	107.8	105.7	106.2	125.6	122.8	98.8	100.7	100.4
032	CONCRETE REINFORCEMENT	110.2	61.5	82.8	95.8	168.0	136.5	93.6	120.0	108.5	99.1	128.6	115.7	95.8	155.8	129.6	93.6	123.6	110.5
033	CAST IN PLACE CONCRETE	101.8	52.5	81.1	103.5	131.0	115.0	98.4	95.4	97.2	92.2	110.4	99.8	103.4	118.9	109.9	96.2	108.5	101.4
3	CONCRETE	112.9	51.3	81.8	97.3	134.9	116.3	92.1	100.1	96.2	84.2	113.6	99.0	97.3	127.9	112.7	90.9	108.1	99.6
4	MASONRY	134.3	49.5	81.6	95.6	130.3	117.2	71.9	104.7	92.3	75.8	113.0	98.9	97.2	126.7	115.5	115.1	110.7	112.4
5	METALS	113.7	70.2	98.0	97.1	128.9	108.6	97.2	113.1	102.9	94.6	129.3	107.1	95.4	121.0	104.6	97.2	116.6	104.2
6	WOOD & PLASTICS	100.7	44.2	71.6	101.8	124.8	113.7	103.0	90.4	96.5	96.1	108.0	102.2	103.7	125.0	114.7	103.0	95.5	99.2
7	THERMAL & MOISTURE PROTECTION	97.4	56.3	78.3	100.6	126.4	112.6	96.5	95.6	96.1	91.5	105.3	97.9	100.4	123.5	111.1	96.2	104.0	99.9
8	DOORS & WINDOWS	98.5	48.0	85.5	105.0	136.4	112.6	99.7	98.8	99.5	88.9	114.4	95.1	104.9	133.5	111.8	99.7	103.9	100.7
092	LATH, PLASTER & GYPSUM BOARD	89.7	42.2	59.1	97.4	125.1	115.3	111.1	89.7	97.3	107.7	107.8	107.8	95.2	125.3	114.6	111.1	94.9	100.7
095	ACOUSTICAL TREATMENT & WOOD FLOORING	96.9	42.2	61.5	91.4	125.1	113.2	94.3	89.7	91.3	88.9	107.8	101.2	91.4	125.3	113.4	94.3	94.9	94.7
096	FLOORING & CARPET	106.2	69.4	97.2	84.2	123.8	93.8	100.8	103.9	101.5	110.0	66.1	99.3	83.7	115.1	91.3	100.8	105.7	102.0
099	PAINTING & WALL COVERINGS	113.2	39.4	69.9	77.2	128.3	107.2	86.8	100.8	95.0	94.7	99.4	97.4	74.8	110.4	95.7	86.8	99.8	94.5
9	FINISHES	99.8	47.9	73.2	85.4	125.6	106.0	95.4	96.6	96.0	94.9	98.7	96.9	84.9	122.1	103.9	95.3	100.7	98.1
10 - 14	TOTAL DIV. 10 - 14	100.0	61.7	91.9	100.0	128.4	106.0	100.0	102.7	100.6	100.0	111.3	102.4	100.0	128.1	105.9	100.0	105.7	101.2
15	MECHANICAL	99.8	45.9	75.7	100.2	122.4	110.1	100.2	99.3	99.8	100.1	100.5	100.3	100.4	109.5	104.4	100.2	105.4	102.5
16	ELECTRICAL	88.1	40.7	56.2	101.8	129.9	120.7	100.7	90.9	94.1	97.1	102.6	100.8	101.4	100.0	100.4	99.6	88.8	92.3
1 - 16	WEIGHTED AVERAGE	104.1	54.7	80.3	97.8	125.0	110.9	96.1	99.1	97.5	93.7	106.9	100.1	97.6	114.9	105.9	98.5	102.8	100.6

DIVISION		ILLINOIS ROCKFORD			ILLINOIS SPRINGFIELD			INDIANA ANDERSON			INDIANA BLOOMINGTON			INDIANA EVANSVILLE			INDIANA FORT WAYNE		
		MAT.	INST.	TOTAL	MAT.	INST.	TOTAL	MAT.	INST.	TOTAL	MAT.	INST.	TOTAL	MAT.	INST.	TOTAL	MAT.	INST.	TOTAL
2	SITE WORK	91.1	96.2	95.1	89.5	96.7	95.0	83.1	94.2	91.7	77.5	95.2	91.1	83.1	130.1	119.2	83.2	94.4	91.8
031	CONCRETE FORMWORK	103.8	111.2	110.1	103.2	97.7	98.5	89.2	84.1	84.8	103.4	79.5	82.9	90.9	85.4	86.2	88.8	79.5	80.8
032	CONCRETE REINFORCEMENT	93.6	151.2	126.1	93.6	120.1	108.5	95.8	84.7	89.5	89.4	84.9	86.9	97.9	81.5	88.7	95.8	84.0	89.2
033	CAST IN PLACE CONCRETE	98.4	106.7	101.9	91.5	99.8	95.0	106.5	85.4	97.7	104.7	82.4	95.4	100.0	91.7	96.5	113.1	87.2	102.2
3	CONCRETE	92.4	117.3	104.9	88.9	103.1	96.1	98.3	85.1	91.6	102.0	81.1	91.4	104.3	86.9	95.5	101.5	83.6	92.5
4	MASONRY	86.3	112.6	102.6	70.6	106.9	93.2	92.2	82.7	86.3	91.5	81.8	85.5	87.6	87.3	87.4	90.2	87.4	88.5
5	METALS	97.2	127.9	108.2	97.2	113.5	103.1	99.2	90.7	96.1	96.1	74.7	88.4	89.9	86.3	88.6	99.2	90.5	96.0
6	WOOD & PLASTICS	103.0	109.1	106.1	102.8	93.5	98.0	98.6	84.2	91.2	115.6	78.2	96.3	91.3	84.6	87.8	98.2	77.8	87.7
7	THERMAL & MOISTURE PROTECTION	96.1	113.3	104.1	96.0	99.4	97.6	98.5	82.2	90.9	93.1	85.4	89.5	96.5	89.6	93.3	97.9	82.2	90.6
8	DOORS & WINDOWS	99.7	119.0	104.4	99.7	100.4	99.9	102.8	84.4	98.4	105.4	80.6	99.4	98.2	82.5	94.4	102.8	78.7	97.0
092	LATH, PLASTER & GYPSUM BOARD	111.1	109.0	109.7	111.1	92.9	99.3	111.3	84.3	93.8	109.4	78.2	89.3	104.1	82.9	90.4	106.0	77.6	87.7
095	ACOUSTICAL TREATMENT & WOOD FLOORING	94.3	109.0	103.8	94.3	92.9	93.4	89.9	84.3	86.3	82.9	78.2	79.9	94.3	82.9	86.9	89.9	77.6	81.9
096	FLOORING & CARPET	100.8	102.8	101.3	101.0	104.0	101.8	90.2	81.6	88.1	103.5	71.0	95.6	97.0	85.5	94.2	90.2	87.0	89.4
099	PAINTING & WALL COVERINGS	86.8	109.2	100.0	86.8	100.5	94.8	89.7	75.7	81.5	90.9	90.6	90.7	97.0	90.2	93.0	89.7	77.0	82.2
9	FINISHES	95.3	108.8	102.2	95.4	98.9	97.2	92.9	82.9	87.8	97.1	79.0	87.8	96.4	85.9	91.0	92.0	80.3	86.0
10 - 14	TOTAL DIV. 10 - 14	100.0	116.3	103.4	100.0	103.9	100.8	100.0	89.3	97.7	100.0	73.3	94.4	100.0	91.9	98.3	100.0	91.2	98.1
15	MECHANICAL	100.2	108.8	104.0	100.2	100.2	100.2	99.8	83.0	92.3	99.8	85.5	93.4	100.0	86.7	94.1	99.8	86.3	93.8
16	ELECTRICAL	99.6	112.1	108.1	100.7	93.8	96.0	83.2	95.3	91.3	101.4	91.5	94.8	96.2	89.3	91.5	83.6	91.0	88.6
1 - 16	WEIGHTED AVERAGE	97.1	112.0	104.3	95.8	100.9	98.3	97.0	87.3	92.3	98.9	84.2	91.8	96.7	91.5	94.2	97.2	86.9	92.2

DIVISION		INDIANA GARY			INDIANA INDIANAPOLIS			INDIANA MUNCIE			INDIANA SOUTH BEND			INDIANA TERRE HAUTE			IOWA CEDAR RAPIDS		
		MAT.	INST.	TOTAL	MAT.	INST.	TOTAL	MAT.	INST.	TOTAL	MAT.	INST.	TOTAL	MAT.	INST.	TOTAL	MAT.	INST.	TOTAL
2	SITE WORK	83.7	95.7	92.9	83.4	98.2	94.8	76.9	95.4	91.2	83.2	94.4	91.8	84.2	129.9	119.4	81.9	93.0	90.4
031	CONCRETE FORMWORK	89.7	102.2	100.4	89.6	89.5	89.5	88.3	83.7	84.3	94.4	77.1	79.6	92.5	81.0	82.7	101.7	75.6	79.4
032	CONCRETE REINFORCEMENT	95.8	94.9	95.3	95.2	87.4	90.8	98.8	84.6	90.8	95.8	71.3	82.0	97.9	78.4	86.9	96.8	79.7	87.1
033	CAST IN PLACE CONCRETE	111.2	102.6	107.6	102.5	89.6	97.1	110.0	80.8	97.8	103.6	84.2	95.5	96.8	88.2	93.2	105.0	76.7	93.1
3	CONCRETE	100.6	101.0	100.8	100.5	88.6	94.5	100.6	83.3	91.9	93.0	80.2	86.6	103.9	83.1	93.4	96.4	77.2	86.7
4	MASONRY	93.6	96.8	95.6	99.6	88.2	92.5	93.5	82.6	86.8	87.5	83.1	84.7	94.5	85.8	89.1	105.1	73.1	85.2
5	METALS	99.2	98.0	98.8	101.0	79.5	93.2	97.7	89.9	94.9	99.2	101.0	99.8	90.6	83.6	88.1	87.9	83.6	86.3
6	WOOD & PLASTICS	97.6	103.5	100.7	96.3	89.9	93.0	100.3	84.0	91.9	98.9	76.1	87.1	94.0	79.7	86.6	106.3	74.7	90.0
7	THERMAL & MOISTURE PROTECTION	97.8	98.9	98.3	97.2	89.8	93.7	94.8	82.2	88.9	97.5	84.9	91.7	96.6	84.5	91.0	97.3	78.4	88.5
8	DOORS & WINDOWS	102.8	97.3	101.5	109.0	88.4	104.0	100.1	83.4	96.0	95.7	76.4	91.0	98.8	80.3	94.3	104.0	76.4	97.3
092	LATH, PLASTER & GYPSUM BOARD	107.0	104.2	105.2	107.0	89.8	95.9	102.9	84.3	90.9	110.8	75.8	88.2	104.1	77.9	87.2	98.1	74.4	82.8
095	ACOUSTICAL TREATMENT & WOOD FLOORING	89.9	104.2	99.1	88.5	89.8	89.4	84.3	84.3	84.3	89.9	75.8	80.8	94.3	77.9	83.7	110.6	74.4	87.1
096	FLOORING & CARPET	90.2	103.1	93.3	90.0	96.7	91.6	96.4	81.6	92.8	90.2	66.3	84.4	97.0	83.8	93.8	130.7	72.0	116.5
099	PAINTING & WALL COVERINGS	89.7	91.4	90.7	89.7	90.6	90.2	90.9	75.7	82.0	89.7	75.0	81.0	97.0	87.2	91.3	115.9	74.0	91.3
9	FINISHES	92.3	101.6	97.0	92.3	91.2	91.8	93.9	82.7	88.2	92.8	74.3	83.3	96.4	82.1	89.0	113.3	74.1	93.2
10 - 14	TOTAL DIV. 10 - 14	100.0	101.6	100.3	100.0	91.2	98.2	100.0	88.6	97.6	100.0	82.2	96.2	100.0	93.0	98.5	100.0	85.1	96.9
15	MECHANICAL	99.8	92.2	96.4	99.8	90.3	95.6	99.7	82.9	92.2	99.8	77.1	89.7	100.0	83.6	92.7	100.2	78.8	90.7
16	ELECTRICAL	90.4	94.4	93.1	101.8	95.2	97.2	89.9	80.9	83.8	96.4	79.6	85.0	93.3	84.9	87.6	93.6	80.5	84.7
1 - 16	WEIGHTED AVERAGE	97.8	96.9	97.4	99.9	90.5	95.4	97.1	84.6	91.1	96.2	82.4	89.5	97.1	88.5	93.0	98.9	79.6	89.6

City Cost Indexes

	DIVISION	IOWA																	
		COUNCIL BLUFFS			DAVENPORT			DES MOINES			DUBUQUE			SIOUX CITY			WATERLOO		
		MAT.	INST.	TOTAL	MAT.	INST.	TOTAL	MAT.	INST.	TOTAL	MAT.	INST.	TOTAL	MAT.	INST.	TOTAL	MAT.	INST.	TOTAL
2	SITE WORK	85.5	90.8	89.6	80.5	97.5	93.6	74.8	98.3	92.9	80.1	90.6	88.2	88.6	95.1	93.6	81.0	94.9	91.7
031	CONCRETE FORMWORK	76.6	67.2	68.5	101.3	88.8	90.6	103.5	75.5	79.5	78.6	63.5	65.7	101.7	56.8	63.2	102.3	60.1	66.2
032	CONCRETE REINFORCEMENT	98.8	75.6	85.7	96.8	90.4	93.2	96.8	78.2	86.3	95.4	81.9	87.8	96.8	68.7	81.0	96.8	82.0	88.4
033	CAST IN PLACE CONCRETE	109.3	69.0	92.4	101.2	89.8	96.4	105.3	80.3	94.8	102.8	69.2	88.7	104.1	59.0	85.2	105.0	55.9	84.4
3	CONCRETE	97.9	70.1	83.9	94.5	89.7	92.1	96.7	78.1	87.3	92.7	69.7	81.1	96.0	60.8	78.2	96.4	63.6	79.9
4	MASONRY	106.2	58.6	76.6	105.4	85.9	93.2	99.7	82.9	89.3	106.0	69.4	83.3	99.3	61.6	75.9	99.4	64.1	77.4
5	METALS	92.9	80.7	88.5	87.9	92.8	89.7	87.8	84.8	86.7	86.4	83.7	85.4	87.9	78.5	84.5	87.9	83.9	86.5
6	WOOD & PLASTICS	78.0	67.9	72.8	106.3	88.1	96.9	108.1	73.5	90.2	80.5	61.2	70.5	106.3	57.2	81.0	107.1	61.4	83.5
7	THERMAL & MOISTURE PROTECTION	96.4	63.8	81.3	96.7	87.6	92.5	97.4	77.2	88.1	96.8	68.0	83.4	96.7	59.4	79.4	96.4	59.5	79.3
8	DOORS & WINDOWS	103.0	69.3	94.8	104.0	87.5	100.0	104.0	75.3	97.1	103.0	69.8	95.0	104.0	61.9	93.8	99.3	69.4	92.0
092	LATH, PLASTER & GYPSUM BOARD	87.6	67.4	74.6	98.1	87.9	91.5	94.3	72.8	80.5	88.1	60.5	70.3	98.1	56.1	71.0	98.1	60.4	73.8
095	ACOUSTICAL TREATMENT & WOOD FLOORING	106.5	67.4	81.2	110.6	87.9	95.9	109.2	72.8	85.6	106.5	60.5	76.6	110.6	56.1	75.3	110.6	60.4	78.1
096	FLOORING & CARPET	104.6	58.8	93.5	115.7	84.6	108.1	115.5	53.7	100.4	119.9	50.1	102.9	116.3	73.9	106.0	117.5	76.2	107.4
099	PAINTING & WALL COVERINGS	106.3	60.7	79.6	111.1	88.1	97.6	111.1	75.4	90.1	114.5	60.7	82.9	112.4	59.0	81.1	112.4	44.1	72.3
9	FINISHES	101.8	64.7	82.8	108.0	87.9	97.7	106.4	70.8	88.2	107.4	59.8	83.0	109.1	60.0	83.9	108.7	61.3	84.4
10 - 14	TOTAL DIV. 10 - 14	100.0	80.5	95.9	100.0	89.9	97.9	100.0	86.7	97.2	100.0	81.8	96.2	100.0	78.5	95.5	100.0	79.1	95.6
15	MECHANICAL	100.2	72.2	87.7	100.2	86.0	94.3	100.2	86.2	94.0	99.8	72.4	87.6	99.8	53.3	79.0	100.2	58.9	81.8
16	ELECTRICAL	101.7	81.2	87.9	91.0	88.1	89.1	94.3	85.9	88.6	99.4	75.0	83.0	93.6	74.1	80.4	93.6	59.4	70.5
1 - 16	WEIGHTED AVERAGE	99.0	73.7	86.8	97.9	89.2	93.7	97.8	83.2	90.8	97.5	73.4	85.9	98.2	67.0	83.1	97.5	67.3	82.9

	DIVISION	KANSAS															KENTUCKY		
		DODGE CITY			KANSAS CITY			SALINA			TOPEKA			WICHITA			BOWLING GREEN		
		MAT.	INST.	TOTAL	MAT.	INST.	TOTAL	MAT.	INST.	TOTAL	MAT.	INST.	TOTAL	MAT.	INST.	TOTAL	MAT.	INST.	TOTAL
2	SITE WORK	106.9	95.2	97.9	86.6	91.8	90.6	96.5	95.1	95.4	89.0	92.5	91.7	90.5	95.3	94.2	71.0	100.3	93.6
031	CONCRETE FORMWORK	96.1	53.8	59.9	103.0	79.5	82.9	91.1	56.2	61.2	101.8	54.1	60.9	98.4	57.0	63.0	82.0	81.0	81.2
032	CONCRETE REINFORCEMENT	101.3	81.9	90.4	96.3	88.7	92.0	100.7	93.7	96.8	93.6	97.5	95.8	93.6	94.3	94.0	88.7	71.5	79.0
033	CAST IN PLACE CONCRETE	114.3	69.1	95.4	89.6	87.0	88.5	99.2	58.3	82.0	93.4	63.2	80.8	87.7	65.5	78.4	91.3	78.8	86.0
3	CONCRETE	107.7	65.9	86.6	90.1	84.5	87.3	95.5	65.3	80.3	89.8	66.8	78.2	86.7	68.3	77.4	93.1	78.6	85.8
4	MASONRY	104.7	54.2	73.3	107.3	83.3	92.4	119.8	52.0	77.7	100.0	65.1	78.3	95.0	64.2	75.9	94.2	80.2	85.5
5	METALS	94.4	89.0	92.4	99.4	92.8	97.0	94.2	92.2	93.5	97.2	95.0	96.4	97.2	93.6	95.9	93.6	79.4	88.5
6	WOOD & PLASTICS	93.9	53.9	73.2	102.8	78.4	90.2	88.8	58.0	72.9	98.8	51.3	74.3	96.2	55.2	75.1	86.9	80.6	83.7
7	THERMAL & MOISTURE PROTECTION	97.3	60.5	80.2	95.0	84.7	90.2	96.7	65.4	82.2	96.7	72.5	85.5	96.3	71.3	84.7	87.4	78.0	83.0
8	DOORS & WINDOWS	99.6	57.7	89.5	98.4	76.2	93.0	99.6	60.3	90.1	99.7	62.2	90.6	99.7	61.6	90.5	97.9	73.0	91.9
092	LATH, PLASTER & GYPSUM BOARD	108.4	52.0	72.0	104.1	77.2	86.8	106.9	56.2	74.2	111.1	49.3	71.2	111.1	53.3	73.8	100.0	80.3	87.3
095	ACOUSTICAL TREATMENT & WOOD FLOORING	87.5	52.0	64.5	94.3	77.2	83.3	87.5	56.2	67.2	94.3	49.3	65.2	94.3	53.3	67.8	90.2	80.3	83.8
096	FLOORING & CARPET	100.1	62.7	91.0	90.0	66.9	84.4	98.0	45.8	85.3	101.7	58.2	91.1	100.8	72.2	93.9	93.0	77.3	89.2
099	PAINTING & WALL COVERINGS	86.8	61.8	72.2	94.7	81.3	86.8	86.8	48.7	64.5	86.8	67.7	75.6	86.8	57.5	69.6	97.0	82.4	88.4
9	FINISHES	94.3	55.8	74.6	93.4	77.0	85.0	92.9	53.0	72.4	95.6	54.8	74.7	95.4	59.1	76.8	93.8	80.6	87.0
10 - 14	TOTAL DIV. 10 - 14	100.0	64.6	92.5	100.0	89.0	97.7	100.0	71.5	94.0	100.0	79.7	95.7	100.0	73.2	94.3	100.0	74.9	94.7
15	MECHANICAL	100.2	60.1	82.4	100.0	83.8	92.8	100.2	45.2	75.7	100.2	69.6	86.6	100.2	67.3	85.5	100.0	84.4	93.1
16	ELECTRICAL	95.4	64.8	74.8	104.5	91.0	95.4	94.9	71.1	78.8	101.6	72.0	81.6	99.3	71.1	80.3	93.6	89.0	90.5
1 - 16	WEIGHTED AVERAGE	99.4	66.7	83.6	98.1	85.6	92.1	98.2	65.0	82.2	97.6	71.9	85.2	96.8	71.9	84.8	95.2	83.8	89.7

	DIVISION	KENTUCKY									LOUISIANA								
		LEXINGTON			LOUISVILLE			OWENSBORO			ALEXANDRIA			BATON ROUGE			LAKE CHARLES		
		MAT.	INST.	TOTAL	MAT.	INST.	TOTAL	MAT.	INST.	TOTAL	MAT.	INST.	TOTAL	MAT.	INST.	TOTAL	MAT.	INST.	TOTAL
2	SITE WORK	77.0	102.7	96.8	68.0	100.2	92.8	82.2	130.0	119.0	103.7	83.8	88.4	112.4	86.1	92.2	114.1	85.8	92.4
031	CONCRETE FORMWORK	92.9	71.0	74.2	91.7	80.5	82.1	86.4	79.2	80.2	78.2	53.4	57.0	96.8	59.2	64.6	96.9	60.2	65.4
032	CONCRETE REINFORCEMENT	97.9	95.8	96.7	97.9	96.4	97.0	88.8	95.3	92.5	98.1	66.0	80.0	100.4	61.8	78.7	100.4	61.7	78.6
033	CAST IN PLACE CONCRETE	98.7	78.8	90.3	95.4	77.2	87.8	94.2	91.2	92.9	95.1	50.4	76.4	91.3	60.9	78.5	96.6	62.6	82.4
3	CONCRETE	95.7	78.8	87.2	94.0	82.5	88.2	101.8	86.6	94.1	88.1	55.8	71.8	92.0	61.1	76.4	94.6	62.1	78.2
4	MASONRY	91.5	60.0	71.9	91.9	78.3	83.4	91.6	65.0	75.1	110.6	53.9	75.4	98.2	64.4	77.2	97.3	64.8	77.1
5	METALS	95.1	89.7	93.2	95.1	89.5	93.1	85.3	90.3	87.1	87.4	75.6	83.2	98.0	74.1	89.4	97.5	74.2	89.1
6	WOOD & PLASTICS	94.0	71.7	82.5	97.3	80.6	88.7	86.8	79.2	82.9	77.3	54.2	65.4	102.6	59.9	80.5	100.4	60.7	79.9
7	THERMAL & MOISTURE PROTECTION	97.0	70.2	84.6	87.5	81.6	84.8	96.5	79.2	88.5	96.0	57.6	78.2	97.3	65.1	82.4	99.9	65.0	83.7
8	DOORS & WINDOWS	98.8	81.7	94.6	98.8	86.5	95.8	96.2	85.3	93.5	99.8	58.5	89.8	103.5	59.9	92.9	103.5	62.3	93.5
092	LATH, PLASTER & GYPSUM BOARD	104.1	69.7	81.9	107.6	80.3	89.9	99.7	77.4	85.3	87.6	53.8	65.8	102.3	59.4	74.6	102.3	60.3	75.2
095	ACOUSTICAL TREATMENT & WOOD FLOORING	94.3	69.7	78.4	94.3	80.3	85.2	82.0	77.4	79.0	100.3	53.8	70.2	97.1	59.4	72.7	97.1	60.3	73.3
096	FLOORING & CARPET	97.9	53.7	87.1	96.3	76.0	91.4	95.2	77.3	90.8	108.5	61.6	97.1	110.8	74.2	101.9	111.1	64.8	99.8
099	PAINTING & WALL COVERINGS	97.0	72.7	82.7	97.0	78.3	86.0	97.0	102.4	100.1	97.1	51.2	70.2	96.8	58.8	74.5	96.8	54.1	71.8
9	FINISHES	96.7	67.4	81.7	96.4	79.0	87.5	92.9	81.2	86.9	98.3	54.5	75.8	102.8	61.9	81.9	102.9	60.4	81.1
10 - 14	TOTAL DIV. 10 - 14	100.0	92.0	98.3	100.0	92.2	98.3	100.0	95.0	98.9	100.0	68.7	93.4	100.0	71.0	93.9	100.0	71.2	93.9
15	MECHANICAL	100.0	60.3	82.3	100.0	83.1	92.5	100.0	66.3	85.0	100.0	47.7	76.7	100.0	54.4	79.6	100.0	65.5	84.6
16	ELECTRICAL	94.4	65.2	74.7	94.4	89.0	90.7	92.8	83.8	86.7	95.9	57.1	69.7	99.0	64.7	75.9	99.0	64.7	75.9
1 - 16	WEIGHTED AVERAGE	96.6	73.4	85.4	95.9	85.7	90.9	95.0	84.1	89.8	96.4	59.2	78.5	99.6	64.8	82.8	99.9	67.0	84.0

City Cost Indexes

		LOUISIANA									MAINE								
	DIVISION	MONROE			NEW ORLEANS			SHREVEPORT			AUGUSTA			BANGOR			LEWISTON		
		MAT.	INST.	TOTAL	MAT.	INST.	TOTAL	MAT.	INST.	TOTAL	MAT.	INST.	TOTAL	MAT.	INST.	TOTAL	MAT.	INST.	TOTAL
2	SITE WORK	103.7	83.6	88.3	113.5	88.2	94.1	102.4	83.5	87.8	92.3	95.7	94.9	92.2	98.1	96.7	90.4	98.1	96.3
031	CONCRETE FORMWORK	77.4	54.3	57.6	96.0	67.5	71.6	100.2	57.5	63.7	96.1	40.8	48.7	89.7	85.1	85.8	96.3	84.9	86.5
032	CONCRETE REINFORCEMENT	97.1	65.9	79.5	100.4	67.3	81.7	96.6	66.0	79.4	95.0	42.7	65.5	95.0	106.7	101.6	116.7	106.6	111.0
033	CAST IN PLACE CONCRETE	95.1	55.6	78.6	95.7	64.7	82.7	93.7	60.0	79.6	87.1	49.2	71.2	87.1	76.0	82.4	97.0	75.9	88.1
3	CONCRETE	87.9	57.9	72.8	94.1	67.1	80.5	88.3	60.9	74.5	107.4	45.7	76.3	106.3	85.4	95.8	109.9	85.2	97.4
4	MASONRY	106.1	51.8	72.4	99.6	62.4	76.5	99.4	50.4	68.9	92.6	46.0	63.7	109.5	67.6	83.5	93.7	67.6	77.5
5	METALS	87.4	74.9	82.9	100.4	77.6	92.2	88.2	74.6	83.3	98.1	75.0	89.8	97.9	82.0	92.2	101.3	81.8	94.3
6	WOOD & PLASTICS	76.3	54.8	65.2	96.1	68.9	82.1	101.8	59.6	80.0	99.0	39.1	68.1	91.8	84.9	88.2	99.0	84.9	91.7
7	THERMAL & MOISTURE PROTECTION	96.0	59.2	78.9	100.8	67.6	85.4	95.3	59.3	78.6	101.7	43.5	74.7	101.5	65.3	84.7	101.4	65.3	84.6
8	DOORS & WINDOWS	99.8	64.0	91.1	102.1	71.0	94.6	97.6	61.6	88.9	106.0	47.7	91.9	105.9	76.1	98.7	109.1	76.1	101.1
092	LATH, PLASTER & GYPSUM BOARD	87.1	54.4	66.0	101.2	68.8	80.3	94.8	59.4	71.9	96.6	36.1	57.6	93.2	83.4	86.9	98.5	83.4	88.8
095	ACOUSTICAL TREATMENT & WOOD FLOORING	100.3	54.4	70.5	97.1	68.8	78.8	101.7	59.4	74.3	93.5	36.1	56.3	92.1	83.4	86.5	101.7	83.4	89.8
096	FLOORING & CARPET	108.2	53.5	94.9	111.6	63.6	99.9	119.1	56.2	103.8	96.9	53.8	86.4	94.7	53.8	84.8	96.9	53.8	86.4
099	PAINTING & WALL COVERINGS	97.1	44.9	66.5	98.8	68.9	81.3	97.1	51.2	70.2	89.3	29.5	54.2	89.3	40.8	60.9	89.3	40.8	60.9
9	FINISHES	98.1	52.6	74.8	103.1	66.9	84.5	102.9	56.4	79.1	95.6	41.0	67.6	94.1	74.4	84.0	97.1	74.4	85.5
10 - 14	TOTAL DIV. 10 - 14	100.0	69.1	93.5	100.0	73.3	94.4	100.0	70.8	93.8	100.0	67.9	93.2	100.0	90.9	98.1	100.0	90.8	98.0
15	MECHANICAL	100.0	54.6	79.7	100.0	64.3	84.1	100.0	57.8	81.2	100.0	32.4	69.8	100.0	79.9	91.0	100.0	79.9	91.0
16	ELECTRICAL	99.0	61.3	73.6	99.3	67.0	77.6	96.9	66.0	76.1	104.6	83.8	90.6	101.3	88.5	92.6	104.7	57.2	72.7
1 - 16	WEIGHTED AVERAGE	96.4	61.3	79.4	100.2	69.5	85.4	96.5	63.4	80.5	100.6	57.2	79.6	100.9	82.0	91.8	101.9	76.8	89.8

		MAINE			MARYLAND						MASSACHUSETTS								
	DIVISION	PORTLAND			BALTIMORE			HAGERSTOWN			BOSTON			BROCKTON			FALL RIVER		
		MAT.	INST.	TOTAL	MAT.	INST.	TOTAL	MAT.	INST.	TOTAL	MAT.	INST.	TOTAL	MAT.	INST.	TOTAL	MAT.	INST.	TOTAL
2	SITE WORK	89.8	98.1	96.2	95.7	93.2	93.8	87.0	88.8	88.4	98.1	104.8	103.2	96.0	100.9	99.8	94.9	101.1	99.6
031	CONCRETE FORMWORK	95.5	84.9	86.4	101.5	76.4	80.0	88.3	77.7	79.1	102.3	134.7	130.1	102.0	119.6	117.1	102.0	117.7	115.4
032	CONCRETE REINFORCEMENT	116.7	106.6	111.0	96.9	85.8	90.7	85.7	74.9	79.6	115.4	169.2	145.7	102.7	168.9	146.1	116.7	151.6	136.4
033	CAST IN PLACE CONCRETE	90.2	75.9	84.2	106.4	81.5	95.9	90.4	67.3	80.7	112.3	142.1	124.8	106.9	136.4	119.2	103.4	138.2	118.0
3	CONCRETE	106.5	85.2	95.8	102.8	81.2	91.9	87.9	74.8	81.3	121.0	142.4	131.7	117.9	133.5	125.8	116.2	130.1	123.2
4	MASONRY	91.6	67.6	76.7	90.5	73.7	80.1	94.7	75.7	82.9	112.5	146.7	133.8	107.6	141.1	128.4	107.3	142.4	129.1
5	METALS	101.3	81.8	94.3	94.9	100.0	96.7	93.9	93.8	93.9	104.2	126.5	112.2	101.2	123.1	109.1	101.2	117.5	107.1
6	WOOD & PLASTICS	99.0	84.9	91.7	101.9	77.7	89.4	87.9	77.5	82.5	103.4	133.8	119.1	102.6	115.4	109.2	102.6	113.0	107.9
7	THERMAL & MOISTURE PROTECTION	101.3	65.3	84.6	94.7	78.6	87.2	93.9	78.2	86.6	101.9	141.0	120.1	101.7	134.7	117.0	101.6	130.0	114.8
8	DOORS & WINDOWS	109.1	76.1	101.1	92.9	82.6	90.4	92.1	78.2	88.7	102.9	138.5	111.6	102.9	126.2	108.5	102.9	121.3	107.3
092	LATH, PLASTER & GYPSUM BOARD	98.5	83.4	88.8	101.8	77.7	86.2	97.6	77.7	84.7	98.5	133.9	121.4	98.5	114.8	109.1	98.5	112.0	107.2
095	ACOUSTICAL TREATMENT & WOOD FLOORING	101.7	83.4	89.8	93.3	77.6	83.1	93.3	77.6	83.1	101.7	133.9	122.6	101.7	114.8	110.2	101.7	112.0	108.3
096	FLOORING & CARPET	96.9	53.8	86.4	90.0	84.0	88.5	85.5	76.4	83.3	96.7	153.0	110.4	97.1	153.0	110.7	96.9	153.0	110.5
099	PAINTING & WALL COVERINGS	89.3	40.8	60.9	100.0	80.8	88.7	100.0	50.0	70.7	90.1	143.3	121.3	89.4	132.9	114.9	89.4	132.9	114.9
9	FINISHES	97.1	74.4	85.5	90.8	78.1	84.3	88.4	74.3	81.2	96.8	139.1	118.5	97.0	126.8	112.2	96.9	125.4	111.5
10 - 14	TOTAL DIV. 10 - 14	100.0	90.8	98.0	100.0	83.2	96.5	100.0	85.1	96.9	100.0	129.5	106.2	100.0	126.4	105.6	100.0	127.1	105.7
15	MECHANICAL	100.0	79.9	91.0	100.0	81.2	91.6	100.0	82.6	92.3	100.0	123.5	110.4	100.0	103.2	101.4	100.0	106.1	102.7
16	ELECTRICAL	104.9	57.2	72.7	102.0	97.4	98.9	98.1	81.1	86.6	99.7	128.2	118.9	99.4	96.7	97.5	98.7	96.7	97.3
1 - 16	WEIGHTED AVERAGE	101.4	76.8	89.5	97.1	85.7	91.6	94.4	81.0	87.9	103.8	130.6	116.7	102.7	116.6	109.4	102.3	115.9	108.9

		MASSACHUSETTS																	
	DIVISION	HYANNIS			LAWRENCE			LOWELL			NEW BEDFORD			PITTSFIELD			SPRINGFIELD		
		MAT.	INST.	TOTAL	MAT.	INST.	TOTAL	MAT.	INST.	TOTAL	MAT.	INST.	TOTAL	MAT.	INST.	TOTAL	MAT.	INST.	TOTAL
2	SITE WORK	92.5	100.8	98.8	96.7	100.9	100.0	95.8	100.9	99.7	94.6	101.1	99.6	97.0	99.6	99.0	96.1	99.8	99.0
031	CONCRETE FORMWORK	91.4	117.1	113.4	101.8	115.9	113.8	98.1	116.0	113.4	102.0	117.7	115.4	98.0	104.2	103.3	98.2	105.7	104.7
032	CONCRETE REINFORCEMENT	93.6	147.7	124.1	115.7	141.5	130.3	116.7	138.5	129.0	116.7	151.6	136.4	96.8	126.6	113.6	116.7	136.9	128.1
033	CAST IN PLACE CONCRETE	97.5	137.4	114.2	107.2	139.5	120.7	98.0	139.6	115.4	100.4	138.2	116.2	106.9	104.4	105.8	100.4	111.6	105.1
3	CONCRETE	107.1	128.8	118.1	117.9	127.9	122.9	107.7	127.2	117.6	114.7	130.1	122.5	109.5	107.5	108.5	108.9	112.6	110.8
4	MASONRY	106.5	142.4	128.8	107.1	141.1	128.2	93.8	137.9	121.2	107.1	142.4	129.0	94.5	101.9	99.1	94.0	111.3	104.8
5	METALS	97.7	115.4	104.1	98.7	113.5	104.0	98.7	109.2	102.5	101.2	117.5	107.1	98.5	99.2	98.8	101.1	103.6	102.0
6	WOOD & PLASTICS	91.5	112.6	102.4	102.6	110.4	106.6	101.3	110.4	106.0	102.6	113.0	107.9	101.3	104.2	102.8	101.3	104.0	102.7
7	THERMAL & MOISTURE PROTECTION	101.2	127.0	113.1	101.7	134.6	117.0	101.4	133.0	116.1	101.7	130.0	114.8	101.5	106.1	103.6	101.4	109.7	105.3
8	DOORS & WINDOWS	99.1	120.2	104.2	102.9	117.5	106.4	109.1	116.8	111.0	102.9	121.3	107.3	109.1	107.3	108.7	109.1	109.6	109.2
092	LATH, PLASTER & GYPSUM BOARD	92.1	112.0	104.9	98.5	109.8	105.8	98.5	109.8	105.8	98.5	112.0	107.2	98.5	103.3	101.6	98.5	103.1	101.5
095	ACOUSTICAL TREATMENT & WOOD FLOORING	92.1	112.0	105.0	101.7	109.8	106.9	101.7	109.8	106.9	101.7	112.0	108.3	101.7	103.3	102.7	101.7	103.1	102.6
096	FLOORING & CARPET	93.6	153.0	108.1	96.9	153.0	110.5	96.9	153.0	110.5	96.9	153.0	110.5	97.1	101.4	98.2	96.7	111.6	100.3
099	PAINTING & WALL COVERINGS	89.4	131.1	113.9	89.4	132.9	114.9	89.3	132.9	114.9	89.4	132.9	114.9	89.3	96.0	93.2	90.7	96.0	93.8
9	FINISHES	92.9	124.9	109.3	96.9	123.9	110.7	96.9	123.9	110.7	96.8	125.4	111.5	97.0	102.7	99.9	96.9	105.5	101.3
10 - 14	TOTAL DIV. 10 - 14	100.0	126.0	105.5	100.0	125.8	105.4	100.0	125.8	105.4	100.0	127.1	105.7	100.0	108.2	101.7	100.0	109.5	102.0
15	MECHANICAL	100.0	106.0	102.6	100.0	104.0	101.8	100.0	118.0	108.0	100.0	106.1	102.7	100.0	90.1	95.5	100.0	96.7	98.5
16	ELECTRICAL	94.6	96.7	96.0	103.8	107.7	106.4	104.7	107.6	106.7	99.7	96.7	97.7	104.7	84.3	90.9	104.7	90.3	95.0
1 - 16	WEIGHTED AVERAGE	99.3	115.2	107.0	102.6	116.2	109.2	101.4	118.0	109.4	102.2	115.9	108.8	101.7	97.6	99.7	101.9	102.4	102.2

City Cost Indexes

DIVISION		MASSACHUSETTS WORCESTER			MICHIGAN ANN ARBOR			MICHIGAN DEARBORN			MICHIGAN DETROIT			MICHIGAN FLINT			MICHIGAN GRAND RAPIDS		
		MAT.	INST.	TOTAL	MAT.	INST.	TOTAL	MAT.	INST.	TOTAL	MAT.	INST.	TOTAL	MAT.	INST.	TOTAL	MAT.	INST.	TOTAL
2	SITE WORK	95.8	100.8	99.7	81.3	94.3	91.3	81.1	94.5	91.4	100.4	96.3	97.2	68.6	93.8	88.0	82.9	88.1	86.9
031	CONCRETE FORMWORK	98.7	113.5	111.4	95.7	103.6	102.4	95.6	116.1	113.1	97.6	116.2	113.5	96.8	99.9	99.4	96.0	82.7	84.6
032	CONCRETE REINFORCEMENT	116.7	157.5	139.7	96.1	118.2	108.5	96.1	118.8	108.9	95.4	118.7	108.6	96.1	117.8	108.3	97.9	85.7	91.0
033	CAST IN PLACE CONCRETE	98.0	133.3	112.8	92.4	116.1	102.3	90.2	119.5	102.5	99.1	119.6	107.7	93.0	96.8	94.6	98.8	92.5	96.2
3	CONCRETE	107.8	127.5	117.7	86.9	111.6	99.4	85.9	118.3	102.2	90.3	116.7	103.6	87.3	103.2	95.3	96.0	86.1	91.0
4	MASONRY	93.8	140.2	122.6	102.6	108.3	106.1	102.4	119.7	113.2	101.3	119.7	112.7	102.6	97.8	99.6	96.2	62.3	75.1
5	METALS	101.1	115.1	106.2	97.7	125.7	107.8	97.8	126.9	108.3	98.3	102.5	99.8	97.8	123.8	107.1	96.0	82.8	91.2
6	WOOD & PLASTICS	101.8	108.3	105.2	91.5	100.9	96.4	91.5	115.8	104.1	94.0	115.8	105.3	91.5	100.9	96.4	95.6	83.9	89.5
7	THERMAL & MOISTURE PROTECTION	101.4	125.1	112.4	93.1	110.2	101.0	92.3	120.2	105.3	90.7	120.2	104.4	91.5	94.9	93.1	92.8	68.6	81.6
8	DOORS & WINDOWS	109.1	122.1	112.2	96.5	105.1	98.6	96.5	112.0	100.3	96.0	113.3	100.2	96.5	101.4	97.7	93.5	75.0	89.0
092	LATH, PLASTER & GYPSUM BOARD	98.5	107.6	104.4	115.9	99.1	105.1	115.9	114.4	115.0	115.9	114.4	115.0	115.9	99.1	105.1	104.1	77.2	86.7
095	ACOUSTICAL TREATMENT & WOOD FLOORING	101.7	107.6	105.5	100.3	99.1	99.5	100.3	114.4	109.5	100.3	114.4	109.5	100.3	99.1	99.5	94.3	77.2	83.2
096	FLOORING & CARPET	96.9	143.5	108.2	95.5	110.7	99.2	95.0	115.7	100.0	95.2	115.7	100.1	95.2	91.5	94.3	96.5	54.0	86.2
099	PAINTING & WALL COVERINGS	89.3	117.1	105.6	96.3	112.1	105.6	96.3	114.9	107.2	98.4	114.9	108.1	96.3	71.2	81.6	97.0	54.2	71.9
9	FINISHES	96.9	118.9	108.2	100.2	105.4	102.9	100.1	116.0	108.3	101.0	116.0	108.7	99.6	95.3	97.4	96.2	74.1	84.9
10 - 14	TOTAL DIV. 10 - 14	100.0	113.2	102.8	100.0	108.1	101.7	100.0	111.2	102.4	100.0	111.2	102.4	100.0	104.7	101.0	100.0	106.3	101.3
15	MECHANICAL	100.0	99.6	99.8	100.0	95.4	98.0	100.0	108.9	104.0	100.0	111.9	105.3	100.0	90.3	95.7	100.0	66.8	85.2
16	ELECTRICAL	104.7	97.3	99.7	94.1	107.9	103.4	94.1	110.6	105.2	95.3	110.5	105.6	94.1	101.5	99.1	93.9	78.3	83.4
1 - 16	WEIGHTED AVERAGE	101.8	112.6	107.0	96.6	105.9	101.1	96.4	113.1	104.5	97.6	111.4	104.3	96.2	99.6	97.8	96.4	76.8	86.9

DIVISION		MICHIGAN KALAMAZOO			MICHIGAN LANSING			MICHIGAN MUSKEGAN			MICHIGAN SAGINAW			MINNESOTA DULUTH			MINNESOTA MINNEAPOLIS		
		MAT.	INST.	TOTAL	MAT.	INST.	TOTAL	MAT.	INST.	TOTAL	MAT.	INST.	TOTAL	MAT.	INST.	TOTAL	MAT.	INST.	TOTAL
2	SITE WORK	83.5	88.2	87.1	89.4	93.7	92.7	83.4	88.5	87.3	70.9	93.6	88.4	79.3	103.6	98.0	78.9	109.8	102.7
031	CONCRETE FORMWORK	94.9	86.7	87.9	99.4	92.4	93.4	96.3	86.2	87.6	95.7	97.9	97.6	97.7	115.9	113.3	98.4	132.4	127.5
032	CONCRETE REINFORCEMENT	97.9	86.9	91.7	96.1	117.5	108.2	97.8	86.5	91.4	96.1	117.1	107.9	90.7	99.5	95.7	90.8	106.5	99.6
033	CAST IN PLACE CONCRETE	100.5	101.4	100.9	92.4	94.6	93.3	98.5	105.1	101.3	91.2	95.3	92.9	103.9	110.2	106.5	102.4	120.4	109.9
3	CONCRETE	98.8	91.1	94.9	87.2	99.1	93.2	95.9	92.1	94.0	86.4	101.7	94.1	94.1	111.4	102.8	94.9	123.4	109.3
4	MASONRY	98.7	85.0	90.2	95.6	91.9	93.3	98.5	81.8	88.2	104.1	82.9	90.9	107.1	115.2	112.1	107.2	128.6	120.5
5	METALS	96.3	85.3	92.3	97.0	123.1	106.4	95.4	84.5	91.5	97.8	122.2	106.6	93.2	119.7	102.8	95.3	125.2	106.1
6	WOOD & PLASTICS	94.0	86.4	90.1	95.3	91.9	93.5	95.6	83.2	89.2	91.5	100.9	96.4	102.6	115.6	109.3	103.1	132.0	118.0
7	THERMAL & MOISTURE PROTECTION	92.5	86.8	89.9	92.7	90.6	91.7	92.5	81.0	87.2	92.0	90.0	91.0	97.3	121.1	108.4	97.2	134.2	114.4
8	DOORS & WINDOWS	93.6	77.5	89.7	96.5	96.4	96.5	94.4	74.7	89.6	96.5	95.6	96.3	100.9	119.4	105.4	102.0	138.4	110.8
092	LATH, PLASTER & GYPSUM BOARD	104.1	79.7	88.4	119.4	89.8	100.3	105.4	76.4	86.7	115.9	99.1	105.1	93.2	116.9	108.5	93.2	133.7	119.4
095	ACOUSTICAL TREATMENT & WOOD FLOORING	94.3	79.7	84.9	100.3	89.8	93.5	99.8	76.4	84.7	100.3	99.1	99.5	87.2	116.9	106.5	87.2	133.7	117.3
096	FLOORING & CARPET	96.5	62.6	88.3	95.5	80.0	91.7	96.5	78.0	92.0	95.5	72.8	89.9	117.3	99.5	113.0	114.4	124.9	116.9
099	PAINTING & WALL COVERINGS	97.0	79.2	86.5	96.3	81.9	87.8	97.0	66.3	79.0	96.3	78.0	85.6	106.2	107.9	107.2	113.5	118.0	116.2
9	FINISHES	96.2	80.8	88.3	101.2	88.4	94.6	97.4	82.0	89.5	100.0	91.3	95.5	101.0	112.8	107.0	100.5	130.2	115.7
10 - 14	TOTAL DIV. 10 - 14	100.0	111.3	102.4	100.0	102.9	100.6	100.0	109.4	102.0	100.8	103.3	101.3	99.2	105.1	100.5	100.0	111.2	102.4
15	MECHANICAL	100.0	83.4	92.6	100.0	90.3	95.7	100.0	89.4	95.3	100.0	84.0	92.9	99.9	106.4	102.8	99.8	115.5	106.8
16	ELECTRICAL	93.5	84.5	87.5	92.8	91.5	91.9	93.8	74.0	80.5	96.3	84.2	88.1	96.9	101.9	100.3	98.0	109.2	105.6
1 - 16	WEIGHTED AVERAGE	96.8	85.7	91.5	96.4	95.5	96.0	96.6	84.6	90.8	96.5	92.9	94.8	97.9	109.9	103.7	98.5	120.4	109.0

DIVISION		MINNESOTA ROCHESTER			MINNESOTA SAINT PAUL			MINNESOTA ST. CLOUD			MISSISSIPPI BILOXI			MISSISSIPPI GREENVILLE			MISSISSIPPI JACKSON		
		MAT.	INST.	TOTAL	MAT.	INST.	TOTAL	MAT.	INST.	TOTAL	MAT.	INST.	TOTAL	MAT.	INST.	TOTAL	MAT.	INST.	TOTAL
2	SITE WORK	78.5	103.2	97.5	81.1	104.1	98.8	74.3	104.1	97.2	110.9	87.4	92.8	115.4	87.2	93.7	107.1	87.2	91.8
031	CONCRETE FORMWORK	98.2	105.8	104.7	88.3	125.3	120.0	79.2	97.4	94.8	100.3	55.5	62.2	77.5	46.5	51.0	94.4	53.2	59.1
032	CONCRETE REINFORCEMENT	90.7	105.8	99.2	87.5	106.4	98.1	100.0	105.4	103.0	95.7	69.5	80.9	103.7	57.7	77.8	95.7	62.6	77.1
033	CAST IN PLACE CONCRETE	100.4	102.2	101.2	103.3	117.2	109.1	95.4	114.7	103.5	108.3	56.4	86.6	108.8	49.4	84.0	106.3	52.5	83.8
3	CONCRETE	92.4	105.4	99.0	96.2	119.3	107.8	87.1	106.0	96.6	96.3	60.3	78.1	98.5	51.6	74.9	94.9	56.5	75.5
4	MASONRY	106.9	106.1	106.4	117.9	128.6	124.6	108.2	107.2	107.6	88.2	51.0	65.1	128.3	48.4	78.7	91.2	48.4	64.6
5	METALS	93.1	123.0	103.9	91.9	124.7	103.7	94.4	122.8	104.6	98.3	86.0	93.9	96.6	81.5	91.2	98.3	83.4	92.9
6	WOOD & PLASTICS	103.1	104.8	104.0	92.2	122.9	108.0	83.2	88.3	85.8	99.5	56.9	77.5	74.0	46.1	59.6	92.6	54.8	73.1
7	THERMAL & MOISTURE PROTECTION	97.1	107.0	101.7	97.0	132.2	113.3	96.6	123.1	108.9	97.4	57.6	78.9	97.3	52.3	76.4	97.1	54.0	77.1
8	DOORS & WINDOWS	100.9	117.0	104.8	98.0	133.5	106.6	95.6	108.1	98.6	97.0	57.5	87.4	96.4	47.9	84.7	97.4	53.8	86.8
092	LATH, PLASTER & GYPSUM BOARD	93.2	105.9	101.4	88.9	124.5	111.9	81.8	88.8	86.3	110.9	56.0	75.5	102.7	44.9	65.4	110.9	53.9	74.1
095	ACOUSTICAL TREATMENT & WOOD FLOORING	87.2	105.9	99.3	84.4	124.5	110.4	68.0	88.8	81.5	100.2	56.0	71.6	94.7	44.9	62.4	100.2	53.9	70.2
096	FLOORING & CARPET	117.1	98.0	112.4	109.9	124.9	113.6	103.8	120.5	107.9	112.8	52.5	98.1	103.6	44.8	89.3	112.8	51.9	98.0
099	PAINTING & WALL COVERINGS	109.0	99.8	103.6	113.5	113.1	113.3	110.9	81.2	93.4	103.1	46.2	69.7	103.1	45.5	69.3	103.1	45.5	69.3
9	FINISHES	101.0	104.2	102.7	98.2	124.3	111.6	93.3	98.5	96.0	105.4	54.1	79.1	100.6	45.9	72.6	105.4	52.2	78.1
10 - 14	TOTAL DIV. 10 - 14	100.0	101.6	100.3	100.0	109.5	102.0	100.0	103.3	100.7	100.0	73.1	94.3	100.0	70.8	93.8	100.0	71.9	94.1
15	MECHANICAL	99.8	103.7	101.5	99.8	112.2	105.3	99.7	104.1	101.7	100.0	53.3	79.2	100.0	46.5	76.1	100.0	46.0	75.9
16	ELECTRICAL	96.9	90.4	92.5	96.0	95.5	95.7	96.2	87.2	90.2	95.9	61.0	72.3	94.8	50.8	65.1	96.4	50.8	65.6
1 - 16	WEIGHTED AVERAGE	97.7	104.3	100.9	97.8	115.2	106.2	95.5	103.4	99.3	98.8	62.6	81.3	100.2	56.1	78.9	98.7	58.0	79.0

City Cost Indexes

	DIVISION	MISSISSIPPI			MISSOURI													
		MERIDIAN			CAPE GIRARDEAU			COLUMBIA			JOPLIN			KANSAS CITY			SPRINGFIELD		
		MAT.	INST.	TOTAL	MAT.	INST.	TOTAL	MAT.	INST.	TOTAL	MAT.	INST.	TOTAL	MAT.	INST.	TOTAL	MAT.	INST.	TOTAL
2	SITE WORK	105.9	87.2	91.5	98.5	94.2	95.2	99.5	95.5	96.5	98.5	96.7	97.1	91.0	94.9	94.0	91.3	95.3	94.4
031	CONCRETE FORMWORK	75.8	45.1	49.5	85.1	87.4	87.0	85.7	66.4	69.2	105.7	62.7	68.9	105.3	94.4	96.0	104.2	61.0	67.2
032	CONCRETE REINFORCEMENT	102.4	62.1	79.7	99.2	95.8	97.3	97.4	97.3	97.3	100.5	78.2	87.9	95.4	98.3	97.0	93.6	97.4	95.7
033	CAST IN PLACE CONCRETE	102.7	52.5	81.6	90.3	94.4	92.0	88.1	76.1	83.1	104.2	77.3	92.9	96.8	98.2	97.4	99.6	68.1	86.4
3	CONCRETE	91.5	52.9	72.0	84.8	93.1	89.0	80.7	78.0	79.3	97.1	72.4	84.6	93.3	97.2	95.2	93.0	71.9	82.3
4	MASONRY	87.8	39.4	57.7	114.4	83.7	95.3	133.3	70.0	93.9	99.0	65.7	78.3	105.9	92.5	97.5	89.3	71.1	78.0
5	METALS	96.6	82.4	91.5	96.3	118.3	104.2	94.6	117.4	102.8	97.3	96.7	97.1	100.9	107.6	103.3	98.0	102.4	99.6
6	WOOD & PLASTICS	72.0	44.2	57.7	84.5	89.0	86.8	88.3	61.8	74.6	104.6	59.8	81.5	104.9	93.3	98.9	103.0	58.1	79.8
7	THERMAL & MOISTURE PROTECTION	96.7	50.6	75.4	92.2	86.8	89.7	91.6	75.3	84.0	98.3	70.0	85.2	97.1	96.5	96.8	95.9	70.4	84.1
8	DOORS & WINDOWS	96.4	47.0	84.4	98.2	89.9	96.2	93.9	83.6	91.4	94.4	73.9	89.4	98.5	96.2	97.9	99.7	70.1	92.5
092	LATH, PLASTER & GYPSUM BOARD	101.7	43.0	63.8	99.5	88.2	92.2	105.0	60.1	76.1	114.4	58.1	78.0	108.6	92.7	98.3	111.1	56.3	75.7
095	ACOUSTICAL TREATMENT & WOOD FLOORING	94.7	43.0	61.2	88.7	88.2	88.4	88.9	60.1	70.2	95.0	58.1	71.1	100.5	92.7	95.4	94.3	56.3	69.7
096	FLOORING & CARPET	102.7	36.4	86.6	101.1	95.3	99.7	107.1	68.0	97.6	115.0	64.1	102.7	94.5	92.6	94.0	109.6	64.1	98.6
099	PAINTING & WALL COVERINGS	103.1	44.9	68.9	94.7	94.3	94.5	94.7	63.8	76.6	90.2	55.7	70.0	95.3	98.0	96.8	89.6	73.9	80.4
9	FINISHES	99.6	42.8	70.5	92.5	89.2	90.8	93.5	64.4	78.6	101.8	61.1	80.9	97.1	94.1	95.6	98.5	61.9	79.8
10 - 14	TOTAL DIV. 10 - 14	100.0	70.6	93.8	100.0	85.1	96.9	100.0	91.9	98.3	100.0	84.3	96.7	100.0	96.9	99.3	100.0	87.2	97.3
15	MECHANICAL	100.0	46.1	76.0	100.0	96.6	98.5	100.1	74.5	88.7	100.2	61.7	83.0	100.0	98.0	99.1	100.2	70.0	86.8
16	ELECTRICAL	94.3	54.5	67.4	94.4	109.9	104.9	94.0	83.5	86.9	89.9	73.3	78.7	104.1	101.5	102.4	100.4	74.0	82.6
1 - 16	WEIGHTED AVERAGE	96.7	55.6	76.8	96.5	97.1	96.8	96.4	81.5	89.2	98.0	73.3	86.1	99.2	97.9	98.6	97.8	75.9	87.2

	DIVISION	MISSOURI						MONTANA										
		ST. JOSEPH			ST. LOUIS			BILLINGS			BUTTE			GREAT FALLS			HELENA		
		MAT.	INST.	TOTAL	MAT.	INST.	TOTAL	MAT.	INST.	TOTAL	MAT.	INST.	TOTAL	MAT.	INST.	TOTAL	MAT.	INST.	TOTAL
2	SITE WORK	92.4	92.0	92.1	97.9	97.8	97.8	79.9	97.5	93.4	85.7	96.2	93.8	89.1	97.0	95.2	90.7	96.9	95.5
031	CONCRETE FORMWORK	105.2	77.6	81.6	103.4	107.5	106.9	94.9	90.2	90.9	80.5	87.9	86.8	101.6	90.5	92.1	101.7	90.5	92.1
032	CONCRETE REINFORCEMENT	94.3	88.4	90.9	90.8	105.1	98.8	96.8	97.9	97.4	105.0	97.7	100.9	96.8	97.9	97.4	100.2	97.7	98.8
033	CAST IN PLACE CONCRETE	96.8	93.7	95.5	90.3	111.4	99.1	115.9	84.8	102.9	119.3	80.9	103.2	126.1	74.4	104.4	128.4	83.2	109.5
3	CONCRETE	93.1	86.4	89.7	85.1	109.6	97.4	101.2	90.0	95.6	101.1	87.6	94.3	106.7	86.5	96.5	108.3	89.5	98.8
4	MASONRY	105.0	77.3	87.8	98.7	108.1	104.5	119.3	97.2	105.6	117.7	95.7	104.0	121.6	101.6	109.2	118.6	98.3	106.0
5	METALS	99.5	101.3	100.1	98.8	124.1	107.9	96.2	96.9	96.5	95.6	96.0	95.7	96.6	96.6	96.6	95.8	96.1	95.9
6	WOOD & PLASTICS	105.4	75.9	90.2	104.2	105.8	105.0	96.9	90.9	93.8	82.7	89.7	86.3	106.1	90.6	98.1	106.3	90.6	98.2
7	THERMAL & MOISTURE PROTECTION	97.8	82.4	90.6	92.3	102.6	97.0	97.2	90.1	93.9	96.5	84.7	91.0	97.4	88.9	93.5	97.4	88.8	93.4
8	DOORS & WINDOWS	99.3	84.3	95.6	95.0	110.5	98.8	103.8	87.4	99.8	100.3	86.6	97.0	104.0	87.3	100.0	103.5	87.5	99.6
092	LATH, PLASTER & GYPSUM BOARD	115.3	74.7	89.1	107.3	105.5	106.1	98.1	91.2	93.6	89.0	89.9	89.6	98.1	90.9	93.4	97.5	90.9	93.2
095	ACOUSTICAL TREATMENT & WOOD FLOORING	99.1	74.7	83.3	92.8	105.5	101.0	110.6	91.2	98.0	107.8	89.9	96.2	110.6	90.9	97.8	107.8	90.9	96.8
096	FLOORING & CARPET	96.8	78.6	92.4	108.5	96.8	105.7	114.0	66.7	102.5	105.7	53.1	92.9	114.0	72.1	103.8	114.0	69.8	103.2
099	PAINTING & WALL COVERINGS	90.9	83.2	86.4	94.7	107.5	102.2	106.3	81.9	92.0	106.3	63.2	81.0	106.3	71.2	85.7	106.3	79.0	90.3
9	FINISHES	98.2	77.7	87.7	96.8	105.1	101.0	107.0	84.9	95.7	102.5	78.8	90.3	107.1	85.0	95.8	106.6	85.5	95.8
10 - 14	TOTAL DIV. 10 - 14	100.0	91.7	98.3	100.0	104.2	100.9	100.0	90.4	98.0	100.0	89.5	97.8	100.0	91.3	98.2	100.0	80.9	96.0
15	MECHANICAL	100.2	79.0	90.8	100.0	108.3	103.7	100.0	90.3	95.8	100.2	83.0	92.5	100.2	82.9	92.5	100.2	81.3	91.8
16	ELECTRICAL	103.5	78.6	86.7	98.0	113.5	108.5	92.4	86.9	88.7	103.7	66.6	78.7	92.4	82.3	85.6	92.4	82.1	85.4
1 - 16	WEIGHTED AVERAGE	99.2	83.5	91.6	96.6	109.1	102.7	100.6	90.9	95.9	100.3	84.5	92.7	101.8	88.6	95.5	101.7	88.1	95.1

	DIVISION	MONTANA			NEBRASKA												NEVADA		
		MISSOULA			GRAND ISLAND			LINCOLN			NORTH PLATTE			OMAHA			CARSON CITY		
		MAT.	INST.	TOTAL	MAT.	INST.	TOTAL	MAT.	INST.	TOTAL	MAT.	INST.	TOTAL	MAT.	INST.	TOTAL	MAT.	INST.	TOTAL
2	SITE WORK	70.5	96.2	90.3	93.6	92.5	92.8	84.5	92.5	90.6	94.4	92.3	92.8	77.0	91.0	87.8	65.0	103.1	94.3
031	CONCRETE FORMWORK	85.1	87.5	87.1	100.2	58.5	64.5	105.8	51.1	59.0	100.0	57.6	63.7	100.6	68.1	72.8	98.7	92.7	93.6
032	CONCRETE REINFORCEMENT	106.8	102.7	104.5	102.0	70.5	84.2	93.6	70.3	80.5	103.2	62.5	80.3	97.9	71.3	83.0	109.3	115.4	112.8
033	CAST IN PLACE CONCRETE	87.9	85.5	86.9	115.0	65.1	94.1	103.9	67.9	88.8	115.0	62.6	93.1	107.7	71.7	92.7	116.3	96.3	107.9
3	CONCRETE	80.3	90.0	85.2	102.6	64.5	83.4	95.2	62.3	78.6	102.7	61.7	82.1	96.5	70.4	83.3	112.9	97.9	105.3
4	MASONRY	144.5	87.9	109.3	107.5	54.0	74.3	97.8	51.2	68.8	92.3	50.7	66.4	103.4	70.4	82.9	133.4	82.8	102.0
5	METALS	95.7	99.1	96.9	94.5	86.3	91.5	97.5	86.0	93.4	94.7	82.3	90.2	100.1	76.4	91.6	104.3	97.3	101.8
6	WOOD & PLASTICS	87.9	90.6	89.3	99.1	56.6	77.2	104.8	46.8	74.9	98.9	56.6	77.1	101.2	68.9	84.5	96.2	91.7	93.9
7	THERMAL & MOISTURE PROTECTION	95.7	92.4	94.1	96.1	62.1	80.4	96.6	56.7	78.1	96.1	57.2	78.0	91.7	69.5	81.4	103.2	90.9	97.5
8	DOORS & WINDOWS	100.4	90.3	97.9	93.2	57.2	84.5	98.9	54.1	88.0	92.5	57.6	84.0	102.8	66.0	93.9	94.8	100.1	96.1
092	LATH, PLASTER & GYPSUM BOARD	91.1	90.9	90.9	107.4	54.8	73.4	111.1	44.6	68.2	107.7	54.8	73.6	117.8	68.3	85.8	88.7	91.3	90.4
095	ACOUSTICAL TREATMENT & WOOD FLOORING	107.8	90.9	96.8	87.5	54.8	66.3	94.3	44.6	62.1	88.9	54.8	66.8	132.8	68.3	91.0	96.9	91.3	93.3
096	FLOORING & CARPET	107.5	83.0	101.6	98.9	44.5	85.7	100.8	46.4	87.6	98.8	46.4	86.1	129.2	55.7	111.3	106.1	82.7	100.4
099	PAINTING & WALL COVERINGS	106.3	71.2	85.7	86.8	52.1	66.5	86.8	52.6	66.8	86.8	63.0	72.9	138.7	63.0	94.3	113.2	99.3	105.0
9	FINISHES	102.6	85.0	93.6	93.5	54.5	73.5	95.7	49.2	71.8	93.7	56.0	74.4	120.7	65.0	92.2	98.3	90.7	94.4
10 - 14	TOTAL DIV. 10 - 14	100.0	77.2	95.2	100.0	78.7	95.5	100.0	77.4	95.2	100.0	70.6	93.8	100.0	78.3	95.4	100.0	125.8	105.4
15	MECHANICAL	100.2	81.6	91.9	100.2	75.6	89.2	100.2	75.6	89.2	100.2	48.9	77.3	99.9	73.4	88.1	99.8	96.9	98.5
16	ELECTRICAL	100.4	77.9	85.2	91.2	56.6	67.9	100.7	56.6	70.9	94.5	56.6	68.9	88.5	82.1	84.2	93.9	89.3	90.8
1 - 16	WEIGHTED AVERAGE	98.7	86.8	93.0	97.5	67.9	83.2	97.9	66.2	82.6	96.9	61.5	79.8	100.5	74.9	88.2	101.8	95.0	98.5

City Cost Indexes

		NEVADA						NEW HAMPSHIRE									NEW JERSEY		
	DIVISION	LAS VEGAS			RENO			MANCHESTER			NASHUA			PORTSMOUTH			CAMDEN		
		MAT.	INST.	TOTAL	MAT.	INST.	TOTAL	MAT.	INST.	TOTAL	MAT.	INST.	TOTAL	MAT.	INST.	TOTAL	MAT.	INST.	TOTAL
2	SITE WORK	65.3	104.3	95.3	65.4	103.1	94.4	95.9	97.0	96.7	98.1	97.0	97.2	92.0	96.5	95.4	101.4	100.9	101.0
031	CONCRETE FORMWORK	94.7	105.2	103.7	99.1	92.7	93.6	97.7	75.5	78.7	98.2	75.5	78.8	83.9	72.3	74.0	98.2	123.8	120.1
032	CONCRETE REINFORCEMENT	101.0	118.9	111.1	101.0	118.5	110.8	116.7	93.8	103.8	116.7	93.8	103.8	93.3	93.7	93.5	116.7	112.9	114.6
033	CAST IN PLACE CONCRETE	110.7	109.0	110.0	118.5	96.3	109.2	101.6	92.3	97.7	99.0	92.3	96.2	94.0	88.2	91.6	86.1	120.3	100.4
3	CONCRETE	108.7	108.5	108.6	112.9	98.5	105.6	112.2	84.8	98.4	111.0	84.8	97.8	101.6	81.8	91.6	104.7	119.2	112.0
4	MASONRY	127.3	97.6	108.9	133.5	82.8	102.0	94.9	102.7	99.8	95.3	102.7	99.9	89.7	95.8	93.5	87.3	124.6	110.5
5	METALS	105.0	100.8	103.5	104.9	98.4	102.5	101.1	87.2	96.1	101.1	87.2	96.1	97.6	85.7	93.3	101.0	99.3	100.4
6	WOOD & PLASTICS	90.8	103.1	97.2	96.6	91.7	94.1	101.3	70.1	85.2	101.3	70.1	85.2	85.6	70.1	77.6	101.3	123.7	112.9
7	THERMAL & MOISTURE PROTECTION	102.8	101.3	102.1	103.2	90.9	97.5	101.3	102.7	101.9	101.6	102.7	102.1	101.2	98.5	99.9	101.1	117.0	108.4
8	DOORS & WINDOWS	95.2	106.9	98.0	95.2	99.5	96.2	109.1	76.4	101.2	109.1	76.4	101.2	110.1	69.0	100.2	109.1	117.0	111.0
092	LATH, PLASTER & GYPSUM BOARD	88.6	103.1	97.9	89.6	91.3	90.7	98.5	68.1	78.9	98.5	68.1	78.9	90.0	68.1	75.9	98.5	123.5	114.6
095	ACOUSTICAL TREATMENT & WOOD FLOORING	102.6	103.1	102.9	101.0	91.3	94.7	101.7	68.1	79.9	101.7	68.1	79.9	92.1	68.1	76.5	101.7	123.5	115.9
096	FLOORING & CARPET	106.1	94.0	103.1	106.1	82.7	100.4	97.1	106.6	99.4	96.9	106.6	99.2	92.1	106.6	95.7	96.9	130.3	105.0
099	PAINTING & WALL COVERINGS	113.2	129.7	122.9	113.2	99.3	105.0	89.3	84.6	86.6	89.3	84.6	86.6	89.3	48.6	65.5	89.3	135.6	116.5
9	FINISHES	99.3	105.2	102.3	99.2	90.7	94.8	97.1	81.2	89.0	97.3	81.2	89.1	92.4	75.4	83.7	97.6	126.8	112.6
10 - 14	TOTAL DIV. 10 - 14	100.0	114.7	103.1	100.0	125.8	105.4	100.0	99.4	99.9	100.0	99.4	99.9	100.0	96.6	99.3	100.0	120.4	104.3
15	MECHANICAL	99.8	109.5	104.1	99.8	97.0	98.5	100.0	83.5	92.6	100.0	83.5	92.6	100.0	79.8	91.0	100.0	117.6	107.8
16	ELECTRICAL	96.0	111.1	106.2	93.9	89.3	90.8	104.9	77.9	86.7	104.7	77.9	86.6	101.4	79.1	86.4	104.7	116.4	112.6
1 - 16	WEIGHTED AVERAGE	101.3	106.4	103.8	102.0	95.1	98.7	102.4	86.5	94.7	102.4	86.5	94.7	99.4	83.6	91.8	101.3	116.1	108.4

		NEW JERSEY															NEW MEXICO		
	DIVISION	ELIZABETH			JERSEY CITY			NEWARK			PATERSON			TRENTON			ALBUQUERQUE		
		MAT.	INST.	TOTAL	MAT.	INST.	TOTAL	MAT.	INST.	TOTAL	MAT.	INST.	TOTAL	MAT.	INST.	TOTAL	MAT.	INST.	TOTAL
2	SITE WORK	117.4	101.3	105.0	101.4	101.4	101.4	121.4	101.3	105.9	115.7	101.3	104.6	102.5	101.5	101.8	86.2	111.0	105.3
031	CONCRETE FORMWORK	109.8	117.8	116.7	98.2	124.5	120.7	96.5	124.0	120.1	97.0	121.5	118.0	97.3	129.2	124.6	97.0	72.1	75.7
032	CONCRETE REINFORCEMENT	89.8	122.2	108.1	116.7	126.3	122.1	116.7	126.3	122.1	116.7	126.3	122.1	116.7	121.1	119.2	101.7	69.7	83.7
033	CAST IN PLACE CONCRETE	94.9	123.7	106.9	86.1	127.3	103.4	97.0	129.8	110.7	109.7	129.7	118.1	96.9	127.5	109.7	108.9	79.3	96.5
3	CONCRETE	108.3	119.7	114.1	104.7	124.5	114.7	109.9	125.3	117.7	116.2	124.2	120.2	109.9	125.6	117.8	108.1	75.3	91.6
4	MASONRY	108.8	117.3	114.1	87.3	127.5	112.3	97.0	126.3	115.2	92.0	126.3	113.3	88.3	124.6	110.9	110.0	73.5	87.3
5	METALS	97.4	106.6	100.7	101.0	106.5	103.0	101.0	109.8	104.2	101.0	109.7	104.2	101.8	104.0	102.6	106.0	91.4	100.7
6	WOOD & PLASTICS	117.9	120.1	119.1	101.3	123.5	112.7	103.1	123.3	113.5	103.1	120.0	111.8	101.3	130.0	116.1	97.1	73.6	85.0
7	THERMAL & MOISTURE PROTECTION	102.0	113.4	107.3	101.1	114.9	107.5	101.4	123.8	111.7	101.8	120.9	110.7	100.0	121.1	109.8	102.2	79.7	91.7
8	DOORS & WINDOWS	110.4	120.5	112.8	109.1	123.7	112.6	115.4	123.5	117.3	115.4	121.2	116.8	109.1	126.4	113.3	95.1	72.4	89.6
092	LATH, PLASTER & GYPSUM BOARD	102.2	119.8	113.5	98.5	123.3	114.5	98.5	123.0	114.3	98.5	119.6	112.1	98.5	130.0	118.8	89.6	72.2	78.4
095	ACOUSTICAL TREATMENT & WOOD FLOORING	92.1	119.8	110.0	101.7	123.3	115.7	101.7	123.0	115.5	101.7	119.6	113.3	101.7	130.0	120.0	101.0	72.2	82.4
096	FLOORING & CARPET	101.2	70.2	93.6	96.9	134.4	106.0	97.1	134.4	106.2	96.9	134.4	106.0	97.1	130.4	105.2	106.1	77.7	99.2
099	PAINTING & WALL COVERINGS	89.2	122.1	108.5	89.3	122.1	108.6	89.2	122.1	108.5	89.2	122.1	108.5	89.3	122.1	108.6	113.2	66.1	85.5
9	FINISHES	98.3	108.7	103.6	97.6	126.1	112.2	98.1	125.7	112.2	97.7	123.8	111.1	97.7	128.9	113.7	99.7	72.5	85.8
10 - 14	TOTAL DIV. 10 - 14	100.0	97.6	99.5	100.0	104.3	100.9	100.0	103.7	100.8	100.0	103.3	100.7	100.0	121.1	104.5	100.0	78.3	95.4
15	MECHANICAL	100.0	110.0	104.4	100.0	124.7	111.0	100.0	122.6	110.1	100.0	123.2	110.3	100.0	122.8	110.2	99.8	77.1	89.7
16	ELECTRICAL	99.5	124.7	116.5	106.3	136.5	126.7	106.1	131.4	123.2	106.3	128.2	121.1	104.9	129.9	121.7	88.3	79.9	82.7
1 - 16	WEIGHTED AVERAGE	102.8	113.4	107.9	101.4	122.2	111.4	103.9	121.4	112.4	104.2	120.4	112.0	102.1	121.5	111.5	100.6	81.1	91.1

		NEW MEXICO												NEW YORK					
	DIVISION	FARMINGTON			LAS CRUCES			ROSWELL			SANTA FE			ALBANY			BINGHAMTON		
		MAT.	INST.	TOTAL	MAT.	INST.	TOTAL	MAT.	INST.	TOTAL	MAT.	INST.	TOTAL	MAT.	INST.	TOTAL	MAT.	INST.	TOTAL
2	SITE WORK	91.6	110.9	106.4	99.5	86.2	89.3	96.7	110.8	107.6	85.5	111.0	105.1	74.8	108.9	101.0	99.1	91.3	93.1
031	CONCRETE FORMWORK	97.0	72.0	75.6	94.5	69.8	73.3	97.0	68.9	72.9	97.0	72.1	75.7	99.9	91.0	92.3	106.2	79.5	83.3
032	CONCRETE REINFORCEMENT	111.0	67.6	86.5	105.1	62.8	81.2	110.2	63.4	83.8	109.1	69.6	86.8	99.0	88.9	93.3	98.0	91.9	94.5
033	CAST IN PLACE CONCRETE	109.5	79.1	96.8	95.3	68.4	84.0	100.9	77.6	91.1	102.9	79.3	93.0	82.4	101.4	90.4	104.3	91.4	98.9
3	CONCRETE	111.9	74.7	93.2	88.3	68.7	78.4	112.4	72.0	92.0	106.2	75.3	90.6	100.8	95.5	98.1	102.2	88.5	95.3
4	MASONRY	124.2	71.6	91.5	110.4	63.3	81.1	125.6	69.1	90.5	114.7	71.4	87.8	93.0	97.9	96.0	108.8	84.9	94.0
5	METALS	105.2	89.6	99.6	99.4	78.1	91.7	105.1	87.5	98.8	105.1	91.2	100.1	99.9	109.8	103.5	95.1	124.2	105.6
6	WOOD & PLASTICS	97.1	73.6	85.0	90.5	72.0	80.9	97.1	69.9	83.1	97.1	73.6	85.0	101.6	89.1	95.1	111.8	76.2	93.4
7	THERMAL & MOISTURE PROTECTION	103.0	78.9	91.8	87.8	70.4	79.7	103.3	77.4	91.3	102.4	79.1	91.6	92.7	95.6	94.1	102.3	88.0	95.7
8	DOORS & WINDOWS	98.1	71.8	91.7	87.1	69.6	82.9	94.1	68.5	87.9	94.3	72.4	89.0	99.7	84.2	95.9	94.4	78.7	90.6
092	LATH, PLASTER & GYPSUM BOARD	88.1	72.2	77.8	89.9	72.2	78.5	88.1	68.4	75.4	88.1	72.2	77.8	100.4	88.4	92.7	107.4	74.7	86.3
095	ACOUSTICAL TREATMENT & WOOD FLOORING	94.2	72.2	80.0	97.8	72.2	81.2	94.2	68.4	77.5	94.2	72.2	80.0	97.1	88.4	91.5	97.1	74.7	82.6
096	FLOORING & CARPET	106.1	77.7	99.2	138.6	52.6	117.7	106.1	70.5	97.4	106.1	77.7	99.2	81.6	88.8	83.4	91.2	84.7	89.6
099	PAINTING & WALL COVERINGS	113.2	72.5	89.3	106.2	48.5	72.3	113.2	72.5	89.3	113.2	65.0	84.9	78.9	83.4	81.5	79.6	70.1	74.0
9	FINISHES	98.5	73.3	85.6	116.6	64.2	89.7	98.9	69.5	83.8	98.3	72.4	85.0	94.6	89.4	91.9	94.7	78.6	86.5
10 - 14	TOTAL DIV. 10 - 14	100.0	78.3	95.4	100.0	73.6	94.4	100.0	77.7	95.3	100.0	78.3	95.4	100.2	95.0	99.1	100.0	91.6	98.2
15	MECHANICAL	99.8	75.1	88.8	100.0	76.5	89.5	99.8	75.2	88.8	99.8	77.1	89.7	100.3	90.8	96.1	100.6	85.5	93.8
16	ELECTRICAL	85.6	78.6	80.9	86.8	65.2	72.2	86.8	78.6	81.3	88.3	77.2	80.8	103.2	92.9	96.2	104.1	78.0	86.5
1 - 16	WEIGHTED AVERAGE	101.8	80.1	91.3	97.8	71.4	85.1	101.8	78.6	90.6	100.2	80.3	90.6	98.5	95.8	97.2	99.4	87.8	93.8

City Cost Indexes

		NEW YORK																	
	DIVISION	BUFFALO			HICKSVILLE			NEW YORK			RIVERHEAD			ROCHESTER			SCHENECTADY		
		MAT.	INST.	TOTAL	MAT.	INST.	TOTAL	MAT.	INST.	TOTAL	MAT.	INST.	TOTAL	MAT.	INST.	TOTAL	MAT.	INST.	TOTAL
2	SITE WORK	104.3	93.7	96.1	119.5	131.6	128.8	143.5	128.8	132.2	119.7	131.7	129.0	78.6	108.6	101.7	74.8	108.9	101.0
031	CONCRETE FORMWORK	103.5	114.1	112.6	90.1	146.9	138.7	110.5	171.7	162.9	95.0	146.9	139.4	103.1	99.6	100.1	105.6	91.1	93.2
032	CONCRETE REINFORCEMENT	101.4	105.7	103.8	99.2	165.1	136.3	100.4	185.1	148.1	101.1	165.1	137.2	102.2	90.0	95.4	97.7	88.9	92.8
033	CAST IN PLACE CONCRETE	105.1	119.2	111.0	97.5	143.1	116.6	123.8	161.6	139.6	95.7	144.9	116.3	100.0	105.4	102.3	95.7	101.4	98.1
3	CONCRETE	103.7	113.4	108.6	106.3	147.8	127.2	127.3	168.8	148.2	105.3	148.4	127.0	110.2	100.9	105.5	107.6	95.6	101.5
4	MASONRY	106.3	117.9	113.5	111.4	150.3	135.6	113.3	166.9	146.6	118.8	153.6	140.4	102.6	101.3	101.8	93.7	97.9	96.3
5	METALS	100.0	96.6	98.8	109.2	133.8	118.1	109.3	143.0	121.5	109.3	133.8	118.1	103.2	110.6	105.9	99.9	109.8	103.5
6	WOOD & PLASTICS	103.6	114.2	109.1	90.0	149.2	120.5	113.4	173.6	144.5	95.2	147.5	122.2	99.9	100.1	100.0	108.6	89.1	98.6
7	THERMAL & MOISTURE PROTECTION	105.2	107.6	106.3	107.2	137.5	121.2	108.7	158.7	131.9	107.2	138.6	121.8	101.8	101.3	101.6	92.9	95.6	94.2
8	DOORS & WINDOWS	94.1	106.9	97.2	91.9	151.2	106.3	100.5	171.5	117.7	91.9	150.3	106.1	99.8	93.7	98.3	99.7	84.2	95.9
092	LATH, PLASTER & GYPSUM BOARD	96.1	114.1	107.7	93.8	150.7	130.5	105.3	175.8	150.8	95.4	149.0	130.0	97.8	99.8	99.1	100.4	88.4	92.7
095	ACOUSTICAL TREATMENT & WOOD FLOORING	92.8	114.1	106.6	80.6	150.7	126.0	102.9	175.8	150.1	80.6	149.0	124.9	95.6	99.8	98.3	97.1	88.4	91.5
096	FLOORING & CARPET	90.8	118.4	97.5	90.8	111.4	95.8	92.0	161.0	108.8	92.1	111.4	96.8	79.8	106.1	86.2	81.6	88.8	83.4
099	PAINTING & WALL COVERINGS	75.6	115.9	99.2	101.9	137.4	122.8	95.3	151.3	128.2	101.9	137.4	122.8	72.8	104.6	91.5	78.9	83.4	81.5
9	FINISHES	93.0	115.9	104.8	104.2	138.9	122.0	108.0	167.6	138.5	104.8	138.7	122.2	94.0	101.8	98.0	94.3	89.4	91.8
10-14	TOTAL DIV. 10 - 14	100.0	106.2	101.3	100.0	126.6	105.6	100.0	151.0	110.8	100.0	127.7	105.9	100.0	96.3	99.2	100.0	95.0	98.9
15	MECHANICAL	100.0	97.8	99.1	99.9	141.8	118.6	100.2	164.2	128.8	99.9	143.5	119.3	100.0	93.6	97.2	100.3	93.1	97.1
16	ELECTRICAL	102.0	101.4	101.6	103.6	149.8	134.8	111.8	168.9	150.3	104.7	149.8	135.1	107.1	98.6	101.4	103.6	97.4	99.4
1-16	WEIGHTED AVERAGE	99.8	105.0	102.3	103.2	142.6	122.2	108.9	160.6	133.9	103.7	143.3	122.8	101.2	100.5	100.9	99.4	97.0	98.2

		NEW YORK																NORTH CAROLINA		
	DIVISION	SYRACUSE			UTICA			WATERTOWN			WHITE PLAINS			YONKERS			ASHEVILLE		
		MAT.	INST.	TOTAL	MAT.	INST.	TOTAL	MAT.	INST.	TOTAL	MAT.	INST.	TOTAL	MAT.	INST.	TOTAL	MAT.	INST.	TOTAL
2	SITE WORK	97.7	108.8	106.2	72.8	108.0	99.8	81.6	110.0	103.4	132.2	127.5	128.6	143.2	127.1	130.8	103.4	73.9	80.7
031	CONCRETE FORMWORK	104.9	89.0	91.3	106.1	78.7	82.7	84.8	85.8	85.6	111.3	132.2	129.2	110.3	142.4	137.8	93.2	48.1	54.6
032	CONCRETE REINFORCEMENT	99.0	92.3	95.2	99.0	81.2	89.0	99.5	71.9	84.0	94.1	151.3	126.4	97.8	109.9	104.6	93.8	45.8	66.8
033	CAST IN PLACE CONCRETE	95.7	97.5	96.5	88.4	92.8	90.3	103.0	97.8	100.8	109.1	134.3	119.6	122.1	134.6	127.3	101.0	55.2	81.8
3	CONCRETE	105.7	93.9	99.7	104.2	85.7	94.9	117.6	88.8	103.1	114.4	136.0	125.3	126.4	133.9	130.1	99.4	52.4	75.7
4	MASONRY	99.4	94.8	96.6	92.4	88.3	89.9	93.5	95.2	94.5	106.5	135.6	124.6	112.9	135.9	127.2	79.4	41.8	56.0
5	METALS	99.8	110.6	103.7	98.0	106.0	100.9	98.0	102.3	99.6	99.4	131.4	110.9	106.4	137.6	117.7	93.7	83.7	90.1
6	WOOD & PLASTICS	108.6	87.0	97.5	108.6	76.4	92.0	85.0	84.4	84.7	115.6	130.5	123.3	114.0	143.6	129.3	95.0	48.9	71.2
7	THERMAL & MOISTURE PROTECTION	100.8	95.8	98.5	92.8	92.6	92.7	93.1	92.2	92.7	109.6	131.7	119.9	110.0	140.7	124.2	95.5	48.5	73.7
8	DOORS & WINDOWS	97.4	83.6	94.1	99.7	72.7	93.1	99.7	75.5	93.8	96.9	141.1	107.7	100.6	155.9	114.0	92.9	47.6	81.9
092	LATH, PLASTER & GYPSUM BOARD	100.4	86.3	91.3	100.4	75.3	84.2	92.5	83.5	86.7	101.4	131.3	120.7	105.0	144.8	130.7	99.7	47.1	65.7
095	ACOUSTICAL TREATMENT & WOOD FLOORING	97.1	86.3	90.1	97.1	75.3	83.0	97.1	83.5	88.3	83.7	131.3	114.5	101.5	144.8	129.5	87.3	47.1	61.2
096	FLOORING & CARPET	83.5	87.5	84.4	81.4	82.9	81.8	74.3	82.9	76.4	88.2	147.1	102.5	87.8	150.1	103.0	89.9	51.0	80.4
099	PAINTING & WALL COVERINGS	84.1	89.0	87.0	78.9	83.9	81.8	78.9	75.1	76.7	92.6	121.0	109.3	92.6	121.0	109.3	105.8	47.8	71.8
9	FINISHES	95.8	88.2	91.9	94.2	79.5	86.7	91.5	83.7	87.5	101.6	133.5	118.0	106.1	141.9	124.4	91.2	48.4	69.2
10-14	TOTAL DIV. 10 - 14	100.0	93.2	98.6	100.0	90.8	98.1	100.0	91.1	98.1	100.0	124.3	105.1	100.0	142.0	108.9	100.0	71.7	94.0
15	MECHANICAL	100.3	93.4	97.2	100.3	84.3	93.2	100.3	87.3	94.5	100.6	123.2	110.7	100.6	125.4	111.6	100.1	53.3	79.3
16	ELECTRICAL	103.6	92.0	95.8	103.6	82.1	89.1	103.6	79.3	87.2	96.1	131.5	119.9	109.3	143.2	132.2	100.7	51.5	67.5
1-16	WEIGHTED AVERAGE	100.3	95.5	97.9	98.6	88.1	93.5	100.0	89.9	95.1	103.0	130.9	116.5	108.0	136.0	121.5	96.1	56.1	76.8

		NORTH CAROLINA																	
	DIVISION	CHARLOTTE			DURHAM			FAYETTEVILLE			GREENSBORO			RALEIGH			WILMINGTON		
		MAT.	INST.	TOTAL	MAT.	INST.	TOTAL	MAT.	INST.	TOTAL	MAT.	INST.	TOTAL	MAT.	INST.	TOTAL	MAT.	INST.	TOTAL
2	SITE WORK	103.8	73.9	80.8	103.5	84.2	88.6	101.6	84.2	88.2	103.4	84.2	88.6	104.6	84.2	88.9	104.5	73.9	81.0
031	CONCRETE FORMWORK	102.1	48.2	55.9	95.4	48.3	55.0	90.3	48.3	54.3	95.5	48.3	55.0	98.7	48.2	55.5	95.0	48.3	55.0
032	CONCRETE REINFORCEMENT	94.2	45.9	67.0	94.2	52.2	70.6	93.3	52.2	70.2	94.2	52.2	70.6	94.2	52.2	70.6	94.5	52.2	70.7
033	CAST IN PLACE CONCRETE	103.5	55.2	83.3	101.2	55.3	82.0	97.7	55.3	79.9	100.3	55.3	81.5	107.1	55.3	85.4	100.5	55.3	81.6
3	CONCRETE	100.8	52.5	76.4	99.1	53.7	76.2	96.5	53.7	75.0	98.7	53.7	76.0	102.3	53.7	77.8	99.2	53.7	76.3
4	MASONRY	82.9	41.8	57.4	81.5	41.8	56.8	85.5	41.8	58.4	81.3	41.7	56.7	88.8	41.8	59.6	68.9	41.8	52.1
5	METALS	95.0	83.8	91.0	95.1	86.5	92.0	94.0	86.5	91.3	95.8	86.5	92.5	95.1	86.5	92.0	94.1	86.5	91.3
6	WOOD & PLASTICS	106.0	48.9	76.6	97.6	48.9	72.5	91.4	48.9	69.5	97.6	48.9	72.5	101.6	48.9	74.4	97.0	48.9	72.2
7	THERMAL & MOISTURE PROTECTION	95.5	49.7	74.3	96.1	49.2	74.3	95.7	49.2	74.1	96.1	49.2	74.3	95.9	48.6	74.0	95.5	49.2	74.0
8	DOORS & WINDOWS	96.7	47.6	84.8	96.7	49.9	85.4	93.0	49.9	82.5	96.7	49.9	85.4	93.7	49.9	83.1	93.0	49.9	82.6
092	LATH, PLASTER & GYPSUM BOARD	106.4	47.1	68.1	106.4	47.1	68.1	100.0	47.1	65.8	106.4	47.1	68.1	109.9	47.1	69.4	100.5	47.1	66.0
095	ACOUSTICAL TREATMENT & WOOD FLOORING	91.4	47.1	62.7	91.4	47.1	62.7	88.7	47.1	61.7	91.4	47.1	62.7	91.4	47.1	62.7	88.7	47.1	61.7
096	FLOORING & CARPET	93.1	51.0	82.8	93.3	51.0	83.0	90.0	51.0	80.5	93.3	51.0	83.0	93.3	51.0	83.0	90.5	51.0	80.9
099	PAINTING & WALL COVERINGS	105.8	47.8	71.8	105.8	47.8	71.8	105.8	47.8	71.8	105.8	47.8	71.8	105.8	47.8	71.8	105.8	47.8	71.8
9	FINISHES	93.8	48.4	70.6	94.0	48.4	70.6	91.5	48.4	69.4	94.0	48.4	70.6	94.5	48.4	70.9	91.7	48.4	69.5
10-14	TOTAL DIV. 10 - 14	100.0	71.7	94.0	100.0	71.7	94.0	100.0	71.7	94.0	100.0	71.7	94.0	100.0	71.7	94.0	100.0	71.7	94.0
15	MECHANICAL	100.1	53.4	79.3	100.1	53.5	79.3	100.1	53.5	79.3	100.1	53.5	79.3	100.1	53.5	79.3	100.1	53.5	79.3
16	ELECTRICAL	100.2	46.2	63.8	98.6	49.3	65.3	93.8	49.3	63.8	99.7	49.3	65.7	99.3	49.3	65.6	100.5	49.3	65.9
1-16	WEIGHTED AVERAGE	97.4	55.3	77.1	97.0	57.4	77.9	95.6	57.4	77.1	97.1	57.3	77.9	97.6	57.3	78.2	95.7	56.3	76.7

City Cost Indexes

DIVISION		NORTH CAROLINA WINSTON-SALEM			NORTH DAKOTA BISMARCK			NORTH DAKOTA FARGO			NORTH DAKOTA GRAND FORKS			NORTH DAKOTA MINOT			OHIO AKRON		
		MAT.	INST.	TOTAL	MAT.	INST.	TOTAL	MAT.	INST.	TOTAL	MAT.	INST.	TOTAL	MAT.	INST.	TOTAL	MAT.	INST.	TOTAL
2	SITE WORK	103.8	84.2	88.7	82.2	95.3	92.3	82.2	95.3	92.3	89.8	95.1	93.9	87.6	95.3	93.5	104.2	108.7	107.7
031	CONCRETE FORMWORK	97.0	48.2	55.2	93.6	60.5	65.3	94.3	61.0	65.8	90.0	55.3	60.3	84.3	60.4	63.8	102.0	100.4	100.6
032	CONCRETE REINFORCEMENT	94.2	45.9	67.0	105.0	72.8	86.8	96.8	72.7	83.2	103.4	65.9	82.2	107.0	72.8	87.7	96.0	96.6	96.4
033	CAST IN PLACE CONCRETE	103.6	55.3	83.3	104.6	64.7	87.9	107.1	67.5	90.5	104.6	65.4	88.2	104.6	62.9	87.1	101.1	108.8	104.3
3	CONCRETE	100.4	52.5	76.2	96.7	65.0	80.7	96.9	66.2	81.4	101.1	61.7	81.2	99.7	64.3	81.8	97.0	101.4	99.2
4	MASONRY	81.5	41.8	56.8	105.9	61.3	78.2	106.0	60.8	77.9	105.9	56.8	75.4	105.4	61.4	78.1	94.9	101.1	98.7
5	METALS	95.0	83.8	91.0	93.5	76.0	87.2	93.4	75.8	87.1	93.5	73.3	86.2	93.8	75.9	87.4	91.0	81.7	87.6
6	WOOD & PLASTICS	97.6	48.9	72.5	86.8	58.2	72.0	86.8	59.1	72.5	82.7	53.5	67.6	76.7	58.2	67.2	97.4	99.5	98.5
7	THERMAL & MOISTURE PROTECTION	96.1	49.2	74.3	97.9	61.5	81.0	98.4	61.5	81.3	98.6	59.4	80.4	98.3	61.4	81.2	108.8	100.9	105.1
8	DOORS & WINDOWS	96.7	48.1	84.9	104.7	55.4	92.7	104.6	55.8	92.8	104.7	51.2	91.7	104.8	55.4	92.8	107.1	98.7	105.0
092	LATH, PLASTER & GYPSUM BOARD	106.4	47.1	68.1	115.5	57.4	78.0	115.5	58.3	78.6	113.4	52.6	74.1	111.3	57.4	76.5	103.1	98.7	100.2
095	ACOUSTICAL TREATMENT & WOOD FLOORING	91.4	47.1	62.7	141.3	57.4	86.9	141.3	58.3	87.5	141.3	52.6	83.8	141.3	57.4	86.9	97.3	98.7	98.2
096	FLOORING & CARPET	93.3	51.0	83.0	114.5	59.0	101.0	114.3	58.1	100.6	112.8	58.1	99.5	110.2	59.2	97.8	113.4	108.5	112.2
099	PAINTING & WALL COVERINGS	105.8	47.8	71.8	106.3	49.1	72.7	106.3	45.1	70.4	106.3	37.5	65.9	106.3	41.1	68.0	103.4	117.7	111.8
9	FINISHES	94.0	48.4	70.6	115.5	58.7	86.4	115.4	58.5	86.3	115.2	53.4	83.5	113.9	57.8	85.1	104.7	103.9	104.3
10-14	TOTAL DIV. 10 - 14	100.0	71.7	94.0	100.0	64.5	92.5	100.0	64.6	92.5	100.0	62.3	92.0	100.0	64.5	92.5	100.0	97.8	99.5
15	MECHANICAL	100.1	53.4	79.3	100.5	67.9	85.9	100.5	61.2	83.0	100.5	59.0	82.0	100.5	61.1	82.9	100.0	102.6	101.2
16	ELECTRICAL	99.7	49.3	65.7	94.3	65.5	74.9	94.2	55.2	67.9	98.9	62.1	74.1	103.9	65.5	78.0	98.7	98.2	98.4
1-16	WEIGHTED AVERAGE	97.2	56.9	77.8	100.1	68.0	84.6	100.1	65.1	83.2	101.1	63.7	83.0	101.1	66.5	84.4	99.6	100.1	99.8

DIVISION		OHIO CANTON			OHIO CINCINNATI			OHIO CLEVELAND			OHIO COLUMBUS			OHIO DAYTON			OHIO LORAIN		
		MAT.	INST.	TOTAL	MAT.	INST.	TOTAL	MAT.	INST.	TOTAL	MAT.	INST.	TOTAL	MAT.	INST.	TOTAL	MAT.	INST.	TOTAL
2	SITE WORK	104.4	107.7	106.9	78.4	111.4	103.8	104.0	108.0	107.1	79.8	99.2	94.7	78.0	111.1	103.4	103.6	107.8	106.9
031	CONCRETE FORMWORK	102.0	89.0	90.9	96.8	84.9	86.6	102.1	107.1	106.4	95.9	88.8	89.8	96.7	86.7	88.1	102.1	89.8	91.6
032	CONCRETE REINFORCEMENT	96.0	81.3	87.7	95.9	82.3	88.3	96.4	97.0	96.7	105.6	83.4	93.1	95.9	80.2	87.0	96.0	96.2	96.1
033	CAST IN PLACE CONCRETE	102.0	105.9	103.6	89.2	88.6	88.9	99.1	116.7	106.5	95.8	95.8	95.8	81.3	91.2	85.5	96.2	100.1	97.8
3	CONCRETE	97.4	92.6	95.0	90.1	85.9	88.0	96.1	107.3	101.7	94.8	89.7	92.3	86.2	86.5	86.3	94.6	93.7	94.1
4	MASONRY	95.8	92.2	93.6	84.8	91.0	88.6	99.8	111.3	106.9	88.5	92.3	90.9	84.2	90.7	88.2	91.6	91.3	91.4
5	METALS	91.0	75.1	85.2	94.9	87.1	92.1	92.3	84.4	89.5	96.2	80.0	90.3	94.2	76.1	87.7	91.5	80.8	87.7
6	WOOD & PLASTICS	97.4	88.2	92.6	97.3	82.6	89.7	96.7	104.8	100.9	95.3	88.0	91.6	99.2	86.3	92.6	97.4	86.7	91.9
7	THERMAL & MOISTURE PROTECTION	109.3	96.7	103.5	93.5	92.2	92.9	107.5	112.8	109.9	104.0	96.4	100.5	98.2	90.1	94.4	109.2	100.3	105.1
8	DOORS & WINDOWS	101.4	82.0	96.7	97.8	80.6	93.6	95.6	102.6	97.3	99.9	83.7	96.0	98.2	80.9	94.0	101.4	92.8	99.3
092	LATH, PLASTER & GYPSUM BOARD	103.1	87.0	92.7	103.8	82.5	90.0	102.2	104.1	103.4	103.0	87.3	92.9	103.8	86.3	92.5	103.1	85.4	91.7
095	ACOUSTICAL TREATMENT & WOOD FLOORING	97.3	87.0	90.6	94.5	82.5	86.7	95.9	104.1	101.2	97.4	87.3	90.9	94.5	86.3	89.2	97.3	85.4	89.6
096	FLOORING & CARPET	113.6	86.5	107.0	85.7	96.1	88.2	113.2	116.5	114.0	96.8	93.5	96.0	88.1	88.6	88.2	113.6	94.0	108.9
099	PAINTING & WALL COVERINGS	103.4	90.4	95.8	100.4	94.6	97.0	103.4	117.7	111.8	98.6	96.2	97.2	100.4	90.0	94.3	103.4	117.7	111.8
9	FINISHES	104.8	88.2	96.3	91.6	87.8	89.6	104.3	110.0	107.2	95.6	90.3	92.9	92.4	87.4	89.8	104.8	93.0	98.7
10-14	TOTAL DIV. 10 - 14	100.0	94.4	98.8	100.0	87.0	97.3	100.0	104.9	101.0	100.0	91.3	98.2	100.0	86.7	97.2	100.0	99.4	99.9
15	MECHANICAL	100.0	88.2	94.8	99.9	91.8	96.3	100.0	106.5	102.9	100.0	93.6	97.2	100.7	87.0	94.6	100.0	92.7	96.8
16	ELECTRICAL	97.2	95.9	96.3	94.9	83.9	87.5	97.8	106.9	103.9	103.5	88.0	93.1	93.5	88.9	90.4	97.2	96.7	96.9
1-16	WEIGHTED AVERAGE	98.9	91.3	95.3	94.8	90.0	92.5	98.4	105.6	101.9	97.5	90.5	94.1	94.6	88.9	91.8	98.4	94.1	96.3

DIVISION		OHIO SPRINGFIELD			OHIO TOLEDO			OHIO YOUNGSTOWN			OKLAHOMA ENID			OKLAHOMA LAWTON			OKLAHOMA MUSKOGEE		
		MAT.	INST.	TOTAL	MAT.	INST.	TOTAL	MAT.	INST.	TOTAL	MAT.	INST.	TOTAL	MAT.	INST.	TOTAL	MAT.	INST.	TOTAL
2	SITE WORK	78.5	110.8	103.4	79.6	100.1	95.3	104.1	108.8	107.7	109.4	87.3	92.4	104.9	88.9	92.6	95.5	83.6	86.4
031	CONCRETE FORMWORK	96.7	87.1	88.4	95.9	99.6	99.1	102.0	91.5	93.0	94.3	48.8	55.3	98.7	67.2	71.7	100.5	44.4	52.5
032	CONCRETE REINFORCEMENT	95.9	80.1	87.0	105.6	87.9	95.6	96.0	90.5	92.9	96.4	84.2	89.5	96.6	84.2	89.6	96.4	47.6	68.9
033	CAST IN PLACE CONCRETE	85.2	90.8	87.6	95.8	106.0	100.1	100.1	107.7	103.3	93.8	60.1	79.7	90.7	60.1	77.9	84.4	45.8	68.2
3	CONCRETE	88.1	86.5	87.3	94.8	99.0	97.0	96.5	96.0	96.2	90.0	59.4	74.5	86.7	67.4	77.0	82.2	46.6	64.3
4	MASONRY	84.5	90.0	87.9	98.2	98.5	98.4	95.0	97.9	96.8	97.7	59.5	74.0	95.2	59.5	73.0	104.9	54.2	73.4
5	METALS	94.2	75.9	87.6	96.0	86.1	92.4	91.0	79.6	86.9	94.1	67.0	84.3	96.2	67.0	85.7	94.0	65.4	83.7
6	WOOD & PLASTICS	99.2	87.3	93.1	95.3	100.9	98.2	97.4	89.2	93.2	95.0	46.4	69.9	99.4	71.4	85.0	101.8	45.8	72.9
7	THERMAL & MOISTURE PROTECTION	98.2	90.0	94.4	106.0	101.3	103.8	109.4	98.9	104.6	96.4	63.3	81.1	96.2	65.8	82.1	96.0	52.2	75.7
8	DOORS & WINDOWS	98.2	78.8	93.5	99.9	94.5	98.6	101.4	89.6	98.5	96.2	59.3	87.3	97.6	72.8	91.6	96.2	45.1	83.8
092	LATH, PLASTER & GYPSUM BOARD	103.8	87.3	93.2	103.0	100.6	101.4	103.1	88.0	93.3	91.3	45.8	62.0	94.8	71.7	79.9	94.0	45.1	62.5
095	ACOUSTICAL TREATMENT & WOOD FLOORING	94.5	87.3	89.9	95.9	100.6	98.9	97.3	88.0	91.3	93.5	45.8	62.6	101.7	71.7	82.2	93.5	45.1	62.1
096	FLOORING & CARPET	88.1	88.6	88.2	95.9	78.3	91.6	113.6	99.1	110.1	116.3	65.9	104.0	119.3	65.9	106.3	120.3	53.1	104.0
099	PAINTING & WALL COVERINGS	100.4	90.0	94.3	98.6	104.4	102.0	103.4	101.1	102.1	97.1	65.2	78.4	97.1	44.3	66.1	97.1	44.2	66.0
9	FINISHES	92.4	87.8	90.1	95.0	96.1	95.6	104.8	93.5	99.0	100.7	52.3	75.9	103.3	64.5	83.4	101.4	46.3	73.2
10-14	TOTAL DIV. 10 - 14	100.0	86.6	97.2	100.0	100.0	100.0	100.0	97.9	99.6	100.0	68.7	93.4	100.0	72.0	94.1	100.0	41.5	87.7
15	MECHANICAL	100.7	86.6	94.4	100.0	99.8	99.9	100.0	90.6	95.8	100.0	64.8	84.3	100.0	64.8	84.3	100.0	37.5	72.1
16	ELECTRICAL	93.5	84.7	87.5	104.1	100.9	102.0	97.2	88.3	91.2	95.4	66.2	75.7	98.1	56.1	69.8	94.8	45.1	61.3
1-16	WEIGHTED AVERAGE	94.8	88.0	91.5	98.0	97.9	98.0	98.8	93.1	96.1	97.2	64.4	81.4	97.5	66.4	82.5	96.3	50.7	74.3

COST INDEXES

596

City Cost Indexes

	DIVISION	OKLAHOMA						OREGON										
		OKLAHOMA CITY			TULSA			EUGENE			MEDFORD			PORTLAND			SALEM		
		MAT.	INST.	TOTAL	MAT.	INST.	TOTAL	MAT.	INST.	TOTAL	MAT.	INST.	TOTAL	MAT.	INST.	TOTAL	MAT.	INST.	TOTAL
2	SITE WORK	105.1	89.5	93.1	102.2	84.5	88.5	95.1	106.8	104.1	104.0	106.5	105.9	96.1	106.8	104.4	95.3	106.8	104.2
031	CONCRETE FORMWORK	100.2	57.4	63.6	100.1	58.6	64.5	101.2	107.2	106.3	95.4	102.4	101.4	102.8	107.6	106.9	102.7	107.3	106.7
032	CONCRETE REINFORCEMENT	96.6	84.2	89.6	96.6	84.1	89.6	111.0	100.3	105.0	102.5	97.9	99.9	106.1	100.6	103.0	112.2	100.5	105.6
033	CAST IN PLACE CONCRETE	90.7	58.7	77.3	92.0	58.3	77.9	96.2	102.8	99.0	99.3	101.9	100.4	103.2	105.0	103.9	99.7	104.9	101.9
3	CONCRETE	86.8	62.7	74.7	87.4	64.1	75.7	113.9	104.1	109.0	121.7	101.2	111.3	116.8	105.1	110.9	115.9	104.9	110.4
4	MASONRY	97.1	61.3	74.9	94.3	59.3	72.6	111.8	104.2	107.1	109.0	99.2	102.9	113.5	107.5	109.8	114.0	107.5	110.0
5	METALS	96.4	67.1	85.8	96.8	83.3	91.9	95.5	100.5	97.3	95.0	98.9	96.4	94.1	101.1	96.6	96.1	100.9	97.8
6	WOOD & PLASTICS	101.8	57.1	78.7	100.3	58.9	78.9	97.6	106.5	102.2	91.2	102.9	97.3	99.6	106.5	103.2	99.6	106.5	103.2
7	THERMAL & MOISTURE PROTECTION	95.4	65.2	81.4	96.0	64.1	81.2	109.7	96.8	103.7	110.5	94.3	103.0	109.5	101.2	105.7	109.5	101.0	105.6
8	DOORS & WINDOWS	97.6	65.1	89.7	97.6	65.4	89.8	101.4	108.4	103.1	104.2	105.7	104.6	98.8	108.4	101.1	100.5	108.4	102.4
092	LATH, PLASTER & GYPSUM BOARD	94.8	56.9	70.4	94.8	58.6	71.4	91.1	106.6	101.1	88.1	103.0	97.7	90.0	106.6	100.8	91.9	106.6	101.4
095	ACOUSTICAL TREATMENT & WOOD FLOORING	101.7	56.9	72.7	101.7	58.6	73.8	122.0	106.6	112.1	120.7	103.0	109.2	122.0	106.6	112.1	130.3	106.6	115.0
096	FLOORING & CARPET	119.3	65.9	106.3	119.1	68.6	106.8	121.2	100.4	116.2	119.0	100.4	114.5	121.2	104.1	117.1	121.2	100.4	116.2
099	PAINTING & WALL COVERINGS	97.1	65.2	78.4	97.1	65.2	78.4	125.4	86.7	102.7	125.4	73.3	94.9	125.4	86.7	102.7	125.4	86.7	102.7
9	FINISHES	103.4	59.1	80.6	102.8	60.7	81.2	117.8	103.9	110.7	117.0	99.1	107.8	117.7	104.7	111.0	119.4	103.9	111.5
10 - 14	TOTAL DIV. 10 - 14	100.0	70.9	93.9	100.0	71.7	94.0	100.0	109.9	102.1	100.0	104.5	101.0	100.0	109.9	102.1	100.0	109.9	102.1
15	MECHANICAL	100.0	65.8	84.7	100.0	66.2	84.9	100.2	95.8	98.3	100.2	93.0	97.0	100.2	104.7	102.2	100.2	95.8	98.3
16	ELECTRICAL	96.9	66.2	76.2	98.1	58.8	71.6	102.4	99.2	100.2	107.9	91.8	97.0	102.3	108.1	106.2	102.0	99.2	100.1
1 - 16	WEIGHTED AVERAGE	97.6	66.7	82.7	97.5	66.8	82.7	104.0	101.8	102.9	105.6	98.0	101.9	104.0	105.7	104.8	104.5	102.3	103.5

	DIVISION	PENNSYLVANIA																	
		ALLENTOWN			ALTOONA			ERIE			HARRISBURG			PHILADELPHIA			PITTSBURGH		
		MAT.	INST.	TOTAL	MAT.	INST.	TOTAL	MAT.	INST.	TOTAL	MAT.	INST.	TOTAL	MAT.	INST.	TOTAL	MAT.	INST.	TOTAL
2	SITE WORK	96.7	108.8	106.0	101.5	108.9	107.2	97.7	109.1	106.5	84.7	107.4	102.2	111.1	96.4	99.8	97.4	111.2	108.0
031	CONCRETE FORMWORK	104.8	103.1	103.3	82.7	89.7	88.7	103.1	95.0	96.2	95.7	90.6	91.3	106.2	130.3	126.8	103.9	103.6	103.7
032	CONCRETE REINFORCEMENT	99.0	108.2	104.2	96.0	94.9	95.4	98.0	90.4	93.7	99.0	91.3	94.7	97.9	120.5	110.6	102.2	105.5	104.1
033	CAST IN PLACE CONCRETE	87.6	99.7	92.7	97.7	91.1	94.9	96.1	97.3	96.6	86.0	93.2	89.0	99.0	124.2	109.6	102.2	102.8	102.4
3	CONCRETE	100.5	104.2	102.3	94.4	92.8	93.6	93.5	96.4	95.0	98.8	93.2	96.0	107.8	125.9	117.0	98.5	105.0	101.8
4	MASONRY	97.5	96.6	96.9	99.3	87.3	91.8	91.0	95.3	93.7	94.8	92.4	93.3	94.5	127.5	115.0	93.8	106.2	101.5
5	METALS	97.9	125.5	107.8	91.7	118.6	101.4	91.8	117.0	100.9	99.7	117.4	106.1	98.9	121.1	106.9	98.7	126.1	108.5
6	WOOD & PLASTICS	108.6	104.0	106.2	81.3	89.2	85.4	104.3	94.0	99.0	99.7	90.8	95.1	110.1	130.1	120.5	105.9	102.8	104.3
7	THERMAL & MOISTURE PROTECTION	100.8	113.1	106.5	99.9	95.8	98.0	100.0	97.2	98.7	103.8	94.1	99.3	99.9	131.4	114.5	96.7	105.3	100.7
8	DOORS & WINDOWS	97.4	105.6	99.4	91.8	99.9	93.8	92.0	91.8	91.9	97.4	99.5	97.9	99.2	134.0	107.6	93.6	110.7	97.8
092	LATH, PLASTER & GYPSUM BOARD	100.4	103.7	102.6	83.7	88.5	86.8	93.4	93.4	93.4	100.4	90.1	93.8	94.4	130.9	117.9	94.1	102.5	99.5
095	ACOUSTICAL TREATMENT & WOOD FLOORING	97.1	103.7	101.4	91.6	88.5	89.6	97.1	93.4	94.7	97.1	90.1	92.6	96.0	130.9	118.6	90.1	102.5	98.1
096	FLOORING & CARPET	83.5	92.1	85.6	78.2	73.1	77.0	84.1	82.3	83.6	83.7	88.0	84.8	78.9	134.8	92.5	92.2	109.9	96.5
099	PAINTING & WALL COVERINGS	84.1	98.9	92.8	80.0	103.1	93.5	86.1	84.1	84.9	84.1	82.0	82.8	89.4	136.7	117.2	87.3	114.1	103.0
9	FINISHES	95.8	100.5	98.2	91.1	87.3	89.2	95.7	91.2	93.4	94.7	88.9	91.8	92.2	131.9	112.5	97.5	105.4	101.6
10 - 14	TOTAL DIV. 10 - 14	100.0	103.2	100.7	100.0	100.9	100.2	100.0	103.8	100.8	100.0	95.7	99.1	100.0	127.6	105.8	100.0	105.5	101.2
15	MECHANICAL	100.3	101.0	100.6	99.9	85.9	93.7	99.9	93.7	97.1	100.3	91.1	96.2	100.0	125.3	111.3	99.9	103.5	101.5
16	ELECTRICAL	103.6	90.6	94.8	88.7	104.0	99.0	91.1	84.3	86.5	102.6	80.8	87.9	98.2	132.5	121.4	96.1	104.0	101.4
1 - 16	WEIGHTED AVERAGE	99.2	102.9	101.0	95.1	96.7	95.9	95.4	96.3	95.8	98.6	94.2	96.5	99.8	124.9	111.9	97.8	107.5	102.5

	DIVISION	PENNSYLVANIA						RHODE ISLAND			SOUTH CAROLINA					
		READING			SCRANTON			YORK			PROVIDENCE			CHARLESTON			COLUMBIA		
		MAT.	INST.	TOTAL	MAT.	INST.	TOTAL	MAT.	INST.	TOTAL	MAT.	INST.	TOTAL	MAT.	INST.	TOTAL	MAT.	INST.	TOTAL
2	SITE WORK	108.4	114.5	113.1	97.2	108.8	106.2	85.5	107.5	102.4	90.4	99.9	97.7	94.3	83.2	85.8	94.0	83.2	85.7
031	CONCRETE FORMWORK	105.7	91.5	93.5	104.9	95.2	96.6	82.5	89.8	88.8	101.0	109.9	108.6	95.4	46.7	53.7	101.1	49.4	56.8
032	CONCRETE REINFORCEMENT	96.3	95.7	95.9	99.0	99.8	99.5	98.0	91.3	94.2	116.7	126.3	122.1	94.2	48.3	68.4	94.2	48.0	68.2
033	CAST IN PLACE CONCRETE	72.4	93.4	81.2	91.6	95.1	93.1	86.2	94.0	89.5	91.9	116.8	102.3	86.0	58.3	74.4	84.3	53.9	71.5
3	CONCRETE	94.6	94.6	94.6	102.4	97.6	100.0	100.5	93.2	96.8	110.5	114.9	112.7	91.7	53.1	72.2	91.3	52.7	71.8
4	MASONRY	96.8	93.7	94.8	97.8	105.6	102.6	95.8	91.9	93.4	103.1	117.8	112.2	88.3	45.5	61.7	87.3	39.8	57.8
5	METALS	96.0	119.5	104.6	99.7	122.0	107.8	97.0	117.5	104.4	101.1	111.7	104.9	95.0	80.4	89.7	95.0	79.7	89.5
6	WOOD & PLASTICS	110.1	89.4	99.4	108.6	93.7	100.9	88.4	88.8	88.6	102.5	107.2	104.9	97.6	46.4	71.2	104.8	50.5	76.8
7	THERMAL & MOISTURE PROTECTION	99.9	109.8	104.5	100.7	108.0	104.1	99.1	106.2	102.4	100.4	109.9	104.8	95.6	52.4	75.6	95.6	50.2	74.6
8	DOORS & WINDOWS	99.2	93.9	97.9	97.4	103.8	99.0	94.2	98.5	95.2	102.9	115.4	105.9	96.7	44.4	84.0	96.7	46.6	84.6
092	LATH, PLASTER & GYPSUM BOARD	103.1	88.8	93.9	100.4	93.1	95.7	94.3	88.1	90.3	98.5	106.5	103.6	106.4	44.5	66.5	106.4	48.7	69.2
095	ACOUSTICAL TREATMENT & WOOD FLOORING	98.8	88.8	92.3	97.1	93.1	94.5	88.9	88.1	88.4	101.7	106.5	104.8	91.4	44.5	61.0	91.4	48.7	63.7
096	FLOORING & CARPET	77.2	90.8	80.5	83.5	92.7	85.7	79.8	88.0	81.8	96.9	124.2	103.5	93.3	50.2	82.8	93.1	50.2	82.7
099	PAINTING & WALL COVERINGS	87.4	92.7	90.5	84.1	90.2	87.7	84.1	82.0	82.8	89.4	120.5	107.7	105.8	48.0	71.9	105.8	48.0	71.9
9	FINISHES	93.3	90.8	92.0	95.8	93.8	94.8	91.2	88.3	89.7	96.8	113.7	105.5	94.2	47.2	70.1	94.1	49.5	71.2
10 - 14	TOTAL DIV. 10 - 14	100.0	100.6	100.1	100.0	99.8	100.0	100.0	96.0	99.2	99.0	109.6	101.2	100.0	70.6	93.8	100.0	71.2	93.9
15	MECHANICAL	100.2	100.3	100.2	100.3	89.2	95.3	100.3	91.8	96.5	100.0	104.0	101.8	100.1	55.6	80.3	100.1	46.8	76.3
16	ELECTRICAL	100.9	83.8	89.3	103.6	88.6	93.4	93.0	80.7	84.8	99.2	100.1	99.8	99.6	42.7	61.2	100.8	45.0	63.2
1 - 16	WEIGHTED AVERAGE	98.2	98.2	98.2	99.8	98.7	99.3	96.8	94.4	95.6	101.2	108.3	104.6	96.3	55.9	76.8	96.3	54.3	76.1

City Cost Indexes

DIVISION		SOUTH CAROLINA									SOUTH DAKOTA								
		FLORENCE			GREENVILLE			SPARTANBURG			ABERDEEN			PIERRE			RAPID CITY		
		MAT.	INST.	TOTAL	MAT.	INST.	TOTAL	MAT.	INST.	TOTAL	MAT.	INST.	TOTAL	MAT.	INST.	TOTAL	MAT.	INST.	TOTAL
2	SITE WORK	104.4	83.2	88.1	99.6	82.8	86.7	99.4	82.8	86.6	78.8	94.5	90.9	77.2	94.5	90.5	77.5	94.2	90.3
031	CONCRETE FORMWORK	78.5	49.4	53.6	95.3	49.5	56.1	99.8	49.5	56.7	94.0	48.1	54.7	92.1	50.4	56.4	105.5	45.9	54.4
032	CONCRETE REINFORCEMENT	93.9	48.3	68.2	93.8	48.4	68.2	93.8	48.4	68.2	103.6	65.8	82.3	103.1	66.5	82.5	96.8	66.7	79.8
033	CAST IN PLACE CONCRETE	76.1	58.2	68.6	76.0	58.2	68.6	76.0	58.2	68.6	99.7	59.6	82.9	96.8	55.0	79.3	96.1	51.7	77.5
3	CONCRETE	93.0	54.2	73.5	91.7	54.3	72.9	92.1	54.3	73.0	94.9	56.6	75.5	92.5	56.1	74.2	92.4	53.0	72.5
4	MASONRY	72.5	45.5	55.7	70.6	45.5	55.0	72.5	45.5	55.7	105.9	63.3	79.4	104.3	53.4	72.7	104.7	50.3	70.9
5	METALS	93.9	80.1	88.9	93.8	80.2	88.9	93.8	80.2	88.9	104.7	74.9	94.0	104.6	74.3	93.7	106.7	74.6	95.2
6	WOOD & PLASTICS	78.4	50.5	64.0	97.2	50.5	73.1	102.2	50.5	75.5	96.8	45.7	70.4	94.6	49.4	71.3	106.1	46.2	75.2
7	THERMAL & MOISTURE PROTECTION	95.9	52.8	75.9	95.9	52.8	75.9	96.0	52.8	76.0	96.2	57.0	78.0	96.4	54.6	77.0	96.9	52.8	76.4
8	DOORS & WINDOWS	92.9	46.6	81.7	92.9	46.6	81.7	92.9	46.6	81.7	99.5	49.4	87.3	103.0	51.7	90.6	104.0	50.0	90.9
092	LATH, PLASTER & GYPSUM BOARD	95.2	48.7	65.2	100.7	48.7	67.1	102.3	48.7	67.7	99.8	44.5	64.1	98.4	48.3	66.1	99.6	45.0	64.4
095	ACOUSTICAL TREATMENT & WOOD FLOORING	88.7	48.7	62.8	87.3	48.7	62.3	87.3	48.7	62.3	108.7	44.5	67.1	107.3	48.3	69.1	112.8	45.0	68.9
096	FLOORING & CARPET	84.5	50.2	76.2	90.9	51.2	81.2	92.6	51.2	82.6	114.9	74.3	105.0	114.0	53.0	99.2	114.0	62.3	101.4
099	PAINTING & WALL COVERINGS	105.8	48.0	71.9	105.8	48.0	71.9	105.8	48.0	71.9	106.3	42.9	69.1	106.3	42.9	69.1	106.3	42.9	69.1
9	FINISHES	90.1	49.5	69.3	92.4	49.7	70.5	93.2	49.7	70.9	107.0	52.1	78.8	106.2	49.9	77.3	107.5	48.4	77.2
10 - 14	TOTAL DIV. 10 - 14	100.0	71.1	93.9	100.0	71.2	93.9	100.0	71.2	93.9	100.0	63.8	92.4	100.0	64.3	92.5	100.0	61.4	91.9
15	MECHANICAL	100.1	46.8	76.3	100.1	47.0	76.4	100.1	47.0	76.4	100.0	44.6	75.3	100.0	44.5	75.3	100.0	41.2	73.8
16	ELECTRICAL	96.5	25.7	48.8	100.0	40.9	60.2	100.0	40.9	60.2	99.7	51.9	67.4	93.6	51.9	65.4	94.2	51.9	65.7
1 - 16	WEIGHTED AVERAGE	94.4	52.0	74.0	94.7	54.6	75.3	95.0	54.6	75.5	100.3	58.9	80.3	99.8	57.6	79.4	100.5	55.9	79.0

DIVISION		SOUTH DAKOTA			TENNESSEE														
		SIOUX FALLS			CHATTANOOGA			JACKSON			JOHNSON CITY			KNOXVILLE			MEMPHIS		
		MAT.	INST.	TOTAL	MAT.	INST.	TOTAL	MAT.	INST.	TOTAL	MAT.	INST.	TOTAL	MAT.	INST.	TOTAL	MAT.	INST.	TOTAL
2	SITE WORK	78.4	96.4	92.3	107.5	98.8	100.8	108.0	95.9	98.7	118.0	87.4	94.5	94.6	87.4	89.1	103.0	93.5	95.7
031	CONCRETE FORMWORK	92.2	48.2	54.5	96.6	56.2	62.0	86.8	40.5	47.2	79.8	58.5	61.5	95.5	58.5	63.8	96.5	63.8	68.5
032	CONCRETE REINFORCEMENT	96.8	67.1	80.0	94.2	52.6	70.8	99.6	51.7	72.6	98.3	52.8	72.7	94.2	52.8	70.9	93.5	63.7	76.7
033	CAST IN PLACE CONCRETE	100.2	59.7	83.2	104.2	57.4	84.6	104.2	40.4	77.5	83.9	64.2	75.6	97.9	58.7	81.5	97.2	69.7	85.7
3	CONCRETE	93.3	56.9	75.0	92.0	57.9	74.8	93.9	44.9	69.2	95.3	61.2	78.1	89.1	59.4	74.1	88.7	67.7	78.1
4	MASONRY	101.6	63.3	77.8	95.4	56.1	71.0	106.2	28.2	57.7	102.7	55.8	73.6	72.7	55.8	62.2	82.5	67.5	73.2
5	METALS	107.2	75.5	95.8	96.8	85.1	92.6	95.3	81.0	90.2	94.5	84.7	90.9	97.0	84.8	92.6	96.0	93.7	95.2
6	WOOD & PLASTICS	94.6	45.7	69.3	95.0	57.4	75.6	82.8	43.0	62.3	70.7	60.9	65.6	87.6	60.9	73.8	93.9	65.1	79.0
7	THERMAL & MOISTURE PROTECTION	96.3	58.4	78.7	103.2	57.9	82.2	101.7	41.2	73.7	97.4	58.8	79.5	95.2	58.2	78.0	100.5	68.4	85.6
8	DOORS & WINDOWS	104.0	49.7	90.9	99.9	56.1	89.3	100.3	46.7	87.3	96.2	59.8	87.4	93.1	59.8	85.0	99.8	66.7	91.8
092	LATH, PLASTER & GYPSUM BOARD	99.6	44.5	64.0	91.5	56.6	69.0	98.9	41.8	62.0	104.0	60.2	75.7	111.4	60.2	78.3	101.7	64.2	77.5
095	ACOUSTICAL TREATMENT & WOOD FLOORING	112.8	44.5	68.5	97.3	56.6	70.9	100.8	41.8	62.5	85.8	60.2	69.2	92.7	60.2	71.6	95.9	64.2	75.4
096	FLOORING & CARPET	114.0	74.3	104.4	96.2	62.7	88.0	88.3	30.3	74.2	90.0	64.4	83.8	95.3	64.4	87.8	90.9	57.2	82.7
099	PAINTING & WALL COVERINGS	106.3	42.9	69.1	99.9	53.1	72.5	92.6	34.7	58.6	97.7	68.0	80.2	97.7	68.0	80.2	92.7	69.0	78.8
9	FINISHES	107.4	52.1	79.1	97.2	57.1	76.7	96.3	38.7	66.8	97.8	60.9	78.9	92.3	60.9	76.2	94.9	62.8	78.4
10 - 14	TOTAL DIV. 10 - 14	100.0	63.9	92.4	100.0	70.2	93.7	100.0	63.1	92.2	100.0	69.4	93.5	100.0	69.5	93.6	100.0	75.9	94.9
15	MECHANICAL	100.0	44.6	75.3	100.1	54.1	79.6	100.1	47.6	76.7	99.9	57.3	80.9	99.9	57.3	80.9	100.0	67.5	85.5
16	ELECTRICAL	93.2	63.5	73.2	102.4	69.2	80.0	98.5	39.6	58.8	90.0	42.3	57.8	99.3	65.0	76.2	97.6	79.8	85.6
1 - 16	WEIGHTED AVERAGE	100.4	61.2	81.4	98.5	65.6	82.6	98.5	51.1	75.6	97.4	61.7	80.2	94.6	65.2	80.4	96.4	74.2	85.7

DIVISION		TENNESSEE			TEXAS														
		NASHVILLE			ABILENE			AMARILLO			AUSTIN			BEAUMONT			CORPUS CHRISTI		
		MAT.	INST.	TOTAL	MAT.	INST.	TOTAL	MAT.	INST.	TOTAL	MAT.	INST.	TOTAL	MAT.	INST.	TOTAL	MAT.	INST.	TOTAL
2	SITE WORK	96.3	101.3	100.2	102.6	83.5	87.9	102.6	84.6	88.7	91.1	85.9	87.1	98.5	81.5	85.4	126.7	81.0	91.5
031	CONCRETE FORMWORK	96.3	68.6	72.6	96.6	55.5	61.4	100.3	62.4	67.9	99.3	67.3	71.9	105.8	73.5	78.2	103.0	53.5	60.6
032	CONCRETE REINFORCEMENT	94.4	64.4	77.5	96.6	58.5	75.1	96.6	58.3	75.0	94.5	66.2	78.5	94.6	60.8	75.5	92.7	55.9	72.0
033	CAST IN PLACE CONCRETE	92.3	68.9	82.5	95.4	51.6	77.0	98.9	61.1	83.1	84.8	63.8	76.0	86.3	69.9	79.4	100.5	58.7	83.0
3	CONCRETE	86.7	69.6	78.1	88.8	55.6	72.1	90.8	61.9	76.2	79.2	66.4	72.8	85.9	70.3	78.0	88.8	57.8	73.1
4	MASONRY	84.2	65.7	72.7	97.4	56.0	71.7	101.1	54.2	71.9	97.5	61.2	74.9	100.4	73.4	83.6	88.1	53.8	66.8
5	METALS	99.4	92.4	96.9	97.4	71.2	88.0	97.4	71.0	87.9	98.0	75.3	89.8	97.2	74.2	88.9	97.5	86.3	93.5
6	WOOD & PLASTICS	90.4	70.1	79.9	95.9	57.1	75.9	99.4	65.1	81.7	97.0	70.4	83.2	106.1	76.3	90.7	106.3	54.3	79.5
7	THERMAL & MOISTURE PROTECTION	97.3	67.0	83.3	96.1	61.6	80.1	98.1	57.0	79.0	94.6	65.7	81.2	96.3	72.1	85.1	97.2	59.0	79.5
8	DOORS & WINDOWS	93.4	68.8	87.4	92.9	58.2	84.5	92.9	59.6	84.8	95.8	69.3	89.4	97.0	69.4	90.3	103.0	52.7	90.8
092	LATH, PLASTER & GYPSUM BOARD	100.9	69.6	80.7	94.8	56.8	70.3	94.8	65.0	75.6	96.1	70.3	79.5	93.8	76.6	82.7	97.3	53.6	69.1
095	ACOUSTICAL TREATMENT & WOOD FLOORING	92.7	69.6	77.7	101.7	56.8	72.6	101.7	65.0	77.9	91.1	70.3	77.6	107.7	76.6	87.6	96.6	53.6	68.7
096	FLOORING & CARPET	98.3	70.2	91.5	119.3	62.4	105.5	119.1	55.8	103.7	98.3	64.2	90.0	118.3	80.3	109.0	110.8	60.7	98.6
099	PAINTING & WALL COVERINGS	102.1	64.0	79.8	95.9	71.5	81.6	95.9	51.1	69.6	100.0	57.3	75.0	89.7	68.9	77.5	115.1	51.2	77.6
9	FINISHES	101.1	68.6	84.4	102.8	58.7	80.2	102.8	60.2	81.0	94.4	65.8	79.7	99.0	74.8	86.5	101.1	54.3	77.1
10 - 14	TOTAL DIV. 10 - 14	100.0	73.4	94.4	100.0	66.7	93.0	100.0	65.9	92.8	100.0	69.5	93.6	100.0	75.2	94.8	100.0	70.6	93.8
15	MECHANICAL	100.0	67.1	85.3	100.0	47.6	76.6	100.0	57.5	81.0	100.0	63.2	83.6	100.0	66.2	84.9	100.0	48.0	76.8
16	ELECTRICAL	101.1	61.8	74.6	98.1	51.1	66.4	99.0	62.0	74.1	97.5	69.9	78.9	95.1	77.7	83.4	94.3	64.0	73.9
1 - 16	WEIGHTED AVERAGE	96.6	72.6	85.0	97.4	58.5	78.6	98.0	63.2	81.2	95.3	68.8	82.5	97.0	73.3	85.5	98.4	61.2	80.5

City Cost Indexes

	DIVISION	TEXAS																
		DALLAS			EL PASO			FORT WORTH			HOUSTON			LAREDO			LUBBOCK		
		MAT.	INST.	TOTAL	MAT.	INST.	TOTAL	MAT.	INST.	TOTAL	MAT.	INST.	TOTAL	MAT.	INST.	TOTAL	MAT.	INST.	TOTAL
2	SITE WORK	126.8	83.2	93.2	103.1	83.6	88.1	102.4	83.8	88.1	126.4	79.3	90.1	91.3	85.6	86.9	132.8	81.7	93.5
031	CONCRETE FORMWORK	97.1	68.9	72.9	97.3	42.5	50.4	99.4	68.5	73.0	92.5	79.7	81.6	90.6	53.7	59.0	98.7	57.7	63.5
032	CONCRETE REINFORCEMENT	96.1	65.3	78.7	96.6	58.3	75.0	96.6	65.0	78.8	97.2	68.0	80.7	94.5	56.3	73.0	95.8	58.2	74.6
033	CAST IN PLACE CONCRETE	100.6	68.3	87.0	97.7	46.5	76.2	93.7	62.5	80.6	88.9	76.8	83.9	77.4	63.2	71.5	95.6	61.1	81.1
3	CONCRETE	90.0	69.6	79.7	90.0	48.1	68.9	88.2	66.3	77.2	85.2	77.9	81.5	79.0	58.4	68.6	87.6	60.9	74.2
4	MASONRY	91.9	65.4	75.5	96.2	53.9	69.9	93.0	61.3	73.3	95.5	74.7	82.6	97.3	60.2	74.3	97.1	50.0	67.8
5	METALS	98.9	90.5	95.9	97.3	69.8	87.4	97.2	74.3	89.0	101.4	94.5	98.9	98.8	70.5	88.6	101.5	87.4	96.4
6	WOOD & PLASTICS	101.7	70.9	85.8	97.4	41.1	68.3	103.9	70.8	86.8	89.9	82.1	85.9	85.1	54.2	69.1	100.2	60.0	79.5
7	THERMAL & MOISTURE PROTECTION	93.1	70.2	82.5	95.7	57.9	78.2	96.6	65.2	82.0	89.0	75.0	82.5	93.5	62.2	79.0	89.7	60.9	76.3
8	DOORS & WINDOWS	106.1	67.4	96.7	92.9	45.8	81.5	87.6	67.3	82.7	105.2	77.0	98.4	96.4	53.4	86.0	105.3	57.4	93.7
092	LATH, PLASTER & GYPSUM BOARD	97.6	70.9	80.4	94.8	40.2	59.6	94.8	70.9	79.4	91.7	82.5	85.7	93.4	53.6	67.7	95.4	59.6	72.3
095	ACOUSTICAL TREATMENT & WOOD FLOORING	101.2	70.9	81.6	101.7	40.2	61.9	101.7	70.9	81.7	110.4	82.5	92.3	91.1	53.6	66.8	104.4	59.6	75.4
096	FLOORING & CARPET	109.4	67.9	99.3	119.3	62.5	105.5	154.8	62.2	132.3	106.3	69.7	97.4	95.2	60.7	86.8	110.3	52.7	96.3
099	PAINTING & WALL COVERINGS	102.6	66.9	81.6	95.9	49.0	68.4	97.1	72.8	82.8	98.8	74.8	84.7	100.0	56.7	74.6	107.3	45.8	71.2
9	FINISHES	102.4	68.8	85.2	102.8	46.2	73.8	114.7	68.2	90.9	105.5	77.7	91.2	93.2	54.9	73.5	104.3	55.4	79.2
10 - 14	TOTAL DIV. 10 - 14	100.0	71.3	93.9	100.0	64.3	92.5	100.0	71.0	93.9	100.0	78.0	95.4	100.0	68.9	93.4	100.0	67.5	93.1
15	MECHANICAL	100.0	68.6	86.0	100.0	46.8	76.3	100.0	67.1	85.3	99.9	76.1	89.3	99.9	56.5	80.5	99.9	54.9	79.8
16	ELECTRICAL	98.9	73.8	82.0	96.9	58.8	71.2	96.9	67.9	77.3	96.9	75.4	82.4	97.5	68.7	78.0	96.5	57.9	70.5
1 - 16	WEIGHTED AVERAGE	99.6	72.9	86.7	97.3	56.0	77.4	97.7	69.1	83.9	99.4	78.4	89.3	95.2	63.5	79.9	100.0	62.1	81.7

	DIVISION	TEXAS												UTAH					
		ODESSA			SAN ANTONIO			WACO			WICHITA FALLS			LOGAN			OGDEN		
		MAT.	INST.	TOTAL	MAT.	INST.	TOTAL	MAT.	INST.	TOTAL	MAT.	INST.	TOTAL	MAT.	INST.	TOTAL	MAT.	INST.	TOTAL
2	SITE WORK	102.6	84.0	88.3	91.1	89.6	89.9	101.4	83.8	87.8	102.1	83.5	87.8	99.2	100.5	100.2	85.7	100.5	97.1
031	CONCRETE FORMWORK	96.6	55.2	61.2	90.6	69.3	72.3	94.5	54.6	60.9	98.8	57.9	63.8	101.7	65.6	70.7	101.7	65.6	70.7
032	CONCRETE REINFORCEMENT	98.8	58.1	75.9	94.5	61.7	76.0	96.6	66.0	79.3	96.6	57.9	74.8	101.4	72.5	85.2	101.4	72.5	85.2
033	CAST IN PLACE CONCRETE	95.4	56.0	78.9	76.0	66.6	72.0	86.1	64.7	77.1	92.0	59.3	78.3	92.0	71.7	83.5	93.4	71.7	84.3
3	CONCRETE	89.1	57.0	72.9	78.3	67.4	72.8	84.4	61.1	72.7	87.3	59.2	73.2	112.0	69.5	90.6	100.8	69.5	85.0
4	MASONRY	97.4	50.0	68.0	97.1	64.6	76.9	94.9	62.8	75.0	95.3	58.6	72.5	120.4	63.9	85.3	113.3	63.9	82.6
5	METALS	97.6	70.5	87.8	99.4	73.7	90.2	97.4	74.2	89.0	97.3	71.7	88.1	105.7	77.2	95.4	106.1	77.2	95.7
6	WOOD & PLASTICS	95.9	56.9	75.8	85.1	72.2	78.4	102.6	52.8	76.9	102.6	59.8	80.5	91.3	65.7	78.1	91.3	65.7	78.1
7	THERMAL & MOISTURE PROTECTION	96.1	55.0	77.1	93.5	67.9	81.6	96.8	61.8	80.6	96.8	62.1	80.7	102.9	71.0	88.1	101.5	71.0	87.4
8	DOORS & WINDOWS	92.9	55.2	83.8	96.4	67.7	89.5	87.6	53.5	79.3	87.6	59.6	80.8	90.0	64.0	83.7	90.0	64.0	83.7
092	LATH, PLASTER & GYPSUM BOARD	94.8	56.5	70.1	93.4	72.1	79.7	94.8	52.3	67.4	94.8	59.6	72.1	89.6	64.4	73.3	89.6	64.4	73.3
095	ACOUSTICAL TREATMENT & WOOD FLOORING	101.7	56.5	72.4	91.1	72.1	78.8	101.7	52.3	69.7	101.7	59.6	74.4	101.0	64.4	77.3	101.0	64.4	77.3
096	FLOORING & CARPET	119.3	52.1	102.9	95.2	61.5	87.0	155.0	48.4	129.1	155.5	66.6	133.9	106.1	56.8	94.1	106.1	56.8	94.1
099	PAINTING & WALL COVERINGS	95.9	45.8	66.5	100.0	56.7	74.6	97.1	47.2	67.9	99.1	74.9	84.9	113.2	60.4	82.2	113.2	60.4	82.2
9	FINISHES	102.8	53.5	77.6	93.2	66.6	79.5	114.7	51.9	82.5	115.0	61.5	87.6	100.9	62.7	81.3	99.8	62.7	80.8
10 - 14	TOTAL DIV. 10 - 14	100.0	67.4	93.1	100.0	73.3	94.4	100.0	68.6	93.4	100.0	64.3	92.5	100.0	80.2	95.8	100.0	80.2	95.8
15	MECHANICAL	100.0	51.2	78.2	99.9	73.5	88.1	100.0	59.9	82.1	100.0	56.8	80.7	99.8	72.7	87.7	99.8	72.7	87.7
16	ELECTRICAL	98.1	58.0	71.0	97.5	68.7	78.0	98.1	66.1	76.5	102.9	62.6	75.8	93.9	70.4	78.0	93.9	70.4	78.0
1 - 16	WEIGHTED AVERAGE	97.4	59.1	78.9	95.2	71.5	83.7	97.4	64.1	81.3	98.2	63.4	81.4	101.8	72.8	87.8	99.6	72.8	86.7

	DIVISION	UTAH						VERMONT						VIRGINIA					
		PROVO			SALT LAKE CITY			BURLINGTON			RUTLAND			ALEXANDRIA			ARLINGTON		
		MAT.	INST.	TOTAL	MAT.	INST.	TOTAL	MAT.	INST.	TOTAL	MAT.	INST.	TOTAL	MAT.	INST.	TOTAL	MAT.	INST.	TOTAL
2	SITE WORK	95.2	98.5	97.7	85.3	100.4	96.9	89.2	96.3	94.7	89.2	96.3	94.7	116.1	85.0	92.2	126.0	84.7	94.2
031	CONCRETE FORMWORK	103.5	65.6	71.1	100.3	65.6	70.6	86.6	60.5	64.2	98.6	60.5	66.0	91.8	74.3	76.8	88.6	73.0	75.2
032	CONCRETE REINFORCEMENT	109.7	72.6	88.8	99.3	72.6	84.3	116.7	75.4	93.4	116.7	75.4	93.4	83.8	89.5	87.0	94.5	81.4	87.1
033	CAST IN PLACE CONCRETE	92.1	71.8	83.6	101.0	71.8	88.7	103.7	65.9	87.9	98.9	65.9	85.0	104.5	82.0	95.1	101.7	78.1	91.8
3	CONCRETE	111.6	69.5	90.4	104.2	69.5	86.7	112.5	65.3	88.7	111.0	65.3	87.9	99.1	81.1	90.0	106.5	77.6	91.9
4	MASONRY	125.3	63.9	87.1	132.2	63.9	89.7	94.9	68.7	78.6	83.0	68.7	74.1	85.8	72.0	77.2	96.5	69.4	79.7
5	METALS	103.1	77.3	93.8	104.9	77.3	95.0	101.8	70.5	90.5	101.1	70.5	90.0	95.1	99.1	96.5	94.0	94.9	94.3
6	WOOD & PLASTICS	93.3	65.7	79.0	91.5	65.7	78.2	86.9	59.6	72.8	101.8	59.6	80.0	96.3	74.4	85.0	91.6	74.4	82.7
7	THERMAL & MOISTURE PROTECTION	105.1	71.0	89.3	103.9	71.0	88.7	101.0	65.2	84.4	100.9	65.2	84.3	95.8	80.4	88.7	96.5	76.9	87.4
8	DOORS & WINDOWS	94.4	64.0	87.0	90.0	64.0	83.7	109.1	54.4	95.8	109.1	54.4	95.8	96.7	77.2	92.0	94.7	74.6	89.9
092	LATH, PLASTER & GYPSUM BOARD	88.9	64.4	73.1	89.6	64.4	73.3	98.5	57.3	71.9	98.5	57.3	71.9	106.4	73.4	85.1	101.6	73.4	83.4
095	ACOUSTICAL TREATMENT & WOOD FLOORING	95.6	64.4	75.4	101.0	64.4	77.3	101.7	57.3	72.9	101.7	57.3	72.9	91.4	73.4	79.7	88.7	73.4	78.8
096	FLOORING & CARPET	106.7	56.8	94.6	105.6	56.8	93.7	96.9	79.2	92.6	96.9	79.2	92.6	93.3	82.9	90.8	91.8	72.3	87.1
099	PAINTING & WALL COVERINGS	113.2	62.9	83.7	113.2	62.9	83.7	89.3	49.0	65.7	89.3	49.0	65.7	117.1	81.7	96.3	117.1	98.0	105.9
9	FINISHES	100.3	63.0	81.2	100.1	63.0	81.1	96.3	62.7	79.1	96.2	62.7	79.0	94.7	76.3	85.3	93.9	75.9	84.7
10 - 14	TOTAL DIV. 10 - 14	100.0	80.2	95.8	100.0	80.2	95.8	100.0	67.0	93.0	100.0	67.0	93.0	100.0	87.5	97.4	100.0	80.0	95.8
15	MECHANICAL	99.8	72.7	87.7	99.9	72.7	87.8	100.0	63.7	83.8	100.0	63.7	83.8	100.1	84.2	93.0	100.1	77.9	90.2
16	ELECTRICAL	94.4	77.4	82.9	94.8	77.4	83.1	105.9	50.6	68.6	104.7	50.6	68.2	99.8	93.3	95.4	96.2	86.8	89.9
1 - 16	WEIGHTED AVERAGE	102.1	73.8	88.4	101.0	74.0	88.0	102.2	65.7	84.6	101.3	65.7	84.1	97.7	84.2	91.2	98.7	80.4	89.9

City Cost Indexes

DIVISION		VIRGINIA															WASHINGTON		
		NEWPORT NEWS			NORFOLK			PORTSMOUTH			RICHMOND			ROANOKE			EVERETT		
		MAT.	INST.	TOTAL	MAT.	INST.	TOTAL	MAT.	INST.	TOTAL	MAT.	INST.	TOTAL	MAT.	INST.	TOTAL	MAT.	INST.	TOTAL
2	SITE WORK	107.3	86.1	91.0	106.4	87.3	91.7	105.6	85.9	90.4	108.0	86.8	91.7	104.2	82.9	87.8	90.5	118.9	112.3
031	CONCRETE FORMWORK	95.4	56.2	61.8	100.7	56.2	62.6	81.3	56.2	59.8	96.4	62.5	67.3	95.2	44.0	51.3	106.8	95.4	97.1
032	CONCRETE REINFORCEMENT	94.2	74.5	83.1	94.2	74.5	83.1	93.9	74.6	83.0	94.2	76.5	84.3	94.2	69.8	80.5	109.4	91.2	99.1
033	CAST IN PLACE CONCRETE	102.3	62.1	85.4	105.3	62.1	87.2	101.3	64.3	85.8	108.8	63.8	90.0	106.1	55.4	84.9	92.9	105.2	98.0
3	CONCRETE	99.7	63.4	81.4	101.5	63.4	82.3	98.1	64.2	81.0	102.9	67.1	84.9	101.5	54.8	78.0	106.5	97.5	102.0
4	MASONRY	89.8	53.9	67.5	97.5	53.9	70.4	94.5	55.0	69.9	86.2	58.3	68.9	89.3	42.5	60.2	135.3	101.6	114.4
5	METALS	95.1	91.7	93.9	94.3	91.8	93.4	94.3	91.4	93.2	95.1	93.6	94.5	94.9	86.2	91.7	102.8	85.9	96.7
6	WOOD & PLASTICS	97.6	57.1	76.7	104.4	57.1	80.0	81.4	57.1	68.9	99.0	65.0	81.4	97.6	43.8	69.8	109.4	93.3	101.1
7	THERMAL & MOISTURE PROTECTION	95.6	54.2	76.4	95.5	54.2	76.3	95.5	54.5	76.5	95.2	58.3	78.1	95.6	49.7	74.3	104.7	96.9	101.1
8	DOORS & WINDOWS	96.7	57.7	87.2	96.7	59.8	87.8	96.8	59.8	87.8	96.7	61.1	88.1	96.7	48.2	84.9	103.2	90.8	100.2
092	LATH, PLASTER & GYPSUM BOARD	106.4	54.6	73.0	106.4	54.6	73.0	96.9	54.6	69.6	106.4	62.7	78.2	106.4	41.8	64.7	99.6	92.6	95.1
095	ACOUSTICAL TREATMENT & WOOD FLOORING	91.4	54.6	67.5	91.4	54.6	67.5	91.4	54.6	67.5	91.4	62.7	72.8	91.4	41.8	59.3	114.5	92.6	100.3
096	FLOORING & CARPET	93.3	48.9	82.5	93.1	48.9	82.3	85.7	48.9	76.7	93.1	72.7	88.1	93.3	43.9	81.3	128.8	100.6	122.0
099	PAINTING & WALL COVERINGS	105.8	52.2	74.4	105.8	54.5	75.7	105.8	45.8	70.6	105.8	67.1	83.1	105.8	40.8	67.6	119.8	82.2	97.7
9	FINISHES	94.0	54.2	73.6	94.0	54.4	73.7	90.3	53.4	71.4	93.9	65.0	79.1	93.9	43.1	67.9	121.4	94.6	107.7
10-14	TOTAL DIV. 10 - 14	100.0	75.5	94.8	100.0	75.5	94.8	100.0	75.5	94.8	100.0	77.1	95.2	100.0	69.1	93.5	100.0	101.3	100.3
15	MECHANICAL	100.1	60.5	82.5	100.1	58.3	81.5	100.1	61.2	82.8	100.1	68.6	86.1	100.1	50.1	77.8	100.0	99.6	99.8
16	ELECTRICAL	99.7	59.9	72.9	99.7	59.7	72.8	96.8	63.4	74.3	100.8	72.6	81.8	99.7	44.5	62.5	103.2	95.1	97.7
1-16	WEIGHTED AVERAGE	97.7	64.9	81.9	98.3	64.7	82.0	96.8	65.8	81.8	98.0	71.4	85.1	97.8	55.2	77.2	106.0	98.4	102.3

DIVISION		WASHINGTON																	
		RICHLAND			SEATTLE			SPOKANE			TACOMA			VANCOUVER			YAKIMA		
		MAT.	INST.	TOTAL	MAT.	INST.	TOTAL	MAT.	INST.	TOTAL	MAT.	INST.	TOTAL	MAT.	INST.	TOTAL	MAT.	INST.	TOTAL
2	SITE WORK	93.6	91.3	91.9	93.9	116.8	111.5	94.3	91.3	92.0	93.3	119.1	113.2	106.2	104.0	104.5	96.5	118.3	113.3
031	CONCRETE FORMWORK	110.7	88.3	91.5	89.7	100.8	99.2	119.3	88.4	92.9	89.7	100.6	99.0	94.2	97.3	96.9	92.2	96.4	95.8
032	CONCRETE REINFORCEMENT	102.7	92.9	97.2	103.3	93.6	97.8	103.4	93.0	97.5	103.3	93.5	97.8	106.3	93.1	98.9	105.9	92.4	98.3
033	CAST IN PLACE CONCRETE	106.5	91.3	100.2	97.4	106.5	101.2	110.4	91.4	102.4	95.4	106.4	100.0	106.6	100.9	104.2	101.9	90.6	97.2
3	CONCRETE	110.2	89.9	100.0	108.7	100.8	104.7	112.7	90.0	101.3	107.7	100.6	104.1	120.3	97.4	108.7	113.4	93.0	103.1
4	MASONRY	111.5	93.8	100.5	128.3	104.0	113.2	113.4	93.8	101.2	128.1	102.6	112.3	130.3	100.8	112.0	119.6	79.1	94.4
5	METALS	93.4	86.1	90.8	104.2	89.8	99.0	93.2	86.3	90.7	103.8	87.7	98.0	102.3	88.9	97.5	102.7	83.9	95.9
6	WOOD & PLASTICS	101.7	86.7	94.0	91.3	98.9	95.2	112.6	86.7	99.2	90.2	98.9	94.7	89.2	96.7	93.0	93.0	98.9	96.0
7	THERMAL & MOISTURE PROTECTION	169.0	88.4	131.6	104.5	100.8	102.8	166.8	88.8	130.7	104.3	100.0	102.3	107.8	89.2	99.2	104.5	84.7	95.3
8	DOORS & WINDOWS	116.4	83.2	108.3	103.3	95.1	101.4	116.2	82.2	107.9	103.8	95.1	101.7	100.3	88.1	97.4	103.4	86.2	99.2
092	LATH, PLASTER & GYPSUM BOARD	119.0	86.2	97.9	93.6	98.5	96.7	122.7	86.2	99.2	96.8	98.5	97.9	98.3	96.6	97.2	96.9	98.5	97.9
095	ACOUSTICAL TREATMENT & WOOD FLOORING	123.4	86.2	99.3	118.6	98.5	105.6	123.4	86.2	99.3	117.3	98.5	105.1	125.7	96.6	106.9	113.2	98.5	103.6
096	FLOORING & CARPET	116.8	56.5	102.2	120.6	100.6	115.8	120.0	85.0	111.5	121.3	104.3	117.2	127.2	77.9	115.2	122.6	80.7	112.4
099	PAINTING & WALL COVERINGS	122.9	80.9	98.3	119.8	91.1	103.0	122.9	84.7	100.5	119.8	91.1	103.0	128.8	79.7	100.0	119.8	84.7	99.2
9	FINISHES	133.1	80.8	106.3	118.8	99.3	108.8	134.7	87.1	110.3	119.2	100.0	109.4	119.4	91.8	105.3	119.0	92.5	105.4
10-14	TOTAL DIV. 10 - 14	100.0	98.3	99.6	100.0	105.0	101.1	100.0	98.3	99.6	100.0	105.0	101.1	100.0	90.1	97.9	100.0	101.8	100.4
15	MECHANICAL	100.6	99.1	100.0	100.0	111.8	105.3	100.6	93.2	97.3	100.1	102.9	101.4	100.3	97.3	99.0	100.1	97.6	99.0
16	ELECTRICAL	102.4	94.1	96.8	102.9	100.1	101.0	93.2	88.9	90.3	102.9	96.4	98.5	115.5	105.1	108.5	107.6	94.1	98.5
1-16	WEIGHTED AVERAGE	108.5	91.3	100.2	105.7	103.4	104.6	108.4	90.1	99.5	105.6	101.0	103.4	108.0	97.4	102.9	106.0	94.2	100.3

DIVISION		WEST VIRGINIA												WISCONSIN					
		CHARLESTON			HUNTINGTON			PARKERSBURG			WHEELING			EAU CLAIRE			GREEN BAY		
		MAT.	INST.	TOTAL	MAT.	INST.	TOTAL	MAT.	INST.	TOTAL	MAT.	INST.	TOTAL	MAT.	INST.	TOTAL	MAT.	INST.	TOTAL
2	SITE WORK	102.6	86.6	90.3	104.4	86.5	90.6	108.5	86.6	91.7	109.2	86.1	91.4	79.5	101.0	96.0	81.5	96.9	93.3
031	CONCRETE FORMWORK	104.1	92.3	94.0	96.1	94.5	94.7	84.2	90.7	89.8	86.4	89.1	88.7	96.5	95.6	95.8	117.2	95.5	98.6
032	CONCRETE REINFORCEMENT	94.2	78.5	85.4	94.2	89.7	91.7	92.9	85.4	88.7	92.2	90.9	91.5	100.2	95.3	97.5	96.8	94.6	95.6
033	CAST IN PLACE CONCRETE	100.1	100.8	100.4	108.0	105.3	106.9	100.9	91.9	97.1	100.9	99.8	100.5	97.5	94.2	96.1	100.8	98.2	99.7
3	CONCRETE	99.2	93.5	96.4	102.5	98.1	100.3	102.0	91.1	96.5	102.1	94.1	98.1	93.7	95.1	94.4	95.5	96.3	95.9
4	MASONRY	88.0	89.9	89.2	89.4	100.0	96.0	75.1	91.8	85.5	97.5	92.7	94.5	92.0	100.2	97.1	112.3	99.2	104.2
5	METALS	95.1	99.1	96.5	95.1	103.8	98.2	93.9	101.4	96.6	94.0	103.8	97.5	92.0	94.8	93.0	94.5	94.7	94.6
6	WOOD & PLASTICS	107.8	92.7	100.0	97.6	93.7	95.6	84.2	89.6	87.0	86.6	87.7	87.1	106.3	95.3	100.6	125.8	95.3	110.0
7	THERMAL & MOISTURE PROTECTION	95.6	87.8	92.0	95.8	91.8	93.9	95.9	86.2	91.4	96.0	88.1	92.4	95.7	89.4	92.8	98.4	90.9	95.0
8	DOORS & WINDOWS	97.9	82.9	94.3	96.7	86.0	94.1	97.3	81.9	93.5	98.1	90.0	96.2	105.3	91.9	102.0	103.9	90.1	100.5
092	LATH, PLASTER & GYPSUM BOARD	106.4	92.2	97.3	106.4	93.3	98.0	98.9	89.1	92.6	99.5	87.1	91.5	108.4	95.7	100.2	93.2	95.7	94.8
095	ACOUSTICAL TREATMENT & WOOD FLOORING	91.4	92.2	92.0	91.4	93.3	92.6	88.7	89.1	89.0	88.7	87.1	87.6	106.5	95.7	99.5	101.4	95.7	97.7
096	FLOORING & CARPET	93.1	96.6	93.9	93.1	110.5	97.3	88.5	94.6	90.0	89.4	100.6	92.2	95.6	75.1	90.6	115.0	102.3	111.9
099	PAINTING & WALL COVERINGS	105.8	87.0	94.8	105.8	90.3	96.7	105.8	100.4	102.6	105.8	86.5	94.5	95.4	84.0	88.7	106.3	77.6	89.5
9	FINISHES	94.0	93.0	93.5	93.8	97.4	95.7	91.2	92.9	92.1	91.6	90.7	91.1	100.7	90.6	95.5	105.2	95.2	100.0
10-14	TOTAL DIV. 10 - 14	100.0	98.2	99.6	100.0	99.3	99.8	100.0	98.6	99.7	100.0	100.4	100.1	100.0	99.1	99.8	100.0	98.0	99.6
15	MECHANICAL	100.1	82.5	92.3	100.1	89.9	95.6	100.1	82.1	92.1	100.1	91.2	96.1	100.0	89.6	95.4	100.5	91.3	96.4
16	ELECTRICAL	99.7	83.9	89.1	99.7	84.2	89.2	100.5	93.5	95.8	95.7	81.3	86.0	102.2	88.7	93.1	93.5	90.0	91.2
1-16	WEIGHTED AVERAGE	97.7	88.7	93.4	97.9	93.0	95.5	96.7	90.2	93.6	97.8	90.7	94.4	97.8	93.3	95.6	99.6	94.0	96.9

City Cost Indexes

DIVISION		WISCONSIN															WYOMING		
		KENOSHA			LA CROSSE			MADISON			MILWAUKEE			RACINE			CASPER		
		MAT.	INST.	TOTAL	MAT.	INST.	TOTAL	MAT.	INST.	TOTAL	MAT.	INST.	TOTAL	MAT.	INST.	TOTAL	MAT.	INST.	TOTAL
2	SITE WORK	86.2	98.5	95.7	74.0	100.9	94.7	81.4	101.7	97.0	82.4	90.7	88.8	81.8	102.3	97.5	86.6	100.3	97.1
031	CONCRETE FORMWORK	111.9	101.1	102.6	78.7	95.8	93.3	98.2	106.6	105.4	101.3	110.1	108.9	98.0	101.1	100.6	99.5	53.7	60.3
032	CONCRETE REINFORCEMENT	109.8	100.0	104.3	98.8	91.7	94.8	102.8	91.9	96.7	102.8	100.4	101.5	102.8	100.0	101.2	108.2	55.7	78.6
033	CAST IN PLACE CONCRETE	115.2	98.9	108.4	87.7	93.9	90.3	103.9	101.4	102.8	103.9	105.6	104.6	103.9	98.5	101.6	103.6	68.3	88.8
3	CONCRETE	104.4	100.1	102.2	84.9	94.4	89.7	96.9	101.7	99.3	97.4	105.7	101.6	96.9	99.9	98.4	106.6	59.9	83.0
4	MASONRY	96.9	105.7	102.4	91.3	100.6	97.1	101.2	110.7	107.1	101.2	115.1	109.9	101.2	105.7	104.0	107.3	49.7	71.5
5	METALS	96.0	99.1	97.1	91.9	93.3	92.4	96.3	94.1	95.5	97.8	90.2	95.1	96.3	99.1	97.3	105.4	68.2	92.0
6	WOOD & PLASTICS	121.5	99.6	110.2	86.1	95.3	90.8	109.3	106.3	107.7	113.0	109.1	111.0	109.5	99.6	104.4	97.5	52.4	74.2
7	THERMAL & MOISTURE PROTECTION	96.7	94.2	95.5	94.9	88.8	92.1	95.8	93.9	94.9	95.1	105.7	100.0	96.3	93.6	95.0	103.0	65.7	85.7
8	DOORS & WINDOWS	101.8	101.5	101.7	105.3	87.3	100.9	106.6	101.0	105.3	106.5	106.7	106.5	106.6	101.5	105.4	94.0	53.4	84.2
092	LATH, PLASTER & GYPSUM BOARD	95.3	100.1	98.4	101.1	95.7	97.6	107.4	107.0	107.1	107.4	109.7	108.9	107.4	100.1	102.7	88.4	50.7	64.0
095	ACOUSTICAL TREATMENT & WOOD FLOORING	86.5	100.1	95.3	102.3	95.7	98.0	95.6	107.0	103.0	95.6	109.7	104.7	95.6	100.1	98.5	95.6	50.7	66.5
096	FLOORING & CARPET	110.1	95.6	106.5	88.5	91.7	89.2	92.9	63.1	85.6	95.7	108.5	98.8	92.9	95.6	93.5	106.1	53.5	93.3
099	PAINTING & WALL COVERINGS	104.3	94.8	98.8	95.4	84.0	88.7	92.8	89.9	91.1	95.5	106.7	102.1	92.7	95.1	94.1	113.2	70.1	87.9
9	FINISHES	102.0	99.7	100.8	96.3	94.1	95.1	99.0	96.9	97.9	100.1	109.7	105.0	99.0	99.7	99.4	98.8	54.7	76.2
10-14	TOTAL DIV. 10-14	100.0	99.3	99.9	100.0	99.3	99.8	100.0	96.5	99.3	100.0	102.5	100.5	100.0	99.3	99.9	100.0	78.4	95.5
15	MECHANICAL	100.3	97.0	98.8	100.0	91.8	96.4	100.0	100.3	100.1	100.0	101.1	100.5	100.0	97.0	98.6	99.8	67.1	85.2
16	ELECTRICAL	93.3	102.4	99.5	102.6	88.7	93.2	92.2	99.7	97.3	93.0	106.1	101.8	91.1	103.0	99.1	93.9	65.7	74.8
1-16	WEIGHTED AVERAGE	99.5	100.0	99.7	95.9	93.8	94.8	98.6	100.4	99.5	99.2	103.3	101.2	98.6	100.4	99.5	100.4	65.7	83.7

DIVISION		WYOMING						CANADA											
		CHEYENNE			ROCK SPRINGS			CALGARY, ALBERTA			EDMONTON, ALBERTA			HAMILTON, ONTARIO			LONDON, ONTARIO		
		MAT.	INST.	TOTAL	MAT.	INST.	TOTAL	MAT.	INST.	TOTAL	MAT.	INST.	TOTAL	MAT.	INST.	TOTAL	MAT.	INST.	TOTAL
2	SITE WORK	86.4	100.3	97.1	89.4	99.8	97.4	105.1	97.9	99.6	106.4	97.9	99.9	111.4	98.1	101.1	111.4	97.8	100.9
031	CONCRETE FORMWORK	99.5	53.8	60.3	105.4	38.0	47.7	119.0	86.6	91.2	116.2	86.6	90.8	118.4	109.9	111.1	118.3	104.3	106.3
032	CONCRETE REINFORCEMENT	101.4	55.8	75.7	110.2	52.1	77.5	160.8	68.4	108.7	160.8	68.4	108.7	174.2	97.4	130.9	122.4	95.5	107.2
033	CAST IN PLACE CONCRETE	103.6	68.3	88.8	104.1	51.0	81.8	144.3	87.9	120.7	144.3	87.9	120.7	157.2	111.2	138.0	157.2	108.3	136.7
3	CONCRETE	105.7	60.0	82.6	107.5	46.5	76.7	137.1	84.0	110.3	136.9	84.0	110.2	145.1	107.6	126.2	138.2	103.8	120.9
4	MASONRY	106.4	52.5	72.9	172.5	40.6	90.6	146.6	87.9	110.1	146.6	87.9	110.1	149.8	113.1	127.0	149.1	109.6	124.6
5	METALS	106.7	68.4	92.9	105.5	67.0	91.6	100.8	85.8	95.4	100.8	85.8	95.4	101.0	96.9	99.5	99.2	96.4	98.2
6	WOOD & PLASTICS	96.5	52.4	73.7	104.4	37.0	69.7	116.7	85.9	100.8	112.2	85.9	98.6	117.6	109.4	113.4	117.6	103.0	110.1
7	THERMAL & MOISTURE PROTECTION	102.9	66.4	86.0	103.6	49.7	78.6	104.5	86.5	96.2	104.5	86.5	96.1	104.5	104.3	104.4	104.5	102.0	103.4
8	DOORS & WINDOWS	94.7	53.4	84.7	101.0	45.1	87.5	91.3	80.3	88.6	91.3	80.5	88.7	91.3	103.2	94.2	92.1	98.6	93.6
092	LATH, PLASTER & GYPSUM BOARD	89.6	50.7	64.5	91.6	34.8	55.0	149.4	85.5	108.2	146.3	85.5	107.1	208.3	109.8	144.7	208.3	103.2	140.5
095	ACOUSTICAL TREATMENT & WOOD FLOORING	102.6	50.7	68.9	95.6	34.8	56.2	101.7	85.5	91.2	101.7	85.5	91.2	101.7	109.8	106.9	101.7	103.2	102.7
096	FLOORING & CARPET	106.1	71.3	97.6	108.3	52.5	94.7	132.2	87.6	121.4	132.2	87.6	121.4	132.2	113.1	127.5	132.2	113.1	127.5
099	PAINTING & WALL COVERINGS	113.0	70.1	87.9	113.2	42.6	71.8	109.9	83.5	94.4	109.9	83.5	94.4	109.9	113.3	111.9	109.9	113.3	111.9
9	FINISHES	100.2	58.4	78.8	99.9	40.3	69.3	119.6	86.9	102.8	119.3	86.9	102.7	127.1	111.4	119.0	127.1	107.2	116.9
10-14	TOTAL DIV. 10-14	100.0	78.5	95.5	100.0	64.6	92.5	100.0	91.0	98.1	100.0	90.7	98.0	100.0	117.3	103.6	100.0	115.6	103.3
15	MECHANICAL	99.8	56.5	80.5	99.8	39.8	73.1	103.0	78.6	92.1	103.0	78.6	92.1	103.0	108.2	105.3	103.0	103.8	103.4
16	ELECTRICAL	93.8	68.5	76.7	92.8	59.0	70.0	113.8	87.5	96.0	113.8	87.5	96.0	126.9	110.9	116.1	126.9	106.8	113.3
1-16	WEIGHTED AVERAGE	100.6	64.9	83.4	105.0	53.6	80.2	110.3	85.9	98.5	110.2	85.9	98.5	113.4	107.3	110.5	112.4	104.0	108.3

DIVISION		CANADA																	
		MONTREAL, QUEBEC			OTTAWA, ONTARIO			QUEBEC, QUEBEC			TORONTO, ONTARIO			VANCOUVER, B C			WINNIPEG, MANITOBA		
		MAT.	INST.	TOTAL	MAT.	INST.	TOTAL	MAT.	INST.	TOTAL	MAT.	INST.	TOTAL	MAT.	INST.	TOTAL	MAT.	INST.	TOTAL
2	SITE WORK	91.6	98.2	96.7	110.9	97.9	100.9	91.2	98.2	96.6	113.1	98.4	101.8	100.6	99.4	99.7	109.4	96.8	99.7
031	CONCRETE FORMWORK	129.0	99.3	103.6	116.7	105.4	107.0	129.0	99.4	103.7	120.2	115.1	115.8	110.5	106.1	106.8	119.1	85.8	90.6
032	CONCRETE REINFORCEMENT	156.2	92.7	120.4	174.2	95.4	129.8	147.4	92.7	116.6	173.3	102.0	133.1	160.8	108.2	131.2	160.8	69.5	109.4
033	CAST IN PLACE CONCRETE	140.1	107.2	126.3	153.3	108.3	134.4	137.5	107.2	124.8	170.5	119.6	149.2	125.5	109.1	118.6	151.2	85.0	123.5
3	CONCRETE	135.2	100.6	117.7	143.0	104.3	123.5	132.7	100.7	116.6	151.6	113.6	132.5	133.3	107.2	120.1	133.6	82.9	108.0
4	MASONRY	145.0	103.0	118.9	149.5	109.1	124.4	144.0	103.0	118.6	150.9	123.0	133.6	145.2	110.6	123.7	147.1	82.5	106.9
5	METALS	101.1	93.3	98.3	101.0	96.4	99.3	101.0	93.4	98.3	101.0	100.0	100.6	101.2	100.1	100.8	100.8	85.4	95.3
6	WOOD & PLASTICS	132.7	99.4	115.5	116.7	105.1	110.7	132.7	99.4	115.5	118.9	113.0	115.9	103.6	103.8	103.7	116.6	87.1	101.4
7	THERMAL & MOISTURE PROTECTION	104.8	102.7	103.8	104.5	101.1	102.9	104.8	102.7	103.8	104.8	112.5	108.4	104.3	105.6	104.9	104.5	86.1	96.0
8	DOORS & WINDOWS	91.3	85.9	90.0	91.3	99.6	93.3	91.3	91.1	91.3	90.5	108.0	94.8	91.3	102.9	94.1	91.3	77.9	88.0
092	LATH, PLASTER & GYPSUM BOARD	149.1	99.5	117.1	259.2	105.3	159.9	215.2	99.5	140.5	144.6	113.5	124.6	152.0	104.0	121.0	138.5	86.8	105.1
095	ACOUSTICAL TREATMENT & WOOD FLOORING	101.7	99.5	100.2	101.7	105.3	104.0	101.7	99.5	100.2	101.7	113.5	109.4	101.7	104.0	103.2	101.7	86.8	92.0
096	FLOORING & CARPET	132.2	115.2	128.1	132.2	111.5	127.2	132.2	115.2	128.1	132.2	119.9	129.2	132.2	112.5	127.4	132.2	82.9	120.2
099	PAINTING & WALL COVERINGS	109.9	106.6	107.9	109.9	105.5	107.3	109.9	106.6	107.9	112.9	123.6	119.2	109.8	120.5	116.1	109.9	72.2	87.8
9	FINISHES	118.7	103.5	110.9	133.8	107.0	120.1	127.4	103.5	115.2	118.9	117.3	118.1	120.1	108.3	114.0	118.1	84.2	100.7
10-14	TOTAL DIV. 10-14	100.0	100.0	100.0	100.0	113.1	102.8	100.0	100.0	100.0	100.0	119.7	104.2	100.0	112.1	102.6	100.0	80.1	95.8
15	MECHANICAL	103.0	93.4	98.8	103.0	104.1	103.5	103.0	93.5	98.8	103.0	114.4	108.1	103.0	105.9	104.3	103.0	87.8	96.2
16	ELECTRICAL	123.6	95.2	104.5	123.6	107.8	113.0	123.6	95.3	104.5	127.0	111.7	116.7	125.6	106.7	112.9	128.9	93.1	104.7
1-16	WEIGHTED AVERAGE	110.5	97.5	104.2	113.6	104.2	109.1	111.0	97.7	104.6	113.4	111.9	112.7	110.5	105.7	108.2	111.0	87.1	99.5

Location Factors

Costs shown in *Means cost data publications* are based on National Averages for materials and installation. To adjust these costs to a specific location, simply multiply the base cost by the factor and divide by 100 for that city. The data is arranged alphabetically by state and postal zip code numbers. For a city not listed, use the factor for a nearby city with similar economic characteristics.

STATE/ZIP	CITY	MAT.	INST.	TOTAL
ALABAMA				
350-352	Birmingham	96.5	77.0	87.1
354	Tuscaloosa	96.2	62.2	79.8
355	Jasper	97.5	53.3	76.2
356	Decatur	96.3	68.4	82.8
357-358	Huntsville	96.1	68.4	82.7
359	Gadsden	97.0	66.2	82.2
360-361	Montgomery	97.1	60.8	79.6
362	Anniston	95.1	53.1	74.8
363	Dothan	96.6	59.5	78.7
364	Evergreen	95.9	61.3	79.2
365-366	Mobile	97.0	68.9	83.4
367	Selma	96.2	59.5	78.5
368	Phenix City	96.9	60.1	79.2
369	Butler	96.3	59.5	78.6
ALASKA				
995-996	Anchorage	133.1	117.7	125.7
997	Fairbanks	129.3	120.7	125.1
998	Juneau	131.2	118.0	124.8
999	Ketchikan	140.6	118.0	129.7
ARIZONA				
850,853	Phoenix	100.6	79.0	90.2
852	Mesa/Tempe	100.6	69.5	85.6
855	Globe	101.4	73.9	88.1
856-857	Tucson	99.4	77.6	88.9
859	Show Low	101.5	74.0	88.2
860	Flagstaff	102.8	78.2	91.0
863	Prescott	100.3	73.6	87.4
864	Kingman	99.1	74.4	87.2
865	Chambers	99.1	74.2	87.1
ARKANSAS				
716	Pine Bluff	95.4	62.0	79.3
717	Camden	93.8	47.5	71.5
718	Texarkana	94.7	53.4	74.8
719	Hot Springs	93.0	46.9	70.7
720-722	Little Rock	95.9	62.3	79.7
723	West Memphis	95.2	64.8	80.5
724	Jonesboro	95.2	64.8	80.5
725	Batesville	93.9	59.1	77.1
726	Harrison	95.3	59.1	77.8
727	Fayetteville	92.4	40.8	67.5
728	Russellville	94.1	56.9	76.1
729	Fort Smith	96.1	60.7	79.0
CALIFORNIA				
900-902	Los Angeles	105.0	116.5	110.6
903-905	Inglewood	101.2	114.3	107.5
906-908	Long Beach	103.0	114.3	108.5
910-912	Pasadena	100.6	114.4	107.2
913-916	Van Nuys	104.5	114.1	109.2
917-918	Alhambra	103.2	114.4	108.6
919-921	San Diego	104.9	109.5	107.1
922	Palm Springs	102.5	112.0	107.1
923-924	San Bernardino	100.1	111.8	105.7
925	Riverside	104.6	112.8	108.6
926-927	Santa Ana	102.3	112.3	107.2
928	Anaheim	104.9	115.1	109.8
930	Oxnard	105.4	113.8	109.4
931	Santa Barbara	104.6	112.9	108.6
932-933	Bakersfield	104.3	107.0	105.6
934	San Luis Obispo	106.2	111.5	108.8
935	Mojave	102.8	108.9	105.8
936-938	Fresno	105.3	112.3	108.7
939	Salinas	107.3	116.7	111.8
940-941	San Francisco	111.0	138.2	124.2
942,956-958	Sacramento	106.9	114.5	110.5
943	Palo Alto	105.0	127.8	116.0
944	San Mateo	108.0	127.1	117.2
945	Vallejo	105.5	127.0	115.9
946	Oakland	109.9	126.5	117.9
947	Berkeley	109.5	127.9	118.4
948	Richmond	109.3	125.3	117.0
949	San Rafael	111.2	125.7	118.2
950	Santa Cruz	110.8	118.4	114.5

STATE/ZIP	CITY	MAT.	INST.	TOTAL
CALIFORNIA (CONT'D)				
951	San Jose	110.1	129.7	119.6
952	Stockton	105.9	113.2	109.4
953	Modesto	106.0	113.3	109.5
954	Santa Rosa	107.2	129.0	117.7
955	Eureka	108.6	112.1	110.3
959	Marysville	107.3	113.7	110.4
960	Redding	108.4	108.9	108.6
961	Susanville	108.6	108.3	108.5
COLORADO				
800-802	Denver	101.9	84.8	93.6
803	Boulder	100.0	69.5	85.3
804	Golden	102.4	76.9	90.1
805	Fort Collins	103.2	77.9	91.0
806	Greeley	100.2	69.1	85.2
807	Fort Morgan	100.7	77.7	89.6
808-809	Colorado Springs	100.7	80.3	90.8
810	Pueblo	102.6	79.2	91.3
811	Alamosa	104.9	70.3	88.2
812	Salida	104.8	70.4	88.2
813	Durango	105.6	66.0	86.5
814	Montrose	103.9	63.3	84.3
815	Grand Junction	106.9	63.7	86.0
816	Glenwood Springs	105.0	75.6	90.8
CONNECTICUT				
060	New Britain	103.0	105.0	104.0
061	Hartford	103.3	105.3	104.3
062	Willimantic	103.8	104.0	103.9
063	New London	100.2	105.8	102.9
064	Meriden	102.9	104.5	103.7
065	New Haven	103.2	105.3	104.2
066	Bridgeport	104.4	102.5	103.5
067	Waterbury	103.7	105.0	104.4
068	Norwalk	103.7	102.7	103.2
069	Stamford	103.9	106.1	105.0
D.C.				
200-205	Washington	99.6	92.0	96.0
DELAWARE				
197	Newark	99.5	97.2	98.4
198	Wilmington	98.8	97.2	98.0
199	Dover	99.5	97.2	98.4
FLORIDA				
320,322	Jacksonville	98.6	68.6	84.1
321	Daytona Beach	98.7	75.9	87.7
323	Tallahassee	99.1	58.6	79.6
324	Panama City	99.6	45.6	73.5
325	Pensacola	99.2	68.5	84.4
326	Gainesville	100.0	64.6	82.9
327-328,347	Orlando	100.4	70.6	86.1
329	Melbourne	100.6	75.1	88.3
330-332,340	Miami	98.0	74.3	86.6
333	Fort Lauderdale	97.9	75.1	86.9
334,349	West Palm Beach	96.8	69.2	83.5
335-336,346	Tampa	99.8	67.6	84.2
337	St. Petersburg	101.5	67.5	85.1
338	Lakeland	98.5	67.3	83.5
339	Fort Myers	98.2	64.2	81.8
342	Sarasota	100.0	64.6	82.9
GEORGIA				
300-303,399	Atlanta	96.9	79.3	88.4
304	Statesboro	96.8	36.9	67.9
305	Gainesville	96.0	52.2	74.9
306	Athens	95.1	64.5	80.3
307	Dalton	96.8	34.8	66.9
308-309	Augusta	95.7	62.7	79.8
310-312	Macon	95.7	67.6	82.2
313-314	Savannah	97.8	65.6	82.3
315	Waycross	97.7	52.0	75.6
316	Valdosta	97.3	55.6	77.1
317	Albany	97.4	61.6	80.1
318-319	Columbus	97.5	59.7	79.2

Location Factors

STATE/ZIP	CITY	MAT.	INST.	TOTAL
HAWAII				
967	Hilo	115.4	130.7	122.8
968	Honolulu	116.0	130.7	123.1
STATES & POSS.				
969	Guam	115.2	47.2	82.4
IDAHO				
832	Pocatello	101.9	84.4	93.5
833	Twin Falls	104.1	54.7	80.3
834	Idaho Falls	101.4	65.2	83.9
835	Lewiston	113.5	90.6	102.4
836-837	Boise	101.9	85.1	93.8
838	Coeur d'Alene	115.5	65.7	91.4
ILLINOIS				
600-603	North Suburban	97.6	119.9	108.4
604	Joliet	97.6	114.9	105.9
605	South Suburban	97.6	119.8	108.3
606	Chicago	97.8	125.0	110.9
609	Kankakee	93.8	107.9	100.6
610-611	Rockford	97.1	112.0	104.3
612	Rock Island	94.7	100.7	97.6
613	La Salle	96.1	103.0	99.4
614	Galesburg	95.7	100.5	98.0
615-616	Peoria	98.5	102.8	100.6
617	Bloomington	95.0	103.8	99.3
618-619	Champaign	98.7	100.9	99.8
620-622	East St. Louis	93.7	106.9	100.1
623	Quincy	95.2	95.9	95.6
624	Effingham	94.6	99.8	97.1
625	Decatur	96.1	99.1	97.5
626-627	Springfield	95.8	100.9	98.3
628	Centralia	92.9	104.6	98.6
629	Carbondale	92.6	100.5	96.4
INDIANA				
460	Anderson	97.0	87.3	92.3
461-462	Indianapolis	99.9	90.5	95.4
463-464	Gary	97.8	96.9	97.4
465-466	South Bend	96.2	82.4	89.5
467-468	Fort Wayne	97.2	86.9	92.2
469	Kokomo	95.3	82.0	88.9
470	Lawrenceburg	93.1	81.9	87.7
471	New Albany	94.7	78.3	86.8
472	Columbus	96.8	85.9	91.6
473	Muncie	97.1	84.6	91.1
474	Bloomington	98.9	84.2	91.8
475	Washington	95.0	88.2	91.8
476-477	Evansville	96.7	91.5	94.2
478	Terre Haute	97.1	88.5	93.0
479	Lafayette	96.6	82.6	89.8
IOWA				
500-503,509	Des Moines	97.8	83.2	90.8
504	Mason City	96.0	65.7	81.4
505	Fort Dodge	96.5	59.9	78.8
506-507	Waterloo	97.5	67.3	82.9
508	Creston	97.1	72.5	85.2
510-511	Sioux City	98.2	67.0	83.1
512	Sibley	96.7	59.5	78.8
513	Spencer	99.2	59.5	80.0
514	Carroll	95.7	67.0	81.9
515	Council Bluffs	99.0	73.7	86.8
516	Shenandoah	95.6	56.6	76.8
520	Dubuque	97.5	73.4	85.9
521	Decorah	96.9	64.7	81.4
522-524	Cedar Rapids	98.9	79.6	89.6
525	Ottumwa	97.0	73.3	85.6
526	Burlington	95.8	61.0	79.0
527-528	Davenport	97.9	89.2	93.7
KANSAS				
660-662	Kansas City	98.1	85.6	92.1
664-666	Topeka	97.6	71.9	85.2
667	Fort Scott	97.0	72.2	85.0
668	Emporia	96.7	65.3	81.5
669	Belleville	98.7	66.7	83.3
670-672	Wichita	96.8	71.9	84.8
673	Independence	98.5	60.3	80.1
674	Salina	98.2	65.0	82.2
675	Hutchinson	93.8	59.3	77.1
676	Hays	97.9	66.7	82.9
677	Colby	98.8	66.7	83.3

STATE/ZIP	CITY	MAT.	INST.	TOTAL
KANSAS (CONT'D)				
678	Dodge City	99.4	66.7	83.6
679	Liberal	97.6	55.4	77.2
KENTUCKY				
400-402	Louisville	95.9	85.7	90.9
403-405	Lexington	96.6	73.4	85.4
406	Frankfort	95.8	80.1	88.2
407-409	Corbin	94.3	52.8	74.3
410	Covington	95.1	91.6	93.4
411-412	Ashland	93.1	99.8	96.4
413-414	Campton	95.2	52.8	74.7
415-416	Pikeville	95.9	70.3	83.6
417-418	Hazard	94.5	52.8	74.4
420	Paducah	93.0	89.3	91.3
421-422	Bowling Green	95.2	83.8	89.7
423	Owensboro	95.0	84.1	89.8
424	Henderson	92.6	93.3	92.9
425-426	Somerset	92.2	52.8	73.2
427	Elizabethtown	91.8	85.7	88.9
LOUISIANA				
700-701	New Orleans	100.2	69.5	85.4
703	Thibodaux	100.5	69.0	85.3
704	Hammond	97.5	67.5	83.0
705	Lafayette	99.7	64.2	82.6
706	Lake Charles	99.9	67.0	84.0
707-708	Baton Rouge	99.6	64.8	82.8
710-711	Shreveport	96.5	63.4	80.5
712	Monroe	96.4	61.3	79.4
713-714	Alexandria	96.4	59.2	78.5
MAINE				
039	Kittery	98.2	61.6	80.6
040-041	Portland	101.4	76.8	89.5
042	Lewiston	101.9	76.8	89.8
043	Augusta	100.6	57.2	79.6
044	Bangor	100.9	82.0	91.8
045	Bath	99.8	56.3	78.8
046	Machias	99.3	67.5	84.0
047	Houlton	99.5	61.3	81.1
048	Rockland	98.4	68.4	83.9
049	Waterville	99.9	57.2	79.3
MARYLAND				
206	Waldorf	97.7	77.2	87.8
207-208	College Park	97.5	81.4	89.8
209	Silver Spring	96.9	80.1	88.8
210-212	Baltimore	97.1	85.7	91.6
214	Annapolis	96.9	82.5	90.0
215	Cumberland	94.0	80.2	87.4
216	Easton	95.6	42.8	70.1
217	Hagerstown	94.4	81.0	87.9
218	Salisbury	96.2	60.2	78.8
219	Elkton	93.2	77.2	85.4
MASSACHUSETTS				
010-011	Springfield	101.9	102.4	102.2
012	Pittsfield	101.7	97.6	99.7
013	Greenfield	99.7	100.9	100.3
014	Fitchburg	98.1	112.6	105.1
015-016	Worcester	101.8	112.6	107.0
017	Framingham	97.8	120.4	108.7
018	Lowell	101.4	118.0	109.4
019	Lawrence	102.6	116.2	109.2
020-022, 024	Boston	103.8	130.6	116.7
023	Brockton	102.7	116.6	109.4
025	Buzzards Bay	96.9	115.2	105.7
026	Hyannis	99.3	115.2	107.0
027	New Bedford	102.2	115.9	108.8
MICHIGAN				
480,483	Royal Oak	94.3	102.2	98.1
481	Ann Arbor	96.6	105.9	101.1
482	Detroit	97.6	111.4	104.3
484-485	Flint	96.2	99.6	97.8
486	Saginaw	96.5	92.9	94.8
487	Bay City	96.0	93.3	94.7
488-489	Lansing	96.4	95.5	96.0
490	Battle Creek	96.5	87.8	92.3
491	Kalamazoo	96.8	85.7	91.5
492	Jackson	95.2	96.5	95.9
493,495	Grand Rapids	96.4	76.8	86.9
494	Muskegan	96.6	84.6	90.8

Location Factors

STATE/ZIP	CITY	MAT.	INST.	TOTAL
MICHIGAN (CONT'D)				
496	Traverse City	94.5	79.1	87.1
497	Gaylord	96.0	85.6	91.0
498-499	Iron mountain	97.9	86.4	92.4
MINNESOTA				
550-551	Saint Paul	97.8	115.2	106.2
553-554	Minneapolis	98.5	120.4	109.0
556-558	Duluth	97.9	109.9	103.7
559	Rochester	97.7	104.3	100.9
560	Mankato	96.4	101.1	98.7
561	Windom	95.3	75.8	85.9
562	Willmar	94.5	77.2	86.1
563	St. Cloud	95.5	103.4	99.3
564	Brainerd	96.0	99.9	97.9
565	Detroit Lakes	98.8	91.0	95.0
566	Bemidji	98.1	97.0	97.5
567	Thief River Falls	97.2	87.8	92.6
MISSISSIPPI				
386	Clarksdale	96.9	36.6	67.8
387	Greenville	100.2	56.1	78.9
388	Tupelo	98.1	46.7	73.3
389	Greenwood	98.3	39.2	69.8
390-392	Jackson	98.7	58.0	79.0
393	Meridian	96.7	55.6	76.8
394	Laurel	98.0	40.7	70.3
395	Biloxi	98.8	62.6	81.3
396	Mccomb	96.4	37.7	68.1
397	Columbus	98.0	46.2	73.0
MISSOURI				
630-631	St. Louis	96.6	109.1	102.7
633	Bowling Green	96.5	93.9	95.2
634	Hannibal	95.3	93.8	94.6
635	Kirksville	97.2	82.0	89.8
636	Flat River	97.5	98.5	98.0
637	Cape Girardeau	96.5	97.1	96.8
638	Sikeston	95.0	89.2	92.2
639	Poplar Bluff	94.5	88.9	91.8
640-641	Kansas City	99.2	97.9	98.6
644-645	St. Joseph	99.2	83.5	91.6
646	Chillicothe	96.2	70.9	84.0
647	Harrisonville	95.8	89.1	92.6
648	Joplin	98.0	73.3	86.1
650-651	Jefferson City	95.2	86.7	91.1
652	Columbia	96.4	81.5	89.2
653	Sedalia	95.7	82.1	89.1
654-655	Rolla	94.8	69.5	82.6
656-658	Springfield	97.8	75.9	87.2
MONTANA				
590-591	Billings	100.6	90.9	95.9
592	Wolf Point	100.9	87.0	94.2
593	Miles City	99.0	90.4	94.8
594	Great Falls	101.8	88.6	95.5
595	Havre	99.6	87.9	94.0
596	Helena	101.7	88.1	95.1
597	Butte	100.3	84.5	92.7
598	Missoula	98.7	86.8	93.0
599	Kalispell	97.8	85.9	92.0
NEBRASKA				
680-681	Omaha	100.5	74.9	88.2
683-685	Lincoln	97.9	66.2	82.6
686	Columbus	96.5	50.9	74.5
687	Norfolk	98.8	68.3	84.1
688	Grand Island	97.5	67.9	83.2
689	Hastings	97.0	61.5	79.9
690	Mccook	96.8	44.4	71.5
691	North Platte	96.9	61.5	79.8
692	Valentine	100.6	48.2	75.3
693	Alliance	99.4	43.9	72.6
NEVADA				
889-891	Las Vegas	101.3	106.4	103.8
893	Ely	102.1	91.0	96.7
894-895	Reno	102.0	95.1	98.7
897	Carson City	101.8	95.0	98.5
898	Elko	100.8	90.5	95.8
NEW HAMPSHIRE				
030	Nashua	102.4	86.5	94.7
031	Manchester	102.4	86.5	94.7

STATE/ZIP	CITY	MAT.	INST.	TOTAL
NEW HAMPSHIRE (CONT'D)				
032-033	Concord	100.2	86.5	93.6
034	Keene	99.3	61.7	81.2
035	Littleton	99.3	65.1	82.8
036	Charleston	98.7	58.1	79.1
037	Claremont	97.8	58.1	78.7
038	Portsmouth	99.4	83.6	91.8
NEW JERSEY				
070-071	Newark	103.9	121.4	112.4
072	Elizabeth	102.8	113.4	107.9
073	Jersey City	101.4	122.2	111.4
074-075	Paterson	104.2	120.4	112.0
076	Hackensack	101.2	116.9	108.8
077	Long Branch	100.8	118.8	109.5
078	Dover	101.6	117.0	109.0
079	Summit	101.7	112.0	106.7
080,083	Vineland	99.1	113.6	106.1
081	Camden	101.3	116.1	108.4
082,084	Atlantic City	100.1	115.1	107.3
085-086	Trenton	102.1	121.5	111.5
087	Point Pleasant	101.5	116.0	108.5
088-089	New Brunswick	101.9	119.2	110.2
NEW MEXICO				
870-872	Albuquerque	100.6	81.1	91.1
873	Gallup	102.0	80.3	91.5
874	Farmington	101.8	80.1	91.3
875	Santa Fe	100.2	80.3	90.6
877	Las Vegas	100.1	80.2	90.5
878	Socorro	99.6	79.8	90.1
879	Truth/Consequences	99.8	74.4	87.6
880	Las Cruces	97.8	71.4	85.1
881	Clovis	100.2	79.5	90.2
882	Roswell	101.8	78.6	90.6
883	Carrizozo	102.5	79.9	91.6
884	Tucumcari	101.2	78.8	90.4
NEW YORK				
100-102	New York	108.9	160.6	133.9
103	Staten Island	105.1	145.0	124.4
104	Bronx	102.4	145.6	123.2
105	Mount Vernon	103.1	132.9	117.5
106	White Plains	103.0	130.9	116.5
107	Yonkers	108.0	136.0	121.5
108	New Rochelle	103.8	133.1	117.9
109	Suffern	103.8	118.8	111.0
110	Queens	103.3	146.4	124.1
111	Long Island City	105.3	146.1	125.0
112	Brooklyn	105.6	144.0	124.1
113	Flushing	106.0	146.1	125.4
114	Jamaica	103.9	146.1	124.3
115,117,118	Hicksville	103.2	142.6	122.2
116	Far Rockaway	106.1	145.3	125.0
119	Riverhead	103.7	143.3	122.8
120-122	Albany	98.5	95.8	97.2
123	Schenectady	99.4	97.0	98.2
124	Kingston	103.6	112.0	107.6
125-126	Poughkeepsie	102.8	117.9	110.1
127	Monticello	101.9	111.7	106.6
128	Glens Falls	93.5	89.2	91.4
129	Plattsburgh	99.2	84.7	92.2
130-132	Syracuse	100.3	95.5	97.9
133-135	Utica	98.6	88.1	93.5
136	Watertown	100.0	89.9	95.1
137-139	Binghamton	99.4	87.8	93.8
140-142	Buffalo	99.8	105.0	102.3
143	Niagara Falls	98.1	103.3	100.6
144-146	Rochester	101.2	100.5	100.9
147	Jamestown	97.4	83.2	90.6
148-149	Elmira	96.8	88.8	92.9
NORTH CAROLINA				
270,272-274	Greensboro	97.1	57.3	77.9
271	Winston-Salem	97.2	56.9	77.8
275-276	Raleigh	97.6	57.3	78.2
277	Durham	97.0	57.4	77.9
278	Rocky Mount	95.5	42.8	70.1
279	Elizabeth City	96.1	45.6	71.7
280	Gastonia	97.2	55.0	76.8
281-282	Charlotte	97.4	55.3	77.1
283	Fayetteville	95.6	57.4	77.1
284	Wilmington	95.7	56.3	76.7
285	Kinston	94.0	42.3	69.0

Location Factors

STATE/ZIP	CITY	MAT.	INST.	TOTAL
NORTH CAROLINA (CONT'D)				
286	Hickory	94.2	41.4	68.7
287-288	Asheville	96.1	56.1	76.8
289	Murphy	95.6	40.4	69.0
NORTH DAKOTA				
580-581	Fargo	100.1	65.1	83.2
582	Grand Forks	101.1	63.7	83.0
583	Devils Lake	101.1	63.7	83.0
584	Jamestown	100.8	63.9	83.0
585	Bismarck	100.1	68.0	84.6
586	Dickinson	101.6	63.7	83.3
587	Minot	101.1	66.5	84.4
588	Williston	100.3	63.7	82.6
OHIO				
430-432	Columbus	97.5	90.5	94.1
433	Marion	94.8	88.2	91.6
434-436	Toledo	98.0	97.9	98.0
437-438	Zanesville	94.8	86.6	90.8
439	Steubenville	96.5	96.3	96.4
440	Lorain	98.4	94.1	96.3
441	Cleveland	98.4	105.6	101.9
442-443	Akron	99.6	100.1	99.8
444-445	Youngstown	98.8	93.1	96.1
446-447	Canton	98.9	91.3	95.3
448-449	Mansfield	96.3	90.5	93.5
450	Hamilton	94.9	90.2	92.6
451-452	Cincinnati	94.8	90.0	92.5
453-454	Dayton	94.6	88.9	91.8
455	Springfield	94.8	88.0	91.5
456	Chillicothe	94.1	94.7	94.4
457	Athens	97.4	77.3	87.7
458	Lima	97.9	88.2	93.2
OKLAHOMA				
730-731	Oklahoma City	97.6	66.7	82.7
734	Ardmore	95.6	65.5	81.1
735	Lawton	97.5	66.4	82.5
736	Clinton	96.9	63.9	81.0
737	Enid	97.2	64.4	81.4
738	Woodward	95.7	64.0	80.4
739	Guymon	97.0	39.4	69.2
740-741	Tulsa	97.5	66.8	82.7
743	Miami	94.6	67.8	81.6
744	Muskogee	96.3	50.7	74.3
745	Mcalester	93.9	59.5	77.3
746	Ponca City	94.5	66.3	80.9
747	Durant	94.6	65.1	80.3
748	Shawnee	96.1	62.1	79.7
749	Poteau	93.7	67.3	81.0
OREGON				
970-972	Portland	104.0	105.7	104.8
973	Salem	104.5	102.3	103.5
974	Eugene	104.0	101.8	102.9
975	Medford	105.6	98.0	101.9
976	Klamath Falls	106.4	97.9	102.3
977	Bend	105.3	99.3	102.4
978	Pendleton	97.8	99.9	98.8
979	Vale	95.4	93.6	94.5
PENNSYLVANIA				
150-152	Pittsburgh	97.8	107.5	102.5
153	Washington	95.2	105.4	100.2
154	Uniontown	95.3	102.6	98.8
155	Bedford	96.4	95.5	96.0
156	Greensburg	96.7	103.5	99.9
157	Indiana	95.3	100.5	97.8
158	Dubois	96.8	96.4	96.6
159	Johnstown	96.4	97.9	97.1
160	Butler	93.2	101.1	97.0
161	New Castle	93.1	101.6	97.2
162	Kittanning	93.7	105.1	99.2
163	Oil City	93.1	94.7	93.9
164-165	Erie	95.4	96.3	95.8
166	Altoona	95.1	96.7	95.9
167	Bradford	96.7	96.1	96.4
168	State College	96.3	98.1	97.2
169	Wellsboro	97.6	92.3	95.0
170-171	Harrisburg	98.6	94.2	96.5
172	Chambersburg	97.0	91.5	94.4
173-174	York	96.8	94.4	95.6
175-176	Lancaster	95.6	93.1	94.4

STATE/ZIP	CITY	MAT.	INST.	TOTAL
PENNSYLVANIA (CONT'D)				
177	Williamsport	93.9	89.8	92.0
178	Sunbury	96.3	92.7	94.5
179	Pottsville	95.3	94.5	94.9
180	Lehigh Valley	97.2	105.4	101.2
181	Allentown	99.2	102.9	101.0
182	Hazleton	96.3	94.7	95.5
183	Stroudsburg	96.4	94.3	95.4
184-185	Scranton	99.8	98.7	99.3
186-187	Wilkes-Barre	95.9	96.5	96.2
188	Montrose	95.5	97.9	96.6
189	Doylestown	95.7	113.2	104.2
190-191	Philadelphia	99.8	124.9	111.9
193	Westchester	96.8	110.1	103.2
194	Norristown	95.5	115.9	105.4
195-196	Reading	98.2	98.2	98.2
RHODE ISLAND				
028	Newport	100.9	108.4	104.5
029	Providence	101.2	108.3	104.6
SOUTH CAROLINA				
290-292	Columbia	96.3	54.3	76.1
293	Spartanburg	95.0	54.6	75.5
294	Charleston	96.3	55.9	76.8
295	Florence	94.4	52.0	74.0
296	Greenville	94.7	54.6	75.3
297	Rock Hill	94.8	39.7	68.2
298	Aiken	95.6	40.4	68.9
299	Beaufort	96.4	44.2	71.2
SOUTH DAKOTA				
570-571	Sioux Falls	100.4	61.2	81.4
572	Watertown	98.8	58.9	79.5
573	Mitchell	97.9	58.9	79.1
574	Aberdeen	100.3	58.9	80.3
575	Pierre	99.8	57.6	79.4
576	Mobridge	98.7	58.9	79.5
577	Rapid City	100.5	55.9	79.0
TENNESSEE				
370-372	Nashville	96.6	72.6	85.0
373-374	Chattanooga	98.5	65.6	82.6
375,380-381	Memphis	96.4	74.2	85.7
376	Johnson City	97.4	61.7	80.2
377-379	Knoxville	94.6	65.2	80.4
382	Mckenzie	97.3	40.8	70.0
383	Jackson	98.5	51.1	75.6
384	Columbia	95.6	56.0	76.5
385	Cookeville	97.0	39.5	69.2
TEXAS				
750	Mckinney	98.7	66.9	83.4
751	Waxahackie	98.8	67.2	83.5
752-753	Dallas	99.6	72.9	86.7
754	Greenville	98.9	49.1	74.9
755	Texarkana	97.8	59.6	79.4
756	Longview	98.4	50.4	75.2
757	Tyler	98.9	61.6	80.9
758	Palestine	95.2	53.5	75.1
759	Lufkin	96.3	60.4	79.0
760-761	Fort Worth	97.7	69.1	83.9
762	Denton	97.5	61.9	80.3
763	Wichita Falls	98.2	63.4	81.4
764	Eastland	96.8	51.9	75.2
765	Temple	95.3	59.2	77.9
766-767	Waco	97.4	64.1	81.3
768	Brownwood	97.5	48.1	73.7
769	San Angelo	97.2	55.1	76.9
770-772	Houston	99.4	78.4	89.3
773	Huntsville	97.9	51.3	75.4
774	Wharton	99.6	55.8	78.5
775	Galveston	97.6	75.9	87.1
776-777	Beaumont	97.0	73.3	85.5
778	Bryan	94.5	70.2	82.7
779	Victoria	99.7	61.3	81.2
780	Laredo	95.2	63.5	79.9
781-782	San Antonio	95.2	71.5	83.7
783-784	Corpus Christi	98.4	61.2	80.5
785	Mc Allen	98.6	57.1	78.6
786-787	Austin	95.3	68.8	82.5
788	Del Rio	98.0	39.6	69.8
789	Giddings	95.2	52.2	74.4
790-791	Amarillo	98.0	63.2	81.2

Location Factors

STATE/ZIP	CITY	MAT.	INST.	TOTAL
TEXAS (CONT'D)				
792	Childress	97.3	60.8	79.7
793-794	Lubbock	100.0	62.1	81.7
795-796	Abilene	97.4	58.5	78.6
797	Midland	100.5	60.6	81.3
798-799,885	El Paso	97.3	56.0	77.4
UTAH				
840-841	Salt Lake City	101.0	74.0	88.0
842,844	Ogden	99.6	72.8	86.7
843	Logan	101.8	72.8	87.8
845	Price	102.5	59.9	81.9
846-847	Provo	102.1	73.8	88.4
VERMONT				
050	White River Jct.	100.8	43.8	73.3
051	Bellows Falls	99.3	46.4	73.7
052	Bennington	99.5	38.7	70.2
053	Brattleboro	100.0	46.4	74.1
054	Burlington	102.2	65.7	84.6
056	Montpelier	99.2	65.7	83.0
057	Rutland	101.3	65.7	84.1
058	St. Johnsbury	100.9	49.8	76.2
059	Guildhall	99.4	49.2	75.2
VIRGINIA				
220-221	Fairfax	97.9	79.4	88.9
222	Arlington	98.7	80.4	89.9
223	Alexandria	97.7	84.2	91.2
224-225	Fredericksburg	96.5	73.1	85.2
226	Winchester	97.2	62.1	80.3
227	Culpeper	97.1	64.6	81.4
228	Harrisonburg	97.3	52.9	75.8
229	Charlottesville	97.6	67.0	82.8
230-232	Richmond	98.0	71.4	85.1
233-235	Norfolk	98.3	64.7	82.0
236	Newport News	97.7	64.9	81.9
237	Portsmouth	96.8	65.8	81.8
238	Petersburg	97.4	71.4	84.9
239	Farmville	96.9	50.7	74.6
240-241	Roanoke	97.8	55.2	77.2
242	Bristol	96.4	52.3	75.1
243	Pulaski	96.1	43.1	70.6
244	Staunton	97.0	45.1	71.9
245	Lynchburg	97.1	57.3	77.9
246	Grundy	96.5	43.1	70.8
WASHINGTON				
980-981,987	Seattle	105.7	103.4	104.6
982	Everett	106.0	98.4	102.3
983-984	Tacoma	105.6	101.0	103.4
985	Olympia	105.5	100.9	103.3
986	Vancouver	108.0	97.4	102.9
988	Wenatchee	106.8	90.9	99.1
989	Yakima	106.0	94.2	100.3
990-992	Spokane	108.4	90.1	99.5
993	Richland	108.5	91.3	100.2
994	Clarkston	107.7	86.7	97.6
WEST VIRGINIA				
247-248	Bluefield	95.2	75.4	85.6
249	Lewisburg	96.7	81.8	89.5
250-253	Charleston	97.7	88.7	93.4
254	Martinsburg	96.7	58.0	78.0
255-257	Huntington	97.9	93.0	95.5
258-259	Beckley	94.9	87.2	91.2
260	Wheeling	97.8	90.7	94.4
261	Parkersburg	96.7	90.2	93.6
262	Buckhannon	96.6	88.6	92.7
263-264	Clarksburg	97.0	88.3	92.8
265	Morgantown	97.2	89.5	93.5
266	Gassaway	96.3	89.3	92.9
267	Romney	96.5	84.9	90.9
268	Petersburg	96.4	85.6	91.2
WISCONSIN				
530,532	Milwaukee	99.2	103.3	101.2
531	Kenosha	99.5	100.0	99.7
534	Racine	98.6	100.4	99.5
535	Beloit	98.5	95.4	97.0
537	Madison	98.6	100.4	99.5
538	Lancaster	96.7	82.9	90.0
539	Portage	95.1	91.1	93.2
540	New Richmond	95.9	87.9	92.1

STATE/ZIP	CITY	MAT.	INST.	TOTAL
WISCONSIN (CONT'D)				
541-543	Green Bay	99.6	94.0	96.9
544	Wausau	95.3	89.0	92.2
545	Rhinelander	98.4	85.1	92.0
546	La Crosse	95.9	93.8	94.8
547	Eau Claire	97.8	93.3	95.6
548	Superior	95.8	92.3	94.1
549	Oshkosh	95.8	86.2	91.2
WYOMING				
820	Cheyenne	100.6	64.9	83.4
821	Yellowstone Nat'l Park	100.0	58.6	80.0
822	Wheatland	101.7	56.2	79.8
823	Rawlins	103.3	53.4	79.2
824	Worland	100.8	53.6	78.0
825	Riverton	102.1	56.8	80.2
826	Casper	100.4	65.7	83.7
827	Newcastle	100.6	53.4	77.9
828	Sheridan	101.7	62.7	82.9
829-831	Rock Springs	105.0	53.6	80.2
CANADIAN FACTORS (reflect Canadian currency)				
ALBERTA				
	Calgary	110.3	85.9	98.5
	Edmonton	110.2	85.9	98.5
BRITISH COLUMBIA				
	Vancouver	110.5	105.7	108.2
	Victoria	113.0	102.4	107.9
MANITOBA				
	Winnipeg	111.0	87.1	99.5
NEW BRUNSWICK				
	Moncton	108.8	75.8	92.9
	Saint John	110.1	81.4	96.2
NEWFOUNDLAND				
	St. John's	114.7	75.0	95.6
NOVA SCOTIA				
	Halifax	109.8	83.3	97.0
ONTARIO				
	Barrie	115.3	102.3	109.1
	Brantford	113.2	108.4	110.9
	Cornwall	113.5	103.5	108.7
	Hamilton	113.4	107.3	110.5
	Kingston	113.5	103.2	108.5
	Kitchener	107.1	101.6	104.5
	London	112.4	104.0	108.3
	North Bay	113.2	101.2	107.4
	Oshawa	113.3	104.7	109.2
	Ottawa	113.6	104.2	109.1
	Owen Sound	115.4	100.8	108.4
	Peterborough	113.2	103.2	108.4
	Sarnia	112.3	109.2	110.8
	St. Catharines	106.5	101.5	104.1
	Sudbury	106.4	101.2	103.9
	Thunder Bay	108.1	101.4	104.9
	Toronto	113.4	111.9	112.7
	Windsor	106.6	104.6	105.6
PRINCE EDWARD ISLAND				
	Charlottetown	112.2	70.4	92.0
QUEBEC				
	Chicoutimi	109.0	97.4	103.4
	Montreal	110.5	97.5	104.2
	Quebec	111.0	97.7	104.6
SASKATCHEWAN				
	Regina	107.5	80.0	94.2
	Saskatoon	107.3	79.8	94.0

Abbreviations

A	Area Square Feet; Ampere	Cab.	Cabinet	d.f.u.	Drainage Fixture Units
ABS	Acrylonitrile Butadiene Stryrene; Asbestos Bonded Steel	Cair.	Air Tool Laborer	D.H.	Double Hung
A.C.	Alternating Current; Air-Conditioning; Asbestos Cement; Plywood Grade A & C	Calc	Calculated	DHW	Domestic Hot Water
		Cap.	Capacity	Diag.	Diagonal
		Carp.	Carpenter	Diam.	Diameter
		C.B.	Circuit Breaker	Distrib.	Distribution
A.C.I.	American Concrete Institute	C.C.A.	Chromate Copper Arsenate	Dk.	Deck
AD	Plywood, Grade A & D	C.C.F.	Hundred Cubic Feet	D.L.	Dead Load; Diesel
Addit.	Additional	cd	Candela	DLH	Deep Long Span Bar Joist
Adj.	Adjustable	cd/sf	Candela per Square Foot	Do.	Ditto
af	Audio-frequency	CD	Grade of Plywood Face & Back	Dp.	Depth
A.G.A.	American Gas Association	CDX	Plywood, Grade C & D, exterior glue	D.P.S.T.	Double Pole, Single Throw
Agg.	Aggregate			Dr.	Driver
A.H.	Ampere Hours	Cefi.	Cement Finisher	Drink.	Drinking
A hr.	Ampere-hour	Cem.	Cement	D.S.	Double Strength
A.H.U.	Air Handling Unit	CF	Hundred Feet	D.S.A.	Double Strength A Grade
A.I.A.	American Institute of Architects	C.F.	Cubic Feet	D.S.B.	Double Strength B Grade
AIC	Ampere Interrupting Capacity	CFM	Cubic Feet per Minute	Dty.	Duty
Allow.	Allowance	c.g.	Center of Gravity	DWV	Drain Waste Vent
alt.	Altitude	CHW	Chilled Water; Commercial Hot Water	DX	Deluxe White, Direct Expansion
Alum.	Aluminum			dyn	Dyne
a.m.	Ante Meridiem	C.I.	Cast Iron	e	Eccentricity
Amp.	Ampere	C.I.P.	Cast in Place	E	Equipment Only; East
Anod.	Anodized	Circ.	Circuit	Ea.	Each
Approx.	Approximate	C.L.	Carload Lot	E.B.	Encased Burial
Apt.	Apartment	Clab.	Common Laborer	Econ.	Economy
Asb.	Asbestos	C.L.F.	Hundred Linear Feet	EDP	Electronic Data Processing
A.S.B.C.	American Standard Building Code	CLF	Current Limiting Fuse	EIFS	Exterior Insulation Finish System
Asbe.	Asbestos Worker	CLP	Cross Linked Polyethylene	E.D.R.	Equiv. Direct Radiation
A.S.H.R.A.E.	American Society of Heating, Refrig. & AC Engineers	cm	Centimeter	Eq.	Equation
		CMP	Corr. Metal Pipe	Elec.	Electrician; Electrical
		C.M.U.	Concrete Masonry Unit	Elev.	Elevator; Elevating
A.S.M.E.	American Society of Mechanical Engineers	CN	Change Notice	EMT	Electrical Metallic Conduit; Thin Wall Conduit
		Col.	Column		
A.S.T.M.	American Society for Testing and Materials	CO_2	Carbon Dioxide	Eng.	Engine, Engineered
		Comb.	Combination	EPDM	Ethylene Propylene Diene Monomer
Attchmt.	Attachment	Compr.	Compressor		
Avg.	Average	Conc.	Concrete	EPS	Expanded Polystyrene
A.W.G.	American Wire Gauge	Cont.	Continuous; Continued	Eqhv.	Equip. Oper., Heavy
AWWA	American Water Works Assoc.	Corr.	Corrugated	Eqlt.	Equip. Oper., Light
Bbl.	Barrel	Cos	Cosine	Eqmd.	Equip. Oper., Medium
B. & B.	Grade B and Better; Balled & Burlapped	Cot	Cotangent	Eqmm.	Equip. Oper., Master Mechanic
		Cov.	Cover	Eqol.	Equip. Oper., Oilers
B. & S.	Bell and Spigot	C/P	Cedar on Paneling	Equip.	Equipment
B. & W.	Black and White	CPA	Control Point Adjustment	ERW	Electric Resistance Welded
b.c.c.	Body-centered Cubic	Cplg.	Coupling	E.S.	Energy Saver
B.C.Y.	Bank Cubic Yards	C.P.M.	Critical Path Method	Est.	Estimated
BE	Bevel End	CPVC	Chlorinated Polyvinyl Chloride	esu	Electrostatic Units
B.F.	Board Feet	C.Pr.	Hundred Pair	E.W.	Each Way
Bg. cem.	Bag of Cement	CRC	Cold Rolled Channel	EWT	Entering Water Temperature
BHP	Boiler Horsepower; Brake Horsepower	Creos.	Creosote	Excav.	Excavation
		Crpt.	Carpet & Linoleum Layer	Exp.	Expansion, Exposure
B.I.	Black Iron	CRT	Cathode-ray Tube	Ext.	Exterior
Bit.; Bitum.	Bituminous	CS	Carbon Steel, Constant Shear Bar Joist	Extru.	Extrusion
Bk.	Backed			f.	Fiber stress
Bkrs.	Breakers	Csc	Cosecant	F	Fahrenheit; Female; Fill
Bldg.	Building	C.S.F.	Hundred Square Feet	Fab.	Fabricated
Blk.	Block	CSI	Construction Specifications Institute	FBGS	Fiberglass
Bm.	Beam			F.C.	Footcandles
Boil.	Boilermaker	C.T.	Current Transformer	f.c.c.	Face-centered Cubic
B.P.M.	Blows per Minute	CTS	Copper Tube Size	f'c.	Compressive Stress in Concrete; Extreme Compressive Stress
BR	Bedroom	Cu	Copper, Cubic		
Brg.	Bearing	Cu. Ft.	Cubic Foot	F.E.	Front End
Brhe.	Bricklayer Helper	cw	Continuous Wave	FEP	Fluorinated Ethylene Propylene (Teflon)
Bric.	Bricklayer	C.W.	Cool White; Cold Water		
Brk.	Brick	Cwt.	100 Pounds	F.G.	Flat Grain
Brng.	Bearing	C.W.X.	Cool White Deluxe	F.H.A.	Federal Housing Administration
Brs.	Brass	C.Y.	Cubic Yard (27 cubic feet)	Fig.	Figure
Brz.	Bronze	C.Y./Hr.	Cubic Yard per Hour	Fin.	Finished
Bsn.	Basin	Cyl.	Cylinder	Fixt.	Fixture
Btr.	Better	d	Penny (nail size)	Fl. Oz.	Fluid Ounces
BTU	British Thermal Unit	D	Deep; Depth; Discharge	Flr.	Floor
BTUH	BTU per Hour	Dis.;Disch.	Discharge	F.M.	Frequency Modulation; Factory Mutual
B.U.R.	Built-up Roofing	Db.	Decibel		
BX	Interlocked Armored Cable	Dbl.	Double	Fmg.	Framing
c	Conductivity, Copper Sweat	DC	Direct Current	Fndtn.	Foundation
C	Hundred; Centigrade	DDC	Direct Digital Control	Fori.	Foreman, Inside
C/C	Center to Center, Cedar on Cedar	Demob.	Demobilization	Foro.	Foreman, Outside

Abbreviations

Fount.	Fountain	J.I.C.	Joint Industrial Council	MD	Medium Duty
FPM	Feet per Minute	K	Thousand; Thousand Pounds;	M.D.O.	Medium Density Overlaid
FPT	Female Pipe Thread		Heavy Wall Copper Tubing	Med.	Medium
Fr.	Frame	K.A.H.	Thousand Amp. Hours	MF	Thousand Feet
F.R.	Fire Rating	KCMIL	Thousand Circular Mils	M.F.B.M.	Thousand Feet Board Measure
FRK	Foil Reinforced Kraft	KD	Knock Down	Mfg.	Manufacturing
FRP	Fiberglass Reinforced Plastic	K.D.A.T.	Kiln Dried After Treatment	Mfrs.	Manufacturers
FS	Forged Steel	kg	Kilogram	mg	Milligram
FSC	Cast Body; Cast Switch Box	kG	Kilogauss	MGD	Million Gallons per Day
Ft.	Foot; Feet	kgf	Kilogram Force	MGPH	Thousand Gallons per Hour
Ftng.	Fitting	kHz	Kilohertz	MH, M.H.	Manhole; Metal Halide; Man-Hour
Ftg.	Footing	Kip.	1000 Pounds	MHz	Megahertz
Ft. Lb.	Foot Pound	KJ	Kiljoule	Mi.	Mile
Furn.	Furniture	K.L.	Effective Length Factor	MI	Malleable Iron; Mineral Insulated
FVNR	Full Voltage Non-Reversing	K.L.F.	Kips per Linear Foot	mm	Millimeter
FXM	Female by Male	Km	Kilometer	Mill.	Millwright
Fy.	Minimum Yield Stress of Steel	K.S.F.	Kips per Square Foot	Min., min.	Minimum, minute
g	Gram	K.S.I.	Kips per Square Inch	Misc.	Miscellaneous
G	Gauss	kV	Kilovolt	ml	Milliliter
Ga.	Gauge	kVA	Kilovolt Ampere	M.L.F.	Thousand Linear Feet
Gal.	Gallon	K.V.A.R.	Kilovar (Reactance)	Mo.	Month
Gal./Min.	Gallon per Minute	KW	Kilowatt	Mobil.	Mobilization
Galv.	Galvanized	KWh	Kilowatt-hour	Mog.	Mogul Base
Gen.	General	L	Labor Only; Length; Long;	MPH	Miles per Hour
G.F.I.	Ground Fault Interrupter		Medium Wall Copper Tubing	MPT	Male Pipe Thread
Glaz.	Glazier	Lab.	Labor	MRT	Mile Round Trip
GPD	Gallons per Day	lat	Latitude	ms	Millisecond
GPH	Gallons per Hour	Lath.	Lather	M.S.F.	Thousand Square Feet
GPM	Gallons per Minute	Lav.	Lavatory	Mstz.	Mosaic & Terrazzo Worker
GR	Grade	lb.; #	Pound	M.S.Y.	Thousand Square Yards
Gran.	Granular	L.B.	Load Bearing; L Conduit Body	Mtd.	Mounted
Grnd.	Ground	L. & E.	Labor & Equipment	Mthe.	Mosaic & Terrazzo Helper
H	High; High Strength Bar Joist;	lb./hr.	Pounds per Hour	Mtng.	Mounting
	Henry	lb./L.F.	Pounds per Linear Foot	Mult.	Multi; Multiply
H.C.	High Capacity	lbf/sq.in.	Pound-force per Square Inch	M.V.A.	Million Volt Amperes
H.D.	Heavy Duty; High Density	L.C.L.	Less than Carload Lot	M.V.A.R.	Million Volt Amperes Reactance
H.D.O.	High Density Overlaid	Ld.	Load	MV	Megavolt
Hdr.	Header	LE	Lead Equivalent	MW	Megawatt
Hdwe.	Hardware	LED	Light Emitting Diode	MXM	Male by Male
Help.	Helpers Average	L.F.	Linear Foot	MYD	Thousand Yards
HEPA	High Efficiency Particulate Air	Lg.	Long; Length; Large	N	Natural; North
	Filter	L & H	Light and Heat	nA	Nanoampere
Hg	Mercury	LH	Long Span Bar Joist, Labor Hours	NA	Not Available; Not Applicable
HIC	High Interrupting Capacity	L.L.	Live Load	N.B.C.	National Building Code
HM	Hollow Metal	L.L.D.	Lamp Lumen Depreciation	NC	Normally Closed
H.O.	High Output	L-O-L	Lateralolet	N.E.M.A.	National Electrical Manufacturers
Horiz.	Horizontal	lm	Lumen		Assoc.
H.P.	Horsepower; High Pressure	lm/sf	Lumen per Square Foot	NEHB	Bolted Circuit Breaker to 600V.
H.P.F.	High Power Factor	lm/W	Lumen per Watt	N.L.B.	Non-Load-Bearing
Hr.	Hour	L.O.A.	Length Over All	NM	Non-Metallic Cable
Hrs./Day	Hours per Day	log	Logarithm	nm	Nanometer
HSC	High Short Circuit	L.P.	Liquefied Petroleum; Low Pressure	No.	Number
Ht.	Height	L.P.F.	Low Power Factor	NO	Normally Open
Htg.	Heating	LR	Long Radius	N.O.C.	Not Otherwise Classified
Htrs.	Heaters	L.S.	Lump Sum	Nose.	Nosing
HVAC	Heating, Ventilation & Air-	Lt.	Light	N.P.T.	National Pipe Thread
	Conditioning	Lt. Ga.	Light Gauge	NQOD	Combination Plug-on/Bolt on
Hvy.	Heavy	L.T.L.	Less than Truckload Lot		Circuit Breaker to 240V.
HW	Hot Water	Lt. Wt.	Lightweight	N.R.C.	Noise Reduction Coefficient
Hyd.;Hydr.	Hydraulic	L.V.	Low Voltage	N.R.S.	Non Rising Stem
Hz.	Hertz (cycles)	M	Thousand; Material; Male;	ns	Nanosecond
I.	Moment of Inertia		Light Wall Copper Tubing	nW	Nanowatt
I.C.	Interrupting Capacity	m/hr; M.H.	Man-hour	OB	Opposing Blade
ID	Inside Diameter	mA	Milliampere	OC	On Center
I.D.	Inside Dimension; Identification	Mach.	Machine	OD	Outside Diameter
I.F.	Inside Frosted	Mag. Str.	Magnetic Starter	O.D.	Outside Dimension
I.M.C.	Intermediate Metal Conduit	Maint.	Maintenance	ODS	Overhead Distribution System
In.	Inch	Marb.	Marble Setter	O.G.	Ogee
Incan.	Incandescent	Mat; Mat'l.	Material	O.H.	Overhead
Incl.	Included; Including	Max.	Maximum	O & P	Overhead and Profit
Int.	Interior	MBF	Thousand Board Feet	Oper.	Operator
Inst.	Installation	MBH	Thousand BTU's per hr.	Opng.	Opening
Insul.	Insulation/Insulated	MC	Metal Clad Cable	Orna.	Ornamental
I.P.	Iron Pipe	M.C.F.	Thousand Cubic Feet	OSB	Oriented Strand Board
I.P.S.	Iron Pipe Size	M.C.F.M.	Thousand Cubic Feet per Minute	O. S. & Y.	Outside Screw and Yoke
I.P.T.	Iron Pipe Threaded	M.C.M.	Thousand Circular Mils	Ovhd.	Overhead
I.W.	Indirect Waste	M.C.P.	Motor Circuit Protector	OWG	Oil, Water or Gas
J	Joule			Oz.	Ounce

Abbreviations

P.	Pole; Applied Load; Projection	SCFM	Standard Cubic Feet per Minute	T.L.	Truckload
p.	Page	Scaf.	Scaffold	T.M.	Track Mounted
Pape.	Paperhanger	Sch.; Sched.	Schedule	Tot.	Total
P.A.P.R.	Powered Air Purifying Respirator	S.C.R.	Modular Brick	T-O-L	Threadolet
PAR	Weatherproof Reflector	S.D.	Sound Deadening	T.S.	Trigger Start
Pc., Pcs.	Piece, Pieces	S.D.R.	Standard Dimension Ratio	Tr.	Trade
P.C.	Portland Cement; Power Connector	S.E.	Surfaced Edge	Transf.	Transformer
P.C.F.	Pounds per Cubic Foot	Sel.	Select	Trhv.	Truck Driver, Heavy
P.C.M.	Phase Contract Microscopy	S.E.R.	Service Entrance Cable	Trlr	Trailer
P.E.	Professional Engineer; Porcelain Enamel; Polyethylene; Plain End	S.E.U.	Service Entrance Cable	Trlt.	Truck Driver, Light
		S.F.	Square Foot	TV	Television
		S.F.C.A.	Square Foot Contact Area	T.W.	Thermoplastic Water Resistant Wire
Perf.	Perforated	S.F.G.	Square Foot of Ground		
Ph.	Phase	S.F. Hor.	Square Foot Horizontal	UCI	Uniform Construction Index
P.I.	Pressure Injected	S.F.R.	Square Feet of Radiation	UF	Underground Feeder
Pile.	Pile Driver	S.F. Shlf.	Square Foot of Shelf	UGND	Underground Feeder
Pkg.	Package	S4S	Surface 4 Sides	U.H.F.	Ultra High Frequency
Pl.	Plate	Shee.	Sheet Metal Worker	U.L.	Underwriters Laboratory
Plah.	Plasterer Helper	Sin.	Sine	Unfin.	Unfinished
Plas.	Plasterer	Skwk.	Skilled Worker	URD	Underground Residential Distribution
Pluh.	Plumbers Helper	SL	Saran Lined		
Plum.	Plumber	S.L.	Slimline	US	United States
Ply.	Plywood	Sldr.	Solder	USP	United States Primed
p.m.	Post Meridiem	SLH	Super Long Span Bar Joist	UTP	Unshielded Twisted Pair
Pntd.	Painted	S.N.	Solid Neutral	V	Volt
Pord.	Painter, Ordinary	S-O-L	Socketolet	V.A.	Volt Amperes
pp	Pages	S.P.	Static Pressure; Single Pole; Self-Propelled	V.C.T.	Vinyl Composition Tile
PP; PPL	Polypropylene			VAV	Variable Air Volume
P.P.M.	Parts per Million	Spri.	Sprinkler Installer	VC	Veneer Core
Pr.	Pair	Sq.	Square; 100 Square Feet	Vent.	Ventilation
P.E.S.B.	Pre-engineered Steel Building	S.P.D.T.	Single Pole, Double Throw	Vert.	Vertical
Prefab.	Prefabricated	SPF	Spruce Pine Fir	V.F.	Vinyl Faced
Prefin.	Prefinished	S.P.S.T.	Single Pole, Single Throw	V.G.	Vertical Grain
Prop.	Propelled	SPT	Standard Pipe Thread	V.H.F.	Very High Frequency
PSF; psf	Pounds per Square Foot	Sq. Hd.	Square Head	VHO	Very High Output
PSI; psi	Pounds per Square Inch	Sq. In.	Square Inch	Vib.	Vibrating
PSIG	Pounds per Square Inch Gauge	S.S.	Single Strength; Stainless Steel	V.L.F.	Vertical Linear Foot
PSP	Plastic Sewer Pipe	S.S.B.	Single Strength B Grade	Vol.	Volume
Pspr.	Painter, Spray	sst	Stainless Steel	VRP	Vinyl Reinforced Polyester
Psst.	Painter, Structural Steel	Sswk.	Structural Steel Worker	W	Wire; Watt; Wide; West
P.T.	Potential Transformer	Sswl.	Structural Steel Welder	w/	With
P. & T.	Pressure & Temperature	St.; Stl.	Steel	W.C.	Water Column; Water Closet
Ptd.	Painted	S.T.C.	Sound Transmission Coefficient	W.F.	Wide Flange
Ptns.	Partitions	Std.	Standard	W.G.	Water Gauge
Pu	Ultimate Load	STK	Select Tight Knot	Wldg.	Welding
PVC	Polyvinyl Chloride	STP	Standard Temperature & Pressure	W. Mile	Wire Mile
Pvmt.	Pavement	Stpi.	Steamfitter, Pipefitter	W-O-L	Weldolet
Pwr.	Power	Str.	Strength; Starter; Straight	W.R.	Water Resistant
Q	Quantity Heat Flow	Strd.	Stranded	Wrck.	Wrecker
Quan.; Qty.	Quantity	Struct.	Structural	W.S.P.	Water, Steam, Petroleum
Q.C.	Quick Coupling	Sty.	Story	WT., Wt.	Weight
r	Radius of Gyration	Subj.	Subject	WWF	Welded Wire Fabric
R	Resistance	Subs.	Subcontractors	XFER	Transfer
R.C.P.	Reinforced Concrete Pipe	Surf.	Surface	XFMR	Transformer
Rect.	Rectangle	Sw.	Switch	XHD	Extra Heavy Duty
Reg.	Regular	Swbd.	Switchboard	XHHW; XLPE	Cross-Linked Polyethylene Wire Insulation
Reinf.	Reinforced	S.Y.	Square Yard		
Req'd.	Required	Syn.	Synthetic	XLP	Cross-linked Polyethylene
Res.	Resistant	S.Y.P.	Southern Yellow Pine	Y	Wye
Resi.	Residential	Sys.	System	yd	Yard
Rgh.	Rough	t.	Thickness	yr	Year
RGS	Rigid Galvanized Steel	T	Temperature; Ton	Δ	Delta
R.H.W.	Rubber, Heat & Water Resistant; Residential Hot Water	Tan	Tangent	%	Percent
		T.C.	Terra Cotta	~	Approximately
rms	Root Mean Square	T & C	Threaded and Coupled	∅	Phase
Rnd.	Round	T.D.	Temperature Difference	@	At
Rodm.	Rodman	T.E.M.	Transmission Electron Microscopy	#	Pound; Number
Rofc.	Roofer, Composition	TFE	Tetrafluoroethylene (Teflon)	<	Less Than
Rofp.	Roofer, Precast	T. & G.	Tongue & Groove; Tar & Gravel	>	Greater Than
Rohe.	Roofer Helpers (Composition)				
Rots.	Roofer, Tile & Slate	Th.; Thk.	Thick		
R.O.W.	Right of Way	Thn.	Thin		
RPM	Revolutions per Minute	Thrded	Threaded		
R.R.	Direct Burial Feeder Conduit	Tilf.	Tile Layer, Floor		
R.S.	Rapid Start	Tilh.	Tile Layer, Helper		
Rsr	Riser	THHN	Nylon Jacketed Wire		
RT	Round Trip	THW.	Insulated Strand Wire		
S.	Suction; Single Entrance; South	THWN	Nylon Jacketed Wire		

Index

A

Abandon catch basin	25
Abatement asbestos	39
ABC extinguisher	245
Abrasive aggregate	76
floor tile	217
stair tread concrete	81
tread	217
ABS DWV pipe	294
Absorption cold generator	318
A/C coils furnace	311
fan coil system	459, 460
rooftop DX	457
rooftop DXVAV	457
self contained	455, 456
self contained VAV	455, 456
Accelerator set	77
Access control	272
door	181
door basement	83
door duct	325
door fire rated	181
door floor	185
door metal	182
door roof	167
door stainless steel	182
floor	242
road and parking area	13
security	272
Accessories bath	249
bathroom	249
door	203
door and window	203
drywall	215
duct	325
roof	167
Accessory boiler	309
drainage	163
fireplace	243
formwork	70
masonry	86
Accordion door	180
partitions	248
Acid proof floor	222
Acoustic ceiling board	219
Acoustical ceiling	219
door	186, 248
enclosure	270
folding partition	248
insulation	220
metal deck	107
panel	220, 248
partition	248
sealant	169, 214
space units	220
suspension system	210
treatment	219
underlayment	220
wallboard	214
window wall	207
Acrylic ceiling	219
latex	77
rubber roofing	160
sign	244
wall coating	225
wallcovering	233
wood block	221
Adhesive	118
cement	223
EPDM	144
neoprene	144
PVC	144
roof	158
wallpaper	233
Adjustable astragal	202
frequency drives	336
Admixture cement	76
concrete	77
water reducing	77
Aerial bucket	19
lift	17
Aggregate abrasive	76
coating	212
spreader	15
stone	65
Air cleaner electronic	323
compressor	17
compressor sprinkler system	307
conditioner direct expansion	318
conditioner fan coil	318
conditioner gas heat	319
conditioner receptacle	347
conditioner removal	33
conditioner rooftop	319
conditioner self-contained	319
conditioner window	320
conditioner wiring	349
conditioning	318
conditioning computer	318
conditioning fan	322
conditioning ventilating	319, 320, 322, 323, 325, 326
cooled condensing unit	320
entraining agent	77
extractor	325
filter	323
filter roll type	323
filtration	39
handler heater	311
handler modular	311
handling fan	322
hose	17
make-up unit	312
register	325
return grille	324
sampling	39
spade	17
supply register	325
tool	17
tube system	280
vent roof	168
Air-compressor mobilization	49
Airless sprayer	39
Alarm burglar	343
exit control	343
fire	343
residential	348
sprinkler	343
water motor	307
Alteration fee	6
Aluminum astragal	202
bench	63
ceiling tile	219
column	105, 140
conduit	472
coping	89, 90
cross	252
diffuser perforated	324
door	184, 186-188
door frame	187
downspout	162
drip edge	163
ductwork	321
edging	53, 54
entrance	187
expansion joint	114, 166
fence	60
flashing	163, 288
foil	145, 146
gravel stop	167
grille	324
gutter	165
ladder	112
light pole	466
louver	242
mansard	165
nail	118
reglet	165
roof	155
sash	189
service entrance cable	333
sheet metal	162
shingle	152
shore	74
siding	156
siding paint	227
sliding door	182
stair	112
stair tread	82
steeple	252
storefront	188
storm door	186
tile	154, 217
transom	187
tube frame	206
tubular	106
weatherstrip	202
window	189, 190, 387
window demolition	37
wire	334
Anchor bolt	86, 103
brick	87
buck	87
channel slot	88
chemical	102
expansion	102
framing	118
hollow wall	103
joist	119
lead screw	102
machine	103
masonry	87
nailing	103
partition	88
rafter	119
rigid	88
sill	119
steel	88
stone	88
wall	102
wedge	103
Angle framing	105
Antenna system	345
T.V.	345
Apartment call system	345
Appliance	256
compactor	484
dishwasher	484
garbage disposer	484
plumbing	306
range	483
range hood	484
refrigerator	484
residential	254, 256, 349
water	305
Appurtenances	62
Apron wood	130
Arch laminated	129
radial	129
Architectural equipment	256
fee	6, 500
panel	127
precast	83
woodwork	136
Area clean-up	41
Armored cable	332
Arrow	55
Asbestos abatement	39
demolition	40
disposal	41
felt	158
removal	39-41
removal process	512
Ash receiver	250
Ashlar stone	95
Asphalt base sheet	158
block	52
block floor	52
coating	145
curb	53
cutting	36
expansion joint	70
felt	158, 159
flashing	163
flood coat	158
paper	145
paver	18
primer	161, 223
rubberized	55
sheathing	126
shingle	152
sidewalk	52
Asphaltic binder	51
concrete	51
emulsion	54
pavement	51
paving	519
wearing course	51
Astragal adjustable	202
aluminum	202
magnetic	202
molding	131
one piece	202
overlapping	202
rubber	202
split	202
steel	202
Athletic equipment	261, 262
room	270
Atomizer water	39
Attic stair	260
ventilation fan	322
Auger hole	24
Auto park drain	285
Automatic flush	285
opener	201
timed thermostat	323
Automotive equipment	255
lift	255
Awning	246
canvas	246
window	192

B

Backer rod	70, 169
Backerboard	144, 217
Backfill	43, 47
compaction	515
dozer	44
planting pit	65
structural	44
trench	46
Backflow preventer	284
preventer solar	313
Backhoe	45
excavation	46
rental	15
Backsplash countertop	132
Backstop basketball	262
electric	262
Backup block	91

Index

Baffle roof ... 168
Bag disposable ... 39
　glove ... 41
Baked enamel door ... 172
　enamel frame ... 174
Balanced door ... 188
Balcony fire escape ... 112
Bale hay ... 49
Ball check valve ... 301
　valve ... 301
　wrecking ... 19
Ballast fixture ... 341
Baluster ... 140
Balustrade painting ... 232
Band molding ... 130
Bank counter ... 252
　equipment ... 252
　window ... 252
Bankrun gravel ... 44
Baptistry ... 252
Bar bell ... 261
　front ... 256
　grab ... 249
　joist ... 106, 107
　panic ... 200
　restaurant ... 266
　touch ... 200
　towel ... 250
　tub ... 249
　Zee ... 216
Barbed wire fence ... 60
Barber equipment ... 253
Barometric damper ... 309
Barricade ... 13, 62
Barrier parking ... 62
　separation ... 40
　waterstop ... 70
　X-ray ... 271
Barriers and enclosures ... 13
Base cabinet ... 136, 138
　carpet ... 224
　column ... 114, 119
　course ... 48
　cove ... 222
　gravel ... 48
　light ... 74
　masonry ... 93
　molding ... 130
　quarry tile ... 217
　resilient ... 222
　road ... 48
　sheet ... 158, 159
　sign ... 74
　sink ... 137
　stone ... 48, 95
　terrazzo ... 218
　vanity ... 139
　wood ... 130, 141
Baseball scoreboard ... 262
Baseboard demolition ... 34
　heat ... 313
　heat electric ... 344
　register ... 325
Basement stair ... 83
Basketball backstop ... 262
　scoreboard ... 262
Bath accessories ... 249
　communal ... 302
　steam ... 270
　whirlpool ... 301
Bathroom ... 301
　accessories ... 249
　exhaust fan ... 322
　faucet ... 285
　fixture ... 301, 302, 304
　heater & fan ... 322

Bathtub ... 301
　bar ... 249
　removal ... 35
Batt insulation ... 147, 148
Battery light ... 340
Bead blast demo ... 31
　casing ... 215
　corner ... 215
　parting ... 132
Beam & girder framing ... 120
　and girder formwork ... 70
　bond ... 86
　bondcrete ... 212
　box ... 127
　ceiling ... 134
　concrete ... 78, 80
　drywall ... 213
　fireproofing ... 150
　grade ... 81
　hanger ... 118
　laminated ... 129
　mantel ... 134
　plaster ... 212
　precast ... 83
　reinforcing ... 75
　removal ... 31
　spandrel ... 70
　steel ... 106
　wood ... 120, 128
Bed molding ... 130
Bedding brick ... 53
　pipe ... 56
Bedpan cleanser ... 286
Beech tread ... 140
Belgian block ... 53
Bell & spigot pipe ... 289
　bar ... 261
Bench aluminum ... 63
　fiberglass ... 62
　folding ... 262
　greenhouse ... 272
　park ... 62
　players ... 63
　wood ... 63
　work ... 263
Bend EMT field ... 328
Berm pavement ... 53
　road ... 53
Bevel siding ... 157
Bicycle trainer ... 261, 262
Bi-fold door ... 173, 179
Binder asphaltic ... 51
Bi-passing closet door ... 179
Birch door ... 179, 180
　molding ... 131
　paneling ... 133
　stair ... 140
　wood frame ... 175
Bit drill ... 25
Bituminous block ... 52
　coating ... 145
　dampproofing ... 145
　expansion joint ... 70
　paver ... 18
　paving ... 519
Blank leaf door ... 178
Blanket insulation ... 147, 314
　sound attenuation ... 220
Blast demo bead ... 31
　floor shot ... 31
Blasting water ... 97
Bleacher telescoping ... 262
Blind ... 266
　exterior ... 135
　window ... 266
Block asphalt ... 52

asphalt floor ... 52
backup ... 91
belgian ... 53
bituminous ... 52
Block, brick and mortar ... 537
Block concrete ... 91-94
　concrete bond beam ... 93
　concrete exterior ... 93
　decorative concrete ... 92
　filler ... 233
　floor ... 221
　glass ... 95
　glazed ... 92
　grooved ... 91
　insulation ... 93
　interlocking ... 92
　lightweight ... 92
　lintel ... 93
　partition ... 92
　profile ... 92
　reflective ... 95
　removal ... 38
　slump ... 92
　split rib ... 92
　wall ... 537
　wall removal ... 38
Blocking carpentry ... 119
　steel ... 119
　wood ... 119, 125
Blockout slab ... 73
Blower pneumatic tube ... 280
Blown in cellulose ... 145
　in fiberglass ... 146
　in insulation ... 145
Blueboard ... 212, 213
　partition ... 215
Bluegrass sod ... 65
Bluestone ... 95
　sill ... 91
　step ... 62
Board ... 337
　& batten fence ... 62
　& batten siding ... 157
　bulletin ... 244
　ceiling ... 219
　control ... 253
　directory ... 244
　dock ... 255
　gypsum ... 213
　insulation ... 147
　paneling ... 134
　sheathing ... 125
　valance ... 137
　verge ... 131
Boiler ... 307
　accessory ... 309
　demolition ... 33
　electric ... 307, 308
　electric steam ... 307
　gas fired ... 308
　gas/oil combination ... 309
　hot water ... 308, 309
　oil fired ... 308
　solid fuel ... 309
　steam ... 308, 309
　wood/coal oil fired ... 309
Bollard ... 105
Bollards pipe ... 62
Bolt anchor ... 86, 103
　expansion ... 102
　steel ... 118
　toggle ... 103
　wedge ... 103
Bolt-on circuit-breaker ... 338
Bond beam ... 86
　performance ... 507, 508

Bondcrete ... 212
Bonding agent ... 77
Bookcase ... 132, 138
Bookshelf ... 252
Boom lift ... 17
　truck ... 19
Booster fan ... 322
Booth painting ... 255
　restaurant ... 266
　telephone ... 249
Boring ... 24
　cased ... 24
　horizontal ... 47
　service ... 47
Borosilicate pipe ... 293
Borrow ... 44
Bottle storage ... 260
Bow window ... 192
Bowstring truss ... 129
Box ... 335
　beam ... 127
　distribution ... 59
　mail ... 247
　out ... 73
　out opening formwork ... 72
　pull ... 335
　stair ... 139
　storage ... 14
　termination ... 345
　vent ... 89
Boxes & wiring device ... 335
Brace cross ... 105
Bracing ... 104, 119
　let-in ... 104
Brass hinge ... 198
　pipe ... 288
　pipe fitting ... 288
Brazed connection ... 335
Break glass station ... 344
Breaker circuit ... 337
　vacuum ... 288
Brick ... 90, 425
　anchor ... 87
　bedding ... 53
　bedding mortar ... 52
Brick, block and mortar ... 537
Brick cart ... 17
　catch basin ... 58
　chimney simulated ... 243
　chimneys ... 535
　concrete ... 92
　demolition ... 31, 38
　economy ... 90
　edging ... 54
　engineer ... 90
　face ... 90
　floor ... 53, 222
　forklift ... 18
　masonry ... 89
　molding ... 131
　paving ... 52
　removal ... 25
　shelf ... 73
　sidewalk ... 53
　sill ... 91
　simulated ... 91
　step ... 62
　veneer ... 94
　veneer demolition ... 39
　vent box ... 89
　wall ... 379
Bridge cranes ... 280
　sidewalk ... 11
Bridging ... 120
Broiler ... 257
Bronze body strainer ... 317

611

Index

expansion joint 114
plaque 244
push-pull plate 200
valve 300
Broom cabinet 137
finish concrete 82
Brown coat 218
Brownstone 96
Bubbler 302
Buck anchor 87
rough 121
Bucket aerial 19
concrete 15
Buggy concrete 15, 81
Builder's risk insurance 501
Building demolition 26
directory 345
disposal 26
greenhouse 272
hardware 197
insulation 145
moving 43
paper 145
permit 8
portable 272
prefabricated 272
sprinkler 307
temporary 14
Built-up roof 158
Bulb incandescent 342
Bulk bank measure excavating ... 45
Bulkhead door 185
formwork 72, 73
Bulldozer 16, 44
Bulletin board 244
Bulletproof glass 205
Bumper dock 255, 256
door 197
rail 112
wall 197
Burglar alarm 343
alarm indicating panel 343
Burlap curing 79
rubbing 82
Burner gas conversion 309
gun type 309
oil 309
residential 309
Bush hammer 82
hammer concrete 82
Butterfly valve 301
Buttress formwork 73
Butyl caulking 170
expansion joint 166
flashing 164
waterproofing 144
BX cable 472

C

Cabinet base 136, 138
broom 137
casework 138
corner base 137
corner wall 137
current transformer 336
demolition 33, 495
door 138
electrical 335
electrical hinged 336
fire equipment 245
hardboard 136
hardware 138
hinge 139
hose rack 245
hotel 250
kitchen 136
laboratory 263
medicine 250
oven 137
shower 241
stain 230
standard wood base 483
storage 263
strip 345
transformer 336
Cabinet unit heater 450
Cabinet varnish 230
wall 137
Cable armored 332
electric 332, 334
jack 20
mineral insulated 332, 333
sheathed nonmetallic 333
sheathed romex 333
termination mineral insulated ... 333
tray 328
Cafe door 177
Caisson 50
concrete 50
foundation 50
Caissons 518
Calcium chloride 77
Call system apartment 345
Canopy 245
door 246
entrance 245
framing 105, 123
Cant roof 122
Canvas awning 246
Cap pile 73, 79, 81
post 119
service entrance 334
Capacitor 340
Capital column 71
Car bumper 112
Carbon black 77
dioxide extinguisher 245
Carpentry finish 130, 134, 136
rough 119
Carpet 224
base 224
cleaning 224
computer room 242
demolition 495
felt pad 224
floor 224
nylon 224
padding 224
removal 31
sheet 224
stair 224
tile 224
urethane pad 224
wool 224
Carrel 252
Carrier ceiling 210
channel 210
fixture 287
Cart brick 17
concrete 15, 81
Carving stone 96
Case display 254
refrigerated 254
work 138
Cased boring 24
evaporator coils 311
Casement window 189, 192, 193
Casework cabinet 138
custom 136
demolition 33
ground 124
painting 230
varnish 230
Cash register 254
Casing bead 215
door 216
wood 130
Cast in place concrete 78
in place pile 50
in place terrazzo 218
iron bench 63
iron casting 114
iron damper 243
iron drain 285
iron fitting 289
iron manhole cover 58
iron miscellaneous 114
iron pipe 289
iron pipe fitting 289, 297
iron radiator 314
iron stair 112
iron stair tread 82, 111
iron trap 287
trim lock 199
Casting 114
construction 114
Catch basin 58
basin brick 58
basin masonry 58
basin precast 58
basin removal 25
door 138
Catwalk 11
Caulking 169, 170
masonry 98
polyurethane 170
sealant 169
Cavity truss reinforcing 87
wall grout 86
wall insulation 146
Cedar closet 133
fence 61
paneling 134
post 141
roof deck 130
roof plank 127
shingle 153
siding 157
stair 139
Ceiling 427
acoustical 219
beam 134
board 219
board acoustic 219
board fiberglass 219
bondcrete 212
carrier 210
demolition 27, 495
diffuser 324
drill 102
drywall 213, 401
eggcrate 219
expansion joint 115
fan 322
finish price sheet 401, 427
framing 120
furring 124, 210
gypsum board 419
hatch 182
insulation 146
integrated 270
lath 211
luminous 219, 220, 342
molding 130
painting 232, 233
plaster 212, 375, 401
price sheet 401
register 325
stair 260
stressed skin 127
support 105
suspended 210, 213, 219
suspended acoustical 418
suspended plaster 417
suspension system 210
tile 219, 220, 376, 402
Cell prison 256
Cellar door 185
wine 260
Cellular concrete 78
deck concrete 83
fill 84
metal deck 107
Cellulose blown in 145
insulation 146
Cement adhesive 223
admixture 76
color 77
flashing 161
grout 48, 86
gunite 80
gypsum 86
liner 59, 60
masonry 86
masonry unit 91-94
mortar 217
Cementitious deck 84
waterproofing 144
Central vacuum 252
Centrifugal fan 322
Ceramic tile 216
tile countertop 133
tile demolition 31
tile floor 216
veneer 94
Certification welding 9
Chain hoist 20
hoist door 184
link fence 13, 60
link fence paint 227
saw 18
trencher 17
Chair barber 253
molding 131
movie 252, 253
rail demolition 34
restaurant 266
Chalkboard 240
freestanding 240
liquid chalk 240
wall hung 240
Chamber decontamination 40
echo 270
Channel carrier 210
frame 172
framing 105
furring 210, 216
siding 157
slot 88
slot anchor 88
slotted 105
Charges disposal 41
Check valve ball 301
Checkout counter 253
scanner 253
supermarket 253
Chemical anchor 102
cleaning masonry 97
dry extinguisher 245
toilet 19
Chiller water 320
Chime door 344

Index

Chimney	89
accessories	243
brick	89
demolition	38, 495
foundation	78
metal	242
screen	243
simulated brick	243
vent	316
vent fitting	316
China cabinet	136
Chipping hammer	17
Church equipment	252
pew	252
Chute linen	280
mail	246
refuse	280
rubbish	27
Chutes	280
C.I.P. concrete	76
Circline fixture	342
Circuit-breaker	337
bolt-on	338
Circular saw	19
Circulating pump	304
Cladding	156
sheet metal	166
Clamp water pipe ground	335
Clapboard painting	226
Clay fire	98
roofing tile	154
tile	154
tile coping	90
Clean tank	42
Cleaner steam	19
Cleaning masonry	97
rug	224
up	21
Cleanout door	243
floor	284
pipe	284
tee	284
Clean-up area	41
Climbing jack	20
Clip plywood	119
Clock timer	348
Closer concealed	201
door	201
electronic	202
floor	201
holder	202
Closet cedar	133
door	173, 179, 180
pole	131
rod	132
water	304
Clothes dryer commercial	254
CMU	91
Coal burning furnace	311
tar pitch	158, 161
Coat brown	218
glaze	232
hook	250
rack	138
scratch	218
tack	54
Coating aggregate	212
bituminous	145
flood	159
glazed	225
roof	161
rubber	145
silicone	145
special	225
spray	145
trowel	145
wall	225
water repellent	145
waterproofing	145
Coffee urn	257
Coil cooling	320
Coiling door	183
grille	183
Cold applied roofing	159
generator absorption	318
planing	54
recycling	54
roofing	159
storage door	183
storage room	270
Coldformed framing	108
Cold-formed joists	107
Collection box lobby	247
Collector solar energy system	312
Colonial door	179, 180
wood frame	175
Color concrete	77
Column	105
aluminum	105
base	114, 119
bondcrete	212
brick	89
capital	71
concrete	78, 80, 83
demolition	38
drywall	213
fireproof	150
formwork	71
lally	105
laminated wood	129
lath	211
pipe	105
plaster	212
precast	83
reinforcing	75
removal	31, 38
tie	88
wood	122, 128, 140
Columns formwork	71
Combination storm door	179, 180
Command dog	13
Commercial door	172, 178, 185
folding partition	248
gutting	32
water heater	306
Common brick	89
nail	118
Communal bath	302
Communicating lockset	198, 199
Compaction	44
backfill	515
soil	43
test Proctor	9
Compactor	256
earth	15
plate	45
residential	256
sheepsfoot	44
tamper	45
Compartments shower	241
toilet	240
Component sound system	344
sprinkler system	307
Components furnace	311
Composite door	172
insulation	149
joist	107
metal deck	107
rafter	122
Composition flooring	225
flooring removal	31
Compressive strength	8
Compressor air	17
reciprocating hermetic	320
Computer air conditioning	318
floor	242
room carpet	242
Concealed closer	201
Concrete	83, 526-530, 532
admixture	77
asphaltic	51
beam	78, 80
block	91-94
block back-up	91
block bond beam	93
block decorative	91, 92
block demolition	28
block exterior	93
block foundation	93
block grout	86
block wall	359, 378
brick	92
broom finish	82
bucket	15
buggy	81
bush hammer	82
caisson	50
cart	15, 81
cast in place	77, 78
cellular	78, 84
cellular deck	83
C.I.P.	76
color	77
column	78, 80
conveyer	15
coping	89
core	24
cost	530
curb	53
curing	52, 77, 79
cutout	28
cutting	37
cylinder	8
darby finish	82
demo	25
demolition	28, 31, 495
drill	24, 102, 329
elevated slab	80
finish	52, 82, 533
float	15
float finish	82
floor	77, 533
footing	79, 81
forms	521-524
formwork	70
foundation	79
furring	124
granolithic finish	82
grout	86
hand trowel finish	82
hardener	77
hole cutting	330
hole drilling	329
hydrodemolition	26
in place	532
insulation	84
integral finish	82
joist	78
lift slab	533
lightweight	78, 79, 84, 535
lintel	83
materials	529
mixer	15
monolithic finish	82
panel	367
patching	80
paver	18
paving	51
pier	78
pile	50
pipe	58, 520
pipe removal	26
placing	80, 531
plank	368
planter	63
precast	83
prestressed precast	534
protection	82
pump	15, 80
ready mix	77
rehabilitation	84
reinforcement	75
removal	25, 38
restoration	84
roof deck	83
sandblasting	82
saw	15, 36
scarify	31
sealer	77
septic tank	59
shingle	154
sidewalk	52
sill	91
slab	78, 81, 366
slabs X-ray	9
spreader	18
stair	79
stair tread	82
stamping	70
structural	76
topping	82
trowel	15
utility vault	56
vibrator	15
wall	79, 81, 358
wheeling	81
Condenser pad	324
Condensing unit air cooled	320
Conductive floor	222
Conductor	332
& grounding	332, 333
wire	334
Conductors	553
Conduit	328
& fitting flexible	331
electrical	328
in slab	328
in slab PVC	328
in trench electrical	329
in trench steel	329
intermediate	328
intermediate steel	328
rigid in slab	328
Cone traffic	13
Connection brazed	335
motor	331
standpipe	307
Connector flexible	284
joist	118
stud	104
timber	118
Construction aids	10
casting	114
management fee	6
temporary	9
time	6
tunnel	49
Contaminated soil	42
Contingencies	6
Continuous hinge	201
Contract closeout	21
Contractor equipment	15
overhead	10, 21
Control board	253

Index

component	323
crack	54
draft	309
expansion	114
joint	86
joint PVC	86
joint rubber	86
package firecycle	307
quality	8
system electronic	324
temporary	13
valve heating	324
Convection oven	259
Convector cover	132
Conveyor	15
system	280
Cooking equipment	256, 257
range	256
Cooler	270
beverage	257
Cooling coil	320
tower	320
towers fiberglass	321
towers stainless	321
Coping	89, 96
aluminum	89, 90
clay tile	90
concrete	89
removal	38
terra cotta	90, 94
Copper cable	332
downspout	162
drum trap	287
DWV tubing	291
fitting	291
flashing	163, 164, 288
gutter	165
pipe	290, 291
reglet	165
roof	161
wall covering	233
wire	334
Corbel formwork	73
Core drill	24
testing	8
Coreboard	214
Cork expansion joint	70
floor	222
tile	222
wall tile	233
Corner base cabinet	137
bead	215
guard	242
wall cabinet	137
Cornice	90
drain	285
molding	130, 131
painting	232
Correspondence lift	280
Corrosion resis. backflow preven	284
resistant fan	322
resistant fitting	293
resistant pipe	293
resistant pipe fitting	293
Corrugated metal pipe	58
roof tile	154
siding	155, 156
Cost mark-up	7
Costs of trees	520
Counter bank	252
checkout	253
door	183
flashing	165
flashing aluminum	404
flashing copper	404
flashing steel	404
top	132, 133, 263
top demolition	33
Countertop backsplash	132
laminated plastic	483
sink	303
Course base	48
wearing	51
Court tennis	60
Cove base	222
base ceramic tile	216
base terrazzo	218
molding	130
molding scotia	130
Cover convector	132
ground	65
stair tread	9
Covers expansion	114
CPVC pipe	294
valve	301
Crack control	54
filling	55
repair	84
Crane crawler	19
hydraulic	19
material handling	19
mobilization	49
rail	280
Crawler crane	19
Crew survey	8
Cross brace	105
wall	252
Crown molding	130, 131
Cubicle shower	303
toilet	240
Culvert reinforced	58
Cupola	244
Curb	53
asphalt	53
concrete	53
edging	53, 102
formwork	72, 73
granite	53
inlet	53
precast	53
prefabricated	324
removal	26
roof	122
seal	54
terrazzo	218
Curing concrete	52, 77, 79
paper	145
Current transformer cabinet	336
Curtain damper fire	325
divider	262
gymnasium divider	262
rod	249
wall	206
Curved stair	139
Custom casework	136
Cut stone	95
Cutoff pile	49
Cutout	27
counter	132
slab	27
Cutting asphalt	36
block	133
concrete	37
saw	36
steel	37, 106
torch	19
Cylinder concrete	8
lockset	198
recore	198, 199

D

Dairy case	254
Damper	325, 326
barometric	309
fireplace	243
foundation vent	89
multi-blade	325
vent	309, 310
Dampproofing bituminous	145
Darby finish concrete	82
Darkroom door	261
sink	261
Data survey	8
Deadbolt	197
Deadlocking latch	197
Deciduous shrub	66
tree	66
Deck cementitious	84
concrete cellular	83
drain	285
metal	107
roof	107, 125, 127
steel	107
wood	127, 130
Decontamination chamber	40
enclosure	40
equipment	39
Decorator device	346
switch	346
Deep therapy room	271
Delicatessen case	254
Delivery charge	48
Demo concrete	25
Demolition	24, 26, 31, 32, 35, 37-39, 43
asbestos	40
baseboard	34
boiler	33
brick	31, 38
building	26
cabinet	33
casework	33
ceiling	27
ceramic tile	31
chimney	38
column	38
concrete	28, 31
concrete block	28
door	28
drywall	27
ductwork	33
electric	29, 30
enclosure	41
fireplace	39
flooring	31
framing	32
furnace	33
glass	37
granite	39
gutter	36
hammer	16
house	26
HVAC	33
joist	32
lath	27
masonry	28, 37, 38
metal deck	36
metal stud	37
millwork	33
paneling	34
partition	37
pavement	25, 26
plaster	27, 37
plumbing	35
plywood	27, 36, 37
post	32
price sheet	495
rafter	32
railing	34
roofing	36, 41
selective	27
siding	36
site	25
steel window	37
stucco	37
terrazzo	31
tile	27
trim	34
wall	37
walls and partitions	37
window	37
wood	27
Demountable partition	247, 412
Detection system	343
tape	56
Detector infra-red	343
motion	343
smoke	344
temperature rise	344
ultrasonic motion	343
Detention equipment	256
Developing tank	261
Device decorator	346
exit	199, 200
GFI	347
load management	339
panic	199
receptacle	347
residential	345
wiring	336
Diamond lath	211
Diaphragm pump	18
Dielectric union	285
Diesel hammer	16
Diffuser ceiling	324
linear	324
opposed blade damper	324
perforated aluminum	324
rectangular	324
steel	324
T-bar mount	324
Dimmer switch	336, 345
Direct expansion A/C	318
Directional sign	62
Directory	244
board	244
building	345
Disappearing stairs	260
Discharge hose	18
Dishwasher	256, 257
Dispenser napkin	250
product	255
soap	249, 250
toilet tissue	249, 250
towel	249, 250
Display case	254
Disposable bag	39
Disposal	26
asbestos	41
building	26
charges	41
field	59
garbage	256
Distribution box	59
fuel	56
system gas	57
Divider curtain	262
strip terrazzo	218
Dock board	255
bumper	255, 256
loading	255
shelter	256
truck	255
Dog command	13

614

Index

Dome drain 285
   fiberglass 72
   wood 127
Door access 181
   accessories 203
   accordion 180
   acoustical 186, 248
   aluminum 187, 188
   and frame demolition 495
   automatic entrance 188
   balanced 188
   bell residential 348
   bell system 344
   bi-fold 173, 179
   bi-passing closet 179
   birch 180
   blind 135
   bulkhead 185
   bumper 197
   cabinet 138
   cafe 177
   canopy 246
   casing 216
   catch 138
   chain hoist 184
   chime 344
   cleanout 243
   closer 201, 394, 423
   closet 173, 179, 180, 416
   coiling 183
   cold storage 183
   combination storm 179
   commercial 172, 178
   composite 172
   counter 183
   darkroom 261
   demolition 28
   double 173
   dutch 179
   dutch oven 243
   entrance 179, 187, 188
   fire 172, 177, 178, 344
   fire rated access 181
   flexible 186
   floor 185
   flush 175, 176, 179
   flush wood 175
   folding accordion 180
   frame 172-174
   frame grout 86
   frame interior 175
   garage 184
   glass 182, 186, 188
   handle 138
   hardboard 179
   hardware 197
   interior louvered 414
   interior solid 414
   kick plate 198
   knob 199
   knocker 203
   labeled 172, 177, 178
   metal 172, 415
   metal access 182
   metal-clad 182
   mirror 205
   molding 131
   moulded 178
   opener 185, 186, 201
   overhead 184
   overhead commercial 184
   panel 178
   paneled 173
   partition 247
   passage 180, 181
   plastic 174
   prefinished 175, 176
   pre-hung 180
   pull 200
   refrigerator 183
   release 345
   removal 28
   residential 173, 175, 179
   residential garage 184
   revolving 261
   rolling 186
   roof 167
   rough buck 122
   sauna 270
   sectional 184
   sectional overhead 184
   shower 241
   sill 132, 174, 203
   sliding 182
   sound retardant 186
   special 181, 186
   special purpose 185
   stain 231
   stainless steel (access) 182
   steel 172, 173
   stop 197, 206, 394, 423
   storm 186
   swing 186
   switch burglar alarm 343
   threshold 175
   varnish 231
   vertical lift 185
   weatherstrip 203
   weatherstrip garage 203
   wood 174-176, 178, 413
Doors & windows interior paint . 230
Dormer gable 124
Dormitory furniture 266
Double acting door 186
   brick 90
   hung window 189, 192, 193
   wall pipe 56, 57
   weight hinge 200
Dowel 88
Dowels reinforcing 76
Downspout 162, 163
   aluminum 162, 403
   copper 162, 403
   elbow 163
   lead-coated copper 162, 403
   steel 162
   steel galvanized 403
   strainer 162
Dozer 16, 44
   backfill 44
   excavating bulk 45
   excavation 45
Draft control 309
   damper vent 309
Drain 285
   cast iron 285
   deck 285
   dome 285
   floor 285
   main 285
Drainage accessory 163
   pipe 58, 293
   sewage 58
   site 58
   trap 287
Drains roof 285
Drawer 139
   kitchen 136
   track 138
   wood 139
Drill bit 25
   ceiling 102
   concrete 24, 102, 329
   core 24
   drywall 102
   earth 24, 50
   hammer 18
   plaster 102
   rig 24
   rock 24
   shop 263
   track 17
   wall 102
   wood 118
Drilling horizontal 47
Drinking fountain 302, 305
   fountain floor rough-in 302
   fountain handicap 302
   fountain wall rough-in 302
Drip edge 163
   edge aluminum 163, 403
   edge steel galvanized 403
Drive pin 104
Driven pile 50
Driveway 52, 490
   removal 25
Drop pan ceiling 219
Drum trap 287
   trap copper 287
Dry pipe sprinkler head 307
   transformer 339
Drycleaner 254
Dryer commercial clothes ... 254
   darkroom 261
   hand 249
   receptacle 347
   residential 254
Drywall 213, 422
   accessories 215
   ceiling 213
   column 213
   cutout 28
   demolition 27, 37
   drill 102
   frame 174
   gypsum 213
   interior surface 392
   nail 118
   painting 232
   partition 214, 215
   prefinished 213
   removal 37
Duck tarpaulin 13
Duct access door 325
   accessories 325
   demolition 495
   flexible insulated 321
   flexible noninsulated 321
   furnace 310
   heater electric 310
   humidifier 314
   insulation 314
   liner 315
   mechanical 321
   mixing box 325
   silencer 326
   underground 343
   utility 343
Ductile iron pipe cement lined ... 56
Ductless split system 319
Ductwork 321, 553
   aluminum 321
   demolition 33
   fabric coated flexible 321
   galvanized 321
   rectangular 321
   removal 33
   rigid 321
Dumbbell 261
Dumbwaiter 276
   electric 276
   manual 276
Dump charge 27
   truck 17
Dumpster 27
Duplex receptacle 336
Dust collector shop 263
   partition 27
Dustproofing 77
Dutch door 179
   oven door 243
DWV pipe ABS 294
   PVC pipe 294
   tubing copper 291

E

Earth compactor 15
   drill 24, 50
   vibrator 44, 46
Earthwork 43
   equipment 43
Ecclesiastical equipment 252
Echo chamber 270
Economizer shower-head water . 303
Economy brick 90
Edge drip 163
   form 72, 73
Edging 53
   aluminum 53
   curb 53, 102
Eggcrate ceiling 219
EIFS 149, 150
Ejector pump 305
Elastomeric roof 160
   waterproofing 144
Elbow aluminum 403
   copper 403
   downspout 163
   pipe 299
Electric backstop 262
   ballast 341
   baseboard heater 344
   boiler 307, 308
   cable 332, 334
   demolition 29, 30
   duct heater 310
   dumbwaiter 276
   fixture 340, 342
   furnace 310
   generator 18
   generator set 340
   heating 344
   hinge 200
   lamp 342
   log 243
   metallic tubing 328
   panelboard 338
   relay 339
   service 337
   stair 260
   switch 339
   unit heater 344
   utilities 343
   water heater 306
   wire 334
Electrical cabinet 335
   conduit 328
   demolition 512
   field bend 328
   installation drilling 329
   knockout 331
   laboratory 263

Index

site work 343
Electronic air cleaner 323
closer 202
control system 324
Elevated floor 78
slab 78, 522
slab concrete 80
slab formwork 72
Elevator 276, 549-551
construction 20
fee 6
options 278
shaft wall 215
Embossed print door 178
Emergency lighting 340
EMT 328
conduit 472
Emulsion adhesive 223
asphaltic 54
pavement 54
Encapsulation 42
pipe 42
Enclosure acoustical 270
decontamination 40
demolition 41
swimming pool 272
telephone 249
Energy circulator air solar 312
system air purger solar 313
system air vent solar 313
system balancing valve solar 313
system control valve solar 313
system controller solar 312
system expansion tank solar 313
system gauge pressure solar 313
system heat exchanger solar 312
system storage tank solar 312
system vacuum relief solar 313
Engineer brick 90
Engineering fee 6
fees 501
Entrance aluminum 187
and storefront 187
canopy 245
door 179, 180, 187, 188
frame 175
lock 197
screen 241
sliding 188
EPDM adhesive 144
roof 160
Epoxy 48
dustproofing 77
fiberglass wound pipe 293
floor 225
grout 48, 80, 216, 217
injection 84
marble chip floor 225
resin 77
terrazzo 225
wall coating 225
Equipment 15, 252, 253
athletic 261
bank 252
barber 253
detention 256
earthwork 43
ecclesiastical 252
fire 307
food service 256
formwork 72
general 7
gymnasium 262
health club 261
insurance 7
laboratory 263
laundry 254
library 252
loading dock 255
maintenance 252
mobilization 47, 49
move 34
parking 255
rental 15, 19, 511
security and vault 252
service station 255
shop 263
stage 253
theater and stage 253
waste handling 256
Erosion control 48
Escape fire 112
Estimating 500
Evaporator coils cased 311
Evergreen shrub 66
tree 66
Excavating bulk bank measure 45
bulk dozer 45
equipment 517
Excavation 43, 45, 56, 516
backhoe 46
dozer 45
footing 487
foundation 488
hand 43, 45, 46
hauling 47
machine 43
planting pit 65
septic tank 59
structural 45, 46
trench 46, 47
utility trench 486
Exercise equipment 262
ladder 262
rope 262
weight 261
Exhaust hood 256
vent 326
Exist. pipelines relining 59
Exit and emergency lighting 340
control alarm 343
device 199, 200
light 340
Expansion anchor 102
bolt 102
control 114
covers 114
joint 70, 114, 115, 166
joint aluminum 114
joint asphalt 70
joint bituminous 70
joint bronze 114
joint ceiling 115
joint cork 70
joint cover 115
joint floor 114
joint neoprene 70
joint polyethylene 70
joint polyurethane 70
joint premolded 70
joint PVC 70
joint roof 115, 166
joint rubber 70
joint wall 114
shield 102
tank 315
Expense office 7
Exposed aggregate 52
Exterior blind 135
concrete block 93
door frame 174
floodlamp 340
insulation 149
insulation finish system 149
lighting fixture 340
molding 130
painting 225
plaster 212
pre-hung door 180
residential door 179
sprinkler 60
surface masonry 392
surface metal 392
surface wood 392
wall price sheet 392
wood frame 175
Extinguisher ABC 245
carbon dioxide 245
chemical dry 245
fire 245
standard 245
Extra work 7
Extractor 16
air 325
industrial 254
Eye wash fountain 302

F

Fabric flashing 164
overlay 54
stile 202
waterproofing 144
welded wire 76
Fabrication metal 111
Fabrications plastic 141
Face brick 90, 536
tile structural 94
wash fountain 302
Facing stone 96
tile 94
Factor 6
Fan 322
air conditioning 322
air handling 322
attic ventilation 322
bathroom exhaust 322
booster 322
ceiling 322
centrifugal 322
coil air conditioning 318
corrosion resistant 322
house ventilation 323
in-line 322
kitchen exhaust 322
paddle 349
residential 349
utility set 322
ventilation 349
ventilator 322
wiring 349
Farm type siding 156
Fascia board 122
board demolition 32
demolition 495
metal 167
wood 131
Fast food equipment 257
Fastener 118
metal 114
timber 118
wood 119
Fastening metal 102
Faucet & fitting 285, 286
bathroom 285
gooseneck 286
medical 286
Fee architectural 6
engineering 6
Felt 159
asphalt 158, 159
carpet pad 224
tarred 159
waterproofing 144
Fence and gate 60
auger, truck mounted 15
board & batten 62
cedar 61
chain link 13, 60
mesh 60
picket paint 227
plywood 13
removal 25
security 61
snow 61
steel 61
temporary 13
tennis 60
treated pine 62
wire 13, 61
Fences 227
Fiber cement shingle 152
cement siding 157
panel mineral 127
reinforcing 76
tube formwork 71
wood 84
Fiberboard insulation 148
Fiberglass bench 62
blown in 146
ceiling board 219
cooling towers 321
cupola 244
dome 72
door 184
formwork 71
insulation 146, 147, 314
panel 13, 155, 220
planter 63
shower stall 241
steeple 252
Fiberglass storage tank 479, 480
Fiberglass tank 315
waterproofing 144
wool 146
Field bend electrical 328
bend EMT 328
disposal 59
office 14
personnel 6, 7
Fieldstone 95
Fill 44, 47
cellular 84
floor 78
gravel 44
Filler block 233
joint 55
strip 202
Fillet weld 104
Filling crack 55
Film equipment 261
Filter air 323
mechanical media 323
Filtration air 39
Fin tube radiation 314
Final cleaning 21
Finish carpentry 130, 134, 136
concrete 52, 82
floor 221, 233
hardware 197
lime 86
nail 118
wall 82

INDEX

Index

Finisher floor 15
Fir column 140
  floor 220
  molding 131
  roof deck 130
  roof plank 127
Fire alarm 343
  call pullbox 344
  clay 98
  damage repair 236
  damper curtain type 325
  door 172, 177, 178, 344
  door frame 174
  equipment 307
  equipment cabinet 245
  escape 112
  escape disappearing 260
  extinguisher 245
  extinguisher portable 245
  horn 344
  hose 307
  hose gate valve 307
  hose nozzle 307
  hose storage cabinet 245
  hose valve 307
  hydrant 307
  protection 245
  protection kitchen 259
  protection system 307
  rated closer 202
  resistant drywall 213, 214
  resistant wall 214
  retardant lumber 136
  retardant plywood 136
  signal bell 343
  sprinkler head 307
  system 307
Firebrick 98
Firecycle system control package 307
Fireplace accessory 243
  box 98
  built-in 243
  damper 243
  demolition 39
  form 243
  free standing 242
  mantel 134
  masonry 98
  prefabricated 242
Fireproofing 150
  plaster 150
  spray 150
Firestop gypsum 210
  wood 121
Firestopping 150, 544
Fitting 284
  cast iron 289
  copper 291
  corrosion resistant 293
  glass 294
  grooved joint pipe 299
  malleable iron 298
  plastic 295
  PVC 295
  steel 297, 299
  vent chimney 316
Fixture ballast 341
  bathroom 301, 302, 304
  carrier 287
  electric 340
  exterior mercury vapor 340
  fluorescent 340-342
  incandescent 341
  incandescent vaportight ... 341
  interior light 340, 341
  lantern 342

metal halide 341
mirror light 341
plumbing 301, 303, 304
removal 35
residential 342, 348
support handicap 287
vandalproof 341
Flagging 222
  slate 53
Flange tie 88
Flashing 162-164, 167
  aluminum 163, 288, 403
  asphalt 163
  butyl 164
  cement 161
  copper 163, 164, 288, 403
  counter 165
  fabric 164
  lead 403
  lead coated 164
  lead-coated copper 403
  masonry 163
  membrane 159
  polyvinyl chloride 403
  PVC 164
  stainless 164
  steel 404
  valley 152
  vent 288
  vent chimney 316
Flat plate formwork 72
  slab formwork 72
Flatbed truck 17
Flexible conduit & fitting 331
  connector 284
  door 186
  ductwork fabric coated 321
  insulated duct 321
Float concrete 15
  finish concrete 82
  glass 204
Floater equipment 7
Floating floor 221
  pin 198
Flood coating 159
Floodlamp exterior 340
Floodlight 18
  pole mounted 340
Floor access 242
  acid proof 222
  and carpet 221
  asphalt block 52
  brick 53, 222
  carpet 224
  ceramic tile 216
  cleaning 21
  cleanout 284
  closer 201
  concrete 77
  conductive 222
  cork 222
  door 185
  drain 285
  elevated 78
  epoxy 225
  epoxy marble chip 225
  expansion joint 114
  fill 78
  finish 233
  finish price sheet 429
  finisher 15
  framing removal 28
  hatch 185
  insulation 146
  marble 96
  nail 118

oak 220
paint 231
pans 522
parquet 221
patching concrete 80
pedestal 242
plank 128
plywood 126
polyethylene 223
quarry tile 217
receptor 286
removal 38
resilient tile 222
rubber 223
sander 18
slate 222
special 225
stain 231
stressed skin 127
subfloor 126
terrazzo 218
tile terrazzo 218
underlayment 126
varnish 231
vinyl 223
wood 220
wood block 221
wood strip 220
Flooring 222, 429
  carpet 375
  composition 225, 375
  demolition 31, 495
  marble 221
  resilient 375
  wood 375
Flue chimney metal 316
  liner 89
  prefab metal 316
  screen 243
Fluid heat transfer 312
Fluorescent fixture 340-342
  lamp 342
Fluoroscopy room 271
Flush automatic 285
  door 175, 176, 179
  tube framing 206
  valve 285
  wood door 175
Flying truss 75
Foam glass insulation 147
  insulation 146
  urethane 170
Foil aluminum 145, 146
  back insulation 148
Folded plate roof 127
Folder laundry 254
Folding accordion door 180
  accordion partition 248
  bench 262
  partition 248
Food mixer 258
  service equipment ... 256, 257
  warmer 258
Football scoreboard 262
Footing concrete 79, 81
  reinforcing 75
  removal 38
  spread 73
Forklift brick 18
Form edge 72, 73
  fireplace 243
  liner 74
  material 521
  polystyrene 73
  slab 108
Forms 522-524

concrete 522-524
slab 522
Formwork 71, 73
  accessory 70
  beam and girder 70
  box out opening 72
  bulkhead 73
  buttress 73
  columns 71
  concrete 70
  corbel 73
  curb 72, 73
  elevated slab 72
  equipment 72
  fiber tube 71
  flat plate 72
  flat slab 72
  girder 70, 71
  interior beam 71
  labor hours 525
  liner 74
  lintel 74
  pilaster 74
  plywood 71-73
  retaining wall 74
  steel frame 72
  structural 70
  trench 73
  void 72
  wall 73
Fossil fuel boiler 308, 309
Foundation caisson 50
  chimney 78
  concrete 79
  concrete block 93
  mat 79, 81
  underdrain 360
  underpin 43
  vent 89
  wall 93
Fountain drinking 302, 305
  eye wash 302
  face wash 302
  wash 304
Frame baked enamel 174
  door 172-174
  drywall 174
  entrance 175
  fire door 174
  labeled 174
  metal 173
  metal butt 174
  roof 106
  steel 173
  welded 174
  window 196
  wood 138, 174
Framing anchor 118
  angle 105
  beam & girder 120
  canopy 105, 123
  channel 105
  coldformed 108
  demolition 32, 495
  heavy 128
  laminated 129
  lightweight 105
  metal 104, 392
  partition 214
  removal 32
  roof truss 130
  sleepers 123
  timber 128
  tube 206
  wall 123
  window wall 105, 206

617

Index

wood 119, 120, 124, 128, 393
Freestanding chalkboard 240
Freezer 254, 258, 270
Freight elevators 548
Friction pile 50
Front end loader 45
shovel 16
Fryer 258
Fuel distribution 56
Full vision door 188
vision glass 204
Furnace A/C coils 311
coal burning 311
components 311
demolition 33
duct 310
electric 310
gas fired 310
hot air 310
oil fired 310
wall 313
wood coal/oil combination . . . 311
Furnishings site/street 62
Furniture 266
and accessories 266
hospital 266
hotel 266
move 34
Furring and lathing 210
ceiling 124, 210
channel 210, 216
metal 210
price sheet 420
steel 210
wall 124, 210
Fusible link closer 201

G

Gable dormer 124
Galley septic 59
Galvanized ductwork 321
roof 155
steel conduit 472
steel reglet 165
Garage door 184
door weatherstrip 203
Garbage disposal 256
Gas boiler HW 451
boiler steam 452
Gas connector 284
conversion burner 309
distribution system 57
fired boiler 308
fired furnace 310
fired space heater 313
generator 340
log 243
pipe 57
station formwork 74
station piping 56
vent 316
water heater 306
Gasket neoprene 170
Gas/oil boiler HW 452
boiler steam 452
Gasoline generator 340
pump 255
Gate fence 60
valve 301
General contractor's overhead . . 502
demolition 512
equipment 7
Generator construction 18
emergency 340
gas 340
set 340
GFI receptacle 347
Girder formwork 70, 71
reinforcing 75
removal 31
steel 106
wood 120, 128
Glass 204-206
bead 206
bead molding 131
block 95
break alarm 343
bulletin board 244
bulletproof 205
demolition 37
door 182, 186-188
door astragal 202
door shower 241
fitting 294
float 204
full vision 204
heat reflective 204
insulating 204
laminated 205
lead 271
low emissivity 204
masonry 95
mirror 205, 250
mosaic 425
pipe 293
pipe fitting 294
railing 113
reflective 205
tempered 204
tile 205
tinted 204
window 205
window wall 207
wire 205
Glasweld 128
Glaze coat 232
Glazed block 92
brick 90
coating 225
wall coating 225
Glazing 204
labor 546
plastic 205
polycarbonate 206
Glove bag 41
Glued laminated 129
laminated construction 129
Gooseneck faucet 286
Gore line 55
Grab bar 249
Gradall 15
Grade beam 81
wall 79
Grader motorized 15
Grading 47
Granite 96
building 96
curb 53
demolition 39
indian 53
paving block 53
sidewalk 53
Granolithic finish 533
finish concrete 82
Grass cloth wallpaper 233
lawn 65
sprinkler 60
Grate precast 52
tree 52
Grating 112
Gravel bankrun 44
base 48
fill 44
stop 167
Grease interceptor 302
Greenhouse 272
cooling 272
Grid spike 119
Griddle 258
Grille air return 324
aluminum 324
coiling 183
convector cover 132
decorative wood 134
painting 231
roll up 184
top coiling 183
window 196
Grinder shop 263
terrazzo 15
Grooved block 91
joint pipe 299
Grooved-joint pipe 299
Ground 124
clamp water pipe 335
cover 65
cover edging 498
rod 334, 335
water monitoring 9
wire 335
Grounding 334
& conductor 333
wire brazed 335
Group wash fountain 304
Grout 86
Grout cavity wall 86
cement 86
concrete 86
concrete block 86
door frame 86
epoxy 48, 80, 216, 217
pressure 48
topping 80
underlayment 80
wall 86
Guard corner 242
gutter 165
service 13
window 114
Guardrail temporary 13
Guards wall & corner 242
Guide rail 62
rail removal 25
rail timber 62
Guide/guard rail 62
Gunite 80
Gutter 165
aluminum 165, 404
copper 165, 404
demolition 36, 495
guard 165
lead coated copper 165
stainless 165
steel 165, 404
strainer 165
vinyl 165
wood 165
Gutting 32
Guying tree 63
Gym mat 262
Gymnasium divider curtain 262
equipment 262
floor 223
floor expansion joint 115
Gypsum block demolition 28
board 213
board accessories 215
board system 212
cement 86
drywall 213
fabric wallcovering 233
firestop 210
lath 210
lath nail 118
partition 215, 247
plaster 212, 547
poured 84
roof plank demolition 36
shaft wall 215
sheathing 126
weatherproof 126

H

H pile 50
Half round molding 131
Hammer bush 82
chipping 17
demolition 16
drill 18
hydraulic 18
pile 16
pile mobilization 49
Hand carved door 177
dryer 249
excavation 43, 45, 46, 56
hole 56
rail 113
split shake 153
trowel finish concrete 82
Handicap drinking fountain 302
fixture support 287
lever 197
opener 201
ramp 79
tub shower 301
Handle door 138
Handling rubbish 27
waste 256
Handrail and railing 112
wood 131, 140
Hanger beam 118
joist 118
Hardboard cabinet 136
door 179
overhead door 184
paneling 133
siding 157
soffit 135
tempered 133
underlayment 126
Hardener concrete 77
Hardware 197
cabinet 138
door 197
finish 197
panic 200
price sheet 394, 395, 423
rough 125
window 197
Hardwood carrel 253
floor 220
grille 134
Hasp 199
Hat and coat strip 250
Hatch ceiling 182
floor 185
roof 167, 168
smoke 168
Hauling charge 47
excavation 47

INDEX

Index

truck	47
Hay bale	49
Hazardous waste cleanup	32
waste disposal	32
waste handling	256
Head sprinkler	307
Header wood	123
Health club equipment	261
Hearth	98
Heat baseboard	313, 471
electric baseboard	344
greenhouse	272
pump	318
pump residential	349
radiant	270
recovery air to air	313
reflective glass	204
temporary	9, 82
transfer fluid	312
Heat-cool piping	317
Heater & fan bathroom	322
air handler	311
contractor	18
electric residential	344
floor mounted space	313
sauna	270
unit	313
water	306
Heating	307-309, 312-316
electric	344
gas fired	445
hot air	310
hydronic	308, 309
oil fired	444
system accessories	313
Heavy framing	128
timber	128
Hemlock column	141
High intensity discharge lamp	342
intensity discharge lighting	341
pressure fixture sodium	341
pressure sodium lighting	341
rib lath	211
rise glazing	204
strength block	91
strength concrete	77
Highway sign	62
Hinge	394, 423
brass	198
cabinet	139
continuous	201
electric	200
hospital	200
paumelle	200
prison	200
residential	198
school	200
security	200
special	200
steel	198
Hinges	546
Hip rafter	122
Hockey scoreboard	262
Hoist	280
and tower	20
automotive	255
contractor	20
lift equipment	19
personnel	20
Holder closer	202
Holdown	118
Hole cutting electrical	330
drilling	102
drilling electrical	329
Hollow core door	175, 180
metal	173
metal door	172
metal frames	545
metal stud partition	211
wall anchor	103
Hood fire protection	259
range	256
Hook coat	250
robe	250
Horizontal boring	47
drilling	47
shore	75
Horn fire	344
Hose air	17
discharge	18
fire	307
rack	307
rack cabinet	245
suction	18
water	18
Hospital door hardware	197
furniture	266
hinge	200
kitchen equipment	260
tip pin	198
Hot air furnace	310
air heating	310
tub	302
water boiler	308, 309
water heating	308, 313
Hotel cabinet	250
furniture	266
lockset	198, 199
House demolition	26
telephone	345
ventilation fan	323
Housewrap	145
Humidification equipment	272
Humidifier duct	314
room	314
Humidifiers	314
HVAC demolition	33
piping specialties	317
removal	33
Hydrant fire	307
removal	25
water	287
Hydrated lime	86
Hydraulic crane	19
elevator	432
hammer	18
jack	20
Hydrocumulator	304
Hydrodemolition concrete	26
Hydronic heating	308, 309
Hypalon neoprene roofing	160

I

Icemaker	258
Impact wrench	17
Inslab conduit	328
Incandescent bulb	342
exterior lamp	342
fixture	341, 342
interior lamp	342
Inclined ladder	112
Indian granite	53
Indicating panel burglar alarm	343
Industrial address system	344
door	185
lighting	341
railing	113
safety fixture	302
window	189
Inert gas	42
Infra-red broiler	257
detector	343
Injection epoxy	84
latex	84
Inlet curb	53
In-line fan	322
Insecticide	49
Inspection technician	9
Insulated panels	149
protectors ADA	314
Insulating glass	204
Insulation	145-147, 314, 315
acoustical	220
batt	147, 148, 393
blanket	147, 314
board	147
building	145
cavity wall	146
ceiling batts	401
cellulose	146
composite	149
concrete	84
duct	314
exterior	149
fiberglass	146, 147, 314
foam	146
foam glass	147
insert	93
isocyanurate	147
masonry	146
mineral fiber	148
pipe	315
polystyrene	146, 147
removal	40
roof	148
roof deck	148
shingle	152
spray	146
urethane	146
vapor barrier	145
vermiculite	146
wall	93, 147
water heater	314
Insurance	6
builder risk	6
equipment	7
public liability	7
Integral finish concrete	82
floor finish	533
waterproofing	77
Integrated ceiling	270
Interceptor	302
grease	302
oil	302
Interior beam formwork	71
door frame	175
light fixture	340, 341
painting	230
pre-hung door	181
residential door	179
wall finish price sheet	425
wood frame	175
Interlocking block	92
Intermediate conduit	328
Interval timer	345
Intrusion system	343
Inverted bucket steam trap	317
tee beam	83
Iron alloy mechanical joint pipe	293
body valve	301
grate	52
Ironer laundry	254
Ironspot brick	222
Irrigation system	60
Island formwork	74
Isocyanurate insulation	147

J

Jack cable	20
hydraulic	20
mud	15
screw	43
Jackhammer	17
Jacking	47
Jalousie	190
Job condition	7
Joint control	86
expansion	70, 114, 115, 166
filler	55
reinforcing	87
roof	167
sealer	169
Jointer shop	263
Joist anchor	119
bar	106, 107
composite	107
concrete	78
connector	118
demolition	32
hanger	118
metal	107
open web	107
removal	32
sister	121
steel	107
wood	121, 128
Joists cold-formed	107
Jumbo brick	90
Jute mesh	48

K

Kalamein door	182
Kennel fence	61
Kettle	258
Kettle/pot tar	19
Keyless lock	199
Keyway	72
Kick plate	113, 198, 394, 423
plate door	198
Kiln dried lumber	136
vocational	263
King brick	90
Kiosk	272
Kitchen cabinet	136
equipment	257
exhaust fan	322
heat recovery	313
selective price sheet	483, 484
sink	303
sink faucet	286
system	476
K-lath	211
Knee action mixing valve	286
Knob door	199
Knocker door	203
Knockout electrical	331
Kraft paper	145

L

Labeled door	172, 177, 178
frame	174
Labor formwork	525
Laboratory cabinet	263
equipment	263
Ladder	18, 112
building	112
exercise	262
reinforcing	87

Index

steel 112
towel 250
Lag screws 103
Lally column 105
Laminate plastic 132
Laminated beam 129
   construction glued 129
   countertop 133
   countertop plastic 132
   framing 129
   glass 205
   roof deck 130
   veneer members 129
   wood 129
Lamp fluorescent 342
   high intensity discharge ... 342
   incandescent exterior 342
   incandescent interior 342
   metal halide 342
   post 114
Lampholder 336
Landfill fees 27
Landing newel 140
   stair 112, 218
Landscape 63
   surface 223
Landscaping 494
Lantern fixture 342
Laser 18
Latch deadlocking 197
   set 198, 199
Latex acrylic 77
   caulking 170
   injection 84
   underlayment 223
Lath 422
   and plaster 210
   demolition 27
   gypsum 210
   metal 211
   rib 211
Lathe shop 263
Lattice molding 131
Lauan door 180
Laundry equipment 254
   faucet 286
   sink 303
   tray 303
Lavatory 302
   faucet 286
   removal 35
   support 287
   vanity top 302
   wall hung 303
Lawn bed preparation 64
   grass 65
Lazy susan 137
Leaching field chamber 59
   pit 59
Lead coated copper downspout . 162
   coated copper gutter 165
   coated downspout 162
   coated flashing 164
   flashing 164
   glass 271
   paint encapsulation 235
   paint remediation methods . 513
   paint removal 235
   pile 16
   plastic 271
   roof 161
   screw anchor 102
   sheets 271
   shielding 270
   wool 70
Lean-to type greenhouse 272

Let-in bracing 104
Letter slot 247
Lever handicap 197
Lexan 206
Liability insurance 502
Library equipment 252
   shelf 252
Lift 280
   aerial 17
   automotive 255
   correspondence 280
   slab 79, 533
   wheelchair 276
Lifter platform 256
Light base 74
   exit 340
   fixture interior 340, 341
   post 342
   stand 39
   support 105
   temporary 9
   tower 18
Lighting 340-342
   darkroom 261
   emergency 340
   exit and emergency 340
   fixture exterior 340
   fluorescent 468
   high intensity 470
   high intensity discharge .. 341
   high pressure sodium 341
   incandescent 469
   industrial 341
   metal halide 341
   outdoor 17
   outlet 348
   residential 348
   strip 341
   track 342
Lightning suppressor 345
Lightweight block 92
   concrete 78, 84, 535
   floor fill 78
   framing 105
Lime finish 86
   hydrated 86
Limestone 65, 96
   coping 89
Line gore 55
Linear diffuser 324
Linen chute 280
Liner cement 59, 60
   duct 315
   formwork 74
   pipe 59
Lint collector 254
Lintel 83, 96, 105, 106
   block 93
   concrete 83
   formwork 74
   precast 83
Load management switch ... 339
Loadbearing studs 108
Loadcenter residential 345
Loader front end 45
   tractor 16
   vacuum 39
Loading dock 255
   dock equipment 255
Loam 44, 48, 64, 65
Lobby collection box 247
Lock electric release 199
   entrance 197
   keyless 199
   tubular 197
Locker metal 245

steel 245
wire mesh 245
Locking receptacle 347
Lockset 394, 423
   communicating 198, 199
   cylinder 198
   hotel 198, 199
   mortise 199
Log electric 243
   gas 243
Louver 242
   aluminum 242
   metal 242
   midget 242
   redwood 134
   ventilation 134
   wall 242
   wood 134
Louvered door 180, 181
Lube equipment 255
Lumber 540, 542
   core paneling 133
   kiln dried 136
   treatment 136
Luminous ceiling .. 219, 220, 342
   panel 219

M

Machine anchor 103
   excavation 43
   trowel finish 82
   welding 19
Magnetic astragal 202
   particle test 9
Mahogany door 177
Mail box 247
   box call system 345
   chute 246
   slot 247
Main drain 285
   office expense 7
Maintenance equipment 252
Make-up air unit 312
Mall front 188
Malleable iron fitting 298
   iron pipe fitting 298
Management fee construction . 6
Manhole 56, 58
   precast 58
   removal 25
Mansard aluminum 165
Mantel beam 134
   fireplace 134
Manual dumbwaiter 276
Maple countertop 133
   wall 270
Marble 95
   coping 90
   countertop 133
   floor 96
   flooring 221
   screen 241
   sill 91
   synthetic 222
   tile 221
Mark-up cost 7
Masonry accessory 86
   anchor 87
   base 93
   brick 89, 222
   catch basin 58
   caulking 98
   cement 86
   cleaning 97, 381

cornice 90
demolition 28, 37, 38, 495
exterior surface 392
fireplace 98, 478
flashing 163
furring 124
glass 95
insulation 146
nail 118
needle 98
pointing 98
reinforced 93
reinforcing 87
removal 25, 38
restoration 98, 381
saw 18
sill 91
step 62
toothing 98
unit 89
veneer 94
ventilator 89
wall 49, 91, 378, 379
wall tie 87
Mat foundation 79, 81
   gym 262
   wall 262
Material handling system 280
   hoist 20
Materials concrete 529
Meat case 254
Mechanical 552
   duct 321
   equipment demolition ... 33
   fee 6
   media filter 323
Medical faucet 286
Medicine cabinet 250
Membrane curing 79
   flashing 159
   roofing 158
   waterproofing 55, 144
Mercury vapor exterior fixture . 340
   vapor lamp 342
Mesh fence 60
   stucco 211
Metal bookshelf 252
   butt frame 174
   chimney 242
   deck 107
   deck composite 107
   deck demolition 36
   door 172, 187, 383
   door frame 187
   door residential 173
   ductwork 321
   exterior surface 392
   fabrication 111
   fascia 167
   fastener 114
   fastening 102
   flue chimney 316
   frame 173
   framed skylight 169
   framing 104
   furring 210
   halide fixture 341
   halide lamp 342
   halide lighting 341
   hollow 173
   jalousie window 190
   joist 107
   lath 211
   locker 245
   louver 242
   ornamental 114

Index

overhead door 184	trim 131	molding 131	and wall covering 225
pan 72	wood 140	paneling 133	balustrade 232
pan ceiling 220	wood transition 221	stair tread 140	booth 255
pipe 56	Money safe 252	threshold 175	casework 230
roof 155	Monitor support 105	Off highway truck 17	ceiling 232, 233
sash 189	Monolithic finish concrete ... 82	Office expense 7	clapboard 226
screen 191	Mop holder strip 250	field 14	cornice 232
sheet 161	roof 159	floor 242	decking 227
shelf 249	Mortar 86	partition 247, 412	drywall 232
shingle 153	Mortar, brick and block ... 537	partition movable 247	exterior 225
siding 155, 156	Mortar cement 217	safe 252	grille 231
soffit 166	mixer 15, 18	system modular 247	interior 230
specialties 114	Portland cement 86	trailer 14	parking stall 55
stair 111, 112	thinset 217	Oil burner 309	pavement 55
stair tread 81	Mortise lockset 199	fired boiler 308	pipe 232
stud 214	Mosaic tile 425	fired furnace 310	plaster 232
stud demolition 37	Motel swimming pool 272	heater temporary 18	reflective 55
support system 210	Motion detector 343	interceptor 302	siding 226
threshold 203	Motor connection 331	water heater 306	sprayer 18
tile 217, 425	generator 18	Olive knuckle hinge 200	steel siding 226
toilet partition 240	support 105	Omitted work 7	stucco 226
window 189, 190	Motorized modulating damper . 326	One piece astragal 202	temporary road 55
Metal-clad door 182	zone valve 324	Open web joist 107	thermoplastic 55
Metallic foil 146	Moulded door 178	Opener automatic 201	trim 232
hardener 77	Mounting board plywood ... 125	door 185, 186, 201	truss 232
waterproofing 77	Movable office partition ... 247	handicap 201	wall 232, 233
Meter socket 337	Move equipment 34	Operating cost equipment .. 15	window 231
water supply 306	furniture 34	Operator 201	Pan metal 72
water supply domestic ... 306	Movie screen 254	Options elevator 278	shower 164
Microtunneling 49	Moving building 43	Ornamental metal 114	slab 78
Microwave detector 343	shrub 65	railing 113	stair 82
oven 256	structure 43	OSHA testing 42	Panel acoustical 220, 248
Mill construction 128	tree 66	Outdoor lighting 17	architectural 127
Millwork 130, 138	Mud jack 15	Outlet box plastic 335	divider 248
demolition 33	Mullion vertical 206	box steel 335	door 178, 179
Mineral fiber ceiling 219	Multi-blade damper 325	lighting 348	fiberglass 13, 155
fiber insulation 148	Multizone air conditioner rooftop	Oven 257	fire 344
fiber panel 127	 319	cabinet 137	luminous 219
insulated cable 332, 333	Municipal swimming pool ... 272	convection 259	partitions 248
roof 159	Muntin window 196	microwave 256	portable 248
siding 127, 128	Mylar tarpaulin 14	Overhaul 27, 47	structural 127
wool blown in 146		Overhead 6	wall 79, 91
Mirror 205, 250	**N**	& profit 7	Panelboard 337
ceiling board 219		and profit 506	electric 338
door 205	Nail 118	commercial door 184	w/circuit-breaker 338
glass 205	Nailer 18	contractor 10, 21, 502	Paneled door 173
light fixture 341	pneumatic 17	door 184, 386	pine door 180
plexiglass 205	steel 121	Overlapping astragal 202	Paneling 133, 134, 425
wall 205	wood 121	Overlay fabric 54	board 134
Mix planting pit 65	Napkin dispenser 250	face door 175, 176, 178	cutout 28
Mixer concrete 15	Needle masonry 98	pavement 54	demolition 34, 495
food 258	Neoprene adhesive 144	Overtime 7	hardboard 133
mortar 15, 18	expansion joint 70, 166	Oxygen lance cutting 37	plywood 133
plaster 18	flashing 164		wood 133
Mixing box duct 325	gasket 170	**P**	Panelized shingle 154
valve 286, 317	roof 160		Panels insulated 149
Mobilization 47, 51	waterproofing 144	P trap 287	prefabricated 149
air-compressor 49	Newel 140	Packaging waste 41	Panic bar 200
equipment 49	No hub pipe 289	Pad condenser 324	device 199, 394, 423
Modification to cost 7	Non-destructive testing ... 9	prefabricated 324	device door hardware .. 197
Modified bitumen roofing ... 544	Non-metallic hardener 77	Padding carpet 224	Paper building 145
Modular air handler 311	sheathed cable 472	Paddle fan 349	curing 79
office 412	Non-removable pin 198	Paint aluminum siding ... 227	sheathing 145
office system 247	Norwegian brick 90	chain link fence 227	Paperhanging 233
Modulating damper motorized .. 326	Nosing rubber 223	doors & windows interior . 230	Paperholder 250
Module tub-shower 301	safety 223	encapsulation lead 235	Parallel bar 262
Moisture content test 9	stair 82, 223	fence picket 227	Parapet wall 380
Molding 130	Nozzle fire hose 307	floor 231	Park bench 62
base 130	Nylon carpet 224, 234	floor concrete 231	Parking barrier 62
brick 131		floor wood 231	barrier precast 62
ceiling 130	**O**	removal 235	control equipment 255
chair 131		siding 227	equipment 255
cornice 131	Oak door frame 174	trim 228	lot asphalt 491
exterior 130	floor 220	walls masonry 229	lot concrete 492
hardboard 134		Painting 425	lots paving 52
pine 130			stall painting 55

621

Index

Parquet floor 221
Particle board siding 157
   board underlayment 126
   core door 176
Parting bead 132
Partition 247, 248
   acoustical 248
   anchor 88
   block 92
   blueboard 215
   bulletproof 252
   concrete block 406
   demolition 37
   demountable 247
   door 247
   drywall 214, 215, 409
   dust 27
   folding 248
   folding leaf 248
   framing 214
   gypsum 215, 247
   metal stud 408, 410
   movable office 247, 412
   office 247
   plaster 411
   portable 248
   sheetrock 214, 215
   shower 241
   steel 247
   stud 211
   support 105
   thin plaster 215
   toilet 240
   wall 214, 215
   wood frame 124
   wood stud 407
Partitions accordion 248
   demountable 247
   panel 248
Passage door 180, 181
Passenger elevators 551
Patch core hole 9
   roof 161
Patching concrete 80
   concrete floor 80
   concrete wall 80
Patio 62
   door 182
Paumelle hinge 200
Pavement 51
   asphaltic 51
   berm 53
   demolition 25, 26
   emulsion 54
   marking 55
   overlay 54
   painting 55
   profiling 54
   pulverization 54
   reclaimation 54
   recycling 54
   replacement 51
Paver bituminous 18
   concrete 18
   floor 222
Pavers 52
Paving and surfacing 51
   asphaltic 519
   block granite 53
   brick 52
   concrete 51
   parking lots 52
Peastone 65
Pedestal floor 242
Pegboard 133
Penetration test 24

Perforated ceiling 219
Performance bond 507, 508
Perlite concrete 84
   insulation 147
   plaster 212
   sprayed 225
Permit building 8
Personal respirator 39
Personnel field 6, 7
   hoist 20
Pew church 252
Phone booth 249
PIB roof 160
Pickup truck 19
Picture window 189, 194
Pier brick 89
   concrete 78
Pilaster formwork 74
   toilet partition 241
   wood column 141
Pile cap 73, 79, 81
   cast in place 50
   concrete 50
   cutoff 49
   driven 50
   driver 16
   driving 49, 511
   friction 50
   H 50
   hammer 16
   load test 50
   mobilization hammer 49
   pipe 50
   sod 65
   steel 50
   steel sheet 43
   step tapered 50
   testing 49
   treated 50
   wood 50, 518
   wood sheet 43
Piling sheet 43
Pin floating 198
   non-removable 198
Pine door 179
   door frame 174
   fireplace mantel 134
   floor 221
   molding 130
   roof deck 130
   shelving 132
   siding 157
   stair 140
   stair tread 139
Pipe 288
   & fittings .. 284-286, 290, 291, 294,
                     295, 297 -300
   and fittings 551
   bedding 56
   bedding trench 56
   bollards 62
   brass 288
   cast iron 289
   cleanout 284
   column 105
   concrete 58, 520
   copper 290, 291
   corrosion resistant 293
   corrugated metal 58
   covering 315
   covering fiberglass 315
   CPVC 294
   double wall 56, 57
   drainage 58, 293
   DWV ABS 294
   DWV PVC 294

elevated installation 288
encapsulation 42
epoxy fiberglass wound 293
fitting brass 288
fitting cast iron 289, 297
fitting copper 291
fitting corrosion resistant 293
fitting DWV 295
fitting grooved joint 299
fitting malleable iron 298
fitting no hub 289
fitting plastic 295, 296
fitting soil 289
fitting steel 299
fitting steel carbon 299
fitting weld steel 299
gas 57
glass 293
grooved joint 299
insulation 315
insulation removal 40
iron alloy mechanical joint 293
liner 59
no hub 289
painting 232
pile 50
plastic 294
plastic, FRP 294
polyethylene 57
PVC 58
rail 112, 113
reinforced concrete 58
removal 26, 36
sewage 58
shock absorber 287
single hub 289
soil 289
stainless 113
steel 296, 297
support framing 105
vitrified clay 58
weld joint 297
Piped utilities 56
Piping demolition 496
   gas station 56
   heat-cool 317
Pit excavation 45
   leaching 59
Pitch coal tar 158
   emulsion tar 54
   pockets 168
Pivoted window 189
Placing concrete 80, 531
Plain tube framing 206
Planer shop 263
Planing cold 54
Plank floor 128
   roof 127
   sheathing 125
Plant bed preparation 65
   screening 16
Planter 63
   concrete 63
   fiberglass 63
Planting 65
   price sheet 497
Plants trees 65
Plaster 422
   and drywall price sheet 422
   beam 212
   ceiling 212
   column 212
   cutout 28
   demolition 27, 37
   drill 102
   ground 124

   gypsum 212, 547
   mixer 18
   painting 232
   partition thin 215
   perlite 212
   thincoat 212
   veneer 212
   wall 212
Plasterboard 213
Plastic convector cover 132
   door 174
   fabrications 141
   faced hardboard 134
   fitting 295
Plastic, FRP pipe 294
Plastic glazing 205
   laminate 132
   laminate door 176
   laminated countertop 132
   lead 271
   outlet box 335
   pipe 294
   pipe fitting 295, 296
   roof ventilator 322
   skylight 168
   valve 301
Plate compactor 45
   glass 204
Plate heat exchanger 453
Plate push-pull 200
   shear 119
   vibrating 45
   wall switch 336
Platform lifter 256
Plating zinc 118
Players bench 63
Plenum silencer 326
Plexiglass 205
   mirror 205
Plug in tandem circuit-breaker . 338
Plugmold raceway 332
Plumbing 284
   appliance 306
   demolition 35
   fixture 301, 303, 304, 552
   fixtures removal 35
   laboratory 263
   system 434-441
Plywood 541
   clip 119
   demolition 27, 36, 37
   fence 13
   floor 126
   formwork 71-73
   joist 128
   mounting board 125
   paneling 133
   sheathing 125
   shelving 132
   sidewalk 13
   siding 157
   sign 244
   soffit 135
   stressed skin 127
   subfloor 126
   treatment 136
   underlayment 126
Pneumatic nailer 17
   tube system 280
Pocket door frame 175
   pitch 168
Pockets pitch 168
Pointing masonry 98
   tuck 98
Poisoning soil 49
Pole closet 131

Index

tele-power ... 332
Police connect panel ... 343
Polycarbonate glazing ... 206
Polyethylene expansion joint ... 70
   floor ... 223
   pipe ... 57
   septic tank ... 59
   tarpaulin ... 13
   waterproofing ... 144
Polystyrene blind ... 135
   ceiling ... 219
   ceiling panel ... 219
   insulation ... 146, 147
Polysulfide caulking ... 170
Polyurethane caulking ... 170
   expansion joint ... 70
   varnish ... 225
Polyvinyl chloride roof ... 160
   soffit ... 166
   tarpaulin ... 13
Pool swimming ... 272
Porcelain tile ... 216
Porch molding ... 131
Portable air compressor ... 17
   building ... 272
   fire extinguisher ... 245
   heater ... 18
   panel ... 248
   partition ... 248
   stage ... 253
Portland cement terrazzo ... 218
Post cap ... 119
   cedar ... 141
   demolition ... 32
   fence ... 60
   lamp ... 114
   light ... 342
   wood ... 122
Postal specialty ... 247
Posts sign ... 62
Potters wheel ... 263
Poured gypsum ... 84
   insulation ... 146
Powder actuat. tools & fasten. ... 104
Power system ... 340
   temporary ... 9
   wiring ... 337
Precast architectural ... 83
   beam ... 83
   catch basin ... 58
   column ... 83
   concrete ... 83
   coping ... 89
   curb ... 53
   grate ... 52
   lintel ... 83
   manhole ... 58
   members ... 534
   parking barrier ... 62
   sill ... 91
   stair ... 83
   terrazzo ... 218
Prefabricated building ... 272
   fireplace ... 242
   panels ... 149
Prefinished door ... 175, 176
   drywall ... 213
   floor ... 221
   shelving ... 132
Preformed roof panel ... 155
   roofing & siding ... 155
Pre-hung door ... 180
Premolded expansion joint ... 70
Preparation lawn bed ... 64
   plant bed ... 65
   surface ... 235-237

Preservative treatment ... 136
Pressure booster pump ... 305
   grout ... 48
   grouting cement ... 48
   valve relief ... 300
   wash ... 237
Prestressed precast concrete ... 534
Pretreatment termite ... 49
Primer asphalt ... 161, 223
Prison fence ... 61
   hinge ... 200
Prisons work in ... 6
Process air handling fan ... 322
Proctor compaction test ... 9
Produce case ... 254
Product dispenser ... 255
   piping ... 57
Profile block ... 92
Profiling pavement ... 54
Project sign ... 14
Projected window ... 189, 190
Projection screen ... 253, 254
Protection fire ... 245
   radiation ... 270
   slope ... 48
   stile ... 202
   termite ... 49
   winter ... 13
   worker ... 39
Protectors ADA insulated ... 314
P&T relief valve ... 300
Public address system ... 344
Pull box ... 335
   door ... 138
Pulverization pavement ... 54
Pump ... 304
   circulating ... 304
   concrete ... 15, 80
   diaphragm ... 18
Pump end suction ... 448
Pump gasoline ... 255
   heat ... 318
   pressure booster ... 305
   rental ... 18
   sewage ejector ... 305
   staging ... 12, 510
   submersible ... 18, 305
   sump ... 257
   trash ... 18
   water ... 18, 56
Purlin roof ... 128
Push button lock ... 198
Push-pull ... 394, 424
   plate ... 200
Putlog ... 12
Puttying ... 236
PVC adhesive ... 144
   conduit in slab ... 328
   control joint ... 86
   DWV pipe ... 294
   expansion joint ... 70
   fitting ... 295
   flashing ... 164
   gravel stop ... 167
   pipe ... 58, 294
   sheet ... 144, 223
   siding ... 156, 157
   waterstop ... 75
Pyrex pipe ... 293

Q

Quality control ... 8
Quarry tile ... 217
Quarter round molding ... 131
Quoins ... 96

R

Raceway ... 328-331
   plugmold ... 332
   wiremold ... 331
   wireway ... 328
Rack coat ... 138
   hose ... 307
Radial arch ... 129
   wall ... 74
Radiant heat ... 270
Radiation fin tube ... 314
   protection ... 270
Radiator cast iron ... 314
Radiography test ... 9
Rafter ... 122
   anchor ... 119
   composite ... 122
   demolition ... 32
   wood ... 122
Rail ... 280
   bumper ... 112
   crane ... 280
   dock shelter ... 256
   guide ... 62
   guide/guard ... 62
   hand ... 113
   pipe ... 112, 113
   wall ... 113
Railing aluminum ... 113
   demolition ... 34
   industrial ... 113
   ornamental ... 113
   steel ... 113
   wood ... 131, 139, 140
Railroad tie ... 54
   tie step ... 62
   track removal ... 26
Raised floor ... 242
Rake topsoil ... 64
Rammer tamper ... 45
Ramp handicap ... 79
Ranch plank floor ... 221
Range cooking ... 256
   hood ... 256
   receptacle ... 336, 347
   restaurant ... 259
Ready mix ... 530
   mix concrete ... 77, 508, 531
   mix cost ... 530
Receptacle air conditioner ... 347
   device ... 347
   dryer ... 347
   duplex ... 336
   GFI ... 347
   locking ... 347
   range ... 336, 347
   telephone ... 348
   television ... 348
   waste ... 250
   weatherproof ... 347
Receptor floor ... 286
Recip. hermetic compressor ... 320
   water chiller ... 320
Reclaimation pavement ... 54
Recore cylinder ... 198, 199
Rectangular diffuser ... 324
   ductwork ... 321
Recycling cold ... 54
   pavement ... 54
Redwood cupola ... 244
   louver ... 134
   paneling ... 134
   siding ... 157
   trim ... 131
   wine cellar ... 260

Refinish floor ... 221
Reflective block ... 95
   glass ... 205
   insulation ... 146
   painting ... 55
   sign ... 62
Refractories ... 97
Refrigerant removal ... 41
Refrigerated case ... 254
   wine cellar ... 260
Refrigeration ... 270
   commercial ... 254, 259
   residential ... 257
Refrigerator door ... 183
Refuse chute ... 280
Register air supply ... 325
   baseboard ... 325
   cash ... 254
Reglet ... 165
   aluminum ... 165, 404
   copper ... 404
   galvanized steel ... 165
   steel ... 404
Rehabilitation concrete ... 84
Reinforced concrete pipe ... 58
   culvert ... 58
   masonry ... 93
   PVC roof ... 160
Reinforcement concrete ... 75
Reinforcing beam ... 75
   column ... 75
   dowels ... 76
   fiber ... 76
   footing ... 75
   girder ... 75
   joint ... 87
   ladder ... 87
   masonry ... 87
   slab ... 75
   steel ... 75
   truss ... 87
   wall ... 75
Relay electric ... 339
Release door ... 345
Relining exist. pipelines ... 59
Removal air conditioner ... 33
   asbestos ... 39-41
   block wall ... 38
   catch basin ... 25
   chain link fence ... 25
   concrete ... 25, 38
   concrete pipe ... 26
   curb ... 26
   driveway ... 25
   fence ... 25
   floor ... 38
   guide rail ... 25
   hydrant ... 25
   insulation ... 40
   lavatory ... 35
   masonry ... 25
   paint ... 235
   pipe ... 26, 36
   pipe insulation ... 40
   plumbing fixtures ... 35
   railroad track ... 26
   refrigerant ... 41
   shingle ... 36
   sidewalk ... 26
   sod ... 65
   steel pipe ... 26
   stone ... 25
   tank ... 42
   tree ... 63
   urinal ... 36
   vat ... 41

Index

water closet . . . 36
water fountain . . . 36
window . . . 37
Remove topsoil . . . 64
Rendering . . . 8
Rental equipment . . . 15, 19
equipment rate . . . 10, 15
generator . . . 18
Repair crack . . . 84
fire damage . . . 236
slate . . . 153
Repellent water . . . 233
Replacement glass . . . 205
pavement . . . 51
sash . . . 197
sliding door . . . 182
windows . . . 194, 546
Resaturant roof . . . 161
Reshoring . . . 75
Residential alarm . . . 348
appliance . . . 254, 256, 349
burner . . . 309
closet door . . . 173
device . . . 345
door . . . 173, 175, 179, 384
door bell . . . 348
dryer . . . 254
elevator . . . 276
fan . . . 349
fixture . . . 342, 348
folding partition . . . 248
garage door . . . 184
greenhouse . . . 272
gutting . . . 32
heat pump . . . 349
heater electric . . . 344
hinge . . . 198
lighting . . . 348
loadcenter . . . 345
lock . . . 198
overhead door . . . 184
refrigeration . . . 257
roof jack . . . 322
service . . . 345
smoke detector . . . 348
stair . . . 140
storm door . . . 186
swimming pool . . . 272
switch . . . 345
transition . . . 322
ventilation . . . 322
wall cap . . . 322
washer . . . 254
water heater . . . 306, 349
wiring . . . 345, 349
Resilient base and accessories . . . 223
floor . . . 222
tile floor . . . 222
Resin epoxy . . . 77
Respirator . . . 39
personal . . . 39
Resquared shingle . . . 153
Restaurant range . . . 259
Restoration concrete . . . 84
masonry . . . 98
window . . . 235
Retaining wall . . . 49, 79
wall formwork . . . 74
Retarder vapor . . . 145
Revolving door . . . 261
Rib lath . . . 211
Ribbed waterstop . . . 75
Ridge board . . . 122
cap . . . 152
vent . . . 168, 242
Rig drill . . . 24
Rigid anchor . . . 88
conduit in-trench . . . 329
in slab conduit . . . 328
insulation . . . 146
Ring split . . . 119
toothed . . . 119
Riser rubber . . . 224
stair . . . 218
terrazzo . . . 218
wood stair . . . 140
Road base . . . 48
berm . . . 53
sign . . . 62
Robe hook . . . 250
Rock drill . . . 24
Rocker switch . . . 336
Rod backer . . . 70, 169
closet . . . 132
curtain . . . 249
ground . . . 334, 335
tie . . . 106
Roll roof . . . 158
roofing . . . 159
type air filter . . . 323
up grille . . . 183
Roller earth . . . 16
vibrating . . . 44, 45
Rolling door . . . 186, 189
service door . . . 186
topsoil . . . 64
tower . . . 12
Roman brick . . . 90
Romex copper . . . 333
Roof accessories . . . 167
accessory price sheet . . . 403, 404
adhesive . . . 158
aluminum . . . 155
baffle . . . 168
beam . . . 129
built-up . . . 158
cant . . . 122, 159
clay tile . . . 154
coating . . . 161
copper . . . 161
CSPE . . . 160
deck . . . 107, 127
deck concrete . . . 83
deck insulation . . . 148
deck laminated . . . 130
deck wood . . . 130
drains . . . 285
elastomeric . . . 160
EPDM . . . 160
expansion joint . . . 115, 166
fiberglass . . . 155
fill . . . 535
flashing vent chimney . . . 317
folded plate . . . 127
frame . . . 106
framing removal . . . 28
hatch . . . 167, 400
insulation . . . 148
jack residential . . . 322
joint . . . 167
lead . . . 161
metal . . . 155
mineral . . . 159
modified bitumen . . . 160
mop . . . 159
nail . . . 118
panel preformed . . . 155
patch . . . 161
PIB . . . 160
plywood . . . 127
polyvinyl chloride . . . 160
purlin . . . 128
rafter . . . 122
reinforced PVC . . . 160
resaturant . . . 161
roll . . . 158
sheathing . . . 125
sheet metal . . . 161
shingle . . . 152
single-ply . . . 160
skylight . . . 168
slate . . . 153
specialties, prefab . . . 166
stainless steel . . . 161
steel . . . 155
stressed skin . . . 127
tile . . . 154
truss . . . 128-130
vent . . . 168
ventilator . . . 168
ventilator plastic . . . 322
walkway . . . 159
wood . . . 127
zinc . . . 162
Roofing & siding preformed . . . 155
built-up . . . 401
cold . . . 159
demolition . . . 36, 41, 496
elastomeric . . . 401
finish price sheet . . . 401
membrane . . . 158
modified bitumen . . . 160
roll . . . 159
sheet metal . . . 161
shingle . . . 401
single ply . . . 160
Rooftop air conditioner . . . 319
multizone air conditioner . . . 319
Room athletic . . . 270
humidifier . . . 314
Root raking & loading . . . 64
Rope exercise . . . 262
Rosewood door . . . 177
Rosin paper . . . 145
Rotary hammer drill . . . 18
Rough buck . . . 121
carpentry . . . 119
hardware . . . 125
stone . . . 95
stone wall . . . 95
Rough-in drinking fountain floor . . . 302
drinking fountain wall . . . 302
sink countertop . . . 303
sink raised deck . . . 303
sink service floor . . . 303
tub . . . 302
Round rail fence . . . 61
Rubber astragal . . . 202
base . . . 222
coating . . . 145
control joint . . . 86
expansion joint . . . 70
floor . . . 223
floor tile . . . 223
nosing . . . 223
riser . . . 224
sheet . . . 223
stair . . . 223
threshold . . . 203
tile . . . 222
tired roller . . . 16
waterproofing . . . 144
Rubberized asphalt . . . 55
Rubbish chute . . . 27
handling . . . 27
Rug cleaning . . . 224

S

Safe office . . . 252
Safety equipment laboratory . . . 263
fixture industrial . . . 302
glass nosing . . . 114
nosing . . . 223
shower . . . 302
switch . . . 339
Salamander . . . 18
Sales tax . . . 8, 507
Salt treatment lumber . . . 136
Sampling air . . . 39
Sand fill . . . 44
Sandblast masonry . . . 97
Sandblasting concrete . . . 82
equipment . . . 18
Sander floor . . . 18
Sanding . . . 236
floor . . . 221
Sandstone . . . 96
Sandwich panel skylight . . . 169
Sanitary base cove . . . 216
Sash aluminum . . . 189
metal . . . 189
replacement . . . 197
security . . . 189
steel . . . 189
wood . . . 196
Sauna . . . 270
door . . . 270
Saw . . . 18
chain . . . 18
circular . . . 19
concrete . . . 15, 36
cutting . . . 36
masonry . . . 18
shop . . . 263
table . . . 263
Scaffold specialties . . . 11, 12
steel tubular . . . 10, 11
Scaffolding . . . 509
tubular . . . 10
Scanner checkout . . . 253
Scarify concrete . . . 31
subsoil . . . 64
School door hardware . . . 197
equipment . . . 261
hinge . . . 200
Scoreboard baseball . . . 262
SCR brick . . . 90
Scrape after damage . . . 236
Scraper . . . 16
mobilization . . . 47
Scratch coat . . . 218
Screed . . . 73
Screen . . . 191
chimney . . . 243
entrance . . . 241
fence . . . 61
metal . . . 191
molding . . . 131
projection . . . 253, 254
security . . . 114, 191
sight . . . 248
squirrel and bird . . . 243
urinal . . . 241
window . . . 191, 197
wood . . . 197
Screened loam . . . 64
topsoil . . . 64
Screening plant . . . 16
Screw jack . . . 43
Screws lag . . . 103
Seal curb . . . 54
pavement . . . 54

INDEX

624

Index

security . . . 202
slurry . . . 55
Sealant . . . 145
acoustical . . . 214
caulking . . . 169
tape . . . 170
Sealcoat . . . 54
Sealer concrete . . . 77
joint . . . 169
Seating movie . . . 253
Sectional door . . . 184
overhead door . . . 184
Security . . . 13
access . . . 272
and vault equipment . . . 252
fence . . . 61
hinge . . . 200
sash . . . 189
screen . . . 114, 191
seal . . . 202
Seeding . . . 65, 520
Selective demolition . . . 27
Self propelled crane . . . 20
Self-closing relief valve . . . 300
Self-contained air conditioner . . . 319
Sentry dog . . . 13
Separation barrier . . . 40
Septic galley . . . 59
system . . . 59, 489
tank . . . 59
tank concrete . . . 59
Service boring . . . 47
electric . . . 337
entrance cable aluminum . . . 333
entrance cap . . . 334
residential . . . 345
sink . . . 303
sink faucet . . . 286
station equipment . . . 255
Set accelerator . . . 77
Sewage drainage . . . 58
ejector pump . . . 305
pipe . . . 58
system . . . 58
Shade . . . 266
Shaft wall . . . 215
Shake wood . . . 153
Shear plate . . . 119
test . . . 9
wall . . . 125
Sheathed nonmetallic cable . . . 333
romex cable . . . 333
Sheathing . . . 125
asphalt . . . 126
gypsum . . . 126
paper . . . 145
plywood . . . 125
roof . . . 125
Sheepsfoot compactor . . . 44
Sheet base . . . 159
carpet . . . 224
floor . . . 225
metal . . . 161
metal aluminum . . . 162
metal cladding . . . 166
metal roofing . . . 161
piling . . . 43
Sheeting wale . . . 43
wood . . . 43, 514
Sheetrock . . . 213
partition . . . 214, 215
removal . . . 37
Sheets lead . . . 271
Shelf bathroom . . . 250
brick . . . 73
library . . . 252
metal . . . 249
Shellac door . . . 231
Shell/tube heat exchanger . . . 453
Shelter dock . . . 256
rail dock . . . 256
Shelving . . . 132
pine . . . 132
plywood . . . 132
prefinished . . . 132
storage . . . 249
wood . . . 132
Shield expansion . . . 102
Shielding lead . . . 270
Shingle . . . 152
aluminum . . . 152
asphalt . . . 152
concrete . . . 154
metal . . . 153
panelized . . . 154
removal . . . 36
roof . . . 152
strip . . . 152
wood . . . 153
Shock absorber . . . 287
absorber pipe . . . 287
absorbing door . . . 186
Shop drawing . . . 8
drill . . . 263
equipment . . . 263
Shoring . . . 43, 74
frame system . . . 75
horizontal . . . 75
installation . . . 74
vertical . . . 75
Shot blast floor . . . 31
Shovel front . . . 16
Shower by-pass valve . . . 286
compartments . . . 241
cubicle . . . 303
door . . . 241
glass door . . . 241
pan . . . 164
partition . . . 241
safety . . . 302
Shower-head water economizer . . . 303
Shrub broadleaf evergreen . . . 66
deciduous . . . 66
evergreen . . . 66
moving . . . 65
Shutter . . . 266
Sidelight . . . 175
Sidewalk . . . 52, 53, 222, 493
asphalt . . . 52
brick . . . 53
bridge . . . 11
concrete . . . 52
removal . . . 26
temporary . . . 13
Siding aluminum . . . 156
bevel . . . 157
cedar . . . 157
demolition . . . 36
fiber cement . . . 157
fiberglass . . . 155
hardboard . . . 157
metal . . . 155, 156
mineral . . . 127, 128
nail . . . 118
paint . . . 227
painting . . . 226
plywood . . . 157
redwood . . . 157
removal . . . 36
steel . . . 156
vinyl . . . 156
wood . . . 157
wood product . . . 157
Sign . . . 14, 62, 244
base . . . 74
directional . . . 62
posts . . . 62
project . . . 14
reflective . . . 62
road . . . 62
traffic . . . 62
Signal bell fire . . . 343
Silencer duct . . . 326
plenum . . . 326
Silicon carbide aggregate . . . 77
Silicone caulking . . . 170
coating . . . 145
water repellent . . . 145
Sill . . . 96, 122
anchor . . . 119
door . . . 132, 174, 203
masonry . . . 91
precast . . . 91
quarry tile . . . 217
stone . . . 95, 97
window . . . 196
Sillcock . . . 286
Silt fence . . . 49
Simulated brick . . . 91
Single hub pipe . . . 289
hung window . . . 189, 190
ply roofing . . . 160
zone rooftop unit . . . 319
Single-ply roof . . . 160
Sink . . . 303
barber . . . 253
base . . . 137
countertop . . . 303
countertop rough-in . . . 303
darkroom . . . 261
kitchen . . . 303
laundry . . . 303
raised deck rough-in . . . 303
removal . . . 35
service . . . 303
service floor rough-in . . . 303
Siren . . . 343
Sister joist . . . 121
Site demolition . . . 25
drainage . . . 58
improvement . . . 60, 62
preparation . . . 43
work electrical . . . 343
Site/street furnishings . . . 62
Skirtboard . . . 140
Skylight . . . 168, 400
plastic . . . 168
removal . . . 36
roof . . . 168
Skyroof . . . 169
Slab blockout . . . 73
concrete . . . 78, 81
cutout . . . 27
elevated . . . 78
form . . . 108
lift . . . 79, 533
on grade . . . 73, 79, 364
pan . . . 78
precast . . . 83
reinforcing . . . 75
textured . . . 79
waffle . . . 78
Slate . . . 97
flagging . . . 53
floor . . . 222
removal . . . 36
repair . . . 153
roof . . . 153
shingle . . . 153
sidewalk . . . 53
sill . . . 91
stair . . . 97
tile . . . 222
Slatwall . . . 234
Sleeper . . . 123, 375
Sleepers framing . . . 123
Slide gate . . . 60
Sliding door . . . 182, 385
entrance . . . 188
glass door . . . 182
mirror . . . 250
panel door . . . 188
window . . . 190, 195
Slop sink . . . 303
Slope protection . . . 48
Slot channel . . . 88
letter . . . 247
Slotted channel . . . 105
Slump block . . . 92
Slurry seal . . . 55
Small tools . . . 8
Smoke detector . . . 344
hatch . . . 168
vent . . . 168
vent chimney . . . 316
Snow fence . . . 61
Soap dispenser . . . 249, 250
holder . . . 250
tank . . . 250
Socket meter . . . 337
Sod . . . 65
Sodium high pressure fixture . . . 341
low pressure fixture . . . 340
Soffit drywall . . . 213
metal . . . 166
plaster . . . 212
plywood . . . 135
stucco . . . 212
vinyl . . . 156
wood . . . 135
Softener water . . . 257
Soil compaction . . . 43
compactor . . . 15
decontamination . . . 42
pipe . . . 289
poisoning . . . 49
preparation . . . 64
stabilization . . . 48
tamping . . . 43
test . . . 9
treatment . . . 49
Solar backflow preventer . . . 313
energy . . . 312, 313
energy circulator air . . . 312
energy system air purger . . . 313
energy system air vent . . . 313
energy system balancing valve . . . 313
energy system collector . . . 312
energy system control valve . . . 313
energy system controller . . . 312
energy system expansion tank . . . 313
energy system gauge pressure . . . 313
energy system heat exchanger . . . 312
energy system storage tank . . . 312
energy system thermometer . . . 313
energy system vacuum relief . . . 313
film glass . . . 205
system solenoid valve . . . 313
Solid core door . . . 176
fuel boiler . . . 309
fuel furnace . . . 311
surfacing . . . 141
wood door . . . 178
Sound attenuation . . . 220

INDEX

Index

movie ... 253
system component ... 344
Spa bath ... 301
Space frame ... 127
heater floor mounted ... 313
heater rental ... 18
Spade air ... 17
Spandrel beam ... 70
Spanish roof tile ... 154
Special coating ... 225
construction ... 272
door ... 181, 186
electrical system ... 343
floor ... 225
hinge ... 200
purpose door ... 185
systems ... 343
wires & fittings ... 334
Specialized equipment ... 263
Specialties ... 249
& accessories, roof ... 166
metal ... 114
scaffold ... 11, 12
Spike grid ... 119
Spiral stair ... 112, 140
Split astragal ... 202
rib block ... 92
ring ... 119
system ductless ... 319
Spotter ... 47
Spray coating ... 145
fireproofing ... 150
insulation ... 146
substrate ... 41
Sprayer airless ... 39
Spread footing ... 73, 79, 356
park soil ... 64
soil conditioner ... 64
topsoil ... 65
Spreader concrete ... 18
Spring bolt astragal ... 202
bronze weatherstrip ... 202
hinge ... 201
Sprinkler alarm ... 343
grass ... 60
head ... 307
system ... 60, 442, 443
system component ... 307
Stabilization soil ... 48
Stage equipment ... 253
portable ... 253
Staging aids ... 10
pump ... 12
swing ... 12
Stain cabinet ... 230
door ... 231
floor ... 231
lumber ... 129
siding ... 157
truss ... 232
Stainless cooling towers ... 321
duct ... 321
flashing ... 164
gutter ... 165
pipe ... 113
reglet ... 165
screen ... 241
steel bolt ... 103
steel gravel stop ... 167
steel hinge ... 198
steel roof ... 161
steel shelf ... 250
steel storefront ... 188
Stair ... 140, 374
basement ... 83, 139
carpet ... 224
ceiling ... 260
climber ... 276
concrete ... 79
demolition ... 496
electric ... 260
fire escape ... 112
landing ... 112, 218
metal ... 111, 112
nosing ... 82, 223
pan ... 82
precast ... 83
railroad tie ... 62
removal ... 32
residential ... 140
riser ... 218
riser vinyl ... 224
rubber ... 223
slate ... 97
spiral ... 140
steel ... 111
stringer ... 122, 218
stringer wood ... 122
temporary protection ... 9
tread ... 82, 95, 223
tread terrazzo ... 218
tread tile ... 217
tread wood ... 140
wood ... 139, 140
Stairlift wheelchair ... 276
Stairs disappearing ... 260
fire escape ... 112
Stairway door hardware ... 197
Stairwork and handrails ... 139
Stall toilet ... 240
type urinal ... 304
urinal ... 304
Stamping concrete ... 70
texture ... 70
Standard extinguisher ... 245
Standpipe connection ... 307
Starter ... 336
board & switch ... 336, 338
Starting newel ... 140
Steam bath ... 270
boiler ... 308, 309
boiler electric ... 307
clean masonry ... 97
cleaner ... 19
jacketed kettle ... 258
trap ... 317
Steamer ... 260
Steel anchor ... 88
astragal ... 202
blocking ... 119
bolt ... 118
bridging ... 120
conduit in slab ... 328
conduit in trench ... 329
conduit intermediate ... 328
corner guard ... 242
cutting ... 37, 106
deck ... 107
diffuser ... 324
door ... 172, 173, 183, 186
downspout ... 162
edging ... 54
estimating ... 538
fence ... 61
fitting ... 297
flashing ... 165
form ... 71
frame ... 173
frame formwork ... 72
furring ... 210
gravel stop ... 167
gutter ... 165
hinge ... 198
joist ... 107, 370
ladder ... 112
lath ... 211
light pole ... 466
lintel ... 106
locker ... 245
lockers ... 548
nailer ... 121
partition ... 247
pile ... 50
pipe ... 296, 297
pipe fitting ... 297, 299
pipe removal ... 26
reinforcing ... 75
roof ... 155
sash ... 189, 545
scaffold tubular ... 10, 11
sheet pile ... 43
shingle ... 153
shore ... 74
siding ... 156
stair ... 111
Steel storage tank ... 481, 482
Steel structural ... 105, 106
stud ... 214
tube ... 105
window ... 189
window demolition ... 37
Steeple ... 252
aluminum ... 252
tip pin ... 198
Step ... 62
bluestone ... 62
brick ... 62
masonry ... 62
railroad tie ... 62
stone ... 96
tapered pile ... 50
Sterilizer barber ... 253
Stile fabric ... 202
protection ... 202
Stone ... 95
aggregate ... 65
anchor ... 88
ashlar ... 95
base ... 48, 95
cast ... 91
cut ... 95
fill ... 44
floor ... 96
ground cover ... 65
paver ... 53
removal ... 25
rough ... 95
sill ... 95, 97
step ... 96
stool ... 97
threshold ... 91
tread ... 95
wall ... 49, 379
Stool cap ... 132
stone ... 97
window ... 91, 96
Stop door ... 131
gravel ... 167
water supply ... 286
Storage bottle ... 260
box ... 14
cabinet ... 263
door cold ... 183
shelving ... 249
Storefront aluminum ... 188
stainless steel ... 188
Storm door ... 186
window ... 190, 191, 390
Stove ... 243, 259
wood burning ... 243, 477
Strainer ... 317
bronze body ... 317
downspout ... 162
gutter ... 165
roof ... 162
wire ... 163
Y type ... 317
Strap hinge ... 201
tie ... 119
Strength compressive ... 8
Stressed skin ... 127
skin roof ... 127
Stringer stair ... 122, 218
stair terrazzo ... 218
Strip cabinet ... 345
filler ... 202
floor ... 220
footing ... 79, 357
lighting ... 341
shingle ... 152
Structural backfill ... 44
concrete ... 76, 532
excavation ... 45, 46
face tile ... 94
fee ... 6
formwork ... 70
panel ... 127
steel ... 105, 106, 369
steel extras ... 539
tile ... 94
welding ... 104
Structure moving ... 43
Stucco ... 212
demolition ... 37
mesh ... 211
painting ... 226
Stud connector ... 104
demolition ... 32
metal ... 214
partition ... 124, 125, 211
price sheet ... 420
steel ... 214
wall ... 124, 214, 215
Studs ... 547
loadbearing ... 108
welded ... 104
Subcontractor O & P ... 7
Subfloor ... 126
plywood ... 126
Subflooring ... 430
Submersible pump ... 18, 56, 305
Submittal ... 8
Subpurlins ... 539
Suction hose ... 18
Sump pump ... 257
Supermarket checkout ... 253
scanner ... 254
Support ceiling ... 105
framing pipe ... 105
lavatory ... 287
light ... 105
monitor ... 105
motor ... 105
partition ... 105
water closet ... 287
Suppressor lightning ... 345
Surface landscape ... 223
preparation ... 235-237
treatment ... 54, 55
Surfacing ... 54
solid ... 141
Surfactant ... 41
Survey crew ... 8
data ... 8

INDEX
626

Index

topographic ... 8
Suspended ceiling ... 210, 213, 219
Suspended space heater ... 449
Suspension system ... 376
   system acoustical ... 210
   system ceiling ... 210
   system ceiling tile ... 402
Swimming pool ... 272
   pool enclosure ... 272
Swing check valve ... 300
   clear hinge ... 200
   door ... 186
   staging ... 12
Swing-up overhead door ... 184
Switch ... 339
   box ... 335
   box plastic ... 335
   decorator ... 346
   dimmer ... 336, 345
   electric ... 339
   general duty ... 339
   load management ... 339
   residential ... 345
   rocker ... 336
   safety ... 339
   time ... 339
   toggle ... 336
Synthetic marble ... 222
Syphon ventilator rotary ... 326
System accessories heating ... 313
   antenna ... 345
   fire ... 307
   irrigation ... 60
   light pole ... 466
   power ... 340
   septic ... 59
   sewage ... 58
   solenoid valve solar ... 313
   special electrical ... 343
   sprinkler ... 60, 307
   tube ... 280
   water ... 56
   wood-metal ... 128

T

Table saw ... 263
   top ... 133
Tack coat ... 54
Tackboard ... 240
Tamper ... 17, 46
   compactor ... 45
   rammer ... 45
Tamping soil ... 43
Tandem roller ... 16
Tank clean ... 42
   darkroom ... 260
   developing ... 261
   disposal ... 42
   expansion ... 315
   fiberglass ... 315
   oil & gas ... 315
   removal ... 42
   septic ... 59
   soap ... 250
   testing ... 9
   water storage solar ... 313
Tape detection ... 56
   sealant ... 170
   temporary ... 55
   underground ... 56
Tar kettle/pot ... 19
   pitch emulsion ... 54
   roof ... 161
Tarpaulin ... 13

duck ... 13
mylar ... 14
polyethylene ... 13
polyvinyl ... 13
Tarred felt ... 159
Tax ... 8
   sales ... 8
   social security ... 8
   unemployment ... 8
Taxes ... 507
T-bar mount diffuser ... 324
Teak floor ... 221
   molding ... 131
   paneling ... 133
Technician inspection ... 9
Tee beam ... 83
   cleanout ... 284
   pipe ... 299
Telephone booth ... 249
   enclosure ... 249
   house ... 345
   receptacle ... 348
Tele-power pole ... 332
Telescoping bleacher ... 262
Television receptacle ... 348
Temperature relief valve ... 300
   rise detector ... 344
Tempered glass ... 204
   hardboard ... 133
Tempering valve ... 300
   valve water ... 317
Temporary building ... 14
   construction ... 9, 10
   control ... 13
   facility ... 13
   fence ... 13
   guardrail ... 13
   heat ... 9, 82
   light ... 9
   oil heater ... 18
   road painting ... 55
   tape ... 55
   toilet ... 19
   utility ... 9
Tennis court ... 60
Termination box ... 345
   mineral insulated cable ... 333
Termite pretreatment ... 49
   protection ... 49
Terne coated flashing ... 165
Terra cotta ... 94
   cotta coping ... 90
   cotta demolition ... 28
Terrazzo ... 218
   base ... 218
   demolition ... 31
   epoxy ... 225
   floor ... 218
   Portland cement ... 218
   precast ... 218
   wainscot ... 218
Test load pile ... 50
   moisture content ... 9
   penetration ... 24
   pile load ... 50
   soil ... 9
   ultrasonic ... 9
Testing ... 8
   OSHA ... 42
   pile ... 49
   tank ... 9
Texture stamping ... 70
Textured slab ... 79
Theater and stage equipment ... 253
Therm. solar energy system ... 313
Thermoplastic painting ... 55

Thermostat ... 323
   automatic timed ... 323
   integral ... 344
   wire ... 350
Thin plaster partition ... 215
   shell construction ... 127
Thincoat plaster ... 212
Thinset ceramic tile ... 216
   mortar ... 217
Threshold ... 203, 395, 424
   door ... 175
   stone ... 91, 96
   wood ... 132
Thru-the-wall A/C ... 461
   heat pump ... 461
Tie adjustable wall ... 87
   column ... 88
   flange ... 88
   rafter ... 122
   railroad ... 54
   rod ... 106
   strap ... 119
   wall ... 87, 88
   wire ... 88
Tile ... 216, 223, 425
   aluminum ... 154
   carpet ... 224
   ceiling ... 219, 220
   ceramic ... 216
   clay ... 154
   cork ... 222
   cork wall ... 233
   demolition ... 27
   facing ... 94
   glass ... 205
   marble ... 221
   metal ... 217
   porcelain ... 216
   quarry ... 217
   roof ... 154
   rubber ... 222
   setting materials ... 217
   slate ... 222
   stainless steel ... 217
   stair tread ... 217
   structural ... 94
   vinyl ... 223
   wall ... 216
   window sill ... 217
Tilling topsoil ... 65
Timber connector ... 118
   fastener ... 118
   framing ... 128
   guide rail ... 62
   heavy ... 128
   laminated ... 129
   roof deck ... 127
Time switch ... 339
Timer clock ... 348
   interval ... 345
   switch ventilator ... 323
Tin clad door ... 182
Tinted glass ... 204
Toaster ... 260
Toggle bolt ... 103
   switch ... 336
Toilet accessory ... 249
   bowl ... 304
   chemical ... 19
   compartments ... 240
   door hardware ... 197
   fixture demolition ... 496
   partition ... 240
   partition removal ... 37
   stall ... 240
   temporary ... 19

tissue dispenser ... 249, 250
trailer ... 19
Tool air ... 17
Tools small ... 8
Toothed ring ... 119
Toothing masonry ... 98
Top coiling grille ... 183
   demolition counter ... 33
   dressing ... 48
   table ... 133
Topographic survey ... 8
Topping concrete ... 82
   epoxy ... 225
   grout ... 80
Topsoil ... 44
   remove ... 64
   screened ... 64
Torch cutting ... 19, 37, 106
Touch bar ... 200
Towel bar ... 250
   dispenser ... 249, 250
Tower cooling ... 320
   crane ... 511
   hoist ... 20
   light ... 18
   rolling ... 12
Track drawer ... 138
   drill ... 17
   lighting ... 342
Tractor ... 16, 44, 46
   loader ... 16
Traffic cone ... 13
   line ... 55
   sign ... 62
Trailer office ... 14
   toilet ... 19
Trainer bicycle ... 261
Transformer ... 339
   & bus-duct ... 339
   cabinet ... 336
   dry type ... 339
Transit ... 19
Transition molding wood ... 221
   residential ... 322
Transom aluminum ... 187
   lite frame ... 174
   windows ... 195
Transplanting ... 63
Trap cast iron ... 287
   drainage ... 287
   grease ... 302
   inverted bucket steam ... 317
   P ... 287
   steam ... 317
Trapezoid windows ... 196
Trash pump ... 18
Tray cable ... 328
   laundry ... 303
Tread abrasive ... 217
   rubber ... 223
   stair ... 82, 95
   stone ... 97
   vinyl ... 223
   wood ... 140
Treadmill ... 262
Treated pile ... 50
   pine fence ... 62
Treatment acoustical ... 219
   lumber ... 136
   plywood ... 136
   preservative ... 136
   surface ... 54
   wood ... 136
Tree ... 66
   and shrub removal ... 63
   deciduous ... 66

Index

Tree evergreen 66
grate 52
guying 63
moving 66
removal 63
Trees plants 65
Trench backfill 46
box 19
excavation 46, 47, 56
formwork 73
utility 46
Trencher chain 17
Trim demolition 34
exterior 131
molding 131
paint 228
painting 232
redwood 131
tile 216
wood 131
Triple brick 90
weight hinge 200
Trowel coating 145
concrete 15
Truck boom 19
dock 255
dump 17
flatbed 17
hauling 47
loading 45
mounted crane 19
off highway 17
pickup 19
rental 17
vacuum 19
Truss bowstring 129
flying 75
painting 232
plate 119
reinforcing 87
roof 128-130
stain 232
varnish 232
wood 130
Tub bar 249
hot 302
redwood 302
rough-in 302
shower handicap 301
Tube framing 206
steel 105
system 280
system air 280
system pneumatic 280
Tubing copper 290
electric metallic 328
Tub-shower module 301
Tubular aluminum 106
fence 61
lock 197
scaffolding 10
steel joist 128
Tuck pointing 98
Tumbler holder 250
Tunnel construction 49
Tunneling 49
Turned column 140
TV antenna 345
Two piece astragal 202

U

Ultrasonic motion detector 343
test 9
Undereave vent 242
Underground duct 343
storage tank removal 512
tape 56
Underlayment 126, 430
acoustical 220
grout 80
latex 223
Underpin foundation 43
Underpinning 43
Unemployment tax 8
Union dielectric 285
Unit heater 313
heater electric 344
masonry 89
Urethane foam 170, 220
insulation 146
wall coating 225
Urinal 304
removal 36
screen 241
stall 304
stall type 304
wall hung 304
Utilities electric 343
piped 56
Utility brick 90
duct 343
electric 343
set fan 322
sitework 343
temporary 9
trench 46
vault 56

V

Vacuum breaker 288
central 252
cleaning 252
loader 39
truck 19
Valance board 137
Valley flashing 152
rafter 122
Valve 300
assembly dry pipe sprinkler . . . 307
ball 301
bronze 300
butterfly 301
CPVC 301
fire hose 307
flush 285
gate 301
heating control 324
iron body 301
mixing 286, 317
motorized zone 324
plastic 301
relief pressure 300
shower by-pass 286
swing check 300
tempering 300
water pressure 300
water supply 286
Vandalproof fixture 341
Vanity base 139
top lavatory 302
Vapor barrier 145
barrier sheathing 126
retarder 145
Vaportight fixture incandescent . 341
Variable frequency drives 336
volume damper 326
Varnish 425
cabinet 230
casework 230
door 231
floor 231, 233
polyurethane 225
truss 232
Vat removal 41
Vault utility 56
Vaulting side horse 262
VCT removal 31
Veneer brick 94
ceramic 94
core paneling 133
granite 96
masonry 94
members laminated 129
plaster 212
removal 39
Venetian terrazzo 218
Vent box 89
chimney 316
chimney all fuel 316
chimney fitting 316
chimney flashing 316
damper 309, 310
draft damper 309
exhaust 326
flashing 288
foundation 89
metal chimney 316
ridge 168, 242
ridge strip 242
roof 168
smoke 168
Ventilating air conditioning . 319, 320, 322 , 323, 325, 326
Ventilation 318
fan 349
louver 134
residential 322
Ventilator fan 322
masonry 89
roof 168
rotary syphon 326
timer switch 323
Verge board 131
Vermiculite insulation 146
Vertical lift door 185
shore 75
Vibrating plate 45
roller 44, 45
Vibrator concrete 15
earth 16, 44, 46
plate 44
Vibratory equipment 15, 16
roller 16
Vinyl blind 135
composition floor 223
faced wallboard 213
floor 223
gutter 165
plastic waterproofing 144
roof 160
siding 156
soffit 156
stair riser 224
stair tread 224
tile 223
tread 223
wall coating 225
wallpaper 233
Vitrified clay pipe 58
Vocational kiln 263
shop equipment 263
Void formwork 72
Volume control damper 326

W

Waffle slab 78
Wainscot molding 131
quarry tile 217
terrazzo 218
Wale sheeting 43
Walk 52
Walkway roof 159
Wall & corner guards 242
aluminum 156
aluminum curtain 206
anchor 102, 103
block 537
bumper 197
cabinet 137, 263
canopy 245
cap residential 322
ceramic tile 216
coating 225, 425
concrete 79, 81
concrete block 359, 378
cross 252
curtain 206
cutout 28
demolition 37, 496
drill 102
drywall 213
expansion joint 114
finish 82
forms 521
formwork 73
foundation 93
framing 123
framing removal 28
furnace 313
furring 124, 210
grout 86
hung lavatory 303
hung urinal 304
hydrant 307
insulation 93, 146, 147
lath 210, 211
louver 242
masonry 49, 91
mat 262
mirror 205
painting 232, 233
panel 79, 91
paneling 133
partition 214, 215
patching concrete 80
plaster 212
radial 74
rail 113
reinforcing 75
removal 38
retaining 49, 79
shaft 215
shear 125
sheathing 125, 126
siding 157
stucco 212
stud 124, 214, 215
switch plate 336
tie 87, 88
tie masonry 87
tile 216
tile cork 233
urn ash receiver 250
window 207
wood frame 382
Wallboard acoustical 214
Wallcovering 233, 425
acrylic 233
gypsum fabric 233

INDEX

628

Index

Wallpaper ... 233
  grass cloth ... 233
  removal ... 233
  vinyl ... 233
Walls and partitions demolition ... 37
Walnut door frame ... 174
  floor ... 221
Wardrobe wood ... 138
Warm air system ... 310
Wash bowl ... 302
  fountain ... 304
  fountain group ... 304
Washer ... 119
  commercial ... 254
  darkroom ... 261
  residential ... 254
Waste handling ... 256
  handling equipment ... 256
  packaging ... 41
  receptacle ... 250
Watchdog ... 13
Watchman service ... 13
Water appliance ... 305
  atomizer ... 39
  blasting ... 97
  chiller ... 320
  closet ... 304
  closet removal ... 36
  closet support ... 287
  cooler ... 305
  distribution system ... 56
  fountain removal ... 36
  heater ... 306, 349
  heater commercial ... 306
  heater electric ... 306
  heater gas ... 306
  heater insulation ... 314
  heater oil ... 306
  heater removal ... 36
  heater residential ... 306
  heater wrap kit ... 314
  heating hot ... 308, 313
  hose ... 18
  hydrant ... 287
  motor alarm ... 307
  pipe ground clamp ... 335
  pressure relief valve ... 300
  pressure valve ... 300
  pump ... 18, 56, 257, 304
  repellent ... 233
  repellent coating ... 145
  repellent silicone ... 145
  softener ... 257
  storage solar tank ... 313
  supply domestic meter ... 306
  supply meter ... 306
  supply valve ... 286
  system ... 56
  tempering valve ... 300, 317
  well ... 56
Waterproofing ... 77, 144
  butyl ... 144
  cementitious ... 144
  coating ... 145
  elastomeric ... 144
  membrane ... 55, 144
  neoprene ... 144
  rubber ... 144
Waterstop ... 75
  barrier ... 70
  PVC ... 75
  ribbed ... 75
Wearing course ... 51
Weatherproof receptacle ... 347
Weatherstrip ... 186, 203
  aluminum ... 202

and seals ... 202
  door ... 203
Weatherstripping ... 395
Weathervanes ... 114
Wedge anchor ... 103
  bolt ... 103
Weight exercise ... 261
  lifting multi station ... 262
Weld fillet ... 104
  joint pipe ... 297
Welded frame ... 174
  structural steel ... 538
  studs ... 104
  wire fabric ... 76
Welder arc ... 263
Welding ... 104
  certification ... 9
  machine ... 19
  structural ... 104
Well ... 56
  water ... 56
Wheel potters ... 263
Wheelbarrow ... 19
Wheelchair lift ... 276
  stairlift ... 276
Whirlpool bath ... 301
Wide throw hinge ... 200
Window ... 189
  air conditioner ... 320
  aluminum ... 189, 190
  awning ... 192
  bank ... 252
  blind ... 135, 266
  casement ... 189, 192, 193
  casing ... 130
  demolition ... 37, 496
  double hung ... 189, 192, 193
  frame ... 196
  glass ... 205
  grille ... 196
  guard ... 114
  hardware ... 197
  industrial ... 189
  metal ... 189, 190
  metal jalousie ... 190
  muntin ... 196
  painting ... 231
  picture ... 189, 194
  pivoted ... 189
  projected ... 189
  removal ... 37
  restoration ... 235
  screen ... 191, 197
  sill ... 91
  sill tile ... 217
  sliding ... 195
  steel ... 189
  stool ... 91, 96
  storm ... 190, 191
  trim set ... 132
  wall ... 207, 391
  wall framing ... 105, 106, 206
  wood ... 192, 193, 195, 196
  wood and plastic ... 192
Windows transom ... 195
  trapezoid ... 196
Wine cellar ... 260
Winter protection ... 13, 82
Wire ... 114
  aluminum ... 334
  copper ... 334
  electric ... 334
  fabric welded ... 76
  fence ... 13, 61
  glass ... 205
  ground ... 335

mesh ... 212
mesh locker ... 245
strainer ... 163
thermostat ... 350
THW ... 334
tie ... 88
window guard ... 114
Wiremold raceway ... 331
  raceway, non-metallic ... 332
Wireway raceway ... 328
Wiring air conditioner ... 349
  device ... 336
  devices price sheet ... 472, 473
  fan ... 349
  power ... 337
  residential ... 345, 349
Wood base ... 130, 141
  beam ... 120, 128
  bench ... 63
  blind ... 135
  block floor ... 221
  block floor demolition ... 31
  blocking ... 119, 125
  burning furnace ... 311
  casing ... 130
  coal/oil combination furnace ... 311
  column ... 122, 128, 140
  cupola ... 244
  deck ... 127, 130
  demolition ... 27
  dome ... 127
  door ... 174-176, 178, 179
  doors ... 545
  drawer ... 139
  exterior surface ... 392
  fascia ... 131
  fastener ... 119
  fiber ... 84
  fiber ceiling ... 219
  fiber sheathing ... 126
  fiber soffit ... 135
  fiber subfloor ... 126
  fiber underlayment ... 126
  floor ... 220, 221
  floor demolition ... 31
  folding partition ... 248
  frame ... 138, 174
  frame wall ... 382
  framing ... 119, 120, 124
  furring ... 124
  girder ... 120
  gutter ... 165
  handrail ... 131
  joist ... 121, 128, 372
  laminated ... 129
  louver ... 134
  molding ... 140
  nailer ... 121
  overhead door ... 184
  panel door ... 178
  paneling ... 133
  partition ... 124
  pile ... 50, 518
  product siding ... 157
  rafter ... 122
  railing ... 140
  roof ... 127
  roof deck ... 127
  roof deck demolition ... 36
  roof truss ... 130
  roof trusses ... 543
  sash ... 196
  screen ... 197
  shake ... 153
  sheathing ... 125
  sheet piling ... 514

sheeting ... 43, 514
shelving ... 132
shingle ... 153
sidewalk ... 52
siding ... 157
siding demolition ... 36
sill ... 123
soffit ... 135
stair ... 139, 140, 543
stair stringer ... 122
storm door ... 180
strip floor ... 220
subfloor ... 126
threshold ... 132
tread ... 140
treatment ... 136
trim ... 131
truss ... 130
veneer wallpaper ... 233
wardrobe ... 138
window ... 192, 193, 195, 196, 388, 389
window demolition ... 37
Wood/coal oil fired boiler ... 309
Wood-metal system ... 128
Woodwork architectural ... 136
Wool fiberglass ... 146
  lead ... 70
Work extra ... 7
  in prisons ... 6
Worker protection ... 39
Workers' compensation ... 503-505
Wrecking ball ... 19
Wrench impact ... 17
Wrestling mat ... 262

X

X-ray barrier ... 271
  concrete slabs ... 9
  protection ... 271

Y

Yellow pine floor ... 221

Z

Z bar suspension ... 210
Zee bar ... 216
Zinc divider strip ... 218
  plating ... 118
  roof ... 162
  terrazzo strip ... 218
  weatherstrip ... 203

Notes

Construction Market Data Group...

R.S. Means Company, Inc., a CMD Group company, the leading provider of construction cost data in North America, supplies comprehensive construction cost guides, related technical publications and educational services.

CMD Group, a leading worldwide provider of proprietary construction information, is comprised of three synergistic product groups crafted to be the complete resource for reliable, timely and actionable construction market data. In North America, CMD Group encompasses: Architects' First Source, an innovative product selection and specification solution in print and on the Internet; Construction Market Data (CMD), the source for construction project information for sales leads, market construction activity information as well as early planning reports for the design community; Associated Construction Publications, with 14 magazines, one of the largest editorial networks dedicated to U.S. highway and heavy construction coverage; Manufacturer's Survey Associates (MSA), the leading estimating and quantity survey firm in the U.S.; R.S. Means, the authority on construction cost data in North America; CMD Canada, the leading supplier of project information, industry news and forecasting data products for the Canadian construction industry and BIMSA/Mexico, the dominant distributor of information on building projects and construction throughout Mexico. Worldwide, CMD Group includes Byggfakta Scandinavia, providing construction market data to Denmark, Estonia, Finland, Norway and Sweden; and Cordell Building Information Services, the market leader for construction cost information in Australia.

Architects' First Source for Products, available in print, on the Means CostWorks CD, and on the Internet, is a comprehensive, product information source. Through an alliance with The Construction Specifications Institute (CSI) and Thomas Register, Architects' First Source also produces CSI's SPEC-DATA® and MANU-SPEC® as well as CADBlocks℠ which deliver manufacturers' technical product data, proprietary specifications, and dimensionally accurate drawings. Together, these products offer commercial building product information for each member of the building team at each stage of the construction process.

Construction Market Data provides complete, accurate and timely project information through all stages of construction. Construction Market Data supplies industry data through productive leads, project reports, contact lists, market penetration analysis and sales evaluation reports. Any of these products can pinpoint a county, look at a state, or cover the country. Data is delivered via paper, e-mail or the Internet.

Construction Market Data Canada serves the Canadian construction market with reliable and comprehensive information services that cover all facets of construction. Core services include: Buildcore Product Source, a preliminary product selection tool available in print and on the Internet; national construction project lead services such as customized CMD Key products, weekly CMD Bulletins and CMD Online; CanaData, statistical and forecasting information; Daily Commercial News, a construction newspaper reporting on news and projects in Ontario; and Journal of Commerce, reporting on products and news in British Columbia and Alberta.

Manufacturers' Survey Associates is a quantity survey and specification service whose experienced estimating staff examines project documents throughout the bidding process and distributes edited information to its clients. Material estimates, edited plans and specifications and distribution of addenda form the heart of the Manufacturers' Survey Associates product line which is available in print and on CD-ROM. In addition, the Market Intelligence Report is a quarterly compilation of actual project specification data that lets building product manufacturers know precisely when and where their products are specified.

Associated Construction Publications are a group of 14 regional magazines focused on highway and heavy construction and cost data. With one of the world's largest editorial staffs dedicated to construction coverage, the magazine group focuses on local and regional news of projects in all phases of construction, precise project volumes, plus material and labor costs. The magazines have a cumulative ABC and BPA audited circulation of 112,000, an estimated pass-along readership of one-half million, and more than 25,000 pages of annual advertising.

Clark Reports is the premier provider of industrial construction project data, noted for providing earlier, more complete project information in the planning and pre-planning stages for all segments of industrial and institutional construction. Comprehensive reporting and tailored information distinguish the Clark Reports products.

Byggfakta Scandinavia AB, founded in 1936, is the parent company for the leaders of customized construction market data for Denmark, Estonia, Finland, Norway and Sweden. Each company fully covers the local construction market and provides information across several platforms including subscription, ad-hoc basis, electronically and on paper.

Cordell Building Information Services, with its complete range of project and cost and estimating services, is Australia's specialist in the construction information industry. Cordell provides in-depth and historical information on all aspects of construction projects and estimation, including several customized reports, construction and sales leads, and detailed cost information among others.

For more information, please visit our website at www.cmdg.com.

CMD Group Corporate Offices
30 Technology Parkway South #100
Norcross, GA 30092-2912
(770) 417-4000
(770) 417-4002 (fax)
www.cmdg.com

Means Project Cost Report

By filling out and returning the Project Description, you can receive a discount of $20.00 off any one of the Means products advertised in the following pages. The cost information required includes all items marked (✔) except those where no costs occurred. The sum of all major items should equal the Total Project Cost.

$20.00 Discount per product for each report you submit.

DISCOUNT PRODUCTS AVAILABLE—FOR U.S. CUSTOMERS ONLY—STRICTLY CONFIDENTIAL

Project Description (No remodeling projects, please.)

- ✔ Type Building _____
- ✔ Location _____
- Capacity _____
- ✔ Frame _____
- ✔ Exterior _____
- ✔ Basement: full ☐ partial ☐ none ☐ crawl ☐
- ✔ Height in Stories _____
- ✔ Total Floor Area _____
- Ground Floor Area _____
- ✔ Volume in C.F. _____
- % Air Conditioned _____ Tons _____
- Comments _____

- Owner _____
- Architect _____
- General Contractor _____
- ✔ Bid Date _____
- Typical Bay Size _____
- ✔ Labor Force: _____ % Union _____ % Non-Union
- ✔ Project Description (Circle one number in each line)
  1. Economy 2. Average 3. Custom 4. Luxury
  1. Square   2. Rectangular 3. Irregular 4. Very Irregular

	✔ Total Project Cost			$
A	✔ General Conditions			$
B	✔ Site Work			$
BS	Site Clearing & Improvement			
BE	Excavation	(	C.Y.)	
BF	Caissons & Piling	(	L.F.)	
BU	Site Utilities			
BP	Roads & Walks Exterior Paving	(	S.Y.)	
C	✔ Concrete			$
C	Cast in Place	(	C.Y.)	
CP	Precast	(	S.F.)	
D	✔ Masonry			$
DB	Brick	(	M)	
DC	Block	(	M)	
DT	Tile	(	S.F.)	
DS	Stone	(	S.F.)	
E	✔ Metals			$
ES	Structural Steel	(	Tons)	
EM	Misc. & Ornamental Metals			
F	✔ Wood & Plastics			$
FR	Rough Carpentry	(	MBF)	
FF	Finish Carpentry			
FM	Architectural Millwork			
G	✔ Thermal & Moisture Protection			$
GW	Waterproofing-Dampproofing	(	S.F.)	
GN	Insulation	(	S.F.)	
GR	Roofing & Flashing	(	S.F.)	
GM	Metal Siding/Curtain Wall	(	S.F.)	
H	✔ Doors and Windows			$
HD	Doors	(	Ea.)	
HW	Windows	(	S.F.)	
HH	Finish Hardware			
HG	Glass & Glazing	(	S.F.)	
HS	Storefronts	(	S.F.)	

J	✔ Finishes			$
JL	Lath & Plaster	(	S.Y.)	
JD	Drywall	(	S.F.)	
JM	Tile & Marble	(	S.F.)	
JT	Terrazzo	(	S.F.)	
JA	Acoustical Treatment	(	S.F.)	
JC	Carpet	(	S.Y.)	
JF	Hard Surface Flooring	(	S.F.)	
JP	Painting & Wall Covering	(	S.F.)	
K	✔ Specialties			$
KB	Bathroom Partitions & Access.	(	S.F.)	
KF	Other Partitions	(	S.F.)	
KL	Lockers	(	Ea.)	
L	✔ Equipment			$
LK	Kitchen			
LS	School			
LO	Other			
M	✔ Furnishings			$
MW	Window Treatment			
MS	Seating	(	Ea.)	
N	✔ Special Construction			$
NA	Acoustical	(	S.F.)	
NB	Prefab. Bldgs.	(	S.F.)	
NO	Other			
P	✔ Conveying Systems			$
PE	Elevators	(	Ea.)	
PS	Escalators	(	Ea.)	
PM	Material Handling			
Q	✔ Mechanical			$
QP	Plumbing	(No. of fixtures	)	
QS	Fire Protection (Sprinklers)			
QF	Fire Protection (Hose Standpipes)			
QB	Heating, Ventilating & A.C.			
QH	Heating & Ventilating	(BTU Output	)	
QA	Air Conditioning	(	Tons)	
R	✔ Electrical			$
RL	Lighting	(	S.F.)	
RP	Power Service			
RD	Power Distribution			
RA	Alarms			
RG	Special Systems			
S	✔ Mech./Elec. Combined			$

Product Name _____

Product Number _____

Your Name _____

Title _____

Company _____

☐ Company
☐ Home   Street Address _____

City, State, Zip _____

☐ Please send _____ forms.

Please specify the Means product you wish to receive. Complete the address information as requested and return this form with your check (product cost less $20.00) to address below.

R.S. Means Company, Inc.,
Square Foot Costs Department
100 Construction Plaza, P.O. Box 800
Kingston, MA 02364-9988

R.S. Means Company, Inc...
a tradition of excellence in Construction Cost Information and Services since 1942.

For more information visit Means Web Site at http://www.rsmeans.com

Table of Contents
Annual Cost Guides, Page 2
Reference Books, Page 6
Seminars, Page 11
Consulting Services, Page 13
Electronic Data, Page 14
New Titles, Page 15
Order Form, Page 16

Book Selection Guide

The following table provides definitive information on the content of each cost data publication. The number of lines of data provided in each unit price or assemblies division, as well as the number of reference tables and crews is listed for each book. The presence of other elements such as an historical cost index, city cost indexes, square foot models or cross-referenced index is also indicated. You can use the table to help select the Means' book that has the quantity and type of information you most need in your work.

Unit Cost Divisions	Building Construction Costs	Mechanical	Electrical	Repair & Remodel.	Square Foot	Site Work Landsc.	Assemblies	Interior	Concrete Masonry	Open Shop	Heavy Construc.	Residential	Light Commercial	Facil. Construc.	Plumbing	Western Construction Costs
1	1099	577	578	770		1025		488	995	1097	1074	425	623	1519	652	1090
2	3393	1440	467	2292		8799		1150	1645	3339	5267	1152	1217	5043	1764	3364
3	1507	90	68	760		1297		191	1913	1483	1470	261	206	1347	43	1487
4	874	27	0	669		767		640	1191	856	670	318	403	1141	0	852
5	1578	179	174	672		823		686	697	1546	1112	480	497	1641	97	1558
6	1398	96	83	1303		476		1316	328	1367	593	1520	1459	1395	59	1752
7	1430	141	90	1368		489		611	455	1428	353	814	1075	1422	151	1429
8	1833	60	0	1857		339		1754	727	1813	9	1096	1146	1967	0	1834
9	1679	50	0	1522		186		1775	322	1627	114	1318	1420	1873	50	1668
10	973	57	31	540		205		813	194	973	0	245	447	971	249	973
11	1036	275	206	602		69		901	34	1019	16	115	235	1033	245	1018
12	355	0	0	48		227		1536	30	346	0	73	69	1538	0	346
13	903	413	200	155		462		356	105	879	323	120	1331	965	240	928
14	365	43	0	262		36		330	0	365	40	9	18	363	17	363
15	2719	15388	703	2284		1962		1772	80	2638	2247	986	1612	12986	11640	2595
16	1550	801	10627	1149		1098		1350	62	1565	1034	707	1305	10207	708	1492
17	459	369	459	1		0		0	0	460	0	0	0	459	369	459
Totals	23151	20006	13686	16254		18260		15669	8778	22801	14322	9639	13063	45870	16284	23208

Assembly Divisions	Building Construction Costs	Mechanical	Electrical	Repair & Remodel.	Square Foot	Site Work Landsc.	Assemblies	Interior	Concrete Masonry	Open Shop	Heavy Construc.	Residential	Light Commercial	Facil. Construc.	Plumbing	Western Construction Costs
1		0	0	202	131	738	775	0	689		752	844	131	89	0	
2		0	0	40	33	35	48	0	49		0	589	32	0	0	
3		0	0	443	1114	0	3064	228	1245		0	1546	806	174	0	
4		0	0	714	1353	0	3172	255	1273		0	2046	1171	26	0	
5		0	0	288	227	0	459	0	0		0	1082	223	25	0	
6		0	0	1006	845	0	1295	1723	152		0	1082	738	330	0	
7		0	0	42	89	0	179	159	0		0	723	33	71	0	
8		2257	149	998	1691	0	2720	926	0		0	1694	1191	1114	2084	
9		0	1346	355	357	0	1283	306	0		0	241	358	319	0	
10		0	0	0	0	0	0	0	0		0	0	0	0	0	
11		0	0	365	465	0	724	153	0		0	0	466	201	0	
12		501	160	539	84	2392	699	0	698		541	0	84	119	850	
Totals		2758	1655	4992	6389	3165	14418	3750	4106		1293	9847	5233	2468	2934	

Reference Section	Building Construction Costs	Mechanical	Electrical	Repair & Remodel.	Square Foot	Site Work Landsc.	Assemblies	Interior	Concrete Masonry	Open Shop	Heavy Construc.	Residential	Light Commercial	Facil. Construc.	Plumbing	Western Construction Costs
Tables	150	46	84	66	4	84	223	59	83	146	55	49	70	86	49	148
Models					102							32	43			
Crews	408	408	408	389		408		408	408	391	408	391	391	389	408	408
City Cost Indexes	yes	yes	yes	yes	yes	yes	yes	yes	yes	yes	yes	yes	yes	yes	yes	yes
Historical Cost Indexes	yes	yes	yes	yes	yes	yes	yes	yes	yes	yes	yes	no	yes	yes	yes	yes
Index	yes	yes	yes	yes	no	yes	yes	yes	yes	yes	yes	yes	yes	yes	yes	yes

Annual Cost Guides

For more information visit Means Web Site at http://www.rsmeans.com

Means Building Construction Cost Data 1999

Available in Both Softbound and Looseleaf Editions

The "Bible" of the industry comes in the standard softcover edition or the looseleaf edition.

Many customers enjoy the convenience and flexibility of the looseleaf binder, which increases the usefulness of *Means Building Construction Cost Data 1999* by making it easy to add and remove pages. You can insert your own cost information pages, so everything is in one place. Copying pages for faxing is easier also. Whichever edition you prefer, softbound or the convenient looseleaf edition, you'll get the *Design/Build Intelligence* newsletter at no extra cost.

$84.95 per copy, Softbound
Catalog No. 60019

$109.95 per copy, Looseleaf
Catalog No. 61019

Means Building Construction Cost Data 1999

Offers you unchallenged unit price reliability in an easy-to-use arrangement. Whether used for complete, finished estimates or for periodic checks, it supplies more cost facts better and faster than any comparable source. Over 21,000 unit prices for 1999. The City Cost Indexes now cover over 930 areas, for indexing to any project location in North America. Order and get the *Design/Build Intelligence* newsletter sent to you FREE. You'll have year-long access to the Means Estimating **Hotline** FREE with your subscription. Expert assistance when using Means data is just a phone call away.

$84.95 per copy
Over 650 pages, illustrated, available Oct. 1998
Catalog No. 60019

Means Building Construction Cost Data 1999

Metric Version

The Federal Government has stated that all federal construction projects must now use metric documentation. The *Metric Version* of *Means Building Construction Cost Data 1999* is presented in metric measurements covering all construction areas. Don't miss out on these billion dollar opportunities. Make the switch to metric today.

$89.95 per copy
Over 650 pages, illustrated, available Nov. 1998
Catalog No. 63019

For more information
visit Means Web Site
at http://www.rsmeans.com

Annual Cost Guides

Means Mechanical Cost Data 1999

• HVAC • Controls

Total unit and systems price guidance for mechanical construction . . . materials, parts, fittings, and complete labor cost information. Includes prices for piping, heating, air conditioning, ventilation, and all related construction.

Plus new 1999 unit costs for:
• Over 3000 installed HVAC/controls assemblies
• "On Site" Location Factors for close to 1,000 cities and towns in the U.S. and Canada
• Crews, labor and equipment

$87.95 per copy
Over 600 pages, illustrated, available Oct. 1998
Catalog No. 60029

Means Plumbing Cost Data 1999

Comprehensive unit prices and assemblies for plumbing, irrigation systems, commercial and residential fire protection, point-of-use water heaters, and the latest approved materials. This publication and its companion, *Means Mechanical Cost Data*, provide full-range cost estimating coverage for all the mechanical trades.

$87.95 per copy
Over 500 pages, illustrated, available Oct. 1998
Catalog No. 60219

Means Electrical Cost Data 1999

Pricing information for every part of electrical cost planning: More than 17,000 unit and systems costs with design tables; clear specifications and drawings; engineering guides and illustrated estimating procedures; complete labor-hour and materials costs for better scheduling and procurement; the latest electrical products and construction methods.
• A Variety of Special Electrical Systems including Cathodic Protection
• Costs for maintenance, demolition, HVAC/ mechanical, specialties, equipment, and more

$87.95 per copy
Over 450 pages, illustrated, available Oct. 1998
Catalog No. 60039

Means Electrical Change Order Cost Data 1999

You are provided with electrical unit prices exclusively for pricing change orders—based on the recent, direct experience of contractors and suppliers. Analyze and check your own change order estimates against the experience others have had doing the same work. It also covers productivity analysis and change order cost justifications. With useful information for calculating the effects of change orders and dealing with their administration.

$89.95 per copy
Over 440 pages, available Oct. 1998
Catalog No. 60239

Means Facilities Maintenance & Repair Cost Data 1999

Published in a looseleaf format, *Means Facilities Maintenance & Repair Cost Data* gives you a complete system to manage and plan your facility repair and maintenance costs and budget efficiently. Guidelines for auditing a facility and developing an annual maintenance plan. Budgeting is included, along with reference tables on cost and management and information on frequency and productivity of maintenance operations.

The only nationally recognized source of maintenance and repair costs. Developed in cooperation with the Army Corps of Engineers.

$199.95 per copy
Over 600 pages, illustrated, available Dec. 1998
Catalog No. 60309

Means Square Foot Costs 1999

It's Accurate and Easy To Use!

• **Updated 1999 price information,** based on nationwide figures from suppliers, estimators, labor experts and contractors.

• "How-to-Use" Sections, with **better, clearer examples** of commercial, residential, industrial, and institutional structures.

• More realistic graphics, offering true-to-life illustrations of building projects.

• More extensive information on using square foot cost data, including **sample estimates** and **alternate pricing methods.**

$99.95 per copy
Over 460 pages, illustrated, available Nov. 1998
Catalog No. 60059

Annual Cost Guides

For more information visit Means Web Site at http://www.rsmeans.com

Means Repair & Remodeling Cost Data 1999
Commercial/Residential

You can use this valuable tool to estimate commercial and residential renovation and remodeling.

Includes: New 1999 costs for hundreds of unique methods, materials and conditions that only come up in repair and remodeling. PLUS:
- 1999 unit costs for over 15,000 construction components
- 1999 installed costs for over 4,000 assemblies
- 1999 costs for 300+ construction crews
- Over 930 "On Site" localization factors for the U.S. and Canada.

$79.95 per copy
Over 600 pages, illustrated, available Oct. 1998
Catalog No. 60049

Means Facilities Construction Cost Data 1999

For the maintenance and construction of commercial, industrial, municipal, and institutional properties. Costs are shown for new and remodeling construction and are broken down into materials, labor, equipment, overhead, and profit. Special emphasis is given to sections on mechanical, electrical, furnishings, site work, building maintenance, finish work, and demolition. More than 40,000 unit costs plus assemblies and reference sections are included.

$209.95 per copy
Over 1100 pages, illustrated, available Nov. 1998
Catalog No. 60209

Means Residential Cost Data 1999

Now contains square foot costs for 30 basic home models with the look of today—plus hundreds of custom additions and modifications you can quote right off the page. With costs for the 100 residential systems you're most likely to use in the year ahead. Complete with blank estimating forms, sample estimates and step-by-step instructions.

$74.95 per copy
Over 550 pages, illustrated, available Dec. 1998
Catalog No. 60179

Means Light Commercial Cost Data 1999

Specifically addresses the light commercial market, which is an increasingly specialized niche in the industry. Aids you, the owner/designer/contractor, in preparing all types of estimates, from budgets to detailed bids. Includes new advances in methods and materials. Assemblies section allows you to evaluate alternatives in the early stages of design/planning.

Over 10,000 unit costs for 1999 ensure you have the prices you need... when you need them.

$76.95 per copy
Over 600 pages, illustrated, available Nov. 1998
Catalog No. 60189

Means Assemblies Cost Data 1999

Means Assemblies Cost Data 1999 takes the guesswork out of preliminary or conceptual estimates. Now you don't have to try to calculate the assembled cost by working up individual components costs. We've done all the work for you.

Presents detailed illustrations, descriptions, specifications and costs for every conceivable building assembly—240 types in all—arranged in the easy-to-use UniFormat system. Each illustrated "assembled" cost includes a complete grouping of materials and associated installation costs including the installing contractor's overhead and profit.

$139.95 per copy
Over 570 pages, illustrated, available Oct. 1998
Catalog No. 60069

Means Site Work & Landscape Cost Data 1999

Means Site Work & Landscape Cost Data 1999 is organized to assist you in all your estimating needs. Hundreds of fact-filled pages help you make accurate cost estimates efficiently.

New for 1999!
- New or expanded demolition features—ceilings, doors, electrical, flooring, HVAC, millwork, plumbing, roofing, walls and windows
- State-of-the-art segmental retaining walls
- Flywheel trenching costs and details
- Expanded wells section
- Thousands of landscape materials, flowers, shrubs and trees

$89.95 per copy
Over 550 pages, illustrated, available Nov. 1998
Catalog No. 60289

For more information visit Means Web Site at http://www.rsmeans.com

Annual Cost Guides

Means Open Shop Building Construction Cost Data 1999

The latest costs for accurate budgeting and estimating of new commercial and residential construction... renovation work... change orders... cost engineering. *Means Open Shop BCCD* will assist you to...
- Develop benchmark prices for change orders
- Plug gaps in preliminary estimates, budgets
- Estimate complex projects
- Substantiate invoices on contracts
- Price ADA-related renovations

$89.95 per copy
Over 650 pages, illustrated, available Nov. 1998
Catalog No. 60159

Means Heavy Construction Cost Data 1999

A comprehensive guide to heavy construction costs. Includes costs for highly specialized projects such as tunnels, dams, highways, airports, and waterways. Information on different labor rates, equipment, and material costs is included. Has unit price costs, systems costs, and numerous reference tables for costs and design. Valuable not only to contractors and civil engineers, but also to government agencies and city/town engineers.

$89.95 per copy
Over 450 pages, illustrated, available Dec. 1998
Catalog No. 60169

Means Building Construction Cost Data 1999
Western Edition

This regional edition provides more precise cost information for western North America. Labor rates are based on union rates from 13 western states and western Canada. Included are western practices and materials not found in our national edition: tilt-up concrete walls, glu-lam structural systems, specialized timber construction, seismic restraints, landscape and irrigation systems.

$89.95 per copy
Over 600 pages, illustrated, available Nov. 1998
Catalog No. 60229

Means Heavy Construction Cost Data 1999
Metric Version

Make sure you have the Means industry standard metric costs for the federal, state, municipal and private marketplace. With thousands of up-to-date metric unit prices in tables by CSI standard divisions. Supplies you with assemblies costs using the metric standard for reliable cost projections in the design stage of your project. Helps you determine sizes, material amounts, and has tips for handling metric estimates.

$89.95 per copy
Over 450 pages, illustrated, available Dec. 1998
Catalog No. 63169

Means Construction Cost Indexes 1999

Who knows what 1999 holds? What materials and labor costs will change unexpectedly? By how much?
- Breakdowns for 305 major cities.
- National averages for 30 key cities.
- Expanded five major city indexes.
- Historical construction cost indexes.

$198.00 per year/$49.50 individual quarters
Catalog No. 60149

Means Interior Cost Data 1999

Provides you with prices and guidance needed to make accurate interior work estimates. Contains costs on materials, equipment, hardware, custom installations, furnishings, labor costs . . . every cost factor for new and remodel commercial and industrial interior construction, plus more than 50 reference tables. For contractors, facility managers, owners.

Newly expanded information on office furnishings.

$89.95 per copy
Over 550 pages, illustrated, available Nov. 1998
Catalog No. 60099

Means Concrete & Masonry Cost Data 1999

Provides you with cost facts for virtually all concrete/masonry estimating needs, from complicated form work to various sizes and face finishes of brick and block, all in great detail. The comprehensive unit cost section contains more than 15,000 selected entries. The assemblies cost section is illustrated with isometric drawings. A detailed reference section supplements the cost data.

$77.95 per copy
Over 520 pages, illustrated, available Dec. 1998
Catalog No. 60119

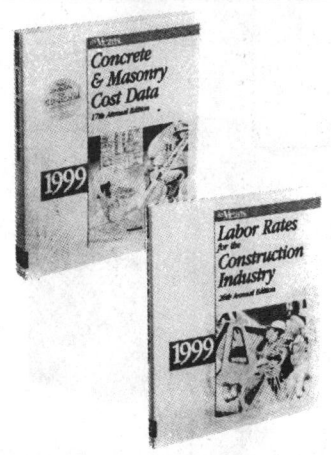

Means Labor Rates for the Construction Industry 1999

Complete information for estimating labor costs, making comparisons and negotiating wage rates by trade for over 300 cities (United States and Canada), 46 construction trades listed by local union number in each city, historical wage rates included for comparison. No similar book is available through the trade.

Each city chart now lists the county and is alphabetically arranged with handy visual flip tabs for quick reference.

$189.95 per copy
Over 330 pages, available Dec. 1998
Catalog No. 60129

Reference Books

For more information visit Means Web Site at http://www.rsmeans.com

Total Productive Facilities Management

By Richard W. Sievert, Jr.

A New Operational Standard for Facilities Management.

The TPFM program incorporates the best of today's cost and project management, quality, and value engineering principles. The book includes:
- Realistic ways to collect and use benchmarking data.
- Value Engineering to find economical answers to the organization's needs.
- Selecting the best scheduling, control, and contracting methods for construction projects.

$79.95 per copy
Over 270 pages, illustrated, Hardcover
Catalog No. 67321

Cyberplaces: The Internet Guide for Architects, Engineers & Contractors

By Paul Doherty

Internet applications for business and project management. Includes book, CD-ROM and Web site.

The CD-ROM offers built-in links to Web sites, tours of captured sites, FREE browser software and a document workshop, plus a test for Continuing Education Credits. **The Web Site** keeps the book current with updates on new technologies, interactive workshops, links to new tools and sites, and reports from top firms.

$59.95 per copy
Over 700 pages, illustrated, Softcover
Catalog No. 67317

Value Engineering: Practical Applications

...For Design, Construction, Maintenance & Operations

By Alphonse Dell'Isola, P.E., leading authority on VE in construction

A tool for immediate application—for engineers, architects, facility managers, owners and contractors. Includes: Making the Case for VE—The Management Briefing, Integrating VE into Planning and Budgeting, Conducting Life Cycle Costing, Integrating VE into the Design Process, and Using VE Methodology in Design Review and Consultant Selection, Case Studies (corporate, commercial, hospital, industrial and civil), an expertly organized VE Workbook, and a Life Cycle cost program on disk.

$79.95 per copy
Over 450 pages, illustrated, Hardcover
Catalog No. 67319

Means Environmental Remediation Estimating Methods

By Richard R. Rast

The first-ever guide to estimating any size environmental remediation project... anywhere in the country.

Field-tested guidelines for estimating 50 standard remediation technologies. This resource will help you: prepare preliminary budgets, develop detailed estimates, compare costs, select solutions, estimate liability, review quotes, and negotiate settlements.

A valuable support tool for **Environmental Restoration** cost data books.

$99.95 per copy
Over 600 pages, illustrated, Hardcover
Catalog No. 64777

The ADA in Practice

(Revised, expanded edition of the award-winning* New ADA: Compliance & Costs)

By Deborah S. Kearney, PhD

Helps you meet and budget for the requirements of the Americans with Disabilities Act. Shows you how to do the job right, by understanding what the law requires, allows, and enforces. Includes an objective "authoritative buyers guide" for 70 ADA-compliant products with specs and purchasing information. With sample evaluation forms and illustrations of ADA-compliant products.

*Winner of the "Distinguished Author of the Year" award from the International Facility Managers Association.

$72.95 per copy
Over 600 pages, illustrated, Softcover
Catalog No. 67147A

Means ADA Compliance Pricing Guide

Gives you detailed cost estimates for budgeting modification projects, including estimates for each of 260 alternates. You get the 75 most commonly needed modifications for ADA compliance, each an assembly estimate with detailed cost breakdown including materials, labor hours and contractor's overhead. 3,000 additional ADA compliance-related unit cost line items allow you to tailor the estimates to your own site conditions and requirements. Costs easily adjusted for 900 cities and towns.

$72.95 per copy
Over 350 pages, illustrated, Softcover
Catalog No. 67310

For more information
visit Means Web Site
at http://www.rsmeans.com

Reference Books

Cost Planning & Estimating for Facilities Maintenance

In this unique book, a team of facilities management authorities shares their expertise at:
- Evaluating and budgeting maintenance operations
- Maintaining & repairing key building components
- Applying *Means Facilities Maintenance & Repair Cost Data* to your estimating

With the special maintenance requirements of the 10 major building types.

$82.95 per copy
Over 475 pages, Hardcover
Catalog No. 67314

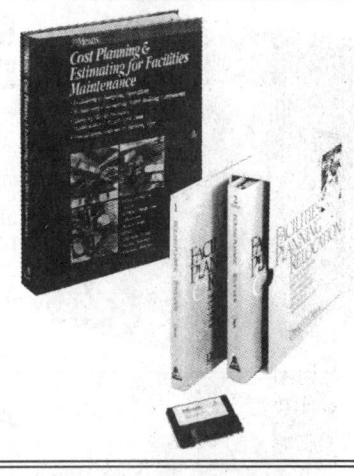

Facilities Planning & Relocation

By David D. Owen

An A–Z working guide—complete with the checklists, schematic diagrams and questionnaires to ensure the success of every office relocation. Complete with a step-by-step manual, 100-page technical reference section, over 50 reproducible forms in hard copy and on computer diskettes.
Winner of the International Facility Managers Assoc. "Distinguished Author of the Year" award.

$109.95 per copy, Textbook-384 pages,
Forms Binder-146 pages, illustrated, Hardcover
Catalog No. 67301

Means Facilities Maintenance Standards

Unique features of this one-of-a-kind working guide for facilities maintenance

A working encyclopedia that points the way to solutions to every kind of maintenance and repair dilemma. With a labor-hours section to provide productivity figures for over 180 maintenance tasks. Included are ready-to-use forms, checklists, worksheets and comparisons, as well as analysis of materials systems and remedies for deterioration and wear.

$159.95 per copy, 600 pages, 205 tables,
checklists and diagrams, Hardcover
Catalog No. 67246

HVAC: Design Criteria, Options, Selection
Expanded Second Edition

By William H. Rowe III, AIA, PE

Includes Indoor Air Quality, CFC Removal, Energy Efficient Systems and Special Systems by Building Type. Helps you solve a wide range of HVAC system design and selection problems effectively and economically. Gives you clear explanations of the latest ASHRAE standards.

$84.95 per copy
Over 600 pages, illustrated, Hardcover
Catalog No. 67306

The Facilities Manager's Reference

By Harvey H. Kaiser, PhD

The tasks and tools the facility manager needs to accomplish the organization's objectives, and develop individual and staff skills. Includes Facilities and Property Management, Administrative Control, Planning and Operations, Support Services, and a complete building audit with forms and instructions, widely used by facilities managers nationwide.

$86.95 per copy, over 250 pages,
with prototype forms and graphics, Hardcover
Catalog No. 67264

Facilities Maintenance Management

By Gregory H. Magee, PE

Now you can get successful management methods and techniques for all aspects of facilities maintenance. This comprehensive reference explains and demonstrates successful management techniques for all aspects of maintenance, repair and improvements for buildings, machinery, equipment and grounds. Plus, guidance for outsourcing and managing internal staffs.

$86.95 per copy
Over 280 pages with illustrations, Hardcover
Catalog No. 67249

Understanding Building Automation Systems

- Direct Digital Control
- Security/Access Control
- Energy Management
- Life Safety
- Lighting

By Reinhold A. Carlson, PE & Robert Di Giandomenico

The authors, leading authorities on the design and installation of these systems, describe the major building systems in both an overview with estimating and selection criteria, and in system configuration-level detail.

$79.95 per copy
Over 200 pages, illustrated, Hardcover
Catalog No. 67284

Maintenance Management Audit

At a time when many companies and institutions are reorganizing or downsizing, this annual audit program is essential for every organization in need of a proper assessment of its maintenance operation. The forms presented in this easy-to-use workbook allow managers to identify and correct problems, enhance productivity, and impact the bottom line. Includes a set of electronic forms on disk.

Now $32.48 per copy, limited quantity
125 pages, spiral bound, illustrated, Hardcover
Catalog No. 67299

Reference Books

For more information visit Means Web Site at http://www.rsmeans.com

Basics For Builders: Plan Reading & Material Takeoff
By Wayne J. DelPico

For Residential and Light Commercial Construction

A valuable tool for understanding plans and specs, and accurately calculating material quantities. Step-by-step instructions and takeoff procedures based on a full set of working drawings.

$35.95 per copy
Over 420 pages, Softcover
Catalog No. 67307

Means Illustrated Construction Dictionary Unabridged Edition

Written in contractor's language, the information is adaptable for report writing, specifications or just intelligent discussion. Contains over 17,000 construction terms, words, phrases, acronyms and abbreviations, slang, regional terminology, and hundreds of illustrations.

$99.95 per copy
Over 700 pages, Hardcover
Catalog No. 67292

Superintending for Contractors:
How to Bring Jobs in On-time, On-Budget
By Paul J. Cook

This book examines the complex role of the superintendent/field project manager, and provides guidelines for the efficient organization of this job. Includes administration of contracts, change orders, purchase orders, and more.

$35.95 per copy
Over 220 pages, illustrated, Softcover
Catalog No. 67233

Means Forms for Contractors
For general and specialty contractors

Means editors have created and collected the most needed forms as requested by contractors of various-sized firms and specialties. This book covers all project phases. Includes sample correspondence and personnel administration.
Full-size forms on durable paper for photocopying or reprinting.

$79.95 per copy
Over 400 pages, three-ring binder, more than 80 forms
Catalog No. 67288

Bidding for Contractors:
How to Make Bids that Make Money
By Paul J. Cook

The author shares the benefit of his more than 30 years of experience in construction project management, providing contractors with the tools they need to develop competitive bids.

Now $17.98 per copy, limited quantity
Over 225 pages with graphics, Softcover
Catalog No. 67180

Means Heavy Construction Handbook

Informed guidance for planning, estimating and performing today's heavy construction projects. Provides expert advice on every aspect of heavy construction work including hazardous waste remediation and estimating. To assist planning, estimating, performing, or overseeing work.

$74.95 per copy
Over 430 pages, illustrated, Hardcover
Catalog No. 67148

Estimating for Contractors:
How to Make Estimates that Win Jobs
By Paul J. Cook

Estimating for Contractors is a reference that will be used over and over, whether to check a specific estimating procedure, or to take a complete course in estimating.

$35.95 per copy
Over 225 pages, illustrated, Softcover
Catalog No. 67160

HVAC Systems Evaluation
By Harold R. Colen, PE

You get direct comparisons of how each type of system works, with the relative costs of installation, operation, maintenance and applications by type of building. With requirements for hooking up electrical power to HVAC components. Contains experienced advice for repairing operational problems in existing HVAC systems, ductwork, fans, cooling coils, and much more!

$84.95 per copy
Over 500 pages, illustrated, Hardcover
Catalog No. 67281

Quantity Takeoff for Contractors:
How to Get Accurate Material Counts
By Paul J. Cook

Contractors who are new to material takeoffs or want to be sure they are using the best techniques will find helpful information in this book, organized by CSI MasterFormat division.

Now $17.48 per copy, limited quantity
Over 250 pages, illustrated, Softcover
Catalog No. 67262

Roofing: Design Criteria, Options, Selection
By R.D. Herbert, III

This book is required reading for those who specify, install or have to maintain roofing systems. It covers all types of roofing technology and systems. You'll get the facts needed to intelligently evaluate and select both traditional and new roofing systems.

Now $31.48 per copy
Over 225 pages with illustrations, Hardcover
Catalog No. 67253

For more information visit Means Web Site at http://www.rsmeans.com

Reference Books

Means Estimating Handbook

This comprehensive reference covers a full spectrum of technical data for estimating, with information on sizing, productivity, equipment requirements, codes, design standards and engineering factors.
Means Estimating Handbook will help you: evaluate architectural plans and specifications, prepare accurate quantity takeoffs, prepare estimates from conceptual to detailed, and evaluate change orders.

$99.95 per copy
Over 900 pages, Hardcover
Catalog No. 67276

Means Repair and Remodeling Estimating Third Edition
By Edward B. Wetherill & R.S. Means

Focuses on the unique problems of estimating renovations of existing structures. It helps you determine the true costs of remodeling through careful evaluation of architectural details and a site visit.
New section on disaster restoration costs.

$69.95 per copy
Over 450 pages, illustrated, Hardcover
Catalog No. 67265A

Successful Estimating Methods:
From Concept to Bid
By John D. Bledsoe, PhD, PE

A highly practical, all-in-one guide to the tips and practices of today's successful estimator. Presents techniques for all types of estimates, *and* advanced topics such as life cycle cost analysis, value engineering, and automated estimating.
Estimate spreadsheets available at Means Web site.

$64.95 per copy
Over 300 pages, illustrated, Hardcover
Catalog No. 67287

Means Productivity Standards for Construction
Expanded Edition *(Formerly* Man-Hour Standards)

Here is the working encyclopedia of labor productivity information for construction professionals, with labor requirements for thousands of construction functions in CSI MasterFormat.
Completely updated, with over 3,000 new work items.

$159.95 per copy
Over 800 pages, Hardcover
Catalog No. 67236A

Means Electrical Estimating Methods Second Edition

Expanded version includes sample estimates and cost information in keeping with the latest version of the CSI MasterFormat. Contains new coverage of Fiber Optic and Uninterruptible Power Supply electrical systems, broken down by components and explained in detail. A practical companion to *Means Electrical Cost Data.*

$62.95 per copy
Over 325 pages, Hardcover
Catalog No. 67230A

Means Mechanical Estimating
Second Edition

This guide assists you in making a review of plans, specs and bid packages with suggestions for takeoff procedures, listings, substitutions and pre-bid scheduling. Includes suggestions for budgeting labor and equipment usage. Compares materials and construction methods to allow you to select the best options for your job.

$64.95 per copy
Over 350 pages, illustrated, Hardcover
Catalog No. 67294

Means Scheduling Manual
Third Edition
By F. William Horsley

Fast, convenient expertise for keeping your scheduling skills right in step with today's cost-conscious times. Covers bar charts, PERT, precedence and CPM scheduling methods. Now updated to include computer applications.

$62.95 per copy
Over 200 pages, spiral-bound, Softcover
Catalog No. 67291

Means Graphic Construction Standards

Means Graphic Construction Standards bridges the gap between design and actual construction methods. With illustrations of unit assemblies, systems and components, you can see quickly which construction methods work best to meet design, budget and time objectives.

$124.95 per copy
Over 540 pages, illustrated, Hardcover
Catalog No. 67210

Means Square Foot Estimating Methods Second Edition
By Billy J. Cox and F. William Horsley

Proven techniques for conceptual and design-stage cost planning. Steps you through the square foot cost process, demonstrating faster, better ways to relate the design to the budget. Now updated to the latest version of UniFormat.

$69.95 per copy
Over 300 pages, illustrated, Hardcover
Catalog No. 67145A

Planning and Managing Interior Projects
By Carol E. Farren

Expert, up-to-date guidance for managing interior installation projects. Includes: project phases; winning client support; space planning and design; budgeting, bidding and purchasing, and more.
For interior designers, architects, facilities professionals.

$76.95 per copy
Over 330 pages, illustrated, Hardcover
Catalog No. 67245

Reference Books

For more information visit Means Web Site at http://www.rsmeans.com

Unit Price Estimating Methods
2nd Edition
$59.95 per copy
Catalog No. 67303

Legal Reference for Design & Construction
By Charles R. Heuer, Esq., AIA
Now $54.98 per copy, limited quantity
Catalog No. 67266

Plumbing Estimating
By Joseph J. Galeno & Sheldon T. Greene
$59.95 per copy
Catalog No. 67283

Structural Steel Estimating
By S. Paul Bunea, PhD
$79.95 per copy
Catalog No. 67241

Business Management for Contractors
How to Make Profits in Today's Market
By Paul J. Cook
Now $17.98 per copy, limited quantity
Catalog No. 67250

Understanding Legal Aspects of Design/Build
By Timothy R. Twomey, Esq., AIA
$79.95 per copy
Catalog No. 67259

Construction Paperwork
An Efficient Management System
By J. Edward Grimes
$52.95 per copy
Catalog No. 67268

Contractor's Business Handbook
By Michael S. Milliner
Now $21.48 per copy, limited quantity
Catalog No. 67255

Basics for Builders: How to Survive and Prosper in Construction
By Thomas N. Frisby
$34.95 per copy
Catalog No. 67273

Successful Interior Projects Through Effective Contract Documents
By Joel Downey & Patricia K. Gilbert
Now $34.98 per copy
Catalog No. 67313

The Building Professional's Guide to Contract Documents
By Waller S. Poage, AIA, CSI, CCS
$64.95 per copy
Catalog No. 67261

Illustrated Construction Dictionary, Condensed
$59.95 per copy
Catalog No. 67282

Managing Construction Purchasing
By John G. McConville, CCC, CPE
Now $31.48 per copy, limited quantity
Catalog No. 67302

Hazardous Material & Hazardous Waste
By Francis J. Hopcroft, PE, David L. Vitale, M. Ed., & Donald L. Anglehart, Esq.
Now $44.98 per copy, limited quantity
Catalog No. 67258

Fundamentals of the Construction Process
By Kweku K. Bentil, AIC
Now $34.98 per copy, limited quantity
Catalog No. 67260

Construction Delays
By Theodore J. Trauner, Jr., PE, PP
$69.95 per copy
Catalog No. 67278

Basics for Builders: Framing & Rough Carpentry
By Scot Simpson
$24.95 per copy
Catalog No. 67298

Interior Home Improvement Costs NEW!
6th Edition
$19.95 per copy
Catalog No. 67308B

Exterior Home Improvement Costs NEW!
6th Edition
$19.95 per copy
Catalog No. 67309B

Concrete Repair and Maintenance Illustrated
By Peter H. Emmons
$64.95 per copy
Catalog No. 67146

How to Estimate with Metric Units
Now $24.98 per copy, limited quantity
Catalog No. 67304

For more information
visit Means Web Site
at http://www.rsmeans.com

Seminars

How to Develop Facility Assessment Programs

This two-day program concentrates on the management process required for planning, conducting, and documenting the physical condition and functional adequacy of buildings and other facilities. Regular facilities condition inspections are one of the facility department's most important duties. However, gathering reliable data hinges on the design of the overall program used to identify and gauge deferred maintenance requirements. Knowing where to look . . . and reporting results effectively are the keys. This seminar is designed to give the facility executive essential steps for conducting facilities inspection programs.

Inspection Program Requirements • Where is the deficiency? • What is the nature of the problem? • How can it be remedied? • How much will it cost in labor, equipment and materials? • When should it be accomplished? • Who is best suited to do the work?

Note: Because of its management focus, this course will not address trade practices and procedures.

Repair and Remodeling Estimating

Repair and remodeling work is becoming increasingly competitive as more professionals enter the market. Recycling existing buildings can pose difficult estimating problems. Labor costs, energy use concerns, building codes, and the limitations of working with an existing structure place enormous importance on the development of accurate estimates. Using the exclusive techniques associated with Means' widely acclaimed **Repair & Remodeling Cost Data**, this seminar sorts out and discusses solutions to the problems of building alteration estimating. Attendees will receive two intensive days of eye-opening methods for handling virtually every kind of repair and remodeling situation . . . from demolition and removal to final restoration.

Mechanical and Electrical Estimating

This seminar is tailored to fit the needs of those seeking to develop or improve their skills and to have a better understanding of how mechanical and electrical estimates are prepared during the conceptual, planning, budgeting and bidding stages. Learn how to avoid costly omissions and overlaps between these two interrelated specialties by preparing complete and thorough cost estimates for both trades. Featured are order of magnitude, assemblies, and unit price estimating. In combination with the use of **Means Mechanical Cost Data**, **Means Plumbing Cost Data** and **Means Electrical Cost Data**, this seminar will ensure more accurate and complete Mechanical/Electrical estimates for both unit price and preliminary estimating procedures.

Unit Price Estimating

This seminar shows how today's advanced estimating techniques and cost information sources can be used to develop more reliable unit price estimates for projects of any size. It demonstrates how to organize data, use plans efficiently, and avoid embarrassing errors by using better methods of checking.

You'll get down-to-earth help and easy-to-apply guidance for:
- making maximum use of construction cost information sources
- organizing estimating procedures in order to save time and reduce mistakes
- sorting out and identifying unusual job requirements to improve estimating accuracy.

Square Foot Cost Estimating

Learn how to make better preliminary estimates with a limited amount of budget and design information. You will benefit from examples of a wide range of systems estimates with specifications limited to building use requirements, budget, building codes, and type of building. And yet, with minimal information, you will obtain a remarkable degree of accuracy.

Workshop sessions will provide you with model square foot estimating problems and other skill-building exercises. The exclusive Means building assemblies square foot cost approach shows how to make very reliable estimates using "bare bones" budget and design information.

Scheduling and Project Management

This seminar helps you successfully establish project priorities, develop realistic schedules, and apply today's advanced management techniques to your construction projects. Hands-on exercises familiarize participants with network approaches such as the Critical Path Method. Special emphasis is placed on cost control, including use of computer-based systems. Through this seminar you'll perfect your scheduling and management skills, ensuring completion of your projects *on time* and *within budget*. Includes hands-on application of **Means Scheduling Manual** and **Means Building Construction Cost Data**.

Facilities Maintenance and Repair Estimating

With our Facilities Maintenance and Repair Estimating seminar, you'll learn how to plan, budget, and estimate the cost of ongoing and preventive maintenance and repair for all your buildings and grounds. Based on R.S. Means' groundbreaking cost estimating book, this two-day seminar will show you how to decide to either contract out or retain maintenance and repair work in-house. In addition, you'll learn how to prepare budgets and schedules that help cut down on unplanned and costly emergency repair projects. Facilities Maintenance and Repair Estimating crystallizes what facilities professionals have learned over the years, but never had time to organize or document. This program covers a variety of maintenance and repair projects, from underground storage tank removal, roof repair and maintenance, exterior wall renovations, and energy source conversions, to service upgrades and estimating energy-saving alternatives.

Managing Facilities Construction and Maintenance

In you're involved in new facility construction, renovation or maintenance projects and are concerned about getting quality work done on time and on or below budget, in Means' seminar **Managing Facilities Construction and Maintenance** you'll learn management techniques needed to effectively plan, organize, control and get the most out of your limited facilities resources.

Learn how to develop budgets, reduce expenditures and check productivity. With the knowledge gained in this course, you'll be better prepared to successfully sell accurate project budgets, timing and manpower needs to senior management . . . plus understand how to evaluate the impact of today's facility decisions on tomorrow's budget.

Call 1-800-448-8182 for more information

Seminars

1999 Means Seminar Schedule

For more information visit Means Web Site at http://www.rsmeans.com

Location	Dates
Las Vegas, NV	March 15 - 18
Washington, DC	April 12 - 15
New Orleans, LA	April TBA
Denver, CO	May 17 - 20
San Francisco, CA	June 14 - 17
Hyannis, MA	September TBA
Washington, DC	September TBA
San Diego, CA	October TBA
Orlando, FL	November TBA

Registration Information

Register Early... Save up to $150! Register 30 days before the start date of a seminar and save $150 off your total fee. *Note: This discount can be applied only once per order. It cannot be applied to team discount registrations or any other special offer.*

How to Register Register by phone today! Means toll-free number for making reservations is: **1-800-448-8182, ext. 701.**

Individual Seminar Registration Fee $875 To register by mail, complete the registration form and return with your full fee to: Seminar Division, R.S. Means Company, Inc., 63 Smiths Lane, Kingston, MA 02364.

Federal Government Pricing All Federal Government employees save 25% off regular seminar price. Other promotional discounts cannot be combined with Federal Government discount.

Team Discount Program Two to four seminar registrations: $760 per person—Five or more seminar registrations: $710 per person—Ten or more seminar registrations: Call for pricing.

Consecutive Seminar Offer One individual signing up for two separate courses at the same location during the designated time period pays only $1,400. You get the second course for only $525 (**a 40% discount**). Payment must be received at least ten days prior to seminar dates to confirm attendance.

Refunds Cancellations will be accepted up to ten days prior to the seminar start. There are no refunds for cancellations postmarked later than ten working days prior to the first day of the seminar. A $150 processing fee will be charged for all cancellations. Written notice or telegram is required for all cancellations. Substitutions can be made at any time before the session starts. **No-shows are subject to the full seminar fee.**

AACE Approved Courses The R.S. Means Construction Estimating and Management Seminars described and offered to you here have each been approved for 14 hours (1.4 recertification credits) of credit by the AACE International Certification Board toward meeting the continuing education requirements for re-certification as a Certified Cost Engineer/Certified Cost Consultant.

AIA Continuing Education R.S. Means is registered with the AIA Continuing Education System (AIA/CES) and is committed to developing quality learning activities in accordance with the CES criteria. R.S. Means seminars meet the AIA/CES criteria for Quality Level 2. AIA members will receive (28) learning units (LUs) for each two day R.S. Means Course.

Daily Course Schedule The first day of each seminar session begins at 8:30 A.M. and ends at 4:30 P.M. The second day is 8:00 A.M.–4:00 P.M. Participants are urged to bring a hand-held calculator since many actual problems will be worked out in each session.

Continental Breakfast Your registration includes the cost of a continental breakfast, a morning coffee break, and an afternoon cola break. These informal segments will allow you to discuss topics of mutual interest with other members of the seminar. (You are free to make your own lunch and dinner arrangements.)

Hotel/Transportation Arrangements R.S. Means has arranged to hold a block of rooms at each hotel hosting a seminar. To take advantage of special group rates when making your reservation be sure to mention that you are attending the Means Seminar. You are of course free to stay at the lodging place of your choice. (**Hotel reservations and transportation arrangements should be made directly by seminar attendees.**)

Important Class sizes are limited, so please register as soon as possible.

Registration Form

Call 1-800-448-8182, ext. 701 to register or FAX 1-781-585-7466

Please register the following people for the Means Construction Seminars as shown here. Full payment or deposit is enclosed, and we understand that we must make our own hotel reservations if overnight stays are necessary.

☐ Full payment of $ _____ enclosed.

Name of Registrant(s)
(To appear on certificate of completion)

_____

_____

_____

P.O. #: _____
GOVERNMENT AGENCIES MUST SUPPLY PURCHASE ORDER NUMBER

Firm Name _____
Address _____
City/State/Zip _____
Telephone No. _____ Fax No. _____
E-Mail Address _____
Charge our registration(s) to: ☐ MasterCard ☐ VISA ☐ American Express ☐ Discover
Account No. _____ Exp. Date _____
Cardholder's Signature _____

Seminar Name	City	Dates

Please mail check to: R.S. MEANS COMPANY, INC., 63 Smiths Lane, P.O. Box 800, Kingston, MA 02364 USA

Consulting Services Group

Proven Solutions for Managing the Costs of Construction and Facility Operations

Business and government leaders go to great lengths today to control costs and increase return on their construction-related activities. But they seldom have an opportunity to achieve optimum success. No matter what the activity... planning and design, new construction, facilities management, or introducing new building technologies... it comes down to the same problem: To control costs one must accurately predict them.

R.S. Means Consulting Services Group has a proven record of success helping businesses meet this challenge while greatly increasing opportunity to maximize return on construction investments. With its extensive, highly specialized experience understanding both construction costs and relational database technology, Means Consulting Services Group offers an unparalleled opportunity for businesses to realize dramatic improvement in their construction/facilities cost control programs.

Recipient of SEARS 1997 Chairman's Award for Innovation

Research and Custom Database Development

- **Custom Database Development**—Means expertise in construction cost engineering and database management can be put to work creating customized cost databases and applications.
- **Data Licensing & Integration**—To enhance applications dealing with construction, any segment of Means vast database can be licensed for use, and harnessed in a format compatible with a previously developed proprietary system.
- **Cost Modeling**—Pre-built custom cost models provide organizations that expend countless hours estimating repetitive work with a systematic time-saving estimating solution.
- **Database Auditing & Maintenance**—For clients with in-house data, Means can help organize it, and by linking it with Means database, fill in any gaps that exist and provide necessary updates to maintain current and relevant proprietary cost data.

Estimating and Cost Analysis

Estimating Service—Means expertise is available to perform construction cost estimates, as well as to develop baseline schedules and establish management plans for projects of all sizes and types. Conceptual, budget and detailed estimates are available.

Benchmarking—Means can run baseline estimates on existing project estimates. Gauging estimating accuracy and identifying inefficiencies improves the success ratio, precision and productivity of estimates.

Project Feasibility Studies—The Consulting Services Group can assist in the review and clarification of the most sound and practical construction approach in terms of time, cost and use.

Litigation Support—Means is available to provide opinions of value and to supply expert interpretations or testimony in the resolution of construction cost claims, litigation and mediation.

Developers of the Dept. of Defense Tri-Services Estimating Database

Staff Assessments, Training and Development

- **Core Curriculum**—Means educational programs, delivered on-site, are designed to sharpen professional skills and to maximize effective use of cost estimating and management tools. On-site training cuts down on travel expenses and time away from the office. The broad curriculum covers such topics as repair, new construction, and conceptual estimating; scheduling and project management; facilities management; metrication; and delivery order contracting (DOC) methods.
- **Custom Curriculum**—Means can custom-tailor courses to meet the specific needs and requirements of clients. The goal is to simultaneously boost skills and broaden cost estimating and management knowledge while focusing on applications that bring immediate benefits to unique operations, challenges, or markets.
- **Staff Assessments and Development Programs**—In addition to custom curricula, Means can work with a client's Human Resources Department or with individual operating units to create programs consistent with long-term employee development objectives.

For more information and a copy of our capabilities brochure, please call 1-800-448-8182 and ask for the Consulting Services Group, or reach us at http://www.rsmeans.com

MeansData™

CONSTRUCTION COSTS FOR SOFTWARE APPLICATIONS
Your construction estimating software is only as good as your cost data.

Software Integration

A proven construction cost database is a mandatory part of any estimating package. We have linked MeansData™ directly into the industry's leading software applications. The following list of software providers can offer you MeansData™ as an added feature for their estimating systems. Visit them on-line at *http://www.rsmeans.com/demo/* for more information and free demos. Or call their numbers listed below.

ACT
Applied Computer Technologies
Facility Management Software
1-910-897-1418

ASSETWORKS, Inc.
Facility Management Software
1-800-659-9001

BSD
Building Systems Design
1-800-875-0047

CDCI
Construction Data Controls, Inc.
1-800-285-3929

CMS
Computerized Micro Solutions
1-800-255-7407

CONAC GROUP
1-604-273-3463

CONSTRUCTIVE COMPUTING, Inc.
1-800-456-2113

ESTIMATING SYSTEMS, Inc.
1-800-967-8572

G2, Inc.
1-800-657-6312

GEAC COMMERCIAL SYSTEMS, Inc.
1-800-851-1115

GRANTLUN CORPORATION
1-602-897-7750

IQ BENECO
1-801-565-1122

MC^2
Management Computer Controls
1-800-225-5622

PRISM COMPUTER CORPORATION
Facility Management Software
1-800-774-7622

PYXIS TECHNOLOGIES
1-914-276-3369

SANDERS SOFTWARE, Inc.
1-404-934-8423

STN, Inc.
Workline Maintenance Systems
1-800-321-1969

TIMBERLINE SOFTWARE CORP.
1-800-628-6583

TMA SYSTEMS, Inc.
Facility Management Software
1-918-494-2890

US COST, Inc.
1-800-955-1385

VERTIGRAPH, Inc.
1-800-989-4243

WINESTIMATOR, Inc.
1-800-950-2374

DemoSource™ One-stop shopping for the latest cost estimating software for just $19.95. This evaluation tool includes product literature and demo diskettes for ten or more estimating systems, all of which link to MeansData™. **Call 1-800-334-3509 to order.**

**FOR MORE INFORMATION ON ELECTRONIC PRODUCTS CALL
1-800-448-8182 OR FAX 1-800-632-6732.**

MeansData™ is a registered trademark of R.S. Means Co., Inc., *A Construction Market Data Group* Company.

For more information visit Means Web Site at http://www.rsmeans.com

New Titles

Residential & Light Commercial Construction Standards
A Unique Collection of Industry Standards That Define Quality in Construction

For Contractors & Subcontractors, Owners, Developers, Architects & Engineers, Attorneys & Insurance Personnel

Compiled from the nation's major building codes, and from scores of publications and reports from professional institutes and other authorities, this one-of-a-kind resource enables you to:

- Set a standard for subcontractors and employees
- Protect yourself against defect claims
- Substantiate your own claim for inferior workmanship
- Resolve disputes
- Overview installation methods
- Answer client questions with an authoritative reference

Assembled by a Nationwide Team of Editors . . . leading contractors, code experts, and professional analysts of construction defects and failures. Includes: paving; concrete & masonry; wood & metal framing; finish carpentry & cabinetry; insulation, ventilation and vapor retarders; roofing, siding & moisture protection; doors & windows; plaster, drywall & ceramic tile

$59.95 per copy
Over 500 pages, Illustrated, Hardcover
Catalog No. 67322

New, Completely Revised Second Edition...

Project Scheduling & Management for Construction
(formerly *Project Planning & Control for Construction*)
by David R. Pierce, Jr.

An up-to-date, very readable guide to scheduling and management. Utilizes the latest Windows-based scheduling and management software—showing you how to quickly compare alternatives to find the most efficient methods and schedules... and the most profitable.

Includes:

- Planning for project success
- Scheduling for optimum speed
- Minimizing downtime & activity conflicts
- **New sample project**—a three story office building—with all scheduling and management details
- Identifying problems before they happen
- Monitoring job progress
- Tips on items easily overlooked

$62.95 per copy
Over 200 pages, Illustrated, Hardcover
Catalog No. 67247A

Means Landscape Estimating Methods Third Edition
by Sylvia Hollman Chattin

An experienced contractor shows you the best way to bid and win jobs—in a down-to-earth, step-by-step guide.

It takes you through deciding whether to bid a job, doing the estimate, and preparing and submitting the bid. The book includes samples of filled-in bid and estimate forms, and reproducible forms you can use for your own jobs. The author explains how to use *Means Site Work & Landscape Cost Data* as a pricing reference.

Once you've won the job, the author shows you how to schedule the work for maximum efficiency and cost savings. Included are insider tips on timing and cost factors you shouldn't overlook, as well as marketing tips for your company.

This new edition features:

- A new sample estimate utilizing the latest methods, materials, and costs
- All new illustrations
- **Two totally new chapters**—Life Cycle Costing and Landscape Maintenance Estimating

$62.95 per copy
Over 250 pages, Illustrated, Hardcover
Catalog No. 67295A

1999 Order Form

ORDER TOLL FREE 1-800-334-3509
OR FAX 1-800-632-6732.

Qty.	Book No.	COST ESTIMATING BOOKS	Unit Price	Total
	60069	Assemblies Cost Data 1999	$139.95	
	60019	Building Construction Cost Data 1999	84.95	
	61019	Building Const. Cost Data–Looseleaf Ed. 1999	109.95	
	63019	Building Const. Cost Data–Metric Version 1999	89.95	
	60229	Building Const. Cost Data–Western Ed. 1999	89.95	
	60119	Concrete & Masonry Cost Data 1999	77.95	
	50140	Construction Cost Indexes 1999	198.00	
	60149A	Construction Cost Index–January 1999	49.50	
	60149B	Construction Cost Index–April 1999	49.50	
	60149C	Construction Cost Index–July 1999	49.50	
	60149D	Construction Cost Index–October 1999	49.50	
	60319	Contr. Pricing Guide: Framing/Carpentry 1999	34.95	
	60339	Contr. Pricing Guide: Resid. Detailed 1999	36.95	
	60329	Contr. Pricing Guide: Resid. Sq. Ft. 1999	39.95	
	64029	ECHOS Assemblies Cost Book 1999	149.95	
	64019	ECHOS Unit Cost Book 1999	99.95	
	60239	Electrical Change Order Cost Data 1999	89.95	
	60039	Electrical Cost Data 1999	87.95	
	60209	Facilities Construction Cost Data 1999	209.95	
	60309	Facilities Maintenance & Repair Cost Data 1999	199.95	
	60169	Heavy Construction Cost Data 1999	89.95	
	63169	Heavy Const. Cost Data–Metric Version 1999	89.95	
	60099	Interior Cost Data 1999	89.95	
	60129	Labor Rates for the Const. Industry 1999	189.95	
	60189	Light Commercial Cost Data 1999	76.95	
	60029	Mechanical Cost Data 1999	87.95	
	60159	Open Shop Building Const. Cost Data 1999	89.95	
	60219	Plumbing Cost Data 1999	87.95	
	60049	Repair and Remodeling Cost Data 1999	79.95	
	60179	Residential Cost Data 1999	74.95	
	60289	Site Work & Landscape Cost Data 1999	89.95	
	60059	Square Foot Costs 1999	99.95	
		REFERENCE BOOKS		
	67147A	ADA in Practice	72.95	
	67310	ADA Pricing Guide	72.95	
	67298	Basics for Builders: Framing & Rough Carpentry	24.95	
	67273	Basics for Builders: How to Survive and Prosper	34.95	
	67307	Basics for Builders: Plan Reading & Takeoff	35.95	
	67180	Bidding for Contractors	17.98	
	67311	Builder's Costs for 100 Home Plans	34.95	
	67261	Building Profess. Guide to Contract Documents	64.95	
	67312	Building Spec Homes Profitably	29.95	
	67250	Business Management for Contractors	17.98	
	67146	Concrete Repair & Maintenance Illustrated	64.95	
	67278	Construction Delays	69.95	
	67268	Construction Paperwork	52.95	
	67255	Contractor's Business Handbook	21.48	
	67314	Cost Planning & Est. for Facil. Maint.	82.95	
	67317	Cyberplaces: The Internet Guide for A/E/C	59.95	
	67230A	Electrical Estimating Methods–2nd Ed.	62.95	
	64777	Environmental Remediation Est. Methods	99.95	
	67160	Estimating for Contractors	35.95	
	67276	Estimating Handbook	99.95	
	67249	Facilities Maintenance Management	86.95	

Qty.	Book No.	REFERENCE BOOKS (Con't)	Unit Price	Total
	67246	Facilities Maintenance Standards	159.95	
	67264	Facilities Manager's Reference	86.95	
	67301	Facilities Planning & Relocation	109.95	
	67288	Forms for Contractors	79.95	
	67260	Fundamentals of the Construction Process	34.98	
	67210	Graphic Construction Standards	124.95	
	67258	Hazardous Material & Hazardous Waste	44.98	
	67148	Heavy Construction Handbook	74.95	
	67308B	Home Improvement Costs–Interior Projects	19.95	
	67309B	Home Improvement Costs–Exterior Projects	19.95	
	67304	How to Estimate with Metric Units	24.98	
	67306	HVAC: Design Criteria, Options, Select.–2nd Ed.	84.95	
	67281	HVAC Systems Evaluation	84.95	
	67282	Illustrated Construction Dictionary, Condensed	59.95	
	67292	Illustrated Construction Dictionary, Unabridged	99.95	
	67295A	Landscape Estimating–3rd Ed.	62.95	
	67266	Legal Reference for Design & Construction	54.98	
	67299	Maintenance Management Audit	32.48	
	67302	Managing Construction Purchasing	31.48	
	67294	Mechanical Estimating–2nd Ed.	64.95	
	67245	Planning and Managing Interior Projects	76.95	
	67283	Plumbing Estimating Methods	59.95	
	67236A	Productivity Standards for Constr.–3rd Ed.	159.95	
	67247A	Project Scheduling & Management for Constr.	62.95	
	67262	Quantity Takeoff for Contractors	17.48	
	67265A	Repair & Remodeling Estimating–3rd Ed.	69.95	
	67322	Residential & Light Commercial Bldg. Standards	59.95	
	67253	Roofing: Design Criteria, Options, Selection	31.48	
	67291	Scheduling Manual–3rd Ed.	62.95	
	67145A	Square Foot Estimating Methods–2nd Ed.	69.95	
	67241	Structural Steel Estimating	79.95	
	67287	Successful Estimating Methods	64.95	
	67313	Successful Interior Projects	34.98	
	67233	Superintending for Contractors	35.95	
	67321	Total Productive Facilities Management	79.95	
	67284	Understanding Building Automation Systems	79.95	
	67259	Understanding Legal Aspects of Design/Build	79.95	
	67303	Unit Price Estimating Methods–2nd Ed.	59.95	
	67319	Value Engineering: Practical Applications	79.95	

MA residents add 5% state sales tax	
Shipping & Handling**	
Total (U.S. Funds)*	

Prices are subject to change and are for U.S. delivery only. *Canadian customers may call for current prices. **Shipping & handling charges: Add 6.5% of total order for check and credit card payments. Add 9% of total order for invoiced orders.

Send Order To: ADDV-1001

Name (Please Print) _____

Company _____

☐ **Company**
☐ **Home**   Address _____

_____

City/State/Zip _____

Phone # _____ P.O. # _____

Mail To: R.S. Means Company, Inc., P.O. Box 800, Kingston, MA 02364-0800   (Must accompany all orders being billed)